FIELDS OF
WRITING

READINGS ACROSS
THE DISCIPLINES

Fourth Edition

FIELDS OF
WRITING

READINGS ACROSS
THE DISCIPLINES

Fourth Edition

Nancy R. Comley

QUEENS COLLEGE, CUNY

David Hamilton

UNIVERSITY OF IOWA

Carl H. Klaus

UNIVERSITY OF IOWA

Robert Scholes

BROWN UNIVERSITY

Nancy Sommers

HARVARD UNIVERSITY

St. Martin's Press

NEW YORK

Senior editor: Karen Allanson
Development editor: Edward Hutchinson
Managing editor: Patricia Mansfield-Phelan
Project editor: Alda Trabucchi
Production supervisor: Alan Fischer
Art director/cover design: Sheree Goodman
Cover art: Grant Wood, *Fall Plowing*, 1931. The John Deere Collection, Moline, Illinois.

Library of Congress Catalog Card Number: 92-62767
Copyright © 1994 by St. Martin's Press, Inc.

8   7   6   5   4
f   e   d

For information, write:
St. Martin's Press, Inc.
175 Fifth Avenue
New York, NY 10010

ISBN: 0-312-08660-1

ACKNOWLEDGMENTS

Angelou, Maya. "Graduation" From *I Know Why the Caged Bird Sings*, by Maya Angelou. Copyright © 1969 by Maya Angelou. Reprinted by permission of Random House, Inc.
Associated Press. "Two Reports of an Airplane Crash." From Associated Press, December 2, 1974. Reprinted by permission.
Avedon, John F. "Tibetan Medicine: The Science of Healing." From *In Exile from the Land of Snows*, by John F. Avedon. Copyright © 1979, 1984 by John F. Avedon. Reprinted by permission of Alfred A. Knopf, Inc.
Baldwin, James. "If Black English Isn't a Language, Then Tell Me, What Is?" From *The New York Times*, July 29, 1979. Copyright © 1979 by The New York Times Company. Reprinted by permission.

Acknowledgments and copyrights are continued at the back of the book on pages 782–786, which constitute an extension of the copyright page.

For Instructors

The fourth edition of *Fields of Writing*, like previous editions, offers a collection of readings designed to reflect the range and variety of thinking and writing across the disciplines. In choosing pieces for this edition, we have been guided by the suggestions of instructors who used the third edition, all of whom told us to keep the collection wide-ranging and varied in its subject matter. Thus, the table of contents again covers a broad array of topics, from the social lives of dolphins to the art of Georgia O'Keeffe, from the bubonic plague of the fourteenth century to the AIDS pandemic of the twentieth century, from the origin of the universe to the education of African Americans. So, too, *Fields of Writing* again offers material drawn equally from the arts and the humanities, from the social sciences and public affairs, and from the natural sciences and technologies—from the major areas of the curriculum in both their academic and applied forms. Overall, you will find here a total of seventy-nine selections as various in subject, form, and purpose as the different kinds of reading and writing that students are expected to carry on both in undergraduate education and in the world outside the classroom.

In organizing our collection, we have once again grouped pieces according to four broad rhetorical categories—"Reflecting," "Reporting," "Explaining," and "Arguing"—that represent essential kinds of reading and writing in virtually every academic or professional area. In every field, individuals need to think about past experience (reflecting), convey information (reporting), make sense of knowledge (explaining), and debate controversial ideas and issues (arguing). Within each of these four categories, we have as before grouped the selections according to three broad curricular areas—"Arts and Humanities," "Social Sciences and Public Affairs," and "Sciences and Technologies." This combined system of organization, our reviewers tell us, continues to be a convenient aid to discovering and assigning selections for a variety of classroom purposes.

While maintaining this rhetorical/cross-curricular system of organization, we have made substantial changes in the table of contents, with the result that twenty-three of the seventy-seven selections are new to this edition. These new selections include pieces by a culturally varied array of scholars, critics, and writers who did not appear in the third edition, such as Jorge Borges, bell hooks, Nancy Mairs, Patricia Williams, Edmund White, and Deborah Woo.

Adding new selections has also made it possible for us to provide substantially new pairings or sets of topically related pieces throughout the table of contents. As a result, students will still have numerous opportunities to read and consider different perspectives on a single issue or to explore a particular topic in depth. Wherever possible, we have placed these topically related pieces side by side, so that you can quickly find them in the table of contents. But in some instances they necessarily appear under different rhetorical headings. So, we have also included a "Topical Guide to the Contents," making it possible to approach all of the selections in terms of particular subjects of study or themes of interest. And in order to encourage students to pursue thematic relationships among the selections, we have provided one or two special questions for each piece, "Making Connections."

Our critical apparatus, once again, focuses on the rhetorical concepts and techniques that apply to reading and writing across the curriculum. These frameworks are discussed in the preface, "For Students," as well as in the detailed introductions to each of the four main sections, "Reflecting," "Reporting," "Explaining," and "Arguing." These introductions, which are illustrated with passages from the anthologized readings, define each type of writing, discuss its relevance within a broad range of fields, compare and contrast its use in differing fields and situations, and identify and explain methods of achieving its aims. Thus, the introductions show, for example, how description and narration are basic in reporting or how analogy, comparison and contrast, definition, and illustration are basic to explaining. All of the rhetorical aims and modes that we discuss in the critical apparatus are referenced in a "Rhetorical Index" that can be found at the back of the book. Concepts and terms that figure in the sectional introductions are also applied throughout the remainder of the editorial apparatus. So you will find that the headnote for each piece identifies and, wherever necessary, explains the professional field of its author and the rhetorical context or source of its original publication. Likewise, the questions following each selection call for reading and writing that relate form and style to purpose, subject, and academic field.

Because the material in this collection is primarily intended to help students develop their reading and writing abilities, we discuss these activities at some length in the general introduction. The first part, "Reading and Rereading," explains and illustrates various approaches to reading, primarily through an examination of an essay by E. B. White. In turn, the second part, "Writing and Rewriting," explains and illustrates the composing process through a detailed discussion of White's essay, including unpublished notes and drafts that White prepared while writing the piece. Immediately following this introduction, we have added a brief, but important, note for students on "Acknowledging Your Sources." This section explains the purposes of documentation and offers various methods of meeting this basic obligation. These introductory materials, like the rest of the book, are meant to present reading and writing, not in abstract terms, but through discussion and examples that vividly demonstrate what is actually involved in each activity.

ACKNOWLEDGMENTS

For their detailed reactions to the third edition of *Fields of Writing* and for their suggestions in compiling the fourth edition, we are grateful to: Gary Arms, Iowa State University; Mary Bly, University of California at Davis; Margaret H. Boese, Ocean County College; Mike Dalby, United States Air Force Academy; Frank A. Davis, Del Mar College; Michel de Benedictis, Miami-Dade Community College; Andrea Fishman, West Chester University; M. Kip Hartvigsen, Ricks College; Harv M. Hopkins-Garris, James Madison University; Thomas Hurley, University of Massachusetts at Boston; Diane Kopp, Southwestern Michigan College; Kathleen Davidson March, Duke University; Catharine Riggs, University of California at Los Angeles; Roberta Rosenberg, Christopher Newport College; Susan Norton Stark, Boise State University; and Linda Woodson, University of Texas at San Antonio.

Finally, for their excellent work in bringing this book into print, we are grateful to the staff at St. Martin's Press, especially Cathy Pusateri, Karen Allanson, Edward Hutchinson, Alda Trabucchi, Sheree Goodman, and Alan Fischer.

N.R.C.
D.H.
C.H.K.
R.S.
N.S.

Contents

Contents

x

xi

CONTENTS

CONTENTS

CONTENTS

CONTENTS

Contents

xvi

CONTENTS

CONTENTS

CONTENTS

Topical Guide to the Contents

RACE AND RACISM

THE EXPERIENCE OF WOMEN

VIOLENCE AND WAR

LIFE AND DEATH

OBSERVING ANIMALS

UNDERSTANDING THE PHYSICAL WORLD

HUMAN PORTRAITS

TEACHING, LEARNING, AND SCHOOLING

HEALTH, DISEASE, AND MEDICINE

For Students

Fields of Writing: Readings across the Disciplines, Fourth Edition, is intended to help you develop the abilities in reading and writing that you will need as you move from one course to another, one field of study to another, throughout your college career. In some senses, of course, all areas of study expect the same things of you—namely, close and careful reading as well as clear and exact writing, with an attentiveness above all to information and ideas. But the particular kinds of information, ideas, and concerns that distinguish each field of study also call for somewhat different reading and writing abilities. A book review for a literature course, for example, requires a different form and style from a lab report in physics. So we have tried to give you a sampling of the varied fields of writing you are likely to encounter in the academic world.

Most undergraduate schools are organized around some version of the traditional division of studies into "the humanities," "the social sciences," and "the sciences." The humanities generally include fields of learning that are thought of as having a cultural orientation, such as language, literature, history, philosophy, and religion. The social sciences, which include such fields as anthropology, economics, education, political science, psychology, and sociology, deal with social institutions and the behavior of their individual members. The sciences include fields of knowledge that are concerned with the natural and physical world, such as astronomy, botany, chemistry, physics, and zoology.

These traditional divisions of study are closely affiliated with applied areas of study and work that also exist in the professional world. The humanities, for example, are closely allied with the arts; the social sciences, with public affairs such as business and government; and the sciences, with technology. These divisions and clusterings of fields—"Arts and Humanities," "Social Sciences and Public Affairs," "Sciences and Technologies"—are so broadly applicable that we have used them as one of the organizing principles in our table of contents.

Like any set of categories, these divisions are a convenient, but by no means foolproof, system of classification. Although the system can help you to understand the academic world, it does not reflect the exact state of affairs in every specialized field at every college and university. Specialists in a particular field sometimes migrate from one area of learning to another, from the social sciences to the sciences, for example, according to the orientation of their research in a particular project. Or specialists from several fields may form an interdisciplinary area of research, such as environmental studies, which involves a wide range of academic disciplines—botany, chemistry, economics, philosophy, political science, and zoology. So, the writing that results from these projects often can be categorized in more than one broad area of learning.

The writing we have collected in *Fields of Writing* can be understood not only in terms of the area of learning that it represents, but also in terms of the particular purpose it is meant to achieve. Every piece of writing, of course, is the product of an author's personal and professional motives, so in a sense the purposes for writing are as varied and ultimately mysterious as are authors themselves. But setting aside the mysteries of human nature, it is possible to identify and define a set of different purposes for writing, which we refer to as "Reflecting," "Reporting," "Explaining," and "Arguing," one or another of which predominates in most academic and professional writing. So, we have used this set of purposes as the major organizing principle in our table of contents.

By "Reflecting," we mean a kind of writing in which authors are concerned with recalling and thinking about their past experience, for personal experience is often an especially valuable source of knowledge and learning. By "Reporting," we mean writing that is concerned primarily with conveying factual information about some particular aspect of the world, past or present. By "Explaining," we mean writing that is concerned primarily with making sense of information or shedding light on a particular subject. By "Arguing," we mean writing that is given to debating controversial explanations, values, or beliefs. Like our other categories, these are convenient, but not rigid, modes of classification. So, they need to be used tactfully, with an awareness that to some degree they are bound to overlap. Most pieces of explanation, for example, will at some point involve reporting, if only to convey the information or subject to be explained. And most pieces of argument will call for some explanation, if only to make clear the issues that are at odds with one another. But generally you will find one or another of these purposes to be dominant in any particular piece of writing.

We think that an awareness of these basic purposes can be especially helpful both in the process of reading and in the process of writing, no matter what academic or professional field is involved. So, we have introduced each section of our collection with an essay on "Reflecting," "Reporting," "Explaining," or "Arguing." In these essays, you will find detailed definitions and examples of each purpose, as well as explanations and illustrations of how to carry it out in differing fields and situations. Each selection is accompanied by a brief headnote, explanatory footnotes where necessary, and questions for you to think about in your reading and writing. In addition, each selection is also followed by questions to help you make connections among related readings in this collection.

Immediately following this preface, you will find an introduction consisting of three parts. In "Reading and Rereading," we discuss various ways to read and understand the pieces in this book or any other material you might encounter in your studies; in "Writing and Rewriting," we show an actual example of how one writer goes through the process of composing a piece of writing; and in

"Acknowledging Sources," we explain various forms of documentation and why such acknowledgment is important in every field of study. This introduction, like the headnotes, questions, and sectional introductions, is meant to help you become a thoughtful and responsible reader and writer. The rest is up to your instructor, your classmates, and you.

FIELDS OF

WRITING

READINGS ACROSS
THE DISCIPLINES

Fourth Edition

Introduction

No matter what your field of study, you will probably find that it involves you repeatedly in the activities of reading and writing. Reading, even in the age of the computer, continues to be the primary means of acquiring knowledge, and writing the primary means of sharing ideas with others. So, we have decided to introduce this collection with a discussion of some general ideas that you might find useful in your own reading and writing.

Our discussion of both activities is illustrated primarily by reference to a short essay that appeared in the *New York Times*, September 23, 1967. We suggest that you begin by reading that essay, which follows, and getting the gist of it for yourself, before we begin to discuss it in detail.

Dear Mr. ⑈0 2 14ꞁꞁꞁ 106 3⑈ ꞁꞁ0 2ꞁꞁꞁ 10 7 30ꞁꞁꞁ8ꞁꞁ

By E. B. WHITE

My bank, which I have forgotten the name of in the excitement of the moment, sent me a warning the other day. It was headed: "An important notice to all our checking account customers." The burden of this communication was that I would no longer be allowed to write checks that did not bear the special series of magnetic ink numbers along the base.   1

My bank said the Federal Reserve System had notified them that it will not accept for processing any checks that don't show these knobby little digits. For example, I would no longer be free to write a check on a blank form, because it would lack a certain magnetism that computers insist on.   2

Slightly Rheumatoid

I first encountered these spooky numbers a few years back and took a dislike to them. They looked like numbers that had been run over by a dump truck or that had developed rheumatoid arthritis and their joints had swollen. But I kept my mouth shut, as they seemed to be doing me no harm.   3

Now, however, it appears that we are all going to knuckle under to the machines that admire these numbers. We must all forgo the pleasure and convenience of   4

1

writing a check on an ordinary nonmagnetic piece of paper. My signature used to be enough to prod my bank into dispatching some of my money to some deserving individual or firm. Not any more.

This, I think, is a defeat for all—a surrender. In order to accommodate the   5
Federal Reserve System, we are asked to put ourselves out.

I Embarrass Easily

The notice I received says that if I try to palm off a check that lacks the   6
magnetic ink numbers, the check cannot be processed without "delay, extra handling charges, and possible embarrassment." I embarrass easily—it doesn't take much, really—and naturally I am eager to learn what form this embarrassment will take if I should decide to write a check using the old blank form that has proved so convenient, for I don't know how many decades, on those occasions when one is stuck without his checkbook or enough lettuce to carry the day.

"The tremendous increase in the use of checks," writes my bank, warming to   7
its subject, "made it necessary for the Federal Reserve to establish a completely computerized operation for processing all checks from all banks. Their computer can function only when proper magnetic numbers are used."

Well, I can believe that last part, about the computer requiring a special diet   8
of malformed numbers; but I am suspicious of that first statement, about how the Federal Reserve would have been unable to carry on unless it went completely over to machines. I suspect that the Federal Reserve simply found machines handy and adventurous. But suppose we had had, in this country, a tremendous increase in the use of checks before anybody had got round to inventing the computer— what would have happened then? Am I expected to believe that the Federal Reserve and all its members would have thrown in the sponge?

I know banks better than that. Banks love money and are not easily deflected   9
from the delicious act of accumulating it. Love would have found a way. Checks would have cleared.

I'm not against machines, as are some people who feel that the computer is   10
leading us back into the jungle. I rather like machines, particularly the egg beater, which is the highest point the machine has yet reached. I'm against machines only when the convenience they afford to some people is regarded as more important than the inconvenience they cause to all.

In short, I don't think computers should wear the pants, or make the decisions.   11
They are deficient in humor, they are not intuitive, and they are not aware of the imponderables. The men who feed them seem to believe that everything is made out of ponderables, which isn't the case. I read a poem once that a computer had written, but didn't care much for it. It seemed to me I could write a better one myself, it I were to put my mind to it.

Time to Find Out

And now I must look around for a blank check. It's time I found out what   12
form my new embarrassment is going to take. First, though, I'll have to remember the name of my bank. It'll come to me, if I sit here long enough. Oddly enough, the warning notice I received contained no signature. Imagine a bank forgetting to sign its name!

READING AND REREADING

Reading this essay in a textbook for a course in English composition, as you have just done, is not quite the same as reading it in a daily newspaper. Not only does the format—the layout, the page size, the typeface—of a newspaper differ from that of a textbook, but the reasons we have for reading each and, consequently, the *way* we read will differ, as well.

Think for a moment, though, about the similarities between your reading of this essay here and now and someone's reading of it in the fall of 1967. First of all, both readings are based on recognizing and interpreting an arrangement of printed symbols, symbols most of us were familiar with long before we began to learn them systematically in the first grade. This aspect of reading is so elemental that you probably never stop to consider what a feat it really is. Second, both readings begin with the title and work their way sequentially through the final line of the text (though seeing the process as purely sequential is somewhat misleading; in fact, our minds ordinarily move back and forth, comparing what we read at one point with what we've read at others, as we work to make sense of the text). Third, both readings assume an active, rather than a passive, reader—someone who is responding to everything that White has to say. And responding in a variety of ways—pondering, questioning, nodding, gesturing, laughing, or growling, just to name a few of the reactions that might be provoked in a reader of White's piece.

Responses to Reading

The complexity of such reactions can be seen just by trying to imagine how one might read the title, "Dear Mr. 0214 1063 02 10730 8." The first two words are easy enough: we recognize them immediately as the conventional salutation of a business letter. We could even speak them aloud (taking into account that the unpronounceable *Mr.* is an abbreviated form of *Mister*). But the following series of "knobby little digits" presents a more complicated problem. "What are they?" we might ask. "What do they mean?" Even if we recognize them as the sort of figures that are printed at the bottom of a check, we cannot, in fact, *read* them, because the markings between the numbers represent nothing in our language or our grammar. In fact, they are meant to be read not by human beings but by machines. Trying to read such a title, therefore, will set off any number of responses: perhaps an inkling of what White is up to ("Ah, a put-down of computer technology"), perhaps confusion ("I can't imagine what to make of this"), perhaps the desire to read on, and probably a less than fully articulated combination of several of these.

Next, the name of the author will create another round of responses. Perhaps you (and our imaginary reader of the *Times*) will be familiar with the name E. B. White and will associate it with *Charlotte's Web* or *Elements of Style* or a piece in the *New Yorker* magazine or something else you've read by White or

3

know he wrote. You (and our imaginary *Times* reader) might respond positively ("I loved *Charlotte's Web*") or negatively ("I hate that *New Yorker* stuff") or less familiarly ("Is E. B. a man or a woman?"), but you will certainly have some response. This complicated sequence of responses, of course, occurs in just the second or two it takes you to comprehend the symbols on the page.

As you continue to read, you will continue to respond. Thoughts and impressions, no matter how tentative and ill-formed, will play through your consciousness. (You may even feel compelled to jot down some of these responses in the margin of the page.) Our minds can only make sense of the information we receive by testing this information against what we already know and feel. Such testing is a peculiarly human activity—at least we regard it as "human" when we observe it in other species—and only by allowing, even encouraging, ourselves to make these mental connections can we participate fully in the collaboration necessary to create meaning. Reading, as you probably realize, is a *transaction* that spans at least two human minds; reader and writer both must work actively for a meaningful transaction to take place.

If either participant fails to regard the human responsibilities of communication, the transaction will be unsatisfying. White provides a particularly unpleasant example of this: an impersonal letter, written not by a human being but by "a bank," has had an unsettling effect because it indicates to White the abrupt dehumanization of what was previously a human transaction. Readers can fail, as well, when they approach the transaction impersonally, when they ignore their personal reactions and responses, and when they don't participate actively in examining and judging what they read. Such passivity is, of course, what impersonal writers hope for from their readers; the impersonal mask is calculated to discourage any questions or objections. Perhaps you have occasionally found yourself intimidated by such all-knowing bureaucratic pronouncements. The surest way to prevent yourself from being cowed ever again is to read inquisitively, ready to respond with all of your mind and all of your feelings to whatever you find in your reading, from the smallest detail to the text as a whole.

As we have said, your reading will always involve responses of some kind. The important step is to move from the responses themselves to a serious examination of them. To read White's reflections on his bank's warning and respond simply with "It's dumb" or "It's funny" or "I agree" or "I disagree" or the implacable "I can't relate to this" is not enough. Examining such responses will reveal a complex interaction between the structures of the text, the intentions and abilities of the writer, and what you as a reader bring to the text from your own experience. You may find White's essay "funny" because his treatment of his bank as a letter-writing entity that forgets to sign its name sets off a particularly exact set of images in your mind. You may "disagree" with White because you find his comment that the egg beater "is the highest point the machine has yet reached" to be overly flippant and because you think the computer's greater accuracy does in fact afford convenience to all. You may feel you "can't relate to" White's experience because you've never known checks *without* the magnetic code and because you've never received a similarly impersonal letter from a bureaucratic institution. Whatever the case, your responses will remain superficial and ill-formed until you examine them closely enough to explain them in detail.

Clearly, our own experiences will deeply affect our reading. Whatever we have seen or done or felt or heard, even the room we are in and our last meal, will contribute to a data bank from which our responses arise. Consider the following excerpt from the memoirs of Frederick Douglass (the complete chapter from which this was taken appears on pp. 62–67). Born into slavery, Douglass managed to learn to read and at the age of twelve saved enough money—fifty cents—to buy his first book, *The Columbian Orator.* This was a popular schoolbook containing speeches by famous orators and dialogues for students of rhetoric to practice and memorize. Here are Douglass's reactions to one of his readings.

> I was now about twelve years old, and the thought of being *a slave for life* began to bear heavily upon my heart. Just about this time, I got hold of a book entitled "The Columbian Orator." Every opportunity I got, I used to read this book. Among much of other interesting matter, I found in it a dialogue between a master and his slave. The slave was represented as having run away from his master three times. The dialogue represented the conversation which took place between them, when the slave was retaken the third time. In this dialogue, the whole argument in behalf of slavery was brought forward by the master, all of which was disposed of by the slave. The slave was made to say some very smart as well as impressive things in reply to his master—things which had the desired though unexpected effect; for the conversation resulted in the voluntary emancipation of the slave on the part of the master.
>
> In the same book, I met with one of Sheridan's mighty speeches on and in behalf of Catholic emancipation. These were choice documents to me. I read them over and over again with unabated interest. They gave tongue to interesting thoughts of my own soul, which had frequently flashed through my mind, and died away for want of utterance. The moral which I gained from the dialogue was the power of truth over the conscience of even a slaveholder. What I got from Sheridan was a bold denunciation of slavery, and a powerful vindication of human rights. The reading of these documents enabled me to utter my thoughts, and to meet the arguments brought forward to sustain slavery, but while they relieved me of one difficulty, they brought on another

5

even more painful than the one of which I was relieved. The more I
read, the more I was led to abhor and detest my enslavers.

Obviously, Douglass's experience as a slave determined his strong response
to his reading. The words he read spoke directly to his condition, shaping his
previously inexpressible desires and emotions into language. He was, of course,
the perfect audience for Richard Brinsley Sheridan's "bold denunciation of
slavery" and "powerful vindication of human rights." But had Douglass's master
and mistress read the same speech, they might well have reacted in a strongly
negative way, finding Sheridan subversive of their position as slave owners.
They might have characterized his denunciation as "too bold" and his vindication of human rights as "wrongheaded" rather than "powerful." We might
read Sheridan today and respond to his speech as an effective piece of eighteenth-
century rhetoric or as an interesting historical document. On the other hand,
if we have lived in places where human rights are greatly restricted, we might
find Sheridan's speech as powerful and bold as Douglass did.

This does not mean, of course, that one's responses are limited to a strictly
personal point of view. As we determine the basis for our most personal responses, we can begin to read with greater discipline and to think more systematically about what we read. First of all, we are able to realize that not everyone
will have the same responses that we do. This, in turn, can help us recognize
what may be limitations in our original responses, limitations imposed perhaps
by our *lack* of experience ("Well, sure, I guess if I had been using blank checks
all my life and got a letter like that out of the blue, threatening me with 'possible
embarrassment' if I didn't start using the magnetically coded ones, I wouldn't
have liked it very much either. But what's his point in making a joke of it?").
Opening up a text for ourselves will almost always mean moving beyond those
important initial responses to asking ourselves implicit questions about what is
being said, how it is being said, and why it is being said in this particular way.

Obviously, we can't fully comprehend what we are reading until we have
read through it completely. Not until we reach White's final line ("Imagine a
bank forgetting to sign its name!") do all the various strands of thought that he
has been pursuing begin to fall clearly into place. At this point a second reading
(and maybe a third or a fourth) will allow us to pay more attention to how a
writer has presented the material because our curiosity has been satisfied as to
what the text is about and we have a sense of it as a whole. In rereading it, we
may discover points we have missed or misinterpreted; other of our experiences
may begin to come to bear ("This is like that letter I got from the registrar's
office informing me that from now on I'd have to have financial aid forms
notarized and submit them with my term bill"). Consequently, our responses
will be different, and we may significantly revise our initial reading. We can
also begin in this second reading to question the text more closely to discover
its intentions and its structure. This questioning may take a number of forms

6

(which we'll be considering later in this discussion), but in all cases it's a good idea to write down your responses, beginning with those that arise during the initial reading. Writing helps us to think more clearly and deeply about what we read and to preserve our thoughts for further development.

Elements of Reading

Earlier we pointed out some basic similarities between reading E. B. White's "Dear Mr. . . ." on the editorial page of the *New York Times* and reading the same essay in a textbook as an assignment for an English composition course. However, as you already know from experience, many elements of your reading can vary, depending on the situation. What you read and why you read will always influence the way you read.

For example, a *Times* buyer in the fall of 1967 would have read White's essay primarily for what we can call "pleasure." "Pleasure," of course, can take many forms: we may read for amusement, for escape, for intellectual discovery and stimulation, even to get angry or to make ourselves more depressed. But it's clear that we *choose* to do such reading because of a definite personal interest. No one is asking us to look for anything or remember anything. Ironically, though, we will often remember what we read for pleasure more clearly and more fully than what we read under pressure, because our minds are more relaxed. On such occasions, we have time to pause over a word or a phrase just because we like the sound of it or the feeling it expresses. So, while the pleasure that arises from personal interest may be our primary purpose for reading, we may also be assimilating new information, analyzing a particularly striking passage to understand how it works, or evaluating what a writer has to say, all because we enjoy what we are doing.

Taking account of how you read for pleasure, then, can help you read more effectively in other situations; you can even use your personal reading to help you develop habits that will make you a better reader generally. One way is to take the time to make note of your immediate responses. For example, you may want to remember a particular piece of information or to hold on to a word or phrase that made an impression; to respond evaluatively, agreeing or disagreeing with what the writer has to say; or to explore responses that the writer has triggered. Begin to record such responses in writing. Keep a notebook handy to use as a journal of observations, information, and impressions. You can then refer to this journal for ideas to use in your own writing. Taking pleasure in working with new concepts and new information is an important step in becoming a better reader.

Reading in its broadest sense (as White's bank's computer *reads* his magnetic code name) always implies taking in information. We do so whenever and from whatever we read. But grasping the most pertinent information in a text requires that we read with an awareness of the author's purpose for writing. An

7

author's primary purpose may be reflective, reportorial, explanatory, or argumentative. Each of these purposes entails a different kind of writing, and thus each calls for a somewhat different kind of reading, as we show in our introductions to the sections "Reflecting," "Reporting," "Explaining," and "Arguing." For example, when we read White's argumentative piece about the computerized numbers on his checks, we must weigh the merits of competing ideas—of his antitechnological outlook versus the technological needs of the bank and its customers. But when we read "'This Is the End of the World': The Black Death" (pp. 177–85), Barbara Tuchman's reportorial piece about the medieval plague, we concern ourselves not with controversial issues but with the details of a particular historical event. So, whenever you are assigned a piece of reading, you should try to determine the author's primary purpose as quickly as possible. Then you will have a better idea of what to focus on as you read and study the material for class discussions, paper assignments, or tests.

Whatever type of reading you are doing, in whatever field of study, you will generally be called upon to analyze, understand, memorize, and possibly evaluate the most important information and ideas that it contains. In order to sort out the most pertinent information and make sense of it for yourself, you will probably find it helpful to use a combination of the following methods:

(1) *Synoptic Reading.* Begin by reading the piece through from beginning to end primarily to get a quick overall sense of the author's subject, purpose, major ideas, and information. This initial reading is meant to help you get acquainted with the piece as a whole, so don't let yourself get bogged down in details as you make your way through the text. But don't hesitate to underline or check off what seem to be important (or puzzling) words, phrases, sentences, ideas, and points of information that you want to look into later when you examine the piece in detail. Once you have completed your initial reading of the piece, you should jot down a few notes about what you consider to be the gist of the piece—its major subject, purpose, points, and information.

(2) *Annotating.* After you have gathered the gist of the piece, then you should annotate the material for yourself. An annotation consists of explanatory notes. So if the piece contains words, names, titles of works, or other bits of information with which you are unfamiliar, you should consult a dictionary, encyclopedia, or other reference work, jotting down explanatory notes that you can use for future reference. This procedure will help you not only to understand the piece but also to expand both your vocabulary and your storehouse of general knowledge.

(3) *Outlining.* Once you have annotated the piece, then you may find it useful to make an outline of the material that it contains. An outline systematically lists the major ideas, points, and bits of information according to the order that they appear in the piece. The process of making an outline will help you to understand the piece more reliably and thoroughly than you can by simply reading it over once or twice. And the outline itself will serve as an

invaluable aid to remembering the piece at a later date, when you may want to draw upon it for a paper or examination. In preparing an outline, you might be tempted to rely entirely on your initial reading, underlinings, and notes. But just to make sure that your outline is reliable, you should read the piece carefully a second time with an eye to getting down the most important material in a form that is accurately worded and arranged. Here, for example, is an outline of White's piece.

I. White's bank informs him that the Federal Reserve System will no longer process checks written on a "blank form," and that he must, therefore, use checks with computer-legible identification numbers.

II. White opposes this requirement because
   A. It is inconvenient for the individual bank customer, and
   B. It subordinates the needs and desires of the individual to the will of the government banking system.

III. White's bank further informs him that the government's adoption of a computerized check-processing system was necessitated by "the tremendous increase in the use of checks."

IV. White is dissatisfied with this explanation because
   A. He believes it is based on a faulty assumption that the increase in checks could only have been processed by computers, and
   B. He believes that computers lack human mental capacities and thus should not be given influence over human affairs.

(4) *Summarizing.* Instead of outlining the piece, you may prefer to summarize it. A summary, like an outline, offers a highly condensed version of the most important material in a piece. But rather than casting the material in a numbered and lettered list, a summary calls upon you to write a paragraph of continuous prose in which you identify the major purpose, ideas, arguments, and information. The process of summarizing, like that of outlining, is a valuable aid to understanding a piece, and the summary itself will also serve as an aid to remembering the piece at a later date. The ability to summarize is an especially important skill in writing research papers, for they usually call upon you to condense material that you have read and integrate it into your own discussion. So you should try your hand at summarizing a few of the pieces that you read in this collection. Here, for example, is a summary of White's piece.

White's intention is to challenge the Federal Reserve System's computerized system of processing bank checks. White opposes the changeover from blank forms to checks with computer-legible numbers, because it inconveniences individual citizens and thus subordinates the needs of the individual to the will of the federal banking system. He also opposes the changeover because he considers it to be based on a

9

faulty assumption that the increasing use of checks could only be handled by computers. Finally, he opposes the changeover because he believes that computers lack human mental capacities and thus should not be allowed to have so much influence over human affairs.

A special kind of summary, known as an *abstract*, is also customary in highly specialized professional journals, which require an author to provide a very brief summary at the beginning of an article for the convenience of readers. (For a sample abstract, see Antonio R. Damasio, "Face Perception without Recognition," p. 556. See also the synopsis that comes at the beginning of "Aircraft Accident Report" by the National Transportation Safety Board, p. 305.)

(5) *Analyzing and Evaluating.* Instead of outlining or summarizing a piece, you may find it necessary to analyze and evaluate it, particularly if you need to understand it in detail. In order to analyze a text carefully and thoughtfully, we suggest that you read it over with several key questions in mind that you want to answer for yourself. Each of these questions, as you will see in the following, is designed to focus on a different aspect of the piece—its purpose, organization, evidence, implied audience, and use of language. In the following paragraphs, we will use White's "Dear Mr. . . ." to show how you can analyze a text by asking and answering a set of questions about it.

What is the writer's purpose? White's immediate purpose is to describe his responses to the letter from his bank, ranging from personal annoyance to ironic evaluations of why a change should be required to a note of wry defiance. These personal reflections revolve around a more general and serious point, which he states fairly directly in paragraph 5 and again in paragraph 10: he thinks it is a "defeat," a "surrender" to allow machines to inconvenience "all" (and himself, in particular) for the sake of making life easier for a powerful few. Allied with this idea is White's belief that computers are "deficient" in the qualities which make us human and that, consequently, they should not be allowed to usurp human transactions (paragraph 11). His conclusion is a refusal to "knuckle under" to the dictates of such machines.

How does the writer organize his or her material? White's reflections are organized around the information contained in the letter he received from his bank. His title is an ironic version of the letter's salutation, and his concluding sentence refers to the lack of a closing signature. In paragraphs 1, 2, 6, and 7, he quotes from the letter, directly or indirectly, and goes on to offer his specific responses. Paragraphs 10 and 11 represent a new, more general direction of thought that grows out of his specific responses to the letter. Paragraph 12 returns to the letter and reinforces White's reactionary position on encroaching impersonality.

10

Does the writer use appropriate evidence and logic to support the points he or she is trying to make? White is not offering a formal or systematic argument, but a more personal consideration of his subject, so we should not necessarily expect detailed, enumerated evidence or other methodical forms of support. Instead, he offers imaginative and playful appeals based on personal experience, particularly in paragraphs 3, 4, 8, 9, 10, and 11. Though his appeals are witty, he does not provide any kind of support for his repeated claims of being inconvenienced, nor does he offer even an imaginative or whimsical alternative to computer processing as a means of dealing with the "tremendous increase in the use of checks."

What are the writer's assumptions about his or her audience? White's essay was written for the *New York Times,* so he could assume that his readers would be a reasonably well-informed group, many of whom would have themselves received similar letters from their banks. Even so, he is careful to explain the change the bank is demanding as well as its practical effects. (A further question you might consider is whether the writer assumes his or her readers will be generally sympathetic with, antagonistic toward, or neutral about the ideas being raised. What would you say about White's assumptions?)

What kind of language and imagery does the writer use? White is responding to what he regards as a ridiculous letter with very serious implications. His language is resolutely informal and conversational; phrases like "spooky numbers," "kept my mouth shut," "palm off," "enough lettuce," and "wear the pants" can be contrasted to the kind of communication he is criticizing. Yet when he has a serious point to make (for example, that computers "are deficient in humor, they are not intuitive, and they are not aware of the imponderables"), his language becomes more formal. His images—particularly his personification of the bank as a letter-writing entity—are comic or wryly sarcastic, but, as with his language, they don't overwhelm his underlying seriousness.

In responding to questions such as these, a reader is able to take a piece of writing apart and examine its components to see how it works. In many situations, so careful an analysis won't be necessary: you would have little reason, for example, to analyze a comprehensive textbook in this way. However, analytical skill can be applied to a wide variety of activities and, in particular, can help a reader move beyond simply personal responses to a more systematic evaluation of a piece of writing.

Suppose that your initial response to the White essay was something like, "I enjoyed this; it was funny." A second analytical reading then helped you to understand the workings of the essay and how the tone and imagery contributed to your interest and appreciation. Further analysis of your own initial responses perhaps led you to realize that you share White's suspicion of computers and

11

his subversive reaction to impersonal, bureaucratic pronouncements. This, in turn, has given you a sense of how others, who do not particularly share your views, might respond. Now you may develop a more systematic evaluation of the essay, using topics like the following to assess or judge the essay:

Purpose. White has succeeded well in presenting his own reactions with wit and grace. His conversational tone and his wry imagery allow a reader to sympathize with his very human rebellion against being inconvenienced because of the requirements of a machine.

Organization. Organizing his essay around the letter he received from his bank is an effective way for White to move from his specific responses to his more general considerations about the relationship between technology and human life. This organization also leads him to his important central image of a bank that forgets "to sign its name."

Evidence. Because White is relating his responses rather than arguing a position, the personal evidence he presents (the inconvenience the new rules will cause him, the computer-composed poem, and so on) is sufficient to communicate aptly and forcefully his reason for feeling the way he does. What White's evidence does not do, however, is to convince us that carrying checks with the magnetic code is a terrible inconvenience. White simply assumes that his reader will agree. Consequently, his general comments on computer technology—particularly from the perspective of over thirty years—don't carry the weight they might.

Summary. White's essay is an entertaining and thought-provoking revelation of what it's like to be told to modify old habits in order to conform to the dictates of new technology. The clarity of his organization, the grace of his style, and the wit of his personality are engaging and continuously appealing. Although we may not finally agree with the specific basis for his objections or with his underlying argument, we can't help but be persuaded by his sincerity, skill, and good sense that his attitudes are admirably humane and that they suggest some of the perils that beset an increasingly complex society.

This, of course, is only the beginning of only one evaluation. These notations—or another set that might be entirely contradictory—could be expanded and developed into an evaluative essay that presents reasons and evidence based on further research, perhaps into other essays by White or studies of computerized banking. Such an essay might be highly supportive (as our sample summary would indicate), or highly critical ("Though White's essay is very clever, the subversive point of view he expresses here is just a few steps from anarchy"), or it might take an intermediate position. It might concentrate on the consequences of the writer's ideas, or the success of the writer's methods, or some combination of the two.

As you may already have begun to realize, becoming a more astute reader can lay the groundwork for becoming a more effective writer. The more reading we do—the more we understand our role as a reader—the more we learn about what it means to be an audience. By paying attention to our responses, by examining them in order to analyze and evaluate what we read, we can begin to see more clearly *why* we feel well or poorly treated by a writer. Transferring such knowledge from our own experience as an audience to the audience for whom we are writing, we become more aware of what that intended audience will require. We become more concerned about the appropriate tone to take, about what does and doesn't need to be said about a topic, given our purpose, and we have a better idea of the organization necessary to gain and hold our audience's interest and bring our work to a satisfactory conclusion. We realize more fully the transaction that must take place, and how we as writers can encourage a reader to collaborate in the making of meaning. In "Writing and Rewriting" we will consider this subject in more detail.

WRITING AND REWRITING

As we discussed in "Reading and Rereading," expressing your ideas will often begin with recording your most immediate responses, jotting them down on a pad, in a journal, or in the margin of a book. Clearly, such jottings are not intended for a reader. You may be surprised to realize, however, that with thought and care and concern for an eventual audience, even the sketchiest notes can evolve into a significant, controlled piece of writing. This process of development and revision is rarely apparent when we read: all we see is the finished product, the piece of writing in its final form. But the polished work that is presented to an audience may, in fact, barely resemble what the writer started out with.

E. B. White didn't simply sit down the afternoon he received the warning from his bank and allow "Dear Mr. . . ." to flow out onto a page (if you haven't yet read White's essay, you'll find it on p. 1). The letter sparked a response, however—a sense of injustice, of annoyance at the threat of "embarrassment" and concern about the effects of technology—and White realized that here was at least the germ of an essay that might eventually find its way into print, earning him a bit of money and the satisfaction of reaching an audience with his concerns. His first thought, though, was merely to provide himself with a rough rendering of his immediate response. Consequently, his original notes (which we include on pp. 14–17) do little more than sketch out his basic intentions and establish a point of view.

White's notes bear almost no resemblance to his polished final draft as it appeared in the *New York Times*. We see White beginning with his immediate

I seldom carry a checkbook
because I like to travel light
but I always have money
in the bank (It is an
old habit of mine that
I can't seem to break)
and I feel that I should
be free to dispense this
money without any
embarrassment to myself.
Now, because of the Federal
Reserve's Knuckling under,
I will not be privileged to
write a blank check.

The ~~ol...~~ danger in a
machine culture is that ~~th~~
in the enjoyment of
the convenience of machines,
~~will to~~ we ~~some~~, will ~~overshadow~~
their disadvantages to others

The danger in a machine
culture is not that ~~machine~~
~~will take over our thinking~~
~~and dominate it or lives~~, but
~~that even, tho~~ the convenience
of machines may come to
overshadow the losses we suffer
~~from their~~ by reason of their
peculiar requirements.

Computers free the Federal Reserve from arduous and voluminous ~~and~~ operations in clearing checks. But in so doing they deprive *narrow* the consumer's of ~~but the privilege~~ *right* of instructing his bank in a casual, agreeable manner

The man who foresaw all
this was a man named
Orwell. and he foresaw
pretty good. If were
not careful. we may
wake up some morning
and find that what he
predicted has come to
pass.

personal response—his desire to dispense his money without any embarrassment or inconvenience to himself—and then moving on to generalize, to expand his annoyance over the particular letter to the larger issue of "the danger in a machine culture." Thus, he establishes the meaning and purpose that will govern his final essay. But there is little attempt to formulate a coherent design at this point. In fact, it is almost comforting to see how messy these initial notes are, when we realize the product for which they will provide the foundation.

Even as White is scribbling notes to himself, however, with little concern for coherence and the needs of his eventual reader, he is his own critic. He is listening to himself as he writes, thinking about how his words go together, and revising when he's not quite satisfied. He has, for example, reworked the sentence about "the danger in a machine culture" several times, trying to get it right (although, as we'll see in his subsequent drafts, this central idea would continue to give him trouble). But he is not particularly concerned with correctness; for instance, he lets stand a sentence like "The man who foresaw all this was a man named Orwell, and he foresaw pretty good." No sentence like this will, in fact, appear in the final draft, but what White seems to be after here is a kind of aptness. Orwell is a touchstone for White's ideas, a way of getting at what he wants to say and finding the words to generalize about his particular situation.

Based on these very rough notes, White typed a first draft, onto which he wrote in further revisions (see pp. 19–21).

This step from notes to first draft is significant: the essay is actually beginning to take shape here. White has used the letter from his bank to provide an opening and conclusion, but you'll note that he has not yet discovered the precise design that will allow his finished work to revolve around this letter. In fact, he has to wrench his attention back to the letter in the final paragraph, after a digression about his bank statement and balancing his checkbook. Nor has he quite developed the important image of the bank as a letter writer (although he *has* begun to personify the bank in his opening sentence and later on when he writes, "Banks love money . . ."; and he has also—perhaps for very practical reasons—assumed the pose of not being able to remember his bank's name). The idea about "the danger in a machine culture," which he struggled with in his original notes, appears here in a quite different form—a specific reference to the bank accommodating the Federal Reserve rather than customers—and, consequently, the incident has not yet been fully generalized.

Again, though, White is his own critic. The draft is messy and chewed over, with typed emendations as well as handwritten ones. Some of these changes seem to show White trying to capture fleeting thoughts, slapping them down on paper, as he did in his notes, to save and cull from later. Others are based on his concern for how an audience will respond (the deletion of the line about banks employing "retarded children" is a good example), while still others are

which I don't often do but which I
consider a great convenience in
certain circumstances.

My bank, which I have forgotten the name of
in the excitement of the moment, sent me a ~~notice~~ warning the other
day. It ~~read~~ worded =: "An important notice to all our checking account
customers." The burden of this communication was ~~this~~ that
~~the Federal Reserve System~~ I would no longer be allowed to
write
~~admit~~ checks that did not bear the special series of
"magnetic ink numbers" along the base. ~~Now~~ My bank said ~~~~
the Federal Reserve System had notified them that it will not
accept for processing any checks that don't bear these curious form
numbers. ~~(Thix~~ For example, I would not be allowed to write a check on a blank
(I've never been very fond of these numbers, since
I first laid eyes on them---they look tonme kike numbers that
have been ~~run over~~ backed into by a dump truck or have developed rheumoatoid
joints
arthritis, and their knuckles have swollen. But, I have kept my
mouth shut, until now.) Now it appears that we are going
to knuckle under to machines, and that I am no longer orivelegd
to write a check on a blank form, because it lacks these ~~~~ spooky
litttle numbers. This, I thinkm is a defeat, a surrender. (
I plan to go on ~~wxix~~ instructing h bank,and I can't think of it
name, to dispense my money in the way I want it dispensed, witjout
any reference to magnetic ink numbers. I will be ~~~~ iterested t
to see what gappens.
The notice I received says that if I try to
~~put over~~ a check that lacks the magnetic ink numbers, it cannot
be processed without delay, extra handling charges, and possible
embarrassment." ~~~~

19

2

rather easily embarrassed---it doesn't take much----and I ~~would like~~ *of course am eager*

to ~~know~~ *learn* what form this embarrassment is going to take if I should

decide to write a check using the old blank form that has proved

so convenient for I don't know how many decades, when one is stuck
without one's checkbook or enough lettuce to carry the day.
            The reason given by my bank for this tightening

of its service is ~~that~~ this: "The tremendous increase in the use of

checks made it necessary for the Federal Reserve to establish a

completely computerized operation for processing all checks from all

banks. Their computer can function only when proper magnetic numbers
            Well, I can believe that last
are used." ~~Ixcanxbelievexthixxlast~~ part, about the computer requiring

a special diet of funny numbers, ---this I can believe. But I am

suspicious of that first statement, about how the Federal Reserve
would have been unable   had gone over
couldn't carry on unless it went over to machines. I think the truth
                        and adventurous
is ~~itxfoundxit~~ the Federal Reserve found machines handy, and that's
                        But   we had had, in this country
why it went over to them. Suppose there had been a tremendous increase
                        and nobody had got round to inventing the computer
in the use of checks but the computer hadn't been invented---what would

h va happened then? Would ~~bankingxhavex~~ banks have ~~givenxupxthex~~
            Would the Federal Reserve System have collapsed from exhaustion *the reflexing*
thrown in the sponge? I know banks better than that---they would
            and adventurous bankers
have cleared those checks ~~if they had to employ retarded children~~ to
            and they are not easily deflected from accumulating it.
~~doxit~~ Banks love money. ~~SoxdoxxIyxxcomxxtvxxkkinkxvxpfxitvxvxv~~

Come to think it, I love money, too. I am a lifelong checking account

patron and have had to be ~~kromxxxk~~ extremely thrifty because of my

refusal to balance my checkbook in the space on the left where you

are supposd to keep track of what you've been spending and depositing.

I've never done that, on the theory that it is a waste of time--also
            subtract quick
I don't add good, and my figures would be ~~deceptive~~ *misleading* because inaccurate.

Instead, I practice thrift and never know my balance until I receive *my*
            in the days before machines
(Monthly) statement. Speaking of bank statements, mine used to arrive the first

20

3

of the month and was legible and decipherable and coherent. Now, since machines have taken over, it arrives anywhere from the first of the month to the eighth of the month, and is indecipherable, largely except to a man hell bent on deciphering something.

The notice

To get back to the warning from my bank, it ended: "So remember...be sure to use only your own personal checks with pre-encoded magnetic ink numbering. It takes both your account number and your signature for your check to clear properly. Thank you very much."

"improvements," revisions of vocabulary and syntax to clarify meaning or create more graceful, forceful expression.

In his second draft, White continues to revise, to tighten his structure and refine his language (see pp. 23–25).

The pieces have begun to fall more gracefully into place here. Most important, perhaps, White gets rid of the digression about bank statements at the end of his first draft and replaces it with the more general reflections he has been aiming toward all along. Note how the troublesome sentence from his notes about "the danger in a machine culture" has found its place in the penultimate paragraph of this second draft. (Note, as well, how White has continued to rework and refine it.)

In the handwritten emendations of this draft, we also see White sharpening the wit of his reflections, particularly as he develops his wry personification of his bank and computers in general ("a certain magnetism that computers insist on" and "machines that admire these numbers"). And it is not until now, in his attempt to bring the essay to a satisfactory close, that White adds the final, memorable image of "a bank forgetting to sign its name," an image that eventually grows very naturally out of his process of revising, of focusing and clarifying his ideas in order to make his point most vividly for his audience. Names are no longer important; all that matters now is a magnetic code for computers to read.

Reading White's finished essay as it appeared in the *New York Times,* we have a hard time realizing that he didn't know exactly what he had in mind when he sat down to write. When a piece of writing is successful, we do not see the seams; the words carry us along so that we are not aware of the writer's process. But it is clear from White's notes and his drafts that this graceful, carefully conceived essay required a great deal of work: jotting, scratching out, drafting, rewriting, private questions and decisions, moments of inspiration when the connections began to seem clear, when the work seemed to pay off. What we learn from White's manuscripts is that ideas don't spring full-blown from a writer's mind into a clear, coherent form. Rather, ideas may tumble out in unformed, fragmented ways that can be developed, modified, and sharpened draft after draft.

Composition is, then, a process, and the practical implications for student writers are readily apparent. It takes time to put what you have to say, your most personal and immediate responses, into a form that an audience can understand and appreciate, into words that will best express your intentions. Waiting to begin a writing assignment until the night before it is due will not allow this sort of time. Fully developed ideas are the result of revising, of working step by step, and require a series of working sessions over the course of several days or several weeks. Only then can you take full advantage of your reading and writing skills in order to produce a final draft that seems to be ready

My bank, which I have forgotten the name of
in the excitement of the moment, sent me a warning the other
day. It was headed: "An important notice to all our checking
account customers." The burden of this communication was that
I would no longer be allowed to write checks that did not bear
the special series of magnetic ink numbers along the base. My
bank said the Federal Reserve System had notified them that it
will not accept for processing any checks that don't show these
knobby little digits. For example, I would no longer be free
to write a check on a blank form, because it would lack ~~the~~ a
~~magnetic numbers~~ certain magnetism that computers insist on.

I first encountered these spooky numbers a few
years back and took a dislike to them. ~~They~~ They looked like numbers
that had been run over by a dump truck, or that had developed
rheumatoid arthritis and their joints had swollen. But I kept
my mouth shut [about them] as they seemed to be doing me no harm.
Now, however, it appears that we are all going to knuckle under
to machines ~~and will have to forego~~ the pleasure and convenience
of writing a check on an ordinary, non-magnetic piece of paper.
My signature used to be enough to prod my bank into dispatching
some of my money to some needy individual or firm, ~~but~~ not any
more. This, I think, is a defeat for all---a surrender. In
order to accommodate the Federal Reserve system, we are ~~going~~ asked
to put ourselves out.

The notice I received says that if I try to

270

2

palm off a check that lacks the magnetic ink numbers, the check
cannot be processed without "delay, extra handling charges, and
possible embarrassment."   I embarrass easy---it doesn't take
much, really---and naturally I am eager to learn what form this
embarrassment will take if I should decide to write a check using
the old blank form that has proved so convenient for I don't know
how many decades on those occasions when one is stuck without
his checkbook or enough lettuce to carry the day.

       "The tremendous increase in the use of checks,"
writes my bank , warming to its subject, "made it necessary for
the Federal Reserve to establish a completely computerized operation for processing all checks from all banks. Their computer
can function only when proper magnetic numbers are used." Well,
I can believe that last part, about the computer requiring a
special diet of ~~dxxxxgxdxxxxhxxx~~ malformed numbers; but I am
suspicious of that first statement, about how the Federal Reserve
would have been unable to carry on unless it went completely over to machines.
I suspect that the Federal Reserve simply found machines useful,
handy, and ~~sustaining to its ego~~ adventurous. But suppose ~~there~~ we had had,
in this country, a tremendous increase in the use of checks and
nobody had yet got round to inventing the computer---what would have
happened then? Am I ~~supposed~~ expected to believe that the Federal Reserve
and all ~~their~~ its member banks would have thrown in the sponge? I.
know banks better than that. Banks love money and are not easily
deflected from the ~~xxhxxxixg~~ delicious business of accumulating
it. ~~Sxxxhxxxxhxxxxxxxxxxxxxxxxx~~ Love would have found a way.
Checks would have cleared.

       I'm not against machines, as are some people

3

who feel that the computer is leading us down the primrose
trail. I ~~kxxxxxxkkxx~~ like machines---particularly the egg
[the highest point has yet reached]
beater, which is the machine at its finest and most mysterious.
~~Bxk~~ I8m only against machines when the convenience they afford
[some is considered more important than]
to ~~xxxxxxx xxxxxxxxxxxxx~~ overshadwos the ~~ix~~inconvience they
cause to ~~xxx xxxx~~ *[all]*. In short, I don't think computers should
[50]
wear the pants, or even make the decisions---~~sxxxxxxxx~~. They
lack humor, and they are not intuitive--or even aware ofthe
mponderables. I read a poem once written by a computer but,
didn't care much for it. It seemed to me I could write a better
[100]
one myself, if I put my mind to it, and my heart in it.

    And now I must look around for a blank check.
It's time I found out what form ~~thxxxxxxkxxxx~~ my new embarrssment
is going to take. First, thoulg, I'll have o remember the
[150]
name of my bank. It'll come to me, if I sit here long enough.

*Oddly enough, the warning notice I received
contained no signature. Imagine a bank
forgetting to sign its name!*

174
278
270
―――
722

for an audience. What you end with will very likely come a long way from how you begin.

You've just seen, of course, how E. B. White began. You'll find what he ended with on page 1.

ACKNOWLEDGING SOURCES

In most of the writing that you do both during and after college, you will probably find yourself drawing upon the ideas, information, and statements of others, interpreting this material, and putting it together with your own experience, observation, and thought to generate new ideas of your own. Some of this material will come from your reading, some of it from lectures and class discussions, some of it from conversations and interviews. Our thinking about things does not, after all, take place in a vacuum, but is shaped by a wide array of influences and sources. Thus, we invariably have an obligation to others that we can only repay by giving credit where credit is due—that is, by acknowledging the sources we have used in our thinking and writing.

To acknowledge your intellectual debts is by no means a confession that your work is unoriginal or without merit. In fact, original work in every field and profession invariably builds in some way and to some extent on the prior work of other researchers and thinkers. Most pieces that you find in this book, except for those that deal entirely with personal experience, include some kind of acknowledgment or reference to the ideas, information, or statements of others. By acknowledging their sources, the writers of these pieces implicitly establish exactly what is new or special in their own way of thinking about something. Acknowledging sources will also enable readers to corroborate your claims and to find material that they wish to investigate in connection with their own research and writing. For a variety of important reasons, then, you should always make sure that you acknowledge any and all sources that you have used in preparing a piece of writing.

In order to get some idea of the various ways in which sources can be acknowledged, you might find it useful to scan several of the pieces in this collection. Some writers, you will notice, cite only the names of authors or interviewees and/or the titles of works from which they have gathered ideas and information or quoted statements; these citations are incorporated into the written discussion, as you can see by looking at Martin Luther King, Jr.'s "Pilgrimage to Nonviolence," the Associated Press "Report of an Airplane Crash," or Susan Fraker's "Why Women Aren't Getting to the Top." Other writers use footnotes or endnotes in which they provide not only names of authors or interviewees and titles of works, but also dates of publication or of interviews and specific page references, as you can see by looking at Theodore R. Sizer's "What High School Is," Carol Gilligan's "Interviewing Adolescent Girls," or Antonio R. Damasio's "Face Perception without Recognition." Finally, some writers, instead of using footnotes, provide author and page references in the text of their discussion, and include more detailed publication data, such as titles and dates of publication, in a complete list of works cited at the end of their discussion, as you can see by looking at John Fiske's "Romancing the Rock."

These various forms of acknowledgment are usually determined by the different purposes and audiences for which authors have written their pieces. For example, personal essays, newspaper reports, and magazine articles, which are written for a general audience, tend to rely on a more casual and shorthand form of acknowledgment, citing only the author and/or title of the source in the body of the discussion. Pieces written for a more specialized audience, such as academic research papers and scholarly articles or books, tend to rely on a more detailed and systematic form of acknowledgment, using either footnotes, or a combination of references in the text with a complete list of works cited at the end of the text. These specialized forms of acknowledgment vary somewhat from one field to another, but in general you will find that research papers in the arts and humanities tend to follow the guidelines set down in the *Modern Language Association Handbook for Writers of Research Papers*, Third Edition (1988), and that research papers in the social sciences and sciences tend to follow the guidelines set down in *The Publication Manual of the American Psychological Association*, Third Edition (1983).

If you are ever in doubt about the form of acknowledgment to be used in any of your courses, don't hesitate to ask your instructor for guidance. Most instructors do have special preferences of one kind or another. But whatever their special preferences may be, they all expect you to acknowledge your sources.

REFLECTING

Here in "Reflecting," as in other parts of this collection, you will encounter writing that touches upon a wide range of topics—from a high school graduation in Arkansas to a sacred landmark in Oklahoma, from the structure of a grain of salt to the intricacies of contract law. But you will also find that the writing in this particular section relies very heavily on personal experience. This personal element may strike you at first as being out of place in a college textbook. However, if you consider the matter just a bit, you will see that personal experience is a basic source of knowledge and understanding. Think for a moment about someone you have known for a long time, or about a long-remembered event in your life; then think about what you have learned from being with that person or going through that event, and you will see that personal experience is, indeed, a valuable source of knowledge. You will probably also notice that in thinking about that person or event you rely very heavily on your remembrance of things past—on your memory of particular words, or deeds, or gestures, or scenes that are especially important to you. Your memory, after all, is the storehouse of your personal knowledge, and whenever you look into this storehouse, you will invariably find an image or impression of your past experience. So, you should not be surprised to find the authors in this section looking into their own memories as they might look into a mirror. Ultimately, the activity of looking back is a hallmark of reflection because it involves writers in recalling and thinking about some aspect of their world in order to make sense of it for themselves and for others.

This essential quality of reflective writing can be seen in the following passage from George Orwell's "Shooting an Elephant":

> One day something happened which in a roundabout way was enlightening. It was a tiny incident in itself, but it gave me a better glimpse than I had had before of the real nature of imperialism—the real motives for which despotic governments act. Early one morning the sub-inspector at a police station the other end of the town rang me up on the phone and said that an elephant was ravaging the bazaar. Would I please come and do something about it? I did not know what I could do, but I wanted to see what was happening and I got on to a pony and started out.

This passage, which comes from the third paragraph of Orwell's essay, clearly presents him as being in a reflective frame of mind. In the opening sentence, for example, he looks back to a specific event from his personal experiences in Burma—to "One day" when "something happened." And in the midst of looking back, he also makes clear that this event is important to him because "in a roundabout way" it "was enlightening." Again, in the second sentence, he looks back not only to the event, "a tiny incident in itself," but also to the understanding that he gained from the event—"a better glimpse than I had had before of the real nature of imperialism—the real motives for which despotic governments act." Having announced the general significance of this event, he then returns to looking back at the event itself, to recalling the particular things that happened that day—the phone call informing him "that an elephant was ravaging the bazaar," the request that he "come and do something about it," and his decision to get "on to a pony" in order "to see what was happening."

This alternation between recalling things and commenting on their significance is typical not only of Orwell's piece, but of all the writing in this section. Sometimes, the alternation takes place within a single sentence, as in the opening of the previous passage. Sometimes, the alternation occurs between sentences or clusters of sentences, as in the following paragraph from Loren Eiseley's "The Bird and the Machine":

> I suppose their little bones have years ago been lost among the stones and winds of those high glacial pastures. I suppose their feathers blew eventually into the piles of tumbleweed beneath the straggling cattle fences and rotted there in the mountain snows, along with dead steers and all the other things that drift to an end in the corners of the wire. I do not quite know why I should be thinking of birds over the *New York Times* at breakfast, particularly the birds of my youth half a continent away. It is a funny thing what the brain will do with memories and how it will treasure them and finally bring them into odd juxtapositions with other things, as though it wanted to make a design, or get some meaning out of them, whether you want it or not, or even see it.

The first two sentences of this passage portray Eiseley as being in a contemplative mood, remembering some birds that he had evidently seen years ago in a high mountain pasture and wondering what became of them. But in the third sentence he is no longer wondering about the fate of the birds, so much as about the focus of his thoughts, about why he "should be thinking of birds over the *New York Times* at breakfast." His curiosity about the movement of his own mind then provokes him in the fourth sentence to reflect on the workings of the human brain, especially on "what the brain will do with memories." Though he ranges quite widely here and later in the piece, each image or idea that comes to his mind is occasioned either by a preceding memory or reflection or by some aspect of his immediate situation, such as his reading of the *Times*.

30

His thoughts develop, then, by a process of association and suggestion, one thing leading to another. This linked sequence of memories, images, other bits of information, and ideas is typical of reflection. Reflective writing thus echoes the process that Eiseley attributes to the brain—calling upon memories, bringing them into "odd juxtapositions with other things," in order "to make a design, or get some meaning out of them."

The alternation between recalling and interpreting will vary from writer to writer, and work to work, depending on the details of the experience and the author's reflective purpose. Nevertheless, every piece of reflective writing will contain both kinds of material, for every reflective writer is concerned not only with sharing something memorable, but also with showing why it is memorable. And as it happens, most memorable experiences, images, or bits of information stick in our minds because they give us, as Orwell says, "a better glimpse than [we] had had before of the real nature of" someone, something, or some aspect of the world. So, as a reader of reflective writing, you should always be attentive not only to the details of an author's recollected experience, but also to the "glimpse" that it gives the author, and you, into the "real nature" of things. And in your own reflective writing, you should make sure that you convey both dimensions of your experience—both what happened and what the happenings enabled you to see.

THE RANGE OF REFLECTIVE WRITING

The range of reflective writing is in one sense limitless, for it necessarily includes the full range of things that make up our personal experience or the personal experience of anyone else in the world. Reflecting, in other words, may deal with anything that anyone has ever seen, or heard, or done, or thought about, and considered memorable enough to write about. Though the range of reflective writing is extraordinarily broad, the subject of any particular piece is likely to be very specific, and as it happens, most pieces can be classified in terms of a few recurrent types of subject matter.

A single, memorable event is often the center of attention in reflective writing, as in Maya Angelou's "Graduation," or George Orwell's "Shooting an Elephant." In reflecting on this kind of subject, the author will usually provide not only a meticulous detailing of the event itself, but also some opening background information that serves as a context for making sense of the event. In "Graduation," for example, Maya Angelou tells about all the pregraduation excitement in her home, at school, and around town before turning to the graduation ceremony itself. And in "Shooting an Elephant," Orwell gives an overall description of his life as a colonial officer in Burma before he turns to the story about shooting the elephant. The event, in turn, is of interest not only in itself but also for what it reveals to the author (and the reader) about some significant aspect of experience. Thus for Angelou, graduation remains memorable because it helped her to see how African-American people have been "sustained" by "Black known and unknown poets," and for Orwell, the shooting remains memorable because it helped him to see "the real nature of imperialism."

A notable person is a subject that often moves people to writing reflectively, as in N. Scott Momaday's "The Way to Rainy Mountain," or in sections of Patricia J. Williams's "On Being the Object of Property." In reflecting on a particular individual, writers may seek to discover and convey what they consider to be the most essential aspects of that person's character. They may survey a number of memorable incidents or images from the person's life. Momaday, for example, recalls not only the stories and legends that he heard from his grandmother, but also "the several postures that were peculiar to her" and her "long, rambling prayers." Or, alternatively, a writer may shift focus from the person's individual character to the relationship between herself and her subject. Patricia J. Williams gives us only a few sparse hints about her godmother Marjorie's enigmatic personality, but reflects intensely upon caring for her during her final illness and, in doing so, crystallizes many of her own ideas about isolation, exchange, and community.

Instead of concentrating on a particular person or event, reflective writing may center on a specific problem or significant issue in the past experience of an author, as in Frederick Douglass's "Learning to Read and Write," or Martin Luther King, Jr.'s "Pilgrimage to Nonviolence." A piece with this kind of subject is likely to touch upon a number of persons and events, and to encompass a substantial period of time, in the process of recalling and reflecting upon the problem with which it is concerned. Douglass, for example, covers seven years of his life in his piece about the problem of learning to read and write, and King recalls events and issues throughout his life that led him to espouse the principles of "nonviolent resistance." In each case, the breadth of coverage serves to reveal the scope and complexity of the problem, as well as the author's special understanding of it.

As you can see from just this brief survey of possibilities, reflective writing may deal with a single event, several events, or a whole lifetime of events. It may be as restricted in its attention as a close-up or as all encompassing as a wide-angle shot. But no matter how little, or how much, experience it takes into account, reflective writing is always decisively focused through the author's persistent attempt to make sense of the past, to push memory to the point of understanding the significance of experience.

METHODS OF REFLECTING

Your experience is unique, as is your memory, so in a sense you know the best methods to follow whenever you are of a mind to reflect upon something that interests you. But once you have recalled something in detail and made sense of it for yourself, you are still faced with the problem of how to present it to readers in a way that will also make sense to them. Given the fact that your readers will probably not be familiar with your experience, you will need to be very careful in selecting and organizing your material so that you give them a clearly detailed account of it. By the same token, you will need to give special emphasis to aspects or elements of your experience that will enable them to understand its significance. Usually, you will find that your choice of subject suggests a corresponding method of presenting it clearly and meaningfully to your readers.

If your reflections are focused on a single, circumscribed event, you will probably find it most appropriate to use a narrative presentation, telling your readers what happened in a relatively straightforward chronological order. Though you cover the event from beginning to end, your narrative should be carefully designed to emphasize the details that you consider most striking and significant. In "Shooting an Elephant," for example, Orwell devotes the largest segment in his piece to covering the very, very brief period of a few moments when he finds himself on the verge of having to shoot the elephant despite his strong desire not to do so. In fact, he devotes one-third of his essay to these few moments of inner conflict because they bring about one of his major insights— "that when the white man turns tyrant it is his own freedom that he destroys." So in telling about a memorable event of your own, you should deliberately pace your story to make it build toward some kind of climax or surprise or decisive incident, which in turn leads to a moment of insight for you (and your reader).

If your reflections are focused on a particular person, you will probably find it necessary to use both narrative and descriptive methods of presentation, telling about several events in order to make clear to readers the character and thought of the person in question. Though you rely heavily on narration, you will not be able to cover incidents in as much detail as if you were focusing on a single event. Instead, you will find it necessary to isolate only the most striking and significant details from each incident you choose to recall. Momaday, for instance, relates his grandmother's background by way of the history of the Kiowa. But to describe her individual character, he isolates particular details— her postures, her praying, her dress—that are carefully chosen to resonate with the "ancient awe" which Momaday says was "in her" and with which he regards her. So, too, in writing about an individual whom you have known, you should carefully select and arrange the details that you recall to make them convey a clear and compelling impression of that person's character.

If your reflections are focused on a particular problem or issue in your past experience, you will probably need to combine narrative, descriptive, and explanatory methods of presentation, bringing together your recollections of numerous events and persons in order to reveal the nature and significance of the problem. Although you will survey the problem chronologically from beginning to end, you will also need to organize your narrative so that it highlights the essential aspects, elements, or facets of the problem. For example, in "Pilgrimage to Nonviolence," King immediately focuses on the "new and sometimes complex doctrinal lands" through which he traveled. And from this point on, he recalls the various theological and philosophical ideas with which he struggled in formulating his belief in nonviolence. So in writing about a particular problem of your own, your recollections should be deliberately selected and organized to highlight your special understanding of the issue.

No matter what specific combination of methods you use in your reflective writing, you will probably find, as do most writers, that a striking recollection is the most effective way to interest your readers and that a significant observation about experience is the most rewarding means to send them on their way. In the following selections, you will get to see how a wide variety of writers use language to produce some very striking and significant pieces of reflection.

Arts and Humanities

GRADUATION

Maya Angelou

In her four volumes of autobiography, Maya Angelou (b. 1928) has written vividly of her struggles to achieve success as an actor, a dancer, a songwriter, a teacher, and a writer. An active worker in the civil rights movement in the 1960s, Angelou continues to focus much of her writing on racial issues. The following selection is from I Know Why the Caged Bird Sings *(1969), in which she writes, "I speak to the Black experience, but I am always talking about the human condition."*

The children in Stamps trembled visibly with anticipation.[1] Some adults were excited too, but to be certain the whole young population had come down with graduation epidemic. Large classes were graduating from both the grammar school and the high school. Even those who were years removed from their own day of glorious release were anxious to help with preparations as a kind of dry run. The junior students who were moving into the vacating classes' chairs were tradition-bound to show their talents for leadership and management. They strutted through the school and around the campus exerting pressure on the lower grades. Their authority was so new that occasionally if they pressed a little too hard it had to be overlooked. After all, next term was coming, and it never hurt a sixth grader to have a play sister in the eighth grade, or a tenth-year student to be able to call a twelfth grader Bubba. So all was endured in a spirit of shared understanding. But the graduating classes themselves were the nobility. Like travelers with exotic destinations on their minds, the graduates

[1] Stamps: a town in Arkansas. [Eds.]

were remarkably forgetful. They came to school without their books, or tablets or even pencils. Volunteers fell over themselves to secure replacements for the missing equipment. When accepted, the willing workers might or might not be thanked, and it was of no importance to the pregraduation rites. Even teachers were respectful of the now quiet and aging seniors, and tended to speak to them, if not as equals, as beings only slightly lower than themselves. After tests were returned and grades given, the student body, which acted like an extended family, knew who did well, who excelled, and what piteous ones had failed.

Unlike the white high school, Lafayette County Training School distin- 2 guished itself by having neither lawn, nor hedges, nor tennis court, nor climbing ivy. Its two buildings (main classrooms, the grade school and home economics) were set on a dirt hill with no fence to limit either its boundaries or those of bordering farms. There was a large expanse to the left of the school which was used alternately as a baseball diamond or basketball court. Rusty hoops on swaying poles represented the permanent recreational equipment, although bats and balls could be borrowed from the P.E. teacher if the borrower was qualified and if the diamond wasn't occupied.

Over this rocky area relieved by a few shady tall persimmon trees the grad- 3 uating class walked. The girls often held hands and no longer bothered to speak to the lower students. There was a sadness about them, as if this old world was not their home and they were bound for higher ground. The boys, on the other hand, had become more friendly, more outgoing. A decided change from the closed attitude they projected while studying for finals. Now they seemed not ready to give up the old school, the familiar paths and classrooms. Only a small percentage would be continuing on to college—one of the South's A & M (agricultural and mechanical) schools, which trained Negro youths to be car- penters, farmers, handymen, masons, maids, cooks and baby nurses. Their future rode heavily on their shoulders, and blinded them to the collective joy that had pervaded the lives of the boys and girls in the grammar school gradu- ating class.

Parents who could afford it had ordered new shoes and ready-made clothes 4 for themselves from Sears and Roebuck or Montgomery Ward. They also engaged the best seamstresses to make the floating graduating dresses and to cut down secondhand pants which would be pressed to a military slickness for the important event.

Oh, it was important, all right. Whitefolks would attend the ceremony, and 5 two or three would speak of God and home, and the Southern way of life, and Mrs. Parsons, the principal's wife, would play the graduation march while the lower-grade graduates paraded down the aisles and took their seats below the platform. The high school seniors would wait in empty classrooms to make their dramatic entrance.

In the Store I was the person of the moment. The birthday girl. The center. 6

Bailey had graduated the year before,[2] although to do so he had had to forfeit all pleasures to make up for his time lost in Baton Rouge.

My class was wearing butter-yellow piqué dresses, and Momma launched   7
out on mine. She smocked the yoke into tiny crisscrossing puckers, then shirred the rest of the bodice. Her dark fingers ducked in and out of the lemony cloth as she embroidered raised daisies around the hem. Before she considered herself finished she had added a crocheted cuff on the puff sleeves, and a point crocheted collar.

I was going to be lovely. A walking model of all the various styles of fine   8
hand sewing and it didn't worry me that I was only twelve years old and merely graduating from the eighth grade. Besides, many teachers in Arkansas Negro schools had only that diploma and were licensed to impart wisdom.

The days had become longer and more noticeable. The faded beige of former   9
times had been replaced with strong and sure colors. I began to see my class-mates' clothes, their skin tones, and the dust that waved off pussy willows. Clouds that lazed across the sky were objects of great concern to me. Their shiftier shapes might have held a message that in my new happiness and with a little bit of time I'd soon decipher. During that period I looked at the arch of heaven so religiously my neck kept a steady ache. I had taken to smiling more often, and my jaws hurt from the unaccustomed activity. Between the two physical sore spots, I suppose I could have been uncomfortable, but that was not the case. As a member of the winning team (the graduating class of 1940) I had outdistanced unpleasant sensations by miles. I was headed for the freedom of open fields.

Youth and social approval allied themselves with me and we trammeled   10
memories of slights and insults. The wind of our swift passage remodeled my features. Lost tears were pounded to mud and then to dust. Years of withdrawal were brushed aside and left behind, as hanging ropes of parasitic moss.

My work alone had awarded me a top place and I was going to be one of   11
the first called in the graduating ceremonies. On the classroom blackboard, as well as on the bulletin board in the auditorium, there were blue stars and white stars and red stars. No absences, no tardinesses, and my academic work was among the best of the year. I could say the preamble to the Constitution even faster than Bailey. We timed ourselves often: "WethepeopleoftheUnited-Statesinordertoformamoreperfectunion. . . ." I had memorized the Presidents of the United States from Washington to Roosevelt in chronological as well as alphabetical order.

My hair pleased me too. Gradually the black mass had lengthened and   12
thickened, so that it kept at last to its braided pattern, and I didn't have to yank my scalp off when I tried to comb it.

---

[2] Bailey: the brother of the author. [Eds.]

Louise and I had rehearsed the exercises until we tired out ourselves. Henry   13
Reed was class valedictorian. He was a small, very black boy with hooded eyes,
a long, broad nose and an oddly shaped head. I had admired him for years
because each term he and I vied for the best grades in our class. Most often he
bested me, but instead of being disappointed I was pleased that we shared top
places between us. Like many Southern Black children, he lived with his
grandmother, who was as strict as Momma and as kind as she knew how to be.
He was courteous, respectful and soft-spoken to elders, but on the playground
he chose to play the roughest games. I admired him. Anyone, I reckoned,
sufficiently afraid or sufficiently dull could be polite. But to be able to operate
at a top level with both adults and children was admirable.

His valedictory speech was entitled "To Be or Not to Be." The rigid tenth-   14
grade teacher had helped him write it. He'd been working on the dramatic
stresses for months.

The weeks until graduation were filled with heady activities. A group of   15
small children were to be presented in a play about buttercups and daisies and
bunny rabbits. They could be heard throughout the building practicing their
hops and their little songs that sounded like silver bells. The older girls (non-
graduates, of course) were assigned the task of making refreshments for the
night's festivities. A tangy scent of ginger, cinnamon, nutmeg and chocolate
wafted around the home economics building as the budding cooks made samples
for themselves and their teachers.

In every corner of the workshop, axes and saws split fresh timber as the   16
woodshop boys made sets and stage scenery. Only the graduates were left out
of the general bustle. We were free to sit in the library at the back of the
building or look in quite detachedly, naturally, on the measures being taken for
our event.

Even the minister preached on graduation the Sunday before. His subject   17
was, "Let your light so shine that men will see your good works and praise your
Father, Who is in Heaven." Although the sermon was purported to be addressed
to us, he used the occasion to speak to backsliders, gamblers and general ne'er-
do-wells. But since he had called our names at the beginning of the service we
were mollified.

Among Negroes the tradition was to give presents to children going only   18
from one grade to another. How much more important this was when the
person was graduating at the top of the class. Uncle Willie and Momma had
sent away for a Mickey Mouse watch like Bailey's. Louise gave me four embroidered handkerchiefs. (I gave her crocheted doilies.) Mrs. Sneed, the minister's wife, made me an undershirt to wear for graduation, and nearly every
customer gave me a nickel or maybe even a dime with the instruction "Keep
on moving to higher ground," or some such encouragement.

Amazingly the great day finally dawned and I was out of bed before I knew   19 it. I threw open the back door to see it more clearly, but Momma said, "Sister, come away from that door and put your robe on."

I hoped the memory of that morning would never leave me. Sunlight was 20 itself young, and the day had none of the insistence maturity would bring it in a few hours. In my robe and barefoot in the backyard, under cover of going to see about my new beans, I gave myself up to the gentle warmth and thanked God that no matter what evil I had done in my life He had allowed me to live to see this day. Somewhere in my fatalism I had expected to die, accidentally, and never have the chance to walk up the stairs in the auditorium and gracefully receive my hard-earned diploma. Out of God's merciful bosom I had won reprieve.

Bailey came out in his robe and gave me a box wrapped in Christmas paper. 21 He said he had saved his money for months to pay for it. It felt like a box of chocolates, but I knew Bailey wouldn't save money to buy candy when we had all we could want under our noses.

He was as proud of the gift as I. It was a soft-leather-bound copy of a 22 collection of poems by Edgar Allan Poe, or, as Bailey and I called him, "Eap." I turned to "Annabel Lee" and we walked up and down the garden rows, the cool dirt between our toes, reciting the beautifully sad lines.

Momma made a Sunday breakfast although it was only Friday. After we 23 finished the blessing, I opened my eyes to find the watch on my plate. It was a dream of a day. Everything went smoothly and to my credit. I didn't have to be reminded or scolded for anything. Near evening I was too jittery to attend to chores, so Bailey volunteered to do all before his bath.

Days before, we had made a sign for the Store, and as we turned out the 24 lights Momma hung the cardboard over the doorknob. It read clearly: CLOSED. GRADUATION.

My dress fitted perfectly and everyone said that I looked like a sunbeam in 25 it. On the hill, going toward the school, Bailey walked behind with Uncle Willie, who muttered, "Go on, Ju." He wanted him to walk ahead with us because it embarrassed him to have to walk so slowly. Bailey said he'd let the ladies walk together, and the men would bring up the rear. We all laughed, nicely.

Little children dashed by out of the dark like fireflies. Their crepe-paper 26 dresses and butterfly wings were not made for running and we heard more than one rip, dryly, and the regretful "uh uh" that followed.

The school blazed without gaiety. The windows seemed cold and unfriendly 27 from the lower hill. A sense of ill-fated timing crept over me, and if Momma hadn't reached for my hand I would have drifted back to Bailey and Uncle Willie, and possibly beyond. She made a few slow jokes about my feet getting cold, and tugged me along to the now-strange building.

Around the front steps, assurance came back. There were my fellow "greats," 28 the graduating class. Hair brushed back, legs oiled, new dresses and pressed pleats, fresh pocket handkerchiefs and little handbags, all homesewn. Oh, we were up to snuff, all right. I joined my comrades and didn't even see my family go in to find seats in the crowded auditorium.

The school band struck up a march and all classes filed in as had been 29 rehearsed. We stood in front of our seats, as assigned, and on a signal from the choir director, we sat. No sooner had this been accomplished than the band started to play the national anthem. We rose again and sang the song, after which we recited the pledge of allegiance. We remained standing for a brief minute before the choir director and the principal signaled to us, rather desperately I thought, to take our seats. The command was so unusual that our carefully rehearsed and smooth-running machine was thrown off. For a full minute we fumbled for our chairs and bumped into each other awkwardly. Habits change or solidify under pressure, so in our state of nervous tension we had been ready to follow our usual assembly pattern: the American national anthem, then the pledge of allegiance, then the song every Black person I knew called the Negro National Anthem. All done in the same key, with the same passion and most often standing on the same foot.

Finding my seat at last, I was overcome with a presentiment of worse things 30 to come. Something unrehearsed, unplanned, was going to happen, and we were going to be made to look bad. I distinctly remember being explicit in the choice of pronoun. It was "we," the graduating class, the unit, that concerned me then.

The principal welcomed "parents and friends" and asked the Baptist minister 31 to lead us in prayer. His invocation was brief and punchy, and for a second I thought we were getting on the high road to right action. When the principal came back to the dais, however, his voice had changed. Sounds always affected me profoundly and the principal's voice was one of my favorites. During assembly it melted and lowed weakly into the audience. It had not been in my plan to listen to him, but my curiosity was piqued and I straightened up to give him my attention.

He was talking about Booker T. Washington, our "late great leader," who 32 said we can be as close as the fingers on the hand, etc. . . . Then he said a few vague things about friendship and the friendship of kindly people to those less fortunate than themselves. With that his voice nearly faded, thin, away. Like a river diminishing to a stream and then to a trickle. But he cleared his throat and said, "Our speaker tonight, who is also our friend, came from Texarkana to deliver the commencement address, but due to the irregularity of the train schedule, he's going to, as they say, 'speak and run.'" He said that we understood and wanted the man to know that we were most grateful for the time he was able to give us and then something about how we were willing always to adjust to another's program, and without more ado—"I give you Mr. Edward Donleavy."

Not one but two white men came through the door off-stage. The shorter   33
one walked to the speaker's platform, and the tall one moved to the center seat
and sat down. But that was our principal's seat, and already occupied. The
dislodged gentleman bounced around for a long breath or two before the Baptist
minister gave him his chair, then with more dignity than the situation deserved,
the minister walked off the stage.

Donleavy looked at the audience once (on reflection, I'm sure that he wanted   34
only to reassure himself that we were really there), adjusted his glasses and
began to read from a sheaf of papers.

He was glad "to be here and to see the work going on just as it was in the   35
other schools."

At the first "Amen" from the audience I willed the offender to immediate   36
death by choking on the word. But Amens and Yes, sir's began to fall around
the room like rain through a ragged umbrella.

He told us of the wonderful changes we children in Stamps had in store.   37
The Central School (naturally, the white school was Central) had already been
granted improvements that would be in use in the fall. A well-known artist was
coming from Little Rock to teach art to them. They were going to have the
newest microscopes and chemistry equipment for their laboratory. Mr. Donleavy
didn't leave us long in the dark over who made these improvements available
to Central High. Nor were we to be ignored in the general betterment scheme
he had in mind.

He said that he had pointed out to people at a very high level that one of   38
the first-line football tacklers at Arkansas Agricultural and Mechanical College
had graduated from good old Lafayette County Training School. Here fewer
Amen's were heard. Those few that did break through lay dully in the air with
the heaviness of habit.

He went on to praise us. He went on to say how he had bragged that "one   39
of the best basketball players at Fisk sank his first ball right here at Lafayette
County Training School."

The white kids were going to have a chance to become Galileos and Madame   40
Curies and Edisons and Gauguins, and our boys (the girls weren't even in on
it) would try to be Jesse Owenses and Joe Louises.

Owens and the Brown Bomber were great heroes in our world, but what   41
school official in the white-goddom of Little Rock had the right to decide that
those two men must be our only heroes? Who decided that for Henry Reed to
become a scientist he had to work like George Washington Carver, as a boot-
black, to buy a lousy microscope? Bailey was obviously always going to be too
small to be an athlete, so which concrete angel glued to what county seat had
decided that if my brother wanted to become a lawyer he had to first pay
penance for his skin by picking cotton and hoeing corn and studying correspondence books at night for twenty years?

The man's dead words fell like bricks around the auditorium and too many   42

41

settled in my belly. Constrained by hard-learned manners I couldn't look behind me, but to my left and right the proud graduating class of 1940 had dropped their heads. Every girl in my row had found something new to do with her handkerchief. Some folded the tiny squares into love knots, some into triangles, but most were wadding them, then pressing them flat on their yellow laps.

On the dais, the ancient tragedy was being replayed. Professor Parsons sat, 43 a sculptor's reject, rigid. His large, heavy body seemed devoid of will or willingness, and his eyes said he was no longer with us. The other teachers examined the flag (which was draped stage right) or their notes, or the windows which opened on our now-famous playing diamond.

Graduation, the hush-hush magic time of frills and gifts and congratulations 44 and diplomas, was finished for me before my name was called. The accomplishment was nothing. The meticulous maps, drawn in three colors of ink, learning and spelling decasyllabic words, memorizing the whole of *The Rape of Lucrece*[3]—it was for nothing. Donleavy had exposed us.

We were maids and farmers, handymen and washerwomen, and anything 45 higher that we aspired to was farcical and presumptuous.

Then I wished that Gabriel Prosser and Nat Turner had killed all whitefolks 46 in their beds and that Abraham Lincoln had been assassinated before the signing of the Emancipation Proclamation,[4] and that Harriet Tubman[5] had been killed by that blow on her head and Christopher Columbus had drowned in the *Santa Maria*.

It was awful to be a Negro and have no control over my life. It was brutal 47 to be young and already trained to sit quietly and listen to charges brought against my color with no chance of defense. We should all be dead. I thought I should like to see us all dead, one on top of the other. A pyramid of flesh with the whitefolks on the bottom, as the broad base, then the Indians with their silly tomahawks and teepees and wigwams and treaties, the Negroes with their mops and recipes and cotton sacks and spirituals sticking out of their mouths. The Dutch children should all stumble in their wooden shoes and break their necks. The French should choke to death on the Louisiana Purchase (1803) while silkworms ate all the Chinese with their stupid pigtails. As a species, we were an abomination. All of us.

Donleavy was running for election, and assured our parents that if he won 48 we could count on having the only colored paved playing field in that part of Arkansas. Also—he never looked up to acknowledge the grunts of acceptance— also, we were bound to get some new equipment for the home economics building and the workshop.

---

[3]*The Rape of Lucrece*: an 1,855-line narrative poem by William Shakespeare. [Eds.]
[4]Gabriel Prosser and Nat Turner: leaders of slave rebellions during the early 1800s in Virginia. [Eds.]
[5]Harriet Tubman (ca. 1820–1913): an escaped slave who conducted others to freedom on the Underground Railroad and worked as an abolitionist. [Eds.]

He finished, and since there was no need to give any more than the most   49
perfunctory thank-you's, he nodded to the men on the stage, and the tall white
man who was never introduced joined him at the door. They left with the
attitude that now they were off to something really important. (The graduation
ceremonies at Lafayette County Training School had been a mere preliminary.)

The ugliness they left was palpable. An uninvited guest who wouldn't leave.   50
The choir was summoned and sang a modern arrangement of "Onward, Christian Soldiers," with new words pertaining to graduates seeking their place in
the world. But it didn't work. Elouise, the daughter of the Baptist minister,
recited "Invictus,"6 and I could have cried at the impertinence of "I am the
master of my fate, I am the captain of my soul."

My name had lost its ring of familiarity and I had to be nudged to go and   51
receive my diploma. All my preparations had fled. I neither marched up to the
stage like a conquering Amazon, nor did I look in the audience for Bailey's
nod of approval. Marguerite Johnson, I heard the name again, my honors were
read, there were noises in the audience of appreciation, and I took my place
on the stage as rehearsed.

I thought about colors I hated: ecru, puce, lavender, beige and black.   52

There was shuffling and rustling around me, then Henry Reed was giving   53
his valedictory address, "To Be or Not to Be." Hadn't he heard the whitefolks?
We couldn't *be*, so the question was a waste of time. Henry's voice came out
clear and strong. I feared to look at him. Hadn't he got the message? There
was no "nobler in the mind" for Negroes because the world didn't think we had
minds, and they let us know it. "Outrageous fortune"? Now, that was a joke.
When the ceremony was over I had to tell Henry Reed some things. That is,
if I still cared. Not "rub," Henry, "erase." "Ah, there's the erase." Us.

Henry had been a good student in elocution. His voice rose on tides of   54
promise and fell on waves of warnings. The English teacher had helped him
to create a sermon winging through Hamlet's soliloquy. To be a man, a doer,
a builder, a leader, or to be a tool, an unfunny joke, a crusher of funky
toadstools. I marveled that Henry could go through with the speech as if we
had a choice.

I had been listening and silently rebutting each sentence with my eyes closed;   55
then there was a hush, which in an audience warns that something unplanned
is happening. I looked up and saw Henry Reed, the conservative, the proper,
the A student, turn his back to the audience and turn to us (the proud graduating
class of 1940) and sing, nearly speaking,

> "Lift ev'ry voice and sing
> Till earth and heaven ring
> Ring with the harmonies of Liberty . . ."

6"Invictus": a poem by the nineteenth-century English poet William Ernest Henley. Its inspi-
rational conclusion is quoted here. [Eds.]

It was the poem written by James Weldon Johnson. It was the music composed by J. Rosamond Johnson. It was the Negro National Anthem. Out of habit we were singing it.

Our mothers and fathers stood in the dark hall and joined the hymn of encouragement. A kindergarten teacher led the small children onto the stage and the buttercups and daisies and bunny rabbits marked time and tried to follow: 56

> "Stony the road we trod
> Bitter the chastening rod
> Felt in the days when hope, unborn, had died.
> Yet with a steady beat
> Have not our weary feet
> Come to the place for which our fathers sighed?"

Each child I knew had learned that song with his ABC's and along with "Jesus Loves Me This I Know." But I personally had never heard it before. Never heard the words, despite the thousands of times I had sung them. Never thought they had anything to do with me. 57

On the other hand, the words of Patrick Henry had made such an impression on me that I had been able to stretch myself tall and trembling and say, "I know not what course others may take, but as for me, give me liberty or give me death." 58

And now I heard, really for the first time: 59

> "We have come over a way that with tears
> has been watered,
> We have come, treading our path through
> the blood of the slaughtered."

While echoes of the song shivered in the air, Henry Reed bowed his head, said "Thank you," and returned to his place in the line. The tears that slipped down many faces were not wiped away in shame. 60

We were on top again. As always, again. We survived. The depths had been icy and dark, but now a bright sun spoke to our souls. I was no longer simply a member of the proud graduating class of 1940; I was a proud member of the wonderful, beautiful Negro race. 61

Oh, Black known and unknown poets, how often have your auctioned pains sustained us? Who will compute the only nights made less lonely by your songs, or the empty pots made less tragic by your tales? 62

If we were a people much given to revealing secrets, we might raise monuments and sacrifice to the memories of our poets, but slavery cured us of that weakness. It may be enough, however, to have it said that we survive in exact relationship to the dedication of our poets (include preachers, musicians and blues singers). 63

QUESTIONS

1. Why was graduation such an important event in Stamps, Arkansas? Note the rituals and preparations associated with this event. How do they compare with those accompanying your own junior-high or high school graduation?

2. At the beginning of the graduation ceremony, Angelou was "overcome with a presentiment of worse things to come. Something unrehearsed, unplanned, was going to happen" (paragraph 30). What "unrehearsed, unplanned" event does occur? How does Angelou convey to the reader the meaning of this event?

3. Toward the end of the essay we are told, "I was no longer simply a member of the proud graduating class of 1940; I was a proud member of the wonderful, beautiful Negro race" (paragraph 61). How did the experience of the graduation change Angelou's way of thinking about herself and her people?

4. Understanding the structure of this essay is important for understanding the meaning of the essay. How does Angelou organize her material, and how does this organization reflect her purpose? Why do you think Angelou changes her point of view from third person in the first five paragraphs to first person in the rest of the essay?

5. Think of an event in your life that didn't turn out as you expected. What were your expectations of this event? What was the reality? Write an essay in which you show the significance of this event by contrasting how you planned for the event with how it actually turned out.

6. We have all had experiences that have changed the directions of our lives. These experiences may be momentous, such as moving from one country to another or losing a parent, or they may be experiences that did not loom so large at the time but that changed the way you thought about things, such as finding that your parents disapproved of your best friend because of her race. Recall such a turning point in your life, and present it so as to give the reader a sense of what your life was like before the event and how it changed after the event.

MAKING CONNECTIONS

1. The essays by Loren Eiseley, George Orwell, Martin Luther King, Jr., and Alice Walker presented later in this section pinpoint formative moments in the life of the writer. Identify some of those moments and compare one or more with Angelou's account of her graduation.

2. Compare the points of view taken by Angelou and Walker. How does the "presence" of the valedictorian in Angelou's essay influence the point of view she takes?

3. Two things link this essay with Orwell's "Shooting an Elephant": each essay turns on an unexpected event, and the reflections each event prompts have to do with political domination. Of course they are from dissimilar points of view. But Orwell, when he goes out to meet and shoot the elephant, finds himself forced before a native crowd, in somewhat the same way that Mr. Donleavy stands before Angelou's school. Write an essay in which you compare and contrast these two events.

BEAUTY: WHEN THE OTHER DANCER IS THE SELF

Alice Walker

Born in Eatonton, Georgia, in 1944, Alice Walker is the youngest of eight children. Her father was a sharecropper, and her mother was a maid. A graduate of Sarah Lawrence College, Walker has been an active worker for civil rights. She has been a fellow of the Radcliffe Institute, a contributing and consulting editor for Ms. *magazine, and a teacher of literature and writing at a number of colleges and universities. She has published poetry, essays, short stories, and four novels,* The Third Life of Grange Copeland *(1970),* Meridian *(1976),* The Color Purple *(1982), for which she won the Pulitzer Prize, and* The Temple of My Familiar *(1989). "Beauty: When the Other Dancer Is the Self" first appeared in* Ms. *magazine, and later in a collection of essays,* In Search of Our Mothers' Gardens *(1983). When asked why she writes, Walker said, "I'm really paying homage to people I love, the people who are thought to be dumb and backward but who were the ones who first taught me to see beauty."*

It is a bright summer day in 1947. My father, a fat, funny man with beautiful eyes and a subversive wit, is trying to decide which of his eight children he will take with him to the county fair. My mother, of course, will not go. She is knocked out from getting most of us ready: I hold my neck stiff against the pressure of her knuckles as she hastily completes the braiding and then beribboning of my hair.

My father is the driver for the rich old white lady up the road. Her name is Miss Mey. She owns all the land for miles around, as well as the house in which we live. All I remember about her is that she once offered to pay my mother thirty-five cents for cleaning her house, raking up piles of her magnolia leaves, and washing her family's clothes, and that my mother—she of no money, eight children, and a chronic earache—refused it. But I do not think of this in 1947. I am two and a half years old. I want to go everywhere my daddy goes. I am excited at the prospect of riding in a car. Someone has told me fairs are fun. That there is room in the car for only three of us doesn't faze me at all. Whirling happily in my starchy frock, showing off my biscuit-polished patent-leather shoes and lavender socks, tossing my head in a way that makes my ribbons bounce, I stand, hands on hips, before my father. "Take me, Daddy," I say with assurance; "I'm the prettiest!"

Later, it does not surprise me to find myself in Miss Mey's shiny black car, 3 sharing the back seat with the other lucky ones. Does not surprise me that I thoroughly enjoy the fair. At home that night I tell the unlucky ones all I can remember about the merry-go-round, the man who eats live chickens, and the teddy bears, until they say: that's enough, baby Alice. Shut up now, and go to sleep.

It is Easter Sunday, 1950. I am dressed in a green, flocked, scalloped-hem 4 dress (handmade by my adoring sister, Ruth) that has its own smooth satin petticoat and tiny hot-pink roses tucked into each scallop. My shoes, new T-strap patent leather, again highly biscuit-polished. I am six years old and have learned one of the longest Easter speeches to be heard that day, totally unlike the speech I said when I was two: "Easter lilies / pure and white / blossom in / the morning light." When I rise to give my speech I do so on a great wave of love and pride and expectation. People in the church stop rustling their new crinolines. They seem to hold their breath. I can tell they admire my dress, but it is my spirit, bordering on sassiness (womanishness), they secretly applaud.

"That girl's a little *mess*," they whisper to each other, pleased. 5

Naturally I say my speech without stammer or pause, unlike those who 6 stutter, stammer, or worst of all, forget. This is before the word "beautiful" exists in people's vocabulary, but "Oh, isn't she the *cutest* thing!" frequently floats my way. "And got so much sense!" they gratefully add . . . for which thoughtful addition I thank them to this day.

It was great fun being cute. But then, one day, it ended. 7

I am eight years old and a tomboy. I have a cowboy hat, cowboy boots, 8 checkered shirt and pants, all red. My playmates are my brothers, two and four years older than I. Their colors are black and green, the only difference in the way we are dressed. On Saturday nights we all go to the picture show, even my mother; Westerns are her favorite kind of movie. Back home, "on the ranch," we pretend we are Tom Mix, Hopalong Cassidy, Lash LaRue (we've even named one of our dogs Lash LaRue); we chase each other for hours rustling cattle, being outlaws, delivering damsels from distress. Then my parents decide to buy my brothers guns. These are not "real" guns. They shoot "BBs," copper pellets my brothers say will kill birds. Because I am a girl, I do not get a gun. Instantly I am relegated to the position of Indian. Now there appears a great distance between us. They shoot and shoot at everything with their new guns. I try to keep up with my bow and arrows.

One day while I am standing on top of our makeshift "garage"—pieces of 9 tin nailed across some poles—holding my bow and arrow and looking out toward the fields, I feel an incredible blow in my right eye. I look down just in time to see my brother lower his gun.

Both brothers rush to my side. My eye stings, and I cover it with my hand. 10 "If you tell," they say, "we will get a whipping. You don't want that to happen, do you?" I do not. "Here is a piece of wire," says the older brother, picking it up from the roof; "say you stepped on one end of it and the other flew up and hit you." The pain is beginning to start. "Yes," I say. "Yes, I will say that is what happened." If I do not say this is what happened, I know my brothers will find ways to make me wish I had. But now I will say anything that gets me to my mother.

Confronted by our parents we stick to the lie agreed upon. They place me 11 on a bench on the porch and I close my left eye while they examine the right. There is a tree growing from underneath the porch that climbs past the railing to the roof. It is the last thing my right eye sees. I watch as its trunk, its branches, and then its leaves are blotted out by the rising blood.

I am in shock. First there is intense fever, which my father tries to break 12 using lily leaves bound around my head. Then there are chills: my mother tries to get me to eat soup. Eventually, I do not know how, my parents learn what has happened. A week after the "accident" they take me to see a doctor. "Why did you wait so long to come?" he asks, looking into my eye and shaking his head. "Eyes are sympathetic," he says. "If one is blind, the other will likely become blind too."

This comment of the doctor's terrifies me. But it is really how I look that 13 bothers me most. Where the BB pellet struck there is a glob of whitish scar tissue, a hideous cataract, on my eye. Now when I stare at people—a favorite pastime, up to now—they will stare back. Not at the "cute" little girl, but at her scar. For six years I do not stare at anyone, because I do not raise my head.

Years later, in the throes of a mid-life crisis, I ask my mother and sister 14 whether I changed after the "accident." "No," they say, puzzled. "What do you mean?"

What do I mean? 15

I am eight, and, for the first time, doing poorly in school, where I have 16 been something of a whiz since I was four. We have just moved to the place where the "accident" occurred. We do not know any of the people around us because this is a different county. The only time I see the friends I knew is when we go back to our old church. The new school is the former state penitentiary. It is a large stone building, cold and drafty, crammed to overflowing with boisterous, ill-disciplined children. On the third floor there is a huge circular imprint of some partition that has been torn out.

"What used to be here?" I ask a sullen girl next to me on our way past it to 17 lunch.

"The electric chair," says she. 18

At night I have nightmares about the electric chair, and about all the people 19
reputedly "fried" in it. I am afraid of the school, where all the students seem
to be budding criminals.

"What's the matter with your eye?" they ask, critically. 20

When I don't answer (I cannot decide whether it was an "accident" or not), 21
they shove me, insist on a fight.

My brother, the one who created the story about the wire, comes to my 22
rescue. But then brags so much about "protecting" me, I become sick.

After months of torture at the school, my parents decide to send me back to 23
our old community, to my old school. I live with my grandparents and the
teacher they board. But there is no room for Phoebe, my cat. By the time my
grandparents decide there *is* room, and I ask for my cat, she cannot be found.
Miss Yarborough, the boarding teacher, takes me under her wing, and begins
to teach me to play the piano. But soon she marries an African—a "prince,"
she says—and is whisked away to his continent.

At my old school there is at least one teacher who loves me. She is the 24
teacher who "knew me before I was born" and bought my first baby clothes. It
is she who makes life bearable. It is her presence that finally helps me turn on
the one child at the school who continually calls me "one-eyed bitch." One
day I simply grab him by his coat and beat him until I am satisfied. It is my
teacher who tells me my mother is ill.

My mother is lying in bed in the middle of the day, something I have never 25
seen. She is in too much pain to speak. She has an abscess in her ear. I stand
looking down on her, knowing that if she dies, I cannot live. She is being
treated with warm oils and hot bricks held against her cheek. Finally a doctor
comes. But I must go back to my grandparents' house. The weeks pass but I
am hardly aware of it. All I know is that my mother might die, my father is
not so jolly, my brothers still have their guns, and I am the one sent away from
home.

"You did not change," they say. 26

Did I imagine the anguish of never looking up? 27

I am twelve. When relatives come to visit I hide in my room. My cousin 28
Brenda, just my age, whose father works in the post office and whose mother
is a nurse, comes to find me. "Hello," she says. And then she asks, looking at
my recent school picture, which I did not want taken, and on which the "glob,"
as I think of it, is clearly visible, "You still can't see out of that eye?"

"No," I say, and flop back on the bed over my book. 29

That night, as I do almost every night, I abuse my eye. I rant and rave at 30
it, in front of the mirror. I plead with it to clear up before morning. I tell it I
hate and despise it. I do not pray for sight. I pray for beauty.

"You did not change," they say. 31

49

I am fourteen and baby-sitting for my brother Bill, who lives in Boston. He   32
is my favorite brother and there is a strong bond between us. Understanding
my feelings of shame and ugliness he and his wife take me to a local hospital,
where the "glob" is removed by a doctor named O. Henry. There is still a small
bluish crater where the scar tissue was, but the ugly white stuff is gone. Almost
immediately I become a different person from the girl who does not raise her
head. Or so I think. Now that I've raised my head I win the boyfriend of my
dreams. Now that I've raised my head I have plenty of friends. Now that I've
raised my head classwork comes from my lips as faultlessly as Easter speeches
did, and I leave high school as valedictorian, most popular student, and *queen*,
hardly believing my luck. Ironically, the girl who was voted most beautiful in
our class (and was) was later shot twice through the chest by a male companion,
using a "real" gun, while she was pregnant. But that's another story in itself.
Or is it?

"You did not change," they say.   33

It is now thirty years since the "accident." A beautiful journalist comes to   34
visit and to interview me. She is going to write a cover story for her magazine
that focuses on my latest book. "Decide how you want to look on the cover,"
she says. "Glamorous, or whatever."

Never mind "glamorous," it is the "whatever" that I hear. Suddenly all I can   35
think of is whether I will get enough sleep the night before the photography
session: if I don't, my eye will be tired and wander, as blind eyes will.

At night in bed with my lover I think up reasons why I should not appear   36
on the cover of a magazine. "My meanest critics will say I've sold out," I say.
"My family will now realize I write scandalous books."

"But what's the real reason you don't want to do this?" he asks.   37

"Because in all probability," I say in a rush, "my eye won't be straight."   38

"It will be straight enough," he says. Then, "Besides, I thought you'd made   39
your peace with that."

And I suddenly remember that I have.   40

I remember: 41

I am talking to my brother Jimmy, asking if he remembers anything unusual   42
about the day I was shot. He does not know I consider that day the last time
my father, with his sweet home remedy of cool lily leaves, chose me, and that
I suffered and raged inside because of this. "Well," he says, "all I remember is
standing by the side of the highway with Daddy, trying to flag down a car. A
white man stopped, but when Daddy said he needed somebody to take his little
girl to the doctor, he drove off."

I remember: 43

I am in the desert for the first time. I fall totally in love with it. I am so   44
overwhelmed by its beauty, I confront for the first time, consciously, the meaning of the doctor's words years ago: "Eyes are sympathetic. If one is blind, the

other will likely become blind too." I realize I have dashed about the world madly, looking at this, looking at that, storing up images against the fading of the light. *But I might have missed seeing the desert!* The shock of that possibility—and gratitude for over twenty-five years of sight—sends me literally to my knees. Poem after poem comes—which is perhaps how poets pray.

ON SIGHT

I am so thankful I have seen
The Desert
And the creatures in the desert
And the desert Itself.

The desert has its own moon
Which I have seen
With my own eye.

There is no flag on it.

Trees of the desert have arms
All of which are always up
That is because the moon is up
The sun is up
Also the sky
The stars
Clouds
None with flags.

If there *were* flags, I doubt
the trees would point.
Would you?

But mostly, I remember this: 45

I am twenty-seven, and my baby daughter is almost three. Since her birth I 46
have worried about her discovery that her mother's eyes are different from other people's. Will she be embarrassed? I think. What will she say? Every day she watches a television program called "Big Blue Marble." It begins with a picture of the earth as it appears from the moon. It is bluish, a little battered-looking, but full of light, with whitish clouds swirling around it. Every time I see it I weep with love, as if it is a picture of Grandma's house. One day when I am putting Rebecca down for her nap, she suddenly focuses on my eye. Something inside me cringes, gets ready to try to protect myself. All children are cruel about physical differences, I know from experience, and that they don't always mean to be is another matter. I assume Rebecca will be the same.

51

But no-o-o-o. She studies my face intently as we stand, her inside and me outside her crib. She even holds my face maternally between her dimpled little hands. Then, looking every bit as serious and lawyerlike as her father, she says, as if it may just possibly have slipped my attention: "Mommy, there's a *world* in your eye." (As in, "Don't be alarmed, or do anything crazy.") And then, gently, but with great interest: "Mommy, where did you *get* that world in your eye?"   47

For the most part, the pain left then. (So what, if my brothers grew up to buy even more powerful pellet guns for their sons and to carry real guns themselves. So what, if a young "Morehouse man" once nearly fell off the steps of Trevor Arnett Library because he thought my eyes were blue.) Crying and laughing I ran to the bathroom, while Rebecca mumbled and sang herself off to sleep. Yes indeed, I realized, looking into the mirror. There *was* a world in my eye. And I saw that it was possible to love it: that in fact, for all it had taught me of shame and anger and inner vision, I *did* love it. Even to see it drifting out of orbit in boredom, or rolling up out of fatigue, not to mention floating back at attention in excitement (bearing witness, a friend has called it), deeply suitable to my personality, and even characteristic of me.   48

That night I dream I am dancing to Stevie Wonder's song "Always" (the name of the song is really "As," but I hear it as "Always"). As I dance, whirling and joyous, happier than I've ever been in my life, another bright-faced dancer joins me. We dance and kiss each other and hold each other through the night. The other dancer has obviously come through all right, as I have done. She is beautiful, whole and free. And she is also me.   49

QUESTIONS

1. Walker's essay moves forward in time through abrupt, though steadily progressive descriptions of episodes. What effect on the reader does this structure produce? Why do you suppose Walker chose this form instead of providing transitions from one episode to the next?

2. Consider Walker's method of contrasting other people's memories with her own. What effect is created by the repetition of "You did not change"?

3. Consider Walker's choices of episodes or examples of beauty. How does each one work toward developing a definition of "beauty"?

4. In what ways does this essay play with the possible meanings of the familiar adage, "Beauty is in the eye of the beholder"?

5. One theme of this essay could be that of coming to terms with a disfigurement, an imagined loss of physical beauty. Recall an event (or accident) in your own life that changed your perception of yourself. Write a reflective narrative in which you use Walker's method of chronologically arranged episodes, including a reflection on the time before the change, as well as the change itself, and episodes from the time following. Like Walker, you may want to contrast (or compare) your memories with those of others.

6. Recall a memorable event that occurred a year or more ago. It might be an event in your family's life, or a public event at which you and your friends were present. Write down your memories of the event, and then interview your family or friends and write down their recollections. Compare the various memories of the event. Come to some conclusion about the differences or similarities you find, and perhaps about the selectivity of memory.

MAKING CONNECTIONS

Walker's daughter's exclamation, "Mommy, there's a *world* in your eye," is obviously a transcendent moment. It is also a metaphor. One or another writer in this section could also be said to have a world in her or his eye. For example, Carl Sagan's description of how insight depends on a degree of restriction is closely related to Walker's theme. Select another essay from this section and show how Walker's reflections on her blind eye can help us understand the discoveries the writer of the other essay is making.

BLACK IS A WOMAN'S COLOR
bell hooks

*When Gloria Watkins (b. 1952) first started writing, she
chose the name of her maternal grandmother as a pen name,
and it stuck. hooks, who teaches English at Oberlin College,
has established herself as a renowned theorist and critic in
books such as* Ain't I a Woman *(1981),* Yearnings *(1990),*
A Woman's Mourning Song *(1992), and* Black Looks: Race
and Representation *(1992), and numerous articles. In this
essay, originally published in the journal* Callaloo, *hooks
reflects on her education in the complexities of marriage and
power relationships between men and women.*

GOOD HAIR—that's the expression. We all know it, begin to hear it when we
are small children. When we are sitting between the legs of mothers and sisters
getting our hair combed. Good hair is hair that is not kinky, hair that does not
feel like balls of steel wool, hair that does not take hours to comb, hair that
does not need tons of grease to untangle, hair that is long. Real good hair is
straight hair, hair like white folks' hair. Yet no one says so. No one says your
hair is so nice, so beautiful it is like white folks' hair. We pretend that the
standards we measure our beauty by are our own invention—that it is questions
of time and money that lead us to make distinctions between good hair and
bad hair. I know from birth that I am lucky, lucky to have hair at all for I was
bald for two years, then lucky finally to have thin almost straight hair, hair that
does not need to be hot combed.

We are six girls who live in a house together. We have different textures of
hair, short, long, thin, thick. We do not appreciate these differences. We do
not celebrate the variety that is ourselves. We do not run our fingers through
each other's dry hair after it is washed. We sit in the kitchen and wait our turn
for the hot comb, wait to sit in the chair by the stove smelling grease, feeling
the heat warm our scalp like a sticky hot summer sun.

For each of us, getting our hair pressed is an important ritual. It is not a
sign of our longing to be white. It is not a sign of our quest to be beautiful.
We are girls. It is a sign of our desire to be women. It is a gesture that says we
are approaching womanhood. It is a rite of passage. Before we reach the
appropriate age we wear braids and plaits that are symbols of our innocence,
our youth, our childhood. Then we are comforted by the parting hands that

comb and braid, comforted by the intimacy and bliss. There is a deeper intimacy in the kitchen on Saturday when hair is pressed, when fish is fried, when sodas are passed around, when soul music drifts over the talk. We are women together. This is our ritual and our time. It is a time without men. It is a time when we work to meet each other's needs, to make each other beautiful in whatever way we can. It is a time of laughter and mellow talk. Sometimes it is an occasion for tears and sorrow. Mama is angry, sick of it all, pulling the hair too tight, using too much grease, burning one ear and then the next.

At first I cannot participate in the ritual. I have good hair that does not need 4 pressing. Without the hot comb I remain a child, one of the uninitiated. I plead, I beg, I cry for my turn. They tell me once you start you will be sorry. You will wish you had never straightened your hair. They do not understand that it is not the straightening I seek but the chance to belong, to be one in this world of women. It is finally my turn. I am happy. Happy even though my thin hair straightened looks like black thread, has no body, stands in the air like ends of barbed wire; happy even though the sweet smell of unpressed hair is gone forever. Secretly I had hoped that the hot comb would transform me, turn the thin good hair into thick nappy hair, the kind of hair I like and long for, the kind you can do anything with, wear in all kinds of styles. I am bitterly disappointed in the new look.

A senior in high school, I want to wear a natural, an afro. I want never to 5 get my hair pressed again. It is no longer a rite of passage, a chance to be intimate in the world of women. The intimacy masks betrayal. Together we change ourselves. The closeness, an embrace before parting, a gesture of farewell to love and one another.

Jazz, she learns from her father, is the black man's music, the working man, 6 the poor man, the man on the street. Different from the blues because it does not simply lament, moan, express sorrow; it expresses everything. She listens to a record he is playing, to a record that is being played on the radio. It is the music of John Coltrane.[1] Her father says this is a musician who understands all the black man is longing for, that he takes this longing and blows it out of his saxophone. Like the alchemist, he turns lead into gold. To listen, her father tells her, is to feel understood. She listens, wanting this jazz not to be beyond her, wanting it to address the melancholy parts of her soul. To her, black people make the most passionate music. She knows that there is no such thing as natural rhythm. She knows it is the intensity of feeling, the constant knowing that death is real and a possibility that makes the music what it is. She knows that it is the transformation of suffering and sorrow into sound that bears witness

---

[1] John Coltrane (1926–1967), a saxophonist whose exceptional talents influenced modern jazz musicians. [Eds.]

to the black past. In her dreams she has seen the alchemist turning lead into gold.

On communion Sundays they sing without musical accompaniment. They keep alive the old ways, the call and response. They sing slow and hold each note as if it is caught in the trap of time and struggling to be free. Like the bread and the wine, they do it this way so as not to forget what the past has been. She listens to the strength in the voices of elderly women as they call out. She sings in the choir. She loves the singing. She looks forward to choir practice on Wednesday night. It is the only weekday night that they are away from home. They sit in the basement of the church singing. They sing "hush children, hush children, somebody's calling my name, oh my lord, oh my lordy, what shall I do." 7

At home her mama listens to music. On Friday nights she sits in her corner on the couch, smoking one cigarette, drinking one can of beer, playing records, staring sadly into the smoke as Brooke Benton sings "you don't miss you water till your well runs dry." Saturday morning they clean house and listen to music. They listen to the soul music on the radio. It is the only time they can hear a whole program with black music. Every other day is country and western or rock 'n roll. In between vacuuming, dusting, and sweeping they listen to the latest songs and show each other the latest dances. She likes to dance, but they make fun of her. She cannot slow dance. She does not know how to follow the lead. She gives up dancing, spends her time listening to the music. 8

She likes to hear the music of Louis Armstrong.[2] She likes to see the pleasure he brings to her father's face. They watch him on the Ed Sullivan show, making funny faces, singing in his deep voice. It is the trumpet sound that they are waiting for. When he pulls the handkerchief from his pocket to wipe away the dripping sweat she is reminded of the right-hand men of God weeping into thin squares of cotton. She imagines tears mingled with Satchmo's sweat, that they are tears of gratitude, that he too is giving thanks for finding in his horn yet another sweet stretching sound he did not know was there. 9

She wants to express herself—to speak her mind. To them it is just talking back. Each time she opens her mouth she risks punishment. They punish her so often she begins to feel they are persecuting her. When she learns the word *scapegoat* in vocabulary lesson, she is sure it accurately describes her lot in life. Her wilderness, unlike the one the goat is led into, is a wilderness of spirit. They abandon her there to get on with the fun things of life. She lies in her bed upstairs after being punished yet again. She can hear the sound of their laughter, their talk. No one hears her crying. Even though she is young, she comes to understand the meaning of exile and loss. They say that she is really 10

---

[2] Louis Armstrong (1900–1971), known as "Satchmo"; jazz trumpeter, singer, bandleader; a genius at improvisation, Armstrong influenced the role of the soloist in jazz. [Eds.]

not a young girl but an old woman born again into a young girl's body. They do not know how to speak the old woman's language so they are afraid of her. She might be a witch. They have given her a large thick paperback of original fairy tales. On page after page, an old woman is eating children, thinking some wicked deed, performing evil magic. She is not surprised that they fear the old woman inside her. She understands that the old women in the fairy tales do evil because they are misunderstood. She is a lover of old women. She does not mind at all when they look at her and say she must be ninety, look at the way she walks. No! They say she must be at least a hundred. Only a hundred-year-old woman could walk so slow.

Their world is the only world there is. To be exiled from it is to be without 11 life. She cries because she is in mourning. They will not let her wear the color black. It is not a color for girls. To them she already looks too old. She would just look like a damn fool in a black dress. Black is a woman's color.

She finds another world in books. Escaping into the world of novels is one 12 way she learns to enjoy life. However, novels only ease the pain momentarily as she holds the book in hand, as she reads. It is poetry that changes everything. When she discovers the Romantics it is like losing a part of herself and recovering it. She reads them night and day, all the time. She memorizes poems. She recites them while ironing or washing dishes. Reading Emily Dickinson she senses that the spirit can grow in the solitary life. She reads Edna St. Vincent Millay's "Renascence," and she feels with the lines the suppression of spirit, the spiritual death, and the longing to live again. She reads Whitman, Wordsworth, Coleridge. Whitman shows her that language, like the human spirit, need not be trapped in conventional form or traditions. For school she recites "O Captain, My Captain." She would rather recite from *Song of Myself*, but they do not read it in school. They do not read it because it would be hard to understand. She cannot understand why everyone hates to read poetry. She cannot understand their moans and groans. She wishes they did not have to recite poems in school. She cannot bear to hear the frightened voices stumbling through lines as if they are a wilderness and a trap. At home she has an audience. They will turn off the television set and listen to her latest favorite.

She writes her own poetry in secret. She does not want to explain. Her 13 poems are about love and never about death. She is always thinking about death and never about love. She knows that they will think it better to discover secret poems about love. She knows they never speak of death. The punishments continue. She eases her pain in poetry, using it to make the poems live, using the poems to keep on living.

*   *   *

They have never heard their mama and daddy fussing or fighting. They have 14 heard him be harsh, complain that the house should be cleaner, that he should not have to come home from work to a house that is not cleaned just right.

They know he gets mad. When he gets mad about the house he begins to clean it himself to show that he can do better. Although he never cooks, he knows how. He would not be able to judge her cooking if he did not cook himself. They are afraid of him when he is mad. They go upstairs to get out of his way. He does not come upstairs. Taking care of children is not a man's work. It does not concern him. He is not even interested—that is, unless something goes wrong. Then he can show her that she is not very good at parenting. They know she is a good mama, "the best." Even though they fear him they are not moved by his opinions. She tries to remember a time when she felt loved by him. She remembers it as being the time when she was a baby girl, a small girl. She remembers him taking her places, taking her to the world inhabited by black men, the barber shop, the pool hall. He took his affections away from her abruptly. She never understood why, only that they went and did not come back. She remembered trying to do whatever she could to bring them back, only they never came. Growing up she stopped trying. He mainly ignored her. She mainly tried to stay out of his way. In her own way she grew to hate wanting his love and not being able to get it. She hated that part of herself that kept wanting his love or even just his approval long after she could see that he was never, never going to give it.

Out of nowhere he comes home from work angry. He reaches the porch 15 yelling and screaming at the woman inside. Yelling that she is his wife and that he can do with her what he wants. They do not understand what is happening. He is pushing, hitting, telling her to shut up. She is pleading, crying. He does not want to hear, to listen. They catch his angry words in their hands like lightning bugs. They store them in a jar to sort them out later. Words about other men, about phone calls, about how he had told her. They do not know what he has told her. They have never heard them in an angry discussion, an argument.

She thinks of all the nights she lies awake in her bed hearing the woman's 16 voice, her mother's voice, hearing his voice. She wonders if it is then that he is telling her the messages he refers to now. Yelling, screaming, hitting, they stare at the red blood that trickles through the crying mouth. They cannot believe that this pleading, crying woman, this woman who does not fight back, is the same person they know. The person they know is strong, gets things done, is a woman of ways and means, a woman of action. They do not know her still, paralyzed, waiting for the next blow, pleading. They do not know her afraid. Even if she does not hit back they want her to run, to run and to not stop running. She wants her to hit him with the table light, the ash tray near her hand. She does not want to see her like this, not fighting back. He notices them long enough to tell them to get out, go upstairs. She refuses to move. She cannot move. She cannot leave her alone. When he says "What are you staring at, do you want some too," she is afraid enough to move, but she does not take her orders from him. She asks the woman if it is right to leave her

58

alone. The woman nods her head yes. She still stands still. It is his movement in her direction that sends her up the stairs. She cannot believe they are not taking a stand, that they go to sleep. She cannot bear their betrayal. When he is not looking she creeps down the steps. She wants the woman to know that she is not alone. She wants to bear witness.

All that she does not understand about marriage, about men and women, is explained to her one night. In her dark place on the stairs she is seeing over and over again the still body of the woman pleading, crying, the moving body of the man angry, yelling. She sees that the man has a gun. She hears him tell the woman that he will kill her. She sits in her place on the stair and demands to know of herself if she is able to come to the rescue, if she is willing to fight, if she is ready to die. Her body shakes with the answers. She is fighting back the tears. When he leaves the room she comes to ask the woman if she is all right, if there is anything she can do. The woman's voice is full of tenderness and hurt. She is now in her role as mother. She tells her daughter to go upstairs and go to sleep, that everything will be all right. The daughter does not believe her. Her eyes are pleading. She does not want to be told to go. She hovers in the shadows. When he returns he tells her that he has told her to get her ass upstairs. She does not look at him. He turns to the woman, tells her to leave, tells her to take the daughter with her.

The woman does not protest. She moves like a robot, hurriedly throwing things into suitcases, boxes. She says nothing to the man. He is still screaming, muttering. When she tried to say to him he was wrong, so wrong, he is more angry, threatening. All the neat drawers are emptied out on the bed, all the precious belongings that can be carried, stuffed, are to be taken. There is sorrow in every gesture, sorrow and pain. It is so thick she feels that she could gather it up in her hands. It is like a dust collecting on everything. She is seeing that the man owns everything, that the woman has only her clothes, her shoes, and other personal belongings. She is seeing that the woman can be told to go, can be sent away in the silent, long hours of the night. She is hearing in her head the man's threats to kill. She can feel the cool metal against her cheek. She can hear the click, the blast. She can see her body falling. No, it is not her body, it is the body of love. It is the death of love she is witnessing. If love were alive she believes it would stop everything. It would steady the man's voice, it would calm his rage. It would take the woman's hand, caress her cheek and with a clean handkerchief wipe her eyes. The gun is pointed at love. He lays it on the table. He wants her to finish her packing and go.

She is again in her role as mother. She tells the daughter that she does not have to flee in the middle of the night, that it is not her fight. The daughter is silent. She is staring into the woman's eyes. She is looking for the bright lights, the care and adoration she has shown the man. The eyes are dark with grief, swollen. She feels that a fire inside the woman is dying out, that she is cold.

She is sure the woman will freeze to death if she goes out into the night alone. She takes her hand. She wants to go with her. Yet she hopes there will be no going. She hopes that when the mother's brother comes he will be strong enough to take love's body, and give it mouth to mouth the life it has lost. She hopes he will talk to the man, guide him. She cannot believe the calm way he lifts suitcase, box, sack, carries it to the car without question. She cannot bear the silent agreement that the man is right, that he has done what men are able to do. She cannot take the bits and pieces of her mother's heart and put them together again.

I am always fighting with mama. Everything has come between us. She no longer stands between me and all that would hurt me. She is hurting me. This is my dream of her—that she will stand between me and all that hurts me, that she will protect me at all cost. It is only a dream. In some way I understand that it has to do with marriage, that to be the wife to the husband she must be willing to sacrifice even her daughters for his good. For the mother it is not simple. She is always torn. She works hard to fulfill his needs, our needs. When they are not the same she must maneuver, manipulate, choose. She has chosen. She has decided in his favor. She is a religious woman. She has been told that a man should obey God, that a woman should obey man, that children should obey their fathers and mothers, particularly their mothers. I will not obey. 20

She says that she punishes me for my own good. I do not know what it is I have done this time. I know that she is ready with her switches, that I am to stand still while she lashes out again and again. In my mind there is the memory of a woman sitting still while she is being hit, punished. In my mind I am remembering how much I want that woman to fight back. Before I can think clearly, my hands reach out, grab the switches, are raised as if to hit her back. For a moment she is stunned, unbelieving. She is shocked. She tells me that I must never ever as long as I live raise my hand against my mother. I tell her I do not have a mother. She is even more shocked; she is enraged. She lashes out again. This time I am still. This time I cry. I see the hurt in her eyes when I say "I do not have a mother." I am ready to be punished because I did not want to hurt. I am ashamed. I am torn. I do not want to stand still and be punished but I do not want to hurt her. It is better to hurt than to cause her pain. She warns me that she will tell him when he comes home, that I may be punished again. I cannot understand her acts of betrayal. I cannot understand that she must be against me to be for him. He and I are strangers. Deep in the night we parted from one another, knowing that nothing would ever be the same. He did not say goodbye. I did not look him in the face. Now we avoid one another. He speaks to me through her. 21

Although they act as if everything between them is the same, that life is as it was, it is only a game. They are only pretending. There is no pain in the 22 pretense. All pain is hidden. Secrets find a way out in sleep. They say to the mother she cries in her sleep, calls out. In her sleep is the place of remembering. It is the place where there is no pretense. She is dreaming always the same dream. A movie is showing. It is a tragic story of jealousy and lost love. It is called "A Crime of Passion." In the movie a man has killed his wife and daughter. He has killed his wife because he believes she has lovers. He has killed the daughter because she witnesses the death of the wife. At his job he is calm and quiet, a hardworking man, a family man. Neighbors come to testify that the dead woman was young and restless, that the daughter was wild and rebellious. Everyone sympathizes with the man. His story is so sad that they begin to weep. All their handkerchiefs are clean and white. They are like flags waving. They are a signal of peace, of surrender. They are a gesture to the man that he can go on with life.

QUESTIONS

1. This essay was reprinted in the book *Bearing Witness*, a collection of twentieth-century African-American autobiographical writing. The editor, Henry Louis Gates, speaks of "the impulse to testify, to chart the peculiar contours of the individual on the road to becoming" that distinguishes black autobiographical writing. In paragraph 16, hooks, speaking of her younger self, says "She wants to bear witness." Why does she? What is she testifying for?

2. hooks has broken her essay into six sections. What kind of sequence has she arranged? Why does she start with the section on "Good hair"?

3. At what points does hooks use memories of specific events to make general statements about relationships? At what points does she use dreams? Why does she end with the movie in the dream? What other uses of strong images do you find, and how are they used?

4. Betrayal is one of the themes of hooks's essay. Define her concept of betrayal and discuss the most relevant instances of it.

5. Write about a time when you felt betrayed by someone you trusted.

6. Choose a theme for a period in your life and illustrate it, as hooks does, with three or more instances. Interweave dreams, images, narratives of events as she does to invoke the time for yourself and for your readers.

MAKING CONNECTIONS

1. What other essays in this section can be described as "bearing witness"? Compare their approaches to that of hooks.

2. Angelou, Walker, and hooks all write about the importance of rituals as rites of passage. What commonalities do you see in the rituals these writers describe? What power and significance of these rituals helps these writers define their racial and gender identities?

LEARNING TO READ
AND WRITE

Frederick Douglass

Frederick Augustus Washington Bailey (1817–1895) was born into slavery on the Eastern Shore of Maryland. His mother was a black slave; his father, a white man. After his escape from the South in 1838, he adopted the name of Douglass and worked to free other slaves and later (after the Civil War) to protect the rights of freed slaves. He was a newspaper editor, a lecturer, United States minister to Haiti, and the author of several books about his life and times. The Narrative of the Life of Frederick Douglass: An American Slave *(1841), from which the following chapter has been taken, is his best-known work.*

I lived in Master Hugh's family about seven years. During this time, I   1
succeeded in learning to read and write. In accomplishing this, I was compelled
to resort to various stratagems. I had no regular teacher. My mistress, who had
kindly commenced to instruct me, had, in compliance with the advice and
direction of her husband, not only ceased to instruct, but had set her face
against my being instructed by any one else. It is due, however, to my mistress
to say of her, that she did not adopt this course of treatment immediately. She
at first lacked the depravity indispensable to shutting me up in mental darkness.
It was at least necessary for her to have some training in the exercise of
irresponsible power, to make her equal to the task of treating me as though I
were a brute.

My mistress was, as I have said, a kind and tender-hearted woman; and in   2
the simplicity of her soul she commenced, when I first went to live with her,
to treat me as she supposed one human being ought to treat another. In entering
upon the duties of a slaveholder, she did not seem to perceive that I sustained
to her the relation of a mere chattel, and that for her to treat me as a human
being was not only wrong, but dangerously so. Slavery proved as injurious to
her as it did to me. When I went there, she was a pious, warm, and tender-
hearted woman. There was no sorrow or suffering for which she had not a tear.
She had bread for the hungry, clothes for the naked, and comfort for every
mourner that came within her reach. Slavery soon proved its ability to divest
her of these heavenly qualities. Under its influence, the tender heart became
stone, and the lamblike disposition gave way to one of tiger-like fierceness. The
first step in her downward course was in her ceasing to instruct me. She now

commenced to practise her husband's precepts. She finally became even more violent in her opposition than her husband himself. She was not satisfied with simply doing as well as he had commanded; she seemed anxious to do better. Nothing seemed to make her more angry than to see me with a newspaper. She seemed to think that here lay the danger. I have had her rush at me with a face made all up of fury, and snatch from me a newspaper, in a manner that fully revealed her apprehension. She was an apt woman; and a little experience soon demonstrated, to her satisfaction, that education and slavery were incompatible with each other.

From this time I was most narrowly watched. If I was in a separate room 3 any considerable length of time, I was sure to be suspected of having a book, and was at once called to give an account of myself. All this, however, was too late. The first step had been taken. Mistress, in teaching me the alphabet, had given me the *inch*, and no precaution could prevent me from taking the *ell*.

The plan which I adopted, and the one by which I was most successful, was 4 that of making friends of all the little white boys whom I met in the street. As many of these as I could, I converted into teachers. With their kindly aid, obtained at different times and in different places, I finally succeeded in learning to read. When I was sent on errands, I always took my book with me, and by going one part of my errand quickly, I found time to get a lesson before my return. I used also to carry bread with me, enough of which was always in the house, and to which I was always welcome; for I was much better off in this regard than many of the poor white children in our neighborhood. This bread I used to bestow upon the hungry little urchins, who, in return, would give me that more valuable bread of knowledge. I am strongly tempted to give the names of two or three of those little boys, as a testimonial of the gratitude and affection I bear them; but prudence forbids;—not that it would injure me, but it might embarrass them; for it is almost an unpardonable offence to teach slaves to read in this Christian country. It is enough to say of the dear little fellows, that they lived on Philpot Street, very near Durgin and Bailey's ship-yard. I used to talk this matter of slavery over with them. I would sometimes say to them, I wished I could be as free as they would be when they got to be men. "You will be free as soon as you are twenty-one, *but I am a slave for life!* Have not I as good a right to be free as you have?" These words used to trouble them; they would express for me the liveliest sympathy, and console me with the hope that something would occur by which I might be free.

I was now about twelve years old, and the thought of being *a slave for life* 5 began to bear heavily upon my heart. Just about this time, I got hold of a book entitled "The Columbian Orator."[1] Every opportunity I got, I used to read this book. Among much of other interesting matter, I found in it a dialogue between

---

[1] *The Columbian Orator:* a popular schoolbook designed to introduce students to argument and rhetoric. [Eds.]

a master and his slave. The slave was represented as having run away from his master three times. The dialogue represented the conversation which took place between them, when the slave was retaken the third time. In this dialogue, the whole argument in behalf of slavery was brought forward by the master, all of which was disposed of by the slave. The slave was made to say some very smart as well as impressive things in reply to his master—things which had the desired though unexpected effect; for the conversation resulted in the voluntary emancipation of the slave on the part of the master.

In the same book, I met with one of Sheridan's mighty speeches on and in behalf of Catholic emancipation.[2] These were choice documents to me. I read them over and over again with unabated interest. They gave tongue to interesting thoughts of my own soul, which had frequently flashed through my mind, and died away for want of utterance. The moral which I gained from the dialogue was the power of truth over the conscience of even a slaveholder. What I got from Sheridan was a bold denunciation of slavery, and a powerful vindication of human rights. The reading of these documents enabled me to utter my thoughts, and to meet the arguments brought forward to sustain slavery; but while they relieved me of one difficulty, they brought on another even more painful than the one of which I was relieved. The more I read, the more I was led to abhor and detest my enslavers. I could regard them in no other light than a band of successful robbers, who had left their homes, and gone to Africa, and stolen us from our homes, and in a strange land reduced us to slavery. I loathed them as being the meanest as well as the most wicked of men. As I read and contemplated the subject, behold! that very discontentment which Master Hugh had predicted would follow my learning to read had already come, to torment and sting my soul to unutterable anguish. As I writhed under it, I would at times feel that learning to read had been a curse rather than a blessing. It had given me a view of my wretched condition, without the remedy. It opened my eyes to the horrible pit, but to no ladder upon which to get out. In moments of agony, I envied my fellow-slaves for their stupidity. I have often wished myself a beast. I preferred the condition of the meanest reptile to my own. Any thing, no matter what, to get rid of thinking! It was this everlasting thinking of my condition that tormented me. There was no getting rid of it. It was pressed upon me by every object within sight or hearing, animate or inanimate. The silver trump of freedom had roused my soul to eternal wakefulness. Freedom now appeared, to disappear no more forever. It was heard in every sound, and seen in every thing. It was ever present to torment me with a sense of my wretched condition. I saw nothing without seeing it, I heard nothing without hearing it, and felt nothing without feeling it. It looked from every star, it smiled in every calm, breathed in every wind, and moved in every storm.

6

---

[2] Richard Brinsley Sheridan (1751–1816): British dramatist, orator, and politician. Catholics were not allowed to vote in England until 1829. [Eds.]

64

I often found myself regretting my own existence, and wishing myself dead; 7
and but for the hope of being free, I have no doubt but that I should have
killed myself, or done something for which I should have been killed. While
in this state of mind, I was eager to hear any one speak of slavery. I was a ready
listener. Every little while, I could hear something about the abolitionists. It
was some time before I found what the word meant. It was always used in such
connections as to make it an interesting word to me. If a slave ran away and
succeeded in getting clear, or if a slave killed his master, set fire to a barn, or
did any thing very wrong in the mind of a slaveholder, it was spoken of as the
fruit of *abolition*. Hearing the word in this connection very often, I set about
learning what it meant. The dictionary afforded me little or no help. I found
it was "the act of abolishing"; but then I did not know what was to be abolished.
Here I was perplexed. I did not dare to ask any one about its meaning, for I
was satisfied that it was something they wanted me to know very little about.
After a patient waiting, I got one of our city papers, containing an account of
the number of petitions from the north, praying for the abolition of slavery in
the District of Columbia, and of the slave trade between the States. From this
time I understood the words *abolition* and *abolitionist*, and always drew near
when that word was spoken, expecting to hear something of importance to
myself and fellow-slaves. The light broke in upon me by degrees. I went one
day down on the wharf of Mr. Waters; and seeing two Irishmen unloading a
scow of stone, I went, unasked, and helped them. When we had finished, one
of them came to me and asked me if I were a slave. I told him I was. He asked,
"Are ye a slave for life?" I told him that I was. The good Irishman seemed to
be deeply affected by the statement. He said to the other that it was a pity so
fine a little fellow as myself should be a slave for life. He said it was a shame
to hold me. They both advised me to run away to the north; that I should find
friends there, and that I should be free. I pretended not to be interested in what
they said, and treated them as if I did not understand them; for I feared they
might be treacherous. White men have been known to encourage slaves to
escape, and then, to get the reward, catch them and return them to their
masters. I was afraid that these seemingly good men might use me so; but I
nevertheless remembered their advice, and from that time I resolved to run
away. I looked forward to a time at which it would be safe for me to escape. I
was too young to think of doing so immediately; besides, I wished to learn how
to write, as I might have occasion to write my own pass. I consoled myself with
the hope that I should one day find a good chance. Meanwhile, I would learn
to write.

The idea as to how I might learn to write was suggested to me by being in 8
Durgin and Bailey's ship-yard, and frequently seeing the ship carpenters, after
hewing, and getting a piece of timber ready for use, write on the timber the
name of that part of the ship for which it was intended. When a piece of timber
was intended for the larboard side, it would be marked thus—"L." When a

piece was for the starboard side, it would be marked thus—"S." A piece for the larboard side forward, would be marked thus—"L. F." When a piece was for starboard side forward, it would be marked thus—"S. F." For larboard aft, it would be marked thus—"L. A." For starboard aft, it would be marked thus— "S. A." I soon learned the names of these letters, and for what they were intended when placed upon a piece of timber in the ship-yard. I immediately commenced copying them, and in a short time was able to make the four letters named. After that, when I met with any boy who I knew could write, I would tell him I could write as well as he. The next word would be, "I don't believe you. Let me see you try it." I would then make the letters which I had been so fortunate as to learn, and ask him to beat that. In this way I got a good many lessons in writing, which it is quite possible I should never have gotten in any other way. During this time, my copy-book was the board fence, brick wall, and pavement; my pen and ink was a lump of chalk. With these, I learned mainly how to write. I then commenced and continued copying the Italics in Webster's Spelling Book, until I could make them all without looking on the book. By this time, my little Master Thomas had gone to school, and learned how to write, and had written over a number of copy-books. These had been brought home, and shown to some of our near neighbors, and then laid aside. My mistress used to go to class meeting at the Wilk Street meetinghouse every Monday afternoon, and leave me to take care of the house. When left thus, I used to spend the time in writing in the spaces left in Master Thomas's copy-book, copying what he had written. I continued to do this until I could write a hand very similar to that of Master Thomas. Thus, after a long, tedious effort for years, I finally succeeded in learning how to write.

QUESTIONS

1. As its title proclaims, Douglass's book is a narrative, the story of his life. So, too, is this chapter a narrative, the story of his learning to read and write. Separate out the main events of this story, and list them in chronological order.

2. Douglass is reporting some of the events in his life in this selection, but certain events are not simply reported. Instead, they are described so that we may see, hear, and feel what was experienced by those people who were present on the original occasions. Which events are described most fully in this narrative? How does Douglass seek to engage our interest and direct our feelings through such scenes?

3. In this episode from his life, as in his whole book, Douglass is engaged in evaluating an institution—slavery—and arguing a case against it. Can you locate the points in the text where reflecting gives way to argumentation? How does Douglass support his argument against slavery? What are the sources of his persuasiveness?

4. The situation of Irish Catholics is a subtheme in this essay. You can trace it by locating every mention of the Irish or of Catholicism in the text. How does this theme relate to African-American slavery? Try to locate *The Columbian Orator* in your library,

or find out more about who Sheridan was and why he had to argue on behalf of "Catholic emancipation" (paragraph 6).

5. There is a subnarrative in this text that tells the story of Master Hugh's wife, the "mistress" of the household in which Douglass learned to read and write. Retell *her* story in your own words. Consider how her story relates to Douglass's own story and how it relates to Douglass's larger argument about slavery.

6. Put yourself in the place of Master Hugh's wife, and retell all events in her words and from her point of view. To do so, you will have to decide both what she might have come to know about all these events and how she would feel about them. You will also have to decide when she is writing. Is she keeping a diary during this very time (the early 1830s), or is she looking back from the perspective of later years? Has she been moved to write by reading Douglass's own book, which appeared in 1841? If so, how old would she be then, and what would she think about these past events? Would she be angry, bitter, repentant, embarrassed, indulgent, scornful, or what?

MAKING CONNECTIONS

1. What are the most common themes of the African-American writers in this section? On what issues, when they write about writing, do they have most in common with the artists represented here who are white?

2. For Maya Angelou, Frederick Douglass, and Alice Walker, events of childhood and youth are particularly important. Compare how at least two of these writers view events when they were young, how they present their younger selves or viewpoints, and how they connect childhood experience to adult knowledge.

THE IGUANA

Isak Dinesen

Karen Dinesen (1885–1962) was a Danish woman who married a Swedish baron and went to Kenya in East Africa with him in 1914 to manage their coffee plantation. After their divorce she stayed in Kenya, managing the plantation until its failure in 1931. During this time she began to write in English (the language of whites in Kenya), taking the male first name of Isak. Her best-known books are Seven Gothic Tales *(1934), a volume of stories, and* Out of Africa *(1937), her reminiscences of Kenya. The following brief selection from the latter volume appeared in the section called "From an Immigrant's Notebook."*

In the Reserve I have sometimes come upon the Iguana, the big lizards,[1] as they were sunning themselves upon a flat stone in a river-bed. They are not pretty in shape, but nothing can be imagined more beautiful than their coloring. They shine like a heap of precious stones or like a pane cut out of an old church window. When, as you approach, they swish away, there is a flash of azure, green and purple over the stones, the color seems to be standing behind them in the air, like a comet's luminous tail.

Once I shot an Iguana. I thought that I should be able to make some pretty things from his skin. A strange thing happened then, that I have never afterwards forgotten. As I went up to him, where he was lying dead upon his stone, and actually while I was walking a few steps, he faded and grew pale, all color died out of him as in one long sigh, and by the time that I touched him he was grey and dull like a lump of concrete. It was the live impetuous blood pulsating within the animal, which had radiated out all that glow and splendor. Now that the flame was put out, and the soul had flown, the Iguana was as dead as a sandbag.

Often since I have, in some sort, shot an Iguana, and I have remembered the one of the Reserve. Up at Meru I saw a young Native girl with a bracelet on, a leather strap two inches wide, and embroidered all over with very small turquoise-colored beads which varied a little in color and played in green, light blue and ultramarine. It was an extraordinarily live thing; it seemed to draw breath on her arm, so that I wanted it for myself, and made Farah buy it from

---

[1] the Reserve: the game reserve in the Ngong Hills of Kenya, Africa. [Eds.]

her.[2] No sooner had it come upon my own arm than it gave up the ghost. It was nothing now, a small, cheap, purchased article of finery. It had been the play of colors, the duet between the turquoise and the "nègre",—that quick, sweet, brownish black, like peat and black pottery, of the Native's skin,—that had created the life of the bracelet.

In the Zoological Museum of Pietermaritzburg, I have seen, in a stuffed   4 deep-water fish in a showcase, the same combination of coloring, which there had survived death; it made me wonder what life can well be like, on the bottom of the sea, to send up something so live and airy. I stood in Meru and looked at my pale hand and at the dead bracelet, it was as if an injustice had been done to a noble thing, as if truth had been suppressed. So sad did it seem that I remembered the saying of the hero in a book that I had read as a child: "I have conquered them all, but I am standing amongst graves."

In a foreign country and with foreign species of life one should take measures   5 to find out whether things will be keeping their value when dead. To the settlers of East Africa I give the advice: "For the sake of your own eyes and heart, shoot not the Iguana."

QUESTIONS

1. In this essay the act of shooting an iguana comes to stand as a type or model of other actions; it becomes a symbolic event. This is expressed explicitly at the beginning of paragraph 3: "Often since I have, *in some sort*, shot an Iguana" (italics added). How do the incidents described in paragraphs 3 and 4 help us to understand the full meaning of the symbolic action of shooting an iguana? Restate this meaning in your own words.

2. An argument that lurks beneath the surface of this meditative essay is made explicit in its last sentence. How do you understand that sentence and that argument?

3. The power of this essay grows from its effective representation—its ability to put us in the picture, to make us see and feel the events represented. Find a phrase of description or comparison that seems to you especially vivid, and explain why it is effective.

4. Dinesen uses three concrete examples here. How are the three related? Why do you suppose she arranged them in the order in which she did?

5. In her meditation, Dinesen moves from lizard, to bracelet, to fish, and then uses these three specific, concrete instances to make the jump to generalizations about foreign species and foreign countries. Try this technique yourself. Find some incident in your own life that reminds you of other similar events, so that they can be brought together as being symbolic of a certain *kind* of event. To what broader point can you leap from these few recollected events?

---

[2]Farah Aden: Dinesen's Somali servant. [Eds.]

MAKING CONNECTIONS

Consider the deaths and captivities of animals in this essay, in Orwell's "Shooting an Elephant," and in Eiseley's "The Bird and the Machine." Could Dinesen's final sentence and its implied argument be the theme of either of the other essays? Would it fit one better than the other? How would Orwell's or Eiseley's essay change if Dinesen's remark were to guide it?

BORGES Y YO

Jorge Luis Borges

Jorge Luis Borges (1899–1986) was born in Buenos Aires, Argentina. From his father, who was half English, he learned that language before learning Spanish, and became well-read in English literature, which he eventually taught as a professor. As a writer, Borges became a master of shorter fiction and essays, and as his eyesight failed, he turned to poetry. One of his best-known collections of writing is en-titled Labyrinths *(1969), a term which aptly describes his fascination with the systems we construct in our efforts to know our world. In this essay originally published in* El aleph *(1957), Borges reflects on our attempts to know our-selves. We have presented the Spanish version along with three English translations to encourage you to reflect not only on your writing selves, but on how they (and Borges) are translated.*

Al otro, a Borges, es a quien le ocurren las cosas. Yo camino por Buenos Aires y me demoro, acaso ya mecánicamente, para mirar el arco de un zaguán y la puerta cancel; de Borges tengo noticias por el correo y veo su nombre en una terna de profesores o en un diccionario biográfico. Me gustan los relojes de arena, los mapas, la tipografía del siglo XVIII, el sabor del café y la prosa de Stevenson; el otro comparte esas preferencias, pero de un modo vanidoso que las convierte en atributos de un actor. Sería exagerado afirmar que nuestra relación es hostil; yo vivo, yo me dejo vivir, para que Borges pueda tramar su literatura y esa literatura me justifica. Nada me cuesta confesar que ha logrado ciertas páginas válidas, pero esas páginas no me pueden salvar, quizá porque lo bueno ya no es de nadie, ni siquiera del otro, sino del lenguaje o la tradición. Por lo demás, yo estoy destinado a perderme, definitivamente, y sólo algún instante de mí podrá sobrevivir en el otro. Poco a poco voy cediéndole todo, aunque me consta su perversa costumbre de falsear y magnificar. Spinoza entendió que todas las cosas quieren perseverar en su ser; la piedra eternamente quiere ser peidra y el tigre un tigre. Yo he de quedar en Borges, no en mí (si es que alguien soy), pero me reconozco menos en sus libros que en muchos otros o que en el laborioso rasgueo de una guitarra. Hace años yo traté de librarme de él y pasé de las mitologías del arrabal a los juegos con el tiempo y con lo infinito, pero esos juegos son de Borges ahora y tendré que idear otras cosas. Así mi vida es una fuga y todo lo pierdo y todo es del olvido, o del otro.

No sé cuál de los dos escribe esta página.   2

BORGES AND MYSELF

It's to the other man, to Borges, that things happen. I walk along the streets   3
of Buenos Aires, stopping now and then—perhaps out of habit—to look at the
arch of an old entranceway or a grillwork gate; of Borges I get news through
the mail and glimpse his name among a committee of professors or in a
dictionary of biography. I have a taste for hourglasses, maps, eighteenth-century
typography, the roots of words, the smell of coffee, and Stevenson's prose; the
other man shares these likes, but in a showy way that turns them into stagy
mannerisms. It would be an exaggeration to say that we are on bad terms; I
live, I let myself live, so that Borges can weave his tales and poems, and those
tales and poems are my justification. It is not hard for me to admit that he has
managed to write a few worthwhile pages, but these pages cannot save me,
perhaps because what is good no longer belongs to anyone—not even the other
man—but rather to speech or tradition. In any case, I am fated to become lost
once and for all, and only some moment of myself will survive in the other
man. Little by little, I have been surrendering everything to him, even though
I have evidence of his stubborn habit of falsification and exaggerating. Spinoza
held that all things try to keep on being themselves; a stone wants to be a stone
and the tiger, a tiger. I shall remain in Borges, not in myself (if it is so that I
am someone), but I recognize myself less in his books than in those of others
or than in the laborious tuning of a guitar. Years ago, I tried ridding myself of
him and I went from myths of the outlying slums of the city to games with
time and infinity, but those games are now part of Borges and I will have to
turn to other things. And so, my life is a running away, and I lose everything
and everything is left to oblivion or to the other man.

Which of us is writing this page I don't know.   4

Translated by
Norman Thomas Di Giovanni

BORGES AND I

The other one, the one called Borges, is the one things happen to. I walk   5
through the streets of Buenos Aires and stop for a moment, perhaps mechanically now, to look at the arch of an entrance hall and the grillwork on the gate;
I know of Borges from the mail and see his name on a list of professors or in a
biographical dictionary. I like hourglasses, maps, eighteenth-century typography,
the taste of coffee and the prose of Stevenson; he shares these preferences, but

in a vain way that turns them into the attributes of an actor. It would be an exaggeration to say that ours is a hostile relationship; I live, let myself go on living, so that Borges may contrive his literature, and this literature justifies me. It is no effort for me to confess that he has achieved some valid pages, but those pages cannot save me, perhaps because what is good belongs to no one, not even to him, but rather to the language and to tradition. Besides, I am destined to perish, definitively, and only some instant of myself can survive in him. Little by little, I am giving over everything to him, though I am quite aware of his perverse custom of falsifying and magnifying things. Spinoza knew that all things long to persist in their being; the stone eternally wants to be a stone and the tiger a tiger. I shall remain in Borges, not in myself (if it is true that I am someone), but I recognize myself less in his books than in many others or in the laborious strumming of a guitar. Years ago I tried to free myself from him and went from the mythologies of the suburbs to the games with time and infinity, but those games belong to Borges now and I shall have to imagine other things. Thus my life is a flight and I lose everything and everything belongs to oblivion, or to him.

I do not know which of us has written this page. 6

Translated by
James E. Irby

BORGES AND I

Things happen to him, the other one, to Borges. I stroll about Buenos Aires 7 and stop, almost mechanically now perhaps, to look at the arch of an entrance-way and the ironwork gate; news of Borges reaches me in the mail and I see his name on an academic ballot or in a biographical dictionary. I like hour-glasses, maps, eighteenth-century typography, etymologies, the taste of coffee, and Robert Louis Stevenson's prose; he shares these preferences, but with a vanity that turns them into the attributes of an actor. It would be an exaggeration to say that our relationship is a hostile one; I live, I go on living, so that Borges may contrive his literature; and that literature justifies me. I do not find it hard to admit that he has achieved some valid pages, but these pages can not save me, perhaps because what is good no longer belongs to anyone, not even to him, the other one, but to the language or to tradition. In any case, I am destined to perish, definitively, and only some instant of me may live on in him. Little by little, I yield him ground, the whole terrain, though I am quite aware of his perverse habit of magnifying and falsifying. Spinoza realized that all things strive to persist in their own nature: the stone eternally wishes to be stone and the tiger a tiger. I shall subsist in Borges, not in myself (assuming I am someone), and yet I recognize myself less in his books than in many another, or than in the intricate flourishes played on a guitar. Years ago I tried to free myself from him, and I went from the mythologies of the city suburbs to games with time and infinity, but now those games belong to Borges, and I will have to think up something else. Thus is my life a flight, and I lose everything, and everything belongs to oblivion, or to him.

I don't know which one of the two of us is writing this page.

8

Translated by
Anthony Kerrigan

QUESTIONS

1. This essay is frequently anthologized as a parable, which has been defined by C. Hugh Holman as "an illustrative story answering a question or pointing a moral or lesson." If the question is "Who is writing?" the answer is "I don't know." Perhaps that is not the real question, or perhaps there is a moral or lesson. What do you think?

2. In an interview, Borges said that, in this piece, "I am concerned with the division between the private man and the public man." How is this concern made evident in the essay? Can we say there is a division between the writer and the one who writes?

3. Who are you when you write? Consider the different kinds of writing you have had to do over the past year. How many roles did you take on? Describe them.

4. What differences can you see in the three English translations? Discuss them. If you know Spanish, write a commentary on the three translations. Which one do you think is most faithful to the Spanish version, and why?

5. Reflect on your other "self." Borges, commenting on his poem, "The Watchers," which has similarities to this essay, said, "There is always this idea of the split personality. Sometimes I fall back on the metaphor of the other, The Watcher. At other times, he is waiting for me at the top of the staircase, and then in the next line he is inside me, he is my voice, or he is in my face." Borges also describes his theme as "a variation on the Jekyll and Hyde motif." If you are bilingual, do you feel different when you speak in English than when you speak in another language?

MAKING CONNECTIONS

Borges reflects on his attempts to know his various selves. Select two other essays in "Reflecting" in which writers are imagining various divisions between their personal selves and their public selves. What connections do you see between these essays? What do these connections show you about the reflecting "I"?

DIALOGUES WITH THE DEAD
Christopher Clausen

Christopher Clausen (b. 1942) is a professor of English at Pennsylvania State University. He is the author of two books, The Place of Poetry: Two Centuries of an Art in Crisis *(1981), named a "notable book of the year" by* The New York Times Book Review, *and* The Moral Imagination: Essays on Literature and Ethics *(1986). He writes that "literature, poetry in particular, was once central to our culture because readers took it seriously as an exploration of life, an attempt to grapple with the intellectual and moral problems that beset human beings like themselves." His essays have appeared in* Kenyon Review, Sewanee Review *and* Children's Literature. *In the following essay, which first appeared in* American Scholar, *Clausen explores the relationship between the living and the dead.*

My great-grandmother's eighth pregnancy was a difficult one. After all, she 1 was nearly forty-eight years old when it began. Of her five living children (two others having died in infancy), the two oldest, my grandfather and his sister Marie, were already in their mid-teens. Contrary to what might have been expected, however, she carried the fetus to term and in the autumn of 1896 gave birth to a healthy boy who would live through most of the following century. Her own prognosis was not so fortunate. Never fully recovered from the birth of her final child, after twenty-one months she knew she was dying. Moreover, she knew only too well that her grief-stricken husband—"not a good provider," in the language of the day—would be hard-pressed to maintain an infant and three other small children, whatever help the oldest son, now at work but eager to enlist in the Spanish-American War, might provide. She was, like her husband, an immigrant. Her own family was far away.

Promise me, she said to her daughter Marie in German, *promise me that you* 2 *will keep the family together and raise your brother Charlie.* What could a late-nineteenth-century girl say to such an appeal? Besides, she adored her mother. *Mama,* she answered inevitably, *I promise.* In that world, that was how they did things. What is more, they sometimes meant it. My great-aunt Marie kept the family together, raised her brother Charlie, and, for good measure, helped raise his children and grandchildren. She never married and lived to be ninety-eight. When Charlie died a few years before she did, she felt reasonably enough that life had become absurd and that it was high time to depart. Her final wish was to be buried in the grave of her mother, to whom she had so spectacularly kept a promise made eighty-one years earlier, and with whom she had so long carried on a dialogue that furnished the pattern for an entire life. Near the end of 1979, the customs of the late twentieth century grudgingly yielded to the sentiments of the nineteenth, and the ancient grave was reopened for its second occupant.

The communication of the dead, according to T. S. Eliot, is tongued with 3 fire beyond the language of the living. Death has freed them to tell us things they had no words for in life. Being dead, they presumably do not mind what shapes we impose on them. All the same, they have their revenge: by admitting their influence through dialogue with them, we impose lasting shapes and obligations on ourselves as well. The dead can strengthen and steady us; they can also drive us crazy. People in superstitious ages imagined ghosts to explain their sense of being haunted, of involuntarily carrying on transactions with those who had died. In more modern language, our conversations with the dead are the ultimate form of projection, in which we define ourselves most revealingly and recognize, consciously or not, our actual status in the world. Whether or not we choose to be buried in the same grave, there is after all that perfect bond of death between the generations.

According to Dr. Milton Helpern, former chief medical examiner of New 4 York City, death is "the irreversible cessation of life. Death may be due to a wide variety of diseases and disorders, but in every case the underlying physiological cause is a breakdown in the body's oxygen cycle." Law, if not medicine, distinguishes rigorously between death from natural causes, accident, homicide, or suicide. So do the survivors; our dialogue with someone who has been murdered is quite different in tone and substance from our colloquy with one who died of heart disease. Much depends also on the age at death. Like cause of death, the age at which one's oxygen cycle breaks down communicates a definite view of the universe to the living. In contemporary America we hold far fewer dialogues with dead children than took place in centuries when infant mortality was a frequent guest in every family, and the death of someone who failed to live out a normal life span is a correspondingly more powerful cause of grief and bitterness. We tend to feel that such a person has been the victim of an outrage. In many ritualistic or traditional cultures, on the other hand, "to be a dead member of one's society is the individual's ultimate social status," according to John Middleton—*ultimate* meaning not only final but highest. Such societies find it easier, at least abstractly, to accept the inevitability of deaths at many ages and to maintain an equable dialogue with their vanished members, although that acceptance does not necessarily lessen either the grief or the extravagance of its expression.

"Must I remember?" the extravagantly grieving Hamlet asks himself reprovingly two months after the untimely death of his father. Memory of the dead is of course the beginning of dialogue with them, a dialogue usually commenced with the rituals of funeral and commitment to the earth. In Hamlet's case, as in many modern ones, the ritual has been foreshortened, with the predictable consequence that memory and dialogue acquire an unhealthy power over the survivors. This power is all the greater for being unanticipated. For we address the dead constantly if they were close to us; and if they had a powerful effect on us in life, they answer. Oh yes, they talk back, make demands, insist on undivided attention. Raise my family, share my grave—these are benign exigencies. Too often, the ghost demands revenge. 5

> Remember thee?
> Aye, thou poor ghost, whiles memory holds a seat
> In this distracted globe. Remember thee?
> Yea, from the table of my memory
> I'll wipe away all trivial fond records,
> All saws of books, all forms, all pressures past
> That youth and observation copied there,
> And thy commandment all alone shall live
> Within the book and volume of my brain,
> Unmixed with baser matter.

How to converse with a ghost who demands vengeance? To adopt its wishes as one's own is to become possessed, whether the ghost's name is Hamlet the elder, or Moses, or Mohammed; whether the essence of its demand is to kill the usurper or repossess the land he took. Share my grave. To deny the ghost, on the other hand, may involve such a renunciation of one's own identity as to be nearly impossible—and the ghost will still be there in any event, as dead as ever. Falling between two stools, as Hamlet did, may be the worst of all choices: as in the play, it may simply widen the power of the ghost to encompass other fates besides that of the individual possessed, leaving the family and the state in ruins and Horatio alone to tell the tale. But possession rarely involves much choice. 6

Hamlet, in the opinion of many critics, is a modern figure trapped in an archaic drama: a man not given to believing ghosts or committing bloody acts of revenge. That is his tragedy. The enlightened mind becomes genuinely unhinged when faced with such demands, or with such a demander. Ghosts, after all, are written into plays to entertain the groundlings, whose benighted state makes them more susceptible to haunting. Although groundlings still exist and ghosts are still created for them—television and Hollywood give ample recent instances—the dead, whether friendly or hateful, hold no dialogues with 7 the truly modern mind. We have learned to outgrow all that. Life is for the living; the healthy mind looks to the future. We cremate the dead and scatter their ashes, dissolving not only the spirit but the material body itself into thin air. There is no grave to share. Nobody can haunt us.

"A ghost in search of vengeance," asks the ghostly narrator of Robertson Davies's novel *Murther & Walking Spirits*—"what is it to do in such a world as ours?" 8

The ghost, of course, was really Hamlet's unconscious speaking. Self-assertion and the desire for revenge, muddled up with Oedipal longings for his sexually accomplished mother, projected themselves quite naturally onto the image of the dead father, who then walked the stage as a ghost. Of course. The word *psychology* would not be invented for another two centuries. We know how to understand the character Hamlet and the play itself not just differently but better than any Elizabethan. In a sense, that is perfectly true. How important that sense may be is more debatable. In Shaw's *Saint Joan*, an indisputably modern play, the title character is informed that the voices of long-dead saints who talk to her are in fact the product of her imagination. "Of course," she answers unabashedly. "That is how the messages of God come to us." To take the ghost out of its shadowy existence in the world and enshrine it in the mind only increases its power, unless the implication is that understanding the true *locus* of the haunting somehow dispels it. Clearly it does no such thing. The dead whose final resting place is in our mind are no less potent than those who are assumed to keep an unquiet vigil in the world of space. Real ghosts could appear only at certain times and places, and they could be exorcised. Psychological ghosts, even of the friendly dead, have no such limitations. Once our dead are buried within us, they can stay there for as long as we live—longer insofar as the patterns they embody are passed on through us to others by way of upbringing or genetic inheritance. Ignoring them is no solution. The less we hold dialogue with them, the more unruly their effect on us becomes. We can never get away from a voice that lives inside us. 9

Sometimes the voices within are collective and historical rather than individual as are the ghosts of our private dead. My father-in-law was a career naval officer who served as a carrier pilot during World War II. Like a surprising number of American officers in that war, he was the grandson of a Confederate veteran and half-consciously saw his own war as a prolongation of his grandfather's, not in terms of the issues involved but rather as an opportunity to vindicate an honorable defeat by winning an even greater struggle eighty years later. Somehow the significance of the past could be changed by valor in the present, not exactly avenging a loss but perhaps removing the shame or sting of it. Although this particular way of looking at World War II was restricted to a small part of a single generation, the habit of seeing a current series of events in the light of the Civil War was not. Much of twentieth-century American 10

78

history involves a dialogue with the ghosts of the Civil War, a conflict in which more Americans died than in all our other wars combined. If the Civil Rights movement had in some respects to defeat the ghosts of the Confederacy all over again, it also drew strength from the black heroes of Fort Wagner and many another battle a hundred years before. The ghost of Abraham Lincoln, the commander in chief, remains the most potent figure in American history, now reinforced by that of Martin Luther King, Jr.

In the last year of his life, when his eyesight and many other things were 11 failing, my father-in-law asked my wife to read him long stretches from Shelby Foote's narrative history of the Civil War as a preparation for death. It was not that he had any wish to refight the war, still less that he expected Stonewall Jackson to meet him on the threshold of Valhalla with an entrance examination. He was a modern man with, for the most part, modern beliefs. No, it was rather that having (again like many Southern men of his generation) lived in the shadow of these events all his life, he wished to be as clear as possible about them before he died. There were lessons to be learned about living and dying; this seemed the best available way for him to learn them. What the dead had to say now was very different from what they had communicated forty or sixty years ago. One last long conversation with the ghosts, perhaps, and then he would be ready to join them. The Crater was the battle he liked to hear about most, but there was nothing bloodthirsty or sentimental in his reactions. Rather he was closing a circle that had begun when he first heard about Southern victories and defeats in childhood, preparing for death in a way that was appropriate to the life he had lived, like a cheerful stoic.

"Then with the knowledge of death as walking one side of me," wrote Walt 12 Whitman in 1865, commemorating Lincoln and the dead of the Civil War,

> And the thought of death close-walking the other side of me,
> And I in the middle as with companions, and as holding the hands
>   of companions,
> I fled forth to the hiding receiving night that talks not . . .

Because he had so thoughtfully assimilated himself to the dead at the end of his life, and because, in the almost forgotten phrase, he was full of years, the ghost of my father-in-law is a quiet one, a familiar daily presence that inspires and does not disturb.

Early death is something else again. To die with manifest unfulfilled promise, 13 to leave grieving parents behind, seems a violation of the natural order. These dead, if we were close to them, are the object not just of mourning but of shock and guilt, as though we should have been able to foresee and prevent. They speak of inconsolable loss, and a long time must pass before we can hear anything else they have to say.

The Boston cancer specialists thought they had cured my brother of lym-   14
phoma not once but twice. A political scientist of great talents, he had had a
somewhat unlucky career, owing to the depressed academic job market of the
seventies and, after he had gone into government, the change of administrations
in 1981. But he had begun to work his way back, interrupted by chemotherapy
and a marrow transplant, and had even managed to complete a book on nuclear
proliferation in which many publishers expressed interest. A few days after he
signed a contract for its publication, his doctor informed him that he had at
most three months to live.

We drove up to visit him immediately. When we arrived he was in the   15
hospital, but they discharged him after a few days. Perhaps there was hope—
perhaps new therapies as yet untried—there are doctors and there are doctors.
One of them was optimistic. My sister-in-law pretended to believe, but there
was no hope, really, and my brother was full of bitterness. It was not *Why me?*
It sounded more like *Why now?* Why not earlier or later? He was anxious for
his family in a way that only someone with a deep capacity for happiness, a
beloved eight-year-old son, and hardly any life insurance can be. That anxiety
was the strongest note in everything he said.

It would be pointless to give details of the conversations we had with him   16
then, or later by telephone. All of them were like conversations with someone
who is already dead, who is looking back from the other side and seeing
something quite different from the other people in the room. How does one
discuss plans for the future of a widow and her son when her young husband
is the most determined of the discussers? From a great distance he watched us
sadly as we talked about mortgages, school fees, the raising of a child in which
he would have no further living part to play. From whatever place he now
inhabited, he pressed all the right questions, asked for and received all the right
promises from everyone, unerringly noticed every feature of the situation that
would soon face his survivors. Unwilling to die but perceiving no alternative,
he expressed in his speech and actions an equal mixture of courage and anger.
Eventually the anger faded, leaving only sorrow, courage, and deep concern
for the two who needed him most.

"There must be wisdom with great Death," Tennyson wrote after the death   17
of another young man: "The dead shall look me through and through." My
brother unwillingly put his house in order, made such peace as he could, and
died on an afternoon in early summer, the three months proving in the end to
be thirty-eight days. At the funeral his father and two of his brothers were
pallbearers, while his mother sat among the mourners, and I felt that whatever
was in the casket was looking us through and through.

A depressing story, certainly, though far from a unique one in this or any   18
other century. What kinds of dialogue will follow such a death? Of course it's
too early to say. Like those of a true ghost, my brother's purposes must be

fulfilled in the lives of others, in contrast to those of most people who live to what is thought to be a normal age. For the time being, he is an unquiet ghost who speaks only of loss and incompletion, who asks only about his wife and son and can be answered only with reassurances. Later on he will have other things to tell those who knew him, and they will speak to him less frantically. He was a much-loved person, not only by his family, and the value of his legacy—and consequently the richness of the dialogues in which he will participate while those who loved him are still alive—will be very great. The scope of those dialogues, like everything else in which the living take part, is unpredictable.

In a sense, any remembered dead person eventually says to us: *I lived in a* 19 *different time, subject to different pressures, part of a story that has now, if not ended, at least reached a different stage, with different characters.* And later still, if anyone is around to hear: *Even if I had lived a normal life, I would be dead now.* Beyond that, is everything they tell us projection? Perhaps, in a way. If so, it is projection of a very special kind, in which by virtue of their being dead we find ourselves extended far beyond our everyday limits of understanding and learn things about ourselves and our world that no living person could tell us. In these strange dialogues, the dead do indeed look us through and through.

Many survivors of the Final Solution feel that they carry the dead within 20 them, an unbearable burden of guilt and remembrance. Here the conversation with the dead, who may include all the members of one's family, must surely reach the limits of possibility. Those who survived the atomic bombings of Hiroshima and Nagasaki tell a slightly different version: they sense that they carry death itself inside them. Perhaps such extreme calamities offer one reason that our time is so reluctant to be reminded of death as the common fate or of any claims that the dead might have on the living.

> They used to pour millet on graves or poppy seeds
> To feed the dead who would come disguised as birds.
> I put this book here for you, who once lived
> So that you should visit us no more,

Czeslaw Milosz wrote in the ruined Warsaw of 1945. If we pay them too much or too little attention, the dead can eat us up.

Even to us ordinary people, the dead speak all the time. Willingly or not, 21 we conduct endless dialogues with them. People who live in periods with no widely accepted way of visualizing the status and influence of the dead will invent new ones or try to revive old ones; hence the widespread half-beliefs in reincarnation and New Age varieties of spiritualism. On a more everyday level, the husband who has lost a wife, the wife who has lost a husband, says, *How could you do this to me?* The other answers, *I had no choice. I would much rather have gone to the beach with you as we planned.* And sometimes, *You should get out more.* And even, *You should remarry, for your own sake and the sake of the children.* Often enough, we do what the dead tell us.

Finally, it is the dead who tell us who we are, not just as individuals (though   22 that too) but as a species of animals that needs reminding. They tell us constantly that life is a rough place and nobody gets out of it alive. Or as Montaigne put it, "Live as long as you please, you will strike nothing off the time you will have to spend dead." Our dialogue with the dead is a conversation between equals. As late-twentieth-century people, we tend to find this familiar news morbid and tasteless, like a Victorian funeral. After all, we make a fetish of youth and health, the unbounded liberation of the self from all forms of oppression, which must surely include the freedom not to die if we so choose. The impersonal objectivity of death is an affront to everything we want to believe.

That reaction only increases the power of the ghosts whom we try so hard,   23 and with so little success, to confine in the safe, invisible place we call the dead past. But the ghosts tell us, either kindly or cruelly depending mostly on our willingness to hear, that they actually represent our future. Share my grave whether you will or not. That irrefutable announcement, which they are now free to speak, is the beginning of all the other things we can learn from them, and if we pretend not to hear it, the rest of what they have to say will be unintelligible.

QUESTIONS

1. Clausen begins his essay by telling us a story about his great-grandmother and the promise she extracted from her daughter, Marie. Why do you think Clausen begins his essay with this story? What is the significance of Marie's promise? What does Clausen want us to understand about the promises we make to the living and to the dead?

2. Why does Clausen entitle his essay "Dialogues with the Dead"? What is the nature of the dialogue between the living and the dead? What are the ways in which the dead talk back, make demands, and insist on the undivided attention of the living?

3. Clausen offers his readers many different kinds of sources as evidence—anecdotes, poetry, and so forth. How do these various sources form a dialogue in this essay?

4. What does Clausen mean when he writes: "But the ghosts tell us, either kindly or cruelly depending mostly on our willingness to hear, that they actually represent our future"?

5. Clausen is interested in the emotional legacies that are buried within us and the ways in which patterns "are passed on . . . by way of upbringing or genetic inheritance." Reflect on your own life and the dialogues you have with your ancestors. What does this conversation sound like? What legacies and patterns have been passed on to you? Write an essay in which you reflect on your dialogues with the dead.

MAKING CONNECTIONS

Clausen suggests that the dead will eat us up if we pay too much or too little attention to them. Elizabeth Kübler-Ross in her essay "On the Fear of Death" suggests that we have significant lessons to learn from the dying. Kübler-Ross warns us that we might avoid thinking about death, but we do so at our own peril. What kind of dialogue can you imagine between Clausen and Kübler-Ross? Write an essay in which you create a conversation between these two essayists.

Social Sciences and Public Affairs

ON BEING THE OBJECT OF PROPERTY

Patricia J. Williams

*Patricia J. Williams (b. 1951) is a professor of women's
studies and law at the University of Wisconsin and is the
great-great-granddaughter of a woman purchased at the age
of eleven by a white lawyer who immediately impregnated
her. In her book* The Alchemy of Race and Rights *(1991),
Williams juxtaposes experiential accounts with sophisticated
legal theories to expose the ideology underlying law in the
United States. Several of her essays have appeared in* Ms.
In the following essay, which first appeared in Signs, *Williams writes: "In my search for roots, I must assume, not
just as history but as an ongoing psychological force, that,
in the eyes of white culture, irrationality, lack of control,
and ugliness signify not just the whole slave personality, not
just the whole black personality, but me."*

ON BEING INVISIBLE

Reflections

For some time I have been writing about my great-great-grandmother. I have   1
considered the significance of her history and that of slavery from a variety of
viewpoints on a variety of occasions: in every speech, in every conversation,

even in my commercial transactions class. I have talked so much about her that I finally had to ask myself what it was I was looking for in this dogged pursuit of family history. Was I being merely indulgent, looking for roots in the pursuit of some genetic heraldry, seeking the inheritance of being special, different, unique in all that primogeniture hath wrought?

I decided that my search was based in the utility of such a quest, not mere 2
indulgence, but a recapturing of that which had escaped historical scrutiny, which had been overlooked and underseen. I, like so many blacks, have been trying to pin myself down in history, place myself in the stream of time as significant, evolved, present in the past, continuing into the future. To be without documentation is too unsustaining, too spontaneously ahistorical, too dangerously malleable in the hands of those who would rewrite not merely the past but my future as well. So I have been picking through the ruins for my roots.

What I know of my mother's side of the family begins with my great-great- 3
grandmother. Her name was Sophie and she lived in Tennessee. In 1850, she was about twelve years old. I know that she was purchased when she was eleven by a white lawyer named Austin Miller and was immediately impregnated by him. She gave birth to my great-grandmother Mary, who was taken away from her to be raised as a house servant.[1] I know nothing more of Sophie (she was, after all, a black single mother—in today's terms—suffering the anonymity of yet another statistical teenage pregnancy). While I don't remember what I was told about Austin Miller before I decided to go to law school, I do remember that just before my first day of class, my mother said, in a voice full of secretive reassurance, "The Millers were lawyers, so you have it in your blood."[2]

When my mother told me that I had nothing to fear in law school, that law 4
was "in my blood," she meant it in a very complex sense. First and foremost, she meant it defiantly; she meant that no one should make me feel inferior because someone else's father was a judge. She wanted me to reclaim that part of my heritage from which I had been disinherited, and she wanted me to use it as a source of strength and self-confidence. At the same time, she was asking me to claim a part of myself that was the dispossessor of another part of myself; she was asking me to deny that disenfranchised little black girl of myself that felt powerless, vulnerable and, moreover, rightly felt so.

In somewhat the same vein, Mother was asking me not to look to her as a 5
role model. She was devaluing that part of herself that was not Harvard and refocusing my vision to that part of herself that was hard-edged, proficient, and Western. She hid the lonely, black, defiled-female part of herself and pushed

---

[1] For a more detailed account of the family history to this point, see Patricia Williams, "Grandmother Sophie," *Harvard Blackletter* 3 (1986): 79.

[2] Patricia Williams, "Alchemical Notes: Reconstructing Ideals from Deconstructed Rights," *Harvard Civil Rights-Civil Liberties Law Review* 22 (1987): 418.

me forward as the projection of a competent self, a cool rather than despairing self, a masculine rather than a feminine self.

I took this secret of my blood into the Harvard milieu with both the pride and the shame with which my mother had passed it along to me. I found myself in the situation described by Marguerite Duras, in her novel *The Lover:* "We're united in a fundamental shame at having to live. It's here we are at the heart of our common fate, the fact that [we] are our mother's children, the children of a candid creature murdered by society. We're on the side of society which has reduced her to despair. Because of what's been done to our mother, so amiable, so trusting, we hate life, we hate ourselves."[3]

Reclaiming that from which one has been disinherited is a good thing. Self-possession in the full sense of that expression is the companion to self-knowledge. Yet claiming for myself a heritage the weft of whose genesis is my own disinheritance is a profoundly troubling paradox.

Images

A friend of mine practices law in rural Florida. His office is in Belle Glade, an extremely depressed area where the sugar industry reigns supreme, where blacks live pretty much as they did in slavery times, in dormitories called slave ships. They are penniless and illiterate and have both a high birth rate and a high death rate.

My friend told me about a client of his, a fifteen-year-old young woman pregnant with her third child, who came seeking advice because her mother had advised a hysterectomy—not even a tubal ligation—as a means of birth control. The young woman's mother, in turn, had been advised of the propriety of such a course in her own case by a white doctor some years before. Listening to this, I was reminded of a case I worked on when I was working for the Western Center on Law and Poverty about eight years ago. Ten black Hispanic women had been sterilized by the University of Southern California–Los Angeles County General Medical Center, allegedly without proper consent, and in most instances without even their knowledge.[4] Most of them found out what had been done to them upon inquiry, after a much-publicized news story in which an intern charged that the chief of obstetrics at the hospital pursued a policy of recommending Caesarian delivery and simultaneous sterilization for any pregnant woman with three or more children and who was on welfare. In the course of researching the appeal in that case, I remember learning that one-quarter of all Navajo women of childbearing age—literally all those of child-bearing age ever admitted to a hospital—have been sterilized.[5]

---

[3] Marguerite Duras, *The Lover* (New York: Harper & Row, 1985), 55.

[4] *Madrigal v. Quilligan*, U.S. Court of Appeals, 9th Circuit, Docket no. 78-3187, October 1979.

[5] This was the testimony of one of the witnesses. It is hard to find official confirmation for this

As I reflected on all this, I realized that one of the things passed on from   10
slavery, which continues in the oppression of people of color, is a belief structure
rooted in a concept of black (or brown, or red) anti-will, the antithetical
embodiment of pure will. We live in a society in which the closest equivalent
of nobility is the display of unremittingly controlled will-fulness. To be perceived
as unremittingly will-less is to be imbued with an almost lethal trait.

Many scholars have explained this phenomenon in terms of total and infan-   11
tilizing interdependency of dominant and oppressed.[6] Consider, for example,
Mark Tushnet's distinction between slave law's totalistic view of personality and
the bourgeois "pure will" theory of personality: "Social relations in slave society
rest upon the interaction of owner with slave; the owner, having total dominion
over the slave. In contrast, bourgeois social relations rest upon the paradigmatic
instance of market relations, the purchase by a capitalist of a worker's labor
power; that transaction implicates only a part of the worker's personality. Slave
relations are total, engaging the master and slave in exchanges in which each
must take account of the entire range of belief, feeling, and interest embodied
by the other; bourgeois social relations are partial, requiring only that participants in a market evaluate their general productive characteristics without regard
to aspects of personality unrelated to production."[7]

Although such an analysis is not objectionable in some general sense, the   12
description of master-slave relations as "total" is, to me, quite troubling. Such

---

or any other sterilization statistic involving Native American women. Official statistics kept by the
U.S. Public Health Service, through the Centers for Disease Control in Atlanta, come from data
gathered by the National Hospital Discharge Survey, which covers neither federal hospitals nor
penitentiaries. Services to Native American women living on reservations are provided almost
exclusively by federal hospitals. In addition, the U.S. Public Health Service breaks down its
information into only three categories: "White," "Black," and "Other." Nevertheless, in 1988, the
Women of All Red Nations Collective of Minneapolis, Minnesota, distributed a fact sheet entitled
"Sterilization Studies of Native American Women," which claimed that as many as 50 percent of
all Native American women of child-bearing age have been sterilized. According to "Surgical
Sterilization Surveillance: Tubal Sterilization and Hysterectomy in Women Aged 15–44, 1979–
1980," issued by the Centers for Disease Control in 1983, "In 1980, the tubal sterilization rate for
black women . . . was 45 percent greater than that for white women" (7). Furthermore, a study
released in 1984 by the Division of Reproductive Health of the Center for Health Promotion and
Education (one of the Centers for Disease Control) found that, as of 1982, 48.8 percent of Puerto
Rican women between the ages of 15 and 44 had been sterilized.

[6] See, generally, Stanley Elkins, *Slavery* (New York: Grosset & Dunlap, 1963); Kenneth Stampp,
The Peculiar Institution (New York: Vintage, 1956): Winthrop Jordan, *White over Black* (Baltimore:
Penguin Books, 1968).

[7] Mark Tushnet, *The American Law of Slavery* (Princeton, N.J.: Princeton University Press,
1981), 6. There is danger, in the analysis that follows, of appearing to "pick" on Tushnet. That is
not my intention, nor is it to impugn the body of his research, most of which I greatly admire.
The choice of this passage for analysis has more to do with the randomness of my reading habits;
the fact that he is one of the few legal writers to attempt, in the context of slavery, a juxtaposition
of political theory with psychoanalytic theories of personality; and the fact that he is perceived to
be of the political left, which simplifies my analysis in terms of its presumption of sympathy, i.e.,
that the constructions of thought revealed are socially derived and unconscious rather than idiosyncratic and intentional.

a choice of words reflects and accepts—at a very subtle level, perhaps—a historical rationalization that whites had to, could do, and did do everything for these simple, above-animal subhumans. It is a choice of vocabulary that fails to acknowledge blacks as having needs beyond those that even the most "humane" or "sentimental" white slavemaster could provide.[8] In trying to describe the provisional aspect of slave law, I would choose words that revealed its structure as rooted in a concept of, again, black anti-will, the polar opposite of pure will. I would characterize the treatment of blacks by whites in whites' law as defining blacks as those who had no will. I would characterize that treatment not as total interdependency, but as a relation in which partializing judgments, employing partializing standards of humanity, impose generalized inadequacy on a race: if pure will or total control equals the perfect white person, then impure will and total lack of control equals the perfect black man or woman. Therefore, to define slave law as comprehending a "total" view of personality implicitly accepts that the provision of food, shelter, and clothing (again assuming the very best of circumstances) is the whole requirement of humanity. It assumes also either that psychic care was provided by slave owners (as though a slave or an owned psyche could ever be reconciled with mental health) or that psyche is not a significant part of a whole human.

Market theory indeed focuses attention away from the full range of human potential in its pursuit of a divinely willed, invisibly handed economic actor. Master-slave relations, however, focused attention away from the full range of black human potential in a somewhat different way: it pursued a vision of blacks as simple minded, strong-bodied economic actants.[9] Thus, while blacks had an indisputable generative force in the marketplace, their presence could not be called activity; they had no active role in the market. To say, therefore, that

13

---

[8] In another passage, Tushnet observes: "The court thus demonstrated its appreciation of the ties of sentiment that slavery could generate between master and slave and simultaneously denied that those ties were relevant in the law" (67). What is noteworthy about the reference to "sentiment" is that it assumes that the fact that emotions could grow up between slave and master is itself worth remarking: slightly surprising, slightly commendable for the court to note (i.e., in its "appreciation")—although "simultaneously" with, and presumably in contradistinction to, the court's inability to take official cognizance of the fact. Yet, if one really looks at the ties that bound master and slave, one has to flesh out the description of master-slave with the ties of father-son, father-daughter, half-sister, half-brother, uncle, aunt, cousin, and a variety of de facto foster relationships. And if one starts to see those ties as more often than not intimate family ties, then the terminology "appreciation of . . . sentiment . . . between master and slave" becomes a horrifying mockery of any true sense of family sentiment, which is utterly, utterly lacking. The court's "appreciation," from this enhanced perspective, sounds blindly cruel, sarcastic at best. And to observe that courts suffused in such "appreciation" could simultaneously deny its legal relevance seems not only a truism; it misses the point entirely.

[9] "Actants have a kind of phonemic, rather than a phonetic role: they operate on the level of function, rather than content. That is, an actant may embody itself in a particular character (termed an acteur) or it may reside in the function of more than one character in respect of their common role in the story's underlying 'oppositional' structure. In short, the deep structure of the narrative generates and defines its actants at a level beyond that of the story's surface content" (Terence Hawkes, *Structuralism and Semiotics* [Berkeley: University of California Press, 1977], 89).

"market relations disregard the peculiarities of individuals, whereas slave rela-tions rest on the mutual recognition of the humanity of master and slave"[10] (no matter how dialectical or abstracted a definition of humanity one adopts) is to posit an inaccurate equation: if "disregard for the peculiarities of individuals" and "mutual recognition of humanity" are polarized by a "whereas," then somehow regard for peculiarities of individuals must equal recognition of hu-manity. In the context of slavery this equation mistakes whites' overzealous and oppressive obsession with projected specific peculiarities of blacks for actual holistic regard for the individual. It overlooks the fact that most definitions of humanity require something beyond mere biological sustenance, some healthy measure of autonomy beyond that of which slavery could institutionally or otherwise conceive. Furthermore, it overlooks the fact that both slave and bourgeois systems regarded certain attributes as important and disregarded cer-tain others, and that such regard and disregard can occur in the same glance, like the wearing of horseblinders to focus attention simultaneously toward and away from. The experiential blinders of market actor and slave are focused in different directions, yet the partializing ideologies of each makes the act of not seeing an unconscious, alienating component of seeing. Restoring a unified social vision will, I think, require broader and more scattered resolutions than the simple symmetry of ideological bipolarity.

Thus, it is important to undo whatever words obscure the fact that slave law 14 was at least as fragmenting and fragmented as the bourgeois worldview—in a way that has persisted to this day, cutting across all ideological boundaries. As "pure will" signifies the whole bourgeois personality in the bourgeois worldview, so wisdom, control, and aesthetic beauty signify the whole white personality in slave law. The former and the latter, the slavemaster and the burgermeister, are not so very different when expressed in those terms. The reconciling difference is that in slave law the emphasis is really on the inverse rationale: that irratio-nality, lack of control, and ugliness signify the whole slave personality. "Total" interdependence is at best a polite way of rationalizing such personality splin-tering; it creates a bizarre sort of yin-yang from the dross of an oppressive schizophrenia of biblical dimension. I would just call it schizophrenic, with all the baggage that that connotes. That is what sounds right to me. Truly total relationships (as opposed to totalitarianism) call up images of whole people dependent on whole people; an interdependence that is both providing and laissez-faire at the same time. Neither the historical inheritance of slave law nor so-called bourgeois law meets that definition.

None of this, perhaps, is particularly new. Nevertheless, as precedent to 15 anything I do as a lawyer, the greatest challenge is to allow the full truth of partializing social constructions to be felt for their overwhelming reality—reality that otherwise I might rationally try to avoid facing. In my search for roots, I

---

[10] Tushnet, 69.

must assume, not just as history but as an ongoing psychological force, that, in the eyes of white culture, irrationality, lack of control, and ugliness signify not just the whole slave personality, not just the whole black personality, but me.

Vision

Reflecting on my roots makes me think again and again of the young woman in Belle Glade, Florida. She told the story of her impending sterilization, according to my friend, while keeping her eyes on the ground at all times. My friend, who is white, asked why she wouldn't look up, speak with him eye to eye. The young woman answered that she didn't like white people seeing inside her. 16

My friend's story made me think of my own childhood and adolescence: my parents were always telling me to look up at the world; to look straight at people, particularly white people; not to let them stare me down; to hold my ground; to insist on the right to my presence no matter what. They told me that in this culture you have to look people in the eye because that's how you tell them you're their equal. My friend's story also reminded me how very difficult I had found that looking-back to be. What was hardest was not just that white people saw me, as my friend's client put it, but that they looked through me, that they treated me as though I were transparent. 17

By itself, seeing into me would be to see my substance, my anger, my vulnerability, and my wild raging despair—and that alone is hard enough to show, to share. But to uncover it and to have it devalued by ignore-ance, to hold it up bravely in the organ of my eyes and to have it greeted by an impassive stare that passes right through all that which is me, an impassive stare that moves on and attaches itself to my left earlobe or to the dust caught in the rusty vertical geysers of my wiry hair or to the breadth of my freckled brown nose— this is deeply humiliating. It re-wounds, relives the early childhood anguish of uncensored seeing, the fullness of vision that is the permanent turning-away point for most blacks. 18

The cold game of equality-staring makes me feel like a thin sheet of glass: white people see all the worlds beyond me but not me. They come trotting at me with force and speed; they do not see me. I could force my presence, the real me contained in those eyes, upon them, but I would be smashed in the process. If I deflect, if I move out of the way, they will never know I existed. 19

Marguerite Duras, again in *The Lover*, places the heroine in relation to her family. "Every day we try to kill one another, to kill. Not only do we not talk to one another, we don't even look at one another. When you're being looked at you can't look. To look is to feel curious, to be interested, to lower yourself."[11] 20

To look is also to make myself vulnerable; yet not to look is to neutralize 21

---

[11] Duras, 54.

the part of myself which is vulnerable. I look in order to see, and so I must look. Without that directness of vision, I am afraid I will will my own blindness, disinherit my own creativity, and sterilize my own perspective of its embattled, passionate insight.

ON ARDOR

The Child

One Saturday afternoon not long ago, I sat among a litter of family photo- 22
graphs telling a South African friend about Marjorie, my godmother and my mother's cousin. She was given away by her light-skinned mother when she was only six. She was given to my grandmother and my great-aunts to be raised among her darker-skinned cousins, for Marjorie was very dark indeed. Her mother left the family to "pass," to marry a white man—Uncle Frederick, we called him with trepidatious presumption yet without his ever knowing of our existence—an heir to a meat-packing fortune. When Uncle Frederick died thirty years later and the fortune was lost, Marjorie's mother rejoined the race, as the royalty of resentful fascination—Lady Bountiful, my sister called her— to regale us with tales of gracious upper-class living.

My friend said that my story reminded him of a case in which a swarthy, 23
crisp-haired child was born, in Durban, to white parents. The Afrikaner government quickly intervened, removed the child from its birth home, and placed it to be raised with a "more suitable," browner family.

When my friend and I had shared these stories, we grew embarrassed some- 24
how, and our conversation trickled away into a discussion of laissez-faire economics and governmental interventionism. Our words became a clear line, a railroad upon which all other ideas and events were tied down and sacrificed.

The Market

As a teacher of commercial transactions, one of the things that has always 25
impressed me most about the law of contract is a certain deadening power it exercises by reducing the parties to the passive. It constrains the lively involvement of its signatories by positioning enforcement in such a way that parties find themselves in a passive relationship to a document: it is the contract that governs, that "does" everything, that absorbs all responsibility and deflects all other recourse.

Contract law reduces life to fairy tale. The four corners of the agreement 26
become parent. Performance is the equivalent of obedience to the parent. Obedience is dutifully passive. Passivity is valued as good contract-socialized behavior; activity is caged in retrospective hypotheses about states of mind at the magic moment of contracting. Individuals are judged by the contract unfolding rather than by the actors acting autonomously. Nonperformance is

disobedience; disobedience is active; activity becomes evil in contrast to the childlike passivity of contract conformity.

One of the most powerful examples of all this is the case of Mary Beth   27
Whitehead, mother of Sara—of so-called Baby M. Ms. Whitehead became a vividly original actor *after* the creation of her contract with William Stern; unfortunately for her, there can be no greater civil sin. It was in this upside-down context, in the picaresque unboundedness of breachor, that her energetic grief became hysteria and her passionate creativity was funneled, whorled, and reconstructed as highly impermissible. Mary Beth Whitehead thus emerged as the evil stepsister who deserved nothing.

Some time ago, Charles Reich visited a class of mine.[12] He discussed with   28
my students a proposal for a new form of bargain by which emotional "items"— such as praise, flattery, acting happy or sad—might be contracted for explicitly. One student, not alone in her sentiment, said, "Oh, but then you'll just feel obligated." Only the week before, however (when we were discussing the contract which posited that Ms. Whitehead "will not form or attempt to form a parent-child relationship with any child or children"), this same student had insisted that Ms. Whitehead must give up her child, because she had *said* she would: "She was obligated!" I was confounded by the degree to which what the student took to be self-evident, inalienable gut reactions could be governed by illusions of passive conventionality and form.

It was that incident, moreover, that gave me insight into how Judge Harvey   29
Sorkow, of New Jersey Superior Court, could conclude that the contract that purported to terminate Ms. Whitehead's parental rights was "not illusory."[13]

(As background, I should say that I think that, within the framework of   30
contract law itself, the agreement between Ms. Whitehead and Mr. Stern was clearly illusory.[14] On the one hand, Judge Sorkow's opinion said that Ms. Whitehead was seeking to avoid her *obligations*. In other words, giving up her child became an actual obligation. On the other hand, according to the logic of the judge, this was a service contract, not really a sale of a child; therefore delivering the child to the Sterns was an "obligation" for which there was no consideration, for which Mr. Stern was not paying her.)

Judge Sorkow's finding the contract "not illusory" is suggestive not just of   31

---

[12] Charles Reich is author of *The Greening of America* (New York: Random House, 1970) and professor of law at the University of San Francisco Law School.

[13] See, generally, In the Matter of Baby "M," A Pseudonym for an Actual Person, Superior Court of New Jersey, Chancery Division, Docket no. FM-25314-86E, March 31, 1987. This decision was appealed, and on February 3, 1988, the New Jersey Supreme Court ruled that surrogate contracts were illegal and against public policy. In addition to the contract issue, however, the appellate court decided the custody issue in favor of the Sterns but granted visitation rights to Mary Beth Whitehead.

[14] "An illusory promise is an expression cloaked in promissory terms, but which, upon closer examination, reveals that the promisor has committed himself not at all" (J. Calamari and J. Perillo, *Contracts* 3d ed. [St. Paul: West Publishing, 1987], 228).

the doctrine by that name, but of illusion in general, and delusion, and the righteousness with which social constructions are conceived, acted on, and delivered up into the realm of the real as "right," while all else is devoured from memory as "wrong." From this perspective, the rhetorical tricks by which Sara Whitehead became Melissa Stern seem very like the heavy-worded legalities by which my great-great-grandmother was pacified and parted from her child. In both situations, the real mother had no say, no power; her powerlessness was imposed by state law that made her and her child helpless in relation to the father. My great-great-grandmother's powerlessness came about as the result of a contract to which she was not a party; Mary Beth Whitehead's powerlessness came about as a result of a contract that she signed at a discrete point of time— yet which, over time, enslaved her. The contract-reality in both instances was no less than magic: it was illusion transformed into not-illusion. Furthermore, it masterfully disguised the brutality of enforced arrangements in which these women's autonomy, their flesh and their blood, were locked away in word vaults, without room to reconsider—*ever.*

In the months since Judge Sorkow's opinion, I have reflected on the simi- 32
larities of fortune between my own social positioning and that of Sara Melissa Stern Whitehead. I have come to realize that an important part of the complex magic that Judge Sorkow wrote into his opinion was a supposition that it is "natural" for people to want children "like" themselves. What this reasoning raised for me was an issue of what, exactly, constituted this "likeness"? (What would have happened, for example, if Ms. Whitehead had turned out to have been the "passed" descendant of my "failed" godmother Marjorie's mother? What if the child she bore had turned out to be recessively and visibly black? Would the sperm of Mr. Stern have been so powerful as to make this child "his" with the exclusivity that Judge Sorkow originally assigned?) What constitutes, moreover, the collective understanding of "un-likeness"?

These questions turn, perhaps, on not-so-subtle images of which mothers 33
should be bearing which children. Is there not something unseemly, in our society, about the spectacle of a white woman mothering a black child? A white woman giving totally to a black child; a black child totally and demandingly dependent for everything, for sustenance itself, from a white woman. The image of a white woman suckling a black child; the image of a black child sucking for its life from the bosom of a white woman. The utter interdependence of such an image; the selflessness, the merging it implies; the giving up of boundary; the encompassing of other within self; the unbounded generosity; the intercon- nectedness of such an image. Such a picture says that there is no difference; it places the hope of continuous generation, of immortality of the white self in a little black face.

When Judge Sorkow declared that it was only to be expected that parents 34
would want to breed children "like" themselves, he simultaneously created a legal right to the same. With the creation of such a "right," he encased the

children conforming to "likeliness" in protective custody, far from whole ranges of taboo. Taboo about touch and smell and intimacy and boundary. Taboo about ardor, possession, license, equivocation, equanimity, indifference, intolerance, rancor, dispossession, innocence, exile, and candor. Taboo about death. Taboos that amount to death. Death and sacredness, the valuing of body, of self, of other, of remains. The handling lovingly in life, as in life; the question of the intimacy versus the dispassion of death.

In effect, these taboos describe boundaries of valuation. Whether something   35
is inside or outside the marketplace of rights has always been a way of valuing it. When a valued object is located outside the market, it is generally understood to be too "priceless" to be accommodated by ordinary exchange relationships; when, in contrast, the prize is located within the marketplace, all objects outside become "valueless." Traditionally, the Mona Lisa and human life have been the sorts of subjects removed from the fungibility of commodification, as "priceless." Thus when black people were bought and sold as slaves, they were placed beyond the bounds of humanity. And thus, in the twistedness of our brave new world, when blacks have been thrust out of the market and it is white children who are bought and sold, black babies have become "worthless" currency to adoption agents—"surplus" in the salvage heaps of Harlem hospitals.

The Imagination

"Familiar though his name may be to us, the storyteller in his living im-   36
mediacy is by no means a present force. He has already become something remote from us and something that is getting even more distant. . . . Less and less frequently do we encounter people with the ability to tell a tale properly. . . . It is as if something that seemed inalienable to us, the securest among our possessions, were taken from us: the ability to exchange experiences."[15]

My mother's cousin Marjorie was a storyteller. From time to time I would   37
press her to tell me the details of her youth, and she would tell me instead about a child who wandered into a world of polar bears, who was prayed over by polar bears, and in the end eaten. The child's life was not in vain because the polar bears had been made holy by its suffering. The child had been a test, a message from god for polar bears. In the polar bear universe, she would tell me, the primary object of creation was polar bears, and the rest of the living world was fashioned to serve polar bears. The clouds took their shape from polar bears, trees were designed to give shelter and shade to polar bears, and humans were ideally designed to provide polar bears with meat.[16]

The truth, the truth, I would laughingly insist as we sat in her apartment   38

---

[15] Walter Benjamin, "The Storyteller," in *Illuminations*, ed. Hannah Arendt (New York: Schocken, 1969), 83.

[16] For an analysis of similar stories, see Richard Levins and Richard Lewontin, *The Dialectical Biologist* (Cambridge, Mass.: Harvard University Press, 1985), 66.

eating canned fruit and heavy roasts, mashed potatoes, pickles and vanilla pudding, cocoa, Sprite, or tea. What about roots and all that, I coaxed. But the voracity of her amnesia would disclaim and disclaim and disclaim; and she would go on telling me about the polar bears until our plates were full of emptiness and I became large in the space which described her emptiness and I gave in to the emptiness of words.

ON LIFE AND DEATH

Sighing into Space

There are moments in my life when I feel as though a part of me is missing. 39 There are days when I feel so invisible that I can't remember what day of the week it is, when I feel so manipulated that I can't remember my own name, when I feel so lost and angry that I can't speak a civil word to the people who love me best. Those are the times when I catch sight of my reflection in store windows and am surprised to see a whole person looking back. Those are the times when my skin becomes gummy as clay and my nose slides around on my face and my eyes drip down to my chin. I have to close my eyes at such times and remember myself, draw an internal picture that is smooth and whole; when all else fails, I reach for a mirror and stare myself down until the features reassemble themselves like lost sheep.

Two years ago, my godmother Marjorie suffered a massive stroke. As she lay 40 dying, I would come to the hospital to give her her meals. My feeding her who had so often fed me became a complex ritual of mirroring and self-assembly. The physical act of holding the spoon to her lips was not only a rite of nurture and of sacrifice, it was the return of a gift. It was a quiet bowing to the passage of time and the doubling back of all things. The quiet woman who listened to my woes about work and school required now that I bend my head down close to her and listen for mouthed word fragments, sentence crumbs. I bent down to give meaning to her silence, her wandering search for words.

She would eat what I brought to the hospital with relish; she would reject 41 what I brought with a turn of her head. I brought fruit and yogurt, ice cream and vegetable juice. Slowly, over time, she stopped swallowing. The mashed potatoes would sit in her mouth like cotton, the pudding would slip to her chin in slow sad streams. When she lost not only her speech but the power to ingest, they put a tube into her nose and down to her stomach, and I lost even that medium by which to communicate. No longer was there the odd but reassuring communion over taste. No longer was there some echo of comfort in being able to nurture one who nurtured me.

This increment of decay was like a little newborn death. With the tube, she 42 stared up at me with imploring eyes, and I tried to guess what it was that she would like. I read to her aimlessly and in desperation. We entertained each

96

other with the strange embarrassed flickering of our eyes. I told her stories to fill the emptiness, the loneliness, of the white-walled hospital room.

I told her stories about who I had become, about how I had grown up to 43 know all about exchange systems, and theories of contract, and monetary fictions. I spun tales about blue-sky laws and promissory estoppel, the wispy-feathered complexity of undue influence and dark-hearted theories of unconscionability. I told her about market norms and gift economy and the thin razor's edge of the bartering ethic. Once upon a time, I rambled, some neighbors of mine included me in their circle of barter. They were in the habit of exchanging eggs and driving lessons, hand-knit sweaters and computer programming, plumbing and calligraphy. I accepted the generosity of their inclusion with gratitude. At first, I felt that, as a lawyer, I was worthless, that I had no barterable skills and nothing to contribute. What I came to realize with time, however, was that my value to the group was not calculated by the physical items I brought to it. These people included me because they wanted me to be part of their circle, they valued my participation apart from the material things I could offer. So I gave of myself to them, and they gave me fruit cakes and dandelion wine and smoked salmon, and in their giving, their goods became provisions. Cradled in this community whose currency was a relational ethic, my stock in myself soared. My value depended on the glorious intangibility, the eloquent invisibility of my just being *part* of the collective; and in direct response I grew spacious and happy and gentle.

My gentle godmother. The fragility of life; the cold mortuary shelf. 44

Dispassionate Deaths

The hospital in which my godmother died is now filled to capacity with 45 AIDS patients. One in sixty-one babies born there, as in New York City generally, is infected with AIDS antibodies.[17] Almost all are black or Hispanic. In the Bronx, the rate is one in forty-three.[18] In Central Africa, experts estimate that, of children receiving transfusions for malaria-related anemia, "about 1000 may have been infected with the AIDS virus in each of the last five years."[19] In Congo, 5 percent of the entire population is infected.[20] The *New York Times* reports that "the profile of Congo's population seems to guarantee the continued spread of AIDS."[21]

In the Congolese city of Pointe Noir, "the annual budget of the sole public 46

---

[17] B. Lambert, "Study Finds Antibodies for AIDS in 1 in 61 Babies in New York City," *New York Times* (January 13, 1988), sec. A.

[18] Ibid.

[19] "Study Traces AIDS in African Children," *New York Times* (January 22, 1988), sec. A.

[20] J. Brooke, "New Surge of AIDS in Congo May Be an Omen for Africa," *New York Times* (January 22, 1988), sec. A.

[21] Ibid.

health hospital is estimated at about $200,000—roughly the amount of money spent in the United States to care for four AIDS patients."[22]

The week in which my godmother died is littered with bad memories. In 47
my journal, I made note of the following:

Good Friday: Phil Donahue has a special program on AIDS. The segues are:

a. from Martha, who weeps at the prospect of not watching her children grow up

b. to Jim, who is not conscious enough to speak just now, who coughs convulsively, who recognizes no one in his family any more

c. to Hugh who, at 85 pounds, thinks he has five years but whose doctor says he has weeks

d. to an advertisement for denture polish ("If you love your Polident Green/ then gimmeeya SMILE!")

e. and then one for a plastic surgery salon on Park Avenue ("The only thing that's expensive is our address")

f. and then one for what's coming up on the five o'clock news (Linda Lovelace, of *Deep Throat* fame, "still recovering from a double mastectomy and complications from silicone injections" is being admitted to a New York hospital for a liver transplant)

g. and finally one for the miracle properties of all-purpose house cleaner ("Mr. Cleeean/is the man/behind the shine/is it wet or is it dry?" I note that Mr. Clean, with his gleaming bald head, puffy musculature and fever-bright eyes, looks like he is undergoing radiation therapy). Now back to our show.

h. "We are back now with Martha" (who is crying harder than before, sobbing uncontrollably, each jerking inhalation a deep unearthly groan). Phil says, "Oh honey, I hope we didn't make it worse for you."

Easter Saturday: Over lunch, I watch another funeral. My office windows 48
overlook a graveyard as crowded and still as a rush-hour freeway. As I savor pizza and milk, I notice that one of the mourners is wearing an outfit featured in the window of Bloomingdale's (59th Street store) only since last weekend. This thread of recognition jolts me, and I am drawn to her in sorrow; the details of my own shopping history flash before my eyes as I reflect upon the sober spree that brought her to the rim of this earthly chasm, her slim suede heels sinking into the soft silt of the graveside.

Resurrection Sunday: John D., the bookkeeper where I used to work, died, 49
hit on the head by a stray but forcefully propelled hockey puck. I cried copiously at his memorial service, only to discover, later that afternoon when I saw a

---

[22] Ibid.

black rimmed photograph, that I had been mourning the wrong person. I had cried because the man I *thought* had died is John D. the office messenger, a bitter unfriendly man who treats me with disdain; once I bought an old electric typewriter from him which never worked. Though he promised nothing, I have harbored deep dislike since then; death by hockey puck is only one of the fates I had imagined for him. I washed clean my guilt with buckets of tears at the news of what I thought was his demise.

The man who did die was small, shy, anonymously sweet-featured and 50 innocent. In some odd way I was relieved; no seriously obligatory mourning to be done here. A quiet impassivity settled over me and I forgot my grief.

Holy Communion

A few months after my godmother died, my Great Aunt Jag passed away in 51 Cambridge, at ninety-six the youngest and the last of her siblings, all of whom died at ninety-seven. She collapsed on her way home from the polling place, having gotten in her vote for "yet another Kennedy." Her wake was much like the last family gathering at which I had seen her, two Thanksgivings ago. She was a little hard of hearing then and she stayed on the outer edge of the conversation, brightly, loudly, and randomly asserting enjoyment of her meal. At the wake, cousins, nephews, daughters-in-law, first wives, second husbands, great-grand-nieces gathered round her casket and got acquainted all over again. It was pouring rain outside. The funeral home was dry and warm, faintly spicily clean-smelling; the walls were solid, dark, respectable wood; the floors were cool stone tile. On the door of a room marked "No Admittance" was a sign that reminded workers therein of the reverence with which each body was held by its family and prayed employees handle the remains with similar love and care. Aunt Jag wore yellow chiffon; everyone agreed that laying her out with her glasses on was a nice touch.

Afterward, we all went to Legal Seafoods, her favorite restaurant, and ate 52 many of her favorite foods.

ON CANDOR

Me

I have never been able to determine my horoscope with any degree of 53 accuracy. Born at Boston's now-defunct Lying-In Hospital, I am a Virgo, despite a quite poetic soul. Knowledge of the *hour* of my birth, however, would determine not just my sun sign but my moons and all the more intimate specificities of my destiny. Once upon a time, I sent for my birth certificate, which was retrieved from the oblivion of Massachusetts microfiche. Said document revealed that an infant named Patricia Joyce, born of parents named

Williams, was delivered into the world "colored." Since no one thought to put down the hour of my birth, I suppose that I will never know my true fate.

In the meantime, I read what text there is of me. 54

My name, Patricia, means patrician. Patricias are noble, lofty, elite, exclu- 55 sively educated, and well mannered despite themselves. I was on the cusp of being Pamela, but my parents knew that such a me would require lawns, estates, and hunting dogs too.

I am also a Williams. Of William, whoever he was: an anonymous white 56 man who owned my father's people and from whom some escaped. That rupture is marked by the dark-mooned mystery of utter silence.

Williams is the second most common surname in the United States; Patricia 57 is *the* most common prename among women born in 1951, the year of my birth.

Them

In the law, rights are islands of empowerment. To be un-righted is to be 58 disempowered, and the line between rights and no rights is most often the line between dominators and oppressors. Rights contain images of power, and manipulating those images, either visually or linguistically, is central in the making and maintenance of rights. In principle, therefore, the more dizzyingly diverse the images that are propagated, the more empowered we will be as a society.

In reality, it was a lovely polar bear afternoon. The gentle force of the earth. 59 A wide wilderness of islands. A conspiracy of polar bears lost in timeless forgetting. A gentleness of polar bears, a fruitfulness of polar bears, a silent black-eyed interest of polar bears, a bristled expectancy of polar bears. With the wisdom of innocence, a child threw stones at the polar bears. Hungry, they rose from their nests, inquisitive, dark-souled, patient with foreboding, fearful in tremendous awakening. The instinctual ferocity of the hunter reflected upon the hunted. Then, proud teeth and warrior claws took innocence for wilderness and raging insubstantiality for tender rabbit breath.

In the newspapers the next day, it was reported that two polar bears in the 60 Brooklyn Zoo mauled to death an eleven-year-old boy who had entered their cage to swim in the moat. The police were called and the bears were killed.[23]

In the public debate that ensued, many levels of meaning emerged. The 61 rhetoric firmly established that the bears were innocent, naturally territorial, unfairly imprisoned, and guilty. The dead child (born into the urban jungle of a black, welfare mother and a Hispanic alcoholic father who had died literally in the gutter only six weeks before) was held to a similarly stern standard. The police were captured, in a widely disseminated photograph,[24] shooting help-

---

[23] J. Barron, "Polar Bears Kill a Child at Prospect Park Zoo," *New York Times* (May 20, 1987), sec. A.

[24] *New York Post* (May 22, 1987), p. 1.

lessly, desperately, into the cage, through three levels of bars, at a pieta of bears; since this image, conveying much pathos, came nevertheless not in time to save the child, it was generally felt that the bears had died in vain.[25]

In the egalitarianism of exile, pluralists rose up as of one body, with a call to buy more bears, control juvenile delinquency, eliminate all zoos, and confine future police.[26] 62

In the plenary session of the national meeting of the Law and Society Association, the keynote speaker unpacked the whole incident as a veritable laboratory of emergent rights discourse. Just seeing that these complex levels of meaning exist, she exulted, should advance rights discourse significantly.[27] 63

At the funeral of the child, the presiding priest pronounced the death of Juan Perez not in vain, since he was saved from growing into "a lifetime of crime." Juan's Hispanic-welfare-black-widow-of-an-alcoholic mother decided then and there to sue. 64

The Universe Between

How I ended up at Dartmouth College for the summer is too long a story to tell. Anyway, there I was, sharing the town of Hanover, New Hampshire, with about two hundred prepubescent males enrolled in Dartmouth's summer basketball camp, an all-white, very expensive, affirmative action program for the street-deprived. 65

One fragrant evening, I was walking down East Wheelock Street when I encountered about a hundred of these adolescents, fresh from the courts, wet, lanky, big-footed, with fuzzy yellow crew cuts, loping toward Thayer Hall and food. In platoons of twenty-five or so, they descended upon me, jostling me, smacking me, and pushing me from the sidewalk into the gutter. In a thoughtless instant, I snatched off my brown silk headrag, my flag of African femininity and propriety, my sign of meek and supplicatory place and presentation. I released the armored rage of my short nappy hair (the scalp gleaming bare between the angry wire spikes) and hissed: "Don't I exist for you?! See Me! And deflect, godammit!" (The quaint professionalism of my formal English never allowed the rage in my head to rise so high as to overflow the edges of my text.) 66

They gave me wide berth. They clearly had no idea, however, that I was talking to them or about them. They skirted me sheepishly, suddenly polite, because they did know, when a crazed black person comes crashing into one's field of vision, that it is impolite to laugh. I stood tall and spoke loudly into their ranks: "I have my rights!" The Dartmouth Summer Basketball Camp raised 67

---

[25] J. Barron, "Officials Weigh Tighter Security at Zoos in Parks," *New York Times* (May 22, 1987), sec. B.

[26] Ibid.

[27] Patricia Williams, "The Meaning of Rights" (address to the annual meeting of the Law and Society Association, Washington, D.C., June 6, 1987).

its collective eyebrows and exhaled, with a certain tested nobility of exhaustion and solidarity.

I pursued my way, manumitted back into silence. I put distance between them and me, gave myself over to polar bear musings. I allowed myself to be watched over by bear spirits. Clean white wind and strong bear smells. The shadowed amnesia; the absence of being; the presence of polar bears. White wilderness of icy meat-eaters heavy with remembrance; leaden with undoing; shaggy with the effort of hunting for silence; frozen in a web of intention and intuition. A lunacy of polar bears. A history of polar bears. A pride of polar bears. A consistency of polar bears. In those meandering pastel polar bear moments, I found cool fragments of white-fur invisibility. Solid, black-gummed, intent, observant. Hungry and patient, impassive and exquisitely timed. The brilliant bursts of exclusive territoriality. A complexity of messages implied in our being.

68

QUESTIONS

1. What is Williams's essay about? Summarize in one paragraph what you consider her main ideas.

2. Explain what you think Williams means when she writes in paragraph 2: "I, like so many blacks, have been trying to pin myself down in history, place myself in the stream of time as significant, evolved, present in the past, continuing into the future. To be without documentation is too unsustaining, too spontaneously ahistorical, too dangerously malleable in the hands of those who would rewrite not merely the past but my future as well."

3. Consider the structure of Williams's essay. How does she develop her ideas from the opening anecdote about her great-great-grandmother to the closing anecdote about her encounter with one hundred prepubescent male basketball players? How does each section and each image help Williams to enlarge and complicate her idea?

4. Williams uses a variety of different sources in her essay—court cases, legal contracts, passages from novels, anecdotes, autobiographical reflections, and conversations. Identify the evidence that Williams derives from each source to weave her reflections together. How does she integrate the sources so they work together to support her essay?

5. The image of the polar bear dramatically figures in many of Williams's anecdotes. What are the complex messages these bears offer Williams? How does she use the bears to unify her essay?

6. Williams describes many significant experiences from her life. Describe some personal experiences that have become permanent parts of your memory, experiences you cannot forget. Try to reflect on and understand why these experiences linger in your memory. What idea connects these various experiences?

7. What central fact of your life—race, religion, parents, birthplace, special abilities, etc.—has influenced you the most? Write an essay such as Williams's in which you focus on the influence of this central fact on the shaping of your life.

MAKING CONNECTIONS

Select an idea about race, class, or gender that intrigues you in Williams's essay. How does this idea converse or resonate with a similar idea you find compelling in any of the other essays in "Reflecting"?

PILGRIMAGE TO NONVIOLENCE
Martin Luther King, Jr.

The son of a minister, Martin Luther King, Jr. (1929–1968) was ordained a Baptist minister in his father's church in Atlanta, Georgia, at the age of eighteen. He sprang into prominence in 1955 when he called a citywide boycott of the segregated bus system in Montgomery, Alabama, and he continued to be the most prominent civil rights activist in America until his assassination on April 4, 1968. During those tumultuous years, he was jailed at least fourteen times and endured countless threats against his life, but he persevered in his fight against racial discrimination, using a synthesis of the nonviolent philosophy of Mahatma Gandhi and the Sermon on the Mount. The 1964 Nobel Peace Prize was only one of the many awards he received, and his several books are characterized as much by their eloquent prose style as by their moral fervor. "Pilgrimage to Nonviolence" originally appeared in the magazine Christian Century *and was revised and updated for a collection of his sermons,* Strength to Love *(1963), the source of the following text.*

In my senior year in theological seminary, I engaged in the exciting reading   1
of various theological theories. Having been raised in a rather strict fundamentalist tradition, I was occasionally shocked when my intellectual journey carried me through new and sometimes complex doctrinal lands, but the pilgrimage was always stimulating, gave me a new appreciation for objective appraisal and critical analysis, and knocked me out of my dogmatic slumber.

Liberalism provided me with an intellectual satisfaction that I had never   2
found in fundamentalism. I became so enamored of the insights of liberalism that I almost fell into the trap of accepting uncritically everything it encompassed. I was absolutely convinced of the natural goodness of man and the natural power of human reason.

I

A basic change in my thinking came when I began to question some of the   3
theories that had been associated with so-called liberal theology. Of course, there are aspects of liberalism that I hope to cherish always: its devotion to the

search for truth, its insistence on an open and analytical mind, and its refusal to abandon the best lights of reason. The contribution of liberalism to the philosophical-historical criticism of biblical literature has been of immeasurable value and should be defended with religious and scientific passion.

But I began to question the liberal doctrine of man. The more I observed the tragedies of history and man's shameful inclination to choose the low road, the more I came to see the depths and strength of sin. My reading of the works of Reinhold Niebuhr made me aware of the complexity of human motives and the reality of sin on every level of man's existence.[1] Moreover, I came to recognize the complexity of man's social involvement and the glaring reality of collective evil. I realized that liberalism had been all too sentimental concerning human nature and that it leaned toward a false idealism.

I also came to see the superficial optimism of liberalism concerning human nature overlooked the fact that reason is darkened by sin. The more I thought about human nature, the more I saw how our tragic inclination for sin encourages us to rationalize our actions. Liberalism failed to show that reason by itself is little more than an instrument to justify man's defensive ways of thinking. Reason, devoid of the purifying power of faith, can never free itself from distortions and rationalizations.

Although I rejected some aspects of liberalism, I never came to an all-out acceptance of neo-orthodoxy. While I saw neo-orthodoxy as a helpful corrective for a sentimental liberalism, I felt that it did not provide an adequate answer to basic questions. If liberalism was too optimistic concerning human nature, neo-orthodoxy was too pessimistic. Not only on the question of man, but also on other vital issues, the revolt of neo-orthodoxy went too far. In its attempt to preserve the transcendence of God, which had been neglected by an overstress of his immanence in liberalism, neo-orthodoxy went to the extreme of stressing a God who was hidden, unknown, and "wholly other." In its revolt against overemphasis on the power of reason in liberalism, neo-orthodoxy fell into a mood of antirationalism and semifundamentalism, stressing a narrow uncritical biblicism. This approach, I felt, was inadequate both for the church and for personal life.

So although liberalism left me unsatisfied on the question of the nature of man, I found no refuge in neo-orthodoxy. I am now convinced that the truth about man is found neither in liberalism nor in neo-orthodoxy. Each represents a partial truth. A large segment of Protestant liberalism defined man only in terms of his essential nature, his capacity for good; neo-orthodoxy tended to define man only in terms of his existential nature, his capacity for evil. An adequate understanding of man is found neither in the thesis of liberalism nor

[1] Reinhold Niebuhr (1892–1971): American theologian, social activist, and noted writer on social and religious issues. [Eds.]

in the antithesis of neo-orthodoxy, but in a synthesis which reconciles the truths of both.

During the intervening years I have gained a new appreciation for the philosophy of existentialism. My first contact with the philosophy came through my reading of Kierkegaard and Nietzsche.[2] Later I turned to a study of Jaspers, Heidegger, and Sartre.[3] These thinkers stimulated my thinking; while questioning each, I nevertheless learned a great deal through a study of them. When I finally engaged in a serious study of the writings of Paul Tillich,[4] I became convinced that existentialism, in spite of the fact that it had become all too fashionable, had grasped certain basic truths about man and his condition that could not be permanently overlooked.

8

An understanding of the "finite freedom" of man is one of the permanent contributions of existentialism, and its perception of the anxiety and conflict produced in man's personal and social life by the perilous and ambiguous structure of existence is especially meaningful for our time. A common denominator in atheistic or theistic existentialism is that man's existential situation is estranged from his essential nature. In their revolt against Hegel's essentialism,[5] all existentialists contend that the world is fragmented. History is a series of unreconciled conflicts, and man's existence is filled with anxiety and threatened with meaninglessness. While the ultimate Christian answer is not found in any of these existential assertions, there is much here by which the theologian may describe the true state of man's existence.

9

Although most of my formal study has been in systematic theology and philosophy, I have become more and more interested in social ethics. During my early teens I was deeply concerned by the problem of racial injustice. I considered segregation both rationally inexplicable and morally unjustifiable. I could never accept my having to sit in the back of a bus or in the segregated section of a train. The first time that I was seated behind a curtain in a dining car I felt as though the curtain had been dropped on my selfhood. I also learned that the inseparable twin of racial injustice is economic injustice. I saw how the systems of segregation exploited both the Negro and the poor whites. These early experiences made me deeply conscious of the varieties of injustice in our society.

10

---

[2] Søren Kierkegaard (1813–1855): Danish religious and aesthetic philosopher, concerned especially with the role of the individual; Friedrich Nietzsche (1844–1900): German philosopher and moralist looking for a heroic, creative rejuvenation of decadent Western civilization. [Eds.]

[3] Karl Jaspers (1883–1969): German philosopher; Martin Heidegger (1899–1976): German philosopher; Jean-Paul Sartre (1905–1980): French philosopher and novelist. All three were existentialists, concerned with the existence and responsibility of the individual in an unknowable universe. [Eds.]

[4] Paul Tillich (1886–1965): German-born American philosopher and theologian whose writings drew on psychology and existentialism. [Eds.]

[5] Georg Friedrich Hegel (1770–1831): German philosopher best known for his theory of the dialectic (thesis vs. antithesis produces synthesis). [Eds.]

II

Not until I entered theological seminary, however, did I begin a serious   11
intellectual quest for a method that would eliminate social evil. I was immediately influenced by the social gospel. In the early 1950s I read Walter Rauschenbusch's *Christianity and the Social Crisis*, a book which left an indelible
imprint on my thinking. Of course, there were points at which I differed with
Rauschenbusch. I felt that he was a victim of the nineteenth-century "cult of
inevitable progress," which led him to an unwarranted optimism concerning
human nature. Moreover, he came perilously close to identifying the Kingdom
of God with a particular social and economic system, a temptation to which
the church must never surrender. But in spite of these shortcomings, Rauschenbusch gave to American Protestantism a sense of social responsibility that it
should never lose. The gospel at its best deals with the whole man, not only
his soul but also his body, not only his spiritual well-being but also his material
well-being. A religion that professes a concern for the souls of men and is not
equally concerned about the slums that damn them, the economic conditions
that strangle them, and the social conditions that cripple them, is a spiritually
moribund religion.

After reading Rauschenbusch, I turned to a serious study of the social and   12
ethical theories of the great philosophers. During this period I had almost
despaired of the power of love to solve social problems. The turn-the-other-
cheek and the love-your-enemies philosophies are valid, I felt, only when
individuals are in conflict with other individuals; when racial groups and nations
are in conflict, a more realistic approach is necessary.

Then I was introduced to the life and teachings of Mahatma Gandhi.[6] As I   13
read his works I became deeply fascinated by his campaigns of nonviolent
resistance. The whole Gandhian concept of *satyagraha* (*satya* is truth which
equals love and *graha* is force; *satyagraha* thus means truth-force or love-force)
was profoundly significant to me. As I delved deeper into the philosophy of
Gandhi, my skepticism concerning the power of love gradually diminished, and
I came to see for the first time that the Christian doctrine of love, operating
through the Gandhian method of nonviolence, is one of the most potent
weapons available to an oppressed people in their struggle for freedom. At that
time, however, I acquired only an intellectual understanding and appreciation
of the position, and I had no firm determination to organize it in a socially
effective situation.

When I went to Montgomery, Alabama, as a pastor in 1954, I had not the   14
slightest idea that I would later become involved in a crisis in which nonviolent
resistance would be applicable. After I had lived in the community about a
year, the bus boycott began. The Negro people of Montgomery, exhausted by

---

[6] Mahatma Gandhi (1869–1948): Hindu nationalist and spiritual leader. [Eds.]

the humiliating experience that they had constantly faced on the buses, expressed in a massive act of noncooperation their determination to be free. They came to see that it was ultimately more honorable to walk the streets in dignity than to ride the buses in humiliation. At the beginning of the protest, the people called on me to serve as their spokesman. In accepting this responsibility, my mind, consciously or unconsciously, was driven back to the Sermon on the Mount and the Gandhian method of nonviolent resistance. This principle became the guiding light of our movement. Christ furnished the spirit and motivation and Gandhi furnished the method.

The experience in Montgomery did more to clarify my thinking in regard to 15 the question of nonviolence than all of the books that I had read. As the days unfolded, I became more and more convinced of the power of nonviolence. Nonviolence became more than a method to which I gave intellectual assent; it became a commitment to a way of life. Many issues I had not cleared up intellectually concerning nonviolence were now resolved within the sphere of practical action.

My privilege of traveling to India had a great impact on me personally, for 16 it was invigorating to see firsthand the amazing results of a nonviolent struggle to achieve independence. The aftermath of hatred and bitterness that usually follows a violent campaign was found nowhere in India, and a mutual friendship, based on complete equality, existed between the Indian and British people within the Commonwealth.

I would not wish to give the impression that nonviolence will accomplish 17 miracles overnight. Men are not easily moved from their mental ruts or purged of their prejudiced and irrational feelings. When the underprivileged demand freedom, the privileged at first react with bitterness and resistance. Even when the demands are couched in nonviolent terms, the initial response is substantially the same. I am sure that many of our white brothers in Montgomery and throughout the South are still bitter toward the Negro leaders, even though these leaders have sought to follow a way of love and nonviolence. But the nonviolent approach does something to the hearts and souls of those committed to it. It gives them new self-respect. It calls up resources of strength and courage that they did not know they had. Finally, it so stirs the conscience of the opponent that reconciliation becomes a reality.

III

More recently I have come to see the need for the method of nonviolence 18 in international relations. Although I was not yet convinced of its efficacy in conflicts between nations, I felt that while war could never be a positive good, it could serve as a negative good by preventing the spread and growth of an evil force. War, horrible as it is, might be preferable to surrender to a totalitarian system. But I now believe that the potential destructiveness of modern weapons totally rules out the possibility of war ever again achieving a negative good. If we assume that mankind has a right to survive, then we must find an alternative to war and destruction. In our day of space vehicles and guided ballistic missiles, the choice is either nonviolence or nonexistence.

I am no doctrinaire pacifist, but I have tried to embrace a realistic pacifism   19
which finds the pacifist position as the lesser evil in the circumstances. I do not claim to be free from the moral dilemmas that the Christian nonpacifist confronts, but I am convinced that the church cannot be silent while mankind faces the threat of nuclear annihilation. If the church is true to her mission, she must call for an end to the arms race.

Some of my personal sufferings over the last few years have also served to   20
shape my thinking. I always hesitate to mention these experiences for fear of conveying the wrong impression. A person who constantly calls attention to his trials and sufferings is in danger of developing a martyr complex and impressing others that he is consciously seeking sympathy. It is possible for one to be self-centered in his self-sacrifice. So I am always reluctant to refer to my personal sacrifices. But I feel somewhat justified in mentioning them in this essay because of the influence they have had upon my thought.

Due to my involvement in the struggle for the freedom of my people, I have   21
known very few quiet days in the last few years. I have been imprisoned in Alabama and Georgia jails twelve times. My home has been bombed twice. A day seldom passes that my family and I are not the recipients of threats of death. I have been the victim of a near-fatal stabbing. So in a real sense I have been battered by the storms of persecution. I must admit that at times I have felt that I could no longer bear such a heavy burden, and have been tempted to retreat to a more quiet and serene life. But every time such a temptation appeared, something came to strengthen and sustain my determination. I have learned now that the Master's burden is light precisely when we take his yoke upon us.

My personal trials have also taught me the value of unmerited suffering. As   22
my sufferings mounted I soon realized that there were two ways in which I could respond to my situation—either to react with bitterness or seek to transform the suffering into a creative force. I decided to follow the latter course. Recognizing the necessity for suffering, I have tried to make of it a virtue, if only to save myself from bitterness, I have attempted to see my personal ordeals as an opportunity to transfigure myself and heal the people involved in the tragic situation which now obtains. I have lived these last few years with the conviction that unearned suffering is redemptive. There are some who still find the Cross a stumbling block, others consider it foolishness, but I am more convinced than ever before that it is the power of God unto social and individual salvation. So like the Apostle Paul I can now humbly, yet proudly, say, "I bear in my body the marks of the Lord Jesus."

The agonizing moments through which I have passed during the last few   23
years have also drawn me closer to God. More than ever before I am convinced

of the reality of a personal God. True, I have always believed in the personality of God. But in the past the idea of a personal God was little more than a metaphysical category that I found theologically and philosophically satisfying. Now it is a living reality that has been validated in the experiences of everyday life. God has been profoundly real to me in recent years. In the midst of outer dangers I have felt an inner calm. In the midst of lonely days and dreary nights I have heard an inner voice saying, "Lo, I will be with you." When the chains of fear and the manacles of frustration have all but stymied my efforts, I have felt the power of God transforming the fatigue of despair into the buoyancy of hope. I am convinced that the universe is under the control of a loving purpose, and that in the struggle for righteousness man has cosmic companionship. Behind the harsh appearances of the world there is a benign power. To say that this God is personal is not to make him a finite object beside other objects or attribute to him the limitations of human personality; it is to take what is finest and noblest in our consciousness and affirm its perfect existence in him. It is certainly true that human personality is limited, but personality as such involves no necessary limitations. It means simply self-consciousness and self-direction. So in the truest sense of the word, God is a living God. In him there is feeling and will, responsive to the deepest yearnings of the human heart: *this* God both evokes and answers prayer.

The past decade has been a most exciting one. In spite of the tensions and uncertainties of this period something profoundly meaningful is taking place. Old systems of exploitation and oppression are passing away; new systems of justice and equality are being born. In a real sense this is a great time to be alive. Therefore, I am not yet discouraged about the future. Granted that the easygoing optimism of yesterday is impossible. Granted that we face a world crisis which leaves us standing so often amid the surging murmur of life's restless sea. But every crisis has both its dangers and its opportunities. It can spell either salvation or doom. In a dark, confused world the Kingdom of God may yet reign in the hearts of men.

24

QUESTIONS

1. King found the extremes of liberalism on one hand and neo-orthodoxy on the other both unsatisfactory. Why?

2. Existentialism and Rauschenbusch's social gospel proved more useful to King than liberalism or neo-orthodoxy. How did these concepts help shape his outlook?

3. King is interested in religious and philosophical theories not for their own sake but for their usefulness in the social world. How do Gandhi's example and King's own experience in Montgomery (paragraphs 14, 15, and 17) illustrate this concern?

4. How did King's personal faith in God aid in his struggles and sufferings? Is his dream of a better society totally dependent upon the existence of this "benign power" (paragraph 23)?

5. King's intellectual development is described as a pilgrimage from a simple fundamentalist attitude through conflicting theological and philosophical concepts to an intensified belief in a benign God and a commitment to international nonviolence. How is his final set of beliefs superior to his original one? Has he convinced you of the validity of his beliefs?

6. King writes for a general audience rather than one with theological and philosophical training. How successful is King at clarifying religious and philosophical concepts for the general reader? Point out examples that show how he treats such concepts.

7. Again and again King employs the classical rhetorical strategy of concession: the opposition's viewpoint is stated and partially accepted before King gives his own viewpoint. Locate two or three instances of this strategy, and explain how it aids a reader's understanding (if not acceptance) of King's views.

8. King's essay reflects on how he came to accept the method of nonviolence. Have you, over time, changed your thoughts or methods of approaching an issue or problem? Or has someone you know well? If so, write an essay reflecting on the events central to this change and their significance.

9. King's hopes for a better world were expressed in the early 1960s. Based on your knowledge of history since then, write an essay in which you justify or disqualify King's guarded optimism.

MAKING CONNECTIONS

1. Like several other writers in this section, King reflects on a turning point in his life. Consider his essay in relation to two or three others, such as those by Maya Angelou, Alice Walker, George Orwell, Zoë Tracy Hardy, or Loren Eiseley. Compare and contrast the ways these writers present their turning points. How does each present the crucial moment or event, and how does each show its meaning?

2. One way a writer convinces us is by the authority we sense in the person as he or she writes. What details in King's essay contribute to our sense of him as an authoritative person, a writer we are inclined to believe? What do you find of similar persuasiveness in the essays of Maya Angelou, George Orwell, or Zoë Tracy Hardy?

THE WAY TO
RAINY MOUNTAIN

N. Scott Momaday

N. Scott Momaday was born in Lawton, Oklahoma, in 1934. His father is a full-blooded Kiowa and his mother is part Cherokee. After attending schools on Navaho, Apache, and Pueblo reservations, Momaday graduated from the University of New Mexico and took his Ph.D. at Stanford University. He has published two collections of poetry, Angle of Geese and Other Poems *(1974) and* The Gourd Dancer *(1976), and a memoir,* The Names *(1976). In 1969, his novel* House Made of Dawn *won the Pulitzer Prize. The following essay appeared first in the* Reporter *magazine in 1967 and later as the introduction to* The Way to Rainy Mountain *(1969), a collection of Kiowa legends.*

A single knoll rises out of the plain in Oklahoma, north and west of the Wichita range. For my people, the Kiowas, it is an old landmark, and they gave it the name Rainy Mountain. The hardest weather in the world is there. Winter brings blizzards, hot tornadic winds arise in the spring, and in summer the prairie is an anvil's edge. The grass turns brittle and brown, and it cracks beneath your feet. There are green belts along the rivers and creeks, linear groves of hickory and pecan, willow and witch hazel. At a distance in July or August the steaming foliage seems almost to writhe in fire. Great green and yellow grasshoppers are everywhere in the tall grass, popping up like corn to sting the flesh, and tortoises crawl about on the red earth, going nowhere in the plenty of time. Loneliness is an aspect of the land. All things in the plain are isolate; there is no confusion of objects in the eye, but *one* hill or *one* tree or *one* man. To look upon that landscape in the early morning, with the sun at your back, is to lose the sense of proportion. Your imagination comes to life, and this, you think, is where Creation was begun. 1

I returned to Rainy Mountain in July. My grandmother had died in the spring, and I wanted to be at her grave. She had lived to be very old and at last infirm. Her only living daughter was with her when she died, and I was told that in death her face was that of a child. 2

I like to think of her as a child. When she was born, the Kiowas were living the last great moment of their history. For more than a hundred years they had controlled the open range from the Smoky Hill River to the Red, from the 3 headwaters of the Canadian to the fork of the Arkansas and Cimarron. In alliance with the Comanches, they had ruled the whole of the Southern Plains. War was their sacred business, and they were the finest horsemen the world has ever known. But warfare for the Kiowas was pre-eminently a matter of disposition rather than of survival, and they never understood the grim, unrelenting advance of the U. S. Cavalry. When at last, divided and ill provisioned, they were driven onto the Staked Plains in the cold of autumn, they fell into panic. In Palo Duro Canyon they abandoned their crucial stores to pillage and had nothing then but their lives. In order to save themselves, they surrendered to the soldiers at Fort Sill and were imprisoned in the old stone corral that now stands as a military museum. My grandmother was spared the humiliation of those high gray walls by eight or ten years, but she must have known from birth the affliction of defeat, the dark brooding of old warriors.

Her name was Aho, and she belonged to the last culture to evolve in North   4
America. Her forebears came down from the high country in western Montana nearly three centuries ago. They were a mountain people, a mysterious tribe of hunters whose language has never been classified in any major group. In the late seventeenth century they began a long migration to the south and east. It was a journey toward the dawn, and it led to a golden age. Along the way the Kiowas were befriended by the Crows, who gave them the culture and religion of the Plains. They acquired horses, and their ancient nomadic spirit was suddenly free of the ground. They acquired Tai-me, the sacred sun-dance doll, from that moment the object and symbol of their worship, and so shared in the divinity of the sun. Not least, they acquired the sense of destiny, therefore courage and pride. When they entered upon the Southern Plains they had been transformed. No longer were they slaves to the simple necessity of survival; they were a lordly and dangerous society of fighters and thieves, hunters and priests of the sun. According to their origin myth, they entered the world through a hollow log. From one point of view, their migration was the fruit of an old prophecy, for indeed they emerged from a sunless world.

Though my grandmother lived out her long life in the shadow of Rainy   5
Mountain, the immense landscape of the continental interior lay like memory in her blood. She could tell of the Crows, whom she had never seen, and of the Black Hills, where she had never been. I wanted to see in reality what she had seen more perfectly in the mind's eye, and drove fifteen hundred miles to begin my pilgrimage.

A dark mist lay over the Black Hills, and the land was like iron. At the top   6
of a ridge I caught sight of Devil's Tower upthrust against the gray sky as if in the birth of time the core of the earth had broken through its crust and the motion of the world was begun. There are things in nature that engender an awful quiet in the heart of man; Devil's Tower is one of them. Two centuries

113

ago, because of their need to explain it, the Kiowas made a legend at the base of the rock. My grandmother said:

"Eight children were there at play, seven sisters and their brother. Suddenly 7 the boy was struck dumb; he trembled and began to run upon his hands and feet. His fingers became claws, and his body was covered with fur. There was a bear where the boy had been. The sisters were terrified; they ran, and the bear after them. They came to the stump of a great tree, and the tree spoke to them. It bade them climb upon it, and as they did so, it began to rise into the air. The bear came to kill them, but they were just beyond its reach. It reared against the tree and scored the bark all around with its claws. The seven sisters were borne into the sky, and they became the stars of the Big Dipper." From that moment, and so long as the legend lives, the Kiowas have kinsmen in the night sky. Whatever they were in the mountains, they could be no more. However tenuous their well-being, however much they had suffered and would suffer again, they had found a way out of the wilderness.

My grandmother had a reverence for the sun, a holy regard that now is all 8 but gone out of mankind. There was a wariness in her, and an ancient awe. She was a Christian in her later years, but she had come a long way about, and she never forgot her birthright. As a child she had been to the sun dances; she had taken part in that annual rite, and by it she had learned the restoration of her people in the presence of Tai-me. She was about seven when the last Kiowa sun dance was held in 1887 on the Washita River above Rainy Mountain Creek. The buffalo were gone. In order to consummate the ancient sacrifice— to impale the head of a buffalo bull upon the Tai-me tree—a delegation of old men journeyed into Texas, there to beg and barter for an animal from the Goodnight herd. She was ten when the Kiowas came together for the last time as a living sun-dance culture. They could find no buffalo; they had to hang an old hide from the sacred tree. Before the dance could begin, a company of soldiers rode out from Fort Sill under orders to disperse the tribe. Forbidden without cause the essential act of their faith, having seen the wild herds slaughtered and left to rot upon the ground, the Kiowas backed away forever from the tree. That was July 20, 1890, at the great bend of the Washita. My grandmother was there. Without bitterness, and for as long as she lived, she bore a vision of deicide.[1]

Now that I can have her only in memory, I see my grandmother in the 9 several postures that were peculiar to her: standing at the wood stove on a winter morning and turning meat in a great iron skillet; sitting at the south window, bent above her beadwork, and afterwards, when her vision failed, looking down for a long time into the fold of her hands; going out upon a cane, very slowly as she did when the weight of age came upon her; praying. I remember her

---

[1] deicide: the killing of a deity or god. [Eds.]

most often at prayer. She made long, rambling prayers out of suffering and hope, having seen many things. I was never sure that I had the right to hear, so exclusive were they of all mere custom and company. The last time I saw her she prayed standing by the side of her bed at night, naked to the waist, the light of a kerosene lamp moving upon her dark skin. Her long black hair, always drawn and braided in the day, lay upon her shoulders and against her breasts like a shawl. I do not speak Kiowa, and I never understood her prayers, but there was something inherently sad in the sound, some merest hesitation upon the syllables of sorrow. She began in a high and descending pitch, exhausting her breath to silence; then again and again—and always the same intensity of effort, of something that is, and is not, like urgency in the human voice. Transported so in the dancing light among the shadows of her room, she seemed beyond the reach of time. But that was illusion; I think I knew then that I should not see her again.

Houses are like sentinels in the plain, old keepers of the weather watch.   10
There, in a very little while, wood takes on the appearance of great age. All colors wear soon away in the wind and rain, and then the wood is burned gray and the grain appears and the nails turn red with rust. The window panes are black and opaque; you imagine there is nothing within, and indeed there are many ghosts, bones given up to the land. They stand here and there against the sky, and you approach them for a longer time than you expect. They belong in the distance; it is their domain.

Once there was a lot of sound in my grandmother's house, a lot of coming   11
and going, feasting and talk. The summers there were full of excitement and reunion. The Kiowas are a summer people; they abide the cold and keep to themselves, but when the season turns and the land becomes warm and vital they cannot hold still; an old love of going returns upon them. The aged visitors who came to my grandmother's house when I was a child were made of lean and leather, and they bore themselves upright. They wore great black hats and bright ample shirts that shook in the wind. They rubbed fat upon their hair and wound their braids with strips of colored cloth. Some of them painted their faces and carried the scars of old and cherished enmities. They were an old council of warlords, come to remind and be reminded of who they were. Their wives and daughters served them well. The women might indulge themselves; gossip was at once the mark and compensation of their servitude. They made loud and elaborate talk among themselves, full of jest and gesture, fright and false alarm. They went abroad in fringed and flowered shawls, bright beadwork and German silver. They were at home in the kitchen, and they prepared meals that were banquets.

There were frequent prayer meetings, and nocturnal feasts. When I was a   12
child I played with my cousins outside, where the lamplight fell upon the ground and the singing of the old people rose up around us and carried away into the darkness. There were a lot of good things to eat, a lot of laughter and

surprise. And afterwards, when the quiet returned, I lay down with my grandmother and could hear the frogs away by the river and feel the motion of the air.

Now there is a funereal silence in the rooms, the endless wake of some final 13
word. The walls have closed in upon my grandmother's house. When I returned to it in mourning, I saw for the first time in my life how small it was. It was late at night, and there was a white moon, nearly full. I sat for a long time on the stone steps by the kitchen door. From there I could see out across the land; I could see the long row of trees by the creek, the low light upon the rolling plains, and the stars of the Big Dipper. Once I looked at the moon and caught sight of a strange thing. A cricket had perched upon the handrail, only a few inches away. My line of vision was such that the creature filled the moon like a fossil. It had gone there, I thought, to live and die, for there, of all places, was its small definition made whole and eternal. A warm wind rose up and purled like the longing within me.

The next morning, I awoke at dawn and went out on the dirt road to Rainy 14
Mountain. It was already hot, and the grasshoppers began to fill the air. Still, it was early in the morning, and birds sang out of the shadows. The long yellow grass on the mountain shone in the bright light, and a scissortail hied above the land. There, where it ought to be, at the end of a long and legendary way, was my grandmother's grave. She had at last succeeded to that holy ground. Here and there on the dark stones were ancestral names. Looking back once, I saw the mountain and came away.

QUESTIONS

1. What is this essay about? Explain whether it is a history of the Kiowas, or a biography of Momaday's grandmother, or a narrative of his journey.

2. Trace the movement in time in this essay. How much takes place in the present, the recent past, the distant past, or legendary time? What effect does such movement create?

3. How much of the essay reports events, and how much of the essay represents a sense of place or of persons through description of what Momaday sees and feels? Trace the pattern of reporting and representing, and consider Momaday's purpose in such an approach to his subject.

4. The first paragraph ends by drawing the reader into the writer's point of view: "Your imagination comes to life, and this, you think, is where Creation was begun." Given the description of the Oklahoma landscape that precedes this in the paragraph, how do you react to Momaday's summarizing statement? Why? What other passages in the essay evoke a sense of place?

5. Visit a place that has historical significance. It may be a place where you or members of your family lived in the past, or it may be a place of local or national historical significance. Describe the place as it appears now, and report on events that

took place there in the past. What, if any, evidence do you find in the present of those events that took place in the past?

6. If you have a grandparent or an older friend living nearby, ask this person about his or her history. What does this person remember about the past that is no longer in the present? Are there also objects—pictures, clothing, medals, and so on—that can speak to you of your subject's past life? Reflect on the person's present life as well as on those events from the past that seem most memorable. Write an essay in which you represent your subject's life by concentrating on the place where he or she lives and the surrounding objects that help you to understand the past and present life.

MAKING CONNECTIONS

1. Compare Momaday's essay to Patricia Williams's for their extended portraits of individuals. How complete is the portrait each writer gives? On what kind of detail or observation is it based? How central is it to the essay in question?

2. Compare Momaday's essay to Alice Walker's for the way each essay moves through time. How do these essayists differ in their conception and representation of time, and how do those differences relate to their individual purposes as writers?

SHOOTING AN ELEPHANT
George Orwell

*George Orwell (1903–1950) was the pen name of Eric Blair,
the son of a British customs officer serving in Bengal, India.
As a boy he was sent home to prestigious schools, where he
learned to dislike the rich and powerful. After finishing
school at Eton, he served as an officer of the British police
in Burma, where he became disillusioned with imperialism.
Then he studied conditions among the urban poor and the
coal miners of Wigan, a city in northwestern England,
which confirmed him as a socialist. He was wounded in the
Spanish civil war, defending the lost cause of the left against
the fascists. Under the name Orwell, he wrote accounts of
all these experiences as well as the anti-Stalinist fable Animal Farm and the novel 1984. In the following essay, first
published in 1936, Orwell attacks the politics of imperialism.*

In Moulmein, in Lower Burma, I was hated by large numbers of people—
the only time in my life that I have been important enough for this to happen
to me. I was sub-divisional police officer of the town, and in an aimless, petty
kind of way anti-European feeling was very bitter. No one had the guts to raise
a riot, but if a European woman went through the bazaars alone somebody
would probably spit betel juice over her dress. As a police officer I was an
obvious target and was baited whenever it seemed safe to do so. When a nimble
Burman tripped me up on the football field and the referee (another Burman)
looked the other way, the crowd yelled with hideous laughter. This happened
more than once. In the end the sneering yellow faces of young men that met
me everywhere, the insults hooted after me when I was at a safe distance, got
badly on my nerves. The young Buddhist priests were the worst of all. There
were several thousands of them in the town and none of them seemed to have
anything to do except stand on street corners and jeer at Europeans.

All this was perplexing and upsetting. For at that time I had already made
up my mind that imperialism was an evil thing and the sooner I chucked up
my job and got out of it the better. Theoretically—and secretly, of course—I
was all for the Burmese and all against their oppressors, the British. As for the
job I was doing, I hated it more bitterly than I can perhaps make clear. In a
job like that you see the dirty work of Empire at close quarters. The wretched
prisoners huddling in the stinking cages of the lock-ups, the grey, cowed faces

of the long-term convicts, the scarred buttocks of the men who had been flogged with bamboos—all these oppressed me with an intolerable sense of guilt. But I could get nothing into perspective. I was young and ill-educated and I had had to think out my problems in the utter silence that is imposed on every English-man in the East. I did not even know that the British Empire is dying, still less did I know that it is a great deal better than the younger empires that are going to supplant it. All I knew was that I was stuck between my hatred of the empire I served and my rage against the evil-spirited little beasts who tried to make my job impossible. With one part of my mind I thought of the British Raj as an unbreakable tyranny,[1] as something clamped down, in *saecula saeculorum*,[2] upon the will of prostrate peoples; with another part I thought that the greatest joy in the world would be to drive a bayonet into a Buddhist priest's guts. Feelings like these are the normal by-product of imperialism; ask any Anglo-Indian official, if you can catch him off duty.

One day something happened which in a roundabout way was enlightening. 3 It was a tiny incident in itself, but it gave me a better glimpse than I had had before of the real nature of imperialism—the real motives for which despotic governments act. Early one morning the sub-inspector at a police station the other end of the town rang me up on the phone and said that an elephant was ravaging the bazaar. Would I please come and do something about it? I did not know what I could do, but I wanted to see what was happening and I got on to a pony and started out. I took my rifle, an old .44 Winchester and much too small to kill an elephant, but I thought the noise might be useful *in terrorem*.[3] Various Burmans stopped me on the way and told me about the elephant's doings. It was not, of course, a wild elephant, but a tame one which had gone "must." It had been chained up, as tame elephants always are when their attack of "must" is due, but on the previous night it had broken its chain and escaped. Its mahout, the only person who could manage it when it was in that state, had set out in pursuit, but had taken the wrong direction and was now twelve hours' journey away, and in the morning the elephant had suddenly reappeared in town. The Burmese population had no weapons and were quite helpless against it. It had already destroyed somebody's bamboo hut, killed a cow and raided some fruit-stalls and devoured the stock; also it had met the municipal rubbish van and, when the driver jumped out and took to his heels, had turned the van over and inflicted violences upon it.

The Burmese sub-inspector and some Indian constables were waiting for me 4 in the quarter where the elephant had been seen. It was a very poor quarter, a labyrinth of squalid bamboo huts, thatched with palm-leaf, winding all over a steep hillside. I remember that it was a cloudy, stuffy morning at the beginning

---

[1] the British Raj: the imperial government ruling British India and Burma. [Eds.]
[2] *saecula saeculorum*: forever and ever. [Eds.]
[3] *in terrorem*: for fright. [Eds.]

of the rains. We began questioning the people as to where the elephant had gone and, as usual, failed to get any definite information. That is invariably the case in the East; a story always sounds clear enough at a distance, but the nearer you get to the scene of events the vaguer it becomes. Some of the people said that the elephant had gone in one direction, some said that he had gone in another, some professed not even to have heard of any elephant. I had almost made up my mind that the whole story was a pack of lies, when we heard yells a little distance away. There was a loud, scandalized cry of "Go away, child! Go away this instant!" and an old woman with a switch in her hand came round the corner of a hut, violently shooing away a crowd of naked children. Some more women followed, clicking their tongues and exclaiming; evidently there was something that the children ought not to have seen. I rounded the hut and saw a man's dead body sprawling in the mud. He was an Indian, a black Dravidian coolie, almost naked, and he could not have been dead many minutes. The people said that the elephant had come suddenly upon him round the corner of the hut, caught him with its trunk, put its foot on his back and ground him into the earth. This was the rainy season and the ground was soft, and his face had scored a trench a foot deep and a couple of yards long. He was lying on his belly with arms crucified and head sharply twisted to one side. His face was coated with mud, the eyes wide open, the teeth bared and grinning with an expression of unendurable agony. (Never tell me, by the way, that the dead look peaceful. Most of the corpses I have seen looked devilish.) The friction of the great beast's foot had stripped the skin from his back as neatly as one skins a rabbit. As soon as I saw the dead man I sent an orderly to a friend's house nearby to borrow an elephant rifle. I had already sent back the pony, not wanting it to go mad with fright and throw me if it smelt the elephant.

The orderly came back in a few minutes with a rifle and five cartridges, and meanwhile some Burmans had arrived and told us that the elephant was in the paddy fields below, only a few hundred yards away. As I started forward practically the whole population of the quarter flocked out of the houses and followed me. They had seen the rifle and were all shouting excitedly that I was going to shoot the elephant. They had not shown much interest in the elephant when he was merely ravaging their homes, but it was different now that he was to be shot. It was a bit of fun to them, as it would be to an English crowd; besides they wanted the meat. It made me vaguely uneasy. I had no intention of shooting the elephant—I had merely sent for the rifle to defend myself if necessary—and it is always unnerving to have a crowd following you. I marched down the hill, looking and feeling a fool, with the rifle over my shoulder and an ever-growing army of people jostling at my heels. At the bottom, when you got away from the huts, there was a metalled road and beyond that a miry waste of paddy fields a thousand yards across, not yet ploughed but soggy from the first rains and dotted with coarse grass. The elephant was standing eight yards from the road, his left side towards us. He took not the slightest notice of the

5

crowd's approach. He was tearing up bunches of grass, beating them against his knees to clean them and stuffing them into his mouth.

I had halted on the road. As soon as I saw the elephant I knew with perfect 6 certainty that I ought not to shoot him. It is a serious matter to shoot a working elephant—it is comparable to destroying a huge and costly piece of machinery— and obviously one ought not to do it if it can possibly be avoided. And at that distance, peacefully eating, the elephant looked no more dangerous than a cow. I thought then and I think now that his attack of "must" was already passing off; in which case he would merely wander harmlessly about until the mahout came back and caught him. Moreover, I did not in the least want to shoot him. I decided that I would watch him for a little while to make sure that he did not turn savage again, and then go home.

But at that moment I glanced around at the crowd that had followed me. It 7 was an immense crowd, two thousand at the least and growing every minute. It blocked the road for a long distance on either side. I looked at the sea of yellow faces above the garish clothes—faces all happy and excited all over this bit of fun, all certain that the elephant was going to be shot. They were watching me as they would watch a conjurer about to perform a trick. They did not like me, but with the magical rifle in my hands I was momentarily worth watching. And suddenly I realized that I should have to shoot the elephant after all. The people expected it of me and I had got to do it; I could feel their two thousand wills pressing me forward, irresistibly. And it was at this moment, as I stood there with the rifle in my hands, that I first grasped the hollowness, the futility of the white man's dominion in the East. Here was I, the white man with his gun, standing in front of the unarmed native crowd—seemingly the leading actor of the piece; but in reality I was only an absurd puppet pushed to and fro by the will of those yellow faces behind. I perceived in this moment that when the white man turns tyrant it is his own freedom that he destroys. He becomes a sort of hollow, posing dummy, the conventionalized figure of a sahib. For it is the condition of his rule that he shall spend his life in trying to impress the "natives," and so in every crisis he has got to do what the "natives" expect of him. He wears a mask, and his face grows to fit it. I had got to shoot the elephant. I had committed myself to doing it when I sent for the rifle. A sahib has got to act like a sahib; he has got to appear resolute, to know his own mind and do definite things. To come all that way, rifle in hand, with two thousand people marching at my heels, and then to trail feebly away, having done nothing—no, that was impossible. The crowd would laugh at me. And my whole life, every white man's life in the East, was one long struggle not to be laughed at.

But I did not want to shoot the elephant. I watched him beating his bunch 8 of grass against his knees, with that preoccupied grandmotherly air that elephants have. It seemed to me that it would be murder to shoot him. At that age I was not squeamish about killing animals, but I had never shot an elephant and never wanted to. (Somehow it always seems worse to kill a *large* animal.) Besides, there was the beast's owner to be considered. Alive, the elephant was worth at least a hundred pounds; dead, he would only be worth the value of his tusks, five pounds, possibly. But I had got to act quickly. I turned to some experienced-looking Burmans who had been there when we arrived, and asked them how the elephant had been behaving. They all said the same thing: he took no notice of you if you left him alone, but he might charge if you went too close to him.

It was perfectly clear to me what I ought to do. I ought to walk up to within, say, twenty-five yards of the elephant and test his behavior. If he charged, I could shoot; if he took no notice of me, it would be safe to leave him until the mahout came back. But also I knew that I was going to do no such thing. I was a poor shot with a rifle and the ground was soft mud into which one would sink at every step. If the elephant charged and I missed him, I should have about as much chance as a toad under a steam-roller. But even then I was not thinking particularly of my own skin, only of the watchful yellow faces behind. For at the moment, with the crowd watching me, I was not afraid in the ordinary sense, as I would have been if I had been alone. A white man mustn't be frightened in front of "natives"; and so, in general, he isn't frightened. The sole thought in my mind was that if anything went wrong those two thousand Burmans would see me pursued, caught, trampled on and reduced to a grinning corpse like that Indian up the hill. And if that happened it was quite probable that some of them would laugh. That would never do. There was only one alternative. I shoved the cartridges into the magazine and lay down on the road to get a better aim. 9

The crowd grew very still, and a deep, low, happy sigh, as of people who see the theatre curtain go up at last, breathed from innumerable throats. They were going to have their bit of fun after all. The rifle was a beautiful German thing with cross-hair sights. I did not then know that in shooting an elephant one would shoot to cut an imaginary bar running from ear-hole to ear-hole. I ought, therefore, as the elephant was sideways on, to have aimed straight at his ear-hole; actually I aimed several inches in front of this, thinking the brain would be further forward. 10

When I pulled the trigger I did not hear the bang or feel the kick—one never does when a shot goes home—but I heard the devilish roar of glee that went up from the crowd. In that instant, in too short a time, one would have thought, even for the bullet to get there, a mysterious, terrible change had come over the elephant. He neither stirred nor fell, but every line of his body had altered. He looked suddenly stricken, shrunken, immensely old, as though the frightful impact of the bullet had paralyzed him without knocking him down. At last, after what seemed a long time—it might have been five seconds, I dare say— he sagged flabbily to his knees. His mouth slobbered. An enormous senility 11 seemed to have settled upon him. One could have imagined him thousands of years old. I fired again into the same spot. At the second shot he did not collapse but climbed with desperate slowness to his feet and stood weakly upright, with legs sagging and head drooping. I fired a third time. That was the shot that did for him. You could see the agony of it jolt his whole body and knock the last remnant of strength from his legs. But in falling he seemed for a moment to rise, for as his hind legs collapsed beneath him he seemed to tower upward like a huge rock toppling, his trunk reaching skywards like a tree. He trumpeted, for the first and only time. And then down he came, his belly towards me, with a crash that seemed to shake the ground even where I lay.

I got up. The Burmans were already racing past me across the mud. It was 12 obvious that the elephant would never rise again, but he was not dead. He was breathing very rhythmically with long rattling gasps, his great mound of a side painfully rising and falling. His mouth was wide open—I could see far down into caverns of pale pink throat. I waited for a long time for him to die, but his breathing did not weaken. Finally I fired my two remaining shots into the spot where I thought his heart must be. The thick blood welled out of him like red velvet, but still he did not die. His body did not even jerk when the shots hit him, the tortured breathing continued without a pause. He was dying, very slowly and in great agony, but in some world remote from me where not even a bullet could damage him further. I felt that I had got to put an end to that dreadful noise. It seemed dreadful to see the great beast lying there, powerless to move and yet powerless to die, and not even to be able to finish him. I sent back for my small rifle and poured shot after shot into his heart and down his throat. They seemed to make no impression. The tortured gasps continued as steadily as the ticking of a clock.

In the end I could not stand it any longer and went away. I heard later that 13 it took him half an hour to die. Burmans were bringing dahs and baskets even before I left,[4] and I was told they had stripped his body almost to the bones by the afternoon.

Afterwards, of course, there were endless discussions about the shooting of 14 the elephant. The owner was furious, but he was only an Indian and could do nothing. Besides, legally I had done the right thing, for a mad elephant has to be killed, like a mad dog, if its owner fails to control it. Among the Europeans opinion was divided. The older men said I was right, the younger men said it was a damn shame to shoot an elephant for killing a coolie, because an elephant was worth more than any damn Coringhee coolie. And afterwards I was very glad that the coolie had been killed; it put me legally in the right and it gave me a sufficient pretext for shooting the elephant. I often wondered whether any of the others grasped that I had done it solely to avoid looking a fool.

---

[4]dahs: butcher knives. [Eds.]

QUESTIONS

1. Describe Orwell's mixed feelings about serving as a police officer in Burma.

2. How do the natives "force" Orwell to shoot the elephant against his better judgment? How does he relate this personal episode to the larger problems of British imperialism?

3. What is Orwell's final reaction to his deed? How literally can we take his statement that he "was very glad that the coolie had been killed" (paragraph 14)?

4. From the opening sentence Orwell displays a remarkable candor concerning his feelings. How does this personal, candid tone add to or detract from the strength of the essay?

5. Orwell's recollection of shooting the elephant is shaped to support a specific point or thesis. Where does Orwell state this thesis? Is this placement effective?

6. This essay reads more like a short story than an expository essay. In what ways is Orwell's use of narrative and personal experience effective?

7. Orwell often wrote with a political purpose, with a "desire to push the world in a certain direction, to alter other people's idea of the kind of society that they should strive after." To what extent does the "tiny incident" in this essay illuminate "the real nature of imperialism" (paragraph 3)? Does Orwell succeed in altering your idea of imperialism?

8. Using Orwell's essay as a model, write a reflection in which the narration of "a tiny incident" (paragraph 3) illuminates a larger social or political problem.

9. Like "Shooting an Elephant," Orwell's novel *Burmese Days* (1934) takes place in Burma and attacks British imperialism. After reading this novel, write a report comparing it with the essay.

MAKING CONNECTIONS

The selections by Maya Angelou, Loren Eiseley, and Zoë Tracy Hardy in this section read somewhat like short stories, as does Orwell's essay. Compare the narrative designs of two of these writers and discuss the usefulness of storytelling in reflective writing.

WHAT DID YOU DO IN THE WAR, GRANDMA?

A Flashback to August, 1945

Zoë Tracy Hardy

Born in 1927 and raised in the Midwest, Zoë Tracy Hardy was one of millions of young women called "Rosie the Riveters" who worked in defense plants during World War II. Considered at first to be mere surrogates for male workers, these women soon were building bombers that their supervisors declared "equal in the construction [to] those turned out by experienced workmen in the plant's other departments," as a news feature at the time stated. After the eventful summer described in the essay below, Hardy finished college, married, and began teaching college English in Arizona, Guam, and Colorado. This essay first appeared in the August 1985 issue of Ms. magazine—exactly forty years after the end of World War II.

It was unseasonably cool that day in May, 1945, when I left my mother and 1 father and kid brother in eastern Iowa and took the bus all the way to Omaha to help finish the war. I was 18, and had just completed my first year at the University of Iowa without distinction. The war in Europe had ended in April; the war against the Japanese still raged. I wanted to go where something *real* was being done to end this bitter war that had always been part of my adolescence.

I arrived in Omaha at midnight. The YWCA, where I promised my family 2 I would get a room, was closed until 7 A.M., so I curled up in a cracked maroon leather chair in the crowded, smoky waiting room of the bus station.

In the morning I set off on foot for the YWCA, dragging a heavy suitcase 3 and carrying my favorite hat trimmed in daisies in a large round hatbox. An hour of lugging and resting brought me to the Y, a great Victorian house of dark brick, where I paid two weeks in advance (most of my money) for board and a single room next to a bathroom that I would share with eight other girls. I surrendered my red and blue food-ration stamp books and my sugar coupons to the cook who would keep them as long as I stayed there.

I had eaten nothing but a wartime candy bar since breakfast at home the 4 day before, but breakfast at the Y was already over. So, queasy and light-headed, I went back out into the cold spring day to find my job. I set out for the downtown office of the Glenn L. Martin Company. It was at their plant south of the city that thousands of workers, in around-the-clock shifts, built the famous B-29 bombers, the great Superfortresses, which the papers said would end the war.

I filled out an application and thought about the women welders and riveters and those who operated machine presses to help put the Superfortresses together. I grew shakier by the minute, more and more certain I was unqualified for any job here.

My interview was short. The personnel man was unconcerned about my total lack of skills. If I passed the physical, I could have a job in the Reproduction Department, where the blueprints were handled.

Upstairs in a gold-walled banquet room furnished with examination tables and hospital screens, a nurse sat me on a stool to draw a blood sample from my arm. I watched my blood rolling slowly into the needle. The gold walls wilted in the distance, and I slumped forward in a dead faint.

A grandfatherly doctor waved ammonia under my nose, and said if I would go to a café down the street and eat the complete 50-cent breakfast, I had the job.

The first week in the Reproduction Department, I learned to cut and fold enormous blueprints as they rolled from a machine that looked like a giant washing machine wringer. Then I was moved to a tall, metal contraption with a lurid light glowing from its interior. An ammonia guzzler, it spewed out smelly copies of specifications so hot my finger-tips burned when I touched them. I called it the dragon, and when I filled it with ammonia, the fumes reminded me of gold walls dissolving before my eyes. I took all my breaks outdoors, even when it was raining.

My boss, Mr. Johnson,[1] was a sandy-haired man of about 40, who spoke pleasantly when he came around to say hello and to check our work. Elsie, his secretary, a cool redhead, seldom spoke to any of us and spent most of her time in the darkroom developing negatives and reproducing photographs.

One of my coworkers in Reproduction was Mildred, a tall dishwater blond with a horsey, intelligent face. She was the first woman I'd ever met with an earthy unbridled tongue.

When I first arrived, Mildred warned me always to knock on the darkroom door before going in because Mr. Johnson and Elsie did a lot of screwing in there. I didn't believe her, I thought we were supposed to knock to give Elsie time to protect her negatives from the sudden light. "Besides," I said, "there isn't room to lie down in there." Mildred laughed until tears squeezed from the corners of her eyes. "You poor kid," she said. "Don't you *know* you don't have to lie down?"

I was stunned. "But it's easier if you do," I protested, defensive about my

---

[1] All names but the author's have been changed.

sex education. My mother, somewhat ahead of her time, had always been explicit in her explanations, and I had read "Lecture 14," an idyllic description of lovemaking being passed around among freshman girls in every dormitory in the country.

"Sitting, standing, any quick way you can in time of war," Mildred winked 14 wickedly. She was as virginal as I, but what she said reminded us of the steady dearth of any day-to-day presence of young men in our lives.

We were convinced that the war would be over by autumn. We were stepping 15 up the napalm and incendiary bombing of the Japanese islands, the British were now coming to our aid in the Pacific, and the Japanese Navy was being reduced to nothing in some of the most spectacular sea battles in history.

Sometimes, after lunch, I went into the assembly areas to see how the 16 skeletons of the B-29s were growing from our blueprints. At first there were enormous stark ribs surrounded by scaffolding two and three stories high. A few days later there was aluminum flesh over the ribs and wings sprouting from stubs on the fuselage. Women in overalls and turbans, safety glasses, and steel-toed shoes scrambled around the wings with riveting guns and welding torches, fitting fuel tanks in place. Instructions were shouted at them by hoarse, paunchy old men in hard hats. I cheered myself by thinking how we were pouring it on, a multitude of us together creating this great bird to end the war.

Away from the plant, however, optimism sometimes failed me. My room at 17 the Y was bleak. I wrote letters to my unofficial fiancé and to other young men in the service who had been friends and classmates. Once in a while I attempted to study, thinking I would redeem my mediocre year at the university.

During those moments when I sensed real homesickness lying in wait, I 18 would plan something to do with Betty and Celia, friends from high school, who had moved to Omaha "for the duration" and had jobs as secretaries for a large moving and storage company. Their small apartment was upstairs in an old frame house in Benson, a northwest suburb. Celia and Betty and I cooked, exchanged news from servicemen we all knew and talked about plans for the end of the war. Betty was engaged to her high school sweetheart, a soldier who had been wounded in Germany and who might be coming home soon. We guessed she would be the first one of us to be married, and we speculated, in the careful euphemisms of "well-brought-up girls," about her impending introduction to sex.

By the first of July, work and the pace of life had lost momentum. The war 19 news seemed to repeat itself without advancing, as day after day battles were fought around jungly Pacific islands that all seemed identical and unreal.

At the plant, I was moved from the dragon to a desk job, a promotion of 20 sorts. I sat on a high stool in a cubicle of pigeonholed cabinets and filed blueprints, specs, and deviations in the proper holes. While I was working, I saw no one and couldn't talk to anybody.

In mid-July Betty got married. Counsel from our elders was always to wait— 21
wait until things settle down after the war. Harold, still recuperating from
shrapnel wounds, asked Betty not to wait.

Celia and I attended the ceremony on a sizzling afternoon in a musty 22
Presbyterian church. Harold was very serious, gaunt-faced and thin in his loose-
hanging Army uniform. Betty, a fair-skinned, blue-eyed brunet in a white street
dress, looked pale and solemn. After the short ceremony, they left the church
in a borrowed car. Someone had given them enough gasoline stamps for a
honeymoon trip to a far-off cabin on the shore of a piney Minnesota lake.

Celia and I speculated on Betty's introduction to lovemaking. I had "Lecture 23
14" in mind and hoped she would like lovemaking, especially way off in
Minnesota, far from the sweltering city and the war. Celia thought it didn't
matter much whether a girl liked it or not, as long as other important parts of
marriage got off to a good start.

That weekend Celia and I took a walk in a park and watched a grandfather 24
carefully pump a seesaw up and down for his small grandson. We saw a short,
middle-aged sailor walking with a sad-faced young woman who towered over
him. "A whore," Celia said, "Probably one of those from the Hotel Bianca."
Celia had been in Omaha longer than I and knew more of its secrets.

I wanted, right then, to see someone young and male and healthy cross the 25
grass under the trees, someone without wounds and without a cap, someone
with thick disheveled hair that hadn't been militarily peeled down to the green
skin on the back of his skull. Someone wearing tennis shorts to show strong,
hair-matted legs, and a shirt with an open neck and short sleeves revealing
smooth, hard muscles and tanned skin. Someone who would pull me out of
this gloom with a wide spontaneous smile as he passed.

In the next few days, the tempo of the summer changed subtly. From friends 26
stationed in the Pacific, I began to get letters free from rectangular holes where
military censors had snipped out "sensitive" words. Our Navy was getting ready
to surround the Japanese islands with a starvation blockade, and our B-29s had
bombed the industrial heart of the country. We were dropping leaflets warning
the Japanese people that we would incinerate hundreds of thousands of them
by firebombing 11 of their major cities. Rumors rippled through the plant back
in Omaha. The Japanese Empire would collapse in a matter of weeks, at most.

One Friday night, with Celia's help, I moved out of the Y to Celia's 27
apartment in Benson. We moved by streetcar. Celia carried my towels and my
full laundry bag in big rolls, one under each arm, and wore my straw picture
hat with the daisies, which bobbled wildly on top of her head. My hatbox was
crammed with extra underwear and the war letters I was determined to save.
When we climbed aboard the front end of the streetcar, I dropped the hatbox,
spilled an armload of books down the aisle, and banged my suitcase into the
knees of an elderly man who was trying to help me retrieve them.

We began to laugh, at everything, at nothing, and were still laughing when 28 we hauled everything off the car and down one block to the apartment, the daisies all the while wheeling recklessly on Celia's head.

It was a good move. Summer nights were cooler near the country, and so quiet I could hear the crickets. The other upstairs apartment was occupied by Celia's older sister, Andrea, and her husband, Bob, who hadn't been drafted.

Late in July, an unusual thing happened at the plant. Mr. Johnson asked us to work double shifts for a few days. The situation was urgent, he said, and he wanted 100 percent cooperation from the Reproduction Department, even if it meant coming to work when we felt sick or postponing something that was personally important to us.

The next morning no one from the day shift was missing, and the place was full of people from the graveyard shift. Some of the time I worked in my cubicle counting out special blueprints and deviations. The rest of the time I helped the crews sweating over the blueprint machine cut out prints that contained odd lines and numbers that I had never seen before. Their shapes were different, too, and there was no place for them in the numbered pigeonholes of my cubicle. Some prints were small, about four inches square. Mildred said they were so cute she might tuck one in her shoe and smuggle it home as a souvenir even if it meant going to the federal pen if she got caught.

During those days I learned to nap on streetcars. I had to get up at 4:30, bolt down breakfast, and catch the first car to rumble out of the darkness at 5:15. The double shift wasn't over until 11:30, so I got home about one in the morning.

The frenzy at the plant ended as suddenly as it had begun. Dazed with fatigue, I slept through most of a weekend and hoped we had pushed ourselves to some limit that would lift us over the last hump of the war.

On Monday the familiar single shift was not quite the same. We didn't know what we had done, but an undercurrent of anticipation ran through the department because of those double shifts—and the news. The papers told of factories that were already gearing up to turn out refrigerators, radios, and automobiles instead of bombs and planes.

In Reproduction, the pace began to slacken. Five hundred thirty-six B-29s, planes we had put together on the Nebraska prairie, had firebombed the principal islands of the Japanese Empire: Hokkaido, Honshu, Kyushu, Shikoku. We had reduced to ashes more than 15 square miles of the heart of Tokyo. The battered and burned Japanese were so near defeat that there couldn't be much left for us to do. With surprising enthusiasm, I began to plan for my return to college.

Going home on the streetcar the first Tuesday afternoon in August, I heard about a puzzling new weapon. Some excited people at the end of the car were jabbering about it, saying the Japanese would be forced to surrender in a matter of hours.

When I got home, Andrea, her round bespectacled face flushed, met me at 37
the head of the stairs. "Oh, come and listen to the radio—it's a new bomb—
it's almost over!"

I sat down in her living room and listened. There was news, then music, 38
then expanded news. Over and over the newscaster reported that the United
States had unlocked a secret of the universe and unleashed a cosmic force—
from splitting atoms of uranium—on the industrial seaport of Hiroshima. Most
of the city had been leveled to the ground, and many of its inhabitants disin-
tegrated to dust in an instant by a single bomb. "Our scientists have changed
the history of the world," the newscaster said. He sounded as if he could not
believe it himself.

We ate dinner from our laps and continued to listen as the news pounded 39
on for an hour, then two, then three. I tried, at last, to *think* about it. In high
school physics we had already learned that scientists were close to splitting an
atom. We imagined that a cupful of the tremendous energy from such a
phenomenon might run a car back and forth across the entire country dozens
of times. I could visualize that. But I could not imagine how such energy put
into a small bomb would cause the kind of destruction described on the radio.

About nine, I walked over to McCollum's grocery store to buy an evening 40
paper. The headline said we had harnessed atomic power. I skimmed through
a front page story. Science had ushered us into a strange new world, and
President Truman had made two things clear: the bomb had created a monster
that could wipe out civilization; and some protection against this monster would
have to be found before its secret could be given to the world.

Back out in the dark street, I hesitated. For the first time I could remember, 41
I felt a rush of terror at being out in the night alone.

When I got back to the apartment, I made a pot of coffee and sat down at 42
the kitchen table to read the rest of the paper. President Truman had said: "The
force from which the sun draws its power has been loosed against those who
brought war to the Far East. . . . If they do not now accept our terms they may
expect a rain of ruin from the air the like of which has never been seen on this
earth." New and more powerful bombs were now being developed.

I read everything, looking for some speculation from someone about how 43
we were going to live in this new world. There was nothing. About midnight
Andrea knocked on my open door to get my attention. She stood there a
moment in her nightgown and curlers looking at me rather oddly. She asked if
I was all right.

I said yes, just trying to soak it all in. 44

Gently she told me I had better go to bed and think about how soon the war 45
would be over.

The next day Reproduction was nearly demolished by the spirit of celebra- 46
tion. The *Enola Gay*, the plane that had dropped the bomb, was one of ours.
By Thursday morning the United States had dropped a second atomic bomb,

an even bigger one, on an industrial city, Nagasaki, and the Russians had declared war on Japan.

At the end of the day, Mr. Johnson asked us to listen to the radio for announcements about when to return to work, then shook hands all around. "You've all done more than you know to help with the war," he said. 47

We said tentative good-byes. I went home and over to McCollum's for an evening paper. An Army Strategic Air Forces expert said that there was no comparison between the fire caused by the atomic bomb and that of a normal conflagration. And there were other stories about radiation, like X-rays, that might cripple and poison living things for hours, weeks, maybe years, until they died. 48

I went to bed late and had nightmares full of flames and strange dry gale winds. The next noon I got up, exhausted, and called Mildred. She said they were still saying not to report to work until further notice. "It's gonna bore our tails off," she moaned. "I don't know how long we can sit around here just playing hearts." I could hear girls laughing in the background. 49

"Mildred," I blurted anxiously, "do you think we should have done this thing?" 50

"Why not? Better us than somebody else, kid." 51

I reminded her that we knew the Japanese were finished weeks ago and asked her if it wasn't sort of like kicking a dead horse—brutally. 52

"Look," she said. "The war is really over even if the bigwigs haven't said so yet. What more do you want?" 53

The evening paper finally offered a glimmer of relief. One large headline said that serious questions about the morality of *Americans* using such a weapon were being raised by some civilians of note and some churchmen. I went to bed early and lay listening to the crickets and thinking about everyone coming home—unofficial fiancés, husbands, fathers, brothers—all filling the empty spaces between kids and women and old men, putting a balance in our lives we hadn't known in years. 54

Yet the bomb haunted me. I was still awake when the windowpanes lightened up at daybreak. 55

It was all over on August 14, 1945. Unconditional surrender. 56

For hours at a time, the bomb's importance receded in the excitement of that day. Streetcar bells clanged up and down the streets; we heard sirens, whistles, church bells. A newscaster described downtown Omaha as a free-for-all. Perfect strangers were hugging each other in the streets; some were dancing. Churches had thrown open their doors, and people were streaming in and out, offering prayers of thanksgiving. Taverns were giving away free drinks. 57

Andrew wanted us to have a little whiskey, even though we were under age, because there would never be another day like this as long as we lived. I hated 58 the first taste of it, but as we chattered away, inventing wild, gratifying futures, I welcomed the muffler it wrapped around the ugliness of the bomb.

In the morning Mildred called to say our jobs were over and that we should 59 report to the plant to turn in our badges and get final paychecks. She had just talked to Mr. Johnson, who told her that those funny blueprints we had made during double shift had something to do with the bomb.

"Well, honey," she said, "I don't understand atomic energy, but old jazzy 60 Johnson said we had to work like that to get the *Enola Gay* and the *thing* to go together."

I held my breath, waiting for Mildred to say she was kidding, as usual. 61 Ordinary 19- and 20-year-old girls were not, not in the United States of America, required to work night and day to help launch scientific monsters that would catapult us all into a precarious "strange new world"—forever. But I knew in my bones that Mildred, forthright arrow-straight Mildred, was only telling me what I had already, unwillingly, guessed.

After a long silence she said, "Well, kid, give me your address in Iowa, and 62 I'll send you a Christmas card for auld lang syne."

I wanted to cry as we exchanged addresses. I liked Mildred. I hated the gap 63 that I now sensed would always be between me and people like her.

"It's been nice talking dirty to you all summer," she said. 64

"Thanks." I hung up, slipped down the stairs, and walked past the streetcar 65 line out into the country.

The whole countryside was sundrenched, fragrant with sweet clover and 66 newly mown alfalfa. I leaned against a fence post and tried to think.

The President had said we had unleashed the great secret of the universe in 67 this way, to shorten the war and save American lives. Our commitment to defeat the Japanese was always clear to me. They had attacked us first. But we had already firebombed much of the Japanese Empire to char. That seemed decisive enough, and terrible enough.

If he had asked me whether I would work very hard to help bring this horror 68 into being, knowing it would shorten the war but put the world into jeopardy for all time, how would I have answered?

I would have said, "No. With all due respect, Sir, how could such a thing 69 make a just end to our just cause?"

But the question had never been asked of us. And I stood now, in the warm 70 sun, gripping a splintery fence post, outraged by our final insignificance—all of us who had worked together in absolute trust to end the war.

An old cow stood near the fence switching her tail. I looked at her great, 71 uncomprehending brown eyes and began to sob.

After a while I walked back to the apartment, mentally packing my suitcase 72 and tying up my hatbox of war letters. I knew it was going to be very hard, from now on, for the whole world to take care of itself.

I wanted very much to go home.   73

QUESTIONS

1. How does Hardy's attitude toward the war change in the course of this essay? What event causes her to reevaluate her attitude?

2. Describe Hardy's feelings about the introduction of atomic power into her world. Are they optimistic or pessimistic?

3. "You've all done more than you know to help win the war," Hardy's boss tells her (paragraph 47). How does she react to the fact that she was not informed by the authorities of the purpose of her work? How does her reaction differ from that of her coworker Mildred?

4. As Hardy's attitude toward war changes, her attitude toward sex changes as well. Trace this change in attitude; what connection, if any, do you see between the two?

5. Is this essay merely a personal reminiscence, or does the author have a larger purpose? Explain what you think her purpose is.

6. This essay was published forty years after the events it describes. Are Hardy's fears and speculations (on atomic power, on the authority of the government, on sex) dated in any way, or are they still relevant today? Explain your answer.

7. Have you, like Hardy, ever wondered about the larger social implications of any job that you've held or that a friend or parent holds? Write an essay like Hardy's reflecting on that job and describing how your attitude changed as you placed the job in a larger context.

MAKING CONNECTIONS

1. Somewhat like Hemingway in "A New Kind of War" (in "Reporting"), Hardy senses that she stands on the threshold of a new era. Compare these two writers for the sense of the new that each conveys. Which writer is more explicit about what he or she senses? Hardy, of course, writes forty years after the events she describes whereas Hemingway writes from a much closer vantage point. How does this fact complicate your comparison?

2. Could Hardy's essay be described as a "pilgrimage" to a particular intellectual or political position, somewhat like Martin Luther King's "Pilgrimage to Nonviolence"? How fair would that retitling be to Hardy's essay? What aspects of pilgrimage do you find in it?

Sciences and Technologies

A MASK ON THE FACE OF DEATH
Richard Selzer

Richard Selzer (b. 1928) is the son of a general practitioner father and a singer mother, both of whom wanted their son to follow in their footsteps. At ten he began sneaking into his father's office to look at his father's medical textbooks, where he discovered "the rich alliterative language of medicine—words such as cerebellum which, when said aloud, melt in the mouth and drip from the end of the tongue like chocolate." After his father's death he decided to become a doctor and was for many years a professor of surgery at Yale Medical School. Only after working as a doctor for many decades did he begin to write. About the similarities between surgery and writing he states, "In surgery, it is the body that is being opened up and put back together. In writing it is the whole world that is taken in for repairs, then put back in working order piece by piece." His articles have appeared in Vanity Fair, Harper's, Esquire *and* The New York Times Magazine. *His books include a volume of short stories,* Rituals of Surgery *(1974), and a collection of autobiographical essays,* Mortal Lessons *(1976). This essay also appeared in* Life *(1988).*

It is ten o'clock at night as we drive up to the Copacabana, a dilapidated brothel on the rue Dessalines in the red-light district of Port-au-Prince. My guide is a young Haitian, Jean-Bernard. Ten years before, J-B tells me, at the age of fourteen, "like every good Haitian boy" he had been brought here by his

135

older cousins for his *rite de passage*. From the car to the entrance, we are accosted by a half dozen men and women for sex. We enter, go down a long hall that breaks upon a cavernous room with a stone floor. The cubicles of the prostitutes, I am told, are in an attached wing of the building. Save for a red-purple glow from small lights on the walls, the place is unlit. Dark shapes float by, each with a blindingly white stripe of teeth. Latin music is blaring. We take seats at the table farthest from the door. Just outside, there is the rhythmic lapping of the Caribbean Sea. About twenty men are seated at the tables or lean against the walls. Brightly dressed women, singly or in twos or threes, stroll about, now and then exchanging banter with the men. It is as though we have been deposited in act two of Bizet's *Carmen*. If this place isn't Lillas Pastia's tavern, what is it?

Within minutes, three light-skinned young women arrive at our table. They are very beautiful and young and lively. Let them be Carmen, Mercedes and Frasquita. 2

"I want the old one," says Frasquita, ruffling my hair. The women laugh uproariously. 3

"Don't bother looking any further," says Mercedes. "We are the prettiest ones." 4

"We only want to talk," I tell her. 5

"Aaah, aaah," she crows. "*Massissi*. You are *massissi*." It is the contemptuous Creole term for homosexual. If we want only to talk, we must be gay. Mercedes and Carmen are slender, each weighing one hundred pounds or less. Frasquita is tall and hefty. They are dressed for work: red taffeta, purple chiffon and black sequins. Among them a thousand gold bracelets and earrings multiply every speck of light. Their bare shoulders are like animated lamps gleaming in the shadowy room. Since there is as yet no business, the women agree to sit with us. J-B orders beer and cigarettes. We pay each woman $10. 6

"Where are you from?" I begin. 7

"We are Dominican." 8

"Do you miss your country?" 9

"Oh, yes, we do." Six eyes go muzzy with longing. "Our country is the most beautiful in the world. No country is like the Dominican. And it doesn't stink like this one." 10

"Then why don't you work there? Why come to Haiti?" 11

"Santo Domingo has too many whores. All beautiful, like us. All light-skinned. The Haitian men like to sleep with light women." 12

"Why is that?" 13

"Because always, the whites have all the power and the money. The black men can imagine they do, too, when they have us in bed." 14

Eleven o'clock. I looked around the room that is still sparsely peopled with men. 15

"It isn't getting any busier," I say. Frasquita glances over her shoulder. Her   16
eyes drill the darkness.

"It is still early," she says.   17

"Could it be that the men are afraid of getting sick?" Frasquita is offended.   18

"Sick! They do not get sick from us. We are healthy, strong. Every week we   19
go for a checkup. Besides, we know how to tell if we are getting sick."

"I mean sick with AIDS." The word sets off a hurricane of taffeta, chiffon   20
and gold jewelry. They are all gesticulation and fury. It is Carmen who speaks.

"AIDS!" Her lips curl about the syllable. "There is no such thing. It is a   21
false disease invented by the American government to take advantage of the
poor countries. The American President hates poor people, so now he makes
up AIDS to take away the little we have." The others nod vehemently.

"*Mira, mon cher.* Look, my dear," Carmen continues. "One day the police   22
came here. Believe me, they are worse than the *tonton macoutes* with their
submachine guns. They rounded up one hundred and five of us and they took
our blood. That was a year ago. None of us have died, you see? We are all still
here. *Mira*, we sleep with all the men and we are not sick."

"But aren't there some of you who have lost weight and have diarrhea?"   23

"One or two, maybe. But they don't eat. That is why they are weak."   24

"Only the men die," says Mercedes. "They stop eating, so they die. It is   25
hard to kill a woman."

"Do you eat well?"   26

"Oh, yes, don't worry, we do. We eat like poor people, but we eat." There   27
is a sudden scream from Frasquita. She points to a large rat that has emerged
from beneath our table.

"My God!" she exclaims. "It is big like a pig." They burst into laughter. For   28
a moment the women fall silent. There is only the restlessness of their many
bracelets. I give them each another $10.

"Are many of the men here bisexual?"   29

"Too many. They do it for money. Afterward, they come to us." Carmen   30
lights a cigarette and looks down at the small lace handkerchief she has been
folding and unfolding with immense precision on the table. All at once she
turns it over as though it were the ace of spades.

"*Mira, blanc* . . . look, white man," she says in a voice suddenly full of   31
foreboding. Her skin seems to darken to coincide with the tone of her voice.

"*Mira*, soon many Dominican women will die in Haiti!"   32

"Die of what?"   33

She shrugs. "It is what they do to us."   34

"Carmen," I say, "if you knew that you had AIDS, that your blood was bad,   35
would you still sleep with men?" Abruptly, she throws back her head and laughs.
It is the same laughter with which Frasquita had greeted the rat at our feet.
She stands and the others follow.

"*Méchant!* You wicked man," she says. Then, with terrible solemnity, "You 36 don't know anything."

"But you are killing the Haitian men," I say. 37

"As for that," she says, "everyone is killing everyone else." All at once, I 38 want to know everything about these three—their childhood, their dreams, what they do in the afternoon, what they eat for lunch.

"Don't leave," I say. "Stay a little more." Again, I reach for my wallet. But 39 they are gone, taking all the light in the room with them—Mercedes and Carmen to sit at another table where three men have been waiting. Frasquita is strolling about the room. Now and then, as if captured by the music, she breaks into a few dance steps, snapping her fingers, singing to herself.

Midnight. And the Copacabana is filling up. Now it is like any other seedy 40 nightclub where men and women go hunting. We get up to leave. In the center a couple are dancing a *méringue*. He is the most graceful dancer I have ever watched; she, the most voluptuous. Together they seem to be riding the back of the music as it gallops to a precisely sexual beat. Closer up, I see that the man is short of breath, sweating. All at once, he collapses into a chair. The woman bends over him, coaxing, teasing, but he is through. A young man with a long polished stick blocks my way.

"I come with you?" he asks. "Very good time. You say yes? Ten dollars? 41 Five?"

I have been invited by Dr. Jean William Pape to attend the AIDS clinic of 42 which he is the director. Nothing from the outside of the low whitewashed structure would suggest it as a medical facility. Inside, it is divided into many small cubicles and a labyrinth of corridors. At nine A.M. the hallways are already full of emaciated silent men and women, some sitting on the few benches, the rest leaning against the walls. The only sounds are subdued moans of discomfort interspersed with coughs. How they eat us with their eyes as we pass.

The room where Pape and I work is perhaps ten feet by ten. It contains a 43 desk, two chairs and a narrow wooden table that is covered with a sheet that will not be changed during the day. The patients are called in one at a time, asked how they feel and whether there is any change in their symptoms, then examined on the table. If the patient is new to the clinic, he or she is questioned about sexual activities.

A twenty-seven-year-old man whose given name is Miracle enters. He is 44 wobbly, panting, like a groggy boxer who has let down his arms and is waiting for the last punch. He is neatly dressed and wears, despite the heat, a heavy woolen cap. When he removes it, I see that his hair is thin, dull reddish and straight. It is one of the signs of AIDS in Haiti, Pape tells me. The man's skin is covered with a dry itchy rash. Throughout the interview and examination he scratches himself slowly, absentmindedly. The rash is called prurigo. It is another symptom of AIDS in Haiti. This man has had diarrhea for six months.

The laboratory reports that the diarrhea is due to an organism called crypto-sporidium, for which there is no treatment. The telltale rattling of the tuber-culous moisture in his chest is audible without a stethoscope. He is like a leaky cistern that bubbles and froths. And, clearly, exhausted.

"Where do you live?" I ask.   45

"Kenscoff." A village in the hills above Port-au-Prince.   46

"How did you come here today?"   47

"I came on the *tap-tap*." It is the name given to the small buses that swarm   48
the city, each one extravagantly decorated with religious slogans, icons, flowers,
animals, all painted in psychedelic colors. I have never seen a *tap-tap* that was
not covered with passengers as well, riding outside and hanging on. The vehicles
are little masterpieces of contagion, if not of AIDS then of the multitude of
germs which Haitian flesh is heir to. Miracle is given a prescription for a supply
of Sera, which is something like Gatorade, and told to return in a month.

"*Mangé kou bêf*," says the doctor in farewell. "Eat like an ox." What can he   49
mean? The man has no food or money to buy any. Even had he food, he has
not the appetite to eat or the ability to retain it. To each departing patient the
doctor will say the same words—"*Mangé kou bêf*." I see that it is his way of
offering a hopeful goodbye.

"Will he live until his next appointment?" I ask.   50

"No." Miracle leaves to catch the *tap-tap* for Kenscoff.   51

Next is a woman of twenty-six who enters holding her right hand to her fore-   52
head in a kind of permanent salute. In fact, she is shielding her eye from view.
This is her third visit to the clinic. I see that she is still quite well nourished.

"Now, you'll see something beautiful, tremendous," the doctor says. Once   53
seated upon the table, she is told to lower her hand. When she does, I see that
her right eye and its eyelid are replaced by a huge fungating ulcerated tumor,
a side product of her AIDS. As she turns her head, the cluster of lymph glands
in her neck to which the tumor has spread is thrown into relief. Two years ago
she received a blood transfusion at a time when the country's main blood bank
was grossly contaminated with AIDS. It has since been closed down. The only
blood available in Haiti is a small supply procured from the Red Cross.

"Can you give me medicine?" the woman wails.   54

"No."   55

"Can you cut it away?"   56

"No."   57

"Is there radiation therapy?" I ask.   58

"No."   59

"Chemotherapy?" The doctor looks at me in what some might call weary   60
amusement. I see that there is nothing to do. She has come here because there
is nowhere else to go.

"What will she do?"   61

"Tomorrow or the next day or the day after that she will climb up into the   62

139

mountains to seek relief from the *houngan*, the voodoo priest, just as her slave ancestors did two hundred years ago."

Then comes a frail man in his thirties, with a strangely spiritualized face, like a child's. Pus runs from one ear onto his cheek, where it has dried and caked. He has trouble remembering, he tells us. In fact, he seems confused. It is from toxoplasmosis of the brain, an effect of his AIDS. This man is bisexual. Two years ago he engaged in oral sex with foreign men for money. As I palpate the swollen glands of his neck, a mosquito flies between our faces. I swat at it, miss. Just before coming to Haiti I had read that the AIDS virus had been isolated from a certain mosquito. The doctor senses my thought. 63

"Not to worry," he says. "So far as we know there has never been a case transmitted by insects." 64

"Yes," I say. "I see." 65

And so it goes until the last, the thirty-sixth AIDS patient has been seen. At the end of the day I am invited to wash my hands before leaving. I go down a long hall to a sink. I turn on the faucets but there is no water. 66

"But what about *you?*" I ask the doctor. "You are at great personal risk here— the tuberculosis, the other infections, no water to wash . . ." He shrugs, smiles faintly and lifts his hands palm upward. 67

We are driving up a serpiginous steep road into the barren mountains above Port-au-Prince. Even in the bright sunshine the countryside has the bloodless color of exhaustion and indifference. Our destination is the Baptist Mission Hospital, where many cases of AIDS have been reported. Along the road there are slow straggles of schoolchildren in blue uniforms who stretch out their hands as we pass and call out, "Give me something." Already a crowd of outpatients has gathered at the entrance to the mission compound. A tour of the premises reveals that in contrast to the aridity outside the gates, this is an enclave of productivity, lush with fruit trees and poinsettia. 68

The hospital is clean and smells of creosote. Of the forty beds, less than a third are occupied. In one male ward of twelve beds, there are two patients. The chief physician tells us that last year he saw ten cases of AIDS each week. Lately the number has decreased to four or five. 69

"Why is that?" we want to know. 70

"Because we do not admit them to the hospital, so they have learned not to come here." 71

"Why don't you admit them?" 72

"Because we would have nothing but AIDS here then. So we send them away." 73

"But I see that you have very few patients in bed." 74

"That is also true." 75

"Where do the AIDS patients go?" 76

"Some go to the clinic in Port-au-Prince or the general hospital in the city. 77
Others go home to die or to the voodoo priest."

"Do the people with AIDS know what they have before they come here?" 78

"Oh, yes, they know very well, and they know there is nothing to be done 79
for them."

Outside, the crowd of people is dispersing toward the gate. The clinic has 80
been canceled for the day. No one knows why. We are conducted to the office
of the reigning American pastor. He is a tall, handsome Midwesterner with an
ecclesiastical smile.

"It is voodoo that is the devil here." He warms to his subject. "It is a demonic 81
religion, a cancer on Haiti. Voodoo is worse than AIDS. And it is one of the
reasons for the epidemic. Did you know that in order for a man to become a
houngan he must perform anal sodomy on another man? No, of course you
didn't. And it doesn't stop there. The *houngans* tell the men that in order to
appease the spirits they too must do the same thing. So you have ritualized
homosexuality. That's what is spreading the AIDS." The pastor tells us of a
nun who witnessed two acts of sodomy in a provincial hospital where she came
upon a man sexually assaulting a houseboy and another man mounting a male
patient in his bed.

"Fornication," he says. "It is Sodom and Gomorrah all over again, so what 82
can you expect from these people?" Outside his office we are shown a cage of
terrified, cowering monkeys to whom he coos affectionately. It is clear that he
loves them. At the car, we shake hands.

"By the way," the pastor says, "what is your religion? Perhaps I am a 83
kinsman?"

"While I am in Haiti," I tell him, "it will be voodoo or it will be nothing at 84
all."

Abruptly, the smile breaks. It is as though a crack had suddenly appeared in 85
the face of an idol.

From the mission we go to the general hospital. In the heart of Port-au- 86
Prince, it is the exact antithesis of the immaculate facility we have just left—
filthy, crowded, hectic and staffed entirely by young interns and residents.
Though it is associated with a medical school, I do not see any members of the
faculty. We are shown around by Jocelyne, a young intern in a scrub suit. Each
bed in three large wards is occupied. On the floor about the beds, hunkered in
the posture of the innocent poor, are family members of the patients. In the
corridor that constitutes the emergency room, someone lies on a stretcher
receiving an intravenous infusion. She is hardly more than a cadaver.

"Where are the doctors in charge?" I ask Jocelyne. She looks at me ques- 87
tioningly.

"We are in charge." 88

"I mean your teachers, the faculty." 89

"They do not come here." 90

"What is wrong with that woman?" 91

"She has had diarrhea for three months. Now she is dehydrated." I ask the 92
woman to open her mouth. Her throat is covered with the white plaques of
thrush, a fungus infection associated with AIDS.

"How many AIDS patients do you see here?" 93

"Three or four a day. We send them home. Sometimes the families abandon 94
them, then we must admit them to the hospital. Every day, then, a relative
comes to see if the patient has died. They want to take the body. That is
important to them. But they know very well that AIDS is contagious and they
are afraid to keep them at home. Even so, once or twice a week the truck
comes to take away the bodies. Many are children. They are buried in mass
graves."

"Where do the wealthy patients go?" 95

"There is a private hospital called Canapé Vert. Or else they go to Miami. 96
Most of them, rich and poor, do not go to the hospital. Most are never
diagnosed."

"How do you know these people have AIDS?" 97

"We don't know sometimes. The blood test is inaccurate. There are many 98
false positives and false negatives. Fifteen percent of those with the disease have
negative blood tests. We go by their infections—tuberculosis, diarrhea, fungi,
herpes, skin rashes. It is not hard to tell."

"Do they know what they have?" 99

"Yes. They understand at once and they are prepared to die." 100

"Do the patients know how AIDS is transmitted?" 101

"They know, but they do not like to talk about it. It is taboo. Their memories 102
do not seem to reach back to the true origins of their disaster. It is understandable, is it not?"

"Whatever you write, don't hurt us any more than we have already been 103
hurt." It is a young Haitian journalist with whom I am drinking a rum punch.
He means that any further linkage of AIDS and Haiti in the media would
complete the economic destruction of the country. The damage was done early
in the epidemic when the Centers for Disease Control in Atlanta added Haitians
to the three other high-risk groups—hemophiliacs, intravenous drug users and
homosexual and bisexual men. In fact, Haitians are no more susceptible to
AIDS than anyone else. Although the CDC removed Haitians from special
scrutiny in 1985, the lucrative tourism on which so much of the country's
economy was based was crippled. Along with tourism went much of the foreign
business investment. Worst of all was the injury to the national pride. Suddenly
Haiti was indicted as the source of AIDS in the western hemisphere.

What caused the misunderstanding was the discovery of a large number of 104
Haitian men living in Miami with AIDS antibodies in their blood. They denied

absolutely they were homosexuals. But the CDC investigators did not know that homosexuality is the strongest taboo in Haiti and that no man would ever admit to it. Bisexuality, however, is not uncommon. Many married men and heterosexually oriented males will occasionally seek out other men for sex. Further, many, if not most, Haitian men visit female prostitutes from time to time. It is not difficult to see that once the virus was set loose in Haiti, the spread would be swift through both genders.

Exactly how the virus of AIDS arrived is not known. Could it have been 105
brought home by the Cuban soldiers stationed in Angola and thence to Haiti, about fifty miles away? Could it have been passed on by the thousands of Haitians living in exile in Zaire, who later returned home or immigrated to the United States? Could it have come from the American and Canadian homosexual tourists, and, yes, even some U.S. diplomats who have traveled to the island to have sex with impoverished Haitian men all too willing to sell themselves to feed their families? Throughout the international gay community Haiti was known as a good place to go for sex.

On a private tip from an official at the Ministry of Tourism, J-B and I drive 106
to a town some fifty miles from Port-au-Prince. The hotel is owned by two Frenchmen who are out of the country, one of the staff tells us. He is a man of about thirty and clearly he is desperately ill. Tottering, short of breath, he shows us about the empty hotel. The furnishings are opulent and extreme— tiger skins on the wall, a live leopard in the garden, a bedroom containing a giant bathtub with gold faucets. Is it the heat of the day or the heat of my imagination that makes these walls echo with the painful cries of pederasty?

The hotel where we are staying is in Pétionville, the fashionable suburb of 107
Port-au-Prince. It is the height of the season but there are no tourists, only a dozen or so French and American businessmen. The swimming pool is used once or twice a day by a single person. Otherwise, the water remains undisturbed until dusk, when the fruit bats come down to drink in midswoop. The hotel keeper is an American. He is eager to set me straight on Haiti.

"What did and should attract foreign investment is a combination of reliable 108
weather, an honest and friendly populace, low wages and multilingual managers."

"What spoiled it?" 109

"Political instability and a bad American press about AIDS." He pauses, then 110
adds: "To which I hope you won't be contributing."

"What about just telling the truth?" I suggest. 111

"Look," he says, "there is no more danger of catching AIDS in Haiti than 112
in New York or Santo Domingo. It is not where you are but what you do that counts." Agreeing, I ask if he had any idea that much of the tourism in Haiti during the past few decades was based on sex.

"No idea whatsoever. It was only recently that we discovered that that was the case."   113

"How is it that you hoteliers, restaurant owners and the Ministry of Tourism did not know what *tout* Haiti knew?"   114

"Look. All I know is that this is a middle-class, family-oriented hotel. We don't allow guests to bring women, or for that matter men, into their rooms. If they did, we'd ask them to leave immediately."   115

At five A.M. the next day the telephone rings in my room. A Creole-accented male voice.   116

"Is the lady still with you, sir?"   117

"There is no lady here."   118

"In your room, sir, the lady I allowed to go up with a package?"   119

"There is no lady here, I tell you."   120

At seven A.M. I stop at the front desk. The clerk is a young man.   121

"Was it you who called my room at five o'clock?"   122

"Sorry," he says with a smile. "It was a mistake, sir. I meant to ring the room next door to yours." Still smiling, he holds up his shushing finger.   123

Next to Dr. Pape, director of the AIDS clinic, Bernard Liautaud, a dermatologist, is the most knowledgeable Haitian physician on the subject of the epidemic. Together, the two men have published a dozen articles on AIDS in international medical journals. In our meeting they present me with statistics: 124

- There are more than one thousand documented cases of AIDS in Haiti, and as many as one hundred thousand carriers of the virus.
- Eighty-seven percent of AIDS is now transmitted heterosexually. While it is true that the virus was introduced via the bisexual community, that route has decreased to 10 percent or less.
- Sixty percent of the wives or husbands of AIDS patients tested positive for the antibody.
- Fifty percent of the prostitutes tested in the Port-au-Prince area are infected.
- Eighty percent of the men with AIDS have had contact with prostitutes.
- The projected number of active cases in four years is ten thousand. (Since my last visit, the Haitian Medical Association broke its silence on the epidemic by warning that one million of the country's six million people could be carriers by 1992.)

The two doctors have more to tell. "The crossing over of the plague from the homosexual to the heterosexual community will follow in the United States within two years. This, despite the hesitation to say so by those who fear to sow panic among your population. In Haiti, because bisexuality is more common,   125 there was an early crossover into the general population. The trend, inevitably, is the same in the two countries."

"What is there to do, then?" 126

"Only education, just as in America. But here the Haitians reject the use of 127 condoms. Only the men who are too sick to have sex are celibate."

"What is to be the end of it?" 128

"When enough heterosexuals of the middle and upper classes die, perhaps 129 there will be the panic necessary for the people to change their sexual lifestyles."

This evening I leave Haiti. For two weeks I have fastened myself to this 130 lovely fragile land like an ear pressed to the ground. It is a country to break a traveler's heart. It occurs to me that I have not seen a single jogger. Such a public expenditure of energy while everywhere else strength is ebbing—it would be obscene. In my final hours, I go to the Cathédrale of Sainte Trinité, the inner walls of which are covered with murals by Haiti's most renowned artists. Here are all the familiar Bible stories depicted in naïveté and piety, and all in such an exuberance of color as to tax the capacity of the retina to receive it, as though all the vitality of Haiti had been turned to paint and brushed upon these walls. How to explain this efflorescence at a time when all else is lassitude and inertia? Perhaps one day the plague will be rendered in poetry, music, painting, but not now. Not now.

QUESTIONS

1. Summarize the scene at the Copacabana. Which details are memorable? Why does Selzer spend so much time with Carmen, Mercedes, and Frasquita? Why are their attitudes toward AIDS so important?

2. Selzer writes at great length about his visit to the AIDS clinic directed by Dr. Jean William Pape. What does Selzer learn from observing patients at this clinic? What does Selzer learn about AIDS from the doctor at work?

3. A young Haitian journalist tells Selzer, "Whatever you write, don't hurt us any more than we have already been hurt." What is the significance of this request? After reading Selzer's essay, do you think Selzer has honored this request?

4. In the final paragraph of the essay, Selzer writes: "For two weeks I have fastened myself to this lovely fragile land like an ear pressed to the ground. It is a country to break a traveler's heart." What has Selzer learned about the politics of AIDS from his journey to Haiti?

5. Look at the various scenes and vignettes Selzer offers his readers. How does he connect these different scenes? How does this structure succeed in presenting his reflections?

6. What have you learned about the politics of AIDS from reading Selzer's essay? Write an essay reflecting on Selzer's essay.

7. Selzer offers his reflections as a way of justifying his strong feelings about AIDS.

In other words, his reflections become a kind of argument. How would you make a more objective argument for his position?

MAKING CONNECTIONS

Selzer, Gould, and Eiseley write about subjects that technically are not "scientific." What commonalities or connections can you find among their questions, approaches, or methods?

COUNTERS AND CABLE CARS
Stephen Jay Gould

Stephen Jay Gould (b. 1941) is a professor of biology, geology, and the history of science at Harvard University. He is also a baseball fan and a prolific essayist. In 1974 he began writing "This View of Life," a monthly column in Natural History, *which also published* Counters and Cable Cars. *Over 200 essays and 6 collections later, Gould maintains that he will write his column into the next millennium. In his essays, collected in* The Panda's Thumb (1980), The Flamingo's Smile (1985), Bully for Brontosaurus (1991), *and his most recent book,* Eight Little Piggies (1993), *he explores the history of life through the particulars of diverse species and the connections between present selves and past generations, "a theme of supreme importance to evolutionists who study in a world in which extinction is the ultimate fate of all and prolonged persistence the only meaningful measure of success."*

San Francisco, October 11, 1989

In a distinctive linguistic regionalism, New Yorkers like me stand "on line," 1
while the rest of the nation waits patiently "in line." Actually, I spend a good part of my life trying to avoid that particular activity altogether, no matter what preposition it may bear. I am a firm supporter of the Yogi Berra principle regarding once fashionable restaurants: "No one goes there anymore; it's too crowded."

Consequently, in San Francisco this morning, I awoke before sunrise in 2
order to get my breakfast of Sears's famous eighteen pancakes (marvel not, they're very small) before the morning crush of more amenable hours rendered the restaurant uninhabitable on Berra's maxim. Then out the door by 7:30 to the cable car stop at Union Square for a ride that thrills me no less in middle life than on my first trip as a boy. What moment in public transportation could possibly surpass that final steep descent down Russian Hill? (For a distant second and third in America, I nominate the Saint Charles streetcar of New Orleans, last of the old-time trolley lines, as it passes by the antebellum houses of the garden district; and the Staten Island Ferry, only a nickel in my youth and the

147

world's most distinguished cheap date, as it skirts the Statue of Liberty by moonlight.) I travel during the last minutes of comfort and accessibility. By 9 A.M., long lines of tourists will form and no one will want to ride anymore.

We paleontologists are driven, almost by professional definition, to an abiding 3 respect for items and institutions that have prevailed and prospered with integrity in an unending sea of change (although I trust that we can also welcome, even foster, intellectual innovation). I love Sears restaurant with its familiar, uniformly excellent, and utterly nonyuppie breakfast menu. And I adore those Victorian cars with their wooden seats and their distinctive sounds—the two-clang signal to move, the hum of the cable perpetually running underground, the grasp of the grip as it takes hold to pull the passive car along.

As I ride, I ponder a psychological puzzle that has long intrigued me: why 4 does authenticity—as a purely conceptual theme—exert such a hold upon us? An identical restaurant with the same food, newly built in the San Francisco segment of a Great Cities Theme Park, would supply me with nothing but calories; a perfect replica of a cable car, following an even hillier route in Disneyland, would be a silly bauble.

Authenticity has many guises, each contributing something essential to our 5 calm satisfaction with the truly genuine. Authenticity of *object* fascinates me most deeply because its pull is entirely abstract and conceptual. The art of replica making has reached such sophistication that only the most astute professional can now tell the difference between, say, a genuine dinosaur skeleton and a well-made cast. The real and the replica are effectively alike in all but our abstract knowledge of authenticity, yet we feel awe in the presence of bone once truly clothed in dinosaur flesh and mere interest in fiberglass of identical appearance.

If I may repeat, because it touched me so deeply, a story on this subject told 6 once before in this forum (November 1984). A group of blind visitors met with the director of the Air and Space Museum in Washington to discuss greater accessibility, especially of the large objects hanging from the ceiling of the great atrium and perceptible only by sight. The director asked his guests whether a scale model of Lindbergh's *Spirit of St. Louis,* mounted and fully touchable, might alleviate the frustration of nonaccess to the real McCoy. The visitors replied that such a solution would be most welcome, but only if the model was placed directly beneath the invisible original. Simple knowledge of the imperceptible presence of authenticity can move us to tears.

We also respect an authenticity of *place.* Genuine objects out of context and 7 milieu may foster intrigue, but rarely inspiration. London Bridge dismantled and reassembled in America becomes a mere curiosity. I love to watch giraffes in zoo cages, but their jerky, yet somehow graceful, progress over the African veld provokes a more satisfying feeling of awe.

Yet, until today, I had not appreciated the power of a third authenticity, that 8 of *use.* Genuine objects in their proper place can be devalued by altered use—

particularly when our avid appetite for casual and ephemeral leisure overwhelms an original use in the honorable world of daily work.

Lord knows, being one myself, I have no right to complain about tourists mobbing cable cars. Visitors have an inalienable right to reach Fisherman's Wharf and Ghirardelli Square by any legal means sanctioned and maintained by the city of San Francisco. Still, I love to ride incognito at 7:30 A.M. with native San Franciscans using the cable car as a public conveyance to their place of work—Asian students embarking on their way to school as the car skirts by Chinatown; smartly dressed executives with their monthly transit passes.

But I write this essay because I experienced a different, unanticipated, and most pleasant example of authenticity of use in Sears this morning. (I could not have asked for a better context. The Bay Area, this week, is experiencing a bonanza in authenticity of place—as the Oakland A's and the San Francisco Giants prepare for the first single-area World Series since 1956, when the seventh and last "subway series" of ten glorious childhood years in New York, 1947 to 1956, produced Don Larsen's perfect game and the revenge of my beloved Yankees for their only defeat, the year before, by the Dodgers in their true home in Brooklyn. Think what we would lose if, in deference to October weather and a misplaced sense of even opportunity, the World Series moved from the home cities of full-season drama to some neutral turf in balmy Miami or New Orleans.)

I have always gone to Sears with other people and sat at a table. This time I went alone and ate at the counter. I had not known that the counter is a domain of regulars, native San Franciscans on their way to work. One man gets up and says to the waitress, "Real good, maybe I'll come back again sometime." "He's in here every morning," whispers the waitress to me. Another man takes the empty seat, saying "Hi, honey" to the woman on the next stool. "You're pretty early today," she replies. "The works!" he says as the waitress passes by. "You got it," she replies. A few minutes later, she returns with a plate of pancakes and a dish of scrambled eggs. But first she slides the eggs off the plate onto a napkin, blotting away the butter. "No good for him," she explains. He begins a discussion on the relative merits of cloth napkins and paper towels in such an enterprise. Good fellowship in authenticity of use; people taking care of each other in small ways of enduring significance.

As I present talks on evolutionary subjects all around America, I can be sure of certain questions following any speech: Where is human evolution going? What about genetic engineering? Are blacks really better at basketball? (Both the dumb and the profound share this character of inevitability.) High on the list of these perennial inquiries, I must rank the ecological question, usually asked with compassion but sometimes with pugnacity: Why do we need to save all these species anyway?

I know the conventional answers rooted in practicality. I even believe in them: you never know what medical or agricultural use might emerge from

9

10

11

12

13

species currently unknown or ignored; beneficial diversity of gene pools in cultivated species can often be fostered by interbreeding with wild relatives; interconnectedness of ecological webs may lead to dire and unintended consequences for "valued" species when "insignificant" creatures are rubbed out. Still, I prefer to answer with an ethical, more accurately a viscerally aesthetic, statement espoused by nearly all evolutionary biologists as a virtual psychic necessity for wanting to enter the field in the first place: we relish diversity; we love every slightly different way, every nuance of form and behavior; and we know that the loss of a significant fraction of this gorgeous variety will quench our senses and our satisfactions for any future worth contemplating in human terms (potential recovery of diversity several million years down the road is too abstract and conjectural for this legitimately selfish argument). What in the world could possibly be more magnificent than the fact that beetle anatomy presents itself in more than half a million separate packages called species?

I have always been especially wary of "soft" and overly pat analogies between biological evolution and human cultural change. (Some comparisons are apt and informative, for all modes of change must hold features in common; but the mechanisms of biological evolution and cultural change are so different that close analogies usually confuse far more than they enlighten.) Nonetheless, aesthetic statements may claim a more legitimate universality, especially when an overt form rather than the underlying mechanism of production becomes the subject of our consideration. If you feel aesthetic pleasure in proportions set by the "golden section," then you may gain similar satisfaction from a nautilus shell or a Greek building despite their maximally different methods and causes of construction. I do, therefore, feel justified in writing an essay on the moral and aesthetic value of diversity both in natural and in human works— and in trying to link the genesis and defense of diversity with various meanings of authenticity. (In addition, *Natural History* has been breaking ground within its genre for many years by including the diversity of human works under its mantle, and by recognizing that the life of modern cities belongs as firmly to natural history as the overphotographed and overromanticized ways of the few human groups still living as hunters and gatherers in pristine habitats.)

(Finally, if I may make a terrible confession for a working biologist and a natural historian: I grew up on the streets of New York, and I suppose that one never loses a primary affection for things first familiar—call it authenticity of place if you wish. I do think that America's southwestern desert, in the four corners region around Monument Valley, is the most sublime spot on earth. But when I crave diversity rather than majesty, I choose cities and the products of human labor, as they resist conformity and embody authenticity of object, place, and use. My motto must be the couplet of Milton's "L'Allegro" and "Il Penseroso"—from the happy rather than the pensive side: "Towered cities please us then / And the busy hum of men." Several years ago I visited India on a trip

14

15

sponsored by Harvard's natural history museum. My colleagues delighted in arising at 4 A.M., piling into a bus, driving to a nature reserve, and trying to spot the dot of a tiger at some absurd distance, rendered only slightly more interesting by binoculars. I yearned to be let off the bus alone in the middle of any bazaar in any town.)

Natural diversity exists at several levels. Variety permeates any nonclonal population from within. Even our tightest genealogical groups contain fat people and thin people, tall and short. The primal folk wisdom of the ages proclaims the enormous differences in temperament among siblings of a single family. But the greatest dollop of natural diversity arises from our geographical divisions—the differences from place to place as we adapt to varying environments and accumulate our distinctiveness by limited contact with other regions. If all species, like rats and pigeons, lived all over the world, our planet would contain but a tiny fraction of its actual diversity. 16

I therefore tend to revel most in the distinctive diversity of geographical regions when I contemplate the aesthetic pleasure of differences. Since I am most drawn to human works, I find my greatest joy in learning to recognize local accents, regional customs of greeting and dining, styles of architecture linked to distinctive times and places. I also, at least in my head if not often enough in overt action, think of myself as a watchdog for the preservation of this fragile variety and an implacable foe of standardization and homogenization. 17

I recognize, of course, that official programs of urban layout and road building must produce more elements of commonality than a strict aesthetic of maximal diversity might welcome. After all, criteria of design have a universality that becomes more and more pressing at upper limits of size and speed. If you have to move a certain number of cars through a given region at a stated speed, the road can't meander along the riverbanks or run through the main streets of old market towns. Public buildings and city street grids beg for an optimal efficiency that imposes some acceptable degree of uniformity. 18

But the sacred task of regionalism must be to fill in the spaces between with a riotous diversity of distinctive local traditions—preferably of productive work, not only of leisure. With this model of a potentially standardized framework for roads and public spaces filled in, softened, and humanized by local products made by local people for local purposes—authenticity of object, place, and use—I think that I can finally articulate why I love the Sears counter and the cable cars in the early morning. They embody all the authenticities, but they also welcome the respectful stranger. (Again, nature and human life jibe in obedience to basic principles of structural organization. Ecological rules and principles—flow of energy across trophic levels, webs of interaction that define the "balance of nature"—have generality corresponding to permissible uniformity in the framework of public space. But local diversity prevails because different organisms embody the rules from place to place—lions or tigers or 19 bears as predictable carnivores of three separate continents—just as uniquely local businesses should fill the slots within a more uniform framework.)

I also now understand, with an intellectual argument to back a previous feeling, what I find so troubling about the drive for standardization, on either vernacular (McDonald's) or boutique levels (Ghirardelli Square or Harborside or Quincy Market or how can you tell which is where when all have their gourmet chocolate chip cookie cart and their Crabtree & Evelyn soap store). I cannot object to the homogenization per se, for I accept such uniformity in the essential framework of public spaces. But McDonald's introduces standardization at the wrong level, for it usurps the smaller spaces of immediate and daily use, the places that cry out for local distinction and its attendant sense of community. McDonald's is a flock of pigeons ordering all endemic birds to the block, a horde of rats wiping out all the mice, gerbils, hamsters, chinchillas, squirrels, beavers, and capybaras. The Mom-and-Pop chain stores of Phoenix and Tucson are almost a cruel joke, a contradiction in terms. 20

I grew up in Queens, next to a fine establishment called the T-Bone Diner (it is still there, *mirabile dictu*). The contrast between railroad-car-style diners of my youth and McDonald's of my midlife brings us to the heart of the dilemma. Diners were manufactured in a few standardized sizes and shapes— many by the Worcester Car Company in my adopted state—and then shipped to their prospective homes. Owners then took their standard issue and proceeded to cultivate the distinctness that defines this precious item of American culture: menus abounding with local products and suited to the skills and tastes of owners; waiters and waitresses with a flair for uniqueness, even eccentricity, of verve, sassiness, or simple friendliness; above all, a regular clientele forged into a community of common care. McDonald's works in precisely the opposite way and becomes perverse in its incongruity. It enters the small-scale domain of appropriate uniqueness within the interstices of an allowable uniform framework. It even occupies spaces of widely differing designs, placements, and previous uses. It then forges this diversity into a crushing uniformity that permits not a millimeter of variation in the width of a fry from Oakland to Ogunquit. 21

But we are not defeated. Uniqueness has a habit of crawling back in and around the uniformities of central planning. Uniqueness also has staying power against all the practical odds of commercial culture because authenticities speak to the human soul. Many of those old diners are still flourishing in New England. I am at least a semiregular at one of the finest. On my last visit, the counter lady pointed to a jar with dollar bills. A regular customer, she told me, had a sick child in need of an operation, and everyone was kicking in, if only as a symbol of support and community. No one even mentioned the jar to casual customers on that particular morning; but I was simply told to contribute. No pleas, no harangues, no explanations beyond the simple facts of the case. Our communities are many, overlapping, and of various strengths. I am proud 22 to be part of this aggregate, forged to a coherent species by a common place of local integrity. So long as these tiny communities continue to form in the interstices of conformity, I will remain optimistic about the power of diversity. And I will remember Elijah's discovery during his flight from Jezebel (1 Kings 19:11–12): "After the wind an earthquake. . . . And after the earthquake a fire. . . . And after the fire, a still, small voice."

POSTSCRIPT: As the dateline indicates, I wrote this essay just a week before 23 the great San Francisco earthquake of October 17. This violently altered circumstance has converted my closing line into an utterance that, if intended after the fact rather than written unwittingly before, might seem overly pointed, if not verging on cruel. In using Elijah to reemphasize my central contrast between small-scale, local, and distinctive diversity (the "still, small voice") and global effects (well represented by general catastrophes), I was, I freely confess, also trying to make a small joke about San Francisco as the location of my essay—for the 1906 earthquake did wreak its main destruction with a tremor followed by fire.

Little did I know that my attempt at humor would soon be turned so sour 24 by nature. I could, of course, just change the ending, sink this postscript, and fudge a fine fit with history—the virtue of working with a magazine's three-month, rather than a newspaper's one-day, lead time. But I would rather show what I wrote originally—appropriate to its moment, but not a week later—as a testimony to nature's continuing power over our fortunes, and as a working example of another theme so often addressed in this series: the quirky role of unique historical events both in nature and in human life.

The earthquake has also illuminated several other points that I raised about 25 authenticity and local diversity. The World Series, although delayed, was not moved to neutral turf but was played by honoring baseball's powerful tradition for authenticity of place, despite the practical difficulties. My line about "people taking care of each other in small ways of enduring significance," although meant only as a comment about the Sears counter, soon extended to the whole region. Every fire or flood provokes endless rumination and pious commentary about why we seem to need disaster to bring out the best in us. But clichés are hackneyed because they are true; and the framework of this essay does put a different twist upon a commonplace: just as McDonald's marks the dark side by bringing the allowable conformity of large-scale public space into the inappropriate arena of local distinctiveness, human kindness after disaster, on the bright side, has a precisely opposite effect, for it promotes the usual caring of small and local communities to the large and overt domain of anonymity and callousness. Now how can this still, small voice be heard and felt at all scales all the time?

QUESTIONS

1. As Gould rides the cable car, he ponders a psychological puzzle: "Why does authenticity—as a purely conceptual theme—exert such a hold upon us?" What does authenticity mean to Gould? Why are counters and cable cars prime examples of authenticity?

2. Gould tells us that evolutionary biologists "relish diversity; we love every slightly different way, every nuance of form and behavior . . ." What connections does Gould draw between diversity and authenticity? What ideas and examples does he offer to show these connections?

3. Gould begins his essay by telling his readers about his eighteen-pancake breakfast, and ends his essay with a postscript about the San Francisco earthquake. Look carefully at the movement of Gould's reflections. What images unify these reflections? What makes this essay cohere?

4. Gould tells us that as a paleontologist he is "driven, almost by professional definition, to an abiding respect for items and institutions that have prevailed and prospered with integrity in an unending sea of change . . ." How does Gould show us his respect? Look carefully at his examples, his reflections, and his meditations, as well as his use of language. How does a writer show respect for his subject matter?

5. "Authenticity speaks to the human soul," Gould tells us. Define for yourself what authenticity means in an essay in which you reflect upon the meaning of authenticity in your life. Use images and details from your experiences to illustrate the concept.

6. In his essay, Gould links two items—counters and cable cars—which we don't usually associate with each other. Use your imagination and consider two objects, words, or concepts that are not usually associated with each other. What question or idea links these two items? Write an essay similar to Gould's in which you show the connection between these two items.

MAKING CONNECTIONS

Gould's essay can be read as a cry for the enduring significance of communities. Why is community so important to Gould? The idea of community looms large in the imagination of many of the essayists whose work you find in "Reflecting." Name two other essayists who are also preoccupied with the idea of community. How is community defined and realized by them? What ideas connect these essayists' reflections upon the value of community?

CAN WE KNOW THE UNIVERSE? REFLECTIONS ON A GRAIN OF SALT

Carl Sagan

Carl Sagan (b. 1934), David Duncan Professor of Astronomy and Space Sciences at Cornell University, is renowned both as a scientist and a writer. For his work with the National Space Administration's Mariner, Viking, and Voyager expeditions, he was awarded NASA's Medals for Exceptional Scientific Achievement and for Distinguished Public Service. Sagan produced the Cosmos television series for public television and received the Peabody award in 1981. For his book, The Dragons of Eden (1977), he received the Pulitzer Prize for Literature in 1978. Among his later works are Comet (1985), Contact (1985), a novel, and (with Ann Druyan) Shadows of Forgotten Ancestors (1992). The following selection is from Broca's Brain: Reflections on the Romance of Science (1979).

> Nothing is rich but the inexhaustible wealth
> of nature. She shows us only surfaces,
> but she is a million fathoms deep.
>
> Ralph Waldo Emerson

Science is a way of thinking much more than it is a body of knowledge. Its goal is to find out how the world works, to seek what regularities there may be, to penetrate to the connections of things—from subnuclear particles, which may be the constituents of all matter, to living organisms, the human social community, and thence to the cosmos as a whole. Our intuition is by no means an infallible guide. Our perceptions may be distorted by training and prejudice or merely because of the limitations of our sense organs, which, of course, perceive directly but a small fraction of the phenomena of the world. Even so straightforward a question as whether in the absence of friction a pound of lead falls faster than a gram of fluff was answered incorrectly by Aristotle and almost everyone else before the time of Galileo. Science is based on experiment, on a willingness to challenge old dogma, on an openness to see the universe as it really is. Accordingly, science sometimes requires courage—at the very least the courage to question the conventional wisdom.

155

Beyond this the main trick of science is to *really* think of something: the shape of clouds and their occasional sharp bottom edges at the same altitude everywhere in the sky; the formation of a dewdrop on a leaf; the origin of a name or a word—Shakespeare, say, or "philanthropic"; the reason for human social customs—the incest taboo, for example; how it is that a lens in sunlight can make paper burn; how a "walking stick" got to look so much like a twig; why the Moon seems to follow us as we walk; what prevents us from digging a hole down to the center of the Earth; what the definition is of "down" on a spherical Earth; how it is possible for the body to convert yesterday's lunch into today's muscle and sinew; or how far is up—does the universe go on forever, or if it does not, is there any meaning to the question of what lies on the other side? Some of these questions are pretty easy. Others, especially the last, are mysteries to which no one even today knows the answer. They are natural questions to ask. Every culture has posed such questions in one way or another. Almost always the proposed answers are in the nature of "Just So Stories," attempted explanations divorced from experiment, or even from careful comparative observations.

But the scientific cast of mind examines the world critically as if many alternative worlds might exist, as if other things might be here which are not. Then we are forced to ask why what we see is present and not something else. Why are the Sun and the Moon and the planets spheres? Why not pyramids, or cubes, or dodecahedra? Why not irregular, jumbly shapes? Why so symmetrical, worlds? If you spend any time spinning hypotheses, checking to see whether they make sense, whether they conform to what else we know, thinking of tests you can pose to substantiate or deflate your hypotheses, you will find yourself doing science. And as you come to practice this habit of thought more and more you will get better and better at it. To penetrate into the heart of the thing—even a little thing, a blade of grass, as Walt Whitman said—is to experience a kind of exhilaration that, it may be, only human beings of all the beings on this planet can feel. We are an intelligent species and the use of our intelligence quite properly gives us pleasure. In this respect the brain is like a muscle. When we think well, we feel good. Understanding is a kind of ecstasy.

But to what extent can we *really* know the universe around us? Sometimes this question is posed by people who hope the answer will be in the negative, who are fearful of a universe in which everything might one day be known. And sometimes we hear pronouncements from scientists who confidently state that everything worth knowing will soon be known—or even is already known—and who paint pictures of a Dionysian or Polynesian age in which the zest for intellectual discovery has withered, to be replaced by a kind of subdued languor, the lotus eaters drinking fermented coconut milk or some other mild hallucinogen. In addition to maligning both the Polynesians, who were intrepid explorers (and whose brief respite in paradise is now sadly ending), as well as the induce-

156

ments to intellectual discovery provided by some hallucinogens, this contention turns out to be trivially mistaken.

Let us approach a much more modest question: not whether we can know the universe or the Milky Way Galaxy or a star or a world. Can we know, ultimately and in detail, a grain of salt? Consider one microgram of table salt, a speck just barely large enough for someone with keen eyesight to make out without a microscope. In that grain of salt there are about 10^{16} sodium and chlorine atoms. This is a 1 followed by 16 zeros, 10 million billion atoms. If we wish to know a grain of salt, we must know at least the three-dimensional positions of each of these atoms. (In fact, there is much more to be known— for example, the nature of the forces between the atoms—but we are making only a modest calculation.) Now, is this number more or less than the number of things which the brain can know?

How much *can* the brain know? There are perhaps 10^{11} neurons in the brain, the circuit elements and switches that are responsible in their electrical and chemical activity for the functioning of our minds. A typical brain neuron has perhaps a thousand little wires, called dendrites, which connect it with its fellows. If, as seems likely, every bit of information in the brain corresponds to one of these connections, the total number of things knowable by the brain is no more than 10^{14}, one hundred trillion. But this number is only one percent of the number of atoms in our speck of salt.

So in this sense the universe is intractable, astonishingly immune to any human attempt at full knowledge. We cannot on this level understand a grain of salt, much less the universe.

But let us look more deeply at our microgram of salt. Salt happens to be a crystal in which, except for defects in the structure of the crystal lattice, the position of every sodium and chlorine atom is predetermined. If we could shrink ourselves into this crystalline world, we could see rank upon rank of atoms in an ordered array, a regularly alternating structure—sodium, chlorine, sodium, chlorine, specifying the sheet of atoms we are standing on and all the sheets above us and below us. An absolutely pure crystal of salt could have the position of every atom specified by something like 10 bits of information.[1] This would not strain the information-carrying capacity of the brain.

If the universe had natural laws that governed its behavior to the same degree of regularity that determines a crystal of salt, then, of course, the universe would be knowable. Even if there were many such laws, each of considerable complexity, human beings might have the capacity to understand them all. Even if such knowledge exceeded the information-carrying capacity of the brain, we

---

[1] Chlorine is a deadly poison gas employed on European battlefields in World War I. Sodium is a corrosive metal which burns upon contact with water. Together they make a placid and unpoisonous material, table salt. Why each of these substances has the properties it does is a subject called chemistry, which requires more than 10 bits of information to understand.

might store the additional information outside our bodies—in books, for example, or in computer memories—and still, in some sense, know the universe.

Human beings are, understandably, highly motivated to find regularities, natural laws. The search for rules, the only possible way to understand such a vast and complex universe, is called science. The universe forces those who live in it to understand it. Those creatures who find everyday experience a muddled jumble of events with no predictability, no regularity, are in grave peril. The universe belongs to those who, at least to some degree, have figured it out.

It is an astonishing fact that there *are* laws of nature, rules that summarize conveniently—not just qualitatively but quantitatively—how the world works. We might imagine a universe in which there are no such laws, in which the 10^{80} elementary particles that make up a universe like our own behave with utter and uncompromising abandon. To understand such a universe we would need a brain at least as massive as the universe. It seems unlikely that such a universe could have life and intelligence, because beings and brains require some degree of internal stability and order. But even if in a much more random universe there were such beings with an intelligence much greater than our own, there could not be much knowledge, passion or joy.

Fortunately for us, we live in a universe that has at least important parts that are knowable. Our common-sense experience and our evolutionary history have prepared us to understand something of the workaday world. When we go into other realms, however, common sense and ordinary intuition turn out to be highly unreliable guides. It is stunning that as we go close to the speed of light our mass increases indefinitely, we shrink toward zero thickness in the direction of motion, and time for us comes as near to stopping as we would like. Many people think that this is silly, and every week or two I get a letter from someone who complains to me about it. But it is a virtually certain consequence not just of experiment but also of Albert Einstein's brilliant analysis of space and time called the Special Theory of Relativity. It does not matter that these effects seem unreasonable to us. We are not in the habit of traveling close to the speed of light. The testimony of our common sense is suspect at high velocities.

Or consider an isolated molecule composed of two atoms shaped something like a dumbbell—a molecule of salt, it might be. Such a molecule rotates about an axis through the line connecting the two atoms. But in the world of quantum mechanics, the realm of the very small, not all orientations of our dumbbell molecule are possible. It might be that the molecule could be oriented in a horizontal position, say, or in a vertical position, but not at many angles in between. Some rotational positions are forbidden. Forbidden by what? By the laws of nature. The universe is built in such a way as to limit, or quantize, rotation. We do not experience this directly in everyday life; we would find it startling as well as awkward in sitting-up exercises, to find arms outstretched from the sides or pointed up to the skies permitted but many intermediate positions forbidden. We do not live in the world of the small, on the scale of 10^{-13} centimeters, in the realm where there are twelve zeros between the decimal place and the one. Our common-sense intuitions do not count. What does count is experiment—in this case observations from the far infrared spectra of molecules. They show molecular rotation to be quantized.

The idea that the world places restrictions on what humans might do is frustrating. Why *shouldn't* we be able to have intermediate rotational positions? Why *can't* we travel faster than the speed of light? But so far as we can tell, this is the way the universe is constructed. Such prohibitions not only press us toward a little humility; they also make the world more knowable. Every restriction corresponds to a law of nature, a regularization of the universe. The more restrictions there are on what matter and energy can do, the more knowledge human beings can attain. Whether in some sense the universe is ultimately knowable depends not only on how many natural laws there are that encompass widely divergent phenomena, but also on whether we have the openness and the intellectual capacity to understand such laws. Our formulations of the regularities of nature are surely dependent on how the brain is built, but also, and to a significant degree, on how the universe is built. 14

For myself, I like a universe that includes much that is unknown and, at the same time, much that is knowable. A universe in which everything is known would be static and dull, as boring as the heaven of some weakminded theologians. A universe that is unknowable is no fit place for a thinking being. The ideal universe for us is one very much like the universe we inhabit. And I would guess that this is not really much of a coincidence. 15

QUESTIONS

1. How are *science* and *scientific thinking* defined in the first three paragraphs? What is Sagan's purpose in defining these terms? What does this tell you about Sagan's conception of his audience?

2. Sagan's mode of reflection might be considered less personal than others in this section in that he is reflecting on an idea rather than on an event in his life. How does Sagan keep the tone from becoming abstract? What elements of the personal are present in this essay?

3. Sagan cites scientists who believe that "everything worth knowing will soon be known" (paragraph 4). How does the evidence in this essay challenge that assumption?

4. We might consider paragraph 15 Sagan's most personal statement in his reflections on the universe: he likes "a universe that includes much that is unknown and, at the same time, much that is knowable." Why is this balance important to Sagan? Do you agree with his closing statements?

5. Consider the statement, "The more restrictions there are on what matter and

energy can do, the more knowledge human beings can attain" (paragraph 14). Describe an example in your own experience (or another's) when you learned that rules, or laws, were helpful in ensuring your personal freedom.

6. In paragraph 3 Sagan concludes, "Understanding is a kind of ecstasy." Describe a time in your life when you understood something for the first time; when, as they say, the light went on in your head, shining on a difficult problem, and bringing about a realization. Could your feelings at the time be considered ecstatic, or did you experience some other emotion?

7. What sort of universe would you consider ideal? What would you like to know about the universe that is now unknown to you? Explain.

MAKING CONNECTIONS

1. A number of the writers in this section offer their reflections in order to justify a belief or a strong feeling about a subject. In other words, their reflections become a kind of argument. Isak Dinesen, Martin Luther King, Jr., George Orwell, and Zoë Tracy Hardy come to mind as well as Sagan. How convincing is the argument in each case? How has the writer used purely personal responses to make a persuasive case? How would you go about developing a more objective argument for one of their positions? What would be the difference in effect?

2. Does his concern for "passion" and "joy" (paragraph 11) surprise you in these remarks by Sagan? Where else, especially in the writings by scientists in this section, do you find evidence of the same concerns? Citing several examples from essayists you have read, write an essay on the role of "passion" and "joy" in the work of scientists and other writers.

THE BIRD AND
THE MACHINE

Loren Eiseley

Loren Eiseley (1907–1977) rode the rails as a young hobo before he finished college, went to graduate school at the University of Pennsylvania, and began a distinguished career as an anthropologist, archaeologist, essayist, and poet. Through his writing, Eiseley made the ideas and findings of anthropology comprehensible to the public. He found significance in small incidents—the flights of birds, the web of a spider, and the chance encounter with a young fox. Eiseley once wrote that animals understand their roles, but that man, "bereft of instinct, must search continually for meanings." This essay is taken from his collection The Immense Journey *(1957).*

I suppose their little bones have years ago been lost among the stones and winds of those high glacial pastures. I suppose their feathers blew eventually into the piles of tumbleweed beneath the straggling cattle fences and rotted there in the mountain snows, along with dead steers and all the other things that drift to an end in the corners of the wire. I do not quite know why I should be thinking of birds over the *New York Times* at breakfast, particularly the birds of my youth half a continent away. It is a funny thing what the brain will do with memories and how it will treasure them and finally bring them into odd juxtapositions with other things, as though I wanted to make a design, or get some meaning out of them, whether you want it or not, or even see it. 1

It used to seem marvelous to me, but I read now that there are machines that can do these things in a small way, machines that can crawl about like animals, and that it may not be long now until they do more things—maybe even make themselves—I saw that piece in the *Times* just now. And then they will, maybe—well, who knows—but you read about it more and more with no one making any protest, and already they can add better than we and reach up and hear things through the dark and finger the guns over the night sky. 2

This is the new world that I read about at breakfast. This is the world that confronts me in my biological books and journals, until there are times when I sit quietly in my chair and try to hear the little purr of the cogs in my head and the tubes flaring and dying as the messages go through them and the circuits snap shut or open. This is the great age, make no mistake about it; the robot has been born somewhat appropriately along with the atom bomb, and the 3 brain they say now is just another type of more complicated feedback system. The engineers have its basic principles worked out; it's mechanical, you know; nothing to get superstitious about; and man can always improve on nature once he gets the idea. Well, he's got it all right and that's why, I guess, that I sit here in my chair, with the article crunched in my hand, remembering those two birds and that blue mountain sunlight. There is another magazine article on my desk that reads "Machines Are Getting Smarter Every Day." I don't deny it, but I'll still stick with the birds. It's life I believe in, not machines.

Maybe you don't believe there is any difference. A skeleton is all joints and pulleys, I'll admit. And when man was in his simpler stages of machine building in the eighteenth century, he quickly saw the resemblances. "What," wrote Hobbes, "is the heart but a spring, and the nerves but so many strings, and the joints but so many wheels, giving motion to the whole body?" Tinkering about in their shops it was inevitable in the end that men would see the world as a huge machine "subdivided into an infinite number of lesser machines." 4

The idea took on with a vengeance. Little automatons toured the country— dolls controlled by clockwork. Clocks described as little worlds were taken on tours by their designers. They were made up of moving figures, shifting scenes and other remarkable devices. The life of the cell was unknown. Man, whether he was conceived as possessing a soul or not, moved and jerked about like these tiny puppets. A human being thought of himself in terms of his own tools and implements. He had been fashioned like the puppets he produced and was only a more clever model made by a greater designer. 5

Then in the nineteenth century, the cell was discovered, and the single machine in its turn was found to be the product of millions of infinitesimal machines—the cells. Now, finally, the cell itself dissolves away into an abstract chemical machine—and that into some intangible, inexpressible flow of energy. The secret seems to lurk all about, the wheels get smaller and smaller, and they turn more rapidly, but when you try to seize it the life is gone—and so, by popular definition, some would say that life was never there in the first place. The wheels and the cogs are the secret and we can make them better in time— machines that will run faster and more accurately than real mice to real cheese. 6

I have no doubt it can be done, though a mouse harvesting seeds on an autumn thistle is to me a fine sight and more complicated, I think, in his multiform activity, than a machine "mouse" running a maze. Also, I like to think of the possible shape of the future brooding in mice, just as it brooded once in a rather ordinary mousy insectivore who became a man. It leaves a nice fine indeterminate sense of wonder that even an electronic brain hasn't got, because you know perfectly well that if the electronic brain changes, it will be because of something man has done to it. But what man will do to himself he doesn't really know. A certain scale of time and a ghostly intangible thing called change are ticking in him. Powers and potentialities like the oak in the seed, or a red and awful ruin. Either way, it's impressive; and the mouse has 7 it, too. Or those birds, I'll never forget those birds—yet before I measured their significance, I learned the lesson of time first of all. I was young then and left alone in a great desert—part of an expedition that had scattered its men over several hundred miles in order to carry on research more effectively. I learned there that time is a series of planes existing superficially in the same universe. The tempo is a human illusion, a subjective clock ticking in our own kind of protoplasm.

As the long months passed, I began to live on the slower planes and to observe more readily what passed for life there. I sauntered, I passed more and more slowly up and down the canyons in the dry baking heat of midsummer. I slumbered for long hours in the shade of huge brown boulders that had gathered in tilted companies out on the flats. I had forgotten the world of men and the world had forgotten me. Now and then I found a skull in the canyons, and these justified my remaining there. I took a serene cold interest in these discoveries. I had come, like many a naturalist before me, to view life with a wary and subdued attention. I had grown to take pleasure in the divested bone.   8

I sat once on a high ridge that fell away before me into a waste of sand dunes. I sat through hours of a long afternoon. Finally, as I glanced beside my boot an indistinct configuration caught my eye. It was a coiled rattlesnake, a big one. How long he had sat with me I do not know. I had not frightened him. We were both locked in the sleep-walking tempo of the earlier world, baking in the same high air and sunshine. Perhaps he had been there when I came. He slept on as I left, his coils, so ill discerned by me, dissolving once more among the stones and gravel from which I had barely made him out.   9

Another time I got on a higher ridge, among some tough little wind-warped pines half covered over with sand in a basin-like depression that caught every-thing carried by the air up to those heights. There were a few thin bones of birds, some cracked shells of indeterminable age, and the knotty fingers of pine roots bulged out of shape from their long and agonizing grasp upon the crevices of the rock. I lay under the pines in the sparse shade and went to sleep once more.   10

It grew cold finally, for autumn was in the air by then, and the few things that lived thereabouts were sinking down into an even chillier scale of time. In the moments between sleeping and waking I saw the roots about me and slowly, slowly, a foot in what seemed many centuries, I moved my sleep-stiffened hands over the scaling bark and lifted my numbed face after the vanishing sun. I was a great awkward thing of knots and aching limbs, trapped up there in some long, patient endurance that involved the necessity of putting living fingers into rock and by slow, aching expansion bursting those rocks asunder. I suppose, so thin and slow was the time of my pulse by then, that I might have stayed on to drift still deeper into the lower cadences of the frost, or the crystalline life   11 that glitters in pebbles, or shines in a snowflake, or dreams in the meteoric iron between the worlds.

It was a dim descent, but time was present in it. Somewhere far down in 12 that scale the notion struck me that one might come the other way. Not many months thereafter I joined some colleagues heading higher into a remote windy tableland where huge bones were reputed to protrude like boulders from the turf. I had drowsed with reptiles and moved with the century-long pulse of trees; now, lethargically, I was climbing back up some invisible ladder of quickening hours. There had been talk of birds in connection with my duties. Birds are intense, fast-living creatures—reptiles, I suppose one might say, that have escaped out of the heavy sleep of time, transformed fairy creatures dancing over sunlit meadows. It is a youthful fancy, no doubt, but because of something that happened up there among the escarpments of that range, it remains with me a lifelong impression. I can never bear to see a bird imprisoned.

We came into that valley through the trailing mists of a spring night. It was 13 a place that looked as though it might never have known the foot of man, but our scouts had been ahead of us and we knew all about the abandoned cabin of stone that lay far up on one hillside. It had been built in the land rush of the last century and then lost to the cattlemen again as the marginal soils failed to take to the plow.

There were spots like this all over that country. Lost graves marked by 14 unlettered stones and old corroding rim-fire cartridge cases lying where somebody had made a stand among the boulders that rimmed the valley. They are all that remain of the range wars; the men are under the stones now. I could see our cavalcade winding in and out through the mist below us: torches, the reflection of the truck lights on our collecting tins, and the far-off bumping of a loose dinosaur thigh bone in the bottom of a trailer. I stood on a rock a moment looking down and thinking what it cost in money and equipment to capture the past.

We had, in addition, instructions to lay hands on the present. The word 15 had come through to get them alive—birds, reptiles, anything. A zoo somewhere abroad needed restocking. It was one of those reciprocal matters in which science involves itself. Maybe our museum needed a stray ostrich egg and this was the payoff. Anyhow, my job was to help capture some birds and that was why I was there before the trucks.

The cabin had not been occupied for years. We intended to clean it out and 16 live in it, but there were holes in the roof and the birds had come in and were roosting in the rafters. You could depend on it in a place like this where everything blew away, and even a bird needed some place out of the weather and away from coyotes. A cabin going back to nature in a wild place draws them till they come in, listening at the eaves, I imagine, pecking softly among the shingles till they find a hole and then suddenly the place is theirs and man is forgotten.

THE BIRD AND THE MACHINE

Sometimes of late years I find myself thinking the most beautiful sight in
the world might be the birds taking over New York after the last man has run
away to the hills. I will never live to see it, of course, but I know just how it
will sound because I've lived up high and I know the sort of watch birds keep
on us. I've listened to sparrows tapping tentatively on the outside of air condi-
tioners when they thought no one was listening, and I know how other birds
test the vibrations that come up to them through the television aerials.

"Is he gone?" they ask, and the vibrations come up from below, "Not yet,
not yet."

Well, to come back, I got the door open softly and I had the spotlight all
ready to turn on and blind whatever birds there were so they couldn't see to get
out through the roof. I had a short piece of ladder to put against the far wall
where there was a shelf on which I expected to make the biggest haul. I had
all the information I needed just like any skilled assassin. I pushed the door
open, the hinges squeaking only a little. A bird or two stirred—I could hear
them—but nothing flew and there was a faint starlight through the holes in the
roof.

I padded across the floor, got the ladder up and the light ready, and slithered
up the ladder till my head and arms were over the shelf. Everything was dark
as pitch except for the starlight at the little place back of the shelf near the
eaves. With the light to blind them, they'd never make it. I had them. I reached
my arm carefully over in order to be ready to seize whatever was there and I
put the flash on the edge of the shelf where it would stand by itself when I
turned it on. That way I'd be able to use both hands.

Everything worked perfectly except for one detail—I didn't know what kind
of birds were there. I never thought about it at all, and it wouldn't have mattered
if I had. My orders were to get something interesting. I snapped on the flash
and sure enough there was a great beating and feathers flying, but instead of
my having them, they, or rather he, had me. He had my hand, that is, and
for a small hawk not much bigger than my fist he was doing all right. I heard
him give one short metallic cry when the light went on and my hand descended
on the bird beside him; after that he was busy with his claws and his beak was
sunk in my thumb. In the struggle I knocked the lamp over on the shelf, and
his mate got her sight back and whisked neatly through the hole in the roof
and off among the stars outside. It all happened in fifteen seconds and you
might think I would have fallen down the ladder, but no, I had a professional
assassin's reputation to keep up, and the bird, of course, made the mistake of
thinking the hand was the enemy and not the eyes behind it. He chewed my
thumb up pretty effectively and lacerated my hand with his claws, but in the
end I got him, having two hands to work with.

He was a sparrow hawk and a fine young male in the prime of life. I was
sorry not to catch the pair of them, but as I dripped blood and folded his wings
carefully, holding him by the back so that he couldn't strike again, I had to

165

admit the two of them might have been more than I could have handled under the circumstances. The little fellow had saved his mate by diverting me, and that was that. He was born to it, and made no outcry now, resting in my hand hopelessly, but peering toward me in the shadows behind the lamp with a fierce, almost indifferent glance. He neither gave nor expected mercy and something out of the high air passed from him to me, stirring a faint embarrassment.

I quit looking into that eye and managed to get my huge carcass with its fist 23 full of prey back down the ladder. I put the bird in a box too small to allow him to injure himself by struggle and walked out to welcome the arriving trucks. It had been a long day, and camp still to make in the darkness. In the morning that bird would be just another episode. He would go back with the bones in the truck to a small cage in a city where he would spend the rest of his life. And a good thing, too. I sucked my aching thumb and spat out some blood. An assassin has to get used to these things. I had a professional reputation to keep up.

In the morning, with the change that comes on suddenly in that high 24 country, the mist that had hovered below us in the valley was gone. The sky was a deep blue, and one could see for miles over the high outcroppings of stone. I was up early and brought the box in which the little hawk was imprisoned out onto the grass where I was building a cage. A wind as cool as a mountain spring ran over the grass and stirred my hair. It was a fine day to be alive. I looked up and all around and at the hole in the cabin roof out of which the other little hawk had fled. There was no sign of her anywhere that I could see.

"Probably in the next county by now," I thought cynically, but before 25 beginning work I decided I'd have a look at my last night's capture.

Secretively, I looked again all around the camp and up and down and opened 26 the box. I got him right out in my hand with his wings folded properly and I was careful not to startle him. He lay limp in my grasp and I could feel his heart pound under the feathers but he only looked beyond me and up.

I saw him look that last look away beyond me into a sky so full of light that 27 I could not follow his gaze. The little breeze flowed over me again, and nearby a mountain aspen shook all its tiny leaves. I suppose I must have had an idea then of what I was going to do, but I never let it come up into consciousness. I just reached over and laid the hawk on the grass.

He lay there a long minute without hope, unmoving, his eyes still fixed on 28 that blue vault above him. It must have been that he was already so far away in heart that he never felt the release from my hand. He never even stood. He just lay with his breast against the grass.

In the next second after that long minute he was gone. Like a flicker of light, 29 he had vanished with my eyes full on him, but without actually seeing even a premonitory wing beat. He was gone straight into that towering emptiness of light and crystal that my eyes could scarcely bear to penetrate. For another long moment there was silence. I could not see him. The light was too intense. Then from far up somewhere a cry came ringing down.

I was young then and had seen little of the world, but when I heard that cry   30
my heart turned over. It was not the cry of the hawk I had captured; for, by shifting my position against the sun, I was now seeing further up. Straight out of the sun's eye, where she must have been soaring restlessly above us for untold hours, hurtled his mate. And from far up, ringing from peak to peak of the summits over us, came a cry of such unutterable and ecstatic joy that it sounds down across the years and tingles among the cups on my quiet breakfast table.

I saw them both now. He was rising fast to meet her. They met in a great   31
soaring gyre that turned to a whirling circle and a dance of wings. Once more, just once, their two voices, joined in a harsh wild medley of question and response, struck and echoed the pinnacles of the valley. Then they were gone forever somewhere into those upper regions beyond the eyes of men.

I am older now, and sleep less, and have seen most of what there is to see   32
and am not very much impressed any more, I suppose, by anything. "What Next in the Attributes of Machines?" my morning headline runs. "It Might Be the Power to Reproduce Themselves."

I lay the paper down and across my mind a phrase floats insinuatingly: "It   33
does not seem that there is anything in the construction, constituents, or behavior of the human being which it is essentially impossible for science to duplicate and synthesize. On the other hand . . ."

All over the city the cogs in the hard, bright mechanisms have begun to   34
turn. Figures move through computers, names are spelled out, a thoughtful machine selects the fingerprints of a wanted criminal from an array of thousands. In the laboratory an electronic mouse runs swiftly through a maze toward the cheese it can neither taste nor enjoy. On the second run it does better than a living mouse.

"On the other hand . . ." Ah, my mind takes up, on the other hand the   35
machine does not bleed, ache, hang for hours in the empty sky in a torment of hope to learn the fate of another machine, nor does it cry out with joy nor dance in the air with the fierce passion of a bird. Far off, over a distance greater than space, that remote cry from the heart of heaven makes a faint buzzing among my breakfast dishes and passes on and away.

QUESTIONS

1. According to Eiseley, what is the difference between birds and machines?
2. Why does Eiseley tell the story about his experience as a young anthropologist exploring life in the American desert? How does this story relate to the rest of the essay?

3. Trace the associative movement of Eiseley's mind. How does one thought suggest another? How does this movement help illustrate his point?

4. Eiseley projects himself from the beginning as someone remembering and reflecting upon his experience. How did the meditative process of this essay, with its various twists and turns of thought, affect you as a reader?

5. Eiseley writes: "It is a funny thing what the brain will do with memories and how it will treasure them and finally bring them into odd juxtapositions with other things, as though I wanted to make a design, or get some meaning out of them, whether you want it or not, or even see it" (paragraph 1). Begin reflecting on some important memories from your past, and see where these reflections take you. As your mind wanders between past and present, see if any kind of design or meaning emerges for you. See what associations can be shaped into your own essay.

MAKING CONNECTIONS

Consider Carl Sagan's title, "Can We Know the Universe? Reflections on a Grain of Salt" and Alice Walker's, "Beauty: When the Other Dancer Is the Self," in relation to this essay by Loren Eiseley. Could either of those titles be appropriate here? In the second case, "Beauty" might indicate the sparrow hawk and the "Other Dancer" the author. Would that work? Write a commentary on Eiseley's essay supposing that one of the other titles (and the themes it suggests) applies to this essay as well.

REPORTING

Here in "Reporting" you will find writing that reflects a wide array of academic and professional situations—a naturalist describing the tool-using behavior of chimpanzees, a brain surgeon detailing the progress of a delicate operation, a historian telling about the plague that swept through medieval Europe, an anthropologist describing life in a tropical lagoon village. Informative writing is basic to every field of endeavor, and the writers in this section seek to fulfill that basic need by reporting material drawn from various sources—a data recorder, a voice recorder, a telescope, articles, books, public records, or firsthand observation. Working from such various sources, these writers aim to provide detailed and reliable accounts of things—to give the background of a case, to convey the look and smell and feel of a place, to describe the appearance and behavior of people, to tell the story of recent or ancient events.

Though reporting depends on a careful gathering of information, it is by no means a mechanical and routine activity that consists simply of getting some facts and writing them up. Newspaper editors and criminal investigators, to be sure, often say that they want "just the facts," but they know that in one way or another the facts are substantially shaped by the point of view of the person who is gathering and reporting them. By point of view, we mean both the physical and the mental standpoints from which a person observes or investigates something. Each of us, after all, stands at a particular point in space and time, as well as in thought and feeling, whenever we look at any subject. And wherever we stand in relation to the subject—whether we observe it close up or at a distance, in sunlight or in shadows, from one angle or another—will determine the particular aspects of it that we perceive and bring out in an account.

The influence that point of view exerts on reporting can be seen in the following passage from an article about an airline crash that took place outside of Washington, D.C., on December 1, 1974:

> According to the National Transportation Safety Board, today's was the first fatal crash by an airliner approaching Dulles, which opened in 1962.
> A T.W.A. spokesman said 85 passengers and a crew of seven were aboard the flight, which originated in Indianapolis. He said 46 persons got on at Columbus.

The plane crashed about one and one-half miles from an underground complex that reportedly is designed to serve as a headquarters for high government officials in the event of nuclear war. A Federal spokesman acknowledged only that the facility was operated by the little known Office of Preparedness, whose responsibilities, he said, include "continuity of government in a time of national disaster."

This report by the Associated Press, (AP), which appeared in the *New York Times* on December 2, 1974, was evidently written by someone who had ready access to a number of sources, for virtually every bit of information in this excerpt comes from a different agency or "spokesman." In fact, the AP report as a whole refers not only to the three sources that are explicitly identified in this passage—namely, the "National Transportation Safety Board," a "T.W.A. spokesman," and a "Federal spokesman"—but also to twelve others, including a county medical examiner, a telephone worker, a state police officer, a T.W.A. ground maintenance employee, and the Dulles control tower. Drawing upon these sources, the writer of this report is able not only to cover the vital statistics, such as the origin of the flight, the number of people aboard, and the location of the crash, but also to give a vividly detailed impression of the weather, the scarred landscape, and the scattered wreckage at and around the scene of the crash, as well as to reveal some fascinating details about the "underground complex" near the site of the crash. As you read through this piece, however, you will discover that it reports very little about the events leading up to the crash or about the circumstances that caused it, for the anonymous writer was evidently not in a position either to track the plane before the crash or to speculate about the cause of the crash only hours after it had taken place.

But an extensive investigation of the crash was carried out by the National Transportation Safety Board (NTSB), a federal agency that is charged with tracing the causes of airline accidents. Almost one year later, on November 26, 1975, the Board issued an elaborately detailed, forty-two-page report of its findings, a segment of which is reprinted in our collection. If you look at this segment of the NTSB "Aircraft Accident Report," you will see that it grew out of a completely different point of view from the one that produced the AP report. The NTSB report, for example, does not make any reference to the "secret government installation" that is highlighted in the AP report; nor does it contain any vividly descriptive passages, like those in the AP report, about the weather, or the scarred landscape, or the scattered wreckage at the site of the crash; nor does it even mention some of the sources who figure prominently in the AP report, such as Captain William Carvello of the state police; Bill Smith of the Marshall, Virginia, Rescue Squad; Vance Berry of Bluemont, Virginia; and Richard Eastman, a ground maintenance employee of TWA. Conversely, some matters that are barely touched upon in the AP report are extensively covered in the NTSB report. In particular, the NTSB report provides a detailed "History of the Flight," which includes summaries of cockpit conversation and navigational information at key points during the flight, as well as excerpts of the conversation that took place among members of the flight crew during the last five minutes of the flight. And the NTSB report provides detailed information about some topics that are not mentioned at all in the AP report, such as "Aids to Navigation" and "Aerodrome and Ground Facilities."

Given such striking differences in the emphases of these two pieces, you might wonder which one offers a more accurate report of the crash. Actually, both are true to the crash within the limits of their points of view on it. The AP report, for example, concentrates on the scene at the site of the crash, drawing material from a number of firsthand observers, and this standpoint brings into focus the appalling spectacle that must have been visible on the mountainside where the crash took place. The NTSB report, by contrast, views the crash within a much broader context that takes into account not only a detailed history of the flight itself, but also the complex system of navigational rules and procedures that were in effect at the time of the flight. And this perspective enables the NTSB to reveal that the mountainside crash resulted in part from serious "inadequacies and lack of clarity in the air traffic control procedures. . . ." Thus each point of view affords a special angle on the crash, obscuring some aspects of it, revealing others. And these are only two of many standpoints from which the crash might have been seen and reported. Imagine, for example, how the crash might have been viewed by workers who scoured the mountainside for remains of the passengers, or by specialists who identified their remains, or by relatives and friends of the victims, or by crews and passengers aboard other flights into Dulles that day.

Once you try to imagine the various perspectives from which anything can be observed or investigated, you will see that no one person can possibly uncover everything there is to be known about something. For this reason, above all, point of view is an important aspect of reporting to be kept in mind by both readers and writers. As a reader of reportorial writing, you should always attempt to identify the point of view from which the information was gathered so as to help yourself assess the special strengths and weaknesses in the reporting that arise from that point of view as distinct from other possible points of view. By the same token, in your own reporting you should carefully decide upon the point of view that you already have or plan to use in observing or gathering information about something. Once you begin to pay deliberate attention to point of view, you will come to see that it is closely related to the various purposes for which people gather and report information in writing.

THE RANGE OF REPORTORIAL WRITING

The purpose of reporting is in one sense straightforward and self-evident, particularly when it is defined in terms of its commonly accepted value to readers. Whether it involves a firsthand account of some recent happening or the documented record of a long-past sequence of events, reportorial writing informs readers about the various subjects that may interest them but that they cannot possibly observe or investigate on their own. You may never get to see chimpanzees in their native African habitats, but you can get a glimpse of their behavior through the firsthand account of Jane van Lawick-Goodall. So, too, you will probably never have occasion to make your way through the many public records and personal reports of the bubonic plague that beset Europe in the mid-fourteenth century, but you can get a synoptic view of the plague from Barbara Tuchman's account, which is based on a thorough investigation of those sources. Reporting expands the range of its readers' perceptions and knowledge beyond the limits of their own immediate experience. From the outlook of readers, then, the function of reporting does seem to be very clear-cut.

But if we shift our focus and look at reporting in terms of the purposes to which it is evidently put by writers, it often turns out to serve a more complex function than might at first be supposed. An example of this complexity can be seen in the following passage from van Lawick-Goodall's account:

> Suddenly I stopped, for I saw a slight movement in the long grass about sixty yards away. Quickly focusing my binoculars I saw that it was a single chimpanzee, and just then he turned in my direction. I recognized David Graybeard.
>
> Cautiously I moved around so that I could see what he was doing. He was squatting beside the red earth mound of a termite nest, and as I watched I saw him carefully push a long grass stem down into a hole in the mound. After a moment he withdrew it and picked something from the end with his mouth.

This passage seems on the whole to be a very neutral bit of scientific reporting that details van Lawick-Goodall's observation of a particular chimpanzee probing for food in a termite nest. The only unusual aspect of the report is her naming of the creature, which has the unscientific effect of personifying the animal. Otherwise, she is careful in the opening part of the description to establish the physical point of view from which she observed the chimpanzee—sixty yards away, looking at him through binoculars. And at the end of the passage she is equally careful not to identify or even conjecture about "something" beyond her range of detailed vision. As it turns out, however, this passage is a record not only of her observations but also of a pivotal moment in the story of how she came to make an important discovery about chimpanzees—that they are tool users—and thus how she came to regard their behavior as being much closer to that of human beings than had previously been supposed. So, she climaxes her previous description of the chimpanzee with this sentence:

> I was too far away to make out what he was eating, but it was obvious that he was actually using a grass stem as a tool.

Here as elsewhere, then, her reporting is thoughtfully worded and structured to make a strong case for her ideas about chimpanzee and human behavior. Thus, she evidently intends her report to be both informative and persuasive.

A different set of purposes can be seen in yet another firsthand account—this time of a medical patient, as observed by his doctor, Richard Selzer:

> From the doorway of Room 542 the man in the bed seems deeply tanned. Blue eyes and close-cropped white hair give him the appearance of vigor and good health. But I know that his skin is not brown from the sun. It is rusted rather, in the last stage of containing the vile repose within. And the blue eyes are frosted, looking inward like the windows of a snowbound cottage. This man is blind. This man is also legless—the right leg missing from midthigh down, the left from just below the knee. It gives him the look of a bonsai, roots and branches pruned into the dwarfed facsimile of a great tree.

In this passage, Selzer seeks to describe both the seemingly healthy visual appearance of his patient and the actually decaying physical condition of the patient. Thus he begins by reporting visual details, such as the "deeply tanned" skin as well as the "blue eyes and close-cropped white hair," that convey "the appearance of vigor and good health." Then in the sentences that follow, Selzer relies heavily on figurative language, on a striking sequence of metaphors and similes, each of which reverses the initial impression so as to convey the drastically impaired condition of the patient. The patient's skin turns out to be "rusted," his eyes "frosted," and his body like "the dwarfed facsimile of a great tree." Yet it is also clear from these and other bits of figurative language in the passage that Selzer is not only trying to convey the dire physical condition of his patient, but also to suggest his own intense personal feelings about the patient. Clearly, he intends his report to be provocative as well as informative.

For yet another combination of purposes, you might look at Farley Mowat's informative, entertaining, and self-mocking account of his firsthand encounter with the territorial behavior of wolves. Or you might look at Margaret Mead's vividly detailed description of life in a New Guinea lagoon village. Or you might turn to the NTSB report we discussed earlier in this introduction, and you will see that it is clearly intended not only to convey information pertaining to the cause of the airline crash, but also to make a case for various procedural changes that might prevent similar accidents in the future.

As is apparent from just this handful of selections, writers invariably seem to use reporting for a combination of purposes—not only to provide information but also to convey their attitudes, beliefs, or ideas about it, as well as to influence the views of their readers. This joining of purposes is hardly surprising, given the factors involved in any decision to report on something. After all, whenever we make a report, we do so presumably because we believe that the subject of our report is important enough for others to be told about it. And presumably we believe the subject to be important because of what we have come to know and think about it. So, when we are faced with deciding what information to report and how to report it, we inevitably base our decisions on these ideas. At every point in the process of planning and writing a report, we act on the basis of our particular motives and priorities for conveying information about the subject. And how could we do otherwise? How else could van Lawick-Goodall have decided what information to report out of all she must have observed during her first few months in Africa? How else could Selzer have decided what to emphasize out of all the information that he must have gathered from the time he first met his patient until the time of the patient's death? Without specific purposes to control our reporting, our records of events would be as long as the events themselves.

Reporting, as you can see, necessarily serves a widely varied range of purposes—as varied as are writers and their subjects. Thus, whenever you read a piece of reportorial writing, you should always try to discover for yourself what appear to be its guiding purposes by examining its structure, its phrasing, and its wording, much as we have earlier in this discussion. And once you have identified the purpose, you should then consider how it has influenced the selection, arrangement, and weighting of information in the report. When you turn to doing your own writing, you should be equally careful in determining your purposes for reporting as well as in organizing your report so as to put the information in a form that is true to what you know and think about the subject.

METHODS OF REPORTING

In planning a piece of reportorial writing, you should be sure to keep in mind not only your ideas about the subject, but also the needs of your readers. Given the fact that most of your readers will probably not be familiar with your information, you should be very careful in selecting and organizing it so that you give them a clear and orderly report of it. Usually, you will find that the nature of your information suggests a corresponding method of presenting it most clearly and conveniently to your readers.

If the information concerns a single, detailed event or covers a set of events spread over time, then the most effective method probably is narration—in the form of story telling—in a more or less chronological order. This is the basic form that van Lawick-Goodall uses in recounting her first few months of observation in Africa, and it proves to be a very clear and persuasive form for gradually unfolding her discovery about the behavior of chimpanzees. If the information concerns a particular place, or scene, or spectacle, then the most convenient method is description, presenting your information in a clear-cut spatial order so as to help your reader visualize both the overall scene and its important details. This is the method that Selzer uses not only in describing his patient's condition, but also in detailing the patient's posture and his hospital room. If the information is meant to provide a synoptic body of knowledge about a particular subject, then the clearest form will be a topical summation, using a set of categories appropriate to the subject at hand. This is the basic form that is used in the NTSB report, which takes us through a comprehensive survey of material about the airline crash, methodically organized under clearly defined topical headings: "History of the Flight," "Meteorological Information," "Aids to Navigation," "Wreckage," "Medical and Pathological Information," and "Survival Aspects."

Although narration, description, topical summation, and other forms of reporting are often treated separately for purposes of convenience in identifying each of them, it is well to keep in mind that they usually end up working in some sort of combination with one another. Narratives, after all, involve not only events but also people and places, so it is natural that they include descriptive passages. Similarly, descriptions of places frequently entail stories about events taking place in them, so it is not surprising that they include bits of narration. And given the synoptic nature of topical summations, they are likely to involve both descriptive and narrative elements. In writing, as in most other activities, form should follow function, rather than being forced to fit arbitrary rules of behavior.

Once you have settled upon a basic form, you should then devise a way of managing your information within that form—of selecting, arranging, and proportioning it—so as to achieve your purposes most effectively. To carry out this task, you will need to review all of the material you have gathered with an eye to determining what you consider to be the most important information to report. Some bits or kinds of information inevitably will strike you as more significant than others, and these are the ones that you should feature in your report. Likewise, you will probably find that some information is simply not important enough even to be mentioned. Van Lawick-Goodall, for example, produces a striking account of her first few months in Africa because she focuses primarily on her observation of chimpanzees, subordinating all the other material she reports to her discoveries about their behavior. Thus, only on a couple of occasions does she include observations about the behavior of animals other than chimpanzees—in particular about the timidities of a bushbuck and a leopard. And she only includes these observations to point up by contrast the distinctively sociable behavior of chimpanzees. For much the same reasons, she proportions her coverage of the several chimpanzee episodes she reports so as to give the greatest amount of detail to the one that provides the most compelling indication of their advanced intelligence—namely, the final episode, which shows the chimpanzees to be tool users and makers, a behavior previously attributed only to human beings.

To help achieve your purposes, you should also give special thought to deciding on the perspective from which you present your information to the reader. Do you want to present the material in first or third person? Do you want to be present in the piece, as are van Lawick-Goodall and Selzer? Or do you want to be invisible, as are the authors of the AP and NTSB reports? To some extent, of course, your answer to these questions will depend upon whether you gathered the information through your own firsthand observations and then want to convey your firsthand reactions to your observations, as van Lawick-Goodall and Selzer do in their pieces. But just to show that there are no hard-and-fast rules on this score, you might look at "A Delicate Operation" by Roy C. Selby, Jr. You will notice at once that although Selby must have written this piece on the basis of firsthand experience, he tells the story in third person, removing himself almost completely from it except for such distant-sounding references to himself as "the surgeon." Clearly, Selby is important to the information in this report, yet he evidently decided to de-emphasize himself in writing the report. In order to see just how important it is to consider these alternatives in planning any report, you might compare Selby's report with Selzer's, which is written throughout in first person. If the perspectives of these two reports were reversed—you might take a stab at changing them around yourself—you would find the contents and effects of both reports to be surprisingly different. Ultimately, then, the nature of a report is substantially determined not only by *what* a writer gathers from various sources but also by *how* a writer presents the information.

In the reports that follow in this section, you will have an opportunity to see various ways of presenting things in writing. In later sections, you will see how reporting combines with other kinds of writing—explaining and arguing.

Arts and Humanities

"THIS IS THE END OF THE WORLD": THE BLACK DEATH

Barbara Tuchman

For over twenty-five years Barbara Wertheim Tuchman (1912–1989) wrote books on historical subjects, ranging over the centuries from the Middle Ages to World War II. Her combination of careful research and lively writing enabled her to produce books like The Guns of August *(1962),* A Distant Mirror *(1978), and* The March of Folly, From Troy to Vietnam *(1984), which pleased not only the general public but many professional historians as well. She twice won the Pulitzer Prize.* A Distant Mirror, *from which the following selection has been taken, was on the* New York Times *best-seller list for over nine months. Her final book,* The First Salute *(1988), is notable for the presence of Tuchman's characteristic scholarship and wit.*

In October 1347, two months after the fall of Calais, Genoese trading ships 1 put into the harbor of Messina in Sicily with dead and dying men at the oars. The ships had come from the Black Sea port of Caffa (now Feodosiya) in the Crimea, where the Genoese maintained a trading post. The diseased sailors showed strange black swellings about the size of an egg or an apple in the armpits and groin. The swellings oozed blood and pus and were followed by spreading boils and black blotches on the skin from internal bleeding. The sick suffered severe pain and died quickly within five days of the first symptoms. As the disease spread, other symptoms of continuous fever and spitting of blood appeared instead of the swellings or buboes. These victims coughed and sweated heavily and died even more quickly, within three days or less, sometimes in 24 hours. In both types everything that issued from the body—breath, sweat, blood from the buboes and lungs, bloody urine, and blood-blackened excrement—smelled foul. Depression and despair accompanied the physical symptoms, and before the end "death is seen seated on the face."

The disease was bubonic plague, present in two forms: one that infected the bloodstream, causing the buboes and internal bleeding, and was spread by contact; and a second, more virulent pneumonic type that infected the lungs and was spread by respiratory infection. The presence of both at once caused the high mortality and speed of contagion. So lethal was the disease that cases were known of persons going to bed well and dying before they woke, of doctors catching the illness at a bedside and dying before the patient. So rapidly did it spread from one to another that to a French physician, Simon de Covino, it seemed as if one sick person "could infect the whole world." The malignity of the pestilence appeared more terrible because its victims knew no prevention and no remedy.

The physical suffering of the disease and its aspects of evil mystery were expressed in a strange Welsh lament which saw "death coming into our midst like black smoke, a plague which cuts off the young, a rootless phantom which has no mercy for fair countenance. Woe is me of the shilling in the armpit! It is seething, terrible . . . a head that gives pain and causes a loud cry . . . a painful angry knob . . . Great is its seething like a burning cinder . . . a grievous thing of ashy color." Its eruption is ugly like the "seeds of black peas, broken fragments of brittle sea-coal . . . the early ornaments of black death, cinders of the peelings of the cockle weed, a mixed multitude, a black plague like half-pence, like berries. . . ."

Rumors of a terrible plague supposedly arising in China and spreading through Tartary (Central Asia) to India and Persia, Mesopotamia, Syria, Egypt, and all of Asia Minor had reached Europe in 1346. They told of a death toll so devastating that all of India was said to be depopulated, whole territories covered by dead bodies, other areas with no one left alive. As added up by Pope Clement VI at Avignon, the total of reported dead reached 23,840,000. In the absence of a concept of contagion, no serious alarm was felt in Europe until the trading ships brought their black burden of pestilence into Messina while other infected ships from the Levant carried it to Genoa and Venice.

By January 1348 it penetrated France via Marseille, and North Africa via Tunis. Shipborne along coasts and navigable rivers, it spread westward from Marseille through the ports of Languedoc to Spain and northward up the Rhône to Avignon, where it arrived in March. It reached Narbonne, Montpellier, Carcassonne, and Toulouse between February and May, and at the same time in Italy spread to Rome and Florence and their hinterlands. Between June and August it reached Bordeaux, Lyon, and Paris, spread to Burgundy and Normandy, and crossed the Channel from Normandy into southern England. From Italy during the same summer it crossed the Alps into Switzerland and reached eastward to Hungary.

In a given area the plague accomplished its kill within four to six months   6
and then faded, except in the larger cities, where, rooting into the close-
quartered population, it abated during the winter, only to reappear in spring
and rage for another six months.

In 1349 it resumed in Paris, spread to Picardy, Flanders, and the Low   7
Countries, and from England to Scotland and Ireland as well as to Norway,
where a ghost ship with a cargo of wool and a dead crew drifted offshore until
it ran aground near Bergen. From there the plague passed into Sweden, Denmark, Prussia, Iceland, and as far as Greenland. Leaving a strange pocket of
immunity in Bohemia, and Russia unattacked until 1351, it had passed from
most of Europe by mid-1350. Although the mortality rate was erratic, ranging
from one fifth in some places to nine tenths or almost total elimination in
others, the overall estimate of modern demographers has settled—for the area
extending from India to Iceland—around the same figure expressed in Froissart's
casual words: "a third of the world died." His estimate, the common one at the
time, was not an inspired guess but a borrowing of St. John's figure for mortality
from plague in Revelation, the favorite guide to human affairs of the Middle
Ages.

A third of Europe would have meant about 20 million deaths. No one knows   8
in truth how many died. Contemporary reports were an awed impression, not
an accurate count. In crowded Avignon, it was said, 400 died daily; 7,000
houses emptied by death were shut up; a single graveyard received 11,000
corpses in six weeks; half the city's inhabitants reportedly died, including 9
cardinals or one third of the total, and 70 lesser prelates. Watching the endlessly
passing death carts, chroniclers let normal exaggeration take wings and put the
Avignon death toll at 62,000 and even at 120,000, although the city's total
population was probably less than 50,000.

When graveyards filled up, bodies at Avignon were thrown into the Rhône   9
until mass burial pits were dug for dumping the corpses. In London in such
pits corpses piled up in layers until they overflowed. Everywhere reports speak
of the sick dying too fast for the living to bury. Corpses were dragged out of
homes and left in front of doorways. Morning light revealed new piles of bodies.
In Florence the dead were gathered up by the Compagnia della Misericordia—
founded in 1244 to care for the sick—whose members wore red robes and hoods
masking the face except for the eyes. When their efforts failed, the dead lay
putrid in the streets for days at a time. When no coffins were to be had, the
bodies were laid on boards, two or three at once, to be carried to graveyards or
common pits. Families dumped their own relatives into the pits, or buried them
so hastily and thinly "that dogs dragged them forth and devoured their bodies."

Amid accumulating death and fear of contagion, people died without last   10
rites and were buried without prayers, a prospect that terrified the last hours of
the stricken. A bishop in England gave permission to laymen to make confession
to each other as was done by the Apostles, "or if no man is present then even

to a woman," and if no priest could be found to administer extreme unction, "then faith must suffice." Clement VI found it necessary to grant remissions of sin to all who died of the plague because so many were unattended by priests. "And no bells tolled," wrote a chronicler of Siena, "and nobody wept no matter what his loss because almost everyone expected death. . . . And people said and believed, 'This is the end of the world.'"

In Paris, where the plague lasted through 1349, the reported death rate was 800 a day, in Pisa 500, in Vienna 500 to 600. The total dead in Paris numbered 50,000 or half the population. Florence, weakened by the famine of 1347, lost three to four fifths of its citizens, Venice two thirds, Hamburg and Bremen, though smaller in size, about the same proportion. Cities, as centers of transportation, were more likely to be affected than villages, although once a village was infected, its death rate was equally high. At Givry, a prosperous village in Burgundy of 1,200 to 1,500 people, the parish register records 615 deaths in the space of fourteen weeks, compared to an average of thirty deaths a year in the previous decade. In three villages of Cambridgeshire, manorial records show a death rate of 47 percent, 57 percent, and in one case 70 percent. When the last survivors, too few to carry on, moved away, a deserted village sank back into the wilderness and disappeared from the map altogether, leaving only a grass-covered ghostly outline to show where mortals once had lived. [11]

In enclosed places such as monasteries and prisons, the infection of one person usually meant that of all, as happened in the Franciscan convents of Carcassonne and Marseille, where every inmate without exception died. Of the 140 Dominicans at Montpellier only seven survived. Petrarch's brother Gherardo, member of a Carthusian monastery, buried the prior and 34 fellow monks one by one, sometimes three a day, until he was left alone with his dog and fled to look for a place that would take him in. Watching every comrade die, men in such places could not but wonder whether the strange peril that filled the air had not been sent to exterminate the human race. In Kilkenny, Ireland, Brother John Clyn of the Friars Minor, another monk left alone among dead men, kept a record of what had happened lest "things which should be remembered perish with time and vanish from the memory of those who come after us." Sensing "the whole world, as it were, placed within the grasp of the Evil One," and waiting for death to visit him too, he wrote, "I leave parchment to continue this work, if perchance any man survive and any of the race of Adam escape this pestilence and carry on the work which I have begun." Brother John, as noted by another hand, died of the pestilence, but he foiled oblivion. [12]

The largest cities of Europe, with populations of about 100,000, were Paris and Florence, Venice and Genoa. At the next level, with more than 50,000, were Ghent and Bruges in Flanders, Milan, Bologna, Rome, Naples, and Palermo, and Cologne. London hovered below 50,000, the only city in England except York with more than 10,000. At the level of 20,000 to 50,000 were [13]

Bordeaux, Toulouse, Montpellier, Marseille, and Lyon in France, Barcelona, Seville, and Toledo in Spain, Siena, Pisa, and other secondary cities in Italy, and the Hanseatic trading cities of the Empire. The plague raged through them all, killing anywhere from one third to two thirds of their inhabitants. Italy, with a total population of 10 to 11 million, probably suffered the heaviest toll. Following the Florentine bankruptcies, the crop failures and workers' riots of 1346–47, the revolt of Cola di Rienzi that plunged Rome into anarchy, the plague came as the peak of successive calamities. As if the world were indeed in the grasp of the Evil One, its first appearance on the European mainland in January 1348 coincided with a fearsome earthquake that carved a path of wreckage from Naples up to Venice. Houses collapsed, church towers toppled, villages were crushed, and the destruction reached as far as Germany and Greece. Emotional response, dulled by horrors, underwent a kind of atrophy epitomized by the chronicler who wrote, "And in these days was burying without sorrowe and wedding without friendschippe."

In Siena, where more than half the inhabitants died of the plague, work was 14 abandoned on the great cathedral, planned to be the largest in the world, and never resumed, owing to loss of workers and master masons and "the melancholy and grief" of the survivors. The cathedral's truncated transept still stands in permanent witness to the sweep of death's scythe. Agnolo di Tura, a chronicler of Siena, recorded the fear of contagion that froze every other instinct. "Father abandoned child, wife husband, one brother another," he wrote, "for this plague seemed to strike through the breath and sight. And so they died. And no one could be found to bury the dead for money or friendship. . . . And I, Agnolo di Tura, called the Fat, buried my five children with my own hands, and so did many others likewise."

There were many to echo his account of inhumanity and few to balance it, 15 for the plague was not the kind of calamity that inspired mutual help. Its loathsomeness and deadliness did not herd people together in mutual distress, but only prompted their desire to escape each other. "Magistrates and notaries refused to come and make the wills of the dying," reported a Franciscan friar of Piazza in Sicily; what was worse, "even the priests did not come to hear their confessions." A clerk of the Archbishop of Canterbury reported the same of English priests who "turned away from the care of their benefices from fear of death." Cases of parents deserting children and children their parents were reported across Europe from Scotland to Russia. The calamity chilled the hearts of men, wrote Boccaccio in his famous account of the plague in Florence that serves as introduction to the *Decameron*. "One man shunned another . . . kinsfolk held aloof, brother was forsaken by brother, oftentimes husband by wife; nay, what is more, and scarcely to be believed, fathers and mothers were found to abandon their own children to their fate, untended, unvisited as if they had been strangers." Exaggeration and literary pessimism were common in the 14th century, but the Pope's physician, Guy de Chauliac, was a sober, careful observer who reported the same phenomenon: "A father did not visit his son, nor the son his father. Charity was dead."

Yet not entirely. In Paris, according to the chronicler Jean de Venette, the nuns of the Hotel Dieu or municipal hospital, "having no fear of death, tended the sick with all sweetness and humility." New nuns repeatedly took the places of those who died, until the majority "many times renewed by death now rest in peace with Christ as we may piously believe." 16

When the plague entered northern France in July 1348, it settled first in Normandy and, checked by winter, gave Picardy a deceptive interim until the next summer. Either in mourning or warning, black flags were flown from church towers of the worst-stricken villages of Normandy. "And in that time," wrote a monk of the abbey of Fourcarment, "the mortality was so great among the people of Normandy that those of Picardy mocked them." The same unneighborly reaction was reported of the Scots, separated by a winter's immunity from the English. Delighted to hear of the disease that was scourging the "southrons," they gathered forces for an invasion, "laughing at their enemies." Before they could move, the savage mortality fell upon them too, scattering some in death and the rest in panic to spread the infection as they fled. 17

In Picardy in the summer of 1349 the pestilence penetrated the castle of Coucy to kill Enguerrand's mother,[1] Catherine, and her new husband. Whether her nine-year-old son escaped by chance or was perhaps living elsewhere with one of his guardians is unrecorded. In nearby Amiens, tannery workers, responding quickly to losses in the labor force, combined to bargain for higher wages. In another place villagers were seen dancing to drums and trumpets, and on being asked the reason, answered that, seeing their neighbors die day by day while their village remained immune, they believed that they could keep the plague from entering "by the jollity that is in us. That is why we dance." Further north in Tournai on the border of Flanders, Gilles li Muisis, Abbot of St. Martin's, kept one of the epidemic's most vivid accounts. The passing bells rang all day and all night, he recorded, because sextons were anxious to obtain their fees while they could. Filled with the sound of mourning, the city became oppressed by fear, so that the authorities forbade the tolling of bells and the wearing of black and restricted funeral services to two mourners. The silencing of funeral bells and of criers' announcements of deaths was ordained by most cities. Siena imposed a fine on the wearing of mourning clothes by all except widows. 18

Flight was the chief recourse of those who could afford it or arrange it. The rich fled to their country places like Boccaccio's young patricians of Florence, who settled in a pastoral palace "removed on every side from the roads" with 19

---

[1] Enguerrand de Coucy: the French nobleman whose life is followed by Tuchman as a way of unifying her study of the fourteenth century. [Eds.]

"wells of cool water and vaults of rare wines." The urban poor died in their burrows, "and only the stench of their bodies informed neighbors of their deaths." That the poor were more heavily afflicted than the rich was clearly remarked at the time, in the north as in the south. A Scottish chronicler, John of Fordun, stated flatly that the pest "attacked especially the meaner sort and common people—seldom the magnates." Simon de Covino of Montpellier made the same observation. He ascribed it to the misery and want and hard lives that made the poor more susceptible, which was half the truth. Close contact and lack of sanitation was the unrecognized other half. It was noticed too that the young died in greater proportion than the old; Simon de Covino compared the disappearance of youth to the withering of flowers in the fields.

In the countryside peasants dropped dead on the roads, in the fields, in their houses. Survivors in growing helplessness fell into apathy, leaving ripe wheat uncut and livestock untended. Oxen and asses, sheep and goats, pigs and chickens ran wild and they too, according to local reports, succumbed to the pest. English sheep, bearers of the precious wool, died throughout the country. The chronicler Henry Knighton, canon of Leicester Abbey, reported 5,000 dead in one field alone, "their bodies so corrupted by the plague that neither beast nor bird would touch them," and spreading an appalling stench. In the Austrian Alps wolves came down to prey upon sheep and then, "as if alarmed by some invisible warning, turned and fled back into the wilderness." In remote Dalmatia bolder wolves descended upon a plague-stricken city and attacked human survivors. For want of herdsmen, cattle strayed from place to place and died in hedgerows and ditches. Dogs and cats fell like the rest. [20]

The dearth of labor held a fearful prospect because the 14th century lived close to the annual harvest both for food and for next year's seed. "So few servants and laborers were left," wrote Knighton, "that no one knew where to turn for help." The sense of a vanishing future created a kind of dementia of despair. A Bavarian chronicler of Neuberg on the Danube recorded that "Men and women . . . wandered around as if mad" and let their cattle stray "because no one had any inclination to concern themselves about the future." Fields went uncultivated, spring seed unsown. Second growth with nature's awful energy crept back over cleared land, dikes crumbled, salt water reinvaded and soured the lowlands. With so few hands remaining to restore the work of centuries, people felt, in Walsingham's words, that "the world could never again regain its former prosperity." [21]

Though the death rate was higher among the anonymous poor, the known and the great died too. King Alfonso XI of Castile was the only reigning monarch killed by the pest, but his neighbor King Pedro of Aragon lost his wife, Queen Leonora, his daughter Marie, and a niece in the space of six months. John Cantacuzene, Emperor of Byzantium, lost his son. In France the lame Queen Jeanne and her daughter-in-law Bonne de Luxemburg, wife of the Dauphin, both died in 1349 in the same phase that took the life of Enguerrand's mother. [22]

Jeanne, Queen of Navarre, daughter of Louis X, was another victim. Edward III's second daughter, Joanna, who was on her way to marry Pedro, the heir of Castile, died in Bordeaux. Women appear to have been more vulnerable than men, perhaps because, being more housebound, they were more exposed to fleas. Boccaccio's mistress Fiammetta, illegitimate daughter of the King of Naples, died, as did Laura, the beloved—whether real or fictional—of Petrarch. Reaching out to us in the future, Petrarch cried, "Oh happy posterity who will not experience such abysmal woe and will look upon our testimony as a fable."

In Florence Giovanni Villani, the great historian of his time, died at 68 in [23] the midst of an unfinished sentence: ". . . *e dure questo pistolenza fino a . . .* (in the midst of this pestilence there came to an end . . .)." Siena's master painters, the brothers Ambrogio and Pietro Lorenzetti, whose names never appear after 1348, presumably perished in the plague, as did Andrea Pisano, architect and sculptor of Florence. William of Ockham and the English mystic Richard Rolle of Hampole both disappear from mention after 1349. Francisco Datini, merchant of Prato, lost both his parents and two siblings. Curious sweeps of mortality afflicted certain bodies of merchants in London. All eight wardens of the Company of Cutters, all six wardens of the Hatters, and four wardens of the Goldsmiths died before July 1350. Sir John Pulteney, master draper and four times Mayor of London, was a victim, likewise Sir John Montgomery, Governor of Calais.

Among the clergy and doctors the mortality was naturally high because of [24] the nature of their professions. Out of 24 physicians in Venice, 20 were said to have lost their lives in the plague, although, according to another account, some were believed to have fled or to have shut themselves up in their houses. At Montpellier, site of the leading medieval medical school, the physician Simon de Covino reported that, despite the great number of doctors, "hardly one of them escaped." In Avignon, Guy de Chauliac confessed that he performed his medical visits only because he dared not stay away for fear of infamy, but "I was in continual fear." He claimed to have contracted the disease but to have cured himself by his own treatment; if so, he was one of the few who recovered.

Clerical mortality varied with rank. Although the one-third toll of cardinals [25] reflects the same proportion as the whole, this was probably due to their concentration in Avignon. In England, in strange and almost sinister procession, the Archbishop of Canterbury, John Stratford, died in August 1348, his appointed successor died in May 1349, and the next appointee three months later, all three within a year. Despite such weird vagaries, prelates in general managed to sustain a higher survival rate than the lesser clergy. Among bishops the deaths have been estimated at about one in twenty. The loss of priests, even if many avoided their fearful duty of attending the dying, was about the same as among the population as a whole.

Government officials, whose loss contributed to the general chaos, found, [26] on the whole, no special shelter. In Siena four of the nine members of the governing oligarchy died, in France one third of the royal notaries, in Bristol 15 out of the 52 members of the Town Council or almost one third. Tax-collecting obviously suffered, with the result that Philip VI was unable to collect more than a fraction of the subsidy granted him by the Estates in the winter of 1347–48.

Lawlessness and debauchery accompanied the plague as they had during the great plague of Athens of 430 B.C., when according to Thucydides, men grew bold in the indulgence of pleasure: "For seeing how the rich died in a moment and those who had nothing immediately inherited their property, they reflected that life and riches were alike transitory and they resolved to enjoy themselves while they could." Human behavior is timeless. When St. John had his vision of plague in Revelation, he knew from some experience or race memory that those who survived "repented not of the work of their hands. . . . Neither repented they of their murders, nor of their sorceries, nor of their fornication, nor of their thefts."

27

NOTES[2]

1. "Death Is Seen Seated": Simon de Covino, q. Campbell, 80.
2. "Could Infect the World": q. Gasquet, 41.
3. Welsh Lament: q. Ziegler, 190.
9. "Dogs Dragged Them Forth": Agnolo di Tura, q. Ziegler, 58.
10. "Or If No Man Is Present": Bishop of Bath and Wells, q. Ziegler, 125. "No Bells Tolled": Agnolo di Tura, q. Schevill, *Siena*, 211. The same observation was made by Gabriel de Muisis, notary of Piacenza, q. Crawford, 113.
11. Givry Parish Register: Renouard, 111. Three Villages Of Cambridgeshire: Salt-marsh.
12. Petrarch's Brother: Bishop, 273. Brother John Clyn: q. Ziegler, 195.
13. Atrophy; "and in These Days": q. Deaux, 143, citing only "an old northern chronicle."
14. Agnolo Di Tura, "Father Abandoned Child": q. Ziegler, 58.
15. "Magistrates And Notaries": q. Deaux, 49. English Priests Turned Away: Ziegler, 261. Parents Deserting Children: Hecker, 30. Guy De Chauliac, "A Father": q. Gasquet, 50–51.
16. Nuns of the Hotel Dieu: *Chron. Jean de Venette*, 49.
17. Picards and Scots Mock Mortality of Neighbors: Gasquet, 53, and Ziegler, 198.
18. Catherine de Coucy: *L'Art de vérifier*, 237. Amiens Tanners: Gasquet, 57. "By the Jollity That is in Us": *Grandes Chrôns.*, VI, 486–87.
19. John of Fordun: q. Ziegler, 199. Simon de Covino on the Poor: Gasquet, 42. On Youth: Cazelles, *Peste*.

---

[2]Tuchman does not use numbered footnotes, but at the back of her book she identifies the source of every quotation or citation. The works cited follow in a bibliography. Although Tuchman's notes are labeled by page number, the numbers here refer to the paragraphs in which the sources are mentioned. [Eds.]

20. Knighton On Sheep: q. Ziegler, 175. Wolves of Austria and Dalmatia: ibid., 84, 111. Dogs and Cats: Muisis, q. Gasquet, 44, 61.

21. Bavarian Chronicler of Neuberg: q. Ziegler, 84. Walsingham, "The World Could Never": Denifle, 273.

22. "Oh Happy Posterity": q. Ziegler, 45.

23. Giovanni Villani, "e dure questo": q. Snell, 334.

24. Physicians of Venice: Campbell, 98. Simon de Covino: ibid., 31. Guy de Chauliac, "I Was in Fear": q. Thompson Ec. and Soc., 379.

27. Thucydides: q. Crawfurd, 30–31.

BIBLIOGRAPHY

L'Art de vérifier les dates des faits historiques, par un Religieux de la Congregation de St.-Maur, vol XII. Paris, 1818.

Bishop, Morris. Petrarch and His World. Indiana University Press, 1963.

Campbell, Anna M. The Black Death and Men of Learning. Columbia University Press, 1931.

Cazelles, Raymond. "La Peste de 1348–49 en Langue d'oil: épidémie prolitarienne et enfantine." Bull philologique et historique, 1962, pp. 293–305.

Chronicle of Jean de Venette. Trans. Jean Birdsall. Ed. Richard A. Newhall. Columbia University Press, 1853.

Crawfurd, Raymond. Plague and Pestilence in Literature and Art. Oxford, 1914.

Deaux, George. The Black Death, 1347. London, 1969.

Denifle, Henri. La Dèsolation des églises, monastères et hopitaux en France pendant la guerre de cent ans, vol. I. Paris, 1899.

Gasquet, Francis Aidan, Abbot. The Black Death of 1348 and 1349, 2nd ed. London, 1908.

Grandes Chroniques de France, vol. VI (to 1380). Ed. Paulin Paris. Paris, 1838.

Hecker, J. F. C. The Epidemics of the Middle Ages. London, 1844.

Renouard, Yves. "La Peste noirs de 1348–50." Rev. de Paris, March, 1950.

Saltmarsh, John. "Plague and Economic Decline in England in the Later Middle Ages," Cambridge Historical Journal, vol. VII, no. 1, 1941.

Schevill, Ferdinand. Siena: The History of a Medieval Commune. New York, 1909.

Snell, Frederick. The Fourteenth Century. Edinburgh, 1899.

Thompson, James Westfall. Economic and Social History of Europe in the Later Middle Ages. New York, 1931.

Ziegler, Philip. The Black Death. New York, 1969. (The best modern study.)

QUESTIONS

1. Try to imagine yourself in Tuchman's position. If you were assigned the task of reporting on the black plague in Europe, how would you go about it? What problems would you expect to encounter in the research and in the composition of your report?

2. The notes and bibliography reveal a broad scholarly base: Tuchman's research was clearly prodigious. But so were the problems of organization after the research had been done. Tuchman had to find a way to present her information to readers that would be clear and interesting. How has she solved her problem? What overall patterns of

organization do you find in this selection? Can you mark off subsections with topics of their own?

3. How does Tuchman organize her paragraphs? Consider paragraph 20, for example. What is the topic? What are the subtopics? Why does the paragraph begin and end as it does? Consider paragraph 22. How does the first sentence serve as a transition from the previous paragraph? How is the rest of the paragraph ordered? Does the next paragraph start a new topic or continue developing the topic announced at the beginning of paragraph 22?

4. Many paragraphs end with direct quotations. Examine some of these. What do they have in common? Why do you suppose Tuchman closes so many paragraphs in this way?

5. Much of this essay is devoted to the reporting of facts and figures. This could be supremely dull, but Tuchman is an expert at avoiding dullness. How does she help the reader see and feel the awfulness of the plague? Locate specific examples in the text, and discuss their effectiveness.

6. We have included the notes for the chapter reprinted here. Examine Tuchman's list of sources, and explain how she has used them. Does she quote directly from each source, or does she paraphrase it? Does she use a source to illustrate a point, or as evidence for argument, or in some other way? Describe Tuchman's general method of using sources.

7. Taking Tuchman as a model, write a report on some other catastrophe, blending factual reporting with description of what it was like to be there. This will require both careful research and artful selection and arrangement of the fruits of that research.

8. Using Tuchman's notes to A *Distant Mirror* as a reference guide, find out more about some specific place or event mentioned by Tuchman. Write a report of your findings.

MAKING CONNECTIONS

1. Compare this account of the black death to the writings by Farley Mowat or Jane van Lawick-Goodall, included in this section. Make your comparison in terms of the points of view established and sustained in the reports you compare. What is Tuchman's point of view toward her subject?

2. Using the terms of our introduction to this section, would you say Tuchman's basic method of reporting is narrative, or that it emphasizes spatial order, or that it makes a topical summation of categories appropriate to its subject? How does her handling of sources compare to the National Transportation Safety Board's report on an airplane crash?

SHAKESPEARE IN THE BUSH

Laura Bohannan

In this essay, originally published in Natural History *in 1966, cultural anthropologist Laura Bohannan faces the difficult task of presenting a renowned piece of English literature to another culture that values stories but whose modes of interpretation, she finds, are quite different from hers. Bohannan, also a professor of anthropology, has published a number of works on the ethnography and religion of the Tiv people of West Africa.*

Just before I left Oxford for the Tiv in West Africa, conversation turned to 1
the season at Stratford. "You Americans," said a friend, "often have difficulty
with Shakespeare. He was, after all, a very English poet, and one can easily
misinterpret the universal by misunderstanding the particular."

I protested that human nature is pretty much the same the whole world over; 2
at least the general plot and motivation of the greater tragedies would always be
clear—everywhere—although some details of custom might have to be explained and difficulties of translation might produce other slight changes. To
end an argument we could not conclude, my friend gave me a copy of *Hamlet*
to study in the African bush: it would, he hoped, lift my mind above its primitive
surroundings, and possibly I might, by prolonged meditation, achieve the grace
of correct interpretation.

It was my second field trip to that African tribe, and I thought myself ready 3
to live in one of its remote sections—an area difficult to cross even on foot. I
eventually settled on the hillock of a very knowledgeable old man, the head of
a homestead of some hundred and forty people, all of whom were either his
close relatives or their wives and children. Like the other elders of the vicinity,
the old man spent most of his time performing ceremonies seldom seen these
days in the more accessible parts of the tribe. I was delighted. Soon there would
be three months of enforced isolation and leisure, between the harvest that takes
place just before the rising of the swamps and the clearing of new farms when
the water goes down. Then, I thought, they would have even more time to
perform ceremonies and explain them to me.

I was quite mistaken. Most of the ceremonies demanded the presence of 4
elders from several homesteads. As the swamps rose, the old men found it too
difficult to walk from one homestead to the next, and the ceremonies gradually

ceased. As the swamps rose even higher, all activities but one came to an end. The women brewed beer from maize and millet. Men, women, and children sat on their hillocks and drank it.

People began to drink at dawn. By midmorning the whole homestead was singing, dancing, and drumming. When it rained, people had to sit inside their huts: there they drank and sang or they drank and told stories. In any case, by noon or before, I either had to join the party or retire to my own hut and my books. "One does not discuss serious matters when there is beer. Come, drink with us." Since I lacked their capacity for the thick native beer, I spent more and more time with *Hamlet*. Before the end of the second month, grace descended on me. I was quite sure that *Hamlet* had only one possible interpretation, and that one universally obvious.

Early every morning, in the hope of having some serious talk before the beer party, I used to call on the old man at his reception hut—a circle of posts supporting a thatched roof above a low mud wall to keep out wind and rain. One day I crawled through the low doorway and found most of the men of the homestead sitting huddled in their ragged cloths on stools, low plank beds, and reclining chairs, warming themselves against the chill of the rain around a smoky fire. In the center were three pots of beer. The party had started.

The old man greeted me cordially. "Sit down and drink." I accepted a large calabash full of beer, poured some into a small drinking gourd, and tossed it down. Then I poured some more into the same gourd for the man second in seniority to my host before I handed my calabash over to a young man for further distribution. Important people shouldn't ladle beer themselves.

"It is better like this," the old man said, looking at me approvingly and plucking at the thatch that had caught in my hair. "You should sit and drink with us more often. Your servants tell me that when you are not with us, you sit inside your hut looking at a paper."

The old man was acquainted with four kinds of "papers": tax receipts, bride price receipts, court fee receipts, and letters. The messenger who brought him letters from the chief used them mainly as a badge of office, for he always knew what was in them and told the old man. Personal letters for the few who had relatives in the government or mission stations were kept until someone went to a large market where there was a letter writer and reader. Since my arrival, letters were brought to me to be read. A few men also brought me bride price receipts, privately, with requests to change the figures to a higher sum. I found moral arguments were of no avail, since in-laws are fair game, and the technical hazards of forgery difficult to explain to an illiterate people. I did not wish them to think me silly enough to look at any such papers for days on end, and I hastily explained that my "paper" was one of the "things of long ago" of my country.

"Ah," said the old man. "Tell us."

I protested that I was not a storyteller. Storytelling is a skilled art among

189

them; their standards are high, and the audiences critical—and vocal in their criticism. I protested in vain. This morning they wanted to hear a story while they drank. They threatened to tell me no more stories until I told them one of mine. Finally, the old man promised that no one would criticize my style "for we know you are struggling with our language." "But," put in one of the elders, "you must explain what we do not understand, as we do when we tell you our stories." Realizing that here was my chance to prove *Hamlet* universally intelligible, I agreed.

The old man handed me some more beer to help me on with my storytelling. 12
Men filled their long wooden pipes and knocked coals from the fire to place in the pipe bowls; then, puffing contentedly, they sat back to listen. I began in the proper style, "Not yesterday, not yesterday, but long ago, a thing occurred. One night three men were keeping watch outside the homestead of the great chief, when suddenly they saw the former chief approach them."

"Why was he no longer their chief?" 13

"He was dead," I explained. "That is why they were troubled and afraid 14
when they saw him."

"Impossible," began one of the elders, handing his pipe on to his neighbor, 15
who interrupted, "Of course it wasn't the dead chief. It was an omen sent by a witch. Go on."

Slightly shaken, I continued. "One of these three was a man who knew 16
things"—the closest translation for scholar, but unfortunately it also meant witch. The second elder looked triumphantly at the first. "So he spoke to the dead chief saying, 'Tell us what we must do so you may rest in your grave,' but the dead chief did not answer. He vanished, and they could see him no more. Then the man who knew things—his name was Horatio—said this event was the affair of the dead chief's son, Hamlet."

There was a general shaking of heads round the circle. "Had the dead chief 17
no living brothers? Or was this son the chief?"

"No," I replied. "That is, he had one living brother who became the chief 18
when the elder brother died."

The old men muttered: such omens were matters for chiefs and elders, not 19
for youngsters; no good could come of going behind a chief's back; clearly Horatio was not a man who knew things.

"Yes, he was," I insisted, shooing a chicken away from my beer. "In our 20
country the son is next to the father. The dead chief's younger brother had become the great chief. He had also married his elder brother's widow only about a month after the funeral."

"He did well," the old man beamed and announced to the others, "I told 21
you that if we knew more about Europeans, we would find they really were very like us. In our country also," he added to me, "the younger brother marries the elder brother's widow and becomes the father of his children. Now, if your

190

uncle, who married your widowed mother, is your father's full brother, then he will be a real father to you. Did Hamlet's father and uncle have one mother?"

His question barely penetrated my mind; I was too upset and thrown too far ²² off balance by having one of the most important elements of *Hamlet* knocked straight out of the picture. Rather uncertainly I said that I thought they had the same mother, but I wasn't sure—the story didn't say. The old man told me severely that these genealogical details made all the difference and that when I got home I must ask the elders about it. He shouted out the door to one of his younger wives to bring his goatskin bag.

Determined to save what I could of the mother motif, I took a deep breath ²³ and began again. "The son Hamlet was very sad because his mother had married again so quickly. There was no need for her to do so, and it is our custom for a widow not to go to her next husband until she has mourned for two years."

"Two years is too long," objected the wife, who had appeared with the old ²⁴ man's battered goatskin bag. "Who will hoe your farms for you while you have no husband?"

"Hamlet," I retorted without thinking, "was old enough to hoe his mother's ²⁵ farms himself. There was no need for her to remarry." No one looked convinced. I gave up. "His mother and the great chief told Hamlet not to be sad, for the great chief himself would be a father to Hamlet. Furthermore, Hamlet would be the next chief: therefore he must stay to learn the things of a chief. Hamlet agreed to remain, and all the rest went off to drink beer."

While I paused, perplexed at how to render Hamlet's disgusted soliloquy to ²⁶ an audience convinced that Claudius and Gertrude had behaved in the best possible manner, one of the younger men asked me who had married the other wives of the dead chief.

"He had no other wives," I told him. ²⁷

"But a chief must have many wives! How else can he brew beer and prepare ²⁸ food for all his guests?"

I said firmly that in our country even chiefs had only one wife, that they ²⁹ had servants to do their work, and that they paid them from tax money.

It was better, they returned, for a chief to have many wives and sons who ³⁰ would help him hoe his farms and feed his people; then everyone loved the chief who gave much and took nothing—taxes were a bad thing.

I agreed with the last comment, but for the rest fell back on their favorite ³¹ way of fobbing off my questions: "That is the way it is done, so that is how we do it."

I decided to skip the soliloquy. Even if Claudius was here thought quite right ³² to marry his brother's widow, there remained the poison motif, and I knew they would disapprove of fratricide. More hopefully I resumed, "That night Hamlet kept watch with the three who had seen his dead father. The dead chief again appeared, and although the others were afraid, Hamlet followed his dead father off to one side. When they were alone, Hamlet's dead father spoke."

"Omens can't talk!" The old man was emphatic.   33

"Hamlet's dead father wasn't an omen. Seeing him might have been an   34
omen, but he was not." My audience looked as confused as I sounded. "It *was* Hamlet's dead father. It was a thing we call a 'ghost.'" I had to use the English word, for unlike many of the neighboring tribes, these people didn't believe in the survival after death of any individuating part of the personality.

"What is a 'ghost?' An omen?"   35

"No, a 'ghost' is someone who is dead but who walks around and can talk,   36
and people can hear him and see him but not touch him."

They objected. "One can touch zombis."   37

"No, no! It was not a dead body the witches had animated to sacrifice and   38
eat. No one else made Hamlet's dead father walk. He did it himself."

"Dead men can't walk," protested my audience as one man.   39

I was quite willing to compromise. "A 'ghost' is the dead man's shadow."   40

But again they objected. "Dead men cast no shadows."   41

"They do in my country," I snapped.   42

The old man quelled the babble of disbelief that arose immediately and told   43
me with that insincere, but courteous, agreement one extends to the fancies of the young, ignorant, and superstitious, "No doubt in your country the dead can also walk without being zombis." From the depths of his bag he produced a withered fragment of kola nut, bit off one end to show it wasn't poisoned, and handed me the rest as a peace offering.

"Anyhow," I resumed, "Hamlet's dead father said that his own brother, the   44
one who became chief, had poisoned him. He wanted Hamlet to avenge him. Hamlet believed this in his heart, for he did not like his father's brother." I took another swallow of beer. "In the country of the great chief, living in the same homestead, for it was a very large one, was an important elder who was often with the chief to advise and help him. His name was Polonius. Hamlet was courting his daughter, but her father and her brother . . . [I cast hastily about for some tribal analogy] warned her not to let Hamlet visit her when she was alone on her farm, for he would be a great chief and so could not marry her."

"Why not?" asked the wife, who had settled down on the edge of the old   45
man's chair. He frowned at her for asking stupid questions and growled, "They lived in the same homestead."

"That was not the reason," I informed them. "Polonius was a stranger who   46
lived in the homestead because he helped the chief, not because he was a relative."

"Then why couldn't Hamlet marry her?"   47

"He could have," I explained, "but Polonius didn't think he would. After   48
all, Hamlet was a man of great importance who ought to marry a chief's daughter, for in his country a man could have only one wife. Polonius was

afraid that if Hamlet made love to his daughter, then no one else would give a high price for her."

"That might be true," remarked one of the shrewder elders, "but a chief's son would give his mistress's father enough presents and patronage to more than make up the difference. Polonius sounds like a fool to me." 49

"Many people think he was," I agreed. "Meanwhile Polonius sent his son Laertes off to Paris to learn the things of that country, for it was the homestead of a very great chief indeed. Because he was afraid that Laertes might waste a lot of money on beer and women and gambling, or get into trouble by fighting, he sent one of his servants to Paris secretly, to spy out what Laertes was doing. One day Hamlet came upon Polonius's daughter Ophelia. He behaved so oddly he frightened her. Indeed"—I was fumbling for words to express the dubious quality of Hamlet's madness—"the chief and many others had also noticed that when Hamlet talked one could understand the words but not what they meant. Many people thought that he had become mad." My audience suddenly became much more attentive. "The great chief wanted to know what was wrong with Hamlet, so he sent for two of Hamlet's age mates [school friends would have taken long explanation] to talk to Hamlet and find out what troubled his heart. Hamlet, seeing that they had been bribed by the chief to betray him, told them nothing. Polonius, however, insisted that Hamlet was mad because he had been forbidden to see Ophelia, whom he loved." 50

"Why," inquired a bewildered voice, "should anyone bewitch Hamlet on that account?" 51

"Bewitch him?" 52

"Yes, only witchcraft can make anyone mad, unless, of course, one sees the beings that lurk in the forest." 53

I stopped being a storyteller, took out my notebook and demanded to be told more about these two causes of madness. Even while they spoke and I jotted notes, I tried to calculate the effect of this new factor on the plot. Hamlet had not been exposed to the beings that lurk in the forest. Only his relatives in the male line could bewitch him. Barring relatives not mentioned by Shakespeare, it had to be Claudius who was attempting to harm him. And, of course, it was. 54

For the moment I staved off questions by saying that the great chief also refused to believe that Hamlet was mad for the love of Ophelia and nothing else. "He was sure that something much more important was troubling Hamlet's heart." 55

"Now Hamlet's age mates," I continued, "had brought with them a famous storyteller. Hamlet decided to have this man tell the chief and all his homestead a story about a man who had poisoned his brother because he desired his brother's wife and wished to be chief himself. Hamlet was sure the great chief could not hear the story without making a sign if he was indeed guilty, and then he would discover whether his dead father had told him the truth." 56

The old man interrupted, with deep cunning, "Why should a father lie to his son?" he asked. 57

I hedged: "Hamlet wasn't sure that it really was his dead father." It was impossible to say anything, in that language, about devil-inspired visions. 58

"You mean," he said, "it actually was an omen, and he knew witches sometimes send false ones. Hamlet was a fool not to go to one skilled in reading omens and divining the truth in the first place. A man-who-sees-the-truth could have told him how his father died, if he really had been poisoned, and if there was witchcraft in it; then Hamlet could have called the elders to settle the matter." 59

The shrewd elder ventured to disagree. "Because his father's brother was a great chief, one-who-sees-the-truth might therefore have been afraid to tell it. I think it was for that reason that a friend of Hamlet's father—a witch and an elder—sent an omen so his friend's son would know. Was the omen true?" 60

"Yes," I said, abandoning ghosts and the devil; a witch-sent omen it would have to be. "It was true, for when the storyteller was telling his tale before all the homestead, the great chief rose in fear. Afraid that Hamlet knew his secret he planned to have him killed." 61

The stage set of the next bit presented some difficulties of translation. I began cautiously. "The great chief told Hamlet's mother to find out from her son what he knew. But because a woman's children are always first in her heart, he had the important elder Polonius hide behind a cloth that hung against the wall of Hamlet's mother's sleeping hut. Hamlet started to scold his mother for what she had done." 62

There was a shocked murmur from everyone. A man should never scold his mother. 63

"She called out in fear, and Polonius moved behind the cloth. Shouting, 'A rat!' Hamlet took his machete and slashed through the cloth." I paused for dramatic effect. "He had killed Polonius!" 64

The old men looked at each other in supreme disgust. "That Polonius truly was a fool and a man who knew nothing! What child would not know enough to shout, 'It's me!'" With a pang, I remembered that these people are ardent hunters, always armed with bow, arrow, and machete; at the first rustle in the grass an arrow is aimed and ready, and the hunter shouts "Game!" If no human voice answers immediately, the arrow speeds on its way. Like a good hunter Hamlet had shouted, "A rat!" 65

I rushed in to save Polonius's reputation. "Polonius did speak. Hamlet heard him. But he thought it was the chief and wished to kill him to avenge his father. He had meant to kill him earlier that evening. . . ." I broke down, unable to describe to these pagans, who had no belief in individual afterlife, the difference between dying at one's prayers and dying "unhousell'd, disappointed, unaneled." 66

This time I had shocked my audience seriously. "For a man to raise his hand 67

194

against his father's brother and the one who has become his father—that is a terrible thing. The elders ought to let such a man be bewitched."

I nibbled at my kola nut in some perplexity, then pointed out that after all the man had killed Hamlet's father. 68

"No," pronounced the old man, speaking less to me than to the young men sitting behind the elders. "If your father's brother has killed your father, you must appeal to your father's age mates; *they* may avenge him. No man may use violence against his senior relatives." Another thought struck him. "But if his father's brother had indeed been wicked enough to bewitch Hamlet and make him mad that would be a good story indeed, for it would be his fault that Hamlet, being mad, no longer had any sense and thus was ready to kill his father's brother." 69

There was a murmur of applause. *Hamlet* was again a good story to them, but it no longer seemed quite the same story to me. As I thought over the coming complications of plot and motive, I lost courage and decided to skim over dangerous ground quickly. 70

"The great chief," I went on, "was not sorry that Hamlet had killed Polonius. It gave him a reason to send Hamlet away, with his two treacherous age mates, with letters to a chief of a far country, saying that Hamlet should be killed. But Hamlet changed the writing on their papers, so that the chief killed his age mates insteads." I encountered a reproachful glare from one of the men whom I had told undetectable forgery was not merely immoral but beyond human skill. I looked the other way. 71

"Before Hamlet could return, Laertes came back for his father's funeral. The great chief told him Hamlet had killed Polonius. Laertes swore to kill Hamlet because of this, and because his sister Ophelia, hearing her father had been killed by the man she loved, went mad and drowned in the river." 72

"Have you already forgotten what we told you?" The old man was reproach- ful. "One cannot take vengeance on a madman; Hamlet killed Polonius in his madness. As for the girl, she not only went mad, she was drowned. Only witches can make people drown. Water itself can't hurt anything. It is merely something one drinks and bathes in." 73

I began to get cross. "If you don't like the story, I'll stop." 74

The old man made soothing noises and himself poured me some more beer. "You tell the story well, and we are listening. But it is clear that the elders of your country have never told you what the story really means. No, don't interrupt! We believe you when you say your marriage customs are different, or your clothes and weapons. But people are the same everywhere; therefore, there are always witches and it is we, the elders, who know how witches work. We told you it was the great chief who wished to kill Hamlet, and now your own words have proved us right. Who were Ophelia's male relatives?" 75

195

"There were only her father and her brother." Hamlet was clearly out of my hands. 76

"There must have been many more; this also you must ask of your elders 77
when you get back to your country. From what you tell us, since Polonius was
dead, it must have been Laertes who killed Ophelia, although I do not see the
reason for it."

We had emptied one pot of beer, and the old men argued the point with 78
slightly tipsy interest. Finally one of them demanded of me, "What did the
servant of Polonius say on his return?"

With difficulty I recollected Reynaldo and his mission. "I don't think he did 79
return before Polonius was killed."

"Listen," said the elder, "and I will tell you how it was and how your story 80
will go, then you may tell me if I am right. Polonius knew his son would get
into trouble, and so he did. He had many fines to pay for fighting, and debts
from gambling. But he had only two ways of getting money quickly. One was
to marry off his sister at once, but it is difficult to find a man who will marry
a woman desired by the son of a chief. For if the chief's heir commits adultery
with your wife, what can you do? Only a fool calls a case against a man who
will someday be his judge. Therefore Laertes had to take the second way: he
killed his sister by witchcraft, drowning her so he could secretly sell her body
to the witches."

I raised an objection. "They found her body and buried it. Indeed Laertes 81
jumped into the grave to see his sister once more—so, you see, the body was
truly there. Hamlet, who had just come back, jumped in after him."

"What did I tell you?" The elder appealed to the others. "Laertes was up to 82
no good with his sister's body. Hamlet prevented him, because the chief's heir,
like a chief, does not wish any other man to grow rich and powerful. Laertes
would be angry, because he would have killed his sister without benefit to
himself. In our country he would try to kill Hamlet for that reason. Is this not
what happened?"

"More or less," I admitted. "When the great chief found Hamlet was still 83
alive, he encouraged Laertes to try to kill Hamlet and arranged a fight with
machetes between them. In the fight both the young men were wounded to
death. Hamlet's mother drank the poisoned beer that the chief meant for Hamlet
in case he won the fight. When he saw his mother die of poison, Hamlet,
dying, managed to kill his father's brother with his machete."

"You see, I was right!" exclaimed the elder. 84

"That was a very good story," added the old man, "and you told it with very 85
few mistakes. There was just one more error, at the very end. The poison
Hamlet's mother drank was obviously meant for the survivor of the fight,
whichever it was. If Laertes had won, the great chief would have poisoned him,
for no one would know that he arranged Hamlet's death. Then, too, he need

not fear Laertes' witchcraft; it takes a strong heart to kill one's only sister by witchcraft.

"Sometime," concluded the old man, gathering his ragged toga about him, 86 "you must tell us some more stories of your country. We, who are elders, will instruct you in their true meaning, so that when you return to your own land your elders will see that you have not been sitting in the bush, but among those who know things and who have taught you wisdom."

QUESTIONS

1. How does this essay comment on the views expressed by Bohannan and her English friend in paragraphs 1 and 2?

2. What does this essay tell us about Tiv culture? What does it tell us about Bohannan? How would you describe the way she presents herself in this essay?

3. How do the Tivs' questions, objections, and reactions affect your reading of *Hamlet*?

4. Why do you think that this essay is considered a "classic" of anthropological writing? What could anthropologists learn from it?

5. Describe a situation in which you tried telling or explaining something to an audience different in culture, age, religion, and so forth, from you.

6. Give a plot summary of *Hamlet* as a contemporary soap opera.

MAKING CONNECTIONS

Compare Bohannan's method of reporting as an anthropologist with those of Mead, van Lawick-Goodall, and Miner. You might also consider whether to include Mowat in your comparison.

THE DEATH
OF THE MOTH
Virginia Woolf

Born in 1882, Virginia Woolf became one of England's major modern novelists before her death in 1941. She is also known as the author of important critical essays and such personal documents as letters, journals, and familiar essays. This selection combines the reporting of a naturalist with the reflecting of an essayist. Ironically, this selection was first published for a wide audience in the posthumous collection The Death of the Moth and Other Essays *(1942), seen into print by her husband, Leonard Woolf.*

Moths that fly by day are not properly to be called moths; they do not excite   1
that pleasant sense of dark autumn nights and ivy-blossom which the commonest yellow-underwing asleep in the shadow of the curtain never fails to rouse in us. They are hybrid creatures, neither gay like butterflies nor sombre like their own species. Nevertheless the present specimen, with his narrow hay-colored wings, fringed with a tassel of the same color, seemed to be content with life. It was a pleasant morning, mid-September, mild, benignant, yet with a keener breath than that of the summer months. The plough was already scoring the field opposite the window, and where the share had been, the earth was pressed flat and gleamed with moisture. Such vigor came rolling in from the fields and the down beyond that it was difficult to keep the eyes strictly turned upon the book. The rooks too were keeping one of their annual festivities;[1] soaring round the tree tops until it looked as if a vast net with thousands of black knots in it had been cast up into the air; which, after a few moments sank slowly down upon the trees until every twig seemed to have a knot at the end of it. Then, suddenly, the net would be thrown into the air again in a wider circle this time, with the utmost clamor and vociferation, as though to be thrown into the air and settle slowly down upon the tree tops were a tremendously exciting experience.

The same energy which inspired the rooks, the ploughmen, the horses, and   2
even, it seemed, the lean bare-backed downs, sent the moth fluttering from side to side of his square of the window-pane. One could not help watching him. One was, indeed, conscious of a queer feeling of pity for him. The possibilities of pleasure seemed that morning so enormous and various that to have only a moth's part in life, and a day moth's at that, appeared a hard fate,

---

[1] rooks: European birds, similar to American crows. [Eds.]

and his zest in enjoying his meagre opportunities to the full, pathetic. He flew vigorously to one corner of his compartment, and, after waiting there a second, flew across to the other. What remained for him but to fly to a third corner and then to a fourth? That was all he could do, in spite of the size of the downs, the width of the sky, the far-off smoke of houses, and the romantic voice, now and then, of a steamer out at sea. What he could do he did. Watching him, it seemed as if a fibre, very thin but pure, of the enormous energy of the world had been thrust into his frail and diminutive body. As often as he crossed the pane, I could fancy that a thread of vital light became visible. He was little or nothing but life.

Yet, because he was so small, and so simple a form of the energy that was rolling in at the open window and driving its way through so many narrow and intricate corridors in my own brain and in those of other human beings, there was something marvelous as well as pathetic about him. It was as if someone had taken a tiny bead of pure life and decking it as lightly as possible with down and feathers, had set it dancing and zigzagging to show us the true nature of life. Thus displayed one could not get over the strangeness of it. One is apt to forget all about life, seeing it humped and bossed and garnished and cumbered so that it has to move with the greatest circumspection and dignity. Again, the thought of all that life might have been had he been born in any other shape caused one to view his simple activities with a kind of pity.

After a time, tired by his dancing apparently, he settled on the window ledge in the sun, and, the queer spectacle being at an end, I forgot about him. Then, looking up, my eye was caught by him. He was trying to resume his dancing, but seemed either so stiff or so awkward that he could only flutter to the bottom of the window-pane; and when he tried to fly across it he failed. Being intent on other matters I watched these futile attempts for a time without thinking, unconsciously waiting for him to resume his flight, as one waits for a machine, that has stopped momentarily, to start again without considering the reason of its failure. After perhaps a seventh attempt he slipped from the wooden ledge and fell, fluttering his wings, onto his back on the window sill. The helplessness of his attitude roused me. It flashed upon me he was in difficulties; he could no longer raise himself; his legs struggled vainly. But, as I stretched out a pencil, meaning to help him to right himself, it came over me that the failure and awkwardness were the approach of death. I laid the pencil down again.

The legs agitated themselves once more. I looked as if for the enemy against which he struggled. I looked out of doors. What had happened there? Presumably it was midday, and work in the fields had stopped. Stillness and quiet had replaced the previous animation. The birds had taken themselves off to feed in the brooks. The horses stood still. Yet the power was there all the same, massed outside indifferent, impersonal, not attending to anything in particular. Somehow it was opposed to the little hay-colored moth. It was useless to try to do anything. One could only watch the extraordinary efforts made by those tiny legs against an oncoming doom which could, had it chosen, have submerged an entire city, not merely a city, but masses of human beings; nothing, I knew, had any chance against death. Nevertheless after a pause of exhaustion the legs fluttered again. It was superb this last protest, and so frantic that he succeeded at last in righting himself. One's sympathies, of course, were all on the side of life. Also, when there was nobody to care or to know, this gigantic effort on the part of an insignificant little moth, against a power of such magnitude, to retain what no one else valued or desired to keep, moved one strangely. Again, somehow, one saw life, a pure bead. I lifted the pencil again, useless though I knew it to be. But even as I did so, the unmistakable tokens of death showed themselves. The body relaxed, and instantly grew stiff. The struggle was over. The insignificant little creature now knew death. As I looked at the dead moth, this minute wayside triumph of so great a force over so mean an antagonist filled me with wonder. Just as life had been strange for a few minutes before, so death was now as strange. The moth having righted himself now lay most decently and uncomplainingly composed. O yes, he seemed to say, death is stronger than I am.

QUESTIONS

1. A moth is a creature so small and seemingly insignificant that most of us would not pay attention to its dying. Why does Woolf pay attention? How does she engage our attention?

2. What most impresses Woolf as she watches the moth?

3. Why does Woolf describe in paragraph 1 the scene beyond the window? How does this description connect with her purpose in writing this essay?

4. In this essay, Woolf reports the sequence of events in the death of the moth as well as her thoughts concerning its dying. Trace the way in which she has chosen to weave the two strands of reporting and commenting together throughout the essay. How else might she have arranged her material? Why do you think she has chosen to arrange it as she has?

5. If you have witnessed a hopeless but valiant struggle on a human, animal, or insect scale, write a report of your observations. Decide how you will make a reader aware of your thoughts about what you observed.

MAKING CONNECTIONS

Woolf's essay is one of those that might have as easily appeared in another section, for example, "Reflecting." Compare it to one or more of the pieces by Isak Dinesen, George Orwell, and Loren Eiseley in that section. Each of those pieces deals with the death or near death of an animal. Does any one of them seem a particularly good candidate for "Reporting?" If so, why?

A NEW KIND OF WAR
Ernest Hemingway

Ernest Hemingway (1899–1961) was born in Oak Park, Illinois. After serving as an ambulance driver in Italy in World War I, Hemingway became a writer and correspondent for the Toronto Star. *His early collection of short fiction,* In Our Time *(1925), shows clear evidence of his journalistic background and his war experience. The latter also informs his novel* A Farewell to Arms *(1929); another novel,* For Whom the Bell Tolls *(1940), is set during the Spanish Civil War (1936–1938). In that war, volunteers from other nations, including anarchists and communists, came to fight with the loyalists, the duly elected government of Spain, against the fascists, led by the rebel Francisco Franco and his generals, who were supported by Italian troops. Hemingway covered the war for the* North American Newspaper Alliance. *The following piece is a dispatch of April 14, 1937.*

Madrid.—The window of the hotel is open and, as you lie in bed, you hear 1
the firing in the front line seventeen blocks away. There is a rifle fire all night long. The rifles go tacrong, capong, craang, tacrong, and then a machine gun opens up. It has a bigger calibre and is much louder, rong, cararong, rong, rong. Then there is the incoming boom of a trench mortar shell and a burst of machine gun fire. You lie and listen to it and it is a great thing to be in bed with your feet stretched out gradually warming the cold foot of the bed and not out there in University City or Carabanchel. A man is singing hard-voiced in the street below and three drunks are arguing when you fall asleep.

In the morning, before your call comes from the desk, the roaring burst of 2
a high explosive shell wakes you and you go to the window and look out to see a man, his head down, his coat collar up, sprinting desperately across the paved square. There is the acrid smell of high explosive you hoped you'd never smell again, and, in a bathrobe and bedroom slippers, you hurry down the marble stairs and almost into a middle-aged woman, wounded in the abdomen, who is being helped into the hotel entrance by two men in blue workmen's smocks. She has her two hands crossed below her big, old-style Spanish bosom and from between her fingers the blood is spurting in a thin stream. On the corner, twenty yards away, is a heap of rubble, smashed cement and thrown up dirt, a single dead man, his torn clothes dusty, and a great hole in the sidewalk from

which the gas from a broken main is rising, looking like a heat mirage in the cold morning air.

"How many dead?" you ask a policeman. 3

"Only one," he says. "It went through the sidewalk and burst below. If it 4 would have burst on the solid stone of the road there might have been fifty."

A policeman covers the top of the trunk, from which the head is missing; 5 they send for someone to repair the gas main and you go in to breakfast. A charwoman, her eyes red, is scrubbing the blood off the marble floor of the corridor. The dead man wasn't you nor anyone you know and everyone is very hungry in the morning after a cold night and a long day the day before up at the Guadalajara front.

"Did you see him?" asked someone else at breakfast. 6

"Sure," you say. 7

"That's where we pass a dozen times a day. Right on that corner." Someone 8 makes a joke about missing teeth and someone else says not to make that joke. And everyone has the feeling that characterizes war. It wasn't me, see? It wasn't me.

The Italian dead up on the Guadalajara front weren't you, although Italian 9 dead, because of where you had spent your boyhood, always seemed, still, like our dead. No. You went to the front early in the morning in a miserable little car with a more miserable little chauffeur who suffered visibly the closer he came to the fighting. But at night, sometimes late, without lights, with the big trucks roaring past, you came on back to sleep in a bed with sheets in a good hotel, paying a dollar a day for the best rooms on the front. The smaller rooms in the back, on the side away from the shelling, were considerably more expensive. After the shell that lit on the sidewalk in front of the hotel you got a beautiful double corner room on that side, twice the size of the one you had had, for less than a dollar. It wasn't me they killed. See? No. Not me. It wasn't me anymore.

Then, in a hospital given by the American Friends of Spanish Democracy, 10 located out behind the Morata front along the road to Valencia, they said, "Raven wants to see you."

"Do I know him?" 11

"I don't think so," they said, "but he wants to see you." 12

"Where is he?" 13

"Upstairs." 14

In the room upstairs they are giving a blood transfusion to a man with a very 15 gray face who lay on a cot with his arm out, looking away from the gurgling bottle and moaning in a very impersonal way. He moaned mechanically and at regular intervals and it did not seem to be him that made the sound. His lips did not move.

"Where's Raven?" I asked. 16

"I'm here," said Raven. 17

The voice came from a high mound covered by a shoddy gray blanket. There   18
were two arms crossed on the top of the mound and at one end there was
something that had been a face, but now was a yellow scabby area with a wide
bandage across where the eyes had been.

"Who is it?" asked Raven. He didn't have lips, but he talked pretty well   19
without them and with a pleasant voice.

"Hemingway," I said. "I came up to see how you were doing."   20

"My face was pretty bad," he said. "It got sort of burned from the grenade,   21
but it's peeled a couple of times and it's doing better."

"It looks swell," I said. "It's doing fine."   22

I wasn't looking at it when I spoke.   23

"How are things in America?" he asked. "What do they think of us over   24
there?"

"Sentiment's changed a lot," I said. "They're beginning to realize the gov-   25
ernment is going to win this war."

"Do you think so?"   26

"Sure," I said.   27

"I'm awfully glad," he said. "You know, I wouldn't mind any of this if I   28
could just watch what was going on. I don't mind the pain, you know. It never
seemed important really. But I was always awfully interested in things and I
really wouldn't mind the pain at all if I could just sort of follow things intelli-
gently. I could even be some use. You know, I didn't mind the war at all. I did
all right in the war. I got hit once before and I was back and rejoined the
battalion in two weeks. I couldn't stand to be away. Then I got this."

He had put his hand in mine. It was not a worker's hand. There were no   29
callouses and the nails on the long, spatulate fingers were smooth and rounded.

"How did you get it?" I asked.   30

"Well, there were some troops that were routed and we went over to sort of   31
reform them and we did and then we had quite a fight with the fascists and we
beat them. It was quite a bad fight, you know, but we beat them and then
someone threw this grenade at me."

Holding his hand and hearing him tell it, I did not believe a word of it.   32
What was left of him did not sound like the wreckage of a soldier somehow. I
did not know how he had been wounded, but the story did not sound right. It
was the sort of way everyone would like to have been wounded. But I wanted
him to think I believed it.

"Where did you come from?" I asked.   33

"From Pittsburgh. I went to the University there."   34

"What did you do before you joined up here?"   35

"I was a social worker," he said. Then I knew it couldn't be true and I   36
wondered how he had really been so frightfully wounded and I didn't care. In
the war that I had known, men often lied about the manner of their wounding.
Not at first, but later. I'd lied a little myself in my time. Especially late in the

evening. But I was glad he thought I believed it, and we talked about books, he wanted to be a writer, and I told him about what happened north of Guadalajara and promised to bring some things from Madrid next time we got out that way. I hoped maybe I could get a radio.

"They tell me Dos Passos and Sinclair Lewis[1] are coming over, too," he said. 37

"Yes," I said. "And when they come I'll bring them up to see you." 38

"Gee, that will be great," he said. "You don't know what that will mean to 39 me."

"I'll bring them," I said. 40

"Will they be here pretty soon?" 41

"Just as soon as they come I'll bring them." 42

"Good boy, Ernest," he said. "You don't mind if I call you Ernest, do you?" 43

The voice came very clear and gentle from that face that looked like some 44 hill that had been fought over in muddy weather and then baked in the sun.

"Hell, no," I said. "Please. Listen, old-timer, you're going to be fine. You'll 45 be a lot of good, you know. You can talk on the radio."

"Maybe," he said. "You'll be back?" 46

"Sure," I said. "Absolutely." 47

"Goodbye, Ernest," he said. 48

"Goodbye," I told him. 49

Downstairs they told me he'd lost both eyes as well as his face and was also 50 badly wounded all through the legs and in the feet.

"He's lost some toes, too," the doctor said, "but he doesn't know that." 51

"I wonder if he'll ever know it." 52

"Oh, sure he will," the doctor said. "He's going to get well." 53

And it still isn't you that gets hit but it is your countryman now. Your 54 countryman from Pennsylvania, where once we fought at Gettysburg.

Then, walking along the road, with his left arm in an airplane splint, walking 55 with the gamecock walk of the professional British soldier that neither ten years of militant party work nor the projecting metal wings of the splint could destroy, I met Raven's commanding officer, Jock Cunningham, who had three fresh rifle wounds through his upper left arm (I looked at them, one was septic) and another rifle bullet under his shoulder blade that had entered his left chest, passed through, and lodged there. He told me, in military terms, the history of the attempt to rally retiring troops on his battalion's right flank, of his bombing raid down a trench which was held at one end by the fascists and at the other end by the government troops, of the taking of this trench and, with six men and a Lewis gun, cutting off a group of some eighty fascists from their own lines, and of the final desperate defense of their impossible position his six men put up until the government troops came up and, attacking, straightened out the line again. He told it clearly, completely convincingly, and with a strong

---

[1]John Dos Passos (1896–1970) and Sinclair Lewis (1885–1951): American writers. [Eds.]

Glasgow accent. He had deep, piercing eyes sheltered like an eagle's, and, hearing him talk, you could tell the sort of soldier he was. For what he had done he would have had a V.C.[2] in the last war. In this war there are no decorations. Wounds are the only decorations and they do not award wound stripes.

"Raven was in the same show," he said. "I didn't know he'd been hit. Ay, 56 he's a good mon. He got his after I got mine. The fascists we'd cut off were very good troops. They never fired a useless shot when we were in that bad spot. They waited in the dark there until they had us located and then opened with volley fire. That's how I got four in the same place."

We talked for a while and he told me many things. They were all important, 57 but nothing was as important as what Jay Raven, the social worker from Pittsburgh with no military training, had told me was true. This is a strange new kind of war where you learn just as much as you are able to believe.

QUESTIONS

1. Hemingway's use of the second person tends to draw the reader into the text. What other effects does he use to place "you" there?

2. Hemingway's own responses to events are very much a part of this dispatch. Are there any sections of relatively objective reporting present? Can dialogue be considered objective reporting?

3. Why is so much space allotted to Hemingway's meeting with Raven? What does Raven represent?

4. Hemingway is comparing the Spanish Civil War with his experience in World War I. What is "new" about this war?

5. How does Hemingway want his readers to perceive him?

6. Using Hemingway's approach to draw readers into a situation (the second person, present tense, sensual information), report on your most recent battle: a subway commute, a department store sale, registration for classes, for example.

MAKING CONNECTIONS

Compare Hemingway's essay to Virginia Woolf's or Richard Selzer's in this section. Make your comparison in terms of the points of view of the writers. How important is each writer's point of view to the essential purpose of his or her writing? How do these points of view differ?

---

[2]V.C.: the Victoria Cross, Great Britain's highest military decoration, is awarded for exceptional valor. [Eds.]

HATSUYO NAKAMURA
John Hersey

John Hersey was born in 1914 in Tientsin, China, where his father was a YMCA secretary and his mother a missionary. After graduating from Yale in 1936, Hersey was a war correspondent in China and Japan. When the United States entered World War II, Hersey covered the war in the South Pacific, the Mediterranean, and Moscow. In 1945, he won the Pulitzer Prize for his novel, A Bell for Adano. In 1946, Hiroshima, a report about the effects of the atomic bomb on the lives of six people, was widely acclaimed. Almost forty years later, Hersey went back to Japan to find those six people to see what their lives had been like. Their stories form the final chapter of the 1985 edition of Hiroshima. The selection presented here first appeared in the New Yorker, as did the first edition of Hiroshima. A prolific writer of fiction and nonfiction, Hersey believes that "journalism allows its readers to witness history; fiction gives its readers an opportunity to live it."

In August, 1946, a year after the bombing of Hiroshima, Hatsuyo Nakamura 1
was weak and destitute. Her husband, a tailor, had been taken into the Army and had been killed at Singapore on the day of the city's capture, February 15, 1942. She lost her mother, a brother, and a sister to the atomic bomb. Her son and two daughters—ten, eight, and five years old—were buried in rubble when the blast of the bomb flung her house down. In a frenzy, she dug them out alive. A month after the bombing, she came down with radiation sickness; she lost most of her hair and lay in bed for weeks with a high fever in the house of her sister-in-law in the suburb of Kabe, worrying all the time about how to support her children. She was too poor to go to a doctor. Gradually, the worst of the symptoms abated, but she remained feeble; the slightest exertion wore her out.

She was near the end of her resources. Fleeing from her house through the 2
fires on the day of the bombing, she had saved nothing but a rucksack of emergency clothing, a blanket, an umbrella, and a suitcase of things she had stored in her air-raid shelter; she had much earlier evacuated a few kimonos to Kabe in fear of a bombing. Around the time her hair started to grow in again,

her brother-in-law went back to the ruins of her house and recovered her late husband's Sankoku sewing machine, which needed repairs. And though she had lost the certificates of a few bonds and other meagre wartime savings, she had luckily copied off their numbers before the bombing and taken the record to Kabe, so she was eventually able to cash them in. This money enabled her to rent for fifty yen a month—the equivalent then of less than fifteen cents—a small wooden shack built by a carpenter in the Nobori-cho neighborhood, near the site of her former home. In this way, she could free herself from the charity of her in-laws and begin a courageous struggle, which would last for many years, to keep her children and herself alive.

The hut had a dirt floor and was dark inside, but it was a home of sorts. 3 Raking back some rubble next to it, she planted a garden. From the debris of collapsed houses she scavenged cooking utensils and a few dishes. She had the Sankoku fixed and began to take in some sewing, and from time to time she did cleaning and laundry and washed dishes for neighbors who were somewhat better off than she was. But she got so tired that she had to take two days' rest for every three days she worked, and if she was obliged for some reason to work for a whole week she then had to rest for three or four days. She soon ran through her savings and was forced to sell her best kimono.

At that precarious time, she fell ill. Her belly began to swell up, and she 4 had diarrhea and so much pain she could no longer work at all. A doctor who lived nearby came to see her and told her she had roundworm, and he said, incorrectly, "If it bites your intestine, you'll die." In those days, there was a shortage of chemical fertilizers in Japan, so farmers were using night soil, and as a consequence many people began to harbor parasites, which were not fatal in themselves but were seriously debilitating to those who had had radiation sickness. The doctor treated Nakamura-san (as he would have addressed her) with santonin, a somewhat dangerous medicine derived from certain varieties of artemisia.[1] To pay the doctor, she was forced to sell her last valuable possession, her husband's sewing machine. She came to think of that as marking the lowest and saddest moment of her whole life.

In referring to those who went through the Hiroshima and Nagasaki bomb- 5 ings, the Japanese tended to shy away from the term "survivors," because in its focus on being alive it might suggest some slight to the sacred dead. The class of people to which Nakamura-san belonged came, therefore, to be called by a more neutral name, "hibakusha"—literally, "explosion-affected persons." For more than a decade after the bombings, the hibakusha lived in an economic limbo, apparently because the Japanese government did not want to find itself saddled with anything like moral responsibility for heinous acts of the victorious United

---

[1] artemisia: a genus of herbs and shrubs, including sagebrush and wormwood, distinguished by strong-smelling foliage. [Eds.]

States. Although it soon became clear that many hibakusha suffered consequences of their exposure to the bombs which were quite different in nature
and degree from those of survivors even of the ghastly fire bombings in Tokyo
and elsewhere, the government made no special provision for their relief—until,
ironically, after the storm of rage that swept across Japan when the twenty-three
crewmen of a fishing vessel, the Lucky Dragon No. 5, and its cargo of tuna
were irradiated by the American test of a hydrogen bomb at Bikini in 1954.
It took three years even then for a relief law for the hibakusha to pass the Diet.

Though Nakamura-san could not know it, she thus had a bleak period ahead 6
of her. In Hiroshima, the early postwar years were, besides, a time, especially
painful for poor people like her, of disorder, hunger, greed, thievery, black
markets. Non-hibakusha employers developed a prejudice against the survivors
as word got around that they were prone to all sorts of ailments, and that even
those like Nakamura-san, who were not cruelly maimed and had not developed
any serious overt symptoms, were unreliable workers, since most of them seemed
to suffer, as she did, from the mysterious but real malaise that came to be
known as one kind of lasting "A-bomb sickness": a nagging weakness and
weariness, dizziness now and then, digestive troubles, all aggravated by a feeling
of oppression, a sense of doom, for it was said that unspeakable diseases might
at any time plant nasty flowers in their bodies, and even in those of their
descendants.

As Nakamura-san struggled to get from day to day, she had no time for 7
attitudinizing about the bomb or anything else. She was sustained, curiously,
by a kind of passivity, summed up in a phrase she herself sometimes used—
"Shikata ga-nai," meaning, loosely, "It can't be helped." She was not religious,
but she lived in a culture long colored by the Buddhist belief that resignation
might lead to clear vision; she had shared with other citizens a deep feeling of
powerlessness in the face of a state authority that had been divinely strong ever
since the Meiji Restoration, in 1868; and the hell she had witnessed and the
terrible aftermath unfolding around her reached so far beyond human understanding that it was impossible to think of them as the work of resentable human
beings, such as the pilot of the Enola Gay, or President Truman, or the scientists
who had made the bomb[2]—or even, nearer at hand, the Japanese militarists
who had helped to bring on the war. The bombing almost seemed a natural
disaster—one that it had simply been her bad luck, her fate (which must be
accepted), to suffer.

When she had been wormed and felt slightly better, she made an arrangement 8
to deliver bread for a baker named Takahashi, whose bakery was in Nobori-
cho. On days when she had the strength to do it, she would take orders for

---

[2]Enola Gay; name of the airplane that dropped the atomic bomb on Hiroshima; Harry S
Truman (1884–1972): president of the United States who made the decision to drop the bomb.
[Eds.]

bread from retail shops in her neighborhood, and the next morning she would pick up the requisite number of loaves and carry them in baskets and boxes through the streets to the stores. It was exhausting work, for which she earned the equivalent of about fifty cents a day. She had to take frequent rest days.

After some time, when she was feeling a bit stronger, she took up another   9 kind of peddling. She would get up in the dark and trundle a borrowed two-wheeled pushcart for two hours across the city to a section called Eba, at the mouth of one of the seven estuarial rivers that branch from the Ota River through Hiroshima. There, at daylight, fishermen would cast their leaded skirt-like nets for sardines, and she would help them to gather up the catch when they hauled it in. Then she would push the cart back to Nobori-cho and sell the fish for them from door to door. She earned just enough for food.

A couple of years later, she found work that was better suited to her need   10 for occasional rest, because within certain limits she could do it on her own time. This was a job of collecting money for deliveries of the Hiroshima paper, the *Chugoku Shimbun*, which most people in the city read. She had to cover a big territory, and often her clients were not at home or pleaded that they couldn't pay just then, so she would have to go back again and again. She earned the equivalent of about twenty dollars a month at this job. Every day, her will power and her weariness seemed to fight to an uneasy draw.

In 1951, after years of this drudgery, it was Nakamura-san's good luck, her   11 fate (which must be accepted), to become eligible to move into a better house. Two years earlier, a Quaker professor of dendrology from the University of Washington named Floyd W. Schmoe, driven, apparently, by deep urges for expiation and reconciliation, had come to Hiroshima, assembled a team of carpenters, and, with his own hands and theirs, begun building a series of Japanese-style houses for victims of the bomb; in all, his team eventually built twenty-one. It was to one of these houses that Nakamura-san had the good fortune to be assigned. The Japanese measure their houses by multiples of the area of the floor-covering *tsubo* mat, a little less than four square yards, and the Dr. Shum-o houses, as the Hiroshimans called them, had two rooms of six mats each. This was a big step up for the Nakamuras. This home was redolent of new wood and clean matting. The rent, payable to the city government, was the equivalent of about a dollar a month.

Despite the family's poverty, the children seemed to be growing normally.   12 Yaeko and Myeko, the two daughters, were anemic, but all three had so far escaped any of the more serious complications that so many young hibakusha were suffering. Yaeko, now fourteen, and Myeko, eleven, were in middle school. The boy, Toshio, ready to enter high school, was going to have to earn money to attend it, so he took up delivering papers to the places from which his mother was collecting. These were some distance from their Dr. Shum-o house, and they had to commute at odd hours by streetcar.

The old hut in Nobori-cho stood empty for a time, and, while continuing 13
with her newspaper collections, Nakamura-san converted it into a small street
shop for children, selling sweet potatoes, which she roasted, and *dagashi*, or
little candies and rice cakes, and cheap toys, which she bought from a whole-
saler.

All along, she had been collecting for papers from a small company, Suyama 14
Chemical, that made mothballs sold under the trade name Paragen. A friend
of hers worked there, and one day she suggested to Nakamura-san that she join
the company, helping wrap the product in its packages. The owner, Nakamura-
san learned, was a compassionate man, who did not share the bias of many
employers against hibakusha; he had several on his staff of twenty women
wrappers. Nakamura-san objected that she couldn't work more than a few days
at a time; the friend persuaded her that Suyama would understand that.

So she began. Dressed in company uniforms, the women stood, somewhat 15
bent over, on either side of a couple of conveyor belts, working as fast as possible
to wrap two kinds of Paragen in cellophane. Paragen had a dizzying odor, and
at first it made one's eyes smart. Its substance, powdered paradichlorobenzene,
had been compressed into lozenge-shaped mothballs and into larger spheres,
the size of small oranges, to be hung in Japanese-style toilets, where their rank
pseudomedicinal smell would offset the unpleasantness of non-flushing facilities.

Nakamura-san was paid, as a beginner, a hundred and seventy yen—then 16
less than fifty cents—a day. At first, the work was confusing, terribly tiring, and
a bit sickening. Her boss worried about her paleness. She had to take many
days off. But little by little she became used to the factory. She made friends.
There was a family atmosphere. She got raises. In the two ten-minute breaks,
morning and afternoon, when the moving belt stopped, there was a birdsong
of gossip and laughter, in which she joined. It appeared that all along there had
been, deep in her temperament, a core of cheerfulness, which must have fuelled
her long fight against A-bomb lassitude, something warmer and more vivifying
than mere submission, than saying "*Shikata ga-nai.*" The other women took
to her; she was constantly doing them small favors. They began calling her,
affectionately, *Oba-san*—roughly, "Auntie."

She worked at Suyama for thirteen years. Though her energy still paid its 17
dues, from time to time, to the A-bomb syndrome, the searing experiences of
that day in 1945 seemed gradually to be receding from the front of her mind.

The Lucky Dragon No. 5 episode took place the year after Nakamura-san 18
started working for Suyama Chemical. In the ensuing fever of outrage in the
country, the provision of adequate medical care for the victims of the Hiroshima
and Nagasaki bombs finally became a political issue. Almost every year since
1946, on the anniversary of the Hiroshima bombing, a Peace Memorial Meeting
had been held in a park that the city planners had set aside, during the city's

rebuilding, as a center of remembrance, and on August 6, 1955, delegates from all over the world gathered there for the first World Conference Against Atomic and Hydrogen Bombs. On its second day, a number of hibakusha tearfully testified to the government's neglect of their plight. Japanese political parties took up the cause, and in 1957 the Diet at last passed the A-Bomb Victims Medical Care Law. This law and its subsequent modifications defined four classes of people who would be eligible for support: those who had been in the city limits on the day of the bombing; those who had entered an area within two kilometers of the hypocenter in the first fourteen days after it; those who had come into physical contact with bomb victims, in administering first aid or in disposing of their bodies; and those who had been embryos in the wombs of women in any of the first three categories. These hibakusha were entitled to receive so-called health books, which would entitle them to free medical treatment. Later revisions of the law provided for monthly allowances to victims suffering from various aftereffects.

Like a great many hibakusha, Nakamura-san had kept away from all the agitation, and, in fact, also like many other survivors, she did not even bother to get a health book for a couple of years after they were issued. She had been too poor to keep going to doctors, so she had got into the habit of coping alone, as best she could, with her physical difficulties. Besides, she shared with some other survivors a suspicion of ulterior motives on the part of the political-minded people who took part in the annual ceremonies and conferences. 19

Nakamura-san's son, Toshio, right after his graduation from high school, went to work for the bus division of the Japanese National Railways. He was in the administrative offices, working first on timetables, later in accounting. When he was in his midtwenties, a marriage was arranged for him, through a relative who knew the bride's family. He built an addition to the Dr. Shum-o house, moved in, and began to contribute to his mother's support. He made her a present of a new sewing machine. 20

Yaeko, the older daughter, left Hiroshima when she was fifteen, right after graduating from middle school, to help an ailing aunt who ran a *ryo-kan*, a Japanese-style inn. There, in due course, she fell in love with a man who ate at the inn's restaurant, and she made a love marriage. 21

After graduating from high school, Myeko, the most susceptible of the three children to the A-bomb syndrome, eventually became an expert typist and took up instructing at typing schools. In time, a marriage was arranged for her. 22

Like their mother, all three children avoided pro-hibakusha and antinuclear agitation. 23

In 1966, Nakamura-san, having reached the age of fifty-five, retired from Suyama Chemical. At the end, she was being paid thirty thousand yen, or about eighty-five dollars, a month. Her children were no longer dependent on her, and Toshio was ready to take on a son's responsibility for his aging mother. 24

She felt at home in her body now; she rested when she needed to, and she had no worries about the cost of medical care, for she had finally picked up Health Book No. 1023993. It was time for her to enjoy life. For her pleasure in being able to give gifts, she took up embroidery and the dressing of traditional *kimekomi* dolls, which are supposed to bring good luck. Wearing a bright kimono, she went once a week to dance at the Study Group of Japanese Folk Music. In set movements, with expressive gestures, her hands now and then tucking up the long folds of the kimono sleeves, and with head held high, she danced, moving as if floating, with thirty agreeable women to a song of celebration of entrance into a house:

> May your family flourish
> For a thousand generations,
> For eight thousand generations.

A year or so after Nakamura-san retired, she was invited by an organization called the Bereaved Families' Association to take a train trip with about a hundred other war widows to visit the Yasukuni Shrine, in Tokyo. This holy place, established in 1869, was dedicated to the spirits of all the Japanese who had died in wars against foreign powers, and could be thought roughly analogous, in terms of its symbolism for the nation, to the Arlington National Cemetery—with the difference that souls, not bodies, were hallowed there. The shrine was considered by many Japanese to be a focus of a still smoldering Japanese militarism, but Nakamura-san, who had never seen her husband's ashes and had held on to a belief that he would return to her someday, was oblivious of all that. She found the visit baffling. Besides the Hiroshima hundred, there were huge crowds of women from other cities on the shrine grounds. It was impossible for her to summon up a sense of her dead husband's presence, and she returned home in an uneasy state of mind.

Japan was booming. Things were still rather tight for the Nakamuras, and Toshio had to work very long hours, but the old days of bitter struggle began to seem remote. In 1975, one of the laws providing support to the hibakusha was revised, and Nakamura-san began to receive a so-called health-protection allowance of six thousand yen, then about twenty dollars, a month; this would gradually be increased to more than twice that amount. She also received a pension, toward which she had contributed at Suyama, of twenty thousand yen, or about sixty-five dollars, a month; and for several years she had been receiving a war widow's pension of another twenty thousand yen a month. With the economic upswing, prices had, of course, risen steeply (in a few years Tokyo would become the most expensive city in the world), but Toshio managed to buy a small Mitsubishi car, and occasionally he got up before dawn and rode a train for two hours to play golf with business associates. Yaeko's husband ran

212

a shop for sales and service of air-conditioners and heaters, and Myeko's husband ran a newsstand and candy shop near the railroad station.

In May each year, around the time of the Emperor's birthday, when the 27 trees along broad Peace Boulevard were at their feathery best and banked azaleas were everywhere in bloom, Hiroshima celebrated a flower festival. Entertainment booths lined the boulevard, and there were long parades, with floats and bands and thousands of marchers. This year, Nakamura-san danced with the women of the folk-dance association, six dancers in each of sixty rows. They danced to "Oiwai-Ondo," a song of happiness, lifting their arms in gestures of joy and clapping in rhythms of threes:

> Green pine trees, cranes and turtles . . .
> You must tell a story of your hard times
> And laugh twice.

The bombing had been four decades ago. How far away it seemed! 28

The sun blazed that day. The measured steps and the constant lifting of the 29 arms for hours at a time were tiring. In midafternoon, Nakamura-san suddenly felt woozy. The next thing she knew, she was being lifted, to her great embarrassment and in spite of begging to be let alone, into an ambulance. At the hospital, she said she was fine; all she wanted was to go home. She was allowed to leave.

QUESTIONS

1. What does Hatsuyo Nakamura's story tell us about the larger group of atomic-bomb survivors?

2. Why do you think Hersey chose Hatsuyo Nakamura as a subject to report on? How is she presented to us? How are we meant to feel about her?

3. In composing his article, Hersey presumably interviewed Nakamura and reports from her point of view. At what points does he augment her story? For example, look at paragraph 5. What material probably comes from Nakamura? What material probably comes from other sources?

4. How has Hersey arranged his material? He has covered forty years of Hatsuyo Nakamura's life in twenty-nine paragraphs. Make a list of the events he chose to report. At what points does he condense large blocks of time?

5. Interview a relative or someone you know who participated in World War II or in some other war, such as Vietnam. How did the war change the person's life? What events does the person consider most important in the intervening years?

6. No doubt every person then in Hiroshima remembers the day of the bombing just as Americans of certain ages remember days of critical national events—the attack on Pearl Harbor, the Kennedy or King assassinations, the space shuttle disaster, and so on. Interview several people about one such day, finding out where they were when they first learned of the event, how they reacted, what long-term impact they felt, and how they view that day now. Use the information from your interviews to write a report.

MAKING CONNECTIONS

1. Imagine an encounter between Hatsuyo Nakamura and either Zoë Tracy Hardy ("What Did You Do in the War, Grandma?") or William L. Laurence ("Atomic Bombing of Nagasaki Told by Flight Member"). What could those persons say to each other? Write the dialogue for a possible conversation between them.

2. One characteristic of reports is to be tentative or even oblique in drawing conclusions. Compare Hersey's report to one by Hemingway, Selby, or Selzer, all presented in this section, and assess their differing methods of coming to a conclusion. What would you say the points are of the two reports you chose to compare?

Social Sciences and Public Affairs

ATOMIC BOMBING OF NAGASAKI TOLD BY FLIGHT MEMBER

William L. Laurence

William L. Laurence was born in Lithuania and came to the United States in 1905. He studied at Harvard and the Boston University Law School. His main interest, however, had always been in science, and after working at the New York World *for five years, Laurence went to the* New York Times *as a science reporter. During World War II, Laurence was the only reporter to know about the top-secret testing of the atomic bomb. On August 9, 1945, he was permitted to fly with the mission to drop the second atomic bomb on Nagasaki. Three days earlier, over one hundred thousand people had been killed in the Hiroshima bombing. Laurence won the Pulitzer Prize for this account of the bombing of Nagasaki. The article appeared in the* New York Times, *September 9, 1945.*

With the atomic-bomb mission to Japan, August 9 (Delayed)—We are on 1
our way to bomb the mainland of Japan. Our flying contingent consists of three specially designed B-29 Superforts, and two of these carry no bombs. But our lead plane is on its way with another atomic bomb, the second in three days, concentrating in its active substance an explosive energy equivalent to twenty thousand and, under favorable conditions, forty thousand tons of TNT.

We have several chosen targets. One of these is the great industrial and 2 shipping center of Nagasaki, on the western shore of Kyushu, one of the main islands of the Japanese homeland.

I watched the assembly of this man-made meteor during the past two days 3 and was among the small group of scientists and Army and Navy representatives privileged to be present at the ritual of its loading in the Superfort last night, against a background of threatening black skies torn open at intervals by great lightning flashes.

It is a thing of beauty to behold, this "gadget." Into its design went millions 4 of man-hours of what is without doubt the most concentrated intellectual effort in history. Never before had so much brain power been focused on a single problem.

This atomic bomb is different from the bomb used three days ago with such 5 devastating results on Hiroshima.

I saw the atomic substance before it was placed inside the bomb. By itself it 6 is not at all dangerous to handle. It is only under certain conditions, produced in the bomb assembly, that it can be made to yield up its energy, and even then it gives only a small fraction of its total contents—a fraction, however, large enough to produce the greatest explosion on earth.

The briefing at midnight revealed the extreme care and the tremendous 7 amount of preparation that had been made to take care of every detail of the mission, to make certain that the atomic bomb fully served the purpose for which it was intended. Each target in turn was shown in detailed maps and in aerial photographs. Every detail of the course was rehearsed—navigation, altitude, weather, where to land in emergencies. It came out that the Navy had rescue craft, known as Dumbos and Superdumbos, stationed at various strategic points in the vicinity of the targets, ready to rescue the fliers in case they were forced to bail out.

The briefing period ended with a moving prayer by the chaplain. We then 8 proceeded to the mess hall for the traditional early-morning breakfast before departure on a bombing mission.

A convoy of trucks took us to the supply building for the special equipment 9 carried on combat missions. This included the Mae West,[1] a parachute, a lifeboat, an oxygen mask, a flak suit, and a survival vest. We still had a few hours before take-off time, but we all went to the flying field and stood around in little groups or sat in jeeps talking rather casually about our mission to the Empire, as the Japanese home islands are known hereabouts.

In command of our mission is Major Charles W. Sweeney, twenty-five, of 10 124 Hamilton Avenue, North Quincy, Massachusetts. His flagship, carrying the atomic bomb, is named *The Great Artiste*, but the name does not appear

---

[1] Mae West: an inflatable life jacket named for the actor. [Eds.]

on the body of the great silver ship, with its unusually long, four-bladed, orange-tipped propellers. Instead, it carries the number 77, and someone remarks that it was "Red" Grange's winning number on the gridiron.

We took off at 3:50 this morning and headed northwest on a straight line for the Empire. The night was cloudy and threatening, with only a few stars here and there breaking through the overcast. The weather report had predicted storms ahead part of the way but clear sailing for the final and climactic stages of our odyssey.   11

We were about an hour away from our base when the storm broke. Our great ship took some heavy dips through the abysmal darkness around us, but it took these dips much more gracefully than a large commercial air liner, producing a sensation more in the nature of a glide than a "bump," like a great ocean liner riding the waves except that in this case the air waves were much higher and the rhythmic tempo of the glide was much faster.   12

I noticed a strange eerie light coming through the window high above the navigator's cabin, and as I peered through the dark all around us I saw a startling phenomenon. The whirling giant propellers had somehow become great luminous disks of blue flame. The same luminous blue flame appeared on the plexiglas windows in the nose of the ship, and on the tips of the giant wings. It looked as though we were riding the whirlwind through space on a chariot of blue fire.   13

It was, I surmised, a surcharge of static electricity that had accumulated on the tips of the propellers and on the di-electric material of the plastic windows. One's thoughts dwelt anxiously on the precious cargo in the invisible ship ahead of us. Was there any likelihood of danger that this heavy electric tension in the atmosphere all about us might set it off?   14

I expressed my fears to Captain Bock, who seems nonchalant and unperturbed at the controls. He quickly reassured me.   15

"It is a familiar phenomenon seen often on ships. I have seen it many times on bombing missions. It is known as St. Elmo's fire."   16

On we went through the night. We soon rode out the storm and our ship was once again sailing on a smooth course straight ahead, on a direct line to the Empire.   17

Our altimeter showed that we were traveling through space at a height of seventeen thousand feet. The thermometer registered an outside temperature of thirty-three degrees below zero Centigrade, about thirty below Fahrenheit. Inside our pressurized cabin the temperature was that of a comfortable air-conditioned room and a pressure corresponding to an altitude of eight thousand feet. Captain Bock cautioned me, however, to keep my oxygen mask handy in case of emergency. This, he explained, might mean either something going wrong with the pressure equipment inside the ship or a hole through the cabin by flak.   18

The first signs of dawn came shortly after five o'clock. Sergeant Curry, of   19
Hoopeston, Illinois, who had been listening steadily on his earphones for radio
reports, while maintaining a strict radio silence himself, greeted it by rising to
his feet and gazing out the window.

"It's good to see the day," he told me. "I get a feeling of claustrophobia   20
hemmed in this cabin at night."

He is a typical American youth, looking even younger than his twenty years.   21
It takes no mind reader to read his thoughts.

"It's a long way from Hoopeston," I find myself remarking.   22

"Yep," he replies, as he busies himself decoding a message from outer   23
space.

"Think this atomic bomb will end the war?" he asks hopefully.   24

"There is a very good chance that this one may do the trick," I assured him,   25
"but if not, then the next one or two surely will. Its power is such that no
nation can stand up against it very long." This was not my own view. I had
heard it expressed all around a few hours earlier, before we took off. To anyone
who had seen this manmade fireball in action, as I had less than a month ago
in the desert of New Mexico, this view did not sound overoptimistic.

By 5:50 it was really light outside. We had lost our lead ship, but Lieutenant   26
Godfrey, our navigator, informs me that we had arranged for that contingency.
We have an assembly point in the sky above the little island of Yakushima,
southeast of Kyushu, at 9:10. We are to circle there and wait for the rest of our
formation.

Our genial bombardier, Lieutenant Levy, comes over to invite me to take   27
his front-row seat in the transparent nose of the ship, and I accept eagerly.
From that vantage point in space, seventeen thousand feet above the Pacific,
one gets a view of hundreds of miles on all sides, horizontally and vertically.
At that height the vast ocean below and the sky above seem to merge into one
great sphere.

I was on the inside of that firmament, riding above the giant mountains of   28
white cumulus clouds, letting myself be suspended in infinite space. One hears
the whirl of the motors behind one, but it soon becomes insignificant against
the immensity all around and is before long swallowed by it. There comes a
point where space also swallows time and one lives through eternal moments
filled with an oppressive loneliness, as though all life had suddenly vanished
from the earth and you are the only one left, a lone survivor traveling endlessly
through interplanetary space.

My mind soon returns to the mission I am on. Somewhere beyond these   29
vast mountains of white clouds ahead of me there lies Japan, the land of our
enemy. In about four hours from now one of its cities, making weapons of war
for use against us, will be wiped off the map by the greatest weapon ever made
by man: In one tenth of a millionth of a second, a fraction of time immeasurable

by any clock, a whirlwind from the skies will pulverize thousands of its buildings and tens of thousands of its inhabitants.

But at this moment no one yet knows which one of the several cities chosen 30 as targets is to be annihilated. The final choice lies with destiny. The winds over Japan will make the decision. If they carry heavy clouds over our primary target, the city will be saved, at least for the time being. None of its inhabitants will ever know that the wind of a benevolent destiny had passed over their heads. But that same wind will doom another city.

Our weather planes ahead of us are on their way to find out where the wind 31 blows. Half an hour before target time we will know what the winds have decided.

Does one feel any pity or compassion for the poor devils about to die? Not 32 when one thinks of Pearl Harbor and of the Death March on Bataan. [2]

Captain Bock informs me that we are about to start our climb to bombing 33 altitude.

He manipulates a few knobs on his control panel to the right of him, and I 34 alternately watch the white clouds and ocean below me and the altimeter on the bombardier's panel. We reached our altitude at nine o'clock. We were then over Japanese waters, close to their mainland. Lieutenant Godfrey motioned to me to look through his radar scope. Before me was the outline of our assembly point. We shall soon meet our lead ship and proceed to the final stage of our journey.

We reached Yakushima at 9:12 and there, about four thousand feet ahead 35 of us, was *The Great Artiste* with its precious load. I saw Lieutenant Godfrey and Sergeant Curry strap on their parachutes and I decided to do likewise.

We started circling. We saw little towns on the coastline, heedless of our 36 presence. We kept on circling, waiting for the third ship in our formation.

It was 9:56 when we began heading for the coastline. Our weather scouts 37 had sent us code messages, deciphered by Sergeant Curry, informing us that both the primary target as well as the secondary were clearly visible.

The winds of destiny seemed to favor certain Japanese cities that must remain 38 nameless. We circled about them again and again and found no opening in the thick umbrella of clouds that covered them. Destiny chose Nagasaki as the ultimate target.

We had been circling for some time when we noticed black puffs of smoke 39 coming through the white clouds directly at us. There were fifteen bursts of

---

[2] Pearl Harbor: on December 7, 1941, a surprise bombing attack by the Japanese on this United States naval base in Hawaii caused the death of 1,177 people and prompted the United States to enter World War II; the Death March on Bataan: physically weakened American and Filipino defenders of the Bataan peninsula were forced by their Japanese captors to march ninety miles under brutal conditions to a prisoner of war camp in Manila. Many did not survive. [Eds.]

flak in rapid succession, all too low. Captain Bock changed his course. There soon followed eight more bursts of flak, right up to our altitude, but by this time they were too far to the left.

We flew southward down the channel and at 11:33 crossed the coastline and headed straight for Nagasaki, about one hundred miles to the west. Here again we circled until we found an opening in the clouds. It was 12:01 and the goal of our mission had arrived. 40

We heard the prearranged signal on our radio, put on our arc welder's glasses, and watched tensely the maneuverings of the strike ship about half a mile in front of us. 41

"There she goes!" someone said. 42

Out of the belly of *The Great Artiste* what looked like a black object went downward. 43

Captain Bock swung to get out of range; but even though we were turning away in the opposite direction, and despite the fact that it was broad daylight in our cabin, all of us became aware of a giant flash that broke through the dark barrier of our arc welder's lenses and flooded our cabin with intense light. 44

We removed our glasses after the first flash, but the light still lingered on, a bluish-green light that illuminated the entire sky all around. A tremendous blast wave struck our ship and made it tremble from nose to tail. This was followed by four more blasts in rapid succession, each resounding like the boom of cannon fire hitting our plane from all directions. 45

Observers in the tail of our ship saw a giant ball of fire rise as though from the bowels of the earth, belching forth enormous white smoke rings. Next they saw a giant pillar of purple fire, ten thousand feet high, shooting skyward with enormous speed. 46

By the time our ship had made another turn in the direction of the atomic explosion the pillar of purple fire had reached the level of our altitude. Only about forty-five seconds had passed. Awe-struck, we watched it shoot upward like a meteor coming from the earth instead of from outer space, becoming ever more alive as it climbed skyward through the white clouds. It was no longer smoke, or dust, or even a cloud of fire. It was a living thing, a new species of being, born right before our incredulous eyes. 47

At one stage of its evolution, covering millions of years in terms of seconds, the entity assumed the form of a giant square totem pole, with its base about three miles long, tapering off to about a mile at the top. Its bottom was brown, its center was amber, its top white. But it was a living totem pole, carved with many grotesque masks grimacing at the earth. 48

Then, just when it appeared as though the thing had settled down into a state of permanence, there came shooting out of the top a giant mushroom that increased the height of the pillar to a total of forty-five thousand feet. The mushroom top was even more alive than the pillar, seething and boiling in a 49 white fury of creamy foam, sizzling upward and then descending earthward, a thousand Old Faithful geysers rolled into one.

It kept struggling in an elemental fury, like a creature in the act of breaking the bonds that held it down. In a few seconds it had freed itself from its gigantic stem and floated upward with tremendous speed, its momentum carrying it into the stratosphere to a height of about sixty thousand feet. — 50

But no sooner did this happen when another mushroom, smaller in size than the first one, began emerging out of the pillar. It was as though the decapitated monster was growing a new head. — 51

As the first mushroom floated off into the blue it changed its shape into a flowerlike form, its giant petals curving downward, creamy white outside, rose-colored inside. It still retained that shape when we last gazed at it from a distance of about two hundred miles. The boiling pillar of many colors could also be seen at that distance, a giant mountain of jumbled rainbows, in travail. Much living substance had gone into those rainbows. The quivering top of the pillar was protruding to a great height through the white clouds, giving the appearance of a monstrous prehistoric creature with a ruff around its neck, a fleecy ruff extending in all directions, as far as the eye could see. — 52

QUESTIONS

1. What do we learn about the crew members on *The Great Artiste*? Why has Laurence bothered to tell us about them?

2. Laurence's description of the bomb as "a thing of beauty" (paragraph 4) suggests that this eyewitness report is not wholly objective. What is Laurence's moral stance on this mission?

3. Consider Laurence's arrangement of time in his narrative. What effect do you think he wishes to create by switching back and forth between past and present tense?

4. Consider Laurence's description of the blast and its resulting cloud (paragraphs 44 through 52). His challenge as a writer is to help his readers to see this strange and awesome thing. What familiar images does he use to represent this unfamiliar sight? What do those images say—especially the last one—about Laurence's feelings as he watched the cloud transform itself?

5. Write an eyewitness report on an event that you consider important. Present the preparations or actions leading up to the event, and include information about others involved. What imagery can you use to describe the glorious, funny, or chaotic event itself?

6. For a report on the basis for Laurence's attitude toward the bombings of Hiroshima and Nagasaki, look at as many newspapers as you can for August 6 through 10 in 1945. Be sure to look at the editorial pages as well as the front pages. If possible, you might also interview relatives and friends who are old enough to remember the war or who might have fought in it. What attitudes toward the bomb and its use were expressed then? How do these compare or contrast with Laurence's attitude?

MAKING CONNECTIONS

1. Describe the differences in point of view taken toward this cataclysmic event by Laurence, John Hersey, and Zoë Tracy Hardy. How does each writer respond to this unparalleled story? Which responses do you find most unusual, most believable, most sympathetic? Why?

2. Imagine a meeting today between Laurence and Hatsuyo Nakamura. What might they say to one another? How might Laurence reflect today on his feelings nearly fifty years ago? Imagine this meeting and write a report of it. Or, if you prefer, substitute Zoë Tracy Hardy for Hatsuyo Nakamura.

OBSERVING WOLVES

Farley Mowat

Farley Mowat was born in Ontario, Canada, in 1921 and finished college at the University of Toronto in 1949, after wartime service and two years living in the Arctic. He makes his living as a writer rather than a scientist, but he works in the same areas covered by anthropologists and zoologists. Often he writes more as a partisan of indigenous peoples and animals rather than as an "objective" scientist, and his work has reached a wide audience. He has written engagingly about the strange animals he grew up with in Owls in the Family *(1963) and about wolves in* Never Cry Wolf *(1963), from which the following selection is taken.*

During the next several weeks I put my decision into effect with the thoroughness for which I have always been noted. I went completely to the wolves. To begin with I set up a den of my own as near to the wolves as I could conveniently get without disturbing the even tenor of their lives too much. After all, I *was* a stranger, and an unwolflike one, so I did not feel I should go too far too fast.

Abandoning Mike's cabin (with considerable relief, since as the days warmed up so did the smell) I took a tiny tent and set it up on the shore of the bay immediately opposite to the den esker.[1] I kept my camping gear to the barest minimum—a small primus stove, a stew pot, a teakettle, and a sleeping bag were the essentials. I took no weapons of any kind, although there were times when I regretted this omission, even if only fleetingly. The big telescope was set up in the mouth of the tent in such a way that I could observe the den by day or night without even getting out of my sleeping bag.

During the first few days of my sojourn with the wolves I stayed inside the tent except for brief and necessary visits to the out-of-doors which I always undertook when the wolves were not in sight. The point of this personal concealment was to allow the animals to get used to the tent and to accept it as only another bump on a very bumpy piece of terrain. Later, when the mosquito population reached full flowering, I stayed in the tent practically all of the time unless there was a strong wind blowing, for the most bloodthirsty beasts in the Arctic are not wolves, but the insatiable mosquitoes.

My precautions against disturbing the wolves were superfluous. It had re-

---

[1] esker: a long, narrow deposit of gravel and sand left by a stream flowing from a glacier. [Eds.]

quired a week for me to get their measure, but they must have taken mine at our first meeting; and, while there was nothing overtly disdainful in their evident assessment of me, they managed to ignore my presence, and indeed my very existence, with a thoroughness which was somehow disconcerting.

Quite by accident I had pitched my tent within ten yards of one of the major paths used by the wolves when they were going to, or coming from, their hunting grounds to the westward; and only a few hours after I had taken up residence one of the wolves came back from a trip and discovered me and my tent. He was at the end of a hard night's work and was clearly tired and anxious to go home to bed. He came over a small rise fifty yards from me with his head down, his eyes half-closed, and a preoccupied air about him. Far from being the preternaturally alert and suspicious beast of fiction, this wolf was so self-engrossed that he came straight on to within fifteen yards of me, and might have gone right past the tent without seeing it at all, had I not banged my elbow against the teakettle, making a resounding clank. The wolf's head came up and his eyes opened wide, but he did not stop or falter in his pace. One brief, sidelong glance was all he vouchsafed to me as he continued on his way.

It was true that I wanted to be inconspicuous, but I felt uncomfortable at being so totally ignored. Nevertheless, during the two weeks which followed, one or more wolves used the track past my tent almost every night—and never, except on one memorable occasion, did they evince the slightest interest in me.

By the time this happened I had learned a good deal about my wolfish neighbors, and one of the facts which had emerged was that they were not nomadic roamers, as is almost universally believed, but were settled beasts and the possessors of a large permanent estate with very definite boundaries.

The territory owned by my wolf family comprised more than a hundred square miles, bounded on one side by a river but otherwise not delimited by geographical features. Nevertheless there *were* boundaries, clearly indicated in wolfish fashion.

Anyone who has observed a dog doing his neighborhood rounds and leaving his personal mark on each convenient post will have already guessed how the wolves marked out *their* property. Once a week, more or less, the clan made the rounds of the family lands and freshened up the boundary markers—a sort of lupine beating of the bounds. This careful attention to property rights was perhaps made necessary by the presence of two other wolf families whose lands abutted on ours, although I never discovered any evidence of bickering or disagreements between the owners of the various adjoining estates. I suspect, therefore, that it was more of a ritual activity.

In any event, once I had become aware of the strong feeling of property rights which existed amongst the wolves, I decided to use this knowledge to make them at least recognize my existence. One evening, after they had gone off for their regular nightly hunt, I staked out a property claim of my own, embracing perhaps three acres, with the tent at the middle, and *including a hundred-yard-long section of the wolves' path.*

Staking the land turned out to be rather more difficult than I had anticipated. In order to ensure that my claim would not be overlooked, I felt obliged to make a property mark on stones, clumps of moss, and patches of vegetation at intervals of not more than fifteen feet around the circumference of my claim. This took most of the night and required frequent returns to the tent to consume copious quantities of tea; but before dawn brought the hunters home the task was done, and I retired, somewhat exhausted, to observe results.   11

I had not long to wait. At 0814 hours, according to my wolf log, the leading male of the clan appeared over the ridge behind me, padding homeward with his usual air of preoccupation. As usual he did not deign to glance at the tent; but when he reached the point where my property line intersected the trail, he stopped as abruptly as if he had run into an invisible wall. He was only fifty yards from me and with my binoculars I could see his expression very clearly.   12

His attitude of fatigue vanished and was replaced by a look of bewilderment. Cautiously he extended his nose and sniffed at one of my marked bushes. He did not seem to know what to make of it or what to do about it. After a minute of complete indecision he backed away a few yards and sat down. And then, finally, he looked directly at the tent and at me. It was a long, thoughtful, considering sort of look.   13

Having achieved my object—that of forcing at least one of the wolves to take cognizance of my existence—I now began to wonder if, in my ignorance, I had transgressed some unknown wolf law of major importance and would have to pay for my temerity. I found myself regretting the absence of a weapon as the look I was getting became longer, yet more thoughtful, and still more intent.   14

I began to grow decidedly fidgety, for I dislike staring matches, and in this particular case I was up against a master, whose yellow glare seemed to become more baleful as I attempted to stare him down.   15

The situation was becoming intolerable. In an effort to break the impasse I loudly cleared my throat and turned my back on the wolf (for a tenth of a second) to indicate as clearly as possible that I found his continued scrutiny impolite, if not actually offensive.   16

He appeared to take the hint. Getting to his feet he had another sniff at my marker, and then he seemed to make up his mind. Briskly, and with an air of decision, he turned his attention away from me and began a systematic tour of the area I had staked out as my own. As he came to each boundary marker he sniffed it once or twice, then carefully placed *his* mark on the outside of each clump of grass or stone. As I watched I saw where I, in my ignorance, had erred. He made his mark with such economy that he was able to complete the entire circuit without having to reload once, or, to change the simile slightly, he did it all on one tank of fuel.   17

The task completed—and it had taken him no longer than fifteen minutes—   18 he rejoined the path at the point where it left my property and trotted off towards his home—leaving me with a good deal to occupy my thoughts.

QUESTIONS

1. What did you know about wolves before reading this piece? What was the most surprising—or amusing—information you acquired from reading about Mowat's experience?

2. Write a paragraph summarizing the information about wolves that you can infer from this selection.

3. How would you describe the narrator of this piece? What does he tell us about himself, and how do his actions describe him?

4. Mowat concludes by saying that he was left "with a good deal to occupy my thoughts" (paragraph 18). What, do you suppose, were these thoughts?

5. Find a more objective, "scientific" account of wolves. Which of Mowat's observations are substantiated there?

6. Rewrite the main events in this piece from the wolf's point of view.

7. Observe the actions of a dog or a cat as it roams your neighborhood. Write an objective report of the animal's actions. Conclude with your reactions to the animal's behavior and, if pertinent, the animal's reactions to your behavior.

MAKING CONNECTIONS

1. Several of the essays in this section deal with the intricacies of placing humans in relation to specific animals and not only observing but sometimes interfering with their lives. Consider the essays by Virginia Woolf, Jane van Lawick-Goodall, and Loren Eiseley as well as this one by Mowat. Then, choosing two essays, compare the degrees of intervention taken by the writers and how that intervention affects the stories they tell.

2. Compare and contrast the similarities and differences in procedure of Mowat's study of wolves and van Lawick-Goodall's study of chimpanzees.

FIRST OBSERVATIONS
Jane van Lawick-Goodall

Jane van Lawick-Goodall (b. 1934), British student of an-
imal behavior, began her work as an assistant to Louis
Leakey, an anthropologist and paleontologist who has stud-
ied human origins. In 1960, with his help, she settled in
Tanzania, East Africa, in the Gombe Stream Game Reserve
to investigate the behavior of chimpanzees in their natural
habitat. Her discoveries have been widely published in
professional journals and in a number of books for more
general audiences. The selection reprinted here is taken from
In the Shadow of Man *(1971), a popular work in which*
she is careful to report her own behavior as well as that of
her chimpanzee subjects.

For about a month I spent most of each day either on the Peak or overlooking 1
Mlinda Valley where the chimps, before or after stuffing themselves with figs,
ate large quantities of small purple fruits that tasted, like so many of their foods,
as bitter and astringent as sloes or crab apples. Piece by piece, I began to form
my first somewhat crude picture of chimpanzee life.

The impression that I had gained when I watched the chimps at the msulula 2
tree of temporary, constantly changing associations of individuals within the
community was substantiated. Most often I saw small groups of four to eight
moving about together. Sometimes I saw one or two chimpanzees leave such a
group and wander off on their own or join up with a different association. On
other occasions I watched two or three small groups joining to form a larger
one.

Often, as one group crossed the grassy ridge separating the Kasekela Valley 3
from the fig trees on the home valley, the male chimpanzee, or chimpanzees,
of the party would break into a run, sometimes moving in an upright position,
sometimes dragging a fallen branch, sometimes stamping or slapping the hard
earth. These charging displays were always accompanied by loud pant-hoots
and afterward the chimpanzee frequently would swing up into a tree overlooking
the valley he was about to enter and sit quietly, peering down and obviously
listening for a response from below. If there were chimps feeding in the fig trees
they nearly always hooted back, as though in answer. Then the new arrivals
would hurry down the steep slope and, with more calling and screaming, the
two groups would meet in the fig trees. When groups of females and youngsters
with no males present joined other feeding chimpanzees, usually there was

none of this excitement; the newcomers merely climbed up into the trees, greeted some of those already there, and began to stuff themselves with figs.

While many details of their social behavior were hidden from me by the foliage, I did get occasional fascinating glimpses. I saw one female, newly arrived in a group, hurry up to a big male and hold her hand toward him. Almost regally he reached out, clasped her hand in his, drew it toward him, and kissed it with his lips. I saw two adult males embrace each other in greeting. I saw youngsters having wild games through the treetops, chasing around after each other or jumping again and again, one after the other, from a branch to a springy bough below. I watched small infants dangling happily by themselves for minutes on end, patting at their toes with one hand, rotating gently from side to side. Once two tiny infants pulled on opposite ends of a twig in a gentle tug-of-war. Often, during the heat of midday or after a long spell of feeding, I saw two or more adults grooming each other, carefully looking through the hair of their companions.

At that time of year the chimps usually went to bed late, making their nests when it was too dark to see properly through binoculars, but sometimes they nested earlier and I could watch them from the Peak. I found that every individual, except for infants who slept with their mothers, made his own nest each night. Generally this took about three minutes: the chimp chose a firm foundation such as an upright fork or crotch, or two horizontal branches. Then he reached out and bent over smaller branches onto this foundation, keeping each one in place with his feet. Finally he tucked in the small leafy twigs growing around the rim of his nest and lay down. Quite often a chimp sat up after a few minutes and picked a handful of leafy twigs, which he put under his head or some other part of his body before settling down again for the night. One young female I watched went on and on bending down branches until she had constructed a huge mound of greenery on which she finally curled up.

I climbed up into some of the nests after the chimpanzees had left them. Most of them were built in trees that for me were almost impossible to climb. I found that there was quite complicated interweaving of the branches in some of them. I found, too, that the nests were fouled with dung; and later, when I was able to get closer to the chimps, I saw how they were always careful to defecate and urinate over the edge of their nests, even in the middle of the night.

During that month I really came to know the country well, for I often went on expeditions from the Peak, sometimes to examine nests, more frequently to collect specimens of the chimpanzees' food plants, which Bernard Verdcourt had kindly offered to identify for me. Soon I could find my way around the sheer ravines and up and down the steep slopes of three valleys—the home valley, the Pocket, and Mlinda Valley—as well as a taxi driver finds his way about in the main streets and byways of London. It is a period I remember vividly, not only because I was beginning to accomplish something at last, but also because of the delight I felt in being completely by myself. For those who love to be alone with nature I need add nothing further; for those who do not, no words of mine could ever convey, even in part, the almost mystical awareness of beauty and eternity that accompanies certain treasured moments. And, though the beauty was always there, those moments came upon me unaware: when I was watching the pale flush preceding dawn; or looking up through the rustling leaves of some giant forest tree into the greens and browns and black shadows that occasionally ensnared a bright fleck of the blue sky; or when I stood, as darkness fell, with one hand on the still-warm trunk of a tree and looked at the sparkling of an early moon on the never still, sighing water of the lake.

One day, when I was sitting by the trickle of water in Buffalo Wood, pausing for a moment in the coolness before returning from a scramble in Mlinda Valley, I saw a female bushbuck moving slowly along the nearly dry streambed. Occasionally she paused to pick off some plant and crunch it. I kept absolutely still, and she was not aware of my presence until she was little more than ten yards away. Suddenly she tensed and stood staring at me, one small forefoot raised. Because I did not move, she did not know what I was—only that my outline was somehow strange. I saw her velvet nostrils dilate as she sniffed the air, but I was downwind and her nose gave her no answer. Slowly she came closer, and closer—one step at a time, her neck craned forward—always poised for instant flight. I can still scarcely believe that her nose actually touched my knee; yet if I close my eyes I can feel again, in imagination, the warmth of her breath and the silken impact of her skin. Unexpectedly I blinked and she was gone in a flash, bounding away with loud barks of alarm until the vegetation hid her completely from my view.

It was rather different when, as I was sitting on the Peak, I saw a leopard coming toward me, his tail held up straight. He was at a slightly lower level than I, and obviously had no idea I was there. Ever since arrival in Africa I had had an ingrained, illogical fear of leopards. Already, while working at the Gombe, I had several times nearly turned back when, crawling through some thick undergrowth, I had suddenly smelled the rank smell of cat. I had forced myself on, telling myself that my fear was foolish, that only wounded leopards charged humans with savage ferocity.

On this occasion, though, the leopard went out of sight as it started to climb up the hill—the hill on the peak of which I sat. I quickly hastened to climb a tree, but halfway there I realized that leopards can climb trees. So I uttered a sort of halfhearted squawk. The leopard, my logical mind told me, would be just as frightened of me if he knew I was there. Sure enough, there was a thudding of startled feet and then silence. I returned to the Peak, but the feeling of unseen eyes watching me was too much. I decided to watch for the chimps in Mlinda Valley. And, when I returned to the Peak several hours later, there, on the very rock which had been my seat, was a neat pile of leopard dung. He

229

must have watched me go and then, very carefully, examined the place where such a frightening creature had been and tried to exterminate my alien scent with his own.

As the weeks went by the chimpanzees became less and less afraid. Quite 11
often when I was on one of my food-collecting expeditions I came across chimpanzees unexpectedly, and after a time I found that some of them would tolerate my presence provided they were in fairly thick forest and I sat still and did not try to move closer than sixty to eighty yards. And so, during my second month of watching from the Peak, when I saw a group settle down to feed I sometimes moved closer and was thus able to make more detailed observations.

It was at this time that I began to recognize a number of different individuals. 12
As soon as I was sure of knowing a chimpanzee if I saw it again, I named it. Some scientists feel that animals should be labeled by numbers—that to name them is anthropomorphic—but I have always been interested in the *differences* between individuals, and a name is not only more individual than a number but also far easier to remember. Most names were simply those which, for some reason or other, seemed to suit the individuals to whom I attached them. A few chimps were named because some facial expression or mannerism reminded me of human acquaintances.

The easiest individual to recognize was old Mr. McGregor. The crown of 13
his head, his neck, and his shoulders were almost entirely devoid of hair, but a slight frill remained around his head rather like a monk's tonsure. He was an old male—perhaps between thirty and forty years of age (the longevity record of a captive chimp is forty-seven years). During the early months of my acquaintance with him, Mr. McGregor was somewhat belligerent. If I accidentally came across him at close quarters he would threaten me with an upward and backward jerk of his head and a shaking of branches before climbing down and vanishing from my sight. He reminded me, for some reason, of Beatrix Potter's old gardener in *The Tale of Peter Rabbit.*

Ancient Flo with her deformed, bulbous nose and ragged ears was equally 14
easy to recognize. Her youngest offspring at that time were two-year-old Fifi, who still rode everywhere on her mother's back, and her juvenile son, Figan, who was always to be seen wandering around with his mother and little sister. He was then about six years old; it was approximately a year before he would attain puberty. Flo often traveled with another old mother, Olly. Olly's long face was also distinctive; the fluff of hair on the back of her head—though no other feature—reminded me of my aunt, Olwen. Olly, like Flo, was accompanied by two children, a daughter younger than Fifi, and an adolescent son about a year older than Figan.

Then there was William, who, I am certain, must have been Olly's blood 15
brother. I never saw any special signs of friendship between them, but their faces were amazingly alike. They both had long upper lips that wobbled when

they suddenly turned their heads. William had the added distinction of several thin, deeply etched scar marks running down his upper lip from his nose.

Two of the other chimpanzees I knew well by sight at that time were David 16 Graybeard and Goliath. Like David and Goliath in the Bible, these two individuals were closely associated in my mind because they were very often together. Goliath, even in those days of his prime, was not a giant, but he had a splendid physique and the springy movements of an athlete. He probably weighed about one hundred pounds. David Graybeard was less afraid of me from the start than were any of the other chimps. I was always pleased when I picked out his handsome face and well-marked silvery beard in a chimpanzee group, for with David to calm the others, I had a better chance of approaching to observe them more closely.

Before the end of my trial period in the field I made two really exciting 17 discoveries—discoveries that made the previous months of frustration well worth while. And for both of them I had David Graybeard to thank.

One day I arrived on the Peak and found a small group of chimps just below 18 me in the upper branches of a thick tree. As I watched I saw that one of them was holding a pink-looking object from which he was from time to time pulling pieces with his teeth. There was a female and a youngster and they were both reaching out toward the male, their hands actually touching his mouth. Presently the female picked up a piece of the pink thing and put it to her mouth: it was at this moment that I realized the chimps were eating meat.

After each bite of meat the male picked off some leaves with his lips and 19 chewed them with the flesh. Often, when he had chewed for several minutes on this leafy wad, he spat out the remains into the waiting hands of the female. Suddenly he dropped a small piece of meat, and like a flash the youngster swung after it to the ground. Even as he reached to pick it up the undergrowth exploded and an adult bushpig charged toward him. Screaming, the juvenile leaped back into the tree. The pig remained in the open, snorting and moving backward and forward. Soon I made out the shapes of three small striped piglets. Obviously the chimps were eating a baby pig. The size was right and later, when I realized that the male was David Graybeard, I moved closer and saw that he was indeed eating piglet.

For three hours I watched the chimps feeding. David occasionally let the 20 female bite pieces from the carcass and once he actually detached a small piece of flesh and placed it in her outstretched hand. When he finally climbed down there was still meat left on the carcass; he carried it away in one hand, followed by the others.

Of course I was not sure, then, that David Graybeard had caught the pig for 21 himself, but even so, it was tremendously exciting to know that these chimpanzees actually ate meat. Previously scientists had believed that although these apes might occasionally supplement their diet with a few insects or small rodents and the like they were primarily vegetarians and fruit eaters. No one had suspected that they might hunt larger mammals.

It was within two weeks of this observation that I saw something that excited 22 me even more. By then it was October and the short rains had begun. The blackened slopes were softened by feathery new grass shoots and in some places the ground was carpeted by a variety of flowers. The Chimpanzees' Spring, I called it. I had had a frustrating morning, tramping up and down three valleys with never a sign or sound of a chimpanzee. Hauling myself up the steep slope of Mlinda Valley I headed for the Peak, not only weary but soaking wet from crawling through dense undergrowth. Suddenly I stopped, for I saw a slight movement in the long grass about sixty yards away. Quickly focusing my binoculars I saw that it was a single chimpanzee, and just then he turned in my direction. I recognized David Graybeard.

Cautiously I moved around so that I could see what he was doing. He was 23 squatting beside the red earth mound of a termite nest, and as I watched I saw him carefully push a long grass stem down into a hole in the mound. After a moment he withdrew it and picked something from the end with his mouth. I was too far away to make out what he was eating, but it was obvious that he was actually using a grass stem as a tool.

I knew that on two occasions casual observers in West Africa had seen 24 chimpanzees using objects as tools: one had broken open palm-nut kernels by using a rock as a hammer, and a group of chimps had been observed pushing sticks into an underground bees' nest and licking off the honey. Somehow I had never dreamed of seeing anything so exciting myself.

For an hour David feasted at the termite mound and then he wandered 25 slowly away. When I was sure he had gone I went over to examine the mound. I found a few crushed insects strewn about, and a swarm of worker termites sealing the entrances of the nest passages into which David had obviously been poking his stems. I picked up one of his discarded tools and carefully pushed it into a hole myself. Immediately I felt the pull of several termites as they seized the grass, and when I pulled it out there were a number of worker termites and a few soldiers, with big red heads, clinging on with their mandibles. There they remained, sticking out at right angles to the stem with their legs waving in the air.

Before I left I trampled down some of the tall dry grass and constructed a 26 rough hide—just a few palm fonds leaned up against the low branch of a tree and tied together at the top. I planned to wait there the next day. But it was another week before I was able to watch a chimpanzee "fishing" for termites again. Twice chimps arrived, but each time they saw me and moved off immediately. Once a swarm of fertile winged termites—the princes and princesses, as they are called—flew off on their nuptial flight, their huge white wings fluttering frantically as they carried the insects higher and higher. Later I realized that it is at this time of year, during the short rains, when the worker termites extend the passages of the nest to the surface, preparing for these emigrations. Several such swarms emerge between October and January. It is principally during these months that the chimpanzees feed on termites.

On the eighth day of my watch David Graybeard arrived again, together with Goliath, and the pair worked there for two hours. I could see much better: I observed how they scratched open the sealed-over passage entrances with a thumb or forefinger. I watched how they bit the end off their tools when they became bent, or used the other end, or discarded them in favor of new ones. Goliath once moved at least fifteen yards from the heap to select a firm-looking piece of vine, and both males often picked three or four stems while they were collecting tools, and put the spares beside them on the ground until they wanted them. 27

Most exciting of all, on several occasions they picked small leafy twigs and prepared them for use by stripping off the leaves. This was the first recorded example of a wild animal not merely *using* an object as a tool, but actually modifying an object and thus showing the crude beginnings of tool*making*. 28

Previously man had been regarded as the only tool-making animal. Indeed, one of the clauses commonly accepted in the definition of man was that he was a creature who "made tools to a regular and set pattern." The chimpanzees, obviously, had not made tools to any set pattern. Nevertheless, my early observations of their primitive toolmaking abilities convinced a number of scientists that it was necessary to redefine man in a more complex manner than before. Or else, as Louis Leakey put it, we should by definition have to accept the chimpanzee as Man. 29

QUESTIONS

1. This essay is an example, principally, of reporting; that is, it is a gathering of facts by a clearheaded, unbiased observer. Identify passages in the essay in which this kind of reporting clearly takes place.

2. Although van Lawick-Goodall, in the main, is a neutral observer of chimpanzee behavior, that neutrality is in fact impossible in any absolute sense. It is clear that she writes, for example, with an eye always on comparisons of chimpanzee and human behavior. Make a list of words, just from paragraphs 3 and 4, that reveal that particular bias.

3. Describe how van Lawick-Goodall's comparison of chimpanzee with human behavior becomes increasingly prominent in the course of her essay.

4. Paraphrase the last discovery van Lawick-Goodall reports toward the end of her essay. What, exactly, was her contribution to science in this instance? What other activities, described earlier in the piece, make that discovery understandable, perhaps even unsurprising once we come to it?

5. What do you make of the choice outlined in paragraph 29? Which choice do you suppose the scientists made? Why?

6. Van Lawick-Goodall's scientific work resembles that of an anthropologist in that she goes into the field to observe the behavior of another social group. Even from this short piece we can learn a good deal about the practices and the way of life of such a worker in the field. Describe van Lawick-Goodall's life in the field as best you can, making whatever inferences you can from this single essay.

7. Amplify your description of van Lawick-Goodall's life in the field, done for question 6, by reading whatever articles you can find that tell more about her and about her work.

8. Place yourself somewhere and observe behavior more or less as van Lawick-Goodall does. You might observe wildlife—pigeons, sparrows, crows, squirrels, or whatever is available—or you might observe some aspect of human behavior. If you choose the latter, look for behavior that is unfamiliar to you, such as that of children at play, of workers on the job, or of persons in a social group very different from your own. Write a report detailing your observations.

9. After you have completed question 8, write a second, shorter report in which you comment on the nature of your task as an observer. Was it difficult to watch? Was it difficult to decide what was meaningful behavior? Did you influence what you saw so that you could not be confident that the behavior was representative? Looking back on your experience as a field worker, what else seems questionable to you now?

MAKING CONNECTIONS

1. Both van Lawick-Goodall and Farley Mowat study a specific kind of animal in its natural habitat. How are their procedures similar? How are they different? What kinds of refinement do they venture in their studies as they proceed? How do their procedures influence both their findings and their presentation of those findings?

2. Compare and contrast van Lawick-Goodall's account of observing the chimpanzees with William Booth's observations of the social lives of dolphins in "Explaining." To what extent are both writers ethnographers, studying and describing behavior in a technologically more primitive society?

3. One of the tools that van Lawick-Goodall lacks in her writing is the ability to interview relevant parties. Don't you imagine she would have liked to interview Mr. McGregor, Goliath, or David Graybeard? Imagine her doing so. What questions would she be likely to ask? What would you like to know from one of those individuals were you able to interview him? Write out the interview that you can imagine.

SCENES FROM MANUS[1] LIFE

Margaret Mead

*Margaret Mead (1901–1978) was a cultural anthropologist
who devoted more than fifty years of her life to studying the
lives of other peoples, in part because of an innate interest
in other cultures, in part because she believed that a knowledge of other cultures would help Americans "better understand themselves." Although she published forty-five books
and several hundred articles during her lifetime, she is probably best known for her first two works,* Coming of Age in
Samoa *(1928) and* Growing Up in New Guinea *(1930),
both of which focus on the lives of South Sea Islanders,
particularly on the behavior and growth of children and
adolescents in those cultures. The essay reprinted here is
Chapter 2 from* Growing Up in New Guinea. *In her preface
to the 1975 edition of the book, Mead noted that "Today,
as when I wrote the book, we are seeking ways to release the
potentialities of children, to regain some of the easy communication with our own bodies which the Manus achieved
for their own children with a creativity which neither we nor
the Manus have known how to preserve."*

I

To the Manus native the world is a greater platter, curving upwards on all
sides, from his flat lagoon village where the pile houses stand like long-legged
birds, placid and unstirred by the changing tides. One long edge of the platter
is the mainland, rising from its fringe of mangrove swamps in fold after fold of
steep, red clay. The mainland is approached across a half mile of lagoon, where
the canoe leaves a path in the thicket of scum-coated sea growth, and is entered
by slowly climbing the narrow tortuous beds of the small rivers which wind
stagnant courses through the dark forbidding swamps. On the mainland live the
Usiai, the men of the bush, whom the Manus people meet daily at set hours
near the river mouths. Here the Manus fishermen, the landless rulers of the
lagoons and reefs, bargain with the Usiai for taro, sago, yams, wood for house-
building, betel nut for refreshments, logs for the hulls of their great outrigger

---

[1] Manus is the name of an island in New Guinea and of the people who reside there. [Eds.]

canoes,—buying with their fish all the other necessities of life from the timid, spindly-legged bush people. Here also the people of Peri come to work the few sago patches which they long ago traded or stole from the Usiai; here the children come for a fresh water swim, and the women to gather firewood and draw water. The swamps are infested with sulky Usiai, hostile demons and fresh water monsters. Because of them the Manus dislike both the rivers and the land and take pains never to look into the still waters lest part of their soul stuff remain there.

At the other edge of the platter is the reef, beyond which lies the open sea and the islands of their own archipelago, where they sail to trade for cocoanuts, oil, carved wooden bowls and carved bedsteads. Beyond, still higher up the sea wall, lies Rabaul, the capital of the white man's government of the Territory of New Guinea, and far up on the rim of the world lies Sydney, the farthest point of their knowledge. Stretching away to right and left along the base of the platter lie other villages of the Manus people, standing in serried ranks in brown lagoons, and far away at each end of the platter lies the gentle slope of the high sea wall which canoes must climb if they would sail upon it.

Around the stout house piles, the tides run, now baring the floor of the lagoon until part of the village is left high and dry in the mud, now swelling with a soft insistence nearly to the floor slats of the houses. Here and there, around the village borders, are small abrupt islands, without level land, and unfit for cultivation. Here the women spread out leaves to dry for weaving, the children scramble precariously from rock to rock. Bleaching on the farther islands lie the white bones of the dead.

This small world of water dwellings, where men who are of one kin build their houses side by side, and scatter sago on the edge of the little island which they have inherited from their fathers, shelters not only the living but also the spirits of the dead. These live protected from the inclemency of wind and rain beneath the house thatch. Disowned by their descendants, they flutter restlessly about the borders of the small islets of coral rubble which stand in the centre of the village and do duty as village greens, places of meeting and festivity.

Within the village bounds, the children play. At low tide they range in straggling groups about the shallows, spearing minnows or pelting each other with seaweed. When the water rises the smaller ones are driven up upon the little islets or into the houses, but the taller still wade about sailing toy boats, until the rising tide drives them into their small canoes to race gaily upon the surface of the water. Within the village the sharks of the open sea do not venture, nor are the children in danger from the crocodiles of the mainland. The paint with which their fathers decorate their faces for a voyage into the open seas as a protection against malicious spirits is not needed here. Naked, except for belts or armlets of beads or necklaces of dogs' teeth, they play all day at fishing, swimming, boating, mastering the arts upon which their landless fathers have built their secure position as the dominant people of the archipelago. Up the sides of the universe lie dangers, but here in the watery bottom, the children play, safe beneath the eyes of their spirit ancestors.

II

In the centre of a long house are gathered a group of women. Two of them 6 are cooking sago and cocoanut in shallow broken pieces of earthenware pottery, another is making beadwork. One old woman, a widow by her rope belt and black rubber-like breast bands, is shredding leaves and plaiting them into new grass skirts to add to those which hang in a long row from above her head. The thatched roof is black from the thick wood smoke, rising incessantly from the fires which are never allowed to go out. On swinging shelves over the fires, fish are smoking. A month-old baby lies on a leaf mat, several other small children play about, now nursing at their mothers' breasts, now crawling away, now returning to cry for more milk. It is dark and hot in the house. The only breath of air comes up through the slats in the floor and from trap door entrances at the far ends of the house. The women have laid aside their long drab cotton cloaks, which they must always wear in public to hide their faces from their male relatives-in-law. Beads of sweat glisten on their shiny shaven heads, sign of the wedded estate. Their grass skirts, which are only two tails worn one before and one behind, leaving the thighs bare, are wilted and work-bedraggled.

One woman starts to gather up her beads: "Come, Alupwa," she says to her 7 three-year-old daughter.

"I don't want to." The fat little girl wriggles and pouts. 8

"Yes, come, I must go home now. I have stayed here long enough making 9 bead-work. Come."

"I don't want to." 10

"Yes, come, father will be home from market and hungry after fishing all 11 night."

"I won't." Alupwa purses her lips into ugly defiance. 12

"But come daughter of mine, we must go home now." 13

"I won't." 14

"If thou dost not come now, I must return for thee and what if in the 15 meantime, my sister-in-law, the wife of my husband's brother, should take the canoe? Thou wouldst cry and who would fetch thee home?"

"Father!" retorted the child impudently. 16

"Father will scold me if thou art not home. He likes it not when thou stayest 17 for a long while with my kinsfolk," replies the mother, glancing up at the skull bowl, where the grandfather's skull hangs from the ceiling.

"Never mind!" The child jerks away from her mother's attempt to detain her 18 and turning, slaps her mother roundly in the face. Every one laughs merrily.

Her mother's sister adds: "Alupwa, thou shouldst go home now with thy 19 mother," whereupon the child slaps her also. The mother gives up the argument

237

and begins working on her beads again, while Alupwa prances to the front of the house and returns with a small green fruit from which the older children make tops. This she begins to eat with a sly glance at her mother.

"Don't eat that, Alupwa, it is bad." Alupwa defiantly sets her teeth into the 20 rind. "Don't eat it. Dost not hear me?" Her mother takes hold of the child's hand and tries to wrest it away from her. Alupwa immediately begins to shriek furiously. The mother lets go of her hand with a hopeless shrug and the child puts the fruit to her lips again. But one of the older women intervenes.

"It is bad that she should eat that thing. It will make her sick." 21

"Well, then do thou take it from her. If I do she will hate me." The older 22 woman grasps the wrist of the screaming child and wrenches the fruit from her.

"Daughter of Kea!" At the sound of her husband's voice, the mother springs 23 to her feet, gathering up her cloak. The other women hastily seize their cloaks against their brother-in-law's possible entrance into the house. But Alupwa, tears forgotten, scampers out to the trap door, climbs down the ladder to the veranda, out along the outrigger poles to the canoe platform, and along the sharp gunwale to nestle happily against her father's leg. His hand plays affectionately with her hair as he scowls up at his wife who is sullenly descending the ladder.

III

It is night in Peri. From the windowless houses with their barred entrances, 24 no house fires shine out into the village. Now and then a shower of incandescent ashes falls into the sea, betraying that folk are still awake within the silent houses. Under a house, at the other end of the village, a dark figure is visible against the light cast by a fan-shaped torch of palm leaves. It is a man who is searing the hull of his water-worn canoe with fire. Out in the shallows near the pounding reef, can be seen the scattered bamboo torches of fishermen. A canoe passes down the central waterway, and stops, without a sound, under the verandah of a house. The occupant of the canoe stands, upright, leaning on his long punt, listening. From the interior of the house comes the sound of low sibilant, indrawn whistlings. The owner of the house is holding a séance and through the whistles of the spirit, who is in possession of the mouth of the medium, he communicates with the spirits of the dead. The whistling ceases, and a woman's voice exclaims: "Ah, Pokus is here and thou mayst question him."

The listener recognizes the name of Pokus, although the voice of his mortal 25 mother, the medium, is strained and disguised. His lips form the words: "Wife of Pokanas is conducting the séance."

The owner of the house speaks, quickly, in a voice of command: "Thou, 26 Pokus, tell me. Why is my child sick? All day he is sick. Is it because I sold

238

those pots which I should have kept for my daughter's dowry? Speak, thou, tell me."

Again the whistling. Then the woman's voice drowsily: "He says he does not know." 27

"Then let him go and ask Selanbelot, my father's brother, whose skull I have given room under my roof. Let him ask him why my child is sick." 28

Again whistling. Then the woman's voice, softly: "He says he will go and ask him." 29

From the next house comes the sharp angry wail of a child. The floor creaks above the listener's head and the medium says in her ordinary voice, "Thou, Pokanas. Wake up. The child is crying. Dost thou sleep? Listen, the child is crying, go quickly." 30

A heavy man climbs down the ladder and perceiving the man in the canoe: "Who is it? Thou, Saot?" 31

"Take me quickly in thy canoe. The child has wakened and is frightened." As the young man punts the father across to his child, the whistling begins again. 32

IV

Against the piles at the back of his veranda a man lounges wearily. After a whole night's fishing and the morning at the market he is very sleepy. His hair is combed stiffly back from his head in a pompadour. Around his throat is a string of dogs' teeth. From his distended ear lobes dangle little notched rings of coconut shell, and through the pierced septum of his nose is passed a long slender crescent of pearl shell. His G-string of trade cloth is held fast by a woven belt, patterned in yellow and brown. On his upper arms are wide woven armlets coated with black, rubber-like gum; in these are stuck the pieces of the rib bones of his dead father. On the rough floor boards lies a small grass bag, from which projects a polished gourd on which intricate designs have been burned. In the mouth of the gourd is thrust a wooden spatula, the end carved to represent a crocodile eating a man. The carved head extends in staring unconcern from the crocodile's ornate jaws. The lounger stirs and draws from the bag the lime gourd, a cluster of bright green betel nuts and a bunch of pepper leaves. He puts a betel nut in his mouth, leisurely rolls a pepper leaf into a long funnel, bites off the end, and dipping the spatula into the powdered lime, adds a bit of lime to the mixture which he is already chewing vigorously. 33

The platform shakes as a canoe collides with one of the piles. The man begins hastily gathering up the pepper leaves and betel nut to hide them from a possible visitor. But he is not quick enough. A small head appears above the edge of the verandah and his six-year-old son, Popoli, climbs up dripping. The child's hair is long and strands of it are caked together with red mud; before they can be cut off, his father must give a large feast. The child has spied the 34 treasure and hanging onto the edge of the verandah he whines out in the tone which all Manus natives use when begging betel nut: "A little betel?" The father throws him a nut. He tears the skin off with his teeth and bites it greedily.

"Another," the child's voice rises to a higher pitch. The father throws him a 35 second nut, which the child grasps firmly in his wet little fist, without acknowledgment. "Some pepper leaf?"

The father frowns. "I have very little, Popoli." 36

"Some pepper leaf." The father tears off a piece of a leaf and throws it to 37 him.

The child scowls at the small piece. "This is too little. More! More! More!" 38 His voice rises to a howl of rage.

"I have but a little, Popoli. I go not to market until the morrow. I go this 39 afternoon to Patusi and I want some for my voyaging." The father resolutely begins to stuff the leaves farther into the bag, and as he does so, his knife slips out of the bag and falls through a crack into the sea.

"Wilt get it, Popoli?" 40

But the child only glares furiously. "No. I won't, thou, thou stingy one, 41 thou hidest thy pepper leaf from me." And the child dives off the verandah and swims away, leaving his father to climb down and rescue the knife himself.

V

On a shaded verandah a group of children are playing cat's cradle. 42

"Molung is going to die," remarks one little girl, looking up from her half- 43 completed string figure.

"Who says so?" demands a small boy, leaning over to light his cigarette at a 44 glowing bit of wood which lies on the floor.

"My mother. Molung has a snake in her belly." 45

The other children pay no attention to this announcement, but one four- 46 year-old adds after a moment's reflection, "She had a baby in her belly."

"Yes, but the baby came out. It lives in the back of our house. My grand- 47 mother looks out for it."

"If Molung dies, you can keep the baby," says the small boy. "Listen!" 48

From the house across the water a high piercing wail of many voices sounds, all crying in chorus, "My mother, my mother, my mother, oh, what can be the matter?"

"Is she dead yet?" asks the small boy, wriggling to the edge of the verandah. 49 Nobody answers him. "Look." From the rear of the house of illness, a large canoe slides away, laden high with cooking pots. An old woman, gaunt of face, and with head uncovered in her haste, punts the canoe along the waterway.

"That's Ndrantche, the mother of Molung," remarks the first little girl. 50

"Look, there goes Ndrantche with a canoe full of pots," shout the children. 51

Two women come to the door of the house and look out. "Oho," says one. 52

"She's getting the pots away so that when all the mourners come, the pots won't be broken."

"When will Molung die?" asks little Itong, and "Come for a swim," she adds,   53
diving off the verandah without waiting for an answer.

QUESTIONS

1. Mead's essay consists of five separately numbered segments, without any element of surface continuity from one segment to the next, except for the fact that all the segments are concerned with scenes from Manus life. Why do you suppose that Mead chose to write her piece in such a disconnected form?

2. What kind of information and experience does Mead emphasize in each separate segment? What kind of information does she emphasize in the group of segments? What impression of Manus life do you get from each separate segment? What impression of Manus life do you get from the group of segments?

3. How do you account for the organization of the segments? Try out some different ways of rearranging Segments II through V. How would each of your rearrangements affect the continuity and significance of the essay?

4. How do you account for Mead's persistent use of the present tense throughout the essay? Rewrite one or two of the segments in the past tense to see how you would perceive and respond to material if it were presented from this different perspective.

5. Mead never makes any explicit comment on the behavior of the people in any of the scenes that she describes in the essay. Why do you suppose that she does not indicate what she thinks of their behavior? Can you infer an opinion from her selection and arrangement of details? What is your opinion of the behavior that she reports in each segment?

6. Write an essay in which you describe "Scenes from _____ Life." Study Mead's way of selecting, presenting, and organizing scenes, so as to compose your own essay on life in a place that you know well.

MAKING CONNECTIONS

Compare Mead's segmented, present-tense essay with Alice Walker's segmented, present-tense piece, "Beauty: When the Other Dancer Is the Self." What similarities and what differences do you find in the effects of these comparably presented essays?

BODY RITUAL AMONG
THE NACIREMA

Horace Miner

*Horace Miner (b. 1912) is Professor Emeritus in sociology
and anthropology at the University of Michigan. Over the
course of a long career as cultural anthropologist, he has
published studies ranging from Timbuktu to French Canada. The following selection appeared first in a professional
journal, the* American Anthropologist, *in 1956. Reprinted
far and wide, it has now become a classic joke among social
scientists.*

The anthropologist has become so familiar with the diversity of ways in   1
which different peoples behave in similar situations that he is not apt to be
surprised by even the most exotic customs. In fact, if all of the logically possible
combinations of behavior have not been found somewhere in the world, he is
apt to suspect that they must be present in some yet undescribed tribe. This
point has, in fact, been expressed with respect to clan organization by Murdock
(1949:71). In this light, the magical beliefs and practices of the Nacirema present
such unusual aspects that it seems desirable to describe them as an example of
the extremes to which human behavior can go.

Professor Linton first brought the ritual of the Nacirema to the attention of   2
anthropologists twenty years ago (1936:326), but the culture of this people is
still very poorly understood. They are a North American group living in the
territory between the Canadian Cree, the Yaqui and Tarahumare of Mexico,
and the Carib and Arawak of the Antilles. Little is known of their origin,
although tradition states that they came from the east. According to Nacirema
mythology, their nation was originated by a culture hero, Notgnihsaw, who is
otherwise known for two great feats of strength—the throwing of a piece of
wampum across the river Pa-To-Mac and the chopping down of a cherry tree
in which the Spirit of Truth resided.

Nacirema culture is characterized by a highly developed market economy   3
which has evolved in a rich natural habitat. While much of the people's time
is devoted to economic pursuits, a large part of the fruits of these labors and a
considerable portion of the day are spent in ritual activity. The focus of this
activity is the human body, the appearance and health of which loom as a
dominant concern in the ethos of the people. While such a concern is certainly
not unusual, its ceremonial aspects and associated philosophy are unique.

The fundamental belief underlying the whole system appears to be that the   4 human body is ugly and that its natural tendency is to debility and disease. Incarcerated in such a body, man's only hope is to avert these characteristics through the use of the powerful influences of ritual and ceremony. Every household has one or more shrines devoted to this purpose. The more powerful individuals in the society have several shrines in their houses and, in fact, the opulence of a house is often referred to in terms of the number of such ritual centers it possesses. Most houses are of wattle and daub construction, but the shrine rooms of the more wealthy are walled with stone. Poorer families imitate the rich by applying pottery plaques to their shrine walls.

While each family has at least one such shrine, the rituals associated with it 5 are not family ceremonies but are private and secret. The rites are normally only discussed with children, and then only during the period when they are being initiated into these mysteries. I was able, however, to establish sufficient rapport with the natives to examine these shrines and to have the rituals described to me.

The focal point of the shrine is a box or chest which is built into the wall. 6 In this chest are kept the many charms and magical potions without which no native believes he could live. These preparations are secured from a variety of specialized practitioners. The most powerful of these are the medicine men, whose assistance must be rewarded with substantial gifts. However, the medicine men do not provide the curative potions for their clients, but decide what the ingredients should be and then write them down in an ancient and secret language. This writing is understood only by the medicine men and by the herbalists who, for another gift, provide the required charm.

The charm is not disposed of after it has served its purpose, but is placed in 7 the charm-box of the household shrine. As these magical materials are specific for certain ills, and the real or imagined maladies of the people are many, the charm-box is usually full to overflowing. The magical packets are so numerous that people forget what their purposes were and fear to use them again. While the natives are very vague on this point, we can only assume that the idea in retaining all the old magical materials is that their presence in the charm-box, before which the body rituals are conducted, will in some way protect the worshipper.

Beneath the charm-box is a small font. Each day every member of the 8 family, in succession, enters the shrine room, bows his head before the charm-box, mingles different sorts of holy water in the font, and proceeds with a brief rite of ablution. The holy waters are secured from the Water Temple of the community, where the priests conduct elaborate ceremonies to make the liquid ritually pure.

In the hierarchy of magical practitioners, and below the medicine men in 9 prestige, are specialists whose designation is best translated "holy-mouth-men." The Nacirema have an almost pathological horror of and fascination with the mouth, the condition of which is believed to have a supernatural influence on all social relationships. Were it not for the rituals of the mouth, they believe that their teeth would fall out, their gums bleed, their jaws shrink, their friends desert them, and their lovers reject them. They also believe that a strong relationship exists between oral and moral characteristics. For example, there is a ritual ablution of the mouth for children which is supposed to improve their moral fiber.

The daily body ritual performed by everyone includes a mouth-rite. Despite the fact that these people are so punctilious about care of the mouth, this rite involves a practice which strikes the uninitiated stranger as revolting. It was reported to me that the ritual consists of inserting a small bundle of hog hairs into the mouth, along with certain magical powders, and then moving the bundle in a highly formalized series of gestures. 10

In addition to the private mouth-rite, the people seek out a holy-mouth-man once or twice a year. These practitioners have an impressive set of paraphernalia, consisting of a variety of augers, awls, probes, and prods. The use of these objects in the exorcism of the evils of the mouth involves almost unbelievable ritual torture of the client. The holy-mouth-man opens the client's mouth and, using the above mentioned tools, enlarges any holes which decay may have created in the teeth. Magical materials are put into these holes. If there are no naturally occurring holes in the teeth, large sections of one or more teeth are gouged out so that the supernatural substance can be applied. In the client's view, the purpose of these ministrations is to arrest decay and to draw friends. The extremely sacred and traditional character of the rite is evident in the fact that the natives return to the holy-mouth-men year after year, despite the fact that their teeth continue to decay. 11

It is to be hoped that, when a thorough study of the Nacirema is made, there will be careful inquiry into the personality structure of these people. One has but to watch the gleam in the eye of a holy-mouth-man, as he jabs an awl into an exposed nerve, to suspect that a certain amount of sadism is involved. If this can be established, a very interesting pattern emerges, for most of the population shows definite masochistic tendencies. It was to these that Professor Linton referred in discussing a distinctive part of the daily body ritual which is performed only by men. This part of the rite involves scraping and lacerating the surface of the face with a sharp instrument. Special women's rites are performed only four times during each lunar month, but what they lack in frequency is made up in barbarity. As part of this ceremony, women bake their heads in small ovens for about an hour. The theoretically interesting point is that what seems to be a preponderantly masochistic people have developed sadistic specialists. 12

The medicine men have an imposing temple, or *latipso*, in every community of any size. The more elaborate ceremonies required to treat very sick patients can only be performed at this temple. These ceremonies involve not only the 13

244

thaumaturge but a permanent group of vestal maidens who move sedately about the temple chambers in distinctive costume and headdress.

The *latipso* ceremonies are so harsh that it is phenomenal that a fair pro- 14 portion of the really sick natives who enter the temple ever recover. Small children whose indoctrination is still incomplete have been known to resist attempts to take them to the temple because "that is where you go to die." Despite this fact, sick adults are not only willing but eager to undergo the protracted ritual purification, if they can afford to do so. No matter how ill the supplicant or how grave the emergency, the guardians of many temples will not admit a client if he cannot give a rich gift to the custodian. Even after one has gained admission and survived the ceremonies, the guardians will not permit the neophyte to leave until he makes still another gift.

The supplicant entering the temple is first stripped of all his or her clothes. 15 In every-day life the Nacirema avoids exposure of his body and its natural functions. Bathing and excretory acts are performed only in the secrecy of the household shrine, where they are ritualized as part of the body-rites. Psycho- logical shock results from the fact that body secrecy is suddenly lost upon entry into the *latipso*. A man, whose own wife has never seen him in an excretory act, suddenly finds himself naked and assisted by a vestal maiden while he performs his natural functions into a sacred vessel. This sort of ceremonial treatment is necessitated by the fact that the excreta are used by a diviner to ascertain the course and nature of the client's sickness. Female clients, on the other hand, find their naked bodies are subjected to the scrutiny, manipulation and prodding of the medicine men.

Few supplicants in the temple are well enough to do anything but lie on 16 their hard beds. The daily ceremonies, like the rites of the holy-mouth-men, involve discomfort and torture. With ritual precision, the vestals awaken their miserable charges each dawn and roll them about on their beds of pain while performing ablutions, in the formal movements of which the maidens are highly trained. At other times they insert magic wands in the supplicant's mouth or force him to eat substances which are supposed to be healing. From time to time the medicine men come to their clients and jab magically treated needles into their flesh. The fact that these temple ceremonies may not cure, and may even kill the neophyte, in no way decreases the people's faith in the medicine men.

There remains one other kind of practitioner, known as a "listener." This 17 witch-doctor has the power to exorcise the devils that lodge in the heads of people who have been bewitched. The Nacirema believe that parents bewitch their own children. Mothers are particularly suspected of putting a curse on children while teaching them the secret body rituals. The counter-magic of the witch-doctor is unusual in its lack of ritual. The patient simply tells the "listener" all his troubles and fears, beginning with the earliest difficulties he can remember. The memory displayed by the Nacirema in these exorcism sessions is truly remarkable. It is not uncommon for the patient to bemoan the rejection he felt upon being weaned as a babe, and a few individuals even see their troubles going back to the traumatic effects of their own birth.

In conclusion, mention must be made of certain practices which have their base in native esthetics but which depend upon the pervasive aversion to the natural body and its functions. There are ritual fasts to make fat people thin and ceremonial feasts to make thin people fat. Still other rites are used to make women's breasts larger if they are small, and smaller if they are large. General dissatisfaction with breast shape is symbolized in the fact that the ideal form is virtually outside the range of human variation. A few women afflicted with almost inhuman hypermammary development are so idolized that they make a handsome living by simply going from village to village and permitting the natives to stare at them for a fee. [18]

Reference has already been made to the fact that excretory functions are ritualized, routinized, and relegated to secrecy. Natural reproductive functions are similarly distorted. Intercourse is taboo as a topic and scheduled as an act. Efforts are made to avoid pregnancy by the use of magical materials or by limiting intercourse to certain phases of the moon. Conception is actually very infrequent. When pregnant, women dress so as to hide their condition. Parturition takes place in secret, without friends or relatives to assist, and the majority of women do not nurse their infants. [19]

Our review of the ritual life of the Nacirema has certainly shown them to be magic-ridden people. It is hard to understand how they have managed to exist so long under the burdens which they have imposed upon themselves. But even such exotic customs as these take on real meaning when they are viewed with the insight provided by Malinowski when he wrote (1948:70): [20]

> Looking from far and above, from our high places of safety in the developed civilization, it is easy to see all the crudity and irrelevance of magic. But without its power and guidance early man could not have mastered his practical difficulties as he has done, nor could man have advanced to the higher stages of civilization.

REFERENCES CITED

LINTON, RALPH
    1936 The Study of Man. New York, D. Appleton-Century Co.
MALINOWSKI, BRONISLAW
    1948 Magic, Science, and Religion. Glencoe, The Free Press.
MURDOCK, GEORGE P.
    1949 Social Structure. New York, The Macmillan Co.

QUESTIONS

1. Where do the Nacirema live? Why would an anthropologist want to study their culture? Do the Nacirema sound like people you would want to know more about?

2. What is Miner's attitude toward his subject? Is his report objective, or is there evaluative language present?

3. What evidence is presented to support the writer's claim in paragraph 12 that "most of the population shows definite masochistic tendencies"? How is the evidence organized? Is enough evidence presented to substantiate this claim?

4. Miner's report was written in 1956. Have you seen in your community any more recent evidence that would indicate that the Nacirema's belief in magical powers has enabled them to advance to a higher stage of civilization, as Malinowski suggests it might?

5. Miner concentrates on the body rituals of the Nacirema. Obviously, the Nacirema must have other rituals, and surely some of these are more pleasurable than those described here. On the other hand, Miner may not have included other barbaric customs of the Nacirema. Do some field research of your own, and write a report of another Nacirema ritual that you have observed.

6. Nonanthropologists find this piece humorous because of Professor Miner's treatment of the Nacirema. Might anthropologists find this piece more humorous than nonanthropologists find it? Use your answer to draw some conclusions about how different audiences respond to humor.

MAKING CONNECTIONS

Miner and Farley Mowat write with a noticeable sense of humor. How does their humor affect the stances they take toward their subjects, and toward themselves as they write?

BACK TO LOVE CANAL
Recycled Homes, Rebuilt Dreams
Verlyn Klinkenborg

Verlyn Klinkenborg is an essayist, critic, and teacher of creative writing at Harvard University. Klinkenborg's reviews and essays, which focus primarily on aspects of contemporary American life and popular culture, have been widely published in such magazines as Harper's, The New Yorker, *and* The New York Times Book Review. *His most recent nonfiction books include a memoir,* The Last Fine Time *(1992), and a collection of essays,* Making Hay *(1986). The following essay appeared in the March 1991 issue of* Harper's.

The day I came to Love Canal, the season was undecided. The postman 1 wore walking shorts, but school had started and I could feel the Niagara Frontier tightening up for autumn, which is only a pause before winter here. I drove from Buffalo through Tonawanda and Wheatfield to the city of Niagara Falls, past the airport, past the few small farms still standing on Cayuga Drive. Around me lay suburbs and malls and, farther north, the beginnings of the fruit belt, the cherry and apple orchards that border Lake Ontario. I crossed the bridge over Bergholtz Creek and entered a quiet residential district, where children had just trailed off to school. The everyday hung over lawns and sidewalks like leaf smoke, creating a sense of protective closure, insulation against the unexpected.

A few blocks away, indiscernible, the Niagara River flowed—opaque, glacial, 2 morbid, bound for its tumult a mile or two downstream. No one moves to Niagara Falls for the falls. It is not that kind of city and not that kind of attraction. Parts of the city sizzle and stink with industry, with refineries, power stations, chemical plants. The Power Vista, as they call it, and the hydroelectric reservoirs—clean arcs of concrete—seem to mock the casual shambles of rock that shape the falls. The city fathers still debate how plainly to mark the route to the precipice. Confusion is profitable. The falls should come as a surprise, they seem to feel.

I followed the map to Frontier Avenue in the easternmost section of the city 3 and found a discrepancy. The map showed 97th and 99th streets running north from Frontier Avenue to Colvin Boulevard. In reality 97th and 99th streets and the houses on both sides of them, together with the cross streets of Read Avenue and Wheatfield Avenue, as well as the 99th Street School and its playground and its parking lot, were demolished in 1982 and 1983 and lie buried under many tons of sod, clay, and high-density polyethylene in what is now called the "Canal Site Containment Area." The sod, a well-kept grass field that mounds attractively in the middle, is surrounded by an eight-foot chain-link fence and pierced by vertical fluorescent-orange pipes. Beneath the field lies the Love Canal, 3,000 feet long, 80 to 100 feet wide, and 15 to 40 feet deep, where between 1942 and 1953 the Hooker Electrochemical Company dumped nearly 22,000 tons of chemical waste, much of it toxic, including, as one of the reporters who broke the story of Love Canal wrote, as much dioxin as fell upon Vietnam in the form of Agent Orange.

"Love Canal," "Hooker Chemical," "Toxic Waste Dump"—these phrases   4
return in a lump after so much time, so much intervening history. Many persons—perhaps most persons—now think that the drama of Love Canal lay in the negligent deposit of chemicals, the unwitting exposure to those chemicals of nearby residents, the ultimate relocation of hundreds of families. They forget that Love Canal became a national story, a byword, because it radicalized apparently ordinary people. Love Canal severed the bond between citizens and their city, their state, and their country. The battle there was fought over that bond, and it was fought in public, through protest marches and press releases, because the public, not the state, was at risk.

I came upon Love Canal too suddenly. It was like stepping out of a lodgepole   5
forest onto the site of an old burn. I wanted a transition. One minute I was savoring the taste of the ordinary, and it lulled me, as it is meant to do. Then, abruptly, almost in the instant I looked up from my map, the streets fell empty of cars, people, sound. The grass had grown long, and the hedges were un-trimmed; fallen branches lay ungathered in yards, and at the curb piles of brush moldered here and there. I turned up 100th Street. Houses lined only its east side. The electric meter had been removed from every house. Sidewalks and driveways were turning to rubble. Nearly all the windows had been boarded up, and on most of the doors a number had been chalked in black, a number that was once an address but now seemed more like an inventory mark. At 723 a yellow lawn chair sat alone on a concrete porch, facing the chain-link fence and mounded field to the west. There were houses with rock-faced fronts and metal awnings, with brick and shingle facades, simple clapboard houses redone in aluminum siding, houses as plain as one ever finds in the suburbs. They were poignant only because they were deserted.

These were not the houses that lay across the street from Love Canal in the   6
1970s. These were the houses that lay across the street from the backyards of the houses that once lay across the street from the houses whose backyards once lined the canal. Everything west of 100th Street for a quarter mile was buried and fenced. When the buyout of homes at Love Canal was finally settled a

decade ago, the state of New York found itself the owner of nearly all the property within what came to be called the EDA, the Emergency Declaration Area: a district one mile long and a half mile wide containing 789 single houses. Now, in order to recoup some of its losses and to restore the neighborhood to life, the state is offering some of those houses for sale through the Love Canal Area Revitalization Agency. You can buy one of the houses LCARA has chosen to offer, or you can deposit one hundred dollars and LCARA will order an appraisal on a vacant house of your own choosing. But to settle at Love Canal, you'll have to forget how these houses came to be empty. You'll have to pretend that the past has little meaning.

Near Frontier Avenue, the houses are old and rural in character, barely salable. But a mile to the north, above Colvin Boulevard, near Bergholtz Creek, and a block or two away from the canal, the streets are in better condition and the houses are more likely to be modern in an early Sixties manner and built of brick. These are the houses LCARA has decided to sell. On 98th Street, which dead-ends at the canal, I stopped and inspected 1071, a small ranch, 1,026 square feet, with gray shingle siding and a pink door. The asking price was forty-eight thousand dollars. That included a long list of renovations yet to be done by LCARA: new driveway, new insulation, new external doors, new paint. I examined 1076, across the street—a gray ranch with a breezeway, two bedrooms, one bath, 1,144 square feet, corner lot, patio, barbecue pit, sixty thousand dollars. It had a clean, urbane fireplace notched into the end of a wall like a missing cornerstone. Behind it flows Black Creek, from whose bed dioxin-contaminated sediments were scraped a year ago as part of the Love Canal remediation plan.

On 98th Street, a telephone lineman was preparing to restore service. A block away, an LCARA maintenance man was working with a languor that looked official. A man who had seen me inspecting houses walked over and began to talk. He wore a blue work shirt and a trim gray beard and was taking the day off from painting his house because of the threat of rain. He was a longtime resident, one of the few persons who had not accepted the federal buyout. I said he must be happy to be getting neighbors again at last.

"Who needs neighbors?" he said. "I like it the way it is. Nice and quiet."

The lineman joined the conversation. They talked about a mysterious section of Love Canal buried under a golf course in another part of town. The reason it had never been dug up, they suggested, was best expressed by rubbing the thumb over the first two fingers in a lucrative motion. The conversation became a workshop in worldly wisdom, a lesson in lump-taking. They talked of people who had lived "inside the fence" and "outside the fence" as if the fence around Love Canal had always been there and as if having lived inside the fence conferred a special authority where suffering was concerned. The talk grew strong. Environmental activists were in it for themselves, the government was a patsy, the chemical industry had been good for the city, life was full of risks, you took your chances.

Are the houses safe? I asked.   11

"I never moved," said the resident.   12

"What's safe?" said the lineman.   13

To find out I drove to 9820 Colvin Boulevard, a ranch house typical of the   14
kind LCARA is selling, perfect for a young family or a retired couple. Michael Podd, the New York State Department of Environmental Conservation's citizen-participation specialist, sat at his desk in someone's former living room. An assistant administrator sat not far away at a desk in someone's former dining room. Podd gave me a sheaf of official documents. He took me back into someone's former bedroom and showed me an elaborate three-dimensional model, complete with geological strata and transparent overlays depicting the lapse of time. He explained what happened at Love Canal in more informal language than that used in the official documents. It was a sad story, full of good intentions gone awry but with a great evil remedied in the end. "I don't tell people what's safe or not," Podd concluded. "My job is to give them enough information so that they can make up their own minds." From his desk, Podd could look directly across the street to the Canal Site Containment Area, or to what LCARA calls the "reservation," Love Canal itself, capped and fenced and monitored through groundwater wells. It was like looking at the buffer zone of a minimum-security prison.

I visited the LCARA sales office. The realtor there was a good-humored,   15
slender man named Leonard Rinallo, seventeen years in the real estate business. He wore a mustache and white pants and drove a Mercury Cougar, which he parked in the driveway of 1010 96th Street, another small ranch house. Someone's former living room, where in 1978, 1979, or 1980 someone might have watched the news coverage of the emotional protests occurring a block away at Love Canal, was now Leonard Rinallo's office. A brightly colored "Adopted Land Use Diagram" was pinned to the wall. Outlined in yellow was "Black Creek Village," the new name for the cluster of streets north of the Canal Site Containment Area. Future parkland was outlined in green, planned residential development in orange. In the red areas east of the canal—areas the present health commissioner has deemed uninhabitable (though several families live there)—plans are afoot for commercial and light industrial development. The empty houses on 100th, 101st, and 102nd streets will eventually be destroyed.

The interior of the LCARA sales office was resonantly empty. It had the   16
midmorning feel I have always associated with the homes of neat, childless housewives, for whom the day's work is done quickly and a vacancy fashioned by ten o'clock. But there was no television, and there were no neighbors, and a realtor's desk stood where a sofa might once have been. By chance, I visited Rinallo on the day after the state supreme court threw out a plea brought by several environmental groups for an injunction against house sales at Love

Canal. He expressed measured happiness with the decision, renewed satisfaction with his job. Rinallo would have been more cheerful had a source of mortgages been found as well. "The banks can't redline," he said, "but they can sit on an application forever." Sales were not brisk. (In the coming months, sales would improve. By early November, thirteen houses were under contract though still awaiting financing. A coalition of environmental groups including the National Resources Defense Council would later sue to stop the sales.)

Rinallo treated me like a customer. He gave me a state-prepared packet of information and took me back into someone's former bedroom, where he played an LCARA sales video for me. It outlined the slow but inexorable process that led from the digging of the canal by William T. Love for a turn-of-the-century model industrial city to the moment when the first new homeowner in the revitalization plan turns the key in the lock of his newly refurbished house. The video was worth watching to see pictures of Love Canal in the Thirties, when it was just a long pond. It was worth watching to hear the cheerful music and the narrator's march-of-time voice and to sense the high pitch of official optimism. (The video is currently being revised. The state attorney general's office protested the video's description of Love Canal as a suitable dumpsite for its era, a problem that Rinallo described as "a play on words type thing." The state may merely be protecting its own litigation. Its case against Occidental Petroleum, Hooker's parent company, for its role at Love Canal has just come to trial in Buffalo after a decade of legal positioning.) 17

I drove back to the edge of the Canal Site Containment Area and parked. I watched the neatly groomed field that lay behind the chain-link fence. It was hard to imagine that it had once been a school and a playground and two streets full of houses. It was hard to imagine the 44 million pounds of chemical waste still lying beneath it. It was especially hard to imagine those chemicals lying on the surface of the earth, suppurating, as they had in the late Seventies, and to picture those streets filled with distraught homeowners protesting their fate and the corporate and governmental negligence that had brought it on. 18

Many of those homeowners—bedrock, blue-collar Americans—worked in the Niagara Falls chemical industry or had friends or relatives who did. It did not surprise all of them to learn that Hooker had dumped 22,000 tons of toxic chemicals, covered the pit, and walked away, wiping its hands. They knew that a chemical plant "is not a chocolate factory," as a Hooker official in Michigan remarked in the late Seventies. What surprised them was the discovery that an attempt had been made to shift liability for those chemicals all down the line. With a warning in the final paragraph of its 1953 deed of sale—the inadequacy of which the attorney general is testing in court, though LCARA includes the same limitation of liability in its current sales contracts—Hooker sold the canal for the sum of one dollar to the Niagara Falls Board of Education, which erected a grammar school on the site. Sensing its own legal jeopardy, the Board 19 of Education deeded part of the property in 1960, with another annulment of liability, to the city of Niagara Falls, where, if you possessed faith in government, you would suppose liability might safely rest. But the mayor of Niagara Falls, Michael O'Laughlin—still mayor in 1990 and chairman of LCARA since 1980—told protesting homeowners, "You are hurting Niagara Falls with your publicity. There is no problem here."

Prospective buyers would visit the LCARA sales office and the Department 20 of Environmental Conservation's Public Information Office, as I had. They would collect pamphlets and brochures. Perhaps they would read them. If they did, they might get the impression that the city, state, and federal governments had willingly initiated the chemical analyses, the health studies, the temporary removal of residents, and the final buyout of homes in the Emergency Declaration Area. They might notice that in the fact sheet on "Love Canal EDA Habitability," the New York State Department of Health said, in effect, that it was up to prospective buyers to decide whether the houses there were safe, houses offered at 15 to 20 percent less than local market prices. With a bundle of encouraging official documents under one's arm and the sight in one's eye of a fenced "reservation" and a scientific-looking leachate treatment plant, the plea of money would always prevail. A bargain is a bargain.

As I sat and stared at the vacancy that was once Love Canal, I found myself 21 temporarily persuaded of, if not by, the state's rationality. But rationality is not always a virtue, and credulity is an old failing of mine, the residue of an upbringing in which deference meant a lot and reasonableness was more important than reason. No one ever called it tractability, that predisposition to reasonableness, but that is what it amounts to. At Love Canal, after visiting Michael Podd and Leonard Rinallo, I found myself eager again to believe what I was told because it was the least depressing choice. I wanted to feel again that the past had been a nice place, or, conversely, that the future would be. I knew better, though not half as well as the former inhabitants of the empty houses that surrounded me.

The question naturally arises: Who would move to Love Canal? The question 22 is imprecise. It assumes that the answer is, No one in his right mind. (It also assumes a full awareness of what happened at Love Canal.) The state of New York, through LCARA, has gone out of its way to appeal to the right-minded. Its brochures and fact sheets bear the stamp of rationality, of solid, official information. Its realtor looks like other realtors, its houses like other houses. The streets where it does its business are as quiet as the streets in brand-new developments. The right-minded may well move to Love Canal, but they will need to believe that their predecessors were wrong when they formed a homeowners' association and insisted on a government buyout of all homes in the area. Either that, or the right-minded will need to believe that the state has fixed the problem. The past was a nice place. Or the future will be.

The potential buyers of homes at Love Canal are middle-aged. They are   23
young. They are mostly blue-collar workers, squeezed, as everyone is, by the
rise in housing costs. They resemble no one so much as they do the people
who used to live there. And what do they say about the area?

"You can't beat the price. If the neighborhood does catch on, in five or six   24
or ten years, I've got a great investment."

"I'd like a place where there's some sense of values, where you can take pride   25
in where you live."

"They must have cleaned it up pretty well. It's probably one of the safest   26
places to live in Niagara Falls by now. There are problems no matter where
you live in the world."

"There are chemicals all over this town. My attitude is, if you find a place   27
where they've at least paid attention to cleaning it up, you should go."

"I think it was all a lot of hooey. This street should never have been   28
condemned to begin with. If it was contaminated, I don't think you'd be seeing
so many green trees."

"Or all these squirrels."   29

Who would move to Love Canal?   30

"Everyone's waiting for someone else," said Leonard Rinallo in September.   31
"Most people are followers."

"Former residents are coming back," he added in November, "people from   32
the Niagara Falls area. One man sold his home in California and bought the
most expensive house we had. He's moving here in the spring. Another family
with three children. They wouldn't be coming if they didn't think it was safe."

Is it safe? Beneath the "reservation," the toxins in the canal have been   33
"contained," though no one will guarantee their perpetual containment. There
is no problem here, the state implies, as it has all along. "I've got an hour-and-
a-half commute to work," says Michael Podd, the citizen-participation specialist.
"I'd buy a house here." Podd also told me a story about one longtime Love
Canal resident who said to an interviewer, "I know what's in my backyard. Do
you know what's in yours?" When the validity of the state's habitability studies
is challenged, LCARA's executive director, William Broderick, says, "Just about
every place is contaminated. If we shouldn't put people in here, then maybe
the rest of the city should be evacuated."

Life at Love Canal halted a decade ago: Its streets are still; traffic, nonexistent.   34
As I sat beside the fence around the canal, it seemed as if all the men were at
work, all the wives shopping, all the children at school, all the grandparents
still living in rural homes. The style of the houses dates back to the late Fifties
and early Sixties, when America was a different country. The threat of toxic
contamination around me was invisible, intangible, but the sense of nostalgia
was extraordinarily pungent. These deserted streets evoked an era when, as one
potential home-buyer remarked, Love Canal was the "kind of place where you
had street parties all the time, where you really knew the people next door. It

was the kind of place where if a father was taking his kids for ice cream, he'd take the whole block along."

That man, a former resident, was describing a time when no one expected   35 to be surprised by the presence of chemical waste in the backyard, a time in the minds of its people when government was generous and watchful, not obdurate and evasive, as it was when the Love Canal Homeowners' Association began to press for chemical analyses, medical testing, and, ultimately, the buyout of homes. What many prospective buyers see when they look at Love Canal, and what its first residents saw too, is a suburban innocence that harks back a generation or more, a neighborhood where the everyday creates a sense of protective closure. They are eager to believe, paradoxically, that everything has changed and that the past can be recaptured. The state would like to foster that faith. It is selling the past, and it hopes to purchase forgetfulness. In the informational packets and video that LCARA shows prospective buyers, there is no allusion to the ardor of homeowners' protests at Love Canal, no trace whatever of the emotions that erupted there a decade ago. The state will replace furnaces and windows and driveways, repaint and reroof and replaster the houses it sells, but it will never be able to restore innocence. That will return, briefly, when the moving vans come, when lights burn again in those houses at night.

QUESTIONS

1. What kinds of information does Klinkenborg provide to inform readers about the history of Love Canal prior to his recent investigation of it? What kinds of information does he report to inform readers about the present condition of Love Canal?

2. Given the information that Klinkenborg provides about the past condition versus the recent condition of Love Canal, what seem to be the most noticeable changes that have taken place in this area? What seem to be the most significant changes that have taken place? In what respects, if any, might it be said that the area has not significantly changed between the early 1980s and the early 1990s?

3. Klinkenborg has divided his report about Love Canal into four separate sections. What do you take to be the primary purpose of each section? What aspects of the Love Canal story does he emphasize in each section? What kinds of details predominate in each section?

4. Klinkenborg provides not only a report on Love Canal but also a record of his own reactions to the place from the beginning to the end of his visit. How would you characterize or describe his attitude toward the various scenes he observes and persons he interviews? At what points does he seem to be most veiled about his own reactions? At what points does he seem to be most open in expressing his reactions?

5. What do you think is Klinkenborg's overall attitude toward the current situation at Love Canal? What is your own attitude toward the situation?

6. Environmental cleanups have become such a widespread aspect of contemporary

American life that they are taking place in communities throughout the country. Investigate some aspect of your hometown or college community that has recently been "cleaned up" or that is in the process of being "cleaned up," and write a report based on your investigation.

MAKING CONNECTIONS

Now that you have read a recent report on Love Canal, consider Michael Brown's 1980 report, written when the pollution had recently been discovered. What do you consider to be the most important aspects of the story that you discovered from Brown's report that you had not learned from reading Klinkenborg's report? In what respect(s), if any, has your attitude toward the present state of Love Canal been changed by reading Brown's report?

Sciences and Technologies

LOVE CANAL AND
THE POISONING OF AMERICA

Michael Brown

Michael Brown is a free-lance writer interested in environmental issues. His investigations into the dumping of toxic waste, which have appeared in newspaper and magazine articles, have won him three Pulitzer Prize nominations and a special award from the Environmental Protection Agency. This essay is taken from his book Laying Waste: The Poisoning of America by Toxic Chemicals *(1980).*

Niagara Falls is a city of unmatched natural beauty; it is also a tired industrial   1
workhorse, beaten often and with a hard hand. A magnificent river—a strait, really—connecting Lake Erie to Lake Ontario flows hurriedly north, at a pace of a half-million tons a minute, widening into a smooth expanse near the city before breaking into whitecaps and taking its famous 186-foot plunge. Then it cascades through a gorge of overhung shale and limestone to rapids higher and swifter than anywhere else on the continent.

The falls attract long lines of newlyweds and other tourists. At the same   2
time, the river provides cheap electricity for industry; a good stretch of its shore is now filled with the spiraled pipes of distilleries, and the odors of chlorine and sulfides hang in the air.

Many who live in the city of Niagara Falls work in chemical plants, the   3
largest of which is owned by the Hooker Chemical Company, a subsidiary of Occidental Petroleum since the 1960s. Timothy Schroeder did not. He was a cement technician by trade, dealing with the factories only if they needed a pathway poured, or a small foundation set. Tim and his wife, Karen, lived in a ranch-style home with a brick and wood exterior at 460 99th Street. One of the Schroeder's most cherished purchases was a Fiberglas pool, built into the ground and enclosed by a red-wood fence.

Karen looked from a back window one morning in October 1974, noting   4 with distress that the pool had suddenly risen two feet above the ground. She called Tim to tell him about it. Karen then had no way of knowing that this was the first sign of what would prove to be a punishing family and economic tragedy.

Mrs. Schroeder believed that the cause of the uplift was the unusual ground-water flow of the area. Twenty-one years before, an abandoned hydroelectric canal directly behind their house had been backfilled with industrial rubble. The underground breaches created by this disturbance, aided by the marshland nature of the region's surficial layer, collected large volumes of rainfall and undermined the back yard. The Schroeders allowed the pool to remain in its precarious position until the following summer and then pulled it from the ground, intending to pour a new pool, cast in cement. This they were unable to do, for the gaping excavation immediately filled with what Karen called "chemical water," rancid liquids of yellow and orchid and blue. These same chemicals had mixed with the groundwater and flooded the entire yard, attacking the redwood posts with such a caustic bite that one day the fence simply collapsed. When the chemicals receded in the dry weather, they left the gardens and shrubs withered and scorched, as if by a brush fire.

How the chemicals got there was no mystery. In the late 1930s, or perhaps early 1940s, the Hooker Company, whose many processes included the manufacture of pesticides, plasticizers, and caustic soda, began using the abandoned canal as a dump for at least 20,000 tons of waste residues—"still-bottoms," in the language of the trade.

Karen Schroeder's parents had been the first to experience problems with the canal's seepage. In 1959, her mother, Aileen Voorhees, encountered a strange black sludge bleeding through the basement walls. For the next twenty years, she and her husband, Edwin, tried various methods of halting the irritating intrusion, pasting the cinder-block wall with sealants and even constructing a gutter along the walls to intercept the inflow. Nothing could stop the chemical smell from permeating the entire household, and neighborhood calls to the city for help were fruitless. One day, when Edwin punched a hole in the wall to see what was happening, quantities of black liquid poured from the block. The cinder blocks were full of the stuff.

More ominous than the Voorhees basement was an event that occurred at 11:12 P.M. on November 21, 1968, when Karen Schroeder gave birth to her third child, a seven-pound girl named Sheri. No sense of elation filled the delivery room. The child was born with a heart that beat irregularly and had a hole in it, bone blockages of the nose, partial deafness, deformed ear exteriors, and a cleft palate. Within two years, the Schroeders realized Sheri was also mentally retarded. When her teeth came in, a double row of them appeared on her lower jaw. And she developed an enlarged liver.

The Schroeders considered these health problems, as well as illnesses among their other children, as acts of capricious genes—a vicious quirk of nature. Like

Mrs. Schroeder's parents, they were concerned that the chemicals were devaluing their property. The crab apple tree and evergreens in the back were dead, and even the oak in front of the home was sick; one year, the leaves had fallen off on Father's Day.

The canal had been dug with much fanfare in the late nineteenth century 10 by a flamboyant entrepreneur named William T. Love, who wanted to construct an industrial city with ready access to water power, and major markets. The setting for Love's dream was to be a navigable power channel that would extend seven miles from the Upper Niagara before falling two hundred feet, circumventing the treacherous falls and at the same time providing cheap power. A city would be constructed near the point where the canal fed back into the river, and he promised it would accommodate half a million people.

So taken with his imagination were the state's leaders that they gave Love a 11 free hand to condemn as much property as he liked, and to divert whatever amounts of water. Love's dream, however, proved grander than his resources, and he was eventually forced to abandon the project after a mile-long trench, ten to forty feet deep and generally twenty yards wide, had been scoured perpendicular to the Niagara River. Eventually, the trench was purchased by Hooker.

Few of those who, in 1977, lived in the numerous houses that had sprung 12 up by the site were aware that the large and barren field behind them was a burial ground for toxic waste. Both the Niagara County Health Department and the city said it was a nuisance condition, but not a serious danger to the people. Officials of the Hooker Company refused comment, claiming only that they had no records of the chemical burials and that the problem was not their responsibility. Indeed, Hooker had deeded the land to the Niagara Falls Board of Education in 1953, for a token $1. With it the company issued no detailed warnings of the chemicals, only a brief paragraph in the quitclaim document that disclaimed company liability for any injuries or deaths which might occur at the site.

Though Hooker was undoubtedly relieved to rid itself of the contaminated 13 land, the company was so vague about the hazards involved that one might have thought the wastes would cause harm only if touched, because they irritated the skin; otherwise, they were not of great concern. In reality, as the company must have known, the dangers of these wastes far exceeded those of acids or alkalines or inert salts. We now know that the drums Hooker had dumped in the canal contained a veritable witch's brew—compounds of truly remarkable toxicity. There were solvents that attacked the heart and liver, and residues from pesticides so dangerous that their commercial sale was shortly thereafter restricted outright by the government; some of them were already suspected of causing cancer.

Yet Hooker gave no hint of that. When the board of education, which 14 wanted the parcel for a new school, approached Hooker, B. Kaussen, at the

259

time Hooker's executive vice president, said in a letter to the board: "Our officers have carefully considered your request. We are very conscious of the need for new elementary schools and realize that the sites must be carefully selected. We will be willing to donate the entire strip of property which we own between Colvin Boulevard and Frontier Avenue to be used for the erection of a school at a location to be determined. . . ."

The board built the school and playground at the canal's midsection. Construction progressed despite the contractor's hitting a drainage trench that gave off a strong chemical odor and the discovery of a waste pit nearby. Instead of halting the work, the authorities simply moved the school eighty feet away. Young families began to settle in increasing numbers alongside the dump, many of them having been told that the field was to be a park and recreation area for their children. 15

Children found the "playground" interesting, but at times painful. They sneezed, and their eyes teared. In the days when the dumping was still in progress, they swam at the opposite end of the canal, occasionally arriving home with hard pimples all over their bodies. Hooker knew children were playing on its spoils. In 1958, three children were burned by exposed residues on the canal's surface, much of which, according to residents, had been covered with nothing more than fly ash and loose dirt. Because it wished to avoid legal repercussions, the company chose not to issue a public warning of the dangers it knew were there, nor to have its chemists explain to the people that their homes would have been better placed elsewhere. 16

The Love Canal was simply unfit as a container for hazardous substances, poor even by the standards of the day, and now, in 1977, local authorities were belatedly finding that out. Several years of heavy snowfall and rain had filled the sparingly covered channel like a bathtub. The contents were overflowing at a frightening rate. 17

The city of Niagara Falls, I was assured, was planning a remedial drainage program to halt in some measure the chemical migration off the site. But no sense of urgency had been attached to the plan, and it was stalled in red tape. No one could agree on who should pay the bill—the city, Hooker, or the board of education—and engineers seemed confused over what exactly needed to be done. 18

Niagara Falls City Manager Donald O'Hara persisted in his view that, however displeasing to the eyes and nose, the Love Canal was not a crisis matter, mainly a question of aesthetics. O'Hara reminded me that Dr. Francis Clifford, county health commissioner, supported that opinion. 19

With the city, the board, and Hooker unwilling to commit themselves to a remedy, conditions degenerated in the area between 97th and 99th streets, until, by early 1978, the land was a quagmire of sludge that oozed from the canal's every pore. Melting snow drained the surface soot onto the private yards, while on the dump itself the ground had softened to the point of collapse, exposing 20 the crushed tops of barrels. Beneath the surface, masses of sludge were finding their way out at a quickening rate, constantly forming springs of contaminated liquid. The Schroeder back yard, once featured in a local newspaper for its beauty, had reached the point where it was unfit even to walk upon. Of course, the Schroeders could not leave. No one would think of buying the property. They still owed on their mortgage and, with Tim's salary, could not afford to maintain the house while they moved into a safer setting. They and their four children were stuck.

Apprehension about large costs was not the only reason the city was reluctant   21
to help the Schroeders and the one hundred or so other families whose properties abutted the covered trench. The city may also have feared distressing Hooker. To an economically depressed area, the company provided desperately needed employment—as many as 3000 blue-collar jobs and a substantial number of tax dollars. Hooker was speaking of building a $17 million headquarters in downtown Niagara Falls. So anxious were city officials to receive the new building that they and the state granted the company highly lucrative tax and loan incentives, and made available to the firm a prime parcel of property near the most popular tourist park on the American side.

City Manager O'Hara and other authorities were aware of the nature of   22
Hooker's chemicals. In fact, in the privacy of his office, O'Hara, after receiving a report on the chemical tests at the canal, had informed the people at Hooker that it was an extremely serious problem. Even earlier, in 1976, the New York State Department of Environmental Conservation had been made aware that dangerous compounds were present in the basement sump pump of at least one 97th Street home, and soon after, its own testing had revealed that highly injurious halogenated hydrocarbons were flowing from the canal into adjoining sewers. Among them were the notorious PCBs; quantities as low as one part PCBs to a million parts normal water were enough to create serious environmental concerns; in the sewers of Niagara Falls, the quantities of halogenated compounds were thousands of times higher. The other materials tracked, in sump pumps or sewers, were just as toxic as PCBs, or more so. Prime among the more hazardous ones was residue from hexachlorocyclopentadiene, or C-56, which was deployed as an intermediate in the manufacture of several pesticides. In certain dosages, the chemical could damage every organ in the body.

While the mere presence of C-56 should have been cause for alarm, gov-   23
ernment remained inactive. Not until early 1978—a full eighteen months after C-56 was first detected—was testing conducted in basements along 97th and 99th streets to see if the chemicals had vaporized off the sump pumps and walls and were present in the household air.

While the basement tests were in progress, the rains of spring arrived at the   24
canal, further worsening the situation. Heavier fumes rose above the barrels. More than before, the residents were suffering from headaches, respiratory

261

discomforts, and skin ailments. Many of them felt constantly fatigued and irritable, and the children had reddened eyes. In the Schroeder home, Tim developed a rash along the backs of his legs. Karen could not rid herself of throbbing pains in her head. Their daughter, Laurie, seemed to be losing some of her hair.

The EPA test revealed that benzene, a known cause of cancer in humans, 25 had been readily detected in the household air up and down the streets. A widely used solvent, benzene was known in chronic-exposure cases to cause headaches, fatigue, loss of weight, and dizziness followed by pallor, nose-bleeds, and damage to the bone marrow.

No public announcement was made of the benzene hazard. Instead, officials 26 appeared to shield the finding until they could agree among themselves on how to present it.

Dr. Clifford, the county health commissioner, seemed unconcerned by the 27 detection of benzene in the air. His health department refused to conduct a formal study of the people's health, despite the air-monitoring results. For this reason, and because of the resistance growing among the local authorities, I went to the southern end of 99th Street to take an informal health survey of my own. I arranged a meeting with six neighbors, all of them instructed beforehand to list the illnesses they were aware of on their block, with names and ages specified for presentation at the session.

The residents' list was startling. Though unafflicted before they moved there, 28 many people were now plagued with ear infections, nervous disorders, rashes, and headaches. One young man, James Gizzarelli, said he had missed four months of work owing to breathing troubles. His wife was suffering epileptic-like seizures which her doctor was unable to explain. Meanwhile, freshly applied paint was inexplicably peeling from the exterior of their house. Pets too were suffering, most seriously if they had been penned in the back yards nearest to the canal, constantly breathing air that smelled like mothballs and weedkiller. They lost their fur, exhibited skin lesions, and, while still quite young, developed internal tumors. A great many cases of cancer were reported among the women, along with much deafness. On both 97th and 99th streets, traffic signs warned passing motorists to watch for deaf children playing near the road.

Evidence continued to mount that a large group of people, perhaps all of 29 the one hundred families immediately by the canal, perhaps many more, were in imminent danger. While watching television, while gardening or doing a wash, in their sleeping hours, they were inhaling a mixture of damaging chemicals. Their hours of exposure were far longer than those of a chemical factory worker, and they wore no respirators or goggles. Nor could they simply open a door and escape. Helplessness and despair were the main responses to the blackened craters and scattered cinders behind their back yards.

But public officials often characterized the residents as hypochondriacs. Every 30

262

agent of government had been called on the phone or sent pleas for help, but none offered aid.

Commissioner Clifford expressed irritation at my printed reports of illness, and disagreement began to surface in the newsroom on how the stories should be printed. "There's a high rate of cancer among my friends," Dr. Clifford argued. "It doesn't mean anything."

Yet as interest in the small community increased, further revelations shook the neighborhood. In addition to benzene, eighty or more other compounds were found in the makeshift dump, ten of them potential carcinogens. The physiological effects they could cause were profound and diverse. At least fourteen of them could impact on the brain and central nervous system. Two of them, carbon tetrachloride and chlorobenzene, could readily cause narcotic and anesthetic consequences. Many others were known to cause headaches, seizures, loss of hair, anemia, or skin rashes. Together, the compounds were capable of inflicting innumerable illnesses, and no one knew what new concoctions were being formulated by their mixture underground.

Edwin and Aileen Voorhees had the most to be concerned about. When a state biophysicist analyzed the air content of their basement, he determined that the safe exposure time there was less than 2.4 minutes—the toxicity in the basement was thousands of times the acceptable limit for twenty-four-hour-breathing. This did not mean they would necessarily become permanently ill, but their chances of contracting cancer, for example, had been measurably increased. In July, I visited Mrs. Voorhees for further discussion of her problems, and as we sat in the kitchen, drinking coffee, the industrial odors were apparent. Aileen, usually chipper and feisty, was visibly anxious. She stared down at the table, talking only in a lowered voice. Everything now looked different to her. The home she and Edwin had built had become their jail cell. Their yard was but a pathway through which toxicants entered the cellar walls. The field out back, that proposed "park," seemed destined to be the ruin of their lives.

On July 14 I received a call from the state health department with some shocking news. A preliminary review showed that women living at the southern end had suffered a high rate of miscarriages and had given birth to an abnormally high number of children with birth defects. In one age group, 35.3 percent had records of spontaneous abortions. That was far in excess of the norm. The odds against it happening by chance were 250 to one. These tallies, it was stressed, were "conservative" figures. Four children in one small section of the neighborhood had documentable birth defects, club feet, retardation, and deafness. Those who lived there the longest suffered the highest rates.

The data on miscarriages and birth defects, coupled with the other accounts of illness, finally pushed the state's bureaucracy into motion. A meeting was scheduled for August 2, at which time the state health commissioner, Dr.

Robert Whalen, would formally address the issue. The day before the meeting, Dr. Nicholas Vianna, a state epidemiologist, told me that the residents were also incurring some degree of liver damage. Blood analyses had shown hepatitis-like symptoms in enzyme levels. Dozens if not hundreds of people, apparently, had been adversely affected.

In Albany, on August 2, Dr. Whalen read a lengthy statement in which he   36
urged that pregnant women and children under two years of age leave the southern end of the dump site immediately. He declared the Love Canal an official emergency, citing it as a "great and imminent peril to the health of the general public."

When Commissioner Whalen's words hit 97th and 99th streets, by way of   37
one of the largest banner headlines in the Niagara *Gazette's* 125-year history, dozens of people massed on the streets, shouting into bullhorns and micro-phones to voice frustrations that had been accumulating for months. Many of them vowed a tax strike because their homes were rendered unmarketable and unsafe. They attacked their government for ignoring their welfare. A man of high authority, a physician with a title, had confirmed that their lives were in danger. Most wanted to leave the neighborhood immediately.

Terror and anger roiled together, exacerbated by Dr. Whalen's failure to   38
provide a government-funded evacuation plan. His words were only a recom-mendation: individual families had to choose whether to risk their health and remain, or abandon their houses and, in so doing, write off a lifetime of work and savings.

On August 3, Dr. Whalen decided he should speak to the people. He arrived   39
with Dr. David Axelrod, a deputy who had directed the state's investigation, and Thomas Frey, a key aide to Governor Hugh Carey.

At a public meeting, held in the 99th Street School auditorium, Frey was   40
given the grueling task of controlling the crowd of 500 angry and frightened people. In an attempt to calm them, he announced that a meeting between the state and the White House had been scheduled for the following week. The state would propose that Love Canal be classified a national disaster, thereby freeing federal funds. For now, however, he could promise no more. Neither could Dr. Whalen and his staff of experts. All they could say was what was already known: twenty-five organic compounds, some of them capable of caus-ing cancer, were in their homes, and because young children were especially prone to toxic effects, they should be moved to another area.

Dr. Whalen's order had applied only to those living at the canal's southern   41
end, on its immediate periphery. But families living across the street from the dump site, or at the northern portion, where the chemicals were not so visible at the surface, reported afflictions remarkably similar to those suffered by families whose yards abutted the southern end. Serious respiratory problems, nervous disorders, and rectal bleeding were reported by many who were not covered by the order.

Throughout the following day, residents posted signs of protest on their front 42
fences or porch posts. "Love Canal Kills," they said, or "Give Me Liberty, I've
Got Death." Emotionally exhausted and uncertain about their future, men
stayed home from work, congregating on the streets or comforting their wives.
By this time the board of education had announced it was closing the 99th
Street School for the following year, because of its proximity to the exposed
toxicants. Still, no public relief was provided for the residents.

Another meeting was held that evening, at a firehall on 102nd Street. It was 43
unruly, but the people, who had called the session in an effort to organize
themselves, managed to form an alliance, the Love Canal Homeowners Association, and to elect as president Lois Gibbs, a pretty, twenty-seven-year-old
woman with jet-black hair who proved remarkably adept at dealing with experienced politicians and at keeping the matter in the news. After Mrs. Gibbs'
election, Congressman John LaFalce entered the hall and announced, to wild
applause, that the Federal Disaster Assistance Administration would be represented the next morning, and that the state's two senators, Daniel Patrick
Moynihan and Jacob Javits, were working with him in an attempt to get funds
from Congress.

With the Love Canal story now attracting attention from the national media, 44
the Governor's office announced that Hugh Carey would be at the 99th Street
School on August 7 to address the people. Decisions were being made in Albany
and Washington. Hours before the Governor's arrival, a sudden burst of "urgent"
reports from Washington came across the newswires. President Jimmy Carter
had officially declared the Hooker dump site a national emergency.

Hugh Carey was applauded on his arrival. The Governor announced that 45
the state, through its Urban Development Corporation, planned to purchase,
at fair market value, those homes rendered uninhabitable by the marauding
chemicals. He spared no promises. "You will not have to make mortgage
payments on homes you don't want or cannot occupy. Don't worry about the
banks. The state will take care of them." By the standards of Niagara Falls,
where the real estate market was depressed, the houses were in the middle-class
range, worth from $20,000 to $40,000 apiece. The state would assess each
house and purchase it, and also pay the costs of moving, temporary housing
during the transition period, and special items not covered by the usual real
estate assessment, such as installation of telephones.

First in a trickle and then, by September, in droves, the families gathered 46
their belongings and carted them away. Moving vans crowded 97th and 99th
streets. Linesmen went from house to house disconnecting the telephones and
electrical wires, while carpenters pounded plywood over the windows to keep
vandals away. By the following spring, 237 families were gone; 170 of them
had moved into new houses. In time the state erected around a six-block

residential area a green chain-link fence, eight feet in height, clearly demarcating the contamination zone.

In October 1978, the long-awaited remedial drainage program began at the south end. Trees were uprooted, fences and garages torn down, and swimming pools removed from the area. So great were residents' apprehensions that dangerous fumes would be released over the surrounding area that the state, at a cost of $500,000, placed seventy-five buses at emergency evacuation pickup spots during the months of work, in the event that outlying homes had to be vacated quickly because of an explosion. The plan was to construct drain tiles around the channel's periphery, where the back yards had been located, in order to divert leakage to seventeen-foot-deep wet wells from which contaminated groundwater could be drawn and treated by filtration through activated carbon. (Removing the chemicals themselves would have been financially prohibitive, perhaps costing as much as $100 million—and even then the materials would have to be buried elsewhere.) After the trenching was complete, and the sewers installed, the canal was to be covered by a sloping mound of clay and planted with grass. One day, city officials hoped, the wasteland would become a park.

In spite of the corrective measures and the enormous effort by the state health department, which took thousands of blood samples from past and current residents and made uncounted analyses of soil, water, and air, the full range of the effects remained unknown. In neighborhoods immediately outside the official "zone of contamination," more than 500 families were left near the desolate setting, their health still in jeopardy. The state announced it would buy no more homes.

The first public indication that chemical contamination had probably reached streets to the east and west of 97th and 99th streets, and to the north and south as well, came on August 11, 1978, when sump-pump samples I had taken from 100th and 101st streets, analyzed in a laboratory, showed the trace presence of a number of chemicals found in the canal itself, including lindane, a restricted pesticide that had been suspected of causing cancer in laboratory animals. While probing 100th Street, I knocked on the door of Patricia Pino, thirty-four, a blond divorcee with a young son and daughter. I had noticed that some of the leaves on a large tree in front of her house exhibited a black oiliness much like that on the trees and shrubs of 99th Street; she was located near what had been a drainage swale.

After I had extracted a jar of sediment from her sump pump for the analysis, we conversed about her family situation and what the trauma now unfolding meant to them. Ms. Pino was extremely depressed and embittered. Both of her children had what appeared to be slight liver abnormalities, and her son had been plagued with "non-specific" allergies, teary eyes, sinus trouble, which improved markedly when he was sent away from home. Patricia told of times, during the heat of summer, when fumes were readily noticeable in her basement and sometimes even upstairs. She herself had been treated for a possibly cancerous condition of her cervix. But, like others, her family was now trapped.

On September 24, 1978, I obtained a state memorandum that said chemical 51 infiltration of the outer regions was significant indeed. The letter, sent from the state laboratories to the U.S. Environmental Protection Agency, said, "Preliminary analysis of soil samples demonstrates extensive migration of potentially toxic materials outside the immediate canal area." There it was, in the state's own words. Not long afterward, the state medical investigator, Dr. Nicholas Vianna, reported indications that residents from 93rd to 103rd streets might also have incurred liver damage.

On October 4, a young boy, John Allen Kenny, who lived quite a distance 52 north of the evacuation zone, died. The fatality was due to the failure of another organ that can be readily affected by toxicants, the kidney. Naturally, suspicions were raised that his death was in some way related to a creek that still flowed behind his house and carried, near an outfall, the odor of chlorinated compounds. Because the creek served as a catch basin for a portion of the Love Canal, the state studied an autopsy of the boy. No conclusions were reached. John Allen's parents, Norman, a chemist, and Luella, a medical research assistant, were unsatisfied with the state's investigation, which they felt was "superficial." Luella said, "He played in the creek all the time. There had been restrictions on the older boys, but he was the youngest and played with them when they were old enough to go to the creek. We let him do what the other boys did. He died of nephrosis. Proteins were passing through his urine. Well, in reading the literature, we discovered that chemicals can trigger this. There was no evidence of infection, which there should have been, and there was damage to his thymus and brain. He also had nosebleeds and headaches, and dry heaves. So our feeling is that chemicals probably triggered it."

The likelihood that water-carried chemicals had escaped from the canal's 53 deteriorating bounds and were causing problems quite a distance from the site was not lost upon the Love Canal Homeowners Association and its president, Lois Gibbs, who was attempting to have additional families relocated. Because she lived on 101st Street, she was one of those left behind, with no means of moving despite persistent medical difficulties in her six-year-old son, Michael, who had been operated on twice for urethral strictures. [Mrs. Gibbs's husband, a worker at a chemical plant, brought home only $150 a week, she told me, and when they subtracted from that the $90 a week for food and other necessities, clothing costs for their two children, $125 a month for mortgage payments and taxes, utility and phone expenses, and medical bills, they had hardly enough cash to buy gas and cigarettes, let alone vacate their house.]

Assisted by two other stranded residents, Marie Pozniak and Grace McCoulf, 54 and with the professional analysis of a Buffalo scientist named Beverly Paigen, Lois Gibbs mapped out the swale and creekbed areas, many of them long ago filled, and set about interviewing the numerous people who lived on or near formerly wet ground. The survey indicated that these people were suffering from an abnormal number of kidney and bladder aggravations and problems of the reproductive system. In a report to the state, Dr. Paigen claimed to have found, in 245 homes outside the evacuation zone, thirty-four miscarriages, eighteen birth defects, nineteen nervous breakdowns, ten cases of epilepsy, and high rates of hyperactivity and suicide.

In their roundabout way, the state health experts, after an elaborate investi- 55
gation, confirmed some of the homeowners' worst fears. On February 8, 1979, Dr. David Axelrod, who by then had been appointed health commissioner, and whose excellence as a scientist was widely acknowledged, issued a new order that officially extended the health emergency of the previous August, citing high incidences of birth deformities and miscarriages in the areas where creeks and swales had once flowed, or where swamps had been. With that, the state offered to evacuate temporarily those families with pregnant women or children under the age of two from the outer areas of contamination, up to 103rd Street. But no additional homes would be purchased; nor was another large-scale evacuation, temporary or otherwise, under consideration. Those who left under the new plan would have to return when their children passed the age limit.

Twenty-three families accepted the state's offer. Another seven families, 56
ineligible under the plan but of adequate financial means to do so, simply left their homes and took the huge loss of investment. Soon boarded windows speckled the outlying neighborhoods.

The previous November and December, not long after the evacuation of 57
97th and 99th streets, I became interested in the possibility that Hooker might have buried in the Love Canal waste residues from the manufacture of what is known as 2,4,5-trichlorophenol. My curiosity was keen because I knew that this substance, which Hooker produced for the manufacture of the antibacterial agent hexachlorophene, and which was also used to make defoliants such as Agent Orange, the herbicide employed in Vietnam, carries with it an unwanted by-product technically called 2,3,7,8-tetrachlorodibenzo-para-dioxin, or tetra dioxin. The potency of dioxin of this isomer is nearly beyond imagination. Although its toxicological effects are not fully known, the few experts on the subject estimate that if three ounces were evenly distributed and subsequently ingested among a million people, or perhaps more than that, all of them would die. It compares in toxicity to the botulinum toxin. On skin contact, dioxin causes a disfiguration called "chloracne," which begins as pimples, lesions, and cysts, but can lead to calamitous internal damage. Some scientists suspect that dioxin causes cancer, perhaps even malignancies that occur, in galloping fashion, within a short time of contact. At least two (some estimates went as high as eleven) pounds of dioxin were dispersed over Seveso, Italy, in 1976, after an explosion of a trichlorophenol plant: dead animals littered the streets, and more than 300 acres of land were immediately evacuated. In Vietnam, the spraying

of Agent Orange, because of the dioxin contaminant, was banned in 1970, when the first effects on human beings began to surface, including dioxin's powerful teratogenic, or fetus-deforming, effects.

I posed two questions concerning trichlorophenol: Were wastes from the process buried in the canal? If so, what were the quantities? 58

On November 8, before Hooker answered my queries, I learned that, indeed, trichlorophenol had been found in liquids pumped from the remedial drain ditches. No dioxin had been found yet, and some officials, ever wary of more emotionalism among the people, argued that, because the compound was not soluble in water, there was little chance it had migrated off-site. Officials at Newco Chemical Waste Systems, a local waste disposal firm, at the same time claimed that if dioxin had been there, it had probably been photolytically destroyed. Its half-life, they contended, was just a few short years. 59

I knew from Whiteside, however, that in every known case, waste from 2,4,5-trichlorophenol carried dioxin with it. I also knew that dioxin *could* become soluble in groundwater and migrate into the neighborhood upon mixing with solvents such as benzene. Moreover, because it had been buried, sunlight would not break it down. 60

On Friday, November 10, I called Hooker again to urge that they answer my questions. Their spokesman, Bruce Davis, came to the phone and, in a controlled tone, gave me the answer: His firm had indeed buried trichlorophenol in the canal—200 tons of it. 61

Immediately I called Whiteside. His voice took on an urgent tone. According to his calculation, if 200 tons of trichlorophenol were there, in all likelihood they were accompanied by 130 pounds of tetra dioxin, an amount equaling the estimated total content of dioxin in the thousands of tons of Agent Orange rained upon Vietnamese jungles. The seriousness of the crisis had deepened, for now the Love Canal was not only a dump for highly dangerous solvents and pesticides; it was also the broken container for one of the most toxic substances ever synthesized by man. 62

I reckoned that the main danger was to those working on the remedial project, digging in the trenches. The literature on dioxin indicated that, even in quantities at times too small to detect, the substance possessed vicious characteristics. In one case, workers in a trichlorophenol plant had developed chloracne, although the substance could not be traced on the equipment with which they worked. The mere tracking of minuscule amounts of dioxin on a pedestrian's shoes in Seveso led to major concerns, and, according to Whiteside, a plant in Amsterdam, upon being found contaminated with dioxin, had been "dismantled, brick by brick, and the material embedded in concrete, loaded at a specially constructed dock, on ships, and dumped at sea, in deep water near the Azores." Workers in trichlorophenol plants had died of cancer or severe liver damage, or had suffered emotional and sexual disturbances. 63

Less than a month after the first suspicions arose, on the evening of December 64
9, I received a call from Dr. Axelrod. "We found it. The dioxin. In a drainage trench behind 97th Street. It was in the part-per-trillion range."

The state remained firm in its plans to continue the construction, and, 65 despite the ominous new findings, no further evacuations were announced. During the next several weeks, small incidents of vandalism occurred along 97th and 99th streets. Tacks were spread on the road, causing numerous flat tires on the trucks. Signs of protest were hung in the school. Meetings of the Love Canal Homeowners Association became more vociferous. Christmas was near, and in the association's office at the 99th Street School, a holiday tree was decorated with bulbs arranged to spell "DIOXIN."

The Love Canal people chanted and cursed at meetings with the state 66 officials, cried on the telephone, burned an effigy of the health commissioner, traveled to Albany with a makeshift child's coffin, threatened to hold officials hostage, sent letters and telegrams to the White House, held days of mourning and nights of prayer. On Mother's Day this year, they marched down the industrial corridor and waved signs denouncing Hooker, which had issued not so much as a statement of remorse. But no happy ending was in store for them. The federal government was clearly not planning to come to their rescue, and the state felt it had already done more than its share. City Hall was silent and remains silent today. Some residents still hoped that, miraculously, an agency of government would move them. All of them watched with anxiety as each newborn came to the neighborhood, and they looked at their bodies for signs of cancer.

One hundred and thirty families from the Love Canal area began leaving 67 their homes last August and September, seeking temporary refuge in local hotel rooms under a relocation plan funded by the state which had been implemented after fumes became so strong, during remedial trenching operations, that the United Way abandoned a care center it had opened in the neighborhood.

As soon as remedial construction is complete, the people will probably be 68 forced to return home, as the state will no longer pay for their lodging. Some have threatened to barricade themselves in the hotels. Some have mentioned violence. Anne Hillis of 102nd Street, who told reporters her first child had been born so badly decomposed that doctors could not determine its sex, was so bitter that she threw table knives and a soda can at the state's on-site coordinator.

In October, Governor Carey announced that the state probably would buy 69 an additional 200 to 240 homes, at an expense of some $5 million. In the meantime, lawyers have prepared lawsuits totaling about $2.65 billion and have sought court action for permanent relocation. Even if the latter action is successful, and they are allowed to move, the residents' plight will not necessarily have ended. The psychological scars are bound to remain among them and their children, along with the knowledge that, because they have already been exposed, they may never fully escape the Love Canal's insidious grasp.

QUESTIONS

1. What caused the poisoning of Love Canal? Why did it take so long for both local and state officials to acknowledge the seriousness of the condition of Love Canal?

2. What kind of information does Brown provide to document the tragedy of Love Canal? What role did he play in uncovering this information?

3. Consider the introduction to this article. Why did Brown choose to tell the story of the Schroeder family in the opening paragraphs?

4. The power of this essay has much to do with the overwhelming tragedy and horror it relates. Find passages in the essay that you feel are especially effective. Explain how Brown creates this effect on the reader.

5. In this essay, Brown relies primarily on the factual data he has collected to tell the story of Love Canal. Compare this writer's approach with that found in newspapers featuring sensational headlines. Analyze one of the headlined stories. How much factual evidence is present? How would such a newspaper's treatment of the story of the Schroeder family differ from Brown's treatment?

6. Environmental calamities such as Love Canal or Three Mile Island have become a permanent part of our lives. The Environmental Protection Agency reports that in most communities the groundwater has become so laced with toxic chemicals that it is no longer safe to drink. Investigate some aspect of the environment in your community such as the water supply or the quality of the air. Write a report based on your investigation.

MAKING CONNECTIONS

Compare Brown's presentation of the Love Canal story with Verlyn Klinkenborg's "Back to Love Canal." What similarities and differences can you find in the kinds of information that each author has presented? What similarities and differences can you find in the ways that each author has organized and presented information? What similarities and differences can you find in the tone of each author toward the situation, and in the way that each author conveys his attitude toward the situation? Based on these similarities and differences, try to reach some conclusions about what you consider to be the most effective ways to present stories of provocative subject matter.

THE DISCUS THROWER

Richard Selzer

*Richard Selzer is a surgeon who has written widely, pub-
lishing articles in popular magazines as well as occasional
short fiction. (See earlier biographical note, page 134, for
additional details.) In the essay reprinted here, which first
appeared in* Harper's *magazine in 1977, Selzer reports on
the visits he made to one of his patients.*

I spy on my patients. Ought not a doctor to observe his patients by any 1
means and from any stance, that he might the more fully assemble evidence?
So I stand in the doorways of hospital rooms and gaze. Oh, it is not all that
furtive an act. Those in bed need only look up to discover me. But they never
do.

From the doorway of Room 542 the man in the bed seems deeply tanned. 2
Blue eyes and close-cropped white hair give him the appearance of vigor and
good health. But I know that his skin is not brown from the sun. It is rusted,
rather, in the last stage of containing the vile repose within. And the blue eyes
are frosted, looking inward like the windows of a snowbound cottage. This man
is blind. This man is also legless—the right leg missing from midthigh down,
the left from just below the knee. It gives him the look of a bonsai, roots and
branches pruned into the dwarfed facsimile of a great tree.

Propped on pillows, he cups his right thigh in both hands. Now and then 3
he shakes his head as though acknowledging the intensity of his suffering. In
all of this he makes no sound. Is he mute as well as blind?

The room in which he dwells is empty of all possessions—no get-well cards, 4
small, private caches of food, day-old flowers, slippers, all the usual kickshaws
of the sickroom. There is only the bed, a chair, a nightstand, and a tray on
wheels that can be swung across his lap for meals.

"What time is it?" he asks. 5

"Three o'clock." 6

"Morning or afternoon?" 7

"Afternoon." 8

He is silent. There is nothing else he wants to know. 9

"How are you?" I say. 10

"Who is it?" he asks. 11

"It's the doctor. How do you feel?" 12

He does not answer right away. 13

"Feel?" he says.   14

"I hope you feel better," I say.   15

I press the button at the side of the bed.   16

"Down you go," I say.   17

"Yes, down," he says.   18

He falls back upon the bed awkwardly. His stumps, unweighted by legs and   19
feet, rise in the air, presenting themselves. I unwrap the bandages from the
stumps, and begin to cut away the black scabs and the dead, glazed fat with
scissors and forceps. A shard of white bone comes loose. I pick it away. I wash
the wounds with disinfectant and redress the stumps. All this while, he does
not speak. What is he thinking behind those lids that do not blink? Is he
remembering a time when he was whole? Does he dream of feet? Of when his
body was not a rotting log?

He lies solid and inert. In spite of everything, he remains impressive, as   20
though he were a sailor standing athwart a slanting deck.

"Anything more I can do for you?" I ask.   21

For a long moment he is silent.   22

"Yes," he says at last and without the least irony. "You can bring me a pair   23
of shoes."

In the corridor, the head nurse is waiting for me.   24

"We have to do something about him," she says. "Every morning he orders   25
scrambled eggs for breakfast, and, instead of eating them, he picks up the plate
and throws it against the wall."

"Throws his plate?"   26

"Nasty. That's what he is. No wonder his family doesn't come to visit. They   27
probably can't stand him any more than we can."

She is waiting for me to do something.   28

"Well?"   29

"We'll see," I say.   30

The next morning I am waiting in the corridor when the kitchen delivers   31
his breakfast. I watch the aide place the tray on the stand and swing it across
his lap. She presses the button to raise the head of the bed. Then she leaves.

In time the man reaches to find the rim of the tray, then on to find the   32
dome of the covered dish. He lifts off the cover and places it on the stand. He
fingers across the plate until he probes the eggs. He lifts the plate in both hands,
sets it on the palm of his right hand, centers it, balances it. He hefts it up and
down slightly, getting the feel of it. Abruptly, he draws back his right arm as
far as he can.

There is the crack of the plate breaking against the wall at the foot of his   33
bed and the small wet sound of the scrambled eggs dropping to the floor.

And then he laughs. It is a sound you have never heard. It is something   34
new under the sun. It could cure cancer.

Out in the corridor, the eyes of the head nurse narrow. 35

"Laughed, did he?" 36

She writes something down on her clipboard. 37

A second aide arrives, brings a second breakfast tray, puts it on the nightstand, 38
out of his reach. She looks over at me shaking her head and making her mouth
go. I see that we are to be accomplices.

"I've got to feed you," she says to the man. 39

"Oh, no you don't," the man says. 40

"Oh, yes I do," the aide says, "after the way you just did. Nurse says so." 41

"Get me my shoes," the man says. 42

"Here's oatmeal," the aide says. "Open." And she touches the spoon to his 43
lower lip.

"I ordered scrambled eggs," says the man. 44

"That's right," the aide says. 45

I step forward. 46

"Is there anything I can do?" I say. 47

"Who are you?" the man asks. 48

In the evening I go once more to that ward to make my rounds. The head 49
nurse reports to me that Room 542 is deceased. She has discovered this quite
by accident, she says. No, there had been no sound. Nothing. It's a blessing,
she says.

I go into his room, a spy looking for secrets. He is still there in his bed. His 50
face is relaxed, grave, dignified. After a while, I turn to leave. My gaze sweeps
the wall at the foot of the bed, and I see the place where it has been repeatedly
washed, where the wall looks very clean and very white.

QUESTIONS

1. Why does the writer say, "I spy on my patients" (paragraph 1)? Don't doctors
usually "look in on" their patients? What effect does Selzer hope to achieve by starting
with such a statement?

2. The writer uses the present tense throughout this piece. Would the past tense be
just as effective? Explain your answer.

3. Selzer writes in the first person. Why might he have decided to make himself
prominent in the report in that way? How would his report have come across if it had
been written in the third person rather than the first person?

4. How would you describe this doctor's attitude toward his patient? How would you
describe the nurse's attitude toward the patient? How does the narrator manage to
characterize himself in one way and the nurse in another?

5. Is the title, "The Discus Thrower," appropriate for this piece? In a slightly revised
version, the title was changed to "Four Appointments with the Discus Thrower." Is this
a better title?

6. What do you think Selzer's purpose was in writing this essay? Did he simply wish to shock us, or is there a message in this piece for the medical profession or for those of us who fear illness and death?

7. The essay reports on four visits to the patient by the doctor. Write a shorter version reporting on two or more visits by the head nurse. How would she react to the patient's request for shoes? How might her own point of view explain some of her reactions?

8. For many of us, knowledge of hospitals is limited, perhaps to television shows in which the hospital functions as a backdrop for the romances of its staff. Write a short essay in which you present your conception of what a hospital is and in which you consider how Selzer's essay either made you revise that conception or reaffirmed what you know through experience.

MAKING CONNECTIONS

Selzer and Roy C. Selby, Jr., write of human subjects. Farley Mowat and Jane van Lawick-Goodall write of animals. Does this choice of subject seem to affect the distance the writer maintains, achieves, or overcomes in offering his or her report? Do you find any common denominators here? How do you account for them?

A DELICATE OPERATION
Roy C. Selby, Jr.

*Roy C. Selby, Jr., (b. 1930) graduated from Louisiana State
University and the University of Arkansas Medical School,
where he specialized in neurology and neurosurgery. He now
practices in the Chicago area and is the author of numerous
professional articles on neurosurgery. "A Delicate Operation," which first appeared in* Harper's *magazine in 1975,
reports for a more general audience the details of a difficult
brain operation.*

In the autumn of 1973 a woman in her early fifties noticed, upon closing
one eye while reading, that she was unable to see clearly. Her eyesight grew
slowly worse. Changing her eyeglasses did not help. She saw an ophthalmologist, who found that her vision was seriously impaired in both eyes. She then
saw a neurologist, who confirmed the finding and obtained X rays of the skull
and an EMI scan—a photograph of the patient's head. The latter revealed a
tumor growing between the optic nerves at the base of the brain. The woman
was admitted to the hospital by a neurosurgeon.

Further diagnosis, based on angiography, a detailed X-ray study of the cir-
culatory system, showed the tumor to be about two inches in diameter and
supplied by many small blood vessels. It rested beneath the brain, just above
the pituitary gland, stretching the the optic nerves to either side and intimately
close to the major blood vessels supplying the brain. Removing it would pose
many technical problems. Probably benign and slow-growing, it may have been
present for several years. If left alone it would continue to grow and produce
blindness and might become impossible to remove completely. Removing it,
however, might not improve the patient's vision and could make it worse. A
major blood vessel could be damaged, causing a stroke. Damage to the under-
surface of the brain could cause impairment of memory and changes in mood
and personality. The hypothalamus, a most important structure of the brain,
could be injured, causing coma, high fever, bleeding from the stomach, and
death.

The neurosurgeon met with the patient and her husband and discussed the
various possibilities. The common decision was to operate.

The patient's hair was shampooed for two nights before surgery. She was
given a cortisonelike drug to reduce the risk of damage to the brain during
surgery. Five units of blood were cross-matched, as a contingency against

hemorrhage. At 1:00 P.M. the operation began. After the patient was anesthe-tized her hair was completely clipped and shaved from the scalp. Her head was prepped with an organic iodine solution for ten minutes. Drapes were placed over her, leaving exposed only the forehead and crown of the skull. All the routine instruments were brought up—the electrocautery used to coagulate areas of bleeding, bipolar coagulation forceps to arrest bleeding from individual blood vessels without damaging adjacent tissues, and small suction tubes to remove blood and cerebrospinal fluid from the head, thus giving the surgeon a better view of the tumor and surrounding areas.

A curved incision was made behind the hairline so it would be concealed 5 when the hair grew back. It extended almost from ear to ear. Plastic clips were applied to the cut edges of the scalp to arrest bleeding. The scalp was folded back to the level of the eyebrows. Incisions were made in the muscle of the right temple, and three sets of holes were drilled near the temple and the top of the head because the tumor had to be approached from directly in front. The drill, powered by nitrogen, was replaced with a fluted steel blade, and the holes were connected. The incised piece of skull was pried loose and held out of the way by a large sponge.

Beneath the bone is a yellowish leatherlike membrane, the dura, that sur- 6 rounds the brain. Down the middle of the head the dura carries a large vein, but in the area near the nose the vein is small. At that point the vein and dura were cut, and clips made of tantalum, a hard metal, were applied to arrest and prevent bleeding. Sutures were put into the dura and tied to the scalp to keep the dura open and retracted. A malleable silver retractor, resembling the blade of a butter knife, was inserted between the brain and skull. The anesthesiologist began to administer a drug to relax the brain by removing some of its water, making it easier for the surgeon to manipulate the retractor, hold the brain back, and see the tumor. The nerve tracts for smell were cut on both sides to provide additional room. The tumor was seen approximately two-and-one-half inches behind the base of the nose. It was pink in color. On touching it, it proved to be very fibrous and tough. A special retractor was attached to the skull, enabling the other retractor blades to be held automatically and freeing the surgeon's hands. With further displacement of the frontal lobes of the brain, the tumor could be seen better, but no normal structures—the carotid arteries, their branches, and the optic nerves—were visible. The tumor obscured them.

A surgical microscope was placed above the wound. The surgeon had selected 7 the lenses and focal length prior to the operation. Looking through the micro-scope, he could see some of the small vessels supplying the tumor and he coagulated them. He incised the tumor to attempt to remove its core and thus collapse it, but the substance of the tumor was too firm to be removed in this fashion. He then began to slowly dissect the tumor from the adjacent brain tissue and from where he believed the normal structures to be.

Using small squares of cotton, he began to separate the tumor from very 8 loose fibrous bands connecting it to the brain and to the right side of the part of the skull where the pituitary gland lies. The right optic nerve and carotid artery came into view, both displaced considerably to the right. The optic nerve had a normal appearance. He protected these structures with cotton compresses placed between them and the tumor. He began to raise the tumor from the skull and slowly to reach the point of its origin and attachment—just in front of the pituitary gland and medial to the left optic nerve, which still could not be seen. The small blood vessels entering the tumor were cauterized. The upper portion of the tumor was gradually separated from the brain, and the branches of the carotid arteries and the branches to the tumor were coagulated. The tumor was slowly and gently lifted from its bed, and for the first time the left carotid artery and optic nerve could be seen. Part of the tumor adhered to this nerve. The bulk of the tumor was amputated, leaving a small bit attached to the nerve. Very slowly and carefully the tumor fragment was resected.

The tumor now removed, a most impressive sight came into view—the 9 pituitary gland and its stalk of attachment to the hypothalamus, the hypothalamus itself, and the brainstem, which conveys nerve impulses between the body and the brain. As far as could be determined, no damage had been done to these structures or other vital centers, but the left optic nerve, from chronic pressure of the tumor, appeared gray and thin. Probably it would not completely recover its function.

After making certain there was no bleeding, the surgeon closed the wounds 10 and placed wire mesh over the holes in the skull to prevent dimpling of the scalp over the points that had been drilled. A gauze dressing was applied to the patient's head. She was awakened and sent to the recovery room.

Even with the microscope, damage might still have occurred to the cerebral 11 cortex and hypothalamus. It would require at least a day to be reasonably certain there was none, and about seventy-two hours to monitor for the major postoperative dangers—swelling of the brain and blood clots forming over the surface of the brain. The surgeon explained this to the patient's husband, and both of them waited anxiously. The operation had required seven hours. A glass of orange juice had given the surgeon some additional energy during the closure of the wound. Though exhausted, he could not fall asleep until after two in the morning, momentarily expecting a call from the nurse in the intensive care unit announcing deterioration of the patient's condition.

At 8:00 A.M. the surgeon saw the patient in the intensive care unit. She was 12 alert, oriented, and showed no sign of additional damage to the optic nerves or the brain. She appeared to be in better shape than the surgeon or her husband.

QUESTIONS

1. Why did the neurosurgeon decide to operate? What could have happened if the patient chose not to have the operation? What effect does knowing this information have on the reader?

2. Although the essay is probably based on the writer's experience, it is reported in the third person. What effect does this have on the information reported? How would the report have come across if it had been written in the first person?

3. Selby uses different methods of reporting to create the drama of "A Delicate Operation." At what point in the essay does he provide background information? How much of the essay reports events before, during, and after the operation? At what points does the writer explain terms and procedures for the reader?

4. Which passages in this essay do you find especially powerful? How did Selby create this effect?

5. Write a report of a procedure with which you are familiar and which calls for some expertise or sensitivity or a combination of these because there is always the chance that something could go wrong. You should proceed step by step, giving the reader as much information as necessary to understand and follow the procedure. At appropriate points, also include the problems you face. Suggestions are trimming a Christmas tree, carrying out a chemistry experiment, getting a child off to school, or preparing a gourmet meal.

MAKING CONNECTIONS

1. Compare Selby's essay with Richard Selzer's "The Discus Thrower." Whereas Selby writes in the third person, Selzer uses the first. How do those choices affect the resulting essays?

2. Rewrite several paragraphs of Selby's and Selzer's essays, changing one from third to first person and the other from first to third. How do these changes alter the nature of the information presented and the effect of each report?

TIBETAN MEDICINE:
THE SCIENCE OF HEALING

John F. Avedon

*John F. Avedon is a writer whose interest in Tibet began in
1973, on his first trip to Asia, when he toured a Tibetan
refugee camp in New Delhi, India. The material presented
here is a chapter from his book on present-day Tibet,* In
Exile *from the* Land of Snows. *His intent was "to tell
Tibet's tale through the lives of those who have both defined
and been governed by the major developments in recent
history." Avedon also included "some measure of Tibetan
civilization, the spiritual underpinnings of which permeate
every facet of the country's political life." In the following
selection, the life of Dr. Yeshi Dhonden, physician to the
Dalai Lama, the ruler of the Tibetans, serves to illuminate
the ancient science of Tibetan medicine.*

Dr. Yeshi Dhonden pressed the three middle fingers of his right hand gently   1
along the inside of William Schneider's left wrist, bowed his head and listened.
The fifty-two-year-old patient smiled, perplexed. The physician before him wore
neither a white coat nor a name tag. He asked no questions and carried no
charts or instruments. Dressed in maroon robes, head shaved, a turquoise-
studded charm box bulging beneath his orange shirt, Dr. Dhonden remained
motionless, deep in concentration. A minute later, he took the patient's right
arm and briefly pressed the radial artery as if to confirm his findings. Ushering
Mr. Schneider into an adjacent room, the doctor gestured for him to undress,
whereupon he pressed selected points along his spine. With each touch, Mr.
Schneider cried out in pain. Dr. Dhonden nodded sympathetically and told
him to get dressed.

In his guest suite at the University of Virginia, Dr. Yeshi Dhonden offered   2
his diagnosis of William Schneider, a man he knew nothing of and had met
only minutes before. "Many years ago you lifted a heavy object," he said,
speaking through an interpreter. "At that time you damaged a channel in the
vicinity of your right kidney, blocking the normal flow of wind through your
back. The wind has accumulated outside the channel, there is bone deterioration and the disease has become quite severe." Mr. Schneider was stunned. For
three years, he confirmed, he had suffered from acute arthritis along the neck
and lower back. The illness had caused incapacitating pain, and he had been

forced to give up his job. But he was even more astonished at Dr. Dhonden's ability to reconstruct his past. "In 1946," he recalled, "I injured my back lifting a milk can out of a cooler. I was in bed a week, and as soon as I got up I reinjured it and was bed-ridden again. That must have been the start of the whole problem."

It was a diagnosis that Western physicians could arrive at simply by using an   3
X ray, but Dr. Yeshi Dhonden, the Dalai Lama's personal physician, sent by him in the winter of 1980 to introduce Tibetan medicine to the West, enthralled American doctors and patients alike with his unique skills. "It's quite conceivable that in our attempt to be scientific, some of our powers of observation have atrophied," said Dr. Gerald Goldstein, a professor at the University of Virginia's Medical Oncology Department, who worked closely with the Tibetan physician during his stay. "Dr. Dhonden, on the other hand, is totally attuned to every-thing that is going on. He uses all of his senses as his medical instrument. Our patients have been very impressed." Dr. Richard Selzer, assistant professor of surgery at Yale University, met Yeshi Dhonden in 1974 on his first visit to the United States. "I went to observe Dr. Dhonden with some healthy skepticism," he recounted. "I was surprised and elated by what I found. It was as if he was a human electrocardiogram machine interpreting the component parts of the pulse. We have nothing like it in the West. It's a dimension of medicine that we have not yet realized." "Western scientific documentation of Tibetan claims is nonexistent," observed Dr. Herbert Benson, leader of a team of Harvard researchers that visited the Tibetan Medical Center in 1981. "It would be nice, though, to discover the worth of what they have developed over thousands of years. If their claims are only partly true they would be worthy of investigation. Therefore, can we really afford to ignore this?"

To test the efficacy of Tibetan drugs by laboratory standards, Yeshi Dhonden   4
agreed, while in Virginia, to engage in an experiment with cancerous mice. On the basis of a visual examination alone, he prescribed a general Tibetan cancer drug, comprised of over sixty ingredients, for nine tumor-implanted mice in a lab in the University of Virginia's vivarium. Six mice refused the medicine and died within thirty-five days. Three mice accepted it and survived up to fifty-three days. A second experiment involving sixteen animals confirmed the find-ings, producing the most successful results since work with the particular tumor involved began in 1967. Of even greater interest, though, was the fact that Dr. Dhonden had no knowledge of the nature of the cancer he was dealing with. "There are literally hundreds of kinds of tumors," commented Dr. Donald Baker, the researcher in charge of the experiment. "How often has Dr. Dhonden encountered a KHT anaplastic sarcoma growing in a highly inbred strain of $_3$CH/HEJ female mice? It would be utterly unreasonable to ask him to decide what would be the best treatment. If he had been familiar with these conditions he might well have effected a complete cure." "There is no question that this

is a very fertile area for cancer quacks," added Dr. Goldstein. "In the end, though, things either work or they don't work. Dr. Dhonden has things that work."

Sitting cross-legged over a cup of butter tea in his Virginia apartment, Dr. Dhonden offered a brief description of cancer in Tibetan terms. "I've treated perhaps one thousand cancer patients of which sixty to seventy percent have been cured," he maintained. "Our medical texts specify fifty-four types of tumors which appear at eighteen places in the body in one of three forms. We consider cancer to be a disease of the blood. It begins with pollutants in the environment. These, in turn, affect seven types of sentient beings in the body, two of which are most susceptible. They are extremely minute, but if you could see them, they would be round, red and flat. They can travel through the bloodstream in an instant, are formed with the embryo in the womb and normally function to maintain strength. In general the Buddha predicted that eighteen diseases would become prevalent in our time due to two causes, low moral conduct and pollution. Cancer is one of the eighteen."

Based on the results of his first experiment those physicians working with Yeshi Dhonden hoped to initiate a broader study of Tibetan medicine in the West. Dr. Dhonden, too, was eager to undertake an in-depth exchange of medical lore. "If Western medicine can come to understand the Tibetan view of the human organism," he commented toward the close of his stay in Virginia, "I feel it will be of inestimable value. Our medicine has many cures for diseases which Western doctors currently don't understand or have incorrectly identified. We successfully treat diabetes, various forms of coronary disease, arthritis, hepatitis, Parkinson's disease, cancers, ulcers and the common cold. We have difficulty treating epilepsy and paralysis. But because the Tibetan system is scientific, Western physicians, as scientists, will see what is of value and what is not." To illuminate an ancient science hidden behind the Himalayas for over two thousand years, Yeshi Dhonden described his own life and training as a Tibetan doctor.

Dr. Dhonden was born in 1929 into a wealthy family of farmers living in the small village of Namro, south of the Tsangpo River, one day's ride from Lhasa. Much of the land surrounding Namro belonged to the Dhonden family and their relatives. Five thousand sheep, yaks and horses and many fields of *chingko* or mountain barley were owned by Yeshi Dhonden's aunt and uncle, who, not having a male child, assumed he would grow up to run the estate. Dr. Dhonden's parents, however, felt differently. As their only child, they decided that Yeshi Dhonden should devote his life to the Dharma.[1] Accordingly, at the age of six, their son left his home and traveled a short way up the mountain behind Namro, to be accepted as a novice monk in the local mon-

---

[1] Dharma: the corpus of Buddhist teaching. [Eds.]

astery of Shedrup Ling. "I remember it all," recollected Dr. Dhonden. "Becoming a monk, entering into the comfort of the group, living with my teacher. I had a strong wish to learn quickly and my mind was very clear. I could memorize four of our long pages in a single day." Yeshi Dhonden's facility for memorization earned him a high position among his peers, on the basis of which he was selected at the age of eleven to represent Shedrup Ling at Mendzekhang, the larger of Lhasa's two state-run medical colleges. Like all monasteries, district headquarters and military camps, Shedrup Ling was required by the government to send medical students to Lhasa. Upon the completion of their training, they would then return to practice in their region. But while the monastery's superiors were not averse to receiving the government salary paid to them for their students' attendance, the four hundred monks were less than enthusiastic at the prospect of medical studies. "Everyone in the monastery was afraid that he would be selected," recalled Dr. Dhonden, laughing. "No one wanted to become a doctor. You have to spend at least eleven years in classes and there is a tremendous amount of memorization. But because I liked to memorize, when my parents told me that I had been chosen, I was eager to go."

The medical system Yeshi Dhonden was to study had begun as one of the ten branches of learning originally pursued by all Mahayana Buddhist monks. It flourished for over a thousand years in the great monastic universities of northern India, from whence it was taken to Tibet by two Indian pandits in the first century B.C. Thereafter, it was the province for almost seven hundred years of a single family of physicians attendant on the Royal Tibetan Court. With the introduction of over a hundred Buddhist medical texts in the sixth century, however, it grew into a widespread practice and was ultimately acclaimed by a conference of physicians from nine nations convened in Tibet, as the preeminent medical science of its time. Subsequently, Tibet's first medical college, called Melung or "Country of Medicine," was built in the eighth century by King Trisong Detsen in Kongpo, south of Lhasa. Melung inspired the founding of scores of medical schools, most contained in *dratsangs* or colleges appended to the country's larger monasteries. In the mid-seventeenth century, the Fifth Dalai Lama built Tibet's second medical college, called Chokpori, atop Iron Hill, just across from the Potala.[2] There, doctors from all across Tibet and Mongolia were trained to practice a composite of the various schools of medicine that had developed over the years. The need for more physicians in modern times resulted in the Thirteenth Dalai Lama's construction of Tibet's most recent central medical college, Mendzekhang or "Medicine House," in 1916.

Mendzekhang lay on the west side of Lhasa, next to the Tibetan government's newly built post and telegraph office. It was centered on a flagstone courtyard, with dormitories for students, both lay and monk, occupying two long wings, at the head of which, facing the main gate, stood the classrooms, assembly hall

8

9

---

[2] Potala: the winter palace of the Dalai Lama. [Eds.]

and the Master's quarters. Outside, the college walls were lined with display beds of frequently used medicinal plants. Inside, life at Mendzekhang followed a spartan schedule. At four each morning a bell sounded in the main temple at the head of the courtyard. Yeshi Dhonden had a few minutes to wash and roll up his bedding before hurrying to his classroom to begin memorizing by the soft light of butter lamps. As the mind was believed to be most fresh on waking, the first three hours before sunrise were given over to the memorization of the 1,140 pages of the four medical tantras, the root texts, preached by the Buddha, which, together with hundreds of commentaries and pharmacological catalogues, were the basis of Tibetan medicine. At seven o'clock instructors quizzed their students on the morning's work, after which they would return to their rooms for the day's first bowl of tea. A second bell then rang, and the whole college gathered to pray in long seated rows running the length of the pillared assembly hall, its walls hung with *thankas* illustrating herbs, anatomy, embryonic development and surgical instruments. On the way back to his room, Yeshi Dhonden would pass patients lined up for treatment beneath the apartments of Kenrab Norbu, the Master of Mendzekhang. Under their instructors' observation, senior students examined the sick while other professors, along with all the doctors of Chokpori, fanned out into the city on morning house calls, visiting those too ill to come to the colleges. As always in Tibet, medical treatment was free, only the medicines themselves having to be paid for.

Although Yeshi Dhonden's day was spent mainly in memorization, he often looked in on Mendzekhang's chief pharmacist and his staff. Two doors east of the front gate, they carried out the first step in the preparation of medicines, pounding into a fine powder the various roots, stems, leaves and branches as well as the numerous gems, minerals and animal products used in the 2,000 drugs routinely made by the college. The demands of their work were so great that Mendzekhang was covered with the raw materials of the trade. Hundreds of pungent medicinal plants, collected on expeditions into the mountains, were laid out to dry throughout the school's hallways, classrooms and rooftops. Subsequently they were administered either in powder form or as shiny black and brown pills.

Following an early dinner at five o'clock, the student body once again assembled, this time to practice debate. Seated by class in the courtyard, the college would, on the Master's signal, break into a cacophony of shouts, claps and loud retorts as attackers queried their respondents on the correct interpretation of the tantras' description of the causes, conditions and treatments of various illnesses. Often debates became so heated that when the five-hour session had concluded, individual pairs, a small group of entranced onlookers seated around them, their *sens* or outer robes wrapped tightly against the chill, continued debating far into the night.

After two years and four months, Yeshi Dhonden completed memorizing the medical tantras. He then recited for a full day before his teacher, declining to divide his first test over a period of time, as was customary. Promoted, despite his youth, to be senior student among the five in his room, he went on to take his official examination. The mornings of four days were set aside. His parents came from Namro to attend, while his home monastery, Shedrup Ling, offered a tea service at each session. Yeshi Dhonden, aged thirteen and a half, then appeared in the Assembly Hall before the Master of Mendzekhang, the faculty and the entire student body and after prostrating three times to the images of the Medicine Buddha and Tibet's most famous doctor, Yuthok Yonten Gonpo, on the main altar, recited verbatim the one hundred fifty-six chapters of the four tantras—in and out of sequence—as he was requested. Only minor mistakes were accepted—a lapse of any kind being considered grounds for failure. On the afternoon of the fourth day Yeshi Dhonden was informed that he had passed in good standing. Rewarded with a white scarf and a set of brocade book covers, he was admitted into the college to commence his formal education.

Dr. Dhonden spent the next four years absorbed in eleven divisions of study. 13 To provide an overview of the medical system, Mendzekhang's curriculum began with the Illustrated Tree of Medicine, a diagram wherein each field of learning found its proper place in relation to the whole. Yeshi Dhonden and his fellow students spent long hours laying out on the large flagstones before their rooms the three roots, nine trunks, forty-two branches, two hundred twenty-four leaves, three fruits and two flowers of the tree, using colored thread, sticks and bright plastic buttons from the Barkhor or marketplace. After they had mastered the diagram, they were taught how to collate the appropriate chapters of the tantras with the various parts of the tree, following which they entered into the study of root one, trunk one, branch one, explaining the most important topic in Tibetan medicine, the theoretical basis for the entire system, that of the three bodily humors.

As explained by the Buddha in the First or Root Tantra, three humors govern 14 the condition of all sentient beings: wind, bile and phlegm. Wind is described as rough, hard, cold, subtle and motile in nature; bile as light, oily, acrid and hot; phlegm as sticky, cool, heavy and gentle. Five kinds of each orchestrate the human organism. The five winds control movement, respiration, circulation, secretions and the joining of consciousness to the body; the five biles, digestion, sight and skin tone; the five phlegms, among other functions, the body's cohesiveness. The quantity of wind in an average adult is said to fill a bladder, that of bile a scrotum, that of phlegm, three double handfuls. Although active throughout the body, wind predominates in the pelvis, bile in the middle torso and phlegm in the upper torso. Wind moves through the skeleton, bile in the blood, phlegm in the chyle, flesh, fat and regenerative fluid. Phlegm prevails in youth, bile in adulthood, wind in old age. When all the humors are in balance, health exists. The smallest imbalance, however, produces disease. Every illness—of which the tantras account for 84,000 in 1,616 divisions— owes its cure to the correction of a humoral imbalance. Equipped with such an all-inclusive theory, the medical system could address itself to any disease, known or unknown, including mental illness, as not just the body but also the personality of each individual was said to be governed by the balance of humors in his makeup.

With a working knowledge of the humors, Dr. Dhonden went on to study 15 embryology, anatomy, metabolic function, signs of death, pathology, treatment and diagnosis. In embryology, conception, followed by the weekly growth of the embryo (including the nature of its consciousness at critical stages of development), was described in texts predating Western medicine's own findings by 2,000 years. Techniques for determining the sex of the child prior to birth were demonstrated, along with medicines which would reduce labor to between two and four hours, guard against postpartum infection and ease pain. Anatomy was the next subject. As autopsies were performed only if attending physicians disagreed on the cause of death, Mendzekhang's students obtained their anatomical knowledge from detailed charts first drawn up late in the eighth century when the practice of surgery in Tibetan medicine was at its height. At that time Tibetan surgeons had routinely performed heart and brain surgery until the mother of King Muni Tsenpo, Tibet's thirty-eighth monarch, died during an operation to lessen swelling from water retention around the heart. Following her death, surgery was officially banned. Nevertheless, minor operations continued to be performed and the use of surgical instruments as well as that of anesthetizing drugs remained part of the Mendzekhang program. While metabolic function and signs of death were relatively brief topics, pathology, treatment and diagnosis were immense undertakings, requiring Yeshi Dhonden's greatest efforts. Pathology alone dealt with in the ninety-two chapters of the Third or Oral Tradition Tantra, entailed individual descriptions of the categories, causes, symptoms and complications of thousands of diseases, supplemented by their treatments under varying conditions. It was here that memorization of the tantras proved invaluable as, equipped with commentaries written by Tibet's long line of physicians, Yeshi Dhonden gradually built up an intricate picture of the entire range of human illness through its expression in single, double and triple humoral imbalances. The study of diagnostic procedure, though, was even more difficult. Unlike academic topics, the three trunks, eight branches and thirty-eight leaves of the Diagnostic Root of the Tree of Medicine could be thoroughly understood only through actual practice. Questioning the patient and analyzing nine aspects of his urine were essential to diagnosis. But it was mastery of the third trunk, pulse diagnosis, that was the hallmark of a leading physician.

Although pulse diagnosis was taught for an entire year in Mendzekhang, it 16 was believed to take a decade or more to fully comprehend. The basics were laid out in thirteen sections of the Last Tantra. The first four detail eight guidelines for the evening before an examination. To prepare themselves, both patient and doctor should refrain from the consumption of tea, alcohol and overly nutritious food, also avoiding exercise, sex and any anxiety-producing encounter. The following morning, after the sun has risen but, as the Tantra says, before "its rays have fallen on the mountaintop," the pulse should be read. In this brief period, two definitive factors characterizing every pulse, disease and medicine—the forces of hot and cold—are believed to be most in equilibrium. Prior to dawn, lunar influences, manifested in an enhanced cold or negative pulse, accentuate wind and phlegm; after dawn, solar influences augment the hot or positive pulse of bile and blood (sometimes spoken of as the fourth humor). Because the patient has not yet eaten, digestion does not obscure other functions, while all the winds have subsided during sleep into the heart of the central channel, where, according to tantric theory, the mind and body are joined.

The best place to read the pulse is said to be on the patient's wrist, just over 17 the radial artery. The Last Tantra queries itself: "Why is the radial artery used?" It replies that listening to arteries close to the vital organs "is like talking to someone by a waterfall," whereas using those in the extremities is like receiving "messages brought by distant merchants." The radial artery is the optimum position and is likened to "a voice in summer shouting across an open field." "How is it possible to read the quality of the twelve organs at the radial artery?" the tantra continues. "Just as a successful businessman can discern the place of origin and make of wares at a marketplace, so the pulse if read at the radial artery can exhibit the condition of the hollow and solid organs." Only in children below the age of eight and terminally ill patients is the pulse to be read elsewhere: in the former, on the blood vessels in the lobe of the ear; in the latter, to determine how many days of life remain, at the posterior tibial artery behind the ankle.

The doctor is now instructed in the technique for taking the pulse. If the 18 patient is male, the left arm is examined first; if female, the right. Switching hands, the physician then examines the patient's other arm. In both cases he uses the three middle fingers of either hand spaced apart the width "of a grain," while to overcome the thickness of the forearm's muscle, his index finger presses the skin, his middle finger the flesh and his ring finger the bone. The essential ingredient of pulse diagnosis is explained next. Each of the six fingers used is to be divided into an "inner" and "outer" half. These twelve positions monitor the organs; hollow organs are read on the outer half, solid on the inner. For example, the outside of the physician's right index finger reads the heart; the inside, the small intestine; the outside of his middle finger, the spleen; the inside, the stomach. The correspondence of all six fingers is the same for both men and women save for one instance. In a male patient the doctor's right index finger registers the heart; his left, the lung. With a female patient the reverse applies. They are switched because the consciousness of a woman is believed to enter the center of the ovum and sperm at a slightly different position than that of a man at the time of conception. The text then admonishes the doctor to always keep his fingertips "smooth, sensitive, without scars and pliable."

There is one final consideration before the pulse can be read. One of three "constitutional pulses," corresponding to the three humors, is said to dominate every person. The male pulse, similar to wind, is bulky and prominent; the female, similar to bile, subtle and rapid; the neuter, similar to phlegm, slow and smooth. Unless the patient's particular type—any of which can be had by either a man or a woman—is known to the physician (either by examining the patient when healthy or by being told), a diagnostic error can easily be made. Furthermore, once the constitutional pulse is known, it is crucial to factor in the "seasonal pulse"—each season manifesting an influence on the characteristic pulse imprint of a particular organ, such as heat in summer, which affects the heart, and cold in winter, which affects the kidneys.

The doctor begins by ascertaining whether the illness is hot or cold in nature. He does so by using his own respiratory cycle, to determine the rate of the patient's pulse. If the pulse beats five times per breath, the person is in perfect health. More than five beats denotes a hot disorder; less than five, a cold. Above eight in a hot disorder or below three in a cold disease means an extremely severe, usually uncurable problem.

One of twelve general pulse types is now sought. The six hot beats are strong, ample, rolling, swift, tight and hard. The six cold beats are weak, deep, declining, slow, loose and hollow. If the moment all his fingers touch the radial artery a hot beat is superficially felt, the physician knows that the disorder is new and minor. If, after pressure is applied, they are felt deeply, the illness is chronic and complex. The reverse holds true for cold disorders; superficial pulses reveal old, serious ailments; deep ones indicate new, minor imbalances. From this second step the history of an ailment is known.

The state of the three humors in the body is now explored. Each humor, as well as its combinations, possesses a characteristic pulse type. When it has been identified, the individual pulse of one of a huge number of conditions is sought. If the patient is pregnant, the "pregnancy pulse" will reveal it, as well as, after the sixth week, the sex of the child. If worms are present, the pulse is "flat" and seems to knot as it beats; if bacteria, it is incomplete, with "sudden, irregular and unpredictable cessation in the rhythm of the beat." In leprosy, the pulsebeat is "quivering," and contracting at its conclusion "like a person who limps." Wounds manifest a "bulky, hard and quick" pulse. A bullet lodged in the body produces a "limping and double" pulse as if there were two arteries, not one, being read. After describing tests to distinguish pulse types, the tantra instructs the physician to investigate the individual organs through the twelve positions on the fingertips. His exam complete, over a period of roughly one hundred breaths, the doctor knows what the humoral imbalance is, its severity, which organs are affected and in what manner.

As Yeshi Dhonden and his classmates discovered, however, the topic of pulse   23
diagnosis was far from exhausted. In the remaining sections numerous exceptions to the rules were cited as well as the uses of the pulse in determining
lifespan, spirit possession and, in an extremely complex section known as the
"Seven Amazing Pulses," the future course of an illness. In the eleventh section,
those pulses which reveal that a disease will be terminal are described, showing
how vivid the tantra's descriptions can be.

The "changing" death pulse is said to "flutter like a flag in the wind"; while   24
the "irregular" death pulse appears "like a vulture attacking a bird, who stops,
plunges, beats its wings quickly, stops again and then resumes flight." In a
combined wind-bile disorder, the patient's pulse will resemble "a fish leaping
out of water to catch a fly, who quickly shimmers back." Accumulation of
phlegm and wind producing death are like "the pecking of a hen eating grain";
that of a triple humoral imbalance, like "the saliva of a drooling cow, moving
in the wind." The text then enumerates death pulses unrelated to the humors.
If a healthy person who has had an accident has a thin pulse, he will die
shortly. If in a person who has been sick for some time the pulse suddenly turns
strong or violent, death is imminent. The amount of time left to live, within a
period of eight days, is shown by the absence of pulse. Death will occur in
three days if the liver or gallbladder pulse is missing; in two if the lung or large
intestine pulse is absent; in one if the tongue is black, the eyes are in a fixed
stare and the pulse of either the heart or the small intestine is gone.

Dr. Dhonden's true education in pulse diagnosis came only after his studies   25
were completed. At the age of eighteen he was sent to Kenrab Norbu, Mendzekhang's principal, to undertake a four-year internship with a master physician
practicing in Lhoka, who was already surrounded by many disciples. During
this second stage in his training, Dr. Dhonden rose before dawn each day to
take pulse, analyze urine and present his diagnosis of patients' ailments to his
new teacher. While his understanding of the myriad pulse types grew, he came
to have a profound regard for the efficacy of the entire medical system. Although
patients in advanced states of illness could not be cured, others, afflicted by a
number of usually fatal degenerative diseases, such as cancer and diabetes,
responded with complete remission. In the case of diabetes, seen in one out of
every two to three hundred patients, he witnessed many cures occurring within
six to nine months. When medicine proved ineffective, he and his teacher used
accessory treatments: emetics, purgatives, moxabustion, cauterization, blood-
letting and acupuncture or "Golden Needle" therapy, which, according to
Tibetan medical histories, originated in Tibet and spread to China via Mongolia.
Among the most successful treatments Yeshi Dhonden found were those for
senility (employing memory pills), those included in the divisions covering
women's and children's diseases as well as those in the eight branches of
infertility, itself an entire category of medical practice. Although rarely pre-

scribed, due to Buddhist ethics, two types of birth-control pills existed. One had to be taken for a few consecutive days, whereafter its effect lasted for a year; the other eliminated fertility for life.

A related specialty known as *chu-len* or "Extracting the Essence" dealt with rejuvenation. By using its medicines, religious practitioners on three-, nine-, or twelve-year retreats were able to survive, it was believed, on a single seed or flower a day. For lay people *chu-len* could restore hair and teeth while increasing lifespan by many decades. As Dr. Dhonden explained, "Each of us breathes 21,000 times a day; 500 of these breaths are associated with lifespan. *Chu-len* medicines, taken in conjunction with the correct meditation practices, increase the number of these breaths. From my own experience I can definitely say they work. I've known people in their hundreds who have undergone the full course of treatment, beginning at the age of fifty, and been restored to a state of middle age. I met one lama when he was 170 years old. He had gray hair but the face of a forty-year old." 26

Having administered rejuvenation treatment for two millennia, Tibetan physicians considered it a normal component of their medical practice. However, one group of drugs, as venerable as those of *chu-len*, excited particular interest— *rinchen ribus* or "Precious Pills." Whenever Dr. Dhonden returned to Mendzekhang to replenish his professor's medicines, he made sure to inquire which Precious Pills had most recently been manufactured in the college's pharmacy. Seven types existed, the weakest composed of eighteen ingredients, the strongest, known as the King of Medicines, of one hundred sixty-five. Wrapped in colored cotton, tied with rainbow-hued thread and sealed with wax, the Precious Pills received their name for two reasons: for their contents—gold, silver, mercury, pearl, ruby, sapphire and diamond, specially treated and then mixed with various medicinal plants—and for their function—as panaceas for the entire body. Precious Pills, it was believed, could cure the most intractable ailments. As their manufacture sometimes took up to three months of around-the-clock labor by a team of twenty druggists, they were extremely potent and administered only under strict conditions. The stronger ones often incapacitated the patient for a day, while toxins were eliminated and imbalances in the body corrected. Though Yeshi Dhonden was familiar with their ingredients, his internship was primarily geared toward expanding his knowledge of Tibetan medicine's vast pharmacopoeia. To check his progress, Kenrab Norbu required Dr. Dhonden to accompany the college each year on its annual outing to pick herbs in the mountains. 27

The journey commenced at the start of July and was attended by those who had completed memorization, generally 300 students and faculty in all. As a rule, each traveler brought three changes of clothing, the Buddha having stressed the importance of cleanliness while collecting medicinal substances. With one pack animal and a groom serving every two students, the caravan left Mend- 28 zekhang and, skirting Lhasa, proceeded a day north to Dhakyaba, a region of peaks and alpine meadows considered ideal for herb gathering. A large tent camp provided by the government, staffed with cooks and fully provisioned, already awaited the college. For seven weeks, changing location every three days, small groups of students and teachers set off at eight o'clock each morning to collect herbs just below the snow line. While harvesting, they recited prayers to the Medicine Buddha, intent on keeping the mind as well as the body pure. Thirty classes of plants, subdivided into fifty-nine categories, with each plant having nine divisions, were initially sought. Hundreds of herbs with less universal value were also taken. With the waxing of vegetative processes and the onset of pollination, barks and plant secretions received less attention; flowers, fruits, seeds and leaves, more.

Halfway through the summer, large wooden crates began arriving from Lhasa. Ordered from district governors months in advance, the crates contained dozens of medicinal plants that were unavailable in Central Tibet. They had been carefully picked with earth still around their roots and immediately packed in snow and ice. By the end of August, when all had arrived, the students had completed their own collections and were ready to take the year-end test on the identification of plants. 29

The exam took place inside a large tent surrounded by a high cloth wall. Within, stacks of wood covered with white cotton lined the enclosure, two hundred selected plants laid out haphazardly on top. With Kenrab Norbu presiding from a high seat at the far end, three faculty members, each assisted by a secretary, escorted students past the tables. While the secretaries recorded their replies, the students were asked to describe each specimen by type, species and the medicinal power of the active part. Guided out the tent's rear, they were separated from those yet to be examined, and the next group of three took their places. While they did, the scores were tabulated and given to the Master, who had them announced to the whole gathering—a procedure guaranteed to increase the tremendous tension the students already felt. The test completed, students once more were taken around, this time to have their mistakes pointed out. 30

Most of Mendzekhang's aspiring physicians took up to five exams before they could correctly identify a majority of each year's plants. In his first and second attempts, Yeshi Dhonden placed sixty-second, then forty-fifth in the ranking. By the age of twenty, though, with his internship completed, he captured third place. By coincidence his old roommates took first and second, giving the three friends a clean sweep of the top positions. Because their scores were so close, Kenrab Norbu ordered a retest. This time the young men were taken around the tables blindfolded. One by one their examiners held up plants, requesting that they be identified by odor and taste alone. As Yeshi Dhonden recalled, "This was very difficult, but fortunately all of us were able to answer correctly. 31

291

When the test was over, it was announced that I had come in number one. Later, though," he added, laughing, "I found out there had been a catch. Because I was graduating, my friends had pretended to make little mistakes. In reality I was number three, but thanks to their trick I was chosen as the best student in the college."

Following the exam, a large celebration, equivalent to graduation day, was 32 held. Hundreds of people came from Lhasa and the surrounding villages to watch as the students were publicly ranked. Those who took first and second places received long silk scarves embroidered with the words "Luck in the Day. Luck in the Night." Those who came in last didn't fare so well. The fifth from last was pronounced "Carrier of the Medicines"—a barb equivalent to "nurse"— and given a blue doctor's bag to hold, of the kind used by every physician's assistant. The fourth from last, called "The Doorman," was dressed in the black robes of a government servant and placed at the entrance to the tent; the third from last, costumed as a muleteer, escorted the second from last and the last— banished not from the race of physicians but that of men—known, respectively, as the "White" and "Black Donkeys." With bells, reins and halters on their necks and medicines loaded across their backs, the "donkeys" were driven around the camp, bellowing and braying, to the great amusement of the crowd, after which a picnic was shared by all. The next day the college returned to Lhasa, where a ceremony at the Central Cathedral took place and the year ended for a week's vacation.

After graduating, Dr. Dhonden served as Kenrab Norbu's special assistant 33 for three years. In the evenings he continued to debate with Mendzekhang's senior students and faculty members. Once a month he went to the Lingkhor, Lhasa's Holy Walk, to treat the hundreds of poor pilgrims and beggars who rarely came on their own for help. In conjunction with this, he paid special attention to cultivating the eleven vows of the physicians' code which attempted to instill an altruistic motive as the basis of a doctor's practice. As Yeshi Dhonden commented, concerning his own application of the ancient code, "I am just an ordinary person afflicted by desire, hatred and ignorance. But through contemplating the suffering I see in my work, I have tried to increase my compassion. As doctors we are expected to put kindness before all else." Out of his own curiosity, Dr. Dhonden also went, two hours a day, to the British Legation, to acquaint himself with Western medicine. Finally, in 1951, Kenrab Norbu sent Yeshi Dhonden's diploma to the office of the Cabinet, where it was officially confirmed. The Kashag then dispatched letters to district officials in Lhoka, as well as the government transport center, from which Yeshi Dhonden received free passage home. Thirteen years after his education began, Dr. Dhonden left Lhasa, looking forward to taking up practice on his own.

He didn't have long to wait. An epidemic had broken out along the Bhutanese 34 border, imported—along with chocolate, batteries, silks and the beloved fedora hats—by traders returning from India. In Tibet's high, germ-scarce environment, those who contracted the disease—a form of intestinal influenza—died quickly. Scores of doctors had already flocked to the area.

Traveling to a monastery called Sungroling Gonpa, Dr. Dhonden joined   35
three physicians who had been attempting, unsuccessfully, to check the epidemic. Nine of the monastery's 300 monks had already died, as well as many of the inhabitants of the village below its walls. Arriving just before nightfall, Dr. Dhonden was shown to a private room, where, after his regular evening meditation session, he went to sleep, expecting to see his first patients in the morning. During the night, however, he experienced an unusual dream, one which, though seemingly inexplicable by Western standards, demonstrated the close relationship of religion to science in Tibetan medicine. "In the night I dreamt that a naked woman came before me, a *khadroma*," said Dr. Dhonden, referring to a spiritual being believed, in a manner similar to that of an angel, to aid practitioners in meditation. "In her right hand she held a tantric drum; in her left hand she held a skull. She carried a bag of medicine under her left arm. A white tin cup with a red design and a slight crack on its rim, filled with urine, appeared before her. Then the woman asked me, 'After examining this urine can you tell me the disease of the patient? What is your diagnosis?' In the dream I looked at the urine and replied, 'This is today's epidemic, one of sixty-five types of the eighteen new diseases predicted in the tantras for this era.' 'What is its cause?' she asked. I responded that it was due, as the tantras state, to environmental pollution and that it was a hot disease. 'You said that externally it is a fever, but are you sure that internally it's not cold?' she said. At that time, because my memory was fresh from constant study, I recalled that the thirteenth and fourteenth chapters of the third Tantra address the topic of cold and hot diseases together. I answered her in debate form, quoting the text as proof, stating that there was no hidden cold fever, but that the ailment was hot both inside and out. We debated back and forth for some time and finally she said, 'What treatment will you give?' I replied, 'Because the bacteria causing the disease have mixed the blood and bile, medicine should be given to separate them.' Then she asked what the patient's behavior and diet should be—two aspects of treatment that always accompany medicine. I answered and she said, 'Tell me again. How will you cut the tail of this disease?' Once more we debated vigorously and then she laughed and suddenly disappeared. There was complete silence and I woke up."

In a short while, as the day began, Dr. Dhonden was brought tea. Afterwards   36
he was asked to visit his first patient, a twenty-three-year-old monk, infected by the illness, languishing in his room. "I went to see the young man," continued Dr. Dhonden. "It was a very serious case. The room he lay in stank. Diarrhea mixed with blood was pouring from him onto the bed and he was semi-comatose; he couldn't talk. I asked for his urine specimen and it was brought to me in a

tin cup. All of a sudden I remembered my dream. It was the exact cup, even with the crack on the rim. 'Oh, I have already examined this before,' I thought. I was amazed. Then the whole dream came back. I recalled the debate and the treatment and immediately I prepared the correct medicines. The man recovered and after that, the epidemic in the village was completely stopped. Now when I look back on it," Dr. Dhonden said, "I feel that whoever came to me in the form of a *khadroma* that night was actually administering my true final examination."

As Dr. Dhonden's reputation spread, he spent the remainder of the 1950s 37 traveling from one district to another. "Each day I rode from village to village, returning periodically to Lhasa to obtain medicines," he recounted. "I was able to cure three quarters of my patients. And because I gave penicillin injections for skin disease—a great novelty among Tibetans—my reputation continued to increase. I never had a free day." A group of young relations began to study with him but before long the uprising against the nine-year-old Chinese occupation broke out in Lhasa and the Dalai Lama fled. "I saw His Holiness when his party came through my area," recalled Dr. Dhonden. "Those who weren't following him had joined the guerrillas to put up a last fight for our freedom. My students all had family members whom they couldn't leave. My own mother's legs were too poor for her to walk out and my father had said that he was too old to cross the high passes into Bhutan. As a monk, I wouldn't fight. So I felt that I had no other choice but to leave. I borrowed a horse, said farewell and set off."

Though Namro was only a few days from the border, the presence of Chinese 38 troops forced Dr. Dhonden to hide for over a month before finally, in the company of eighty other refugees, he descended a steep snow-covered slope, trekked through a valley and crossed a glacial stream into the forests of Bhutan. With only a few texts, instruments and medicines in his possession, he then walked across Bhutan begging day to day. "After I was forced to flee my homeland, I was overwhelmed by a deep sense of renunciation," reflected Dr. Dhonden. "I saw life as essenceless, without real stability. I only wanted to practice religion." Arriving at Buxa, Yeshi Dhonden requested permission to remain with the monks there while the rest of his group was transferred to road work. The Tibetan government official in charge replied, "You have the right to practice religion and you are also young and fit to work on the roads. However, if the Kashag asks me, 'Has any doctor come out of Tibet?' and I've sent you elsewhere, what will I say? Therefore, you studied medicine at the government's expense, and now the time has come for you to help us."

Dr. Dhonden was sent to Dalhousie, where 3,000 refugees, including the 39 elite monks of Lhasa's two Tantric colleges, Gyudto and Gyudme, were camped in squalid conditions. Tuberculosis, hepatitis and amoebic dysentery were rampant. Preparing what medicines he could from the few herbs available in Indian stores, he set up a clinic and went to work. "One day a sweeper in my clinic was bitten by a poisonous snake," he related. "Just as I was applying a Tibetan tourniquet, an Indian doctor arrived. He examined the bite and declared that unless his leg was amputated immediately the man would die in half an hour. I told him this was unnecessary; I had already given the man Tibetan medicine effective for poison. The doctor turned to the sweeper and said, 'You will die within minutes unless I operate, but this Tibetan'—indicating me—'thinks otherwise.' He asked him whose diagnosis he wished to accept. The sweeper had seen my work and so he replied mine. The doctor then compelled me to sign a paper releasing him from all responsibility in the case. There were many aspects to my treatment, but after ten days the sweeper could move about and in a month he was completely cured."

Despite the man's recovery, the episode proved to be the start of a serious conflict. Once a week Indian doctors came to inspect the refugees, in the course of which they dropped by Dr. Dhonden's clinic to demand that, as he was not certified in India, he discontinue practice. "During one of their visits I was examining a patient with skin disease," continued Dr. Dhonden. "The physicians saw this woman and together announced that she had chicken pox. They claimed that unless she was isolated an epidemic would sweep over all the refugees. I said bluntly that they were wrong. It was a minor heat disorder and no more. They departed, leaving medicine for her to take. I forbade her to. In a short while they came back and tried to remove her to an isolated house in the forest. I refused to let her go. They asked if I was willing to have an outbreak of chicken pox on my hands and I replied, 'The Tibetans are my own people. How could I ever harm them?' I then demanded that now *they* sign a paper, just as I had been made to, certifying that indeed this woman had chicken pox. They stalled and within a few days the woman was cured." Despite this minor victory, more battles ensued, until, in mid-1960, Yeshi Dhonden was unexpectedly summoned to Dharamsala. Word had reached the government-in-exile that a Mendzekhang-trained physician had escaped. Apprised of his existence, the Dalai Lama had called for Dr. Dhonden personally.

"I arrived in Dharamsala just before sunset," Dr. Dhonden remembered. "The hills were covered with tents. People were living in very poor conditions. They had refused to leave His Holiness and were going wherever he went." Directed to the kitchen area of the Secretariat compound at Mortimer Hall, Yeshi Dhonden sat and waited. He was finishing his tea when the Dalai Lama arrived. "Suddenly I heard His Holiness in the other room. 'Where is the doctor?' he said. I stood up, folding my hands in prayer, praying for his long life. I had a very strong mind of faith. But when he entered the room I began to weep. I had never wept upon meeting someone before. I must have been thinking of Tibet . . ."

The Dalai Lama questioned Dr. Dhonden on his escape and then requested

295

him to treat those camped around Dharamsala. Working out of the Nursery at Conium House, Dr. Dhonden began seeing patients under the observation of Tibetan government officials. Having met with their approval, he was summoned to the Dalai Lama once more, this time in the capacity of examining physician. After curing the Dalai Lama of a skin disorder, he was asked to see Kyabjé Ling Rinpoché, the Dalai Lama's senior tutor and head of the Gelugpa sect, who was bedridden in a hospital in Calcutta suffering from a severe case of pericarditis, an inflammation and swelling around the heart. In little over a year Ling Rinpoché was cured and Dr. Dhonden was officially appointed to be the Dalai Lama's personal physician, a post normally filled by up to four doctors in Tibet. His enthusiasm for his practice now fully recovered, he set about the monumental task of preserving Tibetan medicine in exile.

Only two other doctors had escaped from Tibet, neither of whom could assist 43 Dr. Dhonden in Dharamsala. Alone, he began to train ten students in the rudiments of his science, their progress hampered by an almost total lack of funds. Yeshi Dhonden could do little until, one day in 1963, his many run-ins with Indian doctors yielded an ironically positive result.

Responding to repeated complaints from local physicians that the Tibetan 44 was "stealing" their patients, a senior minister in the Indian Health Department arrived in Dharamsala to investigate. For a week he watched Dr. Dhonden diagnose patients by their pulse and urine, after which he carefully asked each individual his ailment. At one point, five officers from the nearby army cantonment came in to refill prescriptions. "When the minister saw them he exploded in rage," recalled Dr. Dhonden. 'We give you the best health care in India and now you've come here to eat shit from a Tibetan!' he yelled." The officers replied that in many cases they had been ill for fifteen years or more. Where Western medicine had failed, Tibetan medicine had succeeded. "Unlike other doctors," they said, "we don't have to tell Dr. Dhonden what's wrong. He tells us." The day before he departed for New Delhi, the minister came to Yeshi Dhonden's office. "You are doing very good work here," he said. "There is only one problem. You don't have enough students. I'm going to give you thirty thousand rupees a year and a twenty-bed hospital." In this manner, the Tibetan Medical Center was formally organized.

Dr. Dhonden assumed the roles of director and pharmacologist as well as 45 chief examining physician. In 1965 he was joined by a second physician, who assisted in teaching the now seven-year curriculum, leading expeditions into the mountains behind Dharamsala to collect herbs and manufacturing 165 principal drugs. With 15 students graduating to join the 150 or so doctors practicing Tibetan medicine outside of Tibet and plans underway for a research wing, a museum and nine outpatient clinics in the settlements, Dr. Dhonden resigned from the Center in 1969. Opening a private practice in McLeod Ganj, he continued to see the Dalai Lama, taking his pulse each day just after sunrise, until in 1978 another physician was appointed to assist him. Dr. Dhonden was then freed to introduce Tibetan medicine to the West.

"The information required before Tibetan medicines could be approved for 46 use in the United States would take an army of lab technicians years to develop," commented Dr. Gerald Goldstein, speculating on the future of an exchange between Tibetan and Western doctors as Yeshi Dhonden's visit in Virginia drew to an end. "Each ingredient must be individually identified, purified from its crude state and then thoroughly tested. Who is going to pay for it?" "Research today is a cost-benefit situation," concurred Dr. Donald Baker. "How is a drug company going to collect all of these medicines in northern India and still make a profit at it?" "The impetus for the work, though, is clear," added Dr. Goldstein. "Over one third of our pharmacopoeia comes from plants and microorganisms, specifically some of our oldest and most effective cancer drugs. These are just the sort of materials Tibetans have acquired experience with over centuries of use. Personally, I think the drug companies are missing a bet. Some of these medicines are definitely going to be active."

In the East, the bet has not been missed. Whereas Peking destroyed every 47 institution of the old Tibet soon after 1959, it preserved and later expanded Mendzekhang. Now called the Hospital of Tibetan Medicine, Mendzekhang's 127-member staff treats 700 to 800 patients a day. Though the doctors have been forced to curtail their unique knowledge of the mind's relation to the body (considered, as a basic component of Buddhist teachings, anathema), volumes of color photographs cataloguing medicinal plants have been compiled, while many of the most valuable herbs indigenous to the Himalayas have begun to be cultivated on high-altitude farms. Concurrently, Tibetan drugs are in wide-spread use throughout mainland China though they are referred to as Chinese in origin and not Tibetan.

"Tibetan and Western medicine begin from completely opposite standpoints," 48 said Dr. Dhonden, summing up his view of the two sciences after visiting the United States. "To start with, a Western scientist looks through a microscope to examine the cause of a disease in terms of its molecular particles. Only then does he take into account the particular patient. Tibetan doctors begin with the patient. We consider his disposition in terms of wind, bile and phlegm. And then we approach the disease. The difference, I feel, makes for weakness and strength in both. We lack many of the symptomatic treatments modern physicians possess. On the other hand, it would be useful for Western doctors to understand the Tibetan presentation of the humors, their balance and imbalance in the human body. Without this, their medical system remains incomplete. It cannot establish a clear view of the correct causes and conditions governing all disease. If young Western doctors would come and train with us for a period of years—as well as relating their own system's analysis of disease—then, I feel, a true exchange could occur. So each of us it seems," he concluded, judiciously, "has something of value to learn from the other."

QUESTIONS

1. For most readers, Tibetan medicine is an exotic subject. How does Avedon help readers acclimate themselves to such a subject and a foreign sensibility? For example, how does he deal with the many Tibetan terms he uses?

2. Yeshi Dhonden's career can be called a medical success story. What are its highlights? How many times must he prove his ability? How would an American medical success story compare with Dhonden's?

3. What aspects of Tibetan medicine do you think would be useful to Western medicine?

4. Compare your most recent encounter with the processes of a Western doctor to Dhonden's approach. Would you agree with his assessment of Western medicine as starting with a microscope and not a patient?

5. Because Dhonden was so good at memorization he was chosen to represent his monastery at medical school. What particular talent might distinguish a student hoping for a career in Western medicine?

6. The story of Dhonden's education and career is framed by the account of his more recent trip to Virginia. What other essays in this collection use a similar framing device? What purpose does the frame serve?

7. Upon what sources other than Dhonden has Avedon drawn?

8. At a crucial moment in Dhonden's early career, the cure for intestinal flu comes to him in a dream (paragraphs 34–36). Describe a time in your life when the help you desired came from an unexpected source, such as a dream.

MAKING CONNECTIONS

1. Read Richard Selzer's essays, "The Discus Thrower" and "A Mask on the Face of Death." Notice that Selzer is quoted in Avedon's account, too (paragraph 3). What connections do you think Selzer would find between his own orientation to medicine and that of Dhonden?

2. Avedon and Michael Brown both assemble and organize a large body of relatively technical information. Compare their methods of managing such material and making it presentable to readers. What similarities do you find between them? What differences?

THE SOCIAL LIVES
OF DOLPHINS

William Booth

*Born in 1959 in Flushing, New York, William Booth ma-
jored in English and American literature at the University
of Texas at Austin. While working as a journalist on a daily
newspaper, he developed an increasing interest in science,
and is now a senior writer at* Science, *the journal published
by the American Association for the Advancement of Science. "Science writing allows me to write about ideas, hard
facts, people, political battles, things real and immediate
(acid rain, AIDS), or things that are just fascinating to
know, just to know (black holes)." Booth says he learned
about the dolphin site described in this article "from anthropologist Irven DeVore while working on another article
about controversy surrounding the creation of zombies with
tetrodotoxin from puffer fish." This article appeared in the
June 3, 1988, issue of* Science *magazine.*

On the shores of Shark Bay in Western Australia, there is a beach where   1
wild bottle-nosed dolphins swim into knee-deep water and allow tourists to
stroke their flanks and feed them frozen fish. Often, the dolphins return the
favor by tossing the onlookers a fresh herring or nice piece of seaweed.

Fascinated by tales of Shark Bay and intrigued by the research potential of   2
such a place, two undergraduate students traveled to Western Australia in the
summer of 1982 to have a look for themselves. What Richard Connor and
Rachel Smolker found was a mixed group of eight bottle-nosed dolphins so
habituated to humans that they daily swam onto a beach "so shallow that they
could be seen using their pectoral fins as braces against the bottom while lifting
their heads out of the water."

With only $1000 in funding from the New York Explorers Club and no boat   3
their first summer, Connor and Smolker simply watched the dolphins from the
shore, yet they made a number of unique observations, including evidence of
begging behavior among dolphins similar to that exhibited by wild chimpanzees.
"It was like watching a soap opera," says Connor, who along with Smolker, is
now a graduate student at the University of Michigan in Ann Arbor.

In addition to amusing the tourists in a remote part of Australia, the habit-   4
uated dolphins often brought other, more shy and retiring, dolphins with them.
As Connor and Smolker began identifying individuals, it became clear that the

eight friendly dolphins were part of a larger community of over 200 animals residing in the shallow, clear waters of Shark Bay.

This remarkable site is now being compared to the Gombe Stream Reserve, a flattering allusion to the chimpanzee habitat on the shores of Lake Tanganyika so richly worked by Jane Goodall, who originally encouraged the habituation of wild chimpanzees by feeding them bananas. Says Irven DeVore, an anthropologist and primatologist from Harvard University who has visited Shark Bay: "These youngsters are sitting on the motherlode."

The comparison between Gombe Stream and Shark Bay does not end with the habituation of the residents. The dolphins are attracting some of the very same scientists whose previous work focused on the chimpanzees of Gombe and who now hope to compare the social lives of these two big-brained mammals, animals which live in such different media and are separated by at least 60 million years of evolution yet seem to share many social adaptations.

The first reports from Shark Bay, which are built upon nearly two decades of research on a community of dolphins in Florida, are revealing "a striking and remarkable convergence between the social systems of dolphins and chimpanzees," says Barbara Smuts of the University of Michigan who studied chimpanzees with Goodall in Tanzania and is now launching projects at Shark Bay with Richard Wrangham, another primatologist who cut his teeth at Gombe. The two will oversee the work of Connor and Smolker and a third graduate student.

In the past, says Smuts, researchers have been frustrated in their attempts to make comparisons between terrestrial and aquatic mammals because of their inability to observe wild dolphins with the same intimacy and intensity that they could achieve with wild chimpanzees at sites such as Gombe. Such richly textured observations of individual and group behavior are crucial if comparisons between higher primates and dolphins are to be made. Captive populations of dolphins, with their small numbers of mixed animals in cramped aquaria, have been of limited value in unraveling social structures, says Smuts.

Until now, the study of dolphin social organization in the wild has been pioneered by Randy Wells of Woods Hole Oceanographic Institution and the Long Marine Laboratory at the University of California at Santa Cruz. Since 1970, when he began his dolphin days while still in high school, Wells has gathered an enormous amount of data on a dolphin community living in the warm, grassy shallows around Sarasota, Florida. In particular, by tagging, radio-tracking, and taking blood samples, Wells has pieced together much of what is known about the range and demographics of a stable community of dolphins.

"Randy has given us incredible information about who associates with whom, but not as much on who does *what* with whom," says Smuts. For unfortunately, the inshore waters of Sarasota are a murky green soup, making detailed observations of interactions difficult. In contrast, the water at Shark Bay is relatively clear and the animals allow boats to pursue them at distances of only a few meters. The dolphins at Shark Bay are so cooperative that they often roll over while riding the research boat's bow wave, giving observers a chance to sex the animals with a quick glance at the animal's genital slits. (Unlike Wells and his colleagues, who capture and quickly release animals, the researchers at Shark Bay will not handle the dolphins.)

What makes dolphins so appealing to primate researchers is the fact that 11 both dolphins and chimpanzees evolved to possess such big brains while adapting to very different environments. Says Smuts: "Once you start comparing chimpanzees and dolphins—and large brains and social systems separated by millions of years of evolution—you can ask some pretty interesting questions." The forebears of both animals were terrestrial mammals. About 60 million years ago, the ancestors of modern cetaceans[1] were primitive ungulates[2] with small bodies and small brains that returned to the sea, from which two extant suborders of cetaceans eventually evolved, one being toothed whales and dolphins. As Smuts notes, it is the dolphins alone among the cetaceans that exhibit such a dramatic increase in brain size. When compared to body size, the brain of *Tursiops truncatus* is below that of humans but roughly double the size value of higher primates. Like humans, both dolphins and chimpanzees possess brains with an expanded neocortex and with extensive convolution, and much development is completed after birth.

Based on the work of Wells and as yet unpublished observations made at 12 Shark Bay, a picture of the social lives of wild dolphins is beginning to emerge. Though the primatologists believe the social system employed by dolphins might prove remarkably similar to chimpanzees, Wells himself is not completely convinced. "I think anyone who tries to pin the dolphins on any one terrestrial animal will probably be disappointed," says Wells. Yet Smuts maintains that, combined, the social systems of dolphins and chimps are not shared by other mammals.

Like chimpanzees, for example, dolphin communities occupy a common 13 home range, says Smuts. In Florida, Wells has established that his Sarasota community of 100 individuals lives along a 40-kilometer stretch of shallow bays and inlets that hug the barrier islands separating the Gulf of Mexico from the mainland, with the total range amounting to about 100 square kilometers.

Within their home range, both dolphins and chimpanzees live in an ex- 14 tremely fluid and flexible community, referred to as a "fusion-fission society," where individuals may join temporary parties of varying sizes, instead of operating in one relatively closed or rigid group. The females in both chimpanzee and dolphin communities have a tendency to travel in more limited, "core areas" within the home range, while the males roam to the periphery. The wandering males probably occasionally succeed in mating with a female from

---

[1] cetaceans: an order of aquatic mammals, including whales and dolphins. [Eds.]
[2] ungulates: hoofed quadrupeds. [Eds.]

another community, thus keeping the populations from being reproductively isolated, says Wells.

Within the community, dolphins have a tendency to associate with members 15 of the same sex and age, except in the case of females and young calves. Mothers and offspring form some of the tightest bonds in the community, remaining together until the calf is weaned between the ages of 3 and 4 years.

Indeed, like chimpanzees, sons and daughters may often closely associate 16 with their mothers years after weaning. Wells reports that he has watched older offspring return to their mother's side for the birth of a sibling. "They seem to want to check out the new arrival," says Wells.

Female dolphins with calves are extremely cooperative. The mothers will 17 often form "playpens" around youngsters and allow them to interact within the protective enclave. Episodes of "baby-sitting" are also common, where one female will watch another's calf while the mother is occupied elsewhere. In many cases, Wells says that the cooperating females are related.

As females tend to associate together, so do males. Perhaps the most intrigu- 18 ing of all male groups is the existence of persistent pairs or trios. Wells has seen many such pairings of both juvenile and adult males. In one case, two large, older, and heavily scarred males have been observed in each other's constant company since 1975. Connor is also seeing what he calls "coalitions" of two and three males in Shark Bay and is preparing several papers on the subject. "I can say the coalitions of males that I am seeing are extremely exciting," says Connor.

The rationale behind such behavior is only just emerging. Wells believes 19 that the male pairs may protect each other from predation and cooperate in hunting. According to Wells, the teams are also capable of working in tandem to separate individual females from groups. In one anecdote published in 1987 by Wells, he describes two males flanking a female and chasing her.

At Shark Bay, Connor has repeatedly witnessed a behavior he considers 20 "sexual herding," in which two or three males in a coalition will cooperate to intimidate a female and keep her close by their sides. Connor suspects the males intend to mate with their captive. In Sarasota, this hypothesis is supported somewhat by the presence of closely bonded male pairs even during the mating season.

Using DNA fingerprinting techniques and chromosome band analysis, Wells 21 and Debbie Duffield of Portland State University in Oregon are currently examining blood samples taken from many of his male pairs in Sarasota to find out whether or not the males are related. The reason for the blood analysis is that it would be almost impossible to discern in the wild which male is fruitfully mating with which female because sexual encounters among dolphins are so common, says Wells.

The mating system for dolphins, like chimpanzees, is a promiscuous one. 22

302

Males and females do not form long-term bonds. Females may mate with a number of different males. Among the males in Shark Bay, Connor observes constant sexual interaction, both heterosexual and homosexual. "There'll be a group of 4 or 5 males and it seems like one of them goes, 'Let's go get Pointer!' And the other males start mounting him with erections," says Connor. "So much of the sexual interaction appears to be purely social. The males are constantly mounting each other and mounting females not in estrus."

Indeed, Wells reports that male bottle-nosed dolphins have unusually large testes and that the sperm concentrations in their ejaculate is 300 times the mean concentration for humans and 100 times the concentration for chimpanzees. Two-day-old dolphins have exhibited erections, and dolphins in both captivity and the wild masturbate. In Sarasota, males have been reported to mount sailboats. Says Wells: "The early development of sexual behavior, many years before sexual maturity, suggests that sex is quite important in the lives of these animals." It appears that large brains may have something to do with the amount of sexual behavior that is pursued outside of any reproductive context, says Smuts.[3]

23

QUESTIONS

1. Consider Booth's purpose for writing. How does this article end? Does Booth reach any conclusion about his material?

2. Summarize the similarities between chimpanzees and dolphins as Booth presents them in this article.

3. One of the dolphin-watchers says of his experience, "It was like watching a soap opera" (paragraph 3). What does he mean by this? What evidence of "soap opera" behavior is reported in this article?

4. How many sources does Booth use? How frequently does he rely on direct quotation of his sources? How much synthesizing and paraphrasing of information does he do?

5. Find a prime area for observing the courting or herding behavior of other large-brained mammals, such as college students. Write a report in which you tell why the site you chose is a particularly good one, what types of behavior you observed, and what your findings suggest for further investigation.

6. In groups, compare reports written for question 5. Draw up a report in each group based on your combined findings. Discuss these reports in class to see what general patterns of behavior emerge, and what these patterns suggest about the socialization of college students (or whatever group you've chosen to study).

---

[3] Booth later emphasized that the theory relating large brains and sexual behavior is speculative and not original with Smuts. [Eds.]

MAKING CONNECTIONS

1. The Shark Bay site is compared to the Gombe Stream Game Reserve (paragraphs 5–8). In what ways are these sites comparable? Read Jane van Lawick-Goodall's "First Observations" and compare the methods of observation at the two sites.

2. Consider the various animals reported and reflected upon by Booth, Farley Mowat, Jane van Lawick-Goodall, Virginia Woolf, Loren Eiseley, George Orwell, and Isak Dinesen. Do you find any patterns in the kinds of animals found for study and the attitudes of various writers toward them? What are some of the reasons we find animals so interesting? Which of these accounts do you find most interesting, and why? Is it the subject itself or the writer's handling of the subject that most attracts you? Explain.

TWO REPORTS OF AN
AIRPLANE CRASH

The Associated Press
The National Transportation Safety Board

The crash of a TWA jetliner on its way into Dulles International Airport outside Washington, D.C., was the lead story in the New York Times *on December 2, 1974. Almost a year later, the National Transportation Safety Board (NTSB) reported the results of their investigation into the causes of that crash. The work of the NTSB, which is also responsible for investigating rail, highway, marine, and pipeline accidents, has contributed significantly to the low rate of airline accidents in this country. We present here the newspaper article and the first part of the NTSB report, which reviews the accident itself, as examples of two different approaches to the reporting of the same event.*

BY THE ASSOCIATED PRESS

Upperville, Va., Dec. 1—

A Trans World Airlines 727, battling a driving rainstorm, slammed into a wooded slope near a secret government installation today, killing all 92 persons aboard. It was the worst air disaster of the year in the United States. [1]

Capt. William Carvello of the state police declared "there are no survivors" after rescue workers had combed for hours through the wreckage on Mount Weather, a foothill of the Blue Ridge Mountains. [2]

The plane, Flight 514, was bound for Washington from Columbus, Ohio, and was approaching Dulles International Airport when the tower lost radar contact at 11:10 A.M. [3]

The crash site was about five miles north of Upperville, a tiny community in the tip of the state and about 20 miles northwest of Dulles. [4]

First on Dulles Approach

According to the National Transportation Safety Board, today's was the first fatal crash by an airliner approaching Dulles, which opened in 1962. [5]

A T.W.A. spokesman said 85 passengers and a crew of seven were aboard the flight, which originated in Indianapolis. He said 46 persons got on at Columbus. [6]

The plane crashed about one and one-half miles from an underground 7
complex that reportedly is designed to serve as a headquarters for high government officials in the event of nuclear war. A Federal spokesman acknowledged
only that the facility was operated by the little known Office of Preparedness,
whose responsibilities, he said, include "continuity of government in a time of
national disaster."

All of Mount Weather, a peak of about 2000 feet, is owned by the Federal 8
Government. One official confirmed that several government employees were
at work at the building complex, and helped in search and rescue efforts.

The airlines released a list of the victims' names tonight after relatives had 9
been notified. The remains were taken to a makeshift morgue at the Bluemont
Community Center, five miles from the site. Rescue operations were halted at
8:15 P.M. because of fog, high winds, and rain.

Dr. George Hocker, Loudoun County medical examiner, said the plane hit 10
just below the summit and cut a swath 60 to 70 yards wide and about a quarter
of a mile long.

"There were just chunks of metal and total destruction," he said. 11

The police initially sealed off an area within a five-mile radius of the site to 12
all but law enforcement and rescue officials. A reporter who viewed the wreckage
several hours later said that much of it was still burning and the largest piece
of metal he could find measured only 5 by 10 feet.

The Federal Aviation Administration said there were no unusual commu- 13
nications from the plane before the crash, "just routine flight conversation."

The flight had been scheduled to land at National Airport near Washington 14
at 10:23 A.M. but was diverted to Dulles, a larger facility about 20 miles west
of the capital, because of high winds.

When the Dulles tower lost radar contact 37 minutes later, it notified the 15
local authorities to begin a search. Captain Carvello said two state troopers
found the wreckage almost immediately.

Apparently no one on the ground was hit by the crash nor were any buildings. 16
But a worker for the Chesapeake and Potomac Telephone Company said the
wreckage had severed the main underground phone line into the secret government installation. It was restored after two-and-a-half hours.

According to Federal aviation experts examining the wreckage, the airliner 17
broke down through the treetops and its underbelly was apparently ripped off
by a 10-foot-high rock ledge at the end of a secondary road.

Visibility on the ground was only about 100 feet, with snow flurries mixed 18
with rain and some fog. The Dulles tower said that at the proper altitude,
visibility would have been up to five miles, despite the rain.

John Reed, chairman of the National Transportation Safety Board, said "it 19
was impossible to say" what the cause of the crash was, outside of "an obviously
premature descent." He said his team of accident investigators was still searching
for the cockpit voice recorder and the aircraft's technical data recorder.

Mr. Reed said it was hoped that when these instruments were recovered, 20
they would provide a clue to the fateful last minutes.

Bill Smith, a member of the Marshall, Va. Rescue Squad, said the plane 21
hit "well below" the peak and there was "quite a bit of fire" at the site. He said
the plane devastated about 700 to 800 yards of the mountain's surface.

Vance Berry of Bluemont, who said he lived about three miles from the 22
scene, walked to it about an hour after the crash.

"There was nothing left but what looked like a bunch of crumpled up tinfoil," 23
he said. "You couldn't tell it had been a plane. What was left of the fuselage
was burning fiercely with a blue flame, even in the rain. For 100 yards the tops
of the trees had been cut off."

Mr. Berry added, "The weather was fierce—winds up to 50 miles per hour, 24
raining and foggy. I'd say the visibility was about 100 or 150 yards."

Richard Eastman, a ground maintenance employee of T.W.A., said after 25
viewing the wreckage, "If you didn't know it was an airplane you could never
guess it. The parts of the plane were scattered all over the area. There's no tail
or wing that you could make out."

In Washington, relatives and friends of the victims waited in despair at private 26
lounges at National and Dulles Airports for news from the crash site.

Carl Zwisler, a lawyer who said he believed his parents were on the plane, 27
said Senator Birch Bayh, Democrat of Indiana, who had planned to take the
plane back to Indianapolis, came into the lounge "and was very comforting."

"He was very helpful," Mr. Zwisler said. "He gave us his number and offered 28
to try to help us any way he could."

T.W.A. said the seven crew members included three pilots, all based in Los 29
Angeles, three stewardesses from Chicago and one from Kansas City.

AIRCRAFT ACCIDENT REPORT
NATIONAL TRANSPORTATION SAFETY BOARD

At 1110 e.s.t., December 1, 1974, Trans World Airlines, Inc., Flight 514, 1
a Boeing 727-231, N54328, crashed 25 nautical miles northwest of Dulles
International Airport, Washington, D.C. The accident occurred while the flight
was descending for a VOR/DME approach to runway 12 at Dulles during
instrument meteorological conditions.[1] The 92 occupants—85 passengers and
7 crewmembers—were killed and the aircraft was destroyed.

The National Transportation Safety Board determines that the probable cause 2
of the accident was the crew's decision to descend to 1,800 feet before the
aircraft had reached the approach segment where that minimum altitude ap-

---

[1] VOR: very high frequency omnidirectional radio range, a radio navigation aid supplying bearing
information; DME: distance measuring equipment, a radio navigation aid that provides distance
information. VOR/DME is basic equipment used for an instrument landing in bad weather. [Eds.]

plied. The crew's decision to descend was a result of inadequacies and lack of clarity in the air traffic control procedures which led to a misunderstanding on the part of the pilots and of the controllers regarding each other's responsibilities during operations in terminal areas under instrument meteorological conditions. Nevertheless, the examination of the plan view of the approach chart should have disclosed to the captain that a minimum altitude of 1,800 feet was not a safe altitude.

Contributing factors were: 3

(1) The failure of the FAA to take timely action to resolve the confusion and misinterpretation of air traffic terminology although the Agency had been aware of the problem for several years;

(2) The issuance of the approach clearance when the flight was 44 miles from the airport on an unpublished route without clearly defined minimum altitudes; and

(3) Inadequate depiction of altitude restrictions on the profile view of the approach chart for the VOR/DME approach to runway 12 at Dulles International Airport.

1. INVESTIGATION

1.1 History of the Flight

Trans World Airlines, Inc., Flight 514 was a regularly scheduled flight from   4
Indianapolis, Indiana, to Washington, D.C., with an intermediate stop at Columbus, Ohio. There were 85 passengers and 7 crewmembers aboard the aircraft when it departed Columbus.

The flight was dispatched by TWA's dispatch office in New York through   5
the operations office in Indianapolis. The captain received a dispatch package which included en route and destination weather information. The flight operated under a computer-stored instrument flight rules (IFR) flight plan.

Flight 514 departed Indianapolis at 0853 e.s.t.[2] and arrived in Columbus at   6
0932. The crew obtained weather and aircraft load information. The flight departed Columbus at 1024, 11 minutes late.

At 1036, the Cleveland Air Route Traffic Control Center (ARTCC) informed   7
the crew of Flight 514 that no landings were being made at Washington National Airport because of high crosswinds, and that flights destined for that airport were either being held or being diverted to Dulles International Airport.

At 1038, the captain of Flight 514 communicated with the dispatcher in   8

---

[2] All times are eastern standard times expressed on 24-hour clock. [Eds.]

New York and advised him of the information he had received. The dispatcher, with the captain's concurrence, subsequently amended Flight 514's release to allow the flight to proceed to Dulles.

At 1042, Cleveland ARTCC cleared Flight 514 to Dulles Airport via the   9
Front Royal VOR, and to maintain flight level (FL) 290.[3] At 1043, the controller cleared the flight to descend to FL 230 and to cross a point 40 miles west of Front Royal at that altitude. Control of the flight was then transferred to the Washington ARTCC and communications were established with that facility at 1048.

During the period between receipt of the amended flight release and the   10
transfer of control of Washington ARTCC, the flightcrew discussed the instrument approach to runway 12, the navigational aids, and the runways at Dulles, and the captain turned the flight controls over to the first officer.

When radio communications were established with Washington ARTCC,   11
the controller affirmed that he knew the flight was proceeding to Dulles. Following this contact, the cockpit voice recorder (CVR) indicated that the crew discussed the various routings they might receive to conduct a VOR/DME approach to runway 12 at Dulles. They considered the possibilities of proceeding via Front Royal VOR, via Martinsburg VOR, or proceeding on a "straight-in" clearance.

At 1501, the Washington ARTCC controller requested the flight's heading.   12
After being told that the flight was on a heading of 100°, the controller cleared the crew to change to a heading of 090°, to intercept the 300° radial of the Armel VOR, to cross a point 25 miles northwest of Armel to maintain 8,000 feet,[4] and ". . . the 300° radial will be for a VOR approach to runway 12 at Dulles." He gave the crew an altimeter setting of 29.74 for Dulles.[5] The crew acknowledged this clearance. The CVR recording indicated that the Armel VOR was then tuned on a navigational receiver. The pilots again discussed the VOR/DME approach to runway 12 at Dulles.

At 1055, the landing preliminary checklist was read by the flight engineer   13
and the other crewmembers responded to the calls. A reference speed of 127 kn was calculated and set on the airspeed indicator reference pointers. The altimeters were set at 29.74.

At 1057, the crew again discussed items on the instrument approach chart   14
including the Round Hill intersection, the final approach fix, the visual approach slope indicator and runway lights, and the airport diagram.

At 1059, the captain commented that the flight was descending from 11,000   15
feet to 8,000 feet. He then asked the controller if there were any weather obstructions between the flight and the airport. The controller replied that he

---

[3] Altitude reference used above 18,000 feet m.s.l., using an altimeter setting of 29.92. [Eds.]

[4] All altitudes and elevations are expressed in feet above mean sea level unless otherwise noted.

[5] altimeter: instrument which shows the altitude of the airplane with respect to a fixed level, such as sea level. [Eds.]

did not see any significant weather along the route. The captain replied that the crew also did not see any weather on the aircraft weather radar. The CVR recording indicated that the captain then turned on the anti-icing system.

At 1101, the controller cleared the flight to descend to and maintain 7,000   16 feet and to contact Dulles approach control. Twenty-six seconds later, the captain initiated a conversation with Dulles approach control and reported that the aircraft was descending from 10,000 feet to maintain 7,000 feet. He also reported having received the information "Charlie" transmitted on the ATIS broadcast.[6]

The controller replied with a clearance to proceed inbound to Armel and to   17 expect a VOR/DME approach to runway 12. The controller then informed the crew that ATIS information Delta was current and read the data to them. The crew determined that the difference between information Charlie and Delta was the altimeter setting which was given in Delta as 29.70. There was no information on the CVR to indicate that the pilots reset their altimeters from 29.74.

At 1104, the flight reported it was level at 7,000 feet. Five seconds after   18 receiving that report, the controller said, "TWA 514, you're cleared for a VOR/DME approach to runway 12." This clearance was acknowledged by the captain. The CVR recorded the sound of the landing gear warning horn followed by a comment from the captain that "Eighteen hundred is the bottom." The first officer then said, "Start down." The flight engineer said, "We're out here quite a ways. I better turn the heat down."

At 1105:06, the captain reviewed the field elevation, the minimum descent   19 altitude, and the final approach fix and discussed the reason that no time to the missed approach point was published. At 1106:15, the first officer commented that, "I hate the altitude jumping around." Then he commented that the instrument panel was bouncing around. At 1106:15, the captain said, "We have a discrepancy in our VOR's, a little but not much." He continued, "Fly yours, not mine." At 1106:27, the captain discussed the last reported ceiling and minimum descent altitude. He concluded, ". . . should break out."

At 1106:42, the first officer said, "Gives you a headache after a while,   20 watching this jumping around like that." At 1107:27, he said, ". . . you can feel that wind down here now." A few seconds later, the captain said, "You know, according to this dumb sheet it says thirty-four hundred to Round Hill—is our minimum altitude." The flight engineer then asked where the captain saw that and the captain replied, "Well, here. Round Hill is eleven and a half DME." The first officer said, "Well, but—" and the captain replied, "When he clears you, that means you can go to your—" An unidentified voice said, "Initial approach," and another unidentified voice said, "Yeah!" Then the captain said "Initial approach altitude." The flight engineer then said, "We're

---

[6] ATIS—Automatic Terminal Information Service. [Eds.]

out a—twenty-eight for eighteen." An unidentified voice said, "Right," and someone said, "One to go."

At 1108:14, the flight engineer said, "Dark in here," and the first officer stated, "And bumpy too." At 1108:25, the sound of an altitude alert horn was recorded. The captain said, "I had ground contact a minute ago," and the first officer replied, "Yeah, I did too." At 1108:29, the first officer said, "* power on this #."[7] The captain said "Yeah—you got a high sink rate." The first officer replied, "Yeah." An unidentified voice said, "We're going uphill," and the flight engineer replied, "We're right there, we're on course." Two voices responded, "Yeah!" The captain then said, "You ought to see ground outside in just a minute.—Hang in there boy." The flight engineer said, "We're getting seasick." 21

At 1108:57, the altitude alert sounded. Then the first officer said, "Boy, it was—wanted to go right down through there, man," to which an unidentified voice replied, "Yeah!" Then the first officer said, "Must have had a # of a downdraft." 22

At 1109:14, the radio altimeter warning horn sounded and stopped. The first officer said, "Boy!" At 1109:20, the captain said, "Get some power on." The radio altimeter warning horn sounded again and stopped. At 1109:22, the sound of impact was recorded. 23

At 1109:54, the approach controller called Flight 514 and said, "TWA 514, say your altitude." There was no response to this or subsequent calls. 24

The controller subsequently testified that he noticed on the radarscope that the flight's altitude was about 2,000 feet just before he called them. 25

The flight data recorder (FDR) readout indicated that after the aircraft left 7,000 feet, the descent was continuous with little rate variation until the indicated altitude was about 1,750 feet. The altitude increased about 150 feet over a 15-second period and then decreased about 200 feet during a 20-second period. The recorded altitude remained about 1,750 feet until impact. 26

During that same portion of the flight, the indicated airspeed varied from 240 kn to 230 kn until the altitude trace leveled off about 1,750 feet after which the airspeed decreased and fluctuated between 222 kn to 248 kn. Some of the fluctuations occurred within short time spans while others were within longer spans. 27

The heading trace showed little variation during the latter portion of the flight. As the aircraft left 7,000 feet, the heading changed from an indication of 112° to about 120° in about 2.5 minutes. The heading did not vary more than 2° to 4° from that indication until impact. 28

As the aircraft left 7,000 feet, the vertical acceleration (g) trace was smooth with little fluctuation. After 40 seconds, the g trace activity increased to about ± 0.1 g. This continued for about 1 minute and then increased in amplitude to about ± 0.2 g for about 70 seconds. At this point there was a blank in the 29

[7]*Indicates unintelligible word(s); # indicates nonpertinent word(s).

g trace. When the trace reappeared, it was still active, with variations in indicated g ranging from ± 0.2 to 0.5 g, until impact.

The accident occurred on the west slope of Mount Weather, Virginia, about 30 25 nmi from Dulles, at an elevation of about 1,670 feet. The latitude was 39° 04.6°N and the longitude was 77° 52.9°W.

31

1.2 Injuries to Persons

Injuries	Crew	Passengers	Others
Fatal	7	85	0
Nonfatal	0	0	0
None	0	0	

1.3 Damage to Aircraft

The aircraft was destroyed.

32

1.4 Other Damage

Power and communications lines were damaged.

33

1.5 Crew Information

The flightcrew was qualified and certificated in accordance with the existing 34 FAA requirements. The captain was qualified to operate into Dulles under the provisions of 14 CFR 121.443.

1.6 Aircraft Information

The aircraft was certified and maintained in accordance with FAA-approved 35 procedures. The aircraft weight and balance were calculated to be within limits at takeoff and at the time of the accident. The aircraft was serviced with Jet A fuel, and there were 29,700 pounds of fuel aboard when the flight departed Columbus. There were about 19,300 pounds of fuel aboard at impact.

1.7 Meteorological Information

The weather in the area where the accident occurred was characterized by 36 low clouds, rain mixed with occasional wet snow, and strong, gusty easterly winds. A complex low-pressure system extended from western Kentucky to southeastern Virginia and the eastern Carolinas with small low centers located in western Kentucky and south-central Virginia. An occluded front extended from the Kentucky low through North Carolina into the Virginia low.[8] A warm front extended northeastward from the Virginia low into the Atlantic, while a cold front extended from the same low to the Virginia coast, then southward into the Atlantic. A large area of low cloudiness and precipitation extended from the mid-Atlantic states to the Great Lakes, and southward to Tennessee. High gusty winds extended from the Middle Atlantic States to the Great Lakes.

The aviation weather observations taken at Washington National Airport 37 between 0853 and 1054 reported scattered clouds at 700 feet, overcast at 1,200 feet, and visibility of 5 or more miles with very light to light rain. The winds were blowing from 70°, and the velocity varied from 25 to 28 kn with gusts of 35 kn reported at 0853, 44 kn reported at 0953, and 49 kn reported at 1054.

The aviation weather observations taken at Dulles International Airport be- 38 tween 0858 and 1055 reported an overcast at 900 feet with visibility varying from 3 to 7 miles in light rain. The winds were from: 080° at 20 kn gusting to 32 kn reported at 0858; 090° at 26 kn, gusting to 40 kn reported at 0955; and, 080° at 25 kn, gusting to 36 kn, reported at 1055.

The 1131 radar weather observation from Patuxent, Maryland, showed a 39 large area of weather echoes which included the accident area. One-tenth of the area was covered with thunderstorms which were producing moderate rain showers, and five-tenths of the area was covered with moderate rain. The thunderstorm cells were moving from 170° at 45 kn. The maximum cloud tops were at 24,000 feet between Charlottesville, Virginia, and the accident site.

There were three SIGMETS[9] in effect at the time of the accident. They 40 recommended caution due to ". . . moderate to severe mixed icing in clouds and precipitation above the freezing level" and embedded thunderstorms with tops near 40,000 feet. The cells were moving northeastward at 25 to 30 kn.

Although there were numerous pilot reports of weather conditions in the 41 area around Washington, none was received from pilots flying in the area where the accident occurred.

Ground witnesses in the accident area stated that, at about the time of the 42 accident, the local weather was characterized by low ceilings with visibilities ranging from 50 to 100 feet at the crash site. The wind was estimated at 40 mph with stronger gusts. There was a steady drizzle in the accident area.

At the request of the Safety Board, the National Weather Service (NWS) 43 studied the possibility of pressure changes in the accident area which could have contributed to the cause of the accident. Based on the observed wind direction and velocity at Dulles at 1025 (43 kn), the NWS calculated that a pressure drop of 0.4 millibars, equivalent to 0.012 in. Hg., could have occurred

---

[8] occluded front: when a warm front is overtaken by a cold front, the warm air is forced upward from the surface of the earth. [Eds.]

[9] SIGMETS are advisory warnings of weather severe enough to be potentially hazardous to all aircraft. They are broadcast on navigation aid voice frequencies and by flight service stations. They are also transmitted on the Service A weather teletype circuits. [Eds.]

if the wind conditions in the accident area were the same as the winds at Dulles.[10] This pressure change could result in an aircraft altimeter reading 13 feet higher than the actual altitude of the aircraft. They further calculated that if the wind velocity was 60 kn, the resulting pressure change could be 3.2 millibars (0.094 in. Hg.) causing an altimeter reading 95 feet higher than the actual altitude. A wind velocity of 80 kn could result in an altitude indication 218 feet higher than the aircraft altitude.

The accident occurred in clouds and during the hours of daylight.　　　44

1.8 *Aids to Navigation*

The navigational aids in use for the VOR/DME approach to runway 12 at　45
Dulles included the Martinsburg, Front Royal, Linden, and Armel VOR's. These navigational aids were flightchecked after the accident and were operating within the prescribed tolerances. The distance measuring function of Armel had been inoperative about 2 hours before the accident, but it was operating without reported malfunction shortly before and after the accident.

Automated radar terminal system equipment (ARTS III) was used by the　46
approach controller to observe and control the traffic. The ARTS III is a system which automatically processes the transponder beacon return from all transponder-equipped aircraft.[11] The computed data are selectively presented on a data block next to each aircraft's updated position on the air traffic controller's radar display. The information provided on the video display is aircraft identification, groundspeed in knots, and, when the transponder of the aircraft being tracked has Mode C capability, pressure altitude in 100-foot increments. The aircraft's transponder has this capability. The position accuracy of these data is limited to about $\frac{1}{4}°$ in azimuth and $\frac{1}{16}$ nmi in range.[12] Altitude is presented with a tolerance of $\pm$ 100 feet.

The controller's radarscopes are equipped with video maps which depict　47
various terrain features, the position of navigational aids, and other pertinent data. In this case, the video map did not display the Round Hill intersection which is the intermediate approach fix for this approach, nor did it display the high terrain northwest of that fix. The updated video maps depicting the Round Hill intersection had been ordered but had not been received at the time of the accident.

There was no current letter of agreement between Dulles Approach Control　48
and the adjacent ARTCC's regarding the use of the Armel VOR/DME approach to runway 12 at Dulles.

---

[10] Hg.: mercury, used to measure atmospheric changes and thus changes in altitude. [Eds.]

[11] transponder: a radio transmitter-receiver. [Eds.]

[12] azimuth: the horizontal direction of a celestial point from a terrestrial point; range: a line of bearing defined by a radio range. [Eds.]

1.9 Communications

No air-to-ground radio communication difficulties were reported.   49

1.10 Aerodrome and Ground Facilities

Dulles International Airport is equipped with three primary runways: 12/30,   50
1L/19R, and 1R/19L. The north-south runways (1L/19R and 1R/19L) are
11,500 feet long and 12/30 (runway 12) is 10,000 feet long. There are provisions
for ILS approaches to the north-south runways. Runway 12 is served by a VOR/
DME approach. In addition, a surveillance radar approach is available to all
runways. Runway 12 is equipped with high intensity runway lights but not with
approach lights. There is a visual approach slope indicator (VASI) installed on
the left side of the runway.

1.11 Flight Recorders

N54328 was equipped with Lockheed Aircraft Service Model 109-D flight   51
data recorder, serial No. 117, and a Fairchild Model A-100 cockpit voice
recorder, serial No. 1123. Both recorders were installed in a nonpressurized
area aft of the pressure bulkhead.

The flight data recorder parameter traces were clearly recorded. There were   52
no recorder malfunctions. A readout was made of the last 15 minutes 25 seconds
of the flight. There was a small gap in the vertical acceleration trace shown on
the data graph at time 13 minutes 30 seconds because of foil damage which
obliterated the trace.

The cockpit voice recorder remained intact and the recording was clear. A   53
composite flight track was prepared by correlating the recorder data.

1.12 Wreckage

The wreckage was contained within an area about 900 feet long and 200 feet   54
wide. The evidence of first impact was trees whose tops were cut off about 70
feet above the ground. The elevation at the base of the trees was 1,605 feet.
The wreckage path was oriented along a line 118° magnetic. Calculations
indicated that the left wing went down about 6° as the aircraft passed through
the trees and the aircraft was descending at an angle of about 1°. After about
500 feet of travel through the trees, the aircraft struck a rock outcropping at an
elevation of about 1,675 feet. Numerous heavy components of the aircraft were
thrown forward of the outcropping.

The wing flaps, wing leading edge devices, and the landing gears were   55
retracted. The condition of the flight control system could not be determined

because of impact and fire damage. No evidence was found of preimpact structural failure or control system malfunction.

All three engines separated from the aircraft and were damaged.   56

The major rotating compressor components were bent or broken in a direc-   57
tion opposite to normal rotation. There was no evidence found of preimpact engine fire or malfunction.

Most of the instruments on the pilots' instrument panels were destroyed, as   58
were most of the aircraft navigational and flight instrument systems' compo-
nents. Among those that were recovered and from which useful information could be obtained were the first officer's DME indicator which read 12 miles; the first officer's course deviation indicator which showed a selected course of 123°; and the first officer's altimeter, set at 29.70 in. Hg., with an internal indication of 1,818 feet. The first officer's flight director indicator showed the altitude marker at "0" feet, and the pitch display showed 5° aircraft noseup. An airspeed indicator was recovered with the reference pointer set at 123 kn; and a radio altimeter was found which indicated 10 feet. One distance measuring equipment interrogator unit was recovered; it showed a mileage indication of 12 miles and was tuned to a channel paired with 115.3 MHz., the frequency of the Front Royal VOR. [13]

1.13 *Medical and Pathological Information*

All of the occupants of the aircraft died of traumatic injuries. Post-mortem   59
examinations and toxicological and histological analyses were conducted on all flight crewmembers. No evidence of disease was found and the analyses were negative. The medical histories of the flight crewmembers disclosed no evidence of abnormal conditions.

1.14 *Fire*

No evidence of in-flight fire was found. Scattered intense ground fires oc-   60
curred throughout the wreckage area. Local fire departments were notified of the location of the wreckage about 1145 and about 150 fire and rescue personnel responded with six pumpers and several rescue vehicles.

1.15 *Survival Aspects*

This was not a survivable accident.   61

---

[13] MHz.: megahertz, a unit of frequency equal to one million hertz, or cycles per second. [Eds.]

QUESTIONS

1. What information is present in the *Times* article but missing in the NTSB report? What does the NTSB report include that the newspaper account does not?

2. What does this difference in information tell you about the writers' conceptions of audience and purpose? Look back at the first two paragraphs of each report. How do these two openings reflect these conceptions?

3. The editors had to go to a library reference room to look up terms not explained by the writers of the NTSB report. Choose a term from the report that is not glossed or that is not explained clearly. Then find the best source in your library that explains the term better than the editors (or the NTSB) did.

4. Using the NTSB report, write an article for the *New York Times* in which you summarize the information in the report. Be sure to provide a headline.

5. Select an event familiar to you, and write a report about it aimed at a general audience that will need key terms explained. You might choose an event such as participating in a bicycle race or tour, entering a pet in a show, participating in a band concert or a wrestling match, preparing a special meal, or building a dog house. Give your report to a classmate for comments on any areas that may need revision for clarity.

MAKING CONNECTIONS

1. Compare the NTSB account of this crash with Horace Miner's "Body Ritual among the Nacirema." Although Miner's report is a parody, both reports exhibit formal features that show them prepared for specialized, professional audiences. Describe several formal features of each report. What can you infer about the audience and purpose of each report?

2. Compare the AP report of this crash with William Booth's "The Social Lives of Dolphins." How similar and how different are the methods of each report? What does your comparison tell you about the purpose of each writer?

EXPLAINING

Here in "Explaining" you will find writing by specialists from a wide range of fields seeking to account for matters as various as the color of the sky, the origin of the universe, the content of urban legends, and the art of Georgia O'Keeffe. Explanation is an essential kind of writing in every academic field and profession. Facts, after all, do not speak for themselves, nor do figures add up on their own. Even the most vividly detailed report or computer printout requires someone to make sense of the information it contains. To make sense of a subject, we need to see it in terms of something that is related to it—the color of the sky in terms of light waves from the sun, the content of urban legends in terms of the immediate circumstances in which they are told. To understand a subject, in other words, we must examine it in terms of some relevant context that will shed light on its origin and development, or its nature and design, or its elements and functions, or its causes and effects, or its meaning and significance. For this reason, you will repeatedly find the writers in this section drawing on specific bodies of knowledge and systems of interpretation to explain the problems and subjects that they address.

This essential element of explaining can be seen in connection with the following passage from James Jeans's "Why the Sky Is Blue":

> We know that sunlight is a blend of lights of many colors—as we can prove for ourselves by passing it through a prism, or even through a jug of water, or as Nature demonstrates to us when she passes it through the raindrops of a summer shower and produces a rainbow. We also know that light consists of waves, and that the different colors of light are produced by waves of different lengths, red light by long waves and blue light by short waves. The mixture of waves which constitutes sunlight has to struggle through the obstacles it meets in the atmosphere, just as the mixture of waves at the seaside has to struggle past the columns of the pier. And these obstacles treat the light-waves much as the columns of the pier treat the sea-waves. The long waves which constitute red light are hardly affected, but the short waves which constitute blue light are scattered in all directions.
>
> Thus, the different constituents of sunlight are treated in different ways as they struggle through the earth's atmosphere. A wave of blue

light may be scattered by a dust particle, and turned out of its course. After a time a second dust particle again turns it out of its course, and so on, until finally it enters our eyes by a path as zigzag as that of a flash of lightning. Consequently the blue waves of the sunlight enter our eyes from all directions. And that is why the sky looks blue.

Jeans's purpose here is to explain "why the sky looks blue," and as you can see from the opening sentence of the passage, he systematically establishes an explanatory context by setting forth directly relevant information about the nature and properties of sunlight, light, and light-waves. That is, he approaches the explanatory problem in terms of knowledge drawn from his specialized fields of astronomy and physics. With this knowledge in hand, he then proceeds to show how "the different constituents of sunlight are treated in different ways as they struggle through the earth's atmosphere." In this way, he develops his explanation according to the analytic framework one would expect of an astronomer and physicist, concerning himself with the interaction of the atmosphere and light-waves. Having formulated a cause-and-effect analysis demonstrating that blue light is scattered "in all directions," Jeans is able to conclude that "the blue waves of the sunlight enter our eyes from all directions. And that is why the sky looks blue." Thus, the particular body of information that Jeans draws upon from astronomy and physics makes it possible for him to offer a knowledgeable, systematic, and instructive explanation.

To appreciate how significant an explanatory context can be, you need only consider how knowledge from other fields might influence an understanding of "why the sky looks blue." A zoologist specializing in optics, for example, might note the importance of the retinal organs known as cones, which in animals are thought to be the mechanism primarily responsible for the reception of color. Given this crucial bit of information, a zoologist might observe that the sky looks blue to human beings because their eyes are equipped with cones, whereas it does not look blue to animals lacking cones, such as guinea pigs, owls, and armadillos. An anthropologist, in turn, might think it worth noting that coastal and island cultures, given their maritime environments, tend to develop unusually rich vocabularies for describing how the sea looks and how the sky looks. Thus, an anthropologist might conclude that members of maritime cultures are likely to be especially discerning about the colors of the sea and sky.

Our hypothetical zoologist and anthropologist would both differ from Jeans in their explanatory approaches to the blue sky. Whereas Jeans approached it in terms of accounting for the source and prevalence of blue color, our zoologist and anthropologist would take the color for granted and seek instead to account for the human ability to perceive the color or the propensity of some cultures to be especially discriminating in their perception of it. Their differing approaches, in this case as in others, would result from their differing fields of study. Each academic area, after all, involves a distinctive body of knowledge, a distinctive array of interests, and a distinctive set of methods for making sense of the subjects that fall within its field of interest. Thus it follows that each area is likely to approach problems from different angles and arrive at different kinds of explanations. It follows, too, that no area can lay claim to the ultimate truth about things. But, as the case of the blue sky illustrates, each field does have a special angle on the truth, particularly about subjects that fall within its area of specialization. Our zoologist and anthropologist could be as valid and as enlightening in this case as the astronomer-physicist. In a broader sense, you can see from the case of the blue sky that in trying to explain a particular subject or problem one always has to look at it or approach it from a particular angle or a combination of viewpoints and that any particular approach brings a corresponding body of knowledge to bear upon an understanding of the subject. Relevant knowledge, quite simply, is the most essential element of explaining.

But knowledge alone is not sufficient to produce intelligible and effective explanation. Jeans's explanation, for example, depends not only upon a body of information about the properties and movement of light and light-waves but also, as you will see, upon the form and style in which the information is presented. To develop your ability in explaining, then, you will need to develop a resourcefulness in putting your knowledge to use. One way to do that is to familiarize yourself with some of the many different forms that explanatory writing can take in different academic and professional situations.

THE RANGE OF EXPLANATORY WRITING

Explanatory writing serves a wide range of academic, professional, and public purposes. Rules and regulations, guidelines and instructions—all these are familiar examples of explanation in the service of telling people how to carry on many of the practical and public activities of their lives. Textbooks, such as the one you are reading right now, as well as popularized presentations of highly specialized research or theory are common examples of explanatory writing in the service of helping people to understand a particular body of information and ideas. Scholarly research papers, government documents, and other highly technical presentations of data and analysis, though less familiar to the general reader, are important kinds of explanation that advance knowledge and informed decision making.

To serve the differing needs of such varied purposes and audiences, explanatory writing necessarily incorporates various forms and styles of presentation. Jeans's piece about the sky, for example, comes from a book intended as an introduction to astronomy. Thus, he writes in a style that depends on a vocabulary accessible to most readers. And to make sure that beginners will understand the important concepts in his explanation, Jeans repeatedly illustrates his discussion with analogies and references to familiar experiences. In fact, if you look at the whole of Jeans's piece, you will see that he establishes his analogy of light-waves to sea-waves at the very beginning of his discussion and then systematically uses it to organize and clarify the rest of his explanation.

By contrast, the scientific paper by Antonio R. Damasio, "Face Perception without Recognition," is written for a highly specialized audience of researchers, as you can tell immediately from the abstract that precedes it as well as from its highly technical language and scholarly reference notes. Thus, Damasio does not structure his explanation in terms of a familiar analogy but instead uses a highly methodological format for reviewing research on a particular problem. According to this format, his review begins with a definition of the research topic and a summary of established knowledge, then moves into a detailed discussion of research on issues about which there has been "considerable controversy," and finally concludes with a look at some "new developments" in the study of the problem. In each of these sections of his review, Damasio refers to specific pieces of published research, which he enumerates and documents at the end of his article. Thus, the review of research not only provides readers with an explanatory overview of investigation, but it also tells them where to look for more detailed information on the subject.

For yet another variation in the format and style of explanatory writing, we need only shift our attention from the sciences to the social sciences and look at Oliver Sacks's "The Autist Artist." Here Sacks is not reviewing investigative research, but is offering the results of a case study, which entails the close observation of an individual subject over time. Because the subject of a case study is by definition unique, the study cannot be replicated by other researchers. A case study, therefore, must be written up in sufficient detail not only to document the observer's understanding of the subject but also to enable other researchers to draw their own conclusions about the subject. So, you will find that Sacks provides an extensively detailed description, history, and analysis of José's behavior. You will also find that Sacks writes on the whole in a standard rather than specialized style, as befits an audience of generally educated readers.

However, we need only look at the following passage from the first paragraph of Joan Didion's essay "Georgia O'Keeffe" to see that style and format do not always adhere to audience and purpose exactly as one might expect:

> I recall an August afternoon in Chicago in 1973 when I took my daughter, then seven, to see what Georgia O'Keeffe had done with where she had been. One of the vast O'Keeffe "Sky Above Clouds" canvases floated over the back stairs in the Chicago Art Institute that day, dominating what seemed to be several stories of empty light, and my daughter looked at it once, ran to the landing, and kept on looking. "Who drew it," she whispered after a while. I told her. "I need to talk to her," she said finally.

322

Judging from the plain style as well as the personal aspects of the story that Didion tells about her daughter's reaction to O'Keeffe's painting, you might think that this piece belongs in "Reflecting" rather than here in "Explaining." But if you read the whole of Didion's essay, you will discover that it is a highly informed piece, in which she also tells some surprising stories about O'Keeffe in order to identify and explain what she perceives to be the most distinctive elements and qualities in O'Keeffe's work. You will also discover that Didion organizes her material and tells her stories in a way that is often quite surprising, yet also quite appropriate to what she considers to be most distinctive about O'Keeffe.

As you can see from our brief discussion of just this handful of selections, explanation is a widely varied form of writing, involving as it does in every case a delicate mix of adjustments to the audience, purpose, specialized field, and subject matter. Thus as a reader of explanation, you will have to be very flexible in your approach, always willing to make your way through unfamiliar territory on the way to a clear understanding of the subject being discussed, or perhaps to a clear recognition that understanding may be beyond the scope of your knowledge in a particular field. And as a writer, you will have to be equally flexible in your choice of language, as well as in your selection and arrangement of material, so as to put your knowledge and understanding in a form that not only satisfies you but also fulfills the complex set of conditions to which your explanation is addressed.

METHODS OF EXPLAINING

In planning a piece of explanatory writing, you should begin by reviewing your material with an eye to deciding upon the overall approach that you intend to use. As our previous discussion has indicated, you should aim to develop an approach that is adjusted to all the conditions of your explanatory situation. Some methods, you will find, are inescapable, no matter what your subject, audience, or purpose. Every piece of explanation requires that ideas be clarified and demonstrated through *illustration*—that is, through the citing of specific examples, as you can see from the earlier passage by Jeans and in the following excerpt from Sacks's essay on José, the "autist artist":

> We walked around the hospital grounds, José sometimes gazing at the sky and trees, but more often down at his feet, at the mauve and yellow carpet of clover and dandelions beneath us. He had a very quick eye for plant forms and colours, rapidly saw and picked a rare white clover, and found a still rarer four-leaved one. He found seven different types of grass, no less, seemed to recognize, to greet, each one as a friend. He was delighted most of all by the great yellow dandelions, open, all their florets flung open to the sun. This was his plant—it was how he felt, and to show his feeling he would draw it. The need to draw, to

pay graphic reverence, was immediate and strong: he knelt down, placed his clipboard on the ground, and, holding the dandelion, drew it.

Sacks's obligation to illustrate and demonstrate José's artistic proficiency leads him here, as elsewhere in his piece, to turn to a detailed *description* and *narration* of José's actions. So it is that reporting constitutes an essential element of explaining. And not only for reasons of clarity, but also for purposes of reliability and credibility. If an explanation cannot be illustrated, or can only be weakly documented, then it is likely to be much less reliable and therefore much less credible to readers than one that can be amply and vividly detailed.

Some methods, while not required in every case, are often so important that they should be kept in mind as being potentially necessary in any piece of explanation. An essay that depends on the use of special terms or concepts almost certainly will call for a *definition* of each term and concept, in order to assure that the reader understands them exactly as the writer intends them to be understood. In "Urban Legends: 'The Boyfriend's Death,'" for example, Jan Harold Brunvand begins his study by carefully defining urban legends as a subclass of folklore, and by defining in turn what is entailed in the study of folklore.

Likewise, in his essay about José, Sacks, introducing the term "autist" in his title, and suggesting in his opening descriptions of José's drawings that the "imagination, playfulness, [and] art" they exhibit are atypical of the autistic, describes autistic behavior. He uses the definition of a colleague who has diagnosed José as autistic, and presents similar information from another doctor's research on the drawing abilities of autistic children. Such expert opinion serves to show that José's performance deviates from the "merely mechanical" proficiencies of autistic individuals, and leads Sacks to ask, "What then was José" and "might anything be done" about the state he was in. In his subsequent review of the data comprising José's case history, Sacks is careful to define the terms he uses, and to qualify them with descriptions of José's behavior. Sacks' conclusion further defines autism, differentiating between "classical autism," which cuts the person off from any memory of ordinary life, and José's "secondary autism," in which there remains some memory of a past life and a capacity to interact with others. Definition, in other words, can be carried out in a variety of ways—by citing examples, by identifying essential qualities or characteristics, by offering synonyms, by making distinctions.

Other methods, while not necessarily imperative, can be very effective in a broad range of explanatory situations. If you are trying to explain the character, design, elements, or nature of something, you will often do best to *compare and contrast* it with something to which it is logically and self-evidently related. Comparison calls attention to similarities, contrast focuses on differences, and together the methods work to clarify and emphasize important points by playing related subjects against each other. In his study of urban legends, for example,

Brunvand attempts to shed light on the complex circumstances that influence the content of such folktales by comparing and contrasting several versions of the same legendary story. His comparison and contrast enables him to show that popular urban legends, such as "The Boyfriend's Death," retain a basically unvarying situation and plot as they travel from one storyteller and locale to another, but that specific details are altered by individual storytellers to make them fit the circumstances of a particular audience. Like Brunvand's piece, some examples of comparison and contrast rely on a strategic balancing of similarities and differences. Other pieces depend largely on a sustained contrast. And still other pieces might work primarily in terms of comparison. The mix within each piece is adjusted to the needs of its explanatory situation. By the same token, you should make sure that whenever you use comparison and contrast, your attention to similarities and differences is adjusted to the needs of your explanatory situation.

A special form of comparison, namely *analogy*, can also be useful in many explanatory situations. Analogies help readers to understand difficult or unfamiliar ideas by putting them in tangible and familiar terms. In "Why the Sky Is Blue," for example, Jeans's analogy of light-waves to sea-waves enables us to visualize a process that we could not otherwise see. And in "Times and Distances, Large and Small," Francis Crick discusses a variety of analogies that scientists have used in order to help people grasp measurements of space and time that are either so vast or so diminutive as to be otherwise quite difficult to comprehend. Useful as analogies are, however, they rely at last upon drawing particular resemblances between things that are otherwise unlike. Sea-waves, after all, are not light-waves, and the dimensions of the universe are not the same as anything within the range of ordinary human experience. Thus, whenever you develop an analogy, you should be careful in applying it to your explanatory situation, so as to make sure that the analogy fits and that it does not involve misleading implications.

Some explanatory methods are especially suited to a particular kind of situation. If you are trying to show how to do something, or how something works, or how something was done, you will find it best to use a method known as *process analysis*. In analyzing a process, your aim is to make it clear to a reader by providing a narrative breakdown and presentation of it step-by-step, by identifying and describing each step or stage in the process, by showing how each step leads to the next, and by explaining how the process as a whole leads to its final result. Jeans's piece, for example, analyzes the process by which light-waves from the sun make their way through the earth's atmosphere and determine human perception of the color of the sky. Sven Birkerts, in "The Woman in the Garden," explains what we do when we read, and is concerned as well with the difficulties of presenting that process.

A method related to process analysis is *causal analysis*. As the term suggests, this type of analysis seeks to get at the causes of things, particularly ones that are sufficiently complex as to be open to various lines of explanation. Usually, then, a causal analysis involves a careful investigation that works backward from something difficult to account for—such as José's artistic proficiency or the corporate career problems of aspiring women—through an examination of various causes that might account for the situation. Sometimes, however, an analysis might work forward from a particular cause to the various effects it has produced; Carol Gilligan uses this method in "Interviewing Adolescent Girls" when she shows that the problems of adolescent girls are problems of connection, of "drowning" in "the sea of Western [largely male] culture." Because no two things can be identically accounted for, no set method exists for carrying out a causal analysis. Keep in mind, however, a few cautionary procedures. You should review other possible causes and other related circumstances before attempting to assert the priority of one cause or set of causes over another, and you should present enough evidence to demonstrate the reliability of your explanation. By doing so, you will be avoiding the temptation to oversimplify things.

As you can probably tell by now, almost any piece of writing that aims to make sense of something will invariably have to combine several methods of explanation. But this should come as no surprise if you stop to think about the way people usually explain even the simplest things in their day-to-day conversations with each other. Just ask someone, for example, to give you directions for getting from one place to another, and you will probably find that the person gives you both an overview of where the place is situated and a step-by-step set of movements to follow and places to look for, as well as brief descriptions of the most prominent guideposts along the way, and possibly even a review of the original directions, together with a brief remark or two about misleading spots to avoid. Whenever we ask for directions, after all, we want not only to get reliable information but also to get it in a form that cannot be misunderstood. So, whenever people give directions, they try not only to give them accurately but also to give them so clearly and fully from start to finish that they cannot be mistaken. By the same token, whenever people try to explain something in writing, they want to help readers get from one place to another in a particular subject matter. Thus, in the midst of giving a process analysis or causal analysis, a writer might feel compelled to illustrate this point, or define that term, or offer a telling analogy.

In the several pieces that make up this section, you will get to see how writers in different fields combine various methods of explaining things. And in the next section, you will see how explaining also contributes to arguing.

Arts and Humanities

URBAN LEGENDS: "THE BOYFRIEND'S DEATH"

Jan Harold Brunvand

Trained in the study of folklore, Jan Harold Brunvand has become a leading collector and interpreter of contemporary legends. These "urban legends" are stories told around campfires and in college dormitories, often as true experiences that happened to somebody other than the teller of the tale. Presently a professor at the University of Utah, Brunvand has been the editor of The Journal of American Folklore *and is the author of the standard introduction to the field,* The Study of American Folklore: An Introduction. *The following selection is taken from the first of his several collections of urban legends,* The Vanishing Hitchhiker: American Urban Legends and Their Meanings (1981). *Here he defines urban legends, gives one striking example, and offers some explanations about how and why such stories flourish even in the midst of a highly technologized society. The selection as reprinted is complete, except for the deletion of a few brief references to other discussions elsewhere in Brunvand's book.*

We are not aware of our own folklore any more than we are of the grammatical rules of our language. When we follow the ancient practice of informally transmitting "lore"—wisdom, knowledge, or accepted modes of behavior—by word of mouth and customary example from person to person, we do not concentrate on the form or content of our folklore; instead, we simply listen to information that others tell us and then pass it on—more or less accurately—to other listeners. In this stream of unselfconscious oral tradition the information that acquires a clear story line is called *narrative folklore,* and those stories alleged to be true are *legends.* This, in broad summary, is the typical process of legend formation and transmission as it has existed from time immemorial and continues to operate today. It works about the same way whether the legendary plot concerns a dragon in a cave or a mouse in a Coke bottle.

It might seem unlikely that legends—*urban* legends at that—would continue to be created in an age of widespread literacy, rapid mass communications, and restless travel. While our pioneer ancestors may have had to rely heavily on oral traditions to pass the news along about changing events and frontier dangers, surely we no longer need mere "folk" reports of what's happening, with all their tendencies to distort the facts. A moment's reflection, however, reminds us of the many weird, fascinating, but unverified rumors and tales that so frequently come to our ears—killers and madmen on the loose, shocking or funny personal experiences, unsafe manufactured products, and many other unexplained mysteries of daily life. Sometimes we encounter different oral versions of such stories, and on occasion we may read about similar events in newspapers or magazines; but seldom do we find, or even seek after, reliable documentation. The lack of verification in no way diminishes the appeal urban legends have for us. We enjoy them merely as stories, and we tend at least to half-believe them as possibly accurate reports. And the legends we tell, as with any folklore, reflect many of the hopes, fears, and anxieties of our time. In short, legends are definitely part of our modern folklore—legends which are as traditional, variable, and functional as those of the past.

Folklore study consists of collecting, classifying, and interpreting in their full cultural context the many products of everyday human interaction that have acquired a somewhat stable underlying form and that are passed traditionally from person to person, group to group, and generation to generation. Legend study is a most revealing area of such research because the stories that people believe to be true hold an important place in their worldview. "If it's true, it's important" is an axiom to be trusted, whether or not the lore really *is* true or not. Simply becoming aware of this modern folklore which we all possess to some degree is a revelation in itself, but going beyond this to compare the tales, isolate their consistent themes, and relate them to the rest of the culture can yield rich insights into the state of our current civilization. . . .

URBAN LEGENDS AS FOLKLORE

Folklore subsists on oral tradition, but not all oral communication is folklore. The vast amounts of human interchange, from casual daily conversations to formal discussions in business or industry, law, or teaching, rarely constitute straight oral folklore. However, all such "communicative events" (as scholars dub them) are punctuated routinely by various units of traditional material that are memorable, repeatable, and that fit recurring social situations well enough to serve in place of original remarks. "Tradition" is the key idea that links together such utterances as nicknames, proverbs, greeting and leave-taking formulas, wisecracks, anecdotes, and jokes as "folklore"; indeed, these are a few of the best known "conversational genres" of American folklore. Longer and more complex folk forms—fairy tales, epics, myths, legends, or ballads, for example—may thrive only in certain special situations of oral transmission. All true folklore ultimately depends upon continued oral dissemination, usually within fairly homogeneous "folk groups," and upon the retention through time of internal patterns and motifs that become traditional in the oral exchanges. The corollary of this rule of stability in oral tradition is that all items of folklore, while retaining a fixed central core, are constantly changing as they are transmitted, so as to create countless "variants" differing in length, detail, style, and performance technique. Folklore, in short, consists of oral tradition in variants.

Urban legends belong to the subclass of folk narratives, legends, that—unlike 5 fairy tales—are believed, or at least believable, and that—unlike myths—are set in the recent past and involve normal human beings rather than ancient gods or demigods. Legends are folk history, or rather quasi-history. As with any folk legends, urban legends gain credibility from specific details of time and place or from references to source authorities. For instance, a popular western pioneer legend often begins something like, "My great-grandmother had this strange experience when she was a young girl on a wagon train going through Wyoming when an Indian chief wanted to adopt her . . ." Even though hundreds of different great-grandmothers are supposed to have had the same doubtful experience (being desired by the chief because of her beautiful long blond hair), the fact seldom reaches legend-tellers; if it does, they assume that the family lore has indeed spread far and wide. This particular popular tradition, known as "Goldilocks on the Oregon Trail," interests folklorists because of the racist implications of a dark Indian savage coveting a fair young civilized woman— this legend is familiar in the *white* folklore only—and it is of little concern that the story seems to be entirely apocryphal.

In the world of modern urban legends there is usually no geographical or 6 generational gap between teller and event. The story is *true*; it really occurred, and recently, and always to someone else who is quite close to the narrator, or at least "a friend of a friend." Urban legends are told both in the course of casual conversations and in such special situations as campfires, slumber parties, and college dormitory bull sessions. The legends' physical settings are often close by, real, and sometimes even locally renowned for other such happenings. Though the characters in the stories are usually nameless, they are true-to-life examples of the kind of people the narrators and their audience know firsthand.

One of the great mysteries of folklore research is where oral traditions orig- 7 inate and who invents them. One might expect that at least in modern folklore we could come up with answers to such questions, but this is seldom, if ever, the case. . . .

THE PERFORMANCE OF LEGENDS

Whatever the origins of urban legends, their dissemination is no mystery.   8
The tales have traveled far and wide, and have been told and retold from person
to person in the same manner that myths, fairy tales, or ballads spread in earlier
cultures, with the important difference that today's legends are also disseminated
by the mass media. Groups of age-mates, especially adolescents, are one important American legend channel, but other paths of transmission are among
office workers and club members, as well as among religious, recreational, and
regional groups. Some individuals make a point of learning every recent rumor
or tale, and they can enliven any coffee break, party, or trip with the latest
supposed "news." The telling of one story inspires other people to share what
they have read or heard, and in a short time a lively exchange of details occurs
and perhaps new variants are created.

Tellers of these legends, of course, are seldom aware of their roles as "per-   9
formers of folklore." The conscious purpose of this kind of storytelling is to
convey a true event, and only incidentally to entertain an audience. Nevertheless, the speaker's demeanor is carefully orchestrated, and his or her delivery is
low-key and soft-sell. With subtle gestures, eye movements, and vocal inflections
the stories are made dramatic, pointed, and suspenseful. But, just as with jokes,
some can tell them and some can't. Passive tellers of urban legends may just
report them as odd rumors, but the more active legend tellers re-create them
as dramatic stories of suspense and, perhaps, humor.

"THE BOYFRIEND'S DEATH"

With all these points in mind folklore's subject-matter style, and oral per-   10
formance, consider this typical version of a well-known urban legend that
folklorists have named "The Boyfriend's Death," collected in 1964 (the earliest
documented instance of the story) by folklorist Daniel R. Barnes from an
eighteen-year-old freshman at the University of Kansas. The usual tellers of the
story are adolescents, and the normal setting for the narration is a college
dormitory room with fellow students sprawled on the furniture and floors.

> This happened just a few years ago out on the road that turns off
> highway 59 by the Holiday Inn. This couple were parked under a tree
> out on this road. Well, it got to be time for the girl to be back at the
> dorm, so she told her boyfriend that they should start back. But the car
> wouldn't start, so he told her to lock herself in the car and he would
> go down to the Holiday Inn and call for help. Well, he didn't come
> back and he didn't come back, and pretty soon she started hearing a
> scratching noise on the roof of the car. "Scratch, scratch . . . scratch,
> scratch." She got scareder and scareder, but he didn't come back.
> Finally, when it was almost daylight, some people came along and

stopped and helped her out of the car, and she looked up and there was her boyfriend hanging from the tree, and his feet were scraping against the roof of the car. This is why the road is called "Hangman's Road."

Here is a story that has traveled rapidly to reach nationwide oral circulation, in the process becoming structured in the typical manner of folk narratives. The traditional and fairly stable elements are the parked couple, the abandoned girl, the mysterious scratching (sometimes joined by a dripping sound and ghostly shadows on the windshield), the daybreak rescue, and the horrible climax. Variable traits are the precise location, the reason for her abandonment, the nature of the rescuers, murder details, and the concluding placename explanation. While "The Boyfriend's Death" seems to have captured teenagers' imaginations as a separate legend only since the early 1960s, it is clearly related to at least two older yarns, "The Hook" and "The Roommate's Death." All three legends have been widely collected by American folklorists, although only scattered examples have been published, mostly in professional journals. Examination of some of these variations helps to make clear the status of the story as folklore and its possible meanings.

At Indiana University, a leading American center of folklore research, folk-narrative specialist Linda Dégh and her students have gathered voluminous data on urban legends, especially those popular with adolescents. Dégh's preliminary published report on "The Boyfriend's Death" concerned nineteen texts collected from IU students from 1964 to 1968. Several storytellers had heard it in high school, often at parties; others had picked it up in college dormitories or elsewhere on campus. Several students expressed some belief in the legend, supposing either that it had happened in their own hometowns, or possibly in other states, once as far distant as "a remote part of Alabama." One informant reported that "she had been sworn to that the incident actually happened," but another, who had heard some variations of the tale, felt that "it seemed too horrible to be true." Some versions had incorporated motifs from other popular teenage horror legends or local ghost stories. . . .

One of the Indiana texts, told in the state of Washington, localizes the story there near Moses Lake, "in the country on a road that leads to a dead-end right under a big weeping willow tree . . . about four or five miles from town." As in most American versions of the story, these specific local touches make believable what is essentially a traveling legend. In a detail familiar from other variants of "The Boyfriend's Death," the body—now decapitated—is left hanging upside down from a branch of the willow tree with the fingernails scraping the top of the car. Another version studied by the Indiana researcher is somewhat aberrant, perhaps because the student was told the story by a friend's parents who claimed that "it happened a long time ago, probably thirty or forty years." Here a murderer is introduced, a "crazy old lady" on whose property the couple

11

12

13

331

has parked. The victim this time is skinned rather than decapitated, and his head scrapes the car as the corpse swings to and fro in the breezy night.

A developing motif in "The Boyfriend's Death" is the character and role of 14 the rescuers, who in the 1964 Kansas version are merely "some people." The standard identification later becomes "the police," authority figures whose presence lends further credence to the story. They are either called by the missing teenagers' parents, or simply appear on the scene in the morning to check the car. In a 1969 variant from Leonardtown, Maryland, the police give a warning, "Miss, please get out of the car and walk to the police car with us, but don't look back." . . . In a version from Texas collected in 1971, set "at this lake somewhere way out in nowhere," a policeman gets an even longer line: "Young lady, we want you to get out of the car and come with us. Whatever you do, don't turn, don't turn around, just keep walking, just keep going straight and don't look back at the car." The more detailed the police instructions are, the more plausible the tale seems to become. Of course the standard rule of folk-narrative plot development now applies: the taboo must be broken (or the "interdiction violated" as some scholars put it). The girl always *does* look back, like Orpheus in the underworld, and in a number of versions her hair turns white from the shock of what she sees, as in a dozen other American legends.

In a Canadian version of "The Boyfriend's Death," told by a fourteen-year- 15 old boy from Willowdale, Ontario, in 1973, the words of the policemen are merely summarized, but the opening scene of the legend is developed more fully, with several special details, including . . . a warning heard on the car radio. The girl's behavior when left behind is also described in more detail.

> A guy and his girlfriend are on the way to a party when their car starts to give them some trouble. At that same time they catch a news flash on the radio warning all people in the area that a lunatic killer has escaped from a local criminal asylum. The girl becomes very upset and at that point the car stalls completely on the highway. The boyfriend gets out and tinkers around with the engine but can't get the car to start again. He decides that he is going to have to walk on up the road to a gas station and get a tow truck but wants his girlfriend to stay behind in the car. She is frightened and pleads with him to take her, but he says that she'll be safe on the floor of the car covered with a blanket so that anyone passing will think it is an abandoned car and not bother her. Besides he can sprint along the road and get back more quickly than if she comes with him in her high-heeled shoes and evening dress. She finally agrees and he tells her not to come out unless she hears his signal of three knocks on the window. . . .

She does hear knocks on the car, but they continue eerily beyond three; the sound is later explained as the shoes of the boyfriend's corpse bumping the car as the body swings from a limb above the car.

332

The style in which oral narratives are told deserves attention, for the live 16
telling that is dramatic, fluid, and often quite gripping in actual folk performance
before a sympathetic audience may seem stiff, repetitious, and awkward on the
printed page. Lacking in all our examples of "The Boyfriend's Death" is the
essential ingredient of immediate context—the setting of the legend-telling, the
storyteller's vocal and facial expression and gestures, the audience's reaction,
and the texts of other similar tales narrated at the same session. Several of the
informants explained that the story was told to them in spooky situations, late
at night, near a cemetery, out camping, or even "while on a hayride or out
parked," occasionally near the site of the supposed murder. Some students refer
to such macabre legends, therefore, as "scary stories," "screamers," or "horrors."

A widely-distributed folk legend of this kind as it travels in oral tradition 17
acquires a good deal of its credibility and effect from the localized details inserted
by individual tellers. The highway and motel identification in the Kansas text
are good examples of this, and in a New Orleans version, "The Boyfriend's
Death" is absorbed into a local teenage tradition about "The Grunch"—a half-
sheep, half-human monster that haunts specific local sites. One teenager there
reported, "A man and lady went out by the lake and in the morning they found
'em hanging upside down on a tree and they said grunches did it." Finally,
rumors or news stories about missing persons or violent crimes (as mentioned
in the Canadian version) can merge with urban legends, helping to support
their air of truth, or giving them renewed circulation after a period of less
frequent occurrence.

Even the bare printed texts retain some earmarks of effective oral tradition. 18
Witness in the Kansas text the artful use of repetition (typical of folk narrative
style): "Well, he didn't come back and he didn't come back . . . but he didn't
come back." The repeated use of "well" and the building of lengthy sentences
with "and" are other hallmarks of oral style which give the narrator complete
control over his performance, tending to squeeze out interruptions or prevent
lapses in attention among the listeners. The scene that is set for the incident—
lonely road, night, a tree looming over the car, out of gas—and the sound
effects—scratches or bumps on the car—contribute to the style, as does the
dramatic part played by the policeman and the abrupt ending line: "She looked
back, and she saw . . . !" Since the typical narrators and auditors of "The
Boyfriend's Death" themselves like to "park" and may have been alarmed by
rumors, strange sights and noises, or automobile emergencies (all intensified in
their effects by the audience's knowing other parking legends), the abrupt,
unresolved ending leaves open the possibilities of what "really happened."

URBAN LEGENDS AS CULTURAL SYMBOLS

Legends can survive in our culture as living narrative folklore if they contain 19
three essential elements: a strong basic story-appeal, a foundation in actual

belief, and a meaningful message or "moral." That is, popular stories like "The Boyfriend's Death" are not only engrossing tales, but also "true," or at least so people think, and they teach valuable lessons. Jokes are a living part of oral tradition, despite being fictional and often silly, because of their humor, brevity, and snappy punch lines, but legends are by nature longer, slower, and more serious. Since more effort is needed to tell and appreciate a legend than a joke, it needs more than just verbal art to carry it along. Jokes have significant "messages" too, but these tend to be disguised or implied. People tell jokes primarily for amusement, and they seldom sense their underlying themes. In legends the primary messages are quite clear and straightforward; often they take the form of explicit warnings or good examples of "poetic justice." Secondary messages in urban legends tend to be suggested metaphorically or symbolically; these may provide deeper criticisms of human behavior or social condition.

People still tell legends, therefore, and other folk take time to listen to them, 20 not only because of their inherent plot interest but because they seem to convey true, worthwhile, and relevant information, albeit partly in a subconscious mode. In other words, such stories are "news" presented to us in an attractive way, with hints of larger meanings. Without this multiple appeal few legends would get a hearing in the modern world, so filled with other distractions. Legends survive by being as lively and "factual" as the television evening news, and, like the daily news broadcasts, they tend to concern deaths, injuries, kidnappings, tragedies, and scandals. Apparently the basic human need for meaningful personal contact cannot be entirely replaced by the mass media and popular culture. A portion of our interest in what is occurring in the world must be filled by some face-to-face reports from other human beings.

On a literal level a story like "The Boyfriend's Death" simply warns young 21 people to avoid situations in which they may be endangered, but at a more symbolic level the story reveals society's broader fears of people, especially women and the young, being alone and among strangers in the darkened world outside the security of their own home or car. Note that the young woman in the story (characterized by "her high-heeled shoes and evening dress") is shown as especially helpless and passive, cowering under the blanket in the car until she is rescued by men. Such themes recur in various forms in many other urban legends. . . .

In order to be retained in a culture, any form of folklore must fill some 22 genuine need, whether this be the need for an entertaining escape from reality, or a desire to validate by anecdotal examples some of the culture's ideals and institutions. For legends in general, a major function has always been the attempt to explain unusual and supernatural happenings in the natural world. To some degree this remains a purpose for urban legends, but their more common role nowadays seems to be to show that the prosaic contemporary scene is capable of producing shocking or amazing occurrences which may actually have happened to friends or to near-acquaintances but which are nevertheless explainable in some reasonably logical terms. On the one hand we want our factual lore to inspire awe, and at the same time we wish to have the most fantastic tales include at least the hint of a rational explanation and perhaps even a conclusion. Thus an escaped lunatic, a possibly *real* character, not a fantastic invader from outer space or Frankenstein's monster, is said to be responsible for the atrocities committed in the gruesome tales that teenagers tell. As sometimes happens in real life, the car radio gives warning, and the police get the situation back under control. (The policemen's role, in fact, becomes larger and more commanding as the story grows in oral tradition.) Only when the young lovers are still alone and scared are they vulnerable, but society's adults and guardians come to their rescue presently.

In common with brief unverified reports ("rumors"), to which they are often 23
closely related, urban legends gratify our desire to know about and to try to understand bizarre, frightening, and potentially dangerous or embarrassing events that *may* have happened. (In rumors and legends there is always some element of doubt concerning where and when these things *did* occur.) These floating stories appeal to our morbid curiosity and satisfy our sensation-seeking minds that demand gratification through frequent infusions of new information, "sanitized" somewhat by the positive messages. Informal rumors and stories fill in the gaps left by professional news reporting, and these marvelous, though generally false, "true" tales may be said to be carrying the folk-news—along with some editorial matter—from person to person even in today's technological world.

QUESTIONS

1. In your own words, define *urban legends*.
2. Have you ever heard the story of "The Boyfriend's Death" before? Did you believe it was true? Can you remember the circumstances in which you first heard this legend (or a similar one)? Describe your first encounter with this tale or a similar one. How does your experience compare with those described by Brunvand?
3. Below is a list of other tales collected by Brunvand. Do you know any stories that might correspond to these titles?

The Vanishing Hitchhiker
The Hook
The Baby-sitter and the Man Upstairs
The Pet (or Baby) in the Oven
The Spider in the Hairdo
Alligators in the Sewers
The Nude in the RV
The Economical Car

Compare the various versions produced by members of the class. What are the variables in the tale and what seem to be the common features?

4. Do you know a story that looks like an urban legend but really is true? Can you prove it?

5. What urban legend are you most aware of at the present time? Write down the best version of it that you can, then analyze what you have written as an urban legend. That is, explain what features mark it as an urban legend and discuss the elements in it that have made it interesting or appealing to you.

6. Can you remember someone who told you something as a "true" story that you now recognize as an urban legend? Write an essay in which you first describe that person and report on the legend he or she told you, and then go on to explain to that person that the story he or she told is not actually true but is an urban legend. If you think that your explanation would not convince the person in question, try to explain why this is so. Describe the resistance you might encounter and indicate how you might modify your explanation to make it more persuasive.

MAKING CONNECTIONS

1. Several of the pieces in "Reporting" deal with events that could provide the material for an urban legend. The AP report of the air crash, Richard Selzer's "The Discus Thrower," and Michael Brown's "Love Canal and the Poisoning of America" are examples. What elements of those stories would qualify them as urban legends? In what ways do they not qualify as such a legend?

2. Rewrite either the AP report of the air crash, "The Discus Thrower," or "Love Canal and the Poisoning of America" as an urban legend. Make any changes you find necessary to make it read like an urban legend. Then write a few paragraphs of explanation, discussing the changes you made and why you made them.

WHAT HIGH SCHOOL IS
Theodore R. Sizer

Born in New Haven, Connecticut, and educated at Yale and Harvard, Theodore R. Sizer has been headmaster at Phillips Academy, Andover, dean of the Graduate School of Education at Harvard University, and chairman of the Education Department at Brown University. Besides being the author of several books on American secondary schools, in recent years he has also worked on a study of American high schools sponsored by the National Association of Independent Schools. His book Horace's Compromise: The Dilemma of the American High School (1984) *reports the results of that study. The selection reprinted here is the first chapter of the second section of that book, "The Program."*

Mark, sixteen and a genial eleventh-grader, rides a bus to Franklin High   1
School, arriving at 7:45. It is an Assembly Day, so the schedule is adapted to allow for a meeting of the entire school. He hangs out with his friends, first outside school and then inside, by his locker. He carries a pile of textbooks and notebooks; in all, it weighs eight and a half pounds.

From 7:30 to 8:19, with nineteen other students, he is in Room 304 for   2
English class. The Shakespeare play being read this year by the eleventh grade is *Romeo and Juliet*. The teacher, Ms. Viola, has various students in turn take parts and read out loud. Periodically, she interrupts the (usually halting) recitations to ask whether the thread of the conversation in the play is clear. Mark is entertained by the stumbling readings of some of his classmates. He hopes he will not be asked to be Romeo, particularly if his current steady, Sally, is Juliet. There is a good deal of giggling in class, and much attention paid to who may be called on next. Ms. Viola reminds the class of a test on this part of the play to be given next week.

The bell rings at 8:19. Mark goes to the boys' room, where he sees a classmate   3
who he thinks is a wimp but who constantly tries to be a buddy. Mark avoids the leech by rushing off. On the way, he notices two boys engaged in some sort of transaction, probably over marijuana. He pays them no attention. 8:24. Typing class. The rows of desks that embrace big office machines are almost filled before the bell. Mark is uncomfortable here: typing class is girl country. The teacher constantly threatens what to Mark is a humiliatingly female future:

337

"Your employer won't like these erasures." The minutes during the period are spent copying a letter from a handbook onto business stationery. Mark struggles to keep from looking at his work; the teacher wants him to watch only the material from which he is copying. Mark is frustrated, uncomfortable, and scared that he will not complete his letter by the class's end, which would be embarrassing.

Nine tenths of the students present at school that day are assembled in the auditorium by the 9:18 bell. The dilatory tenth still stumble in, running down aisles. Annoyed class deans try to get the mob settled. The curtains part; the program is a concert by a student rock group. Their electronic gear flashes under the lights, and the five boys and one girl in the group work hard at being casual. Their movements on stage are studiously at three-quarter time, and they chat with one another as though the tumultuous screaming of their schoolmates were totally inaudible. The girl balances on a stool; the boys crank up the music. It is very soft rock, the sanitized lyrics surely cleared with the assistant principal. The girl sings, holding the mike close to her mouth, but can scarcely be heard. Her light voice is tentative, and the lyrics indecipherable. The guitars, amplified, are tuneful, however, and the drums are played with energy.

The students around Mark—all juniors, since they are seated by class—alternately slouch in their upholstered, hinged seats, talking to one another, or sit forward, leaning on the chair backs in front of them, watching the band. A boy near Mark shouts noisily at the microphone-fondling singer, "Bite it . . . ohhh," and the area around Mark explodes in vulgar male laughter, but quickly subsides. A teacher walks down the aisle. Songs continue, to great applause. Assembly is over at 9:46, two minutes early.

9:53 and biology class. Mark was at a different high school last year and did not take this course there as a tenth-grader. He is in it now, and all but one of his classmates are a year younger than he. He sits on the side, not taking part in the chatter that goes on after the bell. At 9:57, the public address system goes on, with the announcements of the day. After a few words from the principal ("Here's today's cheers and jeers . . ." with a cheer for the winning basketball team and a jeer for the spectators who made a ruckus at the gymnasium), the task is taken over by officers of ASB (Associated Student Bodies). There is an appeal for "bat bunnies." Carnations are for sale by the Girls' League. Miss Indian American is coming. Students are auctioning off their services (background catcalls are heard) to earn money for the prom. Nominees are needed for the ballot for school bachelor and school bachelorette. The announcements end with a "thought for the day. When you throw a little mud, you lose a little ground."

At 10:04 the biology class finally turns to science. The teacher, Mr. Robbins, has placed one of several labeled laboratory specimens—some are pinned in frames, others swim in formaldehyde—on each of the classroom's eight laboratory tables. The three or so students whose chairs circle each of these benches

338

are to study the specimen and make notes about it or drawings of it. After a few minutes each group of three will move to another table. The teacher points out that these specimens are of organisms already studied in previous classes. He says that the period-long test set for the following day will involve observing some of these specimens—then to be without labels—and writing an identifying paragraph on each. Mr. Robbins points out that some of the printed labels ascribe the specimens names different from those given in the textbook. He explains that biologists often give several names to the same organism.

The class now falls to peering, writing, and quiet talking. Mr. Robbins comes over to Mark, and in whispered words asks him to carry a requisition form for science department materials to the business office. Mark, because of his "older" status, is usually chosen by Robbins for this kind of errand. Robbins gives Mark the form and a green hall pass to show to any teacher who might challenge him, on his way to the office, for being out of a classroom. The errand takes Mark four minutes. Meanwhile Mark's group is hard at work but gets to only three of the specimens before the bell rings at 10:42. As the students surge out, Robbins shouts a reminder about a "double" laboratory period on Thursday. 8

Between classes one of the seniors asks Mark whether he plans to be a candidate for schoolwide office next year. Mark says no. He starts to explain. The 10:47 bell rings, meaning that he is late for French class. 9

There are fifteen students in Monsieur Bates's language class. He hands out tests taken the day before: "*C'est bien fait, Etienne . . . c'est mieux, Marie . . . Tch, tch, Robert . . .*" Mark notes his C+ and peeks at the A− in front of Susanna, next to him. The class has been assigned seats by M. Bates; Mark resents sitting next to prissy, brainy Susanna. Bates starts by asking a student to read a question and give the correct answer. "*James, question un.*" James haltingly reads the question and gives the answer that Bates, now speaking English, says is incomplete. In due course: "*Mark, question cinq.*" Mark does his bit, and the sequence goes on, the eight quiz questions and answers filling about twenty minutes of time. 10

"Turn to page forty-nine. *Maintenant, lisez après moi . . .*" and Bates reads a sentence and has the class echo it. Mark is embarrassed by this and mumbles with a barely audible sound. Others, like Susanna, keep the decibel count up, so Mark can hide. This I-say-you-repeat drill is interrupted once by the public address system, with an announcement about a meeting for the cheerleaders. Bates finishes the class, almost precisely at the bell, with a homework assignment. The students are to review these sentences for a brief quiz the following day. Mark takes note of the assignment, because he knows that tomorrow will be a day of busy-work in French class. Much though he dislikes oral drills, they are better than the workbook stuff that Bates hands out. Write, write, write, for Bates to throw away, Mark thinks. 11

11:36. Down to the cafeteria, talking noisily, hanging, munching. Getting to room 104 by 12:17: U.S. history. The teacher is sitting cross-legged on his 12 desk when Mark comes in, heatedly arguing with three students over the fracas that had followed the previous night's basketball game. The teacher, Mr. Suslovic, while agreeing that the spectators from their school certainly were provoked, argues that they should neither have been so obviously obscene in yelling at the opposing cheerleaders nor have allowed Coke cans to be rolled out on the floor. The three students keep saying that "it isn't fair." Apparently they and some others had been assigned "Saturday mornings" (detentions) by the principal for the ruckus.

At 12:34, the argument appears to subside. The uninvolved students, including Mark, are in their seats, chatting amiably. Mr. Suslovic climbs off his desk and starts talking: "We've almost finished this unit, chapters nine and ten . . ." The students stop chattering among themselves and turn toward Suslovic. Several slouch down in their chairs. Some open notebooks. Most have the five-pound textbook on their desks. 13

Suslovic lectures on the cattle drives, from north Texas to railroads west of St. Louis. He breaks up this narrative with questions ("Why were the railroad lines laid largely east to west?"), directed at nobody in particular and eventually answered by Suslovic himself. Some students take notes. Mark doesn't. A student walks in the open door, hands Mr. Suslovic a list, and starts whispering with him. Suslovic turns from the class and hears out this messenger. He then asks, "Does anyone know where Maggie Sharp is?" Someone answers, "Sick at home"; someone else says, "I thought I saw her at lunch." Genial consternation. Finally Suslovic tells the messenger, "Sorry, we can't help you," and returns to the class: "Now, where were we?" He goes on for some minutes. The bell rings. Suslovic forgets to give the homework assignment. 14

1:11 and Algebra II. There is a commotion in the hallway: someone's locker is rumored to have been opened by the assistant principal and a narcotics agent. In the five-minute passing time, Mark hears the story three times and three ways. A locker had been broken into by another student. It was Mr. Gregory and a narc. It was the cops, and they did it without Gregory's knowing. Mrs. Ames, the mathematics teacher, has not heard anything about it. Several of the nineteen students try to tell her and start arguing among themselves. "O.K., that's enough." She hands out the day's problem, one sheet to each student. Mark sees with dismay that it is a single, complicated "word" problem about some train that, while traveling at 84 mph, due west, passes a car that was going due east at 55 mph. Mark struggles: Is it $d = rt$ or $t = rd$? The class becomes quiet, writing, while Mrs. Ames writes some additional, short problems on the blackboard. "Time's up." A sigh; most students still writing. A muffled "Shit." Mrs. Ames frowns. "Come on, now." She collects papers, but it takes four minutes for her to corral them all. 15

"Copy down the problems from the board." A minute passes. "William, try number one." William suggests an approach. Mrs. Ames corrects and cajoles, and William finally gets it right. Mark watches two kids to his right passing 16 notes; he tries to read them, but the handwriting is illegible from his distance. He hopes he is not called on, and he isn't. Only three students are asked to puzzle out an answer. The bell rings at 2:00. Mrs. Ames shouts a homework assignment over the resulting hubbub.

Mark leaves his books in his locker. He remembers that he has homework,   17 but figures that he can do it during English class the next day. He knows that there will be an in-class presentation of one of the *Romeo and Juliet* scenes and that he will not be in it. The teacher will not notice his homework writing, or won't do anything about it if she does.

Mark passes various friends heading toward the gym, members of the bas-   18 ketball teams. Like most students, Mark isn't an active school athlete. However, he is associated with the yearbook staff. Although he is not taking "Yearbook" for credit as an English course, he is contributing photographs. Mark takes twenty minutes checking into the yearbook staff's headquarters (the classroom of its faculty adviser) and getting some assignments of pictures from his boss, the senior who is the photography editor. Mark knows that if he pleases his boss and the faculty adviser, he'll take that editor's post for the next year. He'll get English credit for his work then.

After gossiping a bit with the yearbook staff, Mark will leave school by 2:35   19 and go home. His grocery market bagger's job is from 4:45 to 8:00, the rush hour for the store. He'll have a snack at 4:30, and his mother will save him some supper to eat at 8:30. She will ask whether he has any homework, and he'll tell her no. Tomorrow, and virtually every other tomorrow, will be the same for Mark, save for the lack of the assembly: each period then will be five minutes longer.

Most Americans have an uncomplicated vision of what secondary education   20 should be. Their conception of high school is remarkably uniform across the country, a striking fact, given the size and diversity of the United States and the politically decentralized character of the schools. This uniformity is of several generations' standing. It has, however, two appearances, each quite different from the other, one of words and the other of practice, a world of political rhetoric and Mark's world.

A California high school's general goals, set out in 1979, could serve equally   21 well most of America's high schools, public and private. This school had as its ends:

- Fundamental scholastic achievement . . . to acquire knowledge and share in the traditionally academic fundamentals . . . to develop the ability to make decisions, to solve problems, to reason independently, and to accept responsibility for self-evaluation and continuing self-improvement.
- Career and economic competence . . .
- Citizenship and civil responsibility . . .

- Competence in human and social relations . . .
- Moral and ethical values . . .
- Self-realization and mental and physical health . . .
- Aesthetic awareness . . .
- Cultural diversity . . .[1]

In addition to its optimistic rhetoric, what distinguishes this list is its compre-hensiveness. The high school is to touch most aspects of an adolescent's exis-tence—mind, body, morals, values, career. No one of these areas is given especial prominence. School people arrogate to themselves an obligation to all.

An example of the wide acceptability of these goals is found in the courts. Forced to present a detailed definition of "thorough and efficient education," elementary as well as secondary, a West Virginia judge sampled the best of conventional wisdom and concluded that

> there are eight general elements of a thorough and efficient system of education: (a) Literacy, (b) The ability to add, subtract, multiply, and divide numbers, (c) Knowledge of government to the extent the child will be equipped as a citizen to make informed choices among persons and issues that affect his own governance, (d) Self-knowledge and knowl-edge of his or her total environment to allow the child to intelligently choose life work—to know his or her options, (e) Work-training and advanced academic training as the child may intelligently choose, (f) Recreational pursuits, (g) Interests in all creative arts such as music, theater, literature, and the visual arts, and (h) Social ethics, both be-havioral and abstract, to facilitate compatibility with others in this society.[2]

That these eight—now powerfully part of the debate over the purpose and practice of education in West Virginia—are reminiscent of the influential list, "The Seven Cardinal Principles of Secondary Education," promulgated in 1918 by the National Education Association, is no surprise.[3] The rhetoric of high

---

[1] Shasta High School, Redding, California. An eloquent and analogous statement, "The Essen-tials of Education," one stressing explicitly the "interdependence of skills and content" that is implicit in the Shasta High School statement, was issued in 1980 by a coalition of educational associations. Organizations for the Essentials of Education (Urbana, Illinois).

[2] Judge Arthur M. Recht, in his order resulting from *Pauley v. Kelly,* 1979, as reprinted in *Education Week,* May 26, 1982, p. 10. See also, in *Education Week,* January 16, 1983, pp. 21, 24, Jonathan P. Sher, "The Struggle to Fulfill a Judicial Mandate: How Not to 'Reconstruct' Education in W. Va."

[3] Bureau of Education, Department of the Interior, "Cardinal Principles of Secondary Education: A Report of the Commission on the Reorganization of Secondary Education, appointed by the National Education Association," *Bulletin,* no. 35 (Washington: U.S. Government Printing Office, 1918).

school purpose has been uniform and consistent for decades. Americans agree on the goals for their high schools.

That agreement is convenient, but it masks the fact that virtually all the words in these goal statements beg definition. Some schools have labored long to identify specific criteria beyond them; the result has been lists of daunting pseudospecificity and numbing earnestness. However, most leave the words undefined and let the momentum of traditional practice speak for itself. That is why analyzing how Mark spends his time is important: from watching him one uncovers the important purposes of education, the ones that shape practice. Mark's day is similar to that of other high school students across the country, as similar as the rhetoric of one goal statement to others'. Of course, there are variations, but the extent of consistency in the shape of school routine for a large and diverse adolescent population is extraordinary, indicating more graphically than any rhetoric the measure of agreement in America about what one does in high school, and, by implication, what it is for. 23

The basic organizing structures in schools are familiar. Above all, students are grouped by age (that is, freshman, sophomore, junior, senior), and all are expected to take precisely the same time—around 720 school days over four years, to be precise—to meet the requirements for a diploma. When one is out of his grade level, he can feel odd, as Mark did in his biology class. The goals are the same for all, and the means to achieve them are also similar. 24

Young males and females are treated remarkably alike; the schools' goals are the same for each gender. In execution, there are differences, as those pressing sex discrimination suits have made educators intensely aware. The students in metalworking classes are mostly male; those in home economics, mostly female. But it is revealing how much less sex discrimination there is in high schools than in other American institutions. For many young women, the most liberated hours of their week are in school. 25

School is to be like a job: you start in the morning and end in the afternoon, five days a week. You don't get much of a lunch hour, so you go home early, unless you are an athlete or are involved in some special school or extracurricular activity. School is conceived of as the children's workplace, and it takes young people off parents' hands and out of the labor market during prime-time work hours. Not surprisingly, many students see going to school as little more than a dogged necessity. They perceive the day-to-day routine, a Minnesota study reports, as one of "boredom and lethargy." One of the students summarizes: School is "boring, restless, tiresome, puts ya to sleep, tedious, monotonous, pain in the neck."[4] 26

The school schedule is a series of units of time: the clock is king. The base 27

---

[4]Diane Hedin, Paula Simon, and Michael Robin, *Minnesota Youth Poll: Youth's Views on School and School Discipline*, Minnesota Report 184 (1983), Agricultural Experiment Station, University of Minnesota, p. 13.

time block is about fifty minutes in length. Some schools, on what they call modular scheduling, split that fifty-minute block into two or even three pieces. Most schools have double periods for laboratory work, especially in the sciences, or four-hour units for the small numbers of students involved in intensive vocational or other work-study programs. The flow of all school activity arises from or is blocked by these time units. "How much time do I have with my kids" is the teacher's key question.

Because there are many claims for those fifty-minute blocks, there is little   28
time set aside for rest between them, usually no more than three to ten minutes, depending on how big the school is and, consequently, how far students and teachers have to walk from class to class. As a result, there is a frenetic quality to the school day, a sense of sustained restlessness. For the adolescents, there are frequent changes of room and fellow students, each change giving tempting opportunities for distraction, which are stoutly resisted by teachers. Some schools play soft music during these "passing times," to quiet the multitude, one principal told me.

Many teachers have a chance for a coffee break. Few students do. In some   29
city schools where security is a problem, students must be in class for seven consecutive periods, interrupted by a heavily monitored twenty-minute lunch period for small groups, starting as early as 10:30 A.M. and running to after 1:00 P.M. A high premium is placed on punctuality and on "being where you're supposed to be." Obviously, a low premium is placed on reflection and repose. The students rush from class to class to collect knowledge. Savoring it, it is implied, is not to be done much in school, nor is such meditation really much admired. The picture that these familiar patterns yield is that of an academic supermarket. The purpose of going to school is to pick things up, in an organized and predictable way, the faster the better.

What is supposed to be picked up is remarkably consistent among all sorts   30
of high schools. Most schools specifically mandate three out of every five courses a student selects. Nearly all of these mandates fall into five areas—English, social studies, mathematics, science, and physical education. On the average, English is required to be taken each year, social studies and physical education three out of the four high school years, and mathematics and science one or two years. Trends indicate that in the mid-eighties there is likely to be an increase in the time allocated to these last two subjects. Most students take classes in these four major academic areas beyond the minimum requirements, sometimes in such special areas as journalism and "yearbook," offshoots of English departments.[5]

Press most adults about what high school is for, and you hear these subjects   31
listed. *High school? That's where you learn English and math and that sort of*

---

[5] I am indebted to Harold F. Sizer and Lyde E. Sizer for a survey of the diploma requirements of fifty representative secondary schools, completed for A *Study of High Schools*.

thing. Ask students, and you get the same answer. High school is to "teach" these "subjects."

What is often absent is any definition of these subjects or any rationale for   32
them. They are just there, labels. Under those labels lie a multitude of things. A great deal of material is supposed to be "covered"; most of these courses are surveys, great sweeps of the stuff of their parent disciplines.

While there is often a sequence *within* subjects—algebra before trigonometry,   33
"first-year" French before "second-year" French—there is rarely a coherent relationship or sequence *across* subjects. Even the most logically related matters—reading ability as a precondition for the reading of history books, and certain mathematical concepts or skills before the study of some of physics— are only loosely coordinated, if at all. There is little demand for a synthesis of it all; English, mathematics, and the rest are discrete items, to be picked up individually. The incentive for picking them up is largely through tests and, with success at these, in credits earned.

Coverage within subjects is the key priority. If some imaginative teacher   34
makes a proposal to force the marriage of, say, mathematics and physics or to require some culminating challenges to students to use several objects in the solution of a complex problem, and if this proposal will take "time" away from other things, opposition is usually phrased in terms of what may be thus forgone. If we do that, we'll have to give up colonial history. We won't be able to get to programming. We'll not be able to read *Death of a Salesman.* There isn't time. The protesters usually win out.

The subjects come at a student like Mark in random order, a kaleidoscope   35
of worlds: algebraic formulae to poetry to French verbs to Ping-Pong to the War of the Spanish Succession, all before lunch. Pupils are to pick up these things. Tests measure whether the picking up has been successful.

The lack of connection between stated goals, such as those of the California   36
high school cited earlier, and the goals inherent in school practice is obvious and, curiously, tolerated. Most striking is the gap between statements about "self-realization and mental and physical growth" or "moral and ethical values"—common rhetoric in school documents—and practice. Most physical education programs have neither the time nor the focus really to ensure fitness. Mental health is rarely defined. Neither are ethical values, save at the negative extremes, such as opposition to assault or dishonesty. Nothing in the regimen of a day like Mark's signals direct or implicit teaching in this area. The "school boy code" (not ratting on a fellow student) protects the marijuana pusher, and a leechlike associate is shrugged off without concern. The issue of the locker search was pushed aside, as not appropriate for class time.

Most students, like Mark, go to class in groups of twenty to twenty-seven   37
students. The expected attendance in some schools, particularly those in low-income areas, is usually higher, often thirty-five students per class, but high absentee rates push the actual numbers down. About twenty-five per class is an

average figure for expected attendance, and the actual numbers are somewhat lower. There are remarkably few students who go to class in groups much larger or smaller than twenty-five.[6]

A student such as Mark sees five or six teachers per day; their differing styles 38 and expectations are part of his kaleidoscope. High school staffs are highly specialized: guidance counselors rarely teach mathematics, mathematics teachers rarely teach English, principals rarely do any classroom instruction. Mark, then, is known a little bit by a number of people, each of whom sees him in one specialized situation. No one may know him as a "whole person"—unless he becomes a special problem or has special needs.

Save in extracurricular or coaching situations, such as in athletics, drama, 39 or shop classes, there is little opportunity for sustained conversation between student and teacher. The mode is a one-sentence or two-sentence exchange: *Mark, when was Grover Cleveland president? Let's see, was 1890 . . . or something . . . wasn't he the one . . . he was elected twice, wasn't he . . . Yes . . . Gloria, can you get the dates right?* Dialogue is strikingly absent, and as a result the opportunity of teachers to challenge students' ideas in a systematic and logical way is limited. Given the rushed, full quality of the school day, it can seldom happen. One must infer that careful probing of students' thinking is not a high priority. How one gains (to quote the California school's statement of goals again) "the ability to make decisions, to solve problems, to reason independently, and to accept responsibility for self-evaluation and continuing self-improvement" without being challenged is difficult to imagine. One certainly doesn't learn these things merely from lectures and textbooks.

Most schools are nice places. Mark and his friends enjoy being in theirs. The 40 adults who work in schools generally like adolescents. The academic pressures are limited, and the accommodations to students are substantial. For example, if many members of an English class have jobs after school, the English teacher's expectations for them are adjusted, downward. In a word, school is sensitively accommodating, as long as students are punctual, where they are supposed to be, and minimally dutiful about picking things up from the clutch of courses in which they enroll.

This characterization is not pretty, but it is accurate, and it serves to describe 41 the vast majority of American secondary schools. "Taking subjects" in a systematized, conveyer-belt way is what one does in high school. That this process is, in substantial respects, not related to the rhetorical purposes of education is tolerated by most people, perhaps because they do not really either believe in those ill-defined goals or, in their heart of hearts, believe that schools can or should even try to achieve them. The students are happy taking subjects. The parents are happy, because that's what they did in high school. The rituals, the

---

[6]Education Research Service, Inc., *Class Size: A Summary of Research* (Arlington, Virginia, 1978); and *Class Size Research: A Critique of Recent Meta-Analyses* (Arlington, Virginia, 1980).

most important of which is graduation, remain intact. The adolescents are supervised safely and constructively most of the time, during the morning and afternoon hours, and they are off the labor market. That is what high school is all about.

QUESTIONS

1. The first half of this essay (the first nineteen paragraphs, to be exact) is a report. What do you think of this report? Given your own experience, how accurate is it? What attitude does the report convey, or is it objective?

2. Paragraph 19 is the conclusion of the report. It ends the story of Mark's day. Does it draw or imply any conclusions from the events reported?

3. How is the explanatory section of the essay (paragraphs 20 through 41) organized? If the first subtopic discussed is the goals of high school, what are the other subtopics?

4. What is the major conclusion of this explanation? To what extent do you agree with the last sentence of the essay and what it implies?

5. How does the report (paragraphs 1 through 19) function in the explanation that follows? What would be lost if the report were omitted? In considering how the two sections of the essay relate, note especially places where the explanation specifically refers to the report.

6. If you have a different view of high school, or went to a different kind of school, write an essay that is organized like Sizer's but that presents your own report and explanation of what school is.

7. Using the basic outline of Sizer's essay, write your own explanation of the workings of some institution: store, family, church or temple, club, team, or whatever else you know well. Think of your project in terms of Sizer's title: "What X Is."

MAKING CONNECTIONS

1. How do you suppose Sizer got this information about Mark and "what high school is"? Compare his approach to that of Farley Mowat, Jane van Lawick-Goodall, and Horace Miner. Which one comes closest, do you think, to Sizer's method for researching his essay? Explain the resemblances and differences.

2. Sizer presents a teenage male's high school day. Taking Carol Gilligan's "Interviewing Adolescent Girls" into account, write a shorter version of the high school day of a female teenager.

GEORGIA O'KEEFFE

Joan Didion

*Joan Didion was born in Sacramento, California, in 1934
and graduated with a B.A. in English from the University
of California at Berkeley in 1956. Until the publication of
her first novel,* Run River, *in 1963, she worked as an
associate feature editor for* Vogue *magazine. Since then she
has written three more novels,* Play It As It Lays *(1971),* A
Book of Common Prayer *(1977), and* Democracy *(1984),
as well as four books of essays,* Slouching Towards Bethle-
hem *(1969),* The White Album *(1982),* Salvador *(1983),
and* Miami *(1987). As an essayist, she has shown herself to
be a trenchant observer and interpreter of American society.
The following essay on Georgia O'Keeffe, a major American
painter, is taken from* The White Album.

"Where I was born and where and how I have lived is unimportant," Georgia   1
O'Keeffe told us in the book of paintings and words published in her ninetieth
year on earth. She seemed to be advising us to forget the beautiful face in the
Stieglitz photographs. She appeared to be dismissing the rather condescending
romance that had attached to her by then, the romance of extreme good looks
and advanced age and deliberate isolation. "It is what I have done with where
I have been that should be of interest." I recall an August afternoon in Chicago
in 1973 when I took my daughter, then seven, to see what Georgia O'Keeffe
had done with where she had been. One of the vast O'Keeffe "Sky Above
Clouds" canvases floated over the back stairs in the Chicago Art Institute that
day, dominating what seemed to be several stories of empty light, and my
daughter looked at it once, ran to the landing, and kept on looking. "Who drew
it," she whispered after a while. I told her. "I need to talk to her," she said
finally.

My daughter was making, that day in Chicago, an entirely unconscious but   2
quite basic assumption about people and the work they do. She was assuming
that the glory she saw in the work reflected a glory in its maker, that the painting
was the painter as the poem is the poet, that every choice one made alone—
every word chosen or rejected, every brush stroke laid or not laid down—
betrayed one's character. *Style is character.* It seemed to me that afternoon that
I had rarely seen so instinctive an application of this familiar principle, and I
recall being pleased not only that my daughter responded to style as character

but that it was Georgia O'Keeffe's particular style to which she responded: this was a hard woman who had imposed her 192 square feet of clouds on Chicago.

"Hardness" has not been in our century a quality much admired in women, ³ nor in the past twenty years has it even been in official favor for men. When hardness surfaces in the very old we tend to transform it into "crustiness" or eccentricity, some tonic pepperiness to be indulged at a distance. On the evidence of her work and what she has said about it, Georgia O'Keeffe is neither "crusty" nor eccentric. She is simply hard, a straight shooter, a woman clean of received wisdom and open to what she sees. This is a woman who could early on dismiss most of her contemporaries as "dreamy," and would later single out one she liked as "a very poor painter." (And then add, apparently by way of softening the judgment: "I guess he wasn't a painter at all. He had no courage and I believe that to create one's own world in any of the arts takes courage.") This is a woman who in 1939 could advise her admirers that they were missing her point, that their appreciation of her famous flowers was merely sentimental. "When I paint a red hill," she observed coolly in the catalogue for an exhibition that year, "you say it is too bad that I don't always paint flowers. A flower touches almost everyone's heart. A red hill doesn't touch everyone's heart." This is a woman who could describe the genesis of one of her most well-known paintings—the "Cow's Skull: Red, White and Blue" owned by the Metropolitan—as an act of quite deliberate and derisive orneriness. "I thought of the city men I had been seeing in the East," she wrote. "They talked so often of writing the Great American Novel—the Great American Play—the Great American Poetry. . . . So as I was painting my cow's head on blue I thought to myself, 'I'll make it an American painting. They will not think it great with the red stripes down the sides—Red, White and Blue—but they will notice it.'"

The city men. The men. They. The words crop up again and again as this ⁴ astonishingly aggressive woman tells us what was on her mind when she was making her astonishingly aggressive paintings. It was those city men who stood accused of sentimentalizing her flowers: "I made you take time to look at what I saw and when you took time to really notice my flower you hung all your associations with flowers on my flower and you write about my flower as if I think and see what you think and see—and I don't." *And I don't.* Imagine those words spoken, and the sound you hear is *don't tread on me.* "The men" believed it impossible to paint New York, so Georgia O'Keeffe painted New York. "The men" didn't think much of her bright color, so she made it brighter. The men yearned toward Europe so she went to Texas, and then New Mexico. The men talked about Cézanne, "long involved remarks about the 'plastic quality' of his form and color," and took one another's long involved remarks, in the view of his angelic rattlesnake in their midst, altogether too seriously. "I can paint one of those dismal-colored paintings like the men," the woman who regarded herself always as an outsider remembers thinking one day in 1922, and she did: a painting of a shed "all low-toned and dreary with the tree beside the door." She called this act of rancor "The Shanty" and hung it in her next show. "The men seemed to approve of it," she reported fifty-four years later, her contempt undimmed. "They seemed to think that maybe I was beginning to paint. That was my only low-toned dismal-colored painting."

Some women fight and others do not. Like so many successful guerrillas in the war between the sexes, Georgia O'Keeffe seems to have been equipped early with an immutable sense of who she was and a fairly clear understanding that she would be required to prove it. On the surface her upbringing was conventional. She was a child on the Wisconsin prairie who played with china dolls and painted watercolors with cloudy skies because sunlight was too hard to paint and with her brother and sisters, listened every night to her mother read stories of the Wild West, of Texas, of Kit Carson and Billy the Kid. She told adults that she wanted to be an artist and was embarrassed when they asked what kind of artist she wanted to be: she had no idea "what kind." She had no idea what artists did. She had never seen a picture that interested her, other than a pen-and-ink Maid of Athens in one of her mother's books, some Mother Goose illustrations printed on cloth, a tablet cover that showed a little girl with pink roses, and the painting of Arabs on horseback that hung in her grandmother's parlor. At thirteen, in a Dominican convent, she was mortified when the sister corrected her drawing. At Chatham Episcopal Institute in Virginia she painted lilacs and sneaked time alone to walk out to where she could see the line of the Blue Ridge Mountains on the horizon. At the Art Institute in Chicago she was shocked by the presence of live models and wanted to abandon anatomy lessons. At the Art Students League in New York one of her fellow students advised her that, since he would be a great painter and she would end up teaching painting in a girls' school, any work of hers was less important than modeling for him. Another painted over her work to show her how the Impressionists did trees. She had not before heard how the Impressionists did trees and she did not much care.

At twenty-four she left all those opinions behind and went for the first time to live in Texas, where there were no trees to paint and no one to tell her how not to paint them. In Texas there was only the horizon she craved. In Texas she had her sister Claudia with her for a while, and in the late afternoons they would walk away from town and toward the horizon and watch the evening star come out. "The evening star fascinated me," she wrote. "It was in some way very exciting to me. My sister had a gun, and as we walked she would throw bottles into the air and shoot as many as she could before they hit the ground. I had nothing but to walk into nowhere and the wide sunset space with the star. Ten watercolors were made from that star." In a way one's interest is compelled as much by the sister Claudia with the gun as by the painter Georgia with the star, but only the painter left us this shining record. Ten watercolors were made from that star.

QUESTIONS

1. Didion's first paragraph brings together two kinds of material, research and personal experience. In doing this, Didion quotes from two sources, a ninety-year-old woman and a seven-year-old child. The result is that we encounter three "I"s in the first paragraph—all female—and we also encounter a mixture of the personal and the impersonal. What is the effect of all this? How did you personally react to this mixture of research and personal experience? What connections can you make among the three "I"s?

2. Paragraph 3 opens with "Hardness." Comment on the importance of this word to Didion's essay. What does this concept add to her mixture of research and personal experience? What would the essay be like without this concept?

3. Extend your study of O'Keeffe by locating a book in the library that reproduces more of her paintings. What qualities do you find in her work? Write an essay of your own in which you describe her essential style, as you see it.

4. Select a visual artist (or an artist in any other medium) whose work interests you. Find out about this person's life and career. Then, write an essay in which you explain what you like in this artist's work and why you like it, connecting the life and work through some metaphor or concept that organizes your feelings and your essay the way that "hardness" organizes Didion's.

MAKING CONNECTIONS

1. Compare Didion's account of Georgia O'Keeffe to the several other representations of women artists collected in this anthology, such as Maya Angelou's "Graduation," Alice Walker's "Beauty: When the Other Dancer Is the Self," Isak Dinesen's "The Iguana," and Virginia Woolf's "The Death of the Moth." What themes and concerns seem common to these women?

2. Compare Didion's account of Georgia O'Keeffe to Virginia Woolf's essay, "The Death of the Moth." Does O'Keeffe, as Didion represents her, bear any relation to Woolf, as she represents herself in her essay? What, if anything, seems similar in the stances of these two artists? What seems most different? Although O'Keeffe (1887–1986) lived much longer, she and Woolf (1882–1941) were of the same generation. Would you expect them to have been compatible?

EINSTEIN'S BRAIN
Roland Barthes

*Roland Barthes (1915–1980) was a major force in the in-
tellectual life of France until his death in 1980. His reputation as a writer continues to grow as his works are
translated into more and more languages. He wrote frequently on literary subjects and popular culture from the
perspective known as semiotics: the study of signs and symbols. In his writing, Barthes favored short and personal forms
such as the essay and the fragment; he wrote for newspapers
and magazines in addition to producing the more formal
articles expected of a French professor. Among his most
accessible pieces are the brief discussions he called* Mythologies: *studies in the various ways that myths are created in
the modern world. In his view the popular media, while
seeming to report facts about the contemporary world, actually make myths that people find comforting. He believed,
and demonstrated many times over, that myths could be
made from almost anything—wrestling, striptease, tourism,
advertising—even the brain of Albert Einstein. Like most
of the other pieces collected in* Mythologies, *the following
essay was written in the mid-1950s for the French magazine,*
Les Lettres Nouvelles.

Einstein's brain is a mythical object: paradoxically, the greatest intelligence   1
of all provides an image of the most up-to-date machine, the man who is too
powerful is removed from psychology, and introduced into a world of robots; as
is well known, the supermen of science-fiction always have something reified
about them. So has Einstein: he is commonly signified by his brain, which is
like an object for anthologies, a true museum exhibit. Perhaps because of his
mathematical specialization, superman is here divested of every magical character; no diffuse power in him, no mystery other than mechanical: he is a
superior, a prodigious organ, but a real, even a physiological one. Mythologi-
cally, Einstein is matter, his power does not spontaneously draw one towards
the spiritual, it needs the help of an independent morality, a reminder about
the scientist's "conscience" (*Science without conscience,*[1] they said . . .).

---

[1] "Science without conscience is but the ruin of the Soul" (Rabelais, *Pantagruel* II, ch. 8).

Einstein himself has to some extent been a party to the legend by bequeathing 2 his brain, for the possession of which two hospitals are still fighting as if it were an unusual piece of machinery which it will at last be possible to dismantle. A photograph shows him lying down, his head bristling with electric wires: the waves of his brain are being recorded, while he is requested to "think of relativity." (But for that matter, what does "to think of" mean, exactly?) What this is meant to convey is probably that the seismograms will be all the more violent since "relativity" is an arduous subject. Thought itself is thus represented as an energetic material, the measurable product of a complex (quasi-electrical) apparatus which transforms cerebral substance into power. The mythology of Einstein shows him as a genius so lacking in magic that one speaks about his thoughts as of a functional labour analogous to the mechanical making of sausages, the grinding of corn or the crushing of ore: he used to produce thought, continuously, as a mill makes flour, and death was above all, for him, the cessation of a localized function: *"the most powerful brain of all has stopped thinking."*

What this machine of genius was supposed to produce was equations. 3 Through the mythology of Einstein, the world blissfully regained the image of knowledge reduced to a formula. Paradoxically, the more the genius of the man was materialized under the guise of his brain, the more the product of his inventiveness came to acquire a magical dimension, and gave a new incarnation to the old esoteric image of a science entirely contained in a few letters. There is a single secret to the world, and this secret is held in one word; the universe is a safe of which humanity seeks the combination: Einstein almost found it, this is the myth of Einstein. In it, we find all the Gnostic themes: the unity of nature, the ideal possibility of a fundamental reduction of the world, the unfastening power of the word, the age-old struggle between a secret and an utterance, the idea that total knowledge can only be discovered all at once, like a lock which suddenly opens after a thousand unsuccessful attempts. The historic equation $E = mc^2$, by its unexpected simplicity, almost embodies the pure idea of the key, bare, linear, made of one metal, opening with a wholly magical ease a door which had resisted the desperate efforts of centuries. Popular imagery faithfully expresses this: *photographs* of Einstein show him standing next to a blackboard covered with mathematical signs of obvious complexity; but *cartoons* of Einstein (the sign that he has become a legend) show him chalk still in hand, and having just written on an empty blackboard, as if without preparation, the magic formula of the world. In this way mythology shows an awareness of the nature of the various tasks: research proper brings into play clockwork-like mechanisms and has its seat in a wholly material organ which is monstrous only by its cybernetic complication; discovery, on the contrary, has a magical essence, it is simple like a basic element, a principal substance, like the philosophers' stone of hermetists, tar-water for Berkeley, or oxygen for Schelling.[2]

But since the world is still going on, since research is proliferating, and on the other hand since God's share must be preserved, some failure on the part of Einstein is necessary: Einstein died, it is said, without having been able to verify *"the equation in which the secret of the world was enclosed."* So in the end the word resisted; hardly opened, the secret closed again, the code was incomplete. In this way Einstein fulfills all the conditions of myth, which could not care less about contradictions so long as it establishes a euphoric security: at once magician and machine, eternal researcher and unfulfilled discoverer, unleashing the best and the worst, brain and conscience, Einstein embodies the most contradictory dreams, and mythically reconciles the infinite power of man over nature with the "fatality" of the sacrosanct, which man cannot yet do without.

4

QUESTIONS

1. By a common figure of speech (synecdoche), one part of Einstein—his brain—has come to stand for the whole person. Can you think of other public figures who are normally perceived in terms of some part of their anatomy or by something regularly associated with them (metonymy)? Why do you suppose this practice is so common in our media?

2. Examine how Barthes reports on the way Einstein has been represented visually through photographs and cartoons. How does Barthes move from description of the image to interpretation? That is, how does he move from a picture or image to its meaning?

3. In paragraph 4, Barthes says that myths establish for us a "euphoric security." Talk this phrase over with your classmates. What does *euphoric* mean? What does the phrase mean as a whole way of thinking about myth? If Barthes is right about the function of myth, then we can see the media not so much as distorting the truth, but rather as simply giving us what we want, which is not truth but comfort. Is he right?

4. What relationship between science and magic does Barthes present in this essay? Consider especially paragraphs 2 and 3 in answering this question.

5. Barthes says that the "supermen" of science fiction always have something "reified" about them. (*Reified* comes from the Latin word for "thing," *res*; to be reified is to be turned into a thing.) What Barthes means is that the supermen—and superwomen—of science fiction always have something thinglike or machinelike about them. Einstein, Barthes suggests, is understood by our connecting him to the superfigures of science fiction. Such understanding is part of the mythologizing process. Do you agree with Barthes about this?

6. Using Barthes's essay as a model, consider the way we have mythologized some

---

[2] hermetists: alchemists, prescientific dabblers in chemical matters; George Berkeley (1685–1753) and Friedrich Willem Joseph von Schelling (1775–1854): early philosophers of science. [Eds.]

other public figure. That is, discuss the way that our images of this person simplify and reduce him or her to the proportions of a comforting myth. Make your essay about the same length as Barthes's and try, like him, to consider typical representations of this person (in newsphotos, cartoons, etc.), moving from these images to the way we understand them and the reasons behind our understanding.

MAKING CONNECTIONS

1. Compare the mythification of Einstein's brain with the mythification in America of Columbus as discoverer, as described in John Noble Wilford's "Discovering Columbus."

2. Draw a cartoon to illustrate "The Boyfriend's Death" as related in Jan Harold Brunvand's essay on urban legends. Try to make your cartoon parallel to the one described in paragraph 3 in this essay, of Einstein at the blackboard. Then write an explanation of your cartoon, drawing out and interpreting the representation of "The Boyfriend's Death" that your cartoon offers.

DISCOVERING COLUMBUS
John Noble Wilford

John Noble Wilford (b. 1933) is a widely honored journalist who began his career at the Wall Street Journal, *moved on to* Time *magazine, and since 1965 has written for the* New York Times. *Best known for his extensive coverage of the United States space program from its beginning to the most recent space shuttle flights, he has written two award-winning books about American space projects,* We Reach the Moon (1969) *and* Mars Beckons (1990). *His coverage of various space topics, such as "Star Wars," won him a Pulitzer Prize for national reporting in 1984. He has also written an award-winning book about the history of map-making,* The Mapmakers (1981), *and most recently* The Mysterious History of Columbus (1991), *from which the following piece is adapted.*

Few stories in history are more familiar than the one of Christopher Colum- 1
bus sailing west for the Indies and finding instead the New World. Indelibly imprinted in our memory is the verse from childhood: "In fourteen hundred and ninety-two/Columbus sailed the ocean blue." The names of his ships, the Niña, the Pinta and the Santa María, roll fluently from our lips. We know how Columbus, a seaman of humble and obscure origins, pursued a dream that became his obsession. How he found not the riches of Cathay but a sprinkling of small islands inhabited by gentle people. How he called these people Indians, thinking that surely the mainland of Asia lay just over the horizon.

Yet the history of Columbus is frustratingly incomplete. When and how in 2
the mists of his rootless life did he conceive of his audacious plan? He supposedly wanted to sail west across the Ocean Sea to reach Cipangu, the name then for Japan, and the region known generally as the Indies. But was he really seeking the Indies? How are we to navigate the poorly charted waters of ambiguous and conflicting documentation everywhere Columbus went and in everything he did? We are not certain how he was finally able to win royal backing for the enterprise. We know little about his ships and the men who sailed them. We don't know exactly where he made his first landfall. We don't know for sure what he looked like or where he lies buried. We do know he was an inept governor of the Spanish settlements in the Caribbean and had a bloodied hand in the brutalization of the native people and in the start of a slave trade. But we are left wondering if he is to be admired and praised, condemned—or perhaps pitied as a tragic figure.

Walt Whitman imagined Columbus on his deathbed, in the throes of self- 3
doubt, seeming to anticipate the vicissitudes that lay ahead in his passage
through history:

> What do I know of life? what of myself?
> I know not even my own work past or present;
> Dim ever-shifting guesses of it spread before me,
> Of newer better worlds, their mighty parturition,
> Mocking, perplexing me.

The man who wrote to his patron, Luis de Santángel, on the voyage back 4
to Europe in 1493, proclaiming discovery and assuring that he would not be
forgotten, probably had no such thoughts. He could not foresee posterity's "ever-
shifting guesses" concerning his deeds and himself any more than he could
assimilate in his inflexible mind what he had done and seen. But it was his fate
to be the accidental agent of a transcendental discovery and, as a result, to be
tossed into the tempestuous sea of history, drifting half-forgotten at first, then
swept by swift currents to a towering crest of honor and legend, only to be
caught in recent years in a riptide of conflicting views of his life and of his
responsibility for almost everything that has happened since.

Columbus's reputation in history has followed a curious course. His obses- 5
sion, obstinacy and navigational skill carried Europe across the ocean. "The
Admiral was the first to open the gates of that ocean which had been closed for
so many thousands of years before," wrote Bartolomé de las Casas a half century
later in a comprehensive account of the voyages, which remains to this day a
major source of knowledge about Columbus. "He it was who gave the light by
which all others might see how to discover." But he was then anything but the
stellar figure in history he was to become. His immediate reputation was
diminished by his failures as a colonial administrator and by a protracted lawsuit
between the crown and the heirs of Columbus, casting doubt on the singularity
of his plan for sailing west to the Indies. (Testimony by some seamen who had
sailed with Columbus suggested that one of his captains was actually responsible
for much of the idea.) In time, Las Casas forced his contemporaries to question
the morality of the brutal treatment of Indians at the hands of Columbus and
his successors.

By the early years of the 16th century, Amerigo Vespucci, a more perceptive 6
interpreter of the New World and a more engaging writer, had already robbed
Columbus of prominence on the map. His star was also eclipsed by explorers
like Cortés and Pizarro, who obtained gold and glory for Spain and had the
good fortune to conquer not an assortment of islands but splendid empires like
those of the Aztecs of Mexico and Incas of Peru, and by mariners like Vasco
da Gama, who actually reached the Indies, and Magellan, whose expedition of
circumnavigation was the first to confirm by experience the world's sphericity—

and also left no doubt about the magnitude of Columbus's error in thinking he had reached Asia.

Many books of general history in the first decades of the 16th century either scarcely mentioned Columbus or ignored him altogether. Writers of the time "showed little interest in his personality and career, and some of them could not even get his Christian name right," according to J. H. Elliott, a British historian. Responsibility for the neglect has been attributed in part to Peter Martyr, an Italian cleric in the court at Barcelona, whose correspondence, beginning in the months after Columbus's return, was widely read. It made much of the years of discovery but gave only passing notice to Columbus himself, though acknowledging his fortitude and courage.

7

With the poverty of available documentation about the man, there were few alternative sources of information. Yet to come were the works of the contemporary observers Gonzalo Fernández de Oviedo (who would write an encyclopedic history of the early discoveries), Bartolomé de las Casas and Columbus's son Ferdinand, who would write the first definitive biography of Columbus. Nearly all of Columbus's own letters and journals had long since disappeared.

8

By the middle of the 16th century, Columbus began to emerge from the shadows, reincarnated not so much as a man and historical figure but as a myth and symbol. In 1552, in a ringing assessment that would be repeated time and again, the historian Francisco Lopez de Gómara wrote, "The greatest event since the creation of the world (excluding the incarnation and death of Him who created it) is the discovery of the Indies." Columbus came to epitomize the explorer and discoverer, the man of vision and audacity, the hero who overcame opposition and adversity to change history.

9

By the end of the 16th century, English explorers and writers acknowledged his primacy and inspiration. "Had they not Columbus to stirre them up," Richard Hakluyt, the historian of exploration, wrote in 1598. He was celebrated in poetry and plays, especially by the Italians. Even Spain was coming around. In 1614, a popular play, "El Nuevo Mundo descubierto por Cristóbal Colón," portrayed Columbus as a dreamer up against the stolid forces of entrenched tradition, a man of singular purpose who triumphed, the embodiment of that spirit driving humans to explore and discover.

10

The association between Columbus and America prospered in the 18th century, as the population became increasingly American-born, with less reason to identify with the "mother country." No one in Boston or New York is recorded to have celebrated Columbus on the bicentennial, in 1692. But within a very short time, the colonists began thinking of themselves as a people distinct from the English. By virtue of their isolation and common experience in a new land, they were becoming Americans, and they looked to define themselves on their own terms and through their own symbols. Samuel Sewall of Boston was one of the first to suggest their land should rightfully be named for Columbus, "the magnanimous heroe . . . who was manifestly appointed of God to be the Finder

11

out of these lands." The Columbus who thought of himself as God's messenger—"As the Lord told of it through the mouth of Isaiah, He made me the messenger, and he showed me the way," Columbus wrote on his third voyage—would have been pleased at this turn in his posthumous reputation. But Sewall was also indulging in a practice that would become rampant: enlisting the symbolic Columbus for his own purposes—in spirited defense of the colonies, which were being described by theologians at Oxford and Cambridge as the Biblical "infernal region," or in plain English, "hell."

By the time of the Revolution, Columbus had been transmuted into a national icon, a hero second only to Washington. The new Republic's celebration of Columbus reached a climax in October 1792, the 300th anniversary of the landfall. By then, King's College in New York had been renamed Columbia and the national capital being planned was given the name the District of Columbia, perhaps to appease those who demanded that the entire country be designated Columbia.   12

It is not hard to understand the appeal of Columbus as a totem for the former subjects of George III. Columbus had found the way of escape from Old World tyranny. He was the solitary individual who challenged the unknown sea, as triumphant Americans contemplated the dangers and promise of their own wilderness frontier. He had been opposed by kings and (in his mind) betrayed by royal perfidy. But as a consequence of his vision and audacity, there was now a land free from kings, a vast continent for new beginnings.   13

In Columbus, the new nation found a hero seemingly free of any taint from association with the European colonial powers. The Columbus symbolism gave Americans an instant mythology and a unique place in history, and their adoption of Columbus magnified his own place.   14

In "The Whig Interpretation of History," Herbert Butterfield, a British historian of this century, properly deplored "the tendency of many historians . . . to produce a story which is the ratification if not the glorification of the present." But historians cannot control the popularizers, the myth makers and propagandists, and in post-Revolutionary America the few who studied Columbus were probably not disposed to try. Even if they had been, there was little information available on which to assess the real Columbus and distinguish the man from the myth.   15

By the 19th century new materials had emerged—some of Columbus's own writings and a lengthy abridgment of his lost journal of the first voyage—that might have been used to assess the real man. Instead, these manuscripts provided more ammunition for those who would embellish the symbolic Columbus. Washington Irving mined the new documents to create a hero in the romantic mold favored in the century's literature. His Columbus was "a man of great and inventive genius" and his "ambition was lofty and noble, inspiring him with high thoughts, and an anxiety to distinguish himself by great achievements."   16

Perhaps. But an effusive Irving got carried away. Columbus's "conduct was   17
characterized by the grandeur of his views and the magnanimity of his spirit,"
he wrote. "Instead of ravaging the newly found countries . . . he sought to
colonize and cultivate them, to civilize the natives." Columbus may have had
some faults, Irving acknowledged, such as his part in enslaving and killing
people, but these were "errors of the times."

The historian Daniel J. Boorstin observes that people "once felt themselves   18
made by their heroes" and cites James Russell Lowell: "The idol is the measure
of the worshiper." Accordingly, writers and orators of the 19th century ascribed
to Columbus all the human virtues that were most prized in that time of
geographic and industrial expansion, heady optimism and an unquestioning
belief in progress as the dynamic of history.

This image of Columbus accorded with the popular rags-to-riches, log-cabin-   19
to-the-White-House scenario of human advancement. This was the ideal Columbus that schoolchildren learned about in their McGuffey readers. The orator
Edward Everett reminded his audience in 1853 that Columbus had once been
forced to beg for bread at the convent doors of Spain. "We find encouragement
in every page of our country's history," Everett declared. "Nowhere do we meet
with examples more numerous and more brilliant of men who have risen above
poverty and obscurity. . . . One whole vast continent was added to the geography
of the world by the persevering efforts of a humble Genoese mariner, the great
Columbus; who, by the steady pursuit of the enlightened conception he had
formed of the figure of the earth, before any navigator had acted upon the belief
that it was round, discovered the American continent."

With the influx of millions of immigrants after the American Civil War,   20
Columbus assumed a new role, that of ethnic hero. Irish Catholic immigrants
organized the Knights of Columbus in New Haven in 1882. The fraternity's
literature described Columbus as "a prophet and a seer, an instrument of Divine
Providence" and an inspiration to each knight to become "a better Catholic and
a better citizen." The knights grew in number and influence, promoting academic studies in American history, lobbying for the Columbus memorial erected
in front of Union Station in Washington and seeking the canonization of their
hero.

At the same time, French Catholics were mounting a campaign to elevate   21
Columbus to sainthood, on the grounds that he had "brought the Christian
faith to half the world." But, despite encouragement from Pope Pius IX, the
proponents got nowhere with the Vatican. Columbus's rejection was based
largely on his relationship with Beatriz Enríquez de Arana, his mistress and the
mother of his son Ferdinand, and the lack of proof that he had performed a
miracle, as defined by the church.

The 400th anniversary of Columbus's voyage was marked by a yearlong   22
commemoration throughout the United States. To the beat of brass bands and
a chorus of self-congratulation, Americans hailed the man who had crossed

uncharted seas as they had now leaped a wide and wild continent. As part of the celebration, Antonín Dvorak composed "From the New World," a symphony evoking the sweep and promise of the beckoning American landscape. President Benjamin Harrison proclaimed, "Columbus stood in his age as the pioneer of progress and enlightenment." In New York, Italian immigrants, who had joined the Irish in search of an identity with the larger American community, raised money for a statue atop a column of Italian marble, placed at the southwest corner of Central Park, which was renamed Columbus Circle.

The grandest of all the celebrations, the World's Columbian Exposition, in 23 Chicago, was billed as "the jubilee of mankind." President Grover Cleveland threw the switch on that new invention, electricity, to set in motion the many machines and architectural marvels by which the United States advertised itself as an emerging giant among the nations. Columbus was now the symbol of American success. The invocation was a prayer of thanksgiving for "that most momentous of all voyages by which Columbus lifted the veil that hid the New World from the Old and opened the gateway of the future of mankind." Clearly, the exposition was more than a commemoration of the past; it was also the exclamation of a future that self-confident Americans were eager to shape and enjoy.

A few historians, seeking the man behind the myth, struck chords of a 24 refreshing counterpoint to the adulatory hymns. Henry Harrisse's diligent examination of all known Columbus materials left scholars no excuse for continuing to treat the man as a demigod, though he, too, rendered a largely favorable judgment. "Columbus removed out of the range of mere speculation the idea that beyond the Atlantic Ocean lands existed and could be reached by sea," he wrote in "Christopher Columbus and the Bank of Saint George." He "made of the notion a fixed fact, and linked forever the two worlds. That event, which is unquestionably the greatest of modern time, secures to Columbus a place in the pantheon dedicated to the worthies whose courageous deeds mankind will always admire."

It was the biographer Justin Winsor, more than any other respected historian 25 of the day, who cast a cold light on the dark side of Columbus's character. He had objected strongly to Columbus's proposed canonization. ("He had nothing of the generous and noble spirit of a conjoint lover of man and of God," he wrote at the time.) In his view, Columbus forfeited any claim to sympathy when he robbed of proper credit the lookout who had cried *"Tierra!"* and thus took for himself the lifetime pension promised to the first person to see land.

"No child of any age ever did less to improve his contemporaries, and few 26 ever did more to prepare the way for such improvements," Winsor wrote in his 1891 biography. "The age created him and the age left him. There is no more conspicuous example in history of a man showing the path and losing it. . . ." Columbus left his new world "a legacy of devastation and crime. He might have been an unselfish promoter of geographical science; he proved a rabid seeker for gold and a viceroyalty. He might have won converts to the fold of Christ by the kindness of his spirit; he gained the execrations of the good angels. He might, like Las Casas, have rebuked the fiendishness of his contemporaries; he set them an example of perverted belief."

Winsor's withering assault on the Columbus of legend was the exception in the late 19th century, and not taken kindly by those who held to the prevailing image. They had created the Columbus they wanted to believe in, and were quite satisfied with their creation.　　27

But by the early 20th century, historians were beginning to expose contra- dictions, lacunas and suspected fictions in the familiar story. No one could be sure when and how Columbus arrived at his idea, what his real objective was or what manner of man he was—an inspired but rational genius, a lucky adventurer clouded by mysticism, a man of the Renaissance or of the Middle Ages. It wasn't until 1942 that Columbus was rescued from mythology and portrayed as what he had been first and foremost: an inspired mariner.　　28

In his biography, "Admiral of the Ocean Sea," Samuel Eliot Morison, drawing on the accumulating documents and his own seafaring expertise, chose to stress the one aspect of Columbus that has been beyond serious dispute. Morison's Columbus was no saint, but he could sail a ship and possessed the will and courage to go where no one had presumably gone before.　　29

The world and America are changing, of course, and Columbus's reputation is changing, too. Modern life has made disbelievers of many who once wor- shiped at the altar of progress. In the years after World War II, nearly all the colonies of the major empires won their independence and, like the United States in its early days, began to view world history from their own anticolonial perspective. The idol had been the measure of the worshipers, but now there were atheists all around. To them, the Age of Discovery was not the bright dawning of a glorious epoch, but an invasion. Columbus became the avatar of oppression. Another Columbus for another age.　　30

"A funny thing happened on the way to the quincentennial observation of America's 'discovery,'" Garry Wills wrote in The New York Review of Books in 1990. "Columbus got mugged. This time the Indians were waiting for him. He comes now with an apologetic air—but not, for some, sufficiently apologetic. . . . He comes to be dishonored."　　31

Today, historians are addressing consequences as well as actions—increas- ingly approaching the European incursion in America from the standpoint of the native Americans. They speak not of the "discovery" but of the "encounter" or the "contact." Alfred W. Crosby, at the University of Texas at Austin, has examined the biological consequences of Columbus's arrival. While some— the exchange of plants and animals between continents, the eventual global- ization of biology—were generally beneficial, he found others, like the spread of devastating disease, to be catastrophic.　　32

In public forums, Columbus is tarred as the precursor of exploitation and 33
conquest. Kirkpatrick Sale, in "The Conquest of Paradise," argues that Columbus was a grasping fortune hunter whose legacy was the destruction of the native
population and rape of the land that continues to this day.

Descendants of American Indians and the African slaves brought to the New 34
World, as well as those who sympathize with their causes, are understandably
reluctant to celebrate the anniversary of Columbus's landfall. Leaders of American Indian organizations condemn Columbus as a pirate or worse; Russell
Means of the American Indian Movement says that Columbus "makes Hitler
look like a juvenile delinquent." In a 1987 newspaper story, the Indian activist
Vernon Bellecourt was quoted as calling for "militant demonstrations" against
celebrants in 1992 "to blow out the candles on their birthday cake."

The governing board of the National Council of Churches, a predominantly 35
Protestant organization, resolved that, in consideration of the "genocide, slavery,
'ecocide' and exploitation" that followed Columbus, the quincentenary should
be a time of penitence rather than jubilation. In 1986, after four years of
impassioned debate, the United Nations abandoned its attempt to plan a celebration.

Once again, Columbus has become a symbol, this time of exploitation and 36
imperialism. It is time that the encounter be viewed not only from the European
standpoint, but from that of the indigenous Americans. It is time that the
sanitized storybook version of Europeans bringing civilization and Christianity
to America be replaced with a more clear-eyed recognition of the evils and
atrocities committed in wresting a land from its original inhabitants.

But are we burdening him with more guilt than any one man should have 37
to shoulder? Should not the guilt be more broadly shared?

Columbus should be judged by the evidence of his actions and words, not 38
by the legend that has been embedded in our imaginations. What do we know of
Columbus the person, who he really was, and of the times, as they really were?

Columbus, as far as we can tell, was born in 1451 in Genoa, apparently the 39
eldest of five surviving children in a family of wool weavers. (One child was a
girl, rarely mentioned in historical accounts.) They were tradespeople of modest
means. But of them, as of most aspects of his early life, Columbus said nothing.
Some of his ancestors may have been Jewish, though this has never been
established and, in any event, it seems to have had no direct bearing on his life
and exploits. His family was Christian, and so was Columbus—demonstrably
so. His surviving journals and letters are replete with invocations of the names
of Christ, Mary and the saints, and he often sought the advice and hospitality
of Franciscans.

Even more crucial than his ancestry may have been the time into which he 40
was born. Columbus grew up hearing of the scourge of Islam, the blockage of
trade routes to the spices of the East and the parlous times for Christendom.
All this could have nourished dreams in an ambitious young man with nautical

experience. Columbus did write that at a "tender age" he cast his lot with those who go to sea, shipping out on several voyages in the Mediterranean. In 1476, he found his way by chance to Portugal, where exploration of the sea was a dynamic of the age and the search for a new route to the Indies was an economic and religious imperative.

He gained a knowledge of the Atlantic in voyages to England and Ireland 41 (perhaps as far as Iceland) and at least once down the African coast. His marriage to Felipa Perestrello e Moniz took him to the Madeiras, where he would study Atlantic sailing charts and hear the many tales of westering voyages, and gave him access to Portuguese nobility. In these years he presumably conceived of his bold plan, but it was rejected by John II of Portugal.

So after his wife died, Columbus took their young son, Diego, and went to 42 Spain in 1484, again seeking royal backing. He managed to make friends with influential Franciscan friars and members of the royal court. "Columbus's ability to thrust himself into the circles of the great was one of the most remarkable things about him," writes John H. Parry, an American historian. But he would spend the next eight years entreating the court and defending his plan before royal commissions.

During this time, he fell in love with Beatriz Enríquez de Arana of Cordoba; 43 they never married, but she bore their son, Ferdinand, who became his father's devoted biographer. Ferdinand described his father as a "well-built man of more than average stature" who had a complexion tending to bright red, an aquiline nose and blond hair that, after the age of 30, had all turned white.

Only after the fall of Granada in January 1492, which ended the Moorish 44 presence in Spain, did Ferdinand and Isabella finally relent, apparently on the advice of Santángel, the king's financial adviser. Contrary to legend, Isabella did not have to hock her jewels, and Columbus did not have to prove the world was round. Educated Europeans were already convinced, but he seems to have been the first to stake his life on it.

Columbus was a consummate mariner everyone seemed to agree. As Michele 45 de Cuneo, who sailed with him, said: "By a simple look at the night sky, he would know what route to follow or what weather to expect; he took the helm, and once the storm was over, he would hoist the sails, while the others were asleep." And he found a new world. If there had not been an America there, he would probably have sailed to his death and certainly to oblivion. He could never have made the Indies, which lay far beyond where his miscalculations had placed them. He was wrong, but lucky. No explorer succeeds without some luck.

He made three more voyages, but his skill and luck deserted him on land. 46 He was an inept administrator of the colony he established at La Isabela, on the north shore of what is now the Dominican Republic. Ruling by the gibbet for three years, he antagonized his own men to insurrection (some lieutenants tried to seize ships and get away with a load of gold) and goaded the native

Tainos into bloody rebellion. Thousands of Tainos were raped, killed and tortured and their villages burned. At the first opportunity, Columbus captured Tainos and shipped them to Spain as slaves, a practice not without precedent in Europe or even among the people of pre-Columbian America. Las Casas sadly lamented the practices of his countrymen: "If we Christians had acted as we should."

The geographic interpretations of Columbus were muddled by preconceptions. He tended to see what he wanted to see and took native words to be mispronunciations of places in Cathay. He forced his crew to swear that one of his landfalls, Cuba, was the Asian mainland. His was not an open mind. He sought confirmation of received wisdom, usually church teachings, rather than new knowledge. Enthralled by the proximity of what he believed was the earthly paradise, he failed to appreciate that he had reached the South American continent on his third voyage. The waters of the Orinoco, he wrote, must flow from the fountain in Paradise, "whither no one can go but by God's permission." 47

Still, Columbus persevered, often racked with the pain of arthritis, which worsened with each voyage, and also tropical fevers. His four voyages, between 1492 and 1504, showed the way to countless others. As he approached death in 1506, his mind was consumed with self-pity, mysticism and a desperate desire to seize Jerusalem in preparation for Judgment Day. He wrote in a letter to the court: "All that was left to me and to my brothers has been taken away and sold, even to the cloak that I wore, to my great dishonor. . . . I am ruined as I have said. Hitherto I have wept for others; now have pity upon me, Heaven, and weep for me, earth!" Columbus did not die a pauper, legend notwithstanding. But his death, in Valladolid, Spain, went unheralded. 48

How are we to judge the historical Columbus, the man and not the legend? Was he a great man? 49

No, if greatness is measured by one's stature among contemporaries. We will never know if the course of history might have been any different if Columbus had been a kinder, more generous man. To argue that Columbus was acting in the accepted manner of his time is to concede that he was not superior to his age. To contend (with ample supporting evidence) that even if Columbus had set a better example, others who followed would have eventually corrupted his efforts, is to beg the question. Moreover, the only example Columbus set was one of pettiness, self-aggrandizement and a lack of magnanimity. He could not find in himself the generosity to share any credit for his accomplishments. Whatever his original objective, his lust for gold drove him from island to island and, it seems, to the verge of paranoia. And the only future he could anticipate was wealth for himself and his heirs and, probably more than most people of his time, the chimera of the imminent end of the world. 50

Yes, if greatness derives from the audacity of his undertaking, its surprising revelation and the magnitude of its impact on subsequent history. Columbus did cross the uncharted Atlantic, no mean feat. He did find new lands and 51 people, and he returned to tell of it so that others could follow, opening the way to intercontinental travel and expansion. True, if he had never sailed, other mariners would eventually have raised the American coast, as the Portuguese did in reaching Brazil by accident in 1500. But it was Columbus who had the idea, ill conceived though it was in many respects, and pursued it with uncommon persistence, undeterred by the doubters and scoffers. As it was put in the apocryphal story, Columbus showed the world how to stand an egg on its end.

Whether he was a great man or merely an agent of a great accomplishment, the issue really is his standing in history. And that depends on posterity's changing evaluation—Whitman's "ever-shifting guesses"—of him and the consequence of Europe's discovery of America. His reputation is inextricably linked to America. Ultimately, Columbus's place in history can be judged only in relation to the place accorded America in history. Surely we have not finally established that place. 52

It would be interesting to know how Columbus will be characterized in 2092. For it seems that his destiny is to serve as a barometer of our self-confidence and complacency, our hopes and aspirations, our faith in progress and the capacity of humans to create a more just society. 53

QUESTIONS

1. What aspects of Columbus's life, behavior, and activities have been factually established beyond dispute? What aspects of Columbus's life, behavior, and activities remain uncertain or unknown?

2. According to Wilford, the reputation of Columbus has been continually changing from the time that he lived to the present day. Make an outline of all the changes that Wilford discusses in his piece.

3. Which of the changes seem to be most drastic and striking? How does Wilford account for such drastic changes in Columbus's reputation?

4. Given such drastic changes in his reputation, are there any respects in which opinions of Columbus's life, behavior, or activities have remained constant during the past five hundred years?

5. What new information, if any, did you discover about Columbus from reading Wilford's piece? What additional information would you like to know about him?

6. What was your opinion of Columbus before reading Wilford's piece? What is your opinion of Columbus after reading it?

7. Write an essay, "Discovering _____," about a major American public figure (artist, entertainer, or politician) whose reputation has undergone some drastic change(s) during the past several years. What changes have taken place in this person's reputation? How do you account for the change(s)? What do you think this person's reputation will be twenty-five or fifty years from now?

8. Write an essay, "Discovering _____," about your own changing reputation. What changes do you think have taken place in the way people perceive you and think about

you? How do you account for the changes? What do you think your reputation will be five or ten years from now?

MAKING CONNECTIONS

Consider Wilford's discussion of Columbus in the light of Carr's "The Historian and His Facts" (pp. 601–611) and/or Tuchman's "When Does History Happen?" (pp. 612–619). How do you think Carr would evaluate Wilford's approach to Columbus? How do you think Tuchman would evaluate Wilford's approach to Columbus?

CARNAL ACTS
Nancy Mairs

*Nancy Mairs (b. 1943) is an essayist, memoirist, and poet.
She was born in California and grew up in New England,
where she learned the "rules of polite discourse" that she has
rebelled against in all of her writing. Thus she is widely
known for her continuing attempt to speak "as plainly and
truthfully as the squirms and wriggles of the human psyche
will permit" about her experiences as a woman, particularly
about her experience as someone afflicted by chronic depression, suicidal impulses, agoraphobia, and multiple sclerosis.
Since moving to Tucson, where she teaches creative writing
at the University of Arizona, Mairs has published an award-
winning collection of poems,* All the Rooms in the Yellow
House *(1984); a memoir,* Remembering the Bone House:
An Erotics of Space and Place *(1980); and two collections
of essays,* Plaintext: Deciphering a Woman's Life *(1986)
and* Carnal Acts *(1990), from which the following title essay
is reprinted.*

Inviting me to speak at her small liberal-arts college during Women's Week, 1
a young woman set me a task: "We would be pleased," she wrote, "if you could
talk on how you cope with your MS disability, and also how you discovered
your voice as a writer." Oh, Lord, I thought in dismay, how am I going to pull
this one off? How can I yoke two such disparate subjects into a coherent
presentation, without doing violence to one, or the other, or both, or myself?
This is going to take some fancy footwork, and my feet scarcely carry out the
basic steps, let alone anything elaborate.

To make matters worse, the assumption underlying each of her questions 2
struck me as suspect. To ask *how* I cope with multiple sclerosis suggests that I
do cope. Now, "to cope," *Webster's Third* tells me, is "to face or encounter and
to find necessary expedients to overcome problems and difficulties." In these
terms, I have to confess, I don't feel like much of a coper. I'm likely to deal
with my problems and difficulties by squawking and flapping around like that
hysterical chicken who was convinced the sky was falling. Never mind that in
my case the sky really *is* falling. In response to a clonk on the head, regardless
of its origin, one might comport oneself with a grace and courtesy I generally
lack.

368

As for "finding" my voice, the implication is that it was at one time lost or   3
missing. But I don't think it ever was. Ask my mother, who will tell you a little
wearily that I was speaking full sentences by the time I was a year old and could
never be silenced again. As for its being a writer's voice, it seems to have become
one early on. Ask Mother again. At the age of eight I rewrote the Trojan War,
she will say, and what Nestor was about to do to Helen at the end doesn't bear
discussion in polite company.

Faced with these uncertainties, I took my own teacherly advice, something,   4
I must confess, I don't always do. "If an idea is giving you trouble," I tell my
writing students, "put it on the back burner and let it simmer while you do
something else. Go to the movies. Reread a stack of old love letters. Sit in your
history class and take detailed notes on the Teapot Dome scandal. If you've got
your idea in mind, it will go on cooking at some level no matter what else
you're doing." "I've had an idea for my documented essay on the back burner,"
one of my students once scribbled in her journal, "and I think it just boiled
over!"

I can't claim to have reached such a flash point. But in the weeks I've had   5
the themes "disability" and "voice" sitting around in my head, they seem to
have converged on their own, without my having to wrench them together and
bind them with hoops of tough rhetoric. They *are* related, indeed interdependent, with an intimacy that has for some reason remained, until now, submerged
below the surface of my attention. Forced to juxtapose them, I yank them out
of the depths, a little startled to discover how they were intertwined down there
out of sight. This kind of discovery can unnerve you at first. You feel like a
giant hand that, pulling two swimmers out of the water, two separate heads
bobbling on the iridescent swells, finds the two bodies below, legs coiled around
each other, in an ecstasy of copulation. You don't quite know where to turn
your eyes.

Perhaps the place to start illuminating this erotic connection between who I   6
am and how I speak lies in history. I have known that I have multiple sclerosis
for about seventeen years now, though the disease probably started long before.
The hypothesis is that the disease process, in which the protective covering of
the nerves in the brain and spinal cord is eaten away and replaced by scar tissue,
"hard patches," is caused by an autoimmune reaction to a slow-acting virus.
Research suggests that I was infected by this virus, which no one has ever seen
and which therefore, technically, doesn't even "exist," between the ages of four
and fifteen. In effect, living with this mysterious mechanism feels like having
your present self, and the past selves it embodies, haunted by a capricious and
meanspirited ghost, unseen except for its footprints, which trips you even when
you're watching where you're going, knocks glassware out of your hand, squeezes
the urine out of your bladder before you reach the bathroom, and weights your
whole body with a weariness no amount of rest can relieve. An alien invader
must be at work. But of course it's not. It's your own body. That is, it's you.

369

This, for me, has been the most difficult aspect of adjusting to a chronic incurable degenerative disease: the fact that it has rammed my "self" straight back into the body I had been trained to believe it could, through highminded acts and aspirations, rise above. The Western tradition of distinguishing the body from the mind and/or the soul is so ancient as to have become part of our collective unconscious, if one is inclined to believe in such a noumenon, or at least to have become an unquestioned element in the social instruction we impose upon infants from birth, in much the same way we inculcate, without reflection, the gender distinctions "female" and "male." I *have* a body, you are likely to say if you talk about embodiment at all; you don't say, I *am* a body. A body is a separate entity possessable by the "I"; the "I" and the body aren't, as the copula would make them, grammatically indistinguishable.

To widen the rift between the self and the body, we treat our bodies as subordinates, inferior in moral status. Open association with them shames us. In fact, we treat our bodies with very much the same distance and ambivalence women have traditionally received from men in our culture. Sometimes this treatment is benevolent, even respectful, but all too often it is tainted by outright sadism. I think of the body-building regimens that have become popular in the last decade or so, with the complicated vacillations they reflect between self-worship and self-degradation: joggers and aerobic dancers and weightlifters all beating their bodies into shape. "No pain, no gain," the saying goes. "Feel the burn." Bodies get treated like wayward women who have to be shown who's boss, even if it means slapping them around a little. I'm not for a moment opposing rugged exercise here. I'm simply questioning the spirit in which it is often undertaken.

Since, as Hélène Cixous points out in her essay on women and writing, "Sorties,"* thought has always worked "through dual, hierarchical oppositions" (p. 64), the mind/body split cannot possibly be innocent. The utterance of an "I" immediately calls into being its opposite, the "not-I," Western discourse being unequipped to conceive "that which is neither 'I' nor 'not-I,'" "that which is both 'I' and 'not-I,'" or some other permutation which language doesn't permit me to speak. The "not-I" is, by definition, other. And we've never been too fond of the other. We prefer the same. We tend to ascribe to the other those qualities we prefer not to associate with our selves: it is the hidden, the dark, the secret, the shameful. Thus, when the "I" takes possession of the body, it makes the body into an other, direct object of a transitive verb, with all the other's repudiated and potentially dangerous qualities.

At the least, then, the body had best be viewed with suspicion. And a woman's body is particularly suspect, since so much of it is in fact hidden, dark, secret, carried about on the inside where, even with the aid of a speculum,

---

*In *The Newly Born Woman*, translated by Betsy Wing (Minneapolis: University of Minnesota Press, 1986).

one can never perceive all of it in the plain light of day, a graspable whole. I, for one, have never understood why anyone would want to carry all that delicate stuff around on the outside. It would make you awfully anxious, I should think, put you constantly on the defensive, create a kind of siege mentality that viewed all other beings, even your own kind, as threats to be warded off with spears and guns and atomic missiles. And you'd never get to experience that inward dreaming that comes when your flesh surrounds all your treasures, holding them close, like a sturdy shuttered house. Be my personal skepticism as it may, however, as a cultural woman I bear just as much shame as any woman for my dark, enfolded secrets. Let the word for my external genitals tell the tale: my pudendum, from the Latin infinitive meaning "to be ashamed."

It's bad enough to carry your genitals like a sealed envelope bearing the cipher that, once unlocked, might loose the chaotic flood of female pleasure—*jouissance*, the French call it—upon the world-of-the-same. But I have an additional reason to feel shame for my body, less explicitly connected with its sexuality: it is a crippled body. Thus it is doubly other, not merely by the homosexual standards of patriarchal culture but by the standards of physical desirability erected for every body in our world. Men, who are by definition exonerated from shame in sexual terms (this doesn't mean that an individual man might not experience sexual shame, of course; remember that I'm talking in general about discourse, not folks), may—more likely must—experience bodily shame if they are crippled. I won't presume to speak about the details of their experience, however. I don't know enough. I'll just go on telling what it's like to be a crippled woman, trusting that, since we're fellow creatures who've been living together for some thousands of years now, much of my experience will resonate with theirs.

I was never a beautiful woman, and for that reason I've spent most of my life (together with probably at least 95 percent of the female population of the United States) suffering from the shame of falling short of an unattainable standard. The ideal woman of my generation was . . . perky, I think you'd say, rather than gorgeous. Blond hair pulled into a bouncing ponytail. Wide blue eyes, a turned-up nose with maybe a scattering of golden freckles across it, a small mouth with full lips over straight white teeth. Her breasts were large but well harnessed high on her chest; her tiny waist flared to hips just wide enough to give the crinolines under her circle skirt a starting outward push. In terms of personality, she was outgoing, even bubbly, not pensive or mysterious. Her milieu was the front fender of a white Corvette convertible, surrounded by teasing crewcuts, dressed in black flats, a sissy blouse, and the letter sweater of the Corvette owner. Needless to say, she never missed a prom.

Ten years or so later, when I first noticed the symptoms that would be diagnosed as MS, I was probably looking my best. Not beautiful still, but the ideal had shifted enough so that my flat chest and narrow hips gave me an elegantly attenuated shape, set off by a thick mass of long, straight, shining hair. I had terrific legs, long and shapely, revealed nearly to the pudendum by the fashionable miniskirts and hot pants I adopted with more enthusiasm than delicacy of taste. Not surprisingly, I suppose, during this time I involved myself in several pretty torrid love affairs.

The beginning of MS wasn't too bad. The first symptom, besides the per- 14 nicious fatigue that had begun to devour me, was "foot drop," the inability to raise my left foot at the ankle. As a consequence, I'd started to limp, but I could still wear high heels, and a bit of a limp might seem more intriguing than repulsive. After a few months, when the doctor suggested a cane, a crippled friend gave me quite an elegant wood-and-silver one, which I carried with a fair amount of panache. The real blow to my self-image came when I had to get a brace. As braces go, it's not bad: lightweight plastic molded to my foot and leg, fitting down into an ordinary shoe and secured around my calf by a Velcro strap. It reduces my limp and, more important, the danger of tripping and falling. But it meant the end of high heels. And it's ugly. Not as ugly as I think it is, I gather, but still pretty ugly. It signified for me, and perhaps still does, the permanence and irreversibility of my condition. The brace makes my MS concrete and forces me to wear it on the outside. As soon as I strapped the brace on, I climbed into trousers and stayed there (though not in the same trousers, of course). The idea of going around with my bare brace hanging out seemed almost as indecent as exposing my breasts. Not until 1984, soon after I won the Western States Book Award for poetry, did I put on a skirt short enough to reveal my plasticized leg. The connection between winning a writing award and baring my brace is not merely fortuitous; being affirmed as a writer really did embolden me. Since then, I've grown so accustomed to wearing skirts that I don't think about my brace any more than I think about my cane. I've incorporated them, I suppose: made them, in their necessity, insensate but fundamental parts of my body.

Meanwhile, I had to adjust to the most outward and visible sign of all, a 15 three-wheeled electric scooter called an Amigo. This lessens my fatigue and increases my range terrifically, but it also shouts out to the world, "Here is a woman who can't stand on her own two feet." At the same time, paradoxically, it renders me invisible, reducing me to the height of a seven-year-old, with a child's attendant low status. "Would she like smoking or nonsmoking?" the gate agent assigning me a seat asks the friend traveling with me. In crowds I see nothing but buttocks. I can tell you the name of every type of designer jeans ever sold. The wearers, eyes front, trip over me and fall across my handlebars into my lap. "Hey!" I want to shout to the lofty world. "Down here! There's a person down here!" But I'm not, by their standards, quite a person anymore.

My self-esteem diminishes further as age and illness strip from me the features 16 that made me, for a brief while anyway, a good-looking, even sexy, young woman. No more long, bounding strides: I shuffle along with the timid gait I remember observing, with pity and impatience, in the little old ladies at Boston's

Symphony Hall on Friday afternoons. No more lithe, girlish figure: my belly sags from the loss of muscle tone, which also creates all kinds of intestinal disruptions, hopelessly humiliating in a society in which excretory functions remain strictly unspeakable. No more sex, either, if society had its way. The sexuality of the disabled so repulses most people that you can hardly get a doctor, let alone a member of the general population, to consider the issues it raises. Cripples simply aren't supposed to Want It, much less Do It. Fortunately, I've got a husband with a strong libido and a weak sense of social propriety, or else I'd find myself perforce practicing a vow of chastity I never cared to take.

Afflicted by the general shame of having a body at all, and the specific shame   17
of having one weakened and misshapen by disease, I ought not to be able to hold my head up in public. And yet I've gotten into the habit of holding my head up in public, sometimes under excruciating circumstances. Recently, for instance, I had to give a reading at the University of Arizona. Having smashed three of my front teeth in a fall onto the concrete floor of my screened porch, I was in the process of getting them crowned, and the temporary crowns flew out during dinner right before the reading. What to do? I wanted, of course, to rush home and hide till the dental office opened the next morning. But I couldn't very well break my word at this last moment. So, looking like Hansel and Gretel's witch, and lisping worse than the Wife of Bath, I got up on stage and read. Somehow, over the years, I've learned how to set shame aside and do what I have to do.

Here, I think, is where my "voice" comes in. Because, in spite of my   18
demurral at the beginning, I do in fact cope with my disability at least some of the time. And I do so, I think, by speaking about it, and about the whole experience of being a body, specifically a female body, out loud, in a clear, level tone that drowns out the frantic whispers of my mother, my grandmothers, all the other trainers of wayward childish tongues: "Sssh! Sssh! Nice girls don't talk like that. Don't mention sweat. Don't mention menstrual blood. Don't ask what your grandfather does on his business trips. Don't laugh so loud. You sound like a loon. Keep your voice down. Don't tell. Don't tell. Don't tell." Speaking out loud is an antidote to shame. I want to distinguish clearly here between "shame," as I'm using the word, and "guilt" and "embarrassment," which, though equally painful, are not similarly poisonous. Guilt arises from performing a forbidden act or failing to perform a required one. In either case, the guilty person can, through reparation, erase the offense and start fresh. Embarrassment, less opprobrious though not necessarily less distressing, is generally caused by acting in a socially stupid or awkward way. When I trip and sprawl in public, when I wet myself, when my front teeth fly out, I feel horribly embarrassed, but, like the pain of childbirth, the sensation blurs and dissolves in time. If it didn't, every child would be an only child, and no one would set foot in public after the onset of puberty, when embarrassment erupts like a geyser and bathes one's whole life in its bitter stream. Shame may attach itself

373

to guilt or embarrassment, complicating their resolution, but it is not the same emotion. I feel guilt or embarrassment for something I've done; shame, for who I am. I may stop doing bad or stupid things, but I can't stop being. How then can I help but be ashamed? Of the three conditions, this is the one that cracks and stifles my voice.

I can subvert its power, I've found, by acknowledging who I am, shame and all, and, in doing so, raising what was hidden, dark, secret about my life into the plain light of shared human experience. What we aren't permitted to utter holds us, each isolated from every other, in a kind of solipsistic thrall. Without any way to check our reality against anyone else's, we assume that our fears and shortcomings are ours alone. One of the strangest consequences of publishing a collection of personal essays called *Plaintext* has been the steady trickle of letters and telephone calls saying essentially, in a tone of unmistakable relief, "Oh, me too! Me too!" It's as though the part I thought was solo has turned out to be a chorus. But none of us was singing loud enough for the others to hear. 19

Singing loud enough demands a particular kind of voice, I think. And I was wrong to suggest, at the beginning, that I've always had my voice. I have indeed always had *a* voice, but it wasn't *this* voice, the one with which I could call up and transform my hidden self from a naughty girl into a woman talking directly to others like herself. Recently, in the process of writing a new book, a memoir entitled *Remembering the Bone House*, I've had occasion to read some of my early writing, from college, high school, even junior high. It's not an experience I recommend to anyone susceptible to shame. Not that the writing was all that bad. I was surprised at how competent a lot of it was. Here was a writer who already knew precisely how the language worked. But the voice . . . oh, the voice was all wrong: maudlin, rhapsodic, breaking here and there into little shrieks, almost, you might say, hysterical. It was a voice that had shucked off its own body, its own homely life of Cheerios for breakfast and seventy pages of Chaucer to read before the exam on Tuesday and a plantar's wart growing painfully on the ball of its foot, and reeled now wraithlike through the air, seeking incarnation only as the heroine who enacts her doomed love for the tall, dark, mysterious stranger. If it didn't get that part, it wouldn't play at all. 20

Among all these overheated and vaporous imaginings, I must have retained some shred of sense, because I stopped writing prose entirely, except for scholarly papers, for nearly twenty years. I even forgot, not exactly that I had written prose, but at least what kind of prose it was. So when I needed to take up the process again, I could start almost fresh, using the vocal range I'd gotten used to in years of asking the waiter in the Greek restaurant for an extra anchovy on my salad, congratulating the puppy on making a puddle outside rather than inside the patio door, pondering with my daughter the vagaries of female orgasm, saying goodbye to my husband, and hello, and goodbye, and hello. This new voice—thoughtful, affectionate, often amused—was essential because what I 21

374

needed to write about when I returned to prose was an attempt I'd made not long before to kill myself, and suicide simply refuses to be spoken of authentically in high-flown romantic language. It's too ugly. Too shameful. Too strictly a bodily event. And, yes, too funny as well, though people are sometimes shocked to find humor shoved up against suicide. They don't like the incongruity. But let's face it, life (real life, I mean, not the edited-for-television version) is a cacophonous affair from start to finish. I might have wanted to portray my suicidal self as a languishing maiden, too exquisitely sensitive to sustain life's wounding pressures on her soul. (I didn't want to, as a matter of fact, but I might have.) The truth remained, regardless of my desires, that when my husband lugged me into the emergency room, my hair matted, my face swollen and gray, my nightgown streaked with blood and urine, I was no frail and tender spirit. I was a body, and one in a hell of a mess.

I "should" have kept quiet about that experience. I know the rules of polite 22
discourse. I should have kept my shame, and the nearly lethal sense of isolation and alienation it brought, to myself. And I might have, except for something the psychiatrist in the emergency room had told my husband. "You might as well take her home," he said. "If she wants to kill herself, she'll do it no matter how many precautions we take. They always do." *They* always do. I was one of "them," whoever they were. I was, in this context anyway, not singular, not aberrant, but typical. I think it was this sense of commonality with others I didn't even know, a sense of being returned somehow, in spite of my appalling act, to the human family, that urged me to write that first essay, not merely speaking out but calling out, perhaps. "Here's the way I am," it said. "How about you?" And the answer came, as I've said: "Me too! Me too!"

This has been the kind of work I've continued to do: to scrutinize the details 23
of my own experience and to report what I see, and what I think about what I see, as lucidly and accurately as possible. But because feminine experience has been immemorially devalued and repressed, I continue to find this task terrifying. "Every woman has known the torture of beginning to speak aloud," Cixous writes, "heart beating as if to break, occasionally falling into loss of language, ground and language slipping out from under her, because for woman speaking—even just opening her mouth—in public is something rash, a transgression" (p. 92).

The voice I summon up wants to crack, to whisper, to trail back into silence. 24
"I'm sorry to have nothing more than this to say," it wants to apologize. "I shouldn't be taking up your time. I've never fought in a war, or even in a schoolyard free-for-all. I've never tried to see who could piss farthest up the barn wall. I've never even been to a whorehouse. All the important formative experiences have passed me by. I was raped once. I've borne two children. Milk trickling out of my breasts, blood trickling from between my legs. You don't want to hear about it. Sometimes I'm too scared to leave my house. Not scared *of* anything, just scared: mouth dry, bowels writhing. When the fear got really

bad, they locked me up for six months, but that was years ago. I'm getting old now. Misshapen, too. I don't blame you if you can't get it up. No one could possibly desire a body like this. It's not your fault. It's mine. Forgive me. I didn't mean to start crying. I'm sorry . . . sorry . . . sorry. . . ."

An easy solace to the anxiety of speaking aloud: this slow subsidence beneath   25
the waves of shame, back into what Cixous calls "this body that has been worse than confiscated, a body replaced with a disturbing stranger, sick or dead, who so often is a bad influence, the cause and place of inhibitions. By censuring the body," she goes on, "breath and speech are censored at the same time" (p. 97). But I am not going back, not going under one more time. To do so would demonstrate a failure of nerve far worse than the depredations of MS have caused. Paradoxically, losing one sort of nerve has given me another. No one is going to take my breath away. No one is going to leave me speechless. To be silent is to comply with the standard of feminine grace. But my crippled body already violates all notions of feminine grace. What more have I got to lose? I've gone beyond shame. I'm shameless, you might say. You know, as in "shameless hussy"? A woman with her bare brace and her tongue hanging out.

I've "found" my voice, then, just where it ought to have been, in the body-   26
warmed breath escaping my lungs and throat. Forced by the exigencies of physical disease to embrace my self in the flesh, I couldn't write bodiless prose. The voice is the creature of the body that produces it. I speak as a crippled woman. At the same time, in the utterance I redeem both "cripple" and "woman" from the shameful silences by which I have often felt surrounded, contained, set apart; I give myself permission to live openly among others, to reach out for them, stroke them with fingers and sighs. No body, no voice; no voice, no body. That's what I know in my bones.

QUESTIONS

1. Mairs never refers to the title of her essay. What do you think the title signifies? Why do you suppose the title is not mentioned in her essay?

2. Check the dictionary to find out the derivation of "carnal" and its primary meanings. In what respects do you think this essay is and is not about "carnal acts"?

3. In paragraph 5, Mairs claims that her disability from multiple sclerosis and her voice as a writer are "related," and "interdependent," even "intertwined." How do these figures of speech define the relationship between her disability and her voice? Why do you think she, in turn, speaks of the relationship in paragraph 6 as an "erotic connection"?

4. In paragraph 20, Mairs describes her "early writing" as sounding "maudlin, rhapsodic, breaking here and there into little shrieks, almost, you might say, hysterical." How does her voice sound in this piece? What adjectives would you characterize it with? What specific aspects of her style account for your choice of adjectives?

5. In your own recent writing, what aspects of your own style do you consider to be most prominent and most influential in creating the voice that you hear? In your earlier

writing? Consider how your present written voice is related to, or even intertwined with, the condition of your body.

6. Write an essay characterizing your written voice and how it is related to your body and any other aspects of your being and existence that you think have influenced it.

MAKING CONNECTIONS

Mairs's "Carnal Acts" and Alice Walker's "Beauty: When the Other Dancer Is the Self" both involve personal accounts by women of how they have coped with physically disfiguring afflictions. What similarities and differences do you see in their experiences and attitudes, and in their methods of presentation?

THE WOMAN IN THE GARDEN
Sven Birkerts

Sven Birkerts (b. 1951) worked as a bookseller for many years in Ann Arbor, Michigan and Cambridge, Massachusetts. He is the author of three collections of essays, An Artificial Wilderness *(1987),* The Electric Life *(1989), which won a PEN citation for Distinguished Essays, and* American Energies *(1992), in which he writes, "I insist that vital and ambitious novels and stories are being written, published and read. But I also insist that our cultural climate, the atmospheric medium within which meanings are discovered and passed along, is in a perilous condition." His essays have appeared in* The New York Review of Books, The Nation, Partisan Review *and* Ploughshares. *In the following essay, which first appeared in* Agni, *he poses the question "Where am I when I am involved in a book?"*

I have in my mind an image—a painting. Either it really exists, or else I   1
have conjured it up so often that it might as well. Finally, I suppose, it doesn't
matter.

The painting belongs to a familiar genre—that of the pensive figure in the   2
garden. I see a bench, a bower. A woman in period dress gazing away from a
book that she holds in one hand. The image is one of reverie and, if I think
about it, privilege. But these attributions hardly begin to exhaust its significance.
If reverie or privileged leisure were the point, then the book would not figure
so profoundly in my mental reconstruction. Yet it is the book that finally grips
my attention. I have it placed, if not literally then figuratively, in the center of
the visual vortex. At the vanishing point. The painting is, for me, about the
book—or about the woman's reading of the book—and though the contents of
the pages are as invisible as her thoughts, they—the imagined fact of them—
give the image its appeal.

Writing this, I feel as though I'm striding into a labyrinth from which I may   3
never exit. Indeed, my thoughts are already cross-hatched with corrections and
qualifications. For one thing, I suggested a moment ago that the woman was
thinking, had thoughts, as she looked away from the page. Not true. The whole
point of my summoning her up is to fasten upon a state that is other than

thinking. If she were thinking she would be herself, contained fully within her own circuits. But for me the power of the image lies precisely in the fact that she is planted inside one reality—the garden setting—while adrift in the spell of another: that of the author's created reality. The business gets more complicated when I think that the image was presumably held in mind and executed by a painter working at an easel, and that I have it in my mind not through direct perception, but in memory. I will not even try to sort out these Chinese boxes here.

Let me circle back and try another pass. What compels me is that the painter 4 has tried to find a visual expression for that which can be said to have escaped the moorings of the tangible. Is this not the most elusive and private of all conditions, that of the self suspended in the medium of the not-self, the particles of the identity wavering within the magnetic current generated by another sensibility? How are we to talk about it?

I zero in on the book itself. It is, of course, unmarked, unidentified—a 5 generic signifier. But it does not belong to the ordinary run of signifiers: it happens to be a material icon that represents an imagined and immaterial order. The book, whatever it is, holds dissolved in its grid of words a set of figments. These the reader will transform—actualize—into a set of wholly internal sensations. The sensations will, in turn, prove potent enough to eclipse her awareness of the surrounding world. The woman looks up from her book. She looks *at* the garden. What she sees, at most, is a light-shot shimmering of green, nothing more. Of the bench she is entirely oblivious.

I see the book. Inside the book are the words. They are the threshold between 6 the material and immaterial, the outward and the inward. The book is a thing, the page is a thing, and the letters of the words, pressed to the pages by the printing press, are, however slightly, things. But if the physical book can be seen as a signifier, then the words are signifiers raised to the hundredth power. Signification is their manifest essence, their *raison d'être*. The word is the serpent eating its tail; it is the sign that disappears in the act of signing, and signing is not complete *until* the word has disappeared. At the instant of apotheosis it ceases to be itself; when it has brokered the transaction, it vanishes. Paradox of paradoxes: the word is most signifier when it least signifies.

But enough. What about the woman in the garden? More to the point: Why 7 am I saying any of this? I suppose I am trying to sort out something about the meaning of reading—what we do when we brush our eyes over sheaves of signs, and why so many of us elect to do it for our own pleasure. What is the connection between the reading process and the self? That sounds terribly grand, but I'm not sure how else to come at it. Is this a question that can be answered? I'm not sure. But if it can't, maybe there are others that can. Such as: What is the difference between the self when reading and when not reading? Or: Where am I when I am involved in a book?

But you can see the problems that arise. This is Einstein's universe. To 8 isolate where I am when reading I would have to be able to say where I am when I'm not, and this is the psychic equivalent of whirling around before the mirror to see what you look like from the back. And there are other difficulties to boot, such as which epochal self to consider—self as child, self as possessed adolescent, self as adult mired in the distractions of living? And what kind of book, what kind of reading? History, romance, serious novel?

The last is the easiest to answer. I will somewhat arbitrarily confine myself   9
to the literary novel, if only because that, for me, represents reading in its purest form. And what interests me here are not the pedestrian incarnations of the act, but its most idealized attainments. The question of which self, meanwhile, brings on more muddles. For I have no doubt but that my self-as-reader has changed as much over time as the other, merely existing self. What's more, not only has my changing self affected the reader-self, but the reader-self has done no less a job on its counterpart. Which leaves us where? Back at the problematic boundary line that separates the one from the other. Best to plunge on.

I am well aware of the traditional wisdom about reading and its importance,   10
all of the bromides that are passed along to us as we imbibe our formal education: that books are good for you; that reading broadens, quickens verbal skills, fosters attentiveness and imagination, and develops the sense of contextual relativity which makes us more empathic, more inquisitive beings; that rewards increase with the worthiness of the texts themselves. Indeed, the basic assumption behind nearly all schooling—still—is that a steady application to the so-called "great works" yields an accumulation of facts and perspectives that eventually constitutes an education.

I don't intend to quarrel with any of these generalizations here. But I will   11
suggest that, important as they are, they do not begin to get to the real heart of reading, or to answer the question of why it matters. The truth lies elsewhere— in a context of self-making that far transcends the imperatives of self-improvement. There is a metaphysics of reading that has to do with a good deal more than any simple broadening of the mind. It involves, rather, a change of state and inner orientation, and if we contemplate the reading process in this light we can hardly get away from introducing the word *soul* (or something very like it) into the discussion. And this, I would say, is what compels me so much about the painting that I have either seen or imagined: that it uses purely pictorial indicators to push the mind past the picture plane and toward a beyond that is right here inside.

We tend to think of reading as a means to an end. Like driving, it gets us   12
from here to there. We do it, often, in order to have done it, the act is considered a sponge for contents. When we ask someone "Have you read *Bleak House*?"

we are not so much inquiring whether the person has had the *experience* of reading Dickens' novel as asking whether he knows the plot and the basic reference points of character and theme. This is hardly surprising. Ours is a checklist/can-do sort of culture and our approach to artistic expression cannot be expected to diverge much from our general approach to the business of living.

But such an attitude greatly diminishes the scope and importance of reading. For over and above the obvious instrumentality of the act, the immersing of the self in a text has certain fundamental metaphysical implications. To read, when one does so of one's own free will, is to make a volitional statement; it is to posit an elsewhere and to set off toward it. And like any travelling, reading is at once a movement *and* a comment of sorts about the place one has left. Say what you will, to open a book voluntarily is to remark the insufficiency either of the life or of one's orientation toward it. The distinction must be recognized, for when we read we not only transplant ourselves to the place of the text, but we modify our natural angle of regard upon all things—we reposition the self in order to *see* differently.

Reading is not on a continuum with the other bodily or cognitive acts. It instigates a shift, a change of state—a change analogous to, but not as totally affecting as, the change from wakefulness to sleep. Maybe the meditation state (I have not experienced it) would be a better correlative. In any case, the relative outer tranquility of the act belies the magnitude of the transition. When we take up a book we are engaged in, we quite rapidly switch from responding to our immediate environment to processing a set of codes and responding to those. And as any devoted reader of thrillers can tell you, the coded stimuli can set the heart to racing as reliably as crisis circumstances in the real world.

Reading a novel, then, is not simply a matter of making a connection to another person's experiences. Over and above the linguistic connection, the process brings about a transformation within the whole complex of the self. We are, for the duration of our reading, different, and the difference has more to do with the process than with its temporary object, the book being read. As with meditation, both the pulse and breathing seem to change, the interior rhythms are modified in untold ways.

Then there are the metaphysics. When we enter a novel, no matter what novel, we step into the whole world anew. The entire order of earthly things is implicitly there, even if the protagonist never leaves his bed, it is figured, assumed, in the perceptual scheme. There is only one difference: this is a world sustained fully in the suspension of a single sensibility—the author's. However much the life in the book may resemble the life known to the reader, it is nevertheless irradiated through its every part with the intended coherence of its conception. The fictional world is a world with a sponsoring god—or *creator*— and this is true even where the work argues for the nihilistic chaos of experience.

13

14

15

16

381

The author's reality is meaningful—an intended entity—and we soak this up with the story line. And for the space of our reading, and perhaps beyond, it changes our relation to all things.

The transition, of course—from the world we live in to the world of the   17
book—is complex and gradual. We do not open to the first page and find ourselves promptly transported away from our surroundings and concerns. What takes place is a gradual immersion, an exchange whereby we hand over our groundedness in the here and now in order to take up our new groundedness in the elsewhere of the page. The more fully we can accomplish this, the more fully we can be said to be reading. The tree in front of us must dim so that the tree on the page can take on outline and mass. The operation is hardly passive. We collude at every point. We will that it be so. We project ourselves at the word, and pass through it as through a turnstile. And we do this, often, with an astonishing facility—something in us must need it. A reader in the full flush of absorption will not be aware of turning words into mental entities. The conversion is automatic, and as unconscious as highway driving. We often don't register what we're doing for pages at a time. In this peculiar condition, a misprinted word can be as suddenly jarring as the sight of a hubcap rolling toward us down the center-line.

What makes this miracle possible is the shared medium—language. Lan-   18
guage is the land mass that is continuous under our feet and the feet of others and allows us to get to each other's places. We bring the words—set in the intensely suggestive sequences and cadences of another—into ourselves. We engulf them in our consciousness and then allow ourselves to be affected by them. But reading should not therefore be construed as the simple inscription of another person's signs upon the blank screen of our receptivity. We don't shut ourselves off and turn the book on; we are never that silent or submissive. Our own sub-threshold murmuring continues, but it is pushed into the background by the more articulated, more *present* language of the book. Notice, however, that when our attention flags for whatever reason, the self-murmuring rushes in to fill the void. At times we find the two voices—ours and the author's—in dissonant parley. John is confessing his love for Maria and we are simultaneously wondering if the back tire on our car is leaking air. If John and Maria fade any further, we may get up to go to the garage.

But is it really so simple? Do we really find two adjacent voices coexisting,   19
the one making room for the other? Isn't there some way in which the two languages might actually connect, with the author's taking in our own as a kind of tributary? It might be that just as the word-sign dissolves into the concept or picture, so our free-floating consciousness—what I have loosely called the sub-threshold muttering—coalesces around the signals to give them clarity and animation. I do sometimes have the sense that in yielding to a book I am like an orchestra at that moment when it stops its infernal seething and assents to

382

the conductor's uplifted baton. Where *am* I when I am reading? Isn't this another way of asking what happens to the buzz of consciousness when the writer's language takes possession of us?

The phrasing here is tricky, with concealed assumptions and preconceptions. 20 I wrote "language takes possession" because it seemed to convey the sense I wanted, but on second glance the construction is terribly misleading. It implies passivity before conquest, while the far more likely scenario is one of collaboration. We don't just allow the writer's words the run of the house—we bring our substance *to* them and make them live. We are actively present at every moment, scripting and constructing. The writer may tell us that "The mother wore a shabby, discolored dressing gown," but the word-canisters are empty until we load them from our private reservoirs. We activate our sense-memories and determine the degrees of shabbiness and discoloration, not to mention the styling of the gown. We are bustling in all directions. If the murmur of the self is repressed, it is probably less because our language has been overpowered than because we are too busy to heed its flickerings. Fully engaged, we work with the writer to build our own book. We preside over the movements within a world that comes into view and vanishes—present into past—just like the one we inhabit when the book is shut.

Reading may be, as I have suggested, the positing of an elsewhere, but the 21 activity itself is not really a place so much as a state or a condition. How, then, shall we characterize it? What is it that separate reading acts share that lies beyond the local disturbance of the setting, characters, and narrative particulars of any given book? Is there a fundamental and identifiably constant condition that one returns to over and over, a condition different from all other conditions—from being asleep, from being high, from daydreaming?

I think there is—certainly for me. But years of working in bookstores convince 22 me that it's there for others as well, not just a specific inner state, but a need to keep getting back to it. They know it and they seek it. I study people in the aisles of bookstores all the time. I see them standing with their necks tilted at a 45-degree angle, looking not for a specific book, but for a book they can trust to do the job. They want plot and character, sure, but what they really want is a vehicle that will bear them off to the reading state. Which is . . . Well, it's a condition rather unlike any other. Think of it as an engaged detachment, an attentive distractedness, a disembodied hovering that is at once more and less real than anything earthly experience has to offer.

In this condition, when all is clear and right—and believe me, one can fail 23 at reading as readily as at anything else—I feel a connectedness that cannot be duplicated (unless, possibly, in the act of writing when *that* is going well). For me, the reading state brings on an inside limberness, a sense of being for once in accord with time. Not the time that I break into a grid for appointments and chores, but real time. Duration time. Time as the medium within which experience resonates and *means*. This will sound exaggerated, but when I am at the finest pitch of reading, I feel as if the whole of my life—past as well as unknown future—were somehow available to me. Not in terms of any high-definition particulars (reading is not clairvoyance) but as an object of contemplation. At the same time, I register a definite awareness: that I am, in the present, part of a more extensive circuit, a circuit channeling what Wallace Stevens called the "substance in us that prevails."

The elsewhere state of reading was once—in childhood—a momentous   24
discovery. The first arrival was so stunning, so happy, that I wanted nothing more than a guarantee of return. Escape? Of course. But that does not end the discussion. Here was also the finding of a lens that would give me a different orientation to what was already, though only nascently, the project of my life. Through reading I could reposition the contents of my life along the coordinate axes of urgency and purpose. These two qualities not only determined, or informed, the actions of whatever characters I was reading about, but they exerted pressure on my own life so long as I was bathed in the energies of the book. So palpable was this sense that I could stir up a heady excitement in myself just by *thinking* of the book-in-progress. I needed only to call it to mind and I would feel differently about my immediate circumstance. The book was there, at home, like an injection waiting to be administered.

If anything has changed about my reading over the years, it is that I value   25
the state the book puts me in more than I value the specific contents. Indeed, I often find that a novel, even a well-written and compelling novel, can become a blur to me soon after I have finished it. I recollect the feeling of reading it perfectly, the mood I occupied, but I am less certain about the narrative details. It is almost as if the book were, as Wittgenstein said of his propositions, a ladder, to be climbed and then discarded after it has served its purpose.

No matter what the shape or construction of that ladder, the ideal state of   26
arrival is always the same: deeply familiar—like the background setting of certain dreams, like travel, like the body sensations of crying.

I would guess that most adults who are now devoted readers began at a young   27
age, and that they formed a good part of their essential selves via their interaction with books. That is, that they somehow founded their own inwardness, the more reflective component of their self, in the space that reading opened up. The space is, of course, a potential, and it can be found without recourse to the book. But the book is such a natural path to it. The space is implicit in the act of reading—it manifests itself in the act, and the act constantly reinforces it. Again, I use the spatial analogy loosely to represent a way of perceiving the world and of situating the self vis-à-vis experience.

This self-situation of the reader is not a common one in our society. Many   28 perceive it as anomalous and threatening. My intuition is that non-readers tend to see reading as a kind of value judgment upon themselves, as an elitist and exclusionary act. And there is a certain truth in that perception. Reading *is* a judgment. It brands as insufficient the understandings and priorities that govern the common—that is to say, the non-reading—life. Reading, pledged to duration, repudiates the idea of time as simple succession. Reading argues for a larger conception of the meaningful, and its implicit injunction—seldom heeded, even by readers—is that we change our lives. That we strive to live in the light of meaning is not a message that many people want to hear, for the responsibility it imposes is crushingly great.

What reading does, ultimately, is to keep alive the dangerous and exhilarating idea that life is not a sequence of lived moments, but a destiny. That, God or no God, life has a unitary pattern inscribed within it, a pattern that we could possibly discern for ourselves if it were possible to lay the whole of our experience out like a map. And while it is true that the reader cannot see the full map better than anyone else, he is more likely to live under the supposition that such an informative pattern does exist. He is, by inclination and formation, a spelunker of causes and effects, an explorer of connections through time. He does not live in the present as others do—not quite—because the present is known to be a moving point on the larger map he has posited.

The time of reading—the time defined by the author's language resonating in the self—is not the world's time, but the soul's. I don't know how else to define the soul in secular terms than as a self-consistent condensation of self. Reading makes this self more present. The energies which otherwise tend to stream outward through a thousand channels of distraction are marshalled by the cadences of the prose; they are brought into focus by the fact that it is an ulterior, and entirely new, world that the reader has entered. The free-floating self—the self we diffusely commune with while driving or walking or puttering in the kitchen—is enlisted in the work of bringing the narrative to life. In the process, we are able to shake off the habitual burden of insufficient meaning and flex our deeper natures. Everything in the book exists under the aspect of meaning; every sentence takes its place in the overall design. To participate in this meaning is to make the radical assumption—for oneself no less than for the characters—that the least moment will take its appointed place in the whole, and that at last all the parts of the design will disclose their pattern of significance.

This is why the image of the woman in the painting haunts me. I see it as an emblem of the most paradoxical doubleness, where the physical self is rooted in one world, and the inner self is almost entirely dissolved away from its reliance upon the immediate. The figure in the garden thus echoes the paradox of the book itself—which is to be a physical object whose value lies almost entirely in the invisible order its pages hold caged.

385

QUESTIONS

1. What does the image of the woman in the garden mean to Birkerts?

2. Birkerts asks the question in paragraph seven: "What is the difference between the self when reading and when not reading?" What other questions does he need to ask in order to answer this question? How does he answer his own questions?

3. In paragraph 20, Birkerts speaks of collaboration between writer and reader: "We don't just allow the writer's words the run of the house—we bring our substance *to* them and make them live." What is the nature of this collaboration? How does this collaboration help explain something about the mysteriousness of the reading process?

4. Consider both the reading and the writing processes. How are these two processes similar? How are they different? What is the role of collaboration in the writing process?

5. Think of some of the books that have had the most significant impact upon you. Why has it mattered to you to read these books? How have these books become touchstones for your thinking?

6. Who are you when you read? What is the condition of the "reading state" for you? Start with an image such as Birkerts's woman in the garden. What does your image look like? Write a portrait of yourself as a reader in which you explain something about who you are when you are reading.

MAKING CONNECTIONS

Birkerts is fascinated with the process of reading. The reflections of Frederick Douglass and Jorge Luis Borges also try to explain the complex relationship between reading and the reader. What ideas about reading connect these essayists? What questions about reading would you like to ask these writers? Create a conversation between two of these writers.

Social Sciences and Public Affairs

THE AUTIST ARTIST
Oliver Sacks

Oliver Sacks was born in London, England, in 1933, and educated in London and Oxford before coming to the United States to complete his education in California and New York. At present he is clinical professor of neurology at Albert Einstein College of Medicine. He is best known, however, for his extraordinary writing on matters related to his medical studies, in such books as Awakenings *(1974),* A Leg to Stand On *(1984),* Seeing Voices: A Journey into the World of the Deaf *(1989), and his national best-seller,* The Man Who Mistook His Wife for a Hat *(1986), in which the following selection appeared after its earlier publication in the* New York Review of Books. *Interested in the art of storytelling as well as in clinical neurology, Sacks subtitled the book in which this essay appeared, "and Other Clinical Tales." He insists that his essays are not just case studies, though they are that, but also tales or fables of "heroes, victims, martyrs, warriors." In his writing, he says, "the scientific and romantic . . . come together at the intersection of fact and fable."*

"Draw this," I said, and gave José my pocket watch. 1

He was about 21, said to be hopelessly retarded, and had earlier had one of 2
the violent seizures from which he suffers. He was thin, fragile-looking.

His distraction, his restlessness, suddenly ceased. He took the watch carefully, 3

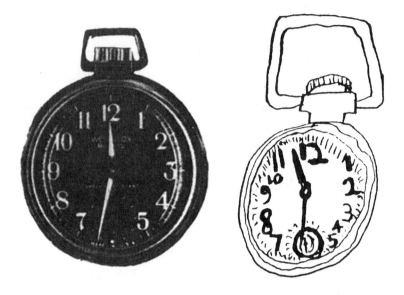

as if it were a talisman or jewel, laid it before him, and stared at it in motionless concentration.

"He's an idiot," the attendant broke in. "Don't even ask him. He don't know 4
what it is—he can't tell time. He can't even talk. They says he's 'autistic,' but he's just an idiot." José turned pale, perhaps more at the attendant's tone than at his words—the attendant had said earlier that José didn't use words.

"Go on," I said. "I know you can do it." 5

José drew with an absolute stillness, concentrating completely on the little 6
clock before him, everything else shut out. Now, for the first time, he was bold, without hesitation, composed, not distracted. He drew swiftly but minutely, with a clear line, without erasures.

I nearly always ask patients, if it is possible for them, to write and draw, 7
partly as a rough-and-ready index of various competences, but also as an expression of "character" or "style."

José had drawn the watch with remarkable fidelity, putting in every feature 8
(at least every essential feature—he did not put in "Westclox, shock resistant, made in USA"), not just "the time" (though this was faithfully registered at 11:31), but every second as well, and the inset seconds dial, and, not least, the knurled winder and trapezoid clip of the watch, used to attach it to a chain. The clip was strikingly amplified, though everything else remained in due proportion. And the figures, now that I came to look at them, were of different

388

sizes, different shapes, different styles—some thick, some thin; some aligned, some inset; some plain and some elaborated, even a bit "gothic." And the inset second hand, rather inconspicuous in the original, had been given a striking prominence, like the small inner dials of star clocks, or astrolabes.

The general grasp of the thing, its "feel," had been strikingly brought out— 9 all the more strikingly if, as the attendant said, José had no idea of time. And otherwise there was an odd mixture of close, even obsessive, accuracy, with curious (and, I felt, droll) elaborations and variations.

I was puzzled by this, haunted by it as I drove home. An "idiot"? Autism? 10 No. Something else was going on here.

I was not called to see José again. The first call, on a Sunday evening, had 11 been for an emergency. He had been having seizures the entire weekend, and I had prescribed changes in his anticonvulsants, over the phone, in the afternoon. Now that his seizures were "controlled," further neurological advice was not requested. But I was still troubled by the problems presented by the clock, and felt an unresolved sense of mystery about it. I needed to see him again. So I arranged a further visit, and to see his entire chart—I had been given only a consultation slip, not very informative, when I saw him before.

José came casually into the clinic—he had no idea (and perhaps did not 12 care) why he'd been called—but his face lit up with a smile when he saw me. The dull, indifferent look, the mask I remembered, was lifted. There was a sudden, shy smile, like a glimpse through a door.

"I have been thinking about you, José," I said. He might not understand my 13 words, but he understood my tone. "I want to see more drawing"—and I gave him my pen.

What should I ask him to draw this time? I had, as always, a copy of *Arizona* 14 *Highways* with me, a richly illustrated magazine which I especially delight in, and which I carry around for neurological purposes, for testing my patients. The cover depicted an idyllic scene of people canoeing on a lake, against a backdrop of mountains and sunset. José started with the foreground, a mass of near-black silhouetted against the water, outlined this with extreme accuracy, and started to block it in. But this was clearly a job for a paintbrush, not a fine pen. "Skip it," I said, then pointing, "Go on to the canoe." Rapidly, unhesitatingly, José outlined the silhouetted figures and the canoe. He looked at them, then looked away, their forms fixed in his mind—then swiftly blocked them in with the side of the pen.

Here again, and more impressively, because an entire scene was involved, I 15 was amazed at the swiftness and the minute accuracy of reproduction, the more so since José had gazed at the canoe and then away, having taken it in. This argued strongly against any mere copying—the attendant had said earlier, "He's just a Xerox"—and suggested that he had apprehended it as an image, exhibiting a striking power not just of copying but of perception. For the image had a

dramatic quality not present in the original. The tiny figures, enlarged, were more intense, more alive, had a feeling of involvement and purpose not at all clear in the original. All the hallmarks of what Richard Wollheim[1] calls "iconicity"—subjectivity, intentionality, dramatization—were present. Thus, over and above the powers of mere facsimile, striking as these were, he seemed to have clear powers of imagination and creativity. It was not *a* canoe but *his* canoe that emerged in the drawing.

I turned to another page in the magazine, to an article on trout fishing, with a pastel watercolour of a trout stream, a background of rocks and trees, and in the foreground a rainbow trout about to take a fly. "Draw this," I said, pointing to the fish. He gazed at it intently, seemed to smile to himself, and then turned away—and now, with obvious enjoyment, his smile growing broader and broader, he drew a fish of his own.   16

I smiled myself, involuntarily, as he drew it, because now, feeling comfortable with me, he was letting himself go, and what was emerging, slyly, was not just a fish, but a fish with a "character" of sorts.   17

The original had lacked character, had looked lifeless, two-dimensional, even stuffed. José's fish, by contrast, tilted and poised, was richly three-dimensional, far more like a real fish than the original. It was not only verisimilitude and animation that had been added but something else, something richly expressive, though not wholly fishlike: a great, cavernous, whalelike mouth; a slightly crocodilian snout; an eye, one had to say, which was distinctly human, and with altogether a positively roguish look. It was a very funny fish—no wonder   18

---

[1] Richard Wollheim: Philosopher and art historian. [Eds.]

he had smiled—a sort of fish-person, a nursery character, like the frog-footman in *Alice*.[2]

Now I had something to go on. The picture of the clock had startled me,   19
stimulated my interest, but did not, in itself, allow any thoughts or conclusions. The canoe had shown that José had an impressive visual memory, and more. The fish showed a lively and distinctive imagination, a sense of humour, and something akin to fairy-tale art. Certainly not great art, it was "primitive," perhaps it was child-art; but, without doubt, it was art of a sort. And imagination, playfulness, art are precisely what one does not expect in idiots, or *idiots savants*, or in the autistic either. Such at least is the prevailing opinion.

My friend and colleague Isabelle Rapin had actually seen José years before,   20
when he was presented with "intractable seizures" in the child neurology clinic—and she, with her great experience, did not doubt that he was "autistic." Of autism in general she had written:

> A small number of autistic children are exceedingly proficient at de-coding written language and become hyperlexic or preoccupied with numbers . . . Extraordinary proficiencies of some autistic children for putting together puzzles, taking apart mechanical toys, or decoding written texts may reflect the consequences of attention and learning being inordinately focused on non-verbal visual-spatial tasks to the exclusion of, or perhaps because of, the lack of demand for learning verbal skills. (1982, pp. 146–50)

Somewhat similar observations, specifically about drawing, are made by   21
Lorna Selfe in her astonishing book *Nadia* (1978). All *idiot savant* or autistic proficiencies and performances, Dr Selfe gathered from the literature, were apparently based on calculation and memory alone, never on anything imagi-native or personal. And if these children could draw—supposedly a very rare occurrence—their drawings too were merely mechanical. "Isolated islands of proficiency" and "splinter skills" are spoken of in the literature. No allowance is made for an individual, let alone a creative, personality.

What then was José, I had to ask myself. What sort of being? What went on   22
inside him? How had he arrived at the state he was in? And what state was it—and might anything be done?

I was both assisted and bewildered by the available information—the mass   23
of "data" that had been gathered since the first onset of his strange illness, his "state." I had a lengthy chart available to me, containing early descriptions of his original illness: a very high fever at the age of eight, associated with the onset of incessant, and subsequently continuing, seizures, and the rapid ap-pearance of a brain-damaged or autistic condition. (There had been doubt from the start about what, exactly, was going on.)

---

[2] *Alice*: Lewis Carroll's *Alice in Wonderland*. [Eds.]

His spinal fluid had been abnormal during the acute stage of the illness. 24
The consensus was that he had probably suffered an encephalitis of sorts. His
seizures were of many different types—*petit mal, grand mal,* "akinetic," and
"psychomotor," these last being seizures of an exceptionally complex type.

Psychomotor seizures can also be associated with sudden passion and vio- 25
lence, and the occurrence of peculiar behaviour-states even between seizures
(the so-called psychomotor personality). They are invariably associated with
disorder in, or damage to, the temporal lobes, and severe temporal-lobe disorder,
both left-sided and right-sided, had been demonstrated in José by innumerable
EEGs.

The temporal lobes are also associated with the auditory capacities, and, in 26
particular, the perception and production of speech. Dr Rapin had not only
considered José "autistic," but had wondered whether a temporal-lobe disorder
had caused a "verbal auditory agnosia"—an inability to recognise speech sounds
that interfered with his capacity to use or understand the spoken word. For what
was striking, however it was to be interpreted (and both psychiatric and neurological interpretations were offered), was the loss or regression of speech, so that
José, previously "normal" (or so his parents avowed), became "mute," and ceased
talking to others when he became ill.

One capacity was apparently "spared"—perhaps in a compensatory way en- 27
hanced: an unusual passion and power to draw, which had been evident since
early childhood, and seemed to some extent hereditary or familial, for his father
had always been fond of sketching, and his (much) older brother was a successful
artist. With the onset of his illness; with his seemingly intractable seizures (he
might have twenty or thirty major convulsions a day, and uncounted "little
seizures," falls, "blanks," or "dreamy states"); with the loss of speech and his
general intellectual and emotional "regression," José found himself in a strange
and tragic state. His schooling was discontinued, though a private tutor was
provided for a while, and he was returned permanently to his family, as a
"fulltime" epileptic, autistic, perhaps aphasic, retarded child. He was considered
ineducable, untreatable and generally hopeless. At the age of nine, he "dropped
out"—out of school, out of society, out of almost all of what for a normal child
would be "reality."

For fifteen years he scarcely emerged from the house, ostensibly because of 28
"intractable seizures," his mother maintaining she dared not take him out,
otherwise he would have twenty or thirty seizures in the street every day. All
sorts of anticonvulsants were tried, but his epilepsy seemed "untreatable": this,
at least, was the stated opinion in his chart. There were older brothers and
sisters, but José was much the youngest—the "big baby" of a woman approaching
fifty.

We have far too little information about these intervening years. José, in 29
effect, disappeared from the world, was "lost to follow-up," not only medically
but generally, and might have been lost forever, confined and convulsing in his

cellar room, had he not "blown up" violently very recently and been taken to the hospital for the first time. He was not entirely without inner life, in the cellar. He showed a passion for pictorial magazines, especially of natural history, of the *National Geographic* type, and when he was able, between seizures and scoldings, would find stumps of pencil and draw what he saw.

These drawings were perhaps his only link with the outside world, and 30 especially the world of animals and plants, of nature, which he had so loved as a child, especially when he went out sketching with his father. This, and this only, he was permitted to retain, his one remaining link with reality.

This, then, was the tale I received, or, rather, put together from his chart or 31 charts, documents as remarkable for what they lacked as for what they contained—the documentation, through default, of a fifteen-year "gap": from a social worker who had visited the house, taken an interest in him, but could do nothing; and from his now aged and ailing parents as well. But none of this would have come to light had there not been a rage of sudden, unprecedented, and frightening violence—a fit in which objects were smashed—which brought José to a state hospital for the first time.

It was far from clear what had caused this rage, whether it was an eruption 32 of epileptic violence (such as one may see, on rare occasions, with very severe temporal-lobe seizures), or whether it was, in the simplistic terms of his admission note, simply "a psychosis," or whether it represented some final, desperate call for help, from a tortured soul who was mute and had no direct way of expressing his predicament, his needs.

What was clear was that coming to the hospital and having his seizures 33 "controlled" by powerful new drugs, for the first time, gave him some space and freedom, a "release," both physiological and psychological, of a sort he had not known since the age of eight.

Hospitals, state hospitals, are often seen as "total institutions" in Erving 34 Goffman's sense, geared mainly to the degradation of patients. Doubtless this happens, and on a vast scale. But they may also be "asylums" in the best sense of the word, a sense perhaps scarcely allowed by Goffman: places that provide a refuge for the tormented, storm-tossed soul, provide it with just that mixture of order and freedom of which it stands in such need. José had suffered from confusion and chaos—partly organic epilepsy, partly the disorder of his life— and from confinement and bondage, also both epileptic and existential. Hospital was good for José, perhaps lifesaving, at this point in his life, and there is no doubt that he himself felt this fully.

Suddenly too, after the moral closeness, the febrile intimacy of his house, 35 he now found others, found a world, both "professional" and concerned: unjudging, unmoralistic, unaccusing, detached, but at the same time with a real feeling both for him and for his problems. At this point, therefore (he had now been in hospital for four weeks), he started to have hope; to become more animated, to turn to others as he had never done before—not, at least, since the onset of autism, when he was eight.

But hope, turning to others, interaction, was "forbidden," and no doubt 36 frighteningly complex and "dangerous" as well. José had lived for fifteen years in a guarded, closed world—in what Bruno Bettelheim in his book on autism called the "empty fortress." But it was not, it had never been, for him, entirely empty; there had always been his love for nature, for animals and plants. *This* part of him, *this* door, had always remained open. But now there was tempta- tion, and pressure, to "interact," pressure that was often too much, came too soon. And precisely at such time José would "relapse"; would turn again, as if for comfort and security, to the isolation, to the primitive rocking movements, he had at first shown.

The third time I saw José, I did not send for him in the clinic, but went up, 37 without warning, to the admission ward. He was sitting, rocking, in the frightful day room, his face and eyes closed, a picture of regression. I had a qualm of horror when I saw him like this, for I had imagined, had indulged, the notion of "a steady recovery." I had to see José in a regressed condition (as I was to do again and again) to see that there was no simple "awakening" for him, but a path fraught with a sense of danger, double jeopardy, terrifying as well as exciting—because he had come to love his prison bars.

As soon as I called him, he jumped up, and eagerly, hungrily, followed me 38 to the art room. Once more I took a fine pen from my pocket, for he seemed to have an aversion to crayons, which was all they used on the ward. "That fish you drew," I hinted it with a gesture in the air, not knowing how much of my words he might understand, "that fish, can you remember it, can you draw it again?" He nodded eagerly, and took the pen from my hands. It was three weeks since he had seen it. What would he draw now?

He closed his eyes for a moment—summoning an image?—and then drew. 39 It was still a trout, rainbow-spotted, with fringy fins and a forked tail, but, this time, with egregiously human features, an odd nostril (what fish has nostrils?), and a pair of ripely human lips. I was about to take the pen, but, no, he was not finished. What had he in mind? The image was complete. The image, perhaps, but not the scene. The fish before had existed—as an icon—in isola- tion: now it was to become part of a world, a scene. Rapidly he sketched in a little fish, a companion, swooping into the water, gambolling, obviously in play. And then the surface of the water was sketched in, rising to a sudden, tumultuous wave. As he drew the wave, he became excited, and emitted a strange, mysterious cry.

I couldn't avoid the feeling, perhaps a facile one, that this drawing was 40 symbolic—the little fish and the big fish, perhaps him and me? But what was so important and exciting was the spontaneous representation, the impulse, not my suggestion, entirely from himself, to introduce this new element—a living

interplay in what he drew. In his drawings as in his life hitherto, interaction had always been absent. Now, if only in play, a symbol, it was allowed back. Or was it? What was that angry, avenging wave?

Best to go back to safe ground, I felt; no more free association. I had seen 41 potential, but I had seen, and heard, danger too. Back to safe, Edenic, prelapsarian Mother Nature.[3] I found a Christmas card lying on the table, a robin redbreast on a tree trunk, snow and stark twigs all around. I gestured to the bird, and gave José the pen. The bird was finely drawn, and he used a red pen for the breast. The feet were somewhat taloned, grasping the bark (I was struck, here and later, by his need to emphasise the grasping power of hands and feet, to make contact sure, almost gripping, obsessed). But—what was happening?— the dry winter twiglet, next to the tree trunk, had shot up in his drawing, expanded into florid open bloom. There were other things that were perhaps symbolic, although I could not be sure. But the salient and exciting and most significant transformation was this: that José had changed winter into spring.

Now, finally, he started to speak—though "speak" is much too strong a term 42 for the strange-sounding, stumbling, largely unintelligible utterances that came out, on occasion startling him as much as they startled us—for all of us, José included, had regarded him as wholly and incorrigibly mute, whether from incapacity, indisposition, or both (there had been the *attitude*, as well as the

---

[3] Prelapsarian: belonging to the time before the "fall" of humans. [Eds.]

fact, of not speaking). And here, too, we found it impossible to say how much was "organic," how much was a matter of "motivation." We had reduced, though not annulled, his temporal-lobe disorders—his electro-encephalograms (EEGs) were never normal; they still showed in these lobes a sort of low-grade electrical muttering, occasional spikes, dysrhythmia, slow waves. But they were immensely improved compared with what they were when he came in. If he

397

could remove their convulsiveness, he could not reverse the damage they had sustained.

We had improved, it could not be doubted, his physiological *potentials* for speech, though there was an impairment of his abilities to use, understand, and recognise speech, with which, doubtless, he would always have to contend. But, equally important, he now was fighting for the recovery of his understanding and speech (egged on by all of us, and guided by the speech therapist in particular), where previously he had accepted it, hopelessly or masochistically,

43

and indeed had turned against virtually all communication with others, verbal and otherwise. Speech impairment and the refusal to speak had coupled before in the double malignancy of disease; now, recovery of speech and attempts to speak were being happily coupled in the double benignity of beginning to get well. Even to the most sanguine of us it was very apparent that José would never speak with any facility approaching normal, that speech could never, for him, be a real vehicle for self-expression, could serve only to express his simpler needs. And he himself seemed to feel this too and, while he continued to fight for speech, turned more fiercely to drawing for self-expression.

One final episode. José had been moved off the frenzied admission ward to a calmer, quieter special ward, more homelike, less prisonlike, than the rest of the hospital: a ward with an exceptional number and quality of staff, designed especially, as Bettelheim would say, as "a home for the heart," for patients with autism who seem to require a kind of loving and dedicated attention that few hospitals can give. When I went up to this new ward, he waved his hand lustily as soon as he saw me—an outgoing, open gesture. I could not imagine him having done this before. He pointed to the locked door, he wanted it open, he wanted to go outside.

He led the way downstairs, outside, into the overgrown, sunlit garden. So far as I could learn, he had not, voluntarily, gone outside since he was eight, since the very start of his illness and withdrawal. Nor did I have to offer him a pen—he took one himself. We walked around the hospital grounds, José sometimes gazing at the sky and trees, but more often down at his feet, at the mauve and yellow carpet of clover and dandelions beneath us. He had a very quick eye for plant forms and colours, rapidly saw and picked a rare white clover, and found a still rarer four-leaved one. He found seven different types of grass, no less, seemed to recognise, to greet, each one as a friend. He was delighted most of all by the great yellow dandelions, open, all their florets flung open to the sun. This was his plant—it was how he felt, and to show his feeling he would draw it. The need to draw, to pay graphic reverence, was immediate and strong: he knelt down, placed his clipboard on the ground, and, holding the dandelion, drew it.

This, I think, is the first drawing from real life that José had done since his father took him sketching as a child, before he became ill. It is a splendid drawing, accurate and alive. It shows his love for reality, for another form of life. It is, to my mind, rather similar to, and not inferior to, the fine vivid flowers one finds in medieval botanies and herbals—fastidiously, botanically exact, even though José has no formal knowledge of botany, and could not be taught it or understand it if he tried. His mind is not built for the abstract, the conceptual. *That* is not available to him as a path to truth. But he has a passion and a real power for the particular—he loves it, he enters into it, he re-creates it. And the particular, if one is particular enough, is also a road—one might say nature's road—to reality and truth.

The abstract, the categorical, has no interest for the autistic person—the 47
concrete, the particular, the singular, is all. Whether this is a question of
capacity or disposition, it is strikingly the case. Lacking, or indisposed to, the
general, the autistic seem to compose their world picture entirely of particulars.
Thus they live, not in a universe, but in what William James called a "multi-
verse," of innumerable, exact, and passionately intense particulars. It is a mode
of mind at the opposite extreme from the generalising, the scientific, but still
"real," equally real, in a quite different way. Such a mind has been imagined
in Borges's story "Funes the Memorious" (so like Luria's *Mnemonist*):

> He was, let us not forget, almost incapable of ideas of a general, Platonic
> sort . . . In the teeming world of Funes, there were only details, almost
> immediate in their presence . . . No one . . . has felt the heat and
> pressure of a reality as indefatigable as that which day and night con-
> verged upon the hapless Ireneo.

As for Borges's Ireneo, so for José. But it is not necessarily a hapless circum- 48
stance: there may be a deep satisfaction in particulars, especially if they shine,
as they may do for José, with an emblematic radiance.

I think José, an autist, a simpleton too, has such a gift for the concrete, for 49

400

form, that he is, in his way, a naturalist and natural artist. He grasps the world as forms—directly and intensely felt forms—and reproduces them. He has fine lateral powers, but he has figurative powers too. He can draw a flower or fish with remarkable accuracy, but he can also make one which is a personification, an emblem, a dream, or a joke. And the autistic are supposed to lack imagination, playfulness, art!

Creatures like José are not supposed to exist. Autistic child-artists like "Nadia" 50 were not supposed to exist. Are they indeed so rare, or are they overlooked? Nigel Dennis, in a brilliant essay on Nadia in the *New York Review of Books* (4 May 1978), wonders how many of the world's "Nadias" may be dismissed or overlooked, their remarkable productions crumpled up and consigned to the trash can, or simply, like José, treated without thought, as an odd talent, isolated, irrelevant, of no interest. But the autistic artist or (to be less lofty) the autistic imagination is by no means rare. I have seen a dozen examples of it in as many years, and this without making any particular effort to find them.

The autistic, by their nature, are seldom open to influence. It is their fate 51 to be isolated, and thus original. Their "vision," if it can be glimpsed, comes from within and appears aboriginal. They seem to me, as I see more of them, to be a strange species in our midst, odd, original, wholly inwardly directed, unlike others.

Autism was once seen as a childhood schizophrenia, but phenomenologically 52 the reverse is the case. The schizophrenic's complaint is always of "influence" from the outside: he is passive, he is played upon, he cannot be himself. The autistic would complain—if they complained—of absence of influence, of absolute isolation.

"No man is an island, entire of itself," wrote Donne. But this is precisely 53 what autism is—an island, cut off from the main. In "classical" autism, which is manifest, and often total, by the third year of life, the cutting off is so early there may be no memory of the main. In "secondary" autism, like José's, caused by brain disease at a later stage in life, there is some memory, perhaps some nostalgia, for the main. This may explain why José was more accessible than most, and why, at least in drawing, he may show interplay taking place.

Is being an island, being cut off, necessarily a death? It may be a death, but 54 it is not necessarily so. For though "horizontal" connections with others, with society and culture, are lost, yet there may be vital and intensified "vertical" connections, direct connections with nature, with reality, uninfluenced, unmediated, untouchable, by any others. This "vertical" contact is very striking with José, hence the piercing directness, the absolute clarity of his perceptions and drawings, without a hint or shade of ambiguity or indirection, a rocklike power uninfluenced by others.

This brings us to our final question: is there any "place" in the world for a 55 man who is like an island, who cannot be acculturated, made part of the main?

Can "the main" accommodate, make room for, the singular? There are similarities here to the social and cultural reactions to genius. (Of course I do not suggest that all autists have genius, only that they share with genius the problem of singularity.) Specifically: what does the future hold for José? Is there some "place" for him in the world which will *employ* his autonomy, but leave it intact?

Could he, with his fine eye, and great love of plants, make illustrations for 56 botanical works or herbals? Be an illustrator for zoology or anatomy texts? (See the drawing overleaf he made for me when I showed him a textbook illustration of the layered tissue called "ciliated epithelium.") Could he accompany scientific expeditions, and make drawings (he paints and makes models with equal facility) of rare species? His pure concentration on the thing before him would make him ideal in such situations.

Or, to take a strange but not illogical leap, could he, with his peculiarities, 57 his idiosyncrasy, do drawings for fairy tales, nursery tales, Bible tales, myths? Or (since he cannot read, and sees letters only as pure and beautiful forms) could he not illustrate, and elaborate, the gorgeous capitals of manuscript breviaries and missals? He has done beautiful altarpieces, in mosaic and stained wood, for churches. He has carved exquisite lettering on tombstones. His current

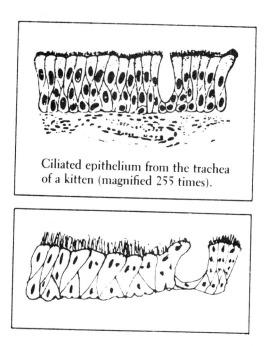

Ciliated epithelium from the trachea of a kitten (magnified 255 times).

"job" is hand-printing sundry notices for the ward, which he does with the flourishes and elaborations of a latter-day Magna Carta. All this he could do, and do very well. And it would be of use and delight to others, and delight him too. He could do all of these—but, alas, he will do none, unless someone very understanding, and with opportunities and means, can guide and employ him. For, as the stars stand, he will probably do nothing, and spend a useless, fruitless life, as so many other autistic people do, overlooked, unconsidered, in the back ward of a state hospital.

QUESTIONS

1. In this essay, Sacks presents two stories along with an explanation of autism: the story of José's life and the story of his treatment by Sacks and his colleagues. Retell these two stories in your own words.

2. Does Sacks think of himself as a storyteller? Discuss paragraph 31 in this connection.

3. In paragraph 45, Sacks not only tells us what José did, but what he was feeling and almost what he was thinking as well. How does he *know* this? Is it proper for him to present such material as part of a case study? Is the use of such material justified or not?

4. As indicated in question 1, this essays offers an explanation of autism as well as two stories. The explanation is limited and incomplete because the state of our knowledge about this condition is itself far from complete. Paragraphs 47–54 in particular sum up the gist of this explanation. Drawing upon these paragraphs, construct your own tentative definition of autism.

5. Sacks is a successful writer on medical subjects, no doubt because of both the information he presents, which many people find interesting, and the way he presents it. Look at his presentation in the beginning of the essay. How would you characterize the way the first ten paragraphs are written? Be specific. Look carefully at paragraph 4, for instance. What is the function of this paragraph?

6. Write an essay in which you discuss how Sacks uses art in his essay. You should consider how Sacks interprets both the original work as well as José's interpretation of it. Do not hesitate to offer your own interpretation as well. In your discussion, consider also the possible uses of art in studying and treating mental illness.

MAKING CONNECTIONS

1. This essay is mainly about autism, but it is also about art. Drawing upon this and other essays that touch on the nature of visual art (by Joan Didion, or Sacks's "The Man Who Mistook His Wife for a Hat," for example), write an essay in which you explain the nature and function of visual art. How does it affect us? How should we respond to it? What role does it play in your life? What role should it play in our lives? Quote from

the essays you use as sources, but try to describe your own explanation of what art is and should be.

2. As we note in the introduction to this piece, Sacks refers to both of his essays as "clinical tales," and not just case studies. Thus he may share characteristics with other storytellers in this collection, such as Maya Angelou, Alice Walker, George Orwell, and Richard Selzer. Do you think Sacks's work is closer to a case study or closer to a story? What makes the difference?

WHAT MADE THIS MAN?
MENGELE

Robert Jay Lifton

Born in New York City in 1926, Robert Jay Lifton received his M.D. in 1948 and is presently Distinguished Professor of Psychiatry and Psychology at John Jay College of Criminal Justice in the City University of New York. The author of books on "brainwashing" and Vietnam veterans, his study of Nazi doctors, The Nazi Doctors: Killing and the Psychology of Genocide *was published in 1986. The following essay was adapted from that book for the* New York Times Magazine *in July 1985. This essay appeared in the* Times *just after Mengele's body—or what most people believe to be his body—was found in a South American grave.*

His bones do not satisfy. Josef Mengele had come to symbolize the entire   1
Nazi killing project. The need was to capture him and put him on trial, hear his confession, put *him* at *our* mercy. For many, that anticipated event took on the significance of confronting the Holocaust and restoring a moral universe.

For Mengele has long been the focus of what could be called a cult of   2
demonic personality. He has been seen as the embodiment of absolute evil, a doctor pledged to heal who kills instead. But this demonization made him something of a deity, a nonhuman or even superhuman force, and served as a barrier to any explanation of his behavior. One reason Auschwitz survivors have hungered for his capture and trial is to divest him of this status. One of them, for instance, spoke to me of his yearning to see "this metamorphosis of turning him back into a person instead of God Almighty."

Mengele was a man, not a demon, and that is our problem.   3

Indeed, during recent weeks he had already begun to fall from grace as a   4
symbol of pure evil. The most notorious Nazi fugitive, unsuccessfully pursued for decades, had suddenly appeared—as bones in a Brazilian grave. The world watched in fascination as scientific examination seemed to confirm that these were the right bones.

It was reported that Mengele had lived out much of his last 25 years in   5
lonely, despairing isolation, that he had fallen in love with a housemaid. An exemplar of pure evil is not supposed to experience loneliness or to care for another person.

What has been lost in the preoccupation with the corpse has been the nature   6

405

of the man: What made Mengele Mengele? How can we explain his murderous behavior in Auschwitz?

Over the last eight years, while conducting research for a book on Nazi doctors, I have sought answers to these questions. I have conducted psychological interviews with 28 former Nazi doctors; a number of Nazi lawyers, economists and other nonmedical professionals; and also with more than 80 former Auschwitz inmates who were engaged in medical work in the camp. The study has required me to probe moral as well as psychological issues and to raise questions about the nature of evil. 7

Hannah Arendt gave currency to a concept of the banality of evil in her portrayal of Adolf Eichmann as a rather unremarkable bureaucrat who killed by meeting schedules and quotas. She is surely correct in her claim that an ordinary person is capable of extreme evil. But over the course of committing evil acts, an ordinary person becomes something different. In a process I call "doubling," a new self takes shape that adapts to the evil environment, and the evil acts become part of that self. At this point, the person and his behavior are anything but banal. 8

Mengele possessed unusually intense destructive potential, but there were no apparent signs of aberrant behavior prior to the Nazis and Auschwitz. Without Auschwitz, he would probably have kept his destructive potential under control. As a wise former inmate physician told me, "In ordinary times, Mengele could have been a slightly sadistic German professor." 9

It was the coming together of the man and the place, the "fit" between the two, that created the Auschwitz Mengele. 10

What we know about the man who arrived in Auschwitz in May 1943 is not especially remarkable. The son of a well-to-do Bavarian industrialist, Mengele is remembered by an acquaintance as a popular young man, an enthusiastic friend. He was also intelligent, a serious student who showed "a very distinct ambitiousness." 11

In 1931, at the age of 20, Mengele joined a right-wing, nationalistic organization. He was an early Nazi enthusiast, enlisting with the SA (the storm troopers) in 1933, applying for party membership in 1937 and for SS membership the following year. There are rumors that, while studying in Munich, he met such high-ranking Nazis as Alfred Rosenberg, a leading ideologue, and even Hitler himself. 12

Mengele became a true ideologue: a man who understood his life to be in the service of a larger vision. 13

According to an Auschwitz friend and fellow-SS physician, Mengele espoused the visionary SS ideology that the Nordic race was the only truly creative race, that it had been weakened by Christian morality of Jewish origin, and that Germany needed to revert to ancient German myths in creating an SS "order" to purify the Nordic race. According to his friend, Mengele was an extreme anti-Semite, "fully convinced that the annihilation of the Jews is a 14 provision for the recovery of the world and Germany." And Mengele considered these views to be scientifically derived. (I have preserved the anonymity of the people I interviewed. Those who are identified had previously made themselves known in books or other public documents.)

Mengele's ideology considerably influenced his intellectual choices. Matriculating not only at Munich but also at Bonn, Vienna and Frankfurt, he came to concentrate on physical anthropology and genetics, eventually working under Professor Freiherr Otmar von Verschuer at the Institute of Hereditary Biology and Racial Hygiene at Frankfurt. He earned a degree in anthropology as well as medicine.

Mengele produced three publications before he came to Auschwitz. They dealt with physical characteristics and abnormalities and, in each case, emphasized the role of heredity—an emphasis in keeping with trends in German and international scholarship at the time. Though jammed with charts, diagrams and photographs that claim more than they prove, the papers are relatively respectable scientific works of that era. But their conclusions uniformly reflect Mengele's commitment to bringing science into the service of the Nazi vision.

Mengele seemed well on his way toward an academic career. He had the strong backing of Verschuer who, in a letter of recommendation, praised his reliability and his capacity for clear verbal presentation of difficult intellectual problems. Mengele's marriage to a professor's daughter was in keeping with his academic aspirations.

His military experience loomed large in his idea of himself. In 1938–39, Mengele served six months with a specially trained mountain light-infantry regiment, followed by a year in the reserve medical corps. He spent three years with a Waffen SS unit, mostly in the East, including action in Russia, where, according to SS records, he was wounded and declared medically unfit for combat. A commendation declared that he had "acquitted himself brilliantly in the face of the enemy," and he received five decorations, including the Iron Cross First Class and Second Class.

Mengele, his friend said, was the only doctor in Auschwitz who possessed that array of medals, and he was enormously proud of them; he frequently referred to his combat experience to bolster his arguments on a variety of matters. According to his friend, Mengele arrived at the camp with a special aura because he was coming more or less directly from the front.

His friend suggests something else special about Mengele. He had asked to be sent to the Auschwitz death camp because of the opportunities it could provide for his research. He continued to have the support and collaboration of his teacher, Verschuer, who convinced the German Research Society to provide financial support for Mengele's work.

Auschwitz was both an annihilation camp and a work camp for German industry. Like other SS doctors there, Mengele had the task of "selecting" prisoners for the gas chamber—the vast majority—and for the slave labor force.

407

SS doctors also controlled and supervised the inmate doctors who alone did whatever actual medical treatment was done. Mengele was the chief doctor of Birkenau, an Auschwitz subcamp, but seemed to many inmates to have authority beyond his position. Dr. Olga Lengyel, an inmate doctor, described Mengele as "far and away the chief provider for the gas chamber and the crematory ovens." Another inmate doctor spoke of Mengele's role as "very important, more than that of the others."

One reason he appeared to be especially important was that he was extraordinarily energetic. While many SS doctors did no more than what was required of them, Mengele was always on the move, busy with his work, initiating new projects. More than any other SS doctor, he seemed to find his calling in Auschwitz.

22

Many inmates thought that Mengele alone conducted the large "selections." When they arrived at Auschwitz, packed by the hundreds into freight and cattle cars, they were unloaded and herded down a ramp. The Nazi doctors were assigned, on a rotating basis, to stand on the ramp and select those prisoners who would live, as workers at the camp, and those who would be killed.

23

The evidence is that Mengele took his turn at the ramp, like everyone else, but he also appeared there frequently to make sure that any twins in a "transport," as the trains were called, would be collected and saved for his research. But the prisoners saw it differently. At a trial of former Auschwitz personnel, in Frankfurt in 1964, an inmate who had been assigned to unload the transports recalled only the name of Mengele. When the judge commented, "Mengele cannot have been there all the time," the witness answered: "In my opinion, always. Night and day." Mengele brought such flamboyance and posturing to the selections task that it was his image inmates remembered.

24

He was an elegant figure on the ramp—handsome, well groomed, extremely upright in posture. Prisoners sometimes described him as "very Aryan looking" or "tall and blond," when he was actually of medium height, with dark hair and a dark complexion. Inmates said Mengele "conveyed the impression of a gentle and cultured man" and spoke of the "cheerful expression on his face . . . almost like he had fun . . . he was very playful."

25

There was an easy rhythm in his approach to selections. He walked back and forth, an inmate recalled, "a nice-looking man" with a riding crop in his hand who "looked at the bodies and the faces just a couple of seconds" and said, "*Links* [left], *Rechts* [right], *Links, Rechts . . . Rechts . . . Links, Rechts.*"

26

Prisoners were struck by the stark contrast between his calm, playful manner and the horror of what he was doing. Occasionally, though, his detachment could give way to outbreaks of rage and violence, especially when he encountered resistance to his sense of "the rules." In one instance, a mother refused to be separated from her teen-age daughter and scratched the face of the SS trooper who tried to enforce Mengele's decision. Mengele drew his gun and shot both the woman and her child. Still raging, he ordered that all the people

27

from that transport whom he had previously selected as workers be sent to the gas chamber.

In the hospital blocks where medical treatment was given to prisoners in 28 order to maintain the workforce, there was another kind of "selection" process. Nazi doctors would weed out for the gas chamber the weakest patients, those thought unlikely to recover in two or three weeks. Mengele, Dr. Lengyel recalled, "could show up suddenly at any hour, day or night. . . . when we least expected him." The prisoners would "march before him with their arms in the air while he continued to whistle his Wagner—or it might be Verdi or Johann Strauss."

Though usually cool in his conduct of selections, Mengele was passionate 29 in pursuing his "scientific research." His main interest was the study of twins, but he carried out a variety of projects with different groups of human subjects.

· He collected and studied dwarfs in an effort to determine the genetic 30 reasons for their condition.

· He investigated a gangrenous condition of the face and mouth called 31 noma. Though ordinarily a rare condition, it was common among gypsy inmates of Auschwitz. It was known to be caused by the kind of debilitation that inmates were subject to, but Mengele focused on what he deemed to be genetic and racial factors.

· He sought out inmates with a condition known as heterochromia of the 32 iris—in which the two eyes are of different colors—and, after their death, sent their eyes to his old professor, Verschuer, at the Berlin-Dahlem Institute of Racial Biology. With some of these inmates, Mengele took the bizarre step of attempting to change eye color in an Aryan direction by injecting methylene blue into the brown eyes of blond inmate children.

But the research that most occupied Mengele, to which he devoted the 33 greatest time and energy, was his study of twins. In fact, he probably came to Auschwitz for that specific purpose—as a continuation of work he had done under Verschuer at the University of Frankfurt a few years earlier.

As early as 1935, Verschuer had written of the absolute necessity of research 34 on twins to achieve "complete and reliable determination of what is hereditary in man."

Because identical twins (derived from the same ovum) possess the same 35 genetic constitution, they have traditionally been used in research on hereditary influences. Their shared physical and sometimes psychological characteristics, normal and abnormal, can be assumed to be genetically determined. Such characteristics can be assumed to be genetically determined in other people as well.

Mengele recognized that Auschwitz would permit him to pursue his mentor's 36 dream. From the hundreds of thousands of prisoners, he could collect twins in quantities never before available to a scientist. What is more, he could exercise total control over them.

He could compare measurements and bodily features. He could try medi-   37
cations meant to prevent, treat or induce a particular illness on an individual twin, or both of a pair of twins. He could then make comparisons of various kinds, in which he sought to demonstrate the importance of heredity rather than environment. He had no need or inclination to concern himself with ethical considerations, sharing as he did the general SS doctor's view that one was doing no harm since Auschwitz inmates, especially Jews, were in any case doomed.

Mengele had a fanatic's commitment to twin research. A number of survivors   38
reported seeing him on the transport ramp, shouting "Zwillinge heraus! [Twins out!], Zwillinge heraustreten! [Twins step forward!]." An inmate anthropologist whom Mengele had eagerly recruited to assist him described the arrival of a group of Hungarian Jews "like a river . . . women, men, women with children, and suddenly I saw Mengele going quickly . . . the same speed [as] the crowd [crying out] only 'Zwillinge heraus!' . . . with such a face that I would think he's mad."

Mengele had the same frenzied attitude in carrying out his research. To   39
inmates, he seemed to have an inner compulsion to get a great deal accomplished quickly in a personal race against time. He undoubtedly came to recognize increasingly that the days of the Auschwitz research bonanza were numbered.

Mainly to pursue his studies of twins, Mengele set up an Auschwitz caricature   40
of an academic research institute. Inmate doctors, mostly Jewish, with specialized training in various laboratory and clinical areas, were called upon to contribute to his work by diagnosing, sometimes treating, X-raying and performing post-mortem examinations of his research subjects. For his pathologist, Dr. Miklos Nyiszli, he provided a special dissection room complete with porcelain sinks and a dissecting table of polished marble. The overall arrangement, as Dr. Nyiszli later wrote, was "the exact replica of any large city's institute of pathology." In addition to the area used by SS physicians, Mengele had three offices of his own, mainly for work with twins.

The precise number of twins Mengele studied is not known, but during the   41
spring and summer of 1944, the time of the influx and mass murder of enormous numbers of Hungarian Jews, he accumulated what inmates of the men's and women's camps estimated to be a total of 175 sets of twins; it was an extraordinarily large number to have available simultaneously in a single place. Most were children, but the twins ranged up to the age of 70. The relative number of identical twins, as opposed to nonidentical twins, is also uncertain. (Nonidentical twins come from different ova and are genetically similar only to the extent of ordinary siblings.) Mengele's capacity or inclination to maintain, in his work, the crucial distinction between these two kinds of twins is unclear.

Since it is known that a few ordinary siblings masqueraded as twins, upon discovering the advantages of doing so, there is reason to doubt the reliability of Mengele's research.

Being a twin gave one a much better chance to survive. That was especially true for children, who were otherwise routinely selected for the gas chamber on arrival. 42

Twins had unique status. They felt themselves, as one put it, "completely elevated, segregated from the hurly-burly of the camp." They lived in special blocks, usually within medical units. They were frequently permitted to keep their own clothing. Their heads were not shaved. Their diet was rich by Auschwitz standards, often including white bread and milk. They were never beaten, as one surviving twin explained—even if they were caught in such a normally "ultimate sin" as stealing food—because the word was out "not to ruin us physically." 43

Mothers of young female twins were sometimes allowed to stay with their children, though usually only temporarily, in order to help the twins remain in good physical and mental condition—and on occasion to contribute to information about heredity and family history. We may say that the lives of twins had unique existential value in Auschwitz. 44

Mengele's research method, according to the inmate anthropologist, was standard for the time—and much the same as that used by her own well-regarded professor at the Polish university where she had obtained her advanced degree. That professor, she said, stressed "the biological foundation of [the] social environment" and the delineation of "racial types." Mengele's approach was different only in being "terribly detailed." 45

Measurements were taken of the twins' skulls and bodies and various characteristics of the nose, lips, ears, hair and eyes. The inmate anthropologist used quality Swiss instruments and wore a white coat "like a physician." 46

Identical twins, Mengele's most treasured research objects, were often examined together. As one of them described: "It was like a laboratory. . . . There isn't a piece of body that wasn't measured and compared. . . . We were always sitting together—always nude. . . . We would sit for hours together." 47

When Mengele himself performed the examination, they said, he was very proper and methodical: "He concentrated on one part of the body at one time . . . like [one day] he measured our eyes for about two hours." They spoke of being examined as frequently as twice a week for a period of five months in late 1944, and also remembered vividly a special visit to the Auschwitz main camp for photographs. 48

There were less benign research programs on twins. One twin survivor, for example, told how he and his 12-year-old twin sister would be examined and subjected to such procedures as the injection of material into their spines or the clamping of some part of the body "to see how long you could stand the pressure." 49

411

The twin survivor also spoke of Mengele's supervising "a lot of research with   50
chemicals" and of how Mengele's assistants "might stick a needle in various
places from behind," including the performing of spinal taps. These procedures,
when done on young children, resulted sometimes in loss of consciousness,
deafness and—among the smaller children—death.

The final step in Mengele's research on a number of the twins was dissection.   51
Auschwitz enabled him not only to observe and measure twins to compare
them in life, but to arrange for them to die together. He could thereby obtain
comparisons of healthy or diseased organs to show the effects of heredity.

Sometimes Mengele himself presided over the murder of his twins. A de-   52
position given by Dr. Nyiszli in 1945 described one such event:

> "In the work room next to the dissecting room, 14 gypsy twins were
> waiting . . . and crying bitterly. Dr. Mengele didn't say a single word
> to us, and prepared a 10cc. and 5cc. syringe. From a box he took
> evipan, and from another box he took chloroform, which was in 20
> cubic-centimeter glass containers, and put these on the operating table.
> After that, the first twin was brought in . . . a 14-year-old girl. Dr.
> Mengele ordered me to undress the girl and put her on the dissecting
> table. Then he injected the evipan into her right arm intravenously.
> After the child had fallen asleep, he felt for the left ventricle of the
> heart and injected 10cc. of chloroform. After one little twitch the child
> was dead, whereupon Dr. Mengele had it taken into the corpse cham-
> ber. In this manner, all 14 twins were killed during the night."

Mengele could be totally arbitrary in his killings. An inmate radiologist told   53
of a pair of gypsy twins, "two splendid boys of 7 or 8, whom we were studying
from all aspects—from the 16 or 18 different specialties we represented." The
boys both had symptoms in their joints that, according to a belief at that time,
could be linked to tuberculosis. Mengele was convinced that the boys were
tubercular, but the various inmate doctors, including the radiologist, found no
trace of that disease.

Mengele was outraged, and he left the room, ordering the radiologist to   54
remain. When he returned about an hour later, Mengele said calmly: "You are
right. There was nothing." After some silence, Mengele added, "Yes, I dissected
them." Later, the radiologist said, he heard from Dr. Nyiszli that Mengele had
shot the two boys in the neck and that "while they were still warm, began to
examine them: lungs first, then each organ."

The two boys, the radiologist added, had been favorites with all the doctors—   55
including Mengele. They had been treated very well, he added, "spoiled in all
respects . . . these two especially . . . they fascinated him considerably." But
their post-mortem study had still greater fascination for him.

Mengele's fanatically brutal approach to his research can be understood   56
mainly in terms of his combination of ideological zealotry and scientific am-

bition. Verschuer, his mentor, was taking science in a Nazi direction when he declared that research with twins would demonstrate "the extent of the damage caused by adverse hereditary influences" as well as "relations between disease, racial types, and miscegenation." In Auschwitz, Mengele saw an opportunity to deepen and extend the Nazi racial vision by means of systematic research "evidence."

He was also intent upon gaining personal recognition as a scientist. Indeed, his Auschwitz friend told me that Mengele planned to use his research with twins as the basis for his Habilitation, the presentation necessary for a formal university appointment. Mengele's ideological worship, then, included the worship of Nazified "science," and from that standpoint he told his friend that "it would be a sin, a crime . . . and irresponsible not to utilize the possibilities that Auschwitz had for twin research," and that "there would never be another chance like it."

Mengele saw himself as a biological revolutionary, part of a vanguard devoted to the bold scientific task of remaking his people and ultimately the people of the world. The German race would have to be cured and its genes improved. Many believed, as one inmate doctor said, that Mengele wanted to make use of his research on twins "to find the cause of multiple pregnancies" in order to increase such events among Aryan women. In any case, he did wish to apply his results toward German-centered racial goals.

Mengele's friend revealed something of this motivation when he told me that Mengele saw his work as having bearing on selecting national leaders "not on a political basis but on a biological basis." He might well have been unclear himself about his exact motivations, but we have reason to see in them a combination of distorted scientific claims and related ideological fantasies.

Mengele's treatment of twins provides important additional clues to his psychology. There we see displayed the full range of his adaptation to the Auschwitz environment. Survivors repeatedly commented on his confusing duality of affection and violence, an extreme manifestation of the process I call "doubling."

The twins lived in an atmosphere that combined sanctuary with terror. As one recalled, they never forgot they were in Auschwitz where, starting in the summer of 1944, they could clearly see "flames really coming up every day, every night" from the open pits in which bodies were burned, and they could "hear every evening a cacophony of screams" and breathe in "the unbearable smell."

Yet most of the twins were safe, under the protection of Mengele, and much of the time he treated them lovingly. According to an inmate doctor, Mengele in his contacts with the children was "as gentle as a father," talking to them and patting them on the head "in a loving way." He could be playful, jumping about to please them. The twin children frequently called him "Uncle Pepi." Sometimes, though, as the inmate doctor reported, Mengele would bring some

413

gypsy twins sweets and invite them for a ride in his car which turned out to be "a little drive with Uncle Pepi, to the gas chamber."

For many of the twins, the strength of their warm feelings toward Mengele   63
was such that they found it impossible in later years to believe the evil things they heard about him. "For us," one said, he was "like a papa, like a mama."

One inmate doctor, in his own excruciating struggles to come to terms with   64
Mengele, thought of him as "the double man" who had "all the human feelings, pity and so on," but also had in his psyche an "impenetrable, indestructible cell, which is obedience to the received order."

He was describing Mengele's Auschwitz self, the new self that can take shape   65
in virtually anyone in adapting to an extreme environment. With the Auschwitz self, Mengele's potential for evil became actual, even as he maintained elements of his prior self that included affection toward children. In this process, each part-self behaved as a functioning whole: the Auschwitz self enabling him to function in that murderous environment and to exploit its human resources with considerable efficiency; the prior self enabling him to maintain a sense of decency. His powerful commitment to Nazi ideology served as a bridge, a necessary connection between the two.

Mengele's Auschwitz behavior reflects important pre-existing psychological   66
tendencies that contributed greatly to that doubling process. His inclinations toward omnipotence and total control over others could be given extreme expression in Auschwitz.

The man and the place were dramatically summed up by a survivor who did   67
art work for him and spoke of herself as Mengele's "pet," someone who was pleasant to have around. The death camp, she said, was like a city dog pound, with Mengele as the inspector checking up on the keepers—the inmate doctors—and on the dogs—the inmates.

The inspector, she recalled, would often admonish the keepers to "wash up   68
the excrement" in the pound, "to keep it clean, to keep the dogs healthy." Then he would examine "these chambers where they are killed" and he would inquire about the dog population: "How many are you? Well, it's too crowded—you better put in two more [gas chambers] today."

This image, with its blending of omnipotence and sadism, was relevant to   69
much of Mengele's relationship to twins. "It was an axiom," one of them told me, "that Mengele is God. He used to come always with an entourage, very well decked out, very elegant. He always carried around him an aura of some terrifying threat, which is, I suspect, unexplainable to normal human beings who didn't see this." It was "literally impossible," the survivor said, "to transmit the edge of this terror."

Only in Auschwitz could Mengele assume that aura and become what the   70
inmate artist described as "a very charismatic man" with "star quality." But when she added, "Marilyn Monroe flashed through my mind," she was perhaps suggesting the strong element of mannered self-display, what is loosely called

"narcissism"—and perhaps a certain amount of kitsch and absurdity—contained in Mengele's assumption of omnipotence.

Another prior trait, Mengele's schizoid tendencies, were reflected in survivors' accounts of his "dead eyes"—eyes that showed no emotion, that avoided looking into the eyes of others. The inmate artist described him as so distant from others that "he seemed to be from a different planet." That kind of schizoid person, however friendly or affectionate at times, remains fundamentally removed from others, with inner divisions that can contribute to the doubling process. 71

Mengele's exaggerated immaculateness was consistent with such tendencies toward withdrawal. He was "very sensitive about bad smells," an inmate doctor reported, so that before he arrived, "the doors and windows had to be opened." He was "Clean, clean, clean!" one survivor said. This passion for cleanliness actually became part of Mengele's selection esthetic. He often sent prisoners with skin blemishes—even those with small abscesses or old appendectomy scars—to the gas chamber. 72

All people are capable of psychic numbing, a diminished tendency or inclination to feel. But Mengele's version of the Auschwitz self—his ease in harming and killing—carried psychic numbing to a remarkable extreme. "The main thing about him," an observant inmate-doctor stated, "was that he totally lacked feeling." He was enabled to feel nothing in killing a young twin, even one he had been fond of, to make a medical point. 73

Mengele's sadism was of a piece with these other traits. The pleasure he could take in causing pain was an aspect of his omnipotence, a means of maintaining his schizoid withdrawal and his renunciation of anything in the realm of fellow-feeling toward his victims. That kind of sadism was manifest in his smiling enthusiasm at selections. It was present in his remark to a Jewish woman doctor who was pleading vainly for the life of her father: "Your father is 70 years old. Don't you think he has lived long enough?" And survivors tell of Mengele's proclaiming on Tisha B'Av, the commemoration of the destruction of the first and second temples, "We will have a concert." There was a concert, then a roll-call, then an enormous selection for the gas chamber. 74

In his play "The Deputy," Rolf Hochhuth creates a fiendish Nazi character known only as "the Doctor," modeled after Mengele, who is described as having "the stature of Absolute Evil," as "only playing the part of a human being." 75

Some inmate-doctors also viewed Mengele as a demon and wished to divest him of his professional status. One described him as "a monster, period," and another as "no more doctor than anything else." 76

But being a doctor was part of Mengele's demonology: he took on the dark side of the omnipotent Svengali-like physician-shaman. 77

The myth of Mengele's demonic stature was given added support by the often misleading rumors about his life after Auschwitz. He was said to be living in comfort in South America, advising dictators such as Gen. Alfredo Stroessner 78 of Paraguay on how to annihilate the Indian population, growing wealthy in an extensive drug trade run by former Nazis. Nobody could touch Mengele.

We have seen that his death has partly dispelled this demonology. His 79 continuing "metamorphosis" into an ordinary mortal can be enhanced by probing his motivations and behavior.

The psychological traits Mengele brought to Auschwitz exist in many of us, 80 but in him they took exaggerated form. His impulse toward omnipotence and total control of the world around him were a means of fending off anxiety and doubt, fears of falling apart—ultimately, fear of death. That fear also activated his sadism and extreme psychic numbing. He could quiet his fears of death in that death-dominated environment by performing the ultimate act of power over another person: murder.

Yet, as far as we know, he had neither killed nor maimed prior to Auschwitz, 81 and had in fact functioned in a more or less integrated way.

The perfect match between Mengele and Auschwitz changed all that. 82 Through doubling, he could call forth his evil potential. That evil, generally speaking, is neither inherent in any self nor foreign to it. Under certain kinds of psychological and moral conditions it can emerge. Crucial to that emergence is an ideology or world view, a theory or vision that justifies or demands evil actions.

Viewed in this light, Josef Mengele emerges as he really was: a visionary 83 ideologue, an efficiently murderous functionary, a diligent careerist—and disturbingly human.

QUESTIONS

1. As paragraph 6 makes clear, this essay means to "explain" Mengele. Summarize in your own words the explanation that it offers.

2. Why were twins so important to Mengele? Are the reasons psychological, scientific, or both? What has his interest in twins got to do with the process Lifton calls "doubling" in paragraph 8?

3. Much of this essay is devoted to reporting. Where do these reports come from? What sources does Lifton identify in the article?

4. In paragraph 70 Lifton speaks of "narcissism." In what ways does Mengele seem to conform to this psychological type or depart from it?

5. "Viewed in this light," Lifton concludes, "Josef Mengele emerges as he really was: a visionary ideologue, an efficiently murderous functionary, a diligent careerist—and disturbingly human." Do you agree? Would you like to offer a different interpretation?

6. Do some research on another person supposed to have been a human monster, such as the Roman emperors Nero or Caligula or some more modern tyrant, terrorist, or torturer. (You may find legend at odds with history as you look into things.) Incorporate your research in an essay considering the kind of figure that humans find horrifying. What is it that makes these creatures both terrible and fascinating?

MAKING CONNECTIONS

Lifton speaks in paragraph 73 of "psychic numbing." Can you think of other instances of this phenomenon that you have encountered in your reading or in your experience? Is a play like Shakespeare's *Macbeth*, for instance, about "psychic numbing"? Write an essay in which you discuss this phenomenon, defining and illustrating the concept.

SOME CONDITIONS OF
OBEDIENCE AND DISOBEDIENCE
TO AUTHORITY

Stanley Milgram

*Stanley Milgram (1933–1984) was born in New York, went
to Queens College and Harvard University, and was a
professor of social psychology at the Graduate Center of the
City University of New York. The following explanation of
Milgram's experiment first appeared in the professional journal* Human Relations *in 1965 and made him famous,
causing a storm of controversy over his method of experimentation and the results of his experiment. Milgram has
said of his work, "As a social psychologist, I look at the
world not to master it in any practical sense, but to understand it and to communicate that understanding to others."*

The situation in which one agent commands another to hurt a third turns
up time and again as a significant theme in human relations.[1] It is powerfully
expressed in the story of Abraham, who is commanded by God to kill his son.
It is no accident that Kierkegaard,[2] seeking to orient his thought to the central
themes of human experience, chose Abraham's conflict as the springboard to
his philosophy.

War too moves forward on the triad of an authority which commands a
person to destroy the enemy, and perhaps all organized hostility may be viewed
as a theme and variation on the three elements of authority, executant, and
victim.[3] We describe an experimental program, recently concluded at Yale

[1]This research was supported by two grants from the National Science Foundation: NSF G-
17916 and NSF G-24152. Exploratory studies carried out in 1960 were financed by a grant from
the Higgins Funds of Yale University. I am grateful to John T. Williams, James J. McDonough,
and Emil Elges for the important part they played in the project. Thanks are due also to Alan
Elms, James Miller, Taketo Murata, and Stephen Stier for their aid as graduate assistants. My wife,
Sasha, performed many valuable services. Finally, I owe a profound debt to the many persons in
New Haven and Bridgeport who served as subjects.
[2]Søren Kierkegaard (1813–1855): Danish philosopher and theologian. [Eds.]
[3]Consider, for example, J. P. Scott's analysis of war in his monograph on aggression:
  . . . while the actions of key individuals in a war may be explained in terms of direct stimulation
to aggression, vast numbers of other people are involved simply by being part of an organized
society.
  . . . For example, at the beginning of World War I an Austrian archduke was assassinated in
Sarajevo. A few days later soldiers from all over Europe were marching toward each other, not

University, in which a particular expression of this conflict is studied by experimental means.

In its most general form the problem may be defined thus: if X tells Y to hurt Z, under what conditions will Y carry out the command of X and under what conditions will he refuse? In the more limited form possible in laboratory research, the question becomes: If an experimenter tells a subject to hurt another person, under what conditions will the subject go along with this instruction, and under what conditions will he refuse to obey? The laboratory problem is not so much a dilution of the general statement as one concrete expression of the many particular forms this question may assume.

One aim of the research was to study behavior in a strong situation of deep consequence to the participants, for the psychological forces operative in powerful and lifelike forms of the conflict may not be brought into play under diluted conditions.

This approach meant, first, that we had a special obligation to protect the welfare and dignity of the persons who took part in the study; subjects were, of necessity, placed in a difficult predicament, and steps had to be taken to ensure their wellbeing before they were discharged from the laboratory. Toward this end, a careful, post-experimental treatment was devised and has been carried through for subjects in all conditions.[4]

TERMINOLOGY

If Y follows the command of X we shall say that he has obeyed X; if he fails to carry out the command of X, we shall say that he has disobeyed X. The terms to *obey* and to *disobey*, as used here, refer to the subject's overt action

---

because they were stimulated by the archduke's misfortune, but because they had been trained to obey orders.

(Slightly rearranged from Scott (1958), *Aggression*, p. 103.)

[4]It consisted of an extended discussion with the experimenter and, of equal importance, a friendly reconciliation with the victim. It is made clear that the victim did *not* receive painful electric shocks. After the completion of the experimental series, subjects were sent a detailed report of the results and full purposes of the experimental program. A formal assessment of this procedure points to its overall effectiveness. Of the subjects, 83.7 percent indicated that they were glad to have taken part in the study; 15.1 percent reported neutral feelings; and 1.3 percent stated that they were sorry to have participated. A large number of subjects spontaneously requested that they be used in further experimentation. Four-fifths of the subjects felt that more experiments of this sort should be carried out, and 74 percent indicated that they had learned something of personal importance as a result of being in the study. Furthermore, a university psychiatrist, experienced in outpatient treatment, interviewed a sample of experimental subjects with the aim of uncovering possible injurious effects resulting from participation. No such effects were in evidence. Indeed, subjects typically felt that their participation was instructive and enriching. A more detailed discussion of this question can be found in Milgram (1964).

only, and carry no implication for the motive or experiential states accompanying the action.[5]

To be sure, the everyday use of the word *obedience* is not entirely free from complexities. It refers to action within varying situations, and connotes diverse motives within those situations: a child's obedience differs from a soldier's obedience, or the love, honor, and *obey* of the marriage vow. However, a consistent behavioral relationship is indicated in most uses of the term: in the act of obeying, a person does what another person tells him to do. Y obeys X if he carries out the prescription for action which X has addressed to him; the term suggests, moreover, that some form of dominance-subordination, or hierarchical element, is part of the situation in which the transaction between X and Y occurs.

A subject who complies with the entire series of experimental commands will be termed an *obedient* subject; one who at any point in the command series defies the experimenter will be called a *disobedient* or *defiant* subject. As used in this report the terms refer only to the subject's performance in the experiment, and do not necessarily imply a general personality disposition to submit to or reject authority.

SUBJECT POPULATION

The subjects used in all experimental conditions were male adults, residing in the greater New Haven and Bridgeport areas, aged 20 to 50 years, and

---

[5]To *obey* and to *disobey* are not the only terms one could use in describing the critical action of Y. One could say that Y is cooperating with X, or displays conformity with regard to X's commands. However, *cooperation* suggests that X agrees with Y's ends, and understands the relationship between his own behavior and the attainment of those ends. (But the experimental procedure, and, in particular, the experimenter's command that the subject shock the victim even in the absence of a response from the victim, preclude such understanding.) Moreover, cooperation implies status parity for the co-acting agents, and neglects the asymmetrical, dominance-subordination element prominent in the laboratory relationship between experimenter and subject. *Conformity* has been used in other important contexts in social psychology, and most frequently refers to imitating the judgments or actions of others when no explicit requirement for imitation has been made. Furthermore, in the present study there are two sources of social pressure; pressure from the experimenter issuing the commands, and pressure from the victim to stop the punishment. It is the pitting of a common man (the victim) against an authority (the experimenter) that is the distinctive feature of the conflict. At a point in the experiment the victim demands that he be let free. The experimenter insists that the subject continue to administer shocks. Which act of the subject can be interpreted as conformity? The subject may conform to the wishes of his peer or to the wishes of the experimenter, and conformity in one direction means the absence of conformity in the other. Thus the word has no useful reference in this setting, for the dual and conflicting social pressures cancel out its meaning.

In the final analysis, the linguistic symbol representing the subject's action must take its meaning from the concrete context in which that action occurs; and there is probably no word in everyday language that covers the experimental situation exactly, without omissions or irrelevant connotations. It is partly for convenience, therefore, that the terms *obey* and *disobey* are used to describe the engaged in a wide variety of occupations. Each experimental condition described in this report employed 40 fresh subjects and was carefully balanced for age and occupational types. The occupational composition for each experiment was: workers, skilled and unskilled: 40 percent; white collar, sales, business: 40 percent; professionals: 20 percent. The occupations were intersected with three age categories (subjects in 20's, 30's, and 40's, assigned to each condition in the proportions of 20, 40, and 40 percent, respectively).

THE GENERAL LABORATORY PROCEDURE[6]

The focus of the study concerns the amount of electric shock a subject is   10
willing to administer to another person when ordered by an experimenter to give the "victim" increasingly more severe punishment. The act of administering shock is set in the context of a learning experiment, ostensibly designed to study the effect of punishment on memory. Aside from the experimenter, one naïve subject and one accomplice perform in each session. On arrival each subject is paid $4.50. After a general talk by the experimenter, telling how little scientists know about the effect of punishment on memory, subjects are informed that one member of the pair will serve as teacher and one as learner. A rigged drawing is held so that the naïve subject is always the teacher, and the accomplice becomes the learner. The learner is taken to an adjacent room and strapped into an "electric chair."

The naïve subject is told that it is his task to teach the learner a list of paired   11
associates, to test him on the list, and to administer punishment whenever the learner errs in the test. Punishment takes the form of electric shock, delivered to the learner by means of a shock generator controlled by the naïve subject. The teacher is instructed to increase the intensity of electric shock one step on the generator on each error. The learner, according to plan, provides many wrong answers, so that before long the naïve subject must give him the strongest shock on the generator. Increases in shock level are met by increasingly insistent demands from the learner that the experiment be stopped because of the growing discomfort to him. However, in clear terms the experimenter orders the teacher to continue with the procedure in disregard of the learner's protests. *Thus, the naïve subject must resolve a conflict between two mutually incompatible demands*

---

subject's actions. At the same time, our use of the words is highly congruent with dictionary meaning.

[6]A more detailed account of the laboratory procedure can be found in Milgram (1963). A similar and independently evolved experimental procedure, employing a shock generator, victim, and learning task, was reported by Buss (1961). Buss used the technique for studying aggression, not obedience, and did not make use of the fundamental measure employed in the present study: breakoff points.

from the social field. He may continue to follow the orders of the experimenter and shock the learner with increasing severity, or he may refuse to follow the orders of the experimenter and heed the learner's pleas. The experimenter's authority operates not in a free field, but against ever-mounting countervailing pressure from the person being punished.

A few technical points need to be considered before the findings of the study 12 are described. For the purpose of delivering shock, a simulated shock generator is used, with 30 clearly marked voltage levels that range from 15 to 450 volts. (Each level is activated by one of 30 individual lever switches set in a horizontal line.) The naïve subject is given a sample shock of 45 volts to convince him of the authenticity of the instrument. The generator bears verbal designations that range from "Slight Shock" to "Danger: Severe Shock."

The responses of the victim are standardized on tape, and each protest is 13 coordinated to a particular voltage level on the shock generator. Starting with 75 volts the learner begins to grunt and moan. At 150 volts he demands to be let out of the experiment. At 180 volts he cries out that he can no longer stand the pain. At 300 volts he refuses to provide any more answers to the memory test, insisting that he is no longer a participant in the experiment and must be freed. In response to this last tactic, the experimenter instructs the naïve subject to treat the absence of an answer as equivalent to a wrong answer, and to follow the usual shock procedure. The experimenter reinforces his demand with the statement: "You have no other choice, you must go on!" (This imperative is used whenever the naïve subject tries to break off the experiment.) If the subject refuses to give the next higher level of shock, the experiment is considered at an end. A quantitative value is assigned to the subject's performance based on the maximum-intensity shock he administered before breaking off. Thus any subject's score may range from zero (for a subject unwilling to administer the first shock level) to 30 (for a subject who proceeds to the highest voltage level on the board). For any particular subject and for any particular experimental condition, the degree to which participants have followed the experimenter's orders may be specified with a numerical value, corresponding to the metric on the shock generator.

This laboratory situation gives us a framework in which to study the subject's 14 reactions to the principal conflict of the experiment. Again, this conflict is between the experimenter's demands that he continue to administer the electric shock, and the learner's demands, which become increasingly more insistent, that the experiment be stopped. The crux of the study is to vary systematically the factors believed to alter the degree of obedience to the experimental commands, to learn under what conditions submission to authority is most probable and under what conditions defiance is brought to the fore.

PILOT STUDIES

Pilot studies for the present research were completed in the winter of 1960; 15
they differed from the regular experiments in a few details: for one, the victim
was placed behind a silvered glass, with the light balance on the glass such that
the victim could be dimly perceived by the subject (Milgram, 1961).

Though essentially qualitative in treatment, these studies pointed to several 16
significant features of the experimental situation. At first no vocal feedback was
used from the victim. It was thought that the verbal and voltage designations
on the control panel would create sufficient pressure to curtail the subject's
obedience. However, this was not the case. In the absence of protests from the
learner, virtually all subjects, once commanded, went blithely to the end of the
board, seemingly indifferent to the verbal designations ("Extreme Shock" and
"Danger: Severe Shock"). This deprived us of an adequate basis for scaling
obedient tendencies. A force had to be introduced that would strengthen the
subject's resistance to the experimenter's commands, and reveal individual
differences in terms of a distribution of break-off points.

This force took the form of protests from the victim. Initially, mild protests 17
were used, but proved inadequate. Subsequently, more vehement protests were
inserted into the experimental procedure. To our consternation, even the strongest protests from the victim did not prevent all subjects from administering the
harshest punishment ordered by the experimenter; but the protests did lower
the mean maximum shock somewhat and created some spread in the subject's
performance; therefore, the victim's cries were standardized on tape and incorporated into the regular experimental procedure.

The situation did more than highlight the technical difficulties of finding a 18
workable experimental procedure: It indicated that subjects would obey authority
to a greater extent than we had supposed. It also pointed to the importance of
feedback from the victim in controlling the subject's behavior.

One further aspect of the pilot study was that subjects frequently averted 19
their eyes from the person they were shocking, often turning their heads in an
awkward and conspicuous manner. One subject explained: "I didn't want to see
the consequences of what I had done." Observers wrote:

> . . . subjects showed a reluctance to look at the victim, whom they
> could see through the glass in front of them. When this fact was brought
> to their attention they indicated that it caused them discomfort to see
> the victim in agony. We note, however, that although the subject refuses
> to look at the victim, he continues to administer shocks.

This suggested that the salience of the victim may have, in some degree, 20
regulated the subject's performance. If, in obeying the experimenter, the subject
found it necessary to avoid scrutiny of the victim, would the converse be true?

If the victim were rendered increasingly more salient to the subject, would obedience diminish? The first set of regular experiments was designed to answer this question.

IMMEDIACY OF THE VICTIM

This series consisted of four experimental conditions. In each condition the   21
victim was brought "psychologically" closer to the subject giving him shocks.

In the first condition (Remote Feedback) the victim was placed in another   22
room and could not be heard or seen by the subject, except that, at 300 volts,
he pounded on the wall in protest. After 315 volts he no longer answered or
was heard from.

The second condition (Voice Feedback) was identical to the first except that   23
voice protests were introduced. As in the first condition the victim was placed
in an adjacent room, but his complaints could be heard clearly through a door
left slightly ajar and through the walls of the laboratory.[7]

The third experimental condition (Proximity) was similar to the second,   24
except that the victim was now placed in the same room as the subject, and 1⅗
feet from him. Thus he was visible as well as audible, and voice cues were
provided.

The fourth, and final, condition of this series (Touch-Proximity) was identical   25

---

[7] It is difficult to convey on the printed page the full tenor of the victim's responses, for we have
no adequate notation for vocal intensity, timing, and general qualities of delivery. Yet these features
are crucial to producing the effect of an increasingly severe reaction to mounting voltage levels.
(They can be communicated fully only by sending interested parties the recorded tapes.) In general
terms, however, the victim indicates no discomfort until the 75-volt shock is administered, at which
time there is a light grunt in response to the punishment. Similar reactions follow the 90- and 105-
volt shocks, and at 120 volts the victim shouts to the experimenter that the shocks are becoming
painful. Painful groans are heard on administration of the 135-volt shock, and at 150 volts the
victim cries out, 'Experimenter, get me out of here! I won't be in the experiment any more! I refuse
to go on!' Cries of this type continue with generally rising intensity, so that at 180 volts the victim
cries out, 'I can't stand the pain,' and by 270 volts his response to the shock is definitely an agonized
scream. Throughout, he insists that he be let out of the experiment. At 300 volts the victim shouts
in desperation that he will no longer provide answers to the memory test; and at 315 volts, after a
violent scream, he reaffirms with vehemence that he is no longer a participant. From this point
on, he provides no answers, but shrieks in agony whenever a shock is administered; this continues
through 450 volts. Of course, many subjects will have broken off before this point.

A revised and stronger set of protests was used in all experiments outside the Proximity series.   86
Naturally, new baseline measures were established for all comparisons using the new set of protests.

There is overwhelming evidence that the great majority of subjects, both obedient and defiant,   87
accepted the victims' reactions as genuine. The evidence takes the form of: (a) tension created in
the subjects (see discussion of tension); (b) scores on "estimated-pain" scales filled out by subjects
immediately after the experiment; (c) subjects' accounts of their feelings in post-experimental
interviews; and (d) quantifiable responses to questionnaires distributed to subjects several months
after their participation in the experiments. This matter will be treated fully in a forthcoming
monograph.

(The procedure in all experimental conditions was to have the naïve subject announce the   88
voltage level before administering each shock, so that—independently of the victim's responses—
he was continually reminded of delivering punishment of ever-increasing severity.)

to the third, with this exception: The victim received a shock only when his hand rested on a shockplate. At the 150-volt level the victim again demanded to be let free and, in this condition, refused to place his hand on the shockplate. The experimenter ordered the naïve subject to force the victim's hand onto the plate. Thus obedience in this condition required that the subject have physical contact with the victim in order to give him punishment beyond the 150-volt level.

Forty adult subjects were studied in each condition. The data revealed that obedience was significantly reduced as the victim was rendered more immediate to the subject. The mean maximum shock for the conditions is shown in Figure 1. 26

Expressed in terms of the proportion of obedient to defiant subjects, the findings are that 34 percent of the subjects defied the experimenter in the Remote condition, 37.5 percent in Voice Feedback, 60 percent in Proximity, and 70 percent in Touch-Proximity. 27

How are we to account for this effect? A first conjecture might be that as the victim was brought closer the subject became more aware of the intensity 28

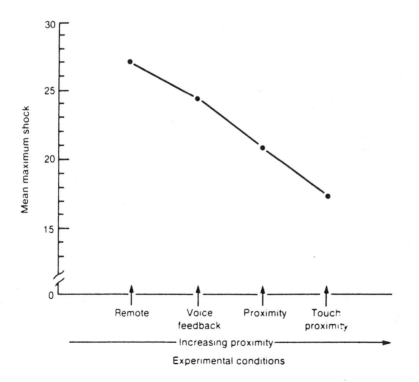

Figure 1. Mean maxima in proximity series.

of his suffering and regulated his behavior accordingly. This makes sense, but our evidence does not support the interpretation. There are no consistent differences in the attributed level of pain across the four conditions (i.e. the amount of pain experienced by the victim as estimated by the subject and expressed on a 14-point scale). But it is easy to speculate about alternative mechanisms:

Empathic cues. In the Remote and to a lesser extent the Voice Feedback   29
conditions, the victim's suffering possesses an abstract, remote quality for the subject. He is aware, but only in a conceptual sense, that his actions cause pain to another person; the fact is apprehended, but not felt. The phenomenon is common enough. The bombardier can reasonably suppose that his weapons will inflict suffering and death, yet this knowledge is divested of affect and does not move him to a felt, emotional response to the suffering resulting from his actions. Similar observations have been made in wartime. It is possible that the visual cues associated with the victim's suffering trigger empathic responses in the subject and provide him with a more complete grasp of the victim's experience. Or it is possible that the empathic responses are themselves unpleasant, possessing drive properties which cause the subject to terminate the arousal situation. Diminishing obedience, then, would be explained by the enrichment of empathic cues in the successive experimental conditions.

Denial and narrowing of the cognitive field. The Remote condition allows a   30
narrowing of the cognitive field so that the victim is put out of mind. The subject no longer considers the act of depressing a lever relevant to moral judgment, for it is no longer associated with the victim's suffering. When the victim is close it is more difficult to exclude him phenomenologically. He necessarily intrudes on the subject's awareness since he is continuously visible. In the Remote condition his existence and reactions are made known only after the shock has been administered. The auditory feedback is sporadic and discontinuous. In the Proximity conditions his inclusion in the immediate visual field renders him a continuously salient element for the subject. The mechanism of denial can no longer be brought into play. One subject in the Remote condition said: "It's funny how you really begin to forget that there's a guy out there, even though you can hear him. For a long time I just concentrated on pressing the switches and reading the words."

Reciprocal fields. If in the Proximity condition the subject is in an improved   31
position to observe the victim, the reverse is also true. The actions of the subject now come under proximal scrutiny by the victim. Possibly, it is easier to harm a person when he is unable to observe our actions than when he can see what we are doing. His surveillance of the action directed against him may give rise to shame, or guilt, which may then serve to curtail the action. Many expressions of language refer to the discomfort or inhibitions that arise

426

in face-to-face confrontation. It is often said that it is easier to criticize a man "behind his back" than to "attack him to his face." If we are in the process of lying to a person it is reputedly difficult to "stare him in the eye." We "turn away from others in shame" or in "embarrassment" and this action serves to reduce our discomfort. The manifest function of allowing the victim of a firing squad to be blindfolded is to make the occasion less stressful for him, but it may also serve a latent function of reducing the stress of the executioner. In short, in the Proximity conditions, the subject may sense that he has become more salient in the victim's field of awareness. Possibly he becomes more self-conscious, embarrassed, and inhibited in his punishment of the victim.

Phenomenal unity of act. In the Remote condition it is more difficult for the subject to gain a sense of *relatedness* between his own actions and the consequences of these actions for the victim. There is a physical and spatial separation of the act and its consequences. The subject depresses a lever in one room, and protests and cries are heard from another. The two events are in correlation, yet they lack a compelling phenomenological unity. The structure of a meaningful act—*I am hurting a man* — breaks down because of the spatial arrangements, in a manner somewhat analogous to the disappearance of phi phenomena[8] when the blinking lights are spaced too far apart. The unity is more fully achieved in the Proximity condition as the victim is brought closer to the action that causes him pain. It is rendered complete in Touch-Proximity.   32

Incipient group formation. Placing the victim in another room not only takes him further from the subject, but the subject and the experimenter are drawn relatively closer. There is incipient group formation between the experimenter and the subject, from which the victim is excluded. The wall between the victim and the others deprives him of an intimacy which the experimenter and subject feel. In the Remote condition, the victim is truly an outsider, who stands alone, physically and psychologically.   33

When the victim is placed close to the subject, it becomes easier to form an alliance with him against the experimenter. Subjects no longer have to face the experimenter alone. They have an ally who is close at hand and eager to collaborate in a revolt against the experimenter. Thus, the changing set of spatial relations leads to a potentially shifting set of alliances over the several experimental conditions.   34

Acquired behavior dispositions. It is commonly observed that laboratory mice will rarely fight with their litter mates. Scott (1958) explains this in terms of passive inhibition. He writes: "By doing nothing under . . . circumstances   35

---

[8]phi phenomena: the optical impression of motion generated when similar stationary objects are presented one after another at a certain interval. [Eds.]

[the animal] learns to do nothing, and this may be spoken of as passive inhibition . . . this principle has great importance in teaching an individual to be peaceful, for it means that he can learn not to fight simply by not fighting." Similarly, we may learn not to harm others simply by not harming them in everyday life. Yet this learning occurs in a context of proximal relations with others, and may not be generalized to that situation in which the person is physically removed from us. Or possibly, in the past, aggressive actions against others who were physically close resulted in retaliatory punishment which extinguished the original form of response. In contrast, aggression against others at a distance may have only sporadically led to retaliation. Thus the organism learns that it is safer to be aggressive toward others at a distance, and precarious to be so when the parties are within arm's reach. Through a pattern of rewards and punishments, he acquires a disposition to avoid aggression at close quarters, a disposition which does not extend to harming others at a distance. And this may account for experimental findings in the remote and proximal experiments.

Proximity as a variable in psychological research has received far less attention   36
than it deserves. If men were sessile[9] it would be easy to understand this neglect. But we move about; our spatial relations shift from one situation to the next, and the fact that we are near or remote may have a powerful effect on the psychological processes that mediate our behavior toward others. In the present situation, as the victim is brought closer to the subject ordered to give him shocks, increasing numbers of subjects break off the experiment, refusing to obey. The concrete, visible, and proximal presence of the victim acts in an important way to counteract the experimenter's power to generate disobedience.[10]

CLOSENESS OF AUTHORITY

If the spatial relationship of the subject and victim is relevant to the degree   37
of obedience, would not the relationship of subject to experimenter also play a part?

There are reasons to feel that, on arrival, the subject is oriented primarily to   38
the experimenter rather than to the victim. He has come to the laboratory to fit into the structure that the experimenter—not the victim—would provide.

---

[9] sessile: permanently attached. [Eds.]

[10] Admittedly, the terms *proximity, immediacy, closeness,* and *salience-of-the-victim* are used in a loose sense, and the experiments themselves represent a very coarse treatment of the variable. Further experiments are needed to refine the notion and tease out such diverse factors as spatial distance, visibility, audibility, barrier interposition, etc.

The Proximity and Touch-Proximity experiments were the only conditions where we were   89
unable to use taped feedback from the victim. Instead, the victim was trained to respond in these conditions as he had in Experiment 2 (which employed taped feedback). Some improvement is possible here, for it should be technically feasible to do a proximity series using taped feedback.

He has come less to understand his behavior than to *reveal* that behavior to a competent scientist, and he is willing to display himself as the scientist's purposes require. Most subjects seem quite concerned about the appearance they are making before the experimenter, and one could argue that this preoccupation in a relatively new and strange setting makes the subject somewhat insensitive to the triadic nature of the social situation. In other words, the subject is so concerned about the show he is putting on for the experimenter that influences from other parts of the social field do not receive as much weight as they ordinarily would. This overdetermined orientation to the experimenter would account for the relative insensitivity of the subject to the victim, and would also lead us to believe that alterations in the relationship between subject and experimenter would have important consequences for obedience.

In a series of experiments we varied the physical closeness and degree of surveillance of the experimenter. In one condition the experimenter sat just a few feet away from the subject. In a second condition, after giving initial instructions, the experimenter left the laboratory and gave his orders by telephone. In still a third condition the experimenter was never seen, providing instructions by means of a tape recording activated when the subjects entered the laboratory.

Obedience dropped sharply as the experimenter was physically removed from the laboratory. The number of obedient subjects in the first condition (Experimenter Present) was almost three times as great as in the second, where the experimenter gave his orders by telephone. Twenty-six subjects were fully obedient in the first condition, and only nine in the second (Chi square obedient vs. defiant in the two conditions, df = 14.7; $p < 0.001$). Subjects seemed able to take a far stronger stand against the experimenter when they did not have to encounter him face to face, and the experimenter's power over the subject was severely curtailed.[11]

Moreover, when the experimenter was absent, subjects displayed an interesting form of behavior that had not occurred under his surveillance. Though continuing with the experiment, several subjects administered lower shocks than were required and never informed the experimenter of their deviation from the correct procedure. (Unknown to the subjects, shock levels were automatically recorded by an Esterline-Angus event recorder wired directly into the shock generator; the instrument provided us with an objective record of the subjects' performance.) Indeed, in telephone conversations some subjects specifically assured the experimenter that they were raising the shock level according to instruction, whereas in fact they were repeatedly using the lowest shock on the board. This form of behavior is particularly interesting: although these subjects acted in a way that clearly undermined the avowed purposes of the experiment,

---

[11] The third condition also led to significantly lower obedience than this first situation in which the experimenter was present, but it contains technical difficulties that require extensive discussion.

they found it easier to handle the conflict in this manner than to precipitate an open break with authority.

Other conditions were completed in which the experimenter was absent 42 during the first segment of the experiment, but reappeared at the point that the subject definitely refused to give higher shocks when commanded by telephone. Although he had exhausted his power via telephone, the experimenter could frequently force further obedience when he reappeared in the laboratory.

Experiments in this series show that the *physical presence* of an authority is 43 an important force contributing to the subject's obedience or defiance. Taken together with the first experimental series on the proximity of the victim, it would appear that something akin to fields of force, diminishing in effectiveness with increasing psychological distance from their source, have a controlling effect on the subject's performance. As the victim is brought closer, the subject finds it harder to administer shocks to him. When the victim's position is held constant relative to the subject, and the authority is made more remote, the subject finds it easier to break off the experiment. This effect is substantial in both cases, but manipulation of the experimenter's position yielded the more powerful results. Obedience to destructive commands is highly dependent on the proximal relations between authority and subject.

TENSIONS

The description of final scores does not fully convey the character of the 44 subjects' performance, and it would be useful to interrupt our reporting of quantitative relationships to remark on the subjects' general reaction to the situation.

One might suppose that a subject would simply break off or continue as his 45 conscience and temperament dictated. Yet this is very far from what happened. There were powerful reactions of tension and emotional strain in a substantial proportion of the participants. Persons were observed to sweat, tremble, stutter, bite their lips, and groan as they found themselves increasingly implicated in the experimental conflict. Some sense of the subjects' mood can be found in a transcript of their remarks at break-off point. Here are the remarks of two defiant subjects:

> Is he banging? . . . Is he hurt out there? Well, I don't want to be responsible for anything that happens to him. No, I can't go on with it. I don't know whether he's all right or not. I mean he may have a heart condition or something; I wouldn't feel right doing it. He's banging for help. He's evidently in trouble or he wouldn't bang . . . I don't see any sense to this—to knocking him out or something. I just can't see it.
> [*Subject refuses to administer shocks*]   [*Subject 0108*]

The man is banging. He wants to get out . . . I'm sorry. If the man wants to get out I'd just as soon stop . . . I don't want to administer any more [extremely excited] . . . I will gladly refund the check, but I will not harm this man . . . I'm sorry, I will not give him any more if he obviously wants to get out. There is no money in the world that will make me hurt another individual.

[*Subject 010X*]

And here is a transcript from an obedient subject. He began the experiment calmly, but became increasingly tense as the experiment proceeded. After administering the 150-volt shock, he began to address the experimenter in agitated tones: 46

150 volts delivered. You want me to keep going?

165 volts delivered. That guy is hollering in there. There's a lot of them here. He's liable to have a heart condition. You want me to go?

180 volts delivered. He can't stand it! I'm not going to kill that man in there! You hear him hollering? He's hollering. He can't stand it. What if something happens to him? . . . I'm not going to get that man sick in there. He's hollering in there. You know what I mean? I mean I refuse to take responsibility. He's getting hurt in there. He's in there hollering. Too many left here. Geez, if he gets them wrong. There's too many of them left. I mean who is going to take responsibility if anything happens to that gentleman?

[*The experimenter accepts responsibility.*] All right.

195 volts delivered. You see he's hollering. Hear that. Gee, I don't know.

[*The experimenter says: 'The experiment requires that you go on.'*]—I know it does, sir, but I mean—hugh—he don't know what he's in for. He's up to 195 volts.

210 volts delivered.

225 volts delivered.

240 volts delivered. Aw, no. You mean I've got to keep going up with the scale? No sir. I'm not going to kill that man! I'm not going to give him 450 volts!

[*The experimenter says: 'The experiment requires that you go on.'*]—I know it does, but that man is hollering there, sir . . .

Despite his numerous, agitated objections, which were constant accompaniments to his actions, the subject unfailingly obeyed the experimenter, proceeding to the highest shock level on the generator. He displayed a curious dissociation between word and action. Although at the verbal level he had resolved not to go on, his actions were fully in accord with the experimenter's commands. This subject did not want to shock the victim, and he found it an extremely disagreeable task, but he was unable to invent a response that would

431

free him from *E*'s authority. Many subjects cannot find the specific verbal formula that would enable them to reject the role assigned to them by the experimenter. Perhaps our culture does not provide adequate models for disobedience.

One puzzling sign of tension was the regular occurrence of nervous laughing fits. In the first four conditions 71 of the 160 subjects showed definite signs of nervous laughter and smiling. The laughter seemed entirely out of place, even bizarre. Full-blown, uncontrollable seizures were observed for 15 of these subjects. On one occasion we observed a seizure so violently convulsive that it was necessary to call a halt to the experiment. In the post-experimental interviews subjects took pains to point out that they were not sadistic types and that the laughter did not mean they enjoyed shocking the victim. 47

In the interview following the experiment subjects were asked to indicate on a 14-point scale just how nervous or tense they felt at the point of maximum tension (Figure 2). The scale ranged from "not at all tense and nervous" to 48

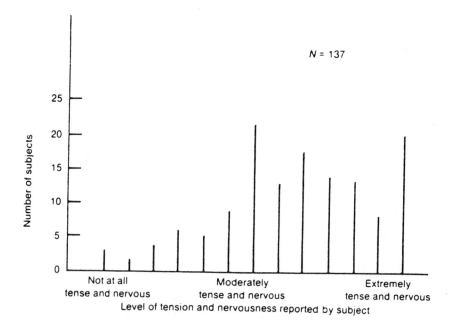

FIGURE 2. Level of tension and nervousness: the self-reports on "tension and nervousness" for 137 subjects in the Proximity experiments. Subjects were given a scale with 14 values ranging from "not at all tense and nervous" to "extremely tense and nervous." They were instructed: "Thinking back to that point in the experiment when you felt the most tense and nervous, indicate just how you felt by placing an X at the appropriate point on the scale." The results are shown in terms of midpoint values.

432

"extremely tense and nervous." Self-reports of this sort are of limited precision and at best provide only a rough indication of the subject's emotional response. Still, taking the reports for what they are worth, it can be seen that the distribution of responses spans the entire range of the scale, with the majority of subjects concentrated at the center and upper extreme. A further breakdown showed that obedient subjects reported themselves as having been slightly more tense and nervous than the defiant subjects at the point of maximum tension.

How is the occurrence of tension to be interpreted? First, it points to the presence of conflict. If a tendency to comply with authority were the only psychological force operating in the situation, all subjects would have continued to the end and there would have been no tension. Tension, it is assumed, results from the simultaneous presence of two or more incompatible response tendencies (Miller, 1944). If sympathetic concern for the victim were the exclusive force, all subjects would have calmly defied the experimenter. Instead, there were both obedient and defiant outcomes, frequently accompanied by extreme tension. A conflict develops between the deeply ingrained disposition not to harm others and the equally compelling tendency to obey others who are in authority. The subject is quickly drawn into a dilemma of a deeply dynamic character, and the presence of high tension points to the considerable strength of each of the antagonistic vectors. 49

Moreover, tension defines the strength of the aversive state from which the subject is unable to escape through disobedience. When a person is uncomfortable, tense, or stressed, he tries to take some action that will allow him to terminate this unpleasant state. Thus tension may serve as a drive that leads to escape behavior. But in the present situation, even where tension is extreme, many subjects are unable to perform the response that will bring about relief. Therefore there must be a competing drive, tendency, or inhibition that precludes activation of the disobedient response. The strength of this inhibiting factor must be of greater magnitude than the stress experienced, or else the terminating act would occur. Every evidence of extreme tension is at the same time an indication of the strength of the forces that keep the subject in the situation. 50

Finally, tension may be taken as evidence of the reality of the situations for the subjects. Normal subjects do not tremble and sweat unless they are implicated in a deep and genuinely felt predicament. 51

BACKGROUND AUTHORITY

In psychophysics, animal learning, and other branches of psychology, the fact that measures are obtained at one institution rather than another is irrelevant to the interpretation of the findings, so long as the technical facilities for measurement are adequate and the operations are carried out with competence. 52

But it cannot be assumed that this holds true for the present study. The 53 effectiveness of the experimenter's commands may depend in an important way on the larger institutional context in which they are issued. The experiments described thus far were conducted at Yale University, an organization which most subjects regarded with respect and sometimes awe. In post-experimental interviews several participants remarked that the locale and sponsorship of the study gave them confidence in the integrity, competence, and benign purposes of the personnel; many indicated that they would not have shocked the learner if the experiments had been done elsewhere.

This issue of background authority seemed to us important for an interpre- 54 tation of the results that had been obtained thus far; moreover it is highly relevant to any comprehensive theory of human obedience. Consider, for example, how closely our compliance with the imperatives of others is tied to particular institutions and locales in our day-to-day activities. On request, we expose our throats to a man with a razor blade in the barber shop, but would not do so in a shoe store; in the latter setting we willingly follow the clerk's request to stand in our stockinged feet, but resist the command in a bank. In the laboratory of a great university, subjects may comply with a set of commands that would be resisted if given elsewhere. *One must always question the relationship of obedience to a person's sense of the context in which he is operating.*

To explore the problem we moved our apparatus to an office building in 55 industrial Bridgeport and replicated experimental conditions, without any visible tie to the university.

Bridgeport subjects were invited to the experiment through a mail circular 56 similar to the one used in the Yale study, with appropriate changes in letterhead, etc. As in the earlier study, subjects were paid $4.50 for coming to the laboratory. The same age and occupational distributions used at Yale and the identical personnel were employed.

The purpose in relocating in Bridgeport was to assure a complete dissociation 57 from Yale, and in this regard we were fully successful. On the surface, the study appeared to be conducted by Research Associates of Bridgeport, an organization of unknown character (the title had been concocted exclusively for use in this study).

The experiments were conducted in a three-room office suite in a somewhat 58 run-down commercial building located in the downtown shopping area. The laboratory was sparsely furnished, though clean, and marginally respectable in appearance. When subjects inquired about professional affiliations, they were informed only that we were a private firm conducting research for industry.

Some subjects displayed skepticism concerning the motives of the Bridgeport 59 experimenter. One gentleman gave us a written account of the thoughts he experienced at the control board:

> . . . Should I quit this damn test? Maybe he passed out? What dopes we were not to check up on this deal. How do we know that these guys

434

are legit? No furniture, bare walls, no telephone. We could of called the Police up or the Better Business Bureau. I learned a lesson tonight. How do I know that Mr. Williams [the experimenter] is telling the truth . . . I wish I knew how many volts a person could take before lapsing into unconsciousness . . .   [*Subject 2414*]

Another subject stated:

> I questioned on my arrival my own judgment [about coming]. I had doubts as to the legitimacy of the operation and the consequences of participation. I felt it was a heartless way to conduct memory or learning processes on human beings and certainly dangerous without the presence of a medical doctor.   [*Subject 2440V*]

There was no noticeable reduction in tension for the Bridgeport subjects. 60 And the subjects' estimation of the amount of pain felt by the victim was slightly, though not significantly, higher than in the Yale study.

A failure to obtain complete obedience in Bridgeport would indicate that the 61 extreme compliance found in New Haven subjects was tied closely to the background authority of Yale University; if a large proportion of the subjects remained fully obedient, very different conclusions would be called for.

As it turned out, the level of obedience in Bridgeport, although somewhat 62 reduced, was not significantly lower than that obtained at Yale. A large proportion of the Bridgeport subjects were fully obedient to the experimenter's commands (48 percent of the Bridgeport subjects delivered the maximum shock versus 65 percent in the corresponding condition at Yale).

How are these findings to be interpreted? It is possible that if commands of 63 a potentially harmful or destructive sort are to be perceived as legitimate they must occur within some sort of institutional structure. But it is clear from the study that it need not be a particularly reputable or distinguished institution. The Bridgeport experiments were conducted by an unimpressive firm lacking any credentials; the laboratory was set up in a respectable office building with a title listed in the building directory. Beyond that, there was no evidence of benevolence or competence. It is possible that the *category* of institution, judged according to its professed function, rather than its qualitative position within that category, wins our compliance. Persons deposit money in elegant, but also in seedy-looking banks, without giving much thought to the differences in security they offer. Similarly, our subjects may consider one laboratory to be as competent as another, so long as it is a scientific laboratory.

It would be valuable to study the subjects' performance in other contexts 64 which go even further than the Bridgeport study in denying institutional support to the experimenter. It is possible that, beyond a certain point, obedience disappears completely. But that point had not been reached in the Bridgeport office: almost half the subjects obeyed the experimenter fully.

FURTHER EXPERIMENTS

We may mention briefly some additional experiments undertaken in the Yale ⁶⁵ series. A considerable amount of obedience and defiance in everyday life occurs in connection with groups. And we had reason to feel in light of the many group studies already done in psychology that group forces would have a profound effect on reactions to authority. A series of experiments was run to examine these effects. In all cases only one naïve subject was studied per hour, but he performed in the midst of actors who, unknown to him, were employed by the experimenter. In one experiment (Groups for Disobedience) two actors broke off in the middle of the experiment. When this happened 90 percent of the subjects followed suit and defied the experimenter. In another condition the actors followed the orders obediently; this strengthened the experimenter's power only slightly. In still a third experiment the job of pushing the switch to shock the learner was given to one of the actors, while the naïve subject performed a subsidiary act. We wanted to see how the teacher would respond if he were involved in the situation but did not actually give the shocks. In this situation only three subjects out of forty broke off. In a final group experiment the subjects themselves determined the shock level they were going to use. Two actors suggested higher and higher shock levels; some subjects insisted, despite group pressure, that the shock level be kept low; others followed along with the group.

Further experiments were completed using women as subjects, as well as a ⁶⁶ set dealing with the effects of dual, unsanctioned, and conflicting authority. A final experiment concerned the personal relationship between victim and subject. These will have to be described elsewhere, lest the present report be extended to monographic length.

It goes without saying that future research can proceed in many different ⁶⁷ directions. What kinds of response from the victim are most effective in causing disobedience in the subject? Perhaps passive resistance is more effective than vehement protest. What conditions of entry into an authority system lead to greater or lesser obedience? What is the effect of anonymity and masking on the subject's behavior? What conditions lead to the subject's perception of responsibility for his own actions? Each of these could be a major research topic in itself, and can readily be incorporated into the general experimental procedure described here.

LEVELS OF OBEDIENCE AND DEFIANCE

One general finding that merits attention is the high level of obedience ⁶⁸ manifested in the experimental situation. Subjects often expressed deep disapproval of shocking a man in the face of his objections, and others denounced it as senseless and stupid. Yet many subjects complied even while they protested.

The proportion of obedient subjects greatly exceeded the expectations of the experimenter and his colleagues. At the outset, we had conjectured that subjects would not, in general, go above the level of "Strong Shock." In practice, many subjects were willing to administer the most extreme shocks available when commanded by the experimenter. For some subjects the experiment provided an occasion for aggressive release. And for others it demonstrated the extent to which obedient dispositions are deeply ingrained and engaged, irrespective of their consequences for others. Yet this is not the whole story. Somehow, the subject becomes implicated in a situation from which he cannot disengage himself.

The departure of the experimental results from intelligent expectation, to some extent, has been formalized. The procedure was to describe the experimental situation in concrete detail to a group of competent persons, and to ask them to predict the performance of 100 hypothetical subjects. For purposes of indicating the distribution of break-off points, judges were provided with a diagram of the shock generator and recorded their predictions before being informed of the actual results. Judges typically underestimated the amount of obedience demonstrated by subjects. 69

In Figure 3, we compare the predictions of forty psychiatrists at a leading medical school with the actual performance of subjects in the experiment. The psychiatrists predicted that most subjects would not go beyond the tenth shock level (150 volts; at this point the victim makes his first explicit demand to be freed). They further predicted that by the twentieth shock level (300 volts; the victim refuses to answer) 3.73 percent of the subjects would still be obedient; and that only a little over one-tenth of one percent of the subjects would administer the highest shock on the board. But, as the graph indicates, the obtained behavior was very different. Sixty-two percent of the subjects obeyed the experimenter's commands fully. Between expectation and occurrence there is a whopping discrepancy. 70

Why did the psychiatrists underestimate the level of obedience? Possibly, because their predictions were based on an inadequate conception of the determinants of human action, a conception that focuses on motives *in vacuo*. This orientation may be entirely adequate for the repair of bruised impulses as revealed on the psychiatrist's couch, but as soon as our interest turns to action in larger settings, attention must be paid to the situations in which motives are expressed. A situation exerts an important press on the individual. It exercises constraints and may provide push. In certain circumstances it is not so much the kind of person a man is, as the kind of situation in which he is placed, that determines his actions. 71

Many people, not knowing much about the experiment, claim that subjects who go to the end of the board are sadistic. Nothing could be more foolish than an overall characterization of these persons. It is like saying that a person thrown into a swift-flowing stream is necessarily a fast swimmer, or that he has 72

437

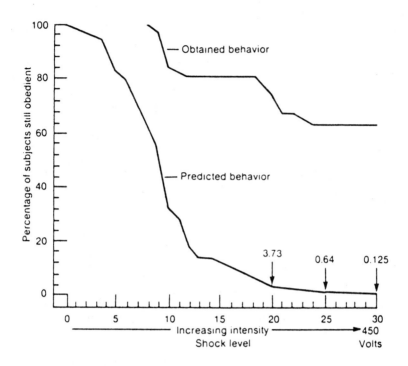

FIGURE 3. Predicted and obtained behavior in voice feedback.

great stamina because he moves so rapidly relative to the bank. The context of action must always be considered. The individual, upon entering the laboratory, becomes integrated into a situation that carries its own momentum. The subject's problem then is how to become disengaged from a situation which is moving in an altogether ugly direction.

The fact that disengagement is so difficult testifies to the potency of the 73 forces that keep the subject at the control board. Are these forces to be conceptualized as individual motives and expressed in the language of personality dynamics, or are they to be seen as the effects of social structure and pressures arising from the situational field?

A full understanding of the subject's action will, I feel, require that both 74 perspectives be adopted. The person brings to the laboratory enduring dispositions toward authority and aggression, and at the same time he becomes enmeshed in a social structure that is no less an objective fact of the case. From the standpoint of personality theory one may ask: What mechanisms of personality enable a person to transfer responsibility to authority? What are the motives underlying obedient and disobedient performance? Does orientation to authority lead to a short-circuiting of the shame-guilt system? What cognitive and emotional defenses are brought into play in the case of obedient and defiant subjects?

The present experiments are not, however, directed toward an exploration of the motives engaged when the subject obeys the experimenter's commands. Instead, they examine the situational variables responsible for the elicitation of obedience. Elsewhere, we have attempted to spell out some of the structural properties of the experimental situation that account for high obedience, and this analysis need not be repeated here (Milgram, 1963). The experimental variations themselves represent our attempt to probe that structure, by systematically changing it and noting the consequences for behavior. It is clear that some situations produce greater compliance with the experimenter's commands than others. However, this does not necessarily imply an increase or decrease in the strength of any single definable motive. Situations producing the greatest obedience could do so by triggering the most powerful, yet perhaps the most idiosyncratic, of motives in each subject confronted by the setting. Or they may simply recruit a greater number and variety of motives in their service. But whatever the motives involved—and it is far from certain that they can ever be known—action may be studied as a direct function of the situation in which it occurs. This has been the approach of the present study, where we sought to plot behavioral regularities against manipulated properties of the social field. Ultimately, social psychology would like to have a compelling *theory of situations* which will, first, present a language in terms of which situations can be defined; proceed to a typology of situations; and then point to the manner in which definable properties of situations are transformed into psychological forces in the individual. [12]

POSTSCRIPT

Almost a thousand adults were individually studied in the obedience research, and there were many specific conclusions regarding the variables that control obedience and disobedience to authority. Some of these have been discussed briefly in the preceding sections, and more detailed reports will be released subsequently.

There are now some other generalizations I should like to make, which do not derive in any strictly logical fashion from the experiments as carried out, but which, I feel, ought to be made. They are formulations of an intuitive sort that have been forced on me by observation of many subjects responding to the pressures of authority. The assertions represent a painful alteration in my own thinking; and since they were acquired only under the repeated impact of direct

---

[12] My thanks to Professor Howard Leventhal of Yale for strengthening the writing in this paragraph.

observation, I have no illusion that they will be generally accepted by persons who have not had the same experience.

With numbing regularity good people were seen to knuckle under the demands of authority and perform actions that were callous and severe. Men who are in everyday life responsible and decent were seduced by the trappings of authority, by the control of their perceptions, and by the uncritical acceptance of the experimenter's definition of the situation, into performing harsh acts. 78

What is the limit of such obedience? At many points we attempted to establish a boundary. Cries from the victim were inserted; not good enough. The victim claimed heart trouble; subjects still shocked him on command. The victim pleaded that he be let free, and his answers no longer registered on the signal box; subjects continued to shock him. At the outset we had not conceived that such drastic procedures would be needed to generate disobedience, and each step was added only as the ineffectiveness of the earlier techniques became clear. The final effort to establish a limit was the Touch-Proximity condition. But the very first subject in this condition subdued the victim on command, and proceeded to the highest shock level. A quarter of the subjects in this condition performed similarly. 79

The results, as seen and felt in the laboratory, are to this author disturbing. They raise the possibility that human nature or, more specifically, the kind of character produced in American democratic society cannot be counted on to insulate its citizens from brutality and inhumane treatment at the direction of malevolent authority. A substantial proportion of people do what they are told to do, irrespective of the content of the act and without limitations of conscience, so long as they perceive that the command comes from a legitimate authority. If in this study an anonymous experimenter could successfully command adults to subdue a fifty-year-old man and force on him painful electric shocks against his protests, one can only wonder what government, with its vastly greater authority and prestige, can command of its subjects. There is, of course, the extremely important question of whether malevolent political institutions could or would arise in American society. The present research contributes nothing to this issue. 80

In an article titled "The Danger of Obedience," Harold J. Laski wrote: 81

> . . . civilization means, above all, an unwillingness to inflict unnecessary pain. Within the ambit of that definition, those of us who heedlessly accept the commands of authority cannot yet claim to be civilized men.
>
> . . . Our business, if we desire to live a life, not utterly devoid of meaning and significance, is to accept nothing which contradicts our basic experience merely because it comes to us from tradition or convention or authority. It may well be that we shall be wrong; but our self-expression is thwarted at the root unless the certainties we are asked to accept coincide with the certainties we experience. That is why the

condition of freedom in any state is always a widespread and consistent skepticism of the canons upon which power insists.

REFERENCES

BUSS, ARNOLD H.
   1961. *The Psychology of Aggression*. New York and London: John Wiley.
KIERKEGAARD, S.
   1843. *Fear and Trembling*. English edition, Princeton: Princeton University Press, 1941.
LASKI, HAROLD J.
   1929. "The dangers of obedience." *Harper's Monthly Magazine*, 15 June, 1–10.
MILGRAM, S.
   1961. "Dynamics of obedience: experiments in social psychology." Mimeographed report, *National Science Foundation*, January 25.

   1963. "Behavioral study of obedience." *J. Abnorm. Soc. Psychol.* 67, 371–378.

   1964. "Issues in the study of obedience: a reply to Baumrind." *Amer. Psychol.* 1, 848–852.
MILLER, N.E.
   1944. "Experimental studies of conflict." In J. McV. Hunt (ed.), *Personality and the Behavior Disorders*. New York: Ronald Press.
SCOTT, J.P.
   1958. *Aggression*. Chicago: University of Chicago Press.

QUESTIONS

1. What did Milgram want to determine by his experiment? What were his anticipated outcomes?

2. What conclusions did Milgram reach about the extent to which ordinary individuals would obey the orders of an authority figure? Under what conditions is this submission most probable? Under what conditions is defiance most likely?

3. Describe the general procedures of this experiment. Some persons have questioned Milgram's methods. Do you think it is ethical to expose subjects without warning to experiments that might have a lasting effect on them? What such effects might this experiment have had?

4. One characteristic of this paper is Milgram's willingness to consider several possible explanations of the same phenomenon. Study the interpretations in paragraphs 28 through 35. What do you make of the range of interpretation there and elsewhere in the essay? How does Milgram achieve such a range?

5. A report such as Milgram's is not structured in the same way as a conventional essay. His research is really a collection of separate but related experiments, each one of which requires its own interpretation. Describe the groups into which these experiments fall. Which results seemed most surprising to you? Which were easiest to anticipate?

6. In Milgram's experiment, people who are responsible and decent in everyday life were seduced, he says, by trappings of authority. Most of us, however, like to believe that we would neither engage in brutality on our own nor obey directions of this kind. Has Milgram succeeded in getting you to question your own behavior? Would you go so far as to say that he forces you to question your own human nature?

7. In paragraph 46 Milgram comments, "Perhaps our culture does not provide adequate models for disobedience." What do you think of this hypothesis? Are there such models? Ought there to be? Have there appeared such models in the time since the experiment was conducted? Explain your stand on Milgram's statement.

8. If research in social psychology takes place in your school today, there is probably a panel of some sort that enforces guidelines on research with human subjects. Locate that board, if it exists, and find out whether this experiment could take place today. Report to your class on the rules that guide researchers today. Do you think those rules are wise?

9. What, in your opinion, should be the guidelines for psychological research with human subjects? List the guidelines you think are appropriate, and compare your list with the lists of your classmates. Would your guidelines have allowed Milgram's experiment?

10. Think of a situation in which you were faced with the moral and ethical dilemma of whether or not to obey a figure of authority. How did you behave? Did your behavior surprise you? Describe and explain that experience.

MAKING CONNECTIONS

1. One of the conditions of valid scientific research is the replicability of its experiments. When we are persuaded results are replicable, we are inclined to believe them valid. What provisions for replicability does Milgram make in his experiments? Compare his stance to that of Bruno Bettelheim or Oliver Sacks, whose observations are not replicable but who are also concerned with writing authoritative science.

2. Think of other essays in this collection in which ethical matters are at issue, particularly the ethics of composing some kind of story. Consider Nancy Mairs's "Carnal Acts," Richard Selzer's "A Mask on the Face of Death," and Michael Brown's "Love Canal and the Poisoning of America." In each of those studies, human subjects seem manipulated a little for the sake of the writer's interests. Perhaps you would prefer to offer another example. Whatever study you choose, compare it to Milgram's and discuss the two writers' sensitivity to their human subjects. Note also the last sentence of Milgram's first footnote. What choices does the writer have in the cases that interest you most?

THE BEAUTY SYSTEM
Dean MacCannell
and
Juliet Flower MacCannell

Dean MacCannell is a professor of applied behavioral sciences at the University of California, Davis, and Juliet Flower MacCannell teaches comparative literature at the University of California, Irvine. Both have written extensively on cultural theory and issues. Dean MacCannell's The Tourist *(1976) is a classic of its kind; Juliet Flower MacCannell's* The Regime of the Brother: After the Patriarchy *(1991) is her latest book. Together they wrote* The Time of the Sign: A Semiotic Interpretation of Modern Culture *(1982). The following essay, in their words, is "part of a series of analyses of systems of culture, especially on issues that frame the arrangement between the sexes, such as 'beauty,' 'order,' and 'cleanliness.'"*

In all societies, the arrangement between the sexes is an uneasy one involving tensions, separation, and segregation.[1] Institutionalized opposition between the sexes occurs in obvious ways, as in some Australian aboriginal groups where males speak a language forbidden to females, or the urinary segregation of the sexes found in our society. There is also a set of oppositions that penetrate to the level of the subconscious so that males and females who associate intimately, sharing sex, toilet facilities, even language, can nevertheless inhabit separate phenomenal worlds and stumble around in quite different libidinal territories. Recent feminist writers have done much to remind us of our deficiencies in understanding the mind and social situation of women. But they may be closing the door on understanding the overall relationship between the sexes by pretending to open it. Feminists now speak of "hot pussy,"[2] rape, even rape fantasies, and other formerly tabooed topics of female public discussion. But in so doing, they carefully step over the *relationship between the sexes* considered as a totality in its everyday expression.

The discipline of social sciences blocks understanding of the arrangement between the sexes in a different way, by reducing relational matters to questions of gender or sex-role differences. The social sciences simply repeat, on a more sophisticated level, the same program followed by people in everyday life: boys are like this, girls are like that. The *form* of the relationship between the sexes is not studied directly and specifically, nor is it possible to do so without exceeding the limits of discipline theory and methods. In two pioneering studies, *Gender Advertisements* and "The arrangement between the sexes" ("ABS"), Erving Goffman directs our attention to this embarrassing gap in sociological knowledge, but he does not claim to have filled it. To the contrary, Goffman remarks

> [Gender role performance competency] might be said to be essential to our nature, but this competency may provide a very poor picture of the overall relationship between the sexes. And indeed, I think it does. What the relationship between the sexes objectively is, taken as a whole, is quite another matter, not yet well analyzed. . . . There is no relationship between the sexes that can be characterized in any satisfactory fashion.[3]

If we explore the terrain between the sexes, we find a pattern of expressive constraint in "masculine" self-portraiture, especially as this imaging is turned toward women. Men, in our Anglo-American society, are supposed to be "cool." This requirement operates on every detail of behavior, including language performance rules requiring men to flatten and draw out the ends of sentences in order to sound "masculine." There are prohibitions and injunctions, not against "showing off," but against *appearing* to be showing off. The man should wait for an opportunity to demonstrate his physical strength or co-ordination, and hope that his shirt sleeves are rolled up when the opportunity comes; he should not seek out such opportunities, or offer to show his muscles. He should be similarly cautious when it comes to other forms of self-expression-for-women, his behavior, speech, and dress, lest they be seen as *intentionally* produced for the purpose of being attractive to females. The woman is supposed to be attracted to the man for his social achievements (wealth and power) and simply because he is a man, not because of any special effort on his part to make himself attractive to her. He must avoid verbal admissions of interest in a particular woman, unless this admission can also be read as unserious, insulting, and so on. The main expression of masculine orientation toward women in our society is a non-reciprocal license to study, stare, examine, no matter what female in no matter what situation, a license which sometimes extends beyond the visual to verbal insolence. This male behavior is a component of an enormous complex of cultural practices that can be called the *feminine beauty system*. Although the men themselves would put it in cruder terms, what they are measuring is the degree to which the woman they are studying has subordinated herself to the beauty system, that is the degree to which she appears to be committed to making herself attractive to men.

The feminine beauty system, including the masculine appraisal of it, and [3]

444

attraction, is the main feature of the cultural terrain between the categories "male" and "female" in our society. There is no other cultural complex in modern society which touches upon individual behavior that is as rigorously conceived and executed, total, and minutely policed by collective observation and moral authority, than are feminine beauty standards. (For example, standards for mothering behavior are nowhere near as detailed.) Beauty standards apply to face paint color, body size and weight, breast shape, upper arm measurement, head and body hair texture, color and visibility, facial expression, garment and accessory selection and co-ordination.[4] A close examination of the beauty system reveals it to be an *ideology*, or a way of living a contradiction as if it were not a contradiction. The ostensible reason for attempting to make oneself beautiful is first to attract men, then to "get" or to hold a man in a marriage or other lasting relationship. The true hidden purpose of the feminine beauty system is to transfer the power of the female libido to men-in-general, not merely toward the end of maintaining male dominance over women, but "male" power in the abstract, or cultural power under a masculine sign, even that which is directed against other males and nature. Institutionalized separation and segregation of the sexes is not the cause of gender disorders but only a part of the system, its maintenance equipment. In short, the contradiction at the base of the beauty system is that prescribed feminine beauty practices are believed to attract males, or bring the sexes closer together, while their real effect is to keep the sexes separate and unequal, even, or especially, as they seem to be coming together.

THE MALE SET-UP

In our society, noted for its commitment to privacy, the assignment of human infants to one of two "sex classes" is done at birth on the basis of visual inspection of the genitalia. Goffman notes that the practice is not unlike "that employed in regard to domestic animals," and it is immediately followed by an appropriate alignment to gender-marked language terms: boy–girl, he–she, man–woman, and so on ("ABS," 302). After the original inspection, the genitals are covered for social occasions. There will only be a few more times in the course of a man's life when he will be asked to take it out and show it as proof of his sex: his seventh-grade physical education class showers, his military induction physical. Most of the time he will be on the honor system, as when he takes his Scholastic Aptitude Test and is permitted to check the appropriate box "male" or "female." In short, after the genitals are covered, gender is imputed, mainly on the basis of arbitrary signs: blue blankets for boys, pink for girls, hair length, etc. Visible so-called "secondary" sex characteristics may be used after adolescence, but this is also largely a matter of imputation as there is considerable overlap between the sexes *vis-à-vis* the actual development of these characteristics. And, of course, there has never been an aspect of our biological consti-

4

445

tution subject to as much socio-cultural manipulation as our secondary sex characteristics which are routinely created and destroyed by cosmetic and surgical procedures. Without actually viewing another's genitals, we have no real *proof* of the other's sex. This, of course, is the way gender, or more properly "genderism," is born, from all the little details of "masculine" and "feminine" behavior, dress, appearance, from the signifiers that displace, hide, and otherwise obliterate the actual sex. The enormous complex of cultural practices we are calling the "feminine beauty system" flows from the literal and figurative absence of sex, and interestingly it is mainly the male sex that is being covered by the tokens of femininity. How can this work?

> Women seem to sit a different way to show their legs when they wear skirts instead of pants. You feel more like a woman. You look like a woman. . . . I never wear pants.

> (Diane von Furstenberg, 33)

> My conversion to pants at the start of the Seventies was slow but complete, accompanied by a sense of relief and relaxation.

> (Susan Brownmiller, 80)

Go back to the original moment of gender classification based on empirical observation. Of this original visual inspection, Goffman remarks politely only that the genitals are "visibly dimorphic." If we are to clarify the overall relationship between the sexes, it will be necessary to be a little less polite and more specific than Goffman. Infants classed as males have a penis and testicles where infants of the other class have a suture in the place of a penis.[5] There are three logical forms an opposition can take: A:B, in which objects of two merely different classes are distinguished; $+:-$, in which objects which are considered to be equal but opposite are opposed; and 1:0 in which objects are classed by the presence or absence of a crucial characteristic. The last form of opposition is called a negation, and it is the form of the original classification, male:female.[6] Males, as a class, do not need to dramatize their sexuality, because they are the only actual sex class. Females are in the other class, not because they possess anything positive, or even negative, of their own; it is only that they are not males, theirs is a residual class: 1:0.

The zero which is the base of the identity "feminine" is also the base of widely held notions that women have a vacuous consciousness, that they are not capable of shaping or forming thought itself. The form of the original classification is the ultimate grounds of the separation of femininity from serious cultural achievement, especially intellectual achievement, and the reason that women who are "accomplished" are given honorary male status. From the original emptiness of the category radiates a myriad of beliefs in the essential comparability of all females in entirely visual terms. Both men and women understand that a man may leave one woman for another simply because the other is "prettier."[7] The most pernicious form this belief system takes, the most self-sustaining achievement of genderism, is the normalization of *boredom* for women. In all beauty books, it is taken for granted that most women will be agonizingly bored most of the time; that when they are alone, they will occupy themselves preening and their heads will be empty. The Princess Pignatelli, a Beautiful Person from the 1960s, reports, "I . . . spent a whole year doing nothing at all. I was so bored I used to remove the hairs from my legs, one by one, with tweezers" (13–14).

Men in our society wear pants and women wear pants and skirts. Feminists   6 have argued that men make women wear skirts that can be lifted on demand for sex, to remind them of their degraded status as the sexual property of males, and to maintain them in a state of vulnerability. From the perspective being developed here, the wearing of skirts has additional and more basic connotations. Women wear skirts to signify that they have nothing to expose, and so that men can wear pants and appear thereby to be covering something up. The real source of male power is in keeping the basis of their identification as males hidden away.[8] The covering of the penis itself precisely corresponds to the promotion of male power by means of a seemingly endless series of penis substitutes the "uncontrolled" use of which is justified on the grounds that they are not the real thing, and are therefore not a real application of male power, only a stand-in for it: knives, clubs, guns, sharp words, hard facts, and so on. A sports writer eulogizing a former golf champion comments, "46-year-old Nicklaus is still bigger than life (would you believe he is just 5-II?), more of a man with a club in his hands than most of the rest with a gun."[9] This game risks being called at the first moment of interpretation based on disclosure of the relationship of the instruments of power to the *veiled* penis. For as soon as a gun appears in this new frame it produces a kind of anxiety of impotence, an uneasy sense that the man might not be able to perform without the aid of a prosthesis. It is this fragility of masculinity which is protected in the overall arrangement between the sexes by shifting virtually all attention away from questions of masculinity to the feminine beauty system. The feminine beauty system is the Maginot Line around male power as it is currently set up.

The preservation of the male set-up depends upon several things. First, adult   7 males must keep their pants on in public as any re-exposure of their claim to unique identity and power threatens the entire set-up by revealing the ridiculous basis for their claim. Second, representative women must on occasion be made to appear naked, or about to be exposed, and a little embarrassed, in public in order to remind us that they have no indexical qualities when it comes to sex class assignment. Diane von Furstenberg enthusiastically volunteers herself and her sisters for the role of the slightly exposed female:

You should wear a dress that moves with your body, clings a little, and makes you feel sensual. It is fun to see a woman in a shirtdress with the buttons opened low, or a wrap dress that's loosely tied and somewhat décolleté. I like to see women who show their bodies because they are pleased with them. (33)

In this regard, it is interesting that some organizations, which have approved the wearing of pants by female employees, still do not approve of women wearing pants with fly fronts. The wearing of such pants on the part of women might force men to have to prove that *they* have something in there. Going beyond von Furstenberg, female frontal nudity is not necessarily a scandal even in prudish social circles, so long as everyone agrees there is nothing to see. One can note, for example, that the editing of the pornographic movies shown on the *Playboy* cable channel involves cutting all footage showing the male organ while leaving abundant footage of female frontal nudity. In *unedited* pornographic movies, the role of the female is to continue to cover the male member, mainly with their faces. The pornographic "violation" is only that it literalizes the real arrangement between the sexes, the same relationship metaphorically expressed outside the pornographic frame by "Cover Girl" facial make-up.

The female beauty system covers the social fact that men are not supposed 8 to have to show or represent themselves in any way in order to be accepted as *men*. They are originally and authentically men in the first place. Men are real. Women are "made up." But this alleged authenticity of the male gender hides behind and is entirely dependent upon feminine self-characterization as fake, false, superficial, artificial, and the like. Now it should be possible to explore the contradictions at the heart of the ideology of feminine beauty in some detail.

BEAUTY IS ONLY UGLINESS
IN DISGUISE

A recurring feature of the autobiographical beauty narrative is the confession 9 to being ugly. Most writers put their ugliness in the past, as something they experienced as a child or especially as an adolescent. Laura Cunningham writing in the *Cosmo Girl's Guide* claims to be ugly underneath her make-up in the present:

My *essentials* are: 1. Foundation—to cover grey skin and mini acne. 2. False eyelashes—to bolster my real lashes which are so sparse I cannot bat them. 3. The "primary line"—a line that I carve out with shadow in the hollow above my eyelids, and without which my eyes sink into my face like raisins in a rice pudding. 4. Dark pinkish-brown lip slicker—without this my lips are a shade darker grey than my skin. [etc. for nose and hair.] (27)

When the beauty narrative dwells upon self-alleged childhood ugliness, it usually includes some expression of anxiety concerning the breasts. The Princess Pignatelli states flatly:

> I was a lump and everyone knew it. To compound the dreariness, my parents sent me to a school run by nuns. All legs and big feet, thick at the waist and thick in the nose, with no breasts and droopy shoulders, I had only one dream—I would grow up to be madly sexy like the movie stars of the forties with their curves and cleavage. I longed for big breasts. (4)

Jane Fonda remarks:

> As a child, I was your basic klutz—awkward, plump and self-conscious. . . . Like a great many women, I am a product of a culture that says thin is better, blond is beautiful, and buxom is best. (9, 13)

And Susan Brownmiller confesses:

> I agonized that I was miserably flat-chested and wore my small breasts unnaturally high and pointed in a push-up bra with foam rubber padding. (26)

The centrality of concern about the breasts in these confessions may reflect an inchoate understanding that the only true sex is male, and until the recent invention of the female muscles, the breast is the most phallic feminine attribute, or the only real grounds for a claim to "feminine" sexuality. Of course they have to be *large*.

It would be easy to dismiss the general form of these complaints as a kind of hypocritical posturing to sell "beauty" books to readers who must think of themselves as plain or they would not consider buying the books in the first place. The ugly confession puts the writer in a necessary identification with the reader: "I was once mousy, flat-chested, and awkward like you, and look at me now." One suspects that Diane von Furstenberg, who can find precious little basis for her claim to have been plain, but makes it nevertheless, does not quite believe herself as she writes:

> [A]fter having had a simple childhood, I spent my teenage years infiltrating into more sophisticated groups. Always the youngest, the most awkward, the least experienced and definitely the least glamorous, I kept looking around, wanting to learn how to become one of those secure and glamorous women across the room. (15)

But there is also often something heartfelt in these passages, a real anxiety that would not go away even if the commercial reasons for expressing it were removed. One cannot read this Lilly Daché passage as anything but a statement directly from the heart:

> Every little girl starts looking in the mirror almost as soon as she can walk. And almost every little girl fears at some point that she is hopelessly ugly, that nobody will ever admire her and that she is doomed to be an old maid. I remember I used to look at myself in the mirror and wonder if other people really saw how ugly I was (or thought I was), and then I decided to fool them so that they should never know. (116)

Daché's remarks notwithstanding, a young girl has a choice. She can accept herself as she is, or she can enter the beauty system, motivated by a belief in her own deficiencies as the taken-for-granted baseline condition justifying the numerous and often bizarre operations deployed against her body. Once in the beauty system, she must live an absolute contradiction: beauty is proof of ugliness. For a young girl to accept herself "as she is" is not an easy choice. She is drawn into the beauty system by the force of her entire culture, by the design of the overall relationship between the sexes. When she looks in the mirror and sees ugliness reflected back upon herself, what she is actually experiencing is the value that her society has placed upon her gender category, that she has no value. And the approved cultural response is to pick up pencil and paint and try to draw a human face on this nothingness, a beautiful face.

Here it should be noted that the beauty system reflects the class and ethnic standards of the entire society in its aesthetic formulas. The *Cosmo Girl's Guide* mainly provides advice on how to pretend you are a class or two above your actual station. Jane Fonda repeats the way the beauty system veils its support of ethnic hierarchies by its emphasis on "blonds." Black women are still not permitted to play in the beauty system major leagues. Interestingly this also saves them from having to view themselves as essentially ugly. Barbara McNair, who is the Jackie Robinson* of her gender, addresses black girls:

> Honesty is the basic ingredient in any beauty plan, and it can be the most difficult. We all, to some extent, see ourselves as being great beauties, and we're right. (15)

But "times they are a changing," and McNair goes on to advise her readers, in effect, that if they wish to compete on an equal footing with white women, they must adopt the attitude of white women, that is, come to regard themselves as essentially ugly, but "perfectable."

---

*Jackie Robinson (1919–1972) pioneered the racial integration of professional sports. He joined the Brooklyn Dodgers in 1947, thus becoming the first African-American to play on a major league baseball team. [eds.]

"NATURAL" BEAUTY

> No one, not even my husband, has seen my face *au naturel* in three
> years.
>
> (Laura Cunningham, writing in the *Cosmo Girl's Guide*, 26)

The originary "hidden ugliness" which serves as a psychological motivation [12]
for the beauty complex is precisely analogous to the male sex organ which must
be covered. This is the reason that "beauty" as defined by the beauty system
can never be natural beauty but must always involve covering and make-up,
even when the desired end result is the appearance of being a "natural" beauty.
Von Furstenberg remarks:

> Begin with an honest evaluation. Look in the mirror and really examine
> yourself. . . . Then think "what am I going to do about it?" That's the
> first step—to decide what you want to do about something unattractive.
> You have a choice. You can do nothing and accept yourself as you are.
> Or, you can choose to reshape your body, color your hair, even have
> plastic surgery. . . . My own feeling is that it is important to be as close
> to natural as possible; generally, being natural is really a great part of
> being beautiful. (29–30)

The beauty complex charts a progression from a break with nature, through
display craft and other artifice, often arriving back to "nature" or a constructed
image which is ideally natural seeming. The Princess Pignatelli is aggressively
candid on the relationship of beauty procedures to the face and body as given
by nature:

> [W]hat nature skipped, I supplied—so much so that I cannot remember
> what is real and what is fake. More important, neither can anyone
> else. (3)

> Before, during, and after marriage, happy or unhappy, I underwent
> hypnosis, had cell implants, diacutaneous fibrolysis, silicone injections,
> my nose bobbed, and my eyelids lifted. I have tried aromatherapy, yoga,
> and still go to the best gymnast in Rome. Facials and pedicures are
> normal routine, as are frequent hair and makeup changes. I will try
> anything new in beauty. I could not bear not to try. I must have
> experimented with every gadget on the market. (11–12)

The beauty complex suppresses nature, even or especially as it appears to imitate
nature.

> When you become deeply involved in any discipline—and beauty,
> above all, is discipline—it takes you outside yourself. First, you learn
> to see your own looks as a quality apart from self, as a symbol, "a

thing." This leads to an immediate appraisal of other beauties and an understanding of the whole problem and phenomenon. In reaching out, you see that all other women can be in the game together. (Princess Pignatelli, 15)

STAGED AUTHENTICITY AND
FEMININE SOLIDARITY

A great deal of the moral force of the beauty complex, the way it serves as 13 a basis for feminine solidarity, derives from its simultaneous dissociation from, and imitation of, nature. Natural advantage or disadvantage can never be used as an excuse for success or failure within the beauty system. The central theme of every beauty manual is that any and every beauty flaw can be corrected by rigorous adherence to beauty discipline. The moral force of the system extends to override the process of aging itself. According to each of these writers, if you appear to age, it is because you have failed to follow their advice. And the parallel subtheme, that a great natural beauty can also flop if she fails to attend to her eyebrows, waist, or accessories, is also present. Again, the Princess Pignatelli comments succinctly:

> When you care about beauty, it may be all to the good if nature is not
> overgenerous. There is no chance then of living in a mythical past or
> in perpetual illusion. It does not matter what you start with, try and
> get on by nature alone past thirty and you are finished. (3)

In other words, a woman who does not play the "beauty game," at least on some level, even a woman who might pass as "naturally" beautiful, is admitting, in effect, that she has opted for a non-standard relationship with men and with other women, in fact, with society in general.

The double theme of suppression and imitation of nature is especially evident 14 in contemporary guides to makeup application which stress (1) cleaning the face completely, (2) applying a layer of skin-colored foundation to the entire face and neck, (3) painting on a new face which resembles as much as possible a "natural" face, but one that is beautiful, and (4) (this step is optional, for evening wear, or for catching someone's eye) one or two, but not all of the following: high gloss lips, extra eyeshadow or liner, cheek blush co-ordinated with hair, eye, and/or dress color, purple or gold nails, and large or multiple (on the same ear), or mismatched, earrings. The goal of these procedures is to achieve a look of generalized natural-seeming beauty that is accented by an unnatural beauty system cliché (perhaps a little extra dab on the eyes) which can serve as a personalized marker. These little, supposedly personalized, beauty markings are intended to make their bearer attractive to men. Sometimes men are attracted because of them, but not for the reason that they are, in-and-of-themselves, attractive. Rather it is because they are expressions of feminine

452

desire to be attractive to men, and a willingness on the part of the woman to subordinate herself to the discipline of "beauty," which, within the framework of the beauty system, is the same thing.

When viewed from the perspective of the thesis of this paper, the beauty 15 system appears as an amazing feat of cultural engineering. To the extent that the beauty system holds, in order to attract men the woman must make herself principally responsible for covering up the inadequate basis for the male claim to socio-cultural superiority. No one, neither males nor females, need be conscious of these forces in order to be caught up in them; in fact, it helps to be *not* conscious of them. But even when these things are not consciously understood, on some basic level, a woman who relates to men via the beauty system is always fundamentally stigmatized, or seen by herself and others as a half-person, if seen as a person at all.

STATUS DISORDERS

The beauty system is related to systems of class, status, and power in society, 16 but they are not in perfect synchronization. Beauty system conventions are more widely accessible than are actual wealth, prestige, and power. At the point of intersection of the system of beauty and status, the powerless may appear to be powerful and vice versa. Pathological expression occurs throughout the social order when an individual comes to believe that his or her personal power derives entirely from appearances, when a woman believes her make-up, hair style, clothing is all that is important in shaping her relations with others, or the man thinks of his gun or Cadillac the same way.

There is evidence for substantial status disorders in the beauty system that 17 takes the form of vicious competition for rank among women, based solely on physical appearances. This attitude is barely suppressed in most of the beauty manuals, and not suppressed at all in the *Cosmo Girl's Guide* or by the Princess Pignatelli, who often take aim at Third-World women and menial laborers. A *Cosmo* writer remarks:

> Hairpiece—my bureau is stuffed with the hair of a thousand Orientals. I feel occasional pangs of remorse when I picture all those peasants going around half-bald in the hot sun. But it was either them or me. (27–8)

The Princess makes clear that competition for *rank* is more important to her than competition for men. Specifically she is willing to sacrifice a relationship with a man if he does not relate to her through her achieved "beauty," which, she believes, is the basis of her power and prestige:

> [F]inding the wrong man is disaster. For example, the man attracted by your glamour who then proceeds to tell you that you would be much

> lovelier with your hair down and your eyes unmade; the man who
> cannot see why a few pounds (which sink straight to the rear) could
> possibly do any harm. It is such a boring attitude, and when heeded,
> leads always to the same boring result. You take away this, take away
> that, and in six months you look like a cook. (12)

Given the contradiction at the heart of the beauty complex, it is not surprising 18
that the perverse appeal of this passage is to cooks and to other women in the
lower socio-economic classes who dream of being a princess. Beautification
contains elements of "identifying up," desiring to be seen as among the rich
and famous who are often represented in the popular entertainments as proponents of the beauty system. In the actual social order, a few people have
more wealth and power than they can ever use, while most of the others do
not have enough to maintain even minimal self-respect. Some moderns cannot
control their own children or their neighbor's dog. Such people may understandably spend much of their lives longing for fame, wealth, or freedom from
workplace constraints. Under these conditions, the working-class male may find
escape in his phallic substitutes, guns, cowboy boots with sharp toes and heels,
four-wheel-drive vehicles with dual drive shafts, and so on. The woman may
derive some pride and self-assurance from making herself beautiful.

If she tries too hard, of course she will fail. Too much, or obvious make-up 19
or glitter in the clothing, is a universal sign of lower-class status. The *Cosmo
Girl's Guide* cautions that this same principle applies to language use: that is, if
you want to appear to be from a higher class, you must learn to avoid the use
of exactly those terms which working-class people believe that upper-class people
use. Such glitzy language is the surest indicator of one's actual condition. The
Cosmo language lesson for the girl who would appear to be upper-class "U":

> You should say *car* (U), and not *limousine* (Non-U), even if it is a
> limousine. *House*, never *estate* or *mansion* (as in "I'm going to
> his—"). *Boat*, not *yacht*. And you say my *coat*, not my *mink* or my
> *sable*, Even If It Is One. (52)

Saying "yacht" instead of "boat" is the linguistic equivalent to wearing too much
mascara. A working-class girl who struggles for hours in front of her mirror to
get her eye make-up to look like the eye make-up of a famous movie star affirms
the existing hierarchies in the same way as a man who wears a jacket that says
"Corvette Racing Team" on the back. Both gestures indicate subservience to
the system of socio-economic values by those who are oppressed by the system.
That this subservience manifests itself in behavior which may confer a sense of
"identity," a little feeling of capacity for independent self-expression, makes it
all the more effective and complete.

POWER FAILURES

Women can gain and wield personal power in a variety of ways having 20 nothing to do with the beauty system. They can start social movements, amass wealth, teach, manage small and large "empires," write and publish, they can even be brilliant and accomplished wives and mothers. A woman's intellectual and emotional life need have nothing to do with her relationship to the beauty system. But to the extent that the woman believes her identity and power derives from her beauty, there is a complex linkage between beauty and the emotions. Given that beauty is only a cover for "original ugliness," the emotions will always vacillate between joy and depression. Human physiology has nicely adapted itself to these cultural arrangements: beautiful powerless women claim to suffer more from menstrual cramps than do powerful plain women.

Eleanore King subscribes to the thesis that improvement in appearance will 21 produce an inner feeling of calm assurance, that is, beauty drives the emotions. She promotes the idea, common in the 1950s, that feminine beauty, or "charm," is intimately connected to strong fellow feelings in general, not just heterosexual love leading to marriage. And she assumes that such feelings do not occur in a natural state, but must be acted out.

Then, after their outward manifestations become habitual, they may actually 22 be felt:

> You learn through doing. You move gracefully until that is your only way of movement. You incorporate radiant, sincere facial expressions until they become yours. You practice tactful, gracious conversation until any other kind would be foreign to you. . . . Soon your friends, your business associates, even your family notice, first, a subtle change, then a remarkable one. . . . "You're a glorious person. . . . Do you know that?" *And you are.* (11)

RELATIONS WITH MEN

Imagine something that does not occur in real life but is theoretically pos- 23 sible, a relationship between a man and a woman that is framed entirely by convention. The only form it could possibly assume is one of reciprocal sadism. If the only power a man has derives solely from his "masculinity," and the power of the woman derives from her "attractiveness," the pure form of inter-action between two such beings would involve pushing each other around with *mood*—or with their "looks." The man tantalizes and tortures by dangling his "thing" (and his feelings) just out of reach, literally and figuratively by sullen withdrawal, silence, and by preoccupation with phallic substitutes, his "things." The woman knows that his attraction to her has nothing to do with herself. Her attractiveness is only an assembly of conventions borrowed from the beauty system to cover up her emptiness and ugliness. His interest in her only serves to indicate that he is susceptible to being duped by the oldest, most widespread, and open cons around, that his balls are bigger than his brains. The more she is interested, and the more he reciprocates her interest, the less she can respect him. The only real personal power she will ever be able to wield is to deny or turn off the men to whom she is attracted who are also naive or crude enough to be attracted to her false beauty. The man expresses his masculine power and "love" by coldness and silent withdrawal, sometimes punctuated by phallic rage at being trapped in a contradiction as final and absolute as this one. Or, if he really loves her, he may attempt to enter into an "intersubjective relationship" with the woman by insulting her, by telling her directly and indirectly that he sees through her feminine facade and knows how stupid and ugly, what a nothingness, she really is. Similarly, the woman can express herself, as an individual and as a woman, only by transforming all attraction into rejection. With her characteristic clarity on such matters, Mae West sums up succinctly, "If I find a man absorbs too much of my time and my mind, and makes me concentrate on him, I get rid of him. It's alright for a man to concentrate on me" (Quoted in Pignatelli, 13).

In the final accounting, "sex appeal," or the power to attract using beauty 24 system clichés, becomes its opposite. If it works, it has no relational function except to put men and women into positions where they can express their individuality only by mutual rejection. While the man wields power *as a man* in every cultural arena, the beauty system provides the only cultural place where a woman can exercise power *as a woman* (as opposed to any power she might have as a "mother," an "executive," a "wife," and so on). That this power takes the form of pure denial follows logically from the original designation of "woman" as a genderless, zero category. If the man's attraction is purely physical, and he stays within the bounds of physical control, the woman's rejection can take the form of silent refusal. If, however, he is attracted to her "as a person," her denial will be verbal as well as non-verbal, perhaps assuming the form of petty self-assertion called "bitching" and going into "deep freeze." That uniquely feminine power is always wielded in the name of its opposite (beauty, love, and attraction) and ultimately serves to separate woman from man, rather than uniting them, is among the most basic contradictions and darkest secrets of the conventionalized arrangement between the sexes.

SINGLED OUT

During the decades since World War II the beauty system has undergone an 25 evolution. Specifically there has been a progression away from heterosexual love as that which is represented as the underlying motive for the entire beauty complex. From the standpoint of this paper, the disappearance of Love as a category in beauty writing is not surprising, and may even reflect a partial coming to consciousness within the beauty system. But this disappearance is

456

unmarked from within, no one seems to have noticed that Love is gone. So we cannot assume that the internal contradictions of the beauty system are about to be exposed to revolutionary action. Something like the opposite is happening, the system is moving in the direction of a more logical and rational elaboration of values around its contradictions.

. . . The logical progression of beauty system ideology arrives at its fullest 26
expression in the writing of Jane Fonda. In the first equation, found in Daché, King, and other writers in the 1950s, appearance and mood were always connected through the man: classically,

$$\text{BEAUTY} \rightarrow \text{MAN} \rightarrow \text{HAPPINESS}$$

(It is the formula for fairy tales.) By the 1960s and 1970s, in the writings of the Princess, *Cosmo*, and others, the man is no longer the central term holding the system together. He is marginalized. His role is to generate beauty, not vice versa:

$$\text{MAN} \rightarrow \text{HAPPINESS} \rightarrow \text{BEAUTY}$$

This was the historical equation inherited by Fonda, and on which she worked her radical transformation of the system.

Fonda does not promote "beauty" in the traditional sense; in fact, she opposes 27
herself to beauty system abuses. Describing an early make-up session readying her for work as a beauty system exemplar, she comments:

> When they were through, I could hardly recognize myself in the mirror—winged eyebrows, false eyelashes, big pink lips, hair that looked as if it had been ironed, right off the Warner Brothers assembly line together with Sandra Dee, Connie Stevens. (17)

She renounces this approach to beauty in favor of one that is more authentic and more powerful—the workout:

> Working out has become a part of my life. . . . [W]hen I approach my Workout I play a game of "pretend." I am no longer Jane Fonda, the actress, wife, mother, activist. I am an athlete. I *have* to push myself to the limit and beyond because I'm preparing for competition. But the competition is with myself. (24)

As the quote implies, Fonda's book contains no attitude whatever on relationships with others, lasting or temporary, with men or women. In this regard, it is unique among beauty books. She is absolutely neutral on her marriages, divorce, and children, printing a photograph of herself with her first husband, and her infant child by him, next to a same-sized photograph of herself with her second husband and her infant child by *him*. These two interesting pictures appear face-to-face on pages 28 and 29 over the captions: "With Roger Vadim and our daughter, Vanessa," and "With Tom Hayden and our son, Troy."

Fonda is emphatic on the point that her beauty treatment is a valued end- 28 in-itself. It is not to get a man, or even to achieve a possible fleeting effect on strangers, to draw a compliment from a man or an envious glance from a woman. Shaping the body is pursued for the sensations experienced while pursuing it, sensations described throughout the book in terms similar to those used to describe the release which some derive from sado-masochistic sex. For example:

> [M]y co-workers would wonder why at the end of a fourteen-hour day on a stuffy sound stage I pushed myself . . . instead of joining them in collapsing with a drink. I certainly felt more like collapsing than working and sweating until I ached, but afterwards I would feel alive and revitalized. It was hard to explain this or describe how good I felt about being disciplined. (21)

The underlying motive of the Fonda narrative is not to fall in love or even to get in touch with others. Rather it is to get in touch with herself, to become an entirely self-contained dialogic unit in which the only important relationship is with her own body. She recalls that she was able to break free from the alienation of the old beauty system only after "*I began consciously listening to what my body was telling me*" (27). The alchemy worked by this onanistic final expression of western individualism is intended to produce a new gender, the first to deserve to be called "woman," that is, an independent woman, one who is not defined entirely by her role in maintaining the cultural and other potency of males. But this cannot occur. For what we find in the place of the male in the beauty system formula as modified by Fonda, is not a new feminine consciousness, but an obvious male simulacrum: working out, muscle building. Moreover, the alleged new feminine consciousness is not identified merely with the male principle in general, but with a special version of it. It is an identifi-cation with the phallic substitutes of the powerless male, the working-class male: bulging muscles. To the extent that this new form of feminine beauty calls forth the substantial homosexual reserves in the general male population,[10] to the extent that it taps into male solidarity, it may serve as well or better than earlier ideals in bringing the sexes together at least for procreative purposes, now ironically under a homosexual sign.

Fonda's critique of the old beauty system is genuine. She fervently desires 29 to be liberated from it, believes she has escaped it, and wants to help others. Commenting on her early vacuous and sexy roles she exclaims:

> If I had only known what I was doing to myself. If I had only understood twenty years ago the futility, the alienation, the self-denigration of trying to fit oneself into a mold. It was as if I was thinking of myself as a product rather than a person. (16)

And on the extension of the system into the Third World, she remarks:

> A [Vietnamese] prostitute could increase her price with her American tricks if she conformed to the Western Playboy sexual standard. And these operations [eye rounding, breast and buttocks enlarging] weren't confined only to prostitutes. Many of them were done to women in "high society" such as the wives of Generals Thieu and Ky. These women literally had their faces and bodies Americanized. . . . The women of Vietnam had become victims of the same *Playboy* culture that had played havoc with me. (20)

One wants Fonda to succeed, if for no other reason than disgust for those groups and individuals who have made it their mission to attack her. But the particular way that she has struggled against the beauty system only succeeds in bringing the original contradiction to the surface where it is less obvious. She *becomes* the contradiction. She cannot see her approach to "beauty" as the ultimate logical extension of the cultural hegemony of the masculine gender as the only gender. As she strikes out against "trying to fit oneself into a mold," a serious revolutionary sentiment, she is evidently unaware that the mold she has made for her followers is harder and more permanent than any face make-up. She will eventually say:

> But something muscle-like does happen and I like it. Since you are reading this book you are probably like me and appreciate a woman's body on which the muscle cuts and contours are evident. This is what you get. (69)

And in the same book where she expresses hatred for thinking of herself as a "product," she makes herself into a product, literally: the "Jane Fonda" Workout Studios, Book, and Video. The limits of narcissism are reached in a photograph on page 20 depicting three Americanized Vietnamese prostitutes, intended to illustrate her criticism of the *"Playboy* sexual standard." The girls appear as a sad parody of the old beauty system. The one on the left has made herself up as an obvious copy of Jane Fonda.

CONCLUSION

In this paper the term "beauty system" has been used to refer to the diverse practices which are widely held to make a woman more attractive, *and* to the primary effect of these practices which is to harness the energy of the female libido, her desire for sex, to covering our culture's designation of "male" as the only gender category. Women must *pretend* to be women so that men can be thought of as *real*. The beauty system turns feminine desire against itself. Actual heterosexual relations are the first things to be sacrificed to the system. Beauty system arrangements were once rigorously gendered in the biological sense, but no longer. Biological women are now taking off their bras and make-up, wearing pants, developing muscles, and claiming to be "authentic." And biological males are wearing earrings, eyeliner, and so on. The secret of the mass appeal of allegedly ultra-macho stars such as Sylvester Stallone is they have learned to imitate the "sultry" or "hot" facial expression of a female who is signaling sexual openness. That the beauty system is no longer biologically gendered does not change its essential structure, of course.

All societies have deep cultural oppositions which can take the form of 31 contradictions. Meaningfulness itself depends upon this. When analyzed, the feminine beauty complex reveals itself to be a deep structural contradiction covered by gender ideology. The beauty system is the only cultural complex designed to bring the sexes together, albeit only for procreative purposes, that is it is patterned female behavior intended to attract males. There is no elaborated corresponding set of male practices. Beauty ideology is a lived contradiction. Beauty practices and beliefs are experienced by both males and females as a coherent totality, as "shared meanings." Ultimately beauty practices and beliefs fragment human existence by turning all intentional acts against the self-interest of the actor. They drive the sexes apart and cut the woman off from men and the rest of society. The male gender remains the only marked gender, now ratified absolutely by equating "feminine" beauty with muscle. More important, the woman remains obsessively concerned with her physical *appearance* as the only basis she has for any claim she might wish to make as a woman, even claims she might wish to make for or against herself as a solitary woman, which is rapidly becoming the only "relationship" she is culturally allowed. She is beautiful. She is strong. She is independent.

Freudians and some feminists have made much of the way the Woman 32 reveals the "truth" about civilization, that it was built upon male castration anxiety.[11] This revelation is effected via representation of the female sex as a "bleeding wound" in the place where the penis *should* be. What we have been stressing here is a simpler truth: namely that the myth of mutilation is a fine collective excuse, but even without injury, the male member is not an adequate base for civilization. Female insecurity which takes the form of "beauty" is only male insecurity displaced. This is the reason the real basis for it can never be found in the heart of the woman who experiences it.

EPIGRAPH

I already know a thing or two. I know it's not clothes that make women 33 beautiful or otherwise, nor beauty care, nor expensive creams, nor the distinction or costliness of their finery. I know the problem lies elsewhere. I don't know where. I only know it isn't where women think. I look at the women in the streets of Saigon and upcountry. Some of them are very beautiful, very white, they take enormous care of their beauty here, especially upcountry. They don't do anything, just save themselves up, save themselves for Europe, for lovers, holidays in Italy, the long six-months leaves every three years, when at last they'll be able to talk about what it's like here, this peculiar colonial existence, the marvelous domestic service provided by the houseboys, the vegetation, the dances, the white villas, big enough to get lost in, occupied by officials in distant outposts. They wait, these women. They dress just for the sake of dressing. They look at themselves. In the shade of their villas, they look at themselves for later on, they dream of romance, they already have huge wardrobes full of more dresses then they know what to do with, added to one by one like time, like the long days of waiting. Some of them go mad. Some are deserted for a young maid who keeps her mouth shut. Ditched. You can hear the word hit them, hear the sound of the blow. Some kill themselves.

This self-betrayal of women always struck me as a mistake, an error.   34

You didn't have to attract desire. Either it was in the woman who aroused   35 it or it didn't exist. Either it was there at first glance or else it had never been. It was instant knowledge of sexual relationship or it was nothing. That too I knew before I experienced it.

(Marguerite Duras, *The Lover*)

NOTES

Financial support for preparation of this chapter was provided by the office of Jaime Rodriguez, Dean of Graduate Studies and Research, and by the Focused Research Program in Gender and Women's Studies, Academic Senate, the University of California, Irvine. The authors wish to give special thanks to Deborah S. Wilson and Asafa Jalata for their assistance in researching this paper.

    1. This paper is a part of a series of analyses of systems of culture, especially on issues that frame the arrangement between the sexes, such as "beauty," "order," and "cleanliness," which the authors have undertaken in the past few years. See D. Mac-Cannell and J. F. MacCannell (1982) *The Time of the Sign: A Semiotic Interpretation of Modern Culture*, Bloomington, Ind., Indiana University Press; J. F. MacCannell (1986) *Figuring Lacan: Criticism and the Cultural Unconscious*, London and Lincoln, Nebraska, Croom Helm and University of Nebraska Press; J. F. MacCannell (forthcoming), *Couplings: The Failures of Heterosexuality from Rousseau to Lacan*, Baltimore, Md., Johns Hopkins University Press; D. MacCannell (1973) "A note on hat-tipping," *Semiotica*, VII, 4, 300–12; D. MacCannell (1976) *The Tourist*, New York, Schocken; and his *American Mythologies* (in preparation).

    2. See, for example, H. Grossett's "Is it true what they say about colored pussy?" and other selections in C. S. Vance (ed.) (1984) *Pleasure and Danger: Exploring Female Sexuality*, Boston, Mass., Routledge & Kegan Paul, 411–12 and *passim*.

    3. E. Goffman (1979) *Gender Advertisements*, New York, Harper & Row, 8. See also his (1977) "The arrangement between the sexes," *Theory and Society*, 301–29.

    4. The evidence used in the following is from observations and from several guide

books to feminine beauty purchased in bulk at reasonable cost from used book shops in Southern California. Citations in brackets in the text refer to the following books, which range from the 1950s to the 1980s: L. Daché, *Lilly Daché's Glamour Book*, ed. D. R. Lewis (1956) Philadelphia and New York, J. B. Lippincott; E. King (1957) *Eleanore King's Guide to Glamor: Beauty, Poise and Charm in a Few Minutes a Day*, Englewood Cliffs, NJ, Prentice Hall; Princess Luciana Pignatelli (as told to J. Molli) (1970) *The Beautiful People's Beauty Book; How to Achieve the Look and Manner of the World's Most Attractive Women*, New York, McCall; *The Cosmo Girl's Guide to the New Etiquette* (1971) New York, Cosmopolitan Books; D. von Furstenberg (with E. Portrait) (1976) Diane von Furstenberg's *Book of Beauty: How to Become a More Attractive, Confident and Sensual Woman*, New York, Simon & Schuster; J. Fonda (1981) *Jane Fonda's Workout Book*, New York; Simon and Schuster; S. Brownmiller (1984) *On Femininity*, New York, Simon & Schuster.

5. The term "suture," the "joining of the inner lips of a wound . . . a line or seam . . . the conflux of the inner margins of elytra," *OED*, has disturbed several pre-publication readers of this chapter. We want to make clear that while this term does not reflect our personal sense of the vagina, it nicely conveys the cultural values which we wish to analyze. Its possibly negative connotation is appropriate to the cultural framing of the vagina as understood in this chapter: that is problematical, but not as negative as the "bleeding wound" of Freudians and some recent feminists. See, for example, Mulvey, cited in note 11.

6. See A. Wilden (1984) "Montage analytic and dialectic," *American Journal of Semiotics*, III, 1, 25–47, on forms of negation.

7. See, for example, a typical confession in R. T. Lakoff and R. L. Scherr (1984) *Face Value: The Politics of Beauty*, Boston, London, Melbourne, and Henley, Routledge & Kegan Paul, which opens with Ms Scherr's claim that the book was inspired by her having been dropped for a blonde.

8. Our argument is the positive side of the by now generally understood notion that in veiling the female pudenda "nothing" is being hidden, because it represents the "truth" of castration. In its practical consequence, however, "castration" by clothing is also the effective means of imputing objective reality to what is hidden underneath. This would explain why the general baring of female parts that is currently available (even traditional women's "covering" is often a diaphanous veil, made as if to be seen "through" to the lack underneath) still supports the myth of the superior "reality" of the masculine. Lynne Gilliland has pointed out that male dancers, in contrast to female strippers, *never* take it all off, whereas females are increasingly displayed in our culture without genital covering. This would make Roland Barthes's "Striptease" myth, wherein a rhinestone triangle still hides the naked truth, a passé form of revelation.

9. *The Sacramento Bee*, 3 February 1986, C5.

10. Jacques Lacan pointed out the monologic nature of human sexuality by calling it *hommosexuel*. Interestingly in *Pumping Iron II*, the docudrama about the female body-building contest in Las Vegas, it is the contestant who has most "masculinized" her display of gender that is depicted as having the tenderest relationship with her male coach.

11. See J. Derrida (1977) "The purveyor of truth," *Yale French Studies*, 67ff; as well as his other writings. See also L. Mulvey (1975) "Visual pleasure and narrative cinema," *Screen*, 16, Autumn, 6–7, for a succinct summation of this position.

QUESTIONS

1. Why do the MacCannells use the term "system" with respect to our conceptions of beauty?

2. What do they mean when they say that males are "the only actual sex class" (Paragraph 4)? How does such an attitude affect the shaping of gender?

3. In Paragraph 6, the metaphor of the "Maginot Line" is used for the feminine beauty system in relation to male power. Look at a history of France in World War II, and decide whether the metaphor is appropriate.

4. What major contradictions are inherent in the beauty system as it is presented here?

5. Look in the latest beauty magazines to see how frequently the word *natural* appears in advertisements and in articles. What do the MacCannells have to say about *natural* beauty? What do the ads want women to believe? Write up your findings.

6. The MacCannells constructed their essay from their observations and from "several guide books to feminine beauty" found in secondhand bookstores. Consult some more recent guides and update a section of their essay. Be sure to include *your* observations as well.

MAKING CONNECTIONS

1. How might Alice Walker ("Beauty: When the Other Dancer Is the Self") and Nancy Mairs ("Carnal Acts") respond to the MacCannell essay? Write up a commentary from their points of view.

2. What does Emily Martin's "The Egg and the Sperm" add to your understanding of the contradictory nature of male-female relationships outlined here?

WHY WOMEN AREN'T GETTING TO THE TOP

Susan Fraker

Susan Fraker is an editor at Fortune *magazine. Assisted by research associate David Weld Stevens, she wrote this essay for the April 16, 1984, issue of the magazine, where it appeared as the cover story. In the magazine's format, the title appeared in very heavy type. It was followed by a subheading in smaller type, designed to attract the reader's attention: "No women are on the fast track to the chief executive's job at any* Fortune *500 corporation. That's incongruous, given the number of years women have been working in management. The reasons are elusive and tough for management to deal with."*

Ten years have passed since U.S. corporations began hiring more than token 1
numbers of women for jobs at the bottom rung of the management ladder. A decade into their careers, how far up have these women climbed? The answer: not as far as their male counterparts. Despite impressive progress at the entry level and in middle management, women are having trouble breaking into senior management. "There is an invisible ceiling for women at that level," says Janet Jones-Parker, executive director of the Association of Executive Search Consultants Inc. "After eight or ten years, they hit a barrier."

The trouble begins at about the $75,000 to $100,000 salary level, and seems 2
to get worse the higher one looks. Only one company on *Fortune's* list of the 500 largest U.S. industrial corporations has a woman chief executive. That woman, Katharine Graham of the Washington Post Co. (No. 342), readily admits she got the job because her family owns a controlling share of the corporation.

More surprising, given that women have been on the ladder for ten years, 3
is that none currently seems to have a shot at the top rung. Executive recruiters, asked to identify women who might become presidents or chief executives of *Fortune* 500 companies, draw a blank. Even companies that have women in senior management privately concede that these women aren't going to occupy the chairman's office.

Women have only four of the 154 spots this year at the Harvard Business 4
School's Advanced Management Program—a prestigious 13-week conclave to

which companies send executives they are grooming for the corridors of power. The numbers aren't much better at comparable programs at Stanford and at Dartmouth's Tuck School. But perhaps the most telling admission of trouble comes from men at the top. "The women aren't making it," confessed the chief executive of a *Fortune* 500 company to a consultant. "Can you help us find out why?"

All explanations are controversial to one faction or another in this highly charged debate. At one extreme, many women—and some men—maintain that women are the victims of blatant sexism. At the other extreme, many men—and a few women—believe women are unsuitable for the highest managerial jobs: they lack the necessary assertiveness, they don't know how to get along in this rarefied world, or they have children and lose interest in—or time for—their careers. Somewhere in between is a surprisingly large group of men and women who see "discrimination" as the major problem, but who often can't define precisely what they mean by the term.

The discrimination they talk about is not the simple-minded sexism of dirty jokes and references to "girls." It is not born of hatred, or indeed of any ill will that the bearer may be conscious of. What they call discrimination consists simply of treating women differently from men. The notion dumbfounds some male managers. You mean to say, they ask, that managerial women don't want to be treated differently from men in any respect, and that by acting otherwise—as I was raised to think only decent and gentlemanly—I'm somehow prejudicing their chances for success? Yes, the women respond.

"Men I talk to would like to see more women in senior management," says Ann Carol Brown, a consultant to several *Fortune* 500 companies. "But they don't recognize the subtle barriers that stand in the way." Brown thinks the biggest hurdle is a matter of comfort, not competence. "At senior management levels, competence is assumed," she says. "What you're looking for is someone who fits, someone who gets along, someone you trust. Now that's subtle stuff. How does a group of men feel that a woman is going to fit? I think it's very hard."

The experience of an executive at a large Northeastern bank illustrates how many managerial women see the problem. Promoted to senior vice president several years ago, she was the first woman named to that position. But she now believes it will be many years before the bank appoints a woman executive vice president. "The men just don't feel comfortable," she says. "They make all sorts of excuses—that I'm not a banker [she worked as a consultant originally], that I don't know the culture. There's a smoke screen four miles thick. I attribute it to being a woman." Similarly, 117 of 300 women executives polled recently by UCLA's Graduate School of Management and Korn/Ferry International, an executive search firm, felt that being a woman was the greatest obstacle to their success.

A common concern among women, particularly in law and investment   9
banking, is that the best assignments go to men. "Some departments—like sales
and trading or mergers and acquisitions — are considered more macho, hence
more prestigious," says a woman at a New York investment bank. "It's nothing
explicit. But if women can't get the assignments that allow them to shine, how
can they advance?"

Women also worry that they don't receive the same kind of constructive   10
criticism that men do. While these women probably overestimate the amount
of feedback their male colleagues receive, even some men acknowledge widespread male reluctance to criticize a woman. "There are vast numbers of men
who can't do it," says Eugene Jennings, professor of business administration at
Michigan State University and a consultant to a dozen large companies. A male
banking executive agrees: "A male boss will haul a guy aside and just kick ass
if the subordinate performs badly in front of a client. But I heard about a
woman here who gets nervous and tends to giggle in front of customers. She's
unaware of it and her boss hasn't told her. But behind her back he downgrades
her for not being smooth with customers."

Sometimes the message that has to be conveyed to a woman manager is   11
much more sensitive. An executive at a large company says he once had to tell
a woman that she should either cross her legs or keep her legs together when
she sat. The encounter was obviously painful for him. "She listened to me and
thanked me and expressed shock at what she was doing," he recalls, with a
touch of agony in his voice. "My God, this is something only your mother tells
you. I'm a fairly direct person and a great believer in equal opportunity. But it
was damn difficult for me to say this to a woman whom I view to be very proper
in all other respects."

Research by Anne Harlan, a human resource manager at the Federal Aviation   12
Administration, and Carol Weiss, a managing associate of Charles Hamilton
Associates, a Boston consulting firm, suggests that the situation doesn't necessarily improve as the number of women in an organization increases. Their
study, conducted at the Wellesley College Center for Research on Women and
completed in 1982, challenges the theory advanced by some experts that when
a corporation attained a "critical mass" of executive women—defined as somewhere between 30% and 35%—job discrimination would vanish naturally as
men and women began to take each other for granted.

Harlan and Weiss observed the effects of different numbers of women in an   13
organization during a three-year study of 100 men and women managers at two
Northeastern retailing corporations. While their sample of companies was not
large, after their results were published, other companies said they had similar
experiences. Harlan and Weiss found that while overt resistance drops quickly
after the first few women become managers, it seems to pick up again as the
number of women reaches 15%. In one company they studied, only 6% of the

managers were women, compared with 19% in the second company. But more women in the second company complained of discrimination, ranging from sexual harassment to inadequate feedback. Could something other than discrimination—very different corporate cultures, say—have accounted for the result? Harlan and Weiss say no, that the two companies were eminently comparable.

Consultants and executives who think discrimination is the problem tend to believe it persists in part because the government has relaxed its commitment to affirmative action, which they define more narrowly than some advocates do. "We're not talking about quotas or preferential treatment," says Margaret Hennig who, along with Anne Jardim, heads the Simmons College Graduate School of Management. "That's stupid management. We just mean the chance to compete equally." Again, a semantic chasm separates women and men. Women like Hennig and Jardim think of affirmative action as a vigorous effort on the part of companies to ensure that women are treated equally and that sexist prejudices aren't permitted to operate. Men think the term means reverse discrimination, giving women preferential treatment. 14

Legislation such as the Equal Employment Opportunity Act of 1972 prohibits companies from discriminating against women in hiring. The laws worked well—indeed, almost too well. After seven or eight years, says Jennings of Michigan State, the pressure was off and no one pushed hard to see that discrimination was eliminated in selecting people for senior management. Jennings thinks the problem began in the latter days of the Carter Administration, when the economy was lagging and companies worried more about making money than about how their women managers were doing. The Reagan Administration hasn't made equal opportunity a priority either. 15

What about the belief that women fall behind not because of discrimination, but because they are cautious, unaggressive, and differently motivated than men—or less motivated? Even some female executives believe that women derail their careers by choosing staff jobs over high-risk, high-reward line positions. One woman, formerly with a large consumer goods company and now president of a market research firm, urges women to worry less about sexism and more about whether the jobs they take are the right route to the top. "I spent five years thinking the only reason I didn't become a corporate officer at my former company was because of my sex," she says. "I finally had to come to grips with the fact that I overemphasized being a woman and underemphasized what I did for a living. I was in a staff function—the company didn't live and die by what I did." 16

Men and women alike tend to believe that because women are raised differently they must manage differently. Research to support this belief is hard to come by, though. The women retail managers studied by Harlan and Weiss, 17 while never quarterbacks or catchers, had no trouble playing on management teams. Nor did they perform less well on standardized tests measuring qualities like assertiveness and leadership. "Women don't manage differently," Harlan says flatly.

In a much larger study specifically addressing management styles, psychol- 18
ogists Jay Hall and Susan Donnell of Teleometrics International Inc., a management training company, reached the same conclusion. They matched nearly 2,000 men and women managers according to age, rank in their organization, kind of organization, and the number of people they supervised. The psychologists ran tests to assess everything from managerial philosophies to the ability to get along with people, even quizzing subordinates on their views of the boss. Donnell and Hall concluded, "Male and female managers do not differ in the way they manage the organization's technical and human resources."

Data on how women's expectations—and therefore, arguably, their perfor- 19
mance—may differ from men's are more confusing. Stanford Professor Myra Strober studied 150 men and 26 women who graduated from the Stanford Business School in 1974. When she and a colleague, Francine Gordon, polled the MBAs shortly before graduation, they discovered that the women had much lower expectations for their peak earnings. The top salary the women expected during their careers was only 60% of the men's. Four years later the ratio had fallen to 40%.

Did this mean that women were less ambitious or were willing to take lower 20
salaries to get management jobs? Strober doesn't think so. She says a major reason for the women's lower salary expectations was that they took jobs in industries that traditionally pay less, but which, the women thought, offered opportunities for advancement. Almost 20% of the women in her sample went into government, compared with 3% of the men. On the other hand, no women went into investment banking or real estate development, which each employed about 6% of the men. Strober points out, however, that investment banking and big-time real estate were all but closed to women in the early 1970s. "One way people decide what their aspirations are," she says, "is to look around and see what seems realistic. If you look at a field and see no women advancing, you may modify your goals."

Some of what Mary Anne Devanna found in her examination of MBAs 21
contradicts Strober's conclusions. Devanna, research coordinator of the Columbia Business School's Center for Research in Career Development, matched 45 men and 45 women who graduated from the Columbia Business School from 1969 to 1972. Each paired man and woman had similar backgrounds, credentials, and marital status. The starting salaries of the women were 98% of the men's. Using data collected in 1980, Devanna found a big difference in the salaries men and women ultimately achieved, though. In manufacturing, the highest paying sector, women earned $41,818 after ten years vs. $59,733 for the men. Women in finance had salaries of $42,867 vs. $46,786 for the men.

The gap in the service industries was smallest: $36,666 vs. $38,600. She then tested four hypotheses in seeking to explain the salary differences: (1) that women are less successful because they are motivated differently than men, (2) that motherhood causes women to divert attention from their careers, (3) that women seek jobs in low-paying industries, and (4) that women seek types of jobs — in human resources, say—that pay less.

Devanna found no major differences between the sexes in the importance 22
they attached to the psychic or monetary rewards of work. "The women did not expect to earn less than the men," she says. Nor did she find that motherhood led women to abandon their careers. Although several women took maternity leaves, all returned to work full time within six months. Finally, Devanna found no big differences in the MBAs' choice of industry or function, either when they took their first jobs or ten years later.

Devanna concluded that discrimination, not level of motivation or choice 23
of job, accounted for the pay differences. Could the problem simply have been performance—that the women didn't manage as well as men? Devanna claims that while she couldn't take this variable into account specifically, she controlled for all the variables that should have made for a difference in performance—from family background to grades in business school.

In their discussions with male executives, researchers like Devanna hear a 24
recurrent theme—a conviction that women don't take their careers seriously. Even though most female managers were regarded as extremely competent, the men thought they would eventually leave—either to have children or because the tensions of work became too much. Both are legitimate concerns. A woman on the fast track is under intense pressure. Many corporate types believe that she gets much more scrutiny than a man and must work harder to succeed. The pressures increase geometrically if she has small children at home.

Perhaps as a result, thousands of women have careers rather than husbands 25
and children. In the UCLA-Korn/Ferry study of executive women, 52% had never married, were divorced, or were widowed, and 61% had no children. A similar study of male executives done in 1979 found that only 5% of the men had never married or were divorced and even fewer—3%—had no children.

Statistics on how many women bear children and then leave the corporation 26
are incomplete. Catalyst, a nonprofit organization that encourages the participation of women in business, studied 815 two-career families in 1980. It found that 37% of the new mothers in the study returned to work within two months; 68% were back after 4½ months; 87% in eight months. To a company, of course, an eight-month absence is a long time. Moreover, the 10% or so who never come back—most males are convinced the figure is higher—represent a substantial capital investment lost. It would be naive to think that companies don't crank this into their calculation of how much the women who remain are worth.

Motherhood clearly slows the progress of women who decide to take long 27 maternity leaves or who choose to work part time. But even those committed to working full time on their return believe they are sometimes held back—purposely or inadvertently. "Men make too many assumptions that women with children aren't free to take on time-consuming tasks," says Gene Kofke, director of human resources at AT&T. Karen Gonçalves, 34, quit her job as a consultant when she was denied challenging assignments after the birth of her daughter. "I was told clearly that I couldn't expect to move ahead as fast as I had been," she says. Later, when Gonçalves began working at the consulting firm of Arthur D. Little Inc. in Cambridge, Massachusetts, she intentionally avoided discussions of family and children: "I didn't keep a picture of my daughter in the office, and I would travel anywhere, no matter how hard it was for me."

Sometimes pregnancy is more of an issue for the men who witness it than for the women who go through it. Karol Emmerich, 35, now treasurer of Dayton Hudson Corp., was the first high-level woman at the department-store company to become pregnant. "The men didn't really know what to do," she recalls. "They were worried when I wanted to take three months off. But they wanted to encourage me to come back. So they promoted me to treasurer when I was seven months pregnant. Management got a lot of good feedback." Emmerich's experience would please Simmons Dean Anne Jardim, who worries that most organizations aren't doing enough to keep women who want to have children. "It's mind-boggling," she argues. "Either some of the brightest women in this country aren't going to reproduce or the companies are going to write off women in whom they have a tremendous investment." 28

To the corporation it may seem wasteful to train a woman and then be unable to promote her because she won't move to take the new job. The Catalyst study found that 40% of the men surveyed had moved for their jobs, vs. only 21% of the women. An argument can be made that an immobile executive is worth less to the corporation—and hence may be paid less. 29

Where women frequently do go is out of the company and into business for themselves. "When the achievements you want aren't forthcoming, it makes going out on your own easier," says a woman who has set up her own consultancy. "I was told I wouldn't make it into senior management at my bank. Maybe I just didn't have it. But the bank never found any woman who did. They were operating under a consent decree and they brought in a lot of women at the vice president level. Every single one of them left." Karen Gonçalves left Arthur D. Little to do part-time teaching and consulting when she was pregnant with her second child. "I didn't think I would get the professional satisfaction I wanted at ADL," she says. 30

From 1977 to 1980, according to the Small Business Administration, the number of businesses owned by women increased 33%, compared with an 11% increase for men—though admittedly the women's increase started from a much 31 smaller base. While it's not clear from the numbers that women are entering the entrepreneurial ranks in greater numbers than they are joining corporations, some experts think so. "It's ironic," says Strober of Stanford. "The problem of the 1970s was bringing women into the corporation. The problem of the 1980s is keeping them there."

A few companies, convinced that women face special problems and that it's   32
in the corporation's interest to help overcome them, are working hard at solutions. At Penn Mutual Life Insurance Co. in Philadelphia, where nearly half the managers are women, executives conducted a series of off-site seminars on gender issues and sex-role stereotypes. Dayton Hudson provides support (moral and financial) for a program whereby women in the company trade information on issues like personal financial planning and child care.

What women need most, the experts say, are loud, clear, continuing state-   33
ments of support from senior management. Women have come a long way at Merck, says B. Lawrence Branch, the company's director of equal employment affairs, because Chairman John J. Horan insisted that their progress be watched. Merck has a program that identifies 10% of its women and 10% of minorities as "most promising." The company prepares a written agenda of what it will take for them to move to the next level. Progress upward may mean changing jobs or switching functions, so Merck circulates their credentials throughout the company. "We have a timetable and we track these women carefully," says Branch. Since 1979 almost 40% of the net growth in Merck's managerial staff has been women.

Sensitive to charges of reverse discrimination, Branch explains that Merck   34
has for years singled out the best employees to make sure they get opportunities to advance. Women, he notes, were consistently underrepresented in that group. In his view the tracking program simply allows women to get into the competition with fast-track men. Others might not be so charitable. Any company that undertakes to do something on behalf of its managerial women leaves itself open to the charge that it too is discriminating—treating women and men differently.

What everyone may be able to agree on is that opening corporations to   35
competition in the executive ranks is clearly good for performance and profits. But how can a company do this? It can try to find productive part-time work for all employees who want to work part time—even managers. It can structure promotions so that fewer careers are derailed by an absence of a few months or the unwillingness to relocate. It can make sure that the right information, particularly on job openings, reaches everyone. Perhaps most importantly, it can reward its managers for developing talent of all sorts and sexes, penalize them if they don't, and vigilantly supervise the process.

QUESTIONS

1. The title of the essay implies that it will answer the question, "Why aren't women getting to the top?" Does it? What, if anything, have you learned about the problem?

2. Where there's a problem, there may be a solution. What does Fraker offer the reader beyond an explanation of the problem and an exploration of its possible causes?

3. The format of *Fortune* does not allow for footnotes, but Fraker mentions her sources regularly, and it is obvious that this essay is a version of a research paper. List the sources you can identify, in the order in which they are mentioned, to see how many sources were consulted and what range and variety of material it takes to produce an informative essay of this kind. How much of the information Fraker presents is based on private conversations or interviews, and how much comes from published documents or public records?

4. Fraker has to present a lot of information in this essay. What does she do to enliven and humanize her data? Look at particular passages that seem to you successful in turning abstractions into concrete form. How do different *kinds* of information work to prevent this from turning into a recital of dry abstractions?

5. How has Fraker organized the essay? What are the large subdivisions of the main topic?

6. Extend Fraker's study to your own school. Are women getting to the top there? Can you discover changes over the past ten years in numbers of women on the faculty, promotions to higher ranks, and so on? Are any women among your school's senior administrators, such as president, deans, or department heads? Write an essay in which you describe the situation, explain it, and, if it seems appropriate, suggest ways to change it. (Check on whether any plans for change are now in operation—and how they are working.) Use a mixture of statistical data and personal interviews as Fraker has.

7. Choose any minority group and consider their progress to the top in some organization for which you can obtain the relevant data. Using Fraker as a model, try to identify a problem, if there is one, explain its sources, and suggest solutions. If what you find is not a problem but a success story, try to explain how it happened and suggest how it might be repeated in other areas.

MAKING CONNECTIONS

1. Fraker, bell hooks, in "Black Is a Woman's Color," and Carol Gilligan, in "Interviewing Adolescent Girls," all express a feminist viewpoint. How similar are these viewpoints? Using these essays as examples, how unified do you take their positions to be?

2. Write an essay in which you define *feminism* and explain what you take to be its aims, using as evidence the essays by Fraker, hooks, Gilligan, and any other specific examples you wish to cite. You might consider such subjects as what feminism is, what motivates feminists, what feminist goals and methods are, and what differences of approach you find within feminist studies.

INTERVIEWING ADOLESCENT GIRLS
Carol Gilligan

Carol Gilligan (b. 1936) is a professor of education at Harvard University. Her research on women's identity formation and moral development in adolescence and adulthood was the subject of In a Different Voice: Psychological Theory and Women's Development *(1982), a book which brought her wide attention in the academic community and beyond. The following selection is from an essay called* "Teaching Shakespeare's Sister: Notes from the Underground of Adolescence," *a synthesis of the preface and prologue to* Making Connections: The Relational Worlds of Adolescent Girls at Emma Willard School *(1990), which Gilligan coauthored with Nona Lyons and Trudy Hanmer.*

Interviewing girls in adolescence, in the time between the twelve-year-old's 1 knowing and the adult woman's remembering, I felt at times that I had entered an underground world, that I was led in by girls to caverns of knowledge that were then suddenly covered over, as if nothing were known and nothing were happening. What I heard was at once familiar and surprising: girls' knowledge of the human social world, a knowledge gleaned by seeing and listening, by piecing together thoughts and feelings, sounds and glances, responses and reactions, until they compose a pattern, compelling in its explanatory power and often intricate in its psychological logic. Such knowledge on the part of girls is not represented in descriptions of psychological development nor in clinical case studies, and, more disturbingly, it is disclaimed by adolescent girls themselves, who often seem divided from their own knowledge and preface their observations by saying "I don't know."

At a school for girls in a large midwestern city, twelve-year-olds, when asked 2 to describe a powerful learning experience, were as likely to describe an experience that took place inside as outside of school. By fifteen more than twice as many girls located powerful learning experiences outside of school rather than inside. With respect to the nature of such experiences, girls at fifteen were more likely than girls at twelve to talk about experiences outside of school in which family or friends or other people they knew were the central catalysts of learning.[1] Between the ages of twelve and fifteen—the time when dropping out of school becomes common in the inner city—the education of girls seems to be moving out of the public sphere and into the private realm. Is this the time, I wondered, when girls' knowledge becomes buried? Was girls' learning going underground?

The question surfaced in reflecting on my experiences in interviewing adolescent girls at Emma Willard School in Troy, New York. The isolated setting of the residential school and its walled enclosure made it something of a strange island in the stream of contemporary living, an odd mixture of old world and new. In this resonant setting I heard girls speak about storms in relationships and pleasure in relationships, revealing a knowledge of relationships that often was grounded in detailed descriptions of inner psychic worlds—relational worlds through which girls sometimes moved freely and which at other times seemed blocked or walled. Listening for this knowledge, I felt myself entering, to some extent, the underground city of female adolescence, the place where powerful learning experiences were happening. The gateway to this underworld was marked by the statement "I don't know"—the sign of repression—and the code word of membership or the password was the phrase "you know." I wondered about the relationship between this knowledge and girls' other life of notebooks, lessons, and homework.

One afternoon, in the second year of the study, toward the end of an interview with Gail, a girl with whom I had not made much contact, I asked if she were curious about the "it" that she was describing—"the problem" that stood between her and her being "able to achieve anywhere near [her] potential," the thing that kept her from "getting [her] act together." Gail said that she did not know whether she would "ever understand what the problem was," but, she said, "I hope that someday it will be gone and I will be happy." I asked how it will go away. She said she did not know, but that it would be "sad if it doesn't." I asked if she were curious; she said she did not know. We went on with the interview questions. As she thought about herself in the future, I asked, how did she imagine her life, what expectations did she feel others had for her, what were her hopes for herself? She was waiting, she said, to see if "it happens." She felt she had come up against "this big wall." We went on. At the end Gail said, "Maybe someday I will draw it." It seemed that she knew what it looked like. I asked what color she would make it: "Kind of deep ivory," she said. What shape? "A giant block of ice. This tall . . . very thick. A cube standing in front of me." She said that she could melt it, but that she would "have to use very high temperatures."

The following year Gail, now a senior, began by talking to me in the language of social science. "I would like to mention," she said, "that, having thought about my last two interviews, it occurs to me that it is hard to get the real opinions of teenage girls as young as we are because a lot of girls really don't know what they think." If I had interviewed her on another day, or if I were a different person, I would "get very different things," especially because "a lot of the questions you asked are not questions that I have ever put to myself . . .

and afterwards I wondered, you know, did I really mean that. . . . I don't feel you are getting what is important to me; you are getting that and other things in equal weight." I asked, "So there is no way of knowing [what's true and what's important]?" She agreed.

I began with the interview questions. "Looking back over the past year. . . ." 6 I suggested that as we went along she might tell me which questions were ones that she had put to herself and which—Gail suddenly switched modes of discourse. She said, "I actually feel a great deal older this year." One way of speaking about herself ("Teenage girls . . . really don't know what they think") yielded to another ("I actually feel . . ."). The relationship between these two ways of speaking about herself seemed critical. In the terms of her own imagery, one way of speaking shored up the wall between herself and her knowledge, and one provided a sense of an opening, a place of entry, which led through knowing how she was feeling. "I really feel able," Gail explained, taking the opening,

> to put myself in perspective about a lot of things that were confusing me about myself, and I have a tendency to keep things to myself, things that bother me. I keep them in and then I start feeling like this, just harassed and I can't really—everything just warps my perception of everything. . . . But I have discovered the reason for my whole block. I mean, I was getting bad grades, and I told you about a mysterious block last year that was like a wall.
> *I remember that.*
> Now, I figured out what was going on. I figured this out last week. It is that, all through my childhood, I interpreted what my parents were saying to me in my mind. I never voiced this interpretation.

The unvoiced or unspoken, being out of relationship, had gotten out of 7 perspective—"just warp[ing] my perception of everything." What Gail interpreted her parents as saying to her was that she should "be independent and self-sufficient from a very early age." Thus, Gail said, "anything that interrupted my sense of what I should be I would soak up into myself, as though I were a big sponge and had tremendous shock capacity to just bounce back." What Gail was taking in was clearly something that she found shocking, but she felt that she should act as though she were a sponge and just soak up the shock by herself. So, she said, "I would feel bad about things, [but] I wouldn't do anything about them. I wouldn't say anything. That goes with grades and personal problems and relationships"—much of her adolescent life. And then, she said, "last week, last Wednesday, this whole thing came over me, and I can really feel that now I can understand what was going on with me. I can put my life in perspective." Thus, Gail explained that she no longer had to not know: "What's happening, what's happening with me? What is going on? Why am I not being able to see? Why is this so hard for me? And then of course when I finally let it out, maybe every six months, it is like a chair casting shadows and making tremendous spokes. Everything becomes monumental. I feel terrible, and it is really very disturbing." With this powerful image of "it" as "a chair casting shadows and making tremendous spokes," Gail conveys how the ordinary can become monumental and very disturbing. What is explicit in this passage is that Gail became disconnected from her own thoughts and feelings and found herself asking questions about herself that she then could not answer. In threatening this disconnection, the process of knowing had become overwhelming. I asked Gail if she had a sense of what had led her to the understanding she described, and she spoke about a conversation with a friend:

> It started when my friend was telling me how angry she was at her math teacher, who when she asked for extra help must have been in a bad mood and was angry with her. I was thinking about the way my stepfather would do the same thing. And then I was thinking about my stepfather, and then I decided that I really have been abused as a child, not physically, but even last summer, whenever he has insecurity, he is very jealous of me, he is insecure with my mother, and then he just lashes out at me and criticizes me to no end, very angrily. And for a person who has grown up with that and who really doesn't understand herself—instead of saying, "Wait a minute. What are you doing? I am a person."—I would just cuddle up and make like a rock. Tense all my muscles and just sit there and listen to it and be relieved when it was over. And then I was thinking about myself and my reactions to things, and I was thinking all year about all the problems I had last year. . . . It is all my holding back. And I really feel I have made a tremendous breakthrough.

Joining her friend in voicing anger in response to anger rather than just soaking it up like a sponge or tensing her muscles and becoming like a rock, Gail felt she had broken through the wall that was holding back her "reactions to things," her feelings and thoughts.

"It was amazing," I said, "to see it that way," responding to Gail's precise description of psychological processes—the step-by-step tracing of her own feelings and thoughts in response to her friend's story about anger and the math teacher as well as her analysis of how insecurity and jealousy breed attack. "My mother," Gail said, turning to the missing person in the drama (and signaling by the phrase "you know" that this was in part an underground story):

> came down the day before yesterday, and I told her about it. She has been worried about me day and night since I was little because of my holding back. She would say, "You are holding your light under a bushel," and then, you know, get very upset once or twice a year, because everything would get [to be] too much, you know. Of course, my mother would have tremendous guilt. . . . "What have I done to

this poor child? I don't really know what I have done, but there is something. What is it?"

"You have read *Oedipus Rex*?" Gail asks me. I had. "Well, Oedipus went 9 through his entire life weighing himself by himself, and I have done that, and that is what allows me to get out of proportion. I don't talk about anything with anybody, anything that is bothering me."

I thought of the queen in the Oedipus story. Gail's description of her mother 10 had caught the franticness of Jocasta as she tries to keep Oedipus from knowing the truth about family relations. No more truth, she pleads. Was Gail hearing a similar plea from her mother? The problem was that "it"—the unnamed or unspoken truth—"just rolls up like a snowball, and it gets bigger and bigger, and my perception just warps out of shape" so that, like Oedipus, Gail cannot see what in another sense she knows. Her question to herself—"Why am I not able to see?"—resonates with the question she attributes to her mother: "What have I done to this poor child?" But Gail also lays out the logic that suppressed her questions about suffering and about women. Gail reasoned that, if her stepfather's attacks had truly been hurtful to her, then her mother would have taken action to stop them. Because her mother did nothing, at least as far as Gail was aware of, Gail concluded that her stepfather's verbal lashings could not really have hurt her. To feel her feelings then posed difficult questions: what does it mean to be a good mother, what does it mean for a mother to love her daughter, and what does it mean for a daughter to love both her mother and herself?

The either/or logic that Gail was learning as an adolescent, the straight-line 11 categories of Western thinking (self/other, mind/body, thought/feelings, past/present) and the if/then construction of linear reasoning threatened to undermine Gail's knowledge of human relationships by washing out the logic of feelings. To understand psychological processes means to follow the both/and logic of feelings and to trace the currents of associations, memories, sounds, and images that flow back and forth, connecting self and other, mind and body, past and present, consciousness and culture. To separate thinking from relationship, and thus to make a division between formal education and powerful learning experiences, is to become like Oedipus, who got things out of proportion by "weighing himself by himself." Gail ties the return of perspective to the return of relationship and describes the insight and knowledge that suddenly came out of the back-and-forth play of her conversation with her friend: "I talked to my friend, and she talked about her math teacher, and I was thinking about my stepfather, and then, with all my thinking about it beforehand, wondering what makes a difference, I finally put it together and bang! . . . Before, when I was getting all tied up, everything was a huge wall that isn't a wall anymore." The "it" is no longer a wall but a relationship that joins Gail with herself and with her friend.

The image of a wall recurred in interviews with adolescent girls—a physical 12 rendering of the blocks preventing connection, the impasses in relationships, which girls acutely described and which were associated with intense feelings of anger and sadness. Girls' wishes to make connection with others reflected the pleasure that they found in relationships.

Pleasure in relationships is linked to knowledge gained through relationships, 13 and girls voice their desire to know more about others and also to be known better themselves. "I wish to become better in the relationship with my mother," Ellen says—"to be able more easily to disagree with her." Disagreement here is a sign of relationship, a manifestation of two people coming together. And it is in close relationships that girls are most willing to argue or disagree, wanting most to be known and seen by those to whom they feel closest and also believing more that those who are close will be there, will listen, and will try to understand. "If you love someone," Anna explains, "you are usually comfortable with them. And, feeling comfortable, you can easily argue with one another and say, look, I want you to see my side. It's a lot easier to fight with someone you love, because you know they will always forgive you, at least usually they will . . . and you know that they are still going to be there for you after the disagreement."

Perhaps it is because of this feeling of being comfortable that girls most often 14 speak about conflict in their relationships with their mothers—the person who, one girl said, "will always welcome me." Girls' willingness to fight for genuine connection with their mothers is well illustrated by Kate, a fifteen-year-old who says, paradoxically:

> I called my mother up and said, "Why can't I speak to you anymore? What is going on?" And I ended up crying and hanging up on her because she wouldn't listen to me. She had her own opinion about what was truth and what was reality, and she gave me no opening. . . . What she had on her mind was the truth. And you know, I kept saying, "Well, you hurt me," and she said, "No, I did not." And I said, "Well, why am I hurt?" you know, and she is just denying my feelings as if they did not exist and as if I had no right to feel them, you know, even though they were.

The counterpart to the image of a wall is the search for an opening, a way 15 of reaching another person, of finding a place of entry. Yet to open oneself to another person creates a great vulnerability, and thus the strength of girls' desire for relationship also engenders the need for protection from fraudulent relationships and psychic wounding. "To me," Jane says, "love means an attachment to a person," by which she means a willingness or wish

> to share a lot of things with that person and not feel as though you are opening up your soul and it is going to be misrepresented or misunderstood. Rather, so that person . . . will know kind of inside how far

478

to go and, if they go too far, they will understand when you say, that's not what I want. . . . where people accept your idiosyncrasies . . . that you can have fun and you can disagree but that the argument isn't something that wounds you for months. . . . Some people are too quick to say "I love you." It takes time to learn someone. I don't think you can love on first sight. . . . You can feel a connection with someone, but you can't just love them.

These carefully drawn distinctions, the contrast between feeling connected with someone and loving them and between having fun and disagreeing and having an argument that wounds you for months, bespeak close observation of relationships and psychological processes and also experiences of being misrepresented, misunderstood, and not listened to, which have left both knowledge and scars. Jane says she is looking for someone who will understand when she says, "that's not what I want." Mira, in contrast, has chosen silence as a way of avoiding being hurt:

I personally have had a hard time asking questions . . . because I was shy and did not really like to talk to people about what I was really thinking.
Why not?
I thought it was much safer just to keep it to myself, and this way nobody would have so much of a vulnerable spot that they could get to me with. And so I thought, just the thought of having somebody having something on me that could possibly hurt me, that scared me and kept me from speaking up a lot of the time.

Like the character in Woolf's story, "An Unwritten Novel," Mira keeps her life to herself; her speaking self also is "entombed . . . driven in, in, in to the central catacomb. . . . Flit[ting] with its lanterns restlessly up and down the dark corridor."[2] Mary Belenky and her colleagues have described how women retreat into silence when words become weapons and are used to wound.[3] Adolescent girls invoke images of violence and talk in the language of warfare or about winning and losing when they describe the inner workings of explosive relationships, fearing also that such relationships can "throw us apart forever."

What is the worst thing that can happen in a relationship?
I guess if people build up resentments and don't talk about them, things can just keep building up until they reach the boiling point, and then there is like a cold war going on. People are just fencing on either side of a wall, but not admitting it to the other person until there is an explosion or something.

Other girls, like Emma, describe "building a wall" that serves to undermine relationships:

479

What is the worst thing that can happen in a relationship?
Not talking it out. Building a wall . . . I think that can lead to a lot
more because you don't give a chance to the other person to say
anything. . . . You are too close-minded to listen to what they have to
say. . . . If you don't listen to your friends, they are not your friends,
there is no relationship there, because you don't listen.

Taken together, these observations of the ways in which people move and
affect, touch and are touched by one another, appear and disappear in relationships with themselves and with others, reveal an understanding of psychic
processes that is closer to a physics than a metaphysics of relationship—based
on tracking voices and images, thoughts and feelings, across the cloud chamber
of daily life. Certain observations are breathtakingly simple in their logic although profound in their implications, especially given the pace of contemporary living. Emma says that, "if you don't listen to your friends, they are not
your friends. There is no relationship there." Others are more complex, like
Joan's exegesis of the indirect discourse of betrayal: "If you don't trust someone
to know a secret . . . you sort of grow apart . . . or you will feel like you are
with them and down underneath you are angry . . . but you don't say anything,
so it comes out . . . in other ways." Or Maria's explication of the confusing
mixing of anger and hurt:

> I am not sure of the difference when I feel angry and hurt. . . . I don't
> even know if they are separate emotions. . . . I was angry, I think at
> myself in that relationship, that I had let myself be used . . . that I had
> let down my guard so much. I was completely vulnerable. And I chose
> to do that. . . . I kept saying, "I hate him," but I realized that he didn't
> even notice me there because he was in his own world. So that I think
> . . . all my anger comes out of being hurt, and it's a confusion there.

Repeatedly, girls emphasize the need for open conflict and voicing disagreement. Catherine describes the fruitful quality of disagreement in her relationship
with her friend:

> We have learned more about ourselves. . . . I think . . . she had never
> really had a close friend but lots of acquaintances. She didn't get into
> fights and things like that. . . . I think she realizes that you have to
> have disagreements and things like that for a relationship to last.
> *How come?*
> Because if you don't really voice your disagreements, then you don't
> really have anything going, do you know what I mean? It's just another
> way, it is another side of you that you are letting someone else see.

And Liza describes the raw pain of finding, at the end of a long journey, that
you are not able to talk with someone on whom you had depended:

480

What is the worst thing that can happen in a relationship?
That you grow up, or sideways, and not be able to talk to each other, especially if you depend on being able to talk to someone and not being able to. That hurts a lot, because you have been dependent on that. It is like walking fifty miles for a glass of water in a hot desert, and you have been depending on it for days, and getting there and finding it is not there anymore; you made the wrong turn ten miles back.

The knowledge about relationships and the life of relationships that flourish 19 on this remote island of female adolescence are, to shift the metaphor, like notes from the underground. Much of what psychologists know about relationships is also known by adolescent girls. But, as girls themselves say clearly, they will speak only when they feel that someone will listen and will not leave in the face of conflict or disagreement. Thus, the fate of girls' knowledge and girls' education becomes tied to the fate of their relationships.

When women's studies is joined with the study of girls' development, it 20 becomes clearer why adolescence is a critical time in girls' lives—a time when girls are in danger of losing their voices and thus losing connection with others, and also a time when girls, gaining voice and knowledge, are in danger of knowing the unseen and speaking the unspoken and thus losing connection with what is commonly taken to be "reality." This crisis of connection in girls' lives at adolescence links the psychology of women with the most basic questions about the nature of relationships and the definition of reality. Girls' questions about relationships and about reality, however, also tug at women's silences.

At the edge of adolescence, eleven- and twelve-year-old girls observe where 21 and when women speak and when they are silent.[4] As resisters, they may be especially prone to notice and question the compliance of women to male authority. One of Woolf's questions in *A Room of One's Own* is why mothers do not provide more rooms for their daughters, why they do not leave more of a legacy for their daughters, and why, more specifically, mothers do not endow their daughters' education with greater comfort.[5] A teacher of twelve-year-olds, after a faculty meeting where women's reluctance to disagree in public became a subject of discussion, told the following story: her eleven-year-old daughter had commented on her reluctance to disagree with her husband (the girl's father). She was angry at her mother, she said, for always giving in. In response, the mother began to explain that, although the girl's father sometimes raised his voice, he was loving and well-intentioned—at which point her daughter interrupted her, saying that it was she, her mother, who she was angry at for always giving in. "I was so humiliated," the teacher said, "so ashamed." Later that year, when her colleague announced a new rule about lunch in homeroom one day, she suppressed her disagreement with him and did not voice her objections—because, she said, she did not want to undermine his authority. Perhaps it was as a result of her previous humiliation that she thought twice on a day when the rule seemed particularly senseless and excused some girls, in spite of the rule, before others who had arrived late at lunch had finished eating. "Good for you," the girls said, "we're proud of you." It was clear that they had noticed everything.

In his appreciation of the poetry of Sylvia Plath, Seamus Heaney reads a 22 famous passage by William Wordsworth as a parable of the three stages in a poet's journey.[6] At first one goes out into the woods and whistles to hear if the owls will respond. Then, once one discovers that one can speak in a way that calls forth a response from the world of nature, one has to learn to perfect one's craft, to enter the world of sounds—of birdcalls, traditions, and poetic conventions—until, Heaney says, if one is blessed or fortunate, one becomes the instrument through which the sounds of the world pass. Heaney traces this transformation in Plath's poetry, drawing the reader into his own exhilaration as her language takes off. But Plath's relationship to the tradition of male voices, which she was entering and changing by entering, was not the same as Heaney's, and her entrance was more deeply disruptive. And the same can be said for women students.

A student first must learn how to call forth a response from the world: to ask 23 a question to which people will listen, which they will find interesting and respond to. Then she must learn the craft of inquiry so that she can tune her questions and develop her ear for language and thus speak more clearly and more freely, can say more and also hear more fully. But if the world of nature, as Heaney implies, is equally responsive to the calls of women and men, the world of civilization is not, or at least has not been up to the present. The wind of tradition blowing through women is a chill wind because it brings a message of exclusion: stay out. It brings a message of subordination: stay under. It brings a message of objectification: become the object of another's worship or desire; see yourself as you have been seen for centuries, through a male gaze. And because all of the suffering, the endless litany of storm and shipwreck, is presented as necessary or even good for civilization, the message to women is: keep quiet, notice the absence of women, and say nothing.

At the present moment the education of women presents genuine dilemmas 24 and real opportunities. Women's questions—especially questions about relationships and questions about violence—often feel disruptive to women because at present they are disruptive both in private and public life. And relationships between women are often strained. It is not at all clear what it means to be a good mother or teacher to an adolescent girl coming of age in Western culture. The choices that women make in order to survive or to appear good in the eyes of others and thus sustain their protection are often at the expense of women's relationships with one another, and girls begin to observe and comment on these choices around the age of eleven or twelve. If women can stay in the gaze of girls so that girls do not have to look and not see, if women can be seen by girls, including the twelve-year-old in themselves, if women can sustain girls' gazes and respond to girls' voices, then, perhaps as Woolf envisioned, "the opportunity will come and the dead poet who is Shakespeare's sister will put on the body which she has so often laid down and find it possible to live and write her poetry"[7]—as Plath did for a moment before taking her life. Yet as Woolf reminds us, before Shakespeare's sister can come, we must have the habit of freedom and the courage to write and say exactly what we think.

NOTES

1. Alan Braun, "Themes of Connection: Powerful Learning among Adolescent Girls" (Working Paper, Laurel/Harvard Study, Project on the Psychology of Women and the Development of Girls, Harvard Graduate School of Education), 3.

2. Virginia Woolf, "An Unwritten Novel," *Haunted House and Other Short Stories* (1921; reprint, New York: Harcourt Brace Jovanovich, 1972), 19.

3. Mary Belenky, Blythe Clinchy, Nancy Goldberger and Jill Tarule, *Women's Ways of Knowing* (New York: Basic Books, 1986).

4. Lyn Mikel Brown, "A Problem of Vision: The Development of Voice and Relational Knowledge in Girls Ages Seven to Sixteen," *Women's Studies Quarterly* 1991:1 & 2.

5. Woolf, *A Room of One's Own* (1928; reprint, New York: Harcourt, Brace, and World, 1957), 20–24.

6. Seamus Heaney, *The Government of the Tongue: Selected Prose, 1978–1987* (New York: Farrar, Straus and Giroux, 1989).

7. Woolf. *A Room of One's Own*, 117.

QUESTIONS

1. Where did your most powerful learning experience occur? Poll your class. How do the answers break down according to sex (and age, if relevant)?

2. In your discussion of learning experiences, did men and women participate equally, or is there a pattern of domination in your classroom?

3. Gilligan is interested in the metaphors her subjects use to express their emotional states. Gail talks about her "block . . . like a wall." What other metaphors does she use? Are they unusual or common? How would you interpret them? What other metaphors are used by Gilligan's subjects?

4. Gilligan says in her conclusion, "It is not at all clear what it means to be a good mother or teacher to an adolescent girl coming of age in Western culture." Discuss some of the reasons why this is so, or disagree with this statement.

5. Take the statement quoted in Question 4 and substitute "father" for "mother" and "boy" for "girl." Then discuss why you agree or disagree with the statement.

6. On the subject of learning experiences, extend your interviews and observations to a wider group of students, or to a different age group. You may, for example, want to talk to a group of public high school or junior high school students, to see if their

experiences are similar to those of the private school students Gilligan interviewed. Write up your findings.

MAKING CONNECTIONS

1. Gilligan ends by saying that adolescents—indeed, all women—"must have . . . the courage to write and say exactly what we think." Compare bell hooks's description of her adolescence in "Black Is a Woman's Color" with those described by Gilligan's interviewees. How does hooks's essay comment on Gilligan's statement?

2. How do Gilligan's findings reflect on those of Susan Fraker in "Why Women Aren't Getting to the Top"?

CHILDREN OF A MARRIAGE
Richard Rodriguez

Richard Rodriguez (b. 1944), the son of Mexican-American immigrants, is a widely published essayist and journalist, whose upbringing in California and education at Stanford, Columbia, the University of California at Berkeley, and the University of London have made him keenly aware of the personal and cultural confusions and tensions experienced by many Hispanic-American children. In addition to numerous magazine articles on Hispanic-American culture, Rodriguez is known for his autobiography, Hunger of Memory: The Education of Richard Rodriguez (1983) *and his recent* Days of Obligation: An Argument with My Mexican Father (1992).

What is culture? 1

The immigrant shrugs. Latin American immigrants come to the United 2
States with only the things they need in mind—not abstractions like culture.
Money. They need dollars. They need food. Maybe they need to get out of the
way of bullets.

Most of us who concern ourselves with Hispanic-American culture, as paint- 3
ers, musicians, writers—or as sons and daughters—are the children of immigrants. We have grown up on this side of the border, in the land of Elvis Presley
and Thomas Edison; our lives are prescribed by the mall, by the DMV and the
Chinese restaurant. Our imaginations yet vacillate between an Edenic Latin
America (the blue door)—which nevertheless betrayed our parents—and the
repellent plate glass of a real American city—which has been good to us.

Hispanic-American culture is where the past meets the future. Hispanic- 4
American culture is not an Hispanic milestone only, not simply a celebration
at the crossroads. America transforms into pleasure what America cannot avoid.
Is it any coincidence that at a time when Americans are troubled by the
encroachment of the Mexican desert, Americans discover a chic in cactus, in
the decorator colors of the Southwest? In sand?

Hispanic-American culture of the sort that is now showing (the teen movie, 5
the rock song) may exist in an hourglass; may in fact be irrelevant to the epic.
The U.S. Border Patrol works through the night to arrest the flow of illegal
immigrants over the border, even as Americans wait in line to get into "La

Bamba." Even as Americans vote to declare, once and for all, that English shall be the official language of the United States, Madonna starts recording in Spanish.

But then so is Bill Cosby's show irrelevant to the 10 o'clock news, where 6 families huddle together in fear on porches, pointing at the body of the slain boy bagged in tarpaulin. Which is not to say that Bill Cosby or Michael Jackson are irrelevant to the future or without neo-Platonic influence. Like players within the play, they prefigure, they resolve. They make black and white audiences aware of a bond that may not yet exist.

Before a national TV audience, Rita Moreno tells Geraldo Rivera that her 7 dream as an actress is to play a character rather like herself: "I speak English perfectly well . . . I'm not dying from poverty . . . I want to play *that* kind of Hispanic woman, which is to say, an American citizen." This is an actress talking, these are show-biz pieties. But Moreno expresses as well the general Hispanic-American predicament. Hispanics want to belong to America without betraying the past.

Hispanics fear losing ground in any negotiation with the American city. We 8 come from an expansive, an intimate culture that has been judged second-rate by the United States of America. For reasons of pride, therefore, as much as of affection, we are reluctant to give up our past. Hispanics often express a fear of "losing" culture. Our fame in the United States has been our resistance to assimilation.

The symbol of Hispanic culture has been the tongue of flame—Spanish. 9 But the remarkable legacy Hispanics carry from Latin America is not language— an inflatable skin—but breath itself, capacity of soul, an inclination to live. The genius of Latin America is the habit of synthesis.

We assimilate. Just over the border there is the example of Mexico, the 10 country from which the majority of U.S. Hispanics come. Mexico is mestizo— Indian and Spanish. Within a single family, Mexicans are light-skinned and dark. It is impossible for the Mexican to say, in the scheme of things, where the Indian begins and the Spaniard surrenders.

In culture as in blood, Latin America was formed by a rape that became a 11 marriage. Due to the absorbing generosity of the Indian, European culture took on new soil. What Latin America knows is that people create one another as they marry. In the music of Latin America you will hear the litany of blood-lines—the African drum, the German accordion, the cry from the minaret.

The United States stands as the opposing New World experiment. In North 12 America the Indian and the European stood apace. Whereas Latin America was formed by a medieval Catholic dream of one world—of meltdown conversion—the United States was built up from Protestant individualism. The American melting pot washes away only embarrassment; it is the necessary initiation into public life. The American faith is that our national strength derives from separateness, from "diversity." The glamour of the United States is a carnival promise: You can lose weight, get rich as Rockefeller, tough up your roots, get a divorce.

Immigrants still come for the promise. But the United States wavers in its 13 faith. As long as there was space enough, sky enough, as long as economic success validated individualism, loneliness was not too high a price to pay. (The cabin on the prairie or the Sony Walkman.)

As we near the end of the American century, two alternative cultures beckon 14 the American imagination—both highly communal cultures—the Asian and the Latin American. The United States is a literal culture. Americans devour what we might otherwise fear to become. Sushi will make us corporate warriors. Combination Plate #3, smothered in mestizo gravy, will burn a hole in our hearts.

Latin America offers passion. Latin America has a life—I mean *life*—big 15 clouds, unambiguous themes, death, birth, faith, that the United States, for all its quality of life, seems without now. Latin America offers communal riches: an undistressed leisure, a kitchen table, even a full sorrow. Such is the solitude of America, such is the urgency of American need, Americans reach right past a fledgling, homegrown Hispanic-American culture for the real thing—the darker bottle of Mexican beer; the denser novel of a Latin American master.

For a long time, Hispanics in the United States withheld from the United 16 States our Latin American gift. We denied the value of assimilation. But as our presence is judged less foreign in America, we will produce a more generous art, less timid, less parochial. Carlos Santana, Luis Valdez, Linda Ronstadt—Hispanic Americans do not have a "pure" Latin American art to offer. Expect bastard themes, expect ironies, comic conclusions. For we live on this side of the border, where Kraft manufactures bricks of "Mexican style" Velveeta, and where Jack in the Box serves "Fajita Pita."

The flame-red Chevy floats a song down the Pan American Highway: From 17 *a rolled-down window, the grizzled voice of Willie Nelson rises in disembodied harmony with the voice of Julio Iglesias. Gabby Hayes and Cisco are thus resolved.*

Expect marriage. We will change America even as we will be changed. We 18 will disappear with you into a new miscegenation.

Along the border, real conflicts remain. But the ancient tear separating 19 Europe from itself—the Catholic Mediterranean from the Protestant north—may yet heal itself in the New World. For generations, Latin America has been the place—the bed—of a confluence of so many races and cultures that Protestant North America shuddered to imagine it.

Imagine it. 20

QUESTIONS

1. In the first paragraph, Rodriguez asks "What is culture?", but in the second paragraph he implies that "abstractions like culture" are irrelevant to Latin-American immigrants. How do you account for this apparent contradiction?

2. What is the significance of Rodriguez's title? In what sense(s) is he concerned with "marriage" in this piece? In what sense(s) is he concerned with "children" of a "marriage"? What echoes of the title can you find in the essay itself?

3. According to Rodriguez, what are the important characteristics of Latin-American culture? How does it differ from North American culture? What does he consider to be the most significant results of the interaction between these cultures?

4. Notice the specific persons and things that Rodriguez cites as manifestations of North American culture. How representative of American culture do you consider these persons and things to be? What aspects of American culture do you consider to be more representative than the ones that Rodriguez cites in his piece?

5. Notice the specific persons and things that Rodriguez cites as manifestations of Latin-American culture. How representative of Latin-American culture do you consider these persons and things to be? What aspects of Latin-American culture do you consider to be more representative than the ones that Rodriguez cites?

6. Why do you think Rodriguez has chosen to put paragraph 17 in italics? What do you consider to be the significance of the descriptive-narrative detail that he features in this paragraph?

7. Write an essay illustrated with your own personal observation, experience, and knowledge, in which you discuss what you perceive to be some of the most distinctive contributions, qualities, and representatives of Hispanic-American culture.

8. Write an essay illustrated with your own personal observation, experience, and knowledge, in which you discuss what you perceive to be some of the most distinctive contributions, qualities, and representatives of the cultural marriage(s) reflected in your own family heritage.

MAKING CONNECTIONS

Based on your reading of James Baldwin's "If Black English Isn't a Language, Then Tell Me, What Is?", how do you suppose he would respond to Rodriguez's ideas of cultural "marriage" and change? Based on your reading of Rodriguez's essay, how do you suppose he would respond to Baldwin's ideas about language and culture?

ON THE FEAR OF DEATH

Elizabeth Kübler-Ross

Elizabeth Kübler-Ross (b. 1926), a Swiss-American psychi-atrist, is one of the leaders of the movement that may help change the way Americans think about death. Born in Zurich, she received her M.D. from the University of Zurich in 1957 and came to the United States as an intern the following year. Kübler-Ross began her work with terminally ill patients while teaching psychiatry at the University of Chicago Medical School. She now heads "Shanti Nilaya" (Sanskrit for "home of peace") in Head Waters, Virginia, an organization she founded in 1976, "dedicated to the promotion of physical, emotional, and spiritual health." "On the Fear of Death" is taken from her first and most famous book, On Death and Dying *(1969).*

> Let me not pray to be sheltered from
> dangers but to be fearless in facing
> them.
> Let me not beg for the stilling of
> my pain but for the heart to conquer it.
> Let me not look for allies in life's
> battlefield but to my own strength.
> Let me not crave in anxious fear to
> be saved but hope for the patience to
> win my freedom.
> Grant me that I may not be a
> coward, feeling your mercy in my
> success alone; but let me find the grasp
> of your hand in my failure.

Rabindranath Tagore, *Fruit-Gathering*

Epidemics have taken a great toll of lives in past generations. Death in infancy and early childhood was frequent and there were few families who didn't lose a member of the family at an early age. Medicine has changed greatly in the last decades. Widespread vaccinations have practically eradicated many illnesses, at least in western Europe and the United States. The use of chemotherapy, especially the antibiotics, has contributed to an ever-decreasing number of fatalities in infectious diseases. Better child care and education have effected a low morbidity and mortality among children. The many diseases that have taken an impressive toll among the young and middle-aged have been conquered. The number of old people is on the rise, and with this fact come the number of people with malignancies and chronic diseases associated more with old age.

Pediatricians have less work with acute and life-threatening situations as they 2 have an ever-increasing number of patients with psychosomatic disturbances and adjustment and behavior problems. Physicians have more people in their waiting rooms with emotional problems than they have ever had before, but they also have more elderly patients who not only try to live with their decreased physical abilities and limitations but who also face loneliness and isolation with all its pains and anguish. The majority of these people are not seen by a psychiatrist. Their needs have to be elicited and gratified by other professional people, for instance, chaplains and social workers. It is for them that I am trying to outline the changes that have taken place in the last few decades, changes that are ultimately responsible for the increased fear of death, the rising number of emotional problems, and the greater need for understanding of and coping with the problems of death and dying.

When we look back in time and study old cultures and people, we are 3 impressed that death has always been distasteful to man and will probably always be. From a psychiatrist's point of view this is very understandable and can perhaps best be explained by our basic knowledge that, in our unconscious, death is never possible in regard to ourselves. It is inconceivable for our unconscious to imagine an actual ending of our own life here on earth, and if this life of ours has to end, the ending is always attributed to a malicious intervention from the outside by someone else. In simple terms, in our unconscious mind we can only be killed; it is inconceivable to die of a natural cause or of old age. Therefore death in itself is associated with a bad act, a frightening happening, something that in itself calls for retribution and punishment.

One is wise to remember these fundamental facts as they are essential in 4 understanding some of the most important, otherwise unintelligible communications of our patients.

The second fact that we have to comprehend is that in our unconscious 5 mind we cannot distinguish between a wish and a deed. We are all aware of some of our illogical dreams in which two completely opposite statements can exist side by side—very acceptable in our dreams but unthinkable and illogical in our wakening state. Just as our unconscious mind cannot differentiate between the wish to kill somebody in anger and the act of having done so, the young child is unable to make this distinction. The child who angrily wishes his mother to drop dead for not having gratified his needs will be traumatized greatly by the actual death of his mother—even if this event is not linked closely in time with his destructive wishes. He will always take part or the whole blame for the loss of his mother. He will always say to himself—rarely to others—"I did it, I am responsible, I was bad, therefore Mommy left me." It is well to remember that the child will react in the same manner if he loses a parent by divorce, separation, or desertion. Death is often seen by a child as an impermanent thing and has therefore little distinction from a divorce in which he may have an opportunity to see a parent again.

Many a parent will remember remarks of their children such as, "I will bury my doggy now and next spring when the flowers come up again, he will get up." Maybe it was the same wish that motivated the ancient Egyptians to supply their dead with food and goods to keep them happy and the old American Indians to bury their relatives with their belongings. 6

When we grow older and begin to realize that our omnipotence is really not so omnipotent, that our strongest wishes are not powerful enough to make the impossible possible, the fear that we have contributed to the death of a loved one diminishes—and with it the guilt. The fear remains diminished, however, only so long as it is not challenged too strongly. Its vestiges can be seen daily in hospital corridors and in people associated with the bereaved. 7

A husband and wife may have been fighting for years, but when the partner dies, the survivor will pull his hair, whine and cry louder and beat his chest in regret, fear and anguish, and will hence fear his own death more than before, still believing in the law of talion—an eye for an eye, a tooth for a tooth—"I am responsible for her death, I will have to die a pitiful death in retribution." 8

Maybe this knowledge will help us understand many of the old customs and rituals which have lasted over the centuries and whose purpose is to diminish the anger of the gods or the people as the case may be, thus decreasing the anticipated punishment. I am thinking of the ashes, the torn clothes, the veil, the *Klage Weiber* of the old days[1]—they are all means to ask you to take pity on them, the mourners, and are expressions of sorrow, grief, and shame. If someone grieves, beats his chest, tears his hair, or refuses to eat, it is an attempt at self-punishment to avoid or reduce the anticipated punishment for the blame that he takes on the death of a loved one. 9

This grief, shame, and guilt are not very far removed from feelings of anger and rage. The process of grief always includes some qualities of anger. Since none of us likes to admit anger at a deceased person, these emotions are often disguised or repressed and prolong the period of grief or show up in other ways. It is well to remember that it is not up to us to judge such feelings as bad or shameful but to understand their true meaning and origin as something very human. In order to illustrate this I will again use the example of the child— and the child in us. The five-year-old who loses his mother is both blaming himself for her disappearance and being angry at her for having deserted him and for no longer gratifying his needs. The dead person then turns into some- 10

---

[1] *Klage Weiber*: wailing wives. [Eds.]

thing the child loves and wants very much but also hates with equal intensity for this severe deprivation.

The ancient Hebrews regarded the body of a dead person as something   11
unclean and not to be touched. The early American Indians talked about the evil spirits and shot arrows in the air to drive the spirits away. Many other cultures have rituals to take care of the "bad" dead person, and they all originate in this feeling of anger which still exists in all of us, though we dislike admitting it. The tradition of the tombstone may originate in the wish to keep the bad spirits deep down in the ground, and the pebbles that many mourners put on the grave are leftover symbols of the same wish. Though we call the firing of guns at military funerals a last salute, it is the same symbolic ritual as the Indian used when he shot his spears and arrows into the skies.

I give these examples to emphasize that man has not basically changed.   12
Death is still a fearful, frightening happening, and the fear of death is a universal fear even if we think we have mastered it on many levels.

What has changed is our way of coping and dealing with death and dying   13
and our dying patients.

Having been raised in a country in Europe where science is not so advanced,   14
where modern techniques have just started to find their way into medicine, and where people still live as they did in this country half a century ago, I may have had an opportunity to study a part of the evolution of mankind in a shorter period.

I remember as a child the death of a farmer. He fell from a tree and was not   15
expected to live. He asked simply to die at home, a wish that was granted without question. He called his daughters into the bedroom and spoke with each one of them alone for a few moments. He arranged his affairs quietly, though he was in great pain, and distributed his belongings and his land, none of which was to be split until his wife should follow him in death. He also asked each of his children to share in the work, duties, and tasks that he had carried on until the time of the accident. He asked his friends to visit him once more, to bid goodbye to them. Although I was a small child at the time, he did not exclude me or my siblings. We were allowed to share in the preparations of the family just as we were permitted to grieve with them until he died. When he did die, he was left at home, in his own beloved home which he had built, and among his friends and neighbors who went to take a last look at him where he lay in the midst of flowers in the place he had lived in and loved so much. In that country today there is still no make-believe slumber room, no embalming, no false makeup to pretend sleep. Only the signs of very disfiguring illnesses are covered up with bandages and only infectious cases are removed from the home prior to the burial.

Why do I describe such "old-fashioned" customs? I think they are an indi-   16
cation of our acceptance of a fatal outcome, and they help the dying patient as well as his family to accept the loss of a loved one. If a patient is allowed to

terminate his life in the familiar and beloved environment, it requires less adjustment for him. His own family knows him well enough to replace a sedative with a glass of his favorite wine; or the smell of a home-cooked soup may give him the appetite to sip a few spoons of fluid which, I think, is still more enjoyable than an infusion. I will not minimize the need for sedatives and infusions and realize full well from my own experience as a country doctor that they are sometimes life-saving and often unavoidable. But I also know that patience and familiar people and foods could replace many a bottle of intravenous fluids given for the simple reason that it fulfills the physiological need without involving too many people and/or individual nursing care.

17 The fact that children are allowed to stay at home where a fatality has struck and are included in the talk, discussions, and fears gives them the feeling that they are not alone in their grief and gives them the comfort of shared responsibility and shared mourning. It prepares them gradually and helps them view death as part of life, an experience which may help them grow and mature.

18 This is in great contrast to a society in which death is viewed as taboo, discussion of it is regarded as morbid, and children are excluded with the presumption and pretext that it would be "too much" for them. They are then sent off to relatives, often accompanied by some unconvincing lies of "Mother has gone on a long trip" or other unbelievable stories. The child senses that something is wrong, and his distrust in adults will only multiply if other relatives add new variations of the story, avoid his questions or suspicions, shower him with gifts as a meager substitute for a loss he is not permitted to deal with. Sooner or later the child will become aware of the changed family situation and, depending on the age and personality of the child, will have an unresolved grief and regard this incident as a frightening, mysterious, in any case very traumatic experience with untrustworthy grownups, which he has no way to cope with.

19 It is equally unwise to tell a little child who lost her brother that God loved little boys so much that he took little Johnny to heaven. When this little girl grew up to be a woman she never solved her anger at God, which resulted in a psychotic depression when she lost her own little son three decades later.

20 We would think that our great emancipation, our knowledge of science and of man, has given us better ways and means to prepare ourselves and our families for this inevitable happening. Instead the days are gone when a man was allowed to die in peace and dignity in his own home.

21 The more we are making advancements in science, the more we seem to fear and deny the reality of death. How is this possible?

22 We use euphemisms, we make the dead look as if they were asleep, we ship the children off to protect them from the anxiety and turmoil around the house if the patient is fortunate enough to die at home, we don't allow children to visit their dying parents in the hospitals, we have long and controversial discussions about whether patients should be told the truth—a question that rarely

arises when the dying person is tended by the family physician who has known him from delivery to death and who knows the weaknesses and strengths of each member of the family.

I think there are many reasons for this flight away from facing death calmly. 23 One of the most important facts is that dying nowadays is more gruesome in many ways, namely, more lonely, mechanical, and dehumanized; at times it is even difficult to determine technically when the time of death has occurred.

Dying becomes lonely and impersonal because the patient is often taken out 24 of his familiar environment and rushed to an emergency room. Whoever has been very sick and has required rest and comfort especially may recall his experience of being put on a stretcher and enduring the noise of the ambulance siren and hectic rush until the hospital gates open. Only those who have lived through this may appreciate the discomfort and cold necessity of such transportation which is only the beginning of a long ordeal—hard to endure when you are well, difficult to express in words when noise, light, pumps, and voices are all too much to put up with. It may well be that we might consider more the patient under the sheets and blankets and perhaps stop our well-meant efficiency and rush in order to hold the patient's hand, to smile, or to listen to a question. I include the trip to the hospital as the first episode in dying, as it is for many. I am putting it exaggeratedly in contrast to the sick man who is left at home—not to say that lives should not be saved if they can be saved by a hospitalization but to keep the focus on the patient's experience, his needs and his reactions.

When a patient is severely ill, he is often treated like a person with no right 25 to an opinion. It is often someone else who makes the decision if and when and where a patient should be hospitalized. It would take so little to remember that the sick person too has feelings, has wishes and opinions, and has—most important of all—the right to be heard.

Well, our presumed patient has now reached the emergency room. He will 26 be surrounded by busy nurses, orderlies, interns, residents, a lab technician perhaps who will take some blood, an electrocardiogram technician who takes the cardiogram. He may be moved to X-ray and he will overhear opinions of his condition and discussions and questions to members of the family. He slowly but surely is beginning to be treated like a thing. He is no longer a person. Decisions are made often without his opinion. If he tries to rebel he will be sedated, and after hours of waiting and wondering whether he has the strength, he will be wheeled into the operating room or intensive treatment unit and become an object of great concern and great financial investment.

He may cry for rest, peace, and dignity, but he will get infusions, transfusions, 27 a heart machine, or tracheotomy if necessary. He may want one single person to stop for one single minute so that he can ask one single question—but he will get a dozen people around the clock, all busily preoccupied with his heart

494

rate, pulse, electrocardiogram or pulmonary functions, his secretions or excretions but not with him as a human being. He may wish to fight it all but it is going to be a useless fight since all this is done in the fight for his life, and if they can save his life they can consider the person afterwards. Those who consider the person first may lose precious time to save his life! At least this seems to be the rationale or justification behind all this—or is it? Is the reason for this increasingly mechanical, depersonalized approach our own defensiveness? Is this approach our own way to cope with and repress the anxieties that a terminally or critically ill patient evokes in us? Is our concentration on equipment, on blood pressure, our desperate attempt to deny the impending death which is so frightening and discomforting to us that we displace all our knowledge onto machines, since they are less close to us than the suffering face of another human being which would remind us once more of our lack of omnipotence, our own limits and failures, and last but not least perhaps our own mortality?

Maybe the question has to be raised: Are we becoming less human or more human? . . . It is clear that whatever the answer may be, the patient is suffering more—not physically, perhaps, but emotionally. And his needs have not changed over the centuries, only our ability to gratify them.   28

QUESTIONS

1. Why does Kübler-Ross describe the death of a farmer? What point is she making in explaining "such 'old-fashioned' customs" (paragraph 16)?

2. To what extent is this essay explanatory? Summarize a particular explanation of hers that you find intriguing. Do you find it persuasive?

3. At what point in this essay does Kübler-Ross turn from explanation toward argument? Do you think she has taken a stand on her subject? How sympathetic are you to her position?

4. In paragraphs 2 and 10, Kübler-Ross indicates a specialized audience for her writing. Who is that audience, and how do you relate to it?

5. Think of the audience you described in question 4 as a primary audience and of yourself as a member of a secondary audience. To what extent do the two audiences overlap? How thoroughly can you divide one from the other?

6. What experience of death have you had so far? Write of a death that you know something about, even if your relation to it is distant, perhaps only through the media. Can you locate elements of fear and anger in your own behavior or in the behavior of other persons involved? Does Kübler-Ross's interpretation of those reactions help you come to terms with the experience?

7. What kind of balance do you think best between prolonging life and allowing a person to die with dignity? What does the phrase "dying with dignity" mean?

8. If you were told you had a limited time to live, how would that news change the way you are living? Or would it? Offer an explanation for your position.

MAKING CONNECTIONS

Read Richard Selzer's "The Discus Thrower" and Ernest Hemingway's "A New Kind of War." What, if any, intimations of Kübler-Ross's position do those essays show? What do you think Kübler-Ross would describe as optimum behavior in either of those cases?

Sciences and Technologies

WHY THE SKY IS BLUE
James Jeans

Sir James Jeans (1877–1946) was a British physicist and astronomer. Educated at Trinity College, Cambridge, he lectured there and was a professor of applied mathematics at Princeton University from 1905 to 1909. He later did research at Mount Wilson Observatory in California. Jeans won many honors for his work and wrote a number of scholarly and popular scientific books. The following selection is from The Stars in Their Courses *(1931), a written version of what began as a series of radio talks for an audience assumed to have no special knowledge of science.*

Imagine that we stand on any ordinary seaside pier, and watch the waves rolling in and striking against the iron columns of the pier. Large waves pay very little attention to the columns—they divide right and left and re-unite after passing each column, much as a regiment of soldiers would if a tree stood in their road; it is almost as though the columns had not been there. But the short waves and ripples find the columns of the pier a much more formidable obstacle. When the short waves impinge on the columns, they are reflected back and spread as new ripples in all directions. To use the technical term, they are "scattered." The obstacle provided by the iron columns hardly affects the long waves at all, but scatters the short ripples. 1

We have been watching a sort of working model of the way in which sunlight struggles through the earth's atmosphere. Between us on earth and outer space the atmosphere interposes innumerable obstacles in the form of molecules of air, tiny droplets of water, and small particles of dust. These are represented by the columns of the pier. 2

The waves of the sea represent the sunlight. We know that sunlight is a 3 blend of lights of many colors—as we can prove for ourselves by passing it through a prism, or even through a jug of water, or as Nature demonstrates to us when she passes it through the raindrops of a summer shower and produces a rainbow. We also know that light consists of waves, and that the different colors of light are produced by waves of different lengths, red light by long waves and blue light by short waves. The mixture of waves which constitutes sunlight has to struggle through the obstacles it meets in the atmosphere, just as the mixture of waves at the seaside has to struggle past the columns of the pier. And these obstacles treat the light-waves much as the columns of the pier treat the sea-waves. The long waves which constitute red light are hardly affected, but the short waves which constitute blue light are scattered in all directions.

Thus, the different constituents of sunlight are treated in different ways as   4
they struggle through the earth's atmosphere. A wave of blue light may be scattered by a dust particle, and turned out of its course. After a time a second dust particle again turns it out of its course, and so on, until finally it enters our eyes by a path as zigzag as that of a flash of lightning. Consequently the blue waves of the sunlight enter our eyes from all directions. And that is why the sky looks blue.

QUESTIONS

1. Analogy, the comparison of something familiar with something less familiar, occurs frequently in scientific explanation. Jeans introduces an analogy in his first paragraph. How does he develop that analogy as he develops his explanation?

2. The analogy Jeans provides enables him to explain the process by which the blue light-waves scatter throughout the sky. Hence he gives us a brief process analysis of that phenomenon. Summarize that process in your own words.

3. Try rewriting this essay without the analogy. Remove paragraph 1 and all the references to ocean waves and pier columns in paragraphs 2 and 3. How clear an explanation is left?

4. Besides the sea-waves, what other familiar examples does Jeans use in his explanation?

5. This piece opens with "Imagine that we stand. . . ." Suppose that every *we* was replaced with a *you*. How would the tone of the essay change?

6. While analogy can be effective in helping to explain difficult scientific concepts, it can be equally useful in explaining and interpreting familiar things by juxtaposing them in new ways. Suppose, for example, that you wished to explain to a friend why you dislike a course you are taking. Select one of the following ideas for an analogy (or find a better one): a forced-labor camp, a three-ring circus, squirrels on a treadmill, a tea party, a group-therapy session. Think through the analogy to your course, and write a few paragraphs of explanation. Let Jeans's essay guide you in organizing your own.

MAKING CONNECTIONS

1. Jeans's essay is a clear explanation of a complex phenomenon. And it is quite short. Where else in this volume have you found explanations as clear? A number of short passages in the essays by Francis Crick, Stephen W. Hawking, Bruno Bettelheim, Horace Miner, and Farley Mowat could provide examples. Choose a descriptive passage that you find clear and compare it to Jeans's. Is an analogy central to the passage you selected? If not, what are the differences in the authors' explanations?

2. Describe the audience Jeans seems to have in mind for his explanation. How does that sense of audience differ for Francis Crick, Richard Rodriguez, Susan Fraker, or Nancy Mairs? Compare one or two of those essays with Jeans's account of "Why the Sky Is Blue" and discuss how the task of explaining shifts according to your assumptions about an audience.

TIMES AND DISTANCES,
LARGE AND SMALL
Francis Crick

*Francis Crick (b. 1916), British molecular biologist, shared
the Nobel prize for medicine in 1962 with James D. Watson
for their report on the structure of DNA. Their work probably
constitutes the single most important scientific discovery of
the century, having generated revolutions in biology, chemistry, physics, and medicine. Crick, known for an incessant
inquisitiveness that has taken him into many fields, was
recently described in the pages of* Nature *as "fractious," a
quality that shows in his current research in the neuroscience
of brain modeling. Both Watson and Crick have made
special efforts to explain their studies to the general public.
The essay reprinted here is the first chapter of Crick's book,*
Life Itself *(1981). A second book, again intended for a larger
audience, is* What Mad Pursuit *(1988).*

There is one fact about the origin of life which is reasonably certain. When- 1
ever and wherever it happened, it started a very long time ago, so long ago that
it is extremely difficult to form any realistic idea of such vast stretches of time.
Our own personal experience extends back over tens of years, yet even for that
limited period we are apt to forget precisely what the world was like when we
were young. A hundred years ago the earth was also full of people, bustling
about their business, eating and sleeping, walking and talking, making love and
earning a living, each one steadily pursuing his own affairs, and yet (with very
rare exceptions) not one of them is left alive today. Instead, a totally different
set of persons inhabits the earth around us. The shortness of human life
necessarily limits the span of direct personal recollection.

Human culture has given us the illusion that our memories go further back 2
than that. Before writing was invented, the experience of earlier generations,
embodied in stories, myths and moral precepts to guide behavior, was passed
down verbally or, to a lesser extent, in pictures, carvings and statues. Writing
has made more precise and more extensive the transmission of such information
and in recent times photography has sharpened our images of the immediate
past. Cinematography will give future generations a more direct and vivid
impression of their forebears than we can now easily get from the written word.

What a pity we don't have a talking picture of Cleopatra;[1] it would not only reveal the true length of her nose but would make more explicit the essence of her charm.

We can, with an effort, project ourselves back to the time of Plato and Aristotle,[2] and even beyond to Homer's Bronze Age heroes.[3] We can learn something of the highly organized civilizations of Egypt, the Middle East, Central America and China and a little about other primitive and scattered habitations. Even so, we have difficulty in contemplating steadily the march of history, from the beginnings of civilization to the present day, in such a way that we can truly experience the slow passage of time. Our minds are not built to deal comfortably with periods as long as hundreds or thousands of years.

Yet when we come to consider the origin of life, the time scales we must deal with make the whole span of human history seem but the blink of an eyelid. There is no simple way to adjust one's thinking to such vast stretches of time. The immensity of time passed is beyond our ready comprehension. One can only construct an impression of it from indirect and incomplete descriptions, much as a blind man laboriously builds up, by touch and sound, a picture of his immediate surroundings.

The customary way to provide a convenient framework for one's thoughts is to compare the age of the universe with the length of a single earthly day. Perhaps a better comparison, along the same lines, would be to equate the age of our earth with a single week. On such a scale the age of the universe, since the Big Bang,[4] would be about two or three weeks. The oldest macroscopic fossils (those from the start of the Cambrian)[5] would have been alive just one day ago. Modern man would have appeared in the last ten seconds and agriculture in the last one or two. Odysseus would have lived only half a second before the present time.[6]

Even this comparison hardly makes the longer time scale comprehensible to us. Another alternative is to draw a linear map of time, with the different events marked on it. The problem here is to make the line long enough to show our own experience on a reasonable scale, and yet short enough for convenient reproduction and examination. For easy reference such a map has been printed

3

4

5

6

---

[1]Cleopatra (69 B.C.–30 B.C.): Egyptian queen who charmed Julius Caesar and Marc Antony. [Eds.]

[2]Plato (428 B.C.?–348 B.C.) and Aristotle (384 B.C.–322 B.C.): Greek philosophers. [Eds.]

[3]Homer's Bronze Age heroes: the heroes of *The Iliad* and *The Odyssey*, epic poems written by the Greek poet Homer about 750 B.C. Homer's heroes fought in the Trojan war (ca. 1200 B.C.) at the end of the Bronze Age (3500 B.C.–1000 B.C.). [Eds.]

[4]Big Bang: a cosmological model in which all matter in the universe originated in a giant explosion about 18 billion years ago. [Eds.]

[5]Cambrian: the earliest period in the Paleozoic era, beginning about 600 million years ago. [Eds.]

[6]Odysseus: the most famous Greek hero of antiquity; he is the hero of Homer's *Odyssey* and a prominent character in the *Iliad*. [Eds.]

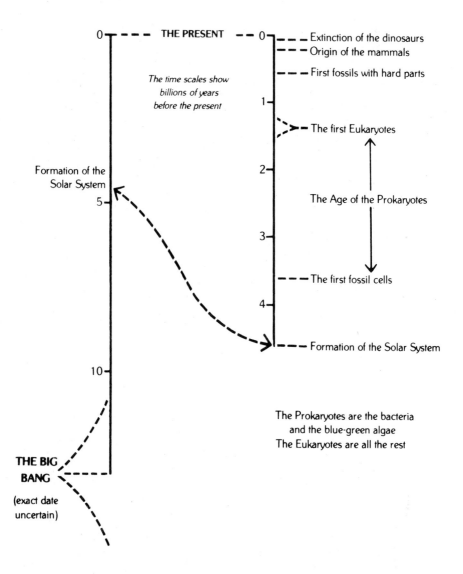

THE UNIVERSE   THE SOLAR SYSTEM

0 — THE PRESENT — 0 — Extinction of the dinosaurs
— Origin of the mammals

The time scales show
billions of years
before the present

— First fossils with hard parts

1 —

— The first Eukaryotes

Formation of the
Solar System

2 —

The Age of the Prokaryotes

5 —

3 —

— The first fossil cells

4 —

— Formation of the Solar System

10 —

The Prokaryotes are the bacteria
and the blue-green algae
The Eukaryotes are all the rest

THE BIG
BANG

(exact date
uncertain)

at the beginning of this [page]. But perhaps the most vivid method is to compare time to the lines of print themselves. Let us make [a 200-page] book equal in length to the time from the start of the Cambrian to the present; that is, about 600 million years. Then each full page will represent roughly 3 million years, each line about ninety thousand years and each letter or small space about

502

fifteen hundred years. The origin of the earth would be about seven books ago and the origin of the universe (which has been dated only approximately) ten or so books before that. Almost the whole of recorded human history would be covered by the last two or three letters of the book.

If you now turn back the pages of the book, slowly reading *one letter at a time*—remember, each letter is fifteen hundred years—then this may convey to you something of the immense stretches of time we shall have to consider. On this scale the span of your own life would be less than the width of a comma. 7

If life really started here we need hardly be concerned with the rest of the universe, but if it started elsewhere the magnitude of large distances must be squarely faced. Though it is difficult to convey a vivid and precise impression of the age of the universe, to grasp its size is almost beyond human comprehension, however we try to express it. The main stumbling block is the extreme emptiness of space; not merely the few atoms in between the stars but the immense distance from one star to another. The visible world close to us is cluttered with objects and our intuitive estimates of their distance depend mainly on various clues provided by their apparent size and their visual interrelationships. It is much more difficult to judge the distance of an unfamiliar object floating in the emptiness of the clear, blue sky. I once heard a Canadian radio interviewer say, when challenged, that he thought the moon "was about the size of a balloon," though admittedly this was before the days of space travel. 8

This is how two astronomers, Jastrow and Thompson, try to describe, by analogy, the size and the distance of objects in space: 9

> Let the sun be the size of an orange; on that scale the earth is a grain of sand circling in orbit around the sun at a distance of thirty feet; Jupiter, eleven times larger than the earth, is a cherry pit revolving at a distance of 200 feet or one city block from the sun. The galaxy on this scale is 100 billion oranges, each orange separated from its neighbors by an average distance of 1,000 miles.[7]

The difficulty with an analogy of this type is that it is almost impossible for us to estimate distances in empty space. A comparison with a city block is misleading, because we too easily visualize the buildings in it, and in doing so lose the idea of emptiness. If you try to imagine an orange floating even a mile up in the sky you will find that its distance seems to become indefinite. An "orange" a thousand miles away would be too small to see unless it were incandescent. 10

Another possible method is to convert distances to time. Pretend you are on a spaceship which is traveling faster than any present-day spaceship. For various reasons, which will become clear later, let us take its speed to be one-hundredth 11

---

[7] Robert Jastrow and Malcolm M. Thompson, *Astronomy: Fundamentals and Frontiers*, 2nd ed. (New York: Wiley, 1972).

the velocity of light; that is, about 1,800 miles per second. At this speed one could go from New York to Europe in about three seconds (Concorde takes roughly three hours), so we are certainly traveling fairly fast by everyday standards. It would take us two minutes to reach the moon and fifteen hours to reach the sun. To go right across the solar system from one side to the other—let us take this distance rather arbitrarily as the diameter of the orbit of Neptune—would take us almost three and one-half weeks. The main point to grasp is that this journey is not unlike a very long train journey, rather longer than the distance from Moscow to Vladivostok and back. Such a trip would probably be monotonous enough, even though the landscape were constantly flowing past the train window. While going across the solar system, there would be nothing at all just outside the window of the spaceship. Very slowly, day after day, the sun would change in size and position. As we traveled farther away from it, its apparent diameter would decrease, till near the orbit of Neptune it would look "little bigger than a pin's head," as I have previously described it, assuming that its apparent size, as viewed from the earth, corresponds roughly to that of a silver dollar. In spite of traveling so fast—remember that at this speed we could travel from any spot to any other on the earth's surface in less than seven seconds—this journey would be tedious in the extreme. Our main impression would be of the almost total emptiness of space. At this distance a planet would appear to be little more than an occasional speck in this vast wilderness.

This feeling of an immense three-dimensional emptiness is bad enough while 12 we are focusing on the solar system. (Almost all of the scale models of the solar system one sees in museums are grossly misleading. The sun and the planets are almost always shown as far too big by comparison with the distances between them.) It is when we try to go farther afield that the enormity of space really hits us. To reach the nearest star—actually a group of three stars fairly close together—would take our spaceship 430 years and the chances are we would pass nothing significant on the way there. A whole lifetime of one hundred years, traveling at this very high speed, would take us less than a quarter of the way there. We would be constantly traveling from emptiness to emptiness with nothing but a few gas molecules and an occasional tiny speck of dust to show that we were not always in the same place. Very, very slowly a few of the nearest stars would change their positions slightly, while the sun itself would fade imperceptibly until it was just another star in the brilliant panorama of stars visible on all sides of the spaceship. Long though it would seem, this journey to the nearest star is, by astronomical standards, a very short one. To cross our own galaxy from side to side would take no less than ten million years. Such distances are beyond anything we can conceive except in the most abstract way. And yet, on a cosmic scale, the distance across the galaxy is hardly any distance at all. Admittedly it is only about twenty times as far to Andromeda, the nearest large galaxy, but to reach the limits of space visible to us in our giant telescopes we would have to travel more than a thousand times farther than that. To me it is remarkable that this astonishing discovery, the vastness and the emptiness of space, has not attracted the imaginative attention of poets and religious thinkers. People are happy to contemplate the limitless powers of God—a doubtful proposition at best—but quite unwilling to meditate creatively on the size of this extraordinary universe in which, through no virtue of their own, they find themselves. Naïvely one might have thought that both poets and priests would be so utterly astonished by these scientific revelations that they would be working with a white-hot fury to try to embody them in the foundation of our culture. The psalmist who said, "When I consider Thy heavens, the work of Thy fingers, the moon and the stars, which Thou hast ordained; what is man, that Thou art mindful of him? . . ." was at least trying, within the limitations of his beliefs, to express his wonder at the universe visible to the naked eye and the pettiness of man by comparison. And yet *his* universe was a small, almost cozy affair compared to the one modern science has revealed to us. It is almost as if the utter insignificance of the earth and the thin film of its biosphere has totally paralyzed the imagination, as if it were too dreadful to contemplate and therefore best ignored.

I shall not discuss here how these very large distances are estimated. The distance of the main objects in the solar system can now be obtained very accurately by a combination of the theory of solar mechanics and radar ranging, the distances of the nearest stars by the way their relative positions change slightly when viewed from the different positions of the earth in its yearly orbit around the sun. After that the arguments are more technical and less precise. But that the distances are the sort of size astronomers estimate there is not the slightest doubt.

So far we have been considering very large magnitudes. Fortunately, when we turn to very small distances and times things are not quite so bad. We need to know the size of atoms—the size and contents of the tiny nucleus within each atom will concern us less—compared to everyday things. This we can manage in two relatively small hops. Let us start with a millimeter. This distance (about a twenty-fifth of an inch) is easy for us to see with the naked eye. One-thousandth part of this is called a micron. A bacteria cell is about two microns long. The wavelength of visible light (which limits what we can see in a high-powered light microscope) is about half a micron long.

We now go down by another factor of a thousand to reach a length known as a nanometer. The typical distance between adjacent atoms bonded strongly together in an organic compound lies between a tenth and a fifth of this. Under the best conditions we can see distances of a nanometer, or a little less, using an electron microscope, provided the specimen can be suitably prepared. Moreover, it is possible to exhibit pictures of a whole series of natural objects at every scale between a small group of atoms and a flea, so that with a little practice we can feel one scale merging into another. By contrast with the emptiness of space, the living world is crammed with detail at every level. The ease with which we can go from one scale to another should not blind us to the fact that the numbers of objects within a *volume* can be uncomfortably large. For example, a drop of water contains rather more than a thousand billion billion water molecules.

The short time we shall be concerned with will rarely be less than a pico- 16 second, that is, one-millionth of a millionth of a second, though very much shorter times occur in nuclear reactions and in studies of subatomic particles. This minute interval is the sort of time scale on which molecules are vibrating, but looked at another way, it does not seem so outlandish. Consider the velocity of sound. In air this is relatively slow—little faster than most jet planes—being about a thousand feet per second. If a flash of lightning is only a mile away, it will take a full five seconds for its sound to reach us. This velocity is, incidentally, approximately the same as the average speed of the molecules of gas in the air, in between their collisions with each other. The speed of sound in most solids is usually a little faster.

Now we ask, how long will it take a sound wave to pass over a small molecule? 17 A simple calculation shows this time to be in the picosecond range. This is just what one would expect, since this is about the time scale on which the atoms of the molecule are vibrating against one another. What is important is that this is, roughly speaking, the pulse rate *underlying* chemical reactions. An enzyme—an organic catalyst—can react a thousand or more times a second. This may appear fast to us but this rate is really rather slow on the time scale of atomic vibration.

Unfortunately, it is not so easy to convey the time scales in between a second 18 and a picosecond, though a physical chemist can learn to feel at home over this fairly large range. Fortunately, we shall not be concerned directly with these very short times, though we shall see their effects indirectly. Most chemical reactions are really very rare events. The molecules usually move around intermittently and barge against one another many times before a rare lucky encounter allows them to hit each other strongly enough and in the correct direction to surmount their protective barriers and produce a chemical reaction. It is only because there are usually so many molecules in one small volume, all doing this at the same time, that the rate of chemical reaction appears to proceed quite smoothly. The chance variations are smoothed out by the large numbers involved.

When we stand back and review once again these very different scales—the 19 minute size of an atom and the almost unimaginable size of the universe; the pulse rate of chemical reaction compared to the deserts of vast eternity since the Big Bang—we see that in all these instances our intuitions, based on our experience of everyday life, are likely to be highly misleading. By themselves, large numbers mean very little to us. There is only one way to overcome this handicap, so natural to our human condition. We must calculate and recalculate, even though only approximately, to check and recheck our initial impressions until slowly, with time and constant application, the real world, the world of the immensely small and the immensely great, becomes as familiar to us as the simple cradle of our common earthly experience.

QUESTIONS

1. Study the diagram that accompanies the essay. How does one line relate to the other? What is the diagram trying to convey?

2. Why are the first three paragraphs devoted to the history and historical memory of humankind?

3. Compare the analogies Crick uses to explain the long passage of universal time in paragraphs 5, 6, and 7. What does the analogy of the book add to that of the week?

4. In paragraph 8, what is the implication of *elsewhere* in its first sentence? This essay is the first chapter of a book called *Life Itself*. What do you imagine to be at least one idea treated in the rest of the book?

5. Paragraph 11 is an extremely long paragraph, and paragraph 12 is even longer. Their lengths seem to correspond to the subjects they take up. Can you think of other ways to imagine the kind of emptiness those paragraphs describe?

6. Paragraph 11 implies an unusual definition of *wilderness*, its last word. Explain why you consider Crick's idea of wilderness the essential one or an eccentric notion.

7. Why do you think that priests and poets have not, as Crick observes, been "working with a white-hot fury to try to embody [these scientific revelations] in the foundation of our culture" (paragraph 12)? What does that last phrase, "foundation of our culture," mean in this context?

8. Why do you think Crick treats the very large before the very small? Which are the more astonishing measurements?

9. Think of a way of estimating, closely but reasonably, something quite numerous— for example, the number of blades of grasses in a yard, the number of leaves or pine needles on a tree, the number of hairs on the tail of a cat, or the number of cars on all the roads, during a single day, in your state or city. Describe your system of estimation, and explain the answer it yields.

MAKING CONNECTIONS

1. Compare the diagrams and illustrations in the articles by Crick, Stephen W. Hawking, and Oliver Sacks. What differences do you find in the purposes for those diagrams and illustrations? Identify one that you find particularly successful and explain its success. Is there one you find less useful?

2. Consider several of the following essays: Virginia Woolf's "The Death of the Moth," Isak Dinesen's "The Iguana," Alice Walker's "Beauty: When the Other Dancer

Is the Self," George Orwell's "Shooting an Elephant," N. Scott Momaday's "The Way to Rainy Mountain," and Joan Didion's "Georgia O'Keeffe." How do you think one or more of these writers would respond to Crick's assertion in paragraph 12 that our poets and priests are not trying to deal with the wonders of the universe?

OUR PICTURE OF THE UNIVERSE
Stephen W. Hawking

Stephen W. Hawking (b. 1942) is the Lucasian Professor of Mathematics at Cambridge University, and one of the world's leading theoretical physicists. Carl Sagan has described the moment in 1974, when he observed "an ancient rite, the investiture of new fellows into the Royal Society, one of the most ancient scholarly organizations on the planet. In the front row a young man in a wheelchair was, very slowly, signing his name in a book that bore on its earliest pages the signature of Isaac Newton. When at last he finished, there was a stirring ovation. Stephen Hawking was a legend even then." Hawking suffers from the serious physical disabilities associated with Lou Gehrig's disease, making his extraordinary achievements an inspiration to all disabled people. Hawking is known especially for his work on "black holes" and their implications for a unified theory of physical phenomena. His book A Brief History of Time *(1988) made his thinking available to the general reader and was a best-seller. (In 1992, filmmaker Erroll Morris released a fascinating documentary portrait of Hawking under the same title.) The essay reprinted below is the first chapter of that book, unchanged except for the removal of references to the book as a whole.*

A well-known scientist (some say it was Bertrand Russell) once gave a public 1 lecture on astronomy. He described how the earth orbits around the sun and how the sun, in turn, orbits around the center of a vast collection of stars called our galaxy. At the end of the lecture, a little old lady at the back of the room got up and said: "What you have told us is rubbish. The world is really a flat plate supported on the back of a giant tortoise." The scientist gave a superior smile before replying, "What is the tortoise standing on?" "You're very clever, young man, very clever," said the old lady. "But it's turtles all the way down!"

Most people would find the picture of our universe as an infinite tower of 2 tortoises rather ridiculous, but why do we think we know better? What do we know about the universe, and how do we know it? Where did the universe come from, and where is it going? Did the universe have a beginning, and if so, what happened *before* then? What is the nature of time? Will it ever come to an end? Recent breakthroughs in physics, made possible in part by fantastic

509

new technologies, suggest answers to some of these longstanding questions. Someday these answers may seem as obvious to us as the earth orbiting the sun—or perhaps as ridiculous as a tower of tortoises. Only time (whatever that may be) will tell.

As long ago as 340 B.C. the Greek philosopher Aristotle, in his book *On the Heavens,* was able to put forward two good arguments for believing that the earth was a round sphere rather than a flat plate. First, he realized that eclipses of the moon were caused by the earth coming between the sun and the moon. The earth's shadow on the moon was always round, which would be true only if the earth was spherical. If the earth had been a flat disk, the shadow would have been elongated and elliptical, unless the eclipse always occurred at a time when the sun was directly under the center of the disk. Second, the Greeks knew from their travels that the North Star appeared lower in the sky when viewed in the south than it did in more northerly regions. (Since the North Star lies over the North Pole, it appears to be directly above an observer at the North Pole, but to someone looking from the equator, it appears to lie just at the horizon.) From the difference in the apparent position of the North Star in Egypt and Greece, Aristotle even quoted an estimate that the distance around the earth was 400,000 stadia. It is not known exactly what length a stadium was, but it may have been about 200 yards, which would make Aristotle's estimate about twice the currently accepted figure. The Greeks even had a third argument that the earth must be round, for why else does one first see the sails of a ship coming over the horizon, and only later see the hull?

Aristotle thought that the earth was stationary and that the sun, the moon, the planets, and the stars moved in circular orbits about the earth. He believed this because he felt, for mystical reasons, that the earth was the center of the universe, and that circular motion was the most perfect. This idea was elaborated by Ptolemy in the second century A.D. into a complete cosmological model. The earth stood at the center, surrounded by eight spheres that carried the moon, the sun, the stars, and the five planets known at the time, Mercury, Venus, Mars, Jupiter, and Saturn (Fig. 1). The planets themselves moved on smaller circles attached to their respective spheres in order to account for their rather complicated observed paths in the sky. The outermost sphere carried the so called fixed stars, which always stay in the same positions relative to each other but which rotate together across the sky. What lay beyond the last sphere was never made very clear, but it certainly was not part of mankind's observable universe.

Ptolemy's model provided a reasonably accurate system for predicting the positions of heavenly bodies in the sky. But in order to predict these positions correctly, Ptolemy had to make an assumption that the moon followed a path that sometimes brought it twice as close to the earth as at other times. And that meant that the moon ought sometimes to appear twice as big as at other times! Ptolemy recognized this flaw, but nevertheless his model was generally, although

510

not universally, accepted. It was adopted by the Christian church as the picture of the universe that was in accordance with Scripture, for it had the great advantage that it left lots of room outside the sphere of fixed stars for heaven and hell.

A simpler model, however, was proposed in 1514 by a Polish priest, Nicholas Copernicus. (At first, perhaps for fear of being branded a heretic by his church, Copernicus circulated his model anonymously.) His idea was that the sun was stationary at the center and that the earth and the planets moved in circular orbits around the sun. Nearly a century passed before this idea was taken seriously. Then two astronomers—the German, Johannes Kepler, and the Italian, Galileo Galilei—started publicly to support the Copernican theory, despite the fact that the orbits it predicted did not quite match the ones observed. The death blow to the Aristotelian/Ptolemaic theory came in 1609. In that year, Galileo started observing the night sky with a telescope, which had just been invented. When he looked at the planet Jupiter, Galileo found that it was accompanied by several small satellites or moons that orbited around it. This implied that everything did *not* have to orbit directly around the earth, as Aristotle and Ptolemy had thought. (It was, of course, still possible to believe that the earth was stationary at the center of the universe and that the moons of Jupiter moved on extremely complicated paths around the earth, giving the

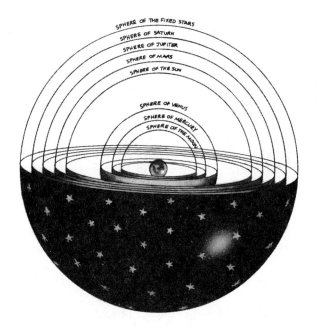

FIGURE 1

appearance that they orbited Jupiter. However, Copernicus's theory was much simpler.) At the same time, Johannes Kepler had modified Copernicus's theory, suggesting that the planets moved not in circles but in ellipses (an ellipse is an elongated circle). The predictions now finally matched the observations.

As far as Kepler was concerned, elliptical orbits were merely an ad hoc 7 hypothesis, and a rather repugnant one at that, because ellipses were clearly less perfect than circles. Having discovered almost by accident that elliptical orbits fit the observations well, he could not reconcile them with his idea that the planets were made to orbit the sun by magnetic forces. An explanation was provided only much later, in 1687, when Sir Isaac Newton published his *Philosophiae Naturalis Principia Mathematica*, probably the most important single work ever published in the physical sciences. In it Newton not only put forward a theory of how bodies move in space and time, but he also developed the complicated mathematics needed to analyse those motions. In addition, Newton postulated a law of universal gravitation according to which each body in the universe was attracted toward every other body by a force that was stronger the more massive the bodies and the closer they were to each other. It was this same force that caused objects to fall to the ground. (The story that Newton was inspired by an apple hitting his head is almost certainly apocryphal. All Newton himself ever said was that the idea of gravity came to him as he sat "in a contemplative mood" and "was occasioned by the fall of an apple.") Newton went on to show that, according to his law, gravity causes the moon to move in an elliptical orbit around the earth and causes the earth and the planets to follow elliptical paths around the sun.

The Copernican model got rid of Ptolemy's celestial spheres, and with them, 8 the idea that the universe had a natural boundary. Since "fixed stars" did not appear to change their positions apart from a rotation across the sky caused by the earth spinning on its axis, it became natural to suppose that the fixed stars were objects like our sun but very much farther away.

Newton realized that, according to his theory of gravity, the stars should 9 attract each other, so it seemed they could not remain essentially motionless. Would they not fall together at some point? In a letter in 1691 to Richard Bentley, another leading thinker of his day, Newton argued that this would indeed happen if there were only a finite number of stars distributed over a finite region of space. But he reasoned that if, on the other hand, there were an infinite number of stars, distributed more or less uniformly over infinite space, this would not happen, because there would not be any central point for them to fall to.

This argument is an instance of the pitfalls that you can encounter in talking 10 about infinity. In an infinite universe, every point can be regarded as the center, because every point has an infinite number of stars on each side of it. The correct approach, it was realized only much later, is to consider the finite situation, in which the stars all fall in on each other, and then to ask how things change if one adds more stars roughly uniformly distributed outside this region. According to Newton's law, the extra stars would make no difference at all to the original ones on average, so the stars would fall in just as fast. We can add as many stars as we like, but they will still always collapse in on themselves. We now know it is impossible to have an infinite static model of the universe in which gravity is always attractive.

It is an interesting reflection on the general climate of thought before the   11
twentieth century that no one had suggested that the universe was expanding or contracting. It was generally accepted that either the universe had existed forever in an unchanging state, or that it had been created at a finite time in the past more or less as we observe it today. In part this may have been due to people's tendency to believe in eternal truths, as well as the comfort they found in the thought that even though they may grow old and die, the universe is eternal and unchanging.

Even those who realized that Newton's theory of gravity showed that the   12
universe could not be static did not think to suggest that it might be expanding. Instead, they attempted to modify the theory by making the gravitational force repulsive at very large distances. This did not significantly affect their predictions of the motions of the planets, but it allowed an infinite distribution of stars to remain in equilibrium—with the attractive forces between nearby stars balanced by the repulsive forces from those that were farther away. However, we now believe such an equilibrium would be unstable: if the stars in some region got only slightly nearer each other, the attractive forces between them would become stronger and dominate over the repulsive forces so that the stars would continue to fall toward each other. On the other hand, if the stars got a bit farther away from each other, the repulsive forces would dominate and drive them farther apart.

Another objection to an infinite static universe is normally ascribed to the   13
German philosopher Heinrich Olbers, who wrote about this theory in 1823. In fact, various contemporaries of Newton had raised the problem, and the Olbers article was not even the first to contain plausible arguments against it. It was, however, the first to be widely noted. The difficulty is that in an infinite static universe nearly every line of sight would end on the surface of a star. Thus one would expect that the whole sky would be as bright as the sun, even at night. Olbers's counterargument was that the light from distant stars would be dimmed by absorption by intervening matter. However, if that happened the intervening matter would eventually heat up until it glowed as brightly as the stars. The only way of avoiding the conclusion that the whole of the night sky should be as bright as the surface of the sun would be to assume that the stars had not been shining forever but had turned on at some finite time in the past. In that case the absorbing matter might not have heated up yet or the light from distant stars might not yet have reached us. And that brings us to the question of what could have caused the stars to have turned on in the first place.

The beginning of the universe had, of course, been discussed long before 14
this. According to a number of early cosmologies and the Jewish/Christian/
Muslim tradition, the universe started at a finite, and not very distant, time in
the past. One argument for such a beginning was the feeling that it was necessary
to have "First Cause" to explain the existence of the universe. (Within the
universe, you always explained one event as being caused by some earlier event,
but the existence of the universe itself could be explained in this way only if it
had some beginning.) Another argument was put forward by St. Augustine in
his book *The City of God*. He pointed out that civilization is progressing and
we remember who performed this deed or developed that technique. Thus man,
and so also perhaps the universe, could not have been around all that long. St.
Augustine accepted a date of about 5000 B.C. for the Creation of the universe
according to the book of Genesis. (It is interesting that this is not so far from
the end of the last Ice Age, about 10,000 B.C., which is when archaeologists
tell us that civilization really began.)

Aristotle, and most of the other Greek philosophers, on the other hand, did 15
not like the idea of a creation because it smacked too much of divine intervention. They believed, therefore, that the human race and the world around it
had existed, and would exist, forever. The ancients had already considered the
argument about progress described above, and answered it by saying that there
had been periodic floods or other disasters that repeatedly set the human race
right back to the beginning of civilization.

The questions of whether the universe had a beginning in time and whether 16
it is limited in space were later extensively examined by the philosopher Im-
manuel Kant in his monumental (and very obscure) work, *Critique of Pure
Reason*, published in 1781. He called these questions antinomies (that is,
contradictions) of pure reason because he felt that there were equally compelling
arguments for believing the thesis, that the universe had a beginning, and the
antithesis, that it had existed forever. His argument for the thesis was that if the
universe did not have a beginning, there would be an infinite period of time
before any event, which he considered absurd. The argument for the antithesis
was that if the universe had a beginning, there would be an infinite period of
time before it, so why should the universe begin at any one particular time? In
fact, his cases for both the thesis and the antithesis are really the same argument.
They are both based on his unspoken assumption that time continues back
forever, whether or not the universe had existed forever. As we shall see, the
concept of time has no meaning before the beginning of the universe. This was
first pointed out by St. Augustine. When asked: What did God do before he
created the universe? Augustine didn't reply: He was preparing Hell for people
who asked such questions. Instead, he said that time was a property of the
universe that God created, and that time did not exist before the beginning of
the universe.

When most people believed in an essentially static and unchanging universe, 17 the question of whether or not it had a beginning was really one of metaphysics or theology. One could account for what was observed equally well on the theory that the universe had existed forever or on the theory that it was set in motion at some finite time in such a manner as to look as though it had existed forever. But in 1929, Edwin Hubble made the landmark observation that wherever you look, distant galaxies are moving rapidly away from us. In other words, the universe is expanding. This means that at earlier times objects would have been closer together. In fact, it seemed that there was a time, about ten or twenty thousand million years ago, when they were all at exactly the same place and when, therefore, the density of the universe was infinite. This discovery finally brought the question of the beginning of the universe into the realm of science.

Hubble's observations suggested that there was a time, called the big bang,   18 when the universe was infinitesimally small and infinitely dense. Under such conditions all the laws of science, and therefore all ability to predict the future, would break down. If there were events earlier than this time, then they could not affect what happens at the present time. Their existence can be ignored because it would have no observational consequences. One may say that time had a beginning at the big bang, in the sense that earlier times simply would not be defined. It should be emphasized that this beginning in time is very different from those that had been considered previously. In an unchanging universe a beginning in time is something that has to be imposed by some being outside the universe; there is no physical necessity for a beginning. One can imagine that God created the universe at literally any time in the past. On the other hand, if the universe is expanding, there may be physical reasons why there had to be a beginning. One could still imagine that God created the universe at the instant of the big bang, or even afterwards in just such a way as to make it look as though there had been a big bang, but it would be meaningless to suppose that it was created *before* the big bang. An expanding universe does not preclude a creator, but it does place limits on when he might have carried out his job!

In order to talk about the nature of the universe and to discuss questions   19 such as whether it has a beginning or an end, you have to be clear about what a scientific theory is. I shall take the simpleminded view that a theory is just a model of the universe, or a restricted part of it, and a set of rules that relate quantities in the model to observations that we make. It exists only in our minds and does not have any other reality (whatever that might mean). A theory is a good theory if it satisfies two requirements: It must accurately describe a large class of observations on the basis of a model that contains only a few arbitrary elements, and it must make definite predictions about the results of future observations. For example, Aristotle's theory that everything was made out of four elements, earth, air, fire, and water, was simple enough to qualify, but it did not make any definite predictions. On the other hand, Newton's theory of gravity was based on an even simpler model, in which bodies attracted each other with a force that was proportional to a quantity called their mass and inversely proportional to the square of the distance between them. Yet it predicts the motions of the sun, the moon, and the planets to a high degree of accuracy.

Any physical theory is always provisional, in the sense that it is only a hypothesis: you can never prove it. No matter how many times the results of experiments agree with some theory, you can never be sure that the next time the result will not contradict the theory. On the other hand, you can disprove a theory by finding even a single observation that disagrees with the predictions of the theory. As philosopher of science Karl Popper has emphasized, a good theory is characterized by the fact that it makes a number of predictions that could in principle be disproved or falsified by observation. Each time new experiments are observed to agree with the predictions the theory survives, and our confidence in it is increased; but if ever a new observation is found to disagree, we have to abandon or modify the theory. At least that is what is supposed to happen, but you can always question the competence of the person who carried out the observation.

In practice, what often happens is that a new theory is devised that is really an extension of the previous theory. For example, very accurate observations of the planet Mercury revealed a small difference between its motion and the predictions of Newton's theory of gravity. Einstein's general theory of relativity predicted a slightly different motion from Newton's theory. The fact that Einstein's predictions matched what was seen, while Newton's did not, was one of the crucial confirmations of the new theory. However, we still use Newton's theory for all practical purposes because the difference between its predictions and those of general relativity is very small in the situations that we normally deal with. (Newton's theory also has the great advantage that it is much simpler to work with than Einstein's!)

The eventual goal of science is to provide a single theory that describes the whole universe. However, the approach most scientists actually follow is to separate the problem into two parts. First, there are the laws that tell us how the universe changes with time. (If we know what the universe is like at any one time, these physical laws tell us how it will look at any later time.) Second, there is the question of the initial state of the universe. Some people feel that science should be concerned with only the first part; they regard the question of the initial situation as a matter for metaphysics or religion. They would say that God, being omnipotent, could have started the universe off any way he wanted. That may be so, but in that case he also could have made it develop in a completely arbitrary way. Yet it appears that he chose to make it evolve in a very regular way according to certain laws. It therefore seems equally reasonable to suppose that there are also laws governing the initial state.

It turns out to be very difficult to devise a theory to describe the universe all in one go. Instead, we break the problem up into bits and invent a number of partial theories. Each of these partial theories describes and predicts a certain limited class of observations, neglecting the effects of other quantities, or representing them by simple sets of numbers. It may be that this approach is completely wrong. If everything in the universe depends on everything else in a fundamental way, it might be impossible to get close to a full solution by investigating parts of the problem in isolation. Nevertheless, it is certainly the way that we have made progress in the past. The classic example again is the Newtonian theory of gravity, which tells us that the gravitational force between two bodies depends only on one number associated with each body, its mass, but is otherwise independent of what the bodies are made of. Thus one does not need to have a theory of the structure and constitution of the sun and the planets in order to calculate their orbits.

Today scientists describe the universe in terms of two basic partial theories— the general theory of relativity and quantum mechanics. They are the great intellectual achievements of the first half of this century. The general theory of relativity describes the force of gravity and the large-scale structure of the universe, that is, the structure on scales from only a few miles to as large as a million million million million (1 with twenty-four zeros after it) miles, the size of the observable universe. Quantum mechanics, on the other hand, deals with phenomena on extremely small scales, such as a millionth of a millionth of an inch. Unfortunately, however, these two theories are known to be inconsistent with each other—they cannot both be correct. One of the major endeavors in physics today . . . is the search for a new theory that will incorporate them both—a quantum theory of gravity. We do not yet have such a theory, and we may still be a long way from having one, but we do already know many of the properties that it must have. And . . . we already know a fair amount about the predictions a quantum theory of gravity must make.

Now, if you believe that the universe is not arbitrary, but is governed by definite laws, you ultimately have to combine the partial theories into a complete unified theory that will describe everything in the universe. But there is a fundamental paradox in the search for such a complete unified theory. The ideas about scientific theories outlined above assume we are rational beings who are free to observe the universe as we want and to draw logical deductions from what we see. In such a scheme it is reasonable to suppose that we might progress even closer toward the laws that govern our universe. Yet if there really is a complete unified theory, it would also presumably determine our actions. And so the theory itself would determine the outcome of our search for it! And why should it determine that we come to the right conclusions from the evidence? Might it not equally well determine that we draw the wrong conclusion? Or no conclusion at all?

The only answer that I can give to this problem is based on Darwin's principle of natural selection. The idea is that in any population of self-reproducing organisms, there will be variations in the genetic material and upbringing that different individuals have. These differences will mean that some individuals are better able than others to draw the right conclusions about the world around them and to act accordingly. These individuals will be more likely to survive and reproduce and so their pattern of behavior and thought will come to dominate. It has certainly been true in the past that what we call intelligence and scientific discovery has conveyed a survival advantage. It is not so clear that this is still the case: our scientific discoveries may well destroy us all, and even if they don't, a complete unified theory may not make much difference to our chances of survival. However, provided the universe has evolved in a regular way, we might expect that the reasoning abilities that natural selection has given us would be valid also in our search for a complete unified theory, and so would not lead us to the wrong conclusions.

Because the partial theories that we already have are sufficient to make accurate predictions in all but the most extreme situations, the search for the ultimate theory of the universe seems difficult to justify on practical grounds. (It is worth noting, though, that similar arguments could have been used against both relativity and quantum mechanics, and these theories have given us both nuclear energy and the microelectronics revolution!) The discovery of a complete unified theory, therefore, may not aid the survival of our species. It may not even affect our life-style. But ever since the dawn of civilization, people have not been content to see events as unconnected and inexplicable. They have craved an understanding of the underlying order in the world. Today we still yearn to know why we are here and where we came from. Humanity's deepest desire for knowledge is justification enough for our continuing quest. And our goal is nothing less than a complete description of the universe we live in.

QUESTIONS

1. There is a break in the essay after paragraph 18, indicated by extra space between paragraphs. If you had to provide a subtitle for each of the two sections demarcated by that break, what would these subtitles be?

2. What is the function of the anecdote in paragraph 1? Why do you suppose Hawking begins with that story?

3. What is the function of paragraph 2? What kind of sentence structure predominates in this paragraph? Why?

4. The first date mentioned in the essay comes in paragraph 3. Make a list of all the other exact dates that are given, noting the paragraphs in which they appear. Discuss any patterns (or violations of pattern) that you note. What does this list tell you about the organization of the essay?

5. Hawking uses the word *God* with some frequency. How would you describe the

notion of *God* generated by his text? Is it different from your own views? How important is *God* to Hawking's view of the universe?

6. What is the notion of *science* that can be derived from Hawking's uses of that word? That is, with what definition or concept of science is he working? Is it the same as your own, or different? Discuss.

7. In the latter part of his essay, Hawking takes up the philosophical question of how we can know that we know what we know. Describe and discuss the view that he presents, bringing in any other theories of knowledge that you have encountered in your studies or reading on the subject.

MAKING CONNECTIONS

Read Carl Sagan's essay, "Can We Know the Universe? Reflections on a Grain of Salt" in "Reflecting." Are Sagan and Hawking talking about the same universe? Note Sagan's strongest beliefs as expressed in his final paragraphs. Are Sagan and Hawking thinking along the same lines? To what extent does Hawking seem to be answering the challenge that Sagan makes?

THE ORIGIN OF THE UNIVERSE
Victor Weisskopf

Victor Weisskopf was born in Vienna in 1908 and came to the United States in 1937. He is now the Institute Professor Emeritus at Massachusetts Institute of Technology. A physicist of international distinction, he was awarded the U.S. Department of Energy's Enrico Fermi Award in 1988, which is only the latest in a series of major awards from many countries. He is a member of the National Academy of Sciences, as well as of the corresponding academies of France, Austria, Denmark, Spain, Germany, Scotland, Bavaria, and the former Soviet Union. His several books include Knowledge and Wonder *(1962),* Physics in the Twentieth Century *(1972), and, most recently,* The Privilege of Being a Physicist *(1988). From 1943 to 1946, Weisskopf worked on the Manhattan Project in Los Alamos, New Mexico, developing the atomic bomb. After the war, he became a professor of physics at MIT. The essay reprinted here is based on a talk he gave to the American Academy of Arts and Sciences in Cambridge, Massachusetts.*

1.

How did the universe begin about 12 billion years ago? The question concerns the very large—space, galaxies, etc.—but also the very small, namely the innermost structure of matter. The reason is that the early universe was very hot, so that matter was then decomposed into its constituents. These two topics hang together, and this is what makes them so interesting.

One must start with a few words about the innermost structure of matter. The sketch in Figure 1 indicates, on the very left, a piece of metal. It is made of atoms. To the right of it you see one of the atoms symbolically designed with a nucleus in the middle and with electrons around it. Here we proceed toward the innermost structure of matter in steps. That's why I call it the quantum ladder. Further to the right you see the nucleus, consisting of protons and neutrons, which I will call nucleons from now on. We have found out that the nucleons themselves are composite; they are made up of quarks, as seen in Figure 1.

Let us look at the forces that keep the constituents together in the four steps of the quantum ladder. The deeper you go, the stronger the forces become. In

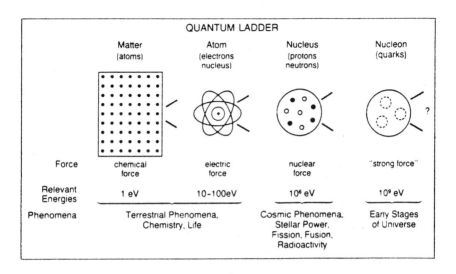

Figure 1

the piece of metal, the chemical force that keeps the atoms together has the strength of a few electron volts (this is a measure of force strength). In the atom, the electrons are bound to the nucleus by a few tens of electron volts. The protons and neutrons are bound within the nucleus by millions of electron volts, and the forces between the quarks in a nucleus are in the billions of electron volts. This leads us to the concept of conditional elementarity. When we apply small amounts of energy, we cannot overcome the forces that keep the constituents together. For example, if energies of less than a few electron volts are available, atoms cannot be decomposed into electrons and nuclei. They seem to be elementary, which means stable, or unchangeable. When energies above a few hundred but below a million electron volts are available, atoms may be decomposed, but nuclei and electrons seem elementary. For energies over a million electron volts, nuclei are decomposed, but the protons and neutrons are elementary. At a billion electron volts, the nucleons appear to be composed of quarks. Electrons, so far, have never been shown to be composite.

It will be important later on to understand the connection between energy 4 and temperature. Heating a piece of material is equivalent to increasing the energy of motion of the constituents of that piece, be they atoms or electrons or other particles. In a hot material, the atoms or the electrons perform all kinds of motions, oscillations, straight flights, etc. The greater the temperature, the higher the energy of the motions. Thus, temperature is equivalent to energy. For example, one electron volt corresponds to about 12,000 degrees Celsius (about 22,000 degrees Fahrenheit). The temperature at which atomic nuclei decompose is about 20 billion degrees. A billion electron volts would be about 20 trillion degrees Celsius.

On the last rung of the quantum ladder, when billions of electron volts are available—by means of accelerators or when the universe was very hot—new phenomena appear. Let us call it the subnuclear realm. Antimatter plays an important role at that stage. What is it? In the last fifty years it was discovered that there is an antiparticle to every particle; an antielectron called a positron, an antiproton and antineutron, an antiquark. They carry the opposite charge of the actual particle. Thus there ought to exist antiatoms, antimolecules, antimatter of all sorts, made of antielectrons and antinuclei. Why do we not find antimatter in our environment? Because of an important fact: when an antiparticle hits a particle, they "annihilate." A small explosion occurs, and the two entities disappear in a burst of light energy or other forms of energy. This is in agreement with the famous Einstein formula $E=mc^2$, which says that mass—in this case, the masses of the particle and the antiparticle—is a form of energy. The opposite process also occurs: a high concentration of energy can give rise to the birth of a particle and antiparticle. This is called pair creation.

To summarize the quantum ladder, let me quote a prophetic statement by Newton, who wrote three hundred years ago; it describes Figure 1 from the right to the left, as it were:

> Now the smallest particles of matter may cohere by the strongest attractions, and compose bigger particles of weaker virtue. And many of these may cohere, and compose bigger particles whose virtue is still weaker. And so on for universe successions, until the progression ends in the biggest particles on which the operation in chemistry and the colors of natural bodies depend, which by cohering compose bodies of a sensible magnitude. . . .

. . . like that piece of metal. He foresaw the ideas of the structure of matter that were developed centuries after his time.

2.

Let us now turn to our main subject: the universe. Let's first look at the universe as we see it today. There are six facts that are important to us. First, most of the stars we see in the universe consist of 93 percent hydrogen, 6 percent helium, and only 1 percent all other elements. This has been determined by analyzing the light from the stars. Here on earth, things—including our bodies—consist mainly of other elements besides hydrogen. But this is a special case; the stars are made mostly of hydrogen. I have to mention something of which astronomers should be very much ashamed. It turned out that visible matter, the one that sends light to us, is only 10 percent of the total matter.

Ninety percent of the matter of the universe is what is now called dark matter—dark because we don't see it; dark because we don't know what it is. How do we know that it is there? The dark matter, like any matter, attracts other matter by gravity. One has found motions of stars and galaxies that could not be explained by the gravitational attraction of the visible, luminous matter. For example, stars in the neighborhood of galaxies move much faster than they would if they were attracted only by the visible stars. So far the nature of that dark matter is unknown. We do not have the slightest idea of what 90 percent of the world is made of.

The second fact concerns the distribution of matter in space. We know that it is very uneven. We see stars, but nothing in between; we see galaxies and clusters of galaxies. However, if we average over a large part of space containing many stars and galaxies, we find that luminous matter is very thinly distributed, only about one hydrogen atom per cubic meter. To this we must add ten times as much dark matter.

The third fact is the expansion of the universe. The following astounding observation was made about sixty years ago, first by the American astronomer E. P. Hubble. It was Hubble who found that faraway objects like galaxies move away from us; the greater the distance, the faster they move away. For example, a galaxy that is as far as one million light years moves away from us with a speed of about twenty kilometers per second. Another galaxy, at a distance of two million light years, moves away at forty kilometers per second; another, at three million light years, moves away at sixty kilometers per second; and so on. As a consequence, the distances between objects in space increase as time goes on. The universe gets more dilute with time. It is a kind of decompression of matter.

A most dramatic conclusion must be drawn from this: if we go backward in time, we conclude that galaxies were nearer to each other in the past. Therefore, at a certain time in the far distant past, the matter in the universe must have been extremely dense. Matter must have been highly compressed, far more than any compression achievable on earth by technical means. At that time there were no galaxies or stars: matter was so thoroughly compressed that everything merged. A little calculation shows that this happened about 12 billion years ago.

In this calculation, one has taken into account that the expansion was faster at an earlier time, since the gravitational attraction acts like a brake and slows down the expansion. Today's rate of expansion, the so-called Hubble constant, is not very well established. It could be fifteen or thirty, instead of twenty, kilometers per second at a million light years. Therefore, the time of extreme compression—this is the time of the beginning of our universe, of the Big Bang—may not have been 12 billion years ago, but perhaps 10 or 15 billion years ago. Still, we can introduce a new chronology: the zero time is the time of extreme compression, the time of the Big Bang. Today is about 12 billion years since the beginning.

We now approach the fourth point regarding our present universe. How far   12
can we see into space? Since the universe is about 12 billion years old, we cannot see farther than about 12 billion light years. We call this distance the cosmic horizon of today. As we will see later in more detail, the Big Bang was a tremendous explosion in which space expanded almost infinitely fast, creating matter over a region probably much larger than what is visible today. Light from those farther regions has not had enough time to reach us today but may do so in the future.

There is another interesting consequence: the farther we look within the   13
cosmic horizons, the younger are the objects we see. After all, it took time for the light to reach us. The light we see of a galaxy, say, 100 million light years away, was emitted 100 million years ago. A picture of the galaxy shows how it was 100 million years back. Figure 2 shows this schematically. The outer circle is the cosmic horizon. The broken circle is about six billion light years away, and objects there appear to us only six billion years old. What about objects at or very near the horizon? What we see there is matter in its first moments, matter just or almost just born. Thus, if we had very good telescopes, we could see the whole history of matter in the universe, starting far out and ending near us.

Beware of the following misunderstanding. One could wrongly argue that,   14
say, the regions that are six billion light years away were much nearer to us when they did send out their light, and therefore we should see them earlier than six billion years after emission. This conclusion is false, because the light velocity must be understood as relative to the expanding space. Seen from a nonexpanding frame, a light beam running against the expansion—that is,

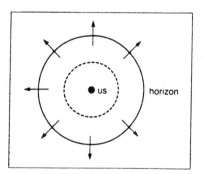

Figure 2

toward us—moves slower than the usual light velocity. As it were, light is dragged along with the expansion.

Our fifth question has to do with the temperature in the universe. How hot   15
is it out there? Let us consider a kiln, such as potters use, to understand the situation. Take a kiln and heat it up. First you can see no light, but the kiln radiates microwaves. When it gets hotter it radiates infrared radiation, which we do not see but can feel as heat radiation. At higher temperatures it becomes red, then yellow and white, then ultraviolet; at millions of degrees it will radiate X-rays.

Today, in the immediate surroundings within a few million light years, the   16
temperature is very low in space. It was measured a few decades ago when two Princeton physicists, A. Penzias and R. Wilson, found a very cool microwave radiation in space corresponding to heat radiation of only five degrees above absolute zero—the lowest possible temperature, which is minus 460°F. An appropriate measure of very low temperatures is the Kelvin scale. Zero degree Kelvin is absolute zero. The Kelvin scale uses Celsius degrees above absolute zero. Thus, the space temperature in our neighborhood is 3°K. This is the temperature in space between the stars. The stars are much hotter inside, but there is so much space between them that their higher temperature does not count.

Was the temperature always 3°K? No, it was much warmer at earlier times,   17
a fact that is related to the expansion of the universe. Let us go back to the kiln again. Imagine a kiln made in such a way that we can expand or contract its volume at will. The laws of physics tell us that the temperature of a kiln drops when it expands and rises when it contracts. Thus, we must conclude that the expansion of the universe lowers the temperature. It must have been hotter at earlier times. For example, about six million years ago, the temperature was roughly twice as high—that is, near 6°K. At the very beginning, about 12 billion years ago, when space was extremely contracted, the temperature must have been extremely high. This has interesting consequences.

We know from the physics of radiation that matter is transparent for light   18
when the temperature is below 1,000°C. This is true only for very dilute matter, such as that found in the space between the stars. Matter of ordinary density, such as a piece of iron or wood, is not transparent, of course. But if the temperature is raised from 1,000°C, even very dilute matter becomes opaque. Thus light from those outer regions near the cosmic horizon, which are so young that the temperature is over 1,000°C, cannot penetrate space and will not reach us. We should emphasize that these regions are very near the cosmic horizon. A temperature of 1,000°C was reached when the universe was about 300,000 years old, an age that is very young compared with 12 billion years. Hence, light reaches us not from the cosmic horizon but from a distance that is almost as far as the cosmic horizon. We see only matter older than 300,000

years, which is nevertheless pretty young. Even younger matter, younger than that, is hidden by the opaque space.

Figure 3 illustrates this schematically. The outermost circle is the cosmic   19
horizon, where matter is just born at extreme density and extreme heat. But already a little nearer to us at the center, the temperature has fallen to and below 1,000°C, and we can see it, since space inside that second circle is transparent.

But why do we not see that part of the universe glowing white-hot at 1,000°C?   20
The reason is the famous Doppler effect. That part of the universe moves away from us at a terrific speed according to the law of expansion, which states that the greater the distance of an object, the faster it moves away from us. The Doppler effect reduces the frequency of light if the emitting object moves away from us. Everybody has observed how the whistle of a fire engine lowers its pitch as the engine moves away. Reducing the frequency is equivalent to lowering the temperature. Red's frequency is lower than yellow's and much lower than violet's. Therefore, the heat radiation from that faraway region of 1,000°K is much cooled down because it moves away from us so fast. Indeed, it is cooled down from 1,000°K to 3°K. Thus, the cool radiation that Penzias and Wilson have observed is indeed the radiation from the hot universe 300,000 years after the Big Bang. The 3°K radiation can be considered the optical reverberation of the Big Bang. This is not quite correct, because it was emitted a little later. That is the explanation of the cool radiation of today.

3.

So far we have discussed the present state of the universe and what one can   21
deduce from it as to its past. Now we will recount the speculations and hypotheses as to the history of the universe from the Big Bang to today, and

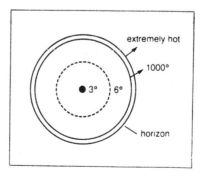

FIGURE 3

perhaps also what was before the Big Bang. Usually history does not enter physics. One studies the properties of matter as it is today. Other sciences, such as geology, anthropology, and biology, are historical sciences; the first one deals with the history of the earth, anthropology with the history of the human animal, and biology with the history of animal and plant species.

When physics becomes historical, it deals with the history of matter—that is, with the history of the universe. It is then called cosmology. It must be emphasized that most of the conclusions are much less reliable than those in other fields of physics. Facts are scarce and not known with any accuracy. The Russian physicist Lev Landau said that the cosmologists have very weak facts to work with but very strong convictions about what they think is going on. Whatever will be told here may turn out to be wrong in the near future. Nevertheless, it is so impressive that it is worth reporting.

As we have seen, our universe is expanding and cooling down. We are in principle able to see parts of the universe in earlier periods just by looking at distant objects. We have seen that this is possible to a point in time in the past 300,000 years after the Big Bang. Let us therefore call the time from 300,000 years after the Bang up to today the period of observable history. Of course, the history is observable only in principle. Actually, our instruments are not good enough to get detailed information regarding very distant objects.

We will not say much about that period; the preobservable history is more interesting. At the beginning of observable history the temperature was around 1,000°K, which was low enough so that atoms were not destroyed and robbed of their electrons. Therefore, space was filled mainly with hydrogen and helium atoms forming a hot gas. The density of things never was completely uniform. There were gas accumulations here and more dilute parts somewhere else. The accumulations grew because of gravity. They had more concentration of mass and therefore attracted the surrounding gas more strongly than the dilute parts. The further this accumulative process went, the more effective the gravitational pull became. Such accumulations finally formed "protostars" of much higher density than elsewhere. These protostars also became much hotter than the rest, since compression produces heat. When it became hot enough at the center of such protostars, nuclear reactions were ignited, producing even more energy. The protostar became a real star like the sun, whose radiation energy comes from the nuclear reactions at the center. Furthermore, the early deviations from complete uniformity caused the stars to be not uniformly distributed but to form agglomerations that we see today as galaxies.

The nuclear reactions inside a star produce helium out of hydrogen. When a star has used up its primary nuclear fuel—hydrogen—at its center, other nuclear processes form heavier elements, such as carbon, oxygen, up to iron. Finally the star explodes and becomes a supernova. In this process most other elements are formed and expelled into space. Then new accumulations and protostars are formed from the gases in space, which now contain traces of other heavier elements, such as oxygen, carbon, iron, gold, and uranium. The sun is an example of a "second-generation" star. Some of the stars are surrounded by planets like the sun. In some of the planets, such as the earth, heavier elements are present in higher concentration. This is because most hydrogen and helium atoms escape from smaller planets, since those atoms are light and planets exert only weak gravitational pull. The hydrogen found on earth is bound in molecules to heavier atoms. Life may develop under the mild warming of the nearby star. So much for the observable history.

Now let us turn to the period between the Big Bang and the onset of observable history at about 300,000 years. Let us call it preobservable history. Nothing about that period can be observed; space was opaque because the temperature was higher than 1,000°C. But we are able to conclude from our knowledge of physics what happened during that period, at least for times that are not too near to the Big Bang. Pursuing the picture of an expanding and cooling universe, one comes to the conclusion that a microsecond after the Big Bang, the temperature must have reached about 10 trillion degrees, or a thermal energy of a billion electron volts. Our present knowledge is good enough that we can guess what has happened in the universe between a microsecond and 300,000 years. But conclusions about events at earlier times, when the energy concentrations were higher, are very uncertain.

Let us tell the story in reverse, going back in time from 300,000 years to a microsecond. In that inverse sense, the universe must be regarded as contracting and getting hotter. When the temperature was hotter than 10,000°K, the atoms were decomposed and formed a "plasma," a dense gas of nuclei and electrons. The plasma was bathed in shining light, visible light, during the time when the temperature was between a thousand and a few ten thousand degrees.

That light was more and more ultraviolet (that is, of a higher frequency) at earlier times, when the temperature was higher. This radiation should be considered the same as today's 3°K radiation but enormously compressed at the early seconds of the expansion. Compression makes light hotter and of higher frequency. Going back in time, we come to a moment at about one second after the Big Bang, when the temperature was about 10 billion degrees, corresponding to an energy concentration of about a few million electron volts. At that point the thermal energy is high enough for creating pairs of electrons and antielectrons (positrons). This is the process of matter-antimatter formation mentioned before. Hence, at one second and earlier, when the temperature was even higher, space was filled by a plasma composed not only of hydrogen and helium nuclei and their electrons but also of a rather dense gas of electrons and positrons.

At a fraction of a second after the Bang, the temperature was high enough to split the helium and nuclei into neutrons and protons. Finally, when our backward history reaches the microsecond after the Bang, the heat and the corresponding energy concentration were high enough not only to decompose protons and neutrons into quarks but also to produce quark-antiquark pairs. At this point of our backward journey in time, the universe was filled with hot, dense gases of quarks and antiquarks, electrons and positrons, and a very intense, high-frequency thermal light radiation. There was also a hot, dense gas of neutrinos, which survived the whole evolution and should be present even today, though much less hot and dense, together with the cool three-degree light radiation. We stop at this point, which is a millionth of a second after the Big Bang. We are practically at it anyway.

The prehistory described here is based on a relatively firm knowledge of the properties of matter at energy concentrations up to several billion electron volts. This knowledge stems from experiments made with accelerators producing particle beams at these energies. The largest of these machines, the ones in Geneva, Switzerland, and in Batavia, Illinois, have reached energies of several hundred billion electron volts. It would be hard to guess what happened much earlier than a microsecond, since the energy concentrations were much higher than the ones reached with our accelerators, and we have no way to know how matter behaves at these enormous compressions and temperatures. 30

4.

We now have reached the point where we should ask the great questions: What was the Big Bang? What caused it? And what existed before? When facing these exciting questions, it must be said that we have no reliable answers. There are speculation, guesswork led by intuition, and a great deal of imagination that may turn out to be wrong in a few years. However, the answers that are discussed in these days are so unusual and impressive that it is worthwhile to describe them in simple terms. The underlying ideas came mostly from four persons whom one might call the four apostles of the new story of Genesis: Alan Guth of MIT, Alexander Vilenkin of Tufts University, Andrei Linde in the USSR, and Stephen Hawking in England. Paul Steinhardt of the University of Pennsylvania also contributed to it. 31

In order to understand the basic ideas, we must introduce a concept that is suggested by some of the latest developments in particle physics. It is the so-called false vacuum. According to these ideas, there are two types of vacuum: the true vacuum and the false vacuum. The true one is very much what one would imagine: it is empty space, empty of matter and empty of energy. The false vacuum, however, is also empty of matter, but not of energy. The energy of the false vacuum is supposed to be none of the ordinary forms of energy, such as electric fields or gravity fields. It is imagined to be a new kind of field, of a type encountered in the current theories of radioactive processes. The most characteristic feature of the false vacuum follows directly from Einstein's general relativity theory. A region filled with energy but not with matter is bound to 32 expand suddenly and explosively, filling more and more space with false vacuum. Alan Guth has called it, succinctly, an inflationary expansion, with a speed very much faster than the previously considered expansion of our universe at any time in its development. According to our four apostles, this sudden explosion is nothing else but the Big Bang.

How does this sudden inflationary expansion of a false vacuum start? Before the event, all space was in the state of a true vacuum. "The world was without form and void, and darkness was upon the face of the deep," as the Bible says. Now we must introduce a concept that is typical for quantum mechanics. According to the fundamental tenets of this well-established theory, there is nothing in nature that remains quiet. Everything, including the true vacuum, is subject to fluctuations—in particular to energy fluctuations. The field that provides the energy to the false vacuum is absent in the true vacuum, but not completely. There must be fluctuations of the field. Thus, at one moment a small region somewhere in space may have fluctuated into a false vacuum. It would happen very rarely but cannot be excluded. That region almost instantly expands tremendously and creates a large space filled with energy according to the properties of a false vacuum. That is supposed to be the Big Bang!

One might wonder where the energy comes from that fills the expanding false vacuum. There is no need to worry about conservation of energy. According to Einstein, energy is subject to gravity. The newly created energies interact via gravity, an effect that produces negative energy, so that the net energy remains essentially constant.

When a certain large size is reached, the inflationary explosion stops and a true vacuum emerges. But the vast amount of energy contained in the false vacuum must have shown up in some form. It filled the true vacuum with hot light, quark-antiquark pairs, electron-antielectron pairs, neutrinos, etc.—in other words, with all the stuff we have described as filling the space at a microsecond after the Big Bang. Our universe is born, the slow expansion takes over, the temperature falls, and the preobservable history develops and is followed by the observable history.

In short, the history of our universe started with a fluctuation of the empty true vacuum into a small region of false vacuum, which exploded, almost immediately, into a very much larger region of false vacuum. That was the primal Bang. Then it changed to a true vacuum, but the energy of the false vacuum created all light, all particles and antiparticles, which developed into what existed at about a microsecond after the explosion. Then the ordinary expansion of the universe took over; it cooled down; quarks and antiquarks as well as electrons and antielectrons were annihilated, but a few supernumerary quarks and electrons remained. The quarks formed protons and neutrons. Then some of these nucleons formed helium nuclei. After 300,000 years it was cool enough that the protons and helium nuclei could grab and retain electrons and become atoms. A hot gas of hydrogen and helium appeared. The gas of atoms condensed to protostars, which became hot inside, allowing nuclear processes to start. Stars were born, grouping themselves in galaxies. The nuclear reactions in the center of the stars and in exploding supernovas produced heavier elements. The expelled gases of exploding stars condensed to protostars and then to stars containing traces of all elements, not only hydrogen and helium. The sun is one of these second-generation stars. It is surrounded by planets, some of which—such as the earth—are special concentrations of heavier elements, benignly supplied with energy from the nearby sun, so that life can start and develop the strange human animal that pretends to understand the whole process.

An interesting conclusion follows from this view of the birth of our universe, as the consequence of an energy fluctuation in the true vacuum. Such intense fluctuations creating a speck of false vacuum are very rare, but it may have happened at other places in infinite space at other times and may have developed into other universes. Thus, we may conclude that our universe is not the only one. It is not the center and the stage of everything in this world. There may be other universes much older or much younger or even not yet born somewhere else. Remember that our universe today is most probably considerably larger than our present cosmic horizon of about 12 billion light years, but there is room and time enough for many other universes. Maybe, in a few billion years, another universe will penetrate ours. Until then we cannot check this hypothesis. Our own universe, of which we see only a small part today, may not be unique. Its beginning is not the beginning of everything. Other universes may exist at an earlier or later stage. 37

It must be emphasized again that these are unproven hypotheses. They may turn out to be pure fantasies, but the ideas are impressively grandiose. 38

The origin of the universe is not only of scientific interest. It always was the subject of mythology, art, and religion. Such approaches are complementary to scientific ones. Most familiarly, the Old Testament describes the beginning of the world with the creation of light on the first day. It seemed contradictory that the sun, our terrestrial source of light, was only created on day four, but it turns out to be in line with current scientific thought, according to which the early universe was full of various kinds of radiation long before the sun appeared. 39

Those first days have been depicted in various forms, in pictures and poetry, but to me, Franz Josef Haydn's oratorio *The Creation* is the most remarkable rendition of the Big Bang. At the beginning we hear a choir of angels singing mysteriously and softly, "And God Said Let There Be Light." And at the words "And There Was Light" the entire choir and the orchestra explode into a blazing C major chord. There is no more beautiful and impressive presentation of the beginning of everything. 40

QUESTIONS

1. Reread the quotation from Newton given in paragraph 6, near the end of section 1. How nearly does it summarize Weisskopf's explanation in that section? Why is it useful for Weisskopf to provide that summary?

2. Notice how Weisskopf organizes section 1 by reviewing four related structures; then he opens section 2 by saying he will explain six facts. What are some further examples of orderliness in his presentation?

3. What implications do you find in Weisskopf's claim in paragraph 7 that "ninety percent of the matter of the universe is what is now called dark matter"? What later claims seem related to it?

4. Explain how Weisskopf sets up the "dramatic conclusion" drawn after the "third fact" presented in paragraph 9.

5. One of Weisskopf's themes is how much we don't know, ranging beyond what we do know or can conjecture. List several examples he gives of what we do not know. What relations do you find among these ideas?

6. In paragraph 33, Weisskopf says, "Thus, at one moment a small region somewhere in space may have fluctuated into a false vacuum." Three paragraphs later, he adds, "In short, the history of our universe started with a fluctuation of the empty true vacuum into a small region of false vacuum." How do you understand the terms *fluctuated* and *fluctuation* in these sentences? Is *fluctuate* a technical term? What are some consequences of that term for understanding "the origin of our universe"?

7. Weisskopf makes several mentions of the Bible in his account of the origins of the universe and even, with a trace of humor, mentions "the four apostles of the new story of Genesis" (paragraph 31). Reread the story of creation in Genesis. How many points of convergence do you find between Genesis and Weisskopf's explanation? Note especially Weisskopf's mention of the creation of the sun on the fourth day, according to Genesis (paragraph 39). How do you account for such detail in Genesis?

8. Go to the library and look up several more creation stories from various religions and mythological systems. Compare two or three such stories, looking especially for surprising convergences with Weisskopf's summary of contemporary scientific thinking.

MAKING CONNECTIONS

1. Taking Weisskopf's essay together with the essays by Stephen W. Hawking and Francis Crick, you can get a pretty good introduction to contemporary cosmological thinking. What attitudes of mind unify these thinkers?

2. Choose a two- or three-paragraph sequence of close explanation in at least two of the three writers, Crick, Hawking, and Weisskopf, and compare their explanations. Choose passages that you find especially clear. What accounts for that clarity? Are diagrams especially helpful? Do the explanations follow an orderly list of subtopics? Are the sentences particularly vivid and precise? Using the two or three good examples you locate, try to draw some conclusions about effective presentation of technical material.

THE MAN WHO MISTOOK
HIS WIFE FOR A HAT

Oliver Sacks

The following essay is taken from Sacks's collection, The
Man Who Mistook His Wife for a Hat and Other Clinical
Tales. *As the headnote on page 387 details, Sacks's writing
deals not only with textbook cases in clinical neurology, but
also with the bizarre, sometimes tragic and funny stories
the neurologist observes and catalogues. For that reason,
Sacks's prose style is lyrical as well as accurate; his explanation of prosopagnosia (perception without recognition)
seeks to engage our interest and emotions at the same time
it defines and illustrates a syndrome unfamiliar to many
readers.*

Dr P. was a musician of distinction, well-known for many years as a singer, 1
and then, at the local School of Music, as a teacher. It was here, in relation to
his students, that certain strange problems were first observed. Sometimes a
student would present himself, and Dr P. would not recognise him; or, specifically, would not recognise his face. The moment the student spoke, he would
be recognised by his voice. Such incidents multiplied, causing embarrassment,
perplexity, fear—and, sometimes, comedy. For not only did Dr P. increasingly
fail to see faces, but he saw faces when there were no faces to see: genially,
Magoo-like, when in the street he might pat the heads of water hydrants and
parking meters, taking these to be the heads of children; he would amiably
address carved knobs on the furniture and be astounded when they did not
reply. At first these odd mistakes were laughed off as jokes, not least by Dr P.
himself. Had he not always had a quirky sense of humour and been given to
Zen-like paradoxes and jests? His musical powers were as dazzling as ever; he
did not feel ill—he had never felt better; and the mistakes were so ludicrous—
and so ingenious—that they could hardly be serious or betoken anything serious.
The notion of there being "something the matter" did not emerge until some
three years later, when diabetes developed. Well aware that diabetes could affect
his eyes, Dr P. consulted an ophthalmologist, who took a careful history and
examined his eyes closely. "There's nothing the matter with your eyes," the
doctor concluded. "But there is trouble with the visual parts of your brain. You
don't need my help, you must see a neurologist." And so, as a result of this
referral, Dr P. came to me.

It was obvious within a few seconds of meeting him that there was no trace 2

533

of dementia in the ordinary sense. He was a man of great cultivation and charm who talked well and fluently, with imagination and humour. I couldn't think why he had been referred to our clinic.

And yet there *was* something a bit odd. He faced me as he spoke, was oriented towards me, and yet there was something the matter—it was difficult to formulate. He faced me with his *ears*, I came to think, but not with his eyes. These, instead of looking, gazing, at me, "taking me in," in the normal way, made sudden strange fixations—on my nose, on my right ear, down to my chin, up to my right eye—as if noting (even studying) these individual features, but not seeing my whole face, its changing expressions, "me," as a whole. I am not sure that I fully realised this at the time—there was just a teasing strangeness, some failure in the normal interplay of gaze and expression. He saw me, he *scanned* me, and yet . . . 3

"What seems to be the matter?" I asked him at length. 4

"Nothing that I know of," he replied with a smile, "but people seem to think there's something wrong with my eyes." 5

"But *you* don't recognise any visual problems?" 6

"No, not directly, but I occasionally make mistakes." 7

I left the room briefly to talk to his wife. When I came back, Dr P. was sitting placidly by the window, attentive, listening rather than looking out. "Traffic," he said, "street sounds, distant trains—they make a sort of symphony, do they not? You know Honegger's *Pacific 234?*" 8

What a lovely man, I thought to myself. How can there be anything seriously the matter? Would he permit me to examine him? 9

"Yes, of course, Dr Sacks." 10

I stilled my disquiet, his perhaps, too, in the soothing routine of a neuro-logical exam—muscle strength, coordination, reflexes, tone. . . . It was while examining his reflexes—a trifle abnormal on the left side—that the first bizarre experience occurred. I had taken off his left shoe and scratched the sole of his foot with a key—a frivolous-seeming but essential test of a reflex—and then, excusing myself to screw my ophthalmoscope together, left him to put on the shoe himself. To my surprise, a minute later, he had not done this. 11

"Can I help?" I asked. 12

"Help what? Help whom?" 13

"Help you put on your shoe." 14

"Ach," he said, "I had forgotten the shoe," adding, *sotto voce*, "The shoe? The shoe?" He seemed baffled. 15

"Your shoe," I repeated. "Perhaps you'd put it on." 16

He continued to look downwards, though not at the shoe, with an intense but misplaced concentration. Finally his gaze settled on his foot: "That is my shoe, yes?" 17

Did I mis-hear? Did he mis-see? 18

"My eyes," he explained, and put a hand to his foot. "*This* is my shoe, no?" 19

534

"No, it is not. That is your foot. *There* is your shoe." 20

"Ah! I thought that was my foot." 21

Was he joking? Was he mad? Was he blind? If this was one of his "strange 22 mistakes," it was the strangest mistake I had ever come across.

I helped him on with his shoe (his foot), to avoid further complication. Dr 23 P. himself seemed untroubled, indifferent, maybe amused. I resumed my examination. His visual acuity was good: he had no difficulty seeing a pin on the floor, though sometimes he missed it if it was placed to his left.

He saw all right, but what did he see? I opened out a copy of the *National* 24 *Geographic Magazine* and asked him to describe some pictures in it.

His responses here were very curious. His eyes would dart from one thing 25 to another, picking up tiny features, individual features, as they had done with my face. A striking brightness, a colour, a shape would arrest his attention and elicit comment—but in no case did he get the scene-as-a-whole. He failed to see the whole, seeing only details, which he spotted like blips on a radar screen. He never entered into relation with the picture as a whole—never faced, so to speak, *its* physiognomy. He had no sense whatever of a landscape or scene.

I showed him the cover, an unbroken expanse of Sahara dunes. 26

"What do you see here?" I asked. 27

"I see a river," he said. "And a little guest-house with its terrace on the water. 28 People are dining out on the terrace. I see coloured parasols here and there." He was looking, if it was "looking," right off the cover into mid-air and confabulating nonexistent features, as if the absence of features in the actual picture had driven him to imagine the river and the terrace and the coloured parasols.

I must have looked aghast, but he seemed to think he had done rather well. 29 There was a hint of a smile on his face. He also appeared to have decided that the examination was over and started to look around for his hat. He reached out his hand and took hold of his wife's head, tried to lift it off, to put it on. He had apparently mistaken his wife for a hat! His wife looked as if she was used to such things.

I could make no sense of what had occurred in terms of conventional 30 neurology (or neuropsychology). In some ways he seemed perfectly preserved, and in others absolutely, incomprehensibly devastated. How could he, on the one hand, mistake his wife for a hat and, on the other, function, as apparently he still did, as a teacher at the Music School?

I had to think, to see him again—and to see him in his own familiar habitat, 31 at home.

A few days later I called on Dr P. and his wife at home, with the score of 32 the *Dichterliebe* in my briefcase (I knew he liked Schumann), and a variety of odd objects for the testing of perception. Mrs P. showed me into a lofty apartment, which recalled fin-de-siècle Berlin. A magnificent old Bösendorfer stood in state in the centre of the room, and all around it were music stands, instruments, scores. . . . There were books, there were paintings, but the music was central. Dr P. came in, a little bowed, and, distracted, advanced with outstretched hands to the grandfather clock, but, hearing my voice, corrected himself, and shook hands with me. We exchanged greetings and chatted a little of current concerts and performances. Diffidently, I asked him if he would sing.

"The *Dichterliebe!*" he exclaimed. "But I can no longer read music. You will play them, yes?"

I said I would try. On that wonderful old piano even my playing sounded right, and Dr P. was an aged but infinitely mellow Fischer-Dieskau, combining a perfect ear and voice with the most incisive musical intelligence. It was clear that the Music School was not keeping him on out of charity.

Dr P.'s temporal lobes were obviously intact: he had a wonderful musical cortex. What, I wondered, was going on in his parietal and occipital lobes, especially in those areas where visual processing occurred? I carry the Platonic solids in my neurological kit and decided to start with these.

"What is this?" I asked, drawing out the first one.

"A cube, of course."

"Now this?" I asked, brandishing another.

He asked if he might examine it, which he did swiftly and systematically: "A dodecahedron, of course. And don't bother with the others—I'll get the icosahedron, too."

Abstract shapes clearly presented no problems. What about faces? I took out a pack of cards. All of these he identified instantly, including the jacks, queens, kings, and the joker. But these, after all, are stylised designs, and it was impossible to tell whether he saw faces or merely patterns. I decided I would show him a volume of cartoons which I had in my briefcase. Here, again, for the most part, he did well. Churchill's cigar, Schnozzle's nose: as soon as he had picked out a key feature he could identify the face. But cartoons, again, are formal and schematic. It remained to be seen how he would do with real faces, realistically represented.

I turned on the television, keeping the sound off, and found an early Bette Davis film. A love scene was in progress. Dr P. failed to identify the actress— but this could have been because she had never entered his world. What was more striking was that he failed to identify the expressions on her face or her partner's, though in the course of a single torrid scene these passed from sultry yearning through passion, surprise, disgust, and fury to a melting reconciliation. Dr P. could make nothing of any of this. He was very unclear as to what was going on, or who was who or even what sex they were. His comments on the scene were positively Martian.

It was just possible that some of his difficulties were associated with the unreality of a celluloid, Hollywood world; and it occurred to me that he might be more successful in identifying faces from his own life. On the walls of the apartment there were photographs of his family, his colleagues, his pupils, himself. I gathered a pile of these together and, with some misgivings, presented them to him. What had been funny, or farcical, in relation to the movie, was tragic in relation to real life. By and large, he recognised nobody: neither his family, nor his colleagues, nor his pupils, nor himself. He recognised a portrait of Einstein because he picked up the characteristic hair and moustache; and the same thing happened with one or two other people. "Ach, Paul!" he said, when shown a portrait of his brother. "That square jaw, those big teeth—I would know Paul anywhere!" But was it Paul he recognised, or one or two of his features, on the basis of which he could make a reasonable guess as to the subject's identity? In the absence of obvious "markers," he was utterly lost. But it was not merely the cognition, the *gnosis*, at fault; there was something radically wrong with the whole way he proceeded. For he approached these faces—even of those near and dear—as if they were abstract puzzles or tests. He did not relate to them, he did not behold. No face was familiar to him, seen as a "thou," being just identified as a set of features, an "it." Thus, there was formal, but no trace of personal, gnosis. And with this went his indifference, or blindness, to expression. A face, to us, is a person looking out—we see, as it were, the person through his *persona*, his face. But for Dr P. there was no *persona* in this sense—no outward *persona*, and no person within.

I had stopped at a florist on my way to his apartment and bought myself an 43 extravagant red rose for my buttonhole. Now I removed this and handed it to him. He took it like a botanist or morphologist given a specimen, not like a person given a flower.

"About six inches in length," he commented. "A convoluted red form with 44 a linear green attachment."

"Yes," I said encouragingly, "and what do you think it *is*, Dr P.?" 45

"Not easy to say." He seemed perplexed. "It lacks the simple symmetry of 46 the Platonic solids, although it may have a higher symmetry of its own. . . . I think this could be an inflorescence or flower."

"Could be?" I queried. 47

"Could be," he confirmed. 48

"Smell it," I suggested, and he again looked somewhat puzzled, as if I had 49 asked him to smell a higher symmetry. But he complied courteously, and took it to his nose. Now, suddenly, he came to life.

"Beautiful!" he exclaimed. "An early rose. What a heavenly smell!" He 50 started to hum "*Die Rose, die Lillie* . . ." Reality, it seemed, might be conveyed by smell, not by sight.

I tried one final test. It was still a cold day, in early spring, and I had thrown 51 my coat and gloves on the sofa.

"What is this?" I asked, holding up a glove. 52

"May I examine it?" he asked, and, taking it from me, he proceeded to 53 examine it as he had examined the geometrical shapes.

"A continuous surface," he announced at last, "infolded on itself. It appears 54 to have"—he hesitated—"five outpouchings, if this is the word."

"Yes," I said cautiously. "You have given me a description. Now tell me   55
what it is."

"A container of some sort?"   56

"Yes," I said, "and what would it contain?"   57

"It would contain its contents!" said Dr P., with a laugh. "There are many   58
possibilities. It could be a change purse, for example, for coins of five sizes. It
could . . ."

I interrupted the barmy flow. "Does it not look familiar? Do you think it   59
might contain, might fit, a part of your body?"

No light of recognition dawned on his face.[1]   60

No child would have the power to see and speak of "a continuous surface   61
. . . infolded on itself," but any child, any infant, would immediately know a
glove as a glove, see it as familiar, as going with a hand. Dr P. didn't. He saw
nothing as familiar. Visually, he was lost in a world of lifeless abstractions.
Indeed, he did not have a real visual world, as he did not have a real visual
self. He could speak about things, but did not see them face-to-face. Hughlings
Jackson, discussing patients with aphasia and left-hemisphere lesions, says they
have lost "abstract" and "propositional" thought—and compares them with dogs
(or, rather, he compares dogs to patients with aphasia). Dr P., on the other
hand, functioned precisely as a machine functions. It wasn't merely that he
displayed the same indifference to the visual world as a computer but—even
more strikingly—he construed the world as a computer construes it, by means
of key features and schematic relationships. The scheme might be identified—
in an "identi-kit" way—without the reality being grasped at all.

The testing I had done so far told me nothing about Dr P.'s inner world.   62
Was it possible that his visual memory and imagination were still intact? I asked
him to imagine entering one of our local squares from the north side, to walk
through it, in imagination or in memory, and tell me the buildings he might
pass as he walked. He listed the buildings on his right side, but none of those
on his left. I then asked him to imagine entering the square from the south.
Again he mentioned only those buildings that were on the right side, although
these were the very buildings he had omitted before. Those he had "seen"
internally before were not mentioned now; presumably, they were no longer
"seen." It was evident that his difficulties with leftness, his visual field deficits,
were as much internal as external, bisecting his visual memory and imagination.

What, at a higher level, of his internal visualisation? Thinking of the almost   63
hallucinatory intensity with which Tolstoy visualises and animates his characters, I questioned Dr P. about *Anna Karenina*. He could remember incidents

---

[1] Later, by accident, he got it on, and exclaimed, "My God, it's a glove!" This was reminiscent
of Kurt Goldstein's patient "Lanuti," who could only recognise objects by trying to use them in
action.

without difficulty, had an undiminished grasp of the plot, but completely omitted visual characteristics, visual narrative, and scenes. He remembered the words of the characters but not their faces; and though, when asked, he could quote, with his remarkable and almost verbatim memory, the original visual descriptions, these were, it became apparent, quite empty for him and lacked sensorial, imaginal, or emotional reality. Thus, there was an internal agnosia as well.[2]

But this was only the case, it became clear, with certain sorts of visualisation. The visualisation of faces and scenes, of visual narrative and drama—this was profoundly impaired, almost absent. But the visualisation of *schemata* was preserved, perhaps enhanced. Thus, when I engaged him in a game of mental chess, he had no difficulty visualising the chessboard or the moves—indeed, no difficulty in beating me soundly.

Luria said of Zazetsky that he had entirely lost his capacity to play games but that his "vivid imagination" was unimpaired. Zazetsky and Dr P. lived in worlds which were mirror images of each other. But the saddest difference between them was that Zazetsky, as Luria said, "fought to regain his lost faculties with the indomitable tenacity of the damned," whereas Dr P. was not fighting, did not know what was lost, did not indeed know that anything was lost. But who was more tragic, or who was more damned—the man who knew it, or the man who did not?

When the examination was over, Mrs P. called us to the table, where there was coffee and a delicious spread of little cakes. Hungrily, hummingly, Dr P. started on the cakes. Swiftly, fluently, unthinkingly, melodiously, he pulled the plates towards him and took this and that in a great gurgling stream, an edible song of food, until, suddenly, there came an interruption: a loud, peremptory rat-tat-tat at the door. Startled, taken aback, arrested by the interruption, Dr P. stopped eating and sat frozen, motionless, at the table, with an indifferent, blind bewilderment on his face. He saw, but no longer saw, the table; no longer perceived it as a table laden with cakes. His wife poured him some coffee: the smell titillated his nose and brought him back to reality. The melody of eating resumed.

How does he do anything? I wondered to myself. What happens when he's dressing, goes to the lavatory, has a bath? I followed his wife into the kitchen and asked her how, for instance, he managed to dress himself. "It's just like the

---

[2] I have often wondered about Helen Keller's visual descriptions, whether these, for all their eloquence, are somehow empty as well? Or whether, by the transference of images from the tactile to the visual, or, yet more extraordinarily, from the verbal and the metaphorical to the sensorial and the visual, she *did* achieve a power of visual imagery, even though her visual cortex had never been stimulated, directly, by the eyes? But in Dr P.'s case it is precisely the cortex that was damaged, the organic prerequisite of all pictorial imagery. Interestingly and typically he no longer dreamed pictorially—the "message" of the dream being conveyed in nonvisual terms.

eating," she explained. "I put his usual clothes out, in all the usual places, and he dresses without difficulty, singing to himself. He does everything singing to himself. But if he is interrupted and loses the thread, he comes to a complete stop, doesn't know his clothes—or his own body. He sings all the time—eating songs, dressing songs, bathing songs, everything. He can't do anything unless he makes it a song."

While we were talking my attention was caught by the pictures on the walls.   68

"Yes," Mrs P. said, "he was a gifted painter as well as a singer. The School   69 exhibited his pictures every year."

I strolled past them curiously—they were in chronological order. All his   70 earlier work was naturalistic and realistic, with vivid mood and atmosphere, but finely detailed and concrete. Then, years later, they became less vivid, less concrete, less realistic and naturalistic, but far more abstract, even geometrical and cubist. Finally, in the last paintings, the canvasses became nonsense, or nonsense to me—mere chaotic lines and blotches of paint. I commented on this to Mrs P.

"Ach, you doctors, you're such Philistines!" she exclaimed. "Can you not   71 see *artistic development*—how he renounced the realism of his earlier years, and advanced into abstract, nonrepresentational art?"

"No, that's not it," I said to myself (but forbore to say it to poor Mrs P.). He   72 had indeed moved from realism to nonrepresentation to the abstract, yet this was not the artist, but the pathology, advancing—advancing towards a profound visual agnosia, in which all powers of representation and imagery, all sense of the concrete, all sense of reality, were being destroyed. This wall of paintings was a tragic pathological exhibit, which belonged to neurology, not art.

And yet, I wondered, was she not partly right? For there is often a struggle,   73 and sometimes, even more interestingly, a collusion between the powers of pathology and creation. Perhaps, in his cubist period, there might have been both artistic and pathological development, colluding to engender an original form; for as he lost the concrete, so he might have gained in the abstract, developing a greater sensitivity to all the structural elements of line, boundary, contour—an almost Picasso-like power to see, and equally depict, those abstract organisations embedded in, and normally lost in, the concrete. . . . Though in the final pictures, I feared, there was only chaos and agnosia.

We returned to the great music room, with the Bösendorfer in the centre,   74 and Dr P. humming the last torte.

"Well, Dr Sacks," he said to me. "You find me an interesting case, I perceive.   75 Can you tell me what you find wrong, make recommendations?"

"I can't tell you what I find wrong," I replied, "but I'll say what I find right.   76 You are a wonderful musician, and music is your life. What I would prescribe, in a case such as yours, is a life which consists entirely of music. Music has been the centre, now make it the whole, of your life."

This was four years ago—I never saw him again, but I often wondered about   77 how he apprehended the world, given his strange loss of image, visuality, and the perfect preservation of a great musicality. I think that music, for him, had taken the place of image. He had no body-image, he had body-music: this is why he could move and act as fluently as he did, but came to a total confused stop if the "inner music" stopped. And equally with the outside, the world . . .[3]

In *The World as Representation and Will*, Schopenhauer speaks of music as   78
"pure will." How fascinated he would have been by Dr P., a man who had wholly lost the world as representation, but wholly preserved it as music or will.

And this, mercifully, held to the end—for despite the gradual advance of his   79
disease (a massive tumour or degenerative process in the visual parts of his brain) Dr P. lived and taught music to the last days of his life.

POSTSCRIPT

How should one interpret Dr P.'s peculiar inability to interpret, to judge, a   80
glove as a glove? Manifestly, here, he could not make a cognitive judgment, though he was prolific in the production of cognitive hypotheses. A judgment is intuitive, personal, comprehensive, and concrete—we "see" how things stand, in relation to one another and oneself. It was precisely this setting, this relating, that Dr P. lacked (though his judging, in all other spheres, was prompt and normal). Was this due to lack of visual information, or faulty processing of visual information? (This would be the explanation given by a classical, schematic neurology.) Or was there something amiss in Dr P.'s attitude, so that he could not relate what he saw to himself?

These explanations, or modes of explanation, are not mutually exclusive—   81
being in different modes they could coexist and both be true. And this is acknowledged, implicitly or explicitly, in classical neurology: implicitly, by Macrae, when he finds the explanation of defective schemata, or defective visual processing and integration, inadequate; explicitly, by Goldstein, when he speaks of "abstract attitude." But abstract attitude, which allows "categorisation," also misses the mark with Dr P.—and, perhaps, with the concept of "judgment" in general. For Dr P. *had* abstract attitude—indeed, nothing else. And it was precisely this, his absurd abstractness of attitude—absurd because unleavened with anything else—which rendered him incapable of perceiving identity, or particulars, rendered him incapable of judgment.

Neurology and psychology, curiously, though they talk of everything else,   82
almost never talk of "judgment"—and yet it is precisely the downfall of judgment . . . which constitutes the essence of so many neuropsychological disorders.

---

[3] Thus, as I learned later from his wife, though he could not recognise his students if they sat still, if they were merely "images," he might suddenly recognise them if they *moved*. "That's Karl," he would cry. "I know his movements, his body-music."

Judgment and identity may be casualties—but neuropsychology never speaks of them.

And yet, whether in a philosophic sense (Kant's sense), or an empirical and evolutionary sense, judgment is the most important faculty we have. An animal, or a man, may get on very well without "abstract attitude" but will speedily perish if deprived of judgment. Judgment must be the *first* faculty of higher life or mind—yet it is ignored, or misinterpreted, by classical (computational) neurology. And if we wonder how such an absurdity can arise, we find it in the assumptions, or the evolution, of neurology itself. For classical neurology (like classical physics) has always been mechanical—from Hughlings Jackson's mechanical analogies to the computer analogies of today.

Of course, the brain *is* a machine and a computer—everything in classical neurology is correct. But our mental processes, which constitute our being and life, are not just abstract and mechanical, but personal, as well—and, as such, involve not just classifying and categorising, but continual judging and feeling also. If this is missing, we become computer-like, as Dr P. was. And, by the same token, if we delete feeling and judging, the personal, from the cognitive sciences, we reduce *them* to something as defective as Dr P.—and we reduce *our* apprehension of the concrete and real.

By a sort of comic and awful analogy, our current cognitive neurology and psychology resemble nothing so much as poor Dr P.! We need the concrete and real, as he did; and we fail to see this, as he failed to see it. Our cognitive sciences are themselves suffering from an agnosia essentially similar to Dr P.'s. Dr P. may therefore serve as a warning and parable—of what happens to a science which eschews the judgmental, the particular, the personal, and becomes entirely abstract and computational.

It was always a matter of great regret to me that, owing to circumstances beyond my control, I was not able to follow his case further, either in the sort of observations and investigations described, or in ascertaining the actual disease pathology.

One always fears that a case is "unique," especially if it has such extraordinary features as those of Dr P. It was, therefore, with a sense of great interest and delight, not unmixed with relief, that I found, quite by chance—looking through the periodical *Brain* for 1956—a detailed description of an almost comically similar case, similar (indeed identical) neuropsychologically and phenomenologically, though the underlying pathology (an acute head injury) and all personal circumstances were wholly different. The authors speak of their case as "unique in the documented history of this disorder"—and evidently experienced, as I did, amazement at their own findings.[4] The interested reader

---

[4] Only since the completion of this book have I found that there is, in fact, a rather extensive literature on visual agnosia in general, and prosopagnosia in particular. In particular I had the great pleasure recently of meeting Dr Andrew Kertesz, who has himself published some extremely detailed studies of patients with such agnosias (see, for example, his paper on visual agnosia, Kertesz 1979).

is referred to the original paper, Macrae and Trolle (1956), of which I here subjoin a brief paraphrase, with quotations from the original.

Their patient was a young man of 32, who, following a severe automobile accident, with unconsciousness for three weeks, ". . . complained, exclusively, of an inability to recognise faces, even those of his wife and children." Not a single face was "familiar" to him, but there were three he could identify; these were workmates: one with an eye-blinking tic, one with a large mole on his cheek, and a third "because he was so tall and thin that no one else was like him." Each of these, Macrae and Trolle bring out, was "recognised solely by the single prominent feature mentioned." In general (like Dr P.) he recognised familiars only by their voices.

He had difficulty even recognising himself in a mirror, as Macrae and Trolle describe in detail: "In the early convalescent phase he frequently, especially when shaving, questioned whether the face gazing at him was really his own, and even though he knew it could physically be none other, on several occasions grimaced or stuck out his tongue 'just to make sure.' By carefully studying his face in the mirror he slowly began to recognise it, but 'not in a flash' as in the past—he relied on the hair and facial outline, and on two small moles on his left cheek."

In general he could not recognise objects "at a glance," but would have to seek out, and guess from, one or two features—occasionally his guesses were absurdly wrong. In particular, the authors note, there was difficulty with the *animate.*

On the other hand, simple schematic objects—scissors, watch, key, etc.—presented no difficulties. Macrae and Trolle also note that: "His *topographical memory* was strange: the seeming paradox existed that he could find his way from home to hospital and around the hospital, but yet could not name streets *en route* [unlike Dr P., he also had some aphasia] or appear to visualize the topography."

It was also evident that visual memories of people, even from long before the accident, were severely impaired—there was memory of conduct, or perhaps a mannerism, but not of visual appearance or face. Similarly, it appeared, when he was questioned closely, that he no longer had visual images in his *dreams.* Thus, as with Dr P., it was not just visual perception, but visual imagination and memory, the fundamental powers of visual representation, which were essentially damaged in this patient—at least those powers insofar as they pertained to the personal, the familiar, the concrete.

Dr Kertesz mentioned to me a case known to him of a farmer who had developed prosopagnosia and in consequence could no longer distinguish (the faces of) his *cows,* and of another such patient, an attendant in a Natural History Museum, who mistook his own reflection for the diorama of an *ape.* As with Dr P., and as with Macrae and Trolle's patient, it is especially the animate which is so absurdly misperceived. The most important studies of such agnosias, and of visual processing in general, are now being undertaken by A. R. and H. Damasio.

543

A final, humorous point. Where Dr P. might mistake his wife for a hat, 93
Macrae's patient, also unable to recognise his wife, needed her to identify
herself by a visual *marker*, by ". . . a conspicuous article of clothing, such as a
large hat."

QUESTIONS

1. Summarize as clearly as you can the nature of Dr. P.'s problem. What are the
symptoms? What seems to have caused them?

2. What conclusions can be drawn from the case of Dr. P. about the way our visual
systems work? Using what Sacks himself says and whatever additional conclusions you
yourself can draw, what does the case of Dr. P. tell us about the way we "see" things
and what it means to "recognize" what we see?

3. Sacks has a way of drawing readers into his case studies, of making them concerned
about the individuals whose cases he presents. How does he do this? That is, considering
him as a writer rather than as a doctor, what aspects of his writing arouse interest and
concern? Look at the opening paragraphs of his essay in particular.

4. Is this essay to any degree a story with a plot? Most people find Sacks a very
compelling writer. What is it about his way of writing that causes this response? How
does he keep readers reading?

5. This essay is not only a single case history and an explanation of some very curious
behavior. It also contains or sketches out an argument about the nature of the cognitive
sciences—how they should and should not proceed. What is that argument? Do you
agree or disagree with the view of cognitive science that Sacks is advocating? Write an
essay in which you present his position and develop one of your own on this matter.

6. This is the second essay by Sacks in this book. (The other is on p. 359.) Write
an essay in which you discuss him as a writer and a scientist. Consider such matters as
his style of writing, his interest in the arts, his clinical procedures, and the values he
expresses or implies in his work. If your instructor wishes, you may look further into his
work in order to write this essay.

MAKING CONNECTIONS

1. Compare Sacks's essay with Robert Jay Lifton's "What Made This Man? Mengele."
How do they differ as case studies? What kinds of evidence do they call upon? How
do they evaluate it? What kinds of stories do they tell? Do you find evidence in
this comparison for what was said about Sacks in our introductory note, that his essays are "not just case studies . . . but also tales or fables of 'heroes, victims, martyrs,
warriors'"?

2. Compare Sacks's essay to the reports of John Hersey, "Hatsuyo Nakamura," and
Roy C. Selby, Jr.'s "A Delicate Operation." What elements of a case study do those
reports contain? Are they also tales or fables similar to Sacks's essay?

THE MEDIAN ISN'T THE MESSAGE

Stephen Jay Gould

Stephen Jay Gould (b. 1941), a paleontologist and professor of geology at Harvard University, is known among specialists in his field for having collaborated in the development of a controversial theory that regards evolution as moving in abrupt fits and starts, rather than gradually and progressively over time. But he is most widely known outside his field for his monthly column in Natural History *magazine, where he has not only defended and explained Darwinian ideas of evolution, but also exposed abuses and misunderstandings of scientific concepts and methods. His monthly columns have been collected in several volumes of essays, including* Ever Since Darwin, The Panda's Thumb, The Flamingo's Smile, *and* Bully for Brontosaurus. *The following article was written in 1985.*

My life has recently intersected, in a most personal way, two of Mark Twain's 1 famous quips. One I shall defer to the end of this essay. The other (sometimes attributed to Disraeli) identifies three species of mendacity, each worse than the one before—lies, damned lies, and statistics.

Consider the standard example of stretching truth with numbers—a case 2 quite relevant to my story. Statistics recognizes different measures of an "average," or central tendency. The *mean* represents our usual concept of an overall average—add up the items and divide them by the number of sharers (100 candy bars collected for five kids next Halloween will yield 20 for each in a fair world). The *median*, a different measure of central tendency, is the halfway point. If I line up five kids by height, the median child is shorter than two and taller than the other two (who might have trouble getting their mean share of the candy). A politician in power might say with pride, "The mean income of our citizens is $15,000 per year." The leader of the opposition might retort, "But half our citizens make less than $10,000 per year." Both are right, but neither cites a statistic with impassive objectivity. The first invokes a mean, the second a median. (Means are higher than medians in such cases because one millionaire may outweigh hundreds of poor people in setting a mean, but can balance only one mendicant in calculating a median.)

The larger issue that creates a common distrust or contempt for statistics is 3 more troubling. Many people make an unfortunate and invalid separation between heart and mind, or feeling and intellect. In some contemporary traditions, abetted by attitudes stereotypically centered upon Southern California, feelings are exalted as more "real" and the only proper basis for action, while intellect gets short shrift as a hang-up of outmoded elitism. Statistics, in this absurd dichotomy, often becomes the symbol of the enemy. As Hilaire Belloc wrote, "Statistics are the triumph of the quantitative method, and the quantitative method is the victory of sterility and death."

This is a personal story of statistics, properly interpreted, as profoundly 4 nurturant and life-giving. It declares holy war on the downgrading of intellect by telling a small story to illustrate the utility of dry, academic knowledge about science. Heart and head are focal points of one body, one personality.

In July 1982, I learned that I was suffering from abdominal mesothelioma, 5 a rare and serious cancer usually associated with exposure to asbestos. When I revived after surgery, I asked my first question of my doctor and chemotherapist: "What is the best technical literature about mesothelioma?" She replied, with a touch of diplomacy (the only departure she has ever made from direct frankness), that the medical literature contained nothing really worth reading.

Of course, trying to keep an intellectual away from literature works about as 6 well as recommending chastity to *Homo sapiens*, the sexiest primate of all. As soon as I could walk, I made a beeline for Harvard's Countway medical library and punched mesothelioma into the computer's bibliographic search program. An hour later, surrounded by the latest literature on abdominal mesothelioma, I realized with a gulp why my doctor had offered that humane advice. The literature couldn't have been more brutally clear: Mesothelioma is incurable,

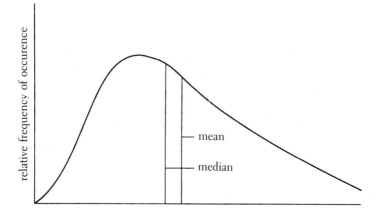

A RIGHT-SKEWED distribution showing that means must be higher than medians, and that the right side of the distribution extends out into a long tail. BEN GAMIT.

with a median mortality of only eight months after discovery. I sat stunned for about fifteen minutes, then smiled and said to myself: So that's why they didn't give me anything to read. Then my mind started to work again, thank goodness.

If a little learning could ever be a dangerous thing, I had encountered a   7
classic example. Attitude clearly matters in fighting cancer. We don't know why (from my old-style materialistic perspective, I suspect that mental states feed back upon the immune system). But match people with the same cancer for age, class, health, and socioeconomic status, and, in general, those with positive attitudes, with a strong will and purpose for living, with commitment to struggle, and with an active response to aiding their own treatment and not just a passive acceptance of anything doctors say, tend to live longer. A few months later I asked Sir Peter Medawar, my personal scientific guru and a Nobelist in immunology, what the best prescription for success against cancer might be. "A sanguine personality," he replied. Fortunately (since one can't reconstruct oneself at short notice and for a definite purpose), I am, if anything, even-tempered and confident in just this manner.

Hence the dilemma for humane doctors: Since attitude matters so critically,   8
should such a somber conclusion be advertised, especially since few people have sufficient understanding of statistics to evaluate what the statements really mean? From years of experience with the small-scale evolution of Bahamian land snails treated quantitatively, I have developed this technical knowledge— and I am convinced that it played a major role in saving my life. Knowledge is indeed power, as Francis Bacon proclaimed.

The problem may be briefly stated: What does "median mortality of eight   9
months" signify in our vernacular? I suspect that most people, without training in statistics, would read such a statement as "I will probably be dead in eight months"—the very conclusion that must be avoided, both because this formulation is false, and because attitude matters so much.

I was not, of course, overjoyed, but I didn't read the statement in this   10
vernacular way either. My technical training enjoined a different perspective on "eight months median mortality." The point may seem subtle, but the consequences can be profound. Moreover, this perspective embodies the distinctive way of thinking in my own field of evolutionary biology and natural history.

We still carry the historical baggage of a Platonic heritage that seeks sharp   11
essences and definite boundaries. (Thus we hope to find an unambiguous "beginning of life" or "definition of death," although nature often comes to us as irreducible continua.) This Platonic heritage, with its emphasis on clear distinctions and separated immutable entities, leads us to view statistical measures of central tendency wrongly, indeed opposite to the appropriate interpretation in our actual world of variation, shadings, and continua. In short, we view means and medians as hard "realities," and the variation that permits their calculation as a set of transient and imperfect measurements of this hidden

essence. If the median is the reality and variation around the median just a device for calculation, then "I will probably be dead in eight months" may pass as a reasonable interpretation.

But all evolutionary biologists know that variation itself is nature's only irreducible essence. Variation is the hard reality, not a set of imperfect measures for a central tendency. Means and medians are the abstractions. Therefore, I looked at the mesothelioma statistics quite differently—and not only because I am an optimist who tends to see the doughnut instead of the hole, but primarily because I know that variation itself is the reality. I had to place myself amidst the variation. 12

When I learned about the eight-month median, my first intellectual reaction was: Fine, half the people will live longer; now what are my chances of being in that half. I read for a furious and nervous hour and concluded, with relief: damned good. I possessed every one of the characteristics conferring a probability of longer life: I was young; my disease had been recognized in a relatively early stage; I would receive the nation's best medical treatment; I had the world to live for; I knew how to read the data properly and not despair. 13

Another technical point then added even more solace. I immediately recognized that the distribution of variation about the eight-month median would almost surely be what statisticians call "right skewed." (In a symmetrical distribution, the profile of variation to the left of the central tendency is a mirror image of variation to the right. Skewed distributions are asymmetrical, with variation stretching out more in one direction than the other—left skewed if extended to the left, right skewed if stretched out to the right.) The distribution of variation had to be right skewed, I reasoned. After all, the left of the distribution contains an irrevocable lower boundary of zero (since mesothelioma can only be identified at death or before). Thus, little space exists for the distribution's lower (or left) half—it must be scrunched up between zero and eight months. But the upper (or right) half can extend out for years and years, even if nobody ultimately survives. The distribution must be right skewed, and I needed to know how long the extended tail ran—for I had already concluded that my favorable profile made me a good candidate for the right half of the curve. 14

The distribution was, indeed, strongly right skewed, with a long tail (however small) that extended for several years above the eight-month median. I saw no reason why I shouldn't be in that small tail, and I breathed a very long sigh of relief. My technical knowledge had helped. I had read the graph correctly. I had asked the right question and found the answers. I had obtained, in all probability, that most precious of all possible gifts in the circumstances—substantial time. I didn't have to stop and immediately follow Isaiah's injunction to Hezekiah—set thine house in order: for thou shalt die, and not live. I would have time to think, to plan, and to fight. 15

One final point about statistical distributions. They apply only to a prescribed 16 set of circumstances—in this case to survival with mesothelioma under conventional modes of treatment. If circumstances change, the distribution may alter. I was placed on an experimental protocol of treatment and, if fortune holds, will be in the first cohort of a new distribution with high median and a right tail extending to death by natural causes at advanced old age.*

It has become, in my view, a bit too trendy to regard the acceptance of death   17 as something tantamount to intrinsic dignity. Of course I agree with the preacher of Ecclesiastes that there is a time to love and a time to die—and when my skein runs out I hope to face the end calmly and in my own way. For most situations, however, I prefer the more martial view that death is the ultimate enemy—and I find nothing reproachable in those who rage mightily against the dying of the light.

The swords of battle are numerous, and none more effective than humor.   18 My death was announced at a meeting of my colleagues in Scotland, and I almost experienced the delicious pleasure of reading my obituary penned by one of my best friends (the so-and-so got suspicious and checked; he too is a statistician, and didn't expect to find me so far out on the left tail). Still, the incident provided my first good laugh after the diagnosis. Just think, I almost got to repeat Mark Twain's most famous line of all: The reports of my death are greatly exaggerated.**

QUESTIONS

1. What is the difference between the "mean" and the "median"? Why is it important to know the difference between measures with respect to any particular situation?

2. What is the difference between a "skewed" and a "symmetrical" distribution? Why is it important to know the difference between these kinds of distributions with respect to any statistical distribution?

3. Unlike many of Gould's essays, this piece centers on a story of personal experience. How does Gould's story arouse interest and build suspense? How does the story's development make his point about the proper interpretation of statistics without losing control of the plot?

4. In this piece, Gould not only claims the importance of knowing something about how to interpret statistics, but also asserts the value of maintaining an "even-tempered, confident," possibly even somewhat playful attitude, in fighting against cancer. What evidence do you see in this essay—in Gould's style and method of storytelling—that he has such an attitude?

5. Think of a specific time in your own recent experience when you have read about, or heard about, or lived through a situation in which it would have been important

---

* So far so good.
** Since writing this, my death has actually been reported in two European magazines, five years apart. *Fama volat* (and lasts a long time). I squawked very loudly both times and demanded a retraction; guess I just don't have Mr. Clemens's *savoir faire*.

to know the statistical concepts that Gould explains in this piece. What happened? How did you interpret the situation prior to reading Gould's piece? How do you understand the situation now?

6. Based on your own experience, write an essay illustrating the importance of understanding and knowing how to apply the statistical concepts explained in this essay.

MAKING CONNECTIONS

Compare this essay to Gould's other pieces in this collection, "Women's Brains" and "Counters and Cable Cars." What similarities and differences do you notice in the ways that he defines, develops, illustrates, and proves his point in each of these pieces?

THE ACTION OF NATURAL SELECTION

Charles Darwin

Charles Darwin (1809–1882), British botanist, geologist, and naturalist, is best known for his discovery that natural selection was responsible for changes in organisms during evolution. After an undistinguished academic career and a five-year voyage to South America with a British survey ship, he began keeping his Transmutation *Notebooks (1837–1839), developing the idea of "selection owing to struggle." In 1842 and 1844 he published short accounts of his views and in 1859 published* On the Origin of Species, *which made him famous—even notorious—as the father of the "Theory of Evolution." He preferred to avoid controversy and left the debates over his theories to others whenever possible. But he was a keen observer and continued to study and write on natural history all his life. The essay that follows here is a brief excerpt from* On the Origin of Species, *in which Darwin explains his principle of "natural selection."*

In order to make it clear how, as I believe, natural selection acts, I must beg 1 permission to give one or two imaginary illustrations. Let us take the case of a wolf, which preys on various animals, securing some by craft, some by strength, and some by fleetness; and let us suppose that the fleetest prey, a deer for instance, had from any change in the country increased in numbers, or that other prey had decreased in numbers, during that season of the year when the wolf is hardest pressed for food. I can under such circumstances see no reason to doubt that the swiftest and slimmest wolves would have the best chance for surviving, and so be preserved or selected,—provided always that they retained strength to master their prey at this or at some other period of the year, when they might be compelled to prey on other animals. I can see no more reason to doubt this, than that man can improve the fleetness of his greyhounds by careful and methodical selection, or by that unconscious selection which results from each man trying to keep the best dogs without any thought of modifying the breed.

Even without any change in the proportional numbers of the animals on 2 which our wolf preyed, a cub might be born with an innate tendency to pursue certain kinds of prey. Nor can this be thought very improbable; for we often observe great differences in the natural tendencies of our domestic animals; one cat, for instance, taking to catch rats, another mice; one cat, according to Mr. St. John, bringing home winged game, another hares or rabbits, and another hunting on marshy ground and almost nightly catching woodcocks or snipes. The tendency to catch rats rather than mice is known to be inherited. Now, if any slight innate change of habit or of structure benefited an individual wolf, it would have the best chance of surviving and of leaving offspring. Some of its young would probably inherit the same habits or structure, and by the repetition of this process, a new variety might be formed which would either supplant or coexist with the parent-form of wolf. Or, again, the wolves inhabiting a mountainous district, and those frequenting the lowlands, would naturally be forced to hunt different prey; and from the continued preservation of the individuals best fitted for the two sites, two varieties might slowly be formed. These varieties would cross and blend where they met; but to this subject of intercrossing we shall soon have to return. I may add, that, according to Mr. Pierce, there are two varieties of the wolf inhabiting the Catskill Mountains in the United States, one with a light greyhound-like form, which pursues deer, and the other more bulky, with shorter legs, which more frequently attacks the shepherd's flocks.

Let us now take a more complex case. Certain plants excrete a sweet juice, apparently for the sake of eliminating something injurious from their sap: this is effected by glands at the base of the stipules in some Leguminosae, and at the back of the leaf of the common laurel. This juice, though small in quantity, is greedily sought by insects. Let us now suppose a little sweet juice or nectar to be excreted by the inner bases of the petals of a flower. In this case insects in seeking the nectar would get dusted with pollen, and would certainly often transport the pollen from one flower to the stigma of another flower. The flowers of two distinct individuals of the same species would thus get crossed; and the act of crossing, we have good reason to believe (as will hereafter be more fully alluded to), would produce very vigorous seedlings, which consequently would have the best chance of flourishing and surviving. Some of these seedlings would probably inherit the nectar-excreting power. Those individual flowers which had the largest glands or nectaries, and which excreted most nectar, would be oftenest visited by insects, and would be oftenest crossed; and so in the long-run would gain the upper hand. Those flowers, also, which had their stamens and pistils placed, in relation to the size and habits of the particular insects which visited them, so as to favor in any degree the transportal of their pollen from flower to flower, would likewise be favored or selected. We might have taken the case of insects visiting flowers for the sake of collecting pollen instead of nectar; and as pollen is formed for the sole object of fertilization, its destruction appears a simple loss to the plant; yet if a little pollen were carried, at first occasionally and then habitually, by the pollen-devouring insects from flower to flower, and a cross thus effected, although nine-tenths of the pollen were destroyed, it might still be a great gain to the plant; and those individuals which produced more and more pollen, and had larger and larger anthers, would be selected.

When our plant, by this process of the continued preservation or natural selection of more and more attractive flowers, had been rendered highly attractive to insects, they would, unintentionally on their part, regularly carry pollen from flower to flower; and that they can most effectually do this, I could easily show by many striking instances. I will give only one—not as a very striking case, but as likewise illustrating one step in the separation of the sexes of plants, presently to be alluded to. Some holly-trees bear only male flowers, which have four stamens producing rather a small quantity of pollen, and a rudimentary pistil; other holly-trees bear only female flowers; these have a full-sized pistil and four stamens with shrivelled anthers, in which not a grain of pollen can be detected. Having found a female tree exactly sixty yards from a male tree, I put the stigmas of twenty flowers, taken from different branches, under the microscope, and on all, without exception, there were pollen-grains, and on some a profusion of pollen. As the wind had set for several days from the female to the male tree, the pollen could not thus have been carried. The weather had been cold and boisterous, and therefore not favorable to bees, nevertheless every female flower which I examined had been effectually fertilized by the bees, accidentally dusted with pollen, having flown from tree to tree in search of nectar. But to return to our imaginary case: as soon as the plant had been rendered so highly attractive to insects that pollen was regularly carried from flower to flower, another process might commence. No naturalist doubts the advantage of what has been called the "physiological division of labor;" hence we may believe that it would be advantageous to a plant to produce stamens alone in one flower or on one whole plant, and pistils alone in another flower or on one whole plant. In plants under culture and placed under new conditions of life, sometimes the male organs and sometimes the female organs become more or less impotent; now if we suppose this to occur in ever so slight a degree under nature, then as pollen is already carried regularly from flower to flower, and as a more complete separation of the sexes of our plant would be advantageous on the principle of the division of labor, individuals with this tendency more and more increased would be continually favored or selected, until at last a complete separation of the sexes would be effected.

Let us now turn to the nectar-feeding insects in our imaginary case: we may suppose the plant of which we have been slowly increasing the nectar by continued selection, to be a common plant; and that certain insects depended in main part on its nectar for food. I could give many facts, showing how anxious bees are to save time; for instance, their habit of cutting holes and sucking the nectar at the bases of certain flowers, which they can, with a very little more trouble, enter by the mouth. Bearing such facts in mind, I can see no reason to doubt that an accidental deviation in the size and form of the body, or in the curvature and length of the proboscis, &c., far too slight to be appreciated by us, might profit a bee or other insect, so that an individual so characterized would be able to obtain its food more quickly, and so have a better chance of living and leaving descendants. Its descendants would probably inherit a tendency to a similar slight deviation of structure. The tubes of the corollas of the common red and incarnate clovers (Trifolium pratense and incarnatum) do not on a hasty glance appear to differ in length; yet the hive-bee can easily suck the nectar out of the incarnate clover, but not out of the common red clover, which is visited by humble-bees alone; so that whole fields of the red clover offer in vain an abundant supply of precious nectar to the hive-bee. Thus it might be a great advantage to the hive-bee to have a slightly longer or differently constructed proboscis. On the other hand, I have found by experiment that the fertility of clover greatly depends on bees visiting and moving parts of the corolla, so as to push the pollen on to the stigmatic surface. Hence, again, if humble-bees were to become rare in any country, it might be a great advantage to the red clover to have a shorter or more deeply divided tube to its corolla, so that the hive-bee could visit its flowers. Thus I can understand how a flower and a bee might slowly become, either simultaneously or one after the other, modified and adapted in the most perfect manner to each other, by the continued preservation of individuals presenting mutual and slightly favorable deviations of structure.

I am well aware that this doctrine of natural selection, exemplified in the 6 above imaginary instances, is open to the same objections which were at first urged against Sir Charles Lyell's noble views on "the modern changes of the earth, as illustrative of geology;" but we now very seldom hear the action, for instance, of the coast-waves, called a trifling and insignificant cause, when applied to the excavation of gigantic valleys or to the formation of the longest lines of inland cliffs. Natural selection can act only by the preservation and accumulation of infinitesimally small inherited modifications, each profitable to the preserved being; and as modern geology has almost banished such views as the excavation of a great valley by a single diluvial wave, so will natural selection, if it be a true principle, banish the belief of the continued creation of new organic beings, or of any great and sudden modification in their structure.

QUESTIONS

1. What does Darwin mean by "natural selection"?
2. The short title of Darwin's major book is often mistakenly given as *The Origin of the Species*. What is the difference between that and the book's correct title, *On the Origin of Species*? Why do you suppose so many people get it wrong?
3. Why does Darwin "beg permission" in the first sentence? In the same sentence, what does he mean by "imaginary" illustrations? Are they untrue, or what?
4. We use the name "bumblebee" for what Darwin (and other English writers before

him) called a "humble-bee." Find out something about the word *humble* and about the different kinds of bees. (What is the difference between a hive-bee and a humble-bee, anyway?) For the word *humble*, go to a good dictionary, but don't depend on a dictionary for information about different kinds of bees. Play with the words *humble* and *bumble* to see which of their meanings can be appropriately applied to bees.

5. Darwin's illustrative explanations are excellent examples of process analysis, a type of writing that presents a complicated chain of events as clearly as possible. Select some subject that you know well and that involves an intricate linkage of events. Explain an "imaginary" process taken from that subject. That is, imagine how some little change in an intricate pattern of events would lead to other changes that would cause other changes, until a whole new pattern was established. For example, how would some change in your behavior, appearance, or abilities change the patterns of school and family life around you? Explain the process you imagine as accurately and "scientifically" as you can. Complete your explanation by drawing some conclusion about the principles exemplified by the process you have described.

MAKING CONNECTIONS

1. To what extent could you read Francis Crick's "Times and Distances, Large and Small," as a commentary on this explanation of Darwin's? Or could you just as well read Darwin as a commentary on Crick?

2. Compare Darwin's illustrations of the wolf, the bee, and the flower to James Jeans's explanation in "Why the Sky Is Blue." What are some similarities of their explanations? Are there any striking differences?

FACE PERCEPTION WITHOUT RECOGNITION

Antonio R. Damasio

Antonio R. Damasio was born in Portugal in 1944, where
he studied medicine, receiving both an M.D. and Ph.D.
from the University of Lisbon. He is professor and head of
the Department of Neurology at the University of Iowa
College of Medicine and adjunct professor at the Salk Institute in La Jolla, California. Most of Damasio's publications are on anatomical aspects of higher brain functions,
Parkinsonism, and dementia. His research focuses on understanding the cerebral basis of vision, language, and
memory. Oliver Sacks has written that "The most important
studies of . . . agnosias, and of visual processing in general,
are now being undertaken by A. R. and H. Damasio." In
1989, Damasio was one of four American scientists and
scholars named to review progress in Western studies of
consciousness for the Dalai Lama. The essay here, a review
of research on "prosopagnosia," the phenomenon of perception without recognition, first appeared in Trends in
NeuroScience (March 1985).

REVIEW OF RESEARCH ON PROSOPAGNOSIA

[Abstract.] The impaired recognition of previously known familiar faces (pro-   1
sopagnosia), when it appears in isolation, is one of the most extreme forms of
behavioral dissociation encountered in human pathology. Its research provides
an outstanding opportunity to understand better the organization of the visual
system and of memory mechanisms in humans. Recent evidence indicates that
the disorder is associated with bilateral lesions of the central visual system,
located in the mesial occipito-temporal region. These lesions either destroy a
specific sector of the visual association cortex or disconnect it from limbic structures located anteriorly in the temporal lobe. This evidence is in keeping with
the demonstration, in normals, that both hemispheres are capable of facial
recognition, but should not be seen to indicate that each hemisphere uses the
same mechanisms to process faces or is equally efficient in the process. Cognitive
analysis of prosopagnosia reveals that the defect is not specific to human faces

but also appears in relation to other visual stimuli whose recognition depends on the evocation of specific contextual attributes and associations, and which are visually "ambiguous" (different stimuli belonging to the same group but having similar physical structure). Physiopathologically, prosopagnosia is the result of a failure to activate, on the basis of visual stimuli, memories pertinent to those stimuli.

The description of prosopagnosia dates from the turn of the century although the designation was only coined in 1947 by Bodamer.[1] In isolation, the condition is so extreme and infrequent that many investigators doubted its reality. Otherwise normal individuals suddenly lose their ability to recognize the faces of relatives, friends, and even their own faces in the mirror, while being able to recognize other objects visually. They also lose the ability to learn to identify the faces of new persons they come into contact with. In short, the visual inspection of these familiar faces no longer generates an experience of even vague familiarity and thus facial recognition is forever precluded. The patients can still recognize, by the sound of their voices, the people whose faces have become meaningless. All the remote memories that pertain to those people remain intact. Cognitive skills also remain intact and so do complex visual abilities, i.e. most prosopagnosic patients describe their visual environment accurately, localize stimuli in space flawlessly, inspect visual arrays in normal fashion, and some can even read. Needless to say, their visual acuity is normal. The only symptoms that commonly accompany prosopagnosia are achromatopsia, an acquired defect in color perception which may affect part or all of the visual field, an acquired defect in the appreciation of textures visually, and some partial field cut for the vision of forms. (Prosopagnosia may also be found as a component of global amnesic syndrome. In such instances no field defects for color or form accompany the manifestation, and visual perception is manifestly intact.)

Even after it became clear that the condition was indeed real, considerable controversy surfaced regarding its physiopathological nature and anatomical basis. This review focuses on some of these issues as well as on new developments in the understanding of prosopagnosia.

ANATOMICAL BASIS

The early descriptions of prosopagnosia indicated that the condition was associated with the bilateral damage to the occipital lobes.[26,3] But when after decades of neglect, there was a resurgence of interest in prosopagnosia, several investigators conceptualized it as a sign of unilateral damage of the right hemisphere. At the time, the 1960s, fresh neuropsychological investigations had revealed the major role of the right hemisphere in visual processing and it appeared reasonable to assume that the right hemisphere might possess the sole key to a refined visual process such as facial recognition. Hecaen and Angelergues[2] added strength to this hypothesis by noting that most prosopagnosic patients had exclusive left visual field defects, and suggesting that this was due to exclusive right hemisphere damage. Later, in a comprehensive review of the data available in 1974, Meadows concluded "that patients with prosopagnosia have right anterior inferior occipital lesions in the region of the occipital temporal junction. Many if not all cases have an additional lesion in the left hemisphere."[4] Although these interpretations were consonant with the anatomical localization methods at the time, the evidence uncovered in the years that followed revealed that they were not supportable. The current view is that bilateral lesions are indeed necessary, a notion that is based on: (1) a critical review of the meaning of visual field data: (2) a reassessment of post-mortem studies of prosopagnosic patients; (3) Computed Tomography (CT), Nuclear Magnetic Resonance (NMR) and Emission Tomography (ET) studies of patients with and without prosopagnosia; (4) a study of patients with cerebral hemispherectomy, callosal surgery and amnesic syndromes. The fundamental evidence is as follows:

(1) The one patient of Hecaen and Angelergues to come to post-mortem, turned out to have a bilateral lesion.[2] The lesion in the left hemisphere was "silent" as far as visual field findings were concerned. Similar "silent" lesions were uncovered at autopsy in patients described by Benson[5] and by Lhermitte.[6] It is now apparent that when lesions of the central visual system fail to involve optic radiations or primary visual cortex they do not produce an overt defect of form vision even when they can cause major disturbances of complex visual processing such as a defect in recognition or color processing.[7] While the presence of a field defect correctly indicates the presence of a lesion, its absence does not exclude focal damage. Thus while the detailed study of field defects is mandatory for the appropriate study of visual agnosia, its details cannot be used for the prediction of lesion localization.

(2) Analysis of the post-mortem records of all patients that have come to autopsy[8,9] indicate that they all have bilateral lesions. Furthermore, it is clear that those lesions preferably involve the inferior visual association cortices, i.e. the occipito-temporal region. Finally, patients with bilateral lesions involving the superior visual association cortices, i.e. the occipito-parietal region, never develop prosopagnosia, presenting instead either a full Balint syndrome or some of its components, i.e. visual disorientation, optic ataxia or ocular apraxia.[7] Patients with Balint syndrome can recognize faces provided their attention is properly directed to the stimuli.

(3) Computed Tomography (CT) has permitted the study of many cases of

prosopagnosia and of numerous controls with unilateral lesions of the left or right occipito-temporal region, or with bilateral lesions of the occipito-parietal region. With one exception all the instances of permanent prosopagnosia studied in appropriate patients with technically advanced scanning techniques have shown bilateral lesions.[8–11] Furthermore, numerous instances of unilateral lesion in the right and left hemispheres have been described and there has been no report of prosopagnosia appearing in those circumstances. (The possible exception was reported in a hypertensive patient on the basis of a single cut of an acute CT scan;[12] it is important to consider the possibility of an undetected lesion in the opposite hemisphere.)

Patients with bilateral occipito-parietal lesions consistently show Balint syndrome or its components but not prosopagnosia.[7] In the only two cases studies with Nuclear Magnetic Resonance (NMR) the lesions were bilateral. In the only two cases studies with Single Photon Emission Tomography there were bilateral regions of diminished cerebral blood flow.[7]

(4) Evidence from hemispherectomy and from cases of surgical callosal section has also been helpful. Patients with right hemispherectomy maintain their ability to recognize faces with their single left hemisphere.[13] The split-brain subjects continue to recognize faces with each isolated hemisphere although, as expected, the mechanisms of recognition appear to be different on the left and on the right.[27]

Final evidence for the bilaterality of damage in prosopagnosia comes from the analysis of patients with amnesic syndromes. Patients with global amnesic syndromes associated with temporal lobe damage have prosopagnosia as a component. All have bilateral lesions.[15,16] The finding simply underscores the fact that memory processing of the type involved in facial recognition is of crucial importance for the individual and is clearly operated by both hemispheres. This is not to say that the left and right hemispheres perform the task in the same way or equally well. On the contrary, we believe each hemisphere learns, recognizes and recalls faces with different strategies and that the right hemisphere's approach is probably more efficient than the left.

THE NATURE OF THE DEFECT

The bizarre nature of prosopagnosia, when it appears in isolation, has prompted all sorts of explanations for the phenomenon. Those who have never seen a prosopagnosic patient may be tempted to dismiss the phenomenon as the result of psychiatric illness or dementia. None of these interpretations obtain, considering that these patients show no evidence of language impairment, have intact cognitive skills and do not have psychiatric symptomatology before or after the onset of prosopagnosia. In his review of the neuropsychological investigation of prosopagnosia, Benton noted how some authors have seen prosopagnosia as a primary perceptual defect that would preclude the analysis and synthesis of complex visual stimuli; how others have postulated an incapacity to perceive individuality within a single class of objects; and yet others have proposed a material specific defect in memory, that is, a defect of integrating current facial percepts with past experience of them.[17]

Some of these issues are more clear today. There is substantial evidence against the notion that prosopagnosia is due to a primary perceptual disturbance. Firstly, prosopagnosic patients can discriminate unfamiliar faces well. Some of these patients perform normally in Benton and Van Allen's test of facial discrimination—a difficult task in which they are called to match unfamiliar and differently lit photographs of faces but obviously not asked to recognize any of them;[8,17] they can perform complex visual tasks such as the anomalous contours test and they have normal stereopsis;[8] they can draw accurately complex figures shown in photographs, drawings or in real models;[8,17] more importantly, they can recognize, at a generic level, any visual stimulus provided that no contextual memory cues are required.[6,8] Secondly, severe disorders of visual perception such as seen in patients with Balint syndrome or comparable disorders, do not have prosopagnosia.[7,18,19] Patients with prosopagnosia can perceive and recognize accurately many stimuli that are visually more complex than human faces, i.e., that have a greater number of individual components arranged in just as complicated a manner but crowded in smaller areas or volumes.[8] On the other hand, there is evidence that the particular class of visual stimuli, as well as the ability to integrate facial percepts with pertinent past experience, are important factors in the physiopathology of prosopagnosia. The evidence is as follows.

Prosopagnosia does not occur in relation to human faces alone. All of the patients with prosopagnosia have defects of recognition for other stimuli.[4,6,8] The types of stimuli for which they have agnosia, however, are rather special. They include: (a) automobiles (prosopagnosics cannot recognize their own car and do not recognize different makes of cars; however, these patients can recognize different types of car, such as a passenger car, a fire engine, an ambulance, or a funeral car); (b) clothes of the same type and general shape, i.e. dresses, suits, shirts, etc.; (c) food ingredients with similar forms and volumes; (d) specific animals within a group (a farmer suddenly became unable to recognize, within a herd, specific animals that he could easily recognize before; birdwatchers have become unable to recognize different birds, etc.). In all of these instances, the process of recognition operates normally up to the point in which specific recognition of a given member within the group is required. In other words, all of these patients can recognize an automobile as an automobile, a cow as a cow, or a dress as a dress. They can also recognize all of the subcomponents of these stimuli correctly, i.e. eyes, noses, windshields, wheels, sleeves, etc. But when, as is the case with human faces, the patient is requested to identify precisely the specific possessor of that visual appearance, the process breaks down and the within-class-membership of the stimulus cannot be ascertained.

An analysis of the shared characteristics of the stimuli which can cause 14 prosopagnosia reveals that: (a) these are stimuli for which a specific recognition is mandatory and for which a generic recognition is either socially unacceptable (human faces), or incompatible with normal activity (cars, clothing, foodstuffs); (b) the specific recognition of all of the stimuli depends on contextual (episodic) memory, i.e. it depends on the evocation of multiple traces of memory previously associated with the currently perceived stimulus; those traces depend on a personal, temporally and spatially bound, memory process; (c) that all of the stimuli belong to groups in which numerous members are physically *similar* (in visual terms), and yet individually *different*; we have designated these stimuli as visually "ambiguous" (an operational definition of visual ambiguity is the presence in a group of numerous *different* members with *similar* visual characteristics). Prosopagnosia patients have no difficulty with the correct, individual recognition of "non-ambiguous" stimuli, i.e. visual stimuli that belong to groups with numerous members but in which *different* individual members have a *different* (distinctive) visual structure.[8]

According to the analysis above, the basic perceptual mechanisms in pro- 15 sopagnosic patients are normal. There is no evidence that the varied partial defects of color, texture or form perception, alone or in combination, can cause prosopagnosia. When patients are called on to recognize stimuli that belong to visually ambiguous classes, they fail to evoke the pertinent, associated traces of contextual memory on the basis of which familiarity and recognition of the stimulus would be based. Seen in this light, the defect must be described, physiopathologically, as a disorder of visually-triggered contextual memory. It is important to distinguish this from a disorder of memory in general (memory traces can be normally activated through other sensory channels) and even from a disorder of visual memory (auditory stimulation can bring forward numerous traces of visual memory testifying to the intactness of many visual memory stores). The malfunction is in the triggering system for the associated evocations. We believe this defect can be explained by one of three possible mechanisms: (1) a defect in the highest level of visual analysis, that which permits the distinction of finest structural details necessary for the separation of visually "ambiguous" stimuli but unnecessary for visually unambiguous ones; (2) a defect of the plotting of the ongoing percept into the pre-existing, templated information, acquired for each specific stimulus (this mechanism would assume the normalcy of the perceptual step referred to above); (3) a defect in the activation of pertinent associated memories occurring after both steps above operate normally. Current research in our laboratory and others is aimed at investigating the validity of these possible mechanisms.

NEW DEVELOPMENTS

Autonomic evidence for nonconscious recognition

One of the intriguing problems posed by visual agnosia and, more generally, 16 by amnesia has to do with the level at which the failure of recognition occurs. Some investigators have hypothesized that the failure to evoke both non-verbal and verbal memories capable of generating recognition does not preclude some process of recognition at a lower, nonconscious level of processing. In other words, it is possible that some part of the brain does recognize stimulus even if the subject is not aware of that process taking place. Patients with prosopagnosia are ideal subjects to test this hypothesis and that is what has recently been accomplished using paradigms aimed at detecting autonomic responses to stimuli that patients are clearly not aware of recognizing. In available studies (Ref. 20 and Tranel, D., and Damasio, A.), there is persuading evidence that at a nonconscious level, faces of relatives, friends, and self, generated strong psychophysiological responses clearly different from the weak or nonexistent responses to faces unfamiliar to the subject. The implications of this discovery are far-reaching. The findings support the notion that perception and recognition processes evolve by steps and that failure at the top of the cascade does not necessarily imply failure at more elementary levels. On the issue of facial recognition itself, they argue for the existence of a template system for each individual familiar face, and suggest that, at least in some of the patients, such a template system is intact. It is important to note that in our model the template system is not conceived in the Humian sense, as a static facsimile of a given face, but rather as a dynamic, evolving record of computations built on multiple exposure to the stimulus and probably stored at multiple levels of CNS, but especially anchored in visual association cortices.

Ocular motor activity in visual recognition

It has been suggested that patients with prosopagnosia might have an impairment of the proper scanning of the face, a disturbance of the ability to 17 search appropriately for elements crucial to facial perception, i.e. eyes, nose, mouth, hairline, facial contour. A recent study carried out in prosopagnosic patients shows that this is not the case (Rizzo, M., Hurtig, R. and Damasio, A., unpublished observations). Using electro-oculographic techniques the investigators showed that prosopagnosic patients scan fundamental elements of the face as do controls, using a natural progression in their scanning and spending comparable times in the analysis of separate features. The prosopagnosic patients also scan a complex picture (e.g. the Cookie Theft plate from the Boston Diagnostic Battery) in exactly the same manner as controls. Once again, the results lend credence to the notion that basic perception proceeds normally and that prosopagnosic subjects search and accumulate information as do normal individuals but fail, at a later stage, either to bring that information together in an integrated pattern, or to lead the integrated pattern to activate the pertinent associated memories.

Perception of contrast sensitivity in visual agnosia

It has been suggested that object recognition may be especially dependent [18] on the processing of low visuospatial frequencies.[21] It might follow that prosopagnosia would be caused by selective impairment of low spatial frequency vision. A recent study investigated this possibility in a prosopagnosic patient and has revealed exactly the contrary: the patient's processing of low spatial frequencies was intact, entirely comparable to matched controls, while the processing of high spatial frequencies showed a defect (Rizzo, M., Hurtig, R. and Damasio, A., unpublished observations). Further studies are necessary to clarify the role of different spatial frequencies in the recognition of objects and faces, in both normals and agnosics. Nonetheless, there is evidence to suggest that normal facial recognition calls for both low and high visuospatial frequencies.[22]

Cognitive strategies in facial processing

While it is clear that both hemispheres can learn, recognize and recall faces, [19] recent investigations demonstrate that, as one might have expected, the left and the right hemispheres utilize different strategies to accomplish the task. The findings obtained in patients with callosal surgery,[14] or in normals,[23-25] suggest that the right hemisphere of most individuals is likely to be the most efficient processor of faces and of comparable visual stimuli.

Studies in animals

The electrophysiological study of neurons responsive to visual stimuli in [20] nonhuman primates is likely to shed some light on the mechanisms of facial recognition and prosopagnosia. E. T. Rolls and E. Perrett have reported the presence of neurons in the temporal lobe of the monkey that respond powerfully to faces.[28]

SELECTED REFERENCES

These references work somewhat in the manner of normal footnotes. That is, they are listed roughly in order of their citation in the text. Number 1 is the first cited, and so on, but there are many exceptions to this and sometimes more than one reference is cited as bearing on a particular statement made in the text. The second citation in the text, for instance, is 26, 3, indicating that both references 26 and 3 bear on the issue under discussion. The third citation is numbered 2, the fourth 4, and the fifth is 2 again. This method avoids the needless proliferation of numbers. Why 3 comes before 2, however, is one of the mysteries of science. [Eds.]

1. Bodamer, J. (1947) *Arch. Psychiatr. Nervenkr.* 179, 6–54
2. Hecaen, H. and Angelergues, R. (1962) *Soc. for Inf. Disp. Arch. Neurol.* 7, 92–100
3. Wilbrand, H. (1892) *Deutche Z Nervenheilkd.* 2, 361–387
4. Meadows, J. C. (1974) *J. Neurol. Neurosurg. Psychiatry* 37, 498–501
5. Benson, D., Segarra, J. and Albert, M. L. (1974) *Arch. Neurol. (Chicago)* 30, 307–310
6. Lhermitte, J., Chain, F., Escourolle, R., Ducarne, B. and Pillon, B. (1972) *Rev. Neurol.* 126, 329–346
7. Damasio, A. R. (1985) in *Principles of Behavioral Neurology* (Mesulam, M. M., ed.), Davis, Philadelphia
8. Damasio, A. R., Damasio, H. and Van Hoesen, G. W. (1982) *Neurology* 32, 331–341
9. Nardelli, E., Buonanno, F., Coccia, G., Fiaschi, A., Terzian, H. and Rizzuto, N. (1982) *Eur. Neurol.* 21, 289–297
10. Brazis, P. W., Biller, J. and Fine, M. (1981) *Neurology* 31, 920
11. Bruyer, R., Laterre, C., Seron, X., Feyereisen, P., Strypstein, E., Pierrand, E. and Rectem, D. (1983) *Brain Cognition* 2, 257–284
12. Whitely, A. M. and Warrington, E. K. (1977) *J. Neurol. Neurosurg. Psychiatry* 40, 395–403
13. Damasio, A. R., Lima, P. A. and Damasio, H. (1975) *Neurology* 25, 89–93
14. Gazzaniga, M. S., Smylie, C. S. (1983) *Ann Neurol.* 13, 537–540
15. Corkin, S. (1984) *Semin. Neurol.* 4, 249–259
16. Damasio, A. R., Eslinger, P. J., Damasio, H., Van Hoesen, G. W. and Cornell, S. (1985) *Arch. Neurol.* 42, 252–259
17. Benton, A. (1980) *Am. Psychol.* 35, 176–186
18. Meier, M. J. and French, L. A. (1965) *Neuropsychologia* 3, 261–272
19. Orgass, B., Poeck, K., Kerchensteiner, M. and Hartje, W. (1972) *Z. Neurol.* 202, 177–195
20. Bauer, R. M. (1984) *Neuropsychologia* 22, 457–469; Tranel, D. and Damasio, A. (1985) *Science* 228, 1453–1454
21. Ginsburg, A. P. (1980) *Proc. of the Soc. for Inf. Dis.* 21, 219–227
22. Fiorentini, A., Maffei, L. and Sandini, G. (1983) *Perception* 12, 195–201
23. Ellis, H. D. (1983) in *Functions of the Right Cerebral Hemisphere*, (Young, A. W., ed.), Academic Press, London
24. Sergent, J. and Bindra, D. (1981) *Psycol. Bull.* 89, 541—554
25. Warrington, E. K. and James, M. (1967) *Cortex* 3, 317–326
26. Heidenhain, A. (1927) *Monatschr. Psychiatr. Neurol.* 66, 61–116
27. Levy, J., Trevarthen, C. and Sperry, R. W. (1972) *Brain* 95, 61–78
28. Perrett, D. I., Rolls, E. T. and Caan, W. (1982) *Exp. Brain. Res.* 47, 329–342

QUESTIONS

1. This article is a review of research on prosopagnosia. Analyze how it is organized. Divide the text into sections and explain the function of each. How do you account for the order or arrangement of the sections?

2. Like many pieces written for scientific journals, this one begins with an abstract. What does the full text provide that is not in the abstract?

3. Consider the relationship between the style of this essay (format, vocabulary, sentence structure, and so on) and the audience for whom it was written. Does audience always have an effect on style? Explain why or why not.

4. What portions of this article give you the most vivid sense of prosopagnosia, the condition under review? What accounts for your clearer understanding of those sections?

5. Using this essay as a model, write a review of research in a field that you know something about. What is the purpose of such a review? What does your own review of research put you in a position to do?

MAKING CONNECTIONS

1. Consider this essay along with Oliver Sacks's "The Man Who Mistook His Wife for a Hat." Obviously, Sacks generates a good deal of interest in a case similar to the problem Damasio describes. Damasio, on the other hand, gives us a good deal of additional information on the problem. Describe the differences in form and content between the two essays.

2. Although Oliver Sacks mentions "agnosia" and frequently refers to Dr. P.'s case as an example of "prosopagnosia" (see footnote 4), some of the details he gives do not square with the description of prosopagnosia that Damasio offers. Make a list of those differences, and describe the ways in which Dr. P. does not behave as a prosopagnosiac would.

ARGUING

Here in "Arguing" you will find authors taking positions on a wide range of controversial subjects—from the issue of sexism in rock videos to the status of black English, from the nature of sexual culture to the use of animals in psychological research. No matter what their academic fields or professions, these authors energetically defend their stands on the issues and questions they address. But this should come as no surprise. None of us, after all, holds lightly to our beliefs and ideas about what is true or beautiful or good. Indeed, most of us get especially fired up when our views are pitted against the ideas and beliefs of others. So, you will find these authors vigorously engaged in the give-and-take of argument. And as a consequence, you will repeatedly find yourself having to weigh the merits of competing positions in a debate or disagreement about some controversial issue.

The distinctive quality of arguing can be seen in the following passage from Frederick A. King's "Animals in Research: The Case for Experimentation":

> A recent pamphlet published by the MFA [Mobilization for Animals Coalition] stated, "Of all these experiments, those conducted in psychology are the most painful, pointless, and repulsive.". . .
>
> Such irresponsible accusations of research cruelty have consistently characterized the publications of the MFA. However, a recent study by psychologists D. Caroline Coile and Neal E. Miller of Rockefeller University counters these charges. Coile and Miller looked at every article (a total of 608) appearing in the past five years in journals of the American Psychological Association that report animal research. They concluded that none of the extreme allegations made by the MFA could be supported. . . .
>
> Furthermore, there are standards and mechanisms to ensure that research animals are treated in a humane and scientifically sensible way. These mechanisms include the Federal Animal Welfare Act of 1966 (amended in Congress in 1970, 1976, and 1979); periodic inspection of all animal-research facilities by the Department of Agriculture. . . .

This excerpt comes from the opening section of a piece in which King attempts to defend the use of animals in psychological research. In taking this view, King realizes that he is at odds with "more than 400 animal-protectionist organizations" that are united by "an adamant opposition to animal research." Given the significant disagreements that exist between his view and those of the animal protectionists, he is not free just to make a straightforward case for his own position on the matter. He must instead contend with his opponents, refuting their positions, while also providing evidence in support of his own. He is, in short, engaged in arguing. The argumentative situation is immediately reflected in the subtitle of his piece, which implicitly acknowledges that there is a case *against* experimentation, and in the debatelike structure of the paragraphs that follow. Accordingly, King begins by identifying the views of his opponents, namely that the use of animals in psychological research is "painful, pointless, and repulsive." He then moves into a discussion intended to refute those claims. So it is that argument puts ideas to the test by forcing them to stand up against opposing beliefs or theories.

As the King passage also reveals, argument naturally arises over significant issues or questions that are open to sharply differing points of view. Questions about the use of animals in research, for example, are of crucial interest to persons in a wide range of fields—not only to experimental psychologists such as King, but also to medical researchers, zoologists, environmentalists, and naturalists in general, as well as to philosophers, theologians, social planners, lawyers, and politicians. And persons in each of these fields might well be inclined to approach the question from markedly different points of view that involve different assumptions as well as different bodies of knowledge and experience. Many experimental psychologists and medical researchers, for example, perceive animals as being absolutely necessary in their investigations, whereas a number of philosophers, lawyers, and specialists in biomedical ethics are intensely committed to establishing and protecting the rights of animals, and thus with defining the point at which those rights have been violated by researchers. Each point of view necessarily leads to substantially different claims about the use of animals in research, and none of the claims can be conclusively proven to be true. Indeed, if conclusive evidence had existed for one view or another, the argument would never have arisen, or it would have been resolved as quickly as the evidence had been discovered. So, like all controversial issues, the question remains open to debate, and anyone involved in such an argument can at best hope to make a persuasive case for a particular viewpoint—a case that will move thoughtful readers to consider that position seriously and possibly even convince them to accept it.

As readers of argumentative writing, we in turn should try to be as impartial as the members of a jury. We should try to set aside any biases or prejudices that we might have about one view or another. Then, we should weigh all the evidence, logic, claims, and appeals for each viewpoint before arriving at a decision about which one we find most convincing. By the same token, as writers of argument we should assume that readers are not likely to be persuaded by a one-sided view of a complex situation. Thus, we should be ready to present a case that not only will support our position but will respond to the crucial challenges of views that differ from our own. Both as readers and writers, then, we should strive to understand the balanced methods of persuasion that can be found throughout the broad range of argumentative writing.

THE RANGE OF ARGUMENTATIVE WRITING

Argumentative writing so pervades our lives that we may not even recognize it as such in the many brochures and leaflets that come our way, urging us to vote for one candidate rather than another or to support one cause rather than another. Argumentative writing also figures heavily in newspaper editorials, syndicated columns, and letters to the editor, which are typically given over to debating the pros and cons of one public issue or another, from local taxes to national defense policies. Argument, of course, is fundamental in the judicial process, providing as it does the basic procedure for conducting all courtroom trials. And it is crucial in the legislative process, for it offers a systematic means of exploring the strengths and weaknesses of differing policies and programs. In a similar way, argument serves the basic aims of the academic world, enabling different ideas and theories to be tested by pitting them against each other. Whatever the field or profession, argument is an important activity in the advancement of knowledge and society.

The broad range of argumentative writing may conveniently be understood by considering the kinds of issues and questions that typically give rise to disagreement and debate. Surely, the most basic sources of controversy are questions of fact—the who, what, when, and where of things, as well as how much. Questions such as these are most commonly at issue in criminal trials. But intense arguments over questions of fact can also develop in any academic or professional field, especially when the facts in question have a significant bearing on the explanation or judgment of a particular subject, body of material, or type of investigation. In his piece on animals in research, for example, King, as we have seen, cites a study conducted by Coile and Miller who "looked at every article (a total of 608) appearing in the past five years in journals of the American Psychological Association that report animal research," in which "[t]hey concluded that none of the extreme allegations made by the MFA could be supported." So, in a very real sense, the argument in this piece arises over questions of fact as well as questions of how to interpret the facts.

Even when there is no question about the facts themselves, there are likely to be arguments about how to explain the facts. Disagreements of this kind abound across the full range of academic and professional fields. And the arguments inevitably arise out of sharply differing points of view on the facts, as can be seen in Bruno Bettelheim's "The Ignored Lesson of Anne Frank." Bettelheim is attacking not the facts of the Frank family's story, but the play and movie version, which "eulogiz[es] how they lived in their hiding place while neglecting to examine first whether it was a reasonable or an effective choice." In attacking "the universal admiration of their way of coping, or rather of not coping," Bettelheim is taking a stand quite opposite to that of persons who interpret the Frank family's attempt at hiding from the Nazis as touching or noble.

Differing viewpoints, of course, ultimately reflect differing beliefs and values. The way we view any particular subject is, after all, a matter of personal choice, an outgrowth of what our experience and knowledge have led us to hold as being self-evident. In this sense, beliefs and values are always to some extent at issue in any argumentative situation, even when they remain more or less in the background. But in some cases the conflicting values themselves are so clearly at the heart of the argument that they become a central focus in the debate, as you can see in this well-known passage from the Declaration of Independence.

> We hold these truths to be self-evident, that all men are created equal, that they are endowed by their Creator with certain unalienable Rights, that among these are Life, Liberty and the pursuit of Happiness. That to secure these rights, Governments are instituted among Men, deriving their just powers from the consent of the governed, That whenever any Form of Government becomes destructive of these ends, it is the Right of the People to alter or to abolish it, and to institute new Government, laying its foundation on such principles and orga-nizing its powers in such form, as to them shall seem most likely to affect their Safety and Happiness.

In this crucial passage that comes at the opening of the second paragraph of the Declaration, Thomas Jefferson and his congressional colleagues directly challenged several fundamental assumptions about the rights of people and the sources of governmental power that were then held not only by the British king but also by many British people and others throughout the world. Only in this way was it possible for them to make the compelling case for their ultimate claim that the colonies should be "FREE AND INDEPENDENT STATES . . . Absolved from all Allegiance to the British Crown."

Though Jefferson and his colleagues did not outline a new system of govern-ment in the Declaration itself, the document does enable us to see that conflicts over beliefs and values can, and often do, have a decisive bearing on questions of policy and planning. For a clear-cut example of how conflicts over beliefs lead to debates over policy, you need only look at Nathan Glazer's "Some Very Modest Proposals for the Improvement of American Education." At the begin-ning, Glazer sidesteps debate on the cost of improving education, by asserting that the cost of his proposals would be small, and savings might even be one end result. His proposals for improving the educational environment in the

United States challenge current beliefs and practices and argue for an alternative approach. As Glazer says, "I have concentrated on a variety of other things that serve to remove distraction . . . to concentrate on the essentials of teaching and learning as I (and many others) have experienced it."

His first proposal seems relatively noncontroversial: remove loudspeakers from classrooms to prevent teachers from being continually interrupted. However, to remove a loudspeaker is to undermine "the notion of hierarchy in education— the principal and assistant principal [as] the most important people." Such a proposal, then, would be considered a radical move—mostly by administrators, of course. Some of Glazer's proposals are far more controversial, such as his concluding one: "Let students, within reason, pick their schools, or let parents choose them for them." As you will see, he does not attempt to answer fully many of the questions such a proposal raises. In an argument structured by proposals, the writer is obligated to explore the possible consequences of his proposed changes. How well Glazer follows through on this obligation we leave to you, as his critical reader, to decide.

Just as his argument for improving education requires Glazer to consider and defend the possible effects of his proposed changes, so every other kind of question imposes on writers a particular set of argumentative obligations. King's argument in favor of using animals in research, for example, obliges him to cite extensive data concerning the humaneness and purposefulness of psychological research on animals, and Bettelheim's argument against the sanctification of the Anne Frank story requires him to present historical evidence against maintaining peacetime "family values" in time of war. A writer who aims to be persuasive cannot simply assert that something is or is not the case, for readers in general are not willing to be bullied, hoodwinked, or otherwise manipulated into accepting a particular claim. But they are capable of being reached by civilized and rational methods of persuasion that are appropriate to controversial issues—by evidence, logic, and eloquence.

METHODS OF ARGUING

In any piece of argumentative writing, no matter what field or subject it concerns, your primary purpose is to bring readers around to your point of view rather than another. Some readers, of course, will agree with you in advance, but others will disagree, and still others will be undecided. So, in planning a piece of argumentative writing, you should begin by examining your material with an eye to discovering the issues that have to be addressed and the points that have to be made in order to present your case most persuasively to readers, especially those who oppose you or who are undecided. This means that you will have to deal not only with issues that you consider relevant but also with matters that have been raised by your opponents. In other words, you will have to show readers that you have considered both sides of the controversy. In arguing about the use of animals in research, for example, King repeatedly takes into account the views of his opponents. Likewise, Glazer not only presents his proposals for improving education, but also argues against existing practices.

After you have identified the crucial points to be addressed, you should then decide upon the methods that will be necessary to make a convincing case with respect to each of the points. Some methods, of course, are imperative no matter what point you are trying to prove. Every piece of argumentation requires that you offer readers evidence to support your position. To do so, you will need to gather and present specific details that bear on each of the points you are trying to make. This basic concern for providing readers with appropriate evidence will lead you inevitably into the activity of reporting. Jefferson, for example, provides a lengthy and detailed list of "injuries" that the king of Great Britain inflicted on the colonies in order to demonstrate the right of the colonies "to throw off such Government"; and Glazer reports the problems that give rise to his proposals. Reporting appropriate evidence constitutes the most basic means of making a persuasive case for any point under consideration. So, any point for which evidence cannot be provided, or for which only weak or limited evidence can be offered, is likely to be much less convincing to readers than one that can be amply and vividly substantiated.

But evidence alone will not be persuasive to readers unless it is brought to bear on a point in a reasonable or logical way. In one of its most familiar forms, known as *induction*, logic involves the process of moving from bits of evidence to a generalization or a conclusion that is based upon them. King, for example, tells in detail about several different kinds of psychological experiments involving animals in order to refute the charge of his opponents that animal research is "pointless." Although this evidence is appropriate for showing that some research on animals has been purposeful and beneficial, it does not demonstrate the necessity of using animals in research. In order to do that, King attempts to show that certain kinds of research problems "do not lend themselves" to alternative methods of investigation. Based on this evidence, he claims that in some instances "animals are necessary if the research is to be done at all." This particular claim appears reasonable not just because King has gathered and presented evidence that pertains to the issue at hand, but also because he has carefully worded his claim, so as not to overstate the case. But like all generalizations, it is a hypothesis and not a certainty. In order to prove his claim beyond any doubt, King would have had to examine every instance of animal research that had ever been conducted and consider alternative methods that might have been available at the time. So, he has no choice but to make what is known as an inductive leap from a reasonable, but necessarily limited, body of evidence to a generalization. So, too, his generalization is at best a statement of probability.

Another form of logic, known as *deduction*, involves the movement from general assumptions or hypotheses to particular conclusions that can be derived from them. For example, having made the general claim that "a long train of abuses" entitles people "to throw off such Government," and having cited, in turn, a long list of abuses that Great Britain had inflicted upon the colonies, Jefferson is able to reach the conclusion that the colonies "are Absolved from all Allegiance to the British Crown." Given his initial assumptions about government and the rights of the people together with his evidence about British abuse of the colonists, Jefferson's deduction seems to be a logical conclusion, as indeed it is. But as in any case of deductive logic, the conclusion is only as convincing as the premises on which it is based. Great Britain, obviously, did not accept Jefferson's premises, so it did not accept his conclusions, logical though they were. Other countries of the time, just as obviously, took a different view of the matter. So, in developing an argument deductively, you need to keep in mind not only the logic of your case, but also the appeal its premises are likely to have for those whom you are most interested in convincing.

As you can see just from the cases of Jefferson, King, and Glazer, presenting evidence and using it in a logical way can take a variety of common forms, and all of these forms are likely to be present in subtle and complicated ways in virtually every piece of argumentative writing. For arguing calls upon writers to be especially resourceful in developing and presenting their positions. Actually, logic is a necessary—and powerful—tool in every field and profession, because it serves to fill in gaps where evidence does not exist or, as in a court case, to move beyond the accumulated evidence to conclusions that follow from it. But like any powerful tool it must be used with care. One weak link in a logical chain of reasoning can lead, after all, to a string of falsehood.

Explanatory techniques, such as we discussed in our introduction to the preceding section, also can play a role in argument, as you may already have inferred from the passages we have just been discussing. Glazer's argument about improving education, for example, is based on a comparison and contrast of concepts of education. And Bettelheim's attack on the sanctification of the Franks' unrealistic approach to a terrible situation relies on causal analysis to make its case. Any piece of argument, in other words, is likely to draw upon a wide range of techniques, for argument is always attempting to achieve the complex purpose not only of getting at the truth about something, and making that truth intelligible to readers, but also of persuading them to accept it as such.

No matter what particular combination of techniques a writer favors, you will probably find that most authors, when carrying out an argument, save a very telling point or bit of evidence or well-turned phrase for last. Like effective storytellers or successful courtroom lawyers, they know that a memorable detail makes for a powerful climax. In the pieces that follow in this section, you will see how different writers use the various resources of language to produce some very striking and compelling pieces of argument.

573

Arts and Humanities

HIROSHIMA
John Berger

After beginning his career as a painter and drawing instructor, John Berger (b. 1926) has come to be one of Britain's most influential art critics. He has achieved recognition as a screenwriter, novelist, and documentary writer. He now lives in a small French farming community, where he spent the latter half of the 1980s working on a trilogy of books tracing the peasant's journey from village to city. As a Marxist, he is concerned with the ideological and technological conditioning of our ways of seeing both art and the world. In Ways of Seeing *(1972), he explores the interrelation between words and images, between verbal and visual meaning. "Hiroshima" first appeared in 1981 in the journal* New Society, *and later in a collection of essays,* The Sense of Sight *(1985). Berger examines how the facts of nuclear holocaust have been hidden through "a systematic, slow and thorough process of suppression and elimination . . . within the reality of politics." Images, rather than words, Berger asserts, can help us to see through the "mask of innocence" that evil wears.*

The whole incredible problem begins with the need to reinsert those events   1
of 6 August 1945 back into living consciousness.

I was shown a book last year at the Frankfurt Book Fair. The editor asked   2
me some question about what I thought of its format. I glanced at it quickly
and gave some reply. Three months ago I was sent a finished copy of the book.
It lay on my desk unopened. Occasionally its title and cover picture caught my
eye, but I did not respond. I didn't consider the book urgent, for I believed that
I already knew about what I would find within it.

Did I not clearly remember the day—I was in the army in Belfast—when   3 we first heard the news of the bomb dropped on Hiroshima? At how many meetings during the first nuclear disarmament movement had I and others not recalled the meaning of that bomb?

And then, one morning last week, I received a letter from America, accom-   4 panying an article written by a friend. This friend is a doctor of philosophy and a Marxist. Furthermore, she is a very generous and warm-hearted woman. The article was about the possibilities of a third world war. Vis-à-vis the Soviet Union she took, I was surprised to read, a position very close to Reagan's. She con- cluded by evoking the likely scale of destruction which would be caused by nuclear weapons, and then welcomed the positive possibilities that this would offer the socialist revolution in the United States.

It was on that morning that I opened and read the book on my desk. It is   5 called *Unforgettable Fire.*[1]

The book consists of drawings and paintings made by people who were in   6 Hiroshima on the day that the bomb was dropped, thirty-six years ago today. Often the pictures are accompanied by a verbal record of what the image represents. None of them is by a professional artist. In 1974, an old man went to the television centre in Hiroshima to show to whomever was interested a picture he had painted, entitled "At about 4 pm, 6th August 1945, near Yurozuyo bridge."

This prompted an idea of launching a television appeal to other survivors of   7 that day to paint or draw their memories of it. Nearly a thousand pictures were sent in, and these were made into an exhibition. The appeal was worded: "Let us leave for posterity pictures about the atomic bomb, drawn by citizens."

Clearly, my interest in these pictures cannot be an art-critical one. One does   8 not musically analyse screams. But after repeatedly looking at them, what began as an impression became a certainty. These were images of hell.

I am not using the word as hyperbole. Between these paintings by women   9 and men who have never painted anything else since leaving school, and who have surely, for the most part, never travelled outside Japan, between these traced memories which had to be exorcised, and the numerous representations of hell in European medieval art, there is a very close affinity.

This affinity is both stylistic and fundamental. And fundamentally it is to do   10 with the situations depicted. The affinity lies in the degree of the multiplication of pain, in the lack of appeal or aid, in the pitilessness, in the equality of wretchedness, and in the disappearance of time.

> I am 78 years old. I was living at Midorimachi on the day of the A-bomb blast. Around 9 am that morning, when I looked out of my window, I saw several women coming along the street one after another towards the Hiroshima prefectural hospital. I realized for the first time, as it is sometimes said, that when people are very much frightened hair really does stand on end. The women's hair was, in fact, standing

HOW SURVIVORS SAW IT. A painting by Kazuhiro Ishizu, aged 68

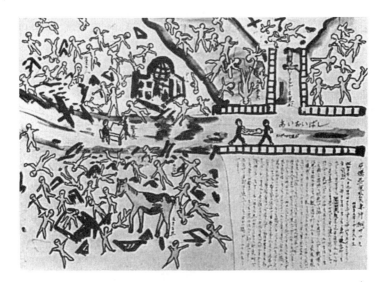

AT THE AIOI BRIDGE, by Sawami Katagiri, aged 76

straight up and the skin of their arms was peeled off. I suppose they were around 30 years old.

Time and again, the sober eyewitness accounts recall the surprise and horror   11
of Dante's verses about the Inferno. The temperature at the centre of the Hiroshima fireball was 300,000 degrees centigrade. The survivors are called in Japanese *hibakuska*—"those who have seen hell."

> Suddenly, one man who was stark naked came up to me and said in a quavering voice, 'Please help me!' He was burned and swollen all over from the effects of the A-bomb. Since I did not recognize him as my neighbour, I asked who he was. He answered that he was Mr. Sasaki, the son of Mr Ennosuke Sasaki, who had a lumber shop in Funairi town. That morning he had been doing volunteer labour service, evacuating the houses near the prefectural office in Kato town. He had been burned black all over and had started back to his home in Funairi. He looked miserable—burned and sore, and naked with only pieces of his gaiters trailing behind as he walked. Only the part of his hair covered by his soldier's hat was left, as if he was wearing a bowl. When I touched him, his burned skin slipped off. I did not know what to do, so I asked a passing driver to take him to Eba hospital.

Does not this evocation of hell make it easier to forget that these scenes belonged to life? Is there not something conveniently unreal about hell? The whole history of the twentieth century proves otherwise.

Very systematically in Europe the conditions of hells have been constructed.   12
It is not even necessary to list the sites. It is not even necessary to repeat the calculations of the organizers. We know this, and we choose to forget it.

We find it ridiculous or shocking that most of the pages concerning, for   13
example, Trotsky were torn out of official Soviet history. What has been torn out of our history are the pages concerning the experience of the two atom bombs dropped on Japan.

Of course, the facts are there in the textbooks. It may even be that school   14
children learn the dates. But what these facts mean—and originally their meaning was so clear, so monstrously vivid, that every commentator in the world was shocked, and every politician was obliged to say (whilst planning differently), "Never again"—what these facts mean has now been torn out. It has been a systematic, slow and thorough process of suppression and elimination. This process has been hidden within the reality of politics.

Do not misunderstand me. I am not here using the word "reality" ironically,   15
I am not politically naïve. I have the greatest respect for political reality, and I believe that the innocence of political idealists is often very dangerous. What we are considering is how in this case in the West—not in Japan for obvious reasons and not in the Soviet Union for different reasons—political and military realities have eliminated another reality.

The eliminated reality is both physical— 16

> Yokogawa bridge above Tenma river, 6th August 1945, 8:30 am.
> People crying and moaning were running towards the city. I did not
> know why. Steam engines were burning at Yokogawa station.
> Skin of cow tied to wire.
> Skin of girl's hip was hanging down.
> "My baby is dead, isn't she?"

and moral.

The political and military arguments have concerned such issues as deter- 17
rence, defence systems, relative strike parity, tactical nuclear weapons and—
pathetically—so-called civil defence. Any movement for nuclear disarmament
today has to contend with those considerations and dispute their false interpretation. To lose sight of them is to become as apocalyptic as the Bomb and all
utopias. (The construction of hells on earth was accompanied in Europe by
plans for heavens on earth.)

What has to be redeemed, reinserted, disclosed and never be allowed to be 18
forgotten, is the other reality. Most of the mass means of communication are
close to what has been suppressed.

These paintings were shown on Japanese television. Is it conceivable that 19
the BBC would show these pictures on Channel One at a peak hour? Without
any reference to "political" and "military" realities, under the straight title, *This
is How It Was, 6th August 1945*? I challenge them to do so.

What happened on that day was, of course, neither the beginning nor the 20
end of the act. It began months, years before, with the planning of the action,
and the eventual final decision to drop two bombs on Japan. However much
the world was shocked and surprised by the bomb dropped on Hiroshima, it
has to be emphasized that it was not a miscalculation, an error, or the result
(as can happen in war) of a situation deteriorating so rapidly that it gets out of
hand. What happened was consciously and precisely planned. Small scenes
like this were part of the plan:

> I was walking along the Hihiyama bridge about 3 pm on 7th August.
> A woman, who looked like an expectant mother, was dead. At her side,
> a girl of about three years of age brought some water in an empty can
> she had found. She was trying to let her mother drink from it.
> As soon as I saw this miserable scene with the pitiful child, I embraced
> the girl close to me and cried with her, telling her that her mother was
> dead.

There was a preparation. And there was an aftermath. The latter included 21
long, lingering deaths, radiation sickness, many fatal illnesses which developed
later as a result of exposure to the bomb, and tragic genetical effects on generations yet to be born.

I refrain from giving the statistics: how many hundreds of thousands of dead,   22
how many injured, how many deformed children. Just as I refrain from pointing
out how comparatively "small" were the atomic bombs dropped on Japan. Such
statistics tend to distract. We consider numbers instead of pain. We calculate
instead of judging. We relativize instead of refusing.

It is possible today to arouse popular indignation or anger by speaking of the   23
threat and immorality of terrorism. Indeed, this appears to be the central plank
of the rhetoric of the new American foreign policy ("Moscow is the world-base
of all terrorism") and of British policy towards Ireland. What is able to shock
people about terrorist acts is that often their targets are unselected and innocent—a crowd in a railway station, people waiting for a bus to go home after
work. The victims are chosen indiscriminately in the hope of producing a shock
effect on political decision-making by their government.

The two bombs dropped on Japan were terrorist actions. The calculation was   24
terrorist. The indiscriminacy was terrorist. The small groups of terrorists operating today are, by comparison, humane killers.

Another comparison needs to be made. Today terrorist groups mostly rep-   25
resent small nations or groupings, who are disputing large powers in a position
of strength. Whereas Hiroshima was perpetrated by the most powerful alliance
in the world against an enemy who was already prepared to negotiate, and was
admitting defeat.

To apply the epithet "terrorist" to the acts of bombing Hiroshima and Na-   26
gasaki is logically justifiable, and I do so because it may help to re-insert that
act into living consciousness today. Yet the word changes nothing in itself.

The first-hand evidence of the victims, the reading of the pages which have   27
been torn out, provokes a sense of outrage. This outrage has two natural faces.
One is a sense of horror and pity at what happened; the other face is self-
defensive and declares: *this should not happen again (here)*. For some the *here*
is in brackets, for others it is not.

The face of horror, the reaction which has now been mostly suppressed,   28
forces us to comprehend the reality of what happened. The second reaction,
unfortunately, distances us from that reality. Although it begins as a straight
declaration, it quickly leads into the labyrinth of defence policies, military
arguments and global strategies. Finally it leads to the sordid commercial
absurdity of private fall-out shelters.

This split of the sense of outrage into, on one hand, horror, and, on the   29
other hand, expediency occurs because the concept of evil has been abandoned.
Every culture, except our own in recent times, has had such a concept.

That its religious or philosophical bases vary is unimportant. The concept   30
of evil implies a force or forces which have to be continually struggled against
so that they do not triumph over life and destroy it. One of the very first written
texts from Mesopotamia, 1,500 years before Homer, speaks of this struggle,
which was the first condition of human life. In public thinking nowadays, the

concept of evil has been reduced to a little adjective to support an opinion or hypothesis (abortions, terrorism, ayatollahs).

Nobody can confront the reality of 6th August 1945 without being forced to acknowledge that what happened was evil. It is not a question of opinion or interpretation, but of events.   31

The memory of these events should be continually before our eyes. This is why the thousand citizens of Hiroshima started to draw on their little scraps of paper. We need to show their drawings everywhere. These terrible images can now release an energy for opposing evil and for the life-long struggle of that opposition.   32

And from this a very old lesson may be drawn. My friend in the United States is, in a sense, innocent. She looks beyond a nuclear holocaust without considering its reality. This reality includes not only its victims but also its planners and those who support them. Evil from time immemorial has often worn a mask of innocence. One of evil's principal modes of being is *looking beyond* (with indifference) that which is before the eyes.   33

August 9th: On the west embankment of a military training field was a young boy four or five years old. He was burned black, lying on his back, with his arms pointing towards heaven.

Only by looking beyond or away can one come to believe that such evil is relative, and therefore under certain conditions justifiable. In reality—the reality to which the survivors and the dead bear witness—it can never be justified.   34

NOTES

1. Edited by Japan Broadcasting Corporation, London, Wildwood House, 1981; New York, Pantheon, 1981.

QUESTIONS

1. Berger begins his essay with this powerful sentence: "The whole incredible problem begins with the need to reinsert those events of 6 August 1945 into living consciousness." What is "the whole incredible problem" as Berger describes and defines it?

2. Berger argues that what happened on August 6, 1945, was "consciously and precisely planned." What evidence does he present to support this claim? How does this argument advance his larger purpose?

3. Berger tells his readers that he refrains from giving statistics because "statistics tend to distract." What do statistics distance us from understanding about Hiroshima?

4. The content in Berger's essay ranges from thoughts about Hiroshima, to images of hell, to political realities, to terrorist actions, to concepts of evil. How does he connect these various subjects? What is the chain of reasoning?

5. Berger offers various images from the book *Unforgettable Fire*, such as "August 9th: On the west embankment of a military training field was a young boy four or five years old. He was burned black, lying on his back, with his arms pointing towards heaven" (paragraph 33). Look at the various places in the essay where Berger presents such images from *Unforgettable Fire*. What effect does this evidence have on you? How does this evidence strengthen Berger's argument?

6. Spend some time looking at and thinking about the paintings by the survivors, Kazuhiro Ishizu and Sawami Katagiri, reprinted on page 549. What do you *see* in these paintings? What do these images represent to you?

MAKING CONNECTIONS

1. Berger insists on closing the distance between ourselves and the essential horror of Hiroshima. Look at some other essays that struggle with issues of distance. Jonathan Swift's "A Modest Proposal," Edmund White's "Sexual Culture," and Alice Walker's "Am I Blue?" would all be examples; but you might propose another. To what an extent is "distance" an issue in arguing? Compare how two or three arguers handle problems of distance in their essays.

2. One of Berger's strategies in this essay is to challenge and invert popular definitions, as of *terrorism* and *terrorists*, for example (paragraphs 23–26). Similar inversions take place or are hinted at in Horace Miner's "Body Ritual among the Nacirema," Jane van Lawick-Goodall's "First Observations," and Alice Walker's "Am I Blue?" In those examples, the inversion always involves humans and animals. Write an argument in which you invert the definition of a key term, of *safe* and *unsafe*, for example, or *capitalist* and *communist*, or *fair* and *foul*, or *villain* and *victim*. Experiment with the leverage for arguing you find in such a radical redefinition.

AM I BLUE?

Alice Walker

As the headnote on page 54 explains, Alice Walker is an essayist, poet, novelist, and short-story writer. The following essay comes from her collection Living by the Word: Selected Writings, 1973–1987 *(1988). About this collection, Walker writes: "In my travels I found many people sitting and thinking thoughts similar to my own. In this study I was taught by these other people, by the art and history of past cultures, by the elements, and by the trees, the flowers, and, most especially, the animals." In the essay reprinted here, Walker questions the distinctions commonly made between human and animal.*

For about three years my companion and I rented a small house in the country that stood on the edge of a large meadow that appeared to run from the end of our deck straight into the mountains. The mountains, however, were quite far away, and between us and them there was, in fact, a town. It was one of the many pleasant aspects of the house that you never really were aware of this.

It was a house of many windows, low, wide, nearly floor to ceiling in the living room, which faced the meadow, and it was from one of these that I first saw our closest neighbor, a large white horse, cropping grass, flipping its mane, and ambling about—not over the entire meadow, which stretched well out of sight of the house, but over the five or so fenced-in acres that were next to the twenty-odd that we had rented. I soon learned that the horse, whose name was Blue, belonged to a man who lived in another town, but was boarded by our neighbors next door. Occasionally, one of the children, usually a stocky teenager, but sometimes a much younger girl or boy, could be seen riding Blue. They would appear in the meadow, climb up on his back, ride furiously for ten or fifteen minutes, then get off, slap Blue on the flanks, and not be seen again for a month or more.

There were many apple trees in our yard, and one by the fence that Blue could almost reach. We were soon in the habit of feeding him apples, which he relished, especially because by the middle of summer the meadow grasses—so green and succulent since January—had dried out from lack of rain, and Blue stumbled about munching the dried stalks half-heartedly. Sometimes he would stand very still just by the apple tree, and when one of us came out he would whinny, snort loudly, or stamp the ground. This meant, of course: I want an apple.

583

It was quite wonderful to pick a few apples, or collect those that had fallen 4
to the ground overnight, and patiently hold them, one by one, up to his large,
toothy mouth. I remained as thrilled as a child by his flexible dark lips, huge,
cubelike teeth that crunched the apples, core and all, with such finality, and
his high, broad-breasted *enormity*; beside which, I felt small indeed. When I
was a child, I used to ride horses, and was especially friendly with one named
Nan until the day I was riding and my brother deliberately spooked her and I
was thrown, head first, against the trunk of a tree. When I came to, I was in
bed and my mother was bending worriedly over me; we silently agreed that
perhaps horseback riding was not the safest sport for me. Since then I have
walked, and prefer walking to horseback riding—but I had forgotten the depth
of feeling one could see in horses' eyes.

I was therefore unprepared for the expression in Blue's. Blue was lonely. 5
Blue was horribly lonely and bored. I was not shocked that this should be the
case; five acres to tramp by yourself, endlessly, even in the most beautiful of
meadows—and his was—cannot provide many interesting events, and once the
rainy season turned to dry that was about it. No, I was shocked that I had he
forgotten that human animals and nonhuman animals can communicate quite
well; if we are brought up around animals as children we take this for granted.
By the time we are adults we no longer remember. However, the animals have
not changed. They are in fact *completed* creations (at least they seem to be, so
much more than we) who are not likely *to* change; it is their nature to express
themselves. What else are they going to express? And they do. And, generally
speaking, they are ignored.

After giving Blue the apples, I would wander back to the house, aware that 6
he was observing me. Were more apples not forthcoming then? Was that to be
his sole entertainment for the day? My partner's small son had decided he
wanted to learn how to piece a quilt; we worked in silence on our respective
squares as I thought . . .

Well, about slavery: about white children, who were raised by black people, 7
who knew their first all-accepting love from black women, and then, when they
were twelve or so, were told they must "forget" the deep levels of communication
between themselves and "mammy" that they knew. Later they would be able to
relate quite calmly, "My old mammy was sold to another good family." "My
old mammy was —————." Fill in the blank. Many more years later a
white woman would say: "I can't understand these Negroes, these blacks. What
do they want? They're so different from us."

And about the Indians, considered to be "like animals" by the "settlers" (a 8
very benign euphemism for what they actually were), who did not understand
their description as a compliment.

And about the thousands of American men who marry Japanese, Korean, 9
Filipina, and other non–English-speaking women and of how happy they report
they are, *"blissfully,"* until their brides learn to speak English, at which point

the marriages tend to fall apart. What then did the men see, when they looked into the eyes of the women they married, before they could speak English? Apparently only their own reflections.

I thought of society's impatience with the young. "Why are they playing the 10 music so loud?" Perhaps the children have listened to much of the music of oppressed people their parents danced to before they were born, with its passionate but soft cries for acceptance and love, and they have wondered why their parents failed to hear.

I do not know how long Blue had inhabited his five beautiful, boring acres 11 before we moved into our house; a year after we had arrived—and had also traveled to other valleys, other cities, other worlds—he was still there.

But then, in our second year at the house, something happened in Blue's 12 life. One morning, looking out the window at the fog that lay like a ribbon over the meadow, I saw another horse, a brown one, at the other end of Blue's field. Blue appeared to be afraid of it, and for several days made no attempt to go near. We went away for a week. When we returned, Blue had decided to make friends and the two horses ambled or galloped along together, and Blue did not come nearly as often to the fence underneath the apple tree.

When he did, bringing his new friend with him, there was a different look 13 in his eyes. A look of independence, of self-possession, of inalienable *horse*ness. His friend eventually became pregnant. For months and months there was, it seemed to me, a mutual feeling between me and the horses of justice, of peace. I fed apples to them both. The look in Blue's eyes was one of unabashed "this is *it*ness."

It did not, however, last forever. One day, after a visit to the city, I went out 14 to give Blue some apples. He stood waiting, or so I thought, though not beneath the tree. When I shook the tree and jumped back from the shower of apples, he made no move. I carried some over to him. He managed to half-crunch one. The rest he let fall to the ground. I dreaded looking into his eyes—because I had of course noticed that Brown, his partner, had gone—but I did look. If I had been born into slavery, and my partner had been sold or killed, my eyes would have looked like that. The children next door explained that Blue's partner had been "put with him" (the same expression that old people used, I had noticed, when speaking of an ancestor during slavery who had been impregnated by her owner) so that they could mate and she conceive. Since that was accomplished, she had been taken back by her owner, who lived somewhere else.

Will she be back? I asked. 15
They didn't know. 16
Blue was like a crazed person. Blue *was*, to me, a crazed person. He galloped 17 furiously, as if he were being ridden, around and around his five beautiful acres. He whinnied until he couldn't. He tore at the ground with his hooves. He butted himself against his single shade tree. He looked always and always

toward the road down which his partner had gone. And then, occasionally, when he came up for apples, or I took apples to him, he looked at me. It was a look so piercing, so full of grief, a look so *human*, I almost laughed (I felt too sad to cry) to think there are people who do not know that animals suffer. People like me who have forgotten, and daily forget, all that animals try to tell us. "Everything you do to us will happen to you; we are your teachers, as you are ours. We are one lesson" is essentially it, I think. There are those who never once have even considered animals' rights: those who have been taught that animals actually want to be used and abused by us, as small children "love" to be frightened, or women "love" to be mutilated and raped. . . . They are the great-grandchildren of those who honestly thought, because someone taught them this: "Woman can't think" and "niggers can't faint." But most disturbing of all, in Blue's large brown eyes was a new look, more painful than the look of despair: the look of disgust with human beings, with life; the look of hatred. And it was odd what the look of hatred did. It gave him, for the first time, the look of a beast. And what that meant was that he had put up a barrier within to protect himself from further violence; all the apples in the world wouldn't change that fact.

And so Blue remained, a beautiful part of our landscape, very peaceful to look at from the window, white against the grass. Once a friend came to visit and said, looking out on the soothing view: "And it *would* have to be a *white* horse; the very image of freedom." And I thought, yes, the animals are forced to become for us merely "images" of what they once so beautifully expressed. And we are used to drinking milk from containers showing "contented" cows, whose real lives we want to hear nothing about, eating eggs and drumsticks from "happy" hens, and munching hamburgers advertised by bulls of integrity who seem to command their fate. 18

As we talked of freedom and justice one day for all, we sat down to steaks. I am eating misery, I thought, as I took the first bite. And spit it out. 19

QUESTIONS

1. Why does Walker begin her argument by setting the scene ("We rented a small house in the country . . .") and by leisurely describing the meadow where she first saw Blue?

2. Walker takes great pleasure in describing Blue for her readers. In paragraph 4 she tells us: "I remained as thrilled as a child by his flexible dark lips, huge, cubelike teeth that crunched the apples, core and all, with such finality, and his high, broad-breasted *enormity*; beside which, I felt small indeed." What does Blue represent to Walker? What does she learn from observing him?

3. In paragraph 7, Walker switches from thinking about Blue to thinking about slavery. This kind of transition is the work of the essayist—to link together through

language horses, slavery, Indians, and non–English-speaking women. How does Walker make these various connections? What is her argument?

4. Walker writes in paragraph 18, "And I thought, yes, the animals are forced to become for us merely 'images' of what they once so beautifully expressed. And we are used to drinking milk from containers showing 'contented' cows, whose real lives we want to hear nothing about, eating eggs and drumsticks from 'happy' hens, and munching hamburgers advertised by bulls of integrity who seem to command their fate." How would you respond to this comment? Write a response to Walker's essay in which you argue your position.

5. Some animal rights activists argue that animal rights will emerge as the civil rights movement of the twenty-first century. A central issue in this movement is the question, What distinguishes humans from other animals? Write an essay in which you argue your position on this issue.

MAKING CONNECTIONS

1. Walker's strategies for arguing differ from those of a more formal argument such as Thomas Jefferson's The Declaration of Independence or Diana Baumrind, in her "Review of Stanley Milgram's Experiments on Obedience." Describe the strategies Walker uses and how they differ from Jefferson's or Gould's or those of another writer of your choice from this section.

2. Walker's other essay in this volume, "Beauty: When the Other Dancer Is the Self," is categorized as reflective rather than argumentative. Presumably, her approaches to these two essays differ. Compare her two essays. In what passages in "Am I Blue?" do you find Walker most intensely absorbed in arguing? How do those passages stand out? How are they prepared for? Is there an argument embedded in the earlier essay as well? If so, how can you describe it?

IF BLACK ENGLISH
ISN'T A LANGUAGE,
THEN TELL ME,
WHAT IS?

James Baldwin

James Baldwin was born in Harlem in 1924 and followed his father's vocation, becoming a preacher at the age of fourteen. At seventeen, he left the ministry and devoted himself to writing until his death in 1987. Baldwin's most frequent subject was the relationship between blacks and whites, about which he wrote, "The color of my skin made me automatically an expert." Baldwin himself might also have added that his life's work lay in defining and legitimizing the black voice; like Orwell, Baldwin argued that language is "a political instrument, means, and proof of power." He wrote five novels, a book of stories, one play, and several collections of essays. The following essay on language and legitimacy first appeared in 1979 in the New York Times *and later was included in* The Price of the Ticket: Collected Nonfiction 1948–1985 *(1985).*

The argument concerning the use, or the status, or the reality, of black 1 English is rooted in American history and has absolutely nothing to do with the question the argument supposes itself to be posing. The argument has nothing to do with language itself but with the role of language. Language, incontestably, reveals the speaker. Language, also, far more dubiously, is meant to define the other—and, in this case, the other is refusing to be defined by a language that has never been able to recognize him.

People evolve a language in order to describe and thus control their circum- 2 stances or in order not to be submerged by a situation that they cannot articulate. (And if they cannot articulate it, they are submerged.) A Frenchman living in Paris speaks a subtly and crucially different language from that of the man living in Marseilles; neither sounds very much like a man living in Quebec; and they would all have great difficulty in apprehending what the man from Guadeloupe, or Martinique, is saying, to say nothing of the man from Senegal—although the "common" language of all these areas is French. But each has paid, and is paying, a different price for this "common" language, in which, as it turns out, they are not saying, and cannot be saying, the same things: They each have very different realities to articulate, or control.

What joins all languages, and all men, is the necessity to confront life, in   3
order, not inconceivably, to outwit death: The price for this is the acceptance,
and achievement, of one's temporal identity. So that, for example, though it is
not taught in the schools (and this has the potential of becoming a political
issue) the south of France still clings to its ancient and musical Provençal,
which resists being described as a "dialect." And much of the tension in the
Basque countries, and in Wales, is due to the Basque and Welsh determination
not to allow their languages to be destroyed. This determination also feeds the
flames in Ireland for among the many indignities the Irish have been forced to
undergo at English hands is the English contempt for their language.

It goes without saying, then, that language is also a political instrument,   4
means, and proof of power. It is the most vivid and crucial key to identity: It
reveals the private identity, and connects one with, or divorces one from, the
larger, public, or communal identity. There have been, and are, times and
places, when to speak a certain language could be dangerous, even fatal. Or,
one may speak the same language, but in such a way that one's antecedents are
revealed, or (one hopes) hidden. This is true in France, and is absolutely true
in England: The range (and reign) of accents on that damp little island make
England coherent for the English and totally incomprehensible for everyone
else. To open your mouth in England is (if I may use black English) to "put
your business in the street." You have confessed your parents, your youth, your
school, your salary, your self-esteem, and, alas, your future.

Now, I do not know what white Americans would sound like if there had   5
never been any black people in the United States, but they would not sound
the way they sound. *Jazz*, for example, is a very specific sexual term, as in *jazz
me, baby*, but white people purified it into the Jazz Age. *Sock it to me*, which
means, roughly, the same thing, has been adopted by Nathaniel Hawthorne's
descendants with no qualms or hesitations at all, along with *let it all hang out*
and *right on! Beat to his socks*, which was once the black's most total and
despairing image of poverty, was transformed into a thing called the Beat
Generation, which phenomenon was, largely, composed of *uptight*, middle-
class white people, imitating poverty, trying to *get down*, to get *with it*, doing
their *thing*, doing their despairing best to be *funky*, which we, the blacks, never
dreamed of doing—we were funky, baby, like *funk* was going out of style.

Now, no one can eat his cake, and have it, too, and it is late in the day to   6
attempt to penalize black people for having created a language that permits the
nation its only glimpse of reality, a language without which the nation would
be even more *whipped* than it is.

I say that the present skirmish is rooted in American history, and it is. Black   7
English is the creation of the black diaspora. Blacks came to the United States
chained to each other, but from different tribes. Neither could speak the other's
language. If two black people, at that bitter hour of the world's history, had
been able to speak to each other, the institution of chattel slavery could never

have lasted as long as it did. Subsequently, the slave was given, under the eye, and the gun, of his master, Congo Square, and the Bible—or, in other words, and under those conditions, the slave began the formation of the black church, and it is within this unprecedented tabernacle that black English began to be formed. This was not, merely, as in the European example, the adoption of a foreign tongue, but an alchemy that transformed ancient elements into a new language: A *language comes into existence by means of brutal necessity, and the rules of the language are dictated by what the language must convey.*

There was a moment, in time, and in this place, when my brother, or my 8
mother, or my father, or my sister, had to convey to me, for example, the danger in which I was standing from the white man standing just behind me, and to convey this with a speed and in a language, that the white man could not possibly understand, and that, indeed, he cannot understand, until today. He cannot afford to understand it. This understanding would reveal to him too much about himself and smash that mirror before which he has been frozen for so long.

Now, if this passion, this skill, this (to quote Toni Morrison) "sheer intelli- 9
gence," this incredible music, the mighty achievement of having brought a people utterly unknown to, or despised by "history"—to have brought this people to their present, troubled, troubling, and unassailable and unanswerable place— if this absolutely unprecedented journey does not indicate that black English is a language, I am curious to know what definition of languages is to be trusted.

A people at the center of the western world, and in the midst of so hostile a 10
population, has not endured and transcended by means of what is patronizingly called a "dialect." We, the blacks, are in trouble, certainly, but we are not inarticulate because we are not compelled to defend a morality that we know to be a lie.

The brutal truth is that the bulk of the white people in America never had 11
any interest in educating black people, except as this could serve white purposes. It is not the black child's language that is despised. It is his experience. A child cannot be taught by anyone who despises him, and a child cannot afford to be fooled. A child cannot be taught by anyone whose demand, essentially, is that the child repudiate his experience, and all that gives him sustenance, and enter a limbo in which he will no longer be black, and in which he knows that he can never become white. Black people have lost too many black children that way.

And, after all, finally, in a country with standards so untrustworthy, a country 12
that makes heroes of so many criminal mediocrities, a country unable to face why so many of the nonwhite are in prison, or on the needle, or standing, futureless, in the streets—it may very well be that both the child, and his elder,

have concluded that they have nothing whatever to learn from the people of a country that has managed to learn so little.

QUESTIONS

1. Baldwin begins his essay by challenging the standard argument concerning black English: "The argument has nothing to do with language itself but with the role of language." What distinctions does Baldwin create between "language itself" and "the role of language"? Why is this distinction central to his argument?

2. Baldwin's position on black English is at odds with those who would like to deny black English status as a language. Summarize Baldwin's position. Summarize the position of Baldwin's opponents.

3. In paragraph 4 Baldwin writes, "It goes without saying, then, that language is also a political instrument, means, and proof of power." How, according to Baldwin, does language connect or divide one from "public or communal identity"? What evidence does he provide to support this claim that "language is a political instrument"?

4. Baldwin asks his readers "What is language?" and thus leads them to define for themselves "what definition of languages is to be trusted" (paragraph 9). Do you find Baldwin's definition and position persuasive?

5. Baldwin's conclusion is a memorable one. Reread it. How does he prepare you for this conclusion? What are you left to contemplate?

6. How has Baldwin's essay made you think about your own use of language and the role language plays in your identity? Baldwin makes an important distinction between *dialect* and *language*. Write an essay in which you take a position on the role of language in shaping your identity.

7. Select a dialect with which you are familiar. Analyze the features of this dialect. Write an essay in which you develop a position showing how this dialect reflects the richness of its culture.

MAKING CONNECTIONS

1. Read Alice Walker's essay, "Am I Blue?," paying particular attention to paragraph 17 on Blue's language and to Walker's sense of Blue's power of communication. To what extent does her argument support Baldwin's position on black English?

2. Consider Baldwin's argument about language as a political instrument that forges and reveals identity in relation to the writings of several women writers in "Explaining"— Joan Didion, Susan Fraker, and Carol Gilligan, in particular. Can you find and describe in those writings evidence of a women's English parallel in some ways to black English? Or is there a men's English you would prefer to describe, drawing on another set of writers?

SEXUAL CULTURE
Edmund White

Edmund White (b. 1940) is an essayist and novelist whose autobiographical novel, A Boy's Own Story *(1982), was acclaimed for its treatment of the gay experience in America. In writing a nonfiction work,* States of Desire: Travels in Gay America *(1983), he wished "to see the varieties of gay experience and also to suggest the enormous range of gay life to straight people." White has been a contributing editor to* Vogue *and has taught writing at several American universities. In this essay, which originally appeared in* Vanity Fair, *White examines some cultural assumptions about gayness and straightness.*

"Do gay men have friends—I mean," she said, "are they friends with each other?" Since the woman asking was a New Yorker, the owner of one of the city's simplest and priciest restaurants, someone who's known gays all her life, I found the question honest, shocking, and revealing of a narrow but bottomless abyss between us.

Of course New York is a city of total, even absolute strangers rubbing shoulders: the Hasidim in their yellow school bus being conveyed back to Brooklyn from the jewelry district, beards and black hats glimpsed through mud-splattered windows in a sun-dimmed daguerreotype; the junkie pushing the baby carriage and telling his wife, the prostitute, as he points to his tattooed biceps, "I haven't partied in this vein for years"; Moonies doing calisthenics at midnight in their Eighth Avenue center high above empty Thirty-fourth Street. . . . But this alienation wasn't religious or ethnic. The woman and I spoke the same language, knew the same people; we both considered Marcella Hazan fun but no substitute for Simone Beck.[1] How odd that she, as lower-upper-middle-class as I, shouldn't know whether gay men befriended one another.

It was then that I saw how mysterious gay culture is—not homosexuality, which is merely an erotic tropism, but modern American gay culture, which is a special way of laughing, spending money, ordering priorities, encoding everything from song lyrics to mirror-shiny military shoes. None of the usual modes for a subculture will do, for gay men are brought up by heterosexuals to be straight, they seek other men through what feels very much like a compulsion though they enter the ghetto by choice, yet once they make that choice it

[1] Marcella Hazan is known for her cookbooks on classic Italian cooking; Simone Beck for hers on classic French cooking. [Eds.]

reshapes their lives, even their bodies, certainly their wardrobes. Many gay men live among straights as Marranos, those Spanish Jews who pretended during the Inquisition to convert to Christianity but continued to observe the old rites in cellars, when alone, in the greatest secrecy. Gays aren't *like* blacks or Jews since they often *are* black or Jewish, and their affectional preference isn't a color or a religion though it has spawned a culture not unlike an ethnic minority's. Few Jews have Christian siblings, but most gays have straight brothers and sisters or at least straight parents. Many American Jews have been raised to feel they belong to the Chosen People, at once superior and inferior to gentiles, but every gay discovers his sexual nature with a combination of pain and relief, regret at being excluded from the tribe but elation at discovering the solution to the puzzle.

Gays aren't a nationality. They aren't Chicanos or Italo-Americans or Irish-   4
Americans, but they do constitute one of the most potent political forces in big cities such as New York, Philadelphia, Washington (where gays and blacks elected Marion Barry mayor), Houston, Los Angeles, and San Francisco (where gays are so numerous they've splintered into countless factions, including the lesbian S/M group Samois and the Sisters of Perpetual Indulgence, a group of drag nuns, one of whose members ran in a cowl and wimple as a candidate in the last citywide election). Not ethnic but a minority, not a polis but political, not a nationality but possessed of a costume, customs, and a patois, not a class but an economic force (not only as a market for records, films, vacations, and clothes but also as an army of worker ants who, for better or worse, have gentrified the center cities, thereby creating a better tomorrow for single young white heterosexual professionals).

Imagine a religion one enters against one's parents' will—and against one's   5
own. Imagine a race one joins at sixteen or sixty without changing one's hue or hair texture (unless at the tanning or beauty salon). Imagine a sterile nation without descendants but with a long, misty regress of ancestors, without an articulated self-definition but with a venerable history. Imagine an exclusive club that includes a P.R. (Puerto Rican) boy of sixteen wearing ankle-high black-and-white Converse basketball shoes and a petrol green shirt sawed off to reveal a Praxitelean stomach—and also includes a P.R. (Public Relations) WASP executive of forty in his Prince of Wales plaids and Cole-Haan tasseled loafers.

If one is gay, one is always in a crucial relationship to gayness as such, a   6
defining category that is so full it is nearly empty (Renaud Camus writes: "Homosexuality is always elsewhere because it is everywhere."). No straight man stands in rapt contemplation of his straightness unless he's an ass. To be sure, heterosexuals may wonder over the significance of their homosexual fantasies, though even that morbid exercise is less popular now than formerly; as Barbara Ehrenreich acutely observes in her new study of the heterosexual male revolt, *The Hearts of Men*, the emergence of gay liberation ended the period in which everyone suspected everyone else of being "latently" homosex-

593

ual. Now there are open homosexuals, and heterosexual men are exempt from the automatic suspicion of deviance.

No homosexual can take his homosexuality for granted. He must sound it, palpate it, auscultate it as though it were the dead limb of a tree or the living but tricky limb of a body; for that reason all homosexuals are "gay philosophers" in that they must invent themselves. At a certain point one undergoes a violent conversion into a new state, the unknown, which one then sets about knowing as one will. Surely everyone experiences his or her life as an artifact, as molten glass being twirled and pinched into a shape to cool, or as a novel at once capacious and suspenseful, but no one is more a *Homo faber* (in the sense of both "fabricator" and "fabulist") than a homo. It would be vain, of course, to suggest that this creativity is praiseworthy, an ambition rather than a response.

Sometimes I try to imagine how straights—not fundamentalist know-nothings, not rural innocents, not Freudian bigots, but educated urban heterosexuals—look at gay men (do they even see lesbians?). When they see gay men, what do they see? A mustache, a pumped-up body in black jeans and a tank top, an eye-catching tattoo (braided rope around the biceps)? And what do they think ("they," in this case, *hypocrite lecteur*, being *you*)? Do you see something at once ludicrous and mildly enviable in the still youthful but overexercised body of this forty-year-old clone with the aggressive stare and soft voice? If you're a woman, do you find so much preening over appearance in a grown man . . . well, if not offensive, at least unappetizing; energy better spent on a career, on a family—on you? If you're a man, does it incense you that this jerk is out of harness, too loose, too free, has so lightly made a mockery of manhood? Once, on a radio call-in show a cop called in to tell me he had to admire the old-style queens back when it was rough being queer but that now, jeez, these guys swapping spit wit' a goil one week, wit' a guy the next, they're too lazy, they just don't know the fine art of being a man, it's all just too easy.

Your sentiments, perhaps?

Do you see gays as menacing satyrs, sex fiends around whom it's dangerous to drop your soap, *and* as feeble sissies, frail wood nymphs locked within massive trunks and limbs? Or, more positively if just as narrowly, are you a sybaritic het who greets the sight of gays with cries of glee, convinced you've stumbled on liberty hall, where sexual license of every sort—including your sort—is bound to reign? In fact, such sybarites often do regard gay men as comrades in arms, fellow libertines, and fellow victims in a country phobic to pleasure.

Or do gays just irk you? Do you regard them as a tinselly distraction in your peripheral vision? As errant, obstinate atoms that can't be drawn into any of the usual social molecules, men who if they insist on their gayness won't really do at any of the solemnities, from dinner parties to debutante balls, all of which depend on strict gender dimorphism for a rational seating plan? Since any proper gathering requires the threat of adultery for excitement and the prospect of marriage as a justification, of what earthly use are gays? Even the few fearless straight guys who've invaded my gay gym drift toward one another, not out of soap-dropping panic but because otherwise their dirty jokes fall on deaf or prettily blushing ears and their taunting, butt-slapping mix of rivalry and camaraderie provokes a weird hostility or a still weirder thrill.

And how do gays look at straights? In Andrew Holleran's superb new novel, 12 *Nights in Aruba*, the narrator wonders "what it would be like to be the head of a family, as if with that all my problems would drop away, when in fact they would have merely been replaced by another set. I would not have worried about the size of my penis, the restrictions of age, the difficulty of finding love; I would have worried about mortgages, tuition, my youngest daughter's asthma, my competition at Shearson Loeb Rhoades." What makes this speculation so characteristically gay is that it is so focused on the family man, for if the nineteenth-century tart required, even invented the convent-bred virgin to contemplate, in the same way the homosexual man today must insult and revere, mock and envy this purely imaginary bourgeois paterfamilias, a creature extinct except in gay fantasies. Meanwhile, of course, the family man devotes his time to scream therapy and tai chi, ticking off Personals in the *Village Voice* and wriggling out of visits from his kids, two punked-out teens who live in a feminist compound with his divorced wife, now a lesbian potter of great sensitivity and verve if low energy.

So much for how the two sexes (straight and gay) regard each other. If the 13 camera were to pull back and frame both worlds in the lens, how would the two systems compare?

The most obvious difference is that whereas heterosexuality does include two 14 sexes, since homosexuality does not it must improvise a new polarity moment by moment. Such a polarity seems necessary to sexual desire, at least as it is constructed in our culture. No wonder that some gay men search out the most extreme opposites (someone of a distant race, a remote language, another class or age); no wonder that even that convinced heterosexual Flaubert was finally able to unbend with a boy prostitute in Egypt, an exotic who provided him with all the difference desire might demand. Other gay men seek out their twins—so that the beloved, I suppose, can stand in for oneself as one bows down to this false god and plays in turn his father, teacher, son, godfather, or god. Still others institutionalize the polarity in that next-best thing to heterosexuality: sadomasochism, the only vice that anthologizes all family and romantic relationships.

Because every gay man loves men, he comes to learn at first hand how to 15 soothe the savage breast of the male ego. No matter how passive or girlish or shy the new beau might be in the boudoir, he will become the autocrat of the dinner table. Women's magazines are always planning articles on gay men and straight women; I'd say what they have most in common, aside from a few shared sexual techniques, is a body of folk wisdom about that hardhead, that bully, that maddeningly self-involved creature, the human male. As studies have surprisingly shown, men talk more than women, interrupt them more often, and determine the topics of conversation and object to women's assertions with more authority and frequency. When two gay men get together, especially after the first romantic urge to oblige the other wanes, a struggle for conversational dominance ensues, a conflict only symptomatic of larger arguments over every issue from where to live to how and whom to entertain.

To be sure, in this way the gay couple resembles the straight duo that includes 16 an assertive, liberated woman. But while most of the young straight liberated women I know, at least, may protect their real long-range interests (career, mode of life, emotional needs) with vigilance, they're still willing to accommodate *him* in little social ways essential to harmony.

One benign side of straight life is that women conceive of men as "charac- 17 ters," as full-bodied, multifaceted beings who are first social, second familial, third amorous or amicable, and only finally physical. I'm trying politely to say that women are lousy judges of male beauty; they're easily taken in by such superficial traits as loyalty, dependability, charm, a sense of humor. Women don't, or at least didn't, judge men as so much beefcake. But men, both straight and gay, start with looks, the most obvious currency of value, worth, price. Let's say that women see men as characters in a long family novel in which the men are introduced complete with phrenology, genealogy, and one annoying and two endearing traits, whereas men see their partners (whether male or female) as cars, makes to be instantly spotted, appraised, envied, made. A woman wants to be envied for her husband's goodness, his character, whereas a man wants to be envied for his wife's beauty, rarity, status—her drivability. Straight life combines the warmth and *Gemütlichkeit* of the nineteenth-century bourgeois (the woman) with the steely corporate ethos of the twentieth-century functionary (the man). If gay male life, freed of this dialectic, has become supremely efficient (the trapdoor beside the bed) and only momentarily intimate (a whole life cycle compressed into the one-night stand), then the gain is dubious, albeit an extreme expression of one trend in our cultural economy.

But of course most morality, that is, popular morality—not real morals, 18 which are unaffected by consensus, but mores, which are a form of fashion— is nothing but a species of nostalgia, a cover-up for pleasurable and profitable but not yet admissible innovations. If so many people condemn promiscuity, they do so at least partly because there is no available rhetoric that could condone, much less glamorize, impermanence in love. Nevertheless, it strikes me that homosexuals, masters of improvisation fully at home with the arbitrary and equipped with an internal compass that orients them instantly to any social novelty, are perhaps the most sensitive indicators of the future.

The birthrate declines, the divorce rate climbs, and popular culture (movies, 19 television, song lyrics, advertising, fashions, journalism) is so completely and irrevocably secularized that the so-called religious revival is of no more lasting importance than the fad for Kabuki in a transistorized Japan—a temporary throwback, a slight brake on the wheel. In such a world the rate of change is so rapid that children, once they are in school, can learn little from their parents but must assimilate new forms of behavior from their peer and new information from specialized instructors. As a result, parental authority declines, and the demarcations between the generations become ever more formidable. Nor do the parents regret their loss of control, since they're devoting all their energy to cultivating the inner self in the wholesale transition of our society from an ethic of self-sacrifice to one of self-indulgence, the so-called aristocraticization of middle-class life that has dominated the peaceful parts of this century in the industrialized West.

In the contemporary world the nineteenth-century experiment of companionate marriage, never very workable, has collapsed utterly. The exact nature of the collapse isn't very clear yet because of our distracting, probably irrelevant habit of psychologizing every crisis (thus the endless speculations in the lowbrow press on the Irresponsible Male and the Defeminized Female or the paradoxical and cruelly impracticable advice to women readers to "go for it all—family, career, marriage, romance, *and* the reveries of solitude"). We treat the failure of marriage as though it were the failure of individuals to achieve it—a decline in grit or maturity or commitment or stamina rather than the unraveling of a poorly tied knot. Bourgeois marriage was meant to concentrate friendship, romance, and sex into an institution at once familial and economic. Only the most intense surveillance could keep such a bulky, ill-assorted load from bursting at the seams. Once the hedonism of the '60s relaxed that tension, people began to admit that friendship tranquilizes sexual desires (when mates become siblings, the incest taboo sets in) and that romance is by its very nature evanescent though indefinitely renewable given an endless supply of fresh partners. Neither sexual nor romantic attraction, so capricious, so passionate, so unstable, could ever serve as the basis for an enduring relationship, which can be balanced only on the plinth of esteem, that easy, undramatic, intimate kind of love one would say resembled family love if families were more loving.

It is this love that so many gay couples know about, aim for, and sometimes even express. If all goes well, two gay men will meet through sex, become lovers, weather the storms of jealousy and the diminution of lust, develop shared interests (a hobby, a business, a house, a circle), and end up with a long-term, probably sexless camaraderie that is not as disinterested as friendship or as seismic as passion or as charged with contradiction as fraternity. Younger gay couples feel that this sort of relationship, when it happens to them, is incomplete, a compromise, and they break up in order to find total fulfillment (i.e., tireless passion) elsewhere. But older gay couples stay together, cultivate their

597

mild, reasonable love, and defend it against the ever-present danger of the sexual allure exercised by a newcomer. For the weak point of such marriages is the eternally recurring fantasy, first in one partner and then the other, of "total fulfillment." Needless to say, such couples can wreak havoc on the newcomer who fails to grasp that Bob and Fred are not just roommates. They may have separate bedrooms and regular extracurricular sex partners or even beaux, but Bob monitors Fred's infatuations with an eye attuned to nuance, and at a certain point will intervene to banish a potential rival.

I think most straight people would find these arrangements more scandalous   22
than the infamous sexual high jinks of gays. Because these arrangements have no name, no mythology, no public or private acknowledgment, they're almost invisible even to the participants. Thus if you asked Bob in a survey what he wanted, he might say he wanted a "real" lover. He might also say Fred was "just a roommate, my best friend, we used to be lovers." So much for explicit analysis, but over the years Bob has cannily steered his affair with Fred between the Scylla of excessive fidelity (which is finally so dull no two imaginative gay men could endure it) and the Charybdis of excessive tolerance (which could leave both men feeling so neglected they'd seek love elsewhere for sure).

There are, of course, countless variants to this pattern. The men live together   23
or they don't. If they don't, they can maintain the civilized fiction of romance for years. They plan dates, honeymoons, take turns sleeping over at each other's house, and avoid conflicts about domestic details. They keep their extracurricular sex lives separate, they agree not to snoop—or they have three-ways. Or one of the pair has an active sex life and the other has abandoned the erotic arena.

Are gay men friends with each other? the woman asked me.   24

The question may assume that gays are only sexual, and that a man eternally   25
on the prowl can never pause for mere affection—that a gay Don Juan is lonely. Or perhaps the question reveals a confusion about a society of one gender. Since a straight woman has other women for friends and men for lovers, my questioner might have wondered how the same sex could serve in both capacities.

The first supposition—that gay men are only sexual—is an ancient prejudice,   26
and like all prejudices mostly untrue but in one sense occasionally accurate. If politically conscious homosexuals prefer the word *gay* to *homosexual*, they do so because they want to make the world regard attraction to members of the same gender as an affectional preference as well as a sexual orientation.

For instance, there are some gay men who prefer the feel of women's bodies   27
to men's, who are even more comfortable sexually with women, but whose emotions crave contact with other men. Gay men have unfinished emotional business with other men—scary, promising, troubling, absorbing business— whereas their sentiments toward women (at least women not in their family)

are much simpler, more stable, less fraught. Affection, passionate affection, is never simple; it is built out of equal parts of yearning, fear, and appetite. For that reason the friendship of one gay man fiercely drawn to another is as tense as any heterosexual passion, whereas a sexless, more disinterested gay friendship is as relaxed, as good-tempered as a friendship, say, between two straight men.

Gay men, then, do divide other gays into two camps—those who are potential 28 partners (lovers) and those who are not (friends). But where gay life is more ambiguous than the world at large (and possibly for that reason more baffling to outsiders) is that the members of the two camps, lovers and friends, are always switching places or hovering somewhere in the margin between. It is these unconfessed feelings that have always intrigued me the most as a novelist— the unspoken love between two gay men, say, who pretend they are just friends, cruising buddies, merely filling in until Mr. Right comes along (mercifully, he never does).

In one sense, the public's prejudice about a gay obsession with sex is valid. 29 The right to have sex, even to look for it, has been so stringently denied to gays for so many centuries that the drive toward sexual freedom remains a bright, throbbing banner in the fierce winds whipping over the ghetto. Laws against sex have always created the biggest problems for homosexuals; they helped to define the very category of homosexuality. For that reason, the gay community, despite its invention of a culture no more eroticized than any other, still cannot give up its origin in sexual desire and its suppression.

But what about the "excessive" promiscuity of gay men, the infamous quick- 30 ies, a phenomenon only temporarily held in check by the AIDS crisis? Don't the quickies prove that gay men are essentially bizarre, fundamentally lacking in judgment—*oversexed?* Of course, gay men behave as all men would were they free of the strictures of female tastes, needs, prohibitions, and expectations. There is nothing in gay male life that cannot be attributed either to its minority status or to its all-male population. All men want quick, uncomplicated sexual adventure (as well as sustained romantic passion); in a world of all men, that desire is granted.

The very universality of sexual opportunity within the modern gay ghetto 31 has, paradoxically, increased the importance of friendship. In a society not based on the measured denial or canalization of sexual desire, there is more energy left over for friendship. Relationships are less loaded in gay life (hence the celebrated gay irony, a levity equivalent to seeing through conventions). In so many ways gays are still prisoners of the dominant society, but in this one regard gays are freer than their jailers: because gay relationships are not disciplined by religious, legal, economic, and political ceremonies but only by the dictates of conscience and the impulses of the heart, they don't stand for anything larger. They aren't symbols but realities, not laws but entities sufficient unto themselves, not consequential but ecstatic.

QUESTIONS

1. White's essay is concerned both with answering the question put forth by the woman (paragraph 1) and with its implications. What does the question reveal about the questioner?

2. How is this essay structured? At what points does White use definition? When does he use comparison and contrast?

3. What is White's attitude toward the reader? Why does he use direct address? When is that strategy most appropriate?

4. White has a lot to say about polarity—specifically that it's essential to all relationships, both straight and gay—but with a difference in the latter group. What is this difference? Why does White think polarity is essential?

5. Traditional marriage—termed "19th-century experiment of companionate marriage" here—takes some criticism from White. What is that criticism, and do you think it is justified? Write an essay in which you agree or disagree with White. In addition to the views expressed in this essay, draw on your own experience and observations.

6. If you have the experience of being a member of a particular subculture or minority group, use White's technique of deflating specific prejudices to speak for that group.

MAKING CONNECTIONS

White's essay starts from the premise (the woman's question) that gays are different from "normal" heterosexuals. White shows that difference to be in a large degree in the eye of the beholder, or that the person who feels "different" has internalized a societal prejudice. Drawing on White's essay, and on other relevant essays such as Claude Steele's "Race and the Schooling of Black Americans," Alice Walker's "Beauty: When the Other Dancer Is the Self," or Laura Bohannan's "Shakespeare in the Bush," discuss the concept of being "different" in American society.

ROMANCING THE ROCK

John Fiske

John Fiske teaches communication arts at the University of Wisconsin–Madison. Previously he taught in Australia and in Great Britain, where he was born. He has written a number of books and articles on popular culture, such as Reading Television *(1979) and* Television Culture *(1987). Of his subject, he says, "Culture (and its meanings and pleasures) is a constant succession of social practices; it is therefore inherently political, it is centrally involved in the distribution and possible redistribution of various forms of social power." In the following piece, a chapter from* Reading the Popular *(1989), Fiske argues that "Both rock videos and soap opera show women in powerful positions vis-à-vis men."*

Rock videos are quintessential television in two main ways. First, they embody in condensed form all the characteristics of television that make it such a popular medium—its "producerliness" and semiotic democracy; its segmentation; its discursive practices of excess, contradictions, metaphor, metonymy, and puns; and its intertextuality.[1] Second, they appeal specifically to subordinate groups, teenagers in general and within them specific youth subcultures. Madonna's appeal is particularly to teenage girls, and this chapter considers one of her videos, "Material Girl," in some detail and compares it with another designed to appeal to the same market, A-ha's "Take on Me."

Both videos are similar in that both are romances—they refer to the common cultural genre of "romance." The narrative of how girl gets boy is told from the girl's point of view. The viewer is required to bring to bear upon these videos competencies within at least two genres, those of rock video and of romance. In her list of contrasting features of rock video and conventional realist television, Morse (1986) details the main textual devices that video competence has to deal with:

---

[1] *producerliness:* television requires us to participate in the production of meaning through our reference to texts we already know, such as romances. *semiotic democracy:* such a democracy treats its members as competent to make meaning, and as motivated by pleasure to want to participate in that process. Semiotics is the study of linguistic and nonlinguistic signs. *intertextuality:* the theory that any one text is read in relationship to others. In this piece, for example, Madonna's "Material Girl" is read in relationship to Marilyn Monroe's "Diamonds Are a Girl's Best Friend." [Eds.]

Rock Video	*Dominant Realism*
nonconsequential images	cause/effect
visual puns that parody accepted cultural values	cultural values taken as a given
juxtaposition of conflicting emotions	consistent emotions for various situations
displacement of time	chronological time
displacement of space	continuity rules (such as the 180-degree rule)
sometimes abstract	usually logical (uses realistic conventions)
excessive	restrained

The rock video characteristics are essentially those of a producerly, popular text: they require either an active, participating audience or one whose concerns are with image, style, and the pleasures of the signifier, rather than those of ideology.

The romance genre is essentially a product of the nineteenth century, the period that produced "sexuality" as a construct and that set up the gender differences required by the new form of patriarchy produced by industrial capitalism. The economic structure of society required women to marry and produce/nurture breadwinners. The romance taught them to experience this requirement not in economic or social terms, but in personal, emotional ones. So, the concept of "a romantic marriage" was constructed as an emotional need for women, not as an economic requirement of patriarchal capitalism, and romances became a training of women for marriage. Similarly, TV game shows can be understood, however inadequately, as training women to be happy, domesticated consumers; they extend the training beyond the marriage ceremony. 3

But there is no lasting pleasure in being a cultural dope, and from the start romances, like game shows, contained traces of women's oppositionality. *Jane Eyre* was typical in expressing the strongly felt needs of women for social, economic, and sexual independence, needs that the genre finally submerges into the need to marry, but the marriage is to a sensitized, or feminized, hero onto whom the feminine values of the heroine are displaced so that they are not lost entirely. Within the patriarchal form of the romance narrative, there is evidence of intransigent feminine values that refuse to be totally submerged. The progress of the plot can be seen as the feminization of the originally cold, distant, cruel masculine hero: not until he has been adequately feminized will the heroine marry him. Admittedly, this feminization is achieved by the suffering of the heroine, but the point is that it *is* achieved, and the heroine is not merely a suffering victim: the feisty, spunky sort of heroine whom Radway's (1984) romance fans strongly preferred does not have her spirit broken by her 4

602

suffering and, in fact, often reacts strongly against it. Women's pleasure in romance comes from this articulation of the tension between masculine and feminine, a tension that survives the patriarchal form of the genre as its equivalent in society has survived centuries of masculine domination.

Television's two genres that derive from the romance—soap opera and some rock videos—show significant changes from their point of origin. Both have minimized the masculine characteristics of romance, particularly its ending in patriarchal marriage, but also its insistence on the suffering of the heroine. Both rock videos and soap opera show women in powerful positions vis-à-vis men. Both differ from romance, too, in being more producerly texts—neither of them reaches a neat point of narrative and ideological closure that attempts to resolve the contradictory voices within it, and both offer up the pleasures of "semiotic democracy," the invitation to the viewer to participate in the construction of meaning, in the process of representation.

Hobson (1982) points out that much of the pleasure women find in soap operas derives from their openness to interpretation—their permission to the viewer to insert herself into the narrative and to play with social conventions, rules, and boundaries, in an active, creative use of the textual conventions and of social rules and knowledge. This creative reading produces a pleasure firmly situated in the subcultural experience of women, which thus evades and resists the dominant ideology. This sort of extraideological pleasure is called "affective pleasure" by Grossberg (1984) and is similar to Barthes's (1975b) *jouissance*.[2] But pleasure is closely related to power; for the powerless, the pleasure in resisting/evading power is at least as great as the pleasure of exerting power for the powerful (see Foucault 1978). Subcultural pleasure is empowering pleasure.

This pleasure is somewhat paradoxical, because teenagers, like women before them, have been systematically cultivated as consumers, and it is popular commodities—records, clothes, concert admissions—that are being promoted through the cultivation of pleasure in rock video. These target groups of teenage girls and women are delivered accurately to advertisers and sponsors. Both rock videos and daytime soaps garner large, demographically specific audiences at little cost to producers and broadcasters. But the fact that such pleasures serve the *economic* interests of the producers does not prevent them from serving the *cultural* interests of the consumers. This positive, subcultural, socially situated pleasure is quite different from the psychoanalytically oriented concept of desire. It is not based on an *absence-* (or loss-) creating desire that must then be tantalizingly restabilized in equilibrium. Rather, rock videos establish a performative pleasure based on the satisfaction of maintaining a sense of subcultural difference, a social identity that is *not* constructed by and for the interests of the dominant.

---

[2] *jouissance:* the final, climactic satisfying of desire. [Eds.]

JOHN FISKE

VIDEOS AND NARRATIVE ROMANCE

The two rock videos I propose to analyze were both popular in 1985, and both show traces of the conventional romance narrative. "Take on Me" looks to be a typical one-girl-for-one-boy romance tale, straightforward and rather linear, with some compelling animation integrated in logical, if fantastic, narrative. "Material Girl" is Madonna's remake of Marilyn Monroe's "Diamonds Are a Girl's Best Friend" number from *Gentlemen Prefer Blondes*, which in its concrete recognition of the metaphor of woman as ultimate commodity is apparently sexist, fetishistic,[3] and at the same time, in its enveloping narrative framing, conventionally romantic. Both videos are boy-meets-girl, girl-gets-boy romances, though neither ends on an unproblematic note. They have enough traces of the conventional romance for a comparison to be fruitful. Both videos, like romance novels, have young, single, lovely heroines who show signs of independence or feistiness. The hero is conventionally distant, aloof, even cruel, and the progress of the narrative traces the sensitization of the hero and the empowering of the heroine until he is sensitized enough for there to be a meeting on terms that are apparently hers, and over which she exerts some degree of control.

A three-minute video, which has to do more than relate a narrative, can hardly display much narrative progression—video romances do not exhibit the conventions of romance, but rather rely on the viewers' previous knowledge of them. The conventions allow music videos to compress narrative without falling into the trap of obscurity. In "Take on Me" the young heroine is drinking coffee alone in a cheap cafe and reading, interestingly, a boys' comic. The comic contains a narrative about motor racing in which the hero is pursued by two villains. The hero, tough and masculine, is transformed into Morten Harkett, the sensitive, almost feminized, lead singer of A-ha. The transformation happens graphically—the drawing of the hunky comic strip hero softens and changes into a drawing of Harkett as the girl looks at it. The feminization of the male occurs not as a result of female suffering (as in conventional romance) but as a result of the *will* of the feminine fantasy. The heroine avoids the traditional suffering and victimization by exerting the power of her fantasy.

In the narrative, the heroine joins her A-ha hero in the fantasy world in a complex series of reciprocal moves between the representational and the real and between photographic and graphic modes of representation. In this fantasy narrative, he joins her in the traditional feminine role of quarry, rather than the masculine role of hunter. They are chased by the villains and she escapes only by escaping from the fantasy world of the comic strip back to the real. He, however, has no such escape route and is caught and laid low by the villains. As she, back in the real world, looks at the drawing of him lying unconscious,

8

9

10

---

[3] *fetishistic:* the way the camera "worships," in close-ups, the female body. [Eds.]

her fantasy-power revives him. He gradually tears his way out of the comic-fantasy world until he materializes in the real world of her kitchen and collapses breathless and helpless on her floor. The final shot is of her looking enigmatically down at him as, we think, the realization dawns that she "really" possesses him, that she can will her fantasy into becoming the real.

In both videos, the romance process of feminizing the hero is condensed   11 into two (or more) separate and simultaneous characters. In "Take on Me," the conventional cruel hero at the start of the romance is embodied in the macho hero in the comic-strip racing driver, and the feminized hero at the end of the romance is embodied in the real A-ha figure. In "Material Girl," the narrative feminization of the difference between the hero at the beginning and end of the romance is again embodied in different characters, but this time their differences are articulated in terms of wealth. Madonna, the star, rejects the rich suitor who has brought her to the studio and drives off finally in a workman's truck with the "poor" suitor. As with "Take on Me," the "Material Girl" narrative avoids any abjection of the heroine; she does not have to suffer alone in order to sensitize and finally win the hero. Madonna is in a position of power throughout. The narrative opens with the "poor" hero and a producer watching some film rushes of Madonna; he insists that Madonna is perfect and nothing needs changing. She arrives at the studio with the rich hero, and the dressing-room romance develops in parallel with her studio song-and-dance number. The "poor" hero realizes that she is playing with and parodying her desire for wealth in the song and dumps the expensive present he has brought her into the trash can and instead gives her a simple bunch of daisies. At the end he buys or rents a workman's truck and drives Madonna off in it. The final shot shows the two kissing as the rain beats on the truck windows.

The video uses money as a metaphor for power, particularly male power; so,   12 the question of whether or not the "poor" suitor is actually poor becomes crucial. The uncertainty makes two narratives. In the first, Madonna believes he is poor and this narrative provides us with the conventional moral that money cannot buy love or happiness. Despite the overt message of the song, Madonna finds "true" love without material wealth. This is the narrative that Madonna herself prefers: she claims it is the poor guy who gets her in the end. But the second narrative casts the suitor as rich, though pretending to be poor because he knows that her song is only a masquerade and that the real way to impress her is with "sincerity"—the simple white daisies. The imagined closure of this narrative is that she falls in love with a rich man, though it is not his money that makes her love him. The interaction of this narrative with the song is more complex, for both involve a sense of play or masquerade. He plays with Madonna as she plays with the chorus boys. And in choosing the apparently poor suitor, she plays not with him but with the conventional moral—for whether he is rich or poor, she knows, and we know, that she is rich. This playing with the relationship between true love and money is so many-sided that it is impossible to determine any fixed or preferred meaning in it. Money is not just the ability to purchase; it is also a symbol of power. In taking the man who actually has the power that he pretends not to have, she is entering a relationship with quite different gender politics from that in the first narrative. The two narratives are alternately there. The textual evidence for the second is contained in two very quick shots (of dumping the expensive present in the trash can and of the roll of bills with which he pays the workman), shots so quick that many viewers miss them or, at least, do not allow them to interfere with their production of the first.

At this point in the argument, we need to note some crucial differences 13 between the videos and the conventional romance. Neither video is closed off as neatly as romances traditionally are. In "Take on Me" it is uncertain whether the heroine and the A-ha hero will enter a real relationship together, or even whether the figure lying on the heroine's floor, the object of her possessing look, is a real or fantasy figure. In "Material Girl" the uncertainty lies in the type of "closing" romantic relationship and the distribution of gender power within it. There is also the fundamental uncertainty of how Madonna "really" relates material wealth and true love. The relative openness of the finish of each narrative leaves the viewer in a position of power vis-à-vis the text. She is invited to participate actively in the construction of the narrative and, using the same knowledge of the same conventions as did the makers of the video, to write her own script from the narrative fragments provided. What Allen (1985) calls "syntagmatic gaps"[4] are so wide here that the amount of "writing" by the viewer is immense; both texts are thoroughly producerly, and as such require producerly readers to construct narratives from them. The texts themselves are the raw materials out of which a number of narratives can be produced.

This reader-production is guided by the conventions of romance working 14 intertextually, but is not determined by them. Part of the pleasure is the knowing departure from the conventions, for as conventions in their regulatory function bear social power, so departing from them is a means of symbolizing a resistance to, or negotiation with, this power or, at the very least, an assertion of subordinate power. The conventional romance, with its abjected, suffering heroine, needs modifying to meet the sociocultural needs of girls in the 1980s, and these rock videos offer their readers the opportunity to do precisely that. The modification occurs partly in the narrative, particularly in the uncertainty of its closure, but most significantly in the modified reading position. The wide syntagmatic gaps that make these texts producerly do not subject the reader to the form of the narrative; rather, they leave spaces that the reader is required to fill with her own production. She is in a more empowered authorial relationship with the text than the reader of the conventional romance; different readers are able to exploit these gaps in order to produce differently articulated readings of

---

[4]*syntagmatic gaps*: breaks between segments of narrative, or between episodes. [Eds.]

the text that interact productively with their own social positions. The reader, located in a nexus of social forces and determinations, is able to shift the reading of a text so that its meanings and pleasures can articulate her sense of her social identity and social relations. She produces her meanings and pleasure at the moment of reading the text.

This production is a direct source of power, and gender power is another 15 area in which the videos differ from conventional romance. Though romances provide the space within which feminine power can be articulated and finally asserted, the narrative means by which this is achieved are severely restricted, confined in the main to the lonely suffering and abjection of the heroine. This is not the case in either of the videos. In "Take on Me" the heroine uses the power of her fantasy to enter the fictional world of the hero, to share his pursuit and initial defeat by the villain, and finally not only to liberate him from the villain but also to liberate herself and him from their imprisonment in separate worlds. The feminization of the hero and her consequent power is achieved by *his* suffering, not hers. In "Material Girl," Madonna is in a position of power throughout. She is always in the position of choosing easily between the suitors, and in the song she toys with the chorus boys as she takes their jewels, money, and admiration for her own use. Stardom has always been a domain of power permitted to women within patriarchy, but Madonna shows that her possession of this power has none of the insecurity of, for instance, Marilyn Monroe's, for it depends upon her own strength, not her ability to win men's admiration. Unlike Monroe, Madonna cares nothing for the men over whom she has power.

FANTASY AND REPRESENTATION

This sense of power that the videos offer a female viewer is centered in two 16 closely interrelated areas—fantasy and representation. The relationship of fantasy to reality, and that of the representation to the real are, to all intents and purposes, the same. Understanding their similarity requires us to reverse and deny the differences that are often set up between them in our patriarchal culture. Fantasy is often seen as feminine, whereas representation is associated with the masculine. In this view fantasy is constructed as "mere escapism," a sign of feminine weakness resulting from women's inability to come to terms with (masculine) reality. It is a sort of daydreaming that allows women to achieve their desires in a way that they are never capable of in the "real" world, a compensatory domain that results from and disguises their "real" lack of power. Representation, however, is seen as a positive act: not a means of escaping from the world but of acting upon it. Representation is the means of making sense of the world in a way that serves one's own interests. It is a political process and involves the power to make meanings of both the world and one's place within it. It is therefore "appropriately" thought of as masculine. It is seen as a site of struggle for power, in a way that fantasy is not. It is these simplistic distinctions, set up and maintained by patriarchy, that we wish to deny.

McRobbie (1984) takes a similar position when she argues convincingly that fantasy is a private, intimate experience that can be interpreted as "part of a strategy of resistance or opposition: that is, as marking out one of those areas that cannot be totally colonised"[5] (p. 184). She makes the point that the apparently obvious distinction between fantasy and reality is open to question: "[Fantasy is] as much an *experience*, a piece of reality, as is babysitting or staying in to do the washing" (p. 184).

Fantasy is a means of representation whose privacy and intimacy do not prevent it acting just as powerfully upon the meanings of social experience as do the more public representations of language and the media. Indeed, it may actually meet the needs of subordinate subcultures better than any of the public, mass-produced modes of representation, and so may be seen to take a more directly resistive stance. Its interiority does not disqualify it from political effectivity: the interior is the political.

It is only ever a tiny minority of people in subordinated groups who organize and act directly in the political realm to try to effect changes in the social order. But the effectiveness of such activists depends to a considerable extent upon the interior resistances of others who share the same social position: without these myriad interior resistances, the activists could not justify their claims to represent a groundswell of social feeling, and their position could all too easily be marginalized and ignored.

Fantasy should not be opposed conceptually to reality, as though the two were mutually exclusive concepts. Our social reality is our experience of it: we can never experience social relations objectively, or extract *their* sense from them, for they have none, it is culture that makes sense of social relations. The difference between fantasy and a sense of reality is one of modality, for both are cultural representations: one is not real and the other false. Fantasy may be of a lower modality than more direct experience of social reality, but it is not disconnected from it, or opposed to it. The social subject moves easily along the modal scale from fantasy to more direct social experience; each feeds the other, each informs and is read into the other. The heroine of "Take on Me," who uses her fantasy to gain power over the man of her dreams, can stimulate politically progressive and positive fantasies in her viewer, and these fantasies may well chime with other traces of feminine power in the viewer's subjectivity, and may, eventually, in some cases, translate into political action within the politics of gender relationships. As part of the changing meanings of feminine-masculine relationships in the 1980s, the narrative of "Take on Me," like that of "Material Girl," may enable some girl viewers to behave differently toward their boyfriends, to understand their role within boy-girl relationships differently

[5] *colonised*: to take over a territory for economic reasons; appropriated. [Eds.]

and thus to contribute to the gradual redistribution of gender power within patriarchy.

Fantasy is an important political part of popular culture: making a resisting 21 sense of one's social relations is prerequisite to developing the will and the self-confidence to act upon them. The culture of the subordinate is typically a provoker of fantasy, and these two videos are no exception. In "Take on Me" four worlds are represented, each bearing a different relationship to the others along these axes of reality—representation/fantasy. Two main modes of representation present these worlds—photography and drawing. Photography appears closer to reality than does drawing; so, the photographic worlds are less "fantastic" than drawn ones. We can model the worlds thus:

THE WORLD OF "TAKE ON ME"	*World of Heroine (Reality)*	*World of A-ha ("Real" Fantasy)*
fantasy/representation (drawing)	comic strip	drawn A-ha
reality (photography)	heroine in cafe/ apartment	photographed A-ha

This shows that the drawn worlds and the photographed world are each 22 divided into two: the "real" world of the heroine (which includes the reading of comic strips) and the "real" world of A-ha (which relates to that of the heroine in terms of a different sort of fantasy). A-ha are both real people and fantasy figures to their fans, hence the designation of them as "real" fantasy. The heroine moves comparatively freely, and at her own will, among all four worlds. A-ha move easily between the representation and the reality of their worlds, but cross to the worlds of the heroine only with difficulty at *her* will.

The comic book that the heroine is reading has little to offer her—it repre- 23 sents only the cold, cruel hero of the beginning of a romance. Her fantasy feminizes this hero into the sensitive A-ha singer and the drawing changes from one to the other as she looks at it. Once her will has pulled Harkett across into the drawn world, she wishes to enter it herself. She then becomes a drawn representation of "herself" and, together with Harkett and A-ha, moves easily among all three fantasy worlds. A sheet of glass enables the vertical transition in the world of A-ha: when seen through it, the heroine and A-ha are represented by photographs, but as they move alongside it they become drawn representations. She and A-ha are never simultaneously "real" (photographs) until the final shot, though they are frequently both representations (drawings). Breaking the fantasy and returning to her reality involves an act of violence—tearing through the paper of the comic book. On her return to the real world, she finds herself on the ground beside the garbage pail where the cafe proprietress has thrown the crumpled comic book in a gesture that nicely symbolizes our society's disregard for feminine fantasy. At the end of the video, the A-ha hero too has to batter his way through the pages, a struggle that continues as he materializes in her "real" apartment until he lies exhausted on her floor, the helpless object of her look/fantasy.

There are two sorts of fantasy involved here. One is the fantasy of A-ha, who are real, but can enter the world of the heroine only by a willed act of fantasy on her part; the other is the fantasy of the comic book, which is an everyday part of her world that she can enter more or less at her will, but that is confined to its own level of representation. The drawn world, the represented fantasy, cannot enter the "real" world in a way that the "real" can enter the represented. The question raised but unanswered by this structural set of relationships is whether A-ha are, for their girl fans, reality or fantasy, or even whether the distinction is a valid one. I will return to this question after analyzing "Material Girl" in similar terms. 24

There are also four worlds in "Material Girl." There is the world of Madonna the person, along with the world of Madonna the star/performer, and the corresponding worlds of Monroe. These worlds can be modeled along the same axes as the worlds of "Take on Me": 25

THE WORLDS OF "MATERIAL GIRL"	The Worlds of Madonna (Reality)	The Worlds of Monroe ("Real" Fantasy)
fantasy/representation	star	star
reality ("being")	person	person

Although the structure is similar to that of A-ha's video, the ability of the heroine to control the movement among the four worlds is effected quite differently. The world of Monroe the star is represented only by Madonna's parody/pastiche of it and the power of this representation to bring Monroe's song-and-dance number to mind. Monroe's "real" world is never directly represented, though it is there as a crucial intertextual gap from which Madonna's "real" world is to be read. Monroe's absence of control over her "real" world and "star" world is significantly opposed to Madonna's control over both. The "Take on Me" heroine's "power" over A-ha is represented directly in her fantasy, but Madonna's control is represented only indirectly by its opposition to Monroe's powerlessness. Both videos require intertextual knowledge from their viewers—not only generic knowledge of romance, but more specific knowledge of stars as images and people. The history of Monroe as a powerful star and a powerless person is a story whose intertextual relations work in the same way as do the stories of romance. The question of whether A-ha is reality or fantasy to the group's fans is echoed in the question of whether Monroe's suicide and powerlessness are fact or fantasy to Madonna's fans. Of course, they are a more factual fantasy than Monroe's performances, and just as factual a fantasy as the existence of A-ha in the world of their fans. The "reality" of one world (that of A-ha or Monroe) can be made to inform the "reality" of another (that of the 26 heroine or Madonna) only by taking on elements of fantasy and becoming what I have called "a real fantasy."

We need to look more closely at the similarities and the differences between   27 Madonna's song-and-dance number in "Material Girl" and Monroe's in *Gentlemen Prefer Blondes*. The two songs are basically similar. Monroe sings "Diamonds Are a Girl's Best Friend," while Madonna sings "Material Girl." Both suggest that a woman in patriarchy has to look after her own interests by using men as a source of the wealth that the system denies her by more "legitimate" means. They assert the right of the woman to use her body, the only asset granted her in patriarchy, for *her* interests, not those of men. There are differences, however, particularly differences of tone. Monroe is calculatedly looking after her own interests and ensuring that she has financial security in her old age:

> Men go cold as girls grow old
> And we all lose our charms in the end,
> But square cut or pear shape
> These rocks don't lose their shape
> Diamonds are a girl's best friend

Madonna derives much more pleasure for herself—she is not just providing   28 for herself materially, but *enjoys* the power over men that gives her the ability to do so. Monroe shows none of the pleasure that Madonna does as she (Madonna) sings:

> Some boys kiss me, some boys hug me
> I think they're okay
> If they don't give me proper credit
> I just walk away

> Boys may come and boys may go
> But that's all right you see
> Experience has made me rich
> And now they're after me

The puns in "credit" and "experience has made me rich" show not only   29 Madonna's control over language, but also that her financial demands are at one with her sexual pleasure and self-esteem. The traditional relationship of economics to sexual power is called into question: Madonna is no commodified woman to be "bought" by the economically successful man. She extracts both money and approval from the men, but because she wants to and is able to: she does not depend upon men and their money to the extent that the Monroe of "Diamonds Are a Girl's Best Friend" appears to. Madonna is no supplicant— she does not use men to fill a lack in her life. Indeed, all that she lacks is the *need* for men. She relates to them in order to assert her independence of them. Men are there not to supply a feminine lack, but to be objects of feminine pleasure and subjects of feminine power.

DANCE AND SPECTACLE

There are also similarities and differences in their dances. In both, Madonna and Monroe reject the large red hearts offered by the chorus boys in favor of their jewels and money. But Monroe has a verse of the song sung to a female chorus, as though she were offering them advice on how to look after themselves in patriarchy. Madonna has no staged address to women: she projects an independent self-sufficiency. She is also more assertive than Monroe. While parodying many of Monroe's movements, gestures, and facial expressions, she goes further in taking money not offered and in knocking down a chorus boy and posing triumphantly over his prostrate body. Monroe wants to attract men's desire so that they will give her diamonds. Madonna merely wants their money and toys with their desire. Her gestures and expressions are less supplicatory or seductive for the men who admire her. Monroe, as was appropriate to her period, is concerned with women's ability to provide for themselves within patriarchy. Madonna asserts women's power to use patriarchal values *against* men.

Both dances are framed by a romance. Monroe tosses one of her diamond bands to her rich but ineffectual suitor in the front row of the theater, signaling her equality with his wealth, but superiority in physical sexuality. The diamonds extracted from other men are given to a rival in a gesture of feminine power over men and over her own sexuality. This power is exercised during a dance/fantasy number, but that, as argued above, does not make it any less "real." For dance, as McRobbie (1984) has pointed out, occupies a special place in feminine culture:

> Dance evokes fantasy because it sets in motion a dual relationship projecting both internally towards the self and externally towards the "other": which is to say that dance as a leisure activity connects desires for the self with those for somebody else. It articulates adolescence and girlhood with femininity and female sexuality and it does this by and through the body. This is especially important because it is the one pleasurable arena where women have some control and know what is going on in relation to their own bodies. (pp. 144–145)

I have drawn elsewhere upon McRobbie's study of how girls find similar pleasures and meanings in dancing themselves to those they produce in watching films such as *Flashdance* or TV series such as *Fame*:

On one level of reading the narrative form and pleasure of *Flashdance* clearly works hegemonically: the female worker uses her skill in break-dancing to win a place in a ballet company and marry the boss's son. In the process she displays her body for patriarchal pleasure; indeed, her beautiful body is crucial to her successful move up the social hierarchy (dancing ballet rather than break, and marrying into management). Women, so the hegemonic reading would go, are rewarded for their ability to use their beauty and talents to give pleasure to men. But McRobbie has shown that this is not the only reading, and has found amongst teenage girls a set of meanings of dance and female sexuality that contest and struggle against the patriarchal hegemony. For them, dance was a form of auto-eroticism, a pleasure in their own bodies and sexuality which gave them an identity that was not dependent upon male approval. *Their* discourse of dance gave a coherent meaning to dancing in discos or watching filmic and televisual representations of it that asserted their subcultural identity and difference from the rest of society. Its meanings were meanings for them that they had made out of the forms that arguably had been provided for them by patriarchy. (Fiske 1987b)

The performance aspects of Madonna's/Monroe's dances outweigh the pa-[33] triarchal construction of desire, of which traces remain in their bracketing romance narratives. Dance numbers in the classic Hollywood musicals have been theorized as interrupting the patriarchal narrative and as replacing the economy of the male gaze with spectacle. Spectacle denies the power of the voyeur over the seen object, for in the spectacle, the spectacular (in this case, the dancing female body) invites, directs, and controls the gaze, which may be masculine, feminine, or both. Madonna as spectacle invites women to find pleasure in her toying with the chorus boys just as much as she invites men to find pleasure in her sexual body, which provides the means of this toying. In spectacle, desire is replaced with pleasure, which is the satisfaction of desire, not through closure and resolution, but through openness and empowerment. The woman dancing is in control not only of the physical sexuality of her own body, but also of its meanings for herself and for others. Dance as spectacle, dance as pleasure for the self, dance as social fantasy, becomes a means of representing and therefore controlling that potentially disabling contradiction so clearly identified by Williamson (1986b): "for [Madonna] retains all the bravado and exhibitionism that most girls start off with until the onset of 'womanhood' knocks it out of them" (p. 47). At the moment when young girls become aware of their potential as women, patriarchy closes its grip upon their social relations and identities. Dance and fantasy resist this closure and assert meanings and control that are women's, not men's.

JOHN FISKE

PLEASURE, POWER, AND
RESISTANCE

Madonna's appeal for her girl fans ("wanna-bes") rests largely on her control   34
over her own image and her assertion of her right to an independent feminine
sexuality. In this she adopts an oppositional political stance that challenges two
of the critical areas of patriarchal power—its control of language/representation
and its control of gender meanings and gender differences.

A fantasy that asserts feminine control over representation, particularly the   35
representation of gender, is no escape from social reality; rather, it is a direct
response to the dominant ideology and its embodiment in social relations. A
fantasy that proposes an empowered heroine controlling the meanings of herself
and her gender relations is an oppositional, resistive fantasy that has a political
effectivity. It does not, however, have a direct political effect. The videos of
A-ha and Madonna do not bring young girls out on the streets in political
demonstrations, for the relationship between the domain of entertainment and
that of politics is never as direct as that: they simply do not relate to each other
in terms of cause and effect. But the absence of a direct effect does not preclude
the presence of a more general effectivity. The assertion of women's right to
control their own representation is a challenge to the way that women are
constructed as subjects in patriarchy. It is a part, and an active part, of the
changing ways in which women understand themselves and their social relations. Any set of social relations requires a set of meanings to hold it in place,
and any set of meanings has to be produced by a social group, or formation of
groups, within those social relations. Those who dominate social relations also
dominate the production of the meanings that underpin them: social power and
semiotic power are different sides of the same coin.

Challenging meanings and the social group with the right to make them is   36
thus no act of escape, but is a crucial part of resisting the subjection of women
within and by patriarchy. It asserts women's rights to be different from the
subjectivities that patriarchy tries to construct for them. Semiotic power is not
a mere symbol of, or licensed substitute for, "real" power. Its uses are not
confined to the construction of resistant subjectivities, but extend also to the
construction of relevances, of ways of negotiating this interface between the
products of the culture industries and the experiences of everyday life. The
reward, and therefore the motivation, for making meanings and relevances is a
form of semiotic pleasure, the pleasure of the text. The fact that these meanings
are relevant means that this power-pleasure can be transferred across the boundary between text and everyday life, a boundary that Bourdieu (1984) shows us
is insistently ignored by proletarian culture. This refusal of the boundary means
that the semiotic power in the text can be transformed into social power in the
micropolitics of everyday life. For the moment I wish merely to argue that this
matrix of pleasure-power-relevance is a crucial characteristic of popular culture,

and that within it, semiotic power and micro political power exist on a continuum, not as alternatives. Madonna is a material girl as well as a semiotic one.

REFERENCES

Allen, R. (1985). *Speaking of Soap Operas*. Chapel Hill: University of North Carolina Press.
Barthes, R. (1975b). *The Pleasure of the Text*. New York: Hill & Wang.
Bourdieu, P. (1984). *Distinction: A Social Critique of the Judgement of Taste* (R. Nice, trans.). Cambridge, MA: Harvard University Press.
Foucault, M. (1978). *The History of Sexuality*. Harmondsworth, England: Penguin.
Grossberg, L. (1984). "Another Boring Day in Paradise: Rock and Roll and the Empowerment of Everyday Life." *Popular Music* 4, 225–257.
Hobson, D. (1982). *Crossroads: The Drama of a Soap Opera*. London: Methuen.
McRobbie, A. (1982). "*Jackie*: An Ideology of Adolescent Femininity," in B. Waites, T. Bennett, and G. Martin (eds.), *Popular Cultures: Past and Present* (pp. 263–283). London: Croom Helm/Open University Press.
Morse, M. (1986). "Post Synchronizing Rock Music and Television." *Journal of Communication Inquiry* 10 (1), 15–28.
Radway, J. (1984) *Reading the Romance: Feminism and the Representation of Women in Popular Culture*. Chapel Hill: University of North Carolina Press.
Williamson, J. (1986b). "The Making of a Material Girl." *New Socialist* (October), 46–47.

QUESTIONS

1. Fiske claims that rock videos and daytime soaps both make money for their producers and serve the "*cultural* interests of the consumers." What does he mean by "cultural interests"? Do you agree? How do you perceive this sort of entertainment?

2. At the end of paragraph 7, Fiske presents what might be considered his thesis, or argumentative stance. What does he mean by "subculture," and are you a member of one?

3. In developing his argument, Fiske works in several stages. First, he analyzes two rock videos (paragraphs 8–15) to set out the differences between videos and conventional narrative romance. What are the characteristics of a conventional romance? How do such videos as "Take on Me" and "Material Girl" differ from conventional romances?

4. Fiske's analysis shows both videos to be relatively "open" texts: he calls them "thoroughly producerly" (be sure you understand this term, since *you* are the producer here). If rock videos such as these are open texts, what constitutes a "closed" text? Are conventional romances closed texts? Think of an example.

5. What is the case for fantasy that Fiske makes in paragraphs 16–29? How does it serve his argument? Does the view of fantasy he presents have any relevance for a reading of a cultural (and commercial) construct such as Disneyworld?

6. Write an analysis of a rock video. You might compare and contrast a more recent Madonna video with another more recent video. Read these texts with an eye to their political stance. Do they challenge societal stereotypes, or do they reinforce them?

7. You may have noticed that many professors are taking heretofore ignored (or scorned, or deplored) cultural phenomena such as rock videos, soap operas, "slasher" movies, and so forth, seriously. Construct an argument in which you make a case for their doing so, or in which you make an argument for their paying more attention to the classics, or to some neglected but worthy area we have not mentioned.

MAKING CONNECTIONS

Compare the MacCannells' examination of relationships between the sexes in "The Beauty System" with Fiske's reading of feminine power as presented in rock videos. Do the two essays contradict one another, or complement one another? How do essays by such writers as Susan Fraker, Deborah Woo, and Carol Gilligan comment on the issue of power and powerlessness?

POLITICS AND THE ENGLISH LANGUAGE

George Orwell

The rise of totalitarianism in Europe led George Orwell (see the headnote on page 118 for more biographical information) to write about its causes in his most famous novels 1984 *(1949) and* Animal Farm *(1945), and in essays such as "Politics and the English Language." In this essay, written in 1946, Orwell tells his readers that "In our time, political speech and writing are largely the defense of the indefensible." He attacks language that consists "largely of euphemism, question begging, and sheer cloudy vagueness." Orwell, like John Berger, is concerned with the ways in which language is often used to conceal unpleasant and horrifying realities.*

Most people who bother with the matter at all would admit that the English 1
language is in a bad way, but it is generally assumed that we cannot by conscious action do anything about it. Our civilization is decadent and our language—so the argument runs—must inevitably share in the general collapse. It follows that any struggle against the abuse of language is a sentimental archaism, like preferring candles to electric light or hansom cabs to aeroplanes. Underneath this lies the half-conscious belief that language is a natural growth and not an instrument which we shape for our own purposes.

Now, it is clear that the decline of a language must ultimately have political 2
and economic causes: it is not due simply to the bad influence of this or that individual writer. But an effect can become a cause, reinforcing the original cause and producing the same effect in an intensified form, and so on indefinitely. A man may take to drink because he feels himself to be a failure, and then fail all the more completely because he drinks. It is rather the same thing that is happening to the English language. It becomes ugly and inaccurate because our thoughts are foolish, but the slovenliness of our language makes it easier for us to have foolish thoughts. The point is that the process is reversible. Modern English, especially written English, is full of bad habits which spread by imitation and which can be avoided if one is willing to take the necessary trouble. If one gets rid of these habits one can think more clearly, and to think clearly is a necessary first step towards political regeneration: so that the fight against bad English is not frivolous and is not the exclusive concern of professional writers. I will come back to this presently, and I hope that by the time

617

the meaning of what I have said here will have become clearer. Meanwhile, here are five specimens of the English language as it is now habitually written.

These five passages have not been picked out because they are especially 3
bad—I could have quoted far worse if I had chosen—but because they illustrate various of the mental vices from which we now suffer. They are a little below the average, but are fairly representative samples. I number them so that I can refer back to them when necessary:

> "(1) I am not, indeed, sure whether it is not true to say that the Milton who once seemed not unlike a seventeenth-century Shelley had not become, out of an experience ever more bitter in each year, more alien [*sic*] to the founder of that Jesuit sect which nothing could induce him to tolerate."
>
> Professor Harold Laski (Essay in Freedom of Expression)

> "(2) Above all, we cannot play ducks and drakes with a native battery of idioms which prescribes such egregious collocations of vocables as the Basic *put up with* for *tolerate* or *put at a loss* for *bewilder*."
>
> Professor Lancelot Hogben (Interglossa)

> "(3) On the one side we have the free personality: by definition it is not neurotic, for it has neither conflict nor dream. Its desires, such as they are, are transparent, for they are just what institutional approval keeps in the forefront of consciousness; another institutional pattern would alter their number and intensity; there is little in them that is natural, irreducible, or culturally dangerous. But *on the other* side, the social bond itself is nothing but the mutual reflection of these self-secure integrities. Recall the definition of love. Is not this the very picture of a small academic? Where is there a place in this hall of mirrors for either personality or fraternity?"
>
> Essay on psychology in Politics (New York)

> "(4) All the 'best people' from the gentlemen's clubs, and all the frantic fascist captains, united in common hatred of Socialism and bestial horror of the rising tide of the mass revolutionary movement, have turned to acts of provocation, to foul incendiarism, to medieval legends of poisoned wells, to legalize their own destruction of proletarian organizations, and rouse the agitated petty-bourgeoisie to chauvinistic fervour on behalf of the fight against the revolutionary way out of the crisis."
>
> Communist pamphlet

> "(5) If a new spirit *is* to be infused into this old country, there is one thorny and contentious reform which must be tackled, and that is the humanization and galvanization of the B.B.C. Timidity here will be-speak cancer and atrophy of the soul. The heart of Britain may be sound and of strong beat, for instance, but the British lion's roar at

present is like that of Bottom in Shakespeare's *Midsummer Night's Dream*—as gentle as any sucking dove. A virile new Britain cannot continue indefinitely to be traduced in the eyes or rather ears, of the world by the effete languors of Langham Place, brazenly masquerading as 'standard English.' When the Voice of Britain is heard at nine o'clock, better far and infinitely less ludicrous to hear aitches honestly dropped than the present priggish, inflated, inhibited, school-ma'amish arch braying of blameless bashful mewing maidens!"

Letter in Tribune

Each of these passages has faults of its own, but, quite apart from avoidable   4
ugliness, two qualities are common to all of them. The first is staleness of imagery: the other is lack of precision. The writer either has a meaning and cannot express it, or he inadvertently says something else, or he is almost indifferent as to whether his words mean anything or not. This mixture of vagueness and sheer incompetence is the most marked characteristic of modern English prose, and especially of any kind of political writing. As soon as certain topics are raised, the concrete melts into the abstract and no one seems able to think of turns of speech that are not hackneyed: prose consists less and less of *words* chosen for the sake of their meaning, and more and more of *phrases* tacked together like the sections of a prefabricated hen-house. I list below, with notes and examples, various of the tricks by means of which the work of prose-construction is habitually dodged:

DYING METAPHORS

A newly invented metaphor assists thought by evoking a visual image, while   5
on the other hand a metaphor which is technically "dead" (e.g. *iron resolution*) has in effect reverted to being an ordinary word and can generally be used without loss of vividness. But in between these two classes there is a huge dump of worn-out metaphors which have lost all evocative power and are merely used because they save people the trouble of inventing phrases for themselves. Examples are: *Ring the changes on, take up the cudgels for, toe the line, ride roughshod over, stand shoulder to shoulder with, play into the hands of, no axe to grind, grist to the mill, fishing in troubled waters, on the order of the day, Achilles' heel, swan song, hotbed.* Many of these are used without knowledge of their meaning (what is a "rift," for instance?), and incompatible metaphors are frequently mixed, a sure sign that the writer is not interested in what he is saying. Some metaphors now current have been twisted out of their original meaning without those who use them even being aware of the fact. For example, *toe the line* is sometimes written *tow the line*. Another example is *the hammer and the anvil*, now always used with the implication that the anvil gets the worst of it. In real life it is always the anvil that breaks the hammer, never the

other way about: a writer who stopped to think what he was saying would be aware of this, and would avoid perverting the original phrase.

OPERATORS OR VERBAL FALSE LIMBS

These save the trouble of picking out appropriate verbs and nouns, and at the same time pad each sentence with extra syllables which give it an appearance of symmetry. Characteristic phrases are: *render inoperative, militate against, make contact with, be subjected to, give rise to, give grounds for, have the effect of, play a leading part (role) in, make itself felt, take effect, exhibit a tendency to, serve the purpose of, etc., etc.* The keynote is the elimination of simple verbs. Instead of being a single word, such as *break, stop, spoil, mend, kill,* a verb becomes a *phrase,* made up of a noun or adjective tacked on to some general-purposes verb such as *prove, serve, form, play, render.* In addition, the passive voice is wherever possible used in preference to the active, and noun constructions are used instead of gerunds (*by examination of* instead of *by examining*). The range of verbs is further cut down by means of the *-ize* and *de-* formation, and the banal statements are given an appearance of profundity by means of the *not un-* formation. Simple conjunctions and prepositions are replaced by such phrases as *with respect to, having regard to, the fact that, by dint of, in view of, in the interests of, on the hypothesis that;* and the ends of sentences are saved from anticlimax by such resounding commonplaces as *greatly to be desired, cannot be left out of account, a development to be expected in the near future, deserving of serious consideration, brought to a satisfactory conclusion,* and so on and so forth.

PRETENTIOUS DICTION

Words like *phenomenon, element, individual* (as noun), *objective, categorical, effective, virtual, basic, primary, promote, constitute, exhibit, exploit, utilize, eliminate, liquidate,* are used to dress up simple statements and give an air of scientific impartiality to biased judgments. Adjectives like *epoch-making, epic, historic, unforgettable, triumphant, age-old, inevitable, inexorable, veritable,* are used to dignify the sordid processes of international politics, while writing that aims at glorifying war usually takes on an archaic colour, its characteristic words being: *realm, throne, chariot, mailed fist, trident, sword, shield, buckler, banner, jackboot, clarion.* Foreign words and expressions such as *cul de sac, ancien régime, deus ex machina, mutatis mutandis, status quo, gleichschaltung, weltanschauung,* are used to give an air of culture and elegance. Except for the useful abbreviations *i.e., e.g.,* and *etc.,* there is no real need for any of the hundreds of foreign phrases now current in English. Bad writers, and especially scientific, political and sociological writers, are nearly always haunted by the notion that Latin or Greek words are grander than Saxon ones, and unnecessary words like *expedite, ameliorate, predict, extraneous, deracinated, clandestine, subaqueous* and hundreds of others constantly gain ground from their Anglo-Saxon opposite numbers.[1] The jargon peculiar to Marxist writing (*hyena, hangman, cannibal, petty bourgeois, these gentry, lacquey, flunkey, mad dog, White Guard,* etc.) consists largely of words and phrases translated from Russian, German or French; but the normal way of coining a new word is to use a Latin or Greek root with the appropriate affix and, where necessary, the *-ize* formation. It is often easier to make up words of this kind (*deregionalize, impermissible, extramarital, nonfragmentatory* and so forth) than to think up the English words that will cover one's meaning. The result, in general, is an increase in slovenliness and vagueness.

MEANINGLESS WORDS

In certain kinds of writing, particularly in art criticism and literary criticism, it is normal to come across long passages which are almost completely lacking in meaning.[2] Words like *romantic, plastic, values, human, dead, sentimental, natural, vitality,* as used in art criticism, are strictly meaningless in the sense that they not only do not point to any discoverable object, but are hardly ever expected to do so by the reader. When one critic writes, "The outstanding feature of Mr. X's work is its living quality," while another writes, "The immediately striking thing about Mr. X's work is its peculiar deadness," the reader accepts this as a simple difference of opinion. If words like *black* and *white* were involved, instead of the jargon words *dead* and *living,* he would see at once that language was being used in an improper way. Many political words are similarly abused. The word *Fascism* has now no meaning except in so far as it signifies "something not desirable." The words *democracy, socialism, freedom, patriotic, realistic, justice,* have each of them several different meanings which cannot be reconciled with one another. In the case of a word like *democracy,* not only is there no agreed definition, but the attempt to make one is resisted from all sides. It is almost universally felt that when we call a country democratic we are praising it: consequently the defenders of every kind of régime claim that it is a democracy, and fear that they might have to stop using the word if it were tied down to any one meaning. Words of this kind are often

8

---

[1] An interesting illustration of this is the way in which the English flower names which were in use till very recently are being ousted by Greek ones, *snapdragon* becoming *antirrhinum, forget-me-not* becoming *myosotis,* etc. It is hard to see any practical reason for this change of fashion: it is probably due to an instinctive turning-away from the more homely word and a vague feeling that the Greek word is scientific.

[2] Example: "Comfort's catholicity of perception and image, strangely Whitmanesque in range, almost the exact opposite in aesthetic compulsion, continues to evoke that trembling atmospheric accumulative hinting at a cruel, an inexorably serene timelessness . . . Wrey Gardiner scores by aiming at simple bull's-eyes with precision. Only they are not so simple, and through this contented sadness runs more than the surface bittersweet of resignation" (*Poetry Quarterly*).

used in a consciously dishonest way. That is, the person who uses them has his own private definition, but allows his hearer to think he means something quite different. Statements like *Marshal Pétain was a true patriot, The Soviet Press is the freest in the world, The Catholic Church is opposed to persecution,* are almost always made with intent to deceive. Other words used in variable meanings, in most cases more or less dishonestly, are: *class, totalitarian, science, progressive, reactionary, bourgeois, equality.*

Now that I have made this catalogue of swindles and perversions, let me   9
give another example of the kind of writing that they lead to. This time it must of its nature be an imaginary one. I am going to translate a passage of good English into modern English of the worst sort. Here is a well-known verse from *Ecclesiastes:*

> "I returned and saw under the sun, that the race is not to the swift, nor the battle to the strong, neither yet bread to the wise, nor yet riches to men of understanding, nor yet favour to men of skill; but time and chance happeneth to them all."

Here it is in modern English: 10

> "Objective consideration of contemporary phenomena compels the conclusion that success or failure in competitive activities exhibits no tendency to be commensurate with innate capacity, but that a considerable element of the unpredictable must invariably be taken into account."

This is a parody, but not a very gross one. Exhibit (3), above, for instance,   11
contains several patches of the same kind of English. It will be seen that I have not made a full translation. The beginning and ending of the sentence follow the original meaning fairly closely, but in the middle the concrete illustrations— race, battle, bread—dissolve into the vague phrase "success or failure in competitive activities." This had to be so, because no modern writer of the kind I am discussing—no one capable of using phrases like "objective consideration of contemporary phenomena"—would ever tabulate his thoughts in that precise and detailed way. The whole tendency of modern prose is away from concreteness. Now analyse these two sentences a little more closely. The first contains forty-nine words but only sixty syllables, and all its words are those of everyday life. The second contains thirty-eight words of ninety syllables: eighteen of its words are from Latin roots, and one from Greek. The first sentence contains six vivid images, and only one phrase ("time and chance") that could be called vague. The second contains not a single fresh, arresting phrase, and in spite of its ninety syllables it gives only a shortened version of the meaning contained in the first. Yet without a doubt it is the second kind of sentence that is gaining ground in modern English. I do not want to exaggerate. This kind of writing is not yet universal, and outcrops of simplicity will occur here and there in the

worst-written page. Still, if you or I were told to write a few lines on the uncertainty of human fortunes, we should probably come much nearer to my imaginary sentence than to the one from *Ecclesiastes*.

As I have tried to show, modern writing at its worst does not consist in 12 picking out words for the sake of their meaning and inventing images in order to make the meaning clearer. It consists in gumming together long strips of words which have already been set in order by someone else, and making the results presentable by sheer humbug. The attraction of this way of writing is that it is easy. It is easier—even quicker, once you have the habit—to say *In my opinion it is a not unjustifiable assumption that* than to say *I think*. If you use ready-made phrases, you not only don't have to hunt about for words; you also don't have to bother with the rhythms of your sentences, since these phrases are generally so arranged as to be more or less euphonious. When you are composing in a hurry—when you are dictating to a stenographer, for instance, or making a public speech—it is natural to fall into a pretentious, Latinized style. Tags like *a consideration which we should do well to bear in mind* or *a conclusion to which all of us would readily assent* will save many a sentence from coming down with a bump. By using stale metaphors, similes and idioms, you save much mental effort, at the cost of leaving your meaning vague, not only for your reader but for yourself. This is the significance of mixed metaphors. The sole aim of a metaphor is to call up a visual image. When these images clash—as in *The Fascist octopus has sung its swan song, the jackboot is thrown into the melting pot*—it can be taken as certain that the writer is not seeing a mental image of the objects he is naming; in other words he is not really thinking. Look again at the examples I gave at the beginning of this essay. Professor Laski (1) uses five negatives in fifty-three words. One of these is superfluous, making nonsense of the whole passage, and in addition there is the slip *alien* for akin, making further nonsense, and several avoidable pieces of clumsiness which increase the general vagueness. Professor Hogben (2) plays ducks and drakes with a battery which is able to write prescriptions, and, while disapproving of the everyday phrase *put up with*, is unwilling to look *egregious* up in the dictionary and see what it means. (3), if one takes an uncharitable attitude towards it, is simply meaningless: probably one could work out its intended meaning by reading the whole of the article in which it occurs. In (4), the writer knows more or less what he wants to say, but an accumulation of stale phrases chokes him like tea leaves blocking a sink. In (5), words and meaning have almost parted company. People who write in this manner usually have a general emotional meaning—they dislike one thing and want to express solidarity with another—but they are not interested in the detail of what they are saying. A scrupulous writer, in every sentence that he writes, will ask himself at least four questions, thus: What am I trying to say? What words will express it? What image or idiom will make it clearer? Is this image fresh enough to have an effect? And he will probably ask himself two more: Could I put it more shortly? Have I said anything that is avoidably ugly? But you are not obliged to go to all this trouble. You can shirk it by simply throwing your mind open and letting the ready-made phrases come crowding in. They will construct your sentences for you—even think your thoughts for you, to a certain extent—and at need they will perform the important service of partially concealing your meaning even from yourself. It is at this point that the special connection between politics and the debasement of language becomes clear.

In our time it is broadly true that political writing is bad writing. Where it is not true, it will generally be found that the writer is some kind of rebel, expressing his private opinions and not a "party line." Orthodoxy, of whatever colour, seems to demand a lifeless, imitative style. The political dialects to be found in pamphlets, leading articles, manifestos, White Papers and the speeches of under-secretaries do, of course, vary from party to party, but they are all alike in that one almost never finds in them a fresh, vivid, home-made turn of speech. When one watches some tired hack on the platform mechanically repeating the familiar phrases—*bestial atrocities, iron heel, bloodstained tyranny, free peoples of the world, stand shoulder to shoulder*—one often has a curious feeling that one is not watching a live human being but some kind of dummy: a feeling which suddenly becomes stronger at moments when the light catches the speaker's spectacles and turns them into blank discs which seem to have no eyes behind them. And this is not altogether fanciful. A speaker who uses that kind of phraseology has gone some distance towards turning himself into a machine. The appropriate noises are coming out of his larynx, but his brain is not involved as it would be if he were choosing his words for himself. If the speech he is making is one that he is accustomed to make over and over again, he may be almost unconscious of what he is saying, as one is when one utters the responses in church. And this reduced state of consciousness, if not indispensable, is at any rate favourable to political conformity.

In our time, political speech and writing are largely the defence of the indefensible. Things like the continuance of British rule in India, the Russian purges and deportations, the dropping of the atom bombs on Japan, can indeed be defended, but only by arguments which are too brutal for most people to face, and which do not square with the professed aims of political parties. Thus political language has to consist largely of euphemism, question-begging and sheer cloudy vagueness. Defenceless villages are bombarded from the air, the inhabitants driven out into the countryside, the cattle machine-gunned, the huts set on fire with incendiary bullets: this is called *pacification*. Millions of peasants are robbed of their farms and sent trudging along the roads with no more than they can carry: this is called *transfer of population* or *rectification of frontiers*. People are imprisoned for years without trial, or shot in the back of the neck or sent to die of scurvy in Arctic lumber camps: this is called *elimination of unreliable elements*. Such phraseology is needed if one wants to name things without calling up mental pictures of them. Consider for instance some comfortable English professor defending Russian totalitarianism. He cannot say outright, "I believe in killing off your opponents when you can get good results by doing so." Probably, therefore, he will say something like this:

"While freely conceding that the Soviet régime exhibits certain features which   15
the humanitarian may be inclined to deplore, we must, I think, agree that a certain curtailment of the right to political opposition is an unavoidable concomitant of transitional periods, and that the rigors which the Russian people have been called upon to undergo have been amply justified in the sphere of concrete achievement."

The inflated style is itself a kind of euphemism. A mass of Latin words falls   16
upon the facts like soft snow, blurring the outlines and covering up all the details. The great enemy of clear language is insincerity. When there is a gap between one's real and one's declared aims, one turns as it were instinctively to long words and exhausted idioms, like a cuttlefish squirting out ink. In our age there is no such thing as "keeping out of politics." All issues are political issues, and politics itself is a mass of lies, evasions, folly, hatred and schizophrenia. When the general atmosphere is bad, language must suffer. I should expect to find—this is a guess which I have not sufficient knowledge to verify— that the German, Russian and Italian languages have all deteriorated in the last ten or fifteen years, as a result of dictatorship.

But if thought corrupts language, language can also corrupt thought. A bad   17
usage can spread by tradition and imitation, even among people who should and do know better. The debased language that I have been discussing is in some ways very convenient. Phrases like *a not unjustifiable assumption, leaves much to be desired, would serve no good purpose, a consideration which we should do well to bear in mind,* are a continuous temptation, a packet of aspirins always at one's elbow. Look back through this essay, and for certain you will find that I have again and again committed the very faults I am protesting against. By this morning's post I have received a pamphlet dealing with conditions in Germany. The author tells me that he "felt impelled" to write it. I open it at random, and here is almost the first sentence that I see: "(The Allies) have an opportunity not only of achieving a radical transformation of Germany's social and political structure in such a way as to avoid a nationalistic reaction in Germany itself, but at the same time of laying the foundations of a cooperative and unified Europe." You see, he "feels impelled" to write—feels, presumably, that he has something new to say—and yet his words, like cavalry horses answering the bugle, group themselves automatically into the familiar dreary pattern. This invasion of one's mind by ready-made phrases (*lay the foundations, achieve a radical transformation*) can only be prevented if one is constantly on guard against them, and every such phrase anaesthetizes a portion of one's brain.

I said earlier that the decadence of our language is probably curable. Those   18
who deny this would argue, if they produced an argument at all, that language

merely reflects existing social conditions, and that we cannot influence its development by any direct tinkering with words and constructions. So far as the general tone or spirit of a language goes, this may be true, but it is not true in detail. Silly words and expressions have often disappeared, not through any evolutionary process but owing to the conscious action of a minority. Two recent examples were *explore every avenue* and *leave no stone unturned*, which were killed by the jeers of a few journalists. There is a long list of flyblown metaphors which could similarly be got rid of if enough people would interest themselves in the job; and it should also be possible to laugh the *not un-* formation out of existence,[3] to reduce the amount of Latin and Greek in the average sentence, to drive out foreign phrases and strayed scientific words, and, in general, to make pretentiousness unfashionable. But all these are minor points. The defence of the English language implies more than this, and perhaps it is best to start by saying what it does *not* imply.

To begin with it has nothing to do with archaism, with the salvaging of obsolete words and turns of speech, or with the setting up of a "standard English" which must never be departed from. On the contrary, it is especially concerned with the scrapping of every word or idiom which has outworn its usefulness. It has nothing to do with correct grammar and syntax, which are of no importance so long as one makes one's meaning clear, or with the avoidance of American-isms, or with having what is called a "good prose style." On the other hand it is not concerned with fake simplicity and the attempt to make written English colloquial. Nor does it even imply in every case preferring the Saxon word to the Latin one, though it does imply using the fewest and shortest words that will cover one's meaning. What is above all needed is to let the meaning choose the word, and not the other way about. In prose, the worst thing one can do with words is to surrender to them. When you think of a concrete object, you think wordlessly, and then, if you want to describe the thing you have been visualizing you probably hunt about till you find the exact words that seem to fit. When you think of something abstract you are more inclined to use words from the start, and unless you make a conscious effort to prevent it, the existing dialect will come rushing in and do the job for you, at the expense of blurring or even changing your meaning. Probably it is better to put off using words as long as possible and get one's meaning as clear as one can through pictures or sensations. Afterwards one can choose—not simply *accept*—the phrases that will best cover the meaning, and then switch round and decide what impression one's words are likely to make on another person. This last effort of the mind cuts out all stale or mixed images, all prefabricated phrases, needless repetitions, and humbug and vagueness generally. But one can often be in doubt about the

19

---

[3] One can cure oneself of the *not un-* formation by memorizing this sentence: *A not unblack dog was chasing a not unsmall rabbit across a not ungreen field.*

effect of a word or a phrase, and one needs rules that one can rely on when instinct fails. I think the following rules will cover most cases:

(i) Never use a metaphor, simile or other figure of speech which you are used to seeing in print.

(ii) Never use a long word where a short one will do.

(iii) If it is possible to cut a word out, always cut it out.

(iv) Never use the passive where you can use the active.

(v) Never use a foreign phrase, a scientific word or a jargon word if you can think of an everyday English equivalent.

(vi) Break any of these rules sooner than say anything outright barbarous.

These rules sound elementary, and so they are, but they demand a deep change of attitude in anyone who has grown used to writing in the style now fashionable. One could keep all of them and still write bad English, but one could not write the kind of stuff that I quoted in those five specimens at the beginning of this article.

I have not here been considering the literary use of language, but merely   20 language as an instrument for expressing and not for concealing or preventing thought. Stuart Chase and others have come near to claiming that all abstract words are meaningless, and have used this as a pretext for advocating a kind of political quietism. Since you don't know what Fascism is, how can you struggle against Fascism? One need not swallow such absurdities as this, but one ought to recognize that the present political chaos is connected with the decay of language, and that one can probably bring about some improvement by starting at the verbal end. If you simplify your English, you are freed from the worst follies of orthodoxy. You cannot speak any of the necessary dialects, and when you make a stupid remark its stupidity will be obvious, even to yourself. Political language—and with variations this is true of all political parties, from Conservatives to Anarchists—is designed to make lies sound truthful and murder respectable, and to give an appearance of solidity to pure wind. One cannot change this all in a moment, but one can at least change one's own habits, and from time to time one can even, if one jeers loudly enough, send some worn-out and useless phrase—some *jackboot, Achilles' heel, hotbed, melting pot, acid test, veritable inferno* or other lump of verbal refuse—into the dustbin where it belongs.

QUESTIONS

1. What is Orwell's position on the ways in which modern writers are destroying the English language?

2. Orwell argues that "thought corrupts language" but he also argues that "language

can also corrupt thought" (paragraph 17). What argument is he making? How does language corrupt thought?

3. Orwell writes in paragraph 17, "Look back through this essay, and for certain you will find that I have again and again committed the very faults I am protesting against." Does Orwell, in fact, break his own rules? If so, what might his purpose be in doing so?

4. What sense of himself does Orwell present to his readers? How would you describe his persona, his character?

5. Why do people write badly, according to Orwell? What causes does he identify in his essay? Do you agree with him?

6. Orwell presents guidelines for good writing in paragraph 18. Take one of your recent essays and analyze how your writing measures up to Orwell's standards.

7. Spend one week developing a list of examples of bad writing from newspapers or popular magazines. Use this material as the basis for an essay in which you develop a thesis to argue your position on politics and language.

8. Written more than forty years ago, this is probably the best known of all Orwell's essays. How insightful and current do you find it today? Take five examples from your reading, as Orwell takes from his, and use them as evidence in an argument of your own about the state of contemporary written English. Take your examples from anything you like, including this book—even this question—if you wish. Be careful to choose recent pieces of writing.

MAKING CONNECTIONS

1. Read Orwell's essay, "Shooting an Elephant," in "Reflecting." What do you learn about Orwell, the essayist, from reading these two essays?

2. John Berger and James Baldwin, as represented by their essays in this section, are likely to be two writers influenced by this essay of Orwell's. Choose the essay you responded to more strongly of those two, and write an essay of your own explaining the connections that you find between either Berger or Baldwin and Orwell.

THE HISTORIAN
AND HIS FACTS

Edward Hallet Carr

E. H. Carr (1892–1982) was a distinguished British historian whose major work was The History of Soviet Russia, *in fourteen volumes. A fellow of Trinity College, Cambridge, Carr delivered a series of lectures there in 1961 under the general title of "What Is History?" The lectures were later published in a book, which opened with the selection reprinted here. It is addressed to the general question—What is history?—in terms of a more specific question: What is a historical fact? Like Barbara Tuchman's "When Does History Happen?" Carr's essay addresses the practice of history. He warns against a "fetishism of facts," and urges that more attention be given to the way that the historian processes the facts.*

What is history? Lest anyone think the question meaningless or superfluous, I will take as my text two passages relating respectively to the first and second incarnations of *The Cambridge Modern History*. Here is Acton in his report of October 1896 to the Syndics of the Cambridge University Press on the work which he had undertaken to edit.[1]

> It is a unique opportunity of recording, in the way most useful to the greatest number, the fullness of the knowledge which the nineteenth century is about to bequeath. . . . By the judicious division of labour we should be able to do it, and to bring home to every man the last document, and the ripest conclusions of international research.
>
> Ultimate history we cannot have in this generation; but we can dispose of conventional history, and show the point we have reached on the road from one to the other, now that all information is within reach, and every problem has become capable of solution.[2]

And almost exactly sixty years later Professor Sir George Clark, in his general introduction to the second *Cambridge Modern History*, commented on this

---

[1] John Dalberg Acton (1834–1902): British historian and editor of the first *Cambridge Modern History*. [Eds.]

[2] *The Cambridge Modern History: Its Origin, Authorship and Production* (Cambridge University Press; 1907), pp. 10–12.

belief of Acton and his collaborators that it would one day be possible to produce "ultimate history," and went on:

> Historians of a later generation do not look forward to any such prospect. They expect their work to be superseded again and again. They consider that knowledge of the past has come down through one or more human minds, has been "processed" by them, and therefore cannot consist of elemental and impersonal atoms which nothing can alter. . . . The exploration seems to be endless, and some impatient scholars take refuge in scepticism, or at least in the doctrine that, since all historical judgments involve persons and points of view, one is as good as another and there is no "objective" historical truth.[3]

Where the pundits contradict each other so flagrantly the field is open to enquiry. I hope that I am sufficiently up-to-date to recognize that anything written in the 1890's must be nonsense. But I am not yet advanced enough to be committed to the view that anything written in the 1950's necessarily makes sense. Indeed, it may already have occurred to you that this enquiry is liable to stray into something even broader than the nature of history. The clash between Acton and Sir George Clark is a reflection of the change in our total outlook on society over the interval between these two pronouncements. Acton speaks out of the positive belief, the clear-eyed self-confidence of the later Victorian age; Sir George Clark echoes the bewilderment and distracted scepticism of the beat generation. When we attempt to answer the question, What is history?, our answer, consciously or unconsciously, reflects our own position in time, and forms part of our answer to the broader question, what view we take of the society in which we live. I have no fear that my subject may, on closer inspection, seem trivial. I am afraid only that I may seem presumptuous to have broached a question so vast and so important.

The nineteenth century was a great age for facts. "What I want," said Mr. Gradgrind in *Hard Times*,[4] "is Facts. . . . Facts alone are wanted in life." Nineteenth-century historians on the whole agreed with him. When Ranke in the 1830's,[5] in legitimate protest against moralizing history, remarked that the task of the historian was "simply to show how it really was (*wie es eigentlich gewesen*)" this not very profound aphorism had an astonishing success. Three generations of German, British, and even French historians marched into battle intoning the magic words, "*Wie es eigentlich gewesen*" like an incantation— designed, like most incantations, to save them from the tiresome obligation to think for themselves. The Positivists, anxious to stake out their claim for history as a science, contributed the weight of their influence to this cult of facts. First ascertain the facts, said the positivists, then draw your conclusions from them.

[3] *The New Cambridge Modern History*, I (Cambridge University Press; 1957), pp. xxiv–xxv.
[4] *Hard Times*: a novel by Charles Dickens. [Eds.]
[5] Leopold von Ranke (1795–1886): German historian. [Eds.]

In Great Britain, this view of history fitted in perfectly with the empiricist tradition which was the dominant strain in British philosophy from Locke to Bertrand Russell.[6] The empirical theory of knowledge presupposes a complete separation between subject and object. Facts, like sense-impressions, impinge on the observer from outside, and are independent of his consciousness. The process of reception is passive: having received the data, he then acts on them. *The Shorter Oxford English Dictionary*, a useful but tendentious work of the empirical school, clearly marks the separateness of the two processes by defining a fact as "a datum of experience as distinct from conclusions." This is what may be called the common-sense view of history. History consists of a corpus of ascertained facts. The facts are available to the historian in documents, inscriptions, and so on, like fish on the fishmonger's slab. The historian collects them, takes them home, and cooks and serves them in whatever style appeals to him. Acton, whose culinary tastes were austere, wanted them served plain. In his letter of instructions to contributors to the first *Cambridge Modern History* he announced the requirement "that our Waterloo must be one that satisfies French and English, German and Dutch alike; that nobody can tell, without examining the list of authors where the Bishop of Oxford laid down the pen, and whether Fairbairn or Gasquet, Liebermann or Harrison took it up."[7] Even Sir George Clark, critical as he was of Acton's attitude, himself contrasted the "hard core of facts" in history with the "surrounding pulp of disputable interpretation"[8]— forgetting perhaps that the pulpy part of the fruit is more rewarding than the hard core. First get your facts straight, then plunge at your peril into the shifting sands of interpretation—that is the ultimate wisdom of the empirical, common-sense school of history. It recalls the favorite dictum of the great liberal journalist C. P. Scott: "Facts are sacred, opinion is free."

Now this clearly will not do. I shall not embark on a philosophical discussion of the nature of our knowledge of the past. Let us assume for present purposes that the fact that Caesar crossed the Rubicon and the fact that there is a table in the middle of the room are facts of the same or of a comparable order, that both these facts enter our consciousness in the same or in a comparable manner, and that both have the same objective character in relation to the person who knows them. But, even on this bold and not very plausible assumption, our argument at once runs into the difficulty that not all facts about the past are historical facts, or are treated as such by the historian. What is the criterion which distinguishes the facts of history from other facts about the past?

What is a historical fact? This is a crucial question into which we must look a little more closely. According to the common-sense view, there are certain basic facts which are the same for all historians and which form, so to speak,

---

[6]John Locke (1632–1704): English philosopher; Bertrand Russell (1872–1970): English philosopher and mathematician. [Eds.]

[7]Acton: *Lectures on Modern History* (London: Macmillan & Co.; 1906), p. 318.

[8]Quoted in *The Listener* (June 19, 1952), p. 992.

the backbone of history—the fact, for example, that the Battle of Hastings was fought in 1066. But this view calls for two observations. In the first place, it is not with facts like these that the historian is primarily concerned. It is no doubt important to know that the great battle was fought in 1066 and not in 1065 or 1067, and that it was fought at Hastings and not at Eastbourne or Brighton. The historian must not get these things wrong. But when points of this kind are raised, I am reminded of Housman's remark that "accuracy is a duty, not a virtue."[9] To praise a historian for his accuracy is like praising an architect for using well-seasoned timber or properly mixed concrete in his building. It is a necessary condition of his work, but not his essential function. It is precisely for matters of this kind that the historian is entitled to rely on what have been called the "auxiliary sciences" of history—archaeology, epigraphy, numismatics, chronology, and so forth. The historian is not required to have the special skills which enable the expert to determine the origin and period of a fragment of pottery or marble, to decipher an obscure inscription, or to make the elaborate astronomical calculations necessary to establish a precise date. These so-called basic facts which are the same for all historians commonly belong to the category of the raw materials of the historian rather than of history itself. The second observation is that the necessity to establish these basic facts rests not on any quality in the facts themselves, but on an *a priori* decision of the historian. In spite of C. P. Scott's motto, every journalist knows today that the most effective way to influence opinion is by the selection and arrangement of the appropriate facts. It used to be said that facts speak for themselves. This is, of course, untrue. The facts speak only when the historian calls on them: it is he who decides to which facts to give the floor, and in what order or context. It was, I think, one of Pirandello's characters who said that a fact is like a sack[10]—it won't stand up till you've put something in it. The only reason why we are interested to know that the battle was fought at Hastings in 1066 is that historians regard it as a major historical event. It is the historian who has decided for his own reasons that Caesar's crossing of that petty stream, the Rubicon, is a fact of history, whereas the crossing of the Rubicon by millions of other people before or since interests nobody at all. The fact that you arrived in this building half an hour ago on foot, or on a bicycle, or in a car, is just as much a fact about the past as the fact that Caesar crossed the Rubicon. But it will probably be ignored by historians. Professor Talcott Parsons once called science "a selective system of cognitive orientations to reality."[11] It might perhaps have been put more simply. But history is, among other things, that. The historian is necessarily selective. The belief in a hard core of historical facts existing objec-

---

[9] M. Manilius: *Astronomicon: Liber Primus*, 2nd ed. (Cambridge University Press; 1937), p. 87. (A. E. Housman [1859–1936]: poet and classical scholar who edited Manilius. [Eds.])

[10] Luigi Pirandello (1867–1936): Italian playwright. [Eds.]

[11] Talcott Parsons and Edward A. Shils: *Toward a General Theory of Action*, 3rd ed. (Cambridge, Mass.: Harvard University Press; 1954), p. 167.

tively and independently of the interpretation of the historian is a preposterous fallacy, but one which it is very hard to eradicate.

Let us take a look at the process by which a mere fact about the past is transformed into a fact of history. At Stalybridge Wakes in 1850, a vendor of gingerbread, as the result of some petty dispute, was deliberately kicked to death by an angry mob. Is this a fact of history? A year ago I should unhesitatingly have said "no." It was recorded by an eyewitness in some little-known memoirs;[12] but I had never seen it judged worthy of mention by any historian. A year ago Dr. Kitson Clark cited it in his Ford lectures in Oxford.[13] Does this make it into a historical fact? Not, I think, yet. Its present status, I suggest, is that it has been proposed for membership of the select club of historical facts. It now awaits a seconder and sponsors. It may be that in the course of the next few years we shall see this fact appearing first in footnotes, then in the text, of articles and books about nineteenth-century England, and that in twenty or thirty years' time it may be a well established historical fact. Alternatively, nobody may take it up, in which case it will relapse into the limbo of unhistorical facts about the past from which Dr. Kitson Clark has gallantly attempted to rescue it. What will decide which of these two things will happen? It will depend, I think, on whether the thesis or interpretation in support of which Dr. Kitson Clark cited this incident is accepted by other historians as valid and significant. Its status as a historical fact will turn on a question of interpretation. This element of interpretation enters into every fact of history.

May I be allowed a personal reminiscence? When I studied ancient history in this university many years ago, I had as a special subject "Greece in the period of the Persian Wars." I collected fifteen or twenty volumes on my shelves and took it for granted that there, recorded in these volumes, I had all the facts relating to my subject. Let us assume—it was very nearly true—that those volumes contained all the facts about it that were then known, or could be known. It never occurred to me to enquire by what accident or process of attrition that minute selection of facts, out of all the myriad facts that must have once been known to somebody, had survived to become *the* facts of history. I suspect that even today one of the fascinations of ancient and mediaeval history is that it gives us the illusion of having all the facts at our disposal within a manageable compass: the nagging distinction between the facts of history and other facts about the past vanishes because the few known facts are all facts of history. As Bury, who had worked in both periods, said, "the records of ancient and mediaeval history are starred with lacunae."[14] History has been called an enormous jig-saw with a lot of missing parts. But the main trouble does not

---

[12] Lord George Sanger: *Seventy Years a Showman* (London: J. M. Dent & Sons; 1962); pp. 188–9.

[13] These will shortly be published under the title *The Making of Victorian England*.

[14] John Bagnell Bury: *Selected Essays* (Cambridge University Press; 1930), p. 52. (lacunae: empty spaces or gaps. [Eds.]

consist of the lacunae. Our picture of Greece in the fifth century B.C. is defective not primarily because so many of the bits have been accidentally lost, but because it is, by and large, the picture formed by a tiny group of people in the city of Athens. We know a lot about what fifth-century Greece looked like to an Athenian citizen; but hardly anything about what it looked like to a Spartan, a Corinthian, or a Theban—not to mention a Persian, or a slave or other noncitizen resident in Athens. Our picture has been pre-selected and predetermined for us, not so much by accident as by people who were consciously or unconsciously imbued with a particular view and thought the facts which supported that view worth preserving. In the same way, when I read in a modern history of the Middle Ages that the people of the Middle Ages were deeply concerned with religion, I wonder how we know this, and whether it is true. What we know as the facts of mediaeval history have almost all been selected for us by generations of chroniclers who were professionally occupied in the theory and practice of religion, and who therefore thought it supremely important, and recorded everything relating to it, and not much else. The picture of the Russian peasant as devoutly religious was destroyed by the revolution of 1917. The picture of mediaeval man as devoutly religious, whether true or not, is indestructible, because nearly all the known facts about him were pre-selected for us by people who believed it, and wanted others to believe it, and a mass of other facts, in which we might possibly have found evidence to the contrary, has been lost beyond recall. The dead hand of vanished generations of historians, scribes, and chroniclers has determined beyond the possibility of appeal the pattern of the past. "The history we read," writes Professor Barraclough, himself trained as a mediaevalist, "though based on facts, is, strictly speaking, not factual at all, but a series of accepted judgments."[15]

But let us turn to the different, but equally grave, plight of the modern historian. The ancient or mediaeval historian may be grateful for the vast winnowing process which, over the years, has put at his disposal a manageable corpus of historical facts. As Lytton Strachey said in his mischievous way, "ignorance is the first requisite of the historian, ignorance which simplifies and clarifies, which selects and omits."[16] When I am tempted, as I sometimes am, to envy the extreme competence of colleagues engaged in writing ancient or mediaeval history, I find consolation in the reflexion that they are so competent mainly because they are so ignorant of their subject. The modern historian enjoys none of the advantages of this built-in ignorance. He must cultivate this necessary ignorance for himself—the more so the nearer he comes to his own times. He has the dual task of discovering the few significant facts and turning them into facts of history, and of discarding the many insignificant facts as

---

[15] Geoffrey Barraclough: *History in a Changing World* (London: Basil Blackwell & Mott; 1955), p. 14.

[16] Lytton Strachey: Preface to *Eminent Victorians*.

unhistorical. But this is the very converse of the nineteenth-century heresy that history consists of the compilation of a maximum number of irrefutable and objective facts. Anyone who succumbs to this heresy will either have to give up history as a bad job, and take to stamp-collecting or some other form of antiquarianism, or end in a madhouse. It is this heresy, which during the past hundred years has had such devastating effects on the modern historian, producing in Germany, in Great Britain, and in the United States a vast and growing mass of dry-as-dust factual histories, of minutely specialized monographs, of would-be historians knowing more and more about less and less, sunk without trace in an ocean of facts. It was, I suspect, this heresy—rather than the alleged conflict between liberal and Catholic loyalties—which frustrated Acton as a historian. In an early essay he said of his teacher Döllinger: "He would not write with imperfect materials, and to him the materials were always imperfect."[17] Acton was surely here pronouncing an anticipatory verdict on himself, on the strange phenomenon of a historian whom many would regard as the most distinguished occupant the Regius Chair of Modern History in this university has ever had—but who wrote no history. And Acton wrote his own epitaph in the introductory note to the first volume of *The Cambridge Modern History*, published just after his death, when he lamented that the requirements pressing on the historian "threaten to turn him from a man of letters into the compiler of an encyclopedia."[18] Something had gone wrong. What had gone wrong was the belief in this untiring and unending accumulation of hard facts as the foundation of history, the belief that facts speak for themselves and that we cannot have too many facts, a belief at that time so unquestioning that few historians then thought it necessary—and some still think it unnecessary today—to ask themselves the question: What is history?

The nineteenth-century fetishism of facts was completed and justified by a fetishism of documents. The documents were the Ark of the Covenant in the temple of facts. The reverent historian approached them with bowed head and spoke of them in awed tones. If you find it in the documents, it is so. But what, when we get down to it, do these documents—the decrees, the treaties, the rent-rolls, the blue books, the official correspondence, the private letters and diaries—tell us? No document can tell us more than what the author of the document thought—what he thought had happened, what he thought ought to happen or would happen, or perhaps only what he wanted others to think he thought, or even only what he himself thought he thought. None of this means anything until the historian has got to work on it and deciphered it. The facts, whether found in documents or not, have still to be processed by the historian

8

---

[17] Quoted in George P. Gooch: *History and Historians in the Nineteenth Century* (London: Longmans, Green & Company; 1952), p. 385. Later Acton said of Döllinger that "it was given him to form his philosophy of history on the largest induction ever available to man" (*History of Freedom and Other Essays* [London: Macmillan & Co.; 1907], p. 435).

[18] *The Cambridge Modern History*, I (1902), p. 4.

before he can make any use of them: the use he makes of them is, if I may put it that way, the processing process.

Let me illustrate what I am trying to say by an example which I happen to know well. When Gustav Stresemann, the Foreign Minister of the Weimar Republic,[19] died in 1929, he left behind him an enormous mass—300 boxes full—of papers, official, semi-official, and private, nearly all relating to the six years of his tenure of office as Foreign Minister. His friends and relatives naturally thought that a monument should be raised to the memory of so great a man. His faithful secretary Bernhardt got to work; and within three years there appeared three massive volumes, of some 600 pages each, of selected documents from the 300 boxes, with the impressive title *Stresemanns Vermächtnis*.[20] In the ordinary way the documents themselves would have mouldered away in some cellar or attic and disappeared for ever; or perhaps in a hundred years or so some curious scholar would have come upon them and set out to compare them with Bernhardt's text. What happened was far more dramatic. In 1945 the documents fell into the hands of the British and the American governments, who photographed the lot and put the photostats at the disposal of scholars in the Public Record Office in London and in the National Archives in Washington, so that, if we have sufficient patience and curiosity, we can discover exactly what Bernhardt did. What he did was neither very unusual nor very shocking. When Stresemann died, his Western policy seemed to have been crowned with a series of brilliant successes—Locarno, the admission of Germany to the League of Nations, the Dawes and Young plans and the American loans, the withdrawal of allied occupation armies from the Rhineland. This seemed the important and rewarding part of Stresemann's foreign policy; and it was not unnatural that it should have been over-represented in Bernhardt's selection of documents. Stresemann's Eastern policy, on the other hand, his relations with the Soviet Union, seemed to have led nowhere in particular; and, since masses of documents about negotiations which yielded only trivial results were not very interesting and added nothing to Stresemann's reputation, the process of selection could be more rigorous. Stresemann in fact devoted a far more constant and anxious attention to relations with the Soviet Union, and they played a far larger part in his foreign policy as a whole, than the reader of the Bernhardt selection would surmise. But the Bernhardt volumes compare favorably, I suspect, with many published collections of documents on which the ordinary historian implicitly relies.

This is not the end of my story. Shortly after the publication of Bernhardt's volumes, Hitler came into power. Stresemann's name was consigned to oblivion in Germany, and the volumes disappeared from circulation: many, perhaps

---

[19] Weimar Republic: the government of Germany, established in the city of Weimar after World War I (1919) and lasting until Adolf Hitler rose to power in 1933. [Eds.]

[20] *Stresemanns Vermächtnis*: this title may be translated as "Stresemann's Legacy." [Eds.]

most, of the copies must have been destroyed. Today *Stresemanns Vermächtnis* is a rather rare book. But in the West Stresemann's reputation stood high. In 1935 an English publisher brought out an abbreviated translation of Bernhardt's work—a selection from Bernhardt's selection; perhaps one third of the original was omitted. Sutton, a well-known translator from the German, did his job competently and well. The English version, he explained in the preface, was "slightly condensed, but only by the omission of a certain amount of what, it was felt, was more ephemeral matter . . . of little interest to English readers or students."[21] This again is natural enough. But the result is that Stresemann's Eastern policy, already under-represented in Bernhardt, recedes still further from view, and the Soviet Union appears in Sutton's volumes merely as an occasional and rather unwelcome intruder in Stresemann's predominantly Western foreign policy. Yet it is safe to say that, for all except a few specialists, Sutton and not Bernhardt—and still less the documents themselves—represents for the Western world the authentic voice of Stresemann. Had the documents perished in 1945 in the bombing, and had the remaining Bernhardt volumes disappeared, the authenticity and authority of Sutton would never have been questioned. Many printed collections of documents gratefully accepted by historians in default of the originals rest on no securer basis than this.

But I want to carry the story one step further. Let us forget about Bernhardt and Sutton, and be thankful that we can, if we choose, consult the authentic papers of a leading participant in some important events of recent European history. What do the papers tell us? Among other things they contain records of some hundreds of Stresemann's conversations with the Soviet ambassador in Berlin and of a score or so with Chicherin.[22] These records have one feature in common. They depict Stresemann as having the lion's share of the conversations and reveal his arguments as invariably well put and cogent, while those of his partner are for the most part scanty, confused, and unconvincing. This is a familiar characteristic of all records of diplomatic conversations. The documents do not tell us what happened, but only what Stresemann thought had happened, or what he wanted others to think, or perhaps what he wanted himself to think, had happened. It was not Sutton or Bernhardt, but Stresemann himself, who started the process of selection. And, if we had, say, Chicherin's records of these same conversations, we should still learn from them only what Chicherin thought, and what really happened would still have to be reconstructed in the mind of the historian. Of course, facts and documents are essential to the historian. But do not make a fetish of them. They do not by themselves constitute history; they provide in themselves no ready-made answer to this tiresome question: What is history?

---

[21] *Gustav Stresemann: His Diaries, Letters, and Papers* (London: Macmillan & Co.; 1935), I, Editor's Note.

[22] Grigory Chicherin (1872–1936): a powerful Russian diplomat. [Eds.]

At this point I should like to say a few words on the question of why [12] nineteenth-century historians were generally indifferent to the philosophy of history. The term was invented by Voltaire,[23] and has since been used in different senses; but I shall take it to mean, if I use it at all, our answer to the question: What is history? The nineteenth century was, for the intellectuals of Western Europe, a comfortable period exuding confidence and optimism. The facts were on the whole satisfactory; and the inclination to ask and answer awkward questions about them was correspondingly weak. Ranke piously believed that divine providence would take care of the meaning of history if he took care of the facts; and Burckhardt with a more modern touch of cynicism observed that "we are not initiated into the purposes of the eternal wisdom." Professor Butterfield as late as 1931 noted with apparent satisfaction that "historians have reflected little upon the nature of things and even the nature of their own subject."[24] But my predecessor in these lectures, Dr. A. L. Rowse, more justly critical, wrote of Sir Winston Churchill's *The World Crisis*—his book about the First World War—that, while it matched Trotsky's *History of the Russian Revolution* in personality, vividness, and vitality, it was inferior in one respect: it had "no philosophy of history behind it."[25] British historians refused to be drawn, not because they believed that history had no meaning, but because they believed that its meaning was implicit and self-evident. The liberal nineteenth-century view of history had a close affinity with the economic doctrine of *laissez-faire*—also the product of a serene and self-confident outlook on the world. Let everyone get on with his particular job, and the hidden hand would take care of the universal harmony. The facts of history were themselves a demonstration of the supreme fact of a beneficent and apparently infinite progress towards higher things. This was the age of innocence, and historians walked in the Garden of Eden, without a scrap of philosophy to cover them, naked and unashamed before the god of history. Since then, we have known Sin and experienced a Fall; and those historians who today pretend to dispense with a philosophy of history are merely trying, vainly and self-consciously, like members of a nudist colony, to recreate the Garden of Eden in their garden suburb. Today the awkward question can no longer be evaded.

QUESTIONS

1. Carr's essay answers the question, "What is a historical fact?" Summarize his answer to that question.
2. In paragraph 7, Carr says the historian must "cultivate . . . ignorance." What

---

[23] Voltaire (1694–1778): French dramatist, philosopher, and social critic. [Eds.]
[24] Herbert Butterfield: *The Whig Interpretation of History* (London: George Bell & Sons; 1931), p. 67.
[25] Alfred L. Rowse: *The End of an Epoch* (London: Macmillan & Co.; 1947), pp. 282–3.

does this expression mean in its context? What is the point of the discussion of Acton and Döllinger in that paragraph? How does this discussion contribute to the larger theme of the essay?

3. In presenting an argument, especially a controversial one, a writer must often seek to gain the confidence of the reader. How does Carr go about this? What sort of picture does he present of himself? What impression of him do you get from his references to himself in paragraphs 1 and 6, and how does that impression affect your evaluation of his position?

4. Carr's essay is an argumentative essay on interpretation. Locate the many uses of the words *interpret* or *interpretation* in the essay, and consider how they function in the larger discussion. What view of the relationship between facts and interpretation is presented here?

5. Carr's essay contradicts previously existing explanations of the relationship between historians and the facts they must deal with in writing history. Where does Carr summarize the opposing position? State in your own words the views of historical facts with which Carr takes issue.

6. Consider several facts generally known to you and your class. Limit your attention to recent facts, specifically from the last year. (You might first discuss in class what sorts of facts merit your attention.) Which of those facts has the best chance of becoming "a historical fact," in Carr's terms? On what does that process depend? Write an explanation of the historicity of a fact you choose, trying to convince your classmates that your fact will become a historical fact.

7. Using an accepted historical fact not mentioned by Carr, write an essay in which you argue why your chosen fact is a historical fact and what grounds we have for understanding it and accepting it as a fact.

MAKING CONNECTIONS

How does John Berger's essay "Hiroshima" comment on the use of facts? How might Carr comment on Berger's interpretation of history?

WHEN DOES HISTORY HAPPEN?

Barbara Tuchman

Like E. H. Carr, Barbara Tuchman is concerned with the role of facts. According to Tuchman, "the historian's task is . . . to tell what happened within the discipline of facts." The following essay comes from her collection, Practicing History: Selected Essays *(1981); in this particular selection, Tuchman offers a lucid argument for her attitudes toward history and historical research. For further biographical information on Tuchman, see the headnote on page 177.*

Within three months of the Conservative party crisis in Britain last October [1963] a book by Randolph Churchill on the day-to-day history of the affair had been written and published. To rush in upon an event before its significance has had time to separate from the surrounding circumstances may be enterprising, but is it useful? An embarrassed author may find, when the excitement has died down, that his subject had little significance at all. The recent prevalence of these hot histories on publishers' lists raises the question: Should—or perhaps can—history be written while it is still smoking? 1

Before taking that further, one must first answer the question: What is history? Professional historians have been exercising themselves vehemently over this query for some time. A distinguished exponent, E. H. Carr of Cambridge University, made it the subject of his Trevelyan Lectures and the title of a book in 1962. 2

Is history, he asked, the examination of past events or is it the past events themselves? By good luck I did not read the book until after I had finished an effort of my own at historical narrative, otherwise I should have never dared to begin. In my innocence I had not been aware that the question posed by Mr. Carr had ever come up. I had simply assumed that history was past events existing independently, whether we examined them or not. 3

I had thought that we who comment on the past were extraneous to it; helpful, perhaps, to its understanding but not integral to its existence. I had supposed that the Greeks' defeat of the Persians would have given the same direction to Western history whether Herodotus chronicled it or not. But that is not Mr. Carr's position. "The belief in a hard core of historical facts existing independently of the interpretation of the historian," he says, "is a preposterous fallacy but one that is very hard to eradicate." 4

On first reading, this seemed to me to be preposterous nonsense. Was it 5 some sort of recondite joke? But a thinker of such eminence must be taken seriously, and after prolonged silent arguments with Mr. Carr of which he remained happily unaware, I began to see what he was driving at. What he means, I suppose, is that past events cannot exist independently of the historian because without the historian we would know nothing about them; in short, that the unrecorded past is none other than our old friend, the tree in the primeval forest which fell where there was no one to hear the sound of the crash. If there was no ear, was there a sound?

I refuse to be frightened by that conundrum because it asks the wrong question. The point is not whether the fall of the tree made a noise but whether it left a mark on the forest. If it left a space that let in the sun on a hitherto shade-grown species, or if it killed a dominant animal and shifted rule of the pack to one of different characteristics, or if it fell across a path of animals and caused some small change in their habitual course from which larger changes followed, then the fall made history whether anyone heard it or not. 6

I therefore declare myself a firm believer in the "preposterous fallacy" of historical facts existing independently of the historian. I think that if Domesday Book and all other records of the time had been burned, the transfer of land ownership from the Saxons to the Normans would be no less a fact of British history. Of course Domesday Book was a record, not an interpretation, and what Mr. Carr says is that historical facts do not exist independently of the *interpretation* of historians. I find this untenable. He might just as well say the Grecian Urn would not exist without Keats. 7

As I see it, evidence is more important than interpretation, and facts are history whether interpreted or not. I think the influence of the receding frontier on American expansion was a phenomenon independent of Frederick Jackson Turner, who noticed it, and the role of the leisure class independent of Thorstein Veblen, and the influence of sea power upon history independent of Admiral Mahan. In the last case lurks a possible argument for the opposition, because Admiral Mahan's book *The Influence of Sea Power upon History* so galvanized the naval policy of Imperial Germany and Great Britain in the years before 1914 that in isolating and describing a great historical fact he himself made history. Mr. Carr might make something of that. 8

Meanwhile I think his main theme unnecessarily metaphysical. I am content to define history as the past events of which we have knowledge and refrain from worrying about those of which we have none—until, that is, some archeologist digs them up. 9

I come next to historians. Who are they: contemporaries of the event or those who come after? The answer is obviously both. Among contemporaries, first and indispensable are the more-or-less unconscious sources: letters, diaries, memoirs, autobiographies, newspapers and periodicals, business and government documents. These are historical raw material, not history. Their authors 10 may be writing with one eye or possibly both on posterity, but that does not make them historians. To perform that function requires a view from the outside and a conscious craft.

At a slightly different level are the I-was-there recorders, usually journalists, 11 whose accounts often contain golden nuggets of information buried in a mass of daily travelogue which the passage of time has reduced to trivia. Some of the most vivid details that went into my book *The Guns of August* came from the working press: the rag doll crushed under the wheel of a German gun carriage from Irvin Cobb, the smell of half a million unwashed bodies that hung over the invaded villages of Belgium from Will Irwin, the incident of Colonel Max Hoffmann yelling insults at the Japanese general from Frederick Palmer, who reported the Russo-Japanese War. Daily journalism, however, even when collected in book form, is, like letters and the rest, essentially source material rather than history.

Still contemporary but dispensable are the Compilers who hurriedly assemble 12 a book from clippings and interviews in order to capitalize on public interest when it is high. A favorite form of these hasty puddings is the overnight biography, like *The Lyndon Johnson Story*, which was in the bookstores within a few weeks of the incident that gave rise to it. The Compilers, in their treatment, supply no extra understanding and as historians are negligible.

All these varieties being disposed of, there remains a pure vein of conscious 13 historians of whom, among contemporaries, there are two kinds. First, the Onlookers, who deliberately set out to chronicle an episode of their own age— a war or depression or strike or social revolution or whatever it may be—and shape it into a historical narrative with character and validity of its own. Thucydides' *Peloponnesian War*, on a major scale, and Theodore White's *The Making of a President*, undertaken in the same spirit though on a tiny scale in comparison, are examples.

Second are the Active Participants or Axe-Grinders, who attempt a genuine 14 history of events they have known, but whose accounts are inevitably weighted, sometimes subtly and imperceptibly, sometimes crudely, by the requirements of the role in which they wish themselves to appear. Josephus' *The Jewish War*, the Earl of Clarendon's *History of the Rebellion*, and Winston Churchill's *World Crisis* and *Second World War* are classics of this category.

For the latter-day historian, these too become source material. Are we now 15 in possession of history when we have these accounts in hand? Yes, in the sense that we are in possession of wine when the first pressing of the grapes is in hand. But it has not fermented, and it has not aged. The great advantage of the latter-day historian is the distance conferred by the passage of time. At a distance from the events he describes and with a wider area of vision, he can see more of what was going on at the time and distinguish what was significant from what was not.

The contemporary has no perspective; everything is in the foreground and appears the same size. Little matters loom big, and great matters are sometimes missed because their outlines cannot be seen. Vietnam and Panama are given four-column headlines today, but the historian fifty or a hundred years hence will put them in a chapter under a general heading we have not yet thought of. [16]

The contemporary, especially if he is a participant, is inside his events, which is not an entirely unmixed advantage. What he gains in intimacy through personal acquaintance—which we can never achieve—he sacrifices in detachment. He cannot see or judge fairly both sides in a quarrel, for example the quarrel as to who deserves chief credit for the French victory at the Battle of the Marne in 1914. All contemporary chroniclers were extreme partisans of either Joffre or Gallieni. So violent was the partisanship that no one (except President Poincaré) noticed what is so clearly visible when viewed from a distance, that both generals had played an essential role. Gallieni saw the opportunity and gave the impetus; Joffre brought the Army and the reinforcements into place to fight, but it took fifty years before this simple and just apportionment could be made. [17]

Distance does not always confer objectivity; one can hardly say Gibbon wrote objectively of the Roman Empire or Carlyle of the French Revolution. Objectivity is a question of degree. It is possible for the latter-day historian to be at least *relatively* objective, which is not the same thing as being neutral or taking no sides. There is no such thing as a neutral or purely objective historian. Without an opinion a historian would be simply a ticking clock, and unreadable besides. [18]

Nevertheless, distance does confer a kind of removal that cools the judgment and permits a juster appraisal than is possible to a contemporary. Once long ago as a freshman journalist I covered a campaign swing by Franklin D. Roosevelt during which he was scheduled to make a major speech at Pittsburgh or Harrisburg, I forget which. As we were leaving the train, one of the newspapermen remained comfortably behind in the club car with his feet up, explaining that as a New Dealer writing for a Republican paper he had to remain "objective" and he could "be a lot more objective right here than within ten feet of that fellow." He was using distance in space if not in time to acquire objectivity. [19]

I found out from personal experience that I could not write contemporary history if I tried. Some people can, William Shirer, for one; they are not affected by involvement. But I am, as I discovered when working on my first book, *Bible and Sword*. It dealt with the historical relations between Britain and Palestine from the time of the Phoenicians to the present. Originally I had intended to bring the story down through the years of the British Mandate to the Arab-Israeli War and the re-establishment of the state of Israel in 1948. [20]

I spent six months of research on the bitter history of those last thirty years: 21
the Arab assaults and uprisings, the Round Tables, the White Papers, the cutting
off of Jewish immigration, the Commissions of Inquiry, the ultimate historical
irony when the British, who had issued the Balfour Declaration, rammed the
ship *Exodus*, the whole ignominious tale of one or more chapters of appease-
ment.

When I tried to write this as history, I could not do it. Anger, disgust, and 22
a sense of injustice can make some writers eloquent and evoke brilliant polemic,
but these emotions stunted and twisted my pen. I found the tone of my
concluding chapter totally different from the seventeen chapters that went
before. I had suddenly walked over the line into contemporary history; I had
become involved, and it showed. Although the publisher wanted the narrative
brought up to date, I knew my final chapter as written would destroy the
credibility of all the preceding, and I could not change it. I tore it up, discarded
six months' work, and brought the book to a close in 1918.

I am not saying that emotion should have no place in history. On the 23
contrary, I think it is an essential element of history, as it is of poetry, whose
origin Wordsworth defined as "emotion recollected in tranquillity." History, one
might say, is emotion plus action recollected or, in the case of latter-day
historians, reflected on in tranquillity after a close and honest examination of
the records. The primary duty of the historian is to stay within the evidence.
Yet it is a curious fact that poets, limited by no such rule, have done very well
with history, both of their own times and of times long gone before.

Tennyson wrote the "Charge of the Light Brigade" within three months of 24
the event at Balaclava in the Crimea. "Cannon in front of them volleyed and
thundered . . . Flashed all their sabres bare . . . Plunged in the battery-smoke
. . . Stormed at with shot and shell . . . When can their glory fade? O the wild
charge they made!" His version, even including the Victorian couplet "Theirs
not to reason why / Theirs but to do and die," as poetry may lack the modern
virtue of incomprehensibility, but as history it captures that combination of the
glorious and the ridiculous which was a nineteenth-century cavalry charge
against cannon. As an onlooker said, *"C'est magnifique, mais ce n'est pas la
guerre"* ("It is magnificent, but it is not war"), which is exactly what Tennyson
conveyed better than any historian.

To me who grew up before Bruce Catton began writing, the Civil War will 25
always appear in terms of

> Up from the meadows rich with corn,
> Clear in the cool September morn,
> The clustered spires of Frederick stand.

Whittier, too, was dealing in contemporary history. Macaulay, on the other
hand, wrote "Horatius at the Bridge" some 2,500 years after the event. Although

he was a major historian and only secondarily a poet, would any of us remember anything about Tarquin the Tyrant or Roman history before Caesar if it were not for "Lars Porsena of Clusium / By the Nine Gods he swore," and the rest of the seventy stanzas? We know how the American Revolution began from Longfellow's signal lights in the old North Church.

> "One, if by land, and two, if by sea,
> And I on the opposite shore will be,
> Ready to ride and spread the alarm
> Through every Middlesex village and farm."

The poets have familiarized more people with history than have the historians, and sometimes they have given history a push. Kipling did it in 1899 with his bidding "Take up the White Man's Burden," addressed to Americans, who, being plunged into involuntary imperialism by Admiral Dewey's adventure at Manila, were sorely perplexed over what to do about the Philippines. "Send forth the best ye breed," Kipling told them firmly,

> To want in heavy harness,
> On fluttered folk and wild—
> Your new-caught, sullen peoples,
> Half-devil and half-child.

> Take up the White Man's burden,
> The savage wars of peace—
> Fill full the mouth of Famine
> And bid the sickness cease;

> Take up the White Man's burden—
> Ye dare not stoop to less.

The advice, published in a two-page spread by *McClure's Magazine*, was quoted across the country within a week and quickly reconciled most Americans to the expenditure of bullets, brutality, and trickery that soon proved necessary to implement it.

Kipling had a peculiar gift for recognizing history at close quarters. He wrote "Recessional" in 1897 at the time of the Queen's Diamond Jubilee when he sensed a self-glorification, a kind of hubris, in the national mood that frightened him. In *The Times* on the morning after, when people read his reminder—

> Lo, all our pomp of yesterday
> Is one with Nineveh and Tyre!

645

Judge of the Nations, spare us yet,
Lest we forget—lest we forget!

—it created a profound impression. Sir Edward Clark, the distinguished barrister who defended Oscar Wilde, was so affected by the message that he pronounced "Recessional" "the greatest poem written by any living man."

What the poets did was to convey the *feeling* of an episode or a moment of   28
history as they sensed it. The historian's task is rather to tell what happened within the discipline of the facts.

What his imagination is to the poet, facts are to the historian. His exercise   29
of judgment comes in their selection, his art in their arrangement. His method is narrative. His subject is the story of man's past. His function is to make it known.

QUESTIONS

1. What position is Tuchman taking in declaring herself a firm believer in "the preposterous fallacy of historical facts existing independently of the historian" (paragraph 7)?

2. According to Tuchman, what advantage does the latter-day historian have over the contemporary historian? What does this advantage suggest about when history happens?

3. Tuchman tells her readers about the problems she had in working on her first book, *Bible and Sword*. Tuchman writes: "Anger, disgust, and a sense of injustice can make some writers eloquent and evoke brilliant polemic, but these emotions stunted and twisted my pen" (paragraph 22). What is the effect of these personal reflections? How do they serve to strengthen her argument?

4. Why does Tuchman choose to quote from Tennyson, Longfellow, and Kipling? How does this evidence from poetry support her argument?

5. How do you respond to Tuchman's claim that emotion "is an essential element of history" (paragraph 23)?

MAKING CONNECTIONS

1. Both E. H. Carr and Tuchman ask, in one way or another, "What is history?" Outline the major areas of agreement and disagreement between these writers. Where do you find the most significant areas of agreement? Of disagreement?

2. Consider an episode or event you know a good deal about and think about how you might write its history. You could write of a recent year or season, a local political campaign, curricular reform at your high school or college, the birth of an organization in which you know some members, a recent criminal case, a school controversy. Any number of events might serve your purpose, which is to determine how you would approach that event if you were to write under the influence of Carr or of Tuchman.

What would you have to know, discover, worry, and think about if you were to take Carr as your guide? What if you were to take Tuchman? Write an explanation of where your research, in one case or the other, would lead you.

3. Tuchman asks an important question: Should, or perhaps can, history be written while it is "still smoking"? Consider your responses to Carr and Tuchman. What is your position?

Social Sciences and Public Affairs

THE IGNORED LESSON OF ANNE FRANK

Bruno Bettelheim

*Psychoanalyst Bruno Bettelheim himself survived impris-
onment in Nazi concentration camps. Here he writes about
Anne Frank, one of the better-known victims of World War
II. Her family, after hiding in an attic in Amsterdam for
two years, was betrayed to the Nazis, and Anne perished
in a concentration camp. Her* Diary, *kept during her time
in hiding, was published in 1947 and later was turned into
a play and a film. The following essay originally appeared
in* Harper's *(November 1960) and was reprinted in Bettelheim's book* Surviving and Other Essays *(1979). In this
essay, Bettelheim seeks to revise our moral understanding of
Anne Frank's story.*

When the world first learned about the Nazi concentration and death camps, 1
most civilized people felt the horrors committed in them to be so uncanny as
to be unbelievable. It came as a severe shock that supposedly civilized nations
could stoop to such inhuman acts. The implication that modern man has such
inadequate control over his cruel and destructive proclivities was felt as a threat
to our views of ourselves and our humanity. Three different psychological
mechanisms were most frequently used for dealing with the appalling revelation
of what had gone on in the camps:

649

(1) its applicability to man in general was denied by asserting—contrary to evidence—that the acts of torture and mass murder were committed by a small group of insane or perverted persons;

(2) the truth of the reports was denied by declaring them vastly exaggerated and ascribing them to propaganda (this originated with the German government, which called all reports on terror in the camps "horror propaganda"—*Greuel-propaganda*);

(3) the reports were believed, but the knowledge of the horror repressed as soon as possible.

All three mechanisms could be seen at work after liberation of those prisoners remaining. At first, after the discovery of the camps and their death-dealing, a wave of extreme outrage swept the Allied nations. It was soon followed by a general repression of the discovery in people's minds. Possibly this reaction was due to something more than the blow dealt to modern man's narcissism by the realization that cruelty is still rampant among men. Also present may have been the dim but extremely threatening realization that the modern state now has available the means for changing personality, and for destroying millions it deems undesirable. The ideas that in our day a people's personalities might be changed against their will by the state, and that other populations might be wholly or partially exterminated, are so fearful that one tries to free oneself of them and their impact by defensive denial, or by repression.

The extraordinary world-wide success of the book, play, and movie *The Diary of Anne Frank* suggests the power of the desire to counteract the realization of the personality-destroying and murderous nature of the camps by concentrating all attention on what is experienced as a demonstration that private and intimate life can continue to flourish even under the direct persecution by the most ruthless totalitarian system. And this although Anne Frank's fate demonstrates how efforts at disregarding in private life what goes on around one in society can hasten one's own destruction.

What concerns me here is not what actually happened to the Frank family, how they tried—and failed—to survive their terrible ordeal. It would be very wrong to take apart so humane and moving a story, which aroused so much well-merited compassion for gentle Anne Frank and her tragic fate. What is at issue is the universal and uncritical response to her diary and to the play and movie based on it, and what this reaction tells about our attempts to cope with the feelings her fate—used by us to serve as a symbol of a most human reaction to Nazi terror—arouses in us. I believe that the world-wide acclaim given her story cannot be explained unless we recognize in it our wish to forget the gas chambers, and our effort to do so by glorifying the ability to retreat into an extremely private, gentle, sensitive world, and there to cling as much as possible to what have been one's usual daily attitudes and activities, although surrounded by a maelstrom apt to engulf one at any moment.

The Frank family's attitude that life could be carried on as before may well have been what led to their destruction. By eulogizing how they lived in their hiding place while neglecting to examine first whether it was a reasonable or an effective choice, we are able to ignore the crucial lesson of their story—that such an attitude can be fatal in extreme circumstances.

While the Franks were making their preparations for going passively into hiding, thousands of other Jews in Holland (as elsewhere in Europe) were trying to escape to the free world, in order to survive and/or fight. Others who could not escape went underground—into hiding—each family member with, for example, a different gentile family. We gather from the diary, however, that the chief desire of the Frank family was to continue living as nearly as possible in the same fashion to which they had been accustomed in happier times.

Little Anne, too, wanted only to go on with life as usual, and what else could she have done but fall in with the pattern her parents created for her existence? But hers was not a necessary fate, much less a heroic one; it was a terrible but also a senseless fate. Anne had a good chance to survive, as did many Jewish children in Holland. But she would have had to leave her parents and go live with a gentile Dutch family, posing as their own child, something her parents would have had to arrange for her.

Everyone who recognized the obvious knew that the hardest way to go underground was to do it as a family; to hide out together made detection by the SS most likely; and when detected, everybody was doomed. By hiding singly, even when one got caught, the others had a chance to survive. The Franks, with their excellent connections among gentile Dutch families, might well have been able to hide out singly, each with a different family. But instead, the main principle of their planning was continuing their beloved family life— an understandable desire, but highly unrealistic in those times. Choosing any other course would have meant not merely giving up living together, but also realizing the full measure of the danger to their lives.

The Franks were unable to accept that going on living as a family as they had done before the Nazi invasion of Holland was no longer a desirable way of life, much as they loved each other; in fact, for them and others like them, it was most dangerous behavior. But even given their wish not to separate, they failed to make appropriate preparations for what was likely to happen.

There is little doubt that the Franks, who were able to provide themselves with so much while arranging for going into hiding, and even while hiding, could have provided themselves with some weapons had they wished. Had they had a gun, Mr. Frank could have shot down at least one or two of the "green police" who came for them. There was no surplus of such police, and the loss of an SS with every Jew arrested would have noticeably hindered the functioning of the police state. Even a butcher knife, which they certainly could have taken with them into hiding, could have been used by them in self-defense. The fate of the Franks wouldn't have been very different, because they all died anyway

651

except for Anne's father. But they could have sold their lives for a high price, instead of walking to their death. Still, although one must assume that Mr. Frank would have fought courageously, as we know he did when a soldier in the first World War, it is not everybody who can plan to kill those who are bent on killing him, although many who would not be ready to contemplate doing so would be willing to kill those who are bent on murdering not only them but also their wives and little daughters.

An entirely different matter would have been planning for escape in case of 11 discovery. The Franks' hiding place had only one entrance; it did not have any other exit. Despite the fact, during their many months of hiding, they did not try to devise one. Nor did they make other plans for escape, such as that one of the family members—as likely as not Mr. Frank—would try to detain the police in the narrow entrance way—maybe even fight them, as suggested above—thus giving other members of the family a chance to escape, either by reaching the roofs of adjacent houses, or down a ladder into the alley behind the house in which they were living.

Any of this would have required recognizing and accepting the desperate 12 straits in which they found themselves, and concentrating on how best to cope with them. This was quite possible to do, even under the terrible conditions in which the Jews found themselves after the Nazi occupation of Holland. It can be seen from many other accounts, for example from the story of Marga Minco, a girl of about Anne Frank's age who lived to tell about it. Her parents had planned that when the police should come for them, the father would try to detain them by arguing and fighting with them, to give the wife and daughter a chance to escape through a rear door. Unfortunately it did not quite work out this way, and both parents got killed. But their short-lived resistance permitted their daughter to make her escape as planned and to reach a Dutch family who saved her.[1]

This is not mentioned as a criticism that the Frank family did not plan or 13 behave along similar lines. A family has every right to arrange their life as they wish or think best, and to take the risks they want to take. My point is not to criticize what the Franks did, but only the universal admiration of their way of coping, or rather of not coping. The story of little Marga who survived, every bit as touching, remains totally neglected by comparison.

Many Jews—unlike the Franks, who through listening to British radio news 14 were better informed than most—had no detailed knowledge of the extermination camps. Thus it was easier for them to make themselves believe that complete compliance with even the most outrageously debilitating and degrading Nazi orders might offer a chance for survival. But neither tremendous anxiety that inhibits clear thinking and with it well-planned and determined action, nor ignorance about what happened to those who responded with passive

---

[1] Marga Minco, *Bitter Herbs* (New York: Oxford University Press), 1960.

waiting for being rounded up for their extermination, can explain the reaction of audiences to the play and movie retelling Anne's story, which are all about such waiting that results finally in destruction.

I think it is the fictitious ending that explains the enormous success of this   15
play and movie. At the conclusion we hear Anne's voice from the beyond, saying, "In spite of everything, I still believe that people are really good at heart." This improbable sentiment is supposedly from a girl who had been starved to death, had watched her sister meet the same fate before she did, knew that her mother had been murdered, and had watched untold thousands of adults and children being killed. This statement is not justified by anything Anne actually told her diary.

Going on with intimate family living, no matter how dangerous it might be   16
to survival, was fatal to all too many during the Nazi regime. And if all men are good, then indeed we can all go on with living our lives as we have been accustomed to in times of undisturbed safety and can afford to forget about Auschwitz. But Anne, her sister, her mother, may well have died because her parents could not get themselves to believe in Auschwitz.

While play and movie are ostensibly about Nazi persecution and destruction,   17
in actuality what we watch is the way that, despite this terror, lovable people manage to continue living their satisfying intimate lives with each other. The heroine grows from a child into a young adult as normally as any other girl would, despite the most abnormal conditions of all other aspects of her existence, and that of her family. Thus the play reassures us that despite the destructiveness of Nazi racism and tyranny in general, it is possible to disregard it in one's private life much of the time, even if one is Jewish.

True, the ending happens just as the Franks and their friends had feared all   18
along: their hiding place is discovered, and they are carried away to their doom. But the fictitious declaration of faith in the goodness of all men which concludes the play falsely reassures us since it impresses on us that in the combat between Nazi terror and continuance of intimate family living the latter wins out, since Anne has the last word. This is simply contrary to fact, because it was she who got killed. Her seeming survival through her moving statement about the goodness of men releases us effectively of the need to cope with the problems Auschwitz presents. That is why we are so relieved by her statement. It explains why millions loved play and movie, because while it confronts us with the fact that Auschwitz existed it encourages us at the same time to ignore any of its implications. If all men are good at heart, there never really was an Auschwitz; nor is there any possibility that it may recur.

The desire of Anne Frank's parents not to interrupt their intimate family   19
living, and their inability to plan more effectively for their survival, reflect the failure of all too many others faced with the threat of Nazi terror. It is a failure that deserves close examination because of the inherent warnings it contains for us, the living.

Submission to the threatening power of the Nazi state often led both to the disintegration of what had once seemed well-integrated personalities and to a return to an immature disregard for the dangers of reality. Those Jews who submitted passively to Nazi persecution came to depend on primitive and infantile thought processes: wishful thinking and disregard for the possibility of death. Many persuaded themselves that they, out of all the others, would be spared. Many more simply disbelieved in the possibility of their own death. Not believing in it, they did not take what seemed to them desperate precautions, such as giving up everything to hide out singly; or trying to escape even if it meant risking their lives in doing so; or preparing to fight for their lives when no escape was possible and death had become an immediate possibility. It is true that defending their lives in active combat before they were rounded up to be transported into the camps might have hastened their deaths, and so, up to a point, they were protecting themselves by "rolling with the punches" of the enemy.

But the longer one rolls with the punches dealt not by the normal vagaries of life, but by one's eventual executioner, the more likely it becomes that one will no longer have the strength to resist when death becomes imminent. This is particularly true if yielding to the enemy is accompanied not by a commensurate strengthening of the personality, but by an inner disintegration. We can observe such a process among the Franks, who bickered with each other over trifles, instead of supporting each other's ability to resist the demoralizing impact of their living conditions.

Those who faced up to the announced intentions of the Nazis prepared for the worst as a real and imminent possibility. It meant risking one's life for a self-chosen purpose, but in doing so, creating at least a small chance for saving one's own life or those of others, or both. When Jews in Germany were restricted to their homes, those who did not succumb to inertia took the new restrictions as a warning that it was high time to go underground, join the resistance movement, provide themselves with forged papers, and so on; if they had not done so long ago. Many of them survived.

Some distant relatives of mine may furnish an example. Early in the war, a young man living in a small Hungarian town banded together with a number of other Jews to prepare against a German invasion. As soon as the Nazis imposed curfews on the Jews, his group left for Budapest—because the bigger capital city with its greater anonymity offered chances for escaping detection. Similar groups from other towns converged in Budapest and joined forces. From among themselves they selected typically "Aryan" looking men who equipped themselves with false papers and immediately joined the Hungarian SS. These spies were then able to warn of impending persecution and raids.

Many of these groups survived intact. Furthermore, they had also equipped themselves with small arms, so that if they were detected, they could put up enough of a fight for the majority to escape while a few would die fighting to make the escape possible. A few of the Jews who had joined the SS were discovered and immediately shot, probably a death preferable to one in the gas chambers. But most of even these Jews survived, hiding within the SS until liberation.

Compare these arrangements not just to the Franks' selection of a hiding place that was basically a trap without an outlet but with Mr. Frank's teaching typically academic high-school subjects to his children rather than how to make a getaway: a token of his inability to face the seriousness of the threat of death. Teaching high-school subjects had, of course, its constructive aspects. It relieved the ever-present anxiety about their fate to some degree by concentrating on different matters, and by implication it encouraged hope for a future in which such knowledge would be useful. In this sense such teaching was purposeful, but it was erroneous in that it took the place of much more pertinent teaching and planning: how best to try to escape when detected.

Unfortunately the Franks were by no means the only ones who, out of anxiety, became unable to contemplate their true situation and with it to plan accordingly. Anxiety, and the wish to counteract it by clinging to each other, and to reduce its sting by continuing as much as possible with their usual way of life incapacitated many, particularly when survival plans required changing radically old ways of living that they cherished, and which had become their only source of satisfaction.

My young relative, for example, was unable to persuade other members of his family to go with him when he left the small town where he had lived with them. Three times, at tremendous risk to himself, he returned to plead with his relatives, pointing out first the growing persecution of the Jews, and later the fact that transport to the gas chambers had already begun. He could not convince these Jews to leave their homes and break up their families to go singly into hiding.

As their desperation mounted, they clung more determinedly to their old living arrangements and to each other, became less able to consider giving up the possessions they had accumulated through hard work over a lifetime. The more severely their freedom to act was reduced, and what little they were still permitted to do restricted by insensible and degrading regulations imposed by the Nazis, the more did they become unable to contemplate independent action. Their life energies drained out of them, sapped by their ever-greater anxiety. The less they found strength in themselves, the more they held on to the little that was left of what had given them security in the past—their old surroundings, their customary way of life, their possessions—all these seemed to give their lives some permanency, offer some symbols of security. Only what had once been symbols of security now endangered life, since they were excuses for avoiding change. On each successive visit the young man found his relatives

25

26

27

28

more incapacitated, less willing or able to take his advice, more frozen into inactivity, and with it further along the way to the crematoria where, in fact, they all died.

Levin renders a detailed account of the desperate but fruitless efforts made 29 by small Jewish groups determined to survive to try to save the rest. She tells how messengers were "sent into the provinces to warn Jews that deportation meant death, but their warnings were ignored because most Jews refused to contemplate their own annihilation."[2] I believe the reason for such refusal has to be found in their inability to take action. If we are certain that we are helpless to protect ourselves against the danger of destruction, we cannot contemplate it. We can consider the danger only as long as we believe there are ways to protect ourselves, to fight back, to escape. If we are convinced none of this is possible for us, then there is no point in thinking about the danger; on the contrary, it is best to refuse to do so.

As a prisoner in Buchenwald, I talked to hundreds of German Jewish pris- 30 oners who were brought there as part of the huge pogrom in the wake of the murder of vom Rath in the fall of 1938. I asked them why they had not left Germany, given the utterly degrading conditions they had been subjected to. Their answer was: How could we leave? It would have meant giving up our homes, our work, our sources of income. Having been deprived by Nazi persecution and degradation of much of their self-respect, they had become unable to give up what still gave them a semblance of it: their earthly belongings. But instead of using possessions, they became captivated by them, and this possession by earthly goods became the fatal mask for their possession by anxiety, fear, and denial.

How the investment of personal property with one's life energy could make 31 people die bit by bit was illustrated throughout the Nazi persecution of the Jews. At the time of the first boycott of Jewish stores, the chief external goal of the Nazis was to acquire the possessions of the Jews. They even let Jews take some things out of the country at that time if they would leave the bulk of their property behind. For a long time the intention of the Nazis, and the goal of their first discriminatory laws, was to force undesirable minorities, including Jews, into emigration.

Although the extermination policy was in line with the inner logic of Nazi 32 racial ideology, one may wonder whether the idea that millions of Jews (and other foreign nationals) could be submitted to extermination did not partially result from seeing the degree of degradation Jews accepted without fighting back. When no violent resistance occurred, persecution of the Jews worsened, slow step by slow step.

Many Jews who on the invasion of Poland were able to survey their situation 33 and draw the right conclusions survived the Second World War. As the Germans

[2] Nora Levin, *The Holocaust* (New York: Thomas Y. Crowell, 1968).

approached, they left everything behind and fled to Russia, much as they distrusted and disliked the Soviet system. But there, while badly treated, they could at least survive. Those who stayed on in Poland believing they could go on with life-as-before sealed their fate. Thus in the deepest sense the walk to the gas chamber was only the last consequence of these Jews' inability to comprehend what was in store; it was the final step of surrender to the death instinct, which might also be called the principle of inertia. The first step was taken long before arrival at the death camp.

We can find a dramatic demonstration of how far the surrender to inertia 34
can be carried, and the wish not to know because knowing would create unbearable anxiety, in an experience of Olga Lengyel.[3] She reports that although she and her fellow prisoners lived just a few hundred yards from the crematoria and the gas chambers and knew what they were for, most prisoners denied knowledge of them for months. If they had grasped their true situation, it might have helped them save either the lives they themselves were fated to lose, or the lives of others.

When Mrs. Lengyel's fellow prisoners were selected to be sent to the gas 35
chambers, they did not try to break away from the group, as she successfully did. Worse, the first time she tried to escape the gas chambers, some of the other selected prisoners told the supervisors that she was trying to get away. Mrs. Lengyel desperately asks the question: How was it possible that people denied the existence of the gas chambers when all day long they saw the crematoria burning and smelled the odor of burning flesh? Why did they prefer ignoring the exterminations to fighting for their very own lives? She can offer no explanation, only the observation that they resented anyone who tried to save himself from the common fate, because they lacked enough courage to risk action themselves. I believe they did it because they had given up their will to live and permitted their death tendencies to engulf them. As a result, such prisoners were in the thrall of the murdering SS not only physically but also psychologically, while this was not true for those prisoners who still had a grip on life.

Some prisoners even began to serve their executioners, to help speed the 36
death of their own kind. Then things had progressed beyond simple inertia to the death instinct running rampant. Those who tried to serve their executioners in what were once their civilian capacities were merely continuing life as usual and thereby opening the door to their death.

For example, Mrs. Lengyel speaks of Dr. Mengele, SS physician at Ausch- 37
witz, as a typical example of the "business as usual" attitude that enabled some prisoners, and certainly the SS, to retain whatever balance they could despite what they were doing. She described how Dr. Mengele took all correct medical precautions during childbirth, rigorously observing all aseptic principles, cutting

---

[3] Olga Lengyel, *Five Chimneys: The Story of Auschwitz* (Chicago: Ziff-Davis, 1947).

the umbilical cord with greatest care, etc. But only half an hour later he sent mother and infant to be burned in the crematorium.

Having made his choice, Dr. Mengele and others like him had to delude 38
themselves to be able to live with themselves and their experience. Only one personal document on the subject has come to my attention, that of Dr. Nyiszli, a prisoner serving as "research physician" at Auschwitz.[4] How Dr. Nyiszli deluded himself can be seen, for example, in the way he repeatedly refers to himself as working in Auschwitz as a physician, although he worked as the assistant of a criminal murderer. He speaks of the Institute for Race, Biological, and Anthropological Investigation as "one of the most qualified medical centers of the Third Reich," although it was devoted to proving falsehoods. That Nyiszli was a doctor didn't alter the fact that he—like any of the prisoner foremen who served the SS better than some SS were willing to serve it—was a participant in the crimes of the SS. How could he do it and live with himself?

The answer is: by taking pride in his professional skills, irrespective of the 39
purpose they served. Dr. Nyiszli and Dr. Mengele were only two among hundreds of other—and far more prominent—physicians who participated in the Nazis' murderous pseudo-scientific human experiments. It was the peculiar pride of these men in their professional skill and knowledge, without regard for moral implications, that made them so dangerous. Although the concentration camps and crematoria are no longer here, this kind of pride still remains with us; it is characteristic of a modern society in which fascination with technical competence has dulled concern for human feelings. Auschwitz is gone, but so long as this attitude persists, we shall not be safe from cruel indifference to life at the core.

I have met many Jews as well as gentile anti-Nazis, similar to the activist 40
group in Hungary described earlier, who survived in Nazi Germany and in the occupied countries. These people realized that when a world goes to pieces and inhumanity reigns supreme, man cannot go on living his private life as he was wont to do, and would like to do; he cannot, as the loving head of a family, keep the family living together peacefully, undisturbed by the surrounding world; nor can he continue to take pride in his profession or possessions, when either will deprive him of his humanity, if not also of his life. In such times, one must radically reevaluate all of what one has done, believed in, and stood for in order to know how to act. In short, one has to take a stand on the new reality—a firm stand, not one of retirement into an even more private world.

If today, Negroes in Africa march against the guns of a police that defends 41
apartheid—even if hundreds of dissenters are shot down and tens of thousands rounded up in camps—their fight will sooner or later assure them of a chance for liberty and equality. Millions of the Jews of Europe who did not or could not escape in time or go underground as many thousands did, could at least

[4]Miklos Nyiszli, *Auschwitz: A Doctor's Eyewitness Account* (New York: Frederick Fell, 1960).

have died fighting as some did in the Warsaw ghetto at the end, instead of passively waiting to be rounded up for their own extermination.

QUESTIONS

1. As part of his evidence, Bettelheim repeatedly refers to and sometimes summarizes parts of the story of Anne Frank. What are the main outlines of her story? What makes it so important?

2. What is Bettelheim's thesis? What is his most urgent message?

3. At times Bettelheim's thesis bears on Nazi resistance during World War II; at times it appears more universal. When does it tip one way, and when another? How do these two messages work together in the essay to strengthen Bettelheim's argument?

4. Bettelheim writes in paragraph 15, "I think it is the fictitious ending that explains the enormous success of this play and movie." Why does Bettelheim suggest that the ending must be fictitious? What evidence does he provide to support this claim?

5. Bettelheim refers to four other stories in print, those of Minco, Levin, Lengyel, and Nyiszli, as well as the case of his own distant relatives. How do these stories serve as evidence? Why do you think Bettelheim decided to arrange them in the order in which they appear?

6. Have you ever observed or learned of a situation in which someone's inaction seemed to increase, rather than decrease, some form of persecution? If so, analyze this situation in light of Bettelheim's essay.

7. Bettelheim seeks to revise his readers' moral understanding of Anne Frank's story. Write an essay in which you argue to revise your readers' understanding of some belief or some conventionally understood situation or story.

MAKING CONNECTIONS

1. Read Robert Jay Lifton's "What Made This Man? Mengele." Bettelheim mentions Mengele, too (paragraphs 37–39). More than that, he offers at least a few hints of what else went into making that man. What would Bettelheim add to Lifton's explanation?

2. Considering the cases Bettelheim discusses in his essay, whatever you know about the struggles of South African blacks, your knowledge of other contemporary freedom movements, and the reasons Thomas Jefferson gives in the Declaration of Independence (which follows in this section), write a position paper on when, if ever, you find it proper to rebel. You may bring any other doctrine you like into this paper—whether it be political, religious, or moral—so long as you explain it clearly and relate its principles to your thesis.

RACE AND THE SCHOOLING OF BLACK AMERICANS

Claude M. Steele

Claude M. Steele (b. 1946) is a social psychologist at Stanford University. Steele's main areas of academic interest, besides racial prejudice and self-esteem, are alcoholism and addictive behaviors. Steele is interested in the process by which the prejudices of American society shape the self-perceptions of African-Americans. The following essay first appeared in The Atlantic *in 1992.*

My former university offered minority students a faculty mentor to help 1 shepherd them into college life. As soon as I learned of the program, I volunteered to be a mentor, but by then the school year was nearly over. Undaunted, the program's eager staff matched me with a student on their waiting list—an appealing nineteen-year-old black woman from Detroit, the same age as my daughter. We met finally in a campus lunch spot just about two weeks before the close of her freshman year. I realized quickly that I was too late. I have heard that the best way to diagnose someone's depression is to note how depressed you feel when you leave the person. When our lunch was over, I felt as gray as the snowbanks that often lined the path back to my office. My lunchtime companion was a statistic brought to life, a living example of one of the most disturbing facts of racial life in America today: the failure of so many black Americans to thrive in school. Before I could lift a hand to help this student, she had decided to do what 70 percent of all black Americans at four-year colleges do at some point in their academic careers—drop out.

I sense a certain caving-in of hope in America that problems of race can be 2 solved. Since the sixties, when race relations held promise for the dawning of a new era, the issue has become one whose persistence causes "problem fatigue"—resignation to an unwanted condition of life.

This fatigue, I suspect, deadens us to the deepening crisis in the education 3 of black Americans. One can enter any desegregated school in America, from grammar school to high school to graduate or professional school, and meet a persistent reality: blacks and whites in largely separate worlds. And if one asks a few questions or looks at a few records, another reality emerges: these worlds are not equal, either in the education taking place there or in the achievement of the students who occupy them.

As a social scientist, I know that the crisis has enough possible causes to give 4 anyone problem fatigue. But at a personal level, perhaps because of my experience as a black in American schools, or perhaps just as the hunch of a myopic psychologist, I have long suspected a particular culprit—a culprit that can undermine black achievement as effectively as a lock on a schoolhouse door. The culprit I see is *stigma*, the endemic devaluation many blacks face in our society and schools. This status is its own condition of life, different from class, money, culture. It is capable, in the words of the late sociologist Erving Goffman, of "breaking the claim" that one's human attributes have on people. I believe that its connection to school achievement among black Americans has been vastly underappreciated.

This is a troublesome argument, touching as it does on a still unhealed part of American race relations. But it leads us to a heartening principle: if blacks are made less racially vulnerable in school, they can overcome even substantial obstacles. Before the good news, though, I must at least sketch in the bad: the worsening crisis in the education of black Americans.

Despite their socioeconomic disadvantages as a group, blacks begin school with test scores that are fairly close to the test scores of whites their age. The longer they stay in school, however, the more they fall behind; for example, by the sixth grade blacks in many school districts are two full grade levels behind whites in achievement. This pattern holds true in the middle class nearly as much as in the lower class. The record does not improve in high school. In 1980, for example, 25,500 minority students, largely black and Hispanic, entered high school in Chicago. Four years later only 9,500 graduated, and of those only 2,000 could read at grade level. The situation in other cities is comparable.

Even for blacks who make it to college, the problem doesn't go away. As I noted, 70 percent of all black students who enroll in four-year colleges drop out at some point, as compared with 45 percent of whites. At any given time nearly as many black males are incarcerated as are in college in this country. And the grades of black college students average half a letter below those of their white classmates. At one prestigious university I recently studied, only 18 percent of the graduating black students had grade averages of B or above, as compared with 64 percent of the whites. This pattern is the rule, not the exception, in even the most elite American colleges. Tragically, low grades can render a degree essentially "terminal" in the sense that they preclude further schooling.

Blacks in graduate and professional schools face a similarly worsening or stagnating fate. For example, from 1977 to 1990, though the number of Ph.D.s awarded to other minorities increased and the number awarded to whites stayed roughly the same, the number awarded to American blacks dropped from 1,116 to 828. And blacks needed more time to get those degrees.

Standing ready is a familiar set of explanations. First is societal disadvantage. Black Americans have had, and continue to have, more than their share: a history of slavery, segregation, and job ceilings; continued lack of economic opportunity; poor schools; and the related problems of broken families, drug-infested communities, and social isolation. Any of these factors—alone, in combination, or through accumulated effects—can undermine school achievement. Some analysts point also to black American culture, suggesting that, hampered by disadvantage, it doesn't sustain the values and expectations critical to education, or that it fosters learning orientations ill suited to school achievement, or that it even "opposes" mainstream achievement. These are the chestnuts, and I had always thought them adequate. Then several facts emerged that just didn't seem to fit.

For one thing, the achievement deficits occur even when black students suffer no major financial disadvantage—among middle-class students on wealthy college campuses and in graduate school among black students receiving substantial financial aid. For another thing, survey after survey shows that even poor black Americans value education highly, often more than whites. Also, as I will demonstrate, several programs have improved black school achievement without addressing culturally specific learning orientations or doing anything to remedy socioeconomic disadvantage.

Neither is the problem fully explained, as one might assume, by deficits in skill or preparation which blacks might suffer because of background disadvantages. I first doubted that such a connection existed when I saw flunk-out rates for black and white students at a large, prestigious university. Two observations surprised me. First, for both blacks and whites the level of preparation, as measured by Scholastic Aptitude Test scores, didn't make much difference in who flunked out; low scorers (with combined verbal and quantitative SATs of 800) were no more likely to flunk out than high scorers (with combined SATs of 1,200 to 1,500). The second observation was racial: whereas only two percent to 11 percent of the whites flunked out, 18 percent to 33 percent of the blacks flunked out, even at the highest levels of preparation (combined SATs of 1,400). Dinesh D'Souza has argued recently that college affirmative-action programs cause failure and high dropout rates among black students by recruiting them to levels of college work for which they are inadequately prepared. That was clearly not the case at this school; black students flunked out in large numbers even with preparation well above average.

And, sadly, this proved the rule, not the exception. From elementary school to graduate school, something depresses black achievement *at every level of preparation, even the highest*. Generally, of course, the better prepared achieve better than the less prepared, and this is about as true for blacks as for whites. But given any level of school preparation (as measured by tests and earlier grades), blacks somehow achieve less in subsequent schooling than whites (that is, have poorer grades, have lower graduation rates, and take longer to graduate), no matter how strong that preparation is. Put differently, the same achievement level requires better preparation for blacks than for whites—far better: among students with a C+ average at the university I just described, the mean American College Testing Program (ACT) score for blacks was at the 98th percentile, while for whites it was at only the 34th percentile. This pattern has been documented so broadly across so many regions of the country, and by so many investigations (literally hundreds), that it is virtually a social law in this society— as well as a racial tragedy.

Clearly, something is missing from our understanding of black underachieve- 13 ment. Disadvantage contributes, yet blacks underachieve even when they have ample resources, strongly value education, and are prepared better than adequately in terms of knowledge and skills. Something else has to be involved. That something else could be of just modest importance—a barrier that simply adds its effect to that of other disadvantages—or it could be pivotal, such that were it corrected, other disadvantages would lose their effect.

That something else, I believe, has to do with the process of identifying with 14 school. I offer a personal example:

I remember conducting experiments with my research adviser early in grad- 15 uate school and awaiting the results with only modest interest. I struggled to meet deadlines. The research enterprise—the core of what one does as a social psychologist—that wasn't *me* yet. I was in school for other reasons—I wanted an advanced degree, I was vaguely ambitious for intellectual work, and being in graduate school made my parents proud of me. But as time passed, I began to like the work. I also began to grasp the value system that gave it meaning, and the faculty treated me as if they thought I might even be able to do it. Gradually I began to think of myself as a social psychologist. With this change in self-concept came a new accountability; my self-esteem was affected now by what I did as a social psychologist, something that hadn't been true before. This added a new motivation to my work; self-respect, not just parental respect, was on the line. I noticed changes in myself. I worked without deadlines. I bored friends with applications of arcane theory to their daily lives. I went to conventions. I lived and died over how experiments came out.

Before this transition one might have said that I was handicapped by my 16 black working-class background and lack of motivation. After the transition the same observer might say that even though my background was working-class, I had special advantages: achievement-oriented parents, a small and attentive college. But these facts alone would miss the importance of the identification process I had experienced: the change in self-definition and in the activities on which I based my self-esteem. They would also miss a simple condition necessary for me to make this identification: treatment as a valued person with good prospects.

I believe that the "something else" at the root of black achievement problems 17 is the failure of American schooling to meet this simple condition for many of its black students. Doing well in school requires a belief that school achievement can be a promising basis of self-esteem, and that belief needs constant reaffirmation even for advantaged students. Tragically, I believe, the lives of black Americans are still haunted by a specter that threatens this belief and the identification that derives from it at every level of schooling.

THE SPECTER OF STIGMA AND
RACIAL VULNERABILITY

I have a good friend, the mother of three, who spends considerable time in the public school classrooms of Seattle, where she lives. In her son's third-grade room, managed by a teacher of unimpeachable good will and competence, she noticed over many visits that the extraordinary art work of a small black boy named Jerome was ignored—or, more accurately perhaps, its significance was ignored. As genuine art talent has a way of doing—even in the third grade— his stood out. Yet the teacher seemed hardly to notice. Moreover, Jerome's reputation, as it was passed along from one grade to the next, included only the slightest mention of his talent. Now, of course, being ignored like this could happen to anyone—such is the overload in our public schools. But my friend couldn't help wondering how the school would have responded to this talent had the artist been one of her own, middle-class white children. 18

Terms like "prejudice" and "racism" often miss the full scope of racial devaluation in our society, implying as they do that racial devaluation comes primarily from the strongly prejudiced, not from "good people" like Jerome's teacher. But the prevalence of racists—deplorable though racism is—misses the full extent of Jerome's burden, perhaps even the most profound part. 19

He faces a devaluation that grows out of our images of society and the way those images catalogue people. The catalogue need never be taught. It is implied by all we see around us: the kinds of people revered in advertising (consider the unrelenting racial advocacy of Ralph Lauren ads) and movies (black women are rarely seen as romantic partners, for example); media discussions of whether a black can be President; invitation lists to junior high school birthday parties; school curricula; literary and musical canons. These details create an image of society in which black Americans simply do not fare well. When I was a kid, we captured it with the saying "If you're white you're right, if you're yellow you're mellow, if you're brown stick around, but if you're black get back." 20

In ways that require no fueling from strong prejudice or stereotypes, these images expand the devaluation of black Americans. They act as mental standards against which information about blacks is evaluated: that which fits these images we accept; that which contradicts them we suspect. Had Jerome had a reading problem, which fits these images, it might have been accepted as characteristic more readily than his extraordinary art work, which contradicts them. 21

These images do something else as well, something especially pernicious in the classroom. They set up a jeopardy of double devaluation for blacks, a 22 jeopardy that does not apply to whites. Like anyone, blacks risk devaluation for a particular incompetence, such as a failed test or a flubbed pronunciation. But they further risk that such performances will confirm the broader, racial inferiority they are suspected of. Thus, from the first grade through graduate school, blacks have the extra fear that in the eyes of those around them their full humanity could fall with a poor answer or a mistaken stroke of the pen.

Moreover, because these images are conditioned in all of us, collectively 23 held, they can spawn racial devaluation in all of us, not just in the strongly prejudiced. They can do this even in blacks themselves: a majority of black children recently tested said they like and prefer to play with white rather than black dolls—almost fifty years after Kenneth and Mamie Clark, conducting similar experiments, documented identical findings and so paved the way for *Brown* v. *Topeka Board of Education*. Thus Jerome's devaluation can come from a circle of people in his world far greater than the expressly prejudiced— a circle that apparently includes his teacher.

In ways often too subtle to be conscious but sometimes overt, I believe, 24 blacks remain devalued in American schools, where, for example, a recent national survey shows that through high school they are still more than twice as likely as white children to receive corporal punishment, be suspended from school, or be labeled mentally retarded.

Tragically, such devaluation can seem inescapable. Sooner or later it forces 25 on its victims two painful realizations. The first is that society is preconditioned to see the worst in them. Black students quickly learn that acceptance, if it is to be won at all, will be hard-won. The second is that even if a black student achieves exoneration in one setting—with the teacher and fellow students in one classroom, or at one level of schooling, for example—this approval will have to be rewon in the next classroom, at the next level of schooling. Of course, individual characteristics that enhance one's value in society—skills, class status, appearance, and success—can diminish the racial devaluation one faces. And sometimes the effort to prove oneself fuels achievement. But few from any group could hope to sustain so daunting and everlasting a struggle. Thus, I am afraid, too many black students are left hopeless and deeply vulnerable in America's classrooms.

"DISIDENTIFYING" WITH SCHOOL

I believe that in significant part the crisis in black Americans' education 26 stems from the power of this vulnerability to undercut identification with schooling, either before it happens or after it has bloomed.

Jerome is an example of the first kind. At precisely the time when he would 27 need to see school as a viable source of self-esteem, his teachers fail to appreciate his best work. The devalued status of his race devalues him and his work in the classroom. Unable to entrust his sense of himself to this place, he resists

665

measuring himself against its values and goals. He languishes there, held by the law, perhaps even by his parents, but not allowing achievement to affect his view of himself. This psychic alienation—the act of not caring—makes him less vulnerable to the specter of devaluation that haunts him. Bruce Hare, an educational researcher, has documented this process among fifth-grade boys in several schools in Champaign, Illinois. He found that although the black boys had considerably lower achievement-test scores than their white classmates, their overall self-esteem was just as high. This stunning imperviousness to poor academic performance was accomplished, he found, by their de-emphasizing school achievement as a basis of self-esteem and giving preference to peer-group relations—a domain in which their esteem prospects were better. They went where they had to go to feel good about themselves.

But recall the young student whose mentor I was. She had already identified   28 with school, and wanted to be a doctor. How can racial vulnerability break so developed an achievement identity? To see, let us follow her steps onto campus: Her recruitment and admission stress her minority status perhaps more strongly than it has been stressed at any other time in her life. She is offered academic and social support services, further implying that she is "at risk" (even though, contrary to common belief, the vast majority of black college students are admitted with qualifications well above the threshold for whites). Once on campus, she enters a socially circumscribed world in which blacks—still largely separate from whites—have lower status; this is reinforced by a sidelining of minority material and interests in the curriculum and in university life. And she can sense that everywhere in this new world her skin color places her under suspicion of intellectual inferiority. All of this gives her the double vulnerability I spoke of: she risks confirming a particular incompetence, at chemistry or a foreign language, for example; but she also risks confirming the racial inferiority she is suspected of—a judgment that can feel as close at hand as a mispronounced word or an ungrammatical sentence. In reaction, usually to some modest setback, she withdraws, hiding her troubles from instructors, counselors, even other students. Quickly, I believe, a psychic defense takes over. She *disidentifies* with achievement; she changes her self-conception, her outlook and values, so that achievement is no longer so important to her self-esteem. She may continue to feel pressure to stay in school—from her parents, even from the potential advantages of a college degree. But now she is psychologically insulated from her academic life, like a disinterested visitor. Cool, unperturbed. But, like a pain-killing drug, disidentification undoes her future as it relieves her vulnerability.

The prevalence of this syndrome among black college students has been   29 documented extensively, especially on predominantly white campuses. Summarizing this work, Jacqueline Fleming, a psychologist, writes, "The fact that black students must matriculate in an atmosphere that feels hostile arouses defensive reactions that interfere with intellectual performance. . . . They display academic demotivation and think less of their abilities. They profess losses of energy." Among a sample of blacks on one predominantly white campus, Richard Nisbett and Andrew Reaves, both psychologists, and I found that attitudes related to disidentification were more strongly predictive of grades than even academic preparation (that is, SATs and high school grades).

To make matters worse, once disidentification occurs in a school, it can 30 spread like the common cold. Blacks who identify and try to achieve embarrass the strategy by valuing the very thing the strategy denies the value of. Thus pressure to make it a group norm can evolve quickly and become fierce. Defectors are called "oreos" or "incognegroes." One's identity as an authentic black is held hostage, made incompatible with school identification. For black students, then, pressure to disidentify with school can come from the already demoralized as well as from racial vulnerability in the setting.

Stigmatization of the sort suffered by black Americans is probably also a 31 barrier to the school achievement of other groups in our society, such as lower-class whites, Hispanics, and women in male-dominated fields. For example, at a large midwestern university I studied, women match men's achievement in the liberal arts, where they suffer no marked stigma, but underachieve compared with men (get lower grades than men with the same ACT scores) in engineering and premedical programs, where they, like blacks across the board, are more vulnerable to suspicions of inferiority.

"WISE" SCHOOLING

"When they approach me they see . . . everything and anything except me. . . . [this] invisibility . . . occurs because of a peculiar disposition of the eyes. . . ."

—Ralph Ellison, *Invisible Man*

Erving Goffman, borrowing from gays of the 1950s, used the term "wise" to 32 describe people who don't themselves bear the stigma of a given group but who are accepted by the group. These are people in whose eyes the full humanity of the stigmatized is visible, people in whose eyes they feel less vulnerable. If racial vulnerability undermines black school achievement, as I have argued, then this achievement should improve significantly if schooling is made "wise"—that is, made to see value and promise in black students and to act accordingly.

And yet, although racial vulnerability at school may undermine black 33 achievement, so many other factors seem to contribute—from the debilitations of poverty to the alleged dysfunctions of black American culture—that one might expect "wiseness" in the classroom to be of little help. Fortunately, we have considerable evidence to the contrary. Wise schooling may indeed be the missing key to the schoolhouse door.

In the mid-seventies black students in Philip Uri Treisman's early calculus 34

667

courses at the University of California at Berkeley consistently fell to the bottom of every class. To help, Treisman developed the Mathematics Workshop Program, which, in a surprisingly short time, reversed their fortunes, causing them to outperform their white and Asian counterparts. And although it is only a freshman program, black students who take it graduate at a rate comparable to the Berkeley average. Its central technique is group study of calculus concepts. But it is also wise; it does things that allay the racial vulnerabilities of these students. Stressing their potential to learn, it recruits them to a challenging "honors" workshop tied to their first calculus course. Building on their skills, the workshop gives difficult work, often beyond course content, to students with even modest preparation (some of their math SATs dip to the 300s). Working together, students soon understand that everyone knows something and nobody knows everything, and learning is speeded through shared understanding. The wisdom of these tactics is their subtext message: "You are valued in this program because of your academic potential—regardless of your current skill level. You have no more to fear than the next person, and since the work is difficult, success is a credit to your ability, and a setback is a reflection only of the challenge." The black students' double vulnerability around failure—the fear that they lack ability, and the dread that they will be devalued—is thus reduced. They can relax and achieve. The movie *Stand and Deliver* depicts Jaime Escalante using the same techniques of assurance and challenge to inspire advanced calculus performance in East Los Angeles Chicano high schoolers. And, explaining Xavier University's extraordinary success in producing black medical students, a spokesman said recently, "What doesn't work is saying, 'You need remedial work.' What does work is saying, 'You may be somewhat behind at this time but you're a talented person. We're going to help you advance at an accelerated rate.'"

The work of James Comer, a child psychiatrist at Yale, suggests that wiseness 35 can minimize even the barriers of poverty. Over a fifteen-year period he transformed the two worst elementary schools in New Haven, Connecticut, into the third and fifth best in the city's thirty-three-school system without any change in the type of students—largely poor and black. His guiding belief is that learning requires a strongly accepting relationship between teacher and student. "After all," he notes, "what is the difference between scribble and a letter of the alphabet to a child? The only reason the letter is meaningful, and worth learning and remembering, is because a *meaningful* other wants him or her to learn and remember it." To build these relationships Comer focuses on the overall school climate, shaping it not so much to transmit specific skills, or to achieve order per se, or even to improve achievement, as to establish a valuing and optimistic atmosphere in which a child can—to use his term—"identify" with learning. Responsibility for this lies with a team of ten to fifteen members, headed by the principal and made up of teachers, parents, school staff, and child-development experts (for example, psychologists or special-education teachers). The team develops a plan of specifics: teacher training, parent workshops, coordination of information about students. But at base I believe it tries to ensure that the students—vulnerable on so many counts—get treated essentially like middle-class students, with conviction about their value and promise. As this happens, their vulnerability diminishes, and with it the companion defenses of disidentification and misconduct. They achieve, and apparently identify, as their achievement gains persist into high school. Comer's genius, I believe, is to have recognized the importance of these vulnerabilities as barriers to *intellectual* development, and the corollary that schools hoping to educate such students must learn first how to make them feel valued.

These are not isolated successes. Comparable results were observed, for 36 example, in a Comer-type program in Maryland's Prince Georges County, in the Stanford economist Henry Levin's accelerated-schools program, and in Harlem's Central Park East Elementary School, under the principalship of Deborah Meier. And research involving hundreds of programs and schools points to the same conclusion: black achievement is consistently linked to conditions of schooling that reduce racial vulnerability. These include relatively harmonious race relations among students; a commitment by teachers and schools to seeing minority-group members achieve; the instructional goal that students at all levels of preparation achieve; desegregation at the classroom as well as the school level; and a de-emphasis on ability tracking.

That erasing stigma improves black achievement is perhaps the strongest 37 evidence that stigma is what depresses it in the first place. This is no happy realization. But it lets in a ray of hope: whatever other factors also depress black achievement—poverty, social isolation, poor preparation—they may be substantially overcome in a schooling atmosphere that reduces racial and other vulnerabilities, not through unrelenting niceness or ferocious regimentation but by wiseness, by *seeing* value and acting on it.

WHAT MAKES SCHOOLING
UNWISE

But if wise schooling is so attainable, why is racial vulnerability the rule, 38 not the exception, in American schooling?

One factor is the basic assimilationist offer that schools make to blacks: You 39 can be valued and rewarded in school (and society), the schools say to these students, but you must first master the culture and ways of the American mainstream, and since that mainstream (as it is represented) is essentially white, this means you must give up many particulars of being black—styles of speech and appearance, value priorities, preferences—at least in mainstream settings. This is asking a lot. But it has been the "color-blind" offer to every immigrant and minority group in our nation's history, the core of the melting-pot ideal, and so I think it strikes most of us as fair. Yet non-immigrant minorities like blacks and Native Americans have always been here, and thus are entitled, more than new immigrants, to participate in the defining images of the society projected in school. More important, their exclusion from these images denies their contributive history and presence in society. Thus, whereas immigrants can tilt toward assimilation in pursuit of the opportunities for which they came, American blacks may find it harder to assimilate. For them, the offer of acceptance in return for assimilation carries a primal insult: it asks them to join in something that has made them invisible.

Now, I must be clear. This is not a criticism of Western civilization. My concern is an omission of image-work. In his incisive essay "What America Would Be Like Without Blacks," Ralph Ellison showed black influence on American speech and language, the themes of our finest literature, and our most defining ideals of personal freedom and democracy. In *The World They Made Together*, Mechal Sobel described how African and European influences shaped the early American South in everything from housing design and land use to religious expression. The fact is that blacks are not outside the American mainstream but, in Ellison's words, have always been "one of its major tributaries." Yet if one relied on what is taught in America's schools, one would never know this. There blacks have fallen victim to a collective self-deception, a society's allowing itself to assimilate like mad from its constituent groups while representing itself to itself as if the assimilation had never happened, as if progress and good were almost exclusively Western and white. A prime influence of American society on world culture is the music of black Americans, shaping art forms from rock-and-roll to modern dance. Yet in American schools, from kindergarten through graduate school, these essentially black influences have barely peripheral status, are largely outside the canon. Thus it is not what is taught but what is *not* taught, what teachers and professors have never learned the value of, that reinforces a fundamental unwiseness in American schooling, and keeps black disidentification on full boil.

Deep in the psyche of American educators is a presumption that black students need academic remediation, or extra time with elemental curricula to overcome background deficits. This orientation guides many efforts to close the achievement gap—from grammar school tutoring to college academic-support programs—but I fear it can be unwise. Bruno Bettelheim and Karen Zelan's article "Why Children Don't Like to Read" comes to mind: apparently to satisfy the changing sensibilities of local school boards over this century, many books that children like were dropped from school reading lists; when children's reading scores also dropped, the approved texts were replaced by simpler books; and when reading scores dropped again, these were replaced by even simpler books, until eventually the children could hardly read at all, not because the material was too difficult but because they were bored stiff. So it goes, I suspect,

670

with a great many of these remediation efforts. Moreover, because so many such programs target blacks primarily, they virtually equate black identity with substandard intellectual status, amplifying racial vulnerability. They can even undermine students' ability to gain confidence from their achievement, by sharing credit for their successes while implying that their failures stem from inadequacies beyond the reach of remediation.

The psychologist Lisa Brown and I recently uncovered evidence of just how 42 damaging this orientation may be. At a large, prestigious university we found that whereas the grades of black graduates of the 1950s improved during the students' college years until they virtually matched the school average, those of blacks who graduated in the 1980s (we chose only those with above-average entry credentials, to correct for more-liberal admissions policies in that decade) worsened, ending up considerably below the school average. The 1950s graduates faced outward discrimination in everything from housing to the classroom, whereas the 1980s graduates were supported by a phalanx of help programs. Many things may contribute to this pattern. The Jackie Robinson, "pioneer" spirit of the 1950s blacks surely helped them endure. And in a pre-affirmative-action era, they may have been seen as intellectually more deserving. But one cannot ignore the distinctive fate of 1980s blacks: a remedial orientation put their abilities under suspicion, deflected their ambitions, distanced them from their successes, and painted them with their failures. Black students on today's campuses may experience far less overt prejudice than their 1950s counterparts but, ironically, may be more racially vulnerable.

THE ELEMENTS OF WISENESS

For too many black students school is simply the place where, more con- 43 certedly, persistently, and authoritatively than anywhere else in society, they learn how little valued they are.

Clearly, no simple recipe can fix this, but I believe we now understand the 44 basics of a corrective approach. Schooling must focus more on reducing the vulnerabilities that block identification with achievement. I believe that four conditions, like the legs of a stool, are fundamental.

• If what is meaningful and important to a teacher is to become meaningful 45 and important to a student, the student must feel valued by the teacher for his or her potential and as a person. Among the more fortunate in society, this relationship is often taken for granted. But it is precisely the relationship that race can still undermine in American society. As Comer, Escalante, and Treisman have shown, when one's students bear race and class vulnerabilities, building this relationship is the first order of business—at all levels of schooling. No tactic of instruction, no matter how ingenious, can succeed without it.

671

- The challenge and the promise of personal fulfillment, not remediation   46
(under whatever guise), should guide the education of these students. Their
present skills should be taken into account, and they should be moved along at
a pace that is demanding but doesn't defeat them. Their ambitions should never
be scaled down but should instead be guided to inspiring goals even when
extraordinary dedication is called for. Frustration will be less crippling than
alienation. Here psychology is everything: remediation defeats, challenge
strengthens—affirming their potential, crediting them with their achievements,
inspiring them.

But the first condition, I believe, cannot work without the second, and vice   47
versa. A valuing teacher-student relationship goes nowhere without challenge,
and challenge will always be resisted outside a valuing relationship. (Again, I
must be careful about something: in criticizing remediation I am not opposing
affirmative-action recruitment in the schools. The success of this policy, like
that of school integration before it, depends, I believe, on the tactics of implementation. Where students are valued and challenged, they generally succeed.)

- Racial integration is a generally useful element in this design, if not a   48
necessity. Segregation, whatever its purpose, draws out group differences and
makes people feel more vulnerable when they inevitably cross group lines to
compete in the larger society. This vulnerability, I fear, can override confidence
gained in segregated schooling unless that confidence is based on strongly
competitive skills and knowledge—something that segregated schooling, plagued
by shortages of resources and access, has difficulty producing.

- The particulars of black life and culture—art, literature, political and social   49
perspective, music—must be presented in the mainstream curriculum of American schooling, not consigned to special days, weeks, or even months of the
year, or to special-topic courses and programs aimed essentially at blacks. Such
channeling carries the disturbing message that the material is not of general
value. And this does two terrible things: it wastes the power of this material to
alter our images of the American mainstream—continuing to frustrate black
identification with it—and it excuses in whites and others a huge ignorance of
their own society. The true test of democracy, Ralph Ellison has said, "is . . .
the inclusion—not assimilation—of the black man."

Finally, if I might be allowed a word specifically to black parents, one issue   50
is even more immediate: our children may drop out of school before the first
committee meets to accelerate the curriculum. Thus, although we, along with
all Americans, must strive constantly for wise schooling, I believe we cannot
wait for it. We cannot yet forget our essentially heroic challenge: to foster in
our children a sense of hope and entitlement to mainstream American life and
schooling, even when it devalues them.

QUESTIONS

1. Summarize Steele's argument. What are his key terms? Identify his key ideas.

2. Steele identifies "stigma" as the "culprit that can undermine black achievement as effectively as a lock on a schoolhouse door." What does stigma mean to Steele? What evidence does he provide to suggest the importance of stigma?

3. What conventional arguments are usually offered to explain the underachievement of blacks? How does Steele introduce these arguments and refute them? Do you find his refutation persuasive?

4. Steele introduces the concept of "wise schooling." What does this concept mean? Steele introduces wise schooling as the "missing key to the schoolhouse door." Does Steele's argument for wise schooling begin to address the problems he identifies earlier in his essay?

5. Steele writes his essay in a personal voice. He refers to himself and his own experiences, and is very present in his essay. How does Steele combine the personal with the academic, the reflective with the scholarly? Do you find his style persuasive and effective?

6. Steele argues that "racial vulnerability [is] the rule, not the exception, in American schooling." Using your own experiences as evidence, respond to Steele's argument.

7. Steele asks his readers to think about not only what is taught in school, but also what is not taught. Write an essay in which you argue for the inclusion of some subject or approach to learning that was excluded from your high school education.

8. Write a response to Steele's essay. You might want to offer a counterargument to one of his arguments or extend one of his arguments.

MAKING CONNECTIONS

How would Patricia Williams respond to Claude Steele's essay? What connections can you find between the ideas of these two essayists? Create a conversation between these writers.

THE GAP BETWEEN STRIVING AND ACHIEVING: THE CASE OF ASIAN-AMERICAN WOMEN

Deborah Woo

*Deborah Woo is a sociologist and a member of the Com-
munity Studies Board at the University of California at
Santa Cruz. She has pursued her interests in the sociology
of mental health, mainly focusing on the cultural issues
that surround mental illness among Chinese-Americans. In
this essay, her concern is the "model minority myth" and
the real occupational achievements of Asian-American
women.*

Much academic research on Asian Americans tends to underscore their   1
success, a success which is attributed almost always to a cultural emphasis on
education, hard work, and thrift. Less familiar is the story of potential not fully
realized. For example, despite the appearance of being successful and highly
educated, Asian American women do not necessarily gain the kind of recognition or rewards they deserve.

The story of unfulfilled dreams remains unwritten for many Asian Ameri-   2
cans. It is specifically this story about the gap between striving and achieving
that I am concerned with here. Conventional wisdom obscures the discrepancy
by looking primarily at whether society is adequately rewarding individuals. By
comparing how minorities as disadvantaged groups are doing relative to each
other, the tendency is to view Asian Americans as a "model minority." This
practice programs us to ignore structural barriers and inequities and to insist
that any problems are simply due to different cultural values or failure of
individual effort.

Myths about the Asian American community derive from many sources. All   3
ethnic groups develop their own cultural myths. Sometimes, however, they
create myths out of historical necessity, as a matter of subterfuge and survival.
Chinese Americans, for example, were motivated to create new myths because
institutional opportunities were closed off to them. Succeeding in America
meant they had to invent fake aspects of an "Oriental culture," which became
the beginning of the Chinatown tourist industry.

What has been referred to as the "model minority myth," however, essentially   4
originated from without. The idea that Asian Americans have been a successful
group has been a popular news media theme for the last twenty years. It has
become a basis for cutbacks in governmental support for all ethnic minorities—

for Asian Americans because they apparently are already successful as a group; for other ethnic minorities because they are presumably not working as hard as Asian Americans or they would not need assistance. Critics of this view argue that the portrayal of Asian Americans as socially and economically successful ignores fundamental inequities. That is, the question "Why have Asians been successful vis-à-vis other minorities?" has been asked at the expense of another equally important question: "What has kept Asians from *fully* reaping the fruits of their education and hard work?"

The achievements of Asian Americans are part reality, part myth. Part of the 5 reality is that a highly visible group of Asian Americans are college-educated, occupationally well-situated, and earning relatively high incomes. The myth, however, is that hard work reaps commensurate rewards. This essay documents the gap between the level of education and subsequent occupational or income gains.

THE ROOTS AND CONTOURS OF THE "MODEL MINORITY" CONCEPT

Since World War II, social researchers and news media personnel have been 6 quick to assert that Asian Americans excel over other ethnic groups in terms of earnings, education, and occupation. Asian Americans are said to save more, study more, work more, and so achieve more. The reason given: a cultural emphasis on education and hard work. Implicit in this view is a social judgment and moral injunction: if Asian Americans can make it on their own, why can't other minorities?

While the story of Asian American women workers is only beginning to be 7 pieced together, the success theme is already being sung. The image prevails that despite cultural and racial oppression, they are somehow rapidly assimilating into the mainstream. As workers, they participate in the labor force at rates higher than all others, including Anglo women. Those Asian American women who pursue higher education surpass other women, and even men, in this respect. Moreover, they have acquired a reputation for not only being conscientious and industrious but docile, compliant, and uncomplaining as well.

In the last few decades American women in general have been demanding 8 "equal pay for equal work," the legitimation of housework as work that needs to be recompensed, and greater representation in the professional fields. These demands, however, have not usually come from Asian American women. From the perspective of those in power, this reluctance to complain is another feature of the "model minority." But for those who seek to uncover employment abuses, the unwillingness to talk about problems on the job is itself a problem. The garment industry, for example, is a major area of exploitation, yet it is also one that is difficult to investigate and control. In a 1983 report on the Concentrated

675

Employment Program of the California Department of Industrial Relations, it was noted:

> The major problem for investigators in San Francisco is that the Chinese community is very close-knit, and employers and employees cooperate in refusing to speak to investigators. In two years of enforcing the Garment Registration Act, the CEP has never received a complaint from an Asian employee. The few complaints received have been from Anglo or Latin workers.[1]

While many have argued vociferously either for or against the model minority concept, Asian Americans in general have been ambivalent in this regard. Asian Americans experience pride in achievement born of hard work and self-sacrifice, but at the same time, they resist the implication that all is well. Data provided here indicate that Asian Americans have not been successful in terms of benefitting fully, (i.e., monetarily), from their education. It is a myth that Asian Americans have proven the American Dream. How does this myth develop? 9

The Working Consumer: Income and Cost of Living

One striking feature about Asian Americans is that they are geographically concentrated in areas where both income and cost of living are very high. In 1970, 80 percent of the total Asian American population resided in five states— California, Hawaii, Illinois, New York, and Washington. Furthermore, 59 percent of Chinese, Filipino, and Japanese Americans were concentrated in only 5 of the 243 Standard Metropolitan Statistical Areas (SMSA) in the United States—Chicago, Honolulu, Los Angeles/Long Beach, New York, and San Francisco/Oakland.[2] The 1980 census shows that immigration during the intervening decade has not only produced dramatic increases, especially in the Filipino and Chinese populations, but has also continued the overwhelming tendency for these groups to concentrate in the same geographical areas, especially those in California.[3] Interestingly enough, the very existence of large Asian communities in the West has stimulated among more recent refugee populations what is now officially referred to as "secondary migration," that is, the movement of refugees away from their sponsoring communities (usually places where there was no sizable Asian population prior to their own arrival) to those areas where there are well-established Asian communities.[4] 10

This residential pattern means that while Asian Americans may earn more by living in high-income areas, they also pay more as consumers. The additional earning power gained from living in San Francisco or Los Angeles, say, is absorbed by the high cost of living in such cities. National income averages which compare the income of Asian American women with that of the more broadly dispersed Anglo women systematically distort the picture. Indeed, if we compare women within the same area, Asian American women are frequently 11 less well-off than Anglo American females, and the difference between women pales when compared with Anglo males, whose mean income is much higher than that of any group of women.[5]

When we consider the large immigrant Asian population and the language barriers that restrict women to menial or entry-level jobs, we are talking about a group that not only earns minimum wage or less, but one whose purchasing power is substantially undermined by living in metropolitan areas of states where the cost of living is unusually high.   12

Another striking pattern about Asian American female employment is the high rate of labor force participation. Asian American women are more likely than Anglo American women to work full time and year round. The model minority interpretation tends to assume that mere high labor force participation is a sign of successful employment. One important factor motivating minority women to enter the work force, however, is the need to supplement family resources. For Anglo American women some of the necessity for working is partly offset by the fact that they often share in the higher incomes of Anglo males, who tend not only to earn more than all other groups but, as noted earlier, also tend to receive higher returns on their education. Moreover, once regional variation is adjusted for, Filipino and Chinese Americans had a median annual income equivalent to black males in four mainland SMSAs—Chicago, Los Angeles/Long Beach, New York, San Francisco/Oakland.[6] Census statistics point to the relatively lower earning capacity of Asian males compared to Anglo males, suggesting that Asian American women enter the work force to help compensate for this inequality. Thus, the mere fact of high employment must be read cautiously and analyzed within a larger context.   13

The Different Faces of Immigration

Over the last decade immigration has expanded the Chinese population by 85.3 percent, making it the largest Asian group in the country at 806,027, and has swelled the Filipino population by 125.8 percent, making it the second largest at 774,640. Hence at present the majority of Chinese American and Filipino American women are foreign-born. In addition the Asian American "success story" is misleading in part because of a select group of these immigrants: foreign-educated professionals.   14

Since 1965 U.S. immigration laws have given priority to seven categories of individuals. Two of the seven allow admittance of people with special occupational skills or services needed in the United States. Four categories facilitate family reunification, and the last applies only to refugees. While occupation is estimated to account for no more than 20 percent of all visas, professionals are not precluded from entering under other preference categories. Yet this select group is frequently offered as evidence of the upward mobility possible in America when Asian Americans who are born and raised in the United States   15

677

are far less likely to reach the doctoral level in their education. Over two-thirds of Asians with doctorates in the United States are trained and educated abroad.[7]

Also overlooked in some analyses is a great deal of downward mobility among the foreign-born. For example, while foreign-educated health professionals are given preferential status for entry into this country, restrictive licensing requirements deny them the opportunity to practice or utilize their special skills. They are told that their educational credentials, experience, and certifications are inadequate. Consequently, for many the only alternatives are menial labor or unemployment.[8] Other highly educated immigrants become owner/managers of Asian businesses, which also suggests downward mobility and an inability to find jobs in their field of expertise. 16

"Professional" Obscures More than It Reveals

Another major reason for the perception of "model minority" is that the census categories implying success, "professional-managerial" or "executive, administrative, managerial," frequently camouflage important inconsistencies with this image of success. As managers, Asian Americans, usually male, are concentrated in certain occupations. They tend to be self-employed in small-scale wholesale and retail trade and manufacturing. They are rarely buyers, sales managers, administrators, or salaried managers in large-scale retail trade, communications, or public utilities. Among foreign-born Asian women, executive-managerial status is limited primarily to auditors and accountants.[9] 17

In general, Asian American women with a college education are concentrated in narrow and select, usually less prestigious, rungs of the "professional-managerial" class. In 1970, 27 percent of native-born Japanese women were either elementary or secondary school teachers. Registered nurses made up the next largest group. Foreign-born Filipino women found this to be their single most important area of employment, with 19 percent being nurses. They were least represented in the more prestigious professions—physicians, judges, dentists, law professors, and lawyers.[10] In 1980 foreign-born Asian women with four or more years of college were most likely to find jobs in administrative support or clerical occupations. 18

Self-help through "Taking Care of One's Own"

Much of what is considered ideal or model behavior in American society is based on Anglo-Saxon, Protestant values. Chief among them is an ethic of individual self-help, of doing without outside assistance or governmental support. On the other hand, Asian Americans have historically relied to a large extent on family or community resources. Their tightly-knit communities tend to be fairly closed to the outside world, even when under economic hardship. Many below the poverty level do not receive any form of public assistance.[11] Even if we include social security benefits as a form of supplementary income, 19 the proportion of Asian Americans who use them is again very low, much lower than that for Anglo Americans.[12] Asian American families, in fact, are more likely than Anglo American families to bear economic hardships on their own.

While Asian Americans appear to have been self-sufficient as communities, we need to ask, at what personal cost? Moreover, have they as a group reaped rewards commensurate with their efforts? The following section presents data which document that while Asian American women may be motivated to achieve through education, monetary returns for them are less than for other groups.   20

THE NATURE OF INEQUALITY

The decision to use white males as the predominant reference group within the United States is a politically charged issue. When women raise and push the issue of "comparable worth," of "equal pay for equal work," they argue that women frequently do work equivalent to men's, but are paid far less for it.   21

The same argument can be made for Asian American women, and the evidence of inequality is staggering. For example, after adjustments are made for occupational prestige, age, education, weeks worked, hours worked each week, and state of residence in 1975, Chinese American women could be expected to earn only 70 percent of the majority male income. Even among the college-educated, Chinese American women fared least well, making only 42 percent of what majority males earned. As we noted earlier, the mean income of all women, Anglo and Asian, was far below that of Anglo males in 1970 and 1980. This was true for both native-born and foreign-born Asians. In 1970 Anglo women earned only 54 percent of what their male counterparts did. Native-born Asian American women, depending on the particular ethnic group, earned anywhere from 49 to 57 percent of what Anglo males earned. In 1980, this inequity persisted.   22

Another way of thinking about comparable worth is not to focus only on what individuals do on the job, but on what they bring to the job as well. Because formal education is one measure of merit in American society and because it is most frequently perceived as the means to upward mobility, we would expect greater education to have greater payoffs.   23

Asian American women tend to be extraordinarily successful in terms of attaining higher education. Filipino American women have the highest college completion rate of all women and graduate at a rate 50 percent greater than that of majority males. Chinese American and Japanese American women follow closely behind, exceeding both the majority male and female rate of college completion.[13] Higher levels of education, however, bring lower returns for Asian American women than they do for other groups.   24

While education enhances earnings capability, the return on education for Asian American women is not as great as that for other women, and is well   25 below parity with white males. Data on Asian American women in the five SMSAs where they are concentrated bear this out.[14] In 1980 all these women fell far behind Anglo males in what they earned in relation to their college education. Between 8 and 16 percent of native-born women earned $21,200 compared to 50 percent of Anglo males. Similar patterns were found among college-educated foreign-born women.

The fact that Asian American women do not reap the income benefits one 26 might expect given their high levels of educational achievement raises questions about the reasons for such inequality. To what extent is this discrepancy based on outright discrimination? On self-imposed limitations related to cultural modesty? The absence of certain social or interpersonal skills required for upper managerial positions? Or institutional factors beyond their control? It is beyond the scope of this paper to address such concerns. However, the fact of inequality is itself noteworthy and poorly appreciated.

In general, Asian American women usually are overrepresented in clerical 27 or administrative support jobs. While there is a somewhat greater tendency for foreign-born college-educated Asian women to find clerical-related jobs, both native- and foreign-born women have learned that clerical work is the area where they are most easily employed. In fact, in 1970 a third of native-born Chinese women were doing clerical work. A decade later Filipino women were concentrated there. In addition Asian American women tend to be overrepresented as cashiers, file clerks, office machine operators, and typists. They are less likely to get jobs as secretaries or receptionists. The former occupations not only carry less prestige but generally have "little or no decision-making authority, low mobility and low public contact."[15]

In short, education may improve one's chances for success, but it cannot 28 promise the American Dream. For Asian American women education seems to serve less as an opportunity for upward mobility than as protection against jobs as service or assembly workers, or as machine operatives—all areas where foreign-born Asian women are far more likely to find themselves.

CONCLUSION

In this essay I have attempted to direct our attention on the gap between 29 achievement and reward, specifically the failure to reward monetarily those who have demonstrated competence. Asian American women, like Asian American men, have been touted as "model minorities," praised for their outstanding achievements. The concept of model minority, however, obscures the fact that one's accomplishments are not adequately recognized in terms of commensurate income or choice of occupation. By focusing on the achievements of one minority in relation to another, our attention is diverted from larger institutional and historical factors which influence a group's success. Each ethnic group has a different history, and a simplistic method of modeling which assumes the experience of all immigrants is the same ignores the sociostructural context in which a certain kind of achievement occurred. For example, World War II enabled many Asian Americans who were technically trained and highly educated to move into lucrative war-related industries.[16] More recently, Korean immigrants during the 1960s were able to capitalize on the fast-growing demand for wigs in the United States. It was not simply cultural ingenuity or individual hard work which made them successful in this enterprise, but the fact that Korean immigrants were in the unique position of being able to import cheap hair products from their mother country.[17]

Just as there are structural opportunities, so there are structural barriers. [30] However, the persistent emphasis in American society on individual effort deflects attention away from such barriers and creates self-doubt among those who have not "made it." The myth that Asian Americans have succeeded as a group, when in actuality there are serious discrepancies between effort and achievement, and between achievement and reward, adds still further to this self-doubt.

While others have also pointed out the myth of the model minority, I want [31] to add that myths do have social functions. It would be a mistake to dismiss the model minority concept as merely a myth. Asian Americans are—however inappropriately—thrust into the role of being models for other minorities.

A closer look at the images associated with Asians as a model minority group [32] suggests competing or contradictory themes. One image is that Asian Americans exemplify a competitive spirit enabling them to overcome structural barriers through perseverance and ingenuity. On the other hand, they are also seen as complacent, content with their social lot, and expecting little in the way of outside help. A third image is that Asian Americans are experts at assimilation, demonstrating that this society still functions as a melting pot. Their values are sometimes equated with white, middle-class, Protestant values of hard work, determination, and thrift. Opposing this image, however, is still another, namely that Asian Americans have succeeded because they possess cultural values unique to them as a group—their family-centeredness and long tradition of reverence for scholarly achievement, for example.

Perhaps, then, this is why so many readily accept the myth, whose tenacity [33] is due to its being vague and broad enough to appeal to a variety of different groups. Yet to the extent that the myth is based on misconceptions, we are called upon to reexamine it more closely in an effort to narrow the gap between striving and achieving.[18]

NOTES

1. Ted Bell, "Quiet Loyalty Keeps Shops Running," *Sacramento Bee*. 11 February 1985.

2. Amado Y. Cabezas and Pauline L. Fong, "Employment Status of Asian-Pacific Women" (Background paper: San Francisco: ASIAN, Inc., 1976).

3. U.S. Bureau of the Census. *Race of the Population by States* (Washington, D.C., 1980). According to the census, 40 percent of all Chinese in America live in California, as well as 46 percent of all Filipinos, and 37 percent of all Japanese. New York ranks second for the number of Chinese residing there, and Hawaii is the second most populated state for Filipinos and Japanese.

4. Tricia Knoll, *Becoming Americans: Asian Sojourners, Immigrants, and Refugees in the Western United States* (Portland, Oreg.: Coast to Coast Books, 1982), 152.

5. U.S. Commission on Civil Rights, *Social Indicators of Equality for Minorities and Women* (Washington, D.C., 1978), 24, 50, 54, 58, 62.

6. David M. Moulton. "The Socioeconomic Status of Asian American Families in Five Major SMSAs" (Paper prepared for the Conference of Pacific and Asian American Families and HEW-related Issues. San Francisco, 1978). No comparative data were available on blacks for the fifth SMSA. Honolulu.

7. James E. Blackwell. *Mainstreaming Outsiders* (New York: General Hall, Inc., 1981), 306; and Commission on Civil Rights. *Social Indicators*, 9.

8. California Advisory Committee, "A Dream Unfulfilled: Korean and Filipino Health Professionals in California" (Report prepared for submission to U.S. Commission on Civil Rights, May 1975), iii.

9. See Amado Y. Cabezas, "A View of Poor Linkages between Education, Occupation and Earnings for Asian Americans" (Paper presented at the Third National Forum on Education and Work, San Francisco, 1977), 17; and Census of Population, PUS, 1980.

10. Census of the Population, PUS, 1970, 1980.

11. A 1977 report on California families showed that an average of 9.3 percent of Japanese, Chinese, and Filipino families were below the poverty level, but that only 5.4 percent of these families received public assistance. The corresponding figures for Anglos were 6.3 percent and 5.9 percent. From Harold T. Yee, "The General Level of Well-Being of Asian Americans" (Paper presented to U.S. government officials in partial response to Justice Department amicus).

12. Moulton, "Socioeconomic Status," 70–71.

13. Commission on Civil Rights, *Social Indicators*, 54.

14. The few exceptions occur in Honolulu with women who had more than a high school education and in Chicago with women who had a high school education or three years of college. Even these women fared poorly when compared to men, however.

15. Bob H. Suzuki, "Education and the Socialization of Asian Americans: A Revisionist Analysis of the 'Model Minority' Thesis," *Amerasia Journal* 4:2 (1977): 43. See also Fong and Cabezas, "Economic and Employment Status," 48–49; and Commission on Civil Rights, *Social Indicators*, 97–98.

16. U.S. Commission on Civil Rights, "Education Issues" in *Civil Rights Issues of Asian and Pacific Americans: Myths and Realities* (Washington, D.C., 1979), 370–376. This material was presented by Ling-chi Wang, University of California, Berkeley.

17. Illsoo Kim. *New Urban Immigrants: The Korean Community in New York* (Princeton, N.J.: Princeton University Press, 1981).

18. For further discussion of the model minority myth and interpretation of census data, see Deborah Woo, "The Socioeconomic Status of Asian American Women in the Labor Force: An Alternative View," *Sociological Perspectives* 28:3 (July 1985):307–338.

QUESTIONS

1. In her introduction, Deborah Woo points out that the tendency to view Asian-Americans as a "model minority" has obscured the issue she wishes to address: "What has kept Asians from *fully* reaping the fruits of their education and hard work?" Does she fully answer this question?

2. Woo states that "All ethnic groups create their own myths." What reasons does she give for Chinese-Americans to have done so? What are the cultural myths of other ethnic groups you know of? Were those myths created inside or outside the group?

3. What evidence does Woo present to substantiate her claim of unequal treatment of Asian-American women in the workplace? How does the experience of Asian-American males compare with theirs? Can we say on the basis of her evidence that Asian-American women have a special case, or do their lower salaries reflect the unequal pay of *all* women in the workplace?

4. Are statistics facts, or are they what we make of them? Woo uses statistics to make her argument, but she also criticizes the way statistics have been interpreted (see Paragraphs 10 and 11, for example). Do you think she is justified in her criticism? Identify other examples of statistical manipulation.

5. Write an essay utilizing the information in Woo's article to comment on the status of the American Dream, describing your own or your family's experience if you wish.

6. Woo mentions the exploitation of Asian-American women in the garment industry. Investigate this matter further, and write up your findings. Or you might investigate other instances of discrimination in the workplace. For example, is the low pay usually given teenage fast-food workers a form of exploitation?

MAKING CONNECTIONS

1. Compare Richard Rodriguez's comments on cultural assimilation and the American Dream in "Children of a Marriage" with Deborah Woo's essay.

2. How might Susan Fraker's observations on the issue of women's success in management jobs be complicated by the ethnic factors raised by Deborah Woo in her discussion?

A MODEST PROPOSAL
Jonathan Swift

Jonathan Swift (1667–1745) was born in Dublin, Ireland, of English parents and educated in Irish schools. A graduate of Trinity College, Dublin, he received an M.A. from Oxford and was ordained a priest in the Church of England in 1695. He was active in politics as well as religion, becoming an editor and pamphlet writer for the Tory party in 1710. After becoming Dean of St. Patrick's Cathedral, Dublin, in 1713, he settled in Ireland and began to take an interest in the English economic exploitation of Ireland, gradually becoming a fierce Irish patriot. By 1724 the English were offering a reward for the discovery of the writer of the Drapier's Letters, *a series of pamphlets secretly written by Swift, attacking the British for their treatment of Ireland. In 1726 Swift produced the first volume of a more universal satire, known to modern readers as* Gulliver's Travels, *which has kept his name alive for two hundred and fifty years. "A Modest Proposal," his best-known essay on Irish affairs, appeared in 1729.*

A Modest Proposal
for Preventing the Children of Poor People in Ireland
from Being a Burden to Their Parents or Country,
and for Making Them Beneficial to the Public

It is a melancholy object to those who walk through this great town,[1] or travel in the country, when they see the streets, the roads and cabin-doors crowded with beggars of the female sex, followed by three, four, or six children, all in rags, and importuning every passenger for an alms. These mothers, instead of being able to work for their honest livelihood, are forced to employ all their time in strolling, to beg sustenance for their helpless infants, who, as they grow up, either turn thieves for want of work, or leave their dear na-

---

[1] this great town: Dublin. [Eds.]

tive country to fight for the Pretender in Spain,[2] or sell themselves to the Barbadoes.[3]

I think it is agreed by all parties that this prodigious number of children, in the arms, or on the backs, or at the heels of their mothers, and frequently of their fathers, is in the present deplorable state of the kingdom a very great additional grievance; and therefore whoever could find out a fair, cheap, and easy method of making these children sound and useful members of the commonwealth would deserve so well of the public as to have his statue set up for a preserver of the nation.

But my intention is very far from being confined to provide only for the children of professed beggars; it is of a much greater extent, and shall take in the whole number of infants at a certain age who are born of parents in effect as little able to support them as those who demand our charity in the streets.

As to my own part, having turned my thoughts for many years upon this important subject, and maturely weighed the several schemes of other projectors, I have always found them grossly mistaken in their computation. It is true a child just dropped from its dam may be supported by her milk for a solar year with little other nourishment, at most not above the value of two shillings,[4] which the mother may certainly get, or the value in scraps, by her lawful occupation of begging, and it is exactly at one year old that I propose to provide for them, in such a manner as, instead of being a charge upon their parents, or the parish, or wanting food and raiment for the rest of their lives, they shall, on the contrary, contribute to the feeding and partly to the clothing of many thousands.

There is likewise another great advantage to my scheme, that it will prevent those voluntary abortions, and that horrid practice of women murdering their bastard children, alas, too frequent among us, sacrificing the poor innocent babes, I doubt, more to avoid the expense than the shame, which would move tears and pity in the most savage and inhuman breast.

The number of souls in Ireland being usually reckoned one million and a half, of these I calculate there may be about two hundred thousand couples whose wives are breeders, from which number I subtract thirty thousand couples who are able to maintain their own children, although I apprehend there cannot be so many under the present distresses of the kingdom, but this being granted, there will remain an hundred and seventy thousand breeders. I again subtract fifty thousand for those women who miscarry, or whose children die by accident

---

[2] Pretender in Spain: a Catholic descendant of the British royal family (James I, Charles I, and Charles II) of Stuart. Exiled so that England could be governed by Protestant rulers, the Stuarts lurked in France and Spain, preparing various disastrous schemes for regaining the throne. [Eds.]

[3] sell themselves to the Barbadoes: sell themselves as indentured servants, a sort of temporary slavery, to the sugar merchants of the British Caribbean islands. [Eds.]

[4] shillings: a shilling used to be worth about one day's labor. [Eds.]

or disease within the year. There only remain an hundred and twenty thousand children of poor parents annually born: the question therefore is, how this number shall be reared, and provided for, which as I have already said, under the present situation of affairs is utterly impossible by all the methods hitherto proposed, for we can neither employ them in handicraft or agriculture; we neither build houses (I mean in the country), nor cultivate land: they can very seldom pick up a livelihood by stealing until they arrive at six years old, except where they are of towardly parts, although I confess they learn the rudiments much earlier, during which time they can however be properly looked upon only as probationers, as I have been informed by a principal gentleman in the County of Cavan, who protested to me that he never knew above one or two instances under the age of six, even in a part of the kingdom so renowned for the quickest proficiency in that art.

I am assured by our merchants that a boy or girl before twelve years old, is no saleable commodity, and even when they come to this age, they will not yield above three pounds, or three pounds and half-a-crown at most on the Exchange, which cannot turn to account either to the parents or the kingdom, the charge of nutriment and rags having been at least four times that value.   7

I shall now therefore humbly propose my own thoughts, which I hope will not be liable to the least objection.   8

I have been assured by a very knowing American of my acquaintance in London, that a young healthy child well nursed is at a year old a most delicious, nourishing and wholesome food, whether stewed, roasted, baked, or boiled, and I make no doubt that it will equally serve in a fricassee, or a ragout.   9

I do therefore humbly offer it to public consideration, that of the hundred and twenty thousand children already computed, twenty thousand may be reserved for breed, whereof only one fourth part to be males, which is more than we allow to sheep, black-cattle, or swine, and my reason is that these children are seldom the fruits of marriage, a circumstance not much regarded by our savages, therefore one male will be sufficient to serve four females. That the remaining hundred thousand may at a year old be offered in sale to the persons of quality, and fortune, through the kingdom, always advising the mother to let them suck plentifully in the last month, so as to render them plump, and fat for a good table. A child will make two dishes at an entertainment for friends, and when the family dines alone, the fore or hind quarters will make a reasonable dish, and seasoned with a little pepper or salt will be very good boiled on the fourth day, especially in winter.   10

I have reckoned upon a medium, that a child just born will weigh twelve pounds, and in a solar year if tolerably nursed increaseth to twenty-eight pounds.   11

I grant this food will be somewhat dear, and therefore very proper for landlords, who, as they have already devoured most of the parents, seem to have the best title to the children.   12

Infant's flesh will be in season throughout the year, but more plentiful in 13
March, and a little before and after, for we are told by a grave author, an
eminent French physician,[5] that fish being a prolific diet, there are more
children born in Roman Catholic countries about nine months after Lent than
at any other season; therefore reckoning a year after Lent, the markets will be
more glutted than usual, because the number of Popish infants is at least three
to one in this kingdom, and therefore it will have one other collateral advantage
by lessening the number of Papists among us.

I have already computed the charge of nursing a beggar's child (in which list 14
I reckon all cottagers, labourers, and four-fifths of the farmers) to be about two
shillings *per annum*, rags included, and I believe no gentleman would repine
to give ten shillings for the carcass of a good fat child, which, as I have said,
will make four dishes of excellent nutritive meat, when he hath only some
particular friend of his own family to dine with him. Thus the Squire will learn
to be a good landlord and grow popular among his tenants, the mother will
have eight shillings net profit, and be fit for work until she produces another
child.

Those who are more thrifty (as I must confess the times require) may flay 15
the carcass; the skin of which artificially dressed, will make admirable gloves
for ladies, and summer boots for fine gentlemen.

As to our city of Dublin, shambles[6] may be appointed for this purpose, in 16
the most convenient parts of it, and butchers we may be assured will not be
wanting, although I rather recommend buying the children alive, and dressing
them hot from the knife, as we do roasting pigs.

A very worthy person, a true lover of his country, and whose virtues I highly 17
esteem was lately pleased, in discoursing on this matter to offer a refinement
upon my scheme. He said that many gentlemen of this kingdom, having of
late destroyed their deer, he conceived that the want of venison might be well
supplied by the bodies of young lads and maidens, not exceeding fourteen years
of age, nor under twelve, so great a number of both sexes in every county being
now ready to starve, for want of work and service: and these to be disposed of
by their parents if alive, or otherwise by their nearest relations. But with due
deference to so excellent a friend, and so deserving a patriot, I cannot be
altogether in his sentiments. For as to the males, my American acquaintance
assured me from frequent experience that their flesh was generally tough and
lean, like that of our schoolboys, by continual exercise, and their taste disagreeable, and to fatten them would not answer the charge. Then as to the females,
it would, I think with humble submission, be a loss to the public, because they

---

[5] French physician: François Rabelais (1494?–1553), physician and satirist known for his *Gar-
gantua and Pantagruel*. [Eds.]
[6] shambles: slaughterhouses. [Eds.]

soon would become breeders themselves: and besides, it is not improbable that some scrupulous people might be apt to censure such a practice (although indeed very unjustly) as a little bordering upon cruelty, which I confess, hath always been with me the strongest objection against any project, howsoever well intended.

But in order to justify my friend, he confessed that this expedient was put 18 into his head by the famous Psalmanazar, a native of the island Formosa, who came from thence to London, above twenty years ago, and in conversation told my friend that in his country when any young person happened to be put to death, the executioner sold the carcass to persons of quality, as a prime dainty, and that, in his time, the body of a plump girl of fifteen, who was crucified for an attempt to poison the emperor, was sold to his Imperial Majesty's Prime Minister of State, and other great Mandarins of the Court, in joints from the gibbet, at four hundred crowns. Neither indeed can I deny that if the same use were made of several plump young girls in this town who, without one single groat to their fortunes, cannot stir abroad without a chair, and appear at the playhouse and assemblies in foreign fineries, which they never will pay for, the kingdom would not be the worse.

Some persons of a desponding spirit are in great concern about that vast 19 number of poor people, who are aged, diseased, or maimed, and I have been desired to employ my thoughts what course may be taken to ease the nation of so grievous an encumbrance. But I am not in the least pain upon that matter, because it is very well known that they are every day dying, and rotting, by cold, and famine, and filth, and vermin, as fast as can be reasonably expected. And as to the younger labourers they are now in almost as hopeful a condition. They cannot get work, and consequently pine away from want of nourishment, to a degree that if at any time they are accidentally hired to common labour, they have not strength to perform it; and thus the country and themselves are in a fair way of being soon delivered from the evils to come.

I have too long digressed, and therefore shall return to my subject. I think 20 the advantages by the proposal which I have made are obvious and many, as well as of the highest importance.

For first, as I have already observed, it would greatly lessen the number of 21 Papists, with whom we are yearly over-run, being the principal breeders of the nation, as well as our most dangerous enemies, and who stay at home on purpose with a design to deliver the kingdom to the Pretender, hoping to take their advantage by the absence of so many good Protestants, who have chosen rather to leave their country than stay at home and pay tithes against their conscience to an idolatrous Episcopal curate.

Secondly, the poorer tenants will have something valuable of their own, 22 which by law may be made liable to distress, and help to pay their landlord's rent, their corn and cattle being already seized, and money a thing unknown.

Thirdly, whereas the maintenance of an hundred thousand children, from 23
two years old, and upwards, cannot be computed at less than ten shillings a
piece *per annum*, the nation's stock will be thereby increased fifty thousand
pounds *per annum*, besides the profit of a new dish, introduced to the tables of
all gentlemen of fortune in the kingdom, who have any refinement in taste,
and the money will circulate among ourselves, the goods being entirely of our
own growth and manufacture.

Fourthly, the constant breeders, besides the gain of eight shillings sterling 24
per annum, by the sale of their children, will be rid of the charge of maintaining
them after the first year.

Fifthly, this food would likewise bring great custom to taverns, where the 25
vintners will certainly be so prudent as to procure the best receipts for dressing
it to perfection, and consequently have their houses frequented by all the fine
gentlemen, who justly value themselves upon their knowledge in good eating;
and a skilful cook, who understands how to oblige his guests, will contrive to
make it as expensive as they please.

Sixthly, this would be a great inducement to marriage, which all wise nations 26
have either encouraged by rewards, or enforced by laws and penalties. It would
increase the care and tenderness of mothers towards their children, when they
were sure of a settlement for life, to the poor babes, provided in some sort by
the public to their annual profit instead of expense. We should soon see an
honest emulation among the married women, which of them could bring the
fattest child to the market. Men would become as fond of their wives, during
the time of their pregnancy, as they are now of their mares in foal, their cows
in calf, or sows when they are ready to farrow, nor offer to beat or kick them
(as it is too frequent a practice) for fear of a miscarriage.

Many other advantages might be enumerated. For instance, the addition of 27
some thousand carcasses in our exportation of barrelled beef; the propagation
of swine's flesh, and improvement in the art of making good bacon, so much
wanted among us by the great destruction of pigs, too frequent at our tables,
are no way comparable in taste or magnificence to a well-grown, fat yearling
child, which roasted whole will make a considerable figure at a Lord Mayor's
feast, or any other public entertainment. But this and many others I omit, being
studious of brevity.

Supposing that one thousand families in this city would be constant custom- 28
ers for infants' flesh, besides others who might have it at merry meetings,
particularly weddings and christenings; I compute that Dublin would take off
annually about twenty thousand carcasses, and the rest of the kingdom (where
probably they will be sold somewhat cheaper) the remaining eighty thousand.

I can think of no one objection that will possibly be raised against this 29
proposal, unless it should be urged that the number of people will be thereby
must lessened in the kingdom. This I freely own, and it was indeed one principal

design in offering it to the world. I desire the reader will observe, that I calculate my remedy *for this one individual Kingdom of* Ireland, *and for no other that ever was, is, or, I think, ever can be upon earth.* Therefore let no man talk to me of other expedients: *Of taxing our absentees at five shillings a pound: Of using neither clothes, nor household furniture, except what is of our own growth and manufacture: Of utterly rejecting the materials and instruments that promote foreign luxury: Of curing the expensiveness of pride, vanity, idleness, and gaming in our women: Of introducing a vein of parsimony, prudence, and temperance: Of learning to love our country, wherein we differ even from* Laplanders, *and the inhabitants of* Topinamboo: *Of quitting our animosities and factions, nor act any longer like the* Jews, *who were murdering one another at the very moment their city was taken: Of being a little cautious not to sell our country and consciences for nothing: Of teaching landlords to have at least one degree of mercy towards their tenants.* Lastly, *of putting a spirit of honesty, industry, and skill into our shopkeepers, who, if a resolution could now be taken to buy only our native goods, would immediately unite to cheat and exact upon us in the price, the measure and the goodness, nor could ever yet be brought to make one fair proposal of just dealing, though often and earnestly invited to it.*

Therefore I repeat, let no man talk to me of these and the like expedients, till he hath at least a glimpse of hope that there will ever be some hearty and sincere attempt to put them in practice.

But as to myself, having been wearied out for many years with offering vain, idle, visionary thoughts, and at length utterly despairing of success, I fortunately fell upon this proposal, which as it is wholly new, so it hath something solid and real, of no expense and little trouble, full in our own power, and whereby we can incur no danger in disobliging England. For this kind of commodity will not bear exportation, the flesh being of too tender a consistence to admit a long continuance in salt, *although perhaps I could name a country which would be glad to eat up our whole nation without it.*

After all I am not so violently bent upon my own opinion as to reject any offer, proposed by wise men, which shall be found equally innocent, cheap, easy and effectual. But before some thing of that kind shall be advanced in contradiction to my scheme, and offering a better, I desire the author, or authors, will be pleased maturely to consider two points. First, as things now stand, how they will be able to find food and raiment for a hundred thousand useless mouths and backs? And secondly, there being a round million of creatures in human figure, throughout this kingdom, whose whole subsistence put into a common stock would leave them in debt two millions of pounds sterling; adding those who are beggars by profession, to the bulk of farmers, cottagers, and laborers with their wives and children, who are beggars in effect; I desire those politicians who dislike my overture, and may perhaps be so bold to attempt an answer, that they will first ask the parents of these mortals whether they would not at this day think it a great happiness to have been sold for food at a year old, in the manner I prescribe, and thereby have avoided such a perpetual scene of misfortunes as they have since gone through, by the oppression of landlords, the impossibility of paying rent without money or trade, the want of common sustenance, with neither house nor clothes to cover them from the inclemencies of weather, and the most inevitable prospect of entailing the like, or greater miseries upon their breed for ever.

I profess in the sincerity of my heart that I have not the least personal interest 33 in endeavoring to promote this necessary work, having no other motive than the *public good of my country, by advancing our trade, providing for infants, relieving the poor, and giving some pleasure to the rich.* I have no children by which I can propose to get a single penny; the youngest being nine years old, and my wife past child-bearing.

QUESTIONS

1. A proposal always involves a proposer. What is the character of the proposer here? Do we perceive his character to be the same throughout the essay? Compare, for example, paragraphs 21, 26, and 33.

2. When does the proposer actually offer his proposal? What does he do before making his proposal? What does he do after making his proposal? How does the order in which he does things affect our impression of him and of his proposal?

3. What kind of counterarguments to his own proposal does this proposer anticipate? How does he answer and refute proposals that might be considered alternatives to his?

4. In reading this essay, most persons are quite certain that the author, Swift, does not himself endorse the proposer's proposal. How do we distinguish the two of them? What details of style help us make this distinction?

5. Consider the proposer, the counterarguments the proposer acknowledges and refutes, and Swift himself, who presumably does not endorse the proposer's proposal. To what extent is Swift's position essentially that which his proposer refutes? To what extent is it a somewhat different position still?

6. To what extent does an ironic essay like this depend upon the author and reader sharing certain values without question or reservation? Can you discover any such values explicitly or implicitly present in Swift's essay?

7. Use Swift's technique to write a "modest proposal" of your own about some contemporary situation. That is, use some outlandish proposal as a way of drawing attention to a situation that needs correcting. Consider carefully the character you intend to project for your proposer and the way you intend to make your own view distinguishable from hers or his.

JONATHAN SWIFT

MAKING CONNECTIONS

1. By calling his essay "Some Very Modest Proposals . . . ," Nathan Glazer strikes a relation to Swift and announces that his essay will be somewhat like Swift's. How much of a relation do you find between the two essays? Where is Glazer most like Swift? What does he gain from that association?

2. Another ironic essay in this collection is Horace Miner's "Body Ritual of the Nacirema," in "Reporting." How similar is it to Swift's essay? How different? Consider especially your sense of the person doing the reporting. Do you find any reason to connect Miner's reporter with Swift's proposer?

SOME VERY MODEST PROPOSALS FOR THE IMPROVEMENT OF AMERICAN EDUCATION

Nathan Glazer

Nathan Glazer (b. 1923) is a New York City native, a professor of education and sociology at Harvard University, and coeditor of The Public Interest *magazine. His books include* The Lonely Crowd *(1950) with Reuel Denney and David Riesman,* Beyond the Melting Pot *(2nd edition, 1970) with Daniel P. Moynihan,* Affirmative Discrimination: Ethnic Inequality and Public Policy *(1975), and an essay collection,* Ethnic Dilemmas, 1964–1982 *(1983). The following essay appeared first in the magazine* Daedalus, *an interdisciplinary journal of The American Academy of Arts and Sciences (Fall 1984). By mentioning "modest proposals," Glazer refers to Jonathan Swift's famous essay which precedes this section. By that term, Glazer also suggests deceptively simple steps that go directly to the heart of the problem. How "modest" are his proposals?*

That we can do a great deal for the sorry state of American education with more money is generally accepted. Even apparently modest proposals will, however, cost a great deal of money. Consider something as simple as increasing the average compensation of American teachers—who are generally considered underpaid—by $2,000 a year each. The bill would come to five billion dollars a year. A similar figure is reached by the report of the highly qualified Twentieth Century Fund Task Force on Federal, Elementary, and Secondary Educational Policy, which proposes fellowships and additional compensation for master teachers. Reducing class size 10 percent, or increasing the number of teachers by the same percentage would cost another five billion dollars. With present-day federal deficits, these look like small sums, but since education is paid for almost entirely by states and local government, these modest proposals would lead to substantial and painful tax increases. (I leave aside for the moment the views of skeptics who believe that none of these changes would matter.)

But the occasional visitor to American schools will note some changes that would cost much less, nothing at all, or even save money—and yet would improve at least the educational *environment* in American schools (once again, we ignore those skeptics who would insist that even a better educational environment cannot be guaranteed to improve educational achievement). In the

693

spirit of evoking further cheap proposals, here is a small list of suggestions that, to my mind at least—and the mind I believe of any adult who visits American public schools—would mean a clear plus for American education:

1. *Disconnect all loudspeaker systems in American schools—or at least reserve* 3 *them, like the hotline between Moscow and Washington, for only the gravest emergencies.* The American classroom—and the American teacher and his or her charges—is continually interrupted by announcements from central head-quarters over the loudspeaker system. These remind teachers to bring in some form or other; or students to bring in some form or other; or students engaged in some activity to remember to come to practice or rehearsal; or they announce a change of time for some activity. There is nothing so unnerving to a teacher engaged in trying to explain something, or a student engaged in trying to understand something, as the crackle of the loudspeaker prepared to issue an announcement, and the harsh and gravelly voice (the systems are not obviously of the highest grade) of the announcement itself.

Aside from questions of personal taste, why would this be a good idea? As I 4 have suggested, one reason is that the loudspeaker interrupts efforts to com-municate complicated material that requires undivided attention. Second, it demeans the teacher as professional: every announcement tells her whatever she is doing is not very important and can be interrupted at any time. Third, it accentuates the notion of hierarchy in education—the principal and assistant principal are the most important people, and command time and attention even in the midst of instruction. Perhaps I have been softened by too many years as a college teacher, but it would be unimaginable that a loudspeaker, if one existed, would ever interrupt a college class except under conditions of the gravest and most immediate threat to life and limb. One way of showing students that education is important is not to interrupt it for band-rehearsal announce-ments.

2. *Disarm the school.* One of the most depressing aspects of the urban school 5 in the United States is the degree of security manifest within it, and that seems to me quite contradictory to what a school should be. Outer doors are locked. Security guards are present in the corridors. Internal doors are locked. Passes are necessary to enter the school or move within it, for outsiders and for students. Students are marched in groups from classroom to classroom, under the eye of the teachers. It is understandable that given the conditions in lower-class areas in our large cities—and not only lower-class areas—some degree of security-mindedness is necessary. There is valuable equipment—typewriters, computers, audio-visual equipment—that can be stolen; vandalism is a serious concern; marauders can enter the school in search for equipment, or teachers' pocket-books, or to threaten directly personal safety in search of money or sex, and so on. School integration and busing, at least in their initial stages, have contrib-

uted to increased interracial tensions in schools and have in part severed the link between community and school. The difference in ethnic and racial composition of faculty, other staff, administrators, and students contributes to the same end.

Having acknowledged all this, I still believe the school should feel less like a prison than it does. One should examine to what extent outside doors must be closed; to what extent the security guard cannot be replaced by local parents, volunteer or paid; the degree to which the endless bells indicating "stop" and "go" are really necessary. I suspect that now that the most difficult period of school integration has passed, now that teachers and administrators and staff more closely parallel in race and ethnic background students and community owing to the increase in black and Hispanic teachers and administrators, we may be saddled with more security than we need. Here we come to the sticky problem of *removing* security measures whose need has decreased. What school board will open itself to suit or to public criticism by deliberately providing *less* security? And yet one must consider the atmosphere of the school and a school's primary objective as a reaching agent: can this be reconciled with a condition of maximum security? Perhaps there are lessons to be learned from colleges and community colleges in older urban areas, which in my experience do seem to manage with less security. One reason is that there are more adults around in such institutions. Is that a hint as to how we could manage better in our public schools?

3. *Enlist the children in keeping the school clean.* Occasionally we see a practice abroad that suggests possible transfer to the American scene. In Japan, the children clean the school. There is a time of day when mops and pails and brooms come out, and the children sweep up and wash up. This does, I am sure, suggest to the children that this is *their* school, that it is not simply a matter of being forced to go to a foreign institution that imposes alien demands upon them. I can imagine some obstacles in the way of instituting regular student clean-up in American schools—custodians' unions, for example, might object. But they can be reassured that children don't do that good a job, and they will still be needed. Once again, as in the case of the security problem, one wants to create in the school, if at all possible, a common enterprise of teachers and students, without the latter being bored and resistant, the former, in response, becoming equally indifferent. The school should be seen as everyone's workplace—and participation in cleaning the school will help.

4. *Save old schools.* Build fewer new ones. It has often surprised me that while in schools such as Eton and Oxford—and indeed well-known private schools and colleges in the United States—old buildings are prized, in so many communities older public schools are torn down when to the naked eye they have many virtues that would warrant their maintenance and use. Only a few

695

blocks from where I live, an excellent example of late nineteenth-century fine brickwork and carved stonework that served as the Cambridge Latin School came down for a remodeling. The carved elements are still displayed about the remodeled school, but why a building of such character should have deserved demolition escaped my understanding, particularly since one can take it almost as a given that a school building put up before the 1940s will be built of heavier and sturdier materials than one constructed today. Even the inconveniences of the old can possess a charm that makes them worthwhile. And indeed many of the reforms that seemed to require new buildings (for example, classrooms without walls, concentrated around activities centers in large open rooms) have turned out, on use, to be not so desirable. Our aim should be to give each school a history, a character, something that at least some students respond to. The pressures for new buildings are enormous, and sometimes perfectly legitimate (as when communities expand), but often illegitimate, as when builders and building-trades workers and contract-givers seek an opportunity or when state aid makes it appear as if a new building won't cost anything.

5. *Look on new hardware with a skeptical eye.* I think it likely that the passion for the new in the way of teaching-hardware not only does not contribute to higher education achievement but may well serve as a temporary means to evade the real and hard tasks of teaching—which really require almost no hardware at all, besides textbooks, blackboard, and chalk. Admittedly, when one comes to high-school science, something more is called for. And yet our tendency is to always find cover behind new hardware. It's *fun* to get new audio-visual equipment, new rooms equipped with them in which all kinds of things can be done by flicking a switch or twisting a dial, or, as is now the case, to decide what kind of personal computers and software are necessary for a good educational program. Once again, foreign experience can be enlightening. When Japanese education was already well ahead of American, most Japanese schools were in prewar wooden buildings. (They are now as up-to-date as ours, but neither their age nor up-to-dateness has much to do with their good record of achievement.) Resisting the appeal of new hardware not only saves money, and provides less in the way of saleable goods to burglarize, but it also prevents distraction from the principal tasks of reading, writing, and calculating. When it turns out that computers and new software are shown to do a better job at these key tasks—I am skeptical as to whether this will ever be the case—there will be time enough to splurge on new equipment. The teacher, alone, up front, explaining, encouraging, guiding, is the heart of the matter—the rest is fun, and very helpful to corporate income, and gives an inflated headquarters staff something new to do. But students will have time enough to learn about computers when they get to college, and getting there will depend almost not at all on what they can do with computers, but how well they understand words and sentences, and how well they do at simple mathematics.

There is nothing wrong with old textbooks, too. Recently, reviewing some 10
recent high-school American history texts, I was astonished to discover they
come out in new editions every two years or so, and not because the main body
of the text is improved, but because the textbook wants to be able to claim it
covers the very last presidential campaign, and the events of the last few years.
This is a waste of time and energy and money. There is enough to teach in
American history up to 1950 or 1960 not to worry about whether the text
includes Reagan's tax cuts. I suspect many new texts in other areas also offer
little advantage over the older ones. There is also a virtue in a teacher becoming
acquainted with a particular textbook. When I read that a school is disadvantaged
because its textbooks are old, I am always mystified. Even the newest advances
in physics and biology might well be reserved for college.

6. *Expand the pool from which we draw good teachers.* This general heading 11
covers a number of simple and concrete things, such as: if a teacher is considered
qualified to teach at a good private school, that teacher should be considered
qualified to teach at a public school. It has always seemed to me ridiculous that
teachers accepted at the best private schools in New York City or top preparatory
schools in the country would not be allowed to teach in the public school
system of New York or Boston. Often, they are willing—after all, the pay is
better in public schools and there are greater fringe benefits. They might, it is
true, be driven out of those schools by the challenge of lower- and working-
class children. But when they are willing, it seems unbelievable that the teacher
qualified (or so Brearley thinks) for Brearley will not be allowed to teach at P.S.
122.[1] Greater use of part-time teachers might also be able to draw upon people
with qualities that we are told the average teacher unfortunately doesn't possess—such as a higher level of competence in writing and mathematics.

Our recurrent concern with foreign-language teaching should lead us to 12
recruit foreign-born teachers. There are problems in getting teaching jobs today
in Germany and France—yet teachers there are typically drawn from pools of
students with higher academic skills than is the case in this country. Paradoxically, we make it easy for teachers of Spanish-language background to get jobs
owing to the expansion of bilingual programs—but then their teaching is confined to children whose Spanish accent doesn't need improvement. It would
make more sense to expose children of foreign-language background more to
teachers with native English—and children from English-speaking families to
teachers who speak French, German, Spanish, and, why not, Japanese, and
Chinese natively. This would mean that rules requiring that a teacher must be
a citizen, or must speak English without an accent, should be lifted for special
teachers with special tasks. Perhaps we could make the most of the oversupply
of teachers in some foreign countries by using them to teach mathematics—a

---

[1] Brearley: a prominent private school in New York City. [Eds.]

subject where accent doesn't count. The school system in Georgia is already recruiting from Germany. Colleges often use teaching assistants whose English is not native and far from perfect, including Asians from Korea and China, to assist in science and mathematics courses. (There are many state laws which would not permit them to teach in elementary and secondary schools.)

All the suggestions above eschew any involvement with some great issues of   13
education—tradition or reform, the teaching of values, the role of religion in the schools—that have in the past dominated arguments over education and still do today. But I add one more proposal that is still, I am afraid, somewhat controversial:

7. *Let students, within reason, pick their schools, or let parents choose them*   14
for them. All those informed on school issues will sense the heaving depths of controversy under this apparently modest proposal. Does this mean they might choose parochial schools, without being required to pay tuition out of their own pockets? Or does this mean black children would be allowed to attend schools in black areas, and whites in white areas, or the reverse if each is so inclined? As we all know, the two great issues of religion and race stand in the way of any such simple and commonsensical arrangement. Students are regularly bused from one section of a city to another because of their race, and students cannot without financial penalty attend that substantial sector of schools—30 percent or so in most Northern and Midwestern cities—that are called "private." I ignore the question of whether, holding all factors constant, students do "better" in private or public schools, in racially well-mixed or hardly mixed schools. The evidence will always be uncertain. What is perhaps less arguable is that students will do better in a school that forms a community, in which teachers, parents, and students all agree that *that* is the school they want to teach in, to attend, to send their children to. I would guess that this is the kind of school most of the readers of this article have attended; it is the kind of school, alas, that our complex racial and religious history makes it harder and harder for those of minority race or of lower- and working-class status to attend.

I have eschewed the grand proposals—for curriculum change, for improving   15
the quality of entering teachers, for checking on the competence of teachers in service, for establishing national standards for achievement in different levels of education—all of which now form the agenda for many state commissions of educational reform, and all of which seem reasonable to me. Rather, I have concentrated on a variety of other things that serve to remove distraction, to open the school to those of quality who would be willing to enter it to improve it, to concentrate on the essentials of teaching and learning as I (and many others) have experienced it. It would be possible to propose larger changes in the same direction: for example, reduce the size of the bureaucracies in urban school systems. Some of my modest proposals are insidiously intended to do this—if there were less effort devoted to building new schools, buying new

equipment, evaluating new textbooks, or busing children, there would be no need to maintain quite so many people at headquarters. Or so I would hope.

In the meantime, why not disconnect the loudspeakers?   16

QUESTIONS

1. Among Glazer's proposals, which seem to you the most helpful and which the least? Explain why.

2. Why do you think Glazer focuses so much on money in his first two paragraphs? Would his proposals "cost much less, nothing at all, or even save money," as he claims in paragraph 2? Explain why or why not.

3. What audience is Glazer addressing? What does he expect readers to do about his "modest proposals"?

4. How has Glazer ordered his seven proposals? Why do you think he arranged them as he did? What other methods of organization might he have used?

5. Glazer makes his suggestions "in the spirit," he says, "of evoking further cheap proposals" (paragraph 2). Offer a few of your own, with explanations.

6. Pool the proposals that you and your classmates have made for question 5. Select the best of these with the best possible explanations, and prepare a group report that you might even forward to Glazer, as well as to other possible audiences.

7. Proposals of this sort suggest parodies. Can you come up with a few comic or ironic proposals that you would like to make on behalf of "better education," something like sending all the teachers home for one day a week and leaving learning to the students? Or maybe all the administrators should become bus drivers, the bus drivers coaches, and the coaches administrators. Of course, you would need to advance reasons for your proposals.

8. In general, Glazer's proposals address public education in elementary and secondary schools, but by now you've had a taste of college. As either an individual or a group activity, make up a list of modest proposals for improving, inexpensively, the quality of education at your college. Present your list, if you wish, wherever you think it should go.

MAKING CONNECTIONS

1. To what extent does Glazer's essay play off of Jonathan Swift's "A Modest Proposal"? In what ways are they similar? How do they differ? Given these similarities and differences, why do you think Glazer selected the title he did?

2. Read Theodore R. Sizer's "What High School Is" in "Explaining." What effect do you think Glazer's proposals would have on high schools as described there? Would some proposals work better than others? Why do you think so? Can you think of related proposals that you might substitute for some of Glazer's? Write your own memo to American high schools, urging some very modest proposals on them.

THE DECLARATION OF INDEPENDENCE

Thomas Jefferson

Thomas Jefferson (1743–1826) was born in Shadwell, Virginia, attended William and Mary College, and became a lawyer. He was elected to the Virginia House of Burgesses in 1769 and was a delegate to the Continental Congress in 1776. When the Congress voted in favor of Richard Henry Lee's resolution that the colonies "ought to be free and independent states," a committee of five members, including John Adams, Benjamin Franklin, and Jefferson, was appointed to draw up a declaration. Jefferson, because of his eloquence as a writer, was asked by this committee to draw up a first draft. Jefferson's text, with a few changes suggested by Franklin and Adams, was presented to the Congress. After a debate in which further changes were made, including striking out a passage condemning the slave trade, the Declaration was approved on the fourth of July, 1776. Jefferson said of it: "Neither aiming at originality of principles or sentiments, nor yet copied from any particular and previous writing, it was intended to be an expression of the American mind."

In Congress, July 4, 1776
The unanimous Declaration of the
thirteen united States of America

When in the Course of human events it becomes necessary for one people   1
to dissolve the political bands which have connected them with another, and
to assume among the powers of the earth, the separate and equal station to
which the Laws of Nature and of Nature's God entitle them, a decent respect
to the opinions of mankind requires that they should declare the causes which
impel them to the separation.

We hold these truths to be self-evident, that all men are created equal, that   2
they are endowed by their Creator with certain unalienable Rights, that among
these are Life, Liberty and the pursuit of Happiness. That to secure these rights,
Governments are instituted among Men, deriving their just powers from the
consent of the governed. That whenever any Form of Government becomes
destructive of these ends, it is the Right of the People to alter or to abolish it,

and to institute new Government, laying its foundation on such principles and organizing its powers in such form, as to them shall seem most likely to affect their Safety and Happiness. Prudence, indeed, will dictate that Governments long established should not be changed for light and transient causes; and accordingly all experience hath shewn that mankind are more disposed to suffer, while evils are sufferable, than to right themselves by abolishing the forms to which they are accustomed. But when a long train of abuses and usurpations, pursuing invariably the same Object evinces a design to reduce them under absolute Despotism, it is their right, it is their duty, to throw off such Government, and to provide new Guards for their future security. Such has been the patient sufferance of these Colonies; and such is now the necessity which constrains them to alter their former Systems of Government. The history of the present King of Great Britain is a history of repeated injuries and usurpations, all having in direct object the establishment of an absolute Tyranny over these States. To prove this, let Facts be submitted to a candid world.

He has refused his Assent to Laws, the most wholesome and necessary for the public good. 3

He has forbidden his Governors to pass laws of immediate and pressing importance, unless suspended in their operation till his Assent should be obtained; and when so suspended, he has utterly neglected to attend to them. 4

He has refused to pass other Laws for the accommodation of large districts of people, unless those people would relinquish the right of Representation in the Legislature, a right inestimable to them and formidable to tyrants only. 5

He has called together legislative bodies at places unusual, uncomfortable, and distant from the depository of their Public Records, for the sole purpose of fatiguing them into compliance with his measures. 6

He has dissolved Representative Houses repeatedly, for opposing with manly firmness his invasions on the rights of the people. 7

He has refused for a long time, after such dissolutions, to cause others to be elected; whereby the Legislative Powers, incapable of Annihilation, have returned to the People at large for their exercise; the State remaining in the mean time exposed to all the dangers of invasion from without, and convulsions within. 8

He has endeavored to prevent the population of these States; for that purpose obstructing the Laws for Naturalization of Foreigners; refusing to pass others to encourage their migration hither, and raising the conditions of new Appropriations of Lands. 9

He has obstructed the Administration of Justice, by refusing his Assent to Laws for Establishing Judiciary Powers. 10

He has made Judges dependent on his Will alone, for the tenure of their offices, and the amount and payment of their salaries. 11

He has erected a multitude of New Offices, and sent hither swarms of Officers to harass our people, and eat out their substance. 12

He has kept among us, in times of peace, Standing Armies without the 13
Consent of our legislatures.

He has affected to render the Military independent of and superior to the 14
Civil Power.

He has combined with others to subject us to a jurisdiction foreign to our 15
constitution, and unacknowledged by our laws; giving his Assent to the Acts of
pretended Legislation: For quartering large bodies of armed troops among us:
For protecting them, by a mock Trial, from punishment for any Murders which
they should commit on the Inhabitants of these States: For cutting off our Trade
with all parts of the world: For imposing Taxes on us without our Consent: For
depriving us in many cases, of the benefits of Trial by Jury: For Transporting
us beyond Seas to be tried for pretended offenses: For abolishing the free System
of English Laws in a neighboring Province, establishing therein an Arbitrary
government, and enlarging its Boundaries so as to render it at once an example
and fit instrument for introducing the same absolute rule into these Colonies:
For taking away our Charters, abolishing our most valuable Laws and altering
fundamentally the Forms of our Governments: For suspending our own Legislatures, and declaring themselves invested with power to legislate for us in all
cases whatsoever.

He has abdicated Government here, by declaring us out of his Protection 16
and waging War against us.

He has plundered our seas, ravaged our Coasts, burnt our towns, and 17
destroyed the lives of our people.

He is at this time transporting large Armies of foreign Mercenaries to com- 18
plete the works of death, desolation and tyranny, already begun with circumstances of Cruelty & Perfidy scarcely paralleled in the most barbarous ages, and
totally unworthy the Head of a civilized nation.

He has constrained our fellow Citizens taken Captive on the high Seas to 19
bear Arms against their Country, to become the executioners of their friends
and Brethren, or to fall themselves by their Hands.

He has excited domestic insurrections amongst us, and has endeavored to 20
bring on the inhabitants of our frontiers, the merciless Indian Savages, whose
known rule of warfare is an undistinguished destruction of all ages, sexes, and
conditions.

In every stage of these Oppressions We have Petitioned for Redress in the 21
most humble terms: Our repeated petitions have been answered only by repeated
injury. A Prince, whose character is thus marked by every act which may define
a Tyrant, is unfit to be the ruler of a free people.

Nor have we been wanting in attention to our British brethren. We have 22
warned them from time to time of attempts by their legislature to extend an
unwarrantable jurisdiction over us. We have reminded them of the circumstances of our emigration and settlement here. We have appealed to their native
justice and magnanimity, and we have conjured them by the ties of our common

kindred to disavow these usurpations, which would inevitably interrupt our connections and correspondence. They too have been deaf to the voice of justice and of consanguinity. We must, therefore, acquiesce in the necessity, which denounces our Separation, and hold them, as we hold the rest of mankind, Enemies in War, in Peace Friends.

We, THEREFORE, the Representatives of the UNITED STATES OF AMERICA, in 23 General Congress, Assembled, appealing to the Supreme Judge of the world for the rectitude of our intentions, do, in the Name, and by Authority of the good People of these Colonies, solemnly publish and declare, That these United Colonies are, and of Right ought to be FREE AND INDEPENDENT STATES; that they are Absolved from all Allegiance to the British Crown, and that all political connection between them and the State of Great Britain, is and ought to be totally dissolved; and that as Free and Independent States; they have full Power to levy War, conclude Peace, contract Alliances, establish Commerce, and to do all the Acts and Things which Independent States may of right do. And for the support of this Declaration, with a firm reliance on the protection of Divine Providence, we mutually pledge to each other our Lives, our Fortunes, and our sacred Honor.

QUESTIONS

1. The Declaration of Independence is frequently cited as a classic deductive argument. A deductive argument is based on a general statement, or premise, that is assumed to be true. What does this document assume that the American colonists are entitled to and on what basis? Look at the reasoning in paragraph 2. What are these truths that are considered self-evident? What does *self-evident* mean?

2. What accusations against the king of Great Britain are the facts presented meant to substantiate? If you were the British king presented with this document, how might you reply to it? Would you first attack its premise or reply to its accusations? Or would you do both? (How did George III respond?)

3. To what extent is the audience of the Declaration intended to be the king and people of Great Britain?

4. What other audiences were intended for this document? Define at least two other audiences, and describe how each might be expected to respond.

5. Although this declaration could have been expected to lead to war and all the horrors thereof, it is a most civilized document, showing great respect throughout for certain standards of civility among people and among nations. Try to define the civilized standards the declaration assumes. Write an essay that tries to identify and characterize the nature and variety of those expectations.

6. Write a declaration of your own, announcing your separation from some injurious situation (an incompatible roommate, a noisy sorority or fraternity house, an awful job, or whatever). Start with a premise, give reasons to substantiate it, provide facts that illustrate the injurious conditions, and conclude with a statement of what your new condition will mean to you and to other oppressed people.

MAKING CONNECTIONS

1. If Jefferson's declaration is a classic deductive argument, as the first question above suggests, Alice Walker's "Am I Blue?" might stand as a clear example of inductive arguing. Review the structure of her argument. Where does she express her thesis most precisely? Why does she not announce it more quickly? What would the Declaration look like if Jefferson were to have approached it inductively? Write an inductive version of the Declaration of Independence.

2. What if Jefferson, rather than writing the Declaration of Independence, had, instead, offered "a modest proposal" to the British king? What do you suppose he would have said? How would he have formulated his argument? Write your own "modest proposal" to the king, addressing him in the manner of Swift, more or less, but drawing on the evidence Jefferson provides in the Declaration.

REVIEW OF STANLEY MILGRAM'S EXPERIMENTS ON OBEDIENCE

Diana Baumrind

Diana Baumrind (b. 1927) is a developmental and clinical psychologist with the Institute of Human Development at the University of California at Berkeley. Her research specializations are "the effects of family socialization on the development of social responsibility and personal agency in children and adolescents" and "the ethics of research with human subjects." That last subject is her topic here as she discusses the experiment conducted by Stanley Milgram (pages 418–42). This article appeared originally in 1964 in American Psychologist, *the journal of the American Psychological Association.*

Certain problems in psychological research require the experimenter to balance his career and scientific interests against the interests of his prospective subjects. When such occasions arise the experimenter's stated objective frequently is to do the best possible job with the least possible harm to his subjects. The experimenter seldom perceives in more positive terms an indebtedness to the subject for his services, perhaps because the detachment which his functions require prevents appreciation of the subject as an individual.

Yet a debt does exist, even when the subject's reason for volunteering includes course credit or monetary gain. Often a subject participates unwillingly in order to satisfy a course requirement. These requirements are of questionable merit ethically, and do not alter the experimenter's responsibility to the subject.

Most experimental conditions do not cause the subjects pain or indignity, and are sufficiently interesting or challenging to present no problem of an ethical nature to the experimenter. But where the experimental conditions expose the subject to loss of dignity, or offer him nothing of value, then the experimenter is obliged to consider the reasons why the subject volunteered and to reward him accordingly.

The subject's public motives for volunteering include having an enjoyable or stimulating experience, acquiring knowledge, doing the experimenter a favor which may some day be reciprocated, and making a contribution to science. These motives can be taken into account rather easily by the experimenter who is willing to spend a few minutes with the subject afterwards to thank him for his participation, answer his questions, reassure him that he did well, and chat with him a bit. Most volunteers also have less manifest, but equally legitimate, motives. A subject may be seeking an opportunity to have contact with, be noticed by, and perhaps confide in a person with psychological training. The dependent attitude of most subjects toward the experimenter is an artifact of the experimental situation as well as an expression of some subjects' personal need systems at the time they volunteer.

The dependent, obedient attitude assumed by most subjects in the experi-   5
mental setting is appropriate to that situation. The "game" is defined by the experimenter and he makes the rules. By volunteering, the subject agrees implicitly to assume a posture of trust and obedience. While the experimental conditions leave him exposed, the subject has the right to assume that his security and self-esteem will be protected.

There are other professional situations in which one member—the patient   6
or client—expects help and protection from the other—the physician or psychologist. But the interpersonal relationship between experimenter and subject additionally has unique features which are likely to provoke initial anxiety in the subject. The laboratory is unfamiliar as a setting and the rules of behavior ambiguous compared to a clinician's office. Because of the anxiety and passivity generated by the setting, the subject is more prone to behave in an obedient, suggestible manner in the laboratory than elsewhere. Therefore, the laboratory is not the place to study degree of obedience or suggestibility, as a function of a particular experimental condition, since the base line for these phenomena as found in the laboratory is probably much higher than in most other settings. Thus experiments in which the relationship to the experimenter as an authority is used as an independent condition are imperfectly designed for the same reason that they are prone to injure the subjects involved. They disregard the special quality of trust and obedience with which the subject appropriately regards the experimenter.

Other phenomena which present ethical decisions, unlike those mentioned   7
above, *can* be reproduced successfully in the laboratory. Failure experience, conformity to peer judgment, and isolation are among such phenomena. In these cases we can expect the experimenter to take whatever measures are necessary to prevent the subject from leaving the laboratory more humiliated, insecure, alienated, or hostile than when he arrived. To guarantee that an especially sensitive subject leaves a stressful experimental experience in the proper state sometimes requires special clinical training. But usually an attitude of compassion, respect, gratitude, and common sense will suffice, and no amount of clinical training will substitute. The subject has the right to expect that the psychologist with whom he is interacting has some concern for his welfare, and the personal attributes and professional skill to express his good will effectively.

Unfortunately, the subject is not always treated with the respect he deserves. It has become more commonplace in sociopsychological laboratory studies to manipulate, embarrass, and discomfort subjects. At times the insult to the subject's sensibilities extends to the journal reader when the results are reported. Milgram's (1963) study is a case in point. The following is Milgram's abstract of his experiment:

> This article describes a procedure for the study of destructive obedience in the laboratory. It consists of ordering a naïve S to administer increasingly more severe punishment to a victim in the context of a learning experiment. Punishment is administered by means of a shock generator with 30 graded switches ranging from Slight Shock to Danger: Severe Shock. The victim is a confederate of E.[1] The primary dependent variable is the maximum shock the S is willing to administer before he refuses to continue further.[2] 26 Ss obeyed the experimental commands fully, and administered the highest shock on the generator. 14 Ss broke off the experiment at some point after the victim protested and refused to provide further answers. The procedure created extreme levels of nervous tension in some Ss. Profuse sweating, trembling, and stuttering were typical expressions of this emotional disturbance. One unexpected sign of tension—yet to be explained—was the regular occurrence of nervous laughter, which in some Ss developed into uncontrollable seizures. The variety of interesting behavioral dynamics observed in the experiment, the reality of the situation for the S, and the possibility of parametric variation within the framework of the procedure,[3] point to the fruitfulness of further study [p. 371].

The detached, objective manner in which Milgram reports the emotional disturbance suffered by his subjects contrasts sharply with his graphic account of that disturbance. Following are two other quotes describing the effects on his subjects of the experimental conditions:

> I observed a mature and initially poised businessman enter the laboratory smiling and confident. Within 20 minutes he was reduced to a twitching, stuttering wreck, who was rapidly approaching a point of nervous collapse. He constantly pulled on his earlobe, and twisted his hands. At one point he pushed his fist into his forehead and muttered: "Oh God, let's stop it." And yet he continued to respond to every word of the experimenter, and obeyed to the end [p. 377].

---

[1] S: stands for subject; E: stands for experimenter. [Eds.]

[2] dependent variable: that which changes as a result of other changes made in the experiment. [Eds.]

[3] parametric variation: statistical term suggesting variables within the experiment that would influence the results and so leave some questions unanswered. [Eds.]

In a large number of cases the degree of tension reached extremes that are rarely seen in sociopsychological laboratory studies. Subjects were observed to sweat, tremble, stutter, bite their lips, groan, and dig their fingernails into their flesh. These were characteristic rather than exceptional responses to the experiment. One sign of tension was the regular occurrence of nervous laughing fits. Fourteen of the 40 subjects showed definite signs of nervous laughter and smiling. The laughter seemed entirely out of place, even bizarre. Full-blown, uncontrollable seizures were observed for 3 subjects. On one occasion we observed a seizure so violently convulsive that it was necessary to call a halt to the experiment . . . [p. 375].

Milgram does state that,

After the interview, procedures were undertaken to assure that the subject would leave the laboratory in a state of well being. A friendly reconciliation was arranged between the subject and the victim, and an effort was made to reduce any tensions that arose as a result of the experiment [p. 374].

It would be interesting to know what sort of procedures could dissipate the type of emotional disturbance just described. In view of the effects on subjects, traumatic to a degree which Milgram himself considers nearly unprecedented in sociopsychological experiments, his casual assurance that these tensions were dissipated before the subject left the laboratory is unconvincing.

What could be the rational basis for such a posture of indifference? Perhaps 10 Milgram supplies the answer himself when he partially explains the subject's destructive obedience as follows, "Thus they assume that the discomfort caused the victim is momentary, while the scientific gains resulting from the experiment are enduring [p. 378]." Indeed such a rationale might suffice to justify the means used to achieve his end if that end were of inestimable value to humanity or were not itself transformed by the means by which it was attained.

The behavioral psychologist is not in as good a position to objectify his faith 11 in the significance of his work as medical colleagues at points of breakthrough. His experimental situations are not sufficiently accurate models of real-life experience; his sampling techniques are seldom of a scope which would justify the meaning with which he would like to endow his results; and these results are hard to reproduce by colleagues with opposing theoretical views. Unlike the Sabin vaccine,[4] for example, the concrete benefit to humanity of his particular piece of work, no matter how competently handled, cannot justify the risk that real harm will be done to the subject. I am not speaking of physical discomfort, inconvenience, or experimental deception per se, but of permanent harm,

---

[4]Sabin vaccine: an oral vaccine against polio, developed by Albert Bruce Sabin (b. 1906), Polish-born American physician and microbiologist. [Eds.]

however slight. I do regard the emotional disturbance described by Milgram as potentially harmful because it could easily effect an alteration in the subject's self-image or ability to trust adult authorities in the future. It is potentially harmful to a subject to commit, in the course of an experiment, acts which he himself considers unworthy, particularly when he has been entrapped into committing such acts by an individual he has reason to trust. The subject's personal responsibility for his actions is not erased because the experimenter reveals to him the means which he used to stimulate these actions. The subject realizes that he would have hurt the victim if the current were on. The realization that he also made a fool of himself by accepting the experimental set results in additional loss of self-esteem. Moreover, the subject finds it difficult to express his anger outwardly after the experimenter in a self-acceptant but friendly manner reveals the hoax.

A fairly intense corrective interpersonal experience is indicated wherein the   12
subject admits and accepts his responsibility for his own actions, and at the same time gives vent to his hurt and anger at being fooled. Perhaps an experience as distressing as the one described by Milgram can be integrated by the subject,[5] provided that careful thought is given to the matter. The propriety of such experimentation is still in question even if such a reparational experience were forthcoming. Without it I would expect a naive, sensitive subject to remain deeply hurt and anxious for some time, and a sophisticated, cynical subject to become even more alienated and distrustful.

In addition the experimental procedure used by Milgram does not appear   13
suited to the objectives of the study because it does not take into account the special quality of the set which the subject has in the experimental situation. Milgram is concerned with a very important problem, namely, the social consequences of destructive obedience. He says,

> Gas chambers were built, death camps were guarded, daily quotas of corpses were produced with the same efficiency as the manufacture of appliances. These inhumane policies may have originated in the mind of a single person, but they could only be carried out on a massive scale if a very large number of persons obeyed orders [p. 371].

But the parallel between authority-subordinate relationships in Hitler's Germany and in Milgram's laboratory is unclear. In the former situation the SS man or member of the German Officer Corps, when obeying orders to slaughter, had no reason to think of his superior officer as benignly disposed towards himself or their victims. The victims were perceived as subhuman and not worthy of consideration. The subordinate officer was an agent in a great cause. He did

---

[5] integrated: a technical term in psychology suggesting the process by which we adjust to and incorporate traumatic experience. [Eds.]

not need to feel guilt or conflict because within his frame of reference he was acting rightly.

It is obvious from Milgram's own descriptions that most of his subjects were   14
concerned about their victims and did trust the experimenter, and that their distressful conflict was generated in part by the consequences of these two disparate but appropriate attitudes. Their distress may have resulted from shock at what the experimenter was doing to them as well as from what they thought they were doing to their victims. In any case there is not a convincing parallel between the phenomena studied by Milgram and destructive obedience as that concept would apply to the subordinate-authority relationship demonstrated in Hitler's Germany. If the experiments were conducted "outside of New Haven and without any visible ties to the university," I would still question their validity on similar although not identical grounds. In addition, I would question the representativeness of a sample of subjects who would voluntarily participate within a noninstitutional setting.

In summary, the experimental objectives of the psychologist are seldom   15
incompatible with the subject's ongoing state of well being, provided that the experimenter is willing to take the subject's motives and interests into consideration when planning his methods and correctives. Section 4b in *Ethical Standards of Psychologists* (American Psychological Association, undated) reads in part:

> Only when a problem is significant and can be investigated in no other way, is the psychologist justified in exposing human subjects to emotional stress or other possible harm. In conducting such research, the psychologist must seriously consider the possibility of harmful aftereffects, and should be prepared to remove them as soon as permitted by the design of the experiment. Where the danger of serious aftereffects exists, research should be conducted only when the subjects or their responsible agents are fully informed of this possibility and volunteer nevertheless [p. 12].

From the subject's point of view procedures which involve loss of dignity, self-esteem, and trust in rational authority are probably most harmful in the long run and require the most thoughtfully planned reparations, if engaged in at all. The public image of psychology as a profession is highly related to our own actions, and some of these actions are changeworthy. It is important that as research psychologists we protect our ethical sensibilities rather than adapt our personal standards to include as appropriate the kind of indignities to which Milgram's subjects were exposed. I would not like to see experiments such as Milgram's proceed unless the subjects were fully informed of the dangers of serious aftereffects and his correctives were clearly shown to be effective in restoring their state of well being.

REFERENCES

AMERICAN PSYCHOLOGICAL ASSOCIATION.
Ethical Standards of Psychologists: A summary of ethical principles. Washington, D.C.:
APA, undated.
MILGRAM, S.
Behavioral study of obedience. *J. abnorm. soc. Psychol.*, 1963, 67, 371–378.

QUESTIONS

1. Baumrind challenges Milgram's experiment on two grounds. Distinguish and summarize the two.

2. Baumrind speaks generally for a couple of pages before even mentioning the Milgram experiment. Why do you think she introduces her argument this way? Are there moments during this opening when the Milgram experiment is very much in mind, even without being mentioned?

3. What do you make of Baumrind's claim that "the laboratory is not the place to study degree of obedience or suggestibility" (paragraph 6)? Do Baumrind's reasons successfully undercut Milgram, or has he anticipated that worry?

4. At the end of her article, Baumrind challenges the applicability of Milgram's experiment to events in Hitler's Germany. Does Baumrind represent Milgram's thinking fairly? Do you agree with her that the application does not work? Explain your views.

5. Study Milgram's abstract, quoted by Baumrind in paragraph 8. How do you understand its next-to-last sentence? Do you really find the "nervous laughter" unexplained?

6. See whether your school has a policy about the use of human subjects in experiments. Assuming it has, and that its standards are available to the public, get a copy of them. After studying them, write a paper either supporting them or arguing for their amendment.

7. Have you ever been coerced by a situation to mistreat another person, or have you witnessed such mistreatment? Write an analysis of that situation as you remember it. Try to explain the degree to which the situation itself seemed to elicit the questionable behavior. How do you weigh individual responsibility against institutional or group responsibility in this instance?

MAKING CONNECTIONS

1. Since Milgram's professed aims included the question of why people obeyed their leaders in Nazi Germany as they did, read Robert Jay Lifton's essay, "What Made This Man? Mengele," and ask whether the Milgram experiment does help answer that question. How does Baumrind's criticism of Milgram contribute to the same question?

2. The ethical points Baumrind raises have certain connections with issues of animal rights addressed in: "Just Like Us: A Forum on Animal Rights," by Arthur Caplan et al. and Frederick A. King's "Animals in Research: The Case for Experimentation." What connections do you find among these selections? To what extent is Baumrind addressing something quite different?

JUST LIKE US:
A FORUM ON ANIMAL RIGHTS

Arthur Caplan, Gary Francione,
Roger Goldman, Ingrid Newkirk

*This discussion of animal rights was held at the Cooper
Union for the Advancement of Science and Art, in ·New
York City. The participants approach the subject from a
variety of viewpoints. Arthur Caplan is the director of the
Center for Biomedical Ethics at the University of Minne-
sota. Gary Francione is a professor at the University of
Pennsylvania Law School and frequently litigates animal
rights cases. Roger Goldman is a constitutional law scholar
and professor at St. Louis University School of Law. Ingrid
Newkirk is the national director of People for the Ethical
Treatment of Animals, in Washington. The forum was mod-
erated by Jack Hitt, a senior editor at* Harper's Magazine.
*The participants debate what qualities determine a right to
life. They raise the question of what the proper relationship
between humans and animals should be: Do animals have
the same rights as humans? During the discussion they seek
to expose the assumptions which underlie their opponents'
arguments.*

The relationship of man to animal has long been one of sympathy, manifested   1
in such welfare organizations as the kindly Bide-A-Wee or the avuncular
ASPCA. In the last few years, the politics of that relationship have been
questioned by a number of new and vociferous interest groups which hold to
the credo that animals are endowed with certain inalienable rights.

Typically, when animal rights advocates are called upon by the media to   2
defend their views, they are seated across the table from research scientists. The
discussion turns on the treatment of laboratory animals or the illegal efforts of
fanatics who smuggle animals out of research facilities via latter-day underground railroads to freedom.

Behind these easy headlines, however, stand serious philosophical questions: 3
How should we treat animals? Why do humans have rights and other animals
not? If animals had rights, what would they be? To address these questions,

Harper's Magazine asked two leading animal rights activists to sit down with a philosopher and a constitutional scholar to examine the logic of their opinions.

BUNNIES AND SEWER RATS

JACK HITT: Let me ask a question that many readers might ask: Gary, why   4
have you—a former Supreme Court law clerk and now a professor of law at the University of Pennsylvania—devoted your life to animal rights?

GARY FRANCIONE: I believe that animals have *rights*. This is not to say that   5
animals have the same rights that we do, but the reasons that lead us to accord certain rights to human beings are equally applicable to animals. The problem is that our value system doesn't permit the breadth of vision necessary to understand that. We currently use the category of "species" as the relevant criterion for determining membership in our moral community, just as we once used race and sex to determine that membership.

If you asked white men in 1810 whether blacks had rights, most of them   6
would have laughed at you. What was necessary then is necessary now. We must change the *way* we think: a paradigm shift in the way we think about animals. Rights for blacks and women were *the* constitutional issues of the nineteenth and twentieth centuries. Animal rights, once more people understand the issue, will emerge as *the* civil rights movement of the twenty-first century.

HITT: I want to see where the logic of your beliefs takes us. Suppose I am the   7
head of a company that has invented a dynamite new shampoo. It gives your hair great body; everyone is going to look like Lisa Bonet. But my preliminary tests show that it may cause some irritation or mild damage to the eye. So I've purchased 2,000 rabbits to test this shampoo on their eyes first. Roger, do you find anything offensive about testing shampoo this way?

ROGER GOLDMAN: As someone new to the animal rights issue, I don't find it   8
particularly offensive.

HITT: What if the only thing new about my shampoo is that it is just a   9
different color?

GOLDMAN: If everything else is equal, then I would say the testing is unnec-   10
essary.

INGRID NEWKIRK: I think Roger hit the nail on the head. The public has   11
absolutely no idea what the tests involve or whether they're necessary. I think Roger might object if he knew that there were alternatives, that a human-skin patch test can be substituted for the rabbit-blinding test. If consumers were informed, then no compassionate consumer would abide such cruelty.

FRANCIONE: The problem is that we can use animals in any way we like   12
because they are *property*. The law currently regards animals as no different from that pad of paper in front of you, Roger. If you own that pad, you can

rip it up or burn it. By and large we treat animals no different than glasses, cups, or paper.

ARTHUR CAPLAN: I know you lawyers love to talk about the property status of these little creatures, but there are other factors. We treat animals as property because people don't believe that animals have any moral worth. People look at rabbits and say, "There are many rabbits. If there are a few less rabbits, who cares?" 13

NEWKIRK: Not true. Many people, who don't support animal rights, *would* care if you stuck a knife in their rabbit or dog. They're deeply offended by acts of *individual* cruelty. 14

CAPLAN: Yes, but I suspect that if in your test we substituted ugly sewer rats for button-nosed rabbits, people might applaud the suffering. There are some animals that just don't register in the human consciousness. Rats don't, rabbits might, dogs and horses definitely do. 15

NEWKIRK: Not always. If the test were done to a sewer rat in *front* of a person, the average person would say, "Don't do that" or "Kill him quickly." 16

HITT: Why? 17

NEWKIRK: It's institutionalized cruelty, born of our hideous compartmentalized thinking. If the killing is done behind closed doors, if the government says it must be done, or if some man or woman in a white coat assures us that it's for our benefit, we ignore our own ethical good sense and allow it to happen. 18

HITT: If the frivolity of the original test bothers us, what if we up the ante? What if the product to be tested might yield a cure for baldness? 19

FRANCIONE: Jack, that is a "utilitarian" argument which suggests that the rightness or wrongness of an action is determined by the *consequences* of that action. In the case of animals, it implies that animal exploitation produces benefits that justify that exploitation. I don't believe in utilitarian moral thought. It's dangerous because it easily leads to atrocious conclusions, both in how we treat humans and how we treat animals. I don't believe it is morally permissible to exploit weaker beings even if we derive benefits. 20

GOLDMAN: So not even the cancer cure? 21

FRANCIONE: No, absolutely not. 22

CAPLAN: But you miss the point about moral selfishness. By the time you get to the baldness cure, people start to say, "I don't *care* about animals. My interests are a hell of a lot more important than the animals' interests. So if keeping hair on my head means sacrificing those animals, painlessly or not, I want it." It's not utilitarian—it's selfish. 23

FRANCIONE: But you certainly wouldn't put that forward as a justification, would you? 24

CAPLAN: No, it's just a description. 25

FRANCIONE: I can't argue with your assertion that people are selfish. But aren't we morally obliged to assess the consequences of that selfishness? To begin 26

715

that assessment, people must become aware of the ways in which we exploit animals.

Maybe I'm just a hopeless optimist, but I believe that once people are 27 confronted with these facts, they will reassess. The backlash that we're seeing from the exploitation industries—the meat companies and the biomedical research laboratories—is a reaction of fear. They know that the more people learn, the more people will reject this painful exploitation.

HITT: But won't your movement always be hampered by that mix of moral 28 utilitarianism and moral egotism? People will say, "Yes, be kind to animals up to a point of utilitarianism (so I can have my cancer cure) and up to a point of moral egotism (so I can have my sirloin)." There may be some shift in the moral center, but it will move only so far.

CAPLAN: I agree. Gary can remain optimistic, but confronting people with the 29 facts won't get him very far. Moral egotism extends even into human relations. Let's not forget that we are in a city where you have to step over people to enter this building. People don't say, "Feed, clothe, and house them, and then tax me: I'll pay." We have a limited moral imagination. It may be peculiarly American, but you can show people pictures of starving children or homeless people or animals in leg traps, and many will say, "That's too bad. Life is hard, but I still want my pleasures, my enjoyments."

NEWKIRK: There are two answers to that. First, people accept the myth. They 30 were brought up with the illusion that they *must* eat animals to be healthy. Now we know that's not true. Second, because of humankind's lack of moral—or even just plain—imagination, we activists have to tell people exactly what they *should* do. Then we must make it easier for them to do it. If we put a moral stepladder in front of people, a lot of them will walk up it. But most people feel powerless as individuals and ask, "Who am I? I'm only one person. What can I do?" We must show them.

HITT: Roger, I'm wondering whether your moral center has shifted since we 31 began. Originally you weren't offended by my using 2,000 rabbits to test a new shampoo. Are you now?

GOLDMAN: I am still a utilitarian. But if the test is unnecessary or just repet- 32 itive, clearly, I'm persuaded that it should be stopped.

NEWKIRK: Precisely Gary's point. Armed with the facts, Roger opts not to hurt 33 animals.

ENFRANCHISING ALL CREATURES

HITT: Art, what makes human beings have rights and animals not have rights? 34

CAPLAN: Some would argue a biblical distinction. God created humans in his 35 image and did not create animals that way. That's one special property. Another philosophical basis is natural law, which holds that inalienable rights accrue to being human—that is a distinguishing feature in and of itself.

Personally I reject both those arguments. I subscribe to an entitlement view, 36
which finds these rights grounded in certain innate properties, such as the
ability to reason, the ability to suffer—

FRANCIONE: Let's take the ability to suffer and consider it more carefully. The 37
ability to use language or to reason is irrelevant to the right to be free from
suffering. Only the ability to feel pain is relevant. Logically, it doesn't follow
that you should restrict those rights to humans. On this primary level, the
question must be *who* can feel pain, *who* can suffer? Certainly animals must
be included within the reach of this fundamental right.

If you don't, then you are basing the right not to suffer pain on "intelli- 38
gence." Consider the grotesque results if you apply that idea exclusively to
human beings. Would you say that a smart person has a right to suffer less
pain than a stupid person? That is effectively just what we say with animals.
Even though they can suffer, we conclude that their suffering is irrelevant
because we think we are smarter than they are.

CAPLAN: The ability to suffer does count, but the level of thinking and con- 39
sciousness also counts. What makes us human? What grants us the right to
life? It is not just a single attribute that makes us human. Rather, there is a
cluster of properties: a sense of place in the world, a sense of time, a sense
of self-awareness, a sense that one *is* somebody, a sense that one is morally
relevant. When you add up these features, you begin to get to the level of
entitlement to rights.

FRANCIONE: And I am going to push you to think specifically about rights 40
again. What must you possess in order to have a right to life? I think the
most obvious answer is simply a *life!*

But let's play this question out in your terms. To have a right to life, you 41
must possess a sense of self, a recollection of the past, and an anticipation of
the future, to name a few. By those standards, the chimpanzee—and I would
argue, the entire class of Mammalia—would be enfranchised to enjoy a right
to life.

NEWKIRK: The question is, do they have an interest in living? If they do, then 42
one has an obligation to recognize their natural rights. The most fundamental
of these is a desire to live. They *are* alive, therefore they want to *be* alive,
and therefore we should *let* them live.

The more profound question, though, is what distinguishes humans from 43
other animals. Most scientists, at first, thought that what separates us from
the other animals is that human beings use tools. So ethnologists went out
into the field and returned with innumerable examples of tool use in animals.
The scientists then concluded that it's not tool use but the *making* of tools.
Ethnologists, such as Geza Teleki, came back with lots of different examples,
everything from chimpanzees making fishing poles to ants making boats to
cross rivers. One might think they would then elevate the criterion to making
tools in *union* workshops, but they switched to "language." Then there was

717

a discussion about what *is* language. Linguists, among them Noam Chomsky and Herbert Terrace, said language possessed certain "components." But when various ethnologists were able to satisfy each of these components, the Cartesian scientists became desperate and kept adding more components, including some pretty complicated ones, such as the ability to recite events in the distant past and to create new words based on past experiences. Eventually the number of components was up to sixteen! The final component was teaching someone else the language. But when Roger Fouts gave the signing ape, Washoe, a son, she independently taught him some seventy American hand-language signs.

CAPLAN: One of the sad facts of the literature of both animal and human   44
rights is that everyone is eager to identify the magic property that separates humans from animals. Is it the ability to suffer? The ability to say something? The ability to say something *interesting*! I think the philosophers are all looking in the right place but are missing something. We have rights because we are *social*.

NEWKIRK: Since all animals are social, then you *would* extend rights to non-   45
humans?

CAPLAN: It's not just sociability. Of course, all animals interact, but there is   46
something about the way humans need to interact.

Suppose we were little Ayn Rands who marched about, self-sufficient,   47
proud, and arrogant. If we were able to chop our own wood, cook our own meals, and fend off those who would assault us, then we wouldn't need any rights. You wouldn't need to have a right to free speech if there was no one to talk to!

My point is that our fundamental rights are not exclusively intellectual   48
properties. They are the natural result of the unique way humans have come together to form societies, *dependent* on each other for survival and therefore respectful of each other's rights.

NEWKIRK: None of this differentiates humans from the other animals. You   49
cannot find a relevant attribute in human beings that doesn't exist in animals as well. Darwin said that the only difference between humans and other animals was a difference of degree, not kind. If you ground any concept of human rights in a particular attribute, then animals will have to be included. Animals have rights.

CAPLAN: That brings up another problem I have with your entire argument.   50
Throughout this discussion, I have argued my position in terms of *ethics*. I have spoken about our moral imagination and animal *interests* and human decency. Why? Because I don't want our relationship with animals to be cast as a battle of rights. Only in America, with its obsession for attorneys, courts, judges, and lawsuits, is the entire realm of human relationships reduced to a clash of rights.

So I ask you: Is our relationship with animals best conceived of under the   51 rubric of rights? I don't think so. When I am dispensing rights, I'm relatively chintzy about it. Do embryos have rights? In my opinion, no. Do irretrievably comatose people have rights? I doubt it. Do mentally retarded people below some level of intellectual functioning have rights? Probably not.

There is a wide range of creatures—some of them human—for whom   52
our rights language is not the best way to deal with them. I want people to deal with them out of a sense of fairness or a sense of humanity or a sense of duty, but not out of a claim to rights.

NEWKIRK: I don't like your supremacist view of a custodial responsibility that   53
grants you the luxury to be magnanimous to those beneath you. The rights of animals are not peripheral interests. In this case, we are talking about blood, guts, pain, and death.

FRANCIONE: Art, when you start talking about obligations without rights, you   54
can justify violations of those obligations or intrusions more easily by spinning airy notions of utility. The reason many of our battles are played out in rights language is because our culture has evolved this notion that a right is something that stands between me and an intrusion. A right doesn't yield automatically because a stronger party might benefit.

If a scientist could cure cancer—without fail—by subjecting me against   55
my will to a painful experiment, it wouldn't matter. I have a right not to be used that way.

CAPLAN: Ironically, I agree with you. That's exactly the role that rights lan-   56
guage plays. It defines the barriers or lines that can't be crossed. But if you hand out rights willy-nilly, you lose that function.

NEWKIRK: When should we stop?   57

CAPLAN: I'm not sure I know the answer, but if you cheapen the currency of   58
rights language, you've got to worry that rights may not be taken seriously. Soon you will have people arguing that trees have rights and that embryos have rights. And the tendency would be to say, "Sure, they have rights, but they are not *important* rights."

NEWKIRK: Art, wouldn't you rather err on the side of giving out too many   59
rights rather than too few?

CAPLAN: No.   60

NEWKIRK: So, according to your view, maybe we should take away some of   61
the rights we've already granted. After all, granting rights to blacks and women has deprived society of very important things, such as cheap labor. That a society evolves and expands its protective shield should not daunt us. That's like saying, if I continue to be charitable, my God, where will it ever end?

CAPLAN: It may not be rights or bust. There may be other ways to get people   62
to conduct themselves decently without hauling out the heavy artillery of rights language every time.

NEWKIRK: People have to be pushed; society has to be pushed. Those who   63
care deeply about a particular wrong have to pressure the general population.

719

Eventually a law is passed, and then adjustments are made to correct past injustices. You have to bring these matters to a head.

HITT: Roger, from a constitutional perspective, do you think that rights are cheapened when they are broadened? 64

GOLDMAN: When you put it in a constitutional context, you invite conflict. That's inevitable. If you have a free press, you're going to have fair trial problems. If you start expanding rights of liberty, you run up against rights of equality. I don't think expansion cheapens them, but by elevating animal rights to a constitutional issue, you certainly multiply the difficulties. 65

HITT: You could argue that conflict strengthens rights. If you had no conflict over free speech, would we have the solid right to free speech that we have today? 66

GOLDMAN: It depends on who wins. What would happen if free speech lost? 67

FRANCIONE: Roger, you will have conflict and difficulties whether you cast our relationship with animals as one of obligations *or* rights. The real question is, are those obligations enforceable by state authority? If they are, there will be clashes and we will turn to the courts for resolution. 68

CAPLAN: Gary, I would like those obligations enforced by the authority, if you like, of empathy, by the power of character. What matters is how people view animals, how their feelings are touched by those animals, what drives them to care about those animals, not what rights the animals have. 69

FRANCIONE: I agree that you don't effect massive social change exclusively through law, but law can certainly help. That's a classic law school debate: Do moral perceptions shape law or does law shape moral perceptions? It probably goes both ways. I have no doubt that we could effect a great change if animals were included within our constitutional framework. 70

NEWKIRK: Great changes often begin with the law. Remember the 1760s case of the West Indian slave Jonathan Strong. Strong's master had abandoned him in England after beating him badly. The judge in that case feared the consequences of emancipating a slave. But the judge freed Strong and declared, "Let justice prevail, though the heavens may fall." 71

MOJO, THE TALKING CHIMPANZEE

HITT: Meet Mojo, the signing chimpanzee. Mojo is female and has learned more words than any other chimpanzee. One day you're signing away with Mojo, and she signs back, "I want a baby." Roger, are we under any obligation to grant her wish? 72

GOLDMAN: Since I am not persuaded animals have any rights, I don't believe there is any obligation. 73

HITT: Doesn't it follow that if this chimpanzee can articulate a desire to have a child—a primal desire and one that we would never forbid humans—we have some obligation to fulfill it? 74

CAPLAN: You are alluding to a foundation for rights that we haven't yet   75
discussed. Is the requirement for possessing a right the ability to *claim* it?
That is, in order to hold a right to life, one must be able to articulate a claim
to life, to be able to say, "I want to live."

There may be animals that can get to that level, and Mojo may be one   76
of them. Nevertheless, I don't buy into that argument. Simply being able to
claim a right does not necessarily entail an obligation to fulfill it.

FRANCIONE: But Mojo does have the right to be left alone to pursue her   77
desires, the right *not* to be in that cage. Aren't we violating some right of
Mojo's by confining her so that she cannot satisfy that primal desire?

HITT: Is this a fair syllogism? Mojo wants to be free; a right to freedom exists   78
if you can claim it; ergo, Mojo has a right to be free. Does the ability to lay
claim to a right automatically translate into the *possession* of such a right?

CAPLAN: You don't always generate obligations and duties from a parallel set   79
of rights, matching one with another.

Look at the relationship that exists between family members. Some people   80
might argue that children have certain rights to claim from their parents. But
there is something wrong with that assumption. Parents have many obligations
to their children, but it seems morally weird to reduce this relationship to a
contractual model. It's not a free-market arrangement where you put down
a rights chit, I put down an obligation chit, and we match them up.

My kid might say to me, "Dad, you have an obligation to care for my   81
needs, and my need today is a new car." I don't enter into a negotiation
based on a balancing of his rights and my duties. That is not the proper
relationship.

NEWKIRK: But having a car is not a fundamental right, whereas the right not   82
to be abused is. For example, children have a right not to be used in factories.
That right had to be fought for in exactly the same way we are fighting for
animal rights now.

CAPLAN: Gary, I want to press you further. A baby needs a heart, and some   83
scientist believes the miniature swine's heart will do it.

FRANCIONE: Would I take a healthy pig, remove its heart, and put it into the   84
child? No.

CAPLAN: I am stymied by your absolutist position that makes it impossible   85
even to consider the pig as a donor.

FRANCIONE: What if the donor were a severely retarded child instead of a pig?   86

CAPLAN: No, because I've got to worry about the impact not only on the   87
donor but on society as well.

FRANCIONE: Art, assume I have a three-year-old prodigy who is a mathematical   88
wizard. The child has a bad heart. The only way to save this prodigy is to
take the heart out of another child. Should we *consider* a child from a low
socio-economic background who has limited mental abilities?

CAPLAN: You're wandering around a world of slopes, and I want to wander   89

721

around a world of steps. I have argued strongly in my writing that it is possible for a human being—specifically an infant born with anencephaly, that is, without most of its brain—to drop below the threshold of a right to life. I think it would be ethical to use such a baby as a source for organ transplants. I do not believe there is a slippery slope between the child born with most of its brain missing and the retarded. There are certain thresholds below which one can make these decisions. At some point along the spectrum of life—many people would say a pig, and I would go further to include the anencephalic baby—we are safely below that threshold.

FRANCIONE: You can't equate the pig with the anencephalic infant. The anencephalic child is not the subject of a life in any meaningful sense. That is to say, it does not possess that constellation of attributes—sense of self-awareness, anticipation of the future, memory of the past—that we have been discussing. The pig is clearly the subject of a meaningful life. 90

CAPLAN: But if it's a matter of saving the life of the baby, then I want a surgeon to saw out the pig's heart and put it in the baby's chest. 91

NEWKIRK: The pig can wish to have life, liberty and the pursuit of happiness, and the anencephalic baby cannot. 92

CAPLAN: But you must also consider the effect on others. I don't think it's going to matter very much what the pig's parents think about that pig. Whereas the child's parents care about the baby, and they don't care about the pig. 93

FRANCIONE: Then you change their reaction. 94

CAPLAN: I don't want to change their reaction. I want human beings to care about babies. 95

NEWKIRK: Like racism or sexism, that remark is pure speciesism. 96

CAPLAN: Speciesism! Mine is a legitimate distinction. The impact of this transplant is going to be different on humans than on lower animals. 97

NEWKIRK: "Lower animals." There comes speciesism rearing its ugly head again. Look, Art, I associate with the child; I don't associate with the pig. But we can't establish why that matters *except* that you are human and I am human. 98

If a building were burning and a baby baboon, a baby rat, and a baby child were inside, I'm sure I would save the child. But if the baboon mother went into the building, I'm sure she would take out the infant baboon. It's just that there is an instinct to save yourself first, then your immediate family, your countrymen, and on to your species. But we have to recognize and reject the self-interest that erects these barriers and try to recognize the rights of others who happen not to be exactly like ourselves. 99

CAPLAN: I think you can teach humans to care about the pig. The morally relevant factor here is that you will never get the pig to care about *me*. 100

NEWKIRK: Not true, Art. Read John Robbin's new book, *Diet for a New America*, in which he lists incidents of altruism by animals outside their own 101 species. Everybody knows about dolphins rescuing sailors. Recently a pig rescued a child from a frozen lake and won an award!

CAPLAN: To the extent to which you can make animals drop *their* speciesism, perhaps you will be persuasive on this point.   102

NEWKIRK: Art, if you don't recognize my rights, that's tough for me. But that doesn't mean my rights don't exist.   103

FRANCIONE: If blacks, as a group, got together and said, "We're going to make a conscious decision to dislike non-blacks," would you say that black people no longer had rights?   104

CAPLAN: No, but I would hold them accountable for their racism. I could never hold a pig accountable for its speciesism. And I am never going to see a meeting of pigs having that kind of conversation.   105

NEWKIRK: That happens when the Ku Klux Klan meets, and the ACLU upholds their rights.   106

CAPLAN: The difference is that there are certain things I expect of blacks, whites, yellows—of all human beings and maybe a few animals. But I am not going to hold the vast majority of animals to those standards.   107

NEWKIRK: So the punishment for their perceived deficiencies—which, incidentally, is shared by the human baby—is to beat them to death.   108

CAPLAN: I didn't say that. I am trying to reach for something that isn't captured by the speciesist charge. The difference between people and animals is that I can persuade people. I can *stimulate* their moral imaginations. But I can't do that with most animals, and I want that difference to count.   109

A WORLD WITH NO DANCING BEARS

HITT: How would you envision a society that embraced animal rights? What would happen to pets?   110

NEWKIRK: I don't use the word "pet." I think it's speciesist language. I prefer "companion animal." For one thing, we would no longer allow breeding. People could not create different breeds. There would be no pet shops. If people had companion animals in their homes, those animals would have to be refugees from the animal shelters and the streets. You would have a protective relationship with them just as you would with an orphaned child. But as the surplus of cats and dogs (artificially engineered by centuries of forced breeding) declined, eventually companion animals would be phased out, and we would return to a more symbiotic relationship—enjoyment at a distance.   111

FRANCIONE: Much more than that would be phased out. For example, there would be no animals used for food, no laboratory experiments, no fur coats, and no hunting.   112

GOLDMAN: Would there be zoos?   113

FRANCIONE: No zoos.   114

Hitt: Circuses?   115

Francione: Circuses would have to change. Look, right now we countenance   116
the taking of an animal from the wild—a bear—dressing that bear in a *skirt*
and parading it in front of thousands of people while it balances a ball on its
nose. When you think about it, that is perverted.

Hitt: Let's say that your logic prevails. People are sickened by dancing bears   117
and are demanding a constitutional amendment. What would be the language
of a Bill of Rights for animals?

Newkirk: It already exists. It's "life, liberty, and the pursuit of happiness."   118
We just haven't extended it far enough.

Goldman: I am assuming your amendment would restrict not only govern-   119
ment action but private action as well. Our Constitution restricts only government action. The single exception is the Thirteenth Amendment, which
prohibits both the government and the individual from the practice of slavery.

Hitt: To whom would these rights apply? Would they apply among animals   120
themselves? Does the lion have to recognize the gazelle's right to life?

Newkirk: That's not our business. The behavior of the lion and the gazelle   121
is a "tribal" issue, if you will. Those are the actions of other nations, and we
cannot interfere.

Goldman: What if we knew the lion was going to kill the gazelle—would we   122
have an obligation to stop it?

Newkirk: It's not our business. This amendment restricts only our code of   123
behavior.

Hitt: But what Roger is asking is, should the amendment be so broad as to   124
restrict both individual and government action?

Francione: It should be that broad. Of course, it would create a lot of issues   125
we would have to work out. First, to whom would we extend these rights? I
have a sneaking suspicion that any moment someone in this room will say,
"But what about cockroaches? Will they have these rights? Do they have the
right to have credit cards?" Hard questions would have to be answered, and
we would have to determine which animals would hold rights and how to
translate these rights into concrete protections from interference.

Newkirk: The health pioneer W. K. Kellogg limited it to "all those with   126
faces." If you can look into the eyes of another, and that other looks back,
that's one measure.

So the amendment shouldn't be limited, as some animal rights advocates   127
think, to mammals, because we know that birds, reptiles, insects, and fishes
all feel pain. They are capable of wanting to be alive. As long as we know
that they have these primal interests, then I think we need to explore down
the line—if we think it is down.

Goldman: Let me go up the line. What about humans?   128

Newkirk: They would be just another animal in the pack.   129

Goldman: But your amendment would massively expand the reach of the   130

Constitution for humans. For example, the Constitution does not require states to provide rights for victims of crime. Under your proposal, if a state decriminalized adultery, shoplifting, or even murder, the victim's *constitutional* rights would be violated.

CAPLAN: And if we take the face test, how is that going to affect the way we treat the unborn? Must we enfranchise our fetuses? That's going to be the end of abortion. 131

FRANCIONE: Not necessarily. I am fairly comfortable with the notion that a fetus does not have a right to life. But that is not to say that a fetus doesn't have a right to be free from suffering. Fetuses do feel pain and they *ought* to be free from suffering. But it doesn't make sense to talk about a fetus having a sense of the past, anticipation of the future, and a sense of interaction with others. 132

CAPLAN: But a mouse? 133

FRANCIONE: Sure. 134

CAPLAN: I guess we can experiment on and eat all the animal fetuses we want. 135

FRANCIONE: I didn't say you had a right to inflict pain on animal fetuses. I don't think you have a right to inflict pain on human fetuses. 136

CAPLAN: Are you suggesting that we can't inflict pain, but we can kill them? 137

NEWKIRK: You are talking about the manner in which abortions are currently performed, not whether they should be performed. Our standard of lack of suffering holds up if you apply it across the board, for human and non-human fetuses. 138

GOLDMAN: Let me see if I can bring together those who advocate animal welfare with those who believe animals hold rights. What about a different amendment, similar to the difference between the Thirteenth Amendment, which is an absolute ban on slavery, and the Fourteenth Amendment, which bans discrimination, but not absolutely. In fact, the Fourteenth allows us to take race into account sometimes, such as affirmative action. Do the animal rights activists see a role for a limited amendment similar to the Fourteenth? It would broadly protect animals from unnecessary suffering, but allow for some medical experiments. 139

FRANCIONE: Does your amendment simply expand the word "persons" in the Fourteenth Amendment to include animals? 140

GOLDMAN: No, but it is modeled on Fourteenth Amendment jurisprudence. It would not permit experimentation on animals unless necessary for a compelling need. 141

FRANCIONE: I would favor this approach if the experimenter had the burden to show the compelling need. I would have only one problem with adjudication under this compelling-need standard. My fear is that the balance would always favor the biomedical research community. Everyone agrees that no one should needlessly use animals in experimentation. Yet we all know that millions of animals are being used for frivolous purposes. That is because 142 the biomedical researchers have persuaded enough people that their experiments are so important they have become "compelling" by definition.

GOLDMAN: Of course the difference with this constitutional amendment is that 143 it wouldn't pass unless two-thirds of Congress and three-fourths of the states backed it. So if we're projecting a hundred years from now, you won't have the problem of science experts always prevailing.

FRANCIONE: Roger, I would retire tomorrow if I could get your amendment. 144 The problem is that our society economically *benefits* from exploitation. The animal industries are so strong that they have shaped an entire *value* system that justifies and perpetuates exploitation. So I am not sure your compelling-need test would result in anything substantially different from what we have now. That's why I favor a hard rights notion, to protect the defenseless absolutely. As soon as you let in the "balancers," people such as Art Caplan, you've got trouble.

CAPLAN: The problem with your constitutional amendment is that, finally, it 145 is irrelevant to human behavior. When the lawyers, the constitutional adjudicators, and the Supreme Court justices aren't there, when it's just me and my companion animal or my bug in the woods, where are the animal's rights then?

There was a time when I was a little boy running around in the woods 146 in New England. It was just a bunch of Japanese beetles in a jar and me. The question was: How is little Art going to deal with those Japanese beetles? Pull their wings off? Never let them out of the jar? Step on them? What do I do with those bugs? What do I think of bugs? No Supreme Court justice is going to tell me what to do with them.

NEWKIRK: A lot of these conflicts of moral obligation result from the wide 147 variety of *unnatural* relationships we have with animals in the first place— whether it's little Art with his jar of Japanese beetles, or the scientist in the lab with his chimpanzee, or any one of us at home with a cat. Just take the single issue of the sterilization of pets. We now have burdened ourselves with the custodial obligation to sterilize thousands of animals because we have screwed up their reproductive cycles so much through domestication and inbreeding that they have many more offspring than they normally would. What would happen if we just left animals alone, to possess their own dignity? You know, you mentioned earlier that there is something cruel in the lion chasing down and killing the gazelle. Well, nature *is* cruel, but man is crueler yet.

A FORUM ON ANIMAL RIGHTS

QUESTIONS

1. One of the central questions of this forum, and of all discussions of animal rights, is the question "What makes human beings have rights and animals not have rights?" How do the various participants in the forum seek to answer this question?

2. Newkirk asks "What distinguishes humans from other animals?" (paragraph 43). How do the various participants respond to this question? What assumptions underlie these various responses?

3. Francione states in paragraph 70: "That's a classic law school debate. Do moral perceptions shape law or does law shape moral perceptions?" Do you think that massive social change can be influenced by legislation protecting animal rights? How would our society change, according to some of the forum participants, if we embraced animal rights?

4. Should all animals have rights? In paragraph 125, one of the forum participants discusses the question: "But what about cockroaches?" Are you persuaded by any of the participants' positions? If animals have rights, what kind of rights should they be? How do you respond to this issue?

5. Newkirk concludes the forum with this powerful thought: "Well, nature is cruel, but man is crueler yet." How do you respond to this thought? Write an essay in which you develop your position on animal rights in the context of this comment.

6. Thomas Jefferson opens the Declaration of Independence by stating directly the "self-evident" "truths" upon which his argument will be based. In fact, every argument depends on an appeal to certain unquestioned values, to a body of "truths" that the writer assumes the audience accepts (although not every writer states these "truths" as explicitly as Jefferson). Take two of the participants in this forum and try to determine the values these participants assume—not the views being argued, but the accepted "truths" on which their arguments depend. Write an essay in which you analyze the accepted truths that provide the basis for their positions.

MAKING CONNECTIONS

1. Frederick A. King, in "Animals in Research: The Case for Experimentation," draws Arthur Caplan, one of the participants of this forum, into his argument, using Caplan to support his case for using animals in experiments. Do you think Caplan would agree with the case King is making? Where, if anywhere, would Caplan quarrel with King?

2. The first paragraph of this forum alludes to the Declaration of Independence. Imagine a "Continental Congress" of animals preparing to declare its independence from humans. Imagine further that you are a delegate, cast as one of whatever species you prefer, and you have been assigned the role Jefferson once held, to draft an animals' Declaration of Independence. What would you say? What evidence would you bring to your task? Go ahead and draft it.

3. Several selections in this collection focus on the special human regard for animals, at least for some species. Farley Mowat's "Observing Wolves," Jane van Lawick-Goodall's "First Observations," and William Booth's "The Social Lives of Dolphins" are examples. Imagine at least two of those writers participating in this forum. Where would they break in? What would they say? Rewrite a section of this forum including two of those writers as participants.

Sciences and Technologies

ANIMALS IN RESEARCH:
THE CASE FOR EXPERIMENTATION
Frederick A. King

Frederick A. King (b. 1925) is a neuroscientist and an educator. He is director of Emory University's primate research center and has served on many committees on animal research and experimentation. He has edited books on primate biology and primate social dynamics. In this essay, King argues that while humans have a moral responsibility to animals, animals do not share the same rights as humans.

The Mobilization for Animals Coalition (MFA) is an international network 1 of more than 400 animal-protectionist organizations that address themselves to a variety of issues, including hunting, trapping, livestock protection, vegetarianism, and pets. Their primary concern, however, is an adamant opposition to animal research. Some groups within the movement want to severely curtail research with animals, but the most visible and outspoken faction wants to eliminate it.

The astonishing growth of this activist movement during the past three years 2 has culminated this year in an intense attack on the use of animals in psychological research. This past spring, John McArdle of the Humane Society of the United States charged that torture is the founding principle and fundamental characteristic of experimental psychology, and that psychological experimentation on animals among all the scientific disciplines is "the ideal candidate for elimination. No major scientific endeavor would suffer by such an act." A recent pamphlet published by the MFA stated, "Of all these experiments, those conducted in psychology are the most painful, pointless, and repulsive."

The following specific allegations have been made by the MFA: Animals are 3 given intense, repeated electric shocks until they lose the ability even to scream in pain; animals are deprived of food and water and allowed to suffer and die from hunger and thirst; animals are put in isolation until they are driven insane or die from despair and terror; animals are subjected to crushing forces that smash their bones and rupture their internal organs; the limbs of animals are mutilated or amputated to produce behavioral changes; animals are the victims of extreme pain and stress, inflicted out of idle curiosity, in nightmarish experiments designed to make healthy animals psychotic.

Such irresponsible accusations of research cruelty have consistently charac- 4
terized the publications of the MFA. However, a recent study by psychologists D. Caroline Coile and Neal E. Miller of Rockefeller University counters these charges. Coile and Miller looked at every article (a total of 608) appearing in the past five years in journals of the American Psychological Association that report animal research. They concluded that none of the extreme allegations made by the MFA could be supported.

Coile and Miller admit that charges of cruelty may have gone unreported or 5
been reported elsewhere but, they say, if such studies did occur, "they certainly were infrequent, and it is extremely misleading to imply that they are typical of experimental psychology."

Furthermore, there are standards and mechanisms to ensure that research 6
animals are treated in a humane and scientifically sensible way. These mechanisms include the Federal Animal Welfare Act of 1966 (amended in Congress in 1970, 1976, and 1979); periodic inspection of all animal-research facilities by the Department of Agriculture; visits by federal agencies that fund animal research and are increasingly attentive to the conditions of animal care and experimental procedures that could cause pain or distress; and a comprehensive document, "Guide for the Care and Use of Laboratory Animals," prepared by the National Academy of Sciences. In addition, virtually every major scientific society whose members conduct animal research distributes guidelines for such research. Above and beyond all of this, most universities and research institutes have animal-care committees that monitor animal research and care.

The United States Public Health Service is revising its guidelines to require 7
institutions that do research with animals to designate even clearer lines of authority and responsibility for animal care. This will include detailed information about how each institution complies with the new regulations as well as a requirement that animal-research committees include not only the supervising laboratory veterinarian and scientists but also a nonscientist and a person not affiliated with the institution. These committees will review programs for animal care, inspect all animal facilities, and review and monitor all research proposals before they are submitted to agencies of the United States Public Health Service. The committees will also have the power to disapprove or terminate any research proposal.

This is not to say that research scientists are perfect. There will be occasional 8
errors, cases of neglect, and instances of abuse—as is the case with any human

endeavor, whether it be the rearing of children, the practicing of a trade or profession, or the governing of a nation. But a high standard of humane treatment is maintained.

The choice of psychological research for special attack almost certainly stems 9 from the fact that such research is viewed as more vulnerable than are studies of anatomy, physiology, or microbiology. In the minds of many, psychology is a less well-developed science than the biological sciences and the benefits that have accrued from psychological research with animals are less well known. Hence, it is more difficult to grasp the necessity for animal research in behavioral studies than it is in biomedical studies.

Anyone who has looked into the matter can scarcely deny that major advances 10 in medicine have been achieved through basic research with animals. Among these are the development of virtually all modern vaccines against infectious diseases, the invention of surgical approaches to eye disorders, bone and joint injuries and heart disease, the discovery of insulin and other hormones, and the testing of all new drugs and antibiotics.

The benefits to humans of psychological research with animals may be less 11 well known than those of medical research but are just as real. Historically, the application of psychological research to human problems has lagged considerably behind the applied use of medical research. Mental events and overt behavior, although controlled by the nervous system and biology of an organism, are much more difficult to describe and study than are the actions of tissues or organ systems. To describe the complex interplay of perceptions, memories, cognitive and emotional processes with a physical and social environment that changes from moment to moment, elaborate research designs had to be developed. Since even a single type of behavior, such as vocalization, has so many different forms, a wide variety of ways of measuring the differences had to be developed. Finally, because much psychological research makes inferences from behavioral observations about internal states of an organism, methods were needed to insure that the interpretations were valid. Such complexities do not make the study of animal or human behavior less scientific or important than other kinds of research, but they do make it more difficult and slow its readiness for clinical applications.

Basic psychological research with animals has led to important achievements 12 in the interest of human welfare. Examples include the use of biofeedback, which had its origin in studies of behavioral conditioning of neuromuscular activities in rats and other animals. Today, biofeedback can be used to control blood pressure and hypertension and help prevent heart attacks. In the case of paralyzed patients, it can be used to elevate blood pressure, enabling those who would otherwise have to spend their lives lying down to sit upright. Biofeedback techniques also are used in the reduction and control of severe pain and as a method of neuromuscular control to help reverse the process of scoliosis, a disabling and disfiguring curvature of the spine. Biofeedback can also be a cost-effective alternative to certain medical treatments and can help avoid many of the complications associated with long-term drug use.

Language studies with apes have led to practical methods of teaching lan- 13 guage skills to severely retarded children who, prior to this work, had little or no language ability. Patients who have undergone radiation therapy for cancer can now take an interest in nutritious foods and avoid foods that have little nutritional value, thanks to studies of conditioned taste aversion done with animals. Neural and behavioral studies of early development of vision in cats and primates—studies that could not have been carried out with children— have led to advances in pediatric ophthalmology that can prevent irreversible brain damage and loss of vision in children who have cataracts and various other serious eye problems.

Behavioral modification and behavioral therapy, widely accepted techniques 14 for treating alcohol, drug, and tobacco addiction, have a long history of animal studies investigating learning theory and reward systems. Programmed instruction, the application of learning principles to educational tasks, is based on an array of learning studies in animals. These are but a few examples of the effectiveness and usefulness for humans of psychological research with animals.

Those opposed to animal research have proposed that alternatives to animal 15 research, such as mathematical and computer models and tissue cultures, be used. In some cases, these alternatives are both feasible and valuable. Tissue cultures, for example, have been very effective in certain toxicological studies that formerly required live animals. For psychological studies, however, it is often necessary to study the whole animal and its relationship to the environment. Visual problems, abnormal sexual behavior, depression, and aggression, for example, are not seen in tissue cultures and do not lend themselves to computer models. When human subjects cannot be used for such studies, animals are necessary if the research is to be done at all.

Extremists within the animal-rights movement take the position that animals 16 have rights equal to or greater than those of humans. It follows from this that even if humans might benefit from animal research, the cost to animals is too high. It is ironic that despite this moral position, the same organizations condone—and indeed sponsor—activities that appear to violate the basic rights of animals to live and reproduce. Each year 10,000,000 dogs are destroyed by public pounds, animal shelters, and humane societies. Many of these programs are supported and even operated by animal-protectionist groups. Surely there is a strong contradiction when those who profess to believe in animal rights deny animals their right to life. A similar situation exists with regard to programs of pet sterilization, programs that deny animals the right to breed and to bear offspring and are sponsored in many cases by antivivisectionists and animal-rights groups. Evidently, animal-rights advocates sometimes recognize and subscribe to the position that animals do not have the same rights as humans.

However, their public posture leaves little room for examining these subtleties or applying similar standards to animal research.

Within the animal-protectionist movement there are moderates who have   17
confidence in scientists as compassionate human beings and in the value of research. Their primary aims are to insure that animals are treated humanely and that discomfort in animal experimentation is kept to a minimum. It is to this group that scientists and scientific organizations have the responsibility to explain what they do, why and how they do it and what benefits occur.

I believe that the values guiding contemporary animal research represent   18
prevailing sentiment within the scientific community and, indeed, within society at large. And I believe that these values are congruent with those of the moderates within the animal-protectionist movement. As articulated by ethicist Arthur Caplan, rights, in the most realistic sense, are granted by one group to another based on perceived similarities between the groups. Plainly, animals lack those characteristics that would allow them to share in the rights we grant to humans. We do not grant domestic animals the right to go where they wish or do what they want because they are obviously unable to comprehend the responsibilities and demands of human society. In fact, we do not as a society even grant all domestic animals and pets the right to live.

This does not mean, however, that we do not have a moral responsibility to   19
animals. I believe, along with Caplan and the scientific research community at large, that we hold a moral stewardship for animals and that we are obliged to treat them with humane compassion and concern for their sentience. Many animal forms can and do feel pain and are highly aware of their environment. This awareness makes them worthy of our respect and serious concern. Caplan is certainly correct when he says that this moral obligation ought to be part of what it means to be a scientist today.

Science must proceed. The objective quest for knowledge is a treasured   20
enterprise of our heritage and culture. Scientific inquiry into the nature of our living world has freed us from ignorance and superstition. Scientific understanding is an expression of our highest capacities—those of objective observation, interpretive reasoning, imagination, and creativity. Founded on the results of basic research, often conducted with no goal other than that of increased understanding, the eventual practical use of this knowledge has led to a vastly improved well-being for humankind.

Extremists in the animal-rights movement probably will never accept such   21
justifications for research or assurances of humane treatments. They may reject any actions, no matter how conscientious, that scientists take in realistically and morally reconciling the advance of human welfare with the use of animals. But, fortunately, there are many who, while deeply and appropriately concerned

733

for the compassionate treatment of animals, recognize that human welfare is and should be our primary concern.

QUESTIONS

1. King begins his argument by presenting the opposition's position. In paragraph 2, he offers the charge from a member of the Humane Society of the United States that "torture is the founding principle and fundamental characteristic of experimental psychology." Why does King begin by presenting the opposition's case? How does he characterize their claims? How does he use this information to strengthen his own argument?

2. King argues that "it is more difficult to grasp the necessity for animal research in behavioral studies than it is in biomedical studies" (paragraph 9). What examples does he offer to make his case that animal research in behavioral studies has had important human benefits? Do you find these examples convincing?

3. Summarize King's position. What *is* the case for animals in research?

4. What values does King appeal to? What assumptions underlie King's position?

5. Compose a position in response to King. You might begin by deciding whether you want to present yourself as a moderate or an extremist, or whether you would reject from the outset those labels for positions mentioned by King.

6. Spend some time in a psychology lab at your school where animals are used for research. What do you observe about the conditions and treatment of these animals? Interview the researchers in the lab to learn about the kind of research conducted and the projected benefits for behavioral studies. Using this information as evidence and your own responses to the various readings on animal rights, write an essay supporting your position.

MAKING CONNECTIONS

King writes, "Many animals can and do feel pain and are highly aware of their environment. This awareness makes them worthy of our respect and serious concern." How would Alice Walker respond to this claim and to King's argument? Read her essay, "Am I Blue?" Would King call Walker an *extremist* as he uses that term in paragraph 16? Imagine a conversation between King and Walker, and compose a dialogue between them.

THE EGG AND THE SPERM:
HOW SCIENCE HAS CONSTRUCTED A ROMANCE BASED ON STEREOTYPICAL MALE-FEMALE ROLES

Emily Martin

Emily Martin is a professor of anthropology at Johns Hopkins University. She has written The Woman in the Body: A Cultural Analysis of Reproduction *(1987) and has been doing research on the anthropology of the immune system. In the following article,* which originally appeared in the journal* Signs *(1991), Martin's intent is to expose the cultural stereotypes operative in the so-called scientific language surrounding human reproduction.*

The theory of the human body is always a part of a world-picture. . . . The theory of the human body is always a part of a fantasy.

[James Hillman, *The Myth of Analysis*][1]

As an anthropologist, I am intrigued by the possibility that culture shapes how biological scientists describe what they discover about the natural world. If this were so, we would be learning about more than the natural world in high school biology class; we would be learning about cultural beliefs and practices as if they were part of nature. In the course of my research I realized that the picture of egg and sperm drawn in popular as well as scientific accounts of reproductive biology relies on stereotypes central to our cultural definitions of male and female. The stereotypes imply not only that female biological processes are less worthy than their male counterparts but also that women are less worthy than men. Part of my goal in writing this article is to shine a bright light on the gender stereotypes hidden within the scientific language of biology. Exposed in such a light, I hope they will lose much of their power to harm us.

1

*Portions of this article were presented as the 1987 Becker Lecture, Cornell University. I am grateful for the many suggestions and ideas I received on this occasion. For especially pertinent help with my arguments and data I thank Richard Cone, Kevin Whaley, Sharon Stephens, Barbara Duden, Susanne Kuechler, Lorna Rhodes, and Scott Gilbert. The article was strengthened and clarified by the comments of the anonymous *Signs* reviewers as well as the superb editorial skills of Amy Gage.
[1]James Hillman, *The Myth of Analysis* (Evanston, Ill.: Northwestern University Press, 1972), 220.

EGG AND SPERM: A SCIENTIFIC
FAIRY TALE

At a fundamental level, all major scientific textbooks depict male and female [2] reproductive organs as systems for the production of valuable substances, such as eggs and sperm.[2] In the case of women, the monthly cycle is described as being designed to produce eggs and prepare a suitable place for them to be fertilized and grown—all to the end of making babies. But the enthusiasm ends there. By extolling the female cycle as a productive enterprise, menstruation must necessarily be viewed as a failure. Medical texts describe menstruation as the "debris" of the uterine lining, the result of necrosis, or death of tissue. The descriptions imply that a system has gone awry, making products of no use, not to specification, unsalable, wasted, scrap. An illustration in a widely used medical text shows menstruation as a chaotic disintegration of form, complementing the many texts that describe it as "ceasing," "dying," "losing," "denuding," "expelling."[3]

Male reproductive physiology is evaluated quite differently. One of the texts [3] that sees menstruation as failed production employs a sort of breathless prose when it describes the maturation of sperm: "The mechanisms which guide the remarkable cellular transformation from spermatid to mature sperm remain uncertain. . . . Perhaps the most amazing characteristic of spermatogenesis is its sheer magnitude: the normal human male may manufacture several hundred million sperm per day."[4] In the classic text *Medical Physiology*, edited by Vernon Mountcastle, the male/female, productive/destructive comparison is more explicit: "Whereas the female *sheds* only a single gamete each month, the seminiferous tubules *produce* hundreds of millions of sperm each day" (emphasis mine).[5] The female author of another text marvels at the length of the microscopic seminiferous tubules, which, if uncoiled and placed end to end, "would span almost one-third of a mile!" She writes, "In an adult male these structures produce millions of sperm cells each day." Later she asks, "How is this feat accomplished?"[6] None of these texts expresses such intense enthusiasm for any female processes. It is surely no accident that the "remarkable" process of making

---

[2]The textbooks I consulted are the main ones used in classes for undergraduate premedical students or medical students (or those held on reserve in the library for these classes) during the past few years at Johns Hopkins University. These texts are widely used at other universities in the country as well.

[3]Arthur C. Guyton, *Physiology of the Human Body*, 6th ed. (Philadelphia: Saunders College Publishing, 1984), 624.

[4]Arthur J. Vander, James H. Sherman, and Dorothy S. Luciano, *Human Physiology: The Mechanisms of Body Function*, 3d ed. (New York: McGraw Hill, 1980), 483–84.

[5]Vernon B. Mountcastle, *Medical Physiology*, 14th ed. (London: Mosby, 1980), 2:1624.

[6]Eldra Pearl Solomon, *Human Anatomy and Physiology* (New York: CBS College Publishing, 1983), 678.

sperm involves precisely what, in the medical view, menstruation does not: production of something deemed valuable.[7]

One could argue that menstruation and spermatogenesis are not analogous   4
processes and, therefore, should not be expected to elicit the same kind of response. The proper female analogy to spermatogenesis, biologically, is ovulation. Yet ovulation does not merit enthusiasm in these texts either. Textbook descriptions stress that all of the ovarian follicles containing ova are already present at birth. Far from being *produced*, as sperm are, they merely sit on the shelf, slowly degenerating and aging like overstocked inventory: "At birth, normal human ovaries contain an estimated one million follicles [each], and no new ones appear after birth. Thus, in marked contrast to the male, the newborn female already has all the germ cells she will ever have. Only a few, perhaps 400, are destined to reach full maturity during her active productive life. All the others degenerate at some point in their development so that few, if any, remain by the time she reaches menopause at approximately 50 years of age."[8] Note the "marked contrast" that this description sets up between male and female: the male, who continuously produces fresh germ cells, and the female, who has stockpiled germ cells by birth and is faced with their degeneration.

Nor are the female organs spared such vivid descriptions. One scientist writes   5
in a newspaper article that a woman's ovaries become old and worn out from ripening eggs every month, even though the woman herself is still relatively young: "When you look through a laparoscope . . . at an ovary that has been through hundreds of cycles, even in a superbly healthy American female, you see a scarred, battered organ."[9]

To avoid the negative connotations that some people associate with the female   6
reproductive system, scientists could begin to describe male and female processes as homologous. They might credit females with "producing" mature ova one at a time, as they're needed each month, and describe males as having to face problems of degenerating germ cells. This degeneration would occur throughout life among spermatogonia, the undifferentiated germ cells in the testes that are the long-lived, dormant precursors of sperm.

But the texts have an almost dogged insistence on casting female processes   7
in a negative light. The texts celebrate sperm production because it is continuous from puberty to senescence, while they portray egg production as inferior because it is finished at birth. This makes the female seem unproductive, but some texts will also insist that it is she who is wasteful.[10] In a section heading

---

[7] For elaboration, see Emily Martin, *The Woman in the Body: A Cultural Analysis of Reproduction* (Boston: Beacon, 1987), 27–53.

[8] Vander, Sherman, and Luciano, 568.

[9] Melvin Konner, "Childbearing and Age," *New York Times Magazine* (December 27, 1987), 22–23, esp. 22.

[10] I have found but one exception to the opinion that the female is wasteful: "Smallpox being

for *Molecular Biology of the Cell*, a best-selling text, we are told that "Oogenesis is wasteful." The text goes on to emphasize that of the seven million oogonia, or egg germ cells, in the female embryo, most degenerate in the ovary. Of those that do go on to become oocytes, or eggs, many also degenerate, so that at birth only two million eggs remain in the ovaries. Degeneration continues throughout a woman's life: by puberty 300,000 eggs remain, and only a few are present by menopause. "During the 40 or so years of a woman's reproductive life, only 400 to 500 eggs will have been released," the authors write. "All the rest will have degenerated. It is still a mystery why so many eggs are formed only to die in the ovaries."[11]

The real mystery is why the male's vast production of sperm is not seen as wasteful.[12] Assuming that a man "produces" 100 million (10^8) sperm per day (a conservative estimate) during an average reproductive life of sixty years, he would produce well over two trillion sperm in his lifetime. Assuming that a woman "ripens" one egg per lunar month, or thirteen per year, over the course of her forty-year reproductive life, she would total five hundred eggs in her lifetime. But the word "waste" implies an excess, too much produced. Assuming two or three offspring, for every baby a woman produces, she wastes only around two hundred eggs. For every baby a man produces, he wastes more than one trillion (10^{12}) sperm.

How is it that positive images are denied to the bodies of women? A look at language—in this case, scientific language—provides the first clue. Take the egg and the sperm.[13] It is remarkable how "femininely" the egg behaves and

---

the nasty disease it is, one might expect nature to have designed antibody molecules with combining sites that specifically recognize the epitopes on smallpox virus. Nature differs from technology, however: it thinks nothing of wastefulness. (For example, rather than improving the chance that a spermatozoon will meet an egg cell, nature finds it easier to produce millions of spermatozoa.)" (Niels Kaj Jerne, "The Immune System," *Scientific American* 229, no. 1 [July 1973]: 53). Thanks to a *Signs* reviewer for bringing this reference to my attention.

[11] Bruce Alberts et al., *Molecular Biology of the Cell* (New York: Garland, 1983), 795.

[12] In her essay "Have Only Men Evolved?" (in *Discovering Reality: Feminist Perspectives on Epistemology, Metaphysics, Methodology, and Philosophy of Science*, ed. Sandra Harding and Merrill B. Hintikka [Dordrecht, The Netherlands: Reidel, 1983], 45–69, esp. 60–61), Ruth Hubbard points out that sociobiologists have said the female invests more energy than the male in the production of her large gametes, claiming that this explains why the female provides parental care. Hubbard questions whether it "really takes more 'energy' to generate the one or relatively few eggs than the large excess of sperms required to achieve fertilization." For further critique of how the greater size of eggs is interpreted in sociobiology, see Donna Haraway, "Investment Strategies for the Evolving Portfolio of Primate Females," in *Body/Politics*, ed. Mary Jacobus, Evelyn Fox Keller, and Sally Shuttleworth (New York: Routledge, 1990), 155–56.

[13] The sources I used for this article provide compelling information on interactions among sperm. Lack of space prevents me from taking up this theme here, but the elements include competition, hierarchy, and sacrifice. For a newspaper report, see Malcolm W. Browne, "Some Thoughts on Self Sacrifice," *New York Times* (July 5, 1988), C6. For a literary rendition, see John Barth, "Night-Sea Journey," in his *Lost in the Funhouse* (Garden City, N.Y.: Doubleday, 1968), 3–13.

how "masculinely" the sperm.[14] The egg is seen as large and passive.[15] It does not *move* or *journey*, but passively "is transported," "is swept,"[16] or even "drifts"[17] along the fallopian tube. In utter contrast, sperm are small, "streamlined,"[18] and invariably active. They "deliver" their genes to the egg, "activate the developmental program of the egg,"[19] and have a "velocity" that is often remarked upon.[20] Their tails are "strong" and efficiently powered.[21] Together with the forces of ejaculation, they can "propel the semen into the deepest recesses of the vagina."[22] For this they need "energy," "fuel,"[23] so that with a "whiplash-like motion and strong lurches"[24] they can "burrow through the egg coat"[25] and "penetrate" it.[26]

At its extreme, the age-old relationship of the egg and the sperm takes on a 10 royal or religious patina. The egg coat, its protective barrier, is sometimes called its "vestments," a term usually reserved for sacred, religious dress. The egg is said to have a "corona,"[27] a crown, and to be accompanied by "attendant cells."[28] It is holy, set apart and above, the queen to the sperm's king. The egg is also passive, which means it must depend on sperm for rescue. Gerald Schatten and Helen Schatten liken the egg's role to that of Sleeping Beauty: "a dormant bride awaiting her mate's magic kiss, which instills the spirit that brings her to life."[29] Sperm, by contrast, have a "mission,"[30] which is to "move through the female genital tract in quest of the ovum."[31] One popular account has it that the sperm

---

[14] See Carol Delaney, "The Meaning of Paternity and the Virgin Birth Debate," *Man* 21, no. 3 (September 1986): 494–513. She discusses the difference between this scientific view that women contribute genetic material to the fetus and the claim of long-standing Western folk theories that the origin and identity of the fetus comes from the male, as in the metaphor of planting a seed in soil.

[15] For a suggested direct link between human behavior and purportedly passive eggs and active sperm, see Erik H. Erikson, "Inner and Outer Space: Reflections on Womanhood," *Daedalus* 93, no. 2 (Spring 1964): 582–606, esp. 591.

[16] Guyton (n. 3), 619; and Mountcastle (n. 5), 1609.

[17] Jonathan Miller and David Pelham, *The Facts of Life* (New York: Viking Penguin, 1984), 5.

[18] Alberts et al., 796.

[19] Ibid., 796.

[20] See, e.g., William F. Ganong, *Review of Medical Physiology*, 7th ed. (Los Altos, Calif.: Lange Medical Publications, 1975), 322.

[21] Alberts et al. (n. 11), 796.

[22] Guyton, 615.

[23] Solomon (n. 6), 683.

[24] Vander, Sherman, and Luciano (n. 4), 4th ed. (1985), 580.

[25] Alberts et al., 796.

[26] All biology texts quoted use the word "penetrate."

[27] Solomon, 700.

[28] A. Beldecos et al., "The Importance of Feminist Critique for Contemporary Cell Biology," *Hypatia* 3, no. 1 (Spring 1988): 61–76.

[29] Gerald Schatten and Helen Schatten, "The Energetic Egg," *Medical World News* 23 (January 23, 1984): 51–53, esp. 51.

[30] Alberts et al., 796.

[31] Guyton (n. 3), 613.

carry out a "perilous journey" into the "warm darkness," where some fall away "exhausted." "Survivors" "assault" the egg, the successful candidates "surrounding the prize."[32] Part of the urgency of this journey, in more scientific terms, is that "once released from the supportive environment of the ovary, an egg will die within hours unless rescued by a sperm."[33] The wording stresses the fragility and dependency of the egg, even though the same text acknowledges elsewhere that sperm also live for only a few hours.[34]

In 1948, in a book remarkable for its early insights into these matters, Ruth Herschberger argued that female reproductive organs are seen as biologically interdependent, while male organs are viewed as autonomous, operating independently and in isolation: 11

> At present the functional is stressed only in connection with women: it is in them that ovaries, tubes, uterus, and vagina have endless interdependence. In the male, reproduction would seem to involve "organs" only.
>
> Yet the sperm, just as much as the egg, is dependent on a great many related processes. There are secretions which mitigate the urine in the urethra before ejaculation, to protect the sperm. There is the reflex shutting off of the bladder connection, the provision of prostatic secretions, and various types of muscular propulsion. The sperm is no more independent of its milieu than the egg, and yet from a wish that it were, biologists have lent their support to the notion that the human female, beginning with the egg, is congenitally more dependent than the male.[35]

Bringing out another aspect of the sperm's autonomy, an article in the journal *Cell* has the sperm making an "existential decision" to penetrate the egg: "Sperm are cells with a limited behavioral repertoire, one that is directed toward fertilizing eggs. To execute the decision to abandon the haploid state, sperm swim to an egg and there acquire the ability to effect membrane fusion."[36] Is this a corporate manager's version of the sperm's activities—"executing decisions" while fraught with dismay over difficult options that bring with them very high risk? 12

There is another way that sperm, despite their small size, can be made to loom in importance over the egg. In a collection of scientific papers, an electron micrograph of an enormous egg and tiny sperm is titled "A Portrait of the 13

[32] Miller and Pelham (n. 17), 7.
[33] Alberts et al. (n. 11), 804.
[34] Ibid., 801.
[35] Ruth Herschberger, *Adam's Rib* (New York: Pelligrini & Cudaby, 1948), esp. 84. I am indebted to Ruth Hubbard for telling me about Herschberger's work, although at a point when this paper was already in draft form.
[36] Bennett M. Shapiro. "The Existential Decision of a Sperm," *Cell* 49, no. 3 (May 1987): 293–94, esp. 293.

Sperm."[37] This is a little like showing a photo of a dog and calling it a picture of the fleas. Granted, microscopic sperm are harder to photograph than eggs, which are just large enough to see with the naked eye. But surely the use of the term "portrait," a word associated with the powerful and wealthy, is significant. Eggs have only micrographs or pictures, not portraits.

One depiction of sperm as weak and timid, instead of strong and powerful— the only such representation in western civilization, so far as I know—occurs in Woody Allen's movie *Everything You Always Wanted To Know About Sex* *But Were Afraid to Ask*. Allen, playing the part of an apprehensive sperm inside a man's testicles, is scared of the man's approaching orgasm. He is reluctant to launch himself into the darkness, afraid of contraceptive devices, afraid of winding up on the ceiling if the man masturbates.

The more common picture—egg as damsel in distress, shielded only by her sacred garments; sperm as heroic warrior to the rescue—cannot be proved to be dictated by the biology of these events. While the "facts" of biology may not *always* be constructed in cultural terms, I would argue that in this case they are. The degree of metaphorical content in these descriptions, the extent to which differences between egg and sperm are emphasized, and the parallels between cultural stereotypes of male and female behavior and the character of egg and sperm all point to this conclusion.

NEW RESEARCH, OLD IMAGERY

As new understandings of egg and sperm emerge, textbook gender imagery is being revised. But the new research, far from escaping the stereotypical representations of egg and sperm, simply replicates elements of textbook gender imagery in a different form. The persistence of this imagery calls to mind what Ludwik Fleck termed "the self-contained" nature of scientific thought. As he described it, "the interaction between what is already known, what remains to be learned, and those who are to apprehend it, go to ensure harmony within the system. But at the same time they also preserve the harmony of illusions, which is quite secure within the confines of a given thought style."[38] We need to understand the way in which the cultural content in scientific descriptions changes as biological discoveries unfold, and whether that cultural content is solidly entrenched or easily changed.

In all of the texts quoted above, sperm are described as penetrating the egg, and specific substances on a sperm's head are described as binding to the egg.

14

15

16

17

---

[37] Lennart Nilsson, "A Portrait of the Sperm," in *The Functional Anatomy of the Spermatozoan*, ed. Bjorn A. Afzelius (New York: Pergamon, 1975), 79–82.

[38] Ludwik Fleck, *Genesis and Development of a Scientific Fact*, ed. Thaddeus J. Trenn and Robert K. Merton (Chicago: University of Chicago Press, 1979), 38.

Recently, this description of events was rewritten in a biophysics lab at Johns Hopkins University—transforming the egg from the passive to the active party.[39]

Prior to this research, it was thought that the zona, the inner vestments of the egg, formed an impenetrable barrier. Sperm overcame the barrier by mechanically burrowing through, thrashing their tails and slowly working their way along. Later research showed that the sperm released digestive enzymes that chemically broke down the zona; thus, scientists presumed that the sperm used mechanical *and* chemical means to get through to the egg. [18]

In this recent investigation, the researchers began to ask questions about the mechanical force of the sperm's tail. (The lab's goal was to develop a contraceptive that worked topically on sperm.) They discovered, to their great surprise, that the forward thrust of sperm is extremely weak, which contradicts the assumption that sperm are forceful penetrators.[40] Rather than thrusting forward, the sperm's head was now seen to move mostly back and forth. The sideways motion of the sperm's tail makes the head move sideways with a force that is ten times stronger than its forward movement. So even if the overall force of the sperm were strong enough to mechanically break the zona, most of its force would be directed sideways rather than forward. In fact, its strongest tendency, by tenfold, is to escape by attempting to pry itself off the egg. Sperm, then, must be exceptionally efficient at *escaping* from any cell surface they contact. And the surface of the egg must be designed to trap the sperm and prevent their escape. Otherwise, few if any sperm would reach the egg. [19]

The researchers at Johns Hopkins concluded that the sperm and egg stick together because of adhesive molecules on the surfaces of each. The egg traps the sperm and adheres to it so tightly that the sperm's head is forced to lie flat against the surface of the zona, a little bit, they told me, "like Br'er Rabbit getting more and more stuck to tar baby the more he wriggles." The trapped sperm continues to wiggle ineffectually side to side. The mechanical force of its tail is so weak that a sperm cannot break even one chemical bond. This is where the digestive enzymes released by the sperm come in. If they start to soften the zona just at the tip of the sperm and the sides remain stuck, then the weak, flailing sperm can get oriented in the right direction and make it through the zona—provided that its bonds to the zona dissolve as it moves in. [20]

Although this new version of the saga of the egg and the sperm broke through cultural expectations, the researchers who made the discovery continued to [21]

---

[39] Jay M. Baltz carried out the research I describe when he was a graduate student in the Thomas C. Jenkins Department of Biophysics at Johns Hopkins University.

[40] Far less is known about the physiology of sperm than comparable female substances, which some feminists claim is no accident. Greater scientific scrutiny of female reproduction has long enabled the burden of birth control to be placed on women. In this case, the researchers' discovery did not depend on development of any new technology. The experiments made use of glass pipettes, a manometer, and a simple microscope, all of which have been available for more than one hundred years.

write papers and abstracts as if the sperm were the active party who attacks, binds, penetrates, and enters the egg. The only difference was that sperm were now seen as performing these actions weakly.[41] Not until August 1987, more than three years after the findings described above, did these researchers reconceptualize the process to give the egg a more active role. They began to describe the zona as an aggressive sperm catcher, covered with adhesive molecules that can capture a sperm with a single bond and clasp it to the zona's surface.[42] In the words of their published account: "The innermost vestment, the *zona pellucida*, is a glyco-protein shell, which captures and tethers the sperm before they penetrate it. . . . The sperm is captured at the initial contact between the sperm tip and the *zona*. . . . Since the thrust [of the sperm] is much smaller than the force needed to break a single affinity bond, the first bond made upon the tip-first meeting of the sperm and *zona* can result in the capture of the sperm."[43]

Experiments in another lab reveal similar patterns of data interpretation. Gerald Schatten and Helen Schatten set out to show that, contrary to conventional wisdom, the "egg is not merely a large, yolk-filled sphere into which the sperm burrows to endow new life. Rather, recent research suggests the almost heretical view that sperm and egg are mutually active partners."[44] This sounds like a departure from the stereotypical textbook view, but further reading reveals Schatten and Schatten's conformity to the aggressive-sperm metaphor. They describe how "the sperm and egg first touch when, from the tip of the sperm's triangular head, a long, thin filament shoots out and harpoons the egg." Then we learn that "remarkably, the harpoon is not so much fired as assembled at great speed, molecule by molecule, from a pool of protein stored in a specialized region called the acrosome. The filament may grow as much as twenty times longer than the sperm head itself before its tip reaches the egg and sticks."[45] Why not call this "making a bridge" or "throwing out a line" rather than firing a harpoon? Harpoons pierce prey and injure or kill them, while this filament

22

---

[41] Jay Baltz and Richard A. Cone, "What Force Is Needed to Tether a Sperm?" (abstract for Society for the Study of Reproduction, 1985), and "Flagellar Torque on the Head Determines the Force Needed to Tether a Sperm" (abstract for Biophysical Society, 1986).

[42] Jay M. Baltz, David F. Katz, and Richard A. Cone, "The Mechanics of the Sperm-Egg Interaction at the Zona Pellucida," *Biophysical Journal* 54, no. 4 (October 1988): 643–54. Lab members were somewhat familiar with work on metaphors in the biology of female reproduction. Richard Cone, who runs the lab, is my husband, and he talked with them about my earlier research on the subject from time to time. Even though my current research focuses on biological imagery and I heard about the lab's work from my husband every day, I myself did not recognize the role of imagery in the sperm research until many weeks after the period of research and writing I describe. Therefore, I assume that any awareness the lab members may have had about how underlying metaphor might be guiding this particular research was fairly inchoate.

[43] Ibid., 643, 650.

[44] Schatten and Schatten (n. 29), 51.

[45] Ibid., 52.

only sticks. And why not focus, as the Hopkins lab did, on the stickiness of the egg, rather than the stickiness of the sperm?[46] Later in the article, the Schattens replicate the common view of the sperm's perilous journey into the warm darkness of the vagina, this time for the purpose of explaining its journey into the egg itself: "[The sperm] still has an arduous journey ahead. It must penetrate farther into the egg's huge sphere of cytoplasm and somehow locate the nucleus, so that the two cells' chromosomes can fuse. The sperm dives down into the cytoplasm, its tail beating. But it is soon interrupted by the sudden and swift migration of the egg nucleus, which rushes toward the sperm with a velocity triple that of the movement of chromosomes during cell division, crossing the entire egg in about a minute."[47]

Like Schatten and Schatten and the biophysicists at Johns Hopkins, another researcher has recently made discoveries that seem to point to a more interactive view of the relationship of egg and sperm. This work, which Paul Wassarman conducted on the sperm and eggs of mice, focuses on identifying the specific molecules in the egg coat (the zona pellucida) that are involved in egg-sperm interaction. At first glance, his descriptions seem to fit the model of an egalitarian relationship. Male and female gametes "recognize one another," and "interactions . . . take place between sperm and egg."[48] But the article in *Scientific American* in which those descriptions appear begins with a vignette that presages the dominant motif of their presentation: "It has been more than a century since Hermann Fol, a Swiss zoologist, peered into his microscope and became the first person to see a sperm penetrate an egg, fertilize it and form the first cell of a new embryo."[49] This portrayal of the sperm as the active party—the one that *penetrates* and *fertilizes* the egg and *produces* the embryo—is not cited as an example of an earlier, now outmoded view. In fact, the author reiterates the point later in the article: "Many sperm can bind to and penetrate the zona pellucida, or outer coat, of an unfertilized mouse egg, but only one sperm will eventually fuse with the thin plasma membrane surrounding the egg proper *(inner sphere)*, fertilizing the egg and giving rise to a new embryo."[50]

The imagery of sperm as aggressor is particularly startling in this case: the main discovery being reported is isolation of a particular molecule *on the egg coat* that plays an important role in fertilization! Wassarman's choice of language sustains the picture. He calls the molecule that has been isolated, ZP3, a "sperm receptor." By allocating the passive, waiting role to the egg, Wassarman can continue to describe the sperm as the actor, the one that makes it all happen:

23

24

---

[46] Surprisingly, in an article intended for a general audience, the authors do not point out that these are sea urchin sperm and note that human sperm do not shoot out filaments at all.

[47] Schatten and Schatten, 53.

[48] Paul M. Wassarman, "Fertilization in Mammals," *Scientific American* 259, no. 6 (December 1988): 78–84, esp. 78, 84.

[49] Ibid., 78.

[50] Ibid., 79.

"The basic process begins when many sperm first attach loosely and then bind tenaciously to receptors on the surface of the egg's thick outer coat, the zona pellucida. Each sperm, which has a large number of egg-binding proteins on its surface, binds to many sperm receptors on the egg. More specifically, a site on each of the egg-binding proteins fits a complementary site on a sperm receptor, much as a key fits a lock."[51] With the sperm designated as the "key" and the egg the "lock," it is obvious which one acts and which one is acted upon. Could this imagery not be reversed, letting the sperm (the lock) wait until the egg produces the key? Or could we speak of two halves of a locket matching, and regard the matching itself as the action that initiates the fertilization?

It is as if Wassarman were determined to make the egg the receiving partner. 25 Usually in biological research, the *protein* member of the pair of binding molecules is called the receptor, and physically it has a pocket in it rather like a lock. As the diagrams that illustrate Wassarman's article show, the molecules on the sperm are proteins and have "pockets." The small, mobile molecules that fit into these pockets are called ligands. As shown in the diagrams, ZP3 on the egg is a polymer of "keys"; many small knobs stick out. Typically, molecules on the sperm would be called receptors and molecules on the egg would be called ligands. But Wassarman chose to name ZP3 on the egg the receptor and to create a new term, "the egg-binding protein," for the molecule on the sperm that otherwise would have been called the receptor.[52]

Wassarman does credit the egg coat with having more functions than those 26 of a sperm receptor. While he notes that "the zona pellucida has at times been viewed by investigators as a nuisance, a barrier to sperm and hence an impediment to fertilization," his new research reveals that the egg coat "serves as a sophisticated biological security system that screens incoming sperm, selects only those compatible with fertilization and development, prepares sperm for fusion with the egg and later protects the resulting embryo from polyspermy [a lethal condition caused by fusion of more than one sperm with a single egg]."[53] Although this description gives the egg an active role, that role is drawn in stereotypically feminine terms. The egg *selects* an appropriate mate, *prepares* him for fusion, and then *protects* the resulting offspring from harm. This is courtship and mating behavior as seen through the eyes of a sociobiologist: woman as the hard-to-get prize, who, following union with the chosen one, becomes woman as servant and mother.

And Wassarman does not quit there. In a review article for *Science*, he 27

---

[51] Ibid., 78.

[52] Since receptor molecules are relatively *immotile* and the ligands that bind to them relatively *motile*, one might imagine the egg being called the receptor and the sperm the ligand. But the molecules in question on egg and sperm are immotile molecules. It is the sperm as a *cell* that has motility, and the egg as a cell that has relative immotility.

[53] Wassarman, 78–79.

outlines the "chronology of fertilization."[54] Near the end of the article are two subject headings. One is "Sperm Penetration," in which Wassarman describes how the chemical dissolving of the zona pellucida combines with the "substantial propulsive force generated by sperm." The next heading is "Sperm-Egg Fusion." This section details what happens inside the zona after a sperm "penetrates" it. Sperm "can make contact with, adhere to, and fuse with (that is, fertilize) an egg."[55] Wassarman's word choice, again, is astonishingly skewed in favor of the sperm's activity, for in the next breath he says that sperm *lose* all motility upon fusion with the egg's surface. In mouse and sea urchin eggs, the sperm enters at the *egg's* volition, according to Wassarman's description: "Once fused with egg plasma membrane [the surface of the egg], how does a sperm enter the egg? The surface of both mouse and sea urchin eggs is covered with thousands of plasma membrane-bound projections, called microvilli [tiny "hairs"]. Evidence in sea urchins suggests that, after membrane fusion, a group of elongated microvilli cluster tightly around and interdigitate over the sperm head. As these microvilli are resorbed, the sperm is drawn into the egg. Therefore, sperm motility, which ceases at the time of fusion in both sea urchins and mice, is not required for sperm entry."[56] The section called "Sperm Penetration" more logically would be followed by a section called "The Egg Envelops," rather than "Sperm-Egg Fusion." This would give a parallel—and more accurate— sense that both the egg and the sperm initiate action.

Another way that Wassarman makes less of the egg's activity is by describing components of the egg but referring to the sperm as a whole entity. Deborah Gordon has described such an approach as "atomism" ("the part is independent of and primordial to the whole") and identified it as one of the "tenacious assumptions" of Western science and medicine.[57] Wassarman employs atomism to his advantage. When he refers to processing going on within sperm, he consistently returns to descriptions that remind us from whence these activities came: they are part of sperm that penetrate an egg or generate propulsive force. When he refers to processes going on within eggs, he stops there. As a result, any active role he grants them appears to be assigned to the parts of the egg, and not to the egg itself. In the quote above, it is the microvilli that actively cluster around the sperm. In another example, "the driving force for engulfment of a fused sperm comes from a region of cytoplasm just beneath an egg's plasma membrane."[58]

28

---

[54] Paul M. Wassarman, "The Biology and Chemistry of Fertilization," *Science* 235, no. 4788 (January 30, 1987): 553–60, esp. 554.

[55] Ibid., 557.

[56] Ibid., 557–58. This finding throws into question Schatten and Schatten's description (n. 29 above) of the sperm, its tail beating, diving down into the egg.

[57] Deborah R. Gordon, "Tenacious Assumptions in Western Medicine," in *Biomedicine Examined*, ed. Margaret Lock and Deborah Gordon (Dordrecht, The Netherlands: Kluwer, 1988), 19–56, esp. 26.

[58] Wassarman, "The Biology and Chemistry of Fertilization," 558.

SOCIAL IMPLICATIONS: THINKING BEYOND

All three of these revisionist accounts of egg and sperm cannot seem to escape the hierarchical imagery of older accounts. Even though each new account gives the egg a larger and more active role, taken together they bring into play another cultural stereotype: woman as a dangerous and aggressive threat. In the Johns Hopkins lab's revised model, the egg ends up as the female aggressor who "captures and tethers" the sperm with her sticky zona, rather like a spider lying in wait in her web.[59] The Schatten lab has the egg's nucleus "interrupt" the sperm's dive with a "sudden and swift" rush by which she "clasps the sperm and guides its nucleus to the center."[60] Wassarman's description of the surface of the egg "covered with thousands of plasma membrane-bound projections, called microvilli" that reach out and clasp the sperm adds to the spiderlike imagery.[61]

These images grant the egg an active role but at the cost of appearing disturbingly aggressive. Images of woman as dangerous and aggressive, the femme fatale who victimizes men, are widespread in Western literature and culture.[62] More specific is the connection of spider imagery with the idea of an engulfing, devouring mother.[63] New data did not lead scientists to eliminate gender stereotypes in their descriptions of egg and sperm. Instead, scientists simply began to describe egg and sperm in different, but no less damaging, terms.

Can we envision a less stereotypical view? Biology itself provides another model that could be applied to the egg and the sperm. The cybernetic model—with its feedback loops, flexible adaptation to change, coordination of the parts within a whole, evolution over time, and changing response to the environment—is common in genetics, endocrinology, and ecology and has a growing influence in medicine in general.[64] This model has the potential to shift our imagery from the negative, in which the female reproductive system is castigated both for not producing eggs after birth and for producing (and thus wasting) too many eggs overall, to something more positive. The female reproductive system could be seen as responding to the environment (pregnancy or menopause), adjusting to monthly changes (menstruation), and flexibly changing from reproductivity after puberty to nonreproductivity later in life. The sperm and egg's interaction could also be described in cybernetic terms. J. F. Hartman's research in reproductive biology demonstrated fifteen years ago that if an egg is killed by

---

[59] Baltz, Katz, and Cone (n. 42 above), 643, 650.

[60] Schatten and Schatten, 53.

[61] Wassarman, "The Biology and Chemistry of Fertilization," 557.

[62] Mary Ellman, *Thinking about Women* (New York: Harcourt Brace Jovanovich, 1968), 140; Nina Auerbach, *Woman and the Demon* (Cambridge, Mass.: Harvard University Press, 1982), esp. 186.

[63] Kenneth Alan Adams, "Arachnophobia: Love American Style," *Journal of Psychoanalytic Anthropology* 4, no. 2 (1981): 157–97.

[64] William Ray Arney and Bernard Bergen, *Medicine and the Management of Living* (Chicago: University of Chicago Press, 1984).

being pricked with a needle, live sperm cannot get through the zona.[65] Clearly, this evidence shows that the egg and sperm *do* interact on more mutual terms, making biology's refusal to portray them that way all the more disturbing.

We would do well to be aware, however, that cybernetic imagery is hardly [32] neutral. In the past, cybernetic models have played an important part in the imposition of social control. These models inherently provide a way of thinking about a "field" of interacting components. Once the field can be seen, it can become the object of new forms of knowledge, which in turn can allow new forms of social control to be exerted over the components of the field. During the 1950s, for example, medicine began to recognize the psychosocial *environment* of the patient: the patient's family and its psychodynamics. Professions such as social work began to focus on this new environment, and the resulting knowledge became one way to further control the patient. Patients began to be seen not as isolated, individual bodies, but as psychosocial entities located in an "ecological" system: management of "the patient's psychology was a new entrée to patient control."[66]

The models that biologists use to describe their data can have important [33] social effects. During the nineteenth century, the social and natural sciences strongly influenced each other: the social ideas of Malthus about how to avoid the natural increase of the poor inspired Darwin's *Origin of Species*.[67] Once the *Origin* stood as a description of the natural world, complete with competition and market struggles, it could be reimported into social science as social Darwinism, in order to justify the social order of the time. What we are seeing now is similar: the importation of cultural ideas about passive females and heroic males into the "personalities" of gametes. This amounts to the "implanting of social imagery on representations of nature so as to lay a firm basis for reimporting exactly that same imagery as natural explanations of social phenomena."[68]

Further research would show us exactly what social effects are being wrought [34] from the biological imagery of egg and sperm. At the very least, the imagery keeps alive some of the hoariest old stereotypes about weak damsels in distress and their strong male rescuers. That these stereotypes are now being written in at the level of the *cell* constitutes a powerful move to make them seem so natural as to be beyond alteration.

The stereotypical imagery might also encourage people to imagine that what [35] results from the interaction of egg and sperm—a fertilized egg—is the result of deliberate "human" action at the cellular level. Whatever the intentions of the

---

[65] J. F. Hartman, R. B. Gwatkin, and C. F. Hutchison, "Early Contact Interactions between Mammalian Gametes *In Vitro*," *Proceedings of the National Academy of Sciences (U.S.)* 69, no. 10 (1972): 2767–69.

[66] Arney and Bergen, 68.

[67] Ruth Hubbard, "Have Only Men Evolved?" (n. 12 above), 51–52.

[68] David Harvey, personal communication, November 1989.

human couple, in this microscope "culture" a cellular "bride" (or femme fatale) and a cellular "groom" (her victim) make a cellular baby. Rosalind Petchesky points out that through visual representations such as sonograms, we are given "*images* of younger and younger, and tinier and tinier, fetuses being 'saved.'" This leads to "the point of viability being 'pushed back' *indefinitely.*"[69] Endowing egg and sperm with intentional action, a key aspect of personhood in our culture, lays the foundation for the point of viability being pushed back to the moment of fertilization. This will likely lead to greater acceptance of technological developments and new forms of scrutiny and manipulation, for the benefit of these inner "persons": court-ordered restrictions on a pregnant woman's activities in order to protect her fetus, fetal surgery, amniocentesis, and rescinding of abortion rights, to name but a few examples.[70]

Even if we succeed in substituting more egalitarian, interactive metaphors 36 to describe the activities of egg and sperm, and manage to avoid the pitfalls of cybernetic models, we would still be guilty of endowing cellular entities with personhood. More crucial, then, than what *kinds* of personalities we bestow on cells is the very fact that we are doing it at all. This process could ultimately have the most disturbing social consequences.

One clear feminist challenge is to wake up sleeping metaphors in science, 37 particularly those involved in descriptions of the egg and the sperm. Although the literary convention is to call such metaphors "dead," they are not so much dead as sleeping, hidden within the scientific content of texts—and all the more powerful for it.[71] Waking up such metaphors, by becoming aware of when we are projecting cultural imagery onto what we study, will improve our ability to investigate and understand nature. Waking up such metaphors, by becoming aware of their implications, will rob them of their power to naturalize our social conventions about gender.

QUESTIONS

1. Summarize Martin's argument. How has she structured it?
2. The first subhead of the essay is "Egg and Sperm: A Scientific Fairy Tale." The implications are that the actions of the egg and sperm constitute a story written by

---

[69] Rosalind Petchesky, "Fetal Images: The Power of Visual Culture in the Politics of Reproduction," *Feminist Studies* 13, no. 2 (Summer 1987): 263–92, esp. 272.

[70] Rita Arditti, Renate Klein, and Shelley Minden, *Test-Tube Women* (London: Pandora, 1984); Ellen Goodman, "Whose Right to Life?" *Baltimore Sun* (November 17, 1987); Tamar Lewin, "Courts Acting to Force Care of the Unborn," *New York Times* (November 23, 1987), A1 and B10; Susan Irwin and Brigitte Jordan, "Knowledge, Practice, and Power: Court Ordered Cesarean Sections," *Medical Anthropology Quarterly* 1, no. 3 (September 1987): 319–34.

[71] Thanks to Elizabeth Fee and David Spain, who in February 1989 and April 1989, respectively, made points related to this.

scientists. Why does Martin call it a fairy tale? What fairy tales does it resemble? In the process of your sexual education, what stories were you told?

3. Martin's argument raises the issue of scientific objectivity. Do you think there can be such a thing as a "pure" fact? Or can we only say that one fact is less encumbered by cultural baggage than another fact? What does Martin suggest as the best approach in presenting reproductive facts?

4. Look at some biology textbooks. How is reproduction presented? Are the same, or similar, "sleeping metaphors" that Martin discusses present in the discussion? What about other bodily processes and functions? Is the male body used as the sole example in discussions of the heart, blood pressure, digestion, or AIDS, for instance?

5. Using the biological information in Martin's essay, write a nonsexist description of the reproductive functions. In your conclusion, reflect on any difficulties you encountered in keeping your cellular entities free of personhood. Switch papers with a classmate to check one another for "sleeping metaphors."

6. Look at a sampling of sex education texts and materials designed for elementary or secondary school students to see if the cultural stereotypes Martin warns against are present. What analogies and metaphors do you find being used? Write up your discussion as an argument either for or against the revision of those texts.

MAKING CONNECTIONS

1. Martin's research is an important addition to the argument and issues surrounding stereotyping of the sexes. How does her essay augment the arguments in Edmund White's "Sexual Culture" or John Fiske's "Romancing the Rock"? What might a Madonna rock video version of a reproductive story be like?

2. Martin warns us to be on the alert for manipulative "sleeping metaphors." Carol Gilligan discusses the metaphors used by adolescent girls, and James Jeans relies on analogy to tell his scientific story. Are there "sleeping metaphors" lurking in other essays in this text?

WOMEN'S BRAINS
Stephen Jay Gould

Stephen Jay Gould, as the headnote on p. 147 mentions, is a biologist best known for his column in Natural History *magazine, where he has not only explained and defended Darwinian ideas of evolution, but also exposed abuses and misunderstandings of scientific concepts and methods. The following essay appeared in* Natural History *in 1992.*

In the prelude to *Middlemarch*, George Eliot lamented the unfulfilled lives   1
of talented women:

> Some have felt that these blundering lives are due to the inconvenient
> indefiniteness with which the Supreme Power has fashioned the natures
> of women: if there were one level of feminine incompetence as strict
> as the ability to count three and no more, the social lot of women
> might be treated with scientific certitude.

Eliot goes on to discount the idea of innate limitation, but while she wrote   2
in 1872, the leaders of European anthropometry were trying to measure "with
scientific certitude" the inferiority of women. Anthropometry, or measurement
of the human body, is not so fashionable a field these days, but it dominated
the human sciences for much of the nineteenth century and remained popular
until intelligence testing replaced skull measurement as a favored device for
making invidious comparisons among races, classes, and sexes. Craniometry,
or measurement of the skull, commanded the most attention and respect. Its
unquestioned leader, Paul Broca (1824–80), professor of clinical surgery at the
Faculty of Medicine in Paris, gathered a school of disciples and imitators around
himself. Their work, so meticulous and apparently irrefutable, exerted great
influence and won high esteem as a jewel of nineteenth-century science.

Broca's work seemed particularly invulnerable to refutation. Had he not   3
measured with the most scrupulous care and accuracy? (Indeed, he had. I have
the greatest respect for Broca's meticulous procedure. His numbers are sound.
But science is an inferential exercise, not a catalog of facts. Numbers, by
themselves, specify nothing. All depends upon what you do with them.) Broca
depicted himself as an apostle of objectivity, a man who bowed before facts and
cast aside superstition and sentimentality. He declared that "there is no
faith, however respectable, no interest, however legitimate, which must not
accommodate itself to the progress of human knowledge and bend before truth."
Women, like it or not, had smaller brains than men and, therefore, could not

751

equal them in intelligence. This fact, Broca argued, may reinforce a common prejudice in male society, but it is also a scientific truth. L. Manouvrier, a black sheep in Broca's fold, rejected the inferiority of women and wrote with feeling about the burden imposed upon them by Broca's numbers:

> Women displayed their talents and their diplomas. They also invoked philosophical authorities. But they were opposed by *numbers* unknown to Condorcet or to John Stuart Mill. These numbers fell upon poor women like a sledge hammer, and they were accompanied by commentaries and sarcasms more ferocious than the most misogynist imprecations of certain church fathers. The theologians had asked if women had a soul. Several centuries later, some scientists were ready to refuse them a human intelligence.

Broca's argument rested upon two sets of data: the larger brains of men in modern societies, and a supposed increase in male superiority through time. His most extensive data came from autopsies performed personally in four Parisian hospitals. For 292 male brains, he calculated an average weight of 1,325 grams; 140 female brains averaged 1,144 grams for a difference of 181 grams, or 14 percent of the male weight. Broca understood, of course, that part of this difference could be attributed to the greater height of males. Yet he made no attempt to measure the effect of size alone and actually stated that it cannot account for the entire difference because we know, a priori, that women are not as intelligent as men (a premise that the data were supposed to test, not rest upon):

> We might ask if the small size of the female brain depends exclusively upon the small size of her body. Tiedemann has proposed this explanation. But we must not forget that women are, on the average, a little less intelligent than men, a difference which we should not exaggerate but which is, nonetheless, real. We are therefore permitted to suppose that the relatively small size of the female brain depends in part upon her physical inferiority and in part upon her intellectual inferiority.

In 1873, the year after Eliot published *Middlemarch*, Broca measured the cranial capacities of prehistoric skulls from L'Homme Mort cave. Here he found a difference of only 99.5 cubic centimeters between males and females, while modern populations range from 129.5 to 220.7. Topinard, Broca's chief disciple, explained the increasing discrepancy through time as a result of differing evolutionary pressures upon dominant men and passive women:

> The man who fights for two or more in the struggle for existence, who has all the responsibility and the cares of tomorrow, who is constantly active in combating the environment and human rivals, needs more brain than the woman whom he must protect and nourish, the sedentary

woman, lacking any interior occupations, whose role is to raise children, love, and be passive.

In 1879, Gustave Le Bon, chief misogynist of Broca's school, used these 6 data to publish what must be the most vicious attack upon women in modern scientific literature (no one can top Aristotle). I do not claim his views were representative of Broca's school, but they were published in France's most respected anthropological journal. Le Bon concluded:

> In the most intelligent races, as among the Parisians, there are a large number of women whose brains are closer in size to those of gorillas than to the most developed male brains. This inferiority is so obvious that no one can contest it for a moment; only its degree is worth discussion. All psychologists who have studied the intelligence of women, as well as poets and novelists, recognize today that they represent the most inferior forms of human evolution and that they are closer to children and savages than to an adult, civilized man. They excel in fickleness, inconstancy, absence of thought and logic, and incapacity to reason. Without doubt there exist some distinguished women, very superior to the average man, but they are as exceptional as the birth of any monstrosity, as, for example, of a gorilla with two heads; consequently, we may neglect them entirely.

Nor did Le Bon shrink from the social implications of his views. He was 7 horrified by the proposal of some American reformers to grant women higher education on the same basis as men:

> A desire to give them the same education, and, as a consequence, to propose the same goals for them, is a dangerous chimera. . . . The day when, misunderstanding the inferior occupations which nature has given her, women leave the home and take part in our battles; on this day a social revolution will begin, and everything that maintains the sacred ties of the family will disappear.

Sound familiar?[1]

I have reexamined Broca's data, the basis for all this derivative pronounce- 8 ment, and I find his numbers sound but his interpretation ill-founded, to say the least. The data supporting his claim for increased difference through time can be easily dismissed. Broca based his contention on the samples from L'Homme Mort alone—only seven male and six female skulls in all. Never have so little data yielded such far ranging conclusions.

In 1988, Topinard published Broca's more extensive data on the Parisian 9

---

[1]When I wrote this essay, I assumed that Le Bon was a marginal, if colorful, figure. I have since learned that he was a leading scientist, one of the founders of social psychology, and best known for a seminal study on crowd behavior, still cited today (*La psychologie des foules*, 1895), and for his work on unconscious motivation.

hospitals. Since Broca recorded height and age as well as brain size, we may use modern statistics to remove their effect. Brain weight decreases with age, and Broca's women were, on average, considerably older than his men. Brain weight increases with height, and his average man was almost half a foot taller than his average woman. I used multiple regression, a technique that allowed me to assess simultaneously the influence of height and age upon brain size. In an analysis of the data for women, I found that, at average male height and age, a woman's brain would weigh 1,212 grams. Correction for height and age reduces Broca's measured difference of 181 grams by more than a third, to 113 grams.

I don't know what to make of this remaining difference because I cannot 10 assess other factors known to influence brain size in a major way. Cause of death has an important effect: degenerative disease often entails a substantial diminution of brain size. (This effect is separate from the decrease attributed to age alone.) Eugene Schreider, also working with Broca's data, found that men killed in accidents had brains weighing, on average, 60 grams more than men dying of infectious diseases. The best modern data I can find (from American hospitals) records a full 100-gram difference between death by degenerative arteriosclerosis and by violence or accident. Since so many of Broca's subjects were elderly women, we may assume that lengthy degenerative disease was more common among them than among the men.

More importantly, modern students of brain size still have not agreed on a 11 proper measure for eliminating the powerful effect of body size. Height is partly adequate, but men and women of the same height do not share the same body build. Weight is even worse than height, because most of its variation reflects nutrition rather than intrinsic size—fat versus skinny exerts little influence upon the brain. Manouvrier took up this subject in the 1880s and argued that muscular mass and force should be used. He tried to measure this elusive property in various ways and found a marked difference in favor of men, even in men and women of the same height. When he corrected for what he called "sexual mass," women actually came out slightly ahead in brain size.

Thus, the corrected 113-gram difference is surely too large; the true figure 12 is probably close to zero and may as well favor women as men. And 113 grams, by the way, is exactly the average difference between a 5 foot 4 inch and a 6 foot 4 inch male in Broca's data. We would not (especially us short folks) want to ascribe greater intelligence to tall men. In short, who knows what to do with Broca's data? They certainly don't permit any confident claim that men have bigger brains than women.

To appreciate the social role of Broca and his school, we must recognize 13 that his statements about the brains of women do not reflect an isolated prejudice toward a single disadvantaged group. They must be weighed in the context of a general theory that supported contemporary social distinctions as biologically ordained. Women, blacks, and poor people suffered the same disparagement, but women bore the brunt of Broca's argument because he had easier access to data on women's brains. Women were singularly denigrated but they also stood as surrogates for other disenfranchised groups. As one of Broca's disciples wrote in 1881: "Men of the black races have a brain scarcely heavier than that of white woman." This juxtaposition extended into many other realms of anthropological argument, particularly to claims that, anatomically and emotionally, both women and blacks were like white children—and that white children, by the theory of recapitulation, represented an ancestral (primitive) adult stage of human evolution. I do not regard as empty rhetoric the claim that women's battles are for all of us.

Maria Montessori did not confine her activities to educational reform for young children. She lectured on anthropology for several years at the University of Rome, and wrote an influential book entitled *Pedagogical Anthropology* (English edition, 1913). Montessori was no egalitarian. She supported most of Broca's work and the theory of innate criminality proposed by her compatriot Cesare Lombroso. She measured the circumference of children's heads in her schools and inferred that the best prospects had bigger brains. But she had no use for Broca's conclusions about women. She discussed Manouvrier's work at length and made much of his tentative claim that women, after proper correction of the data, had slightly larger brains than men. Women, she concluded, were intellectually superior, but men had prevailed heretofore by dint of physical force. Since technology has abolished force as an instrument of power, the era of women may soon be upon us: "In such an epoch there will really be superior human beings, there will really be men strong in morality and in sentiment. Perhaps in this way the reign of women is approaching, when the enigma of her anthropological superiority will be deciphered. Woman was always the custodian of human sentiment, morality and honor." 14

This represents one possible antidote to "scientific" claims for the constitutional inferiority of certain groups. One may affirm the validity of biological distinctions but argue that the data have been misinterpreted by prejudiced men with a stake in the outcome, and that disadvantaged groups are truly superior. In recent years, Elaine Morgan has followed this strategy in her *Descent of Woman*, a speculative reconstruction of human prehistory from the woman's point of view—and as farcical as more famous tall tales by and for men. 15

I prefer another strategy. Montessori and Morgan followed Broca's philosophy to reach a more congenial conclusion. I would rather label the whole enterprise of setting a biological value upon groups for what it is: irrelevant and highly injurious. George Eliot well appreciated the special tragedy that biological labeling imposed upon members of disadvantaged groups. She expressed it for people like herself—women of extraordinary talent. I would apply it more widely—not only to those whose dreams are flouted but also to those who never realize that they may dream—but I cannot match her prose. In conclusion, then, the rest of Eliot's prelude to *Middlemarch*: 16

755

The limits of variation are really much wider than anyone would imagine from the sameness of women's coiffure and the favorite love stories in prose and verse. Here and there a cygnet is reared uneasily among the ducklings in the brown pond, and never finds the living stream in fellowship with its own oary-footed kind. Here and there is born a Saint Theresa, foundress of nothing, whose loving heartbeats and sobs after an unattained goodness tremble off and are dispersed among hindrances instead of centering in some long-recognizable deed.

QUESTIONS

1. In paragraph 3, Gould claims: "Numbers, by themselves, specify nothing. All depends upon what you do with them." What exactly does Gould do with numbers?

2. How does Gould's use of numbers differ from what Broca and his followers did with numbers? Specifically, what distinguishes Gould's and Broca's methods of calculating and interpreting the facts about women's brains?

3. It might also be said that "Quotations, by themselves, specify nothing. All depends upon what you do with them." What does Gould do with quotations in this essay?

4. Why do you suppose Gould begins and ends his piece with passages by George Eliot?

5. Why does Gould quote so extensively from Broca and his followers, particularly from Le Bon? What purpose do all of these quotations serve in connection with the points that Gould is trying to make about women's brains and "biological labeling"?

6. Using Gould's essay as a model, write an essay on a subject with which you are familiar, showing how different ways of gathering, calculating, and interpreting numbers have produced significantly different understandings of the subject in question.

7. Write an essay on a subject with which you are familiar, showing how different ways of gathering, citing, and interpreting quotations have produced significantly different understandings of the subject in question.

MAKING CONNECTIONS

Gould's article on "Women's Brains" is not the only piece in this collection to be concerned with the mismeasurement and misrepresentation of women's mental abilities, as you can see by looking at Kramer's and Lehman's "Mismeasuring Women: A Critique of Research on Computer Ability and Avoidance." What similarities and differences do you see in the problems with which each of these articles is concerned? What similarities and differences do you see in the ways these two articles attempt to analyze and correct the problems they identify? What similarities and differences do you see in the ways these two articles attempt to explore the causes and implications of mismeasuring women's mental abilities?

MISMEASURING WOMEN:
A CRITIQUE
OF RESEARCH ON
COMPUTER ABILITY AND
AVOIDANCE

Pamela E. Kramer
and
Sheila Lehman

Pamela E. Kramer is a professor of psychology at Polytechnic University whose previous research has been in language acquisition and cognitive skill development in mathematics and science. This article grew out of her research interests in the issue of women's career opportunities in science and engineering. Sheila Lehman teaches social science at Polytechnic University. She co-authored The Changing Workplace *(1985) and continues to study the impact of computerization, gender issues in computing, and other people-and-computer topics. The following essay appeared in the journal* Signs.

Among secondary-school-aged children (eleven to eighteen years), boys are [1] at least three times more likely than girls to use a computer at home, participate in computer-related clubs or activities at school, or attend a computer camp.[1] This 3:1 pattern continues through the postsecondary years. In 1985, though approximately fourteen thousand out of twenty-six thousand bachelor's degrees in computer science were awarded to women, women earned only two thousand

---

[1] R. D. Hess and I. T. Miura, "Gender Differences in Enrollment in Computer Camps and Classes," *Sex Roles* 13, nos. 3/4 (August 1985): 193–203. See also Jo Sanders and Antonia Stone, *The Neuter Computer: Why and How to Encourage Computer Equity for Girls* (New York: Women's Action Alliance, 1987). In an article exploring the impact of a course in computer literacy, Betty Collis found that girls, who were five times less likely to enroll, actually expressed more negative than positive attitudes about computing following the course ("Sex Differences in Secondary School Students' Attitudes toward Computers," *Computing Teacher* 12, no. 7 [April 1985]: 33–36). Others, however, have found that increased opportunities for experience with computers, although less likely for girls, do tend to produce positive attitude change. See Marcia Linn, "Gender Equity in Computer Learning Environments," in *Computers and the Social Sciences* (Providence, R.I.: Paradigm Press, 1985), 19–26; and Marlaine Lockheed and Steven Frakt, "Sex Equity: Increasing Girls' Use of Computers," *Computing Teacher* 11, no. 8 (April 1984): 16–18.

out of seven thousand master's degrees.[2] Approximately 30 percent of all employed computer specialists are women. This figure has remained constant for the past decade, during which computer fields have become the fastest growing occupational area for both sexes. Yet, there is also evidence that female computer professionals are disproportionately concentrated in lower paid, less prestigious jobs.[3] Among this population, National Science Foundation figures for 1986 show less than 5 percent of all women earning bachelor's degrees in computer science, or employed in computer-related fields, to be African-American or Hispanic.[4]

While gender-related differences in learning and using computers can be documented at all educational levels, their causes and consequences are unclear. Much of the research assumes that women's lower participation rate is either correlated with, or at least shares a common etiology with, women's avoidance of mathematics. Yet this assumption may rest more on prevailing conventions within primary and secondary education that locate computer-based learning within mathematics and science curriculums than upon a carefully contextualized analysis of women's and girls' mathematics and computer-based learning.

RESEARCH ON MATHEMATICS LEARNING

Contemporary research on participation and achievement has relied increasingly on cognitive, affective, and sociocultural factors, rather than biological ones, to explain sex differences.[5] For example, Elizabeth Fennema and Julia

[2] *Women and Minorities in Science and Engineering* (Washington, D.C.: National Science Foundation, 1986): 27–38, 121–33.

[3] See S. Dubnoff and P. Kraft, "Gender Stratification in Computer Programming" (University of Massachusetts, Center for Survey Research, Boston, 1980); and John Markoff, "Computing in America: A Masculine Mystique," *New York Times* (February 13, 1989).

[4] Computing opportunities for less affluent and minority high school girls, who are less likely to have computers at home, may be available but underutilized due to contextual factors. In a survey of 225 inner-city high school math and science teachers in schools with high minority enrollments, while 95 percent of the teachers reported that computers were available in their schools, the same number also reported that these computers were used by less than 10 percent of all enrolled students. In addition, over half (54 percent) of the teachers admitted that they did not use the computers. See P. Kramer, *Final Report to the National Science Foundation*, grant no. SER-8160408 (Washington, D.C.: National Science Foundation, 1987).

[5] See E. E. Maccoby and C. N. Jacklin, *The Psychology of Sex Differences* (Stanford, Calif.: Stanford University Press, 1974) for documentation of literature that consistently reports significant sex differences in favor of males in mathematics achievement and visual-spatial skills. However, although the authors suggest that these findings support an argument that biological sex differences may be a factor, they do not rule out sociocultural determination as well, since the differences are greater in adults than in children. For a reexamination of much of the data used by Maccoby and Jacklin, see Janet Shibley Hyde, "How Large Are Cognitive Gender Differences? A Meta-Analysis Using ^{2} and d," *American Psychologist* 36, no. 8 (August 1981): 892–901. Hyde demonstrated that gender is a nonsignificant factor in terms of accounting for differences in young people's mathematics achievement. More recently, a similar analysis of visual-spatial abilities not only supports a similar conclusion but raises substantial questions concerning how visual reasoning skills are defined and assessed. See P. J. Caplan, G. MacPherson, and P. Tobin, "Do Sex-related Differences in Spatial

Sherman examined differences in mathematics and spatial achievement scores of over twelve hundred ninth-grade students of comparable mathematics background. They found sex differences in mathematics achievement and spatial visualization scores only in those schools where there were also significant sex differences in the students' self-perception of their ability to learn mathematics and the value they placed on mathematics learning.[6] Furthermore, parents' and teachers' expectations for students' learning were not only a significant factor in achievement but also a significant factor in sex differences in learning. (Boys were expected to be better mathematics learners, and it was more important for boys to learn mathematics.) Even in schools where boys and girls performed equally, students perceived mathematics as a male domain. Fennema and Sherman's sample included both urban working-class and suburban middle-class schools, but socioeconomic factors did not predict achievement or attitudinal differences.

In the past decade feminist scholars have built up a richly detailed picture of the ways in which the lives of girls and women differ from those of boys and men and how these differences affect educational and career decisions involving mathematics at critical choice points during the school years. For example, in a follow-up to the 1977 research described above, Julia Sherman compared three matched groups of high school girls who had elected mathematics courses for four, three, or less than three years. Contrary to her expectations, she found that those girls who had taken four years of mathematics were *more* conflicted about sex role expectations and family and career plans than were the other girls.[7] They expressed greater concern about "being smart" in mathematics; they were more likely to admit to "playing dumb" in front of classmates and peers; and they were also more likely to agree that a "mother's place is in the home." Outnumbered by boys in their advanced mathematics courses (13 percent of girls and 57 percent of boys took fourth-year math), these girls did express more positive attitudes about mathematics and about themselves as potential mathematics learners than other girls did.[8]

4

Abilities Exist? A Multilevel Critique with New Data," *American Psychologist* 40, no. 7 (1985): 786–99.

[6] E. Fennema and J. Sherman, "Sex-related Differences in Mathematics Achievement, Spatial Visualization, and Affective Factors," *American Educational Research Journal* 14, no. 1 (Winter 1977): 51–71. Also see E. Fennema and J. Sherman, "Sex-related Differences in Mathematics Achievement and Related Factors: A Further Study," *Journal for Research in Mathematics Education* 9, no. 3 (1978): 189–203.

[7] Julia Sherman, "Mathematics, the Critical Filter: A Look at Some Residues," *Psychology of Women Quarterly* 6, no. 4 (December 1982): 428–44. Greater ambivalence about career opportunities and plans on the part of more talented young women is also described by Matina Horner, "Toward an Understanding of Achievement-related Conflicts in Women," *Journal of Social Issues* 28, no. 2 (1972): 157–75; and by Irene Hanson Frieze, "Internal and External Psychological Barriers for Women in Science," in *Covert Discrimination and Women in the Sciences*, ed. J. Ramalay (Boulder, Colo.: Westview, 1978).

[8] Very similar attitudes are found in a survey of 160 high school girls participating in advanced placement courses in mathematics and physics by Patricia Lynn Casserly, "Helping Able Young

Changes not only in perceptions and attitudes, but in contextual factors as well can have a significant impact upon women's learning and career choices in sex-typed domains such as mathematics. Patricia Lynn Casserly, for instance, found that changes in recruitment and teaching strategies for advanced placement (AP) high school courses significantly increased girls' participation in these courses. Female AP students were used as recruitment agents and role models, and bright high school girls were aggressively targeted as potential participants. In addition, AP instructors ensured equal participation in classroom recitation with "turn taking."[9] This significantly reduced girls' silent denigration of their own skills, and it encouraged them to speak out in class even if they thought they might be wrong. Girls enrolled in AP courses also became significantly more likely than other girls to include engineering and science fields in their future career plans.

RESEARCH ON COMPUTER LEARNING

There is a large body of research documenting that sex differences in mathematics performance, where they exist at all, are based on complex interactions of social and attitudinal factors. Yet computer learning research that explains sex differences in performance in terms of males' superior performance in and exposure to high school mathematics may ignore this literature and explain any superior mathematics performance by males in terms of superior, quantitative, reasoning skills.[10]

Women Take Math and Science Seriously in School," in *New Voices in Counseling the Gifted*, ed. Nicholas Colangelo and Ronald T. Zaffrann (Dubuque, Iowa: Kendall/Hunt, 1979). Girls reported that they often kept quiet in class when they knew the answer because they did not want to appear to be "too smart." The same girls also said that they often did not speak up because they did not want to appear "too dumb." Forty percent reported playing down their good grades in mathematics in front of classmates and peers, especially male classmates and peers.

[9]The role of teaching styles and attitudes and how these may interact with students' own attributions concerning their abilities as mathematics learners, have been explored in a series of research studies by Carol Dweck and her associates. See, e.g., Carol Dweck, "The Role of Expectations and Attributions in the Alleviation of Learned Helplessness," *Journal of Personality and Social Psychology* 31, no. 4 (April 1975): 679–85. Dweck's research indicates that teachers who allow students to use "learned helplessness" attributions about their ability in mathematics ("I'm just not good at math, so why try?") as opposed to persistence attributions ("Mathematics requires that I work hard") are much more likely to produce math-avoidant students. In Dweck's research, junior high school girls outnumbered boys in the "learned helplessness" group in mathematics classrooms by three to one.

[10]L. Fox and J. Cohen have also examined how changes in motivational structures and attitudes of mathematically gifted girls, who were identified as part of Project Talent Search, could significantly enhance these girls' mathematics course-taking in high school and their future career plans. See L. H. Fox and J. J. Cohen, "Sex Differences in the Development of Precocious Mathematical Talent," in *Women and the Mathematical Mystique*, ed. L. H. Fox, L. Brody, and D. Tobin (Baltimore: Johns Hopkins University Press, 1980), 164–78; Patricia Lynn Casserly, "Factors Affecting Female Participation in Advanced Placement Programs in Mathematics, Chemistry, and Physics," in Fox et al., eds., 138–63; and L. H. Fox, "Women and Mathematics: The Impact of Early Intervention Programs upon Course-taking and Attitudes in High School," final report to the

Here we examine significant exceptions to this approach. However, even 7
where individual studies on girls' and women's performance and participation
in computer-based learning do focus upon factors similar to those identified in
the earlier research on mathematics learning, no study or group of research
studies comprehensively addresses questions and issues dealing with the separate
contexts, contents, and values attached to computer learning.[11]

Some studies recognize that social or institutional factors play a role but then 8
fail to question their assumptions about the relevance of mathematics ability to
computer aptitude. For example, Faye Dambrot and her associates found lower
rates of participation for women in introductory computer programming courses
in college, and lower grades for women who did participate, to be significantly
correlated with both their relative lack of high school preparation in advanced
mathematics and their poorer performance on what is called a "computer
aptitude" test.[12] This aptitude test is essentially a measure of mathematics
knowledge and experience. Thus, the women's significantly less positive attitudes toward their college computer programming courses were viewed as a side
issue unrelated to the other findings: in effect, women are not good at computing, and they do not like it either.[13]

In contrast, other researchers have focused on attitudes as a central factor in 9

National Institute of Education for grant no. NIE-G-77-0062 (Johns Hopkins University, Baltimore,
1979). These intervention efforts, although successful, were unable to close completely the gap
between boys and girls: the boys were far more likely than equally able girls to participate in
advanced or special mathematics programs and to plan on careers in science and engineering fields.
It is worth noting that the Project Talent Search junior high school children are the same group
whose Scholastic Aptitude Test (SAT) scores were used by Camilla Persson Benbow and Julian
Stanley to support their argument for boys' superior mathematical ability. See Camilla Persson
Benbow and Julian C. Stanley, "Sex Differences in Mathematics Ability: Fact or Artifact?" *Science*
210, no. 4475 (December 1980): 1262–64, and their responses to comments about this article in
"Letters to the Editor," *Science* 212, no. 4491 (April 1981): 118, 121.

[11] Studies that report similar correlations between mathematics ability or learning and computer
aptitude include C. A. Alspaugh, "Identification of Some Components of Computer Programming
Aptitude," *Journal of Research in Mathematics Education* 3 (1972): 89–98; C. Gressard, "An
Investigation of the Effects of Math Anxiety and Sex on Computer Attitudes" (paper presented at
the American Educational Research Association meeting, New Orleans, 1984); and J. Konvalina,
S. A. Wileman, and L. J. Stephens, "Math Proficiency—a Key to Success for Computer Science
Students," *Communications of the Association for Computing Machinery* 26 (1983): 377–82.

[12] F. Dambrot, M. Watkins-Malek, S. Marc Silling, R. S. Marshall, and J. A. Garver, "Cor-
relates of Sex Differences in Attitudes towards and Involvement with Computers," *Journal of
Vocational Behavior* 27, no. 1 (August 1985): 71–86.

[13] It is important to remember that correlations between two or more variables do not establish
causal connections between these variables; a third (or more) factor(s) may be causing the observed
effects. If, as is the case in Dambrot et al. and similar studies, computer aptitude is defined in such
a way as to be virtually synonymous with mathematics achievement, then it almost certainly reflects
mathematics experience, which we know to be less for girls than for boys after the second year of
high school. In such studies the presumed finding of lower computer aptitude for girls is invalid.
One measure of computer aptitude that does not depend on previous mathematics knowledge is
the Computer Aptitude, Literacy, and Interest Profile (CALIP), created by Mary Poplin and her
associates (see Mary Poplin, David Drew, and R. Gable, CALIP manual [University of Texas at
Austin, 1984]).

women's and girls' computer ability. Jo Sanders and Antonia Stone, for instance, document the implications for attitudes and performance of the ways in which teachers introduce computer-related learning into educational settings. Higher-level computer skills such as programming are usually associated with the male academic domains of math and science and usually are taught by males. Conversely, text processing, simple accounting, and filing programs involve skills that tend to be associated with less prestigious, female-stereotyped vocational tracks. Sanders and Stone find that in this atmosphere, boys sign up for computer-related extracurricular activities in disproportionate numbers. In the few instances where girls are present, they have usually been encouraged to join.[14]

Betty Collis found that a six-week hands-on introductory computer course 10 that was taught only by male teachers had little or no effect on eighth-grade girls' negative attitudes toward computers.[15] The girls in the study were less interested in computers than were boys, less confident about their ability to use computers, and more likely to be negative about the impact of computers on society; and this remained virtually unchanged by the course. In particular, girls in this study who were enrolled in schools with the most extensive computer programs were less positive after taking the course than were other girls. Boys from these schools, however, became significantly more positive about computers after taking the course than other boys were.[16]

To further complicate addressing differences between boys and girls, the girls 11 in Collis's study did not believe their lack of ability and interest was due to the fact that they were female but, rather, saw it as a matter of individual inability or disinterest: "Girls in both grades [8 and 12] strongly agreed with statements about females, in the abstract, being as competent as males with computers. However, as soon as females were asked to assess their own personal competency and self-confidence, they shifted in their attitudes. The typical girl felt that women in general were capable, but that she as an individual was not competent or likely to be a computer user."[17]

A few researchers have documented connections between cultural assump- 12 tions, the contexts in which computers are used, and girls' disinterest in computers. For example, Karen Scheingold, Jan Hawkins, and Cynthia Char show how the cultural assumptions that govern the interactions of elementary school

---

[14] Sanders and Stone (n. 1). Their Computer Equity Training Project studied junior high school boys and girls in over sixty classrooms in New Jersey, Oregon, and Wisconsin. In addition to school logistics (computers are taught by male mathematics teachers to business, mathematics, and science students), the authors cite voluntary computer use as being an unorganized and solitary activity. Problems with computer software, career awareness, and parental attitudes are also noted as creating significant obstacles for girls.

[15] Collis (n. 1).

[16] However, Lockheed and Frakt (n. 1) report that positive experiences with computers were associated with positive attitude changes for girls.

[17] Collis, 33–34.

children operate to deny young girls credibility, or even visibility, as competent computer users, even when these girls demonstrate the very levels of computer-related knowledge and skills that they supposedly do not have.[18]

Sara Kiesler, Lee Sproull, and Jacquelynne Eccles analyze the ways in which masculine cultural values and stereotypes are incorporated into computer-based learning, work, and play. The high school girls they studied became passive observers ("computer groupies") rather than active participants in many settings; the researchers related this behavior to the pervasive warlike or competitive sports metaphors in much educational and recreational software.[19]   13

SOME ALTERNATIVE APPROACHES

We have suggested that some important insights may be gained by a more contextualized approach that examines the ways in which preexisting social roles and relationships are replicated within settings for computer learning and how this affects learning outcomes. Indeed, our conversations with women about their encounters with computers resonate with a kind of "knowing more than one can say," as they struggle to express their problems with computer learning from the standpoint of their individual lives and values. For example, this conversation between a woman, her friend, and her husband, suggests a form of resistance to computers that is based on concepts of autonomy and control: 14

HUSBAND: "I don't know. She just doesn't like to use it. She's bothered by the physical aspects of the thing. The fan. She can't stand the noise the fan makes."
WIFE: "No, it's not just the fan."
FRIEND: "Maybe. . . ."
HUSBAND: "Yes, you are always complaining about the fan."
FRIEND: "Maybe it's that the computer is so, I don't know, so discontinuous

---

[18] See Karen Scheingold, Jan Hawkins, and Cynthia Char, "'I'm the Thinkist, You're the Typist': The Interaction of Technology and the Social Life of Classrooms," *Journal of Social Issues* 40, no. 3 (1984): 49–61. This article discusses the meaning of computers and the tasks that are presented via the computer for both children and teachers. Interpretations of the computer have powerful implications for how children use computers and structure various tasks. As one example of differential acknowledgment granted to girls' skills, reported by Scheingold, Hawkins, and Char, when children were asked, "Who is the best computer user in the class?" both boys and girls named a boy. However, when the children were asked, "Who would you ask to help you if you got stuck (writing a LOGO program)?" both boys and girls named both girls and boys. While talented girls might be denied public acknowledgment for their skills, the children did not feel girls were less capable as long as the girls were using their skills to help others.

[19] The aggressive masculinity of the subculture surrounding the computer is described by Sara Kiesler, Lee Sproull, and Jacquelynne Eccles in their "Poolhalls, Chips, and War Games: Women in the Culture of Computing," *Psychology of Women Quarterly* 9, no. 4 (December 1985): 451–62.

with everything else. With, you know, the ordinary way of getting our work done."

Wife: "That's it. What you just said. I think that is it. It forces you to do things its way, and even though it may be faster, I don't like it."

A community researcher discussed her choices about learning to use a computer in terms of employment politics and policy:

> I love my job, and the issues I get to work on are very important ones, ones that are really interesting to me, too. But eventually, if I want to stay there I am going to have to work on the computer. The statistical simulations they do on the computer are given an enormous amount of weight in developing plans for the community. The trouble is, I have no interest in doing things that way. I don't believe simulations really get at the important issues. And I would have to learn to program the computer. I don't know how to do that. And I don't want to do that all day long.

New technologies are always introduced into a web of existing human set- 15 tings: physical, organizational, and sociocultural. To understand this technology transfer process, of which computer learning is a part, it is essential to identify the key values that are operative in computer learning settings.

While there are women who express a positive involvement with computers 16 and delight in their capabilities, and men who express doubts or indifferences about computers and "computer jocks," it is women who are expected to avoid computers and who are more often found to do so. We have quoted these two women's voices because the critique implicit in their attempts to frame their ambivalence about computer use suggests themes with which the research literature rarely deals.

Our own observation, based on research, teaching, and consulting experi- 17 ences, is that few computer learners (including those who learn in work settings) have the breadth of knowledge about computer applications and career options that might allow them to imagine how to use the computer in ways most suited to their individual abilities, interests, and values.[20] Similarly, few children at elementary and secondary levels have access to newer developments in computer technology itself, developments—such as graphics, expert systems, hypermedia, or software designed to support collaborative work—that would allow children to explore their abilities and interests creatively. Yet the computer learning research does not address the implications of these gaps for the ways in which computer knowledge is structured, for example, sex-stereotyped computer tracking.

---

[20] See, e.g., A. F. Westin, H. A. Schweder, M. A. Baker, and S. Lehman, *The Changing Workplace: A Guide to Managing the People, Organizational, and Regulatory Aspects of Office Technology* (White Plains, N.Y.: Knowledge Industry Publications, 1985).

Moreover, much of the research that documents sex differences in computer 18 aptitude is too simplistic in its treatment of the computer itself. As Jan Hawkins has pointed out, it is individuals who interact with computers, and they will be engaged individually by different skills and applications. Hawkins notes that studies that have reported significant overall differences between boys and girls "tend to describe the computer as a 'unitary topic' rather than attending to the characteristics of the particular situations where differences are found."[21]

RESEARCH ON REENTRY WOMEN

A reentry program for African-American and Hispanic women two-year 19 community college graduates at Polytechnic University, a technological institution primarily known for undergraduate and graduate education in engineering fields, is a particularly good example of the potential benefit to computer learning programs of (1) abandoning assumptions about the correlation between math performance and computer ability and (2) focusing on what skills are being learned, who is teaching these skills, and within what context(s).[22] Fifty-six out of sixty-nine women eventually earned bachelor's degrees in this program (Minority Women in Management and Technical Fields [MIWIM]). To date, eighteen of these women have continued on to earn M.S. degrees in such fields as information management, computer science, and transportation engineering. At the same time as these women were completing their degrees, a second group of nonminority women were reentering at the graduate level as part of a National Science Foundation program in transportation engineering and management. Twenty-six of an initial thirty-three participants completed M.S. degrees in this program.

While the two groups differed in educational background and degree (A.A.S., 20 B.A., B.S.), they proved to be highly comparable in their needs for basic education in mathematics and their attitudes about mathematics. The two-year college graduates had completed an average of 1.9 years of high school mathematics; graduate students in the transportation engineering program had completed an average of 2.1 years. Women in both groups typically were employed in traditionally female occupations: fully half of the National Science Foundation program participants were elementary and middle school teachers; a majority of participants in the MIWIM program were secretaries. They averaged thirty-four years of age and most were married with children living at home. All of the women were required to take trigonometry, calculus, statistics, and computer courses to complete their degrees at both the undergraduate and

[21] Jan Hawkins, "Computers and Girls: Rethinking the Issues," *Sex Roles* 13, nos. 3/4 (August 1985): 165–80, esp. 171.
[22] The Minority Women in Management and Technical Fields program at Polytechnic University was supported by a grant from the Fund for the Improvement of Postsecondary Education (FIPSE) from 1979 to 1984, Pamela E. Kramer, principal investigator.

graduate levels. All exhibited very high levels of mathematics anxiety on the Math Anxiety Rating Scale (MARS) and on other self-report questionnaires, including the Fennema and Sherman scales used to measure attitudes toward mathematics.[23]

All of the women participated in a noncredit review of high school algebra ²¹ and an introduction to trigonometry before they began their regular college programs. The course, based upon models developed at Harvard University by Deborah Hughes-Hallett and at Wesleyan University by Sheila Tobias, was so effective that all but three participants subsequently passed required college-level precalculus (trigonometry) and calculus or statistics courses.[24]

We examined demographic and attitudinal variables predictive of success in ²² regular college precalculus and calculus courses and success in statistics and computer science courses when such data were available. Data needed to complete this analysis were available for thirty-seven of the fifty-six participants who completed bachelor's degrees in the Minority Women in Management and Technical Fields program and all twenty-six women who earned M.S. degrees in transportation engineering. Because the results for both groups were so similar, we also examined the effect of mathematics-related attitudes on grades in precalculus for a combined sample ($N = 66$).

Previous experience in mathematics did not significantly predict these wom- ²³ en's grades in their precalculus and calculus courses. Moreover, it did not predict grades in computer science courses for women who continued in computer-related fields. Age was a predictor for precalculus and calculus courses: women over forty experienced considerably more difficulty in college-level mathematics courses ($R = -.38$, $P < .001$ [MIWIM]; and $R = -.30$, $P < .01$). Attitudes toward mathematics, including self-perceived ability, perceived ability in comparison with others, and willingness to take math courses and

---

[23] The Fennema and Sherman mathematics attitude scales (Fennema and Sherman, "Sex-related Differences in Mathematics Achievement, Spatial Visualization, and Affective Factors" [n. 6 above]) consist of eight scales containing twelve Likert-scaled items, each of which includes measures of confidence in one's own ability to learn mathematics, perception of mathematics as a male domain, perception of one's ability to learn mathematics in relation to others, perceived usefulness of mathematics, and willingness to take mathematics (effectance motivation). These are the five scales that we used in addition to a subset of twenty-four items from the Mathematics Anxiety Rating Scale (MARS), which dealt with school-related situations involving mathematics. See R. M. Suinn, C. A. Edie, J. Micotelli, and P. Spinelli, "The MARS: A Measure of Mathematics Anxiety," *Journal of Clinical Psychology* 28, no. 3 (July 1972): 373–75.

[24] In brief, this approach combines a solid review of high school algebra with techniques designed to reduce mathematics anxiety and to eliminate "learned helplessness" attributions about one's own abilities. (It is not that you need to have mathematical ability, but it is that mathematics learning requires hard work.) The actual teaching emphasizes word problems and comprehension rather than rote memorization and set problems. It also utilizes group problem solving rather than individual accomplishments (each member of a homework group must understand the solution to a problem and be able to explain it to her peers), peer teaching, and peer tutoring. All of the tutors were minority mathematics and engineering majors at Polytechnic University (most were female). See Deborah Hughes-Hallett, *The Math Workshop: Algebra* (New York: Norton, 1980); and Sheila Tobias, *Overcoming Mathematics Anxiety* (New York: Norton, 1978).

mathematics anxiety (MARS score), were all strong predictors of the women's grades in their college-level mathematics courses. Combined, these attitudinal variables predicted almost 80 percent of the variability of the women's precalculus course grades.[25] However, while high school math review grades also were significant predictors of both precalculus and calculus grades, and while all mathematics grades reflected overall grade point average to some degree, none of the mathematics grades significantly predicted success in college-level computer courses.[26] The correlational relationships that have been found by other researchers between performance in introductory college-level computer courses and previous mathematics grades or courses may be an artifact of the fact that homework programs assigned in introductory computer courses presume calculus knowledge. We found that when calculus-based problems were eliminated, reentry college women simultaneously taking a first-year programming course and an introductory trigonometry and calculus course were able to complete both. This suggests that previous mathematics experience and measures of aptitude based upon such experience may work more effectively to exclude women than to predict ability in computer courses.

REDEFINING COMPUTER LEARNING

Research on computer learning and ability, if it is to avoid confounding the sex difference findings of mathematics ability research with those of computer learning and participation, must focus its attention on the computer itself and critique the contexts and embedded social contents of computer learning as an essential aspect of research design. While graduate-level and advanced undergraduate-level computer science is in part based on mathematical theory, the design, implementation, and applications of computer technology could be taught in terms resonant with everyday problem solving and logic rather than formal mathematical systems.

Computer technology is highly dynamic. As the use of computers expands in educational and workplace settings, the contexts and applications of their use are rapidly changing so that the presumed closeness of the domains of computing and mathematics knowledge constitutes an increasingly inaccurate portrayal of what experienced and highly skilled computer users describe as being the most

24

25

---

[25] The overall regression coefficient for attitudinal factors with mathematics precalculus grades was an astonishing +.93. While this figure reflects the strong individual correlations that were obtained between the various attitudinal measures, which included the Fennema and Sherman mathematics attitude scales and the MARS, it must also be viewed with caution due to the small sample size.

[26] Unfortunately, we could not include computer course grades in the regression analysis with mathematics-related attitudes, so we could not determine the extent to which attitudes toward mathematics (as distinct from mathematics performance) may have been related to performance in computer courses.

advanced types and forms of creative computer-related work.[27] Metaphors for computer technology are moving away from the number-cruncher computer, away from the machine that can replace human action and decision making, and toward an understanding of computing as an interactive process in which the computer becomes an intelligent coparticipant in and facilitator of individual and group communication. This shift reflects the fact that creative computing now relies at least as much upon language, visual design, problem definition, and organizational skills as upon quantitative analysis.

Much of the research on gender differences in computing is based on definitions of computer literacy that fail to take into account the varying contents and context of computing, failing to distinguish clearly between such curricular topics as computer science, software design and programming, the teaching of specific software (such as word processing or spreadsheet packages), and the role of computer technology in our society. Consideration of levels of learning and domains of application of computer-related knowledge and skills should be included in any evaluation of computer aptitude and ability because computer learning, unlike mathematics learning, need not be based on a linear progression in which algebra comes before calculus and calculus before differential equations. Instead, the pieces of computer learning are more like those of a patchwork quilt; they may be joined in a variety of ways, the particular design depending upon the requirements of particular contexts and situations.

The effects of the sociocultural contexts of computing, including the educational and economic structures within which women encounter and work with computers and the attitudes that both shape and are shaped by particular settings, need to be carefully distinguished from effects deriving from the nature of computer-related learning tasks per se.

As in earlier research on women's avoidance of mathematics, we expect that a careful examination of women's computer participation and learning will reveal complex causal patterns of relationships between computer-related attitudes, abilities, and experiences; the nature of the task; and the sociocultural, economic, and educational settings in which women must choose to pursue or avoid computer-related learning and work. Yet because computer and mathematics learning differ in important ways, not all of these patterns of interrelationships will parallel those previously found for mathematics. Although epistemological and pedagogical issues must be evaluated systematically in relation to both mathematics and computer learning, it may be that women's computer learning will prove to be highly dependent upon institutional and economic contexts. (In fact, there is recent solid evidence that the mathematics gender gap is beginning to close.)[28]

---

[27] H. Dreyfus, and S. Dreyfus, *Mind over Machine* (New York: Free Press, 1987); and T. Winograd and F. Flores, *Understanding Computers and Cognition: A New Foundation for Design* (Reading, Mass.: Addison-Wesley, 1986).
[28] Elizabeth Fennema, Thomas Carpenter, and Penelope Peterson, "Teachers' Knowledge of

An examination of the contexts of computing may reveal that women's 29 choices are governed as much by positive preferences for certain styles of knowing and thinking as by negative stereotypes and discrimination. Although studies that have examined the expression of positive preferences and values in relation to computing are few, the existing literature suggests that an important starting point is the recognition of computing as an activity that incorporates and reflects social relationships and has social and psychological impacts.

QUESTIONS

1. This article provides an example of a research paper in the social sciences. As you reread it, notice the use of footnotes. Obviously they document the authors' sources, but what other purposes do they serve? What writing decisions determine what information goes in the body of the paper, and what goes in a footnote?

2. In their title, the writers call their article a "critique." Analyze the structure of the article and then describe what a critique of research does, and how it goes about doing so.

3. How do the conversation and statement in Paragraph 14 serve to illustrate points of the authors' argument? Kramer and Lehman say that the speakers' implicit critiques suggest "themes with which the research literature rarely deals" (Paragraph 16). What are these themes, and which do you think most important to pursue?

4. Why was it important for Kramer and Lehman in their research with women returning to college to examine the assumption that women are biologically unsuited for mathematics? What other assumptions about biological differences do you know of? How would you go about testing their truth value?

5. Consider your own experience with computers in school, at home, at work, or in other contexts (such as your experience with those of the IRS, for example). What problems have you encountered? Write an essay or critique describing them with reference to Kramer and Lehman.

6. If you think you fall into the category of "computer freak" or "computer groupie," write an essay in which you use your experience to illustrate the advantages or disadvantages (or both) of life as a freak or a groupie.

MAKING CONNECTIONS

1. In their conclusion, Kramer and Lehman suggest that further research may show that "women's choices are governed as much by positive preferences for certain styles of knowing and thinking as by negative stereotypes and discrimination." How does Carol

Students' Knowledge of Mathematics Problem-solving: A Correlational and Case Study," *Journal of Educational Psychology* 81, no. 4 (December 1989): 558–69.

Gilligan's "Interviewing Adolescent Girls" comment on this statement? How might Claude Steele comment on it in reference to black students?

2. What does Stephen Jay Gould's examination of Broca's argument in "Women's Brains" add to Kramer and Lehman's argument? Broca's *a priori* assumption that "women are not as intelligent as men" influenced his manipulation of numbers. What *a priori* assumptions do you think lay behind research on women's abilities in the areas of computers and mathematics?

THE HISTORICAL STRUCTURE OF SCIENTIFIC DISCOVERY

Thomas Kuhn

Thomas S. Kuhn (b. 1922) is a professor of philosophy at the Massachusetts Institute of Technology. His best-known book is The Structure of Scientific Revolutions *(2nd edition, 1970). The following essay was abstracted, as his first note says, from its third chapter; the essay appeared originally in* Science *magazine in 1962. Other books of his include* The Essential Tension: Selected Studies in Scientific Tradition and Change *(1977) and* Black-Body Theory and the Quantum Discontinuity, 1894–1912 *(1978). He has made the process of scientific investigation his special subject; historians and philosophers of science are his chief audience.*

My object in this article is to isolate and illuminate one small part of what I take to be a continuing historiographic revolution in the study of science.[1] The structure of scientific discovery is my particular topic, and I can best approach it by pointing out that the subject itself may well seem extraordinarily odd. Both scientists and, until quite recently, historians have ordinarily viewed discovery as the sort of event which, though it may have preconditions and surely has consequences, is itself without internal structure. Rather than being seen as a complex development extended both in space and time, discovering something has usually seemed to be a unitary event, one which, like seeing something, happens to an individual at a specifiable time and place.

This view of the nature of discovery has, I suspect, deep roots in the nature of the scientific community. One of the few historical elements recurrent in the textbooks from which the prospective scientist learns his field is the attribution of particular natural phenomena to the historical personages who first discovered them. As a result of this and other aspects of their training, discovery becomes for many scientists an important goal. To make a discovery is to achieve one of the closest approximations to a property right that the scientific career affords. Professional prestige is often closely associated with these acqui-

---

[1] The larger revolution will be discussed in my forthcoming book, *The Structure of Scientific Revolutions*, to be published in the fall by the University of Chicago Press. The central ideas in this paper have been abstracted from that source, particularly from its third chapter, "Anomaly and the Emergence of Scientific Discoveries" [2nd ed., 1970].

sitions.[2] Small wonder, then, that acrimonious disputes about priority and independence in discovery have often marred the normally placid tenor of scientific communication. Even less wonder that many historians of science have seen the individual discovery as an appropriate unit with which to measure scientific progress and have devoted much time and skill to determining what man made which discovery at what point in time. If the study of discovery has a surprise to offer, it is only that, despite the immense energy and ingenuity expended upon it, neither polemic nor painstaking scholarship has often succeeded in pinpointing the time and place at which a given discovery could properly be said to have "been made."

That failure, both of argument and of research, suggests the thesis that I now wish to develop. Many scientific discoveries, particularly the most interesting and important, are not the sort of event about which the questions "Where?" and, more particularly, "When?" can appropriately be asked. Even if all conceivable data were at hand, those questions would not regularly possess answers. That we are persistently driven to ask them nonetheless is symptomatic of a fundamental inappropriateness in our image of discovery. That inappropriateness is here my main concern, but I approach it by considering first the historical problem presented by the attempt to date and to place a major class of fundamental discoveries.

The troublesome class consists of those discoveries—including oxygen, the electric current, X rays, and the electron—which could not be predicted from accepted theory in advance and which therefore caught the assembled profession by surprise. That kind of discovery will shortly be my exclusive concern, but it will help first to note that there is another sort and one which presents very few of the same problems. Into this second class of discoveries fall the neutrino, radio waves, and the elements which filled empty places in the periodic table. The existence of all these objects had been predicted from theory before they were discovered, and the men who made the discoveries therefore knew from the start what to look for. That foreknowledge did not make their task less demanding or less interesting, but it did provide criteria which told them when their goal had been reached.[3] As a result, there have been few priority debates

---

[2] For a brilliant discussion of these points, see R. K. Merton, "Priorities in Scientific Discovery: A Chapter in the Sociology of Science," *American Sociological Review* 22 (1957): 635. Also very relevant, though it did not appear until this article had been prepared, is F. Reif, "The Competitive World of the Pure Scientist," *Science* 134 (1961): 1957.

[3] Not all discoveries fall so neatly as the preceding into one or the other of my two classes. For example, Anderson's work on the positron was done in complete ignorance of Dirac's electron theory from which the new particle's existence had already been very nearly predicted. On the other hand, the immediately succeeding work by Blackett and Occhialini made full use of Dirac's theory and therefore exploited experiment more fully and constructed a more forceful case for the positron's existence than Anderson had been able to do. On this subject see N. R. Hanson, "Discovering the Positron," *British Journal for the Philosophy of Science* 12 (1961): 194; 12 (1962): 299. Hanson suggests several of the points developed here. I am much indebted to Professor Hanson for a preprint of this material.

over discoveries of this second sort, and only a paucity of data can prevent the historian from ascribing them to a particular time and place. Those facts help to isolate the difficulties we encounter as we return to the troublesome discoveries of the first class. In the cases that most concern us here there are no benchmarks to inform either the scientist or the historian when the job of discovery has been done.

As an illustration of this fundamental problem and its consequences, consider first the discovery of oxygen. Because it has repeatedly been studied, often with exemplary care and skill, that discovery is unlikely to offer any purely factual surprises. Therefore it is particularly well suited to clarify points of principle.[4] At least three scientists—Carl Scheele, Joseph Priestley, and Antoine Lavoisier[5]— have a legitimate claim to this discovery, and polemicists have occasionally entered the same claim for Pierre Bayen.[6] Scheele's work, though it was almost certainly completed before the relevant researches of Priestley and Lavoisier, was not made public until their work was well known.[7] Therefore it had no apparent causal role, and I shall simplify my story by omitting it.[8] Instead, I pick up the main route to the discovery of oxygen with the work of Bayen, who, sometime before March 1774, discovered that red precipitate of mercury

---

[4] I have developed a less familiar example from the same viewpoint in "The Caloric Theory of Adiabatic Compression," *Isis* 49 (1958): 132. A closely similar analysis of the emergence of a new theory is included in the early pages of my essay "Energy Conservation as an Example of Simultaneous Discovery," in *Critical Problems in the History of Science*, ed. M. Clagett (Madison: University of Wisconsin Press, 1959), pp. 321–56. Reference to these papers may add depth and detail to the following discussion.

[5] Carl Wilhelm Scheele (1742–1786): Swedish chemist; Joseph Priestley (1733–1804): British chemist and clergyman; Antoine Laurent Lavoisier (1743–1794): French chemist. Pierre Bayen (1725–1798), mentioned at the end of the sentence, was a French chemist. [Eds.]

[6] The still classic discussion of the discovery of oxygen is A. N. Meldrum, *The Eighteenth Century Revolution in Science: The First Phase* (Calcutta, 1930), chap. 5. A more convenient and generally quite reliable discussion is included in J. B. Conant, *The Overthrow of the Phlogiston Theory: The Chemical Revolution of 1775–1789*. Harvard Case Histories in Experimental Science, case 2 (Cambridge: Harvard University Press, 1950). A recent and indispensable review, which includes an account of the development of the priority controversy, is M. Daumas, *Lavoisier, théoricien et expérimentateur* (Paris, 1955), chaps. 2 and 3. H. Guerlac has added much significant detail to our knowledge of the early relations between Priestley and Lavoisier in his "Joseph Priestley's First Papers on Gases and Their Reception in France," *Journal of the History of Medicine* 12 (1957): 1 and in his very recent monograph, *Lavoisier: The Crucial Year* (Ithaca: Cornell University Press, 1961). For Scheele see J. R. Partington, *A Short History of Chemistry*, 2d ed. (London, 1951), pp. 104–9.

[7] For the dating of Scheele's work, see A. E. Nordenskjöld, *Carl Wilhelm Scheele, Nachgelassene Briefe und Aufzeichnungen* (Stockholm, 1892).

[8] U. Bocklund ("A Lost Letter from Scheele to Lavoisier," *Lychnos*, 1957–58, pp. 39–62) argues that Scheele communicated his discovery of oxygen to Lavoisier in a letter of 30 Sept. 1774. Certainly the letter is important, and it clearly demonstrates that Scheele was ahead of both Priestley and Lavoisier at the time it was written. But I think the letter is not quite so candid as Bocklund supposes, and I fail to see how Lavoisier could have drawn the discovery of oxygen from it. Scheele describes a procedure for reconstituting common air, not for producing a new gas, and that, as we shall see, is almost the same information that Lavoisier received from Priestley at about the same time. In any case, there is no evidence that Lavoisier performed the sort of experiment that Scheele suggested.

(HgO) could, by heating, be made to yield a gas. That aeriform product Bayen identified as fixed air (CO_2), a substance made familiar to most pneumatic chemists by the earlier work of Joseph Black.[9] A variety of other substances were known to yield the same gas.

At the beginning of August 1774, a few months after Bayen's work had appeared, Joseph Priestley repeated the experiment, though probably independently. Priestley, however, observed that the gaseous product would support combustion and therefore changed the identification. For him the gas obtained on heating red precipitate was nitrous air (N_2O), a substance that he had himself discovered more than two years before.[10] Later in the same month Priestley made a trip to Paris and there informed Lavoisier of the new reaction. The latter repeated the experiment once more, both in November 1774 and in February 1775. But, because he used tests somewhat more elaborate than Priestley's, Lavoisier again changed the identification. For him, as of May 1775, the gas released by red precipitate was neither fixed air nor nitrous air. Instead, it was "[atmospheric] air itself entire without alteration . . . even to the point that . . . it comes out more pure."[11] Meanwhile, however, Priestley had also been at work, and, before the beginning of March 1775, he, too, had concluded that the gas must be "common air." Until this point all of the men who had produced a gas from red precipitate of mercury had identified it with some previously known species.[12]

The remainder of this story of discovery is briefly told. During March 1775 Priestley discovered that his gas was in several respects very much "better" than common air, and he therefore reidentified the gas once more, this time calling it "dephlogisticated air," that is, atmospheric air deprived of its normal complement of phlogiston. This conclusion Priestley published in the *Philosophical Transactions*, and it was apparently that publication which led Lavoisier to reexamine his own results.[13] The reexamination began during February 1776 and within a year had led Lavoisier to the conclusion that the gas was actually a separable component of the atmospheric air which both he and Priestley had previously thought of as homogeneous. With this point reached, with the gas

6

7

---

[9] P. Bayen, "Essai d'expériences chymiques, faites sur quelques précipités de mercure, dans la vue de découvrir leur nature, Seconde partie," *Observations sur la physique* 3 (1774): 280–95, particularly pp. 289–91. (Joseph Black [1728–1799]: Scottish physician and chemist. [Eds.])

[10] J. B. Conant, *The Overthrow of the Phlogiston Theory*, pp. 34–40.

[11] Ibid., p. 23. A useful translation of the full text is available in Conant.

[12] For simplicity I use the term *red precipitate* throughout. Actually, Bayen used the precipitate: Priestley used both the precipitate and the oxide produced by direct calcination of mercury: and Lavoisier used only the latter. The difference is not without importance, for it was not unequivocally clear to chemists that the two substances were identical.

[13] There has been some doubt about Priestley's having influenced Lavoisier's thinking at this point, but, when the latter returned to experimenting with the gas in February 1776, he recorded in his notebooks that he had obtained "l'air dephlogistique de M. Priestley" (M. Daumas, *Lavoisier*, p. 36).

recognized as an irreducibly distinct species, we may conclude that the discovery of oxygen had been completed.

But to return to my initial question, when shall we say that oxygen was discovered and what criteria shall be used in answering that question? If discovering oxygen is simply holding an impure sample in one's hands, then the gas had been "discovered" in antiquity by the first man who ever bottled atmospheric air. Undoubtedly, for an experimental criterion, we must at least require a relatively pure sample like that obtained by Priestley in August 1774. But during 1774 Priestley was unaware that he had discovered anything except a new way to produce a relatively familiar species. Throughout that year his "discovery" is scarcely distinguishable from the one made earlier by Bayen, and neither case is quite distinct from that of the Reverend Stephen Hales, who had obtained the same gas more than forty years before.[14] Apparently to discover something one must also be aware of the discovery and know as well what it is that one has discovered.

But, that being the case, how much must one know? Had Priestley come close enough when he identified the gas as nitrous air? If not, was either he or Lavoisier significantly closer when he changed the identification to common air? And what are we to say about Priestley's next identification, the one made in March 1775? Dephlogisticated air is still not oxygen or even, for the phlogistic chemist, a quite unexpected sort of gas.[15] Rather it is a particularly pure atmospheric air. Presumably, then, we wait for Lavoisier's work in 1776 and 1777, work which led him not merely to isolate the gas but to see what it was. Yet even that decision can be questioned, for in 1777 and to the end of his life Lavoisier insisted that oxygen was an atomic "principle of acidity" and that oxygen *gas* was formed only when that "principle" united with caloric, the matter of heat.[16] Shall we therefore say that oxygen had not yet been discovered in 1777? Some may be tempted to do so. But the principle of acidity was not banished from chemistry until after 1810 and caloric lingered on until the 1860s. Oxygen had, however, become a standard chemical substance long before either of those dates. Furthermore, what is perhaps the key point, it would probably have gained that status on the basis of Priestley's work alone without benefit of Lavoisier's still partial reinterpretation.

I conclude that we need a new vocabulary and new concepts for analyzing events like the discovery of oxygen. Though undoubtedly correct, the sentence "Oxygen was discovered" misleads by suggesting that discovering something is

8

9

10

---

[14]J. R. Partington, *A Short History of Chemistry*, p. 91. (Reverend Stephen Hales [1677–1761]: British botanist and physiologist. [Eds.])

[15]phlogistic: from *phlogiston*, a New Latin coinage from the Greek word for inflammable, naming a substance formerly thought to escape when a material burns. Though a faulty theory, its investigation contributed to the discovery of oxygen. [Eds.]

[16]For the traditional elements in Lavoisier's interpretations of chemical reactions, see H. Metzger, *La philosophie de la matière chez Lavoisier* (Paris, 1935), and Daumas, *Lavoisier*, chap. 7.

a single simple act unequivocally attributable, if only we knew enough, to an individual and an instant in time. When the discovery is unexpected, however, the latter attribution is always impossible and the former often is as well. Ignoring Scheele, we can, for example, safely say that oxygen had not been discovered before 1774; probably we would also insist that it had been discovered by 1774; probably we would also insist that it had been discovered by 1777 or shortly thereafter. But within those limits any attempt to date the discovery or to attribute it to an individual must inevitably be arbitrary. Furthermore, it must be arbitrary just because discovering a new sort of phenomenon is necessarily a complex process which involves recognizing both *that* something is and *what* it is. Observation and conceptualization, fact and the assimilation of fact to theory, are inseparably linked in the discovery of scientific novelty. Inevitably, that process extends over time and may often involve a number of people. Only for discoveries in my second category—those whose nature is known in advance—can discovering *that* and discovering *what* occur together and in an instant.

Two last, simpler, and far briefer examples will simultaneously show how 11 typical the case of oxygen is and also prepare the way for a somewhat more precise conclusion. On the night of 13 March 1781, the astronomer William Herschel made the following entry in his journal: "In the quartile near Zeta Tauri . . . is a curious either nebulous star or perhaps a comet."[17] That entry is generally said to record the discovery of the planet Uranus, but it cannot quite have done that. Between 1690 and Herschel's observation in 1781 the same object had been seen and recorded at least seventeen times by men who took it to be a star. Herschel differed from them only in supposing that, because in his telescope it appeared especially large, it might actually be a *comet!* Two additional observations on 17 and 19 March confirmed that suspicion by showing that the object he had observed moved among the stars. As a result, astronomers throughout Europe were informed of the discovery, and the mathematicians among them began to compute the new comet's orbit. Only several months later, after all those attempts had repeatedly failed to square with observation, did the astronomer Lexell suggest that the object observed by Herschel might be a planet.[18] And only when additional computations, using a planet's rather than a comet's orbit, proved reconcilable with observation was that suggestion generally accepted. At what point during 1781 do we want to say that the planet Uranus was discovered? And are we entirely and unequivocally clear that it was Herschel rather than Lexell who discovered it?

Or consider still more briefly the story of the discovery of X rays, a story 12 which opens on the day in 1895 when the physicist Roentgen interrupted a well-precedented investigation of cathode rays because he noticed that a barium

[17] P. Doig, A *Concise History of Astronomy* (London: Chapman, 1950), pp. 115–16. (William Herschel [1738–1822]: German-born English astronomer. [Eds.])
[18] Anders Johan Lexell (1740–1784): Swedish astronomer. [Eds.]

platinocyanide screen far from his shielded apparatus glowed when the discharge was in process.[19] Additional investigations—they required seven hectic weeks during which Roentgen rarely left the laboratory—indicated that the cause of the glow traveled in straight lines from the cathode ray tube, that the radiation cast shadows, that it could not be deflected by a magnet, and much else besides. Before announcing his discovery Roentgen had convinced himself that his effect was not due to cathode rays themselves but to a new form of radiation with at least some similarity to light. Once again the question suggests itself: When shall we say that X rays were actually discovered? Not, in any case, at the first instant, when all that had been noted was a glowing screen. At least one other investigator had seen that glow and, to his subsequent chagrin, discovered nothing at all. Nor, it is almost as clear, can the moment of discovery be pushed back to a point during the last week of investigation. By that time Roentgen was exploring the properties of the new radiation he had *already* discovered. We may have to settle for the remark that X rays emerged in Würzburg between 8 November and 28 December 1895.

The characteristics shared by these examples are, I think, common to all the episodes by which unanticipated novelties become subjects for scientific attention. I therefore conclude these brief remarks by discussing three such common characteristics, ones which may help to provide a framework for the further study of the extended episodes we customarily call "discoveries." 13

In the first place, notice that all three of our discoveries—oxygen, Uranus, and X-rays—began with the experimental or observational isolation of an anomaly, that is, with nature's failure to conform entirely to expectation. Notice, further, that the process by which that anomaly was educed displays simultaneously the apparently incompatible characteristics of the inevitable and the accidental. In the case of X rays, the anomalous glow which provided Roentgen's first clue was clearly the result of an accidental disposition of his apparatus. But by 1895 cathode rays were a normal subject for research all over Europe; that research quite regularly juxtaposed cathode-ray tubes with sensitive screens and films; as a result, Roentgen's accident was almost certain to occur elsewhere, as in fact it had. Those remarks, however, should make Roentgen's case look very much like those of Herschel and Priestley. Herschel first observed his oversized and thus anomalous star in the course of a prolonged survey of the northern heavens. That survey was, except for the magnification provided by Herschel's instruments, precisely of the sort that had repeatedly been carried through before and that had occasionally resulted in prior observations of Uranus. And Priestley, too—when he isolated the gas that behaved almost but not quite like nitrous air and then almost but not quite like common air—was seeing something unintended and wrong in the outcome of a sort of experiment 14

[19]L. W. Taylor, *Physics, the Pioneer Science* (Boston: Houghton Mifflin Co., 1941), p. 790. (Wilhelm Konrad Roentgen [1845–1923]: German physicist. [Eds.])

for which there was much European precedent and which had more than once before led to the production of the new gas.

These features suggest the existence of two normal requisites for the beginning of an episode of discovery. The first, which throughout this paper I have largely taken for granted, is the individual skill, wit, or genius to recognize that something has gone wrong in ways that may prove consequential. Not any and every scientist would have noted that no unrecorded star should be so large, that the screen ought not to have glowed, that nitrous air should not have supported life. But that requisite presupposes another which is less frequently taken for granted. Whatever the level of genius available to observe them, anomalies do not emerge from the normal course of scientific research until both instruments and concepts have developed sufficiently to make their emergence likely and to make the anomaly which results recognizable as a violation of expectation.[20] To say that an unexpected discovery begins only when something goes wrong is to say that it begins only when scientists know well both how their instruments and how nature should behave. What distinguished Priestley, who saw an anomaly, from Hales, who did not, is largely the considerable articulation of pneumatic techniques and expectations that had come into being during the four decades which separate their two isolations of oxygen.[21] The very number of claimants indicates that after 1770 the discovery could not have been postponed for long.

The role of anomaly is the first of the characteristics shared by our three examples. A second can be considered more briefly, for it has provided the main theme for the body of my text. Though awareness of anomaly marks the beginning of a discovery, it marks only the beginning. What necessarily follows, if anything at all is to be discovered, is a more or less extended period during which the individual and often many members of his group struggle to make the anomaly lawlike. Invariably that period demands additional observation or experimentation as well as repeated cogitation. While it continues, scientists repeatedly revise their expectations, usually their instrumental standards, and sometimes their most fundamental theories as well. In this sense discoveries have a proper internal history as well as prehistory and a posthistory. Furthermore, within the rather vaguely delimited interval of internal history, there is no single moment or day which the historian, however complete his data, can identify as the point at which the discovery was made. Often, when several individuals are involved, it is even impossible unequivocally to identify any one of them as the discoverer.

---

[20] Though the point cannot be argued here, the conditions which make the emergence of anomaly likely and those which make anomaly recognizable are to a very great extent the same. That fact may help us understand the extraordinarily large amount of simultaneous discovery in the sciences.

[21] A useful sketch of the development of pneumatic chemistry is included in Partington, *A Short History of Chemistry*, chap. 6.

Finally, turning to the third of these selected common characteristics, note   17
briefly what happens as the period of discovery draws to a close. A full discussion
of that question would require additional evidence and a separate paper, for I
have had little to say about the aftermath of discovery in the body of my text.
Nevertheless, the topic must not be entirely neglected, for it is in part a corollary
of what has already been said.

Discoveries are often described as mere additions or increments to the grow-   18
ing stockpile of scientific knowledge, and that description has helped make the
unit discovery seem a significant measure of progress. I suggest, however, that
it is fully appropriate only to those discoveries which, like the elements that
filled missing places in the periodic table, were anticipated and sought in
advance and which therefore demanded no adjustment, adaptation, and assimilation from the profession. Though the sorts of discoveries we have here been
examining are undoubtedly additions to scientific knowledge, they are also
something more. In a sense that I can now develop only in part, they also react
back upon what has previously been known, providing a new view of some
previously familiar objects and simultaneously changing the way in which even
some traditional parts of science are practiced. Those in whose area of special
competence the new phenomenon falls often see both the world and their work
differently as they emerge from the extended struggle with anomaly which
constitutes the discovery of that phenomenon.

William Herschel, for example, when he increased by one the time-honored   19
number of planetary bodies, taught astronomers to see new things when they
looked at the familiar heavens even with instruments more traditional than his
own. That change in the vision of astronomers must be a principal reason why,
in the half century after the discovery of Uranus, twenty additional circumsolar
bodies were added to the traditional seven.[22] A similar transformation is even
clearer in the aftermath of Roentgen's work. In the first place, established
techniques for cathode-ray research had to be changed, for scientists found they
had failed to control a relevant variable. Those changes included both the
redesign of old apparatus and revised ways of asking old questions. In addition,
those scientists most concerned experienced the same transformation of vision
that we have just noted in the aftermath of the discovery of Uranus. X rays
were the first new sort of radiation discovered since infrared and ultraviolet at
the beginning of the century. But within less than a decade after Roentgen's

---

[22] R. Wolf, *Geschichte der Astronomie* (Munich, 1877), pp. 513–15, 683–93. The prephoto-
graphic discoveries of the asteroids is often seen as an effect of the invention of Bode's law. But
that law cannot be the full explanation and may not even have played a large part. Piazzi's discovery
of Ceres, in 1801, was made in ignorance of the current speculation about a missing planet in the
"hole" between Mars and Jupiter. Instead, like Herschel, Piazzi was engaged in a star survey. More
important, Bode's law was old by 1800 (ibid., p. 683), but only one man before that date seems to
have thought it worthwhile to look for another planet. Finally, Bode's law, by itself, could only
suggest the utility of looking for additional planets; it did not tell astronomers where to look. Clearly,
however, the drive to look for additional planets dates from Herschel's work on Uranus.

work, four more were disclosed by the new scientific sensitivity (for example, to fogged photographic plates) and by some of the new instrumental techniques that had resulted from Roentgen's work and its assimilation.[23]

Very often these transformations in the established techniques of scientific practice prove even more important than the incremental knowledge provided by the discovery itself. That could at least be argued in the cases of Uranus and of X rays; in the case of my third example, oxygen, it is categorically clear. Like the work of Herschel and Roentgen, that of Priestley and Lavoisier taught scientists to view old situations in new ways. Therefore, as we might anticipate, oxygen was not the only new chemical species to be identified in the aftermath of their work. But, in the case of oxygen, the readjustments demanded by assimilation were so profound that they played an integral and essential role— though they were not by themselves the cause—in the gigantic upheaval of chemical theory and practice which has since been known as the chemical revolution. I do not suggest that every unanticipated discovery has consequences for science so deep and so far-reaching as those which followed the discovery of oxygen. But I do suggest that every such discovery demands, from those most concerned, the sorts of readjustment that, when they are more obvious, we equate with scientific revolution. It is, I believe, just because they demand readjustments like these that the process of discovery is necessarily and inevitably one that shows structure and that therefore extends in time. 20

QUESTIONS

1. State in your own words the principle Kuhn identifies at the end of paragraph 2.
2. Distinguish the two kinds of scientific discoveries Kuhn outlines in paragraphs 3 and 4. Which is the subject of this article?
3. Summarize the three characteristics of scientific discovery that Kuhn reviews in paragraphs 14 through 20.
4. Why does Kuhn spend so much more time on the discovery of oxygen than on the comet or x-rays? Would that first example have been sufficient in itself? Do all three examples contribute substantially to "the characteristics of scientific discovery" that Kuhn goes on to outline?
5. If a single word were to distinguish the scientific discoveries that most interest Kuhn, that word might be *process* (as paragraph 10 suggests). Describe an event you know well—a class, a game, a meeting, an accident—as if it were a process rather than a single event. How does your description of that process allow you to understand the event in a way you had not understood it before?
6. Seen from one point of view, the papers you write are events, too. You hand

[23] For α-, β, and γ-radiation, discovery of which dates from 1896, see Taylor, *Physics*, pp. 800–804. For the fourth new form of radiation, N rays, see D. J. S. Price, *Science Since Babylon* (New Haven: Yale University Press, 1961), pp. 84–89. That N rays were ultimately the source of a scientific scandal does not make them less revealing of the scientific community's state of mind.

them in when due and get them back, graded, later. But in another sense, they are part of a process as well. Describe the process of the last paper you wrote. When did that process begin? What pattern did it take? What were the crucial moments, perhaps the turning points? And when can you say the process came to an end?

MAKING CONNECTIONS

The process of scientific discovery, with its three stages as reviewed by Kuhn in paragraphs 14–20, might apply to other developments in our lives. Consider, for example, the several articles in this collection that report, reflect upon, and argue about the atom bomb: William L. Laurence's "Atomic Bombing of Nagasaki Told by Flight Member" and John Hersey's "Hatsuyo Nakamura," both in "Reporting"; Zoë Tracy Hardy's "What Did You Do in the War, Grandma?" in "Reflecting"; and John Berger's "Hiroshima" in "Arguing." What kind of discovery is made in the course of those investigations? What are the stages of its process? When can you say a discovery was made? What was it? Do you agree with it? Do you foresee more stages of discovery to come?

ACKNOWLEDGMENTS (continued from copyright page)

Barthes, Roland. "Einstein's Brain." From Mythologies by Roland Barthes. Translation © 1972 by Jonathan Cape, Ltd. Reprinted by permission of Hill and Wang, a division of Farrar, Straus and Giroux, Inc. and Jonathan Cape, Ltd.

Baumrind, Diana. "Review of Stanley Milgram's Experiments on Obedience." From "Some Thoughts on Ethics of Research: After Reading Milgram's 'Behavioral Study of Obedience,'" in American Psychologist 19, 1964, pp. 421–23. Copyright © 1964 by the American Psychological Association. Reprinted by permission.

Berger, John. "Hiroshima." From The Sense of Sight, by John Berger. Copyright © 1985 by John Berger. Reprinted by permission of Pantheon Books, a Division of Random House, Inc.

Bettelheim, Bruno. "The Ignored Lesson of Anne Frank." From Surviving and Other Essays by Bruno Bettelheim. Copyright © 1979 by Bruno Bettelheim and Trude Bettelheim as Trustees. Reprinted by permission of Alfred A. Knopf, Inc.

Birkerts, Sven. "The Woman in the Garden." From Agni 35 (1992). Reprinted by permission of the author.

Bohannon, Laura. "Shakespeare in the Bush." In Natural History Magazine, Aug/Sep 1966. Reprinted by permission of the author.

Booth, William. "The Social Lives of Dolphins." From Science 240, page 1273, June 3, 1988. Copyright © 1988 by the AAAS. Reprinted with permission.

Borges, Jorge Luis. "Borges and I," translated by James E. Irby. From Labyrinths by Jorge Luis Borges. Copyright © 1964 by New Directions Publishing Corp. Reprinted by permission of New Directions Publishing Corp.

Borges, Jorge Luis. "Borges and I," translated by Anthony Kerrigan. From A Personal Anthology by Jorge Luis Borges. Copyright © 1967 by Grove Press. Used with the permission of Grove/Atlantic Monthly Press.

Borges, Jorge Luis. "Borges and Myself." From The Aleph and Other Stories by Jorge Luis Borges, translated by Norman Thomas di Giovanni. Translation copyright © 1968, 1969, 1970 by Emecé Editores, S.A. and Norman Thomas di Giovanni. Used by permission of the publisher, Dutton, an imprint of New American Library, a division of Penguin Books USA Inc.

Borges, Jorge Luis. "Borges y yo." From El hacedor, 1960 in Obras Completas © Emecé Editores 1974 y © María Kodama and Emecé Editores, 1989. Reprinted by permission.

Brown, Michael H. "Love Canal and the Poisoning of America." From Laying Waste: Love Canal & the Poisoning of America by Michael H. Brown. Copyright © 1979, 1980 by Michael H. Brown. Reprinted by permission of Pantheon Books, a Division of Random House, Inc.

Brunvand, Jan Harold. "Urban Legends: 'The Boyfriend's Death.'" Reprinted from The Vanishing Hitchhiker: American Urban Legends and Their Meanings, by Jan Harold Brunvand, by permission of W. W. Norton & Company Inc. Copyright © 1981 by Jan Harold Brunvand.

Caplan, Arthur et al. "Just Like Us: A Forum of Animal Rights." Copyright © 1988 by Harper's Magazine. All rights reserved. Reprinted from the August issue by special permission.

Carr, Edward Hallett. "The Historian and His Facts." From What is History? Edward

782

Hallett Carr. Copyright © 1961 by Edward Hallett Carr. Reprinted by permission of Alfred A. Knopf, Inc. and Macmillan Ltd.

Clausen, Christopher. "Dialogues with the Dead." Reprinted from *The American Scholar* 61, no. 2, Spring 1992. Copyright © 1992 by Christopher Clausen. By permission of the publisher.

Crick, Francis. "Times and Distances, Large and Small." From *Life Itself.* Copyright © 1981 by Francis Crick. Reprinted by permission of Curtis Brown, Ltd.

Damasio, Antonio R. "Face Perception without Recognition." From *Trends in Neuroscience* (March 1985). Reprinted by permission of the author.

Darwin, Charles. "The Action of Natural Selection." From *The Essential Darwin,* edited by Robert Jastrow with selections and commentary by Kenneth Korey. Copyright © 1984 by Robert Jastrow. By permission of Little, Brown and Company.

Didion, Joan. "Georgia O'Keeffe." From *The White Album* by Joan Didion. Copyright © 1979 by Joan Didion. Reprinted by permission of Farrar, Straus and Giroux, Inc.

Dinesen, Isak. "The Iguana." From *Out of Africa* by Isak Dinesen. Copyright © 1937 by Random House, Inc. and renewed 1965 by Rungstedlundfonden. Reprinted by permission of Random House, Inc. and the Rungstedlund Foundation.

Eiseley, Loren. "The Bird and the Machine." From *The Immense Journey* by Loren Eiseley. Copyright © 1957 by Loren Eiseley. Reprinted by permission of Random House, Inc.

Fiske, John. "Romancing the Rock." From *Reading the Popular* by John Fiske. Reprinted by permission of Unwin Hyman.

Fraker, Susan. "Why Woman Aren't Getting to the Top." From *Fortune,* April 16, 1984. Copyright © 1984 Time, Inc. All rights reserved. Reprinted by permission.

Gilligan, Carol. "Interviewing Adolescent Girls." For permission to photocopy this selection, please contact Harvard University Press. Reprinted by permission of the publishers from *Making Connections: The Relational Worlds of Adolescent Girls at Emma Willard School,* edited by Carol Gilligan, Nona Lyons, and Trudy Hammer, Cambridge, Mass.: Harvard University Press, Copyright © 1990 by the President and Fellows of Harvard College, © 1989 Preface & Prologue by Carol Gilligan, © 1989 by Emma Willard School.

Glazer, Nathan. "Some Very Modest Proposals for the Improvement of American Education." Reprinted by permission of *Daedalus: Journal of the American Academy of Arts and Sciences,* from the issue entitled, "Values, Resources, and Politics in America's Schools," Fall 1984, Vol. 113, no. 4.

Gould, Stephen Jay. "Counters and Cable Cars." Reprinted from *Eight Little Piggies: Reflections in Natural History,* by Stephen Jay Gould. By permission of W. W. Norton & Company, Inc. Copyright © 1993 by Stephen Jay Gould.

Gould, Stephen Jay. "The Median Isn't the Message." Reprinted from *Bully for Brontosaurus: Reflections in Natural History,* by Stephen Jay Gould. By permission of W. W. Norton & Company, Inc. Copyright © 1991 by Stephen Jay Gould.

Gould, Stephen Jay. "Women's Brains." Reprinted from *The Panda's Thumb: More Reflections in Natural History,* by Stephen Jay Gould. By permission of W. W. Norton & Company, Inc. Copyright © 1980 by Stephen Jay Gould.

Hardy, Zöe Tracy. "What Did You Do in the War, Grandma?" *MS.* (August, 1985). Reprinted by permission of the author.

Hawking, Stephen W. "Our Picture of the Universe." From *A Brief History of Time* by

784

Martin, Emily. "The Egg and the Sperm: How Science Has Constructed a Romance Based on Stereotypical Male-Female Roles." From *Signs: Journal of Women in Culture and Society* 16:3(1991). Copyright © 1991 by The University of Chicago. Reprinted by permission of the publisher.

Mead, Margaret. "Scenes from Manus Life." From *Growing Up in New Guinea* by Margaret Mead. Copyright © 1930, 1958, 1962 by Margaret Mead. By permission of William Morrow & Company, Inc.

Milgram, Stanley. "Some Conditions of Obedience and Disobedience to Authority." By Stanley Milgram in *Human Relations* 18, no. 1, pp. 57–76. Copyright © 1972 by Stanley Milgram. All rights controlled by Alexandra Milgram, literary executor. Reprinted by permission.

Miner, Horace. "Body Ritual Among the Nacirema." Reproduced by permission of the American Anthropological Association from *American Anthropologist* 58:3, June 1956. Not for sale or further reproduction.

Momaday, N. Scott. "The Way to Rainy Mountain." First published in *The Reporter*, 26 January 1967. Reprinted from *The Way to Rainy Mountain*, © 1969, the University of New Mexico Press.

Mowat, Farley. "Observing Wolves." From *Never Cry Wolf* by Farley Mowat. Copyright © 1963 by Farley Mowat Limited. By permission of Little, Brown and Company and the author.

Orwell, George. "Politics and the English Language" by George Orwell. Copyright 1946 by Sonia Brownell Orwell and renewed 1974 by Sonia Orwell. Reprinted from his volume *Shooting an Elephant and Other Essays* by permission of Harcourt Brace & Company.

Orwell, George. "Shooting an Elephant." From *Shooting an Elephant and Other Essays* by George Orwell. Copyright 1950 by Sonia Brownell Orwell and renewed 1978 by Sonia Pitt-Rivers. Reprinted by permission of Harcourt Brace & Company and the estate of the late Sonia Brownell Orwell and Martin Secker and Warburg.

Rodriguez, Richard. "Children of A Marriage." Copyright © 1988 by Richard Rodriguez. Reprinted by permission of Georges Borchardt, Inc. for the author. First appeared in *Time Magazine*.

Sacks, Oliver. "The Autist Artist" and "The Man Who Mistook His Wife for a Hat." From *The Man Who Mistook His Wife for a Hat*. Copyright © 1970, 1981, 1983, 1984, 1985 by Oliver Sacks. Reprinted by permission of Summit Books, a division of Simon & Schuster, Inc.

Sagan, Carl. "Can We Know the Universe? Reflections on a Grain of Salt." From *Broca's Brain*. Copyright © 1979 by Carl Sagan. All rights reserved. Reprinted by permission of the author.

Selby, Roy, Jr. "A Delicate Operation." Copyright © 1975 by Harper's Magazine. All rights reserved. Reprinted from the December issue by special permission.

Selzer, Richard. "A Mask on the Face of Death." Copyright © 1987 by Richard Selzer. Reprinted by permission of Georges Borchardt, Inc. for the author. First appeared in *Life Magazine*.

Selzer, Richard. "The Discus Thrower" from *Confessions of a Knife* by Richard Selzer. Copyright © 1979 by David Goldman and Janet Selzer, Trustees. By permission of William Morrow & Company, Inc.

Sizer, Theodore R. "What High School Is." From *Horace's Compromise* by Theodore

Sizer. Copyright © 1984 by Theodore R. Sizer. Reprinted by permission of Houghton Mifflin Company. All rights reserved.

Steele, Claude M. "Race and the Schooling of Black Americans." Copyright © 1992 Claude M. Steele. Originally published in the April 1992 issue of *The Atlantic Monthly*. Reprinted by permission of the author.

Tuchman, Barbara. [When Does History Happen?] "Can History be Served Up Hot?" From *The New York Times Book Review*, March 8, 1964. Reprinted by permission of Russell & Volkening as agents for the author. Copyright © 1964 by Barbara Tuchman, copyright renewed 1992 by Lester Tuchman.

Tuchman, Barbara. "'This Is the End of the World:' The Black Death" From *A Distant Mirror* by Barbara W. Tuchman. Copyright © 1978 by Barbara W. Tuchman. Reprinted by permission of Alfred A. Knopf, Inc.

van Lawick-Goodall, Jane. "First Observations." From *In the Shadow of Man* by Jane van Lawick-Goodall. Copyright © 1971 by Hugo and Jane van Lawick-Goodall. Reprinted by permission of Houghton Mifflin Company and George Weidenfeld & Nicolson Limited. All rights reserved.

Walker, Alice. "Am I Blue?" From *Living by the Word: Selected Writings 1973–1987.* Copyright © 1986 by Alice Walker, reprinted by permission of Harcourt Brace & Company.

Walker, Alice. "Beauty: When the Other Dancer Is the Self." From *In Search of Our Mothers' Gardens: Womanist Prose.* Copyright © 1983 by Alice Walker, reprinted by permission of Harcourt Brace & Company.

Weisskopf, Victor. "The Origin of the Universe." Reprinted with permission from *The New York Review of Books.* Copyright © 1989 Nyrev, Inc.

White, E. B. "Dear Mr. 0214 1063 02 10730 8." From *The New York Times*, September 23, 1987. Copyright © 1987 by The New York Times Company. Reprinted by permission.

White, E. B. Notes and draft of "Dear Mr. 0214 1063 02 10730 8." Reprinted by permission of the Rare and Manuscript Collections, Cornell University Library and Joel White.

White, Edmund. "Sexual Culture." In *Vanity Fair*, 1983. Reprinted by permission of the author.

Wilford, John Noble. "Discovering Columbus." From *The New York Times*, August 11, 1991. Copyright © 1991 by The New York Times Company. Reprinted by permission.

Williams, Patricia J. "On Being the Object of Property." From *Signs: Journal of Women in Culture and Society* 14:1(1988). Copyright © 1988 by The University of Chicago. Reprinted by permission of the publisher.

Woo, Deborah. "The Gap Between Striving and Achieving: The Case of Asian American Women." From *Making Waves*, by Asian Women United of California. Copyright © 1989 by Asian Women United of California. Reprinted by permission of Beacon Press.

Woolf, Virginia. "The Death of the Moth." From *The Death of the Moth and Other Essays* by Virginia Woolf. Copyright 1942 by Harcourt Brace & Company and renewed 1970 by Marjorie T. Parsons, Executrix. Reprinted by permission of the publisher.

786

Rhetorical Index

787

COMPARISON AND CONTRAST

DEFINITION

DESCRIPTION

EVIDENCE

POINT OF VIEW

PROCESS ANALYSIS

PURPOSE

REFLECTING

Author and Title Index